Let's Go Publications

Let's Go: Alaska & the Pacific Northwest 2001
Let's Go: Australia 2001
Let's Go: Austria & Switzerland 2001
Let's Go: Boston 2001 **New Title!**
Let's Go: Britain & Ireland 2001
Let's Go: California 2001
Let's Go: Central America 2001
Let's Go: China 2001
Let's Go: Eastern Europe 2001
Let's Go: Europe 2001
Let's Go: France 2001
Let's Go: Germany 2001
Let's Go: Greece 2001
Let's Go: India & Nepal 2001
Let's Go: Ireland 2001
Let's Go: Israel 2001
Let's Go: Italy 2001
Let's Go: London 2001
Let's Go: Mexico 2001
Let's Go: Middle East 2001
Let's Go: New York City 2001
Let's Go: New Zealand 2001
Let's Go: Paris 2001
Let's Go: Peru, Bolivia & Ecuador 2001 **New Title!**
Let's Go: Rome 2001
Let's Go: San Francisco 2001 **New Title!**
Let's Go: South Africa 2001
Let's Go: Southeast Asia 2001
Let's Go: Spain & Portugal 2001
Let's Go: Turkey 2001
Let's Go: USA 2001
Let's Go: Washington, D.C. 2001
Let's Go: Western Europe 2001 **New Title!**

Let's Go *Map Guides*

Amsterdam	New Orleans
Berlin	New York City
Boston	Paris
Chicago	Prague
Florence	Rome
Hong Kong	San Francisco
London	Seattle
Los Angeles	Sydney
Madrid	Washington, D.C.

Coming Soon: Dublin and Venice

Let's Go

MIDDLE EAST
2001

Jimmy Davis editor
Naz Fatemeh Firoz editor
Amélie Cherlin editor

researcher-writers
Joe Chase
Sarah Eltantawi
Rita Hamad
Arthur Koski-Karell
Elizabeth White

Filip Wojciechowski map editor

Macmillan

HELPING LET'S GO If you want to share your discoveries, suggestions, or corrections, please drop us a line. We read every piece of correspondence, whether a postcard, a 10-page email, or a coconut. Please note that mail received after May 2001 may be too late for the 2002 book, but will be kept for future editions. **Address mail to:**

> **Let's Go: Middle East**
> **67 Mount Auburn Street**
> **Cambridge, MA 02138**
> **USA**

Visit Let's Go at **http://www.letsgo.com,** or send email to:

> **feedback@letsgo.com**
> **Subject: "Let's Go: Middle East"**

In addition to the invaluable travel advice our readers share with us, many are kind enough to offer their services as researchers or editors. Unfortunately, our charter enables us to employ only currently enrolled Harvard students.

Published in Great Britain 2001 by Macmillan, an imprint of Macmillan Publishers Ltd, 25 Eccleston Place, London, SW1W 9NF, Basingstoke and Oxford.
Associated companies throughout the world
www.macmillan.com

Maps by David Lindroth copyright © 2001, 2000, 1999, 1998, 1997, 1996, 1995, 1994, 1993, 1992, 1991, 1990, 1989, 1988 by St. Martin's Press.

Published in the United States of America by St. Martin's Press.

ISBN: 0-333-90137-1
First edition
10 9 8 7 6 5 4 3 2 1

Let's Go: Middle East is written by Let's Go Publications, 67 Mount Auburn Street, Cambridge, MA 02138, USA.

CONTENTS

MAPS

✚ Hospital	✈ Airport	🏛 Museum	▲ Mountain
Police	Bus Station	Hotel/Hostel	Park
Post Office	Train Station	Camping	
Tourist Office	METRO STATION	Food & Drink	Beach
Bank	Ferry Landing	Shopping	
Embassy/Consulate	Church	Arts & Entertainment	Water
Site or Point of Interest	Synagogue	Nightlife	
Telephone Office	Mosque	Internet Café	N
Theater	Castle	Pedestrian Zone	The Let's Go thumb always points NORTH.

RESEARCHER-WRITERS

Joe Chase   *Lebanon*

Committed to making us the only travel guide with updated coverage of South Lebanon, our (no-ordinary) Joe braved army check points, crazed taxi drivers, and sling shots to put us on top. Hard-core traveler *par excellence,* Joe redefined the word "budget." Über-budget Joe's daring attitude translated into plenty of entertaining stories back here in Cambridge.

Sarah Eltantawi   *Syria*

This Egypto-California gal always found time in her already packed schedule to seek out quiet nooks, enjoy the sunset, or sip a nice cup of tea. Super-cool and super-confident, Sarah's inner strength kept her going strong on a lengthy, rough-and-tumble itinerary. Always ultra-conscientious, Sarah blew through Syria before being forced to take a breather (and polish up her already stellar copy) when Assad's funeral shut down Damascus for two weeks.

Rita Hamad   *Islamic Cairo, Aswan, Nile Delta, and the Suez Canal*

Whether battling nasty old fools or nasty old *fuul,* Rita always kept her cool. Lovely Rita sweet-toothed maid revamped our guide's pastry offerings, making sure to sample all the *basbouseh, ba'laweh,* and *kinafeh* along the way. Never one to waste a moment, Rita even wrote up copy while stranded on a *felucca* in the middle of the Nile. In the fight against long-windedness, Rita came out on top; her copy was always short and sweet—just like her.

Arthur Koski-Karell   *Cairo, Alexandria, Luxor, and the Western Desert Oases*

A two-time *Let's Go* vet, Art found that his close encounters with one-legged deviants and desiccated corpses only enriched his experience. One could say that Art was overly dedicated to his job, going so far as to crawl into tombs in order to research them adequately. He was our own little Herodotus, checking and re-checking all historical facts. No hydrophobe and not wishing to be outdone by Rita, Art wrote copy afloat in his flooded hotel room.

Elizabeth White   *Jordan and the Sinai Peninsula*

Battling bad puns and poorly disguised brothels from one end of the desert to the other, this former associate editor of *Let's Go: Europe* knew how to sift through the kitschy sands of the Sinai to unearth *Let's Go* gold (or at least Dahab). Liz's itinerary had her snorkeling one day and working on her tan the next, but when duty called, she skipped off to the Levant on a moment's notice to dish up some of the best coverage of Jordan this book has seen.

Risha K. Lee	*Editor, Israel*
Elizabeth Daniel	*Editor, Turkey*
Siobhan Quinlan	*Associate Editor, Turkey*

Jamie Colbert	*Golan Heights, Gaza, Negev, and Tzfat*
Caitlin Aiko Harrington	*Western Mediterranean, Konya*
Peter Henninger	*İstanbul and Northwestern Turkey*
Inga Hunter	*Northwestern Turkey and Aegean Coast*
Andrew Laming	*Eastern Black Sea Coast and Eastern Anatolia*
Amy Levin	*Mediterranean Coast, Dead Sea, Tel Aviv-Jaffa, and Galilee*
Rachel I. Mason	*Jerusalem, Dead Sea, and West Bank*
Alexander D. Schrank	*North Central Anatolia, Ankara, and the Black Sea Coast*
Selin Tüysüzoğlu	*Cappadocia, Northern Cyprus, and Eastern Mediterranean*

ACKNOWLEDGMENTS

These books don't just put themselves together, you know. They are assembled by machine.

TEAM M.E. THANKS: A haiku. Dear Olivia, you're the best ME we know; now please go to sleep. Thanks to our fabulous R-Ws who made it all happen. Special thanks to Abu Amaal, Dima Reda, and Patrick Gaffney for being honorary researchers. Aarup, Ankur, Anup, Chris B., Alice, Chris R., and everyone at 67 Mt. Auburn St., your keen eyes saved us in the end.

AMÉLIE THANKS: Dima, thanks for helping me come up with good phrases to hurl at felucca captains. Patrick, your help with all things Jordanian was invaluable. Abu Amaal, nice job. Nazette, format manual be damned, with you it was entertainment *before* sights.

JIMMY THANKS: my loving family Mommy, Daddy, Max, Mirele, and Annie. My covers in crime, setting new standards for editing vigilance, Naz, Amélie, and Olivia. Senatorial Thomas Windom, Paul Dilley and his arsenal of Coptic manuscripts, Risha Lee and her Israeli singin', and Marla Kaplan for one long conversation. Jeff Fowler, Benji Flusberg, Dan Saken, Sara Arbogast, and Josh Lambert for your support, and Laura Beth Deason for her advice. Special thanks to Ethan Lebowitz, David Brickman, and Ben Galper. Finally, Herb Snerfler and the Fly for a kickin' party.

NAZ THANKS: Mom and Dad, your loving support keeps me going. Bobbie and Unna, I couldn't have asked for cooler sisters. Parker, thank you for your advice. Kaya and Olivia, your encouragement and understanding eased all that team ME stormed through this summer. Alex, thanks for being a great officemate, especially at the earliest hours of the morning. Amélie and Risha, you are the best podmates, and the best impersonators.

Editors
Amélie Cherlin, Jimmy Davis, Naz Fatemeh Firoz
Managing Editor
Olivia L. Cowley
Map Editor
Filip Wojciechowski

Publishing Director
Kaya Stone
Editor-in-Chief
Kate McCarthy
Production Manager
Melissa Rudolph
Cartography Manager
John Fiore
Editorial Managers
Alice Farmer, Ankur Ghosh,
Aarup Kubal, Anup Kubal
Financial Manager
Bede Sheppard
Low-Season Manager
Melissa Gibson
Marketing & Publicity Managers
Olivia L. Cowley, Esti Iturralde
New Media Manager
Daryush Jonathan Dawid
Personnel Manager
Nicholas Grossman
Photo Editor
Dara Cho
Production Associates
Sanjay Mavinkurve, Nicholas Murphy, Rosalinda Rosalez, Matthew Daniels, Rachel Mason, Daniel Visel
Some Design
Matthew Daniels
Office Coordinators
Sarah Jacoby, Chris Russell

Director of Advertising Sales
Cindy Rodriguez
Senior Advertising Associates
Adam Grant, Rebecca Rendell
Advertising Artwork Editor
Palmer Truelson

President
Andrew M. Murphy
General Manager
Robert B. Rombauer
Assistant General Manager
Anne E. Chisholm

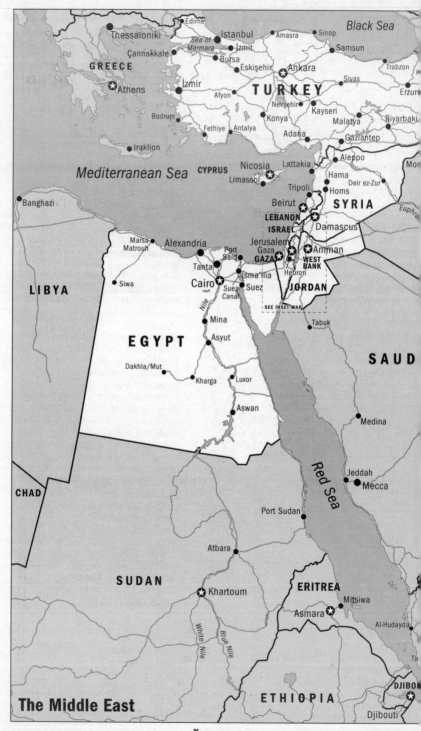

The Middle East

X

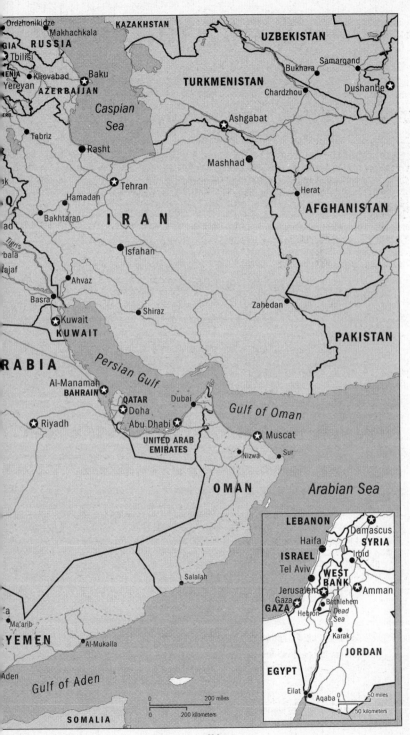

HOW TO USE THIS BOOK

Let's Go: Middle East is a guide to the backpacker's Middle East, overland from Egypt to Turkey and everything in between. If *Let's Go: Middle East* were an animal, it would be a camel. Like a camel, *Let's Go* gets you where you want to go. Like a camel, this book is intelligent, dependable, and on top of things. Like a camel, this book is a delightful shade of yellow. Unlike a camel, this book does not spit.

THE ORGANIZATION OF THIS BOOK

INTRODUCTORY MATERIAL. With that said, meet your camel. The Middle East is huge and may seem daunting to navigate. *Let's Go: Middle East* is also huge and may seem daunting to navigate—don't worry it isn't. First up is **Discover the Middle East,** which includes several sample itineraries maneuvering through everything from ancient plunder to modern wonder. **Essentials** comes next, and lists everything that is... well, essential to making your trip as smooth as possible. Familiarize yourself with the three major world religions, born in the Middle East, by reading our **History of Religion** section, prefaced with the **History of the Middle East,** an overview covering the region's last 10,000 years.

THE "MEAT" (NOT PORK). Next up is coverage of the sights and sounds of seven countries in the Middle East, arranged alphabetically. Along with coverage of **Israel,** you'll find full coverage of the **West Bank** and **Gaza. Cyprus** follows on the heels of **Turkey,** with trips to the cities of Limassol and Paphos, easy ferry trips from Haifa, Israel. Don't miss our exclusive coverage of **South Lebanon,** a region just recently opened up to tourists. Each country chapter begins with general information on the country, including historical and cultural information to help you fit in. Find your way through camel markets or *souqs* in the **Getting Around** section. The **Orientation** section untangles city streets, while **Practical Information** tells you how to get your laundry done, medical assistance, and even check email in the desert. **Accommodations, Food, Sights,** and **Entertainment** sections guide you to the best beds, meals, castles, and discos. At the beginning of every chapter, find out all you need to know to move from one place to another in **Border Crossings.**

APPENDIX. Understand what everyone else around you is saying by checking out the Appendix, which not only includes handy phrases in **Arabic, Hebrew,** and **Turkish,** but also lists holidays, festivals, and telephone codes. To figure out what *zaghrouta* means, flip back to the **Glossary** at the end of the Appendix.

A FEW NOTES ABOUT LET'S GO FORMAT

Our researchers have ranked everything in order of preference, giving a ▨**thumb** to the truly spic-'n'-span rooms, super-scrumptious restaurants, the most soothing *hammams*, the most slow-paced *sheesha* parlors...you get the picture. The phone code for a region or city appears opposite its name and is denoted by the ☎ icon.

Well, that's about it. Travel in the Middle East, like travel on a camel, can be bumpy and requires a lot of water, so drink up, saddle up, and let's get going. We'll help you get over the hump.

A NOTE TO OUR READERS The information for this book was gathered by *Let's Go* researchers from May through August of 2000. Each listing is based on one researcher's opinion, formed during his or her visit at a particular time. Those traveling at other times may have different experiences since prices, dates, hours, and conditions are always subject to change. You are urged to check the facts presented in this book beforehand to avoid inconvenience and surprises.

DISCOVER THE MIDDLE EAST

Gertrude Bell, one of the most famous travelers to the Middle East (see **An English-woman in Arabia,** p. 489), said, "Few such moments of exhilaration can come as that which stands at the threshold of wild travel." The Middle East is, without a doubt, adventure country *par excellence*. Wide expanses of desert dotted with lush green oases, colorful underwater seascapes, and hidden cities carved in stone inspire exploration in the grand tradition of Lawrence of Arabia and Indiana Jones. The Middle East's long-standing and dynamic socio-political canvas is just as colorful as its landscape: ancient civilizations have left rich archaeological records of human struggle and achievement that are no less compelling than the contemporary drama of the Middle East peace process. Five of the seven wonders of the ancient world, numerous relics from three major faiths, and the first written alphabet are only pieces of the historical puzzle. The challenges of politics today range from the preservation of Bedouin traditional lifestyles in modern nation-states like Egypt to the attempts at peace between Israel and the Palestinians. Despite the vast diversity of political views, religious beliefs, and economic status in the region, all of its inhabitants adhere to one very strong belief: the profound importance of hospitality. As a traveler, you will encounter difficulties navigating shifty bus schedules, phantom trains, and stubborn camels. You will take in the Pyramids at Giza, gasp in awe at the lost city of Petra in Jordan, and admire Cappadocia's natural splendor in Turkey. And yet, at the end of the journey, your most striking memory is most likely to be sipping a cup of *ahwa* (coffee) while discussing the meaning of life with a spice vendor in a small corner of a *souq* (market).

FACTS AND FIGURES

PERCENTAGE OF WONDERS OF THE ANCIENT WORLD IN THE MIDDLE EAST: 71.4%

LARGEST BURIAL GROUND IN THE WORLD: Valley of the Mummies, spanning six miles and holding about 10,000 mummies

SINKING RATE OF THE DEAD SEA: 13 inches per year

QUALITY OF PRAYER DURING RAMADAN INSIDE THE DOME OF THE ROCK: 10,000 times more valuable than in any other mosque

WHEN TO GO

Take into account **holidays** when arranging your itinerary (for a list of religious and national holidays, see the **Appendix,** p. 699). In Muslim countries, many businesses close on Fridays. They may close during the afternoon on holidays, but are generally open in the morning. The most important event and the one most likely to complicate travel is **Ramadan** (Nov. 27-Dec. 26 in 2000; Nov. 17-Dec. 15 in 2001), the annual month-long fast during which Muslims abstain from food and drink from dawn to dusk. During this time, most restaurants are closed until sundown. Shops may be open for a few hours in the morning and a short time after *iftar*, the breaking of the fast; government services are either closed entirely or open only in the morning. It would be rude to smoke or eat in public at this time. In Israel, most businesses and public facilities close Friday afternoons for Shabbat, the Jewish sabbath, and reopen at sundown on Saturdays. They also close for Jewish holy days, which begin at sunset on the previous day.

Also think about when everyone else in the region is vacationing. Egypt's high and low seasons depend partly on the region: Cairo is a year-round mob scene, while summertime is partytime in Alexandria and on the Mediterranean and Red Sea beaches. In the Sinai, Oases, and Upper Egypt, reasonable temperatures make winter the high season, but younger travelers revel in summertime bargains. North Americans and students favor summer for visiting Israel and the West Bank; Europeans prefer winter. Jordan's peak seasons are spring and autumn, while Syria and Lebanon receive more visitors in the summer. High tourist season runs between late June and early September in Turkey and Cyprus, bringing throngs of vacationers to Turkey's western coastal regions. If you can stand the climate, off-season travel means smaller crowds, lower prices, and greater local hospitality. For a general temperature chart, see **When to Go,** p. 8. For country-specific temperature charts, see the **Essentials** section for each country.

THINGS TO DO

The Middle East gets a lot of mileage from its historical centrality. But while the Middle East's ancient ruins, religious traditions, and authentic *souqs* are delectable slices of the past upon a backpacker's silver platter, the region contains more than just history. Beirut and Tel Aviv offer hopping, cosmopolitan club scenes, while the sandy shores of the Sinai Peninsula provide a backdrop to satisfy the most reverent beach bunnies. For more specific regional attractions, see **Highlights of the Region,** at the beginning of each chapter.

SUN OF A BEACH

Much of the Middle East embraces the Mediterranean Sea, and cradled in its arms are some amazing beaches. Bodacious **Bodrum** (p. 648) in Turkey is known the world over for its sizzling beaches (matched only by equally sizzling nightlife). For other perspectives on the Mediterranean: party on down with sun-soaked hipsters at youthful **Tel Aviv** (p. 319) in Israel; kick back for a few days in **Jounieh** (p. 526) in Lebanon and **Herzliya** (p. 334) in Israel; and be sure to hop over to the endless, sparkling beaches of **Cyprus** (p. 693), in the heart of the Mediterranean. Don't let the heat get to you: try banana boating, jet-skiing, or parasailing at the intersection of four countries in **Eilat** (p. 418), Israel. Savor the lazy daze of summer in Egypt at **Dahab** (p. 187), one of the many beachside treasures along the coasts of the **Sinai Peninsula** (p. 171), known the world over as a scuba paradise. Tired of jam-packed sands and jammin' discos? Weary travelers can create their own resort and hire a *felucca* to troll down the Nile (p. 209). Continuing northwest, they'll fall into the embrace of countless stretches of undiscovered emerald coast throughout the Middle East: **Marsa Matrouh** (p. 161) in Egypt offers spectacular Mediterranean serenity without the Mediterranean crowds.

SHOP 'TIL YOU DROP

Bargaining is a fact of life in the Middle East, so it makes sense that the region is a shopper's paradise. Almost every city has a *souq*, an outdoor bazaar that sells everything from spices to stilettos. Grab silver and spice and everything nice at the Grand Bazaar in **İstanbul** (p. 616), Turkey; head to **Beirut** (p. 516), Lebanon, for leather and gold; browse the intricately carved boxes and gold jewelry in **Damascus** (p. 566), Syria; and **Cairo** (p. 80), Egypt, is the place for tapestries and *sheeshas*. For less luxurious goods, head to **Petra** (p. 491), Jordan, for beautiful pottery or trek out to the camel markets in **Birqash** (p. 131) or **Daraw** (p. 237), Egypt. At the other extreme, high-end fashions can be found in the sparkling new malls and boutiques of Beirut, while **Israel** (p. 266) is also a haven for shoppers in search of modern luxuries: grab a pair of the world-famous *Naot* sandals anywhere in the country, and pamper yourself with **Dead Sea** (p. 397) mud baths and facial scrubs.

AIN'T NO MOUNTAIN HIGH ENOUGH...

Although the Middle East is better known for rising temperatures than rising peaks, there are many options for the alpine- and hiking-inclined. The **Negev Desert** (p. 406) and **Golan Heights** (p. 389) in Israel offer subtropical paths that cut through cliffside caves and breathtaking *wadis*. No trekking itinerary would be complete without a climb up steep **Mount Sinai** (p. 176) in Egypt. Those interested in ascending the Bible's most famous mountain might also try **Mount Ararat** in Turkey, where Noah's Ark came to rest (p. 690). For those of the skiing persuasion, Lebanon (known as "Little Switzerland" by those in the snow) boasts world-class skiing facilities at the twin resort towns of **Faqra** and **Faraya** (p. 528).

...AIN'T NO VALLEY LOW ENOUGH

What goes up must come down. Take a hike and check out the largest natural crater in the world, **Makhtesh Ramon** (p. 416) in Israel. The depths of the **Dead Sea**, from either the **Israeli** (p. 397) or the **Jordanian** (p. 485) side, may seem like another great place to get down, but be content with floating peacefully on the famed locale's surface.

▧ LET'S GO PICKS

BEST BODY-TO-TOMB RATIO: Nowadays, one body per tomb is standard, but the ancients of **Bab al-Dhira,** Jordan (p. 490), held a slightly different perspective. Their specialized shaft tombs contain 25 bodies a pop.

BEST CRATER: When it slammed into Israel many millennia ago, an asteroid created **Makhtesh Ramon** (p. 416). Measuring a mind-boggling 40km long, 9km wide, and 400m deep, it contains geological formations found nowhere else in the world.

BEST PLACE TO LOOK, NOT TOUCH: Find your inner fish in the legions of brilliantly colored creatures as you flit through coral at the **Yemeniyyeh Reef** in Aqaba (p. 503) or the Red Sea in **Dahab** (p. 187), which rank among the world's best for scoping fish.

BEST WONDER OF THE WORLD: Five of the Seven Wonders of the Ancient World are in the Middle East, but if you only have time for one, head over to the **Pyramids at Giza** in Egypt (p. 130).

BEST CAFE FREQUENTED BY A NOBEL LAUREATE: Smoke *sheesha* and read *Palace Walk* amidst the bustle of Khan al-Khalili at **Fishawi's** (p. 129), the famous teahouse where Naguib Mahfouz spent endless *Arabian Nights and Days.*

BEST MAN-MADE LAKE: The imposing Aswan High Dam doubled Egypt's electrical output. It also created the 200m-deep **Lake Nasser** (p. 248), the world's largest artificial lake.

BEST SEMITIC LANGUAGE: Tongue-tied? Head to Ma'alula (p. 578) in Syria, where **Aramaic**, the language in which Jesus preached, is still spoken.

BEST REASON TO FINISH YOUR SPINACH: For the sweet tooth in you, dream your way into **El 'Abd** in Cairo (p. 100) for the creamiest whopping three scoops of ice cream you've ever had. **Arafat Sweets** (p. 445) glazes the stickiest buns in Gaza City.

BEST TOILET SEAT VIEW: Speaking of buns, don't miss valuable sight-seeing minutes while on the can. The **Nabatean Museum** (p. 497) offers stunning, stall-side views of Petra, Jordan.

BEST MESSY FESTIVAL: Slide on over to the **Kırkpınar Grease Wrestling Festival** in Edirne, Turkey (p. 629), where competitors from all over Turkey don giant leather breeches, slather themselves in oil, and hit the mats.

BEST MONOCHROME ESTABLISHMENT: No more singing the blues. Spend your blue period in the cheerfully decorated **Ambassador Hotel** in Syria (p. 598).

SUGGESTED ITINERARIES

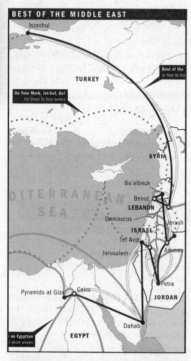

BEST OF THE MIDDLE EAST

Duke once swung it in 4/4 time. Next up is **Amman,** Jordan (p. 458), an excellent jumping off point to the rock-hewn wonders of **Jerash** (p. 473) and lost **Petra** (p. 491). Check in at Amman again on the way over to Israel, where your visit won't be complete without a stopover in **Jerusalem** (p. 278). Whether it's mosques, churches, or nightclubs, Jerusalem beats most other cities in the region. Plan to spend a few days here at least, if only to rest up before heading out to **Tel Aviv,** "The City That Never Takes a Break" (p. 319). Before you get down at the city's cutting edge cut-a-rug hotspots, treat your homesick taste buds to a panoply of non-falafel foods in any of the city's ethnic neighborhoods. Cross over to the **Sinai Peninsula** (p. 171) and tan your tired limbs in **Dahab** (p. 187) before diving into the azure depths of the Red Sea for some of the best snorkeling in the world. Finish your whirlwind tour of the region in equally tempestuous **Cairo** (p. 80) where beautiful, historic neighborhoods are sprawled out in the shadow of the **Pyramids at Giza** (p. 130).

1. BEST OF THE MIDDLE EAST (4-5 WEEKS)

For those who want to sample everything the Middle East has to offer and more, this is for you. Start your journey in **İstanbul** (p. 616), where you can wander through old markets and bargain for gold, spices, and carpets amidst mosques and Ottoman palaces. Let Aya Sofia, the church transformed into a mosque and then finally into a museum, and the Blue Mosque take you from the past to the present. After a few heated days of sightseeing, cool off at a *hammam* (Turkish bath) before hopping a bus to **Damascus,** Syria (p. 566), the oldest continually inhabited city in the world. Shake it on over to fun 'n' funky **Beirut** (p. 516) in Lebanon. Party until dawn, then catch a breather at **Ba'albeck** (p. 540), the unforgettable home of some righteous ruins and host to an internationally-known jazz festival where Ella and the

2. ON YOUR MARK, JET-SET, GO! (3-4 WEEKS)

Jet-set like a pro while boning up on your ancient history with this supersonic tour of the Mediterranean. Dive into the sea of mosques and spice markets in **İstanbul** (p. 616), immerse yourself in one of the city's many famous *hammams,* then make a splash at the many bars and "nomadic" discotheques. Head south to the massive classical ruins at **Ephesus** (p. 640), a notable ancient city which boasts a concentration of art and architecture surpassed only by Rome and Athens. Continue along the coast to the secluded coves and beaches of sunny **Bodrum** (p. 648). After partying until dawn in the city's many discotheques, shake it on over to **Antalya** (p. 660) and the **Turquoise Riviera,** Turkey's premiere tourist resort. Take a breather in the charming markets and tea gardens of **Antakya** (p. 663), then cross the border into Syria. Check out the birthplace of ancient and modern alphabets at **Ugarit**

(p. 591) before day-tripping to the spectacular Crusader castle at **Crac des Chevaliers** (p. 586). Ease your way back into modern life on the streets of leisurely **Tripoli** (p. 532), where you're sure to be taken in by the city's famed Lebanese sweets and even more famous Lebanese hospitality. Take a breath of fresh air at **Bcharré** (p. 538), a tranquil mountain town 1400 meters above sea level. After stopping over at the ever-popular **Cedars of Lebanon** (p. 539) for world-class skiing and snowboarding in the winter, party on down at any one of the many hipster cafes, casinos, and discos in thrill-a-minute **Beirut** (p. 516) and its hip sister **Jounieh** (p. 526). Pass through the oldest continually inhabited city in the world, **Damascus,** Syria (p. 566), then muscle your way through the crowded traffic circles of **Amman,** Jordan (p. 458). Mud-bathe and float your way along the **Dead Sea** (p. 485) en route to the calm seaside port of **Haifa** in Israel (p. 338). Lay out on serene beaches with even more laid-back locals before heading to **Tel Aviv** (p. 319), a city that lives for the moment, grooving on beaches, in boutiques, and in booty-shaking dance halls. Ferry over to **Cyprus** (p. 693), where you can wander along unforgettable beaches and breezy mountains and trek through twisted streets in search of ancient ruins. Finish your Mediterranean tour in the warm embrace of the vibrant seaside city of **Alexandria,** Egypt (p. 144), and be sure to travel a few hours west to the sleepy resorts and busy markets of the town of **Marsa Matrouh** (p. 161).

3. WALK LIKE AN EGYPTIAN (4 WEEKS)

This is your chance to take part in a timeless adventure through the past and present. Hop on a train from Cairo to **Aswan** (p. 237), a city famous for its alabaster. You will love Aswan's unique Nubian flavor, which plays a large part in the surrounding villages and the comprehensive Nubian Museum, as well as its proximity to the ruins at Philae. Once you've had enough of Aswan, book a flight down to **Abu Simbel** (p. 250) to see some of the most awe-inspiring colossal remains in the world. Next on the ruins list is **Luxor** (p. 212), once the capital of ancient Egypt. It would take the rest of this page to list all that Luxor has to offer; make sure to see the Valley of the Kings or the tomb of Queen Nefertari. Though pricey, the latter attraction is Egypt's prized possession. Take a break from all the ruins by taking a leisurely *felucca* cruise up the Nile. Once you reach the town of Asyut, go west, pardner, and trek through the unforgettable desert oases, starting in the White Desert outside lush **Dakhla** (p. 257), then pause in **Farafra** (p. 256) before exploring the hot springs of **Bahariyya** (p. 253). Emerge from the

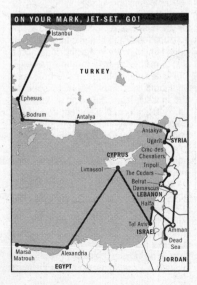

ON YOUR MARK, JET-SET, GO!

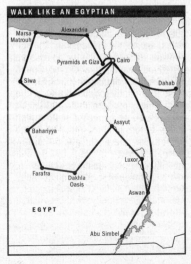

WALK LIKE AN EGYPTIAN

vast expanses of the western desert into bustling **Cairo** (p. 80), the largest city in the Middle East and Africa. The labyrinthine streets of the city are filled with beautiful mosques and churches, frenzied *souqs* where bargains abound, and a mile-a-minute nightlife unlike anything else in Egypt. The majestic pyramids at **Giza** (p. 130) are also an easy daytrip from the city. The cosmopolitan calm of **Alexandria** (p. 144) may seem a shock after Cairo, but you'll fall easily enough into the beachside city's evening-strolling, *sheesha*-smoking pace. Head west from Alexandria and discover the dazzling Mediterranean gem that is **Marsa Matrouh** (p. 161), a resort town rarely visited by tourists except as a base to the verdant **Siwa Oasis** (p. 165). Return to Cairo and catch a bus to the **Sinai Peninsula** (p. 171), where you can find your inner fish by diving and snorkeling through world-famous coral reefs, and kick back with the nomadic Bedouin near **Dahab** (p. 187).

4. OLDIES BUT GOODIES
(4 WEEKS)

If you've always wanted to jump in a time machine, now you can: journey back in time to the ancient Levant. Begin in Syria, where the ancient trade center of **Aleppo** (p. 595) has wowed visitors since Ottoman times with its colossal Citadel and covered *souqs*. Springboard from Aleppo to the **Basilica of St. Simeon** (p. 600), a sacred stopover for Christian pilgrims since the 4th century, and **Ebla** (p. 601), the oldest of the old cities. The queen of **Palmyra** (p. 580), in central Syria, once rebelled against the Romans, and the stupendous ruins of her city have also resisted the wear and tear of time. Spend a few days in **Damascus** (p. 566), the oldest continually inhabited city in the world—now a modern metropolis, but once the majestic capital of the Umayyad Empire—before jumping the border into Lebanon, where everything is but a day-hop from **Beirut** (p. 516). The Roman ruins and Crusader Castle in **Byblos** (p. 529) have toughed it out through centuries of bombardment; the town itself is so old that even the ancients considered it an ancient city. The Roman Temple of Bacchus in **Ba'albeck** (p. 540), east of Beirut, is one of the most celebrated in the world, and the Deir al-Maroun fortress in neighboring **Hermel** (p. 543) satisfies the independent explorer. Near the southern town of Sur, archaeologists have unearthed **Tyre** (p. 548), one of the great Phoenician city-states. Cut through **Amman,** Jordan (p. 458), and shimmy over to **Jerusalem** (p. 278), whose timeless wonders speak for themselves. Head for the **Dead Sea** region, the lowest point on earth (p. 485) and explore King Herod's palace in **Masada** (p. 402). Hungry for more Herod? His greatest achievement was the splendid city of **Caesarea** (p. 353), where Pontius Pilate ordered Christ's crucifixion in 33 CE. Back in Jordan, adventure like Lawrence of Arabia in 1500-year-old desert castles near **Azraq** (p. 481), then journey down the King's Highway to the Nabatean city of **Petra** (p. 491), whose rocky glory was lost to the world for centuries.

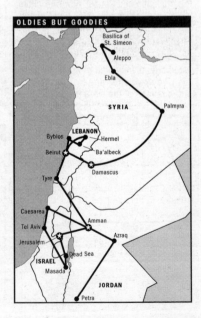

OLDIES BUT GOODIES

5. BEST OF TURKEY
(3 WEEKS)

THE BEST OF TURKEY

Turkey is quite large, but here is what you need to see. Begin in **İstanbul** (p. 616), the traditional gateway to Turkey. You'll bargain for Turkish Delight at the Grand Bazaar (p. 627), marvel at luxurious Ottoman palaces, and stand awed in Aya Sofia (p. 624). For post-sightseeing sweets, tea, and backgammon, head to one of İstanbul's chic waterfront cafes. Need a break from the city? The Bosphorus ferry will take you past stately waterfront mansions, stopping for fresh fish sandwiches and fried mussels along the way. **Edirne** (p. 629), the quietly proud former Ottoman capital, is now the capital of tea gardens and breathtaking architecture, including the finest mosque in all of Turkey. Then step off the beaten track and enjoy the serene beaches and small-town atmosphere of **Bozcaada** (p. 634), an Aegean island that has been producing wine since antiquity. Speaking of antiquity, the sparkling Aegean Coast houses the sun-bleached ruins of some of the ancient world's most powerful cities, including **Bergama** (p. 636) and the eternally-popular **Ephesus** (p. 640). **Kuşadası** (p. 636) lends new meaning to the phrase "Mediterranean party town,"

but it's really **Bodrum** (p. 648) that knows how to boogie down every night, all night. On the morning after, head to the secluded blue lagoon in **Ölüdeniz** (p. 657) to recover. Allow the waterfalls and butterflies of the nearby **Butterfly Valley** (p. 657) to enchant you before continuing along the Turkish Riviera. **Kaş** (p. 657) hosts the Mediterranean's only seal colony. Then on to **Demre** (p. 658) to explore the Basilica of St. Nicholas, a.k.a. Santa Claus. Scramble among the rock tombs of nearby **Myra** (p. 658). In **Göreme** (p. 670) and **Ürgüp** (p. 675) end your Turkish visit with the grand finale that is **Cappadocia:** a fantasy-world of underground cities, cave churches, and fairy chimneys.

ESSENTIALS

FACTS FOR THE TRAVELER

WHEN TO GO

AVERAGE TEMPERATURE AND PRECIPITATION											
	JANUARY			APRIL			JULY			OCTOBER		
	°C	°F	mm	°C	°F	mm	°C	°F	mm	°C	°F	mm
Cairo (Egypt)	13.8	56.8	5.1	21.4	70.5	1.5	27.9	82.2	0	23.7	74.7	1
Jerusalem (Israel)	8.1	46.6	132	15.7	60.3	28	23.5	74.3	0	20.3	68.5	13
Amman (Jordan)	7.9	46.2	63	15.8	60.4	17	25.1	77.2	0	20.2	68.4	6
Damascus (Syria)	6.5	43.7	39	16.6	50.9	13	26.7	80.1	0	18.9	60.6	9
Beirut (Lebanon)	13.5	56.3	195	18.5	65.3	48z	27.1	80.8	1	23.8	74.8	35
Istanbul (Turkey)	5.6	42.1	95	11.4	52.5	44	23.3	73.9	19	15.6	60.1	53
Limassol (Cyprus)	11.5	52.7	105	17.0	62.6	22	26.4	79.5	1	22.4	72.3	24

The Middle East experiences hot, dry summers and cool, wet winters. Travel during the spring or autumn to avoid excessive heat and rain. For country-specific information on when to go, see the Essentials section for individual countries.

DOCUMENTS AND FORMALITIES

ENTRANCE REQUIREMENTS.
Passport (p. 8). Required for all travelers.
Visa (p. 10). Required for citizens of Western countries.
Letter of Invitation. Not required.
Inoculations: (p. 20). Polio, hepatitis A, immune globulin (IG), typhoid, and cholera vaccines. Malaria pills recommended.
Work Permit/Visa (p. 10). Required.
Driving Permit (p. 37). Required for all countries, but rules may not be enforced.

CONSULAR SERVICES

For information on Middle Eastern **embassies and consulates** abroad as well as foreign embassies and consulates in the Middle East, see the Essentials section of individual country chapters.

PASSPORTS

REQUIREMENTS. Citizens of Australia, Canada, Ireland, New Zealand, South Africa, the UK, and the US need valid passports to enter Middle Eastern countries and to reenter their own countries. Most countries do not allow entrance if the holder's passport expires within six months; returning home with an expired passport is illegal, and may result in a fine.

PHOTOCOPIES. Be sure to photocopy the page of your passport with your photo, passport number, and other identifying information, as well as any visas, travel insurance policies, plane tickets, or traveler's check serial numbers. Carry one set of copies in a safe place, apart from the originals, and leave another set at home. Consulates also recommend that you carry an expired passport or an official copy of your birth certificate separate from other documents.

LOST PASSPORTS. If you lose your passport, immediately notify the local police and the nearest embassy or consulate of your home government. To expedite its replacement, you will need to know all information previously recorded and show ID and proof of citizenship. In some cases, a replacement may take weeks to process, and it may be valid only for a limited time. Any visas stamped in your old passport will be irretrievably lost. In an emergency, ask for immediate temporary traveling papers that will permit you to reenter your home country. Your passport is a public document belonging to your nation's government. You may have to surrender it to a foreign government official, but if you don't get it back in a reasonable amount of time, inform the nearest mission of your home country.

NEW PASSPORTS. File any new passport or renewal applications well in advance of your departure date. Most passport offices offer rush services for a steep fee, which may not even reach you in time. Citizens living abroad who need a passport or renewal should contact the nearest consular service of their home country.

Australia: Info ☎ 13 12 32; email passports.australia@dfat.gov.au; www.dfat.gov.au/passports. Apply for a passport at a post office, passport office (in Adelaide, Brisbane, Canberra, Darwin, Hobart, Melbourne, Newcastle, Perth, or Sydney), or overseas diplomatic mission. Passports AUS$128 (32-page) or AUS$192 (64-page); valid for 10 years. Children AUS$64 (32-page) or AUS$96 (64-page); valid for five years.

Canada: Canadian Passport Office, Department of Foreign Affairs and International Trade, Ottawa, ON K1A 0G3 (☎(613) 994-3500 or (800) 567-6868; www.dfait-maeci.gc.ca/passport). Applications available at post offices, passport offices, and Canadian missions. Passports CDN$60; valid for 5 years (non-renewable).

Ireland: Pick up an application at a *Garda* station or post office, or request one from a passport office. Apply by mail to the Department of Foreign Affairs, Passport Office, Molesworth St., Dublin 2 (☎(01) 671 1633; fax 671 1092; www.irlgov.ie/iveagh), or the Passport Office, Irish Life Building, 1A South Mall, Cork (☎(021) 27 25 25). Passports IR£45; valid for 10 years. Under 18 or over 65 IR£10; valid for 3 years.

New Zealand: Send applications to the Passport Office, Department of International Affairs, P.O. Box 10526, Wellington, New Zealand (☎(0800) 22 50 50 or (4) 474 81 00; fax (4) 474 80 10; email passports@dia.govt.nz; www.passports.govt.nz). Standard processing time is 10 working days. Passports NZ$80; valid for 10 years. Children NZ$40; valid for five years. Three day "urgent service" NZ$160; children NZ $120.

South Africa: Department of Home Affairs. Passports are issued only in Pretoria, but all applications must still be submitted or forwarded to the nearest South African consulate. Processing time is 3 months or more. Passports around SAR80; valid for 10 years. Under 16 around SAR60; valid for five years. For more information, http://usaembassy.southafrica.net/VisaForms/Passport/Passport2000.html.

United Kingdom: Info ☎(0870) 521 0410; www.open.gov.uk/ukpass/ukpass.htm. Get an application from a passport office, main post office, travel agent, or online (for UK residents only) at www.ukpa.gov.uk/forms/f_app_pack.htm. Then apply by mail to or in person at a passport office. Passports UK£28; valid for 10 years. Under 15 UK£14.80; valid for five years. The process takes about 4 weeks; faster service (by personal visit to the offices listed above) costs an additional £12.

United States: Info ☎(202) 647-0518; www.travel.state.gov/passport_services.html. Apply at any federal or state courthouse, authorized post office, or US Passport Agency (in most major cities); see the "US Government, State Department" section of the telephone book or a post office for addresses. Processing takes 3-4 weeks. New passports US$60; valid for 10 years. Under 16 US$40; valid for 5 years. Passports may be renewed by mail or in person for US$40. Add US$35 for 3-day expedited service.

VISAS, INVITATIONS, AND WORK PERMITS

VISAS. As of August 2000, citizens of Australia, Canada, Ireland, New Zealand, South Africa, the UK, and the US need a visa—a stamp, sticker, or insert in your passport specifying the purpose of your travel and the permitted duration of your stay—in addition to a valid passport for entrance to Middle Eastern countries; citizens of South Africa do not need visas in Egypt. Price, cost, and other visa details for each Middle Eastern country can be found in the country-specific essentials section. US citizens can take advantage of the **Center for International Business and Travel (CIBT;** ☎(800) 925-2428), which secures visas for travel to almost all countries for a variable service charge.

Be sure to double-check on entrance requirements at the nearest embassy or consulate for up-to-date information before departure. US citizens can also consult www.pueblo.gsa.gov/cic_text/travel/foreign/foreignentryreqs.html.

VISA REQS		AUS	IRE	NZ	SA	UK	US
	EGYPT	Y	Y	Y	N	Y	Y
	ISRAEL	Y	Y	Y	Y	Y	Y
	JORDAN	Y	Y	Y	Y	Y	Y
	LEBANON	Y	Y	Y	Y	Y	Y
	SYRIA	Y	Y	Y	Y	Y	Y
	TURKEY	Y	Y	Y	Y	Y	Y
	CYPRUS	Y	Y	Y	Y	Y	Y

WORK PERMITS. Admission as a visitor does not include the right to work, which is authorized only by a special business visa and/or work permit. Entering Middle Eastern countries to study requires a special permit. For more information, see **Alternatives to Tourism,** p. 42.

IDENTIFICATION

When you travel, carry two or more forms of identification on your person, including at least one photo ID; a passport combined with a driver's license or birth certificate is usually adequate. Many establishments, especially banks, may require several IDs in order to cash traveler's checks. Never carry all your forms of ID together; split them up in case of theft or loss. It is useful to bring extra passport-size photos to affix to the various IDs or passes you may acquire along the way.

STUDENT AND TEACHER IDENTIFICATION. The **International Student Identity Card (ISIC),** the most widely accepted form of student ID, provides discounts on sights, accommodations, food, and transport. The ISIC is preferable to an institution-specific card (such as a university ID) because it is more likely to be recognized (and honored) abroad. All cardholders have access to a 24-hour emergency helpline for medical, legal, and financial emergencies (in North America call ☎(877) 370-ISIC, elsewhere call US collect ☎+1 (715) 345-0505), and US cardholders are also eligible for insurance benefits (see **Insurance,** p. 24). Many student travel agencies issue ISICs, including STA Travel in Australia and New Zealand; Travel CUTS in Canada; USIT in the Republic of Ireland and Northern Ireland; SASTS in South Africa; Campus Travel and STA Travel in the UK; Council Travel (www.counciltravel.com/idcards/default.asp) and STA Travel in the US (see p. 30). The card is valid from September of one year to December of the following year and costs AUS$15, CDN$15, or US$20. Applicants must be degree-seeking students of a secondary or post-secondary school and must be of at least 12 years of age. Because of the proliferation of fake ISICs, some services (particularly airlines) require additional proof of student identity, such as a school ID or a letter attesting to your student status, signed by your registrar and stamped with your school seal. The **International Teacher Identity Card (ITIC)** offers the same insurance coverage as well as similar but limited discounts. The fee is AUS$13, UK£5, or US$20. For more info, contact the **International Student Travel Confederation (ISTC),** Herengracht 479, 1017 BS Amsterdam, Netherlands (☎+31 (20) 421 28 00; fax 421 28 10; email istcinfo@istc.org; www.istc.org).

YOUTH IDENTIFICATION. The International Student Travel Confederation issues a discount card to travelers who are 26 years old or under, but are not students. This one-year **International Youth Travel Card** (**IYTC;** formerly the **GO 25** Card) offers many of the same benefits as the ISIC. Most organizations that sell the ISIC also sell the IYTC (US$20).

CUSTOMS

Upon entering the Middle East, you must declare certain items from abroad and pay a duty on the value of those articles that exceed the allowance established by customs service. Keeping receipts for purchases made abroad will help establish values when you return. Make a list, including serial numbers, of carried valuables from home; if you register this list with customs before your departure and have an official stamp it, you will avoid import duty charges and ensure an easy passage upon your return. Upon returning home, you must declare all articles acquired abroad and pay a **duty** on the value of articles that exceed the allowance established by your country's customs service. Goods and gifts purchased at **duty-free** shops abroad are not exempt from duty or sales tax at your point of return; you must declare these items as well. For more specific information on customs requirements, contact the customs information center in your country.

MONEY

CURRENCY AND EXCHANGE

As a general rule, it's cheaper to convert money at your Middle East destination than at home. You should bring enough foreign currency, however, to last for the first 24 to 72 hours of a trip to avoid being penniless should you arrive after bank hours or on a holiday. Travelers from the US can get foreign currency from the comfort of home: **International Currency Express** (☎(888) 278-6628; www.foreign-money.com) delivers foreign currency or traveler's checks overnight (US$15) or second-day (US$12) at competitive exchange rates.

When changing money abroad, try banks that have at most a 5% margin between their buy and sell prices. You lose money with every transaction, so convert large sums (unless the currency is depreciating rapidly), but no more than you'll need.

If you use traveler's checks or bills, carry some in small denominations (the equivalent of US$50 or less) for times when you are forced to exchange money at disadvantageous rates, but bring a range of denominations since charges may be levied per check cashed. Store your money in a variety of forms; ideally, you should carry some cash, traveler's checks, and an ATM and/or credit card. Travelers should also consider carrying US dollars (about US$50 worth), which are often preferred by local tellers. In the Middle East, US currency is often preferred to local, but avoid using US money when you can. Throwing dollars around for preferential treatment may be offensive, and it can attract thieves. It also marks you as a foreigner and invites many locals to jack up prices.

TRAVELER'S CHECKS

Traveler's checks (**American Express** and **Visa**) are one of the safest and least troublesome means of carrying funds. Several agencies and banks sell them for a small commission. Each agency provides refunds if your checks are lost or stolen, and many provide additional services, such as toll-free refund hotlines abroad, emergency message services, and stolen credit card assistance.

Buying traveler's checks in the currency of the country you are visiting can be an exercise in futility in the Middle East. Lebanon and Syria accept only specific types of traveler's checks. **American Express** is the most widely recognized, and in some cities it is the only type accepted by businesses and banks. All other countries accept checks much more widely. The most readily accepted checks are in US dollars and British pounds (the German mark will sometimes be taken as well); checks in other currencies won't get you very far—if a place will exchange it, you'll probably get a terrible rate.

While traveling, keep check receipts and records of which checks you've cashed separate from the checks themselves. Also leave a list of check numbers with someone at home. Never countersign checks until you're ready to cash them, and always bring your passport with you to cash them. If your checks are lost or stolen, immediately contact a refund center (of the company that issued your checks) to be reimbursed; they may require a police report verifying the loss or theft. Less-touristed countries may not have refund centers at all, in which case you might have to wait to be reimbursed. Ask about toll-free refund hotlines and the location of refund centers when purchasing checks, and always carry emergency cash.

American Express: Call ☎(800) 251 902 in Australia; in New Zealand ☎(0800) 44 10 68; in the UK ☎(0800) 52 13 13; in the US and Canada ☎(800) 221-7282. Elsewhere call US collect ☎+1 (801) 964-6665; www.aexp.com. Traveler's checks are available at 1-4% commission at AmEx offices and banks, commission-free at AAA offices (see p. 37). *Cheques for Two* can be signed by either of two people traveling together.

Citicorp: In the US and Canada call ☎(800) 645-6556; in Europe, the Middle East, or Africa call the UK ☎+44 (020) 7508 7007; elsewhere call US collect ☎+1 (813) 623-1709. Traveler's checks available in seven currencies at 1-2% commission. Call 24hr.

Thomas Cook MasterCard: In the US and Canada call ☎(800) 223-7373; in the UK call ☎(0800) 62 21 01; elsewhere call UK collect ☎+44 (1733) 31 89 50. Checks available in 13 currencies at 2% commission. Thomas Cook offices cash checks commission-free. The only Thomas Cook offices are in Cairo, Alexandria, and Port Said, all in Egypt. The Cairo office is at 33 Nabil al-Wakkad St. (☎(202) 414 12 60; fax 417 13 63).

Visa: In the US call ☎(800) 227-6811; in the UK call ☎(0800) 89 50 78; elsewhere call UK collect ☎+44 (1733) 31 89 49. Call for the location of their nearest office.

CREDIT CARDS

Where they are accepted, credit cards often offer superior exchange rates—up to 5% better than the retail rate used by banks and other currency exchange establishments. Credit cards may also offer services such as insurance or emergency help, and are sometimes required to reserve hotel rooms or rental cars. **MasterCard** and **Visa** are the most welcomed; **American Express** cards work at some ATMs and at AmEx offices and major airports. Budget travelers will find that few of the establishments they frequent accept credit cards; aside from the occasional splurge, you will probably reserve use of your credit card for financial emergencies.

Credit cards are also useful for **cash advances,** which allow you to withdraw currency from associated banks and ATMs throughout the Middle East instantly. Check the individual country listings for country-specific information on credit card acceptance. Note that transaction fees for all credit card advances (up to US$10 per advance, plus 2-3% extra on foreign transactions after conversion) tend to make credit cards a more costly way of withdrawing cash than ATMs or traveler's checks. In an emergency, however, the transaction fee may prove worth the cost. To be eligible for an advance, you'll need to get a **Personal Identification Number (PIN)** from your credit card company (see **Cash (ATM) Cards,** below). Be sure to check with your credit card company before you leave home; in certain circumstances, companies have started to charge foreign transaction fees.

CREDIT CARD COMPANIES. Visa (US ☎(800) 336-8472) and **MasterCard** (US ☎(800) 307-7309) are issued in cooperation with banks and other organizations. **American Express** (US ☎(800) 843-2273) has an annual fee of up to US$55. AmEx cardholders may cash personal checks at AmEx offices abroad, access an emergency medical and legal assistance hotline (24hr.; in North America call ☎(800) 554-

2639, elsewhere call US collect ☎+1 (202) 554-2639), and enjoy American Express Travel Service benefits (including plane, hotel, and car rental reservation changes; baggage loss and flight insurance; mailgram and international cable services; and held mail). The **Discover Card** (in US call ☎(800) 347-2683, elsewhere call US ☎+1 (801) 902-3100) offers small cashback bonuses on most purchases, but it is not nearly as accepted in the Middle East.

CASH (ATM) CARDS

Cash cards—popularly called ATM cards—are fairly widespread in the Middle East. Depending on the system that your home bank uses, you can most likely access your personal bank account from abroad. ATMs get the same wholesale exchange rate as credit cards, but there is often a limit on the amount of money you can withdraw per day (around US$500), and unfortunately computer networks sometimes fail. There is typically also a surcharge of US$1-5 per withdrawal. Be sure to memorize your PIN code in numeric form since machines elsewhere often don't have letters on their keys. Also, if your PIN is longer than four digits, ask your bank whether you need a new number.

The two major international money networks are **Cirrus** (US ☎(800) 424-7787) and **PLUS** (US ☎(800) 843-7587). To locate ATMs around the world, call the above numbers, or consult www.visa.com/pd/atm or www.mastercard.com/atm. The following banks accept Cirrus cards: in Egypt, Banque Misr; in Israel, Bank Hapoalim, Bank Mizrahi, and Bank Yhav; in Lebanon, Crédit Libanais, Bank Lebanon, and Gulf Bank; in Turkey, Türkiye is Bankansi and Yapi ve Kredi Bankasi. The following banks accept PLUS cards: in Egypt, Banque Misr and Egyptian British Bank; in Israel, Bank Hapoalim, Discount Bank, Bank Leumi, and Bank Mizrahi; in Jordan, Housing Bank; in Lebanon, Credit Libanais and British Bank of the Middle East; in Turkey, Türkiye is Bankansi and Yapi ve Kredi Bankasi; in Cyprus, Bank of Cyprus and Cyprus Popular Bank.

Visa TravelMoney is a system allowing you to access money from any Visa ATM, common in major Middle Eastern cities outside of Syria. You deposit an amount before you travel (plus a small administration fee), and you can withdraw up to that sum. The cards, which give you the same favorable exchange rate for withdrawals as a regular Visa, are especially useful if you plan to travel to many countries. Check with your local bank. **Road Cash** (US ☎(877) 762-3227; www.roadcash.com) issues cards in the US with a minimum US$300 deposit.

GETTING MONEY FROM HOME

AMERICAN EXPRESS. Cardholders can withdraw cash from their checking accounts at any major AmEx office and many representative offices (up to US$1000 every 21 days; no service charge; no interest). AmEx "Express Cash" only works in Israel, where there are AmEx ATM's. Withdrawals from any AmEx ATM are automatically debited from the cardholder's checking account or line of credit. Green card holders may withdraw up to US$1000 in any seven-day period (2% transaction fee; minimum US$2.50; maximum US$20). To enroll in Express Cash, cardmembers may call ☎(800) 227-4669 in the US; elsewhere call the US collect ☎+1 (336) 668-5041. AmEx national numbers are the AmEx office numbers in each country. Consult the country-specific sections for those listings.

WESTERN UNION. Travelers from the US, Canada, and the UK can wire money abroad through Western Union's international money transfer services. In the US, call ☎(800) 325-6000; in Canada, ☎(800) 235-0000; in the UK, ☎(0800) 833 833; in Egypt ☎(202) 356 05 61; in Israel ☎(9722) 629 05 21; in Jordan, ☎(9626) 461 90 42; in Lebanon ☎(9611) 39 10 00; in Turkey ☎(90212) 213 19 58; and in Cyprus ☎(357) 237 52 82. Western Union does not wire money to Syria. To wire money within the US using a credit card (V, MC, Discover), call ☎(800) CALL-CASH (225-5227). The rates for sending cash are generally US$10-11 cheaper than with a credit card, and the money is usually available at the place you're sending it to within an hour. To locate the nearest Western Union location, consult www.westernunion.com.

FEDERAL EXPRESS. Some people choose to send money abroad in cash via FedEx to avoid transmission fees and taxes. In the US and Canada, call ☎(800) 463-3339; in the UK, ☎(0800) 12 38 00; in Ireland, ☎(800) 53 58 00; in Australia, 13 26 10; in New Zealand, ☎(0800) 73 33 39; and in South Africa, ☎(021) 551 76 10. While FedEx is reliable, note that this method is illegal and somewhat risky.

US STATE DEPARTMENT (US CITIZENS ONLY). In dire emergencies, the US State Department forwards money within hours to the nearest consular office, which will then disburse it according to instructions for a US$15 fee. Contact the Overseas Citizens Service, American Citizens Services, Consular Affairs, Room 4811, US Department of State, Washington, D.C. 20520 (☎(202) 647-5225; nights, Sundays, and holidays 647-4000; http://travel.state.gov).

MONEY. If you stay in hostels and prepare simple meals for yourself, expect to spend about US$15 per person per day. Starting prices for budget accommodations run anywhere from US$3 per night in an Istanbul hostel to US$15 per night in Beirut. A basic sit-down meal costs at least US$2. Carry cash with you, and have small bills on hand while visiting sights or wandering the streets of a town. Most officials like *bakhsheesh* (see below) and most stores, *service* drivers, and the like cannot (or won't bother to) make change. No one to whom you are giving *bakhsheesh* will give you change. Keep small bills separately from larger bills, so that people cannot point to your stash and demand more.

TIPPING AND BARGAINING

Bargaining and tipping (called *bakhsheesh* in the Middle East) will be encouraged (at times expected) everywhere you go in the Middle East. There are three kinds of *bakhsheesh*. The most common is similar to tipping—a small reward for a small service. *Bakhsheesh* becomes most useful when used to procure special favors. The second kind of *bakhsheesh* is the giving of alms. There are beggars everywhere in the Middle East who are willing to bestow rhetorical blessings in return for a little charity. There are also those who insist on opening a door before you can get to it or snatch your baggage from your hands and then demand *bakhsheesh*. Don't feel obligated to give money in these situations. The final form of *bakhsheesh* is simply a bribe, a bad idea. Don't bribe government officials. For country-specific information on *bakhsheesh*, consult individual country listings.

EGYPT. *Bakhsheesh* is your key to happiness in Egypt. The standard tip in a restaurant is usually included in the bill as a 10-15% service charge. Anything more on top of the bill is not expected. Taxi or *service* drivers do not expect tips. *Bakhsheesh* is also useful when sightseeing, as many places do not provide tour guides. The alternative is to find a local to show you around for some *bakhsheesh*. Egypt is a great place to bargain; use your skills in the bazaars.

ISRAEL. Tipping in Israel is increasingly moving toward American standards, but for the time being, a 10% tip will suffice in restaurants, bars, and hotels. Check whether a service charge is already included in the bill: in restaurants, gratuity is frequently included for parties of six or more. Taxis are for the most part metered. Taxi drivers do not expect tips but accept them. Bargaining in Israel is the norm. There are very few places where you can't bargain: the "no's" are limited for the most part to department stores, drug stores, and supermarkets. Ask hostel owners if they offer any "discounts." Chances are they'll knock 5% or 10% of the price. Do not bargain in restaurants with fixed-price menus, or in stores where prices are barcoded as opposed to hand-labeled.

JORDAN. The appropriate tip in a restaurant is about 15%, and it is often included in the bill. For transportation, don't feel obligated to tip *service* drivers, but make sure to tip taxi drivers if you haven't already agreed on a price. Usually, metered taxis do not require an extra service charge. Like most Middle Eastern countries, bargaining is also crucial in Jordan for getting the best possible price.

LEBANON. In restaurants, gratuity is often included, but if not, 15-20% is expected. It is not the norm to tip *service* drivers in Lebanon.

SYRIA. Gratuity is never included in restaurant bills in Syria, and 10% is adequate for both restaurants and drivers. Be prepared to bargain your way around Syria. It takes practice, but pays off in the end.

TURKEY. Tips are usually not expected, and Turkish salaries do not take tipping into account as a form of income. Leaving a bit of small change, however, at your table after a meal or with a taxi driver is appreciated as a friendly gesture and a sign of gratitude. Bargaining occurs in outdoor food markets, bazaars, and some carpet and souvenir shops. Walk-in stores that stock conventional goods such as groceries, pharmaceuticals, and clothes have fixed prices.

TAXES

In general, figuring out exactly how taxes operate in the Middle East is tricky. Sometimes, tourists may be the only ones who must pay taxes, for the extra money is already included in the bill. Other times, the extra fees included with taxes may be added on to a bill at the last minute. It is best to ask all hotels (and even restaurants) about the taxes they may charge. In **Egypt,** there is no sales tax. In **Lebanon,** taxes are easily negotiable. They are the first part of a price to go, especially at hotels where taxes are the most hefty. **Israel** offers a VAT (Value Added Tax) refund to tourists purchasing more than US$50 worth of goods at a shop approved by the Ministry of Tourism. You must be a foreign passport holder who is not an Israeli citizen, and you must pay for your purchase in foreign currency (cash or international credit cards). Approved stores will be so-marked: look for a the Ministry of Tourism insignia or a sign reading "V.A.T. Refund." In **Jordan,** a 13% tax (as well as a 10% service charge) is added to hotel and restaurant prices. Both are usually already added to the bill, though some hotels may add on the extra charges at the end. Taxes are nonexistent in **Syria.** Not all shops participate, but **Turkey** does have a 10-20% value-added tax (VAT) known as the *katma değer vergisi* or KDV. It is included in the prices of most goods and services (including meals, lodging, and car rentals). Before you buy, check if the KDV is included in the price to avoid paying it twice. Theoretically, it can be reclaimed at most points of departure, but this requires much persistence. An airport tax of $15 is levied only on international travelers, but it is usually included in the cost of the ticket.

SAFETY AND SECURITY

The number one concern for most travelers planning a trip to the Middle East is safety. There are regions in the Middle East in which travel remains unsafe; however, the most important thing to do keep updated on current events. Good sources for information are newspapers, television, and websites on travel safety run by your home country (www.state.gov for the US, www.dfait-maeci.gc.ca for Canada, www.fco.gov.uk for the UK, and www.dfat.gov.au for Australia). For country specifics, see individual chapters and **Terrorism** (p. 17).

BLENDING IN

Tourists are particularly vulnerable to crime because they often carry large amounts of cash and are not as street savvy as locals. To avoid unwanted attention, try to blend in as much as possible. Respecting local customs (in some cases, dressing more conservatively) may placate would-be hecklers. The gawking camera-toter is a more obvious target than the low-profile traveler. This is particularly tricky in the Middle East because the dress code and attitudes often differ drastically from Western norms; read over the *Let's Go* introduction to a country before getting off the plane.

Familiarize yourself with your surroundings before setting out; if you must check a map on the street, duck into a cafe or shop. Also, carry yourself with confidence, as an obviously bewildered bodybuilder is more likely to be harassed than a stern and confident 98-pound weakling. If you are traveling alone, be sure that someone at home knows your itinerary and **never admit that you're traveling alone.** Men and women should make an effort to dress respectably; see the **Dress and Etiquette** and **Women Travelers** section at the start of each country chapter, as well as **Essentials: Women Travelers** (p. 38).

> **FURTHER INFORMATION: SAFETY AND SECURITY.**
> *Fielding's The World's Most Dangerous Places,* edited by Kathy Knoles (US$22), gives detailed descriptions of dangerous destinations around the world. *Don't Go!: 51 Reasons Not to Travel Abroad, But If You Must...176 Tactics for Coping With Discomforts, Distress and Danger,* by Hannah Blank (US$11), provides great tips for taking care of oneself on the road. For specific information on US State Department travel warnings, consult both the country's chapter in this book as well as the State Department's web page at travel.state.gov/travel warnings.html.

PROTECTING YOURSELF (AND YOUR WALLET)

Find out about unsafe areas from tourist offices, the manager of your hotel or hostel, or a local whom you trust. You may want to carry a **whistle** to scare off attackers or attract attention; also memorize emergency numbers for the city or area. Whenever possible, *Let's Go* warns of unsafe neighborhoods and areas, but there are some good general tips to follow. When walking at night, stick to busy, well-lit streets and avoid dark alleyways. Do not attempt to cross through parks, parking lots or other large, deserted areas. The distribution of people can reveal a great deal about the relative safety of the area; look for children playing, women walking in the open, and other signs of an active community. Keep in mind that a district can change drastically from block to block. There are really only a few regions in the Middle East where violent crime against foreigners is a serious threat, and there are a few simple precautions travelers can take (see **Protecting Your Valuables,** p. 18). However, while many places have **pickpockets,** the most common thievery is simple scamming. Trust your instincts: if you feel you are getting something for nothing, be wary. On the other hand, if you feel that something is reasonably priced by Western standards, know that you may very well be paying too much for it. Labor and materials cost much less in most of the Middle East than they do in the Western world, and prices should reflect that.

GETTING AROUND

If you are using a **car,** learn local driving signals and wear a seatbelt. Children under 40 pounds should ride only in a specially designed carseat, available for a small fee from most car rental agencies. Study route maps before you hit the road, and if you plan on spending a lot of time on the road, you may want to bring spare parts. If your car breaks down, wait for the police to assist you. For long drives in desolate areas, invest in a cellular phone. Be sure to park your vehicle in a garage or well traveled area, and use a steering wheel locking device in larger cities. **Sleeping in your car** is one of the most dangerous (and often illegal) ways to get your rest. For info on the perils of **hitchhiking,** see p. 38.

SELF DEFENSE

There is no sure-fire way to avoid all the threatening situations you might encounter when you travel, but a good self-defense course will give you concrete ways to react to unwanted advances. **Impact, Prepare, and Model Mugging** can refer you to local self-defense courses in the US (☎(800) 345-5425) and Vancouver (☎(604) 878-3838). Workshops (2-3hr.) start at US$50; full courses run US$350-500.

TRAVEL ADVISORIES. The following government offices provide travel information and advisories by telephone, by fax, or via the world wide web:

Australian Department of Foreign Affairs and Trade: ☎(2) 6261 1111; www.dfat.gov.au.

Canadian Department of Foreign Affairs and International Trade (DFAIT): In Canada call ☎(800) 267-6788; elsewhere call ☎+1 (613) 944-6788; www.dfait-maeci.gc.ca. Call for their free booklet, *Bon Voyage...But.*

New Zealand Ministry of Foreign Affairs: ☎(04) 494 85 00; fax 494 85 11; www.mft.govt.nz/trav.html.

United Kingdom Foreign and Commonwealth Office: ☎(020) 7238 4503; fax 7238 4545; www.fco.gov.uk.

US Department of State: ☎(202) 647-5225, auto faxback (202) 647-3000; http://travel.state.gov. For *A Safe Trip Abroad,* call ☎(202) 512-1800.

ESSENTIALS

TERRORISM

Although the Middle East has long been known for centuries-old political and religious conflicts, travel in the region is relatively safe for a cautious traveler exercising common sense. Those planning to visit the region for longer periods of time should register with their home country's embassy in each destination country to obtain updated information on travel and security in specific areas.

EGYPT. Traveling in Egypt is safe except for **Middle Egypt** and the **Egyptian frontiers.** Since the summer of 1998, the US government has warned against traveling in Middle Egypt (especially near the governates of Minya, Asyut, Sohag, and just north of Qena), where terrorist attacks by extremist groups have occurred since the mid-1990s. Although there have been no attacks on foreign tourists since 1998, these areas should be considered risky (*Let's Go* has not sent researchers to these areas). Those wishing to visit areas near Egypt's frontiers should also be aware of the dangers of off-road travel and the possible threat of **landmines** (now marked by barbed wire) from previous conflicts. The dangerous areas of Egypt's "frontier" include: the oases near the Libyan border (except for the relatively safe Siwa Oasis); off-road areas in the Sinai; and sights south of Aswan near the Sudanese border (an area known as the disputed "Ha'ib Triangle" area). Travel to the first two regions cannot be complete without permission from the Travel Permits Department of the Ministry of the Interior in Cairo.

ISRAEL AND THE PALESTINIAN TERRITORIES. Terrorists in **Israel** target public transportation and crowded areas. Most bus bombings in Israel occur in the early morning rush hour. If your plans are flexible, try to avoid bus travel at this time. As terrorism has sadly become a part of life in the country, Israelis look at abandoned purses and backpacks in a different light. Don't leave anything unattended. Alert authorities if you see an abandoned package.

Traveling in the **Palestinian territories** can be dangerous, especially in a car with the yellow license plates that identify the vehicle as Israeli. Jewish travelers should avoid identifying themselves as such. Simply placing a baseball cap over a *kippah* can prevent stares and hostility. Be aware of potential unrest in the West Bank by staying up to date with the news and contacting the consular division of the United States Consulate General, at 27 Nablus Rd. in East Jerusalem.

JORDAN. Travel in Jordan is relatively safe. Amman (via the King Hussein/Allenby Bridge) and Aqaba (by way of Eilat) are the only safe gateways into Israel from anywhere in the Levant. See **Jordan: Border Crossings** (p. 454) for detailed information on travel between Jordan and Israel.

LEBANON. As of July 9, 1999, the US Department of State has issued a **travel warning** for Lebanon. In June 1998, the US Embassy in Beirut was the target of a rocket-propelled grenade attack, and the security situation in the city of **Sidon** has recently deteriorated, including the issuance from the Sidon area of an anti-American threat of undetermined credibility. Americans are cautioned to avoid travel into Sidon and adjacent Palestinian refugee camps until security stabilizes. As an added precaution, American air carriers are prohibited from the use of the **Beirut International Airport** due to continuing concern about passenger and aircraft security arrangements.

Since the Israeli withdrawal on May 24, 2000, Southern Lebanon (namely the southern suburbs of Beirut as far north as the Na'ameh Hills and sections of the Beqa'a Valley) is still a dangerous place to travel because of continuing political instability (for details, see **Lebanon: Modern History,** p. 507). **Ba'albeck** (home of Hizbullah headquarters, p. 540) is safe and comfortable for travel.

SYRIA. Traveling in Syria is very safe. The main problem travelers encounter involves traveling to Syria after visiting **Israel.** The Syrian government rigidly enforces restrictions on prior travel to Israel: authorities will refuse admission to travelers whose passports have Israeli stamps, Jordanian entry cachets or cachets from other countries that suggest prior travel to Israel, or whose passports do not bear any entry stamps from a country adjacent to Israel that the traveler has just visited. Although Syria is included on the US Department of State's list of state sponsors of **terrorism,** there is no record of terrorist attacks against foreigners or of a terrorist presence anywhere in Syria; the Syrian government has also repeatedly stated their commitment to protect foreigners.

TURKEY. The **PKK** (Workers' Party of Kurdistan) and the DHKP/C (formerly Dev Sol) commit most of the terrorist acts in Turkey, which have historically not targeted tourists. The PKK vowed to stop targeting civilians and declared a cease-fire in August 1999. Terrorist activities increased after the capture of PKK leader Abdullah Öcalan (see **Turkey: In The News,** p. 610). Since the autumn of 1999, however, tourism has been on the rise. *Let's Go* does not recommend that women travel alone in **Eastern Anatolia.** Incidents of terrorism are frequent in **southeastern Turkey,** which is under martial law because some provinces are in a state of civil war with Kurdish guerillas fighting for freedom. Although access to Mt. Ararat is officially prohibited, it is still possible to get near it. In most militarized cities, **roads close** during certain parts of the day. Photographs of military installations, bridges, and power stations are prohibited.

FINANCIAL SECURITY

PROTECTING YOUR VALUABLES
Street crime is not common in the Middle East, except in larger cities like Beirut. There are a few steps you can take to minimize the financial risk associated with traveling. First, **bring as little with you as possible.** Leave expensive watches, jewelry, cameras, and electronic equipment (like your Discman) at home; chances are you'd break them, lose them, or get sick of lugging them around anyway. Second, buy a few combination **padlocks** to secure your belongings either in your pack—which you should **never leave unattended**—or in a hostel or train station locker. Third, **carry as little cash as possible;** instead, carry traveler's checks and credit cards, keeping them in a **money belt** (not a "fanny pack") along with your passport and ID cards. Fourth, **keep a small cash reserve separate from your primary stash.** This should entail about US$50 (US$ is best) sewn into or stored in the depths of your pack, along with your traveler's check numbers and important photocopies.

CON ARTISTS AND PICKPOCKETS
Among the more colorful aspects of large cities are **con artists.** They often work in groups, and children are the most effective. They possess an innumerable range of ruses. Beware of certain classics: sob stories that require money, rolls of bills "found" on the street, mustard spilled (or saliva spit) onto your shoulder to distract you while they snatch your bag. Especially in Egypt, where thriving tourism

has existed for years and it is often the only source of income, hustlers have fine-tuned the con into an art form (see **Scam Wars, Episode I,** p. 97).

Don't ever hand your passport to someone whose authority is questionable (ask to accompany them to a police station if they insist), and **don't ever let your passport out of your sight.** Similarly, don't let your bag out of sight; never trust a "station-porter" who offers to carry your bag or stow it in the baggage compartment or a "new friend" who wants to guard your bag while you buy a train ticket or use the restroom. Beware of **pickpockets** in crowds, especially on public transportation. Also, be alert in public telephone booths. If you say your calling card number, do so very quietly; if you punch it in, make sure no one can look over your shoulder.

ACCOMMODATIONS AND TRANSPORTATION

Never leave your belongings unattended; crime occurs in even the most demure-looking hostel or hotel. Bring your own **padlock** for hostel lockers, and don't ever store valuables in a locker.

Be particularly careful on **buses** and **trains;** horror stories abound about determined thieves who wait for travelers to fall asleep. Carry your backpack in front of you where you can see it. When traveling with others, sleep in alternate shifts. When alone, use good judgement in selecting a train compartment: never stay in an empty one and use a lock to secure your pack to the luggage rack. Try to sleep on top bunks with your luggage stored above you (if not in bed with you), and keep important documents and other valuables on your person.

If traveling by **car,** don't leave valuables (such as radios or luggage) in it while you are away. If your tape deck or radio is removable, hide it in the trunk or take it with you. If it isn't, at least conceal it. Similarly, hide baggage in the trunk, even though savvy thieves can tell if a car is heavily loaded by the way it sits on its tires.

DRUGS AND ALCOHOL

You are subject to the laws of the country in which you travel, not to those of your home country. **Illegal drugs** (including marijuana) are best avoided. Penalties for possession, use, or trafficking in illegal drugs are severe throughout the Middle East and include severe fines and jail time. Egypt and Syria may impose the **death penalty** on anyone convicted of smuggling or selling. Consulates can do no more than bring floral arrangements to prisoners, provide a list of attorneys, and inform family and friends. If you carry **prescription drugs** while you travel, it is vital to have a copy of the prescriptions themselves readily accessible at country borders.

Although there is an Islamic law forbidding **alcohol,** many people drink anyway. You may be asked to purchase alcohol for not-so-devout Muslims; unless they are underage, it is legal to do so if you are of age. The drinking age in **Egypt** is 21. It is strictly enforced in areas like Islamic Cairo, but may be quite lenient in other areas. In general, keep such practices to yourself and be careful. The drinking age in **Israel** is 18, and for the first time, bars are beginning to enforce it. Eilat in particular has begun to card stringently; a foreign driver's license usually serves as adequate identification. Many clubs in Israel have higher minimum drinking ages to target an older clientele. In **Jordan** and **Syria,** the drinking age is 18, but it doesn't seem to be enforced anywhere. The drinking age in **Lebanon** is also 18, but it is only strictly enforced in heavily Muslim areas, like Tyre and Ba'albeck. Since Islam prohibits the consumption of alcohol, it is improper to drink in the more traditional towns of **Turkey** and during the holy period of Ramadan. In all countries, **public drunkenness** can jeopardize your safety and earn the disdain of locals.

HEALTH AND INSURANCE

Common sense is the simplest prescription for good health while traveling. Travelers complain most often about their feet and their gut, so take precautionary measures: drink lots of fluids to prevent dehydration and constipation, wear sturdy, broken-in shoes and clean socks, and use talcum powder to keep your feet dry.

BEFORE YOU GO

Preparation can help minimize the likelihood of contracting a disease and maximize the chances of receiving effective health care in the event of an emergency. For tips on packing a basic **first-aid kit** and other health essentials, see p. 25.

In your **passport**, write the names of any people you wish to be contacted in case of a medical emergency, and also list any allergies or medical conditions of which you would want doctors to be aware. Matching a prescription to a foreign equivalent is not always easy, safe, or possible. Carry up-to-date, legible prescriptions or a statement from your doctor stating the medication's trade name, manufacturer, chemical name, and dosage. While traveling, be sure to keep all medication with you in your carry-on luggage.

IMMUNIZATIONS AND PRECAUTIONS

Take a look at your **immunization** records before you go; if you are coming from a tropical area with a risk of yellow fever or cholera, such as Sub-Saharan Africa, you may be required to show certificates of up-to-date vaccinations to enter some countries. Travelers over two years old should be sure that the following vaccines are up to date: Measles, Mumps, and Rubella (MMR); Diptheria, Tetanus, and Pertussis (DTP or DTap); Polio (OPV); Haemophilus Influenza B (HbCV); and Hepatitis B (HBV). A booster of Tetanus-diptheria (Td) is recommended once every 10 years, and adults should consider an additional dose of Polio vaccine if they have not already had one during their adult years. Hepatitis A vaccine and/or Immune Globulin (IG) is recommended for travelers to the Middle East as well. If you will be spending more than four weeks in Egypt, Jordan, Lebanon, or Syria you should consider the typhoid vaccine. Travelers to Syria and southern Turkey should also take malaria pills. For recommendations on immunizations and prophylaxis, consult the CDC (p. 20) in the US or the equivalent in your home country, and be sure to check with a doctor for guidance.

USEFUL ORGANIZATIONS AND PUBLICATIONS

The US **Centers for Disease Control and Prevention** (**CDC**; ☎ (877) FYI-TRIP; www.cdc.gov/travel) is an excellent source of information for travelers and maintains an international fax information service. The CDC's comprehensive booklet, *Health Information for International Travelers*, an annual rundown of disease, immunization, and general health advice, is free online or US$22 via the Government Printing Office (☎ (202) 512-1800). The **US State Department** (http://travel.state.gov) compiles Consular Information Sheets on health, entry requirements, and other issues for various countries. For quick information on health and other travel warnings, call the **Overseas Citizens' Services** (☎ (202) 647-5225; after-hours 647-4000), contact a US passport agency, embassy, or consulate abroad or send a self-addressed, stamped envelope to the Overseas Citizens' Services, Bureau of Consular Affairs, #4811, US Department of State, Washington, D.C. 20520. For information on medical evacuation services and travel insurance firms, see http://travel.state.gov/medical.html. The **British Foreign and Commonwealth Office** also gives health warnings for individual countries (www.fco.gov.uk).

For detailed information on travel health, including a country-by-country overview of diseases, try the **International Travel Health Guide**, Stuart Rose, MD (Travel Medicine, US$20; www.travmed.com). For general health info, contact the **American Red Cross** (☎ (800) 564-1234).

MEDICAL ASSISTANCE ON THE ROAD. Most Middle Eastern hospitals do not have the high quality of medical treatment found in North America, Europe, or Australia, and few doctors speak English. Jordan and Syria are a step above the other Middle Eastern countries, but only in Israel, where medicine is socialized, are city hospitals on par with Western standards in training and technology. Many large hotels throughout the Middle East have English-speaking doctors on-call, who can either treat travelers or refer them to the nearest city hospital. Pharma-

FURTHER READING: USEFUL ORGANIZATIONS. For a country by-country overview of diseases, try the **International Travel Health Guide**, Stuart Rose, MD (Travel Medicine, $20). Information is also available at Travel Medicine's website (www.travmed.com). For general health information, contact the **American Red Cross.** The ARC publishes *First-Aid and Safety Handbook* (US$5) available for purchase by calling or writing to the American Red Cross, 285 Columbus Ave., Boston, MA 02116-5114 (☎800-564-1234, M-F 8:30am-4:30pm). Useful **web pages** include CDC Travel Information's *Health Information for Travelers to the Middle East* (www.cdc.gov/travel/mideast.htm) and the United States State Department's *Tips for Travelers to the Middle East and North Africa* (travel.state.gov/tips_mid-east%26nafrica.html).

cies are absolutely everywhere in the Middle East; many countries even have rotating 24-hour pharmacy duties.

If you are concerned about being able to access medical support while traveling, there are special support services you may employ. The *MedPass* from **Global Emergency Medical Services (GEMS)**, 2001 Westside Dr., #120, Alpharetta, GA 30004, USA (☎(800) 860-1111; fax (770) 475-0058; www.globalems.com), provides 24-hour international medical assistance, support, and medical evacuation resources. The **International Association for Medical Assistance to Travelers** (IAMAT; US ☎(716) 754-4883, Canada ☎(416) 652-0137, New Zealand ☎(03) 352 2053; www.sentex.net/~iamat) has free membership, lists English-speaking doctors worldwide, and offers detailed info on immunization requirements and sanitation. If your regular **insurance** policy does not cover travel abroad, you may wish to purchase additional coverage (see p. 24).

Those with medical conditions (diabetes, allergies to antibiotics, epilepsy, heart conditions) may want to obtain a stainless-steel **Medic Alert** ID tag (first-year US$35, $15 annually thereafter), which identifies the condition and gives a 24-hour collect-call number. Contact the Medic Alert Foundation, 2323 Colorado Ave, Turlock, CA 95382, USA (☎(800) 825-3785; www.medicalert.org).

ON THE ROAD

ENVIRONMENTAL HAZARDS

Heat exhaustion and dehydration: Heat exhaustion, characterized by dehydration and salt deficiency, can lead to fatigue, headaches, and wooziness. Avoid it by drinking plenty of fluids, eating salty foods (e.g. crackers), and avoiding dehydrating beverages (e.g. alcohol, coffee, tea, and caffeinated soda). Continuous heat stress can eventually lead to heatstroke, characterized by a rising temperature, severe headache, and cessation of sweating. Victims should be cooled off with wet towels and taken to a doctor.

Sunburn: If you're prone to sunburn, bring sunscreen with you (it's often more expensive and hard to find when traveling), and apply it liberally and often to avoid burns and risk of skin cancer. If you are planning on spending time near water, in the desert, or in the snow, you are at risk of getting burned, even through clouds. If you get sunburned, drink more fluids than usual and apply Calamine or an aloe-based lotion.

PREVENTING DISEASE

INSECT-BORNE DISEASES. Be aware of insects in wet or forested areas, while hiking, and especially while camping. Mosquitoes are most active from dusk to dawn. Use insect repellents, such as DEET. Wear long pants and long sleeves and buy a mosquito net. Wear shoes and socks, and tuck long pants into socks. Soak or spray your gear with permethrin, which is licensed in the US for use on clothing. Natural repellents can be useful supplements: taking vitamin B-12 pills regularly can eventually make you smelly to insects, as can garlic pills. Malaria is transmitted by Anopheles mosquitoes that bite at night. Incubation period varies; it could take months for an infected person to show symptoms. Early symptoms include fever, chills, aches, and fatigue, followed by high fever and sweating, sometimes with vomiting and diarrhea. See a doctor for any flu-like sickness that occurs after travel in a risk area, and get tested immediately. Left untreated, malaria can cause anemia, kidney failure, coma, and death, and is an especially serious threat to pregnant women. There are a number of oral prophylactics to protect against the disease. Western doctors prescribe mefloquine (sold under the name Lariam) or doxycycline. Be aware that these drugs can have very serious side effects, including slowed heart rate and nightmares.

FOOD- AND WATER-BORNE DISEASES. Be sure that everything you eat is cooked properly and that the water you drink is clean. In the Middle East, where the risk of contracting traveler's diarrhea or forms of food poisoning is high, never drink unbottled water that you have not treated. To purify your own water, bring it to a rolling boil or treat it with iodine tablets, available at any camping goods store. In risk areas, don't brush your teeth with tap water or rinse your toothbrush under the faucet, and keep your mouth closed in the shower. Salads and uncooked vegetables (including lettuce and coleslaw) are also full of untreated water. Other culprits are raw shellfish, unpasteurized milk, and sauces containing raw eggs. Insist on having any lukewarm meats or meat-sauces reheated, and anything slightly undercooked put back on the grill. Peel all fruits and vegetables yourself, and beware of watermelon, which is often injected with impure water. Watch out for food, fruit, or juices from markets or street vendors that may have been washed in dirty water or fried in rancid cooking oil. Always wash hands before eating and after using the restroom to minimize the risk of Hepatitis A; bring a quick-drying antibacterial hand cleaner. Your bowels will thank you.

■ **Traveler's diarrhea** results from drinking untreated water or eating uncooked foods, and can last 3 to 7 days. Symptoms include nausea, bloating, urgency, and malaise. If the nasties hit you, eat quick-energy, non-sugary foods with protein and carbohydrates to keep your strength up. Over-the-counter remedies may counteract the problems, but they can complicate serious infections. **Avoid anti-diarrheals** if you suspect that you are at risk for other diseases. If possible, avoid taking such medication unless strictly necessary (i.e., before embarking on an overnight bus trip), as how long your stools remain loose is an important diagnostic clue that remains unclear for those using anti-diarrheals. The most dangerous side effect of diarrhea is **dehydration.** The simplest and most effective anti-dehydration formula is 8oz. of (clean) water with a ½ tsp. of sugar or honey and a pinch of salt. Soft drinks without caffeine or salted crackers are also good. Down several of these remedies a day, rest, and wait for the disease to run its course. If you develop a fever or if your symptoms don't go away after 4 or 5 days, consult a doctor. If children develop traveler's diarrhea, see a doctor, as treatment is different.

Dysentery results from a serious intestinal infection caused by certain bacteria. The most common type is bacillary dysentery, also called shigellosis. Symptoms include bloody diarrhea or bloody stools mixed with mucus, fever, and abdominal pain and tenderness. Bacillary dysentery generally only lasts a week, but it is highly contagious. Amoebic dysentery develops more slowly, with no fever or vomiting. However, it is a more serious disease, and may cause long-term damage if left untreated. A stool test can determine which kind you have, so you should seek medical help immediately. If you are traveling in high-risk regions (especially rural areas) obtain a prescription before you leave home.

Hepatitis A (distinct from B and C, see below) is a **high risk** in the Middle East. Hep A is a viral infection of the liver acquired primarily through contaminated water, ice, shellfish, or unpeeled fruits and vegetables, and also from sexual contact. Symptoms include fatigue, fever, loss of appetite, nausea, dark urine, jaundice, vomiting, aches and pains, and light stools. Ask your doctor about the vaccine Havrix, or ask to get an injection of immune globulin (IG).

Parasites such as microbes and tapeworms also often hide in unsafe water and food. **Giardia**, for example, is acquired by drinking untreated water from streams or lakes all over the world. Symptoms of parasitic infections in general include swollen glands or lymph nodes, fever, rashes or itchiness, digestive problems, eye problems, anal itching and anemia. Boil your water, wear shoes, avoid bugs, and eat only cooked food.

Schistosomiasis (also called **bilharzia**) is a parasitic disease caused by a flatworm. The larvae mature inside freshwater snails and escape back into the water, where they can infect humans by penetrating unbroken skin. Avoid swimming in fresh water areas. If your skin is exposed to untreated water, rub it immediately and vigorously with a towel and/or rubbing alcohol. You may notice an itchy localized rash; later symptoms include fever, painful urination, diarrhea, loss of appetite, night sweats, and a hive-like rash on the body. Schistosomiasis can be treated with prescription drugs.

Typhoid fever is common in villages and rural areas in the Middle East. While mostly transmitted through contaminated food and water, it may also be acquired by direct contact with another person. Symptoms include fever, headaches, fatigue, loss of appetite, constipation, and a rash on the abdomen or chest. Antibiotics can treat typhoid, but the CDC recommends vaccinations (70-90% effective) if you will be hiking, camping, or staying in small cities or rural areas.

OTHER INFECTIOUS DISEASES

Rabies is transmitted through the saliva of infected animals. It is fatal if untreated. Avoid contact with animals, especially strays. If you are bitten, wash the wound thoroughly and seek immediate medical care. Once you begin to show symptoms (thirst and muscle spasms), the disease is in its terminal stage. A rabies vaccine is available but is only semi-effective. Three shots must be administered over one year.

Hepatitis B is a viral infection of the liver transmitted through the transfer of bodily fluids, by sharing needles, or by having unprotected sex. Its incubation period varies and can be much longer than the 30-day incubation period of Hepatitis A. Symptoms may not show until many years after infection. The CDC recommends the Hepatitis B vaccination for health-care workers, sexually active travelers, and anyone planning to seek medical treatment abroad. Vaccination consists of a three-shot series given over a period of time, and should begin six months before traveling.

Hepatitis C is like Hepatitis B, but the modes of transmission are different. Intravenous drug users, those with occupational exposure to blood, hemodialysis patients, or recipients of blood transfusions are at the highest risk, but the disease can also be spread through sexual contact and sharing of items like razors and toothbrushes, which may have traces of blood on them.

AIDS, HIV, STDS

Acquired Immune Deficiency Syndrome (AIDS) is a growing problem around the world. The World Health Organization estimates that there are around 30 million people infected with the HIV virus, and women now represent 40% of all new HIV infections. The easiest mode of HIV transmission is through direct blood-to-blood contact with an HIV-positive person; never share intravenous drug, tattooing, or other needles. The most common mode of transmission is sexual intercourse. Health professionals recommend the use of latex condoms—take a supply with you before you depart for your trip. For more information on AIDS, call the **US Centers for Disease Control's** 24-hour hotline at ☎(800) 342-2437, or contact the **Joint United Nations Programme on HIV/AIDS (UNAIDS)**, 20 av. Appia 20, CH-1211 Geneva 27, Switzerland (☎+41 (22) 791 36 66; fax 791 41 87). Council's brochure, *Travel Safe: AIDS and International Travel*, is available at all Council Travel offices and on their website (www.ciee.org/Isp/safety/travelsafe.htm). Note that Egypt screens incoming travelers who will spend more than 60 days in the country for AIDS and deny entrance to those who test HIV-positive. Contact the nearest Egyptian consulate for up-to-date information.

Sexually transmitted diseases (STDs) such as gonorrhea, chlamydia, genital warts, syphilis, and herpes are easier to catch than HIV, and some can be just as deadly. **Hepatitis B** and **C** are also serious sexually-transmitted diseases (see **Other Infectious Diseases**, p. 23). Warning signs for STDs include: swelling, sores, bumps, or blisters on sex organs, rectum, or mouth; burning and pain during urination and bowel movements; itching around sex organs; swelling or redness in the throat, flu-like symptoms with fever, chills, and aches. If these symptoms develop, see a doctor immediately. When having sex, condoms may protect you from certain STDs, but oral or even tactile contact can lead to transmission.

WOMEN'S HEALTH

Women traveling in unsanitary conditions are vulnerable to **urinary tract** and **bladder infections,** common and severely uncomfortable bacterial diseases that cause a burning sensation and painful and sometimes frequent urination. To try to avoid these infections, drink plenty of vitamin-C-rich juice and plenty of clean water, and urinate frequently, especially right after intercourse. See a doctor if symptoms persist: untreated, these infections can lead to kidney infections, sterility, and death.

Vaginal yeast infections are treatable but uncomfortable illnesses likely to flare up in hot and humid climates. Wearing loosely fitting trousers or a skirt and cotton underwear helps. Bring supplies from home if you are prone to infection, as they may be difficult to find on the road. Some travelers opt for a natural alternative such as eating plain yogurt several times a day if other remedies are unavailable.

Tampons and **pads** are sometimes hard to find when traveling, so take supplies along. **Reliable contraceptive devices** may also be difficult to find. Women on the pill should bring enough to allow for possible loss or extended stays. Bring a prescription, since forms of the pill vary a good deal. Women who use a diaphragm should bring enough contraceptive jelly. Though condoms are increasingly available, you might want to bring your favorite brand before you go, as availability and quality vary. For further reading about women's health issues, check out *Handbook for Women Travellers*, by Maggie and Gemma Moss (Piatkus Books, US$15).

Women considering an **abortion** abroad should contact the **International Planned Parenthood Federation (IPPF),** Regent's College, Inner Circle, Regent's Park, London NW1 4NS (☎ (020) 7487 7900; fax 7487 7950; www.ippf.org), for more information. Abortion is legal in Turkey. In Israel, Jordan, and Egypt it is only permitted on limited health grounds. In Lebanon and Syria it is illegal.

INSURANCE

Travel insurance covers four basic areas: medical/health problems, property loss, trip cancellation/interruption, and emergency evacuation. **Medical insurance** (especially university policies) often covers costs incurred abroad; check with your provider. Medicare does not cover foreign travel. Canadians are protected by their home province's health insurance plan for up to 90 days after leaving the country; check with the provincial Ministry of Health or Health Plan Headquarters for details. **Homeowners' insurance** (or your family's coverage) often covers theft during travel and loss of travel documents (passport, plane ticket, etc.) up to US$500. **ISIC** and **ITIC** provide basic insurance benefits, including US$100 per day of in-hospital sickness for a maximum of 60 days, US$3000 of accident-related medical reimbursement, and US$25,000 for emergency medical transport (see **Identification,** p. 10). Cardholders have access to a toll-free 24-hour helpline whose multilingual staff can provide assistance in medical, legal, and financial emergencies overseas (☎ (800) 626-2427 in the US and Canada; elsewhere call the US collect ☎ (713) 267-2525. **American Express** (☎ (800) 528-4800) grants most cardholders automatic car rental insurance (collision and theft, but not liability) and ground travel accident coverage of US$100,000 on flight purchases made with the card.

INSURANCE PROVIDERS. Council and **STA** (see p. 30) offer a range of plans that can supplement your basic coverage. Other private insurance providers in the **US and Canada** include: **Access America** (☎ (800) 284-8300); **Berkely Group/Carefree Travel Insurance** (☎ (800) 323-3149; www.berkely.com); **Globalcare Travel Insurance** (☎ (800) 821-2488; www.globalcare-cocco.com); and **Travel Assistance International** (☎ (800) 821-2828; www.worldwide-assistance.com). Providers in the **UK** include **Campus Travel** (☎ (01865) 258 000) and **Columbus Travel Insurance** (☎ (020) 7375 0011). In **Australia**, try **CIC Insurance** (☎ 9202 8000).

PACKING

Pack light: lay out only what you absolutely need, then take half the clothes and twice the money. The less you have, the less you have to lose (or store, or carry on your back). Any extra space will be useful for any souvenirs or items you might pick up along the way.

Clothing: don't forget the obvious: it's always a good idea to bring a rain jacket (Gore-Tex is a miracle fabric that's both waterproof and breathable). Natural fibers are better than synthetics in the heat. Dark colors hide dirt, but light colors deflect sun. In many areas (especially holy sites), both men and women should cover their knees and upper arms to avoid offending local rules of modesty. Leave jeans at home: bring along khakis or light cotton trousers. Well-cushioned sneakers are good for walking. Lace-up leather shoes with firm grips provide better support and social acceptability than athletic shoes. A double pair of socks—light absorbent cotton inside and thick wool outside—will cushion feet, keep them dry, and help prevent blisters. If you only want to bring one pair, the best all-around footwear are sneakers-cum-hiking boots. Talcum powder in your shoes and on your feet can prevent sores, and moleskin is great for blisters. You should also bring a comfortable pair of waterproof sandals, as sneakers get very hot and uncomfortable when the temperature skyrockets.

Luggage: if you plan to cover most of your itinerary by foot, a sturdy **frame backpack** is unbeatable. **Internal-frame packs** mold better to your back, keep a lower center of gravity, and can flex adequately on difficult hikes that require a lot of bending and maneuvering. **External-frame packs** are more comfortable for long hikes over even terrain (like city streets) since they keep the weight higher and distribute it more evenly. In addition to your main vessel, a small backpack, rucksack, or courier bag is useful as a **daypack** for sightseeing expeditions.

First-aid kit: for a basic first-aid kit, pack bandages, aspirin or other painkiller, antibiotic cream, a thermometer, a Swiss Army knife, tweezers, moleskin, decongestant, motion-sickness remedy, diarrhea or upset-stomach medication (Pepto Bismol or Imodium), an antihistamine, sunscreen, insect repellent, burn ointment, and a syringe for emergencies (get an explanatory letter from your doctor).

Electric current: in the Middle East, electricity is 220 volts AC, enough to fry any 110V North American appliance. Most outlets are made for round prongs, so even if your machine has a built-in converter, you'll also need an **adapter** to change the plug shape.

Other Useful Items: an umbrella; sealable plastic bags; alarm clock; waterproof matches; sun hat; needle and thread; safety pins; sunglasses; pocketknife; plastic water bottle; compass; string; towel; padlock; whistle; rubber bands; flashlight; cold-water soap; earplugs; electrical tape (for patching tears); tweezers; garbage bags; flip-flops for the shower; a money-belt for carrying valuables; deodorant; razors; tampons; and condoms (see AIDS, HIV, and STDs, p. 23).

ACCOMMODATIONS

HOSTELS

Hostels are generally dorm-style accommodations in single-sex large rooms with bunk beds, although some hostels do offer private rooms for families and couples. The downside to traveling in the Middle East is that there aren't very many hostels. Those that do exist sometimes have kitchens and utensils for your use, bike or moped rentals, storage areas, and laundry services (but not facilities). A bed in a hostel will average around US$6-12. Some **colleges and universities** also open their residence halls to travelers when school is not in session, or even during term-time. These dorms are often close to student areas—good sources for information on things to do—and are usually very clean. Getting a room may take a couple of phone calls and require advanced planning, but rates tend to be low, and many offer free local calls. You can access university lodging worldwide by checking out *Campus Lodging Guide (18th Ed.)*, B&J Publications (US$15).

HOSTELLING INTERNATIONAL

Joining the youth hostel association in your own country (listed below) automatically grants you membership privileges in **Hostelling International (HI),** a federation of national hosteling associations. Only Egypt and Israel have HI hostels and only Israeli hostels accept reservations via the **International Booking Network** (Australia ☎ (02) 9261 1111; Canada ☎ (800) 663-5777; England and Wales ☎ (1629) 58 14 18; Northern Ireland ☎ (1232) 32 47 33; Republic of Ireland ☎ (01) 830 17 66; NZ ☎ (09) 379 42 24; Scotland ☎ (541) 55 32 55; US ☎ (800) 909-4776). HI's umbrella organization's web page (www.iyhf.org), which lists the web addresses and phone numbers of all national associations, can be a great place to begin researching hostelling in a specific region.

CAMPING AND THE OUTDOORS

Camping is a viable option in many areas of the Middle East, in particular in Egypt, Jordan, Israel, Lebanon, and Turkey. It is generally free or close to free, but typically it will not be organized by a central camping agency, meaning that it is almost entirely unregulated. Always check with the local tourist agency, police, and other travelers before setting up camp to find out if there are certain places where camping is illegal. For information on hiking and camping, contact these companies for a free catalog: **Sierra Club Books,** 85 Second St. 2nd fl., San Francisco, CA 94105-3441, USA (☎ (415) 977-5500; www.sierraclub.org/books); **The Mountaineers Books,** 1001 SW Klickitat Way, #201, Seattle, WA 98134, USA (☎ (800) 553-4453 or (206) 223-6303; www.mountaineersbooks.org).

DESERT SAFETY

Stay hydrated. The vast majority of life-threatening desert situations can be avoided by following this simple advice. Prepare yourself for an emergency, however, by always packing a first-aid kit, a reflector, a whistle, high energy food, and extra water for any hike. Dress in light, natural fibers. If spending the night in the desert, remember that temperatures drop dramatically at night.

Spring and fall are the most temperate season for hikes. In summer, most of the day will be in the shade with the Bedouin until the sun calms down, and in winter you'll freeze. The nights are frigid year-round. You may be able to rent blankets from the Bedouin, but don't count on it; bring a sweater and a warm sleeping bag.

Check **weather forecasts** and pay attention to the skies when hiking, since weather patterns can change suddenly. Whenever possible, let someone know when and where you are going hiking, either a friend, your hostel, a park ranger, or a local hiking organization. Do not attempt a hike beyond your ability—you may be endangering your life. See **Health,** p. 19, for information about outdoor ailments and basic medical concerns.

KEEPING IN TOUCH

MAIL

SENDING MAIL TO THE MIDDLE EAST

Airmail letters under 1 oz. between North America and the Middle East or Turkey and Cyprus take five to seven days and typically cost under a US$1, or CDN$0.95 up to 20g. Allow at least five to seven business days from Australia (postage AUS$1.50 for up to 50 grams) and four to 10 days from the UK ($0.65 for up to 20g). Envelopes should be marked "air mail" or "par avion."

RECEIVING MAIL IN THE MIDDLE EAST

There are several ways to arrange picking up letters sent from friends and relatives while you are abroad.

General Delivery: Mail can be sent to the Middle East through **Poste Restante** (the international phrase for General Delivery) to almost any city or town with a post office, though Poste Restante does not exist in Lebanon. Address letters to: Name, Poste Restante, City, COUNTRY. In Turkey, the address must either say *Markaz Postane* (Central Post Office), or specify which office should receive the mail. It is best to use the largest post office in the area, as mail may be sent there regardless of what is written on the envelope. When possible, it is safer and quicker to send mail express or registered. When picking up your mail, bring a form of photo ID, preferably a passport. There is generally no surcharge; if there is, it should not exceed the cost of domestic postage. If there is nothing, have them check under your first name.

American Express: AmEx's travel offices throughout the world will act as a mail service for cardholders. Under this free **Client Letter Service** they will hold mail for up to 30 days and forward upon request. Address the letter in the manner shown above. Some offices will offer these services to non-cardholders (especially those who have purchased AmEx traveler's checks); call ahead to make sure. Check the **Practical Information** section of the countries you plan to visit; *Let's Go* lists AmEx office locations for most large cities. A complete list is available free from AmEx (☎(800) 528-4800).

Express Mail: If regular airmail is too slow, **Federal Express** and **DHL** can move your mail quickly but will charge through the nose for their services. From New York, a half-pound letter costs US$32.50 plus tax to Cairo, Beirut, Tel Aviv or Istanbul, and is guaranteed to arrive in four business days. Rates from non-US locations are similarly expensive (London to Cairo costs US$48 and takes two days; Sydney to Cairo US$73.29, four days). Mail within the Middle East is not much cheaper: Dubai to Cairo runs US$24.38 and takes two days. Cheaper **Global Priority Service** is an excellent alternative, though it only services Cyprus, Israel, and Turkey ($5 up to 4lb., otherwise $9).

ESSENTIALS

ESSENTIALS

SENDING MAIL HOME

Aerogrammes, printed sheets that fold into envelopes and travel via airmail, are available at post offices. Mark them "airmail" or "par avion." Most post offices will charge exorbitant fees or simply refuse to send aerogrammes with enclosures. Delivery time averages four to 21 days. Costs for Europe, North America, and Australia are similar (about US$0.60); costs for Africa and Arab countries are lower.

TELEPHONES

CALLING THE MIDDLE EAST FROM HOME

To call the Middle East direct from home, dial:

1. The **international access code** of your home country. These include: Australia 0011; Ireland, New Zealand, or the UK 00; South Africa 09; Canada and the US 011.

2. The **country code** for the nation you are calling. Country and city codes are sometimes listed with a zero in front (e.g., 033), but after dialing the international access code, drop successive zeros (with an access code of 011 and country code of 033, dial 011 33). For individual country codes, see the **Phone Facts** box of each chapter.

3. The **city code** (see the city's **Practical Information** section) and local number.

CALLING HOME FROM THE MIDDLE EAST

A **calling card** is your best and cheapest bet. Calls are billed collect or to your account. **MCI WorldPhone** also provides access to MCI's Traveler's Assist, which gives legal and medical advice, exchange rate information, and translation services. Calling card use is limited in Jordan. **To obtain a calling card** from your national telecommunications service before you leave home, contact the appropriate company. In **Australia,** call Telstra **Australia Direct** (☎13 22 00); in **Canada,** call Bell Canada **Canada Direct** (☎(800) 565-4708); in **Ireland,** call Telecom Éireann **Ireland Direct** (☎800 250 250); in **New Zealand,** call **Telecom New Zealand** (☎800 000 000); in **South Africa,** contact **Telkom South Africa** (☎09 03); in the **UK,** call British Telecom **BT Direct** (☎800 34 51 44). In the **US,** your options are **AT&T** (☎(888) 288-4685), **Sprint** (☎(800) 877 4646), or **MCI** (☎(800) 444 4141).

You can usually make **direct international calls** from pay phones. Look for pay phones in public areas, especially train stations, as private pay phones are often more expensive. In-room hotel calls invariably include an arbitrary and sky-high surcharge than can run as much as US$0.75 per minute, or a flat fee of around US$10. If you do dial direct, first insert the appropriate amount of money or a pre-paid phonecard, then dial the international access code for the target country, and then dial the country code and number of your home. **Country codes** include: Australia 61; Ireland 353; New Zealand 64; South Africa 27; UK 44; US and Canada 1.

CALLING WITHIN THE MIDDLE EAST
In addition to coin-operated public phones, you can also buy **prepaid phonecards,** which carry a certain amount of phone time depending on the card's denomination. Phone rates tend to be highest in the morning, lower in the evening, and lowest on Sundays and late at night.

TIME DIFFERENCES
Greenwich Mean Time (GMT) is five hours ahead of New York time, eight hours ahead of Vancouver and San Francisco time, two hours behind Johannesburg time, 10 hours behind Sydney time, and 12 hours behind Auckland time. All the countries in this guide are two hours ahead of GMT.

EMAIL AND INTERNET
The **Cybercafe Guide** (www.cyberiacafe.net/cyberia/guide/ccafe.htm) and the **Cybercafe Search Engine** (www.cybercaptive.com) can help you find cybercafes in the Middle East, but don't despair if it doesn't list cafes in your target town: they are cropping up so quickly that no index is current. In Egypt, Lebanon, Israel, and Turkey there should be no trouble finding Internet access. In Jordan, only the big cities have Internet access. It is difficult to find any Internet access in Syria. One money-saving strategy is to befriend college students and ask if you can use their campus terminals. One hour usually costs between $2 and $5. For specific information on Internet access, refer to the **Essentials** section of country chapters.

GETTING THERE

BY PLANE
When it comes to airfare, a little effort can save you a bundle. If your plans are flexible enough to deal with the restrictions, courier fares are the cheapest. Tickets bought from consolidators and standby seating are also good deals, but last-minute specials, airfare wars, and charter flights often beat these fares. The key is to hunt around, to be flexible, and to ask persistently about discounts. Students, seniors, and those under 26 should never pay full price for a ticket.

DETAILS AND TIPS
Timing: Airfares to the Middle East peak between mid-June and late Sept.; holidays are also expensive. The cheapest times to travel are early Nov. to mid-Dec. and early Jan. to the end of Mar. Midweek (M-Th morning) round-trip flights run US$40-50 cheaper than weekend flights, but they are generally more crowded and less likely to permit frequent-flier upgrades. Traveling with an "open return" ticket can be pricier than fixing a return date when buying the ticket.

Route: Round-trip flights are by far the cheapest; "open-jaw" (arriving in and departing from different cities, e.g. London-Paris and Rome-London) tickets tend to be pricier. Patching one-way flights together is the most expensive way to travel. Traveling from hub to hub (e.g. New York to Cairo) will win a more competitive fare than flying to or from smaller cities.

Round-the-World (RTW): If the Middle East is only one stop on a more extensive globe-hop, consider a RTW ticket. Tickets usually include at least 5 stops and are valid for about a year; prices range from US$1200-5000. Try **Northwest Airlines/KLM** (☎(800) 447-4747; www.nwa.com) or **Star Alliance**, a consortium of 13 airlines including United Airlines (☎(800) 241-6522; www.star-alliance.com).

Gateway Cities: Flights between capitals or regional hubs offer the cheapest fares. The cheapest gateway cities in the Middle East are typically Cairo, Istanbul, and Tel Aviv.

Boarding: Confirm international flights by phone within 72hr. of departure. Most airlines require that passengers arrive at the airport at least 2hr. before departure. One carry-on item and two checked bags is the norm for non-courier flights.

Fares: Sample round-trip fares from **New York** include: Cairo (US$800-1200); Istanbul (US$450-600); Beirut (US$1100-1500); Tel Aviv (US$700-1100); and Amman (US$800-1300). From **London:** Cairo (US$500-900); Istanbul (US$320-500); Beirut (US$600-900); Tel Aviv (US$310-500); and Amman (US$800-1100). From **Sydney:** Cairo (US$1400-1800); Istanbul (US$1200-1500); Beirut (US$1500-1600); Tel Aviv (US$1250-1600); and Amman (US$1800-2100).

BUDGET AND STUDENT TRAVEL AGENCIES

While knowledgeable agents specializing in flights to the Middle East can make your life easy and help you save, they may not spend the time to find you the lowest possible fare—they get paid on commission. Students and under-27ers holding **ISIC and IYTC cards** (see p. 3), respectively, qualify for big discounts from student travel agencies. Most flights from budget agencies are on major airlines, but in peak season some may sell seats on less reliable chartered aircraft.

usit world (www.usitworld.com). Over 50 **usit campus** branches in the UK (www.usitcampus.co.uk), including 52 Grosvenor Gardens, **London** SW1W 0AG (☎(0870) 240 10 10); **Manchester** (☎(0161) 273 17 21); and **Edinburgh** (☎(0131) 668 33 03). Nearly 20 **usit now** offices in Ireland, including 19-21 Aston Quay, O'Connell Bridge, **Dublin** 2 (☎(01) 602 16 00; www.usitnow.ie), and **Belfast** (☎(02890) 32 71 11; www.usitnow.com). Offices also in Athens, Auckland, Brussels, Frankfurt, Johannesburg, Lisbon, Luxembourg, Madrid, Paris, Sofia, and Warsaw.

Council Travel (www.counciltravel.com). US offices include: Emory Village, 1561 N. Decatur Rd., **Atlanta**, GA 30307 (☎(404) 377-9997); 273 Newbury St., **Boston**, MA 02116 (☎(617) 266-1926); 1160 N. State St., **Chicago**, IL 60610 (☎(312) 951-0585); 931 Westwood Blvd., Westwood, **Los Angeles**, CA 90024 (☎(310) 208-3551); 254 Greene St., **New York**, NY 10003 (☎(212) 254-2525); 530 Bush St., **San Francisco**, CA 94108 (☎(415) 566-6222); 424 Broadway Ave E., **Seattle**, WA 98102 (☎(206) 329-4567); 3301 M St. NW, **Washington, D.C.** 20007 (☎(202) 337-6464). **For US cities not listed,** call ☎(800) 2-COUNCIL (226-8624). In the UK, 28A Poland St. (Oxford Circus), **London**, W1V 3DB (☎(020) 7437 7767).

CTS Travel, 44 Goodge St., **London** W1 (☎(020) 7636 0031; fax 7637 5328; email ctsinfo@ctstravel.com.uk).

STA Travel, 6560 Scottsdale Rd. #F100, Scottsdale, AZ 85253 (☎(800) 777-0112; fax (602) 922-0793; www.sta-travel.com). A student and youth travel organization with over 150 offices worldwide. Ticket booking, travel insurance, railpasses, and more. US offices include: 297 Newbury St., **Boston**, MA 02115 (☎(617) 266-6014); 429 S. Dearborn St., **Chicago**, IL 60605 (☎(312) 786-9050); 7202 Melrose Ave., **Los Angeles**, CA 90046 (☎(323) 934-8722); 10 Downing St., **New York**, NY 10014 (☎(212) 627-3111); 4341 University Way NE, **Seattle**, WA 98105 (☎(206) 633-5000); 2401 Pennsylvania Ave., Ste. G, **Washington, D.C.** 20037 (☎(202) 887-0912); 51 Grant Ave., **San Francisco**, CA 94108 (☎(415) 391-8407). In the UK, 11 Goodge St., **London** WIP 1FE (☎(020) 7436

7779 for North American travel). In New Zealand, 10 High St., **Auckland** (☎(09) 309 04 58). In Australia, 366 Lygon St., **Melbourne** Vic 3053 (☎(03) 9349 4344).

Travel CUTS (Canadian Universities Travel Services Limited), 187 College St., **Toronto,** ON M5T 1P7 (☎(416) 979 24 06; fax 979 81 67; www.travelcuts.com). Forty offices across Canada. In the UK, 295-A Regent St., **London** W1R 7YA (☎(020) 7255 1944).

COMMERCIAL AIRLINES

FLIGHT PLANNING ON THE INTERNET. The Web is a great place to look for travel bargains—it's fast, it's convenient, and you can spend as long as you like exploring options without driving your travel agent insane.

Many airline sites offer special last-minute deals on the Web. Try **Cape to Cairo** (www.capecairo.com), **Cheap Tickets** (www.cheaptickets.com), **NOW Voyager** (www.nowvoyagertravel.com), **Travac** (www.travac.com), or **Travel Avenue** (www.travelavenue.com) for low fares to the Middle East. Other sites do the legwork and compile the deals for you—try www.bestfares.com, www.one-travel.com, www.lowestfare.com, and www.travelzoo.com.

STA (www.sta-travel.com) and **Council** (www.counciltravel.com) provide quotes on student tickets, while **Expedia** (msn.expedia.com) and **Travelocity** (www.travelocity.com) offer full travel services. **Priceline** (www.priceline.com) allows you to specify a price, and obligates you to buy any ticket that meets or beats it; be prepared for antisocial hours and odd routes. **Skyauction** (www.skyauction.com) allows you to bid on both last-minute and advance-purchase tickets.

Just one last note—to protect yourself, make sure that the site uses a secure server before handing over any credit card details. Happy hunting!

The commercial airlines' lowest regular offer is the **APEX** (Advance Purchase Excursion) fare, which provides confirmed reservations and allows "open-jaw" tickets. Generally, reservations must be made seven to 21 days ahead of departure, with seven- to 14-day minimum-stay and up to 90-day maximum-day restrictions. These fares carry hefty cancellation and change penalties (fees rise in summer). Book peak-season APEX fares early; by May you will have a hard time getting your desired departure date. Use **Microsoft Expedia** (expedia.msn.com) or **Travelocity** (www.travelocity.com) to get an idea of the lowest published fares, then use the resources outlined here to try and beat those fares. Low-season fares should be appreciably cheaper than the **high-season** (mid-June to Sept.) ones listed here.

TRAVELING FROM NORTH AMERICA

Basic round-trip fares to the Middle East range from roughly US$450-1500: to Cairo, US$800-1200; to Istanbul, US$450-600; to Beirut, US$1100-1500; to Tel Aviv, US$700-1100; to Amman, US$800-1300. Standard commercial airlines like American and United will probably offer the most convenient flights, but they may not be the cheapest, unless you manage to grab a special promotion or airfare war ticket. You will probably find flying one of the following "discount" airlines a better deal, if any of their limited departure points is convenient for you.

Lufthansa (☎(800) 399-5838; www.lufthansa-usa.com) has a wide variety of routes covering all major hubs of the Middle East via Frankfurt.

Air France (☎(800) 237-2747; www.airfrance.com) covers much of the Middle East mainly through Paris.

TWA (☎(800) 892-4141; www.twa.com) flies to some, but not all, Middle Eastern cities, like Cairo and Amman.

EgyptAir (☎(800) 334-6787; www.egyptair.com.eg) has the most routes within the country, and also serves major cities like New York and Los Angeles.

Royal Jordanian (☎(800) 755-6732; www.rja.com.jo) not only flies to all major Middle Eastern hubs, but also has extensive service to many smaller airports as well.

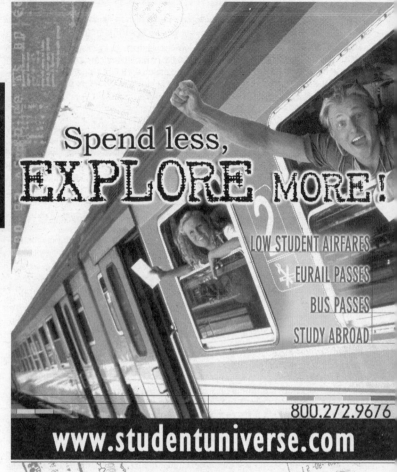

TRAVELING FROM THE UK AND IRELAND

Basic round-trip fares to the Middle East range from roughly US$300-1100: to Cairo, US$500-900; to Istanbul, US$320-500; to Beirut, US$600-900; to Tel Aviv, US$310-500; to Amman, US$800-1100. Standard commercial centers like American and United will probably offer the most convenient flights, but they may not be the cheapest, unless you manage to grab a special promotion or airfare war ticket. You will probably find flying one of the following "discount" airlines a better deal, if any of their limited departure points is convenient for you.

British Airways (☎ (845) 773 33 77; www.british-airways.com) has daily flights to nearly all major Middle Eastern cities, including Cairo, Istanbul, Beirut, and Amman. Most flights originate from London.

British Mediterranean Airways (☎ (845) 773 33 77; www.british-airways.com/inside/wrld-wide/partners/franchise/docs/bmed.shtml) serves European cities to the Middle East.

Austrian Airways (☎ (171) 434 73 80; www.aua.com) connects to all major Middle Eastern cities via Vienna.

EgyptAir (☎ (171) 734 94 90; www.egyptair.com.eg) serves the United Kingdom to the Middle East on a daily basis.

Royal Jordanian (☎ (171) 878 63 00; www.rja.com.jo) provides connections between many cities in Europe and the Middle East through Amman.

TRAVELING FROM AUSTRALIA AND NEW ZEALAND

Basic round-trip fares to the Middle East range from roughly US$1200-2100: to Cairo, US$1400-1800; to Istanbul, US$1200-1500; to Beirut, US$1500-1600; to Tel Aviv, US$1250-1600; to Amman, US$1800-2100. Standard commercial centers like American and United will probably offer the most convenient flights, but they may not be the cheapest, unless you manage to grab a special promotion or airfare war ticket. You will probably find flying one of the following "discount" airlines a better deal, if any of their limited departure points is convenient for you.

Qantas Air (☎ 13 13 13; www.qantas.com.au) flies from a variety of departure cities in Australia and New Zealand to London, from which connecting flights to the Middle East are easy to find.

Air New Zealand (☎ (02) 92 23 46 66; www.airnz.com) has reasonable fares from Auckland to London, and often special sales at much lower prices. Again, it is necessary to find connecting flights to the Middle East.

EgyptAir (☎ (612) 232 66 77; www.egyptair.com.eg) is one of the few airlines serving Cairo from Australia and New Zealand.

TRAVELING FROM SOUTH AFRICA

Basic round-trip fares to the Middle East range from roughly US$600-1600: to Cairo, US$800-1400; to Istanbul, US$600-1000; to Beirut, US$700-1200; to Tel Aviv, US$600-900; to Amman, US$1100-1600. Standard commercial centers like American and United will probably offer the most convenient flights, but they may not be the cheapest, unless you manage to grab a special promotion or airfare war ticket. You will probably find flying one of the following "discount" airlines a better deal, if any of their limited departure points is convenient for you.

South African (☎ (11) 978 10 00; www.saa.co.za) serves mostly Africa, but also connects to some cities in the Middle East.

Lufthansa (☎ (011) 484 47 11; www.lufthansa.com) reliably offers direct flights to Cairo and Istanbul from South Africa, as well as provides connecting flights to the Middle East through Eastern Europe.

British Airways (☎ (011) 441 86 00; www.british-airways.com/regional/sa) has flights from Johannesburg and Cape Town to places in Europe with easy connections to the Middle East.

KLM (☎ (11) 881 96 96; www.klm.com) serves South Africa to the Middle East through Europe.

ESSENTIALS

AIR COURIER FLIGHTS

Those who travel light should consider courier flights. Couriers help transport cargo on international flights by using their checked luggage space for freight. Generally, couriers must travel with carry-ons only and deal with complex flight restrictions. Most flights are round-trip only, with short fixed-length stays (usually one week) and a limit of a one ticket per issue. Most also operate only out of major gateway cities, mostly in North America. Round-trip courier fares from the US to the Middle East run about US$400-750. Most flights leave from New York, Los Angeles, San Francisco, or Miami in the US; and from Montreal, Toronto, or Vancouver in Canada. Generally, you must be over 21 (in some cases 18). In summer, the most popular destinations usually require an advance reservation of about two weeks (you can usually book up to two months ahead). Super-discounted fares are common for "last-minute" flights (three to 14 days ahead).

Air Courier Association (☎(800) 282-1202; www.aircourier.org) provides their members with a list of opportunities and courier brokers worldwide for an annual fee.

International Association for Air Travel Couriers, 20 South Dixie Hwy., PO Box 1349, Lake Worth, FL 33460 (☎(561) 582-8320; email iaatc@courier.org; www.courier.org) is another group that provides information on courier flights.

Now Voyager Travel, 74 Varick St. Suite 307, New York, NY 10013 (☎(212) 431-1616; www.nowvoyagertravel.com) offers both discount courier and non-courier fares.

TICKET CONSOLIDATORS

Ticket consolidators, or **"bucket shops,"** buy unsold tickets in bulk from commercial airlines and sell them at discounted rates. The best place to look is in the Sunday travel section of any major newspaper (such as the *New York Times*), where many bucket shops place tiny ads. Call quickly, as availability is typically extremely limited. Not all bucket shops are reliable, so insist on a receipt that gives full details of restrictions, refunds, and tickets, and pay by credit card (in spite of the 2-5% fee) so you can stop payment if you never receive your tickets. For more info, see www.travel-library.com/air-travel/consolidators.html or pick up Kelly Monaghan's *Air Travel's Bargain Basement* (Intrepid Traveler, US$8).

TRAVELING FROM THE US AND CANADA

Travel Avenue (☎(800) 333-3335; www.travelavenue.com) will search for cheap flights from anywhere for a fee. **NOW Voyager,** 74 Varick St., #307, New York, NY 10013 (☎(212) 431-1616; fax 219-1793; www.nowvoyagertravel.com) arranges discounted flights, mostly from New York, to Barcelona, London, Madrid, Milan, Paris, and Rome. Other consolidators worth trying are **Interworld** (☎(305) 443-4929; fax 443-0351); **Pennsylvania Travel** (☎(800) 331-0947); **Rebel** (☎(800) 227-3235; email travel@rebeltours.com; www.rebeltours.com); **Cheap Tickets** (☎(800) 377-1000; www.cheaptickets.com); and **Travac** (☎(800) 872-8800; fax (212) 714-9063; www.travac.com). Yet more consolidators on the web include the **Internet Travel Network** (www.itn.com); **SurplusTravel.com** (www.surplustravel.com); **Travel Information Services** (www.tiss.com); **TravelHUB** (www.travelhub.com); and **The Travel Site** (www.thetravelsite.com). These are just suggestions to get you started in your research; *Let's Go* does not endorse any of these agencies. As always, be cautious, and research companies before you hand over your credit card number.

TRAVELING FROM THE UK, AUSTRALIA, AND NEW ZEALAND

In London, the **Air Travel Advisory Bureau** (☎(020) 76 36 50 00; www.atab.co.uk) can provide names of reliable consolidators and discount flight specialists. From Australia and New Zealand, look for consolidator ads in the travel section of the *Sydney Morning Herald* and other papers.

CHARTER FLIGHTS

Charters are flights a tour operator contracts with an airline to fly extra loads of passengers during peak season. Charter flights fly less frequently than major airlines, make refunds particularly difficult, and are almost always fully booked. Schedules and itineraries may also change or be cancelled at the last moment (as late as 48 hours before the trip, and without a full refund), and check-in, boarding, and baggage claim are often much slower. However, they can also be cheaper.

Discount clubs and **fare brokers** offer members savings on last-minute charter and tour deals. Study contracts closely; you don't want to end up with an unwanted overnight layover. **Travelers Advantage,** Stamford, CT, USA (☎(800) 548-1116; www.travelersadvantage.com; US$60 annual fee includes discounts, newsletters, and cheap flight directories) specializes in European travel and tour packages.

FURTHER READING

The Worldwide Guide to Cheap Airfare, Michael McColl. Insider Publications (US$15).

Discount Airfares: The Insider's Guide, George Hobart. Priceless Publications (US$14).

The Official Airline Guide, an expensive tome available at many libraries, has flight schedules, fares, and reservation numbers.

Air Traveler's Handbook (www.cs.cmu.edu/afs/cs/user/mkant/Public/Travel/airfare.html).

GETTING AROUND

BY BUS OR TRAIN

BY BUS

EGYPT. Though inexpensive, buses in Egypt can be slow, crowded, and hot. Companies include **Superjet**, **West Delta Bus Company**, and **East Delta Bus Company**. West Delta has a deluxe branch called **Golden Arrow** with vehicles sporting A/C, refreshments, and bathrooms. Air-conditioned East Delta buses serve the Sinai.

ISRAEL. Buses are the most popular and convenient means of travel in Israel. Except for the **Dan Company** and the Arab buses serving the West Bank, Galilee, and Gaza, the **Egged Bus Cooperative** has a monopoly on intercity and most intracity buses. Students with ISIC receive a 10% discount on some fares. Buses are sometimes crowded, especially during rush hours and on Saturday nights after Shabbat.

JORDAN. The government owns a monopoly on intercity bus service, so the **Jordan Express Tourist Transport (JETT)** is your only option. Buses (infrequently) cover popular routes, including daily trips from Amman to Aqaba, Petra, Ma'an, the King Hussein/Allenby Bridge, Damascus, and Cairo. The air-conditioned JETT luxury coaches cost about 20% more than regular buses. Booking ahead is necessary.

LEBANON. Intracity buses all cost L₤500 and are surprisingly easy to use. Over 20 different lines criss-cross the city, and are ideal for going to well-traveled destinations such as Cola Bridge, the National Museum, Dawra, or the Pigeon Rocks (Raouche). Stand on the proper side of busy streets and shout your destination as the bus slows down. Intracity buses finish their runs around 7 or 8pm; after that you're left with *service* or private taxis.

SYRIA. **Karnak,** the government-run bus company, has extensive routes and low fares on orange-and-white, air-conditioned buses. Buses occasionally depart on schedule, and reservations are required. **Pullman** buses are a step below Karnak. Over 50 private bus companies now operate in Syria; they have ship-shape coaches and competitive prices. Reservations are a good idea for these buses too. All tickets must be bought at the stations, as drivers do not handle money. **Micro-**

buses (MEEK-ro-bus) are easy, cheap, and relatively hassle-free. Fees in Damascus are set, but vary elsewhere depending on your destination; ask the person next to you (not the driver) how much to pay or wait to see what other people pay.

TURKEY. Frequent, modern, and cheap buses run between all sizeable cities. In large cities, the *otogar* (bus station) is often quite a distance from the city center, but many bus companies have branch offices downtown. Free shuttles called *servis* take ticketed passengers to the otogar. Buy tickets in advance from local offices, or purchase them directly at the station. You will need to go from booth to booth to piece together a complete schedule; one company may not divulge competitors schedules. Many lines provide a 10% discount to ISIC-carrying students. Fares may increase during summer and religious holidays. Seats are assigned and passengers are expected to remain in their assigned seats for the duration of the trip. Road safety is a serious concern in Turkey, so *Let's Go* strongly recommends that you only travel on reputable bus lines, particularly for long trips. Although these are comparatively the most expensive tickets, they are still cheap. The extra money you pay allows the companies to take safety precautions such as giving the drivers rest breaks. Reputable companies include: Varan, Ulusoy, and Kamıl Ko. Whenever possible, *Let's Go* quotes prices from these companies.

BY TRAIN

EGYPT. Egypt's railway system was the first established in both the Arab world and in Africa. Schedules and signs in the train stations are never in English, but can be obtained from the tourist office or from ticket windows. If lines are long and you're in a hurry, try boarding the train without a ticket—the conductor will usually sell one on board for an additional fee.

Trains offer student discounts (ISIC card required) of up to 50%, with an average discount of about 30%. **Air-conditioned second-class** cars are comfortably small, with reclining seats. Avoid the dangerous **third class**. **Second-class sleeper cars** might be more comfortable for trips of ten hours or more but are overpriced. Reserve space in a sleeper at the wagon-lit offices in Cairo, Luxor, Aswan, and Alexandria. Seats for Cairo-Alexandria (especially in summer) and Cairo-Upper Egypt (especially in winter) trips should be reserved a day or two in advance. Reserve a week in advance during the last week of Ramadan and the following week, as well as before Eid al-Adha.

ISRAEL. Rail service in Israel is useful only for travel along the northern coast. Trains are slightly cheaper than buses, but they too stop during Shabbat. Avoid traveling on Friday afternoons when the trains are most crowded. Students with an ISIC enjoy a 50% discount.

JORDAN. Intracity trams of any kind do not exist in Jordan. The minibuses that roam the country are cheap and a great means of transportation (and many times air-conditioned).

LEBANON. There are no operating trains in Lebanon. It is best to use other means of transportation.

SYRIA. Strictly speaking, trains connect some cities in Syria. Frankly speaking, roller skates would serve you better. Trains are slow, crowded, and dirty, and in most places they drop you off about 30km out of town. Use the buses.

TURKEY. Trains run directly to Istanbul from Athens and Bucharest. Some lines may be suspended due to political crises in the Balkans. Eurail passes are not valid in Turkey, but InterRail passes are. The Under 26 InterRail Pass (from UK159) allows either 15 days or one month of unlimited travel within one, two, three, or all of the seven zones into which InterRail divides Europe; the cost is determined by the number of zones the pass covers. The Over 26 InterRail Pass (also zone-based) offers unlimited second-class travel for 22 days for UK229. Overall, however, trains are slothfully slow and very expensive. Use the buses.

BY CAR

Driving is extremely dangerous in the Middle East. You should be prepared as a pedestrian, passenger, or driver for unorthodox and aggressive moves. Egypt has the highest rate of frequency of car accidents; Turkey has also achieved international notoriety for its unfortunate driving records. **Wear a seatbelt.** Child safety seats are usually not available: strap on children's seatbelts and don't let kids sit in the front seat, if possible. In many regions, road conditions necessitate driving more slowly and cautiously than you would at home. For long drives in desolate areas, invest in a cellular phone.

Sleeping in your car is one of the most dangerous (and often illegal) ways to get your rest. If your car breaks down, wait for the police to assist you.

DRIVING PERMITS AND CAR INSURANCE

INTERNATIONAL DRIVING PERMIT (IDP)

If you plan to drive while in the Middle East, you must be over 18. *Let's Go* also suggests purchasing an International Driving Permit (IDP): Egypt and Syria require one, while Israel, Jordan, Lebanon, and Turkey recommend one. The degree of enforcement of these rules varies from country to country. Even for the countries where an IDP is not required, it may be a good idea to get one anyway, in case you're in an accident or stranded and the police do not know English; information on the IDP is printed in ten languages, including Spanish, French, Chinese, Italian, Portuguese, Swedish, Arabic, Russian, and German.

Your IDP, valid for one year, must be issued in your own country before you depart. An application for an IDP usually needs to include one or two photos, a current local license, an additional form of identification, and a fee.

Australia: Contact your local Royal Automobile Club (RAC) or the National Royal Motorist Association (NRMA) if in NSW or the ACT (☎(08) 94 21 44 44; www.rac.com.au/travel). Permits AUS$15.

Canada: Contact any Canadian Automobile Association (CAA) branch office or write to CAA, 1145 Hunt Club Rd., #200, K1V 0Y3. (☎(613) 247 01 17; www.caa.ca/CAAInternet/travelservices/internationaldocumentation/idptravel.htm). Permits CDN$10.

Ireland: Contact the nearest Automobile Association (AA) office or write to the UK address below. Permits IR£4. The Irish Automobile Association, 23 Suffolk St., Rockhill, Blackrock, Co. Dublin (☎(01) 677 94 81), honors most foreign automobile memberships (24hr. breakdown and road service ☎(800) 66 77 88; toll-free in Ireland).

New Zealand: Contact your local Automobile Association (AA) or their main office at Auckland Central, 99 Albert St. (☎(9) 377 46 60; www.nzaa.co.nz). Permits NZ$8.

South Africa: Contact the Travel Services Department of the Automobile Association of South Africa at P.O. Box 596, 2000 Johannesburg (☎(11) 799 14 00; fax 799 14 10; http://aasa.co.za). Permits SAR28.50.

UK: To visit your local AA Shop, contact the **AA Headquarters** (☎(0990) 44 88 66), or write to: The Automobile Association, International Documents, Fanum House, Erskine, Renfrewshire PA8 6BW. To find the location nearest you that issues the IDP, call ☎(0990) 50 06 00 or (0990) 44 88 66. For more info, see www.theaa.co.uk/motoringandtravel/idp/index.asp. Permits UK£4.

US: Visit any American Automobile Association (AAA) office or write to AAA Florida, Travel Related Services, 1000 AAA Drive (mail stop 100), Heathrow, FL 32746 (☎(407) 444-7000; fax 444-7380). You don't have to be a member to buy an IDP. Permits US$10. AAA Travel Related Services (☎(800) 222-4357) provides road maps, travel guides, emergency road services, travel services, and auto insurance.

CAR INSURANCE

Selective credit cards cover standard insurance (American Express, Gold/Platinum Visa, Gold/Platinum Mastercard), with American Express providing the most coverage. If you rent, lease, or borrow a car, you will need a **green card,** or **International Insurance Certificate,** to certify that you have liability insurance and that it applies abroad. Green cards can be obtained at car rental agencies, car dealers (for those leasing cars), some travel agents, and some border crossings. Rental agencies may require you to purchase theft insurance in countries that they consider to have a high risk of auto theft.

BY PLANE

AIRCRAFT SAFETY. The airlines of the developing world do not always meet safety standards. The *Official Airline Guide* (www.oag.com) and many travel agencies can tell you the type and age of aircraft on a particular route. This can be especially useful in the Middle East, where less reliable equipment is often used for inter-city travel. The **International Airline Passengers Association** (US ☎ (972) 404-9980, safety office open M-F 9-11am; UK ☎ (208) 681 65 55) provides region-specific safety information. The **Federal Aviation Administration** (www.faa.gov) reviews the airline authorities for countries whose airlines enter the US, the **US State Department** (☎ (202) 647-5225; http://travel.state.gov/travel_warnings.html) has travel advisories that sometimes involve foreign carriers, especially when terrorist bombings may be a threat.

BY THUMB

Let's Go strongly urges you to consider the risks before you choose to hitchhike. We do not recommend hitchhiking as a safe means of transportation.

ADDITIONAL INFORMATION

SPECIFIC CONCERNS

WOMEN TRAVELERS

Women traveling alone in the Middle East are uncommon, and therefore perceived as vulnerable if doing so. Women exploring on their own inevitably face some additional safety concerns, but it's easy to be adventurous without taking undue risks. If you are concerned, consider staying in hostels which offer single rooms that lock from the inside or in religious organizations with rooms for women only. Communal showers in some hostels are safer than others; check them before settling in. Stick to centrally located accommodations and avoid solitary late-night treks or metro rides.

When traveling, always carry extra money for a phone call, bus, or taxi. **Hitching** is never safe for lone women, or even for two women traveling together. Choose train compartments occupied by other women or couples; ask the conductor to put together a women-only compartment if he or she doesn't offer to do so first. Look as if you know where you're going (even when you don't) and approach older women or couples for directions if you're lost or feel uncomfortable.

Generally, the less you look like a tourist, the better off you'll be. Dress conservatively, especially in rural areas. Trying to fit in can be effective, but dressing to the style of an obviously different culture may cause you to be ill at ease and a conspicuous target. Wearing a conspicuous **wedding band** may help prevent unwanted overtures. Some travelers report that carrying pictures of a "husband" or "children" is extremely useful to help document marriage status. Even a mention of a husband waiting back at the hotel may be enough in some places to discount your potentially vulnerable, unattached appearance. Women will find themselves approached much less frequently when escorted by a male over the age of 14, but should be wary of claiming to be "friends" with someone: the concept of friendship between men and women in the Arab world differs greatly from its counterpart in the West. Many Arabs see male-female relationships as euphemisms for something more ("friends with benefits," so to speak), and men often think that a woman's speaking to them implies sexual advance. Some hotels frown upon unmarried couples sharing a room and some have been known not to allow it, especially if one of the people is a native.

Foreign women in the Middle East are guaranteed to attract a great deal of attention. While it is not necessary for women to dress in traditional Arab clothing, they should cover their bodies as much as possible, especially their legs and upper arms. Stay away from the following items of clothing: short skirts, shorts, short athletic gear such as biking shorts, midriff-baring halter tops, v-neck blouses that descend more than an inch or two from the neck, tank tops, visible bra straps, and shirts stretched tight across the bodice. In secular havens like Tel Aviv and Beirut, locals dress in many fashions, from the long, draping dresses of Muslim conservatives to hip-hugging hotpants.

Your best answer to verbal harassment is no answer at all; feigning deafness, sitting motionless, and staring straight ahead at nothing in particular will do a world of good. The extremely persistent can sometimes be dissuaded by a firm, loud, and very public "Go away!" in the appropriate language (for useful phrases to use, see **Kiss My As(wan),** p. 243). Don't hesitate to seek out a police officer or a passerby if you are being harassed. Memorize the emergency numbers in places you visit and consider carrying a whistle or airhorn on your keychain. A self-defense course will not only prepare you for a potential attack, but will also raise your level of awareness of your surroundings as well as your confidence (see **Self Defense,** p. 16). Also be sure you are aware of the specific **health concerns** that women face when traveling (see p. 24).

FURTHER READING

A Journey of One's Own: Uncommon Advice for the Independent Woman Traveler, Thalia Zepatos. Eighth Mountain Press (US$17).

Adventures in Good Company: The Complete Guide to Women's Tours and Outdoor Trips, Thalia Zepatos. Eighth Mountain Press (US$7).

Active Women Vacation Guide, Evelyn Kaye. Blue Panda Publications (US$18).

Travelers' Tales: Gutsy Women, Travel Tips and Wisdom for the Road, Marybeth Bond. Traveler's Tales (US$8).

TRAVELING ALONE

There are many benefits to traveling alone, including independence and greater opportunities to interact with the residents of the region you're visiting. On the other hand, any solo traveler is a more vulnerable target of harassment and street theft. Lone travelers need to be well-organized and look confident at all times. Try not to stand out as a tourist, and be especially careful in deserted or very crowded areas. If questioned, never admit that you are traveling alone. Maintain regular contact with someone at home who knows your itinerary.

For more tips, pick up *Traveling Solo* by Eleanor Berman (Globe Pequot, US$17) or subscribe to **Connecting: Solo Travel Network,** P.O. Box 29088, Delamont RPO, Vancouver, BC V6J 5C2 (☎/fax (604) 737-7791; www.cstn.org; membership US$25-35), or the **Travel Companion Exchange,** P.O. Box 833, Amityville, NY 11701, USA (☎ (631) 454-0880 or (800) 392-1256; www.whytravelalone.com; US$48).

OLDER TRAVELERS

Discounts for senior citizens in the Middle East are few and far between, existing solely in Turkey, Israel, and Jordan. That being said, if you don't see a senior citizen price listed, ask, and you may be delightfully surprised.

ElderTreks, 597 Markham St., Toronto, ON M6G 2L7 (☎(800) 741 79 56 or (416) 588 50 00; fax 588 98 39; email eldertreks@eldertreks.com; www.eldertreks.com). Adventure travel programs for the 50+ traveler in Turkey.

Elderhostel, 75 Federal St., Boston, MA 02110, USA (☎(617) 426-7788 or (877) 426-2166; email registration@elderhostel.org; www.elderhostel.org). Organizes 1- to 4-week "educational adventures" in Turkey, Israel, and Jordan on varied subjects for those 55+.

The Mature Traveler, P.O. Box 50400, Reno, NV 89513, USA (☎(775) 786-7419, credit card orders (800) 460-6676). Deals, discounts, and travel packages for the 50+ traveler. Subscription$30.

Walking the World, P.O. Box 1186, Fort Collins, CO 80522, USA (☎(970) 498-0500; fax 498-9100; email walktworld@aol.com; www.walkingtheworld.com), organizes trips for 50+ travelers to Turkey.

FURTHER READING

No Problem! Worldwise Tips for Mature Adventurers, Janice Kenyon. Orca Book Publishers (US$16).

A Senior's Guide to Healthy Travel, Donald L. Sullivan. Career Press (US$15).

Unbelievably Good Deals and Great Adventures That You Absolutely Can't Get Unless You're Over 50, Joan Rattner Heilman. Contemporary Books (US$13).

BISEXUAL, GAY, AND LESBIAN TRAVELERS

The Middle East is not a particularly rainbow-friendly locale—even though men hold hands in the street, this reflects a different cultural attitude about male physicality, not homosexuality (see **I Wanna Hold Your Hand,** p. 78). No one is out of the closet in any public fashion except in Beirut, Haifa, and Tel Aviv; although homosexuality is legal in Turkey, it is not prevalent. A few gay bars here and there do not mean that any same-sex public displays of affection will be socially acceptable—they may even be illegal in some areas.

Listed below are contact organizations, mail-order bookstores and publishers which offer materials addressing some specific concerns. **Out and About** (www.planet.com) offers a bi-weekly newsletter addressing travel concerns. More information on Israel's gay-friendly attitude can be found in the **Special Concerns** section of the Israel coverage (p. 278).

Gay's the Word, 66 Marchmont St., London WC1N 1AB (☎(020) 72 78 76 54; email sales@gaystheword.co.uk; www.gaystheword.co.uk). The largest gay and lesbian bookshop in the UK, with both fiction and non-fiction titles. Mail-order service available.

Giovanni's Room, 345 S. 12th St., Philadelphia, PA 19107, USA (☎(215) 923-2960; fax 923-0813; www.queerbooks.com). An international lesbian/feminist and gay bookstore with mail-order service (carries many of the publications listed below).

International Gay and Lesbian Travel Association, 4331 N. Federal Hwy., #304, Fort Lauderdale, FL 33308, USA (☎(954) 776-2626; fax 776-3303; www.iglta.com). An organization of over 1350 companies serving gay and lesbian travelers worldwide.

International Lesbian and Gay Association (ILGA), 81 rue Marché-au-Charbon, B-1000 Brussels, Belgium (☎/fax +32 (2) 502 24 71; www.ilga.org). Not a travel service; provides political information, such as homosexuality laws of different countries.

FURTHER READING

Spartacus International Gay Guide. Bruno Gmunder Verlag. (US$33).

Damron's Accommodations and *The Women's Traveller.* Damron Travel Guides (US$14-19). For more info, call US ☎(415) 255-0404 or (800) 462-6654 or check their website (www.damron.com).

Ferrari Guides' Gay Travel A to Z, Ferrari Guides' Men's Travel in Your Pocket, Ferrari Guides' Women's Travel in Your Pocket, and *Ferrari Guides' Inn Places.* Ferrari Guides (US$14-16). For more info, call ☎(602) 863-2408 or (800) 962-2912 or try www.q-net.com.

The Gay Vacation Guide: The Best Trips and How to Plan Them, Mark Chesnut. Citadel Press (US$15).

TRAVELERS WITH DISABILITIES

The chaotic traffic and bumpy, frequently unpaved roads that make vehicular travel in the Middle East an annoyance make travel prohibitively difficult for travelers with disabilities. People in the Middle East are fairly ignorant of disabilities, and few places are handicapped accessible. **Israel** has taken several steps toward making the businesses and sights in and around their modernized cities more accessible to disabled travelers.

Those with disabilities should inform airlines and hotels of their disabilities when making arrangements for travel; some time may be needed to prepare special accommodations. Call ahead to restaurants, hotels, parks, and other facilities to find out about the existence of ramps, the widths of doors, the dimensions of elevators, etc. **Guide dog owners** should inquire as to the specific quarantine policies of each destination country. At the very least, they will need to provide a certificate of immunization against rabies.

USEFUL ORGANIZATIONS

Mobility International USA (MIUSA), P.O. Box 10767, Eugene, OR 97440, USA (☎(541) 343-1284 voice and TDD; fax 343-6812; email info@miusa.org; www.miusa.org). Sells *A World of Options: A Guide to International Educational Exchange, Community Service, and Travel for Persons with Disabilities* (US$35).

Moss Rehab Hospital Travel Information Service (☎(215) 456-9600 or (800) CALL-MOSS; email netstaff@mossresourcenet.org; www.mossresourcenet.org). An information resource center on travel-related concerns for those with disabilities.

Society for the Advancement of Travel for the Handicapped (SATH), 347 Fifth Ave., #610, New York, NY 10016 (☎(212) 447-7284; www.sath.org). An advocacy group that publishes the quarterly travel magazine *OPEN WORLD* (free for members, US$13 for nonmembers). Also publishes a wide range of info sheets on disability travel facilitation and destinations. Annual membership US$45, students and seniors US$30.

TOUR AGENCIES

Directions Unlimited, 123 Green Ln., Bedford Hills, NY 10507, USA (☎(914) 241-1700 or (800) 533-5343). Specializes in arranging individual and group vacations, tours, and cruises for the physically disabled.

FURTHER READING

Resource Directory for the Disabled, Richard Neil Shrout. Facts on file (US$45).

MINORITY TRAVELERS

People of all skin colors will find less an active racism in the Middle East than an ignorance about different people. **Ethnic Asians** may attract stares, especially in untouristed areas. In some regions of the Middle East, **black or dark-skinned travelers** may find that they encounter some negative attention. This response arises largely from the fact that Africans have traditionally been seen as interlopers. **Blondes** attract curiosity in the Middle East, since native blondes are nonexistent.

All over the Middle East, the highly explosive ethnic and religious tensions mean that people will likely be curious about your origins. People may ask where your father comes from and which religion you practice (or were raised to practice). In particular, travelers with Biblical names or German-sounding surnames may be asked if they are **Jewish.** Jewish travelers should avoid revealing their religion in volatile areas, as it could result in tension or even confrontation.

TRAVELERS WITH CHILDREN

Family vacations often require that you slow your pace, and always require that you plan ahead. When deciding where to stay, remember the special needs of young children; if you pick a small hotel, call ahead and make sure it's child-friendly. If you rent a car, make sure the rental company provides a car seat for younger children. Be sure that your child carries some sort of ID in case of an emergency or in case he or she gets lost.

Children under two generally fly for 10% of the adult airfare on international flights (this does not necessarily include a seat). International fares are usually discounted 25% for children from two to 11. Finding a private place for **breast feeding** is often a problem while traveling, so pack accordingly.

FURTHER READING

Backpacking with Babies and Small Children, Goldie Silverman. Wilderness Press (US$10).

How to take Great Trips with Your Kids, Sanford and Jane Portnoy. Harvard Common Press (US $10).

Have Kid, Will Travel: 101 Survival Strategies for Vacationing With Babies and Young Children, Claire and Lucille Tristram. Andrews and McMeel (US$9).

Adventuring with Children: An Inspirational Guide to World Travel and the Outdoors, Nan Jeffrey. Avalon House Publishing ($15).

Trouble Free Travel with Children, Vicki Lansky. Book Peddlers (US$9).

DIETARY CONCERNS

The Middle East is definitely a meat munching place, but there's always falafel and hummus, and eggs are sold scrambled or hard-boiled in all the local markets. You won't find tofu or soybeans anywhere but in Israel or in an expat-type store in Beirut. Many restaurants in Israel are vegetarian because of the kosher restriction on mixing milk and meat. To address dietary concerns at restaurants ("I am a vegetarian"), see the **Phrasebook,** p. 702.

The North American Vegetarian Society, P.O. Box 72, Dolgeville, NY 13329, USA (☎ (518) 568-7970; email navs@telenet.com; www.navs-online.org), publishes information about vegetarian travel, including *Transformative Adventures, a Guide to Vacations and Retreats* (US$15) and *Vegetarian Asia* (US$10).

Travelers who keep **kosher** should contact synagogues in larger cities for information on kosher restaurants. Your own synagogue or college Hillel should have access to lists of Jewish institutions across the region. If you are strict in your observance, you may have to prepare your own food on the road. **The Jewish Travel Guide,** which lists synagogues, kosher restaurants, and Jewish institutions in over 100 countries, is available in Europe from Vallentine Mitchell Publishers, Newbury House 890-900, Eastern Ave., Newbury Park, Ilford, Essex IG2 7HH, UK (☎ (020) 85 99 88 66; fax 85 99 09 84) and in the US ($16.95 + $4 S&H) from ISBS, 5804 NE Hassallo St., Portland, OR 97213 (☎ (800) 944-6190).

FURTHER READING

The Vegetarian Traveler: Where to Stay if You're Vegetarian, Jed Civic. Larson Pub. (US$16).

ALTERNATIVES TO TOURISM

For an extensive listing of "off-the-beaten-track" and specialty travel opportunities, try the **Specialty Travel Index,** 305 San Anselmo Ave., #313, San Anselmo, CA 94960, USA (☎ (888) 624-4030 or (415) 455-1643; www.spectrav.com; US$6). **Transitions Abroad** (www.transabroad.com) publishes a bi-monthly on-line newsletter for work, study, and specialized travel abroad.

STUDYING ABROAD

Whether spending a summer, term, or semester abroad, the Middle East is a good place to learn a new language, as well as appreciate a rich culture and history. Though most study programs for foreigners in the Middle East focus on intense language instruction, others offer classes in subjects like Middle Eastern studies and international affairs. Cairo, Tel Aviv, Amman, Beirut, Damascus, and Istanbul are home to universities and programs that welcome students from the West.

Be sure to apply early for a student visa, as application processing is Jurassic in its inefficiency. A visa is required for most Middle Eastern countries for both short and long stays; if unsure of visa requirements, consult an embassy or the university of interest. An excellent place to find the Middle Eastern institution best suited to your study abroad needs is **Amideast Study Abroad,** 1730 M St. NW, #1100, Washington, D.C., 20036 (☎(202) 776-9600; email inquiries@amideast.org; www.amideast.org).

UNIVERSITIES

Most American undergraduates enroll in programs sponsored by US universities. Those relatively fluent in Arabic or Hebrew may find it cheaper to enroll directly in a local university (though getting credit may be more difficult). Though most universities in the Middle East offer language intensive courses, some schools that offer study abroad programs to foreigners are listed below.

School for International Training, College Semester Abroad, Admissions, Kipling Rd., P.O. Box 676, Brattleboro, VT 05302, USA (☎(800) 336-1616 or (802) 258-3267; www.sit.edu). Semester- and year-long programs focusing on peace and conflict studies in Israel and Jordan run US$9900-12,600.

Council on International Educational Exchange (CIEE), 205 East 42nd St., New York, NY 10017 (☎(888) 268-6245 or (800)-407-8839; www.ciee.org/study) sponsors work, volunteer, academic, and internship programs in Jordan and Turkey.

International Association for the Exchange of Students for Technical Experience (IAESTE), 10400 Little Patuxent Pkwy. #250, Columbia, MD 21044, USA (☎(410) 997-3068; www.aipt.org). Operates 8- to 12-week programs in Egypt, Israel, Jordan, Lebanon, Syria, and Turkey for college students who have completed two years of technical study. US$50 application fee.

American University of Beirut (AUB), Bliss St., P.O. Box 11-0236, **Beirut,** Lebanon (☎(01) 350 000, 340 460, 374 374, 374 444; fax 351 706; www.aub.edu.lb), or 850 Third Ave., 18th Fl., **New York,** NY 10022-6297 (☎(212) 583-7600; fax 583-7650). The black-clad hipsters that haunt most Beirut hotspots all hail exclusively from AUB, which offers programs in everything from philosophy to poultry science, with classes conducted in English. Tuition is about L£15,000,000 per semester (12 credits), and about L£565,000 per credit.

LANGUAGE SCHOOLS

The majority of foreign students who travel to the Middle East do so to study another language. These programs are run by foreign universities, independent international or local organizations, and divisions of a variety of Middle Eastern universities. They generally cost anywhere from US$400-$12,000 per semester (depending on the country) and may include room and board. Listed below are schools that offer study abroad programs to foreigners, organized by country.

EGYPT: Studying in Egypt means attending the **American University in Cairo (AUC),** 113 Qasr al-Aini St. AUC offers semester, year, and summer programs in intensive Arabic and undergraduate and graduate degree study conducted in English. Tuition for 2000-2001 is US$11338 per semester plus US$1730 for housing; US$5356 for the summer session (2 months) plus US$940 for housing. Contact the Office of Student Affairs, American University in Cairo, 420 Fifth Ave., 3rd fl., New York, NY 10018 (☎(212) 730-8800; email aucegypt@aucnyo.edu). **Center of Arabic Study Abroad (CASA)** is a private organization with a branch at AUC that offers a well-respected Arabic program to graduate students. Enrollment in classes is only by a series of examinations. Contact CASA, 428-B Candler Library, Emory University, Atlanta, GA 30322 (email casa@mail.jhuwash.jhu.edu; www.sais-jhu.edu/languages/casa).

JORDAN: University of Jordan offers a 6-level intensive program in Arabic (Modern Standard) for non-native speakers. All levels are offered regularly and concurrently during the fall (Sept.-Jan.), spring (Jan.-June), and summer (June-Aug.). Tuition fees for the fall and spring are JD340, for the summer JD205. For more information, contact University of Jordan, Amman 11942, Jordan (☎(06) 535 50 00; fax 535 55 22; www.ju.edu.jo).

ISRAEL: Before the study abroad semester begins, there is a 4-9 week *ulpan* to learn Hebrew, and university programs are preceded by *mekhina*, a year of intensive Hebrew at **Hebrew University of Jerusalem**, 11 E. 69th St., New York, NY 10021 (☎(212) 472-2288; fax 517-4548). For more information, contact British Friends of the Hebrew University, 126 Albert St., London NW1 7NE (☎(0207) 691 14 78; fax 691 15 01; email students@fhu.org.uk). More programs for foreign students are provided by **Tel Aviv University,** Office of Academic Affairs, 360 Lexington Ave., New York, NY 10017 (☎(212) 687-5651; fax 687-4085), or Ramat Aviv, Tel Aviv 69978 (☎(03) 640 83 17; fax 640 67 22) and **Haifa University,** 220 5th Ave., New York, NY 10001 (☎(212) 631-7471; fax 685-7883), or University of Haifa, Haifa 31905 (☎(04) 824 07 66; email rcbs702@uvm.haifa.ac.il; www.haifa.ac.il).

SYRIA: Arabic Teaching Institute for Foreigners in Damascus offers beginning and intermediate classes in Modern Standard Arabic. Tuition is US$600 for either the 8-month winter course (Oct.-May) or the 3-month summer course (Jun.-Sept.) and does not include housing, transportation, food, or living expenses. For more information, contact the Institute at Villat Sharqiyah (Eastern Villas), P.O. Box 9340, Damascus, Syria (☎(11) 22 15 38). **The National Council on US-Arab Relations** offers a six-week "Summer in Syria" program in Aleppo for US$3400 that allows students to earn up to seven hours of college credit—four of which are for intensive Arabic (the remaining credits can be earned in anything from international policy to comparative literature). The cost includes roundtrip airfare, tuition, transportation, room and board. For more information, contact the Council at 1140 Connecticut Ave. NW, Suite 1210, Washington, D.C. 20036 (☎(202) 293-0801; email info@ncusar.org).

TURKEY: Summer Program at Boğaziçi University, Istanbul, offers two or three seven-week classes on the culture, language, and history of Turkey, Central Asia, and the Middle East. Contact the Study Abroad Office, 115 International Studies Building, 910 S. 5th St., Champaign, IL 61820 (☎(217) 333-6322; email saoşuiuc.edu). **TÖMER,** 18/1 Ziya Gökalp Cad., Kızılay, Ankara (☎(312) 435 97 81; fax 433 81 90) is a university whose goal is to teach the Turkish language and culture. It has 13 branches across Turkey, including Istanbul, Antalya, Bursa, and İzmir. Contact **Pitzer College** in Turkey, Office of External Studies, Pitzer College, 1050 N. Mills Ave., Claremont, CA 91711 (☎(909) 621-8104; fax 621-0518; www.pitzer.edu/academics/ilcenter/externalstudies/turkey.htm) to learn more about their four-month field study program.

FURTHER READING AND RESOURCES

www.studyabroad.com

Academic Year Abroad 2000/2001. Institute of International Education Books (US$45).

Vacation Study Abroad 2000/2001. Institute of International Education Books (US$43).

Peterson's Study Abroad 2001. Peterson's (US$30).

Peterson's Summer Study Abroad 2001. Peterson's (US$30)

WORKING ABROAD

A special type of visa and/or a working permit is required in order to work as a foreigner in the Middle East. For travel purposes other than tourism, a special entry visa is required in Egypt; Israel requires a work visa, as well. In Jordan, Lebanon, and Turkey, working permits are required. If on a diplomatic or business related trip, special visas or permits may not be necessary. Contact the Ministry of the Interior of interest for more information. Friends in the Middle East can often help expedite work permits or arrange work-for-accommodations swaps.

Few foreigners work in the Middle East because acquiring a work visa or permit is often a bureaucratic nightmare. Being an **English speaker** does wonders for your marketability (tutoring or teaching English is your best bet). Some travelers in the Sinai work for hotels or dive centers in **Na'ama Bay** (see p. 184). A note on **archaeological digs:** although they abound in this area, most sites offer hard work, menial labor, and no pay (the Archaeological Institute of America listed below is an excellent source for finding more rewarding digs). **Volunteer** jobs are readily available almost everywhere, particularly at Israeli **kibbutzim**.

COUNTRY-SPECIFIC RESOURCES

Egypt: **Work permits** can be obtained through any Egyptian consulate, or from the Ministry of the Interior. Some people look for temporary jobs upon arrival in Na'ama Bay or Alexandria. **American Field Service (AFS)** runs the Egyptian Society for Intercultural Exchange, (ESIE), which sponsors summer-, semester-, and year-long homestay exchange programs in Egypt for current students and short-term service projects for adults. Has programs for nearly every country of origin, and financial aid is available. Contact ESIE at 10 al-Thawra St., Apt. 5, Mohandiseen, Giza, Egypt (☎(2) 360 61 42; fax 337 60 01; email info-egypt@afs.org; www.afs.org/partners/egyhome.htm).

Israel: A special **work visa** is required. Volunteers often work at one of Israel's 250 **kibbutzim,** communal settlements whose members divide work and profits equally. Volunteers work 6-8 hour days per week, with a few days off per month, and receive a small monthly allowance in addition to room and board; the work is generally in agriculture, industry, or service. To apply, contact the main **Kibbutz Aliya Office** at 633 3rd Ave., 21st fl., New York, NY 10017 (☎(800) 247-7852; fax (212) 318-6134; email kibbutzdsk@aol.com). Applicants must be ages 18-35 with no children. **Moshavim** are agricultural communities in which farms and homes are privately owned and operated. You will receive free lodging with a family or with other workers. In return, you work a six-day week, at least eight hours per day. Workers are paid about US$300 per month, and are expected to pay for their own food. Applicants must be ages 18-35 and physically fit. Write the kibbutzim or contact **Volunteers Moshavim Movement,** 19 Leonardo da Vinci St., Tel Aviv (☎(03) 695 84 73).

Jordan: Get **work permits** from the Ministry of Labor. It's difficult for foreigners to find jobs in **Jordan;** a combination of perfect English and business or banking skills is optimal. Positions must be arranged before arrival in order to get a work visa. **Residence permits** are required for stays of more than 3 months.

Lebanon: People who seek to work in Lebanon must acquire a special **work visa.** Contact the nearest Lebanese embassy for details. **UNIPAL (Universities Trust for Educational Exchange with Palestinians)** sends volunteers to teach English to Palestinians and help with handicapped children in the West Bank, Gaza Strip, and Lebanon. Contact BCM Unipal, London, UK WC1N 3XX (☎(191) 386 7124).

Syria: Work for foreigners is scarce in Syria. A **residence permit** is required, as visitors on tourist visas are not allowed to work. The **American Language Center Damascus** employs 40 native speakers to teach English at their special learning facility in Damascus. Contact ALCD c/o USIS, P.O. Box 29, Damascus, Syria (☎(11) 332 72 36) or ALCD c/o USIS, Department of State, Washington, D.C. 20521-6110.

Turkey: Finding work in Turkey is difficult, as the government even restricts employment to citizens. Foreigners who wish to work in Turkey must obtain a **work permit,** issued by the Ministry of the Interior; contact a Turkish diplomatic mission for more information.

TEACHING ENGLISH

International Schools Services, Educational Staffing Program, P.O. Box 5910, Princeton, NJ 08543, USA (☎(609) 452-0990; www.iss.edu). Recruits teachers and administrators for American and English schools in the Middle East. US$150 application fee.

Office of Overseas Schools, US Department of State, Room H328, SA-1, Washington, D.C. 20522 (☎(202) 261-8200; fax 261-8224; www.state.gov/www/about_state/schools/). Keeps a comprehensive list of schools abroad and agencies that arrange placement for Americans to teach abroad.

ELS Language Centers/Middle East employs many English as a First Language (EFL) teachers in full- and part-time work in Egypt and Jordan. Contact them at their main office, P.O. Box 3079, Abu Dhabi, UAE (email elsme@emirates.net.ae).

ARCHAEOLOGICAL DIGS

Archaeological Institute of America, 656 Beacon St., Boston, MA 02215, USA (☎(617) 353-9361; www.archaeological.org). The *Archaeological Fieldwork Opportunities Bulletin* (US$16 for non-members) lists field sites throughout the Middle East. Purchase the bulletin from Kendall/Hunt Publishing, 4050 Westmark Dr., Dubuque, IA 52002, USA (☎(800) 228-0810).

VOLUNTEERING

Volunteer jobs are readily available, and many provide room and board in exchange for labor. You can sometimes avoid high application fees by contacting the individual workcamps directly.

Earthwatch, 680 Mt. Auburn St., Box 403, Watertown, MA 02272, USA (☎(800) 776-0188 or (617) 926-8200; www.earthwatch.org). Arranges 1- to 3-week programs in Turkey to promote conservation of natural resources. Programs average US$1600.

Habitat for Humanity International, 121 Habitat St., Americus, GA 31709, USA (☎(800) 334-3308; www.habitat.org). Offers international opportunities in Egypt to live with and build houses in a host community. Costs range US$1200-3500.

Volunteers for Peace, 1034 Tiffany Rd., Belmont, VT 05730, USA (☎(802) 259-2759; www.vfp.org). Arranges placement in workcamps in Israel and Turkey. Annual *International Workcamp Directory* US$20. Registration fee US$200. Free newsletter.

FURTHER READING

International Jobs: Where they Are, How to Get Them, Eric Koocher. Perseus Books (US$17).

How to Get a Job in Europe, Robert Sanborn. Surrey Books (US$22).

Work Abroad: The Complete Guide to Finding a Job Overseas, Clayton Hubbs. Transitions Abroad (US$16).

International Directory of Voluntary Work, Louise Whetter. Vacation Work Publications (US$16).

Teaching English Abroad, Susan Griffin. Vacation Work (US$17).

Overseas Summer Jobs 2001, Work Your Way Around the World, and *The Directory of Jobs and Careers Abroad.* Peterson's (US$17-18 each).

OTHER RESOURCES

Let's Go tries to cover all aspects of budget travel, but we can't put *everything* in our guides. Listed below are books and websites that can serve as jumping off points for your own research.

TRAVEL BOOK PUBLISHERS AND BOOKSTORES

Hippocrene Books, Inc., 171 Madison Ave., New York, NY 10016 (☎(212) 685-4371; orders ☎(718) 454-2366; www.netcom.com/~hippocre). Free catalog. Publishes travel guides, foreign language dictionaries, and language learning guides.

Hunter Publishing, 130 Campus Dr., Edison, NJ 08818, USA (☎(800) 255-0343; www.hunterpublishing.com). Has an extensive catalog of travel books, guides, language learning tapes, and quality maps.

Rand McNally, 150 S. Wacker Dr., Chicago, IL 60606, USA (☎(800) 234-0679 or (312) 332-2009; www.randmcnally.com), publishes road atlases (each US$10).

Adventurous Traveler Bookstore, 245 S. Champlain St., Burlington, VT 05401, USA (☎(800) 282-3963 or (802) 860-6776; www.adventuroustraveler.com).

Travel Books & Language Center, Inc., 4437 Wisconsin Ave. NW, Washington, D.C. 20016 (☎(800) 220-2665 or (202) 237-1322; www.bookweb.org/bookstore/travelbks). Over 60,000 titles from around the world.

THE WORLD WIDE WEB

Almost every aspect of budget travel (with the most notable exception, of course, being experience) is accessible via the web. Even if you don't have Internet access at home, seeking it out at a public library or at work would be well worth it; within 10min. at the keyboard, you can make a reservation at a hostel in Egypt, Turkey, or Israel, get advice on travel hotspots or experiences from other travelers who have just returned from the Middle East, or find out exactly how much a train from Alexandria to Luxor costs.

Listed here are some budget travel sites to start off your surfing; other relevant web sites are listed throughout the book. Because website turnover is high, use search engines (such as www.yahoo.com) to strike out on your own. But in doing so, keep in mind that most travel web sites simply exist to get your money.

LEARNING THE ART OF BUDGET TRAVEL

How to See the World: www.artoftravel.com. A compendium of great travel tips, from cheap flights to self defense to interacting with local culture.

Rec. Travel Library: www.travel-library.com. A fantastic set of links for general information and personal travelogues.

Shoestring Travel: www.stratpub.com. An e-zine focusing on budget travel.

INFORMATION ON THE MIDDLE EAST

CIA World Factbook: www.odci.gov/cia/publications/factbook/index.html. Tons of vital statistics on geography, government, economy, and people of the Middle East.

Foreign Language for Travelers: www.travlang.com. Provides free online translating dictionaries and lists of phrases in Arabic, Turkish, Hebrew, or for kicks, your Aramaic.

MyTravelGuide: www.mytravelguide.com. Country overview, with everything from history to transportation to live web cam coverage of the Middle East.

Geographia: www.geographia.com. Describes the highlights, culture, and people of the Middle East.

Atevo Travel: www.atevo.com/guides/destinations. Detailed introductions, travel tips, and suggested itineraries.

Columbus Travel Guides: http://www.travel-guides.com/navigate/world.asp. Helpful practical information.

LeisurePlanet: www.leisureplanet.com/TravelGuides. Good general background.

TravelPage: www.travelpage.com. Links to official tourist office sites throughout the Middle East.

PlanetRider: www.planetrider.com/Travel_Destinations.cfm. A subjective list of links to the "best" websites covering the culture and tourist attractions of the Middle East.

Arabnet: www.arab.net. A one-stop guide to the Middle East (except Israel) with extensive country-specific resources on geographic, political, and historical elements. Though the page is not strongly political, it regularly features often inflammatory pro-Arab statements; Israel's absence further discredits Arabnet as a neutral news source.

AND OUR PERSONAL FAVORITE...

Let's Go: www.letsgo.com. Our recently revamped website features photos and streaming video, info about our books, a travel forum buzzing with stories and tips, and links that will help you find everything you could ever want to know about the Middle East.

THE MIDDLE EAST: LIFE AND TIMES

The Middle East is home to what was once one of the lushest river valleys in the world, the **Fertile Crescent** between the Tigris and Euphrates River, and it is there that human civilization originated, almost 10,000 years ago. Simple stone sickles used to harvest wild wheat have been found as early as the 9th millennium BCE, but the critical step was the invention of agriculture in Mesopotamia in the 7th millennium BCE, which was followed by a series of basic inventions in the same area in succeeding millennia, beginning with irrigation and pottery, and later the wheel and systems of writing. In the same period, techniques of metal working were developed: first copper, then bronze, and finally iron. These technological advances produced an archaeological surplus that led to substantial population growth and the development of the earliest cities, such as Jericho.

THE ANCIENT EMPIRES (3000-1200 BCE)

While there is a rich archaeological record of the early development of civilization in this area, including excavations of the ancient city of **Jericho** dating back (as a village) to 6500 BCE, historical records are first found in the 3rd millennium BCE, with the introduction of writing to the area. The beginning of the historical period was marked by constant rivalry between the city-states of the **Akkadians** of central Mesopotamia, who were Semites, and those of the **Sumerians,** who were not. The Sumerians were dominant until the 24th century BCE. In the ensuing Semitic period, **Sargon the Ancient** established the world's first empire, which was ended by the invasion of Guti barbarians in about 2250 BCE, who were finally expelled by the Sumerians a century later. Sargon's empire was reestablished by the Sumerians under the famous 3rd dynasty of the **Kings of Ur** and overrun a century later by the **Amorites,** Arabian nomads coming up from the south. After a period of anarchy, the Amorite leader **Hammurabi** created the 3rd Mesopotamian empire in the 18th century BCE. The **Code of Hammurabi** was the first attempt to develop a comprehensive written legal code of laws and is best remembered for its "eye for an eye" system of punishment. Around the same time, Babylonian mathematicians discovered the famous **"Theorem of Pythagoras,"** named after a Greek who rediscovered it 13 centuries later.

Meanwhile, in the west across the Red Sea, the Kingdoms of **Upper** and **Lower Egypt** were united early in the 3rd millennium under the first dynasty of the **Old Kingdom** of Egypt. The Old Kingdom split apart into independent kingdoms in 2250 BCE, only to be reunited two centuries later by the Theban princes of the 11th dynasty, the founders of the so-called **Middle Kingdom.** The Middle Kingdom was brought down by invasions of Semitic nomads from the east, the **Hyksos,** in about 1700 BCE. The Egyptians applied the technologies developed in Mesopotamia and made innovations of their own. They depended on irrigation to harness the fertility of the Nile River and were the first to build in stone, beginning with the pyramid of Zoser in the 27th century BCE, followed by the massive pyramid of Cheops.

In Anatolia (modern Turkey) and the region of modern Syria, another powerful kingdom was established by the **Hittites,** which flourished after 2000 BCE. The Egyptians, Hittites, and Babylonians vied for influence in the region of modern Israel and Lebanon, with the Egyptians generally in control. Periods of armed conflict alternated with extensive periods where trade was dominant.

In 1580 BCE, Egypt was liberated from the foreign domination of the Hyksos by the princes of Thebes, whose 18th dynasty founded the **New Kingdom.** They also regained Palestine at this time and made incursions into Syria. In Mesopotamia, things were unsettled after major invasions by Iranians with a military innovation, the horse-drawn chariot. The semitic **Assyrians** built up a powerful state with ties to the Hittites, and the Amorites were replaced by the **Aramaeans,** whose alphabet was later adopted by the Hebrews. This alphabet is still used for printed Hebrew, while a version of the original Hebrew alphabet is used in hand writing. The Aramaean language eventually became widely used in the region of Palestine, and is the language that was spoken by Jesus.

About 1375 BCE, the first monotheistic religion appeared in the area, introduced into Egypt by the pharaoh **Akhenaton.** This brief religious revolution ended at his death with the victory of the traditional priesthood. After some disruption caused by this period of religious controversy, Egypt expanded again, becoming active in Syria. In a critical battle, pharaoh **Ramses II** was defeated by the Hittites at Kadesh east of Hama, Syria, in the year 1280. The peace treaty signed between the Egyptians and the Hittites after this battle is the oldest surviving peace treaty. Hebrews worked as slaves of Ramses II, and it is speculated that the Exodus of the Hebrews from Egypt took place under this pharaoh. At this time, Palestine was under Amorite control.

TURMOIL IN THE FERTILE CRESCENT (1200-549)

About 1200 BCE, barbarians from Europe poured into Anatolia, wiped out the Hittite state, and invaded Syria. A few years later, more invaders poured down the coast of Palestine and were beaten back from Egypt with difficulty, settling finally along the coast of Palestine. Palestine takes its name from a version of the name of one of these peoples, the **Philistines.** This was the end of Egyptian dominance in Palestine. After losing Palestine, Egypt also lost control of its southern territory, **Nubia.**

About 1000 BCE, new technology involving the manufacture of iron weapons surfaced. At this time, the **Aramaeans** overran the whole Fertile Crescent, sweeping away the second Assyrian empires, and became the dominant force in Mesopotamia. The **Phoenicians** of Lebanon and the **Hebrews** of Palestine broke the power of the coastal Philistines, who were finally conquered under the leadership of **David** in 975. Under David and Solomon, the Hebrew state dominated the neighboring principalities including Damascus. On the death of Solomon, however, these tributaries revolted, and the state split in two. At this point, the state of Damascus dominated the kingdoms of Israel and Judah, but the main power in the area was the reestablished Assyrian empire, again controlling the Fertile Crescent, while Egypt remained relatively weak.

Under the emperor **Tiglath-Pileser III** (745-728 BCE) and his successors, the **Assyrians** reached the peak of their power. Their empire included all of the area of modern Israel and Syria and the bulk of Egypt, together with a slice of Anatolian territory. A patch of Phoenician territory around the city of Tyre remained independent. The Kingdom of Israel was conquered by **Sargon II** (721-705 BCE), and all ten tribes were deported; at this point, they vanish from the annals of history. The **Babylonians** formed an alliance with the **Iranians,** who had consolidated their control over neighboring Iran. A decade of war ended in a defini-

6500 BCE
Stone Age town in present-day Jericho

3100-2183
Old Kingdom

2713-2494
Pyramids at Giza and Sphinx built

2370
Sargon the Ancient

2290-2250
Guti invasions

2000
Iranians arrive in Iran, Greeks in Greece, and Hittites in Anatolia

1991-1786
Middle Kingdom

1875
Assyrians

1755
Code of Hammurabi

1720
Hyksos

1580
Egypt liberated from Hyksos domination

1573-1180
New Kingdom

1380
Hittite empire spans all of Anatolia and Jerusalem

1375
First monotheistic religion

1280
Treaty of Kadesh

1200
Barbarian invaders wipe out Hittite state

1190
Philistines settle in Palestine

MIDDLE EAST

1000-962
David

962-931
Solomon

931
Judea splits into
North and South
kingdoms

721
Assyrians invade
Northern Kingdom

721-705
Sargon II

586
Nebuchadnezzar
deports Jews to
Babylon

550-330
Achaemenids

539
Cyrus the Great
conquers Babylon

325
Alexander the
Great defeats Per-
sian Empire

301-121
Seleucids

121 BCE-224 CE
Parthians

224-651
Sassanians

622
Muhammad flees
Mecca to Medina

638
Jerusalem
becomes holy city
of Islam

661-750
Umayyad Dynasty

749-1258
Abbasid Dynasty

tive victory for the allies, with a Babylonian empire replacing the Assyrian one, while the Iranians moved deep into Anatolia. Meanwhile, Egypt regained its freedom, and **Pharaoh Necho** tried to seize the opportunity to regain control of Palestine and Syria, but was thoroughly defeated by the Babylonian emperor **Nebuchadnezzar** in 605 BCE. In 586, Nebuchadnezzar deported the last two Hebrew tribes from Judah to Babylonia.

THE NEW EMPIRES (549-334)

The alliance with the Iranians had let the genie out of the bottle. In 549 BCE, Emperor **Cyrus II** assumed control of Persia, which was already the most powerful state in the region, and by 539, he had incorporated the whole of the Babylonian empire into his domains. He allowed the two tribes of Judah, then in Babylonia, to return home again. His son, **Cambyses II**, conquered Egypt, at which point the massive Persian empire covered the whole of the Middle East, from Egypt to the borders of India, as well as Thrace (northern Greece). Egypt revolted and regained its independence about 400 BCE, but for the time being, the rest of the empire held firm. This empire remained the dominant force in the region until the arrival of Alexander the Great.

The Greek counteroffensive was not long in coming. After some preliminary campaigns on the European side, **Alexander the Great** arrived in Asia in 334 BCE and quickly conquered the whole of the Persian Empire and more. Though the empire he founded split up politically on his death, the impact of Greek culture on the area was profound for many centuries to come, until at least the time of Muhammad.

EUROPE ENTERS STAGE LEFT (334 BCE-1453 CE)

In 334 BCE, young general **Alexander of Macedon** (356-323 BCE) invaded Anatolia; nine years later, he defeated the Persian Empire. Not content with the entire Middle East, Alexander pushed on, extending his empire from Greece to the Khyber Pass in India. After his death, his empire broke up into "successor states." Battling over territory, **Seleucus** defeated **Antigonus** at the **Battle of Ipsus** (301 BCE) and became ruler of much of the Middle East. His successors, the Seleucid kings (301-121 BCE), controlled most of Syria, Anatolia, Mesopotamia, and Iran. These kings had no official policy of Hellenization, but Greek culture dramatically impacted the Middle Eastern peoples. The **Parthians** replaced the Seleucid kings, ruling from 121 BCE until 224 CE, when the Sassanian Period began. The **Sassanians** ruled as an extension of the Roman Empire. As politically humdrum as the Parthian Period, the Sassanian Period marked the large-scale introduction of Western religion into the Middle East. Zoroastrianism and **Christianity** gradually replaced local religions and cults.

In the early 7th century, an Arab merchant named **Muhammad** began preaching in the city of **Mecca**. In 622, Muhammad fled persecution in Mecca for the city of **Medina**, where he preached until his death. After his death, his followers continued his preaching. At first, **Islam** spread slowly because of well-organized Christian and Jewish communities, but soon Islam stretched throughout the entire Middle East.

Muhammad's flight marked the dawn of the **Arabo-Islamic Period,** when Islam became the key, unifying Middle Eastern empires until the 13th century. Beginning in 630, Muslims assumed control of the Middle East. The **Umayyads** (661-750) ruled with Damascus as their capital. By 756, they had spread west, toward North Africa. The **Abbasids** (749-1258) replaced the Umayyads farther east, while the **Zaydi** dynasty prevailed in the southern Arabian Peninsula.

In 1099, **Godfrey of Bouillon** crusaded into the Middle East, incorporating parts of what are now Israel, Jordan, and Syria into the **Christian Kingdom of Jerusalem.** Over the next two hundred years, three more Crusades left the land pock-marked with castles. Aided by these castles, the Crusaders staved off attacks from Muslim forces until the end of the 12th century when **Salah al-Din** led the **Mamluks** to reconquer what is now Syria. For the next three centuries, the Mamluks remained the dominant power in the Middle East.

OTTOMANS RULE (1453-1798)

Simultaneous with Salah al-Din's victory over the Crusaders, **Seljuk Turks** began migrating throughout the Middle East, gnawing away at the **Byzantine Empire.** In 1453, the Seljuks gained the ultimate prize when strategically vital Constantinople fell to **Mehmet the Conqueror** after a 54-day siege. Under his successor **Selim I** (1512-1520), Ottoman armies conquered Palestine, Egypt, Arabia, and present-day Syria. In a single, tremendous military campaign, the Ottoman Sultan became guardian of the three holy places of Islam: Mecca, Medina, and Jerusalem.

Because of transportation and communication difficulties in this far-flung empire, the Ottoman state was relatively decentralized. The Ottoman governor granted local leaders autonomy under his national government, and his contact with satellite provinces was usually limited to issues of tax collection and military conscription. In this heterogeneous empire, the hinterland regions developed independently, a situation that would later contribute to the ultimate decline of the empire.

By the 17th century, the **Ottoman Empire** was already experiencing the pull of its outer extremities. Spurred by revenue from piracy, Libya broke free from Ottoman rule and began enjoying greater autonomy. By 1744, Muslim factions also spurned Ottoman rule. **Muhammad ibn Saud,** a prominent sheikh, and **Muhammad ibn Abd al-Wahhab,** a preacher of a form of Islam called **Wahhabism,** united in the **first Saudi Empire.** By 1802, the Saudi-led Wahhabis captured Mecca, and the Saudi empire reached its peak, spanning most of modern-day Saudi Arabia and southern Iraq.

FRACTURE AND COLONIZATION (1798-1947)

Mired in internal conflicts throughout the Middle Ages, European powers experienced a military, economic, cultural, and intellectual boom during the Enlightenment. With the dawn

1099
First Crusade

1291
Rise of the Mamluks

1636
Libya breaks free from Ottoman rule

1798
Napoleon conquers the Mamluks

1802
Wahhabbis capture Mecca

1805
Muhammad Ali defeats British forces

1820
Start of British and French colonization of the Middle East

1860
Ottomans establish Christian settlement in Lebanon

1881
Bardo Treaty: Tunisia established as a French protectorate

1917
Balfour Declaration

1921
Emirate of Trans-Jordan established

1922-1932
British end protectorates in Egypt, Yemen, & Morocco

1936
Anglo-Egyptian Treaty

1946
British evacuate Syria and Jordan

1947
British evacuate Suez Canal

MIDDLE EAST

1948
State of Israel
declared. War of
Independence

1949
Jerusalem divided
under Israeli and
Jordanian rule.
Israel admitted to
the UN

1956
Sinai Campaign

1963
Syrian Ba'ath Party
established

1967
Six-Day War

1968-1970
War of Attrition

1970
Black September

1973
Yom Kippur War

1978
Camp David
Accords

1979
Israel-Egypt
peace treaty

1987
Intifada begins

1990-91
Gulf War

1994
Palestinian self-
government in
Gaza and Jericho

1995
Rabin assassi-
nated

2000
Israel withdraws
from Lebanon

of the 19th century, European powers turned toward the Middle East; their intervention hastened the Ottoman Empire's slow decline. In 1798, **Napoleon's** armies defeated the Mamluk forces at Imbaba. Great Britain ousted Napoleon by 1802, losing to **Muhammad Ali** three years later, but the European intrusion remained significant. Napoleon's victory marked the first European conquest of a major Arab country in Islamic history and signaled the fall of the Middle East as a world political power.

Great Britain and France began a string of colonizations extending to the early 20th century. Between the 1820s and 1870s, the British signed protection treaties with the Gulf States and established colonies in Somalia and the Sudan. But their biggest conquest came in 1882. Spurred on by Egypt's newfound commercial significance due to the Suez Canal, Great Britain pressured Egyptian ruler **Tawfiq Pasha** to relinquish control of the Egyptian government. Not to be out-imperialized by its rival, France also entered the fray. In 1830, France invaded Algiers, beginning a 132-year occupation. The **Bardo Treaty of 1881 (Treaty of Kasser Said)** acknowledged Tunisia as a French protectorate. Joint British and French intervention pressured the Ottoman Empire into establishing a Christian settlement in 1860 in what would become Lebanon.

World War I marked the end of the Ottoman Empire and the rise of the **Mandate System.** Allying itself with Germany and the Austro-Hungarian Empire, the Ottoman Empire collapsed when British forces invaded Mesopotamia and occupied Baghdad in 1917. Following the war, the British promised the Arabs their independence, while the **Balfour Declaration** pledged support for a Jewish national state. These various promises made by the British and French resulted in a muddled system of mandates. The newly created **League of Nations** awarded the Western European powers control over the territories from which the Ottomans had been expelled, with the stated purpose of preparing these countries for independence. Great Britain was given a mandate over Palestine (which included modern-day Israel, Jordan, the West Bank, and Gaza) and Iraq, while France was accorded what are now Syria and Lebanon.

Throughout the interwar years, the British relinquished mandate control in the face of increasing Arab nationalism. In 1921, **Emir Abdullah** established the **Emirate of Trans-Jordan** as a self-governing territory under British mandate. The British also ended their protectorates of Egypt (1922), Yemen (1925), and Morocco (1932). Egypt became a puppet kingdom before the **Anglo-Egyptian Treaty** (1936) honored Egypt as an independent nation under **King Farouk.**

World War II and its aftermath provided the final impetus for Britain to end colonial rule. In 1946, the British evacuated both Syria and Jordan, thereby creating modern-day states, and by 1947, British troops had evacuated the **Suez Canal.** France, however, did not give up as easily. French colonialists remained in Algeria until **General Charles de Gaulle** declared a referendum, allowing the Algerians to vote on their own fate. The Algerians voted almost unanimously for independence, though they remained under French rule until President **Ahmed ibn Bella** issued the **Evian Accords** in 1962.

NATIONALISM AND RELIGIOUS CONFLICT (1947-2000)

ESCALATION

Britain successfully withdrew from both Syria and Jordan, but nothing could have prepared it for dealing with Palestine. Exhausted from centuries of colonial rule, Great Britain submitted the question of Palestine to the newly formed United Nations. The UN General Assembly voted in 1947 to partition Palestine into two states, Jewish and Arab. The Jewish leadership accepted the resolution with some reluctance, while Palestinian Arab leaders and the governments of neighboring Arab states rejected the plan, denying the UN's authority to divide and distribute territories they considered to be Arab patrimony. As the British prepared to evacuate Palestine in accordance with the UN's **partition plan,** Jews and Arabs clashed in sporadic skirmishes, purchased arms overseas, and planned for full-scale war.

On May 14, 1948, the British mandate over Palestine ended, and the head of the Jewish Agency, **David Ben-Gurion,** declared the independence of the State of Israel. The next day, a combined army of Syrian, Iraqi, Lebanese, Saudi, Egyptian, and Jordanian troops marched in from the north, west, and south. When the dust settled with armistices in early 1949, Israel had secured not only its UN-allotted territory, but also some land in the north and in the West Bank designated for Palestine by the UN. Thousands of Palestinian refugees crowded into camps in the West Bank, Gaza, and Jordan, but to them, Jordanian rule was only marginally better than any other foreign occupation.

Egypt, weakened by struggles between Wafdist nationalists and the monarchy, fell into shambles after its 1948 loss to Israel. In 1952, following a bloody confrontation between British soldiers and Egyptian police officers, a group of young army officers, led by charismatic heartthrob **Colonel Gamal Abd al-Nasser,** seized power from corrupt King Farouk. Nasser's cabinet instituted major economic reforms and foreign policy changes, while avoiding the bilateral alignments of the Cold War. Nasser hoped to unify the Arabic-speaking masses into one state powerful enough to resist imperial encroachments and to take control of Palestine. He also intensified the guerilla campaign against Israel from bases in the Gaza Strip. In 1956, the US attempted to curtail Nasser's power by withdrawing its offer to finance the Aswan High Dam. Rather than yield to the snub, Nasser nationalized the previously international Suez Canal to use its revenues for the dam. On October 24, 1956, Jordan, Syria, and Egypt established a joint military command directed against Israel.

Israel, Britain, and France devised a scheme to take the canal. Israel would attack Egypt with French logistical support; a Franco-British "peace-keeping" force would follow. Initially, the conspiracy worked, but they had not considered world reaction to their plan. The US and the Soviet Union, both furious, applied intense diplomatic pressure. When Israel, Britain, and France withdrew their troops to placate the US, Nasser was heralded as the savior of the Arab world.

In 1963, a Syrian coup interrupted the Egyptian-Syrian joyride, giving way to the Syrian Ba'ath party (led by **Hafez al-Assad**), which split off from the larger Ba'ath party in February 1966 and began focusing its efforts on developing Syrian nationalism (rather than pan-Arabism) and maintaining power.

Meanwhile, from bases sanctioned by the governments of Jordan, Syria, and Lebanon, the **Palestinian Liberation Organization (PLO)** raided Israel; in return, Israel hit Palestinian refugee camps. This cycle of raids and reprisals came to a head with a Syrian-Israeli air battle in April 1967. When Syria's hard-line government turned up the rhetoric, Nasser stepped in, concentrating the Egyptian army in the Sinai and successfully demanding the withdrawal of the UN buffer-zone troops stationed there since 1956. Israeli Prime Minister **Levi Eshkol** warned that a blockade would be taken as an act of aggression, but Nasser, under pressure from Syria and Saudi Arabia, initiated a blockade on May 22, 1967.

When Jordan, Iraq, and Syria deployed troops along Israel's borders, Israel launched a preemptive strike against air fields in the Sinai, obliterating the Egyptian air force before it got off the ground. Eshkol warned King Hussein not to interfere, but Hussein opened fire on the UN headquarters in Jerusalem and began bombarding Jewish Jerusalem. In response, Israeli forces broke through the Jordanian lines, simultaneously attacking Janin in the North. East Jerusalem and the Old City fell to Israel on June 7, and by June 9, all parties had accepted the ceasefire. Shortly afterward, Israel annexed East Jerusalem, the Sinai Peninsula (all the way to the Suez Canal), Gaza Strip, West Bank, and Golan Heights.

Staggered by yet another defeat, the Palestinians decided it was up to them to carry on the struggle. In 1969, **Yassir Arafat,** leader of the Palestinian organization **FATAH,** took over the PLO from its pro-Nasser leadership. The Arafat-led PLO sought liberation through propaganda and guerilla warfare. Unfortunately, factionalism became a constant feature of Palestinian politics. Though FATAH consistently sought to maintain contact with all Arab regimes, the regimes constantly manipulated factions against one another. The 1967 War, which had created 400,000 more Palestinian refugees, compounded the problem. With this influx of Palestinians, the Jordanian government and the PLO were thrown together in a tense relationship: King Hussein wanted to hold secret peace negotiations with the Israelis, while the PLO hoped to use Jordan as a base for attacks on Israeli-held territory. In September 1970, the conflicting ambitions of King Hussein and Arafat exploded. Infuriated by the hard-line PLO hijacking of a number of commercial airlines (to protest the exclusion of Palestinians from negotiations between Israel, Egypt, and Jordan), King Hussein declared war on the PLO. Martial law was imposed during the war, and fighting between Jordanian and PLO troops took over 3000 lives. September 1970 became known among Palestinians as **Black September.** After Arab League mediation and Nasser's personal intervention, an agreement was forged, requiring the PLO to move its headquarters to Lebanon.

Nasser died suddenly of a heart attack that same September, and Vice President **Anwar Sadat** assumed control of Egypt, promptly dismantling Nasser's legacy of state socialism. In 1968, with the help of Soviet military instruction and supplies, Egypt launched the War of Attrition against Israel. But within a few years, the war became too heavy a burden for Egypt to bear. In order to alleviate his country's financial crisis, Sadat sought to reopen the lucrative Suez Canal and reclaim the desperately needed Sinai oil fields.

On October 6, 1973, the day of **Yom Kippur** (the Day of Atonement), Egypt and Syria launched a surprise assault. In the war's first three days, Egyptian troops crossed the Suez Canal and captured footholds on the Eastern Bank, while in the North, five Syrian divisions swept through the Golan Heights. Within a matter of days, as the Arab armies moved beyond their Soviet-supplied ground-to-air missile cover, Israel launched a series of fierce missile attacks that stopped the Arab advance. On October 17, with the assistance of a US emergency airlift, Israeli tanks broke through the Egyptian line and crossed the Suez Canal onto the mainland. Ultimately, Egypt, Jordan, and Syria decided to participate in the **Geneva Peace Conference** (convened on December 21, 1973) for the settlement of the conflict under the auspices of the US and the Soviet Union.

All parties finally agreed to disengage forces by May 1974, and the subsequent Sinai I and II agreements returned much of the Sinai to Egypt. However, both sides had suffered huge losses. Israeli public uproar over the government's lack of preparation prompted Prime Minister **Golda Meir** to resign in April. Israel maintained its borders, but the aura of invincibility it had earned over the years had dissipated.

In October 1974, the Arab League declared that the PLO—not Jordan—was "the sole legitimate representative of the Palestinian people." This incensed King Hussein, but when the other 20 Arab nations assented to PLO representation in the League, he was forced to agree. In November 1974, the UN General Assembly granted the PLO observer status in the UN.

DETENTE

Throughout the 1970s, an increasing number of Israelis settled in the occupied territories. On November 11, 1976, the UN Security Council condemned this West Bank policy and demanded that Israel follow the Geneva Convention's rules regarding occupied territories. Although Prime Minister Yitzḥak Rabin (of the left-leaning Israeli Labor Party) discouraged permanent West Bank settlement, the next government (after 1977), under Prime Minister **Menaḥem Begin** of the right-wing Likud bloc, invested money and effort in new settlements.

Eager to regain the Sinai, Sadat decided to seek unilateral peace with Israel. In October 1977, he declared that he would go to Jerusalem to make peace. The next month, Sadat was officially welcomed to Jerusalem. By September 1978, Begin and Sadat had forged an agreement with the help of US President **Jimmy Carter.** The most successful and lasting stipulation was Israel's agreement to relinquish the Sinai in exchange for peace and full diplomatic relations with Egypt. After the **Camp David Accords,** early hopes that other Arab states would negotiate with Israel evaporated. The PLO, Syria, and Jordan were adamant about guarantees for the Palestinians; more distant Arab states issued statements of disapproval, but felt no need to interfere. Egypt, viewed as a traitor to Palestine by many, was left isolated and turned to the US for financial support. Islamists, whom Sadat had courted in his battles against the Nasserist left, objected to this open alliance with the West. In October 1981, in response to his cracking down on Islamic fundamentalists, Sadat was assassinated. The Egyptian government acted swiftly to crush an Islamist riot in Asyut, and **Hosni Mubarak,** Sadat's Vice President, was sworn in.

Though he stuck to the terms of the Camp David accords, Mubarak held Israel at arm's length, keeping the diplomatic air cool for most of the 1980s in an attempt to reintegrate Egypt with the rest of the Arab world. In 1984, Egypt restored relations with the USSR and was readmitted to the Islamic Conference. In 1988, the Arab League invited Egypt to rejoin, dropping demands that Egypt sever ties with Israel.

On June 6, 1982, Israel invaded Lebanon. The attack, dubbed "Operation Peace for Galilee" by Defense Minister **Ariel Sharon,** was supposedly intended to create a protective buffer zone; it is generally accepted, however, that the attack aimed to wipe out PLO forces operating from Palestinian refugee camps that had been attacking northern Israel. When the Israeli army, after surrounding the PLO in Beirut, began shelling the city at an enormous civilian cost, Israeli citizens joined in the world-wide chorus of condemnation. Under an agreement negotiated by the US, most fighting ended in 1983, and Israel withdrew in 1985, but maintained a strip of southern Lebanese territory as a security zone.

In the summer of 1988, King Hussein suddenly dropped his claims to the West Bank and ceased assisting in the administration of the territories, which Jordan had been doing since 1967. Arafat seized the opportunity to secure a PLO role in negotiations by renouncing terrorism, recognizing Israel's right to exist, and proposing an independent Palestinian state. Israeli Prime Minister Yitzḥak Shamir presented his own proposal, but refused to negotiate with the PLO. With increasing Palestinian uprisings and no progress, the US and the PLO terminated their discussions in the summer of 1989.

TO THE BARGAINING TABLE

On August 2, 1990, Iraqi troops marched into Kuwait, marking the beginning of the Gulf Crisis. Early on, Iraqi President **Saddam Hussein** had slyly suggested "linkage" as a way of solving the Gulf crisis—that is, he would withdraw from Kuwait when Israel withdrew from the West Bank, Gaza, and the Golan, and when Syria withdrew from Lebanon. This gesture, along with promises to liberate Palestine, won Saddam the support of Palestinians. In fighting that lasted from January 16 to February 28, 1991, a coalition formed by the US, various European countries, Egypt, Syria, Saudi Arabia, and the other Gulf states disabled Baghdad and forced Iraq to withdraw from Kuwait. During the conflict, 39

Iraqi SCUD missiles fell on Tel Aviv and Haifa, cheered on by Arafat and the Palestinian population. Israel, under pressure from the US, and fearful of an Arab-Israeli conflagration and chaos in Jordan, did not retaliate.

The Gulf Crisis demonstrated the need for a comprehensive peace in the region. When the cease-fire was announced, hope was high that parties such as Israel and Syria—for the first time on the same side of a regional conflict—could be brought to the bargaining table. On October 30, 1991, the Madrid peace conference was convened with Israel carrying on separate negotiations with Syria, Lebanon, Egypt, and a joint Jordanian-Palestinian delegation. However, this unprecedented gathering was quickly bogged down by discussions of **UN Resolution 242,** Palestinian autonomy and rights, Jerusalem, Israeli settlements, and the PLO's political scope. Then, almost a year later, Israel and the PLO surprised the world by announcing that representatives meeting secretly in Oslo had successfully negotiated an agreement on a framework for peacefully solving the Israeli-Palestinian conflict. The Declaration of Principles on Interim Self-Government Arrangements (the **DOP**—also known as the **Oslo Accord**) was signed on the White House lawn on September 13, 1993, with President **Bill Clinton** presiding over the ceremony. The DOP provided mutual recognition between Israel and the PLO, as well as a plan for the implementation of Palestinian autonomy in the Gaza Strip and the Jericho Area, with the autonomous areas to be expanded in stages over a five-year transitional period. The transitional period, according to the DOP, was to be followed by an agreement on final status of refugees, settlements, security arrangements, borders, foreign relations, and Jerusalem.

The DOP was followed by the negotiation and signing of several other Israeli-Palestinian agreements. The **Gaza-Jericho Agreement** provided the details for Israeli withdrawal from these two areas and the creation of a **Palestinian Authority (PA)** headed by Yassir Arafat and a 24-member council. Following the implementation of the Gaza/Jericho Agreement, the two sides signed the Early Empowerment Agreement that transferred several spheres of government in the West Bank to the PA. Finally, the **Wye River Interim Agreement** promised that Israel would withdraw from parts of the West Bank and dismantle certain settlements.

THE QUEST FOR PEACE

Since the Oslo Accords, obstacles continue to obstruct the peace process. On November 4, 1995, 25-year-old Yigal Amir, a Jewish right-wing university student, shot and killed Israel's Prime Minister Yitzḥak Rabin. Rabin had just finished delivering a rousing speech for peace in front of 100,000 Israelis at one of the largest rallies Tel Aviv had ever seen. The May 1996 election of **Benjamin Netanyahu,** leader of the conservative Likud party, marked a turn away from Rabin's peace-oriented politics. The militant Islamic organization **Hamas** dealt another blow to the peace process with the suicide bombing of a crowded Jerusalem market on July 30, 1997.

In May of 1999, Labor candidate **Ehud Barak** was elected prime minister, promising to make the resolution of the peace talks his primary concern. Over the next twelve months, Barak held simultaneous negotiations with the Syrians, Palestinians, and Lebanese. Barak promised to withdraw from Lebanon by June 1, 2000, but Israeli forces preemptively withdrew under heavy Lebanese-Hizbullah fire on May 24, 2000. Negotiations with the Palestinians and Syrians have yet to bear similar results. Many on both sides feel that they are getting the raw end of the deal. Some Israelis argue that they are giving up their defensive territorial depth in exchange for pieces of paper that can be torn up in a moment. Some Palestinians fear that Israel will never grant them total independence and interpret the current process as a "sell-out" on the part of their leadership. In the end, both sides hope that, counter to the Middle East's volatile history, they can forge a lasting peace.

RELIGION IN THE MIDDLE EAST

The Middle East is home to the three major monotheistic religions: **Judaism, Christianity,** and **Islam.** The **Druze, Baha'i, Karaites,** and **Samaritans** also call the Middle East home.

ISLAM

The Arabic word *islam* translates, in its general sense, as "submission," and the basic tenet of Islam is submission to the will of God **(Allah).** Islam has its roots in revelations received from 610 to 622 CE by **Muhammad,** who was informed of his prophetic calling by the angel Gabriel. These revelations, the **Qur'an** ("recitation"), form the core of Islam. Muslims believe the Arabic text is perfect, immutable, and untranslatable—the words of God embodied in human language. Consequently, the Qur'an appears throughout the Muslim world (the majority of which is non-Arabic speaking) in Arabic. Muhammad is seen as the "seal of the prophets," the last of a chain of God's messengers that includes Jewish and Christian figures such as Abraham, Moses, and Jesus.

It is believed that Muhammad received the Qur'an during the month of **Ramadan.** Fasting during this holy month is the fourth pillar of Islam. Between dawn and sunset, Muslims are not permitted to smoke, have sexual intercourse, or let any food or water pass their lips; exceptions are made for pregnant or menstruating women, the sick, and travelers—they must make up the fast at a later date. Fasting is meant to teach Muslims to resist temptation and thereby control all their unchaste urges, better understand the plight of the poor, and be more thankful for the food with which God has provided them. As soon as the evening *adhan* is heard, Muslims break the fast and begin a night of feasting, visits to friends and relatives, and revelry. In busy metropolises like Cairo, the city stays up until just before dawn, but in quieter areas, a neighbor may circulate to houses, banging a drum and waking people for the *suhur*, a small meal eaten just before dawn in an attempt to avoid extreme hunger upon waking.

HISTORY OF ISLAM

Muhammad rapidly gathered followers to his evolving faith. Staunchly monotheistic Islam met with ample opposition in polytheistic Arabia, leading to persecution in Muhammad's native city of **Mecca.** In 622, he and his followers fled to the nearby city of **Medina,** where he was welcomed as mediator of a long-standing blood feud. This *hijra* (emigration) marks the starting point of the Islamic calendar. In 630, Mecca surrendered to the Muslims, making Muhammad the most powerful man in Arabia and leading numerous Meccans to voluntarily convert to the new faith. This established the pattern for *jihad* ("struggle"), referring first and foremost to the spiritual struggle against one's own desires, then to the struggle to make one's own Muslim community as righteous as possible, and lastly to the struggle against outsiders wishing to harm the Muslim community.

Prophet Muhammad is not believed to be divine, but rather a human messenger of God's word. His actions are sanctified because God chose him to be the recipient of revelation; several verses of the Qur'an demand obedience to the Prophet. The stories and traditions surrounding the Prophet's life have been passed on as *sunna*, and those who follow the *sunna* (from which the term "Sunni" is derived) in addition to the teachings of the Qur'an are considered especially devout. The primary source for *sunna* is *Hadith*, a collection of sayings and deeds attributed to Muhammad. A *hadith* had to go through a rigorous verification process before it was accepted as true; the tale had to be verified (preferably by those who saw the action) and the greatest weight was given to testimony by Muhammad's followers and relatives.

SUNNIS, SHI'A, AND SUFIS

Muhammad's nephew and son-in-law 'Ali was the catalyst for the major split in the Muslim world. When 'Ali was murdered in 661, the *Shi'at 'Ali* ("Partisans of 'Ali" or **Shi'a**) believed he was the only legitimate successor to Muhammad, thus separating themselves from Sunni Muslims. Shi'ism is a faith with a sharp focus on divinely chosen leaders (or *imams*) who are blood descendants of the Prophet through 'Ali and his wife, the Prophet's daughter Fatima.

In the 10th century, Sunni Muslim scholars *(ulama)* proclaimed "the gates of *ijtihad* (individual judgment)" closed; new concepts and interpretations could no longer stand on their own but had to be legitimized by tradition. *Ijtihad* continues today, though not on the scale that it did during the first centuries of Islam. There have been numerous reform movements throughout the Islamic world, including the Wahhabbi movement on the Arabian Peninsula, the movement of the thinker Jamal al-Din al-Afghani in the Middle East, and Muhammad Iqbal in South Asia. There are four main schools of thought in the Islamic legal system, and the applicability of *sharia*, or Islamic law, is a subject of much strife in a number of Muslim countries, which have seen challenges to entrenched governments by movements carrying the banner of Islam.

Sufism is a mystical movement within Islam, and Sufis stress the goal of unity with God. They are organized in hierarchical orders that prescribe different ways of life to reach God; some preach total asceticism, while others seem almost hedonistic in their pursuit of pleasure. Sufi *sheikhs* (masters) and saints are reputed to perform miracles, and their tombs are popular pilgrimage destinations. Jalal al-Din Rumi founded the famous order of the "whirling dervishes," who spin to produce a state of mind conducive to unity with God.

FIVE PILLARS OF ISLAM

Allahu akbar. Allahu akbar. Ash-hadu an la ilaha illa Allah. Ash-hadu anna Muhammadan rasul Allah. "God is great. God is great. I swear that there is no god but God. I swear that Muhammad is God's Messenger." These words are the first lines of the Islamic call to prayer *(adhan)*, which emanates five times a day from live or recorded *muezzins* perched atop the minarets of mosques. The first two lines glorify God and the next two lines form the **testimony of faith** *(shahadah)*, which is the first of the five pillars of Islam. These words reflect the unity of God *(tawhid)* and the special place of Muhammad as God's final messenger. Any person who wishes to convert to Islam may do so by repeating these lines three times. Enemies of Islam often memorized the lines before going into battle as an emergency survival tactic.

The second pillar is **prayer** *(salat)*, performed five times per day facing Mecca. Prayers, preceded by ablutions (ritual cleansing), begin with a declaration of intent and consist of a set cycle of prostrations. The Arabic word for Friday *(yom al-jum'a)* means "the day of gathering," and communal prayer is encouraged on this day.

TWIST AND SHOUT Known to Westerners as **whirling dervishes,** the **Sufi** sect of Islam began in Konya, Turkey, during the mid-13th century. The origin of the word Sufi is a mystery. Some think that it derives from the root *suf* (wool), used to describe the woolen garments worn by the first members of the sect. Another theory is that Sufi came from the Greek *sophos*, meaning wisdom. The Persian word *darwish* literally means the "sill of the door"—hence, *dervish* would refer to the Sufi who is at the doorstep of paradise or enlightenment. The dervishes hope to cast off mundane worries and reach a higher spiritual plane through their perpetually whirling dance. The ritual is an entrancing display of color and devotion, a dizzying spin during which the dervish throws off cloak after cloak of earthly possession, eventually left with the soaring white fabric of his inner robe. Their spiritual dance likely inspired the "spinners" made famous at Grateful Dead concerts.

The third pillar is **alms** *(zakat)*. Because all belongs to God, wealth is only held in trust by people, and *zakat* represents the bond between members of the community. Through the required giving of alms to those less fortunate, the contributor is purified from selfishness. *Zakat* has been historically administered as a tax, and the level of giving is determined as a percentage of the surplus wealth and earnings of the individual.

The fourth pillar of Islam is **fasting** *(sawm)*, required for the entire month of Ramadan, the most holy month of the Islamic lunar calendar. It is believed that during this month, the Qur'an was revealed to the Prophet Muhammad by the angel Gabriel. Muslims fast from sunrise until sunset every day of Ramadan. Ramadan ends with Eid al-Fitr, a day of celebration, feasting, and praise of God.

The last pillar is **pilgrimage** *(hajj)*, required once in a lifetime only for those who are financially and physically able to journey to Mecca and Medina during the last month of the Muslim calendar. Worship is focused around the **Ka'aba**, which Muslims believe to be the first house of worship built by the first man (Adam, under instructions from God). While the *Hajj* is essentially a re-creation of the actions of the Prophet Muhammad, it also unites Muslims and stresses the equal status of all who submit to God. Everyone from Gulf princes to Cairene street-sweepers must wrap themselves in white cloth, remove all accessories, and perform the same rituals. If you travel during the *Hajj*, expect delays and pandemonium in airports.

JUDAISM

Neither theologians nor historians can pinpoint a date for the founding of Judaism, but the religion has been evolving for at least four millennia. According to the Bible, **Abraham** first established a covenant with God through his self-circumcision at the ripe old age of 99. This act is symbolically repeated with each generation of Jewish males, but now a ritual circumciser (the *moyel*) performs the honors on the eighth day of life. Abraham's grandson, Jacob, fathered 12 sons from whom the 12 tribes of the nation of Israel descended. Abraham, his son Isaac, and his grandson Jacob are believed to be buried with their wives (Sarah, Rebecca, and Leah) in the Cave of the Machpelach in Hebron. This site is holy to both Judaism and Islam because Abraham's son Ishmael is believed to be the ancestor of Muslims.

The Bible says that the Israelite nation was founded during the generation spent wandering with Moses in the Sinai desert en route to the Holy Land. This generation received the Torah, the central text of Judaism, at Mount Sinai. The disparate tribes had united by the 3rd millennium BCE under **Yahweh** (a warlike version either of the Canaanite deity El or the storm god Ba'al). Once the Israelite kingdom was formed, worship was centralized in the capital, Jerusalem.

Historians estimate the present form of the **Torah** to be 2500 years old. The Written Torah (a.k.a. the **Pentateuch,** or the Books of Moses), which consists of the first five books of the Bible, formed the template for the Oral Torah, a series of interpretations and teachings codified in 200 CE as the *Mishnah*. The *Mishnah*, along with the *Gemara*, is the basis of the Babylonian and Jerusalem *Talmuds*, finalized during the 5th century CE. The *Talmud* was the springboard for a new series of interpretations and teachings that continue to build upon each other.

In Judaism, faith in God is central, but the energy of Jewish life is concentrated on observing the commandments. The Torah contains 613 **mitzvot** (commandments), including directives for ritual observances and instructions concerning moral behavior. Over the ages, rabbis have interpreted and expanded these *mitzvot*. This entire set of laws is called *halakha* ("the way"). Much of modern Jewish life revolves around the **synagogue.** The *aron ha-kodesh* ("Holy Ark") houses the Torah scrolls and determines the orientation of the synagogue. Synagogues normally face Jerusalem; within Jerusalem, they face the Temple Mount. Above the *aron ha-kodesh* hangs a flickering *ner tamid* ("eternal flame"). Most orthodox synagogues contain a *meḥitza*, a divider between men's and women's sections, which have separate entrances. Men should cover their heads when entering; there is often a box of *kippot*, ritual skullcaps, by the entrance.

CHRISTIANITY

Christianity began in Judaea among the Jewish followers of **Jesus.** The most significant sources on the life of Jesus are the **Gospels.** Scholars agree that the "synoptic gospels" of Mark, Matthew, and Luke were written in that order some time after 70 CE, drawing on an oral tradition that recorded the words of Jesus. The Gospel of John was written about 100 CE but has roots as old as the others. These sources provide a history influenced by the experiences of the church fathers and the belief that Jesus was the **Messiah** ("anointed one").

Various historical events date the birth of Jesus between 7 and 4 BCE. The Bible says that Jesus was conceived and brought forth by Mary, a virgin, making him a product of God's creative power and free from humanity's original sin. According to Matthew, **Bethlehem** was the birthplace of Jesus, and Mary and Joseph moved to **Nazareth** to protect him. Jesus was baptized in the Jordan River by **John the Baptist,** a popular evangelist later hailed as the reincarnation of the 9th-century BCE prophet **Elijah,** herald of the Messiah. Jesus later preached in the Galilee, speaking for the poor and the righteous, most notably in the Sermon on the Mount (Matthew 5-7). After about three years of preaching, Jesus went to Jerusalem, where the **Passion,** the events of his death, took place. On Good Friday, he carried his cross down the **Via Dolorosa** until he reached the hill of Golgotha (or Calvary), now marked by the Church of the Holy Sepulchre, where he was crucified. According to the Gospels, three days after Jesus' crucifixion, on what is now celebrated as Easter, Mary and two other women went to Jesus' tomb to anoint his body and discovered the tomb empty. An angel announced that Jesus had been resurrected; Jesus subsequently appeared to the Apostles and performed miracles. The **Resurrection** is the point of departure for the Christian faith, the beginning of an age when the faithful await Christ's *parousia*, or second coming.

At first, Christianity was a sect of Judaism, accepting the Hebrew Bible. However, the sect's defining tenet—that Jesus was the Messiah—severed it from mainstream Judaism. **St. Paul** (originally Saul of Tarsus) successfully adapted the faith of Christianity to meet the spiritual needs of the largest body of converts: former pagans. The incorporation of ancient festivals, such as the winter solstice, helped draw the common people to the new religion, and the usage of Platonic doctrines converted many intellectuals. The Christian faith was officially legitimized by the Edict of Milan, issued by Emperor Licinius in 313 CE. In 325 CE, **Emperor Constantine** made Christianity the official religion of the struggling Roman Empire. Constantine also summoned the first of seven Ecumenical Councils, held in Nicaea, to elaborate and unify the content of the faith. The Council of Nicaea came up with an explicit creed, declaring that Jesus Christ was of the same essence as the Father and that there were three equal parts to God. This crucial doctrine of the **Trinity,** which is only implicitly supported in the Gospels, maintains that the Father, Son, and Holy Spirit are distinct persons yet represent one God.

Despite these unifying dicta, the Christian community suffered many schisms through the centuries. The **Egyptian (Coptic) Church** broke off in the 3rd century (see below), when other eastern branches began to drift away from western Christianity. In 1054, the **Great Schism** split Christendom into the western Roman Catholic Church and the Eastern Orthodox Church. Whereas Rome upheld the universal jurisdiction and infallibility of the Pope, Orthodoxy stressed the infallibility of the church as a whole. In 1517, German monk **Martin Luther** sparked the **Reformation,** which split northern Europe from Roman Catholicism and led to the development of **Protestantism.** Protestantism is itself composed of many sects, which generally believe in salvation through faith rather than good works. Eastern Orthodoxy, too, is divided into multiple nationalist traditions (Greek, Russian, Armenian).

THE COPTIC CHURCH

The term "Copt" is derived from the Greek word for Egyptian, *Ægyptos*, shortened in its Egyptian pronunciation to *qibt*. Copts in Egypt usually have tattoos of a domed cathedral or a tiny cross on their wrists. Of 58 million Egyptians, five to seven million are Copts, most of whom live in Cairo or Middle Egypt. Portions of the liturgy are still in Coptic, though most of the service is in Arabic.

St. Mark introduced Christianity to Egypt in 62 CE. Mass conversions transformed Alexandria into a Christian spiritual center, but Roman persecution also increased. The bloodiest days passed under Diocletian, who murdered so many Christians that the Copts date their Martyr's Calendar from 284 CE, the beginning of his reign. In 451 CE, the Alexandrian branch of the Church declared independence from Constantinople, forming the **Coptic Orthodox Church.**

Byzantine Emperor **Justinian** sought to restore unity by exiling Coptic clergy to isolated monasteries. Copts welcomed the Persians as liberators when they captured Egypt in 619. Since the 7th century, the community has lived as a religious minority in an Islamic state. Relations between the Copts and the Muslims have vacillated throughout history. Recently, the Copts felt besieged by Egypt's vocal Islamists, and acts of violence are often aimed at Coptic population centers.

Coptic Christianity served as a link between the Roman/Pharaonic and Islamic eras, leaving its own mark on modern Egypt. Coptic art incorporates the influences of pharaonic and Hellenistic cultures. The Coptic cross borrows from the *ankh,* the hieroglyphic sign for "life" (vaguely resembling the human form), as well as from the crucifix on Golgotha. Embroidered tapestries and curtains displaying nymphs and centaurs descend from Greco-Roman mythology. Islamic art often borrows from the Coptic style. Many of Cairo's mosques were engineered by Coptic architects, and some are even converted Coptic churches.

These churches usually have one of three shapes: cruciform, circular (to represent the globe, the spread of Christianity, and the eternal nature of the Word), or ark-shaped (the Ark of the Covenant and Noah's Ark are symbols of salvation). Above Coptic altars hang ostrich eggs, symbolizing Resurrection (life out of lifelessness) and thus God's eternal love and care.

OTHER FAITHS

THE DRUZE

The faith of the Druze, a staunchly independent sect of Shi'ite Muslims, centers around a hierarchy of individuals who are the sole custodians of a religious doctrine hidden from the rest of the world. Many Druze consider themselves a separate ethnicity as well as a religious group, while others consider themselves Arabs. The Druze believe that the word of God is revealed only to a divinely chosen few, and that these blessed few must be followed to the ends of the earth. Wherever the Druze settle, however, they generally remain loyal to their host country. Israel has a Druze population of about 85,000, Syria 500,000, and Lebanon 300,000.

The religion was founded in 1017 CE by an Egyptian chieftain, **al-Darazi,** who drew upon various beliefs in the Muslim world at the time, especially from Shi'ism. The Druze believe that God was incarnated in human forms, the final incarnation being the Fatimid Caliph al-Hakim. The Druze have suffered a history of persecution and repression for their beliefs, which may partially explain the group's refusal to discuss its religion. The late 1600s was a period of prosperity, however, and under **Emir Fakr al-Din** the Druze kingdom extended from Lebanon to Gaza and the Golan Heights. In 1830, a Druze revolt against the Egyptian pasha was crushed, along with all but two of the 14 Druze villages in the Carmel. In the 1860s, Ottoman rulers encouraged the Druze to return to the Carmel.

Because the Druze will not discuss their religion, most of what Westerners know about them comes from British "explorers" who fought their way into villages and stole holy books. As far as outsiders know, Jethro, father-in-law of Moses, is their most revered prophet. The most important holiday falls in late April. In Israel, Druze gather in the holy village of Ḥittim, near Tiberias. Devout Druze are forbidden to smoke, drink alcohol, or eat pork, but many young Druze do not adhere strictly to these prohibitions. Some Druze believe in reincarnation.

THE BAHA'I

This movement began in Teheran in 1863 CE, when Mirza Hussein 'Ali renamed himself **Baha'ullah** ("Glory of God") and began preaching non-violence and the unity of all religions. Baha'ullah's arrival had been foretold in 1844 by the Persian **Sa'id 'Ali Muhammad** (or **al-Bab,** "the gateway"), the first prophet of the Baha'i religion. Baha'ullah was exiled to Palestine, where he continued to teach in Acre (Akko). Al-Bab is buried in Haifa, which is now home to a large Baha'i population.

Baha'ullah's teachings, which incorporate elements of major Eastern and Western religions, fill over 100 volumes. Baha'i believe in a Supreme Being, accepting Jesus, Buddha, Muhammad, and Baha'ullah as divine prophets. The scripture includes the Bible, the Qur'an, and the Bhagavad Gita. A central doctrine of the faith regards their vision of the future: Baha'ullah prophesied a "flowering of humanity," an era of peace and enlightenment. Before this new age can arrive, however, the world must experience dreadful events to give civilization the impetus to reform itself. The Baha'i espouse trans-racial unity, sexual equality, global disarmament, and the creation of a world community. The faith currently boasts nearly six million adherents, with two million converts in the last decade.

THE KARAITES

The small sect of Jews known as the Karaites dwell principally in Ashdod, Be'er Sheva, and the Tel Aviv suburb of Ramla. The community, whose existence dates to the 9th century CE, numbers about 15,000 today. Formed out of the political and religious turmoil following the Muslim invasion, Karaites adhere strictly to the five books of the Torah and reject all later Jewish traditions. They are generally cohesive and have their own religious courts.

THE SAMARITANS

Currently, the Samaritan community is a small one, with roughly 550 adherents divided between Nablus (on the West Bank) and Ashkelon (a suburb of Tel Aviv). Originally the residents of Samaria, Samaritans consider themselves the original Israelites, descended from the tribes of Joseph (Manasseh and Ephraim), from whom other Israelites learned monotheism. The religion is seen by non-members as an offshoot of Judaism marked by literal interpretation of the Samaritan version of the Old Testament and the exclusion of later Jewish interpretation (the Mishnah, the Talmud, and all books of the Hebrew Bible after Joshua). A gradual, centuries-long separation between the two religions culminated with the destruction of the Samaritan temple on Mount Gerizim by the Hasmonean king **John Hyrcanus** in 128 BCE. The mountain is still the most holy site of the Samaritan religion. Centuries of persecution by the various rulers of Palestine and thousands of deaths in a 529 CE uprising against Byzantine rule shrank the community further. While the Rabbinate does not recognize Samaritans as Jews, the Israeli government applies the Law of Return (granting settlement rights) to them.

EGYPT مصر

CURRENCY

US$1=3.47 EGYPTIAN POUNDS (E£)	E£1=US$0.29
CDN$1=E£2.31	E£1=CDN$0.43
EUR1=E£3.21	E£1=EUR0.31
UK£1=E£5.15	E£1=UK£0.19
IR£1=E£4.09	E£1=IR£0.25
AUS$1=E£1.97	E£1=AUS$0.51
NZ$1=E£1.58	E£1=NZ$0.63
SAR1=E£0.49	E£1=SAR2.02
NIS1 (NEW ISRAELI SHEKEL)=E£0.83	E£1=NIS1.21
JD1 (JORDANIAN DINAR)=E£4.86	E£1=NIS1.21

PHONE CODES   Country Code: 20. International Dialing Prefix: 00.

The Arab Republic of Egypt (*Gomhoriyyat Misr al-'Arabiyya*, or simply *Misr*) is home to wonders of man and nature of a scale that belie its 5000 years of recorded history. A quarter of the Arab world lives in Egypt, despite the fact that the driest desert in the world, the Western Desert, makes up almost all (97%) of the country's land mass. The Nile, the longest and most fertile river in the world, stretches its arms across this region full of ancient temple ruins and glittering desert oases, welcoming the Mediterranean with the open hands of its Delta. The Nile Delta cradles several jewels in its palm: the breathtaking Pyramids at Giza (and their predecessor at Saqqara, the oldest monument in the world); the dizzying streets and dazzling mosques of Cairo, the largest city in the Middle East and Africa; and cosmopolitan Alexandria, once home to the greatest library in the world. The mainland of Egypt is divided into Upper Egypt in the south (including Aswan, Luxor, and Nubia, the region where African and Egyptian culture merge), Middle Egypt, and Lower Egypt in the north. This orientation comes from the fact that the Nile flows upstream from the south toward the Mediterranean. The Sinai Peninsula is its own rugged wonderland: at its heart, hikers trudge through desert containing some of the oldest and most sacred religious sites in the world; along the coast, scuba divers plunge into the azure depths of the Red Sea, known as one of the planet's premiere underwater sightseeing spots.

Egypt is a budget traveler's paradise. The sights are stunning, the culture is fascinating, and bargains are a way of life. However, travel here requires plenty of time, stamina, and patience. Most travelers find that with a relaxed attitude, the difficulties of navigating the hassles are surpassed by the intensity and beauty of the experiences Egypt has to offer.

LIFE AND TIMES

Egypt is home to one of the principal civilizations of the ancient Middle East and one of the earliest urban and literate societies in the world. Its culture had an important influence on both ancient Israel and ancient Greece, which in turn helped to form the civilization of the modern West. Perhaps the most important quality that typifies this civilization is continuity. Life in the Nile Valley was greatly determined by the behavior of the River. The pattern of inundation and falling water, of high Nile and low Nile, established the Egyptian year and controlled the lives of the Egyptians, who were mainly tied to a life on the land.

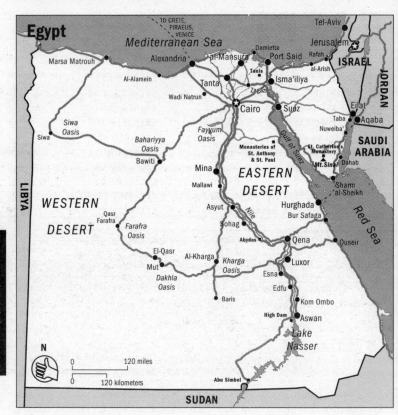

Egypt has always been a transit hub—westward along the coast of North Africa, northwest to Europe, northeast to the Levant, south along the Nile to Africa, and southeast to the Indian Ocean and the Far East. This natural advantage was enhanced in 1869 by the opening of the Suez Canal, connecting the Mediterranean Sea to the Red Sea. The concern of the European powers to safeguard the Suez Canal for strategic and commercial reasons has probably been the single most important influence on the history of Egypt since the 19th century.

HISTORY

ANCIENT HISTORY (2925 BCE-642 CE)

According to the famous **Narmer Palette** (an ancient mascara holder discovered along the Nile in 1898 CE), **King Menes** was the first true pharaoh of Egypt, uniting Upper (southern) and Lower (northern) Egypt in 2925 BCE. His kingdom, centered at Hierakonpolis, is one of the longest lasting and most powerful in all of history, enduring until Narmer was fatally mauled by a hippopotamus.

OLD KINGDOM. The pharaohs of the **Old Kingdom** (2575-2130 BCE) built a new capital at Memphis as Imhotep, history's first recorded architect, began constructing the step pyramids at Saqqara—the forerunners of the self-indulgent mausolea at Giza. Most view this era as the pinnacle of ancient Egyptian civilization: at a time when even China had scarcely emerged from the Stone Age, Egyptians had invented writing and papyrus, forged a national economy, recorded the history of eight dynasties of pharaohs, and built some of history's most impressive struc-tures (all on the faith and labor of the peasantry). Believed to be earthly manifesta-tions of the falcon-god **Horus,** the all-powerful pharaohs feared only death; their most magnificent monuments represent attempts to defeat this ultimate enemy.

MIDDLE KINGDOM. The rise of **Mentuhotep II** ushered in the **Middle Kingdom** (1938-1600 BCE), an era of conservatism and order; nevertheless, internal political rivalries began to weaken the Egyptian dynasties in the 18th century BCE. Taking advantage of this vulnerable state, the chariot-riding **Hyksos** from the North pene-trated the desert citadels at Thebes and ravished the Egyptian countryside.

NEW KINGDOM. Upon the expulsion of the Hyksos by the ever-plotting Theban princes almost a century later, Egypt was resurrected as the **New Kingdom** (1539-1075 BCE). Thebes became the center of a theocratic police state. The high priests of the sun (now embodied in the god **Amun**) wielded unimaginable power, often controlling the pharaoh himself. Egypt "modernized" its formerly primitive army by adapting the bronze weapons and horse-drawn chariots of the Hyksos and immediately proceeded to invade Africa, Palestine, and Syria. Now an empire ruled by warrior-kings, Egypt established control over most of the eastern Medi-terranean. Trade in wood, olive oil, and slaves brought stability and prosperity, though the rivalry between the pharaoh and priests of Amun brought disruption.

Despite this success and the achievements of aggressive pharaohs such as Thut-mosis III and the monumentally egotistical **Ramses II,** the New Kingdom slowly crumbled, and a slew of invaders had their way with it. When **Alexander the Great** arrived in 332 BCE, he freed the Egyptians from Persian rule and was declared the son of Amun and the legitimate pharaoh of Egypt by the Oracle of Amun in the Siwa Oasis (oh yeah, he also founded a dinky little town and named it after him-self: Alexandria). In 48 BCE, more than a century after Rome made its first over-tures to the ever-feuding Ptolemies (descendants of Alexander's successor, Ptolemy), **Julius Caesar** came to Egypt and made similar advances to **Cleopatra VII,** Queen of Egypt. She accepted an alliance with Caesar that left her secure until his assassination four years later. Cleopatra also formed a politico-sexual alliance with **Marc Antony,** one of the three men vying to succeed Caesar. While Antony was otherwise occupied, third wheel **Octavian** grabbed the empire for himself in 30 BCE, ruthlessly crushing the affair and the Ptolemaic dynasty at the **Battle of Actium.** At the height of the battle, both Cleopatra and Antony withdrew. The two fled to Alexandria but could do little more than await the arrival of the victorious Octavian. Alexandria was captured and Antony and Cleopatra committed sui-cide—he by falling on his sword, she probably by the bite of an asp.

The Egypt of Imperial Rome and Byzantium was characterized by political sta-bility and an increasingly entrenched bureaucracy (two traditions that modern Egypt has embraced wholeheartedly). During this period, Egypt was also the breadbasket of the Mediterranean, supplying most of the grain needed to support the empire's growing urban population. Christianity arrived in Egypt around 40 CE with **St. Mark** and helped maintain relative social tranquility. Some argument arose over the personage of Jesus Christ: the **Copts** worshiped him only as a divine fig-ure, whereas the church at Constantinople believed he was both divine and human. This long-festering argument exploded in 451 CE when the Copts were excommunicated and forced to set up their own church in Alexandria. The mod-ern-day Coptic minority in Egypt is descended from these original dissidents (see **Religion and Ethnicity,** p. 68).

MEDIEVAL HISTORY (639-1798 CE)

Medieval Egyptian history opened and closed with outsiders' conquests: the Arab invasion led by **'Amr ibn al-'As** in 639 CE and the Napoleonic expedition of 1798 CE marked the beginning and end of an era. This era was one in which Egypt cast off the heritage of the past to embrace a new language and religion. To facilitate the

E G Y P T

slow process of Arabization, the **Umayyad** and **Abbasid** caliphates adopted policies of tolerance toward Copts and other non-Muslims, as long as they paid their taxes.

A relatively short period of Egyptian history arose in 868 CE when Ahmad ibn Tulun came to power and established the **Tulunid dynasty.** Though initially stable because of strong military and expansionist policies, the death of the dynasty in 905 created chaos, to be left unresolved by the **Ikhshidid dynasty.** In 969, the **Fatimids** came to power as one of the most influential families in the history of Egypt. They enacted grand policies of Islamization, while also improving trade by means of low tariffs and good relations with merchants. The fall of Fatimid rule in 1171 came with the rise in power of **Salah al-Din,** a commander from Syria. He restored Egypt to Abbasid allegiance and helped empower the Ayyubid dynasty. The Ayyubids were popular among the Egyptians, but internal strife characterized their reign. The Ayyubids assigned family members to rule provinces, but instead of solidifying their power, this delegation led to unwanted struggle.

The only real security for Ayyubid Egypt lay in its independent military strength. As a result, one of the last sultans, **al-Malik al-Salih Ayyub** was even forced to purchase Turkish slaves, **Mamluks,** to man his armies. But after the death of al-Salih Ayyub in 1250 CE, the Mamluks were able to exploit a palace feud and elevate a member of their own ranks to the sultanate. Their rule lasted for two and a half centuries and brought Egypt to the peak of its evolution in the medieval period.

From 1250 to 1517, the Mamluks, a group of non-Arab, non-Muslims, established a regime not only protecting Muslims, but also saving Muslim territory. Arabic became the national language, while the military established a haven for Muslims in Syria and Egypt. Under the Mamluks, mosques, colleges, hospitals, and monasteries were built, and encyclopedias, chronicles, and dictionaries were written. The **Ottomans** conquered the region in 1517, ending the Mamluks' 300 year reign and ushering in their own three-century-long rule.

MODERN HISTORY (1798-1997 CE)

FROM THE FRENCH TO THE BRITISH OCCUPATION. Napoleon's invading forces ended Ottoman control of Egypt in 1798 CE, but the French invasion was too short-lived and too universally loathed to have any major impact at the time. However, as the first European conquest of an Arab country in the history of Islam, the invasion signaled the fall of Islam as a world political power.

Europe was still looking for a shortcut to the mysteries (and trade possibilities) of India, and all eyes turned to the Suez. The British and Ottomans fought for control of the country, with the latter winning out and building the Suez Canal in 1869. The rigid Ottoman Empire began to grow flaccid in the later years of the 19th century, when the Brits took over (prompting Mustafa Kamal to found an Egyptian nationalist movement). The Egyptian economy during the British occupation and World War I was so completely focused on the exportation of cotton to England's rheumatic textile mills that grain had to be imported to feed the rural population.

THE KINGDOM OF EGYPT. After World War I ended, the nationalist *Wafd* ("delegation") party was formed, demanding complete autonomy from Britain; the deportation in 1918 of *Wafd* leader, Sa'ad Zaghloul, showed that the British had other plans. Though they eventually recognized Egypt's independence in 1922, they maintained control through puppet-king **Fouad I.** Not content to have his strings pulled by far-distant imperialists, Fouad struggled successfully for some power of his own; soon the British, Fouad, and the popularly supported *Wafd* party were all fighting for control of Egypt. The Anglo-Egyptian Treaty of 1936 ended the three-way tug-of-war for control by granting Egypt independence but allowing for continued British occupation of the Suez Canal Zone.

Egypt again came to center stage as an Allied base of operations during World War II. The decisive Allied victory at the **Battle of al-Alamein** (just outside Alexandria) allowed the Allies to sweep into North Africa and halt the advances of Nazi General Edwin Rommel's Afrika Korps once and for all. Resentment toward the

British reached a fever pitch during and after World War II as Egyptians rioted against being forced to participate in a war they had nothing to do with. Continued rioting and striking led the British to finally leave Alexandria and the Suez in 1947.

The newborn Egyptian government didn't wait long before taking its first, hesitant steps. In 1948, Egypt and the entire Arab world was humiliated when a joint Arab army was easily defeated by the smaller army of the new state of Israel. Several young officers were so outraged at the incompetence of their elder leaders that they formed the **Free Officers** coalition and staged a bloodless coup of the government on July 26, 1952. The king, Farouk, was forced to abdicate, all political parties and Constitution were abolished, and General Muhammad Naguib was elected Prime Minister (although the government was really controlled by a nine-member Revolutionary Command Council led by Colonel **Gamal Abd al-Nasser**).

THE NASSER REGIME. Nasser officially assumed presidency of the Egyptian Arab Republic in 1956. Equal parts brilliant strategist and power-obsessed dictator, he gained popularity because of his dedication to the plight of the *fellaheen* (peasant) majority in Egypt. One of Nasser's first major political moves was the controversial nationalization of the Suez Canal after a lack of Western financial support for the **Aswan High Dam**. During his presidency, Arabic nationalism was born, reached its peak, and died out; as a result, Nasser's name is synonymous with **Pan-Arabism.** In 1958, Egypt and Syria made a bold nationalist move by uniting to form the United Arab Republic; this ended during the **Six-Day War** (July 5–10) of 1967, when Israeli armies managed to gain control of the Sinai Peninsula (as well as other strategic locations). Three years later, the crumbling movement for Pan-Arabism was dealt a fatal blow with the death of Nasser on September 28, 1970.

THE SADAT REGIME. Following Nasser's death, Vice President **Anwar Sadat** was elected President by a landslide (and a lack of opposition). Sadat set up Egypt as a "democratic, socialist state," although in reality it was an election-legitimated authoritarian regime (which it remains to this day). The president serves a six-year term and is almost inevitably reelected for additional terms. The legislative branch of government consists of the 444-member **People's Assembly**, half of whom must be workers or peasants and a whopping 30 of whom must be women.

On October 6, 1973 (Yom Kippur), Sadat attacked Israeli forces in the Sinai. Although this **October War** ended in a stalemate, the Arab world experienced an incredible morale boost. On November 17, 1977, Sadat continued with his surprise movements and made a visit to Jerusalem to discuss peace settlements. The West embraced Sadat as the paragon of Arab-Israeli moderation and conciliation, awarding him (and Israeli Prime Minister Menaḥem Begin) the **Nobel Peace Prize** the next year for his work in the peace process and at the Camp David Accords. Although Sadat was building himself up in terms of foreign relations, his domestic support was crumbling: never the debonair figurehead as Nasser had been, many Arabs saw him as a sellout and a yes-man to Western interests. Sadat was assassinated at a military parade in October 1981.

EGYPT AFTER SADAT. Current President **Hosni Mubarak,** elected in 1981, continued his predecessor's policies with less derring-do and more domestic sensitivity. Mubarak was responsible for developing Egypt's growing tourism industry, resuming diplomatic and trade relations with moderate Arab countries, and bandaging the wounds made by the flamboyant swathe Sadat cut through Arab politics. Mubarak's support of Saudi Arabia and Kuwait in the **Gulf War** in 1990-1991 was important in revitalizing Egypt's position as the center of Middle Eastern politics. The most significant political threat to President Mubarak's regime continues to be internal Arab dissidents, in the form of the Islamist parties. Sadat was assassinated by militants who wanted to overthrow the Egyptian government and establish an Islamic republic in its place. Mubarak has consistently appeased Islamic moderates (who are in the majority anyway) in order to isolate militants: alcohol was banned on EgyptAir flights, the American show *Dallas* was taken off television, and an Islamic newspaper, *al-Liwa' al-Islami*, was initiated. The past several years have seen a rise in Islamist-generated violence, with militants based in Middle Egypt striking at the status quo via attacks on government figures and assassinations of secularist intellectuals. The deadliest attack by Islamist militants involved the death of 58 tourists at Luxor on November 17, 1997, leading the government to drastically tighten security throughout the country.

IN THE NEWS

The **Library at Alexandria** is set to reopen in Spring 2001, nearly five millennia after Ptolemy I first commissioned the construction of the building. The ancient library was the center of scholarly debate and research in the ancient world and may even have achieved its goal of housing every book known to exist at the time under one roof. The Library of Celsus, a similarly prestigious collection of up to 12,000 scrolls, competitively existed in **Ephesus,** Turkey (see p. 640), at the time of Alexandria's peak. Covered in inscriptions recording important events, the library was built in memory of Gaius Julius Celsus by his son. The Library at Alexandria was mysteriously burned down near the end of the Roman Empire. The purpose of the new edifice is almost as unclear as the cause of the fire so many years ago. Egyptian authorities have assured scholars that the library is being built to foster the research of scholars in the Middle East, and consequently, Arab countries have helped pick up a third of the library's US$150 million cost. These funds will be used to collect over 8 million books and manuscripts, and to construct a science museum, a planetarium, and a school for library studies. Many scholars and diplomats have criticized the project in private as a governmental propaganda machine, a library offering a multitude of resources to the public but not really fostering or even tolerating the sort of radical intellectual inquiry the original library did. Press censorship in Egypt is very widespread: books and news articles are frequently banned, and many scholars doubt that the government will allow them to research or publish works criticizing Middle Eastern and Arabic policies. For another look at the *Bibliotheka Alexandria* controversy, see **A Library Long Overdue,** p. 154.

CULTURE

RELIGION AND ETHNICITY

Islam is constitutionally established as the official religion of Egypt, with over 90% of the population belonging to the **Sunni Muslim** sect. Western mores do not apply, especially in matters of family and sex. The visibility and freedom of most Egyptian women is limited. Egypt is one of the most important centers of Islamic theological study in the world, and Cairo's **al-Azhar University** (p. 110) is at its heart. Al-Azhar is the oldest continuously operating university in the world and has graduated Islamic scholars from every Muslim country on earth since it was first founded in 972 CE.

Orthodox Christians (who belong to the **Coptic Church**) make up Egypt's largest and most significant religious minority, with population estimates somewhere between three and seven million. The relationship between the Copts and the Muslim government has always been strained, but with the rise of Muslim fundamentalism, tensions between the Muslim majority and the Coptic minority have erupted in acts of vandalism. Another one million or so members of the Egyptian population are Roman Catholics, Greek and Armenian Orthodox Christians, Protestants, and Jews. These groups thrived in colonial times but have dwindled in number due to emigration.

LANGUAGE

One of the earliest forms of writing was Egyptian **hieroglyphs** (sacred carvings). Alongside this pictorial system developed the **hieratic,** an abbreviated cursive script that retained only the vital characteristics of the pictures. After the 22nd Dynasty, scribes began using the sacred hieratic writing in a secular context, lead-

MEET THE GODS

The ancient Egyptians didn't play that monotheism game. Here's a brief rundown of their many deities:

AMUN "The Hidden One." Amun is typically portrayed as a ram-horned man with blue-colored flesh. In the New Kingdom he became associated with the sun-god Ra, and "Amun-Ra" became the king of the gods and a father figure to the pharaohs.

ANUBIS The jackal-headed god of cemeteries and embalming, whose black skin represents either the silt of the Nile or mummy flesh treated with chemicals. He is usually depicted weighing the hearts of the dead (the heart was considered the center of intellect and emotions) against Maat, the feather of truth.

ATON The sun at noon, usually depicted as a disk from which rays extend ending in outstretched hands holding *ankhs* (a Coptic cross). The heretical 18th dynasty pharaoh Akhenaton worshiped Aton as the one and only god, with the pharaoh as his one and only priest.

GEB The earth god, usually depicted as a reclining man holding up his sister-wife Nut (the sky goddess). He divided Egypt in two, giving Lower Egypt to his son Osiris and Upper Egypt to his son Seth.

HAPY The symbol of the Nile's annual flooding. He is depicted as a seaweed-tressed man with breasts and a rounded abdomen (representing fertility).

HATHOR The daughter of Ra, the goddess of joy and love, and the protectoress of women and travelers. She usually hangs out on tomb walls sporting cow horns with a sun disk between them.

HORUS The hawk-headed sky god and son of Isis and Osiris. When Seth cut out his eyes (they were later glued back on with divine saliva), they came to represent perfection and were known as a guard against evil (the *wedjat* eye).

ISIS Another sister-wife (to Osiris), usually depicted with a throne on her head. She is the protectoress and healer of children.

KHNUM Ram-headed potter god who sculpted both gods and men out of clay. He is known for controlling the Nile's annual flood.

KHONSU As the moon god, this young man holds the posture of a mummy wearing a moon disk on his shoulders. He is the son of Mut and Amun, thus completing the Theban triad. Also revered as the god of time and known as a lover of games.

MAAT The personification of cosmic order, usually depicted as a woman wearing an ostrich feather on her head.

MUT Symbolic mother of the pharaoh and Thebes' principal goddess (wife of Amun), who often appears as a lion-headed woman wearing a vulture-shaped headdress.

NUT Cow-shaped goddess of the sky and yet another sister-wife (to Geb), usually depicted stretched across the ceiling of a tomb, swallowing the sun and making the night. She is the mother of Osiris, Isis, Seth, and Nephthys.

OSIRIS The mummified god of the underworld and fertility and brother of Isis. Seth was so bitter when Geb divided up Egypt that he dismembered his brother Osiris and buried his body parts across Egypt. Isis collected the pieces and bandaged them together, making the first mummy; as a thank-you gift, Osiris fathered Horus by Isis before he headed for Duat (the underworld) to rule as lord and judge of the dead.

RA Don't step to Ra, the falcon-headed sun god with a sun disc upon his head who is so powerful that other gods often merge with him to enhance their own powers (Amun-Ra). He rides across the sky in his solar boat, rising from Duat (the underworld) in the east and reentering the land of the dead in the west.

SETH God of chaotic forces, synonymous with evil in much of Egyptian mythology. He performs his one good deed when he spears the evil snake Apophis as the boat of Ra begins its entry into the underworld every evening.

THOTH The ibis-headed scribe god, inventor of writing, and divine reckoner of time. Thoth sometimes took the form of a great white baboon with a giant penis.

EGYPT

ing to the rise of a form known as Enchorial or **Demotic.** Eventually, even the sacred *Book of the Dead* (a compilation of spells and cult rituals) was translated into this script. Modern scholars owe much of their knowledge of ancient Egyptian linguistics to the **Rosetta Stone,** a stone tablet dating from around 200 BCE that contains the same passage celebrating the crowning of King Ptolemy V recorded in hieroglyphic, Demotic, and Greek writing. **Coptic,** today used only in liturgy, is a derivation of ancient Egyptian that uses Greek letters plus six letters of Demotic.

Since the Islamic conquest, the primary language of Egypt has been Arabic. Modern **Egyptian Arabic** differs greatly from classical Arabic, and the Egyptian dialect varies significantly from that used in other Arab nations.

THE ARTS

LITERATURE. Most of the writings of the ancient Egyptians, such as the *Book of the Dead,* deal with magic and religion. The ancients dabbled in poetic love songs as well. Modern literature in Egypt is synonymous with the name of Cairene novelist **Naguib Mahfouz.** In 1988, Mahfouz became the first Arab to win the Nobel Prize for literature. Mahfouz's major work in the 1950s was *The Cairo Trilogy (Palace Walk, Palace of Desire,* and *Sugar Street),* which seamlessly depicts the life of three generations in Cairo from World War I to the 1950s. His classic allegory *Children of Gebelawi* (1959), banned throughout the Arab world except in Lebanon, retells the stories of the Qur'an in a modern-day Cairo setting.

Notable among more contemporary authors is Alexandrene novelist and essayist **Edward al-Kharrat,** who is considered the father of modernism in Egyptian literature. His popular novels *City of Saffron* (1989) and *Girls of Alexandria* (1993) are both available in translation. Doctor, feminist, and novelist **Nawal al-Saadawi** stands out among women authors with her extensive writings (including the notable works *The Circling Song* and *The Naked Face of Arab Women*) on the liberation of the Arab female psyche, sexuality, and legal position. Her works were once considered so controversial they were banned in her native country, and she herself has been imprisoned for a year and forbidden from practicing medicine in Egypt because of the perceived danger she poses to society.

Many non-Egyptians have written accounts of their travels and experiences within the country. In *The Innocents Abroad,* Mark Twain describes his misadventures in Egypt and other countries. For an engrossing—if oversexed—account of Alexandrene life, don't miss Lawrence Durrell's multi-narrator epic, *The Alexandria Quartet.* For an eye-opening account of early Western explorers roaming the Nile, read Alan Moorehead's *The White Nile* and its companion volume, *The Blue Nile,* which includes hair-raising chapters on the French invasion of Egypt and the rise of Muhammad 'Ali. Michael Ondaatje's award-winning *The English Patient* contains sensual and incredibly accurate descriptions of early desert expeditions in the area.

VISUAL ARTS. Egypt has had a near monopoly on the Arabic entertainment industry for most of the second half of the 20th century, ranking behind only Hollywood (United States) and Bollywood (India) in its prolific output. Egyptian films range from skillfully done modern dramas to comedies pitting down-and-out students against evil capitalists and bumbling police officers, with a smattering of southern Egyptians (portrayed as idiots) thrown in for comic relief.

The 50s and 60s were the golden age of Egyptian cinema, when Alexandrene **Omar Sharif** *(Doctor Zhivago, Funny Girl)* ruled as an international film superstar and his former wife Fatin Hamama presided as queen of Arab cinema. The musicals of that period are still very popular, featuring well-dressed hipsters knitting their brows in consternation over the cruelty of love, the generation gap, and the difficulty of college examinations. Controversial auteur **Yusef Chahine** (credited with discovering Omar Sharif in a Cairo cafe and catapulting him to fame with 1954's *Blazing Sun*) has gained international acclaim for his lushly filmed, genre-bending masterpieces that tackle everything from sexual discovery to the hypocrisy of Western society. *The Emigrant* (1994) was initially banned in Egypt for depicting images of the Prophet Muhammad (which is forbidden in the Muslim religion), but became a box office hit once the ban was lifted. His recent work includes *Destiny* (1997), which attacks modern Islamic fundamentalism by recounting the persecution of the Islamic philosopher Averroes.

The levying of heavy entertainment taxes in the 70s and the general atmosphere of profiteering in the 80s served to drastically lower the standards of modern Egyptian cinema to somewhere below chintzy tragicomedy. A new guard of young directors has begun to revitalize the industry by tackling such once-taboo topics as social conditions, terrorism, and the country's volatile relationship with Israel.

MUSIC. Traditional Egyptian folk music incorporates nasal horns churning out repetitive melodies to the incessant beat of drums. **Nubian music** (called *musiqa nubiyya* in Aswan) is equally enthralling. In general, it eliminates the horns and focuses on slow drumbeats and chanting choruses. The music blaring from taxis, *ahwas*, and homes throughout Egypt is a slightly updated version of this traditional classical music. Egypt is the capital of the Arab music industry and the promised land for aspiring artists from all over the Arab world. Sayyid Darwish and the legendary **Muhammad Abd al-Wahhab** began as early as the 1910s and 20s to integrate Western instrumentation and techniques into Arabic song. Like Egyptian cinema, this type of music had its heyday in the 50s and 60s but shows no signs of waning in popularity today. In the 60s, the emphasis fell on strong, beautiful voices to unite Arabic music's disparate elements, and several "greats" of Egyptian music emerged. The greatest of these was the unmistakable and unforgettable **Umm Kulthum.** Her rags-to-riches story begins in the provinces, where her father dressed her up as a boy to sing with him at religious festivals; it ends in 1975 with a funeral that was bigger than President Nasser's five years earlier. In the interim, Umm Kulthum gave speeches, starred in musical films, and sang everything from post-revolutionary propaganda songs to love ballads. Travelers in Egypt cannot and should not escape without hearing Umm Kulthum's voice and seeing her sunglasses-clad face on a television screen or wall mural. Music in the 80s and 90s saw a wholesale incorporation of Western influences. Modern Egyptian pop is totally danceable, mostly pre-packaged, and rarely long-lived. Among these transitory teen dreams, **Amr Diab** has endured. His upbeat songs provide sing-along material at weddings, parties, and discos.

FOOD AND DRINK

The Egyptian breakfast of choice is **fuul** ("fool")—cooked, mashed fava beans blended with garlic, lemon, olive oil, and salt, eaten with bread and vegetables. What's known as falafel elsewhere—chick peas and/or fava beans mashed, shaped into balls, and fried—is called **ta'amiyya** in Egypt, and both *ta'amiyya* and *fuul* are sold at street stands everywhere. Street vendors also sell *kibdeh* (liver) sandwiches, which don't score high on the smell test but go down quite scrumptiously.

PUFF THE MAGIC SHEESHA In Egypt, relaxation has become synonymous with gurgling and puffing noises accompanied by the smell of sugary honey, apple, or rose tobacco. The instrument of pleasure is a popular smoking apparatus known in Egypt as a *sheesha* (elsewhere as an *argeileh* or *nargilah*), plain or ornately colored and decorated with feathers. It consists of a snake-like tube and a small bowl filled with burning coals, tobacco, and spices. Water vapor carries the tobacco smoke through the one-meter tube and into the mouth, making each puff smooth and sweet. The *sheesha* is thought to have been introduced in Egypt by the Turks, and became fashionable among the elite during the late 17th century. For a long time *sheesha* smoking remained an upper-class pleasure, but as of late the apple and honey puffs of smoke have ushered in a veritable national pastime.

Shawarma made its way from the Levant to Egypt only recently; it is supposed to be sinfully fatty lamb rolled into a pita with vegetables and *tahina*, but Egyptians will slap any sort of meat into bogus French bread and call it *shawarma*. Popular **kushari** is a cheap, filling meal of pasta, lentils, and dried onions in tomato sauce.

At times you might feel that all you will ever get to eat will be *kofta*, kebab, and chicken. These carnivorous joys are almost always served with salads, bread or rice, and *tahina*, a sesame-based sauce. *Kofta* is spiced ground beef grilled on skewers; kebab is chunks of lamb cooked the same way. Chicken is either fried (without batter), roasted on a rotisserie, or skewered, grilled, and called *shish tawouq*. Fried and stuffed pigeon *(hamam)* is a source of national pride, particularly in Alexandria, but most travelers are content to leave the dish, served whole, for the birds. *Biftek* (sometimes called *veal panné* on restaurant menus) is a thinly sliced veal, breaded and fried. You can get feta cheese with a year-long shelf life in no-refrigeration-needed packs—great for long road trips or cheap breakfasts. The brand *La Vache Qui Rit* (The Laughing Cow) is so popular that it has been adopted as a disparaging nickname for President Hosni Mubarak.

Fatir are flaky, chewy, doughy delights, filled with anything and everything and eaten either as a meal or for dessert. Other desserts include *ba'laweh* and rice pudding flavored with rose-water *(roz bel laban)*. Egypt's ruby-red watermelons *(butteekh)*, though sometimes known to be color-enhanced with non-potable water, still make a juicy, hydrating communal snack. Also try the unbelievable **figs** *(teen)*, and in late summer, the papaya-like *teen shoki* (cactus fruit).

A popular drink among travelers is **'asab**, sugar cane juice, said to increase sexual prowess. Egyptians themselves are coffee and tea fiends. Egyptian tea is taken without milk and enough sugar to make it syrupy. Egyptians prefer **ahwa** (Arabic coffee). Especially when you are in Upper Egypt, try *karkadeh*, a red drink made by brewing hibiscus flowers and served hot or cold. Egypt brews its own beer, **Stella,** which costs between E£5 and E£8 in restaurants and bars, as well as the surprisingly good **Sakara,** usually a pound or two more.

FACTS AND FIGURES

OFFICIAL NAME: Arab Republic of Egypt

GOVERNMENT: Democratic, Socialist State

CAPITAL: Cairo

LAND AREA: 1,001,449 sq. km.

GEOGRAPHY: Fertile Nile valley flanked by the Western and Eastern Deserts

CLIMATE: Hot and dry; mild temperatures with winter rains along Mediterranean; freezing temperature Nov.-Feb.

MAJOR CITIES: Alexandria, Aswan, Luxor, Port Said, Suez

POPULATION: 65,000,000; Nile Valley 95%, rural 5%

LANGUAGE: Arabic, English, French

RELIGIONS: Muslim (94%), Copt (6%)

AVERAGE INCOME PER CAPITA: US$2850

MAJOR EXPORTS: Oil, cotton, textiles, metal products, and chemicals

---

ESSENTIALS

WHEN TO GO

Egypt's high and low seasons depend partly on the region: Cairo is a year-round mob scene, while summertime (approximately May-Sept.) is partytime in Alexandria and on the Mediterranean and Red Sea beaches. In the Sinai, Oases, and Upper Egypt, reasonable temperatures make winter (approximately Oct.-Mar.) the high season, especially for wealthier tourists; younger travelers will revel in summertime bargains. In southern Egypt, summer temperatures often reach 49°C (120°F) and can push 55°C (131°F). Fortunately, it's dry—your body's cooling system should know what to do. Winter is perfect across the country. In arid Cairo, pollution makes summer afternoons hellish. Alexandria is temperate year-round, though quite humid. The Red Sea coast is comfortably warm in winter and hot but dry in summer; higher elevations in the Sinai can be freezing in winter and on summer nights.

AVERAGE TEMPERATURE AND PRECIPITATION

	°C	°F	mm	°C	°F	mm	°C	°F	mm	°C	°F	mm
Alexandria	14.7	58.5	52	19.3	66.7	3.7	26.3	79.3	0	24.3	75.7	7.6
Aswan	16.6	61.9	0	27.1	80.8	0	33.9	93.0	0	29.1	84.4	0
Cairo	13.8	56.8	5.1	21.4	70.5	25	27.9	82.2	0	23.7	74.7	1.0
Hurghada	15.6	60.1	0.1	22.4	72.3	0.1	29.5	85.1	0	25.0	77.0	0.2
Luxor	13.9	57.0	0	25.5	77.9	0	32.5	90.5	0	26.5	79.7	0.8

DOCUMENTS AND FORMALITIES

EGYPT'S CONSULAR SERVICES ABROAD

Egypt's embassies and consulates abroad include:

Australia Embassy: 1 Darwin Ave., Yarralumla, Canberra, ACT 2600 (☎(02) 62 73 44 37; fax 62 73 42 79). **Consulate:** 124 Exhibition St., 9th floor, Melbourne, Victoria 3000 (☎(03) 96 54 86 34 or 96 54 88 69; fax 96 50 83 62). **Consulate:** 112 Glen More Rd., Paddington, NSW 2021 (☎(02) 93 32 33 88; fax 93 32 32 88).

Canada Embassy: 454 Laurier Ave. E., Ottawa, ON K1N 6R3 (☎(613) 234-4931; fax 234-6347). **Consulate:** 630 Rene-Levesque, ste. 2302, Montreal, QU H3B 1S6 (☎(514) 861-6340; fax 861-6343).

Ireland Embassy: 12 Clyde Rd., Dublin 4 (☎(01) 660 65 66 or 660 67 18; fax 668 37 45; email embegypt@Indigo.ie).

UK Embassy: 26 South St., London, W1Y 6DD (☎(020) 7499 3304; fax 7491 1542). **Consulate:** 2 Lowndes St., London, SW1 (☎(020) 7235 7919 or 7235 9777; fax 7235 5684).

US Embassy: 3521 International Court NW, Washington, D.C. 20008 (☎(202) 895-5400; fax 244-4319). **Consulate:** 1110 2nd Avenue, New York, NY 10022 (☎(212) 759-7120, 759-7121, 759-7122; fax 308-7643).

CONSULAR SERVICES IN EGYPT

Embassies and consulates of other countries in Egypt include:

Australian Embassy: World Trade Center, Corniche al-Nil, Bulaq, Cairo (☎(02) 575 04 44; fax 578 16 38; email dima-cairo@dfat.gov.au).

Canadian Embassy: 5 al-Sarayah al-Cobrah Sq., Garden City, Cairo (☎(02) 794 31 10; fax 796 35 48).

Ireland Embassy: 3 Abu al-Feda St., Zamalek, Cairo (☎(02) 340 82 64, 340 85 47, 341 46 53; fax 341 28 63).

South African Embassy: 21/23 Giza St., 18th Floor, Giza, Cairo (☎(02) 571 72 34, 571 72 35, 571 72 38, 571 72 39; fax 571 72 41; email saembcai@gega.net).

UK Embassy: 7 Ahmed Ragheb St., Garden City, Cairo (☎(02) 794 0850, 794 0852, 794 0853; fax 794 08 59). **Consulate:** 1 Nile St., Luxor (☎(95) 382 838).

US Embassy: 5 Latin America St., Garden City, Cairo. (☎(02) 355 73 71; fax 357 32 00; email cacairo@state.gov; www.usis.egnet.net).

EGYPT

ENTRY REQUIREMENTS

PASSPORT. Non-Egyptian visitors arriving in Egypt are required to be in possession of a **valid passport.** Travelers with an Israeli stamp on their passports are allowed to enter the country.

VISA AND PERMIT INFO. A **visa** (US$15) is required to enter Egypt. **Visas** can be easily obtained in advance by submitting an application to the nearest embassy or consulate (may be acquired online) and waiting approximately five business days, though processing tends to take notoriously longer. In case of emergencies, visas can be obtained at the airport in Cairo as well as the Port of Alexandria, and with some restrictions at the borders. An Egyptian visa does not permit the holder to work. When applying, you can request a **multiple-entry visa** for travel in and out of Egypt, allowing you to reenter any number of times while the visa is valid. Visits to Sinai from Israel or Jordan can be made on a free, two-week **Sinai-only visa,** available at borders. Generally, all items brought into the country are exempt from taxes. There is no formal declaration for personal items, but passengers may be asked to open their bags for customs officials when leaving the airport.

UPON ARRIVAL. Upon arrival at the **Cairo International Airport,** purchase a US$15 visa stamp at one of the six currency exchanges. These are good for one month, but renewable at police stations or at passport offices in major towns if you provide one photograph, E£12, and (officially) receipts showing that at least US$200 has been changed into Egyptian currency. Reports vary on the strictness of this last rule. There is a 13-day grace period after the 30-day visa expires; if you still fail to renew your visa during this time, you will face (at least) a E£100 penalty upon departure. If your visa has been expired for more than a couple weeks, you will be treated to an all-expenses paid trip to the interrogation rooms of the Egyptian immigration office in Cairo.

There are several options for getting downtown. Taxis are the simplest, but the most expensive (at most E£25); only take those that leave from the official stand, as they are monitored 24 hours a day by tourist police. Taxis will most likely drop you off at Tahrir Sq. (center of Cairo), and you can get anywhere from there. **Minibus** #27 (٢٧) and **bus** #400 (٤٠٠) go to Tahrir Sq. from the Airport's old terminal for 50pt (piasters). Gem Travel also runs a 24-hour **shuttle bus** to downtown (US$4).

All **trains** into Cairo stop at Ramses Station. **Bus** #160 (١٦٠) runs from there to Tahrir Sq. Black and white **taxis** to Tahrir Sq. cost E£2. The **Metro,** opposite the station, runs to Tahrir Sq. for 50pt. To walk (30min.), climb the pedestrian overpass and walk south on Ramses St., away from the Ramses II statue.

Buses from Israel usually drop passengers off at 'Abbasiyya Station. To reach Tahrir Sq. from 'Abbasiyya Station, hop into a southbound black and white cab (E£4-5) or walk left down Ramses St. as you leave the station; go beyond the overpass, and to the first bus stop on the right. From here many buses travel to Tahrir Sq. Buses from Jordan usually drop you off at **Abd al-Munem Riad Station.** To reach Tahrir Sq. from here, walk right onto Gala'a St. as you exit, until you come to the Corniche al-Nil. At the corniche take a left onto Tahrir St.

Some hotels, as well as a tour guide by the name of **Mr. Salah Muhammad** (☎/fax 298 06 50; samo@intouch.com), offer **free 24-hour shuttle service** (reserve ahead of time by email) from the airport to downtown Cairo for visitors who will stay at their establishments or take Muhammad's tour of the Pyramids at Giza, Memphis, Saqqara, and the carpet school at Harania (E£40, not including entrance fees to sights, E£5 *Let's Go* discount if you book with him). For more information on the package, see **Pyramids at Giza,** p. 102.

BORDER CROSSINGS

TO JORDAN. A **ferry** shuttles between the port at **Nuweiba** and **Aqaba.** Nobody really knows what time the ferries leave, but the latest schedule had them both leaving daily at 3pm. **Taxis** from Nuweiba or Tarabin to the port cost E£5. The ticket office for the ferries is in a small white building 100m south of the port, past a bakery. The slow ferry takes three hours barring technical difficulties and costs US$33, payable in dollars or Egyptian pounds; a faster, less crowded, and more punctual **speedboat** takes an hour and runs at US$43. Show up a few hours before the earliest possible departure time to deal with customs and ticketing. For general ferry information, call 52 00 52 or 52 03 60. Jordanian **visas** can be obtained on board (Australia JD16, Canada JD36, Ireland JD11, New Zealand JD16, South Africa free, UK JD23, US JD33). There is no Egyptian departure tax.

TO ISRAEL. The most convenient option is **Taba** to **Eilat** (border open 24hr.). *Service* drop you right at the border, but the East Delta bus stop leaves a 200m walk north to the promised land. See the **Transportation** sections of towns in the Sinai for information on transportation to Taba. On the Israeli side, **bus** #15 runs daily every 15 minutes from the border checkpoint to Eilat until about 11pm except on Fridays, when the last bus is at 5:30pm (NIS3.20). **Taxis** (US$6 to downtown) also go to Eilat. Rented **cars** are not allowed to cross in either direction.

At the border you will be issued a free visa, the length of which is entirely determined by the border guards' mood and your appearance (min. one week, max. three months). You will have to pay a E£2 exit tax if you have traveled beyond the Sinai. The walk through the stations shouldn't take more than an hour. Keep your Israeli entrance card—you'll need it to leave the country. Israeli customs will often let you walk right through their station, but make sure to stop there because you can't pass the final checkpoint without the customs stamp on your gate pass.

POINTERS FOR ENTERING ISRAEL If you plan on traveling to Syria or Lebanon, have Israeli authorities stamp a separate piece of paper—you will not be allowed to enter these countries if there is an Israeli visa in your passport. Authorities will not let you leave Egypt without stamping your passport, so make any trips to Syria or Lebanon beforehand.

Change money at decent rates at either the Taba Hilton or a bank in Eilat. **Al-Arish** is also a convenient crossing point. There is an E£18 Egyptian exit fee and E£10 charge for transfer into Israel. To enter Egypt at Rafah, you need a full Egyptian visa (not just a Sinai only), which cannot be obtained at the border.

GETTING AROUND

Public transportation in Egypt is more prevalent and more pervasive than that of other Arab countries, but transportation to obscure sights may still be difficult to find (particularly in the summer, the off-season for tourism). Before that camel, Peugeot, or minibus spirits you off to a Nilometer or distant praying baboon statue, make sure it's up for the ride back.

BY PLANE. Egypt is served by **EgyptAir** (☎ (02) 76 52 00); see **Cairo: Flights** (p. 81) for locations, prices, and destinations. Check **Airplanes** listings in other cities for EgyptAir offices and flight details. EgyptAir's main office in the US is at 720 Fifth Ave., Suite 505, New York, NY 10019 (☎ (800) 334-6787). **Air Sinai** (☎ (02) 76 09 48; 77 29 49), in the courtyard of the Nile Hilton, serves the Sinai and Israel.

BY TRAIN. Egypt's railway system was the first established in both the Arab world and in Africa, and it shows. Schedules and signs in the train stations are rarely in English, but can be obtained from the tourist office or from ticket windows; fellow passengers can also help you. If lines are long and you're in a hurry, try boarding the train without a ticket—the conductor will usually sell one on board for an additional fee, even if the train is full.

Trains offer student discounts (ISIC card required) of up to 50%, with an average discount of about 30%. **Air-conditioned 2nd-class** cars are comfortably small with reclining seats; shelling out more for first-class means only slightly larger seats and loud, braying Egyptian movies. Avoid the dangerous **3rd-class. Second-class sleeper cars,** available on some regular trains, might be more comfortable for trips of 10 hours or more but are overpriced. Reserve space in a sleeper at the wagon-lit offices in Cairo, Luxor, Aswan, and Alexandria. Seats for Cairo-Alexandria and Cairo-Upper Egypt trips should be reserved a day or two in advance. Reserve a week in advance during the last week of Ramadan and the following week, as well as Eid al-Adha.

BY BUS. Buses are inexpensive (despite not offering student discounts) but often slow, crowded, and the air-conditioning can turn into a cruel, cruel joke. Companies include **Superjet,** West Delta Bus Company, and East Delta Bus Company. **West Delta** has a deluxe branch called **Golden Arrow** with vehicles sporting A/C, refreshments, and bathrooms; unfortunately, they often show Egyptian soap operas with women shrieking at unsustainable volumes. Air-conditioned **East Delta** buses serve locales throughout the Sinai.

BY TAXI. The flexibly-scheduled *service* taxis (known as *taxi bin-nafar* in Middle and Upper Egypt and *taxi ugra* in Lower Egypt) depart when full or when passengers have agreed to split the price of a full carload. The intracity version of *service* is the **minibus.** Cheap **private taxis** are only convenient in Cairo (black and white) and Alexandria (black and yellow or orange). Hail private taxis on the street instead of in front of a tourist trap, train station, or large hotel, and don't take a taxi if the driver approaches you. Never ask the driver for the fare: open the door as you are paying with folded bills and leave the taxi without looking to the driver for approval. Have exact change and small bills ready. "Special" means rip-off: if this word is mentioned in your presence, repeat *La* ("No").

BY CAR. Renting a car is a useful option only in the Sinai and the desert oases. Rentals run about US$35 per day without an driver from the company, and US$50 with one. Make all necessary arrangements before leaving your home country. If you plan to drive, remember to obtain the necessary permits: an International Driver's Permit is required in Egypt, but many places are pretty lax about this (as they are about age requirements; for more on driving in the Middle East, see p. 37).

 ROAD TRAVEL ADVISORY. Highway travel in Egypt is incredibly dangerous: Egypt has one of the highest road casualty rates in the world. **Intracity travel** is just as scary: at night, cars race by at 100kmph (60mph) without headlights. Avoid *service* after sundown. Check with local tourism authorities or the Ministry of the Interior before venturing in private transport off main roads, particularly in the following areas: the Western Desert (especially near the Libyan and Sudanese borders), along the Suez Canal and Red Sea Coast, and in the Sinai. If you need a permit, apply at the Ministry of the Interior in Cairo at 110 Qasr al-'Aini St. (☎354 83 00).

BY THUMB. Egypt is mostly untraveled desert; never count on getting a ride—you'll die of dehydration first. *Let's Go* does not recommend hitchhiking. Hitching is not common in the highly populated parts of Egypt. In recent years, the newspapers have been full of crimes perpetrated by hitchhikers along the roads between Cairo and Alexandria, making most drivers reluctant to pick people up anyway. Rides are reportedly easy to obtain in isolated areas (such as along the Great Desert Road) or for short jaunts in remote parts of the Nile Valley (where public transportation is difficult to find). Many drivers who pick up hitchhikers expect money anyway, so public transportation should be used where it is available.

TOURIST SERVICES AND MONEY

TOURIST OFFICES. Wherever you may be, Egyptian tourism offices are probably not too hard to find. More than 30 offices are spread throughout cities like Alexandria, Port Said, Fayyum, Luxor, Aswan, and the North and South Sinai, with the main office in Cairo (Misr Travel Tower, 'Abbasiyya Sq.; ☎ (02) 285 45 09 or 284 19 70; fax 285 43 63). Tourism services provided within Egypt are abundantly found in all major cities across the world. English is spoken and maps are available.

CURRENCY AND EXCHANGE. The **Egyptian Pound** (E£), pronounced gin-EEH in Arabic, is divided into 100 **piasters** (pt), also called *irsh* (plural u-ROOSH). Coins come in denominations of 5pt (٥), 10pt (١٠), and 20pt (٢٠) (the last two look similar, so check the Arabic numbering). **Save exchange receipts** in case authorities ask for them when you are leaving the country. You are not allowed to carry more than E£1000 into or out of Egypt. Outside of Cairo, most credit cards are useless, although ATMs can be found (most accept Cirrus and PLUS cards). Traveler's checks are not widely accepted in Egypt, except at ritzy hotels or AmEx offices.

PRICES. A brief lesson in Egyptian Arabic: After *min fadlak* (please) and *shukran* (thank you), the most important word to know is **khawaga** (kha-WA-ga), because you are one. *Khawaga* means "tourist," and implies "clueless and rich." Aside from those in hotels and restaurants, most prices are not posted, which means that *khawagas* may be charged more than Egyptians. Being a *khawaga* has a positive side, as Egypt's reliance on its tourist industry means more lax rules for *khawagas* than for natives. Avoid souvenir shops and kiosks near tourist attractions at all costs. When shopping, the key word is **bargain.**

Another word to remember is **bakhsheesh,** the art of tipping: baggage handlers, guards, and bathroom and parking attendants expect to receive a tip of 50pt-E£1. For a detailed breakdown of the different types of *bakhsheesh* and the attitudes toward it in the Middle East, see **Tipping and Bargaining** in **Essentials** (p. 14).

Prices depend upon competition: in towns with heavier tourist traffic, you may spend as little as E£8 per night for clean, comfortable surroundings, while lower-quality accommodations in a town with few hotels and even fewer visitors can cost anywhere from E£10-25. Prices also vary between high and low season. The high season in Alexandria is June to August, in the Nile Valley October to April. There is a hotel tax which varies by location, averaging around 21%. Unless otherwise noted, prices include tax but exclude breakfast. Food costs should not exceed US$10 daily.

BUSINESS HOURS. On **Friday,** the Muslim day of communal prayer, most government offices, banks, and post offices are closed. Bank hours are ordinarily Sunday to Thursday 8:30am to 2pm (although some banks in big cities are open daily), with money exchange available daily 8:30am to noon and 4 to 8pm. Foreign banks keep longer hours, usually Sunday to Thursday 8am to 3pm. Other establishments, such as restaurants, remain open seven days a week. Store hours are ordinarily Saturday to Thursday 9am to 9pm, with many also open Friday. Government offices are open 9am to 2pm, though workers often leave before official closing times. Archaeological sites and other points of interest are typically open 8am to 5pm (4pm in winter), though in summer sites are open 6am to early afternoon.

During the month-long holiday of Ramadan (running from approximately November 17 to December 15 in 2001), some restaurants close entirely. Others open only after sundown, when the streets empty and everyone sits down to *iftar*, the breaking of the daily fast. Most shops close at about 3:30pm during Ramadan and re-open from 8 to 11pm. Egyptians sit down for the second meal of Ramadan (*suhur*, pronounced su-HOOR) in the middle of the night, about 2 to 3am.

HEALTH AND SAFETY

EMERGENCY	Police: ☎ 122. Ambulance: ☎ 122. Fire: ☎ 122.

MEDICAL EMERGENCIES. Luxury hotels may have resident doctors, and other hotels can usually get someone dependable in an emergency. You can also ask

I WANNA HOLD YOUR HAND Egyptian men may seem particularly affectionate to many travelers: they kiss each other on the cheeks, hold hands when strolling through bazaars, and even sit on each other's laps. Soldiers walk with a man on one arm and an AK-47 on the other. These amorous displays are merely manifestations of friendship and brotherhood in Egypt, as is evidenced by the very reserved manner in which Egyptian men treat their women. Women are considered very clean and chaste, and marriage is preceded by a strict courtship of two to three years.

your embassy for a list of recommended physicians and pharmacists. Even big-city **pharmacies** do not carry Western brand-name drugs, but most Egyptian brands are equally effective and cheaper. Pharmacists in Egypt are authorized to write prescriptions (and are more lax about refills than most Western countries) and also able to give injections. There should be at least one pharmacy in each town, although finding a 24-hour store may prove difficult in small towns.

HEALTH. Called Montezuma's Revenge in Mexico and Pharaoh's Revenge in Egypt, an upset stomach can spoil any holiday. A change in water and diet can result in diarrhea and nausea. Stay away from raw fruit and vegetables, and drink plenty of liquids, especially bottled water, which is inexpensive and readily availabe. This will help you avoid amebic dysentery, ingested with unclean food or drink. Though malaria is not common to Egypt, rabies is endemic. Stay away from stray dogs around monuments. Rabies can be contracted not only from a bite, but also from saliva of the sick animal contacting an open wound. It is fatal if not treated in time. Medical treatment or help is available wherever you see a **red crescent,** the symbol of medical services in Egypt equivalent to the red cross seen in other countries. It designates hospitals, ambulances, and other medical services.

WOMEN TRAVELERS. Foreign women traveling alone will be harassed by Egyptian men—and so will foreign men. Egypt is not a place to visit if you want to be left alone, but **harassment** has more to do with socioeconomic inequality and cultural misunderstanding than gender-based hostility. Harassment can take many forms, from overzealous salesmanship to touchy-feely *service* drivers, and from mildly sinister "hellos" to frightening and potentially harmful physical contact. The media has not helped the situation: movies and television tend to depict Western women as free and easy, and the racy nature of much Egyptian cinema has drastically altered expectations about how men and women should interact. Ignorance is bliss; the best way to deal with harassers is simply to ignore them. If they prove to be persistent, raise your voice and threaten to call the police. For more tips, see **Women Travelers,** p. 38.

MINORITY TRAVELERS. No matter what color you are, if you're clearly not Egyptian, be ready to stand out. Egyptian citizenry are known to stare and comment on those who look different than they do. Just remain calm.

BGLT TRAVELERS. As a country populated mainly by traditional Muslims, Egypt does not condone homosexual behavior. Be careful how you act in public—save displays of affection for somewhere safe.

ACCOMMODATIONS & CAMPING

Traveling in the Middle East with a partner is wise, especially for women. Women will find it useful to travel with a fellow male, under the pretense that the two are married. Hostels and hotels usually refuse to offer rooms to couples who are not married. Wearing a wedding band can help prevent unwanted headaches. Prices for a bed can be as low as US$1 or as high as a couple hundred dollars, depending on whether the bed is in a hostel or hotel.

HOSTELS. Whether it is the perplexity of the pyramids, the chaos of Cairo, or the soothing Nile sunset, a hostel will help you get there. Hostels in Egypt are open at all hours of the night. This luxury only costs around US$1.50-7.40 per night, including breakfast. All hostels except for those in Aswan, Asyut, Damanhur, Fayyum, Sohag, and Tanta have self-catering facilities.

HOTELS. Like hostels, some Egyptian hotels charge as little as US$2, that is, if sleeping on the roof of an otherwise shoddy establishment is enticing. With a little searching, a comfortable, safe bed could be yours for US$10. Egypt also proudly offers **five-star** hotels. If the sun gets too hot or the post offices too crowded, stop by these air-conditioned palaces, relax and send some letters home, or even treat yourself to some nice clothes from their self-contained malls. A service charge of 12% applies to hotels as well as a 5-7% sales tax. A further 1-4% tax is sometimes added to upper-end accommodations, so it is possible to find that a 23% tax has been added to the price of mid-range or top-end hotel rooms.

CAMPING. Egypt's oases are unspoiled refuges from the modern world. Endless sand and sky make the Sahara oases perfect for exploration. Wade through date-laden palms and golden-white sand during the day, then savor Bedouin-style meals around a campfire and enjoy the tranquility of bedding down a desert tent at night. Experience **Bahariyya Oasis,** surrounded by black hills of ferruginous quartzite and dolorite, the unique landscape of the erosion in the **White Desert, Bawiti Village's** natural spring hewn from rock, and the oases of Farafra, Dakhla, and al-Kharga.

KEEPING IN TOUCH

MAIL. Airmail letters and postcards from Egypt to any destination outside the Middle East cost E£1.25. Most hotels sell stamps, though a 10pt surcharge may be added. The most dependable place to receive mail is at American Express offices, but this privilege is reserved for cardholders; **Poste Restante** is also available in major cities. Two or three weeks delivery time is normal. For faster service that won't break the bank, seek out **Express Mail Service (EMS),** available almost everywhere. It takes 3 to 20 days to the US and 3 to 15 days to Europe. To send packages by **Federal Express,** contact the office at 1079 Corniche al-Nil, Garden City, Cairo (☎ (02) 357 13 00 or 355 10 63; fax 357 13 18).

TELEPHONES. Long-distance and **international calls** can be made from most government telephone offices (*maktab al-telephonat; centrale* in Alexandria), open 24 hours and packed at night. Most cities accept Sphinx-emblazoned **phone cards** (E£10, 20, 30, or 40), sold at convenience stores for use at green and yellow **Menatel** phones. Rates are lower at night. Major hotels have good connections but can be expensive. For AT&T **collect calls,** USADirect, or World Connect, call ☎ (02) 510 02 00 (AT&T) from anywhere in Egypt, or simply 510 02 00 from Cairo. To reach a Sprint operator outside Cairo, call ☎ 356 477 or 354 622; outside other cities in Egypt, call ☎ (02) 356 47 77 or 354 46 22. Call ☎ (02) 355 57 70 for MCI WorldPhone or collect calls and drop the (02) if calling from Cairo. Call ☎ (02) 365 36 43 for CanadaDirect calls using a Bell Canada calling card; Kiwis should call ☎ (02) 365 37 64 to reach their island home direct, while Brits should call ☎ (02) 365 36 44 to reach theirs. Again, drop the (02) dialing prefix from all access codes if calling from Cairo. You can also call from gray, coin-operated public pay phones for long-distance or **local calls** (10pt per 3min. from public phone, 50pt per 3min. from private phones in establishments).

INTERNET ACCESS. In Cairo, Alexandria, and decent-sized towns, Internet access is roughly E£7-10 per hour. Getting online elsewhere in Egypt is slow and expensive: Dahab is upward of E£15 per hour and Aswan gouges at 50pt per minute.

CUSTOMS AND ETIQUETTE

Keep your soles out of sight. Bottoms of feet resting anywhere but on the ground is disrespectful. Before entering mosques, remove shoes and have socks ready.

Women must cover their heads and arms, and stand behind men. Outside of mosques, women usually congregate with other females, lining up with other women to buy tickets and sitting at the front of buses and trains. For men, speaking to unknown Egyptian women is a breach of etiquette and should be avoided.

It is customary for Egyptians to refuse the first invitation of an offering; tourists should do the same. If ever invited to a home but unable to attend, the householder will often press for a promise from you to visit in the future, usually for a meal. If you make such a promise, keep it. Failing to arrive will humiliate your host. It is also offensive to offer *bakhsheesh* to professionals, businessmen, or others who would consider themselves your equals.

In terms of what to avoid, Egypt prohibits alcohol, drugs, and pork. If you need to drink in the presence of others, ask first. Explicit sexual material, like magazines, photographs, tapes, or records is illegal and subject to confiscation.

HOLIDAYS AND FESTIVALS

Government offices and banks close for Islamic holidays, but most tourist facilities remain open. The month of Ramadan can be a wonderful (if occasionally inconvenient) time to visit, especially in festive Cairo and Alexandria. Along with the regular Islamic festivals, the two Sufi rituals of **Zikr** and **Zar** are not to be missed (both rituals are practiced on Fridays in populous areas). In the former, a group of dancers whirl themselves into a frenzy; in the latter, women dance in a group, primarily as an exorcism rite. The Coptic celebrations of Easter and Christmas are tranquil affairs marked by special church services. The festival known as **Sham al-Nissim** falls on the first Monday after Coptic Easter, but has developed into a secular celebration. Sham al-Nissim was originally an outdoor spring festival in which ancient Egyptians and enslaved Jews feasted on pungent *fisikh* (dried and salted fish) as equals; the highlight of the festival was the ritual casting of a young woman into the Nile. *Fisikh* is still eaten at modern celebrations, but the young women stay dry; even the ritual of throwing a doll into the Nile has all but disappeared from the present-day festivities. See the **Appendix** (p. 699) for a comprehensive list of religious and national holidays' dates.

CAIRO القاهرة ☎ 02

I arrived at length at Cairo, mother of cities and seat of Pharaoh the tyrant, boundless in multitude of buildings, peerless in beauty and splendor, the meeting-place of comer and goer, the halting-place of feeble and mighty, whose throngs surge as waves of the sea.
    —Ibn Battuta

Cairo has been the greatest city in the Middle East and Africa for nearly all of the past millennium. In 2600 BCE, the pharaohs of the Old Kingdom chose the sandy plateau just above the Nile Delta for their ancient capital of Memphis, one of the world's earliest urban settlements and Egypt's capital until the beginning of the first century CE (when St. Mark introduced Christianity to Egypt in the face of intense Roman opposition). For the next 600 years, the Coptic Church that grew out of St. Mark's teaching marked the wrists of its faithful with tattoos and left even more enduring marks in the churches of Old Cairo. The early decades of the 7th century CE found Cairo in the throes of power struggles between the Persian and Byzantine empires. Memphis and Babylon (the glitzy settlement across the Nile) changed hands many times, and warfare near Babylon drove urban dwellers to the villages until the city lay bereft and deserted by the time of the Arab conquest in 641 CE. The leader of the Arab invaders, 'Amr ibn al-'As, set up camp at

Fustat, the seed of modern Cairo. The Arabs were responsible for giving the city its name: Fatimid leader Gawhar al-Sikelli dubbed it *al-Qahira*, "The Conqueror."

The city swelled so much in size and grandeur under the Fatimids and their descendants that it soon became known as *Misr*, the Arabic name for all of Egypt. During Cairo's Golden Age, it became one of the most advanced cultural centers west of China. Although various conquerors had their way with Cairo throughout the Middle Ages, it remained far more populous than any city in Europe. The Ottomans, however, reduced Cairo to the status of a provincial center in 1516. After a brief affair with Napoleon in the late 1700s, Cairo made a grand entrance upon the 19th-century scene thanks to a face-lift by the Albanian Muhammad 'Ali and his European-educated descendants, the *khedives*, whose penchant for the extravagant resulted in streets dotted with glittering Turkish-style mosques and palaces.

The political upheaval of the Middle East has affected Cairo in the 20th century as well. Modern political and economic centralization is driving thousands of rural Egyptians into the arms of the "Mother of the World" (*Umm al-Dunya*, as the medieval Arabs called Cairo), and she is struggling to cope with the needs of her growing brood. Expansion has led to over-crowded neighborhoods, clogged thoroughfares, and urban pollution. Places where pharaohs and kings once lounged now teem with barking street merchants and silver-tongued con artists. Cairo's tumultuous present is only the current incarnation of its tumultuous past. Amid tangled webs of unlabeled streets and the dizzying calls of hawkers, Cairenes frequent their favorite *sheesha* halls, navigate labyrinthine bazaars, and descend on hundreds of places of worship. Patience and curiosity will allow you to overcome the city's cluttered eccentricities, so that you too might be conquered by the power of Egypt's greatest city.

HIGHLIGHTS OF CAIRO AND ENVIRONS

Don't miss the glorious complex of **Sultan Hassan** (p. 107), the **Mausoleum and Mosque of Qaytbay** (p. 114), and the immense **Citadel** (p. 108).

The **Egyptian Museum** (p. 122) showcases an unsurpassed collection of ancient treasures, including the famous loot from **Tutankhamun's tomb.**

A riddle from the **Sphinx** (p. 104): how can you visit Egypt without seeing the **Pyramids at Giza** (p. 130)? See where the whole pyramid craze got started by checking out Imhotep's **Step Pyramid** of Zoser-Netcherikhe at Saqqara (p. 132).

☒ GETTING THERE AND AWAY

FLIGHTS. Flights leave from **Cairo International Airport** (☎291 42 55 or 291 42 66), in Heliopolis. **EgyptAir,** with offices at 6 'Adly St. (☎391 12 56) and in the Nile Hilton (☎576 52 00 or 577 24 10; reservations and info ☎392 74 44 or 392 72 05). Outbound flights to: **Aswan** (E£1150), **Hurghada** (E£900), **Luxor** (E£830), **Sharm al-Sheikh** (E£1000), the **Sinai** (E£1000), **Suez** (E£610), and **Wadi Gadid** (E£900). **Air Sinai,** in the Nile Hilton (☎577 29 49; open daily 9am-5pm), has outbound flights to **Tel Aviv** (E£630; round-trip for trips of 3-30 days E£895, longer trips E£1165). It is very difficult (and expensive) to get flights out of Cairo to international destinations on short notice; reserve in advance. For information on traveling to and from Cairo International Airport, see **Entry Requirements,** p. 74.

TRAINS. Ramses Station is the main train station. (Metro: Mubarak. ☎575 35 55. Ticket windows open daily 8am-10pm.) The **tourist office,** past the entrance on the left, can write out your destination and other details in Arabic to avoid confusion. (Open daily 8am-8pm.) Which line you stand in at the ticket window depends upon whether you are reserving a seat in advance or trying to buy a ticket for the same day (often impossible). Women (and men traveling with women) should take advantage of the special **women's line** that may form at crowded times, which is much shorter and faster than the corresponding men's line. In addition, women are permitted (and expected) to push to the front of any line, head held high. Students receive a **30% discount** on almost all fares with an **ISIC card.** The trains enter their berths at least half an hour before departure time. None of the train numbers or destinations are in English, but other travelers and the tourist police may lend a hand. In summer, prices fluctuate and there are no student discounts.

There are two types of trains to **Alexandria,** both air-conditioned—a **French line** (3hr.; every 1½-2hr 10 per day; first-class E£20, 2nd-class E£12) and a faster **Spanish line** (2hr.; 8, 9am, noon, 2, 3, 6, 7pm; first-class E£22, 2nd-class E£17). Outbound trains also to: **Aswan** (13-16hr.; 7:30 and 10am; first-class E£63, 2nd-class E£39); **Luxor** (9-12hr.; 7:30 and 10am; first-class E£53, 2nd-class E£33); and **Port Said** (4½hr.; 6:35, 8:45, 11:30am, 2:30, 6:30pm; E£18). Trains to Luxor and Aswan stop in Minya, Sohag, Asyut, and Qena.

> Travel agents in the downtown area have been known to add airport taxes (there is no departure tax from Cairo) and other fees to tickets. You should demand receipts for every pound you hand over and have them give you written estimates, including all taxes, for every flight you purchase.

The area just outside the train station is chaotic, despite (or maybe because of) the numerous traffic police and streetlights. Avoid crossing the treacherous roads by using the convenient tunnels of the Mubarak Metro station. Before heading underground, however, be sure to catch a glimpse of the massive **Statue of Ramses II,** standing calm amidst the storm.

BUSES. The bus system in Egypt is a four-wheeled version of the government bureaucracy—things are always changing, no one has any real idea of what's going on, yet somehow it all works out. Taking a bus can be quite a fuss in Cairo (as in much of the Middle East), as schedules shift daily, prices fluctuate, and drop-off points change without warning. Check a day or two before you need to take a bus to make sure it's going where you want for a price you're willing to pay. The buses themselves are quite nice—frequently air-conditioned, often serving food, and always equipped with large, comfortable seats. Make reservations in person a day or two in advance for popular destinations.

Cairo's intercity bus terminal has shifted locations frequently in the past years (even recent schedules can be out of date). Unless otherwise noted, buses leave from **Turgoman Station (Mahattat Turgoman)** near Ramses Sq. Outbound buses to:

Alexandria and the Mediterranean Coast: Superjet (☎290 90 13) goes to **Alexandria** (3hr., every 30min. 5:30am-11pm, E£55) and **Marsa Matrouh** (5hr., 8am, E£37). Buses also run to **Siwa** from both destinations.

The Canal Zone: The **East Delta Bus Co.** (☎576 22 93) travels to: **Isma'ilia** (2hr., every 30min. 6:30am-7pm, E£6); **Port Said** (2hr., every hr. 6:30am-7pm, E£15); and **Suez** (2hr., every 30min. 6:30am-7pm, E£6).

Hurghada: Superjet (8:30am and 2:30pm, E£47; 11pm, E£52) and the **Upper Egypt Bus Co.** (9am, 12:30, 3, 9:40, 11:30pm, midnight; E£45.50).

The Levant: The **East Delta Bus Co.** sends buses to **Jordan** and **Syria** (8pm, E£114) and **Turkey** (8pm, E£310.50). **Superjet** leaves from al-Maza Sq. to **Jordan** (M, Tu, Th, Sa 6am; E£231) and **Syria** (Sa 10pm, E£310.50).

The Sinai: The **East Delta Bus Co.** (☎576 22 93) runs buses to: **Dahab** (8hr.; 7:30am, 1, 4:30, 11:30pm; E£55); **Nuweiba** (8hr., 7:30am and 10pm, E£50-55); and **Taba** (9hr.; 7:30am, E£50; 10pm, E£70). **Superjet** (☎290 90 13) runs buses to **Sharm al-Sheikh** (7hr., 11pm, E£55).

Tel Aviv and **Jerusalem:** Buses leave daily from the Cairo Sheraton. Make reservations a day in advance at the **Sheraton** or at **Misr Travel,** on the first block of Tala'at Harb St.

Upper Egypt: The **Upper Egypt Bus Co.** sends buses to: **Abu Ramad** (11pm, E£65); **Aswan** (13hr., 5:30am, E£55); **Farafra** (7½hr., 10am and noon, E£40); **Kharga** (12hr., 8am, E£40); **Luxor** (9hr., 9pm, E£50); and **Quseir** (10pm, E£55).

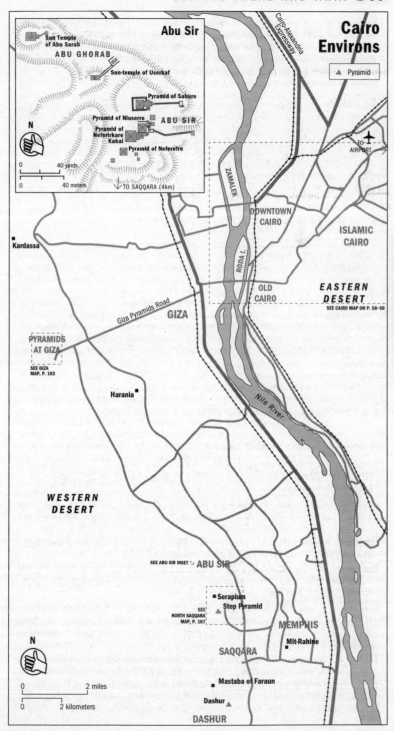

Cairo Environs

▲ Pyramid

Cairo-Alexandria Expressway

TO AIRPORT

ZAMALEK

DOWNTOWN CAIRO

ISLAMIC CAIRO

RODA

OLD CAIRO

EASTERN DESERT

SEE CAIRO MAP ON P. 58–59

EGYPT

■ Kardassa

Giza Pyramids Road

GIZA

PYRAMIDS AT GIZA

SEE GIZA MAP, P. 103

Harania ■

Nile River

WESTERN DESERT

SEE ABU SIR INSET ■ ABU SIR

■ Serapium
Step Pyramid ▲

SEE NORTH SAQQARA MAP, P. 107

MEMPHIS

■ Mit-Rahine

N

SAQQARA

0   2 miles

0   2 kilometers

■ Mastaba of Faraun

Dashur ▲

DASHUR

Abu Sir

Sun Temple of Abu Sarab

ABU GHORAB

Sun-temple of Userkaf

Pyramid of Sahure

Pyramid of Niuserre

ABU SIR

Pyramid of Neferirkare Kakai

Pyramid of Neferefre

N

0   40 yards

0   40 meters

TO SAQQARA (4km)

SERVICE. *Service* leaving from Ramses Station travel outbound to: **Alexandria** (E£10-12), **al-Arish** (E£15), **Isma'ilia** (E£6), **Port Said** (E£9), and **Suez** (E£5-7). *Service* from Giza Sq. travel outbound to: **Alexandria** (E£11) from in front of the Nile Hilton; **Fayyum** (E£5) from the train station; **Wadi Natrun** (about E£10) from Kolali Sq.; and **Mansoura** (E£9), **Tanta** (E£6), **Zagazig** (E£5), and the rest of the Delta from Ahmed Hilmi Sq. Station.

CAR RENTAL. If you're a daredevil or a maniac (or both), driving in Cairo is for you. **Avis** (☎ 354 86 98 or 354 74 00) has branches throughout the city. The branch at Cairo International Airport is open 24 hours (☎ 265 24 29). Join the millions of middle-class Egyptians driving Suzuki Swifts for E£166 per day, including insurance, taxes, and the first 100km. Most branches are open daily 8am-3:30pm. **Hertz** (☎ 347 41 72 or 347 22 38) has branches at Cairo International Airport (☎ 265 24 30), Ramses Hilton (☎ 574 44 00), Semiramis Intercontinental Hotel (☎ 794 32 39), and Forte Grand Hotel (☎ 383 03 83). They have Toyota Corollas for E£188 per day with unlimited mileage and air-conditioning. All branches open daily 9am-5pm.

▐▀ GETTING AROUND

METRO. The Cairo Metro is the fastest and cleanest ticket in town—worlds away from the rest of Cairo's bumpy and grumpy public transport. It was completed in 1987 as a joint project with the French and the Japanese, and is the only subway system in all of Africa. Trains run along the main line, a 40km route linking the southern industrial district of Helwan to al-Marj in Heliopolis, with a number of stops downtown (look for the giant red "M" signs). An additional line connecting Shubra was recently added; other lines to Giza, Imbaba, and al-Azhar are still under construction. Trains run about every six minutes (5:30am-1am; in winter 5:30am-midnight; 50pt-E£1). Save the ticket for exiting. The stations downtown are **Mubarak** (Ramses Sq. and Railway Station), **Orabi** (Orabi St. and Ramses St.), **Nasser** (26 July St. and Ramses St.), **Sadat** (Tahrir Sq.), **Sa'ad Zaghloul** (Mansour St. and Isma'il Abaza St.), **Sayyida Zeinab** (Mansour St. and 'Ali Ibrahim St.), **al-Malik al-Saleh** (Salah Salem Rd.), and **Mari Girgis** (Old Cairo). Rush hour is before 9am and from 2-5pm. Although women can ride in any compartment, the first one is exclusively for women and the second is reserved for women until 4pm.

MICROBUSES. Microbuses follow set routes to certain destinations, but tend to be flexible as long as all passengers are going to the same area. Stops are sometimes marked by a wooden shelter. If you don't have a basic command of Arabic, stick to the numbered, fixed routes. Microbuses go from **'Ataba Sq.** to Ramses Sq., Tahrir Sq., Northern Cemetery, Zamalek, Islamic Cairo, and Heliopolis. From **Tahrir Sq.**, microbuses leave for Heliopolis, Giza Sq., Doqqi, Mohandiseen, the Pyramids, and the airport terminals. Fares (25pt-E£1.50) depend on the length of the route.

MINIBUSES. Minibuses operate along many of the same routes as city buses. Although more expensive (50pt-E£1.50), minibuses are far more comfortable, and the orange-and-white ones operate on natural gas instead of unleaded. Minibus numbers appear in Arabic only. Beware: numbers with a strike through them travel different routes from their ordinary counterparts (e.g. 39 goes to Abd al-Munem Riad, ~~39~~ goes to AUC).

BUSES. Few foreigners use the bus system, and with good reason: although very cheap (25-50pt), the buses are hot, cramped, and full of pickpockets. Buses never come to a full stop, so passengers must jump out the back to exit. Numbers and destinations are always in Arabic. Buses run 5:30am-12:30am (during Ramadan 6:30am-6:30pm and 7:30pm-2am), except for buses **#400** (٤٠٠) and **#400** (٤٠٠), which have 24-hour service to both **airport terminals** from Tahrir Sq. and Ramses Sq., respectively. Cairo's local bus depot is **Abd al-Munem Riad Station,** which is north of the Egyptian Museum just below the towering, triangular Ramses Hilton. Several buses depart from the front of the old **Arab League Building,** to the west of the Mugamm'a along Tahrir St., adjacent to the bridge. Other bus stations are at **'Ataba Sq.** (to the Citadel, the Manial Palace, Giza, and Tahrir Sq.), and at **Giza Sq.** (to the Pyramids, airport, and Citadel).

MINIBUS ROUTES

FROM THE NILE HILTON:

#16 (١٦): al-Gala'a Bridge–Agouza

#27 (٢٧): Masr al-Gadida–Airport

#30 (٣٠): Nasser City–'Abbasiyya Sq.–Ramses Sq.–Abd al-Munem Riad 2

#32 (٣٢): Hai al-Tamin–Mugamm'a–Ramses Sq.–'Abbasiyya

#35 (٣٥): 'Abbasiyya–Abd al-Munem Riad 2–Roxy–al-Hijaz Sq.

#49 (٤٩): Falaki Sq.–Tahrir Sq.–Zamalek

#50 (٥٠): Ramses Sq.–'Ataba Sq.–Citadel

FROM TAHRIR SQUARE:

#77 (٧٧), **102** (١٠٢), **103** (١٠٣): Bulaq al-Dakrur–Khan al-Khalili–al-Darasa

#183 (١٨٣): Giza

#52 (٥٢), **56** (٥٦): Bab al-Luq–Tahrir Sq.–Ma'adi–Old Cairo

#54 (٥٤): Bab al-Luq–Rifa'i Mosque–Ibn Tulun Mosque–Citadel–S. Cemetery

#55 (٥٥): Ma'adi–Bab al-Luq

#58 (٥٨): Ramses Sq.–Manial

#77 (٧٧): Bulaq al-Dakrur–Khan al-Khalili–al-Darasa

#84 (٨٤): 'Ataba/Tahrir Sq.–Doqqi–Giza

FROM 'ATABA SQUARE:

#26 (٢٦): Roxy–Tahrir Sq.–Doqqi–Giza

#48 (٤٨): Zamalek

#93 (٩٣): Mazalat–'Ataba Sq.–Basatin

BUS ROUTES

FROM ABD AL-MUNEM RIAD STATION:

#8 (٨): Tahrir Sq.–Qasr al-'Aini–Manial–Giza–Mena House Hotel (Pyramids)

#63 (٦٣), **66** (٦٦): al-Azhar–Khan al-Khalili

#72 (٧٢): Sayyida Zeinab–Citadel–Imam al-Shafi'i Mausoleum

#82 (٨٢), **182** (١٨٢): Imam al-Shafi'i Mausoleum–S. Cemetery–Citadel

#99 (٩٩): Agouza–Sudan St.–Lebanon Sq. (Midan Lubnan)

#128 (١٢٨): 'Abbasiyya Sq.–'Ain Shams

#173 (١٧٣), **194** (١٩٤), **609** (٦٠٩): Tahrir Sq.–Citadel

#174 (١٧٤): Ramses–Sayyida Zeinab–Ibn Tulun–Sultan Hassan–Citadel

#400 (٤٠٠): Old Cairo Airport via Heliopolis (Roxy Sq.)

#403 (٤٠٣): Citadel–Sultan Hassan

#666 (٦٦٦): al-Gaili Museum

#900 (٩٠٠): Tahrir Sq.–Qasr al-'Aini–Manial (Youth Hostel)–Cairo University–Giza–Pyramids–Holiday Inn Hotel

#923 (٩٢٣): Basatin–Giza Sq.

#949 (٩٤٩): New Cairo Airport

FROM THE ARAB LEAGUE BUILDING:

#13 (١٣): Zamalek–Bab al-Luq

#19 (١٩), **203** (٢٠٣): Doqqi

#102 (١٠٢): Mazalat–Doqqi

#166 (١٦٦): 'Ataba Sq.–Doqqi

#815-173 (٨١٥-١٧٣): Medinat al-Talaba

FROM 'ATABA SQUARE:

#214 (٢١٤): Qanatir

#404 (٤٠٤): Citadel–Tahrir Sq.–Medinat al-Talaba

#801 (٨٠١), **951** (٩٥١): Citadel–Abd al-Munem Riad

#904 (٩٠٤): Mugamm'a–Pyramids

FROM GIZA SQUARE:

#3 (٣): Pyramids

#30 (٣٠): Ramses Station

#949 (٩٤٩): Airport (both terminals)

FROM RAMSES STATION:

#30 (٣٠): Pyramids

#160 (١٦٠): Citadel–Tahrir Sq.

EGYPT

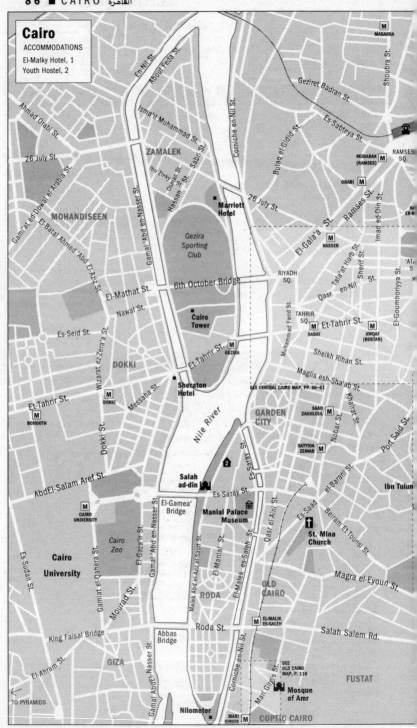

Cairo

ACCOMMODATIONS

El-Malky Hotel, 1
Youth Hostel, 2

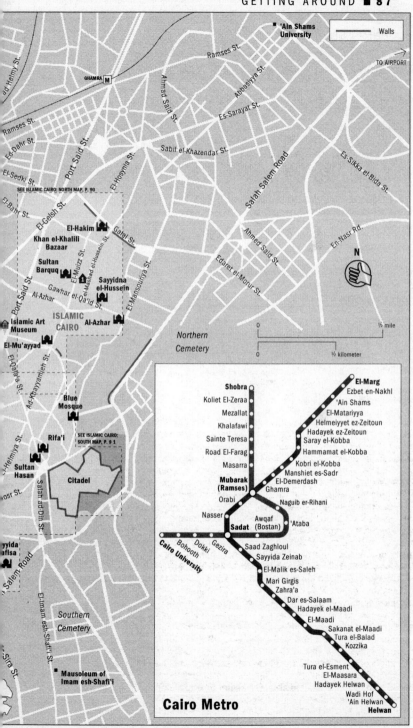

Cairo Metro

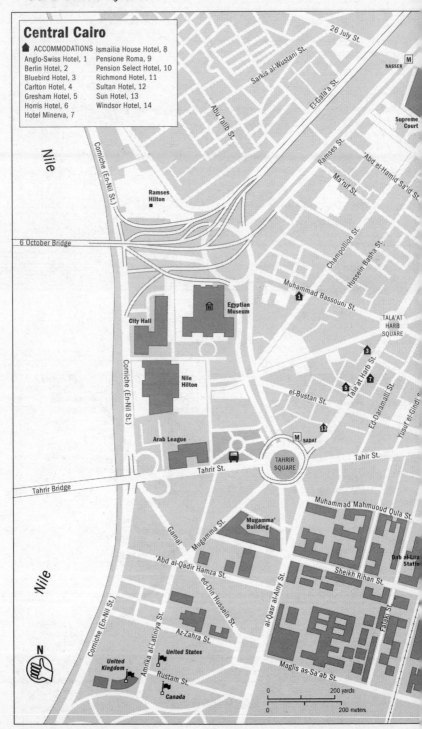

Central Cairo

ACCOMMODATIONS
Anglo-Swiss Hotel, 1
Berlin Hotel, 2
Bluebird Hotel, 3
Carlton Hotel, 4
Gresham Hotel, 5
Horris Hotel, 6
Hotel Minerva, 7
Ismailia House Hotel, 8
Pensione Roma, 9
Pension Select Hotel, 10
Richmond Hotel, 11
Sultan Hotel, 12
Sun Hotel, 13
Windsor Hotel, 14

Nile

26 July St.
Sarkis al-Wustani St.
El-Gala'a St.
NASSER M
Supreme Court
Comiche (En-Nil St.)
Abu Talib St.
Ramses St.
'Abd el-Hamid Sa'id St.
Ma'ruf St.
Ramses Hilton
6 October Bridge
Champollion St.
Hussein Basha St.
Muhammad Bassouni St.
City Hall
Egyptian Museum
TALA'AT HARB SQUARE
Tala'at Harb St.
Ed-Daramalli St.
Yusuf el-Gindi St.
Nile Hilton
el-Bustan St.
Comiche (En-Nil St.)
Arab League
M SADAT
Tahir St.
TAHRIR SQUARE
Tahir St.
Tahrir St.
Tahrir Bridge
Muhammad Mahmuoud Qula St.
Gamal
Mugamma St.
Mugamma' Building
Bab al-Lau Station
Nile
'Abd al-Qadir Hamza St.
ed-Din Hussein St.
Sheikh Rihan St.
al-Qasr al-Ainy St.
Falaki St.
Comiche (En-Nil St.)
Amrika al-Latiniya St.
Az-Zahra St.
United States
United Kingdom
Rustam St.
Canada
Maglis as-Sa'ab St.
N
0   200 yards
0   200 meters

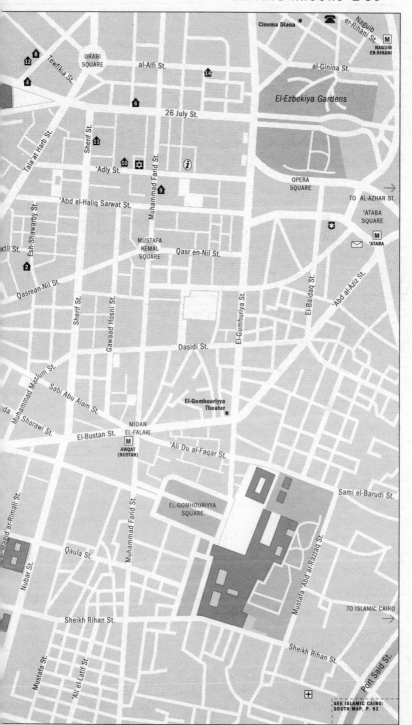

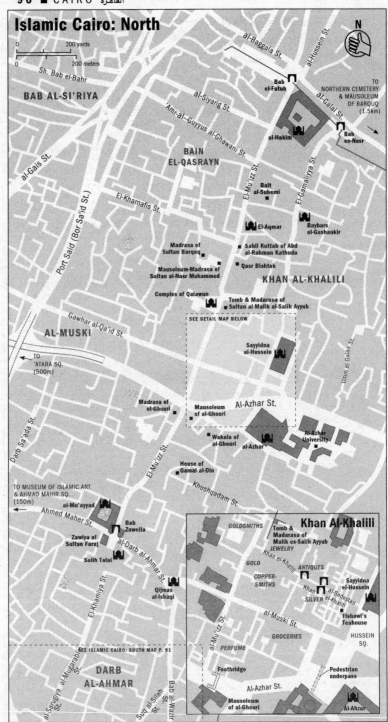

Islamic Cairo: North

0   200 yards

0   200 meters

N

TO
NORTHERN CEMETERY
& MAUSOLEUM
OF BARQUQ
(1.5km)

al-Baggala St.

al-Hussein St.

Sh. Bab el-Bahr

BAB AL-SI'RIYA

al-Siyarig St.

'Amr-al-Guyyus al-Ghawani St.

Bab
el-Futuh

al-Galal St.

Bab
en-Nasr

al-Hakim

al-Gais St.

**BAIN
EL-QASRAYN**

El-Mu'izz St.

El-Gamaliyya St.

El-Kharnafis St.

Bait
al-Suhemi

Port Said (Bor Sa'id St.)

El-Aqmar

Baybars
al-Gashankir

Madrasa of
Sultan Barquq

Sabil Kuttab of Abd
al-Rahman Kathuda

Mausoleum-Madrasa of
Sultan al-Nasr Muhammed

Qasr Bishtak

KHAN AL-KHALILI

Complex of Qalawun

Tomb & Madrasa of
Sultan al-Malik al-Salih Ayyub

Gawhar al-Qa'id St.

SEE DETAIL MAP BELOW

AL-MUSKI

Sayyidna
al-Hussein

TO
'ATABA SQ.
(500m)

Umm el-Gulan St.

Madrasa of
el-Ghouri

Mausoleum
of al-Ghouri

Al-Azhar St.

El-Mu'izz St.

Wakala of
al-Ghouri

al-Azhar

Al-Azhar
University

Darb sa'ada St.

House of
Gamal al-Din

Khushqadam St.

TO MUSEUM OF ISLAMIC ART
& AHMAD MAHIR SQ.
(150m)

al-Mu'ayyad

Ahmed Maher St.

Bab
Zuweila

Zawiya of
Sultan Faraj

al-Darb al-Ahmar St.

Salih Talai

El-Khamiya St.

Qijmas
al-Ishaqi

SEE ISLAMIC CAIRO: SOUTH MAP P. 91

al-Saruga-al-Mugarabin St.

Suq al-Silah St.

Bab al-Wazir

**DARB
AL-AHMAR**

Khan Al-Khalili

GOLDSMITHS

Tomb &
Madarasa of
Malik es-Salih Ayyub

Khan el-Khalili

JEWELRY

ANTIQUES

GOLD

COPPER-
SMITHS

Khan al-Bedestan

Sayyidna
el-Hussein

al-Muizz St.

SILVER al-Khalili

Fishawl's
Teahouse

al-Muski St.

HUSSEIN
SQ.

GROCERIES

PERFUME

Footbridge

Pedestrian
underpass

Al-Azhar St.

Mausoleum
of al-Ghouri

Al-Azhar

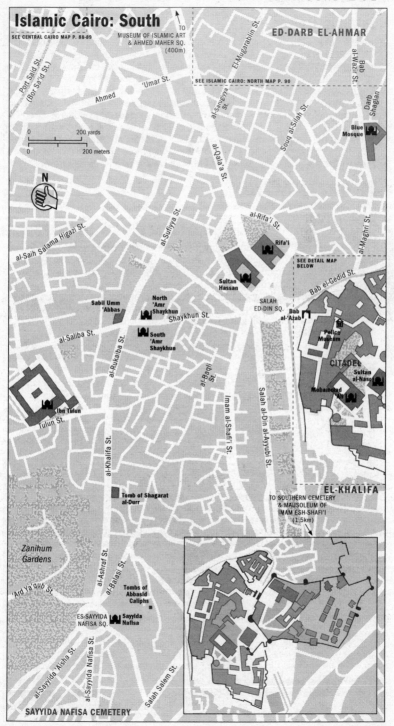

Islamic Cairo: South

SEE CENTRAL CAIRO MAP P. 88-89

TO
MUSEUM OF ISLAMIC ART
& AHMED MAHER SQ.
(400m)

ED-DARB EL-AHMAR

Port Said St.
(Bor Sa'id St.)

'Umar St.

Ahmed

El-Mugarabilin St.

SEE ISLAMIC CAIRO: NORTH MAP P. 90

al-Sangiya St.

al-Qala'a St.

Souq al-Silah St.

Bab al-Wazir St.

Darb Shaglan

Blue Mosque

al-Maghn St.

0   200 yards
0   200 meters

N

al-Saih Salama Higazi St.

al-Sufiyya St.

al-Rifa'i St.

Rifa'i

SEE DETAIL MAP BELOW

Bab el-Gedid St.

Sultan Hassan

SALAH ED-DIN SQ.

Bab al-Azab

Police Museum

Sabil Umm 'Abbas

North 'Amr Shaykhun

Shaykhun St.

CITADEL

al-Saliba St.

South 'Amr Shaykhun

al-Rukaiba St.

al-Barli St.

Sultan al-Nasri

Muhammad Ali

Ibn Tulun

Tulun St.

al-Khalifa St.

Imam al-Shafi'i St.

Salah al-Din al-Ayyubi St.

EL-KHALIFA

Tomb of Shagarat al-Durr

TO SOUTHERN CEMETERY
& MAUSOLEUM OF
IMAM ESH-SHAFI'I
(1.5km)

Zanihum Gardens

al-Ashraf St.

al-Balasi St.

'Ard Ya'qub St.

Tombs of Abbasid Caliphs

ES-SAYYIDA NAFISA SQ.

Sayyida Nafisa

al-Sayyida Nafisa St.

al-Sayyida 'Aisha St.

Salah Salem St.

SAYYIDA NAFISA CEMETERY

TAXIS. Avoid the expensive tourist-hunting taxis in front of major hotels. Stick to the **black-and-white taxis** that collect passengers along the way. To hail a taxi, pick a thoroughfare headed in the general direction you wish to travel, stand on the side of the street, stretch out your arm, and scream out your destination as it goes by. If the driver is interested, he'll stop. Meters have been installed in all taxis, but drivers rarely use them due to outdated gas costs and the prohibitive price of getting them fixed. Feel free to haggle about the price, or walk away if you can't agree on a fair price. Do not expect drivers to speak English; use landmarks and either say or show a written copy of your destination in Arabic. For more information, see **Taxis,** p. 76. Rides in the downtown area (Ramses Sq., Tahrir Sq., Zamalek, and Islamic Cairo) should cost about E£3-5. Trips to the pyramids are about E£15; those to Ma'adi and Heliopolis run around E£8-10. A taxi to or from the airport should cost no more than E£20-25. Wanna be a **playah?** Hire a Mercedes for E£30 per hour from Limousine Misr (☎285 06 25).

✺ ORIENTATION

DOWNTOWN

At the center of it all is **Tahrir Sq.** (Midan Tahrir), one of the many central districts planned by British and French colonialists. Buses depart for every metropolitan destination. Facing the square to the north is the sandstone **Egyptian Museum;** adjacent to it on the west side of the square is the **Nile Hilton.** Entrances to the Sadat Metro station ring the square. At the southern end of the square is the massive, concave **Mugamm'a Building,** headquarters of the Egyptian bureaucracy. The placid gardens and excellent bookstore of the **American University in Cairo (AUC)** are directly to the east of the Mugamm'a Building across Qasr al-'Aini St. A few blocks east on Tahrir St. is the Bab al-Luq public bus depot.

> The area in the immediate vicinity of Tahrir Sq. has been the scene of some **pickpocketing** by youngsters who may barely reach waist-level. Be wary of large, playful groups of local kids in and around the Square, as it is easy to get distracted. Much of the rest of Cairo is theft-free at any time of day.

The three most important streets coming out of Tahrir Sq. are Qasr al-'Aini St., Qasr al-Nil St., and Tala'at Harb St. **Qasr al-'Aini St.** runs south from Tahrir Sq. and ends at **Old Cairo** (also known as Coptic Cairo), the historic and spiritual center of the Copts (Egyptian Eastern Orthodox Christians). The American University in Cairo (AUC), Parliament, and some of the city's most beautifully preserved 19th-century colonial mansions line Qasr al-'Aini St. Just south of Tahrir Sq., sandwiched between Qasr al-'Aini St. and the Nile, foreign embassies and banks cluster along the streets of the serene **Garden City** residential area. Farther south, the exclusive district of **Ma'adi** serves as home for many of Cairo's expatriates. **Qasr al-Nil St.** begins in front of the Nile Hilton, cuts through Tala'at Harb Sq., and continues on to **Mustafa Kamal Sq.** In between lie many of Cairo's Western-style stores, banks, travel agents, and the AmEx office. **Tala'at Harb St.** runs from the northeast side of Tahrir Sq. through **Tala'at Harb Sq.** toward Orabi Sq. and 26 July St. **Ramses Sq.** to the north (west of Orabi Sq.) and **'Ataba Sq.** (east of Orabi Sq., at the end of 26 July St.) form a rough triangle with Tala'at Harb Sq. enclosing the main business and shopping district, which is crammed with travel agents, banks, restaurants, clothing stores, and budget hotels. Due north of Tahrir Sq. lies **Abd al-Munem Riad Sq.,** the starting point of **Ramses St.** and the city's main public bus depot. Heading northeast away from the Nile, Ramses St. runs up to **Ramses Sq.,** the Cairo train station (called **Ramses Station**), and the Mubarak Metro station. South of Ramses Sq. off Ramses St. is the Mahattat Turgoman **(Turgoman Bus Station),** where buses to other parts of Egypt come and go. Farther out on Ramses St. are the **Cairo Stadium** and **Heliopolis,** a fashionable suburb where President Mubarak lives. Heading east from 'Ataba Sq., al-Azhar St. and al-Muski St. (a long shopping strip) both lead to the northern end of Islamic Cairo and the Northern Cemetery.

A TRIP DOWN MEMORY LANE Street names in Egypt are used repeatedly (the most popular is no doubt **Tahrir**, or "Liberation"). Most of these names have historical significance (for details, see **Modern History**, p. 66).

26 July Street: Commemorates the 1953 non-violent coup in which General Naguib and his Free Officers overthrew the king.

6 October Street: The date in 1973 when President Anwar Sadat staged a surprise attack on Israeli forces in the Sinai, earning him incredible popular support.

Sa'ad Zaghloul Street: Its namesake was the leader of the nationalist movement during World War I.

Salah al-Din Street: Salah al-Din al-Ayyubi (a.k.a. Saladin) assumed control of Egypt in 1171, fortified Cairo, and built its Citadel. His reign was a golden age for Egypt, and he is revered as one of the great heroes of Islam.

Tala'at Harb Street: Egypt's most famous economist, Muhammad Tala'at Harb, founded the country's first national bank (now the ubiquitous Misr Bank), which was the first bank in the world to conduct business in Arabic (as it still does).

ISLAMIC CAIRO

Islamic Cairo was the heart of the city in the Middle Ages and is home to many mosques. It occupies an area southeast of downtown Cairo, marked by the **Citadel** and **Mosque of Ibn Tulun** in the south and the **al-Azhar Mosque and University** in the north. Although this district was not laid out with urban planning in mind, there are a few key streets and areas, the first of which is **Salah al-Din Sq.** (Midan Salah al-Din). Both the **Sultan Hassan Mosque** and **Rifa'i Mosque** border this square, as does the gargantuan Citadel. **Salah al-Din St.** runs south to the Southern Cemetery, while **al-Qala'a St.** is a main north-south thoroughfare. Branching off of al-Qala'a and heading toward **al-Azhar** and **Khan al-Khalili** is **al-Mu'izz St.**, once the main avenue of the city. Finally, al-Azhar St. connects Islamic Cairo to 'Ataba Sq. and circumnavigates Khan al-Khalili and al-Azhar.

OTHER NEIGHBORHOODS

The main bridge crossing the Nile from the downtown area is **Tahrir Bridge,** connecting Tahrir Sq. to the southern tip of Gezira Island. The northern half is Cairo's ritziest residential area, **Zamalek,** home to expats and quality restaurants. South of Zamalek is **Roda Island,** site of the Manial Palace Museum and the Nilometer. Past Tahrir Bridge on the western bank of the Nile, the Cairo Sheraton Hotel presides over the residential neighborhood of **Doqqi,** home to a handful of embassies. North of Doqqi lies **Mohandiseen** (Engineer's City), built in the late 1950s by Nasser as a neighborhood for engineers. South of Doqqi, past the Cairo Zoo and across the Giza Bridge, is **Giza Sq.** Southwest is **Pyramids Rd.,** where overpriced bars run from the square all the way to the **Pyramids of Giza.**

The major streets in Cairo are sometimes labeled in both English and Arabic, but a good **map** is helpful (most find they need a map more in-depth than that provided by the Egyptian Tourist Authority). Maps cost E£10-30 and are available at most bookstores (p. 93). *Egypt Today* (E£9) publishes up-to-date street listings. Look for their *Dining Guide* and *Travel & Recreation Guide* (E£15 a piece).

▐ PRACTICAL INFORMATION

A reliable directory for goods and services is the *Cairo Telephone List*, published by the Ma'adi Women's Guild and available for E£20 at the American Chamber of Commerce, Marriott Hotel #1541, Zamalek (☎340 88 88).

TOURIST AND FINANCIAL SERVICES

Tourist Office: The **Egyptian Tourist Authority (ETA)** has offices scattered throughout the city. All are very helpful, provide free maps and info, and can make reservations or write out destinations in Arabic. Locations include: **Cairo International Airport** (☎415 74 75), at the entrance and next to the duty-free shops. Open 24hr. **Giza** (☎385 02 59), in front of Mena House Hotel. Open 24hr. **Railway Station** (☎579 07 67), on the left at the station's main entrance. Open daily 8am-8pm. **5 'Adly St.** (☎391 34 54), a 20 minute walk from Tahrir Sq. Follow Tala'at Harb St. and turn right on 'Adly St. The office is three blocks down on your left, marked "Tourist Police." Open daily 8:30am-8pm. If you want someone who speaks English well, your best bet is the 'Adly location.

Student Cards: Medical Scientific Center, 103 Mathaf al-Manial St., on Roda Island (☎363 88 15). South of the Manial Palace across the street from Kentucky Fried Chicken (look for the ISIC sign). Great source of information for travelers. Provides ISIC and Go25 cards (E£25; bring a photo). Student volunteer staff speaks excellent English and will quote prices for sights and entertainment. The center gives out free maps and pamphlets, and organizes excursions to see the Pyramids and Sufi dancing.

EMBASSIES AND CONSULATES:

Australia, World Trade Center 11-12th floors, 1191 Corniche al-Nil (☎575 04 44), in Bulaq. Past the 26 July Bridge. Passports generally replaced in five working days (32-page passports AUS$128, 64-page AUS$192, payable in E£ only). Immediate replacement in case of emergency. Open Su-W 8:30am-noon and 1:30-4pm, Th 8:30am-1:30pm.

Canada, 3rd floor of Arab-African Bank Building, 5 Midan al-Saraya al-Kobr (☎794 31 10 or 794 31 19, emergencies ☎796 36 44), in Garden City. Passports replaced within one week for E£140. Open Su-Th 9am-4pm.

Israel, 6 Ibn al-Malik St. (☎361 03 80 or 361 04 58), in Doqqi. Cross over to Doqqi from Roda Island on University Bridge (al-Gam'a). The street to the right and parallel to the bridge is Ibn al-Malik. Security guards by the entrance will ask to see your passport. Visas E£65. Open Su-Th 10am-12:30pm.

Jordan, 6 al-Goheina St. (☎348 55 66, 348 61 69, 348 75 43, or 349 99 12), in Doqqi. Two blocks west of the Cairo Sheraton. Visas (photograph required) free for Australians, E£28 for New Zealanders, E£63 for Brits, E£231 for Americans, E£91 for Canadians. Same-day service. Open Sa-Th 9am-2pm; arrive early to avoid the crowd.

Lebanon, 22 al-Mansour Muhammad St. (☎332 28 23, 332 28 24, or 332 28 25), in Zamalek. Photograph required for passports. Visas E£123. Any evidence of having been to Israel prohibits obtaining a Lebanese visa. Consular services open M-Th and Sa 9:30am-12:30pm.

South Africa, 21 and 23 Giza St., 18th floor of the Nile Tower (☎571 72 38 or 571 72 39), in Giza. File applications for new passports here; they're sent to South Africa for processing. Entire process takes eight weeks. In the meantime, you are issued a one-page Emergency Passport good for three months (E£50). Open Su-Th 8am-5pm; consular services Su-Th 9am-noon.

Syria, 18 Abd al-Rahim Sabri St. (☎337 70 20), in Doqqi. Bring two photographs for a visa. Visas, free for Australians and New Zealanders, E£182 for Brits, E£195 for Canadians, and E£211 for Americans, take anywhere from one day to one week for processing, depending on nationality. You are advised to apply for visas in your home country. Americans are sometimes denied visas at Syrian embassies in other Arab countries. Evidence of travel to Israel prohibits obtaining a Syrian visa. Open Sa-Th 9am-2pm.

UK, 7 Ahmed Ragheb St. (☎794 08 50), in Garden City. Also handles **New Zealand** affairs. Will replace passports within four days and only accepts E£ (32-page passports E£270, 48-page E£330). Open Su-Th 9am-1pm.

US, 5 Latin America St. (☎794 82 11, emergencies ☎795 73 71), in Garden City. Two blocks south of Tahrir Sq. For the consulate, enter on Lazoughli St. around the block. Lost or stolen passports replaced overnight for US$60 or E£ equivalent (US$60 for renewal). Open Su-Th 8am-noon.

Passport Office: Mugamm'a Building, 2nd floor (☎792 69 00). The massive concave gray edifice at the southern side of Tahrir Sq. was constructed during Nasser's flirtation with the Soviets, and the spirit of the Cold War lives on in its bureaucratic inefficiency. First, buy forms at window 42, then get stamps at 41, then go to windows 23-29 to culminate the visa extension process. Having what you want written down in Arabic beforehand helps. Registration open Sa-Th 8am-8pm, visa extensions 8am-1pm. For fewer crowds, check the 2nd floor of the **Ministry of Economy and Foreign Trade Building,** 8 'Adly St. (☎390 43 63), next to the EgyptAir office. Bring a passport photo for visa extensions (2-6 months E£10, 1 year E£40). Open Sa-Th 8am-1:30pm.

Currency Exchange: Banks and exchange services litter the downtown area. **Bank Misr** (☎391 75 71) has branches at major hotels, with a main office downtown at 151 Muhammad Farid St. All open Sa-Th 8:30am-2pm and 6-9pm. **Cairo Barclay's International Bank,** 12 Sheikh Yusef Sq., Garden City (☎794 94 15 or 794 94 22), three blocks south of Tahrir Sq. along Qasr al-'Aini St., accepts traveler's checks and has worldwide money transfer services. Open Su-Th 8:30am-2pm; Ramadan 10am-1pm. Foreign banks closed F-Sa, but most Egyptian banks open Sa. Money wired to Egypt through **Citibank,** 4 Ahmed Basha St., Garden City (☎795 18 73 or 795 18 74; open Su-Th 8:30am-2pm) or **Western Union,** 1081 Corniche al-Nil, Garden City (☎797 13 00 or 797 13 74; open Su-Th 9am-8:30pm), in the FedEx office.

ATM: **Egyptian British Banks** have machines that accept V, PLUS, Global Access, and Express Net cards. Locations in Semiramis Intercontinental, Zamalek Marriott, Cairo Sheraton, and Ramses and Nile Hiltons.

Thomas Cook: 17 Mahmoud Bassouni St. (☎574 37 76, 574 39 55, or 574 39 67; fax 576 27 50). Half a block west of Tala'at Harb Sq. Other offices throughout the city. Travel agency, money transfers, currency exchange, and cash advances on V and MC. Cashes traveler's checks. Open daily 8am-5pm.

American Express: 15 Qasr al-Nil (☎574 79 91, 574 79 92, or 574 79 96). Off Tala'at Harb Sq., opposite EgyptAir toward Ramses St. Members can have money sent to the office and have mail held there. Cashes traveler's checks. Open Su-Th 9am-4pm; Ramadan 9am-3:30pm. Other locations at the Nile Hilton (☎578 50 01, 578 50 02, or 578 50 03), Marriott Hotel (☎341 01 36), Pullman Ma'adi (☎790 78 51), and in Mohandiseen, 4 Syria St. (☎570 79 08 or 570 79 14).

LOCAL SERVICES

Luggage Storage: Avoid the unreliable Ramses Station lockers. Get bilingual written proof of having stored anything at a hotel. Make sure that "storage" in budget hotels is a safe at the front desk and not just a hallway.

English-Language Bookstores: Used Books, left of the statue by the Cairo Puppet Theater near 'Ataba Sq. Metro: 'Ataba. Among books on dialectical materialism and US Boy Scout manuals are titles for as low as E£4. **AUC Bookstore,** 113 Qasr al-'Aini St. (☎797 53 77), in the Hill House at the American University in Cairo. University texts, classic novels, Arab literature in translation, maps, and guide books. US passport needed to enter the campus. Open Su-Th 8:30am-5pm, Sa 10:30am-5pm. V, MC. **Lehnert and Landrock,** 44 Sherif St. (☎393 53 24), between 'Adly St. and 26 July St. "L&L" offers a superb, wide-ranging selection of guidebooks, maps, histories, and postcards. Open M-F 10am-2pm and 4-9pm, Sa 9am-11pm. V, MC.

Newspapers and Magazines: The *Egyptian Gazette, al-Ahram Weekly,* and *Middle East Times* are Egypt's English newspapers. *Egypt Today,* a monthly magazine (E£7), is handy for current restaurant and entertainment listings. All are sold at **The Reader's Corner,** 33 Abd al-Khaleq Sarwat St., downtown. Open M-Sa 10am-7pm. Many hotels and street stands from Tahrir Sq. to Tala'at Harb Sq. sell foreign language publications.

American Cultural Center: 5 Latin America St., Garden City (☎794 96 01 or 576 27 04; library ☎795 05 32 or 797 34 12), inside the US Embassy, across from the British Embassy. Tourists in Egypt for at least 12 months are eligible to join no matter what their nationality (bring two photographs and a passport). Members can borrow books and watch videos. All American citizens have access to the A/C library's collection of popular magazines and books on America. Occasional free films and lectures. Call ☎797 33 66 for a schedule. Open Su-F 10am-4pm; in winter M-F 10am-4pm.

Markets: Seoudi Market, 25 Midan al-Missaha St., Doqqi (☎348 84 40 or 348 84 41); 20 Hijaz St., Mohandiseen (☎346 03 91); and 15 Ahmad Hishmat St., Zamalek (☎341 35 86 or 340 03 70). A fully stocked supermarket with fair prices. All open daily 9am-2am. **Sunny Supermarket,** 11 al-'Aziz 'Osman St., Zamalek (☎342 11 21), next door to the Mayfair Hotel south of 26 July St. Impressive array of Egyptian and Western products for not-quite-budget prices. Sunny's also has a bulletin board where you can find information on anything from Arabic lessons to apartments for rent. Open daily 8am-10pm.

Laundromat: Circle Cleaning, 24 26 July St. (☎576 08 55), near the Supreme Court and the intersection with Tala'at Harb St. Open daily 9am-9pm. You're better off doing it yourself or paying a maid in your hotel to do your load (the laundromat can be a madhouse). 50pt per piece is reasonable.

Swimming Pools: Fontana Hotel (☎592 21 45 or 592 23 21), in Ramses Sq. has a teal-tiled pool on its 7th-floor patio (E£15 per day). Cairo's sporting clubs also sell day passes for E£20: the **Gezira Sporting Club** (☎340 60 00), in front of the Marriott Hotel in Zamalek; the **Ma'adi Sporting Club,** 8 al-Nadi Sq. (☎790 54 55); and the **Heliopolis Sporting Club,** 17 al-Merghany St. (☎291 00 65). Sometimes the guards insist that you enter with a club member. Day passes at 5-star hotels up to E£30.

EMERGENCY AND COMMUNICATIONS

Emergency: Police: ☎122, 126, or 303 41 22. **Fire:** ☎125 or 391 01 15.

Tourist Police: 5 'Adly St. (☎390 19 44 or 390 60 28, emergencies ☎126). In the same building as the Tourist Office. Also at Cairo International Airport (☎247 25 84), the Manial Palace Hotel in Giza (☎385 02 59), and Ramses Station.

Late-Night Pharmacies: Victoria Pharmacy, 90 Qasr al-'Aini St. (☎794 86 04). **Isaaf Pharmacy** (☎574 33 69) on Ramses St. and 26 July St. **Seif Pharmacy,** 76 Qasr al-'Aini (☎794 26 78). **Zamalek Pharmacy,** 3 Shagarat al-Durr (☎340 24 06).

Hospitals: The best-equipped is **Al-Salaam International Hospital** (☎524 02 50), Ma'adi, Corniche al-Nil. **Anglo-American Hospital** (☎340 61 62 or 340 61 65), Zamalek, on Botanical Garden St. below the Cairo Tower. **Cairo Medical Center** (☎258 05 66, 258 02 17, or 258 10 03), in Heliopolis at Roxy Sq.

Fax Office: You may send and receive faxes at the business office of the **Ramses Hilton** (fax 575 71 52 or 578 22 21). They charge according to destination for sending and E£4 per page to receive. Most telephone offices can send faxes.

Telephones: Main Telephone Office, on Ramses St., one block north of 26 July St. Other offices in Zamalek, Airport, Ma'adi, Tahrir Sq., 'Adly St., and Alfy St. (under the Windsor Hotel). All open 24hr. **Collect calls** and **credit card calls** are available at the USADirect, UKDirect, CanadaDirect, and JapanDirect phones in the lobbies of the Ramses Hilton, and the Marriott and Semiramis Hotels (for access numbers, see **Keeping in Touch,** p. 79). For a 25% surcharge, you can easily make international calls at the business service offices in the Meridien, Sheraton, and Nile Hilton hotels. Open 24hr. **Directory Assistance:** ☎140.

Internet Access: The **Internet Egypt Cafe** in the Nile Hilton Mall (☎578 04 44; www.internetegypt.com) has a room with fierce A/C and several banks of computers. 15min. minimum E£3, 30min. E£6, 1hr. E£10. There is also a small but serviceable Internet cafe on al-Fadil St., one block north of the Berlin Hotel. 30min. E£7; 1hr. E£12.

Post Office: 55 Sarwat St. (☎391 26 14), in 'Ataba Sq. under the dome. Often crowded, but blissfully empty before closing. Packages require export license, available from airport, hotels, and tourist shops. Open Sa-Th 8am-7pm; Ramadan 9am-3pm. Most in Cairo sell stamps and have EMS. **24hr. Express Mail (EMS)** on Bidek St. One convenient branch is at 13 Metitte Bash St. in Tahrir Sq. (☎575 43 13), opposite the Egyptian Museum. Open Sa-Th 9am-9pm. Stamps sold and letters mailed at major hotels.

Federal Express: 1081 Corniche al-Nil, 8th floor, Garden City (☎792 33 01), opposite the Meridien Hotel on the east bank of the Nile. Open 8am-8pm.

▮ ACCOMMODATIONS

Downtown Cairo, on and around **Tala'at Harb St.,** is littered with dozens of budget hotels and dorms occupying the upper floors of colonial buildings. All prices listed below include breakfast, and all rooms have fans and 24-hour hot water unless otherwise noted. "Hotels" and "hostels" are close cousins in Egypt. Many hotels

SCAM WARS, EPISODE I Never underestimate the power of the con side; the most notorious of these, the **hotel scam**, begins the moment you step off the plane. Have two or three hotels in mind and avoid taking a taxi or otherwise making verbal contact (besides a polite no) with anyone who offers you anything at the airport. Do not believe anyone who claims your first two or three hotels are closed, whether they are taxi drivers, "tour guides," or even (underpaid) tourist police. Simply find another driver, get dropped off at a nearby landmark, or refuse payment. When in Cairo (or any other city) do not let yourself be taken to a hotel by a taxi driver or "hotel manager;" this only succeeds in inflating the price due to hefty commissions, and in bringing you to a seedy establishment that indulges in this practice. Fear and ignorance: these are the paths to the con side. Avoid them at all costs. The second con is the dreaded **tour con.** Even at reputable hotels, the management may push tours of high cost and low quality. Always check with the tourist office for a list of fair prices. Several hotels in Cairo offer day tours to Aswan and Luxor: these are the most likely to be rip-offs. Skip the middleman and contact **Amigo Tours,** in the Isis Hotel in Aswan (☎(097) 31 68 43). Inclusive multiple day trips (excluding train fare) cost US$65-145. As with any tour, seek to pay the balance directly to the tour company and only after you arrive at your destination, whether it be Alexandria or Alderon.

have dorm beds available and many hostels have single or double rooms. Most maids will do your laundry (usually about 50pt per article). If you're in Cairo for a while or during low season, bargain for a reduced rate. Single-sex groups should have no problem renting a **flat** (E£500-2000 per month), but building owners often frown upon renting to coed groups. The billboards at the AUC entrance and the Sunny Market in Zamalek list available apartments.

BUDGET

Anglo-Swiss Hotel, 14 Champollion St., 6th fl. (☎575 14 97), two blocks west of Tala'at Harb Sq. From Tahrir Sq., turn right on Champollion in the northeastern end of the square next to the museum, by the parking lot. The hotel will be to your left at the intersection with Mahmoud Bassouni St. Play the piano in the sunny dining hall or watch some TV in a pleasant living room before retiring to quiet, large rooms with shared baths, most with balconies. Friendly management, but not the most reputable fellows around. French spoken. Singles E£20; doubles E£30. Student discount.

Hotel Minerva, 39 Tala'at Harb St. (☎392 06 00, 392 06 01, or 392 06 02), one block toward Tala'at Harb Sq. from 26 July St. Reception is four doors past the Bamboo Clothing Store on your right. Beautifully renovated bathrooms, vast balconies, and new light fixtures add a touch of elegance. Often full. Singles E£20; doubles E£30; triples E£45.

Isma'ilia House Hotel, 1 Tahrir Sq., 8th fl. (☎796 31 22), by an exit of the Sadat Metro station toward AUC. A warm, convenient hotel with diligent management. The rooms are fairly standard, but have stupendous views of Tahrir Sq. Dorm beds E£15; singles E£20, with shower E£25; doubles E£40, with bath E£50.

Youth Hostel (HI), 135 Malik Abd al-'Aziz al-Sa'ud St., Roda Island (☎364 07 29; fax 98 41 07). Metro: Sayyida Zeinab. Exit to the right and walk straight to the Nile. Cross the Sayala Bridge and continue straight across Roda Island to the Nile's main channel. Turn left just before the University (al-Gam'a) bridge (with Salah al-Din mosque to your right); the hostel is 10m away on the left. This 1970s building shows its age, but is clean and quiet; a nice island retreat from downtown. A bit isolated from tourist sights (but not the Nilometer!). No lockout. Curfew 11pm. Call ahead for reservations. Single-sex triples and quads E£24; nonmembers E£4 extra.

Sun Hotel, 2 Tala'at Harb St., 9th fl. (☎578 17 86). Worshiped by budget travelers for its convenient location, less than a block from the Metro on the left as you leave Tahrir Sq. Features satellite TV, a kitchen, and a small but lively lobby area with crammed couches. Comfortable beds in rooms with (ironically) dim lighting. Bargain for longer stays. Dorm beds E£15; singles E£25; doubles E£40; triples E£51.

Pension Select Hotel, 19 'Adly St., 8th fl. (☎393 37 07), next to a synagogue. High above the street noise, the Select offers spacious 3-bed dorms that are quiet and off the beaten path. Dorm beds E£15; singles E£25; doubles E£30; triples E£45.

Bluebird Hotel, 42 Tala'at Harb St., 6th fl. (☎575 63 77), opposite 'Adly St. heading toward Ramses St. A fairly clean and well-maintained option. Rooms are interestingly decorated, particularly the one with a tapestry of several cats. Separate-sex baths, satellite TV, and common kitchen. Singles E£15; doubles E£30; triples E£45.

Gresham Hotel, 20 Tala'at Harb St. (☎575 90 43; email heshatut@yahoo.com), just off Tala'at Harb Sq. Clean rooms and baths, but not all come with fans. Be cautious of offered tours. Singles E£25, with bath and A/C E£35; doubles E£40, with bath and A/C E£45; triples E£55, with bath and A/C E£65; quads E£70, with bath and A/C E£80.

Horris Hotel, 5 26 July St. (☎591 04 78, 591 05 47, or 591 08 55). Enter from Alfy St. behind Cinema Diana. Modern building with a barren bar and rooms with bath, A/C, and TV. Upper floors have flowery balconies with views blossoming out over Cairo. Singles E£45; doubles E£85; triples E£100; add tax and service charge.

Sultan Hotel, 4 Souq al-Tawfiqia St., 1st and 5th fl. (☎577 22 58), off Tala'at Harb St. on the market street parallel to 26 July St. Bedrooms need a makeover, but helpful staff and unbeatable price compensate. The 5th-floor rooms are less crowded, cheaper, and breezier. Couples sharing a room must be married or brother and sister, and have the same name on their passports to prove it. Single women may feel uncomfortable. Free six-day luggage storage. Breakfast not included, but guests may use the kitchen, and the nearby fruit market is cheap and good. Dorm beds E£6-8; doubles E£25.

A BIT SWANKIER

🏨 **Windsor Hotel,** 19 Alfy St. (☎591 58 10 or 591 52 77; fax 592 16 21; email wdoss@link.com.eg; www.windsorcairo.com). Clean facilities with excellent service in an atmosphere of old-time grandeur. The swank lives on with free access to facilities at the chichi Gezira Club in Zamalek, included in the price of a room. The Barrel Bar (named for the furniture, which is made of barrels) was once the British Officers' Club. Monty Python's Michael Palin hung out here while filming *Around the World in Eighty Days*. Rooms have A/C, towels, crisp sheets, and comfy beds. Singles with shower E£70, with shower and toilet E£100; doubles with shower E£100, with shower and toilet E£130. Prices include breakfast, tax, and 25% *Let's Go* discount. 5% credit card service charge.

🏨 **Berlin Hotel,** 2 al-Shawarby St. (☎/fax 395 75 02; email berlinhotelcairo@hotmail.com). From Tala'at Harb Sq., walk up Qasr al-Nil toward Mustafa Kamal Sq.; the entrance to this new hotel is on a pedestrian-only street. Friendly proprietor Hisham is generous with his wealth of information and advice. Elegant rooms boast private showers, full-length velvet curtains, and freshly painted walls. A neighboring fitness club offers weights, sauna, and massage at a discounted rate for hotel guests. Internet access and Net-2-Phone available starting at E£3 per minute. Breakfast included. Hotel can arrange transportation from airport. Singles with fan E£45, with A/C E£60; doubles with fan E£60, with A/C E£80; triples E£90.

Carlton Hotel, 21 26 July St. (☎575 50 22; fax 575 53 23), beside the Cinema Rivoli and near the vegetable market and intersection of Tala'at Harb St. and 26 July St. Friendly management tries hard to maintain the 1930s glory of this aging institution and succeeds, though pricey rooms are often vacant. Each room comes with satellite TV, A/C, and furnished balconies. Dinner is served nightly on the rooftop garden, complete with stunning views. Singles E£85; doubles E£95.

Richmond Hotel, 41 Sherif St. (☎393 93 58), just south of 26 July St. A newly restored hotel with beautiful art deco furniture. Clean rooms (some with balconies) come with fan and breakfast. Singles E£30; doubles E£45; triples E£60.

El-Malky Hotel, 4 al-Mashhad al-Hussein St. (☎592 88 04; fax 589 67 00), next to al-Hussein Mosque and Khan al-Khalili market. In the heart of Islamic Cairo, away from the downtown bustle, but in the thick of the shopping bustle. You'll get used to the *muezzin* call to prayer five times a day. Savory singles with TV, fridge, and A/C E£30, with bath E£45; dreamy doubles E£55, with bath E£60.

Mayfair Hotel, 9 'Aziz 'Osman St., Zamalek (☎340 73 15), parallel to Hassan Sabri St., on corner of Ibn Zinki St. Two blocks south of 26 July St. Tidy rooms with balconies amid the leafy calm of Zamalek, but close enough to downtown. Some rooms have A/C, all have fans. Management can be insistent on tours. Singles E£30, with shower E£45; doubles E£40, with shower E£60. Prices include breakfast and 10% *Let's Go* discount.

Pension Roma, 169 Muhammad Farid St. (☎391 10 88 or 391 13 40), one block south of 26 July St. and two blocks east of Tala'at Harb St. Turn right on 'Adly St. and left after the synagogue; look for the hotel's green sign above the Gattegno department store, between 'Ataba and Nasser Metro stations. This classic *pensione* is beautifully designed, clean, and well-kept; rooms may have a breezy balcony, but no fans. Towels, toilet paper, and soap provided. Fan rental E£2.50. Free storage. Singles E£25; doubles E£50, with shower E£55; triples E£65, with shower E£72.

🗂 FOOD

Sticking with the same old *fuul* and *ta'amiyya* will only require 40pt to fill your stomach. A good place for *kushari* (servings E£1.50-3, depending on size) is **al-Tahrir,** on Tahrir St. near Bab al-Luq or on Abd al-Haliq Sarwat St. near Tala'at Harb St. **Lux,** on 26 July St., is another tasty choice. Wash it all down with **fruit juice,** on sale anywhere you see bags of fruit hanging around a storefront. Drink at your own risk: the hygiene of juice stores is questionable. At places without waiters, pay first and then exchange your receipt for food.

A sit-down meal is often relatively cheap by Western standards and is usually worth the small investment. Even at more expensive restaurants, you can create a handsome meal out of hummus, *baba ghanoush* (grilled eggplant dip), and salad for under E£5. *Fatir,* a filo dough-like bread stuffed and topped with vegetables, meats, or sweets is far tastier than the imitations of Italian pizza in town and usually cheaper at E£5-10. A 5% **sales tax** on food and a 10-12% **service charge** at sit-down restaurants are both added to the bill. A small **tip** (E£1) is still in order.

While eating local food is an essential component of the Egyptian experience, you might want to try the cleaner, faster, A/C Western fast-food chains lined up in a row across from AUC on Mahmoud St. **Pizza Hut** offers slices for E£1.90 each. (☎796 26 28. Open daily 9am-4am, delivery until 3am.) Next door, **Kentucky Fried Chicken** is a bit cheaper but serves buns instead of the biscuits so treasured by the Colonel and his cohorts. The **McDonald's** by AUC offers combos for E£8.50. (☎795 81 31. Open daily 10am-2am.) All have free delivery up to two kilometers away.

DOWNTOWN

RESTAURANTS

🍽 **Felfela,** 15 Hoda Sha'rawi St. (☎392 27 51 or 392 28 33), off Tala'at Harb St., one block south of Tala'at Harb Sq. Opened by model Amina Zaghloul in 1958, this joint will leave you feeling like you just walked into an Amazon rainforest. Cool air from the ceiling fans and light from the stained glass ceilings filter down through the bamboo and vines, delighting the customers who sit amongst live birds and aquariums at tables made of huge tree stumps. Full meal of *wara 'einab* (stuffed grape leaves) E£12; stuffed pigeon E£17. Also delicious is *om 'ali,* a pastry baked with milk, honey, and raisins (E£5.75). If you don't have time for a sit-down meal, drop by their **take-out station** around the corner at 15 Tala'at Harb St. Both open daily 6am-midnight.

🍽 **'Ali Hassan al-Hati,** 3 Midan Halim Basha (☎591 60 55), between Alfy St. and 26 July St., one block south of the Windsor Hotel. High ceilings, crystal chandeliers, and a name recognized by your average person-on-the-street. Try the generous *fatteh*—garlic, meat, or vegetables poured over crunchy baked bread and covered with a yogurt sauce (E£5). Open daily noon-midnight.

Restaurant al-Hati, 8A 26 July St. (☎391 88 29). The glitzier younger sibling of 'Ali Hassan, complete with marble tiles and mirrors. The lunch special (*kofta*, kebab, oriental rice or macaroni, salad, bread, and dessert) will fill you up, and certainly won't let you down (E£16.5). Take-out available. Open daily noon-midnight. V, MC, AmEx.

Le Bistro, 8 Hoda Sha'rawi St. (☎392 76 94), down the street from Felfela. Walk down the stairs to enter the restaurant. Serves up well prepared bistro food in an airy bistro setting. Entrees are a good deal at E£15-20. Open daily noon-midnight. AmEx.

Restaurant Cairo, the second restaurant on the left side of the street that forks to the right from Orabi Sq. The staff may forget about you, but you won't forget about the food: the half chicken (E£5.5), soup (E£1.5), and stuffed pigeon with salad and bread (E£10) are delicious. Open 24hr.

Peking, 14 Saraya al-Azbakia St. (☎591 23 81), behind Cinema Diana between Alfy St. and 26 July St. One of Cairo's most popular Chinese restaurants. Pamper yourself with the complimentary steaming hand towels before a full meal with appetizer, three dishes, and dessert—don't miss the honey-walnut Tarte Lee (E£40-45). Alcohol served. Free delivery. Open daily noon-midnight. V, MC, AmEx. **Other branches:** Mohandiseen (☎349 98 60), New Ma'adi (☎516 42 18), and Heliopolis (☎418 56 12).

Fu-Shing, 28 Tala'at Harb St. (☎576 61 84), in an alleyway running west from the street. Walk up the stairs past the Arabic and Chinese calligraphy. Exotic items (like purple seaweed soup, E£4) and a diverse array of vegetarian options make this Chinese restaurant a delicious escape from the ho-hum(mus) street vendor fare. Entrees E£10-20. Open daily noon-10pm.

Cafe Riche, 17 Tala'at Harb St. (☎392 97 93). This cafe-restaurant may intimidate budget travelers from the outside, but step inside for a diverse selection of foods ranging from traditional Arabic to modern Western. Pasta steams for E£8, rib eye steak goes for E£28, and stuffed quail flies for E£24. Open daily 10am-1am. V, MC, AmEx.

CAFES

■ **El-'Abd,** 25 Tala'at Harb St. (☎392 44 07), opposite the Arab Bank building. This upscale bakery provides the perfect antidote to Cairo's heat—a whopping three-scoop ice-cream cone (E£1.50). Ask to sample any of the pastries. Open daily 8:30am-12:30am. Another **branch** on 26 July St., one block east of Tala'at Harb St.

J. Groppi, west side of Tala'at Harb Sq. This confectionery opened its doors to Europeans and Europeanized Egyptians in 1891 and hasn't changed its decor since. A great place for a date (chocolate-covered or not). The mango and apricot jams are a tart retort to the excellent Turkish coffee. Open daily 7am-midnight.

La Poire, 18 Latin America St. (☎355 15 09), across the street from the British Embassy in Garden City. Come for the extensive selection of ice cream flavors (E£1.75 per scoop) but stay for the croissants, eclairs, and sticky-sweet *ba'laweh* (about E£1.50 per serving)—and don't leave until you're *poire*-shaped. Open daily 7am-midnight.

Brazilian Coffee Shop, 38 Tala'at Harb St., at the intersection with 'Adly St. A/C restaurant upstairs from the Miami Cinema serves cappuccino and espresso (E£2 each). A great place to read the morning paper with your favorite middle management chums. Chicken sandwich E£5. Open daily 6am-midnight.

ZAMALEK

RESTAURANTS

■ **Didos Al Dente,** 26 Bahgat Basha 'Ali St. (☎340 91 17). Walking north along the western corniche, take a right onto Anis Basha St.; Didos Al Dente is two blocks ahead on your left. Although the fans do a bad job of fending off the heat, your wallet will think the prices are pretty cool. A wide selection of pastas with 18 different sauces (spaghetti starts at E£5), plus tempting Arab-Italian side dishes such as *insalata al-funghi*. Open daily noon-1:30am.

Maison Thomas, 157 26 July St. (☎340 70 57), on the right near the base of the bridge as you come into Zamalek from Cairo. Hip French/Italian bistro filled with hanging salami and wheels of cheese evoke the Mediterranean's other coast. Salads (E£10-13), baguette sandwiches, and pizzas (E£13-37) are delicious and generously proportioned. Gorge yourself like a pig on their numerous pork options. Free delivery. Open 24hr.

Hana Korean Restaurant, 21 Ma'had al-Swissry St. (☎340 18 46), in al-Nil Zamalek Hotel. Take a right off 26 July St. onto Hassan Sabri St. (also called Brazil St.). This A/C haven, popular among tourists and expats, serves up shark-fin soup (E£9) and *bulgogi*, tender slices of beef you barbecue right at the table (E£21). Stella (E£6) is everyone's favorite lady. Open daily 11:30am-11pm.

Bon Appetit, 2 Isma'il Muhammad St. (☎340 43 82 or 340 91 08), one block from the Flamenco Hotel on the west side of Zamalek. This place is not Julia Child's hangout, but it is the cleanest place in town to try brain (E£8) or tongue (E£7.70) sandwiches. These are just appetizers; main courses average E£30. Open daily 9am-1am. V, MC, AmEx.

CAFES

▨ **Simonds,** 112 26 July St. (☎340 94 36), just east of the intersection with Hassan Sabri St. The New York Chic feel lures an eclectic mix of locals and foreign emissaries who sip on *café au lait* (E£2.20) and freshly-squeezed orange juice (E£2.25) while munching on pastries (under E£2). A huge selection of savory desserts. Open daily 7am-9pm.

Mandarin Koedar, 17 Shagarat al-Durr St. (☎340 50 10). Take a right off 26 July St. at the Misr Gas Station onto Shagarat al-Durr St., then follow the crooked lane for 200m. Cool to the core: a wide selection of ice cream (E£1.75 per scoop) and pastries served up in an arctic A/C setting. Open daily 9am-11pm.

MOHANDISEEN

RESTAURANTS

Le Tabasco, 8 'Ammen Sq. (☎336 55 83). One of the best restaurants in Cairo. Dim candlelight and soft jazz *(ooh la la!)* accompany a weekly-changing pricey menu: appetizers E£10-24, pasta E£12-17, main dishes E£21-34. Recent menu selections include *cascadilla* (grilled tomato soup), frogs' legs Provençale, prawns in spicy garlic sauce, and fresh pear crepes. Reservations required. Open daily 1pm-1am. V, MC, AmEx.

Al-Omda, 6 al-Gaza'ir St. (☎346 22 47), down an unmarked staircase a few doors from the Atlas Hotel on Gam'at al-Duwal St. Grape leaves (E£8-15) are almost as expensive as full meals (E£10-15). Dine-in (A/C), delivery. Open daily noon-3am.

Prestige Pizza, 43 Geziret al-'Arab (☎347 03 83), just east of Wadi al-Nil St. Coming from Gam'at al-Duwal St., turn right before Al-Ahli Bank. The ice cream is often warmer than the pies, so stick to the generous "normal" size pizzas E£12, "prestige" size E£17. Cover E£7. Open daily noon-2am. V, MC, AmEx.

Coffee Roastery, 46 Nadi Seid St. (☎349 88 82). An Egyptian expat living in San Francisco exported this cafe to Cairo. Sip on a caffe latte (E£4) while reading through *Time, Newsweek,* or Egyptian teenybopper magazines. Open daily 8am-midnight. V, MC, AmEx.

ISLAMIC CAIRO (KHAN AL-KHALILI)

RESTAURANTS

Egyptian Pancakes, 7 al-Azhar Sq. (☎590 86 23), half block from the intersection of al-Azhar St. and Gohar al-Qa'it St. Tired of the same old *kushari* and kebab? Small (E£10), medium (E£12), or large (E£15) pancakes topped with sweets (honey, coconut, or raisins) or meats (hot dog, tuna, or "turkey cock"). Open 24hr.

Coffee Shop Naguib Mahfouz, 5 al-Badistante Ln. (☎590 37 88), two blocks west of al-Hussein Mosque. Not on *Sugar St.* as you might think. This pricey restaurant is a calm oasis of delectable food in the maddening bustle of Khan al-Khalili. Engage in *Small Talk on the Nile* as you sip on fresh fruit juices (said to be the favorites of Nobel laureate Mahfouz, who was once a regular here). No doubt he also appreciated the clean restrooms and nightly live music. No *Autumn Quail,* but you can try a Lebanese kebab

(E£39) or *tabbouleh* (E£6.50). Minimum charge E£10 per person, E£2 music charge. Open daily 10am-2am. V, MC, AmEx.

Al-Gamhorya, on al-Azhar St., one block east of the green pedestrian overpass at the al-Ghouri Mosque and Mausoleum. A perfect *kushari* stop-off (E£1). Single women may feel uncomfortable among the mostly male clientele. Open daily 9am-11pm.

GIZA

RESTAURANTS

The food situation in Giza is bleak, and it's best either to wait until you get back downtown or bring a bag lunch (as many Egyptians do). There are several **food stands** near the sound and light show auditorium, as well as a **Pizza Hut.**

Pyramids Shishkebab Restaurant (☎385 10 78), two blocks from the Sphinx Rest House along the main road, has a cheap *ta'amiyya* and *shawarma* stand outside and serves up traditional salads, *fuul,* and falafel inside. E£1-4 per item; meat dishes are more expensive. Open daily 10am-3am.

Khan al-Khalili Coffee Shop (☎383 68 28), in the Mena House Oberoi Hotel at the end of Pyramid St., is a sleek spot to sip coffee or mint tea for E£3.50. Open 24hr.

🔘 SIGHTS

Four thousand years of history have been stitched together on the streets of Egypt's capital in a dusty quilt of dynasties past laced heavily with the musk of a metropolitan future. Start your journey through time at the **Pyramids at Giza** (below). In **Islamic Cairo** (p. 105), the devout prostrate themselves before some of the Muslim world's most revered sites while small-time capitalists haggle in the nearby ancient bazaar. In the **Cities of the Dead** (p. 113), mausolea and tombs listen to the struggles of the city's poor and the whispers of the gloried dead. Christian and Jewish communities center in the **Coptic Cairo** district of **Old Cairo** (p. 116), while the remains of **al-Fustat** (p. 118) house the earliest Egyptian mosque. **Modern Cairo** (p. 119) rushes to embrace the future, while the city's **museums** (p. 122) strain to weave together its millennia of history.

PYRAMIDS AT GIZA (AL-AHRAM) الاهرام

*Take **minibus** #183 (١٨٣, 40pt) from Tahrir Sq., #26 (٢٦) from 'Ataba Sq., #84 (٨٤) from the Nile Hilton, or the faster **microbus** (50pt). The last stop is often one kilometer from the Pyramids; cross the street and follow the main road to get there. The easiest and most comfortable way back is on a special tour bus that leaves outside the tourist office every 10-15 minutes (E£2.50). Hotel managers in Cairo can arrange **tours,** but be sure to compare prices. **Mr. Salah Muhammad** (☎/fax 298 06 50; email samo@intouch.com) offers chauffeur-driven tours of Memphis, Saqqara, the carpet school at Harania, and the Pyramids at Giza for E£40 (E£35 for Let's Go users who book a tour in advance), including a guide. Entrance fees excluded (leave at 9am, return at 5pm). Although sunrise at the Pyramids is impressive, guards won't let you in until regular hours of operation. Site open daily 8:30am-5pm; in winter 9am-4pm. Pyramids and Sphinx complex E£20, students E£10. The two smaller pyramids E£10, students E£5. The Great Pyramid E£20, students E£10; limited to the first 100 visitors who appear at 8:30am and 1pm.*

 SIGHTSEEING STRATEGY The best time to visit the Pyramids is on Friday when some of the pious hagglers take the day off (most other attractions are closed anyway). Be wary of going before 9:30am from November to March; fog shrouds the pyramids in the morning and crowds tend to pick up as the day progresses. Be warned that you can't get inside the Pyramids or boat museum after 5pm. Good shoes are key for those who plan on internal climbing; external climbing is no longer permitted.

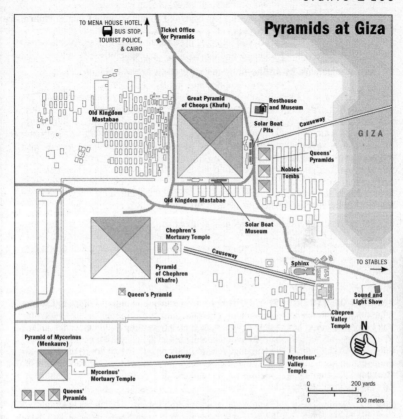

Pyramids at Giza

TO MENA HOUSE HOTEL,
BUS STOP,
TOURIST POLICE,
& CAIRO

Ticket Office
for Pyramids

Great Pyramid
of Cheops (Khufu)

Resthouse
and Museum

Old Kingdom
Mastabae

Solar Boat
Pits

Causeway

GIZA

Queens'
Pyramids

Nobles'
Tombs

Old Kingdom Mastabae

Solar Boat
Museum

Chephren's
Mortuary Temple

Causeway

Sphinx

TO STABLES

Pyramid
of Chephren
(Khafre)

Queen's Pyramid

Sound and
Light Show

Chepren
Valley
Temple

N

Pyramid of Mycerinus
(Menkaure)

Causeway

Mycerinus'
Valley
Temple

Mycerinus'
Mortuary Temple

Queens'
Pyramids

0   200 yards
0   200 meters

EGYPT

A 12th-century Arab historian once said, "all things fear time, but time fears the Pyramids." Originally constructed to honor the pharaohs in death, these three massive stone monoliths are also monuments to generations of slaves who devoted their lives to the pyramids. While treasure has been plundered by grave robbers and museum curators, the edifices still tower over the desert, oblivious to the throngs below. Since everyone wants to see these awe-inspiring testaments to human achievement, nowhere else is Egypt's ravenous tourism industry so persistent. For a solid mile leading up to the pyramids, souvenir shops, alabaster factories, and papyrus museums conspire to pawn off "ancient" artifacts manufactured while you wait. At the foot of the pyramids, an army of hustlers not unlike a biblical swarm of locusts hounds you: Bedouin imposters rent camels and Arabian "race" horses, children peddle tourist dreck at inflated prices, and self-appointed guides approach at every turn. A stern *"la shukran"* ("no thanks") can prove useful at the Pyramids, even with the man who claims to be the mayor of Giza (he isn't). That said, don't let the racket deter you from spending at least a few hours exploring one of the seven wonders of the ancient world.

The three main pyramids at Giza were built for three pharaohs from the 4th dynasty: **Cheops** (Khufu), **Chephren** (Khafre), and **Mycerinus** (Menkaure), a father-son-grandson trio that reigned during the 26th century BCE. The pyramids are lined up in descending order of chronology and size, from Cheops to Mycerinus. All three entrances face north and the bases are aligned with the four cardinal points. The smaller, surrounding pyramids belonged to the pharaohs' wives and children. Each of the pyramids was once attached to its own funerary complex, which included a riverside pavilion and a mortuary temple where the pharaoh's cult could continue for eternity. A long, narrow causeway linked the mortuary temple with the neighboring waters of the Nile. Attendants brought the mummy of the deceased ruler across the Nile by boat, up the causeway in a solemn procession, and deposited it in its sacred resting place at the heart of the pyramid.

GREAT PYRAMID OF CHEOPS. Built around 2550 BCE, the Pyramid of Cheops is the first pyramid you'll encounter upon entering the site. It initially stood 146m high, but over the course of four and a half millennia its height has decreased by 9m. While experts still debate the exact technology used in its construction, they generally agree that it took 10,000 people about 11 years and 2.3 million limestone blocks to build it. The total weight of Cheops is estimated at six million tons. One dubious story recounts that Cheops hired his daughter out as a courtesan and required each of her admirers to give her a stone for her dad's grave. Considering that this pyramid took 3¼ million cubic yards of stone, even a life of 100 years of perfect health and romantic popularity would have provided only enough stone for the tip of the pyramid. Stairs lead up the side to the entrance into the empty tomb, which is marked by neatly carved graffiti left by 18th-century tourists.

PYRAMID OF CHEPHREN. The middle member of the Giza trio is three meters shorter than the Pyramid of Cheops, although it actually looks a bit taller because it's positioned on a higher plateau. Portions of the limestone casing that originally covered the monument still sheathe its apex, making it Egypt's most splendid pyramid. Also notice the granite on the summit; Chephren wanted to add a layer of granite atop the limestone, but died before he could start the addition.

PYRAMID OF MYCERINUS. The Pyramid of Mycerinus is small compared to its relatives. Legend has it that instead of devoting his attention to his death chamber, Mycerinus lavished his energy on his daughter, attempting to become her lover. After the grief-filled girl hanged herself, she was buried in a golden cow which was brought into the light of the sun once a year, in accordance with her dying wish. At the pyramid's northeast corner are the quarried remains of the **Mortuary Temple of Mycerinus.** Farther away, the ruins of the unexcavated Valley Temple of Mycerinus lie swathed in a blanket of sand.

SPHINX. Hewn almost entirely from rock, the Sphinx's poised figure is 80m long and 22m tall. His enigmatic smile is at once friendly and unnerving, leading Egyptians to call him **Abu al-Hul** (Father of Terror). Many centuries have aged the Sphinx, and the Ottomans didn't help things when they used him for target practice. A recent renovation project has just been completed, and the Sphinx now enters its 5th millennium in fine form.

Opinion is divided over the Sphinx's identity. Some believe that the face is a portrait of Chephren, whose pyramid lies directly behind it, while others maintain that the features represent local deity, Horan. Those who subscribe to the former theory believe that the Sphinx emerged from a sturdy knoll facing Chephren's complex. Failing to flatten it, architects transformed the knoll into the figure that lounges on the sand today. Another tale tells how Chephren, living a life of luxury, fell asleep by the sphinx's foot while hunting. The Sphinx spoke out and said, "I shall make thee Pharaoh if thou wilt dig me out of the sand." This theory does not sit well with archaeologists, who suggest that the body and head of the sphinx were carved at different times; they are not proportional to one another and have completely different erosion styles. Egyptian folklore asserts that Abu al-Hul is a half-human, half-tiger creature who protects the tombs from thieves. Whichever explanation you accept, the majesty of the Sphinx remains indisputable.

At the foot of the Sphinx, just around the corner to the south, sits the I-shaped **Valley Temple of Chephren,** discovered in 1853. Sixteen great pillars, each 15m high, support the roof of this edifice, leading up to the ever-smiling pyramid guard.

SOLAR BOAT MUSEUM. This zucchini-shaped work of postmodern architecture is against the south side of the Pyramid of Cheops. It holds the well-preserved

MIDNIGHT MARAUDERS During the full moon, more adventurous travelers have been known to make nighttime excursions to the pyramids by horseback. Both **SA** and **AA stables** stay open later around this time (call ahead to confirm) to accommodate those interested in seeing the pyramids under the stars. The desert sands reflect much of the moon's light, making it rather easy to navigate. The dark outlines of the pyramids themselves are an unforgettable sight against the purple backdrop of Cairo's sky. Rates are about the same as those in the day (E£15-20 per hour), but getting to the stables after dark is more difficult. Have a taxi drop you off near the stables (E£15) or take a series of microbuses from Doqqi. Go when the moon is full or very nearly so to ensure that there is enough light and go only in a group. Women especially should not venture out to Giza alone after dark.

Solar Boat of Cheops, one of the oldest boats in existence. It was used to transport Cheops's body and then buried so his soul could use it in the afterlife. Outside, his mortuary temple is little more than a few column segments and foundations. *(Open daily 9am-4:30pm. E£20, students E£10. Camera privileges E£10, video E£100.)*

CAMEL AND HORSE RIDING. Innumerable animals are available for rent, and their owners will approach incessantly. An hour ride on a horse or camel should cost around E£10. For longer rides and more reliable beasts, walk beyond the Sphinx and turn right after the auditorium where the sound and light show takes place. You'll find a row of reputable establishments, including **AA Stables** (☎385 05 31; open daily 5am-8pm) and **SA Stables.** (☎385 06 26. Open 7am-11pm.) They both provide professional equipment (such as boots or hats) for a reasonable rate. Although the tourist police post prices for an hour-long ride at E£12 for a horse and E£10 for a camel, the going price at these establishments is closer to E£20 for a guided trek on either. E£5-10 is a fair price without a guide (in the unlikely occasion that the owner agrees), but only confident equestrians should inquire as some mounts only obey hieroglyphs and may gallop swiftly off into the desert, ignoring their rider's hysterical yells.

SOUND AND LIGHT SHOW. As far as entertainment goes, it's the Pyramids or bust (unless you find fending off hustlers entertaining). The **sound and light show,** featuring lasers, is E£35 for a tourist seat. Call ☎385 28 80 or check *Egypt Today* to find out when the Sphinx will reveal its secrets in the language of your choice. English shows are at 8:30pm, and 6:30pm in winter. If it's solitude you seek, the people in the stables next to the Sphinx can arrange overnight expeditions through the dunes for E£20-45.

ISLAMIC CAIRO

Ibn Khaldun once said, "[H]e who has not seen Cairo cannot know the grandeur of Islam." The resplendent mosques and monuments of Cairo's medieval district rank among the world's finest examples of Islamic architecture. Unlike Damascus and Baghdad (the two other Middle Eastern capitals of the medieval Islamic world), Cairo was spared the devastation of Mongol invasions. A trip through the narrow winding streets of Islamic Cairo will not only teach you about Islamic architecture, but offer a glimpse at a way of life whose habits and pleasures have endured through time, like the domes and minarets above.

GENERAL ADVICE

It takes at least two days to explore Islamic Cairo, and the area holds riches enough to fill many more. **William Lyster** and **SPARE (Society for the Preservation of Architectural Resources in Egypt)** publish a superb set of four 3-D maps of Islamic Cairo (E£10 per map). The *City Map of Cairo* (E£10) has an indexed map of

EGYPT

Islamic Cairo. For in-depth descriptions and history, try *Islamic Monuments in Cairo: A Practical Guide,* by Caroline Williams (E£100). That book and most maps are available at the AUC Bookstore (p. 95).

Many of the important monuments charge entrance fees (E£6-12, half-price with ISIC). At free sights (mosques in particular), you will be expected to give *bakhsheesh* (E£1 should be adequate). At the biggest mosques, the man who "guards" your shoes while you are inside usually expects compensation of some kind. Students purchasing discounted tickets should only pay 50pt-E£1 in *bakhsheesh,* rather than paying the difference between the regular ticket and the student one. Where permitted, climbing the minaret is included in the ticket price. Opening hours are estimates at best, so declare your interest to whomever is around and someone will let you in; a tour of Islamic Cairo confined to unlocked doors will miss many of the city's treasures.

Most "ornamental" mosques, or those no longer used for regular prayer, are open daily from 8am to 5pm. Other mosques are open from dawn until dusk, but visitors are not welcome during prayer times. Wait a few minutes after the congregation has finished before entering. There are often separate entrances for men and women. Night visitors are often not permitted, although some travelers rave about watching the sunset paint Cairo dusty pink from atop a minaret. Avoid visiting on Fridays (noon-2pm), when the Muslim community gathers for afternoon prayer. Certain highly venerated mosques—namely, Sayyida Hussein, Sayyida Zeinab, and Sayyida Nafisa—are believed to contain the remains of descendants of Muhammad and are officially closed to non-Muslims.

As in the rest of Cairo, visitors must dress modestly in Islamic Cairo; revealing clothing will attract a great deal of unsolicited and unfriendly attention and will prevent admission to many mosques. Residents consider shorts, miniskirts, and exposed shoulders disrespectful. Women are encouraged to cover their hair in the mosques; when head coverings are required, they can usually be rented for a few piasters. In some mosques (such as Muhammad 'Ali) an entire *galabiyya* is provided for free. It is important to avoid sandals and wear clothes that you don't mind getting dirty: just as Islamic Cairo is full of charm, so are its streets full of trash and semi-dry dung. Since you will often be asked to remove your shoes, socks are a good idea. Bring a plastic bag for your shoes to avoid the 50pt charged by custodians to watch them while you are touring. Never wear shoes in a mosque, or even place the soles on a mosque floor.

 SIGHTSEEING STRATEGY. Although each of the following sights can be visited individually, *Let's Go* has divided Islamic Cairo into four easily navigable regions (each of which can be visited in a leisurely **half-day** walking tour): **Southern Islamic Cairo** and the **Mosque of Ibn Tulun** (p. 106), the **Citadel** (p. 108), **Central Islamic Cairo** (p. 109), and **North al-Mu'izz St. and the Walls** (p. 111). A stopover at **al-Azhar University** (p. 110) and the bazaar at **Khan al-Khalili** (p. 110) can easily be tacked on to any of these trips.

SOUTHERN ISLAMIC CAIRO

MOSQUE OF IBN TULUN. Built in 879 CE, the fortress-like Mosque of Ibn Tulun is the largest and third-oldest of Cairo's Islamic monuments. If you stand on Qadri St., the entrance is around the left side: once inside the gate, the **Gayer-Anderson Museum** (p. 123) is to your left and the mosque's courtyard is straight ahead. The serene courtyard covers almost seven acres and has six *mihrabs* indicating the direction to Mecca. In the center of the courtyard, an ablution fountain (*mayda'a*) added in 1296 CE by a Mamluk sultan is still used for washing before prayer time. The mosque (like many other early Islamic monuments) has pared-down decorative elements and an arcade-encompassed courtyard design based on the house of the Prophet Muhammad.

The mosque is named after Ahmed ibn Tulun, who served as the Abbasid governor of Egypt until he broke from the sultanate and established an independent city-state, Qatai'i, with its capital around this mosque. The minaret and its unusual external staircase (a harrowing climb ending in a great view) were probably modeled after the Great Mosque of Samarra in Iraq. A less substantiated theory explains that it was built before it became clear that the *muezzin* could see impure things during his ascent to the top of the minaret. His glimpses of unveiled women relaxing in their homes led architects to build inner stairwells with hopes that the *muezzin* would stay more focused on prayer. *(Take minibus #54 (٥٤) or bus #72 (٧٢) from Tahrir Sq., or take the Metro to Sayyida Zeinab and then bus #501 (٥٠١), 35pt) to Qadri St., which leads to Ibn Tulun. Coming from Giza, take bus #923 (٩٢٣); from the Pyramids, take bus #905 (٩٠٥); or share a taxi (E£5) to "Masjid Ibn Tulun." Open daily 8am-6pm; in winter 8am-5pm; Ramadan 8am-4pm. E£6, students E£3.)*

TOMB OF SHAGARAT AL-DURR. Heading east on Tulun St., turn right onto al-Khalifa St. to find the small Tomb of Shagarat al-Durr on your left. Built in 1250 CE, the tomb is the burial place of a politically prominent Muslim woman (one of only a dozen women to have ruled in the Muslim world) and the last Ayyubid building constructed in Cairo. Shagarat al-Durr (Tree of Pearls) was a slave who rose to power after marrying al-Salih Ayyub, the final ruling member of Salah al-Din's Ayyubid Dynasty. After having her son murdered, Shagarat al-Durr declared herself queen and governed Egypt alone for 80 days before marrying the leader of the Mamluk forces and engineering the succession of the Mamluk Dynasty. The renegade couple managed to rule happily until the queen discovered that her new husband was considering a second marriage and had him murdered as well. Not to be outdone, the prospective second wife avenged the death of her lover by beating Shagarat al-Durr to death with a pair of wooden clogs and then hurling her body from the top of the nearby Citadel, leaving her corpse to the jackals and dogs. The remains were put together in this small, rather unremarkable tomb. Even so, the wall mosaics are worth the *bakhsheesh* (E£1).

If you continue on al-Ashraf Khalifa St. you will find the Mosque of Sayyida Nafisa (see p. 115). Retrace your steps to the left to return to the Mosque of Ibn Tulun. From the main entrance of Ibn Tulun, head left and take a right at the intersection with Khodairi St., which eventually turns into al-Saliba St.

SABIL UMM 'ABBAS. On the left side of Saliba St. is Sabil Umm 'Abbas, an Islamic endowment that became the home of the **Life and Culture Center** in 1990. Tucked away in Islamic Cairo, the artists rarely get visitors and are anxious to share their passions with interested travelers. The medieval exterior inscribed with Islamic calligraphy contrasts with the interior works of contemporary Egyptian artists, which include paintings, textile designs, silk screens, and remarkable lamp shades. *(Open Sa-Th 9am-2pm. Free.)*

MOSQUE AND KHANQAH OF 'AMR SHAYKHUN. Walk north on al-Saliba St. past the intersection with al-Siyuqiyya St. to find these two buildings facing each other on opposite sides of the street, complete with matching facades, doors, and minarets. The entrance to the mosque (the building on the right as you walk north on al-Saliba St.) is up an alley—pop in to check out the amazing stained glass windows installed to keep out evil *djinns*. General Shaykhun is buried in the *khanqah*, parts of which are undergoing renovations. Slip up the stairway near the door to explore the long hallways of cells where Sufi mystics once lived.

▨SULTAN HASSAN COMPLEX. Even compared with the mosque of Muhammad 'Ali which it faces, this masterpiece from the Mamluk era is still impressive. Unlike the Pyramids at Giza, which convey the mighty power of the pharaohs with their own might and size, the majesty of Sultan Hassan's complex stands in complete opposition to his weak rule. The only time Sultan Hassan ever slipped out from under the thumb of the Mamluk generals who controlled him was in 1356 CE, when he built this massive *madrasa* and mausoleum; unfortunately, the generals murdered him when they found out his construction costs had nearly broken the bank. The spacious interior courtyard is surrounded by four vaulted arcades known as *irwans*, each of which once housed one of the four schools of judicial thought in Sunni Islam. On either side of the easternmost *mihrab*, massive, bronze doors open onto the beautifully decorated mausoleum: the inlaid marble-work is the finest in Cairo. *(To reach Sultan Hassan and the Rifa'i Mosque (as well as the Citadel), continue down Saliba St. to Salah al-Din Sq. From Tahrir Sq., take bus #173 (١٧٣) or #194 (١٩٤) or minibus #72 (٧٢). From the southern edge of 'Ataba Sq., take Muhammad 'Ali St., which becomes al-Qala'a (Citadel) St. To get back to Tahrir Sq., take bus #194 (١٩٤) or #609 (٦٠٩). Open Sa-Th 8am-6pm, F 9-11am and 2-5pm; Oct.-Mar. Sa-Th 8am-5pm, F 9-11am and 2-5pm; Ramadan Sa-Th 8am-4pm, F 9-11am and 2-4pm. E£12, students E£6.)*

RIFA'I MOSQUE. Next door to the Sultan Hassan complex stands the enormous Rifa'i Mosque, built by the mother of Khedive Isma'il, who is buried here with her son and grandsons King Fouad and King Farouk (Egypt's last monarch). In the room next to Farouk lies the tomb of Muhammad Reza Pahlavi, the last Shah of Iran. Rifa'i's stupendous size and polished interior will make your neck sore. Near the ticket window is a pleasant lawn—a great place to catch your breath before moving on to other sights. *(Same directions, hours, and prices as Sultan Hassan Complex.)*

CITADEL (AL-QALA'A)

*From Tahrir Sq., take **bus** #82 (٨٢), 83 (٨٣), or 609 (٦٠٩). From 'Ataba Sq., take **bus** #401 (٤٠١) or **minibus** #50 (٥٠) or 55 (٥٥). Enter from either the northern or southern gate. From Hassan and Rifa'i, head right (south) along the wall and circle the Citadel. The entrance is on Salah Salem St. Single women should not visit alone. Open daily 8am-6pm; Oct.-Mar. 8am-5pm; Ramadan 8am-4pm; closed Friday during prayer; entrance locked 1hr. before closing. E£20, students E£10, including all museums and mosques.*

Crowned by the dome and tall minarets of the Muhammad 'Ali mosque, the mind-bogglingly enormous Citadel *(al-Qala'a)* watches over the tumult of Islamic Cairo's tangled alleys. Construction was begun by Salah al-Din in 1176 CE, and the building has been continually expanded and modified since then (most notably by the Mamluks and Muhammad 'Ali). Almost all the rulers of Egypt from the 13th century until 1874 lived here. The complex contains three large mosques and four operating museums: as you walk around the curved road from the Citadel gate, the massive **Mosque of Muhammad 'Ali** will be on your left and the **Mosque of Sultan al-Nasser** on your right; several courtyards away is the third mosque, the **Mosque of Suleiman Basha.** To the southwest of the Mosque of Muhammad 'Ali is the **Qasr al-Gowhara** (Diamond Palace).

MOSQUE OF MUHAMMAD 'ALI. The mosque of Muhammad 'Ali is easy to spot from anywhere in the Citadel. Those flying into Cairo can see its silver domes glistening in the sun. In 1830, 'Ali leveled the western surface of the Citadel, filled in the famous 13th-century Mamluk palace Qasr al-Ablaq, and built his mosque on the ruins as a reminder of Turkish domination. Modeled after the Aya Sophia, the Mosque is a perennial favorite of postcard-makers and tourists, but is disparaged by art historians as a third-rate copy of the great Ottoman mosques in Istanbul. The edifice is also known as the Alabaster Mosque because it is covered inside and out with the clearest alabaster, hauled over from Beni Suef. Only one outer face remains bare: when Muhammad 'Ali died, so did the funding.

The mosque is entered through a courtyard presided over by an ornate (and non-functional) gingerbread-house-like clock of French design. In 1845, when Muhammad 'Ali presented France with the obelisk from Luxor Temple (which now stands in the Place de la Concorde in Paris), King Louis Philippe thanked the ruler by presenting him with this clock. Egyptians have always been somewhat ticked off about getting a dud of a clock in return for a first-rate obelisk, but this didn't stop Muhammad 'Ali from decorating the interior of his mosque in a 19th-century French-salon-inspired style, complete with lavish Parisian architectural details (visible mostly on the five main domes and 15 mini-domes), a chandelier, and 365 tiny lanterns. Much more impressive is the view from the terrace by the exit of the mosque, where you can see all of Cairo and the Pyramids at Giza sprawled out before you. At prayer time, the simultaneous calls to prayer from each of the thousands of mosques in Cairo join together in a haunting, almost otherworldly chorus.

MOSQUE OF SULEIMAN BASHA. The Turkish-inspired Mosque of Suleiman Basha was the first Ottoman mosque in Cairo, built in 1527 by one of the Ottoman governors who headed the Janissary corps. The small-domed mosque, also known as **Sariat al-Gabal** (Mountain Palace), has a cozy prayer hall decorated with different calligraphic styles and a courtyard consisting of four *irwans*.

MOSQUE OF SULTAN AL-NASSER. This is one of the few major buildings in the Citadel to escape the hand of architectural busybody Muhammad 'Ali (although the interior was stripped by Sultan Selin several hundred years before 'Ali arrived). The mosque is well-known for the tile decoration on its minarets, constructed by Iranian craftsmen. Go through the gate with two flags on your left to enter another courtyard with superb views of Cairo and the mosques below.

QASR AL-GOWHARA (THE DIAMOND PALACE). This half-palace was built in full in 1811 by Muhammad 'Ali and named after one of his wives. In 1974, a burglary attempt resulted in a fire that destroyed half of the palace. The surviving half consists of a large reception room (in the excessive French style 'Ali loved), where 'Ali received 500 of his closest Mamluk allies before having them murdered on their way out. Also on display are a few of the gold- and silver-adorned tapestries from the Ka'aba in Mecca; Mecca presented Egypt with one of these tapestries every year until 1961. Only punch-drunk Muhammad 'Ali fans should walk over to the **Carriage (Hantour) Museum,** which houses carriages of the great one's family.

CENTRAL ISLAMIC CAIRO

From Salah al-Din Sq., walk north along the Citadel for 100m until Bab al-Wazir St.

BLUE MOSQUE (MOSQUE OF AQSUNQUR). This 14th-century edifice owes its name to the colored Syrian tiles that line the interior, added in 1652 by a Turkish governor homesick for Istanbul's grand tiled mosques, and not to the words scrawled in blue marker on the main door. The prayer hall to the right has one of the oldest marble *minbars* (pulpits) in the Islamic world. The top of the minaret is a great vantage point for viewing the Citadel to the south, Khan al-Khalili to the north, and the southern end of the City of the Dead to the east. *(On Bab al-Wazir St., several blocks down and on the right. Open daily 8am-6pm; in winter 8am-5pm; Ramadan 8am-4pm. E£6, students E£3.)*

MOSQUE OF QIJMAS AL-ISHAQI. This mosque, dedicated to the Chief of the Royal Stable and Chargé d'Affaires for the pilgrimage to Mecca, is on al-Darb al-Ahmar (Red Way), which commemorates Muhammad 'Ali's massacre of the Mamluks. Its unremarkable exterior gives no inkling of the serene, colorfully lit interior of inlaid marble and wood set with complicated ivory patterns. Under the prayer mats in the east *irwan* lies an ornate marble mosaic floor, an example of geometric Mamluk design (tip the custodian to uncover it for you). *(Head two blocks north of Bab al-Wazir St., where it joins with another street and becomes al-Darb al-Ahmar. To get into the mosque, gesture to the locals and they will retrieve the custodian. Open daily 8am-4pm. Free, but bakhsheesh is appropriate.)*

BAB ZUWEILA. Bab Zuweila is the most impressive of the three remaining gates into Fatimid Cairo, named after the Berber tribe that once guarded it. Egyptians also call it *Bawwabat al-Metwali* (Gate of the Tax Collector) after the civil servant who used to wait for victims there. Nowadays you are more likely to get mobbed by ragged children selling cigarettes. It is topped by two minarets from the Mosque of al-Mu'ayyad, symbolizing Cairo's transformation from the heart of Fatimid-era military operations to the center of the Islamic world. *(The gate is at the intersection of al-Darb al-Ahmar and al-Mu'izz St.)*

MOSQUE OF AL-MU'AYYAD. The Mamluk ruler al-Mu'ayyad was once imprisoned on the site of this mosque; upon becoming Sultan, he tore down the prison and built this house of worship over it between 1415 and 1420. The huge door may remind you of those at the Sultan Hassan Mosque: in fact, it was taken from there. The arcaded building has a lovely garden and excellent inlaid marblework in the prayer hall. Give the guard *bakhsheesh* and he will let you climb the minaret for a spectacular view of Islamic Cairo. *(Go north through Bab Zuweila; the mosque is on the left. Open daily 8:30am-9pm. E£6, students E£3.)*

AL-AZHAR UNIVERSITY

Al-Azhar University is the oldest continuously operating university in the world and the foremost Islamic theological center. Established in 972 CE by the Fatimids (who belonged to the Shi'a Muslim sect), it rose to pre-eminence in the 15th century as a center for the study of Qur'anic law and doctrine. It is still considered to be the final arbiter on all doctrinal issues related to Sunni Islam, the sect to which the focus of study at al-Azhar was shifted once the Ayyubids came to power. Both the University and the Mosque of al-Azhar stand just a few steps from the midpoint of al-Mu'izz St. at the end of al-Azhar St., facing the square.

AL-AZHAR MOSQUE. To reach the central courtyard of this arcaded mosque, enter through the double arched gate and pass under the **Minaret of Qaytbay** (built in 1469). Although the stucco decoration of the courtyard's facade is a reconstruction, the *mihrab* in the central aisle is the original. The **library,** just left of the main entrance, holds over 80,000 manuscripts. For about E£1, the caretaker will allow you to climb one of the locked **minarets** for a fantastic view of Cairo and Khan al-Khalili below you. *(Open Sa-Th 7:30am-9pm, F 9am-noon and 2-7pm. E£12, students E£6. Women without head coverings must cover their heads at the entrance.)*

THE UNIVERSITY. Around the corner from the mosque is where al-Azhar's 8000 students take classes from October to May. Students sit on the plush red carpets of the mosque's *riwaq* (arcaded aisle around the central courtyard) cramming for exams. The theological curriculum has remained virtually unchanged since the Mamluk era (physics and medicine are more recent arrivals). Women, though allowed in the mosque, may not study at al-Azhar; they attend a sister school near 'Abbasiyya Sq. The university uses the Socratic method of teaching, with a professor seated in the center of a circle of students. Give a small consideration to the caretaker and he'll show you the **tomb** of the university's founder.

SAYYIDNA AL-HUSSEIN MOSQUE. The Sayyidna al-Hussein Mosque was built in the Turkish style (note the pencil minarets) by Khedive Isma'il in the 1870s. It is highly revered throughout the Islamic world as the resting place of the skull of Hussein, grandson of the Prophet Muhammad. The head is rumored to have been transported to Cairo in a green silk bag in 1153, almost 500 years after the death of its owner in the Battle of Karbala in Iraq. On *'Eid Mawlid al-Nabi* (Birthday of the Prophet), the President of Egypt traditionally comes to pray at Sayyidna al-Hussein while boisterous festivities take place in the square. During Ramadan, this square is the best place to witness the breaking of the fast after evening prayers (about 8pm). Restaurants display their fare half an hour before prayers begin, and famished patrons stampede to the tables afterward. After blood-sugar levels return to normal, the square erupts in celebration. *(Across al-Hussein Sq., 100m north of al-Azhar Mosque. Closed to non-Muslims.)*

KHAN AL-KHALILI AND ENVIRONS

KHAN AL-KHALILI BAZAAR. Khan al-Khalili, just west of al-Hussein Sq., is the largest and most notorious bazaar in Egypt. The Mamluk prince Gharkas al-Khalili established the market in the 1380s. Today it is still a requisite stop for countless tour buses, whose occupants pour forth to find that perfect little gift for friends and family back home. Revel in the free-market frenzy as you pass through the copperware, perfume, spice, gold, silver, and *sheesha* sections of this massive bazaar. Though the tacky souvenirs are often overpriced, the time-honored institution of bargaining still thrives. Be ferocious if you intend to strike a good deal (often a third of the starting price, if not less); pretending to walk away usually elicits a discount. But be forewarned that there is an unwritten consensus among Khan shopkeepers that they will not go below certain prices. If you are allowed to walk away after making a bid, you probably won't get a better price elsewhere. The farther you go from the heart of the market, the more authentic the wares become. A word of warning: Khan al-Khalili is a **thieves'** paradise: many a hard-won bargain has been rendered futile by a wallet disappearance. Also, be sure not to enter shops with any hustlers whom you meet in the street; the store will inflate the prices to include the hustler's commission. After a hard day's worth of bargaining, Cairenes stay up late into the night at the Khan's many sidewalk cafes. Among the most renowned of these is **Fishawi's**, which offers respite from the market bustle with flavored *sheesha* and exotic juices (see **Ahwas**, p. 129). Although women traveling alone will be safe, they should be prepared to deal with men who come a little too close to whisper unsolicited "compliments".

AL-MUSKI ST. Slightly less tourist-ridden, but more crowded and dirtier than Khan's bazaar, this long bazaar is where Egyptians come to shop for everyday items like men's cologne, shoes, cloth, furniture, pillowcases, and food. Al-Muski stretches from al-Mu'izz St. all the way to Port Said St., running parallel to and one block north of al-Azhar St. It is also a convenient route between downtown and Islamic Cairo. For more places to shop in Cairo, see **Shopping**, p. 126.

AL-GHOURI COMPLEX. This al-Mu'izz St. complex consists of a *madrasa* and mosque (currently closed for renovations) across the street from a **mausoleum**, where whirling dervishes enchant visitors (W and Sa 9pm; see **Performing Arts**, p. 124). Al-Ghouri also hosts plays every once in a while; stop by and ask the guards about the calendar. From the *madrasa*, mausoleum, and mosque, head east on al-Azhar St., then right onto Sheikh Muhammad Abduh St. At No. 3 (on your right), you'll see the magnificently preserved *wikala* (built in 1505), now transformed into a center for handicrafts and folkloric arts. *(Mausoleum and wikala open Sa-Th 9am-9pm. Both E£6, students E£3.)*

NORTHERN AL-MU'IZZ STREET AND THE WALLS

To minimize mileage in this area, walk from al-Azhar up al-Mu'izz St., through both Bab al-Futuh and Bab al-Nasser. Return by way of al-Gamaliyya St., which runs roughly parallel to al-Mu'izz St. from Bab al-Nasser past the Mosque of al-Hussein to the square in front of al-Azhar. Expect to shell out about E£15 to each of the sites below.

The section of al-Mu'izz St. between al-Azhar Mosque and Bab al-Futuh was once known as *Bayn al-Qasrayn* ("between the two palaces," also the title of one of Naguib Mahfouz's novels) after the two Fatimid palaces that once stood here. Although those palaces were destroyed by the rulers of later dynasties, the area is still lined with many Fatimid and early Mamluk architectural attractions, and a brisk walk through this part of al-Mu'izz St. is a wonderful way to see stunning Islamic architecture from the outside. This area is also home to a **bazaar** for restaurant supplies that is locally known as the best place to buy reasonably priced *sheesha* pipes. Forget that gaudy and overpriced tourist junk in the heart of Khan al-Khalili and shop here alongside *ahwa* owners for authentic *sheeshas* (E£15-45).

COMPLEX OF SULTAN AL-MALIK AL-SALIH AYYUB. The last ruler of Salah al-Din's Ayyubid Dynasty and the husband of Shagarat al-Durr (whose tomb lies nearby in Islamic Cairo, p. 107), Sultan Ayyub built this tomb, *madrasa*, and mosque in the 13th century. You'll recognize it by its square minaret pointing resolutely heavenward. The *madrasa* has ornate arched windows in the shape of boat keels. The custodian has keys to the adjacent domed mosque. *(Proceed north on al-Mu'izz St. from the intersection with Gohar al-Qa'id St. After passing four small side streets, you can see the tomb and madrasa on your right; the entrance is off a small alley on the right.)*

EGYPT

COMPLEX OF SULTAN QALAWUN. The Mamluk Sultan Qalawun sponsored the construction of this impressive mausoleum, *madrasa*, and hospital in 1284 (prior to his death en route to attack the Crusader fortress in Akko). Although the Mamluks and the Crusaders didn't get along very well, their architectural styles did— note the Romanesque windows borrowed from the Crusaders and their Levantine castles. Only the three high *irwans* of the original *muristan* (mental hospital) remain. The ornate stucco work inside is original, though the undersides of the arches have been restored. The exquisite wood screen separating the tomb from the rectangular forecourt is also untouched. Before the 14th century, Egypt was the world's center for glasswork, and the Qalawun mausoleum offers especially dazzling glass mosaic work. *(On al-Mu'izz St. Complex open daily 8am-6pm. To gain access to the mausoleum, hunt down the guard, purchase a ticket, and have him unlock the door. E£6, students E£3. Video cameras are not allowed without written permission from a tourist office; the nearest one is on al-Darb al-Asfar, next to Beit al-Suheimi.)*

COMPLEX OF SULTAN BARQUQ. Barquq, the first of the Circassian Mamluk sultans, rose to power in the 14th century through a series of assassinations. His **mosque** was erected in 1386, a century after Qalawun's complex, and the difference in style is striking. The inner courtyard has four *irwans*, the largest and most elaborate of which doubles as a prayer hall. Its beautiful timber roof has been restored and painted in rich hues of blue and gold. Four porphyry columns (quarried in pharaonic times from mountains near the Red Sea) support the ceiling, while the floor is decorated with disks of marble that are actually slices of Greek and Roman columns (Egypt has no indigenous marble). *Bakhsheesh* gets you into the Sultan's **tomb,** constructed of high-quality inlaid marble with an elegant green and gold vine motif decorating the drum of the dome. *(On al-Mu'izz St., next door to the complex of Sultan al-Nasser Muhammad. Open daily 10am-7pm. E£6, students E£3.)*

MOSQUE OF AL-AQMAR. This small but architecturally important Fatimid-era mosque was built in 1125 CE, the first Cairene mosque to have the stone-facade-and-shell motif (found within its keel-arched niche) that became popular during that era. Al-Aqmar means "the moons" and refers to the way the stone facade sparkles in the moonlight. The northern corner is typical of later Cairene architecture; the height of the niche is just about equal to that of a loaded camel, and it was intended to make the turn onto the side street easier for the hump-backed creatures to negotiate. *(Bear left at the fork in al-Mu'izz St. and continue north along al-Mu'izz to the next right-hand side street. Mosque of al-Aqmar is on the corner.)*

BEIT AL-SUHEIMI AND ENVIRONS. The 16th-century Beit al-Suheimi was built by Suheimi, the *sheikh* of al-Azhar Mosque, for himself and his various wives. The house, Cairo's finest old building, is under renovation, but should be open within the next year. Artisans have already restored finely carved wood ceilings and ornately colorful stained-glass windows. Tile mosaics and marble floors will soon be uncovered. The *khanqah* known as **Baybars al-Gashankir** is nearby. Erected in 1310, it is the oldest surviving example of a *khanqah* in Cairo. *(Proceeding north from al-Aqmar Mosque, turn right onto al-Darb al-Asfar and follow the winding alley about 50m. The doorway on the left marked with a small, green plaque is the entrance to Beit al-Suheimi. Walk along al-Darb al-Asfar away from al-Mu'izz St. and you'll eventually come to al-Gamaliyya St. Across the street is the Baybars al-Gashankir.)*

NORTHERN WALLS. Islamic Cairo is bordered on the north by the remains of the Fatimid walls. Built in 1087, these colossal fortifications are the best surviving examples of pre-Crusader Islamic military architecture. Three of the rampart's original gates still stand: **Bab al-Nasser** ("Victory Gate," at the top of al-Gamaliyya St.) and **Bab al-Futuh** ("Conquest Gate," literally "Opening Gate," at the north end of al-Mu'izz St. in front of al-Hakim Mosque) are connected by a stretch of wall so thick it accommodates a tunnel; these walls once wrapped around the Fatimid city to **Bab Zuweila.** Look for graffiti left by French soldiers at the end of the 18th century during the Napoleonic invasion, and then check out the spiffed-up sections of the walls restored by more Frenchies at the end of the 20th.

AL-HAKIM MOSQUE. The Fatimid-era al-Hakim Mosque was built between 990 and 1010 and remains the second largest mosque in Cairo. The grandson of thoroughfare namesake al-Mu'izz, al-Hakim is often referred to as the "Mad Caliph"; he was actually the inspiration for the crazy Ali-Hakim in Rodgers and Hammerstein's famous musical *Oklahoma!*. Al-Hakim's unpredictable rages meant death to Christians, Jews, his enemies, his friends, and, on one occasion, all the dogs in Cairo. He ensured the confinement of women by forbidding cobblers to make shoes for them. He even banned the cooking of *mulukhiga* (a green vegetable eaten throughout Egypt), renaming it *mulukhiyya* (meaning "royal") and restricting its consumption to his family. He was assassinated soon after he announced that he was an incarnation of God. His chief theologian, al-Darazi, fled to Syria and founded the Druze sect there. The mosque was recently restored (amid great controversy) by the Aga Khan Foundation, making it suitable not only for prayer, but also for ballroom and discotheque dancing; the Foundation chose not to restore the mosque to its original glory but instead jazzed it up with chandeliers and a neon *mihrab*. *(Just inside the walls between Bab al-Nasser and Bab al-Futuh. Entrance off al-Mu'izz St. Open daily 9am-6pm. E£6, students E£3. Climbing minaret permitted.)*

CITIES OF THE DEAD

The Cities of the Dead teem with life, serving as home to some of Cairo's finest Islamic architecture along with several thousand (living and breathing) Cairenes. The areas to the northeast and south of the Citadel contain hundreds of spectacular tombs and mausolea; unlike their more pious Islamic predecessors, Mamluk sultans spared no expense in the construction of their final resting places (perhaps they knew that their dynasties would not survive). During the late 1960s, a serious housing shortage for lower-income Egyptians (combined with migration from the countryside to the city) created the trend of occupying burial chambers. Unlike most graveyards, the Cities of the Dead have streets, house numbers (which are not even found in Cairo's city center), and even a regular bus system and postal service. The modern residents of the medieval necropoles dwell amid the funerary architecture, and many households have even incorporated the grave markers into their houses and yards. Tombs frequently serve as clotheslines and soccer goals. On Fridays, the gravesites swarm with visitors arriving to pay their respects to the deceased. Many of the plots are enclosed by walls, encompassing an adjoining chamber and small house where families pray for their ancestors on holy days. The Egyptian custom of picnicking at the family tomb on feast days may be an ancient holdover from pharaonic times, when the corpse was believed to require nourishment for good health in the afterlife. Visitors are not permitted in the mosques on Fridays or during prayers.

NORTHERN CEMETERY

Go east along al-Azhar St. from al-Azhar Mosque, hugging the wall on your left. When the road forks, turn left under the overpass; this leads to the southern section of the northern necropolis. Bus #176 (١٧٦) from 'Ataba Sq. stops in front of the Mausoleum of Barquq. Bus #77 (٧٧) or 904 (٩٠٤) from Tahrir Sq. stops in the cemetery.

The Northern Cemetery, northeast of al-Azhar, has broad avenues and courtyards containing the finest monuments of the Cities of the Dead. Posh modern mausolea sit alongside structures dating from the later Mamluk period (14-16th centuries).

TOMBS OF TULBAY AND TUGHAY. These tombs were erected in honor of two wives of Sultan al-Nasser Muhammad. Tughay was renowned for her beauty and piety, and her grieving husband constructed an appropriately fine tomb for her. The base of the dome is decorated with tiles in the Iranian style, fashionable after a peace was reached with Iran two decades prior to the tombs' construction. Egypt's penchant for the cosmopolitan during that era is evidenced by the use of arabesques and Chinese peony designs on the central *mihrab*. Although the harems of the Mamluk sultans were frequently hotbeds of intrigue and jealousy (and even more frequently just hot beds), Sultana Tulbay was quite close to Sultana Tughay and built her tomb next to that of her deceased friend. *(From al-Azhar St., turn right at the first long street, and walk one block south. Facing the tombs with your back to the long street, Tughay's tomb is on the right; Tulbay's is on the left.)*

◼MAUSOLEUM AND MOSQUE OF QAYTBAY. Enter the complex through the marble northern doorway, passing through a rectangular sanctuary that affords the best view of the polychromatically striped brickwork of the complex (whose likeness graces the Egyptian one-pound note). Qaytbay was a Mamluk slave who rose through the ranks of the army to become leader of Egypt near the end of the 15th century, ruling for 28 years. Qaytbay was not without enemies, so he watched his back, designing his **mausoleum** with three secret doors for quick escapes. Apparently his efforts paid off—Qaytbay was the only Mamluk ruler not to be assassinated. Qaytbay designed the prayer niche to require devotees to pray over the ruler's remains in order to face Mecca. The mausoleum also contains two black stones bearing footprints said to be those of the Prophet Muhammad. The **mosque** itself has a remarkable dome (with an unusual echo effect that the caretaker will demonstrate) that uses both geometric and arabesque designs. *(Upon leaving the alley, turn left and walk 2 blocks, then turn right at the first major street (there will be a small domed tomb on the left opposite the start of the street). Follow this street for 3 blocks; turn left up the lane with a stone arch, around 40m down the lane. This is the gate of Qaytbay's complex. Open daily 9am-9:30pm. E£6, students E£3. Bakhsheesh required to climb the minaret).*

COMPLEX OF SULTAN ASHRAF BARSBAY. Originally intended as a *khanqah*, the 15th-century **mosque** of Sultan Ashraf Barsbay has meticulously fashioned marble mosaic floors; lift the prayer mats to see the colorful tilework. Barsbay pulled out all the stops to construct his combined mosque, *khanqah* and mausoleum complex in 1432. Adjoining the mosque to the north is Barsbay's **mausoleum,** a domed chamber containing his remains and those of his slaves, an elaborately decorated *mihrab*, and gleaming mother-of-pearl and marble mosaics. The dome decorations are complex geometric designs, which replace the chevrons used in earlier tombs (such as that of Barquq). The wooden *minbar* is one of the best in Cairo. *(Three blocks north of the Qaytbay complex and 50m south of the Mausoleum of Barquq, along the cemetery's main thoroughfare. Open daily 9am-sunset. Free.)*

MAUSOLEUM OF BARQUQ. Like the mausoleum of Sultan Barsbay, this mausoleum (identified by its twin domes and minarets) was built in 1411 as a *khanqah* for Sufi mystics. There are limited decorations in the mausoleum: excessive ornamentation was seen as a distraction from the contemplation of the full glory of Allah. This asceticism did not apply to Barquq's mausoleum in the northern corner, which has the largest stone domes in Cairo, though not as intricate as those of Barsbay and Qaytbay. Behind the mosque is a modern military cemetery. *(North of the Barsbay complex. Open daily 8am-6pm; in winter 8am-5pm. E£6, students E£3.)*

TOMBS. Built in 1456 CE, the **Tomb of Barsbay al-Bagasi** is decorated with an intricate geometrical design resembling a tulip, a variation on the Moroccan motif of *dari w ktaf* (cheek and shoulder). The nearby **Tomb of Emir Suleiman** was built about 90 years later; its dome is decorated with a series of zig-zag stripes. *(In front of the Mausoleum of Barquq. To get back to 'Ataba or Tahrir Sq., either take bus #167 (١٦٧) from the bus stop in the square to the west of Barquq's complex or ask someone for help and they'll tell you which bus goes downtown. Free, but caretaker will expect a E£1-2 of bakhsheesh.)*

SOUTHERN CEMETERY

The Southern Cemetery is a sprawling expanse of tombs from the Fatimid period to the present, where the silence is disturbed only by occasional noise from the squatters who inhabit the area (and make it unsafe for women to travel here at night). The entire region is easily accessible by foot from the Mosque of Ibn Tulun, Sultan Hassan, or the Citadel. From Ibn Tulun or Sultan Hassan, proceed east to Salah al-Din Sq., just southeast of the Citadel, then head directly south following the southern slope of the Citadel. When you reach the traffic circle, walk under the overpass and take the right-hand fork, al-Qadiriyya St., which becomes **Imam al-Shafi'i St.**, the main thoroughfare in the cemetery. You can also take bus #82 (٨٢) or #182 (١٨٢) or minibus #54 (٥٤) from Tahrir Sq.

MAUSOLEUM OF IMAM AL-SHAFI'I. The Southern Cemetery's most impressive edifice is the celebrated Mausoleum of Imam al-Shafi'i. The largest Islamic mortuary chamber in Egypt, the mausoleum was erected in 1211 by Salah al-Din's brother and successor in honor of the great Imam al-Shafi'i, founder of one of the four schools of judicial thought of Sunni Islam. Shafi'i Islam is still the dominant judicial school in Egypt and much of East Africa. In 1178, Salah al-Din built a large monument over the grave of Imam al-Shafi'i, which is currently housed within the 13th-century mausoleum and often crowded with Muslims offering prayers. The teak memorial depicts the Imam himself, and is one of the finest surviving pieces of Ayyubid wood-carving. Two mosques adjoin the tomb chamber. The 1190 mosque is closed to non-Muslims. The 1763 mosque, open to all, remains a center of worship and has a distinctive boat that holds grain for birds on its dome. *(Bus #72 (٧٢) from Abd al-Munem Riad Station goes to the Mausoleum. Open daily 6am-7pm. Free, but E£1 bakhsheesh appropriate.)*

TOMB OF THE FAMILY OF MUHAMMAD 'ALI. Just as Muhammad 'Ali spent plenty of time and money on his country, he put an equal amount of effort into providing for his family (especially their remains). His favorite wife, Tulun, her sons, and their families are all buried in these marble tombs, directly behind the tomb of the Imam Shafi'i. Like 'Ali's mosque, which is criticized by art historians as being a third-rate imitation of the mosques of Istanbul, the tombs fail stylistically, decorated in gaudy colors and outlandish designs. The headpieces on each tomb indicate the gender and rank of the deceased. *(Known to most public transportation drivers by its Arabic name, Haush al-Basha. Open daily 9am-9pm. E£6, students E£3.)*

MOSQUE OF SAYYIDA NAFISA. Those approaching the Southern Cemetery can't miss Sayyida Nafisa's tall, single minaret and ornate dome on the western edge. The mosque is Egypt's third-holiest Islamic shrine and one of Cairo's three congregational mosques. It honors the great-great-great-granddaughter of the Prophet, who died in 824 CE and began attracting droves of pilgrims to her tomb soon after. So many mausolea were erected in the immediate vicinity of her tomb that historians suspect that it was this shrine that sparked the development of the Southern Cemetery. Although the mosque is closed to non-Muslims, the beautiful white dome, the well-kept exterior, and nearby grassy lawns merit a visit.

TOMBS OF ABBASID CALIPHS. Adjoining the Mosque of Sayyida Nafisa on the eastern side are the less-than-impressive Tombs of Abbasid Caliphs. At the peak of their authority, the Abbasid caliphs ruled the entire Muslim world (except Spain) from Baghdad. The last reigning caliph fled Baghdad in 1258 after invading Mongols toppled the regime. The Mamluk sultan welcomed the caliph upon his arrival in Egypt and went so far as to exalt the deposed ruler in an effort to legitimize his own rule. Subsequent Mamluk rulers continued to harbor a succession of caliphs, all the while preventing them from gaining any real power. Finally, the sultan in Istanbul declared himself caliph in 1517, thereby consolidating the authority of the Ottoman Sultanate. The Abbasid caliphs have since been deposed, but members of the family are still buried within the 13th-century mausoleum. *(Caretaker will unlock the gates for E£1 bakhsheesh.)*

EGYPT

OLD CAIRO

Old Cairo is a remarkable testament to the religious tolerance of the Islamic dynasties: mosques, Coptic churches, and a synagogue all coexist here peacefully; indeed, the region known as Old Cairo consists of Christian **Coptic Cairo** (below) and heavily Islamic **al-Fustat** (p. 118). Al-Fustat was once the site of the first Islamic capital of Egypt, but today much of Old Cairo is the center of Cairo's Jewish community. Although most of the Jewish population left in 1949 and 1956, approximately 30 families still inhabit this quarter and worship at the ancient **Ben-Ezra Synagogue** (p. 117). The easiest way to reach Old Cairo is to take the **Metro** from Tahrir Sq. toward Helwan to Mari Girgis station (50pt). Although all of these sites can be visited separately, visiting them in the order they are presented makes for an excellent and easily navigable daytrip around Coptic Cairo and al-Fustat.

COPTIC CAIRO

Ancient Egypt inspires images of towering pyramids, hieroglyphs, and mummy cases dripping with jewels. Many mistakenly assume that this ancient pharaonic era shifted directly into the Islamic age of mosques and medieval fortifications. However, the interim period between Cleopatra and the caliphs was the time of the Roman conquest, which led to the spread of Christianity and the conversion of the Emperor Constantine in 324 CE. Indeed, Christianity was the dominant faith in Egypt for 300 years (from the fall of the pagan Romans to the arrival of Islam), and currently some five to seven million Christian Copts live in Egypt, mostly in Coptic Cairo or in Middle Egypt (see **Religion and Ethnicity,** p. 68).

Most of Cairo's Coptic churches are tucked away from the street, and the older structures have simple entrances. Though the churches do not charge admission and hardly require any *bakhsheesh* (indeed, this neighborhood is pleasantly free of the hustlers that infest other sections of Cairo), all have donation boxes. Those seeking serenity should avoid the churches on Sundays or the church saint's day, when hundreds of Coptic Cairenes and their children migrate from church to church, receiving blessings and pronouncing their faith. Renovations of the churches and other structures in Coptic Cairo began in the summer of 2000; entrance to these buildings, however, is still allowed. (*Open daily 9:30am-5pm; mass daily 7-9am. No photography.*)

COPTIC MUSEUM. Directly across from the Mari Girgis Metro station is the Coptic Museum, home to the world's largest and finest collection of Coptic art, texts, textiles, metalwork, and iconographic materials. For more details, see the complete listing for the Coptic Museum on p. 123.

Hmm, call home or eat lunch?
With  you can do both.

Nathan Lane for YOU^{SM}.

No doubt, traveling on a budget is tough. So tear out this wallet guide and keep it with you during your travels. With YOU, calling home from overseas is affordable and easy.

If the wallet guide is missing, call collect 913-624-5336 or visit www.youcallhome.com for YOU country numbers.

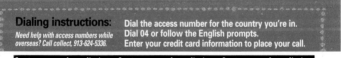

Dialing instructions:
Need help with access numbers while overseas? Call collect, 913-624-5336.

Dial the access number for the country you're in.
Dial 04 or follow the English prompts.
Enter your credit card information to place your call.

Country	Access Number	Country	Access Number	Country	Access Number
Australia **v**	1-800-551-110	Israel **v**	1-800-949-4102	Spain **v**	900-99-0013
Bahamas **+**	1-800-389-2111	Italy **+ v**	172-1877	Switzerland **v**	0800-899-777
Brazil **v**	000-8016	Japan **+ v**	00539-131	Taiwan **v**	0080-14-0877
China **+ ▲ v**	108-13	Mexico **u v**	001-800-877-8000	United Kingdom **v**	0800-890-877
France **v**	0800-99-0087	Netherlands **+ v**	0800-022-9119		
Germany **+ v**	0800-888-0013	New Zealand **▲ v**	000-999		
Hong Kong **v**	800-96-1877	Philippines **T v**	105-16		
India **v**	000-137	Singapore **v**	8000-177-177		
Ireland **v**	1-800-552-001	South Korea **+ v**	00729-16	*Service provided by Sprint*	

v Call answered by automated Voice Response Unit.   **+** Public phones may require coin or card.
▲ May not be available from all payphones.   **u** Use phones marked with "LADATEL" and no coin or card is required.
T If talk button is available, push it before talking.

Pack the Wallet Guide

and save 25% or more* on calls home to the U.S.

It's lightweight and carries heavy savings of 25% or more*
over AT&T USA Direct and MCI WorldPhone rates. So take this
YOU wallet guide and carry it wherever you go.

To save with YOU:

- Dial the access number of the country you're in (see reverse)
- Dial 04 or follow the English voice prompts
- Enter your credit card info for easy billing

Service provided by Sprint

TRAJAN'S GATE AND BATTLEMENTS. In front of the Coptic Museum (directly across from the Mari Girgis Metro station) is Cairo's only substantial classical ruin, the **Iron Gate** of the Roman emperor Trajan's fortress of Babylon (built during the first century CE), and parts of the Roman battlements that accompanied it. This massive fortress once covered 60 acres, and the Muslims could only capture it when the Coptic Patriarch Cyrus ordered the defenders to surrender. A massive tower and gate offer a hint of the scale of the original fortress. *(Open 24hr. Free.)*

CHURCH OF THE VIRGIN (AL-MU'ALLAQA CHURCH). This beautiful Coptic church is on your left as you face the Mari Girgis Metro station. The church is referred to as *Mu'allaqa* ("Hanging") because it was suspended 13m above the ground between two bastions of the fortress of Babylon. The building itself is ark-shaped, its roof held up by eight pillars on each side (one for every member of Noah's family, all of whom have the ark to thank for their salvation). Pointed arches and colorful geometric patterns enliven the main nave; in the center, an elegant pulpit (used only on Palm Sunday) rests on 13 slender columns—one for Christ and each of his disciples. The conspicuous black marble symbolizes Judas Iscariot, the Bible's most famous traitor, and ostrich eggs representing the Resurrection hang overhead. Over 100 icons decorate the chapel.

This church holds a special place in the annals of Coptic history, thanks to its involvement in the miracle of Mokattam Mountain. A doubtful caliph issued an ultimatum to Pope Ibrahim ibn al-Zar'a and the Coptic population—prove that the faithful can move mountains or die. The Copts in the area prayed for three days and three nights in the Church of the Virgin until, on the third night, their communal bowing and wailing of *Kyrie eleison* (Greek: "Lord, have mercy.") supposedly shook the earth and moved Mokattam a few inches. *(Coptic orthodox masses W 7-9am, F 8-11am, Su 6-8:30am and 9-11am.)*

■ CHURCH OF MARI GIRGIS (CHURCH OF ST. GEORGE). This Greek Orthodox church, built in the 6th century, is across the street from the Coptic Museum. Erected over one of the towers of the Fortress of Babylon, this church is dedicated to the Roman soldier George, whose famed tussle with a dragon is shown in a large relief in the courtyard. The current church was built in 1909, and its steps spiraling into the air represent the infinity of God. This church and the nunnery of St. George nearby (where a chain-wrapping ceremony commemorating the torture of St. George is sometimes performed) both claim to house the chains used to torture the saint. The small doorway to the right of the staircase leads to a room where you can try on the chains for yourself. *(From the Mari Girgis station, take a left. The entrance is along the wall on the right. Open daily 8am-noon and 2-5pm. Free.)*

OLD CAIRO PROPER

As you face the Church of St. George, a staircase to the left on Mari Girgis St. descends into an alley leading into Old Cairo proper. The churches here have their own quiet beauty, but the real charm of Old Cairo is in its twisting alleys. These narrow passages, barely marred by souvenir vendors, are cool and quiet. The sun bakes the ancient brick as the occasional local ducks around the corner or underneath an arch to enjoy a smoke or visit a friend.

BEN-EZRA SYNAGOGUE. This is the oldest synagogue in Egypt and the temple of the country's few remaining Jewish families. Jews established the synagogue in the 7th century BCE because Moses supposedly used the site for prayer before the exodus. The Copts eventually took over the site (which explains why the temple is designed very much like the nearby Coptic churches), but in 1115 CE, the caliph returned the Coptic Church to the Jewish community. The temple is beautifully decorated, combining Islamic geometric patterns with the Star of David. The ceiling dates from the Coptic occupation of the site and is in an exquisite arabesque style. The structure directly in front of the entrance is a cenotaph (empty tomb) commemorating Ben-Ezra, and the staircase behind it is the pulpit where the rabbi stands. Jewish history buffs can check out the collection in the library. *(With your* *back to the Church of St. Barbara, the Ben-Ezra Synagogue is approximately 25m to the left. The library is directly behind the synagogue, at the end of the path to the right of the main entrance. ☎359 26 95. No photography.)*

CHURCHES OF ST. BARBARA, ST. CYRUS, AND ST. JOHN. St. Cyrus and St. John were torn apart by wild beasts during the notorious persecution of Christians by the Roman emperor Diocletian, but the only wild beast in the church now is an occasional wandering cat. Legend holds that when the caliph discovered that both Christian churches were being restored, he ordered the architect to destroy one of them. Unable to choose, the architect paced back and forth between the two buildings until he died of exhaustion; the caliph was so moved he allowed both to stand.

The eponymous saint of the **Church of St. Barbara** was killed by her father when she sanctimoniously attempted to convert him. Her bones rest in the tiny chapel accessible through a door to the right as you enter her church. St. Catherine's bones supposedly lie here as well (see **St. Catherine's,** p. 178). An inlaid wooden *iconostasis* from the 13th century graces the church's ornate interior of carved wood and metalwork. Most of the furniture is now in the Coptic Museum, p. 123. *(At the end of the alley leading in to Old Cairo proper and to the left.)*

AL-FUSTAT الفستات

To reach al-Fustat, take the Metro to Mari Girgis (50pt). With your back to the station, head north along Mari Girgis St. until you see the minarets of the Mosque of Amir on your right. Buses #92 (٩٢), 94 (٩٤), and 134 (١٣٤) also run from Tahrir Sq., stopping right beside the Mosque of Amir. If you take a taxi to the outskirts of Old Cairo (E£2-3), ask to go to Misr al-Qadima or Gami' Amir.

Adjoining Coptic Cairo to the north are the partially excavated remains of al-Fustat, one of the oldest Islamic settlements and the capital of Egypt during its first 250 years as a Muslim country. Al-Fustat was the name of a garrison town that some historians say comes from *fossatum*, the Latin word for an entrenchment. A different account of the founding of al-Fustat holds that the conquering general Amir sent word to the caliph in Medina that the magnificent Roman port of Alexandria would be the perfect place for the capital of Egypt. To Amir's dismay, the caliph preferred to establish his outposts along desert trade routes, which were invulnerable to the naval attacks of seafaring Christians. The disappointed general returned to Babylon to find that a white dove had nested in his tent during his absence. Interpreting this as a divine omen, Amir founded the new capital of Egypt on the site of his tent, and dubbed it al-Fustat (City of the Tent). The military camp soon grew into a prosperous city with large houses, running water, and a sophisticated sewer system. Al-Fustat remained the capital of Egypt until the Fatimids established the neighboring city of al-Qahira ("The Conqueror"; see **Cairo**, p. 80) in 969 CE. In 1168, Crusader King Amalric of Jerusalem invaded al-Qahira, and the resident Fatimids burned al-Fustat to the ground to prevent it from falling into the hands of the Crusaders. The ruins were quickly scavenged for building materials, and al-Fustat's days of importance ended ignominiously as the city garbage dump.

As a result, the present-day architectural remains of al-Fustat are insubstantial, and a stroll through the site reveals little more than traces of cisterns, drains, cesspools, and rubbish. The main reason to visit al-Fustat (aside from a few interesting churches) is the **Mosque of Amir,** Egypt's first mosque. Al-Fustat sprawls over the large area behind the mosque. If you venture out to this district in the heat of summer, bring plenty of water. It is best to avoid the area at night, since it is isolated and lacks police protection.

MOSQUE OF AMIR. The present-day Mosque of Amir ibn al-'As, Egypt's first mosque, occupies the site of the original building of 642 CE, and is four times the size of its predecessor. The oldest portion of the current mosque is its crumbling southeastern minaret, added during the Ottoman period. The mosque has been rebuilt countless times over the centuries, most recently in 1983. There is little historically or architecturally interesting about the current building, especially in comparison with the nearby Coptic churches. Architectural fragments, thousands of pieces of fine Islamic pottery, and imported Chinese porcelain have all been discovered here, but most pieces are currently displayed at the Islamic Museum and in the new Islamic Ceramics Museum (p. 124). Behind the Mosque of 'Amir is the **pottery district,** which provides the clay pots used to store water throughout Cairo. Watch modern-day artisans at work feeding smoke-belching kilns with leather scraps and garbage, but ask before you take a picture or be slapped with a E£5 fee by your subjects. *(Open daily 9am-5pm. E£6, students E£3.)*

OTHER SIGHTS. Walk straight down the street directly opposite the entrance to the Mosque of Amir to **Deir Abu Seiffein,** a complex of three 8th-century Coptic churches. The wooden entrance to the churches is about 500m ahead on the right. *Odass,* or liturgy, read in Coptic Su 6-10am, W 8am-noon, and F 7-11am. (Open daily 8am-5pm.) The oldest church with the finest icons in Deir Abu Seiffein is the **Church of St. Mercurius Felopatir** (or the Church of Abu Seiffein), dating from the 4th century but extensively restored during the Middle Ages. St. Mercurius Felopatir, a Roman Christian soldier, was beheaded by his kind because of his religious beliefs, even after he aided in fending off Berber attacks. The martyr is also referred to as Abu Seiffein ("two swords") because an angel gave him a heavenly sword to go with his military saber.

The church has an impressive **iconostasis,** constructed of ebony, ivory, and cedar, that separates the front vestibule from the nave. The elaborate, gabled roof is an impressive feat of Coptic carpentry, as every piece is fitted to the next without screws or nails. Use your charm (or, failing that, *bakhsheesh*) to persuade the caretaker to let you into the **Chamber of St. Barsoum,** where the saint supposedly lived with a cobra for 25 years. Upstairs are the ancient and equally miniscule churches of St. George of Rome, St. John the Baptist, and the 144,000 Martyrs, all of which were rediscovered when the plaster was accidentally chipped away from multiple layers of icons. At press time, the chapels were closed for renovation.

Down the street is the late 4th-century **Church of St. Shnouda,** dedicated to one of the most famous Coptic saints. This chapel contains seven altars and two fine iconostases of red cedar and ebony. The smallest of the three main structures at Deir Abu Seiffein is the early 8th-century **Church of the Holy Virgin,** a one-room chapel crammed with rare icons, paintings, and three altars. Across the Nile on Roda Island is a particularly interesting variation on the ubiquitous Cairene **Nilometer** (glorified stairwells built to measure the depth of the Nile). The Abbasids constructed this particular Nilometer around 850 CE and carved Qur'anic verses about water on the interior walls. The Ottomans lent a hand by adding a dome in the 19th century. If both entrances to the Nilometer are locked, use *bakhsheesh* or ask one of the many children playing nearby to pester the custodian.

MODERN CAIRO

The heart of Cairo beats in **Tahrir Sq.** (Liberation Sq.), with the **Egyptian Museum** on the northern side, the **Mugamm'a** on the southern, and cars speeding suicidally in between. However, the many Cairenes careening through the streets will tell you that the city's "downtown" is not only centered in Tahrir Sq., but also in the many squares surrounding it, particularly **Tala'at Harb Sq.** and **'Ataba Sq.** You'll find yourself surrounded by an architectural wonderland whose more cosmopolitan, French-influenced flavor may come as a welcome relief from the dusty ancient quarters and Mamluk mosques of much of the rest of the city. To truly escape the hubbub, head to the quieter corners of the downtown area: the posh suburb of **Zamalek** beckons from the middle of the Nile and the small suburbs of **Heliopolis** and **Garden City** are but a few steps away.

TAHRIR SQ.

One block up from Tahrir Sq. at the intersection with Bustan St. are two particularly fine old buildings. On the southern side of the intersection is the **4 Tala'at Harb**

EGYPT

St. apartment building, elaborately decked out from its foundation to its richly decorated dome. Across the street, the more restrained and newly renovated **Muhammad 'Ali Club** glistens in the Cairo sun; look for the carved faces in the moldings. The **Sakakini Palace,** north of Modern Cairo at the Ghamra stop of the Metro, is easily visible from the heart of the city. The merchant Sakakini struck it rich when he sent a caravan of camels to the rat-infested Suez Canal; to celebrate his luck, he built this ornate palace and festooned it with a bizarre assortment of statuary. You can get a good view from the outside, but for a little *bakhsheesh* the caretaker will show you around the decaying interior.

TALA'AT HARB SQ.

Just north of Tahrir Sq. is Tala'at Harb Sq., named after the founder of the Egyptian National Bank and ringed with buildings in a variety of European styles. On the west side of the square is **J. Groppi's** (see p. 100), once *the* place to see and be seen (although the only things to see there now are the fabulous Italian mosaics at the entrance), whose lip-smacking pastries used to be exported to Europe's elite. The cafe's frequent concerts and dances during the colonial period were the hottest ticket in Cairo and always a top priority on Victorian social calendars. Although the Revolution brought that world to an abrupt end, Groppi's still remains as a stodgy reminder of Cairo's faded glory. Further up Tala'at Harb St. is the **Cinema Metro,** a beautiful movie palace from the 1930s that often shows English-language films as well as Arabic flicks. Farther north, Tala'at Harb St. intersects with 26 July St. West of Tala'at Harb St. is the **Sha'ar Ha-Shama'im Synagogue.** The name of this Jewish temple means "Gate of the Sky," and its architecture is truly heavenly with decorations that recall the styles of the 1920s, when it was built. (Open Sa. Free.) One block to the north of 'Adly St. on Tala'at Harb St. is the faux leaf-encrusted brick of the massive **Davins Bryan Building,** which once outfitted explorers. To the south is **St. Joseph's Church,** the center of the city's Catholic community.

'ATABA SQ.

To the west of downtown is 'Ataba Sq. and the **Ezbekiya Gardens.** Although they are now fenced in and look like little more than a lawn with a few small palm trees, the Gardens were for many centuries the magnificent, verdant center of the city's social life. A patch of thick trees remains in the southern corner to hint at what it once was, first under the Mamluks and then during the colonial period (when it was redesigned by the landscape architects of the Bois de Boulogne in Paris). In the northeast corner of 'Ataba Sq., just past the skyscraper with an antenna, are the beautiful double domes of the **Sedanoni Department Store.** Although it was built to rival the *prêt-à-porter* extravaganza Au Printemps in Paris, nationalization has left the store with shoddily constructed and hideously ugly *prêt-à-jeter* fashions. The building's interior is still impressive, with a huge open center and a staggeringly large cut-glass chandelier.

ZAMALEK

The quiet, tree-lined streets of the island of Zamalek are a great place to take a breather from the noisy hustle-and-bustle of the rest of Cairo. The city was first settled in the colonial era, when the **Gezira Club** in the north was a second home to the British elite. A walking tour of the sights in and around Zamalek is a cosmopolitan change of pace from the ancient sites and medieval architecture that characterize the rest of Cairo. Spend an afternoon browsing the galleries and exhibitions at the opera complex at the southern end of the island (particularly those at the **Egyptian Modern Art Museum,** p. 123), stopping at the many cafes along the way. When the sun sets, head for the restaurants scattered around the island for some of Cairo's best and most unusual food (see p. 100).

CAIRO MARRIOTT. The building that now houses the Cairo Marriott, along the east bank of Zamalek, was built in 1869 to house Empress Eugenie (wife of Napoleon III) during the grand opening of the Suez Canal. Around the same time, it hosted the first performance of Giuseppe Verdi's opera *Aida,* long regarded as the seminal work in the grand tradition of Egyptian fetishization (rivaled by Lawrence Durrell's *The Alexandria Quartet*). Across the river to the west are **houseboats** that were home to cabarets and nightclubs during World War II. One was owned by a bellydancer (employed by the Germans) who used her charms to acquire secrets from British agents.

CAIRO TOWER. The Cairo Tower dominates the city's skyline and has an excellent (if pricey) view of the city. Commissioned by Nasser and completed in 1961, it was built entirely by Egyptian engineers to commemorate the industrial rise in Egypt. At 187m, the tower is 60 stories high and 50m taller that the Great Pyramid at Giza. A rotating restaurant on the top floor sells expensive drinks and meals. *(Open daily 9am-1am; lines form at sunset. E£30.)*

HELIOPOLIS

This suburb of Cairo was founded in 1906 by the Belgian industrialist Edouard Empain as a community for foreigners in Egypt. Its broad avenues and odd architecture (a strange Euro-Islamic fusion) make it an interesting short trip out of central Cairo. The highlight of Heliopolis is **Empain's Palace.** To get there, head south on Shahid Tayyar Nazih Khalifa. The estate is a strange riot of carved elephants and Cambodian motifs that you can explore on your own (simply *bakhsheesh* the caretaker and he will let you wander around). The massive building behind the high wall in Heliopolis is the **Palace of the President.** Down Cleopatra St. across from the Pres's res are the beautifully decorated offices of the **Heliopolis Company,** who planned the suburb. Al-Ahram St. is home to several cheap cafeterias that were once major hangouts for Allied troops during World War II, as well as a **basilica** just past the cafeterias. Although modeled on the Aya Sophia, it looks more like a jelly mold. At night, Heliopolis comes alive as residents come home from work to flood the shops, malls, and cafes on Roxy St.

GARDEN CITY

Just southwest of Tahrir, historic Garden City has fine examples of **British colonial architecture,** housing a large part of Cairo's expat population. It is rumored that the wide, shady streets were intentionally constructed in this maze-like pattern for security purposes. The recently renovated **Qasr al-Aini Hospital,** the first hospital in Cairo, built by the French, lies in west Garden City on the northern end of Roda Island. In northeast Garden City is **Maglis al-Sha'ab** (the parliament), close to the **Mugamm'a** building. Along the Nile are a plethora of **embassies,** including those of the US and UK, as well as five-star hotels, such as **Shephards** and the **Semiramis.**

MOHANDISEEN

Originally built in the 1960s to house Egypt's *mohandiseen* (engineers), this district is now home to many expats and has some of the best bars and restaurants in Cairo. Its main boulevard, **Gam'at al-Duwal al-Arabiya,** is lined with palm trees, fast food joints, and duty-free shops where you can purchase Swiss chocolates, Mexican tequila, and American cigarettes, among other foreign goods. To purchase duty-free products you must bring your **passport.**

🏛 MUSEUMS

EGYPTIAN MUSEUM

In the heart of Tahrir Sq., accessible by any transportation. Open daily 9am-4:30pm. E£20, students E£10. Mummies: E£60, students E£30.

The multi-storied behemoth that is the Egyptian Museum building seems small in comparison to the astounding size and scope of the collection inside. The world's unrivaled warehouse of pharaonic treasures is filled with precarious stacks of exquisite mummy cases that open onto rooms filled with thousands of statuettes and gilded treasures (including those from the tomb of King Tutankhamun). Legend has it that if you spend one second at every exhibited item, it will take six months of non-stop viewing to see everything. Although the heavily touristed areas (such as the Tutankhamun and Akhenaton rooms) are very well-labeled, many descriptions are unhelpfully banal ("Pot," "Clay"), and some of the most puzzling items have no explanation at all. Although the crowded rooms are impressive, some of the smaller, infrequently visited side rooms are equally fascinating and far from the maddening tourist crowd. Unless you choose to buy the E£100 catalog, the first item to check out should be the wall map to the left of the entrance or the CD-ROM display to the right of the entrance. Flash photography is not permitted, but the museum is fairly well-lit and the exhibits are breath-taking, so bring along a camera.

🖾**TUTANKHAMUN ROOM.** Of all the collections in the museum, the treasures from **Tutankhamun's tomb** are the best-displayed and most popular. Originally squeezed into less than 100 cubic meters, the booty now occupies a quarter of the second floor. The eastern corridor contains decorated furniture, golden statues, delicate alabaster lamps, weapons, amulets, fossilized undergarments, and other bare necessities for a King of the Underworld. **Room #4** displays the famous gold of Tutankhamun, glittering all over coffins and funeral masks, as well as an astounding collection of amulets, scarabs, and jewelry. One elegant mask is made with more than 4kg of solid gold inlaid with quartz and lapis lazuli. In the hallway sit the king's internal organs, each in its own gilded coffin. The countless souvenir versions of these items, sold in tacky *souqs* and found on gaudy t-shirts and fake papyri, only make the originals look more impressive.

NARMER PALETTE. In the small glass case opposite the entrance (and surrounded by mobs of tourists with their guides) is the Narmer Palette, a stone slab commemorating the unification of Upper and Lower Egypt in about 3100 BCE by the mythical founder of pharaonic dynasties, King Narmer or Menes (see **Ancient History,** p. 64). From here, navigate the first floor in a clockwise direction around the central courtyard to get a sampling of pharaonic art from the Old Kingdom to the Greco-Roman period. Walking down the west corridor, you can visit the three rooms off to the right for a few minutes each. The first two rooms feature the best of the Old Kingdom, including a diarite statue of Chephren and a wooden statue named "Sheikh al-Balad" by workers who discovered that it resembled their boss. The third room displays limestones from the Middle Kingdom.

AKHENATON ROOM. In the Akhenaton room (at the rear of the first floor) are statues of the heretical pharaoh who introduced Egypt to a form of monotheism centered around the worship of the sun god and life-giver Aton. Aton was represented as a disk with rays that ended in hands that sometimes held *ankhs,* the Egyptian symbol for life. Artwork from this period is recognizable for its distinctly realistic portraits (versus the very stiff and stylized portraits of other periods) and grotesquely feminine body shapes; read more about Akhenaton-era hijinks by sticking your head between the legs of the king's shapely statue to get a view of the informational plaque. Past the Akhenaton room are a collection of **statues** from the New Kingdom. In the northeast corner room, look for a painting of **Ramses II** displaying his prowess as he clutches the cowering enemies of Egypt by their hair.

GREEK AND ROMAN ROOMS. Down the hall from the painting are the Greek and Roman rooms, where Classical art sits side-by-side with such oddities as a statue of a nude woman with the legs and tail of a chicken. Around the corner toward the entrance is a remarkable statue of **Alexander the Great:** the body is in the stiff pharaonic style, while the head is carved in the style of Greek naturalism.

MUMMY ROOM. The controversial mummy room is in the southeastern corner of the second floor. Former president Sadat closed the famed room in 1981 because the display offended some Islamist groups who felt it was disrespectful toward the dead. The reopening of the room was delayed by the mummies' continued decomposition, which left them offensive to just about everyone. Now restored and lodged in a dimly lit, air-conditioned room, the mummies might offend your budget (E£60, students E£30) and will not enhance your understanding of the mummification process in any way, as there are absolutely no descriptions. For more on mummies, see **Mummy Dearest,** p. 219.

OTHER ROOMS. The west corridor has unlabeled, oblong **mummy cases** in layers, and room #37 has square mummy cases used in the Middle Kingdom. The **papyri** in the middle of the second floor put those sold in the streets to shame, while the fine gold jewelry collection in the back will make you think the stylish necklace you bought at Khan al-Khalili is tacky. At the opposite end of Level II from the gold of Tutankhamun is the modest **Tomb of Yuya and Thuyu,** more typical of the tombs in which most Egyptians rested for eternity. Animal-rights activists may cringe in nearby room #53, where mummified remains of cats, birds, and monkeys repose in frozen honor. In 2000, an exhibit commemorating the millennium, presented by the International Congress of Egyptologists, was arranged to the left of the Greco-Roman rooms on the first floor; exhibits include items excavated within the past two years by Russian, French, and other foreign archaeology teams.

COPTIC MUSEUM

Directly across from the Mari Girgis Metro station. ☎ 363 97 42 or 362 87 66. Open daily 9am-5pm. E£16, students E£8. Camera privileges E£10, video E£100.

The 14,000 textiles, paintings, icons, and other pieces in the Coptic Museum make up the world's finest collection of Coptic art. In the 19th-century Roman fortress of Babylon (Qasr al-Shama), the museum's halls are paved with spotless white marble, and elegant wooden *mashrabiyya* (interlaced woodwork) screens cover the windows. The museum displays a variety of architectural fragments brought from the sanctuary of St. Menas at Maryut and the monastery of St. Jeremiah at Saqqara, along with Coptic textiles from the 2nd century and various metalworks. The most impressive room is a collection of icons on the second floor, which has many superb paintings in a variety of styles; compare an icon of the Virgin Mary suckling the baby Jesus and a carving of the Egyptian goddess Isis suckling her son Horus. The oldest is a fresco dating from the 3rd century. The Library of Gnostics, next to the textiles, contains 7000 volumes of apocryphal works from the 13th and 14th centuries, while the Nag Hammadi Library houses 12 Coptic Gnostic codices from the 4th century. Unlike most museums in Cairo, the collection at the Coptic Museum is well-labeled in French and English.

OTHER MUSEUMS

Egyptian Modern Art Museum (☎ 341 66 67), in the Opera Complex, Zamalek. Cross the bridge from Tahrir Sq. or take the Metro to the Opera. Tastefully exhibited Egyptian paintings in a variety of media and 20th-century styles. A welcome reminder that Cairo's art is not confined to tombs or mummy cases. Open Tu-Su 10am-1pm and 5-9pm. Free.

Gayer-Anderson Museum, 4 Ibn Tulun St. (☎ 364 78 22), just in front of the Ibn Tulun Mosque. Originally two separate buildings, these 16th- and 18th-century mansions were merged when Major Gayer-Anderson, an English art collector, arrived in the 1930s and proceeded to fill his home with eclectic artifacts and furniture. When he left Egypt in the 1940s, he gave the mansion and its contents to the Egyptian government. To

Egyptians, it is mysteriously known as "The House of the Cretan Woman." You may recognize some rooms from the James Bond flick *The Spy Who Loved Me*. Open daily 9am-5pm. E£16, students E£8. Camera privileges E£10, video E£25.

Islamic Art Museum (☎390 99 30), in Bab al-Khalaq Sq., at the intersection of Port Said, Muhammad 'Ali, and Ahmed Maher St. The hiding place of many of the artifacts missing from the mosques, mausolea, and *madaris* of Cairo. Also contains Islamic art from much of the rest of the Middle East. Don't miss miniature paintings and gold-leaf Qur'ans in the calligraphy room at the back. Open Sa-Th 9am-4pm, F 9-11am and 2-4pm; in winter F 9-11:30am and 1:30-4pm. E£16, students E£8.

Mahmoud Khalil Museum, 1 Kafour St., Giza (☎336 23 76), 200m from the Cairo Sheraton. A fantastic collection (housed in an A/C mansion) consisting almost exclusively of paintings by such 19th-century European greats as Monet, Van Gogh, Degas, and Toulouse-Lautrec. Open Sa-Th 10am-5:30pm. E£25, students E£10.

Manial Palace Museum (☎388 74 95), in the north half of Roda Island, close to the Sayyida Zeinab Metro station. This complex was built in the 19th century by the prolific Muhammad 'Ali, and like many of his other buildings reflects an Ottoman influence (particularly the must-see residential palace) from floor to ceiling. The macabre hunting museum is filled with disembodied animal heads. Open Sa-Th 9am-4pm, F 9am-1pm and 2-4pm. E£10, students E£5. Camera privileges E£10, video E£20.

Mugamm'a al-Funun Center of Arts (☎340 82 11), on the corner of Ma'had al-Swissry St. and 26 July Bridge, Zamalek. Rotates exhibitions of works by contemporary Egyptian and foreign artists, many of which are on sale (E£800+). Also screens films. Nile-side serenity doesn't get any better than the garden here. Open Sa-Th 10am-1:30pm. Free.

Mukhtar Museum (☎340 25 19), after Tahrir Bridge and just before al-Gala'a Bridge on Tahrir St. in Zamalek. Built by architect Ramses Wissa Wassef, this museum is devoted to the works of sculptor Mahmoud Mukhtar (1891-1934), a representative of a group of Egyptians working toward independence from European powers. The museum's most famous piece is the *Awakening of Egypt*. You might recognize Mukhtar's style from his sculpture in front of the Cairo Zoo or the statue of the man with a raised hand at the base of the Tahrir Bridge. Open Tu-Su 10am-1pm and 5-9pm. E£1, students 50pt.

Museum of Islamic Ceramics, al-Gezira Arts Center, 1 Sheikh Marsafy St., Zamalek (☎341 86 72), next to the southwest corner of the Marriott Hotel. Proof that less is more, this superb new museum houses an exquisite collection of well-labeled ancient Islamic and contemporary ceramics in the well-organized, A/C rooms of a converted Ottoman Palace. Open Sa-Th 10am-1pm. Free.

🎬 ENTERTAINMENT

CINEMAS

Cairo has a few cinemas that run English-language films four to six months behind their release in the US; *al-Ahram* (Sa-Th 50pt; F 75pt) has listings, but in Arabic. All of these air-conditioned theaters are packed with Egyptian hipsters on Thursday nights. Films usually run at 1, 3:30, 6:30, and 9pm, with a midnight showing on Thursdays and a morning showing on Fridays (E£10, in winter E£20). Two convenient locations are the Metro Cinema (☎393 75 66), on Suleiman Basha St. near Tala'at Harb Sq., and Kareem Cinema, 15 Imad al-Din St. (☎592 48 30).

PERFORMING ARTS

DANCE

▨ Mausoleum al-Ghouri (☎510 08 23), on al-Mu'izz St., just south of the pedestrian overpass near al-Azhar University in Islamic Cairo. This renovated 500-year-old palace hosts free Sufi music and whirling dervishes (spinning at over 100rpm) on Wednesday and Saturday nights (9pm, in winter 8pm). Also hosts plays every once in a while; stop by and ask the guards about the calendar. Arrive early to the hour-long show, as seats fill up fast, and bring water (all that whirling generates quite a lot of heat).

Balloon Theater (☎347 74 57 or 347 17 18), on al-Nil St. at the Zamalek Bridge, Agouza. Regular performances of Rida's Troupe, one of the best Egyptian folk dance companies. Tickets E£10-30. Shows daily 9:30pm.

Falafel Restaurant (☎577 74 44), at Ramses Hilton (behind Egyptian Museum). Serves up a scrumptious but expensive *prix-fixe* dinner (E£105) that includes a fabulous folk dancing show by the Hassan Troupe. Show starts 10pm. Open Sa-Th 9pm-midnight.

Coquillage (☎340 61 26), at the foot of Tahrir Bridge, Zamalek, connected to Qasr al-Nil Casino. A coffee shop by day, lavish hall of stained glass with Arabic dancing and singing by night. Fettuccine with chicken (E£35) dazzles the taste buds and the hour-long variety show dazzles the eyes and ears after 11pm. Open 24 hr. V, MC.

Nile Maxim Cruise (☎342 48 33), at the Marriott Hotel in Zamalek. This glitzy Nile cruiser with chandeliers, mirrors, enormous windows, and jacked-up A/C is a great place to enjoy superb meals at jacked-up prices (E£65-105). Let the belly dancers, Sufi dancers, and lounge lizards entertain you for two hours. Daily 8 and 11pm. Call for reservations. V, MC.

MUSIC AND THEATER

Cairo Opera Complex (☎339 81 44), in Gezira, southern Zamalek. This massive complex hosts the Cairo Symphony Orchestra, outdoor jazz performances, and visiting operas. Casual open-air performances held every day at 9pm. Jacket and tie required for the opera performances (travelers have been known to borrow snazzy clothing from kind hostel workers). Tickets for the small hall cost as little as E£5 with student ID (main hall E£15). Check *al-Ahram* for details. Box office open daily 10am-3pm and 4-9pm.

El-Gomhoriyya Theater, 12 Gomhoriyya St. (☎390 77 07), at the intersection of al-Gomhoriyya St. and Abd al-'Aziz St. Performances by the Arabic Music Troupe and the Cairo Symphony Orchestra, usually on Friday evenings.

Wallace Theater (☎357 54 51), in the American University in Cairo New Campus, on Muhammad Mahmoud St. near the McDonald's off Tahrir Sq. Features two plays in English per year. AUC also hosts a variety of concerts, from jazz to chamber music, and free movie festivals at the library. Open fall-spring. Call or check bulletin boards around the Old Campus (near the AUC bookstore).

Cairo Puppet Theater (☎591 09 54 or 591 83 67), in Ezbekiya Gardens near 'Ataba Sq. World-famous shadow puppets put on performances in Arabic, but are universally understood. W-M 7:30pm and matinee F and Su 10:30am. E£5.

British Council, 192 al-Nil St., Agouza (☎303 15 14), one block south of 26 July St., next to Balloon Theater. Sponsors free performances by visiting British and Egyptian artists and sometimes presents films. Call for information on upcoming events. Large library (open M-Sa 10am-8pm) has CD and video equipment and a traveler-oriented teaching center. Internet E£5 per hr. Office open Su-Th 9am-3pm.

Egyptian Center for International Cultural Cooperation, 11 Shagarat al-Durr St., Zamalek (☎341 54 19). Free art exhibitions, Arabic language courses, lectures, tours, and performances. Open Sa-Th 9:30am-8pm.

PLEASURE TRIPS

Consider hiring a swallow-winged **felucca** and lazing on the river during the day or night. Most *feluccas* can accommodate up to eight people comfortably. The more passengers, the cheaper; bargain for a good rate. *Feluccas* for hire dock just south of the Qasr al-Nil (Tahrir) Bridge on the east bank. Across the corniche (on the water) from the Meridian Hotel, shrewd negotiators can snag a boat for E£5 during the day, E£7 in the evening. A nominal tip (E£1-2) is expected at the cruise's end. Travelers seeking multi-day cruises (especially popular in Upper Egypt, near Luxor and Aswan) should see **Tips on Traveling by Felucca,** p. 210. **Hantours** (horse carriages) are also enjoyable, especially on a breezy evening. Avoid those in front of major hotels, and don't pay more than E£10 for a 30-minute ride.

EGYPT

OUTDOOR DIVERSIONS

GIZA ZOO. With wide walkways, families picnicking, and children playing soccer, the Giza Zoo doubles as a park. Nevertheless, for less than one pound you can take pictures with the animals, feed them (20pt a pop), and get close enough to the lions to get goose bumps on the back of your neck. *(Right in front of you as you cross the University Bridge (al-Gam'a) west into Giza. Open daily 9am-4pm. 25pt. Camera privileges 20pt.)*

PHARAONIC VILLAGE (AL-QARIA AL-FARA'ONIYA). This Disney-fied village was founded by former Egyptian ambassador Dr. Ragab (who claims to be the papyrus king of Egypt). Visitors board motorboats and chug through canals past statues of the gods and historically reconstructed scenes of ancient papyrus-making, temple wall-painting, and mummification. All this is described in detail by a guide speaking the language of your choice. Disembark to view a temple, houses, and King Tut's tomb reconstructed to appear as it did when Howard Carter discovered it in 1922. The price is steep, but it buys information without hassle. It's definitely (and only) worth it if you're not going to see the real thing in Luxor. *(5km south of downtown, on Jacob's Island in Giza. ☎571 86 75. Open daily 9am-9pm; in winter 9am-5pm. E£55, students E£40, groups of 10 or more E£30 per person. Lunch E£17.)*

FUTBOL MATCHES. You can catch a *futbol* (soccer) game at the stadium on Ramses St., in Nasser toward the airport. From September through May, local rivals Zamalek and Ahly take on teams from farther afield. Be cautious of the people next to you; if their team scores, they may set off a firecracker. First- and 2nd-class seats are E£25 and E£10, respectively, but if you're more interested in seeing ballistic fans than athletes, grab a bleacher seat for E£5. *(Games start at 3 or 9pm—check al-Ahram or ask around. Get tickets at the two teams' box offices: Zamalek's is south of 26th July St. in Mohandiseen; Ahly's is in Gezira next to the Cairo Tower.)*

EGYPTIAN CIRCUS. Although Cairo is a three-ring circus, you may want to check out the real deal at the Egyptian Circus in Agouza between the British Council and the Balloon Theater. *(For specific directions to these landmarks, see **Performing Arts,** p. 124. ☎347 06 12 or 347 05 03. Daily shows start at 9:30pm and run for about 3hr. E£21-51.)*

FOURTH OF JULY. On July 4 (or the closest weekend thereabouts), homesick Americans come together at the Cairo American Primary and Secondary School in Ma'adi. Drop by if you miss hearing pure, unbroken American English, but don't count on getting any free food; freebies tend to be limited to two soft drinks and a slice of watermelon per person. Each attendee of the event also receives a free ticket to the raffles held throughout the evening (last year's prizes included return tickets to any destination in the US and other luxury vacations). Bring your US passport—your taxes have already footed the bill—and a swimsuit. Call the American embassy (☎354 82 11) for hours and directions. Be persistent if your inquiries are met with confusion.

SHOPPING

Cairo's biggest and most famous market is **Khan al-Khalili** (see p. 110). Navigating the maze of passages and alleyways that lie within the khan may seem like madness, but there is a method to it. Most gold, copper, and antique dealers lie along Khan al-Khalili St., which changes to al-Badestani St. as it heads east. Perfumes, spices, and cloth can be found a few blocks farther south, between al-Azhar St. and al-Muski St.

In the market south of **Sayyida Zeinab,** each alley offers different wares. Take the Metro to Sayyida Zeinab, then walk five minutes toward the minarets of the Sayyida Mosque. Other major markets are northeast of **'Ataba Sq.** and in **Bulaq.** For 'Ataba Sq. from Tahrir Sq., go eastward along Tahrir St., then up Abd al-'Aziz St.; for Bulaq take bus #46 (٤٦). The **Souq al-Tawfiqia** runs between Ramses and Tala'at

VENI, VIDI, VENDI Buying and selling in the Egyptian capital transcends mundane business—it's an intricate give-and-take that has evolved over centuries. Think of it as a game to be relished, not a battle to be won. Bargaining is a given: no price is set in stone, and successful merchants enjoy the haggling (just remember that the shopkeepers do this for a living and have the benefit of experience). If you play hardball, the vendors will not lower the price—chatting will bring you more success. Theatrics, rather than stubbornness, get results. Walk away in disbelief several times. Do a brief Mexican hat-dance while you weigh the pros and cons of the purchase. Never get too enthusiastic about the object in question. Instead, point out flaws in workmanship and design. Have a friend discourage you from your purchase—if you seem to be reluctant, the merchant will want to drop the price to interest you again. Your starting price should be no more than one-third to one-half the asking price.

Harb St., one block north of 26 July St. Produce stalls stand beside kitchen-equipment booths, all laid out in brilliant displays. On summer days, hose-wielding shopkeepers water the shop entrances to reduce heat and settle the dust.

If bargaining doesn't appeal to you, you can head to one of Cairo's **department stores,** such as the upscale 'Umar Effendi. Be forewarned that ever since the Egyptian government nationalized the department stores, the shops have had little to offer other than out-of-date, outlandishly tacky clothes in various brown-and-orange combos. More expensive shopping centers lure foreigners and wealthy Egyptians with higher-quality goods. The **World Trade Center** on the corniche, north of the Ramses Hilton, is the biggest. A bit less expensive is the **al-Yamama Center** (affectionately called the Yo Mama Center by expats), at 3 Dr. Taha Hussein St. in Zamalek, where you can watch music videos or sporting events on the large-screen TV in the ground-floor cafe. For assuredly high-quality versions of wares found in the khan (copper, antiques, papyrus), and a minimum of bargaining, try Ma'adi's tree-lined **Road Nine** (Metro: Ma'adi).

CLOTHING AND TEXTILES. At the **tent-makers' bazaar,** south of Bab Zuweila in Islamic Cairo, you can commission the making of a Bedouin tent (far out of a budget traveler's price range) or buy appliqué pillowcases (E£20) and bedcovers (E£300). The **Nomad Gallery,** 14 Saraya al-Gezira, Zamalek, near the Marriott, is known for its top-quality jewelry, textiles, and crafts. They're not big bargainers, but their prices are as low as they go at the tent-makers bazaar. (☎341 19 17. Open M-Sa 10am-3pm. V, MC, AmEx.) Closer to the khan, **Khan Misr Tulun,** across from the Ibn Tulun Mosque, sells quality handicrafts from all parts of Egypt and Africa. Run by a friendly French-Egyptian couple, their selection includes Nagada textiles, a traditional industry incorporating contemporary styles restored in the last decade with international help. (☎365 22 27. Open M-F 9am-5pm.) The best places to shop for woven **rugs** are indubitably the stores along **Saqqara Rd.,** near the Pyramids, where Harania artists weave up a storm (see p. 131).

There's a colorful **used clothing market** daily at the east end of 26 July Bridge. The stands hawk modern and vintage Western clothing as well as some traditional Egyptian garb. Women tired of getting hissed at can pick up a used *galabiyya* here or splurge on a new one (E£30-50) at the market south of al-Ghouri Mosque and Khan al-Khalili on al-Mu'izz St. Casual clothing for several well-known Western outlets is made in Egypt, and you may want to take advantage of the slightly lower but fixed prices. Most of these goods are available in boutiques on the main streets and in department stores. On Friday mornings there's a **junk market** at the Mausoleum of Imam al-Shafi'i, where many bizarre items are bought and sold.

 The touts in the street of Khan al-Khalili who try to get you into stores also get a commission. To make up for the commission, the store owner raises the price. You'll never get a good price at a store to which a hustler has brought you.

JEWELRY AND METALWARE. Cairo is a center of the jewel trade, and prices here tend to be markedly lower than in the West. Often, gold or silver jewelry can be made to order for barely more than the cost of the metal itself. Never ask for the price first. Look at a piece of jewelry carefully and then ask the shopkeeper to weigh it in front of you. Inquire about the grade of gold or silver; gold weights under 18 karat are rare in Egypt. Always make sure you see the stamp on both gold and silver items. One of the best shopping areas is in the **Khan al-Khalili Souq al-Fidha** (silver market), where you can find Turkish, pharaonic, and Nubian designs in addition to more modern creations; be sure to shop around. Ceramic plates and trays of varying sizes and designs are available throughout the khan for E£15-20, while a *sheesha* should cost about E£30-35. For the best *sheeshas* in Cairo, however, bypass the junk sold at the khan and head to the **restaurant supply bazaar** on al-Mu'izz St. (see p. 111). Copper or brass mugs, coffeepots, and ashtrays are available, but nothing is as old as the shopkeeper claims.

PAPYRUS. The "papyrus" sold throughout Cairo is usually banana leaf, a cheap look-alike. Real papyrus can be scrunched up and will not retain any wrinkles, while banana leaf crackles and stays crunched. Handpainted papyrus is even rarer; if anything even vaguely looks like a print, it is. A smudged artist's signature is the usual tip-off. To see the real stuff at correspondingly higher prices, head to **Dr. Rayab's Papyrus Factory,** a right turn off the al-Gala'a Bridge heading west from Tahrir Sq. Another authentic option is the **Sa'id Delta Papyrus Center,** 21 al-Ghouria St., 3rd floor (☎512 07 47), by Darb al-Ahmar near the Umayyad Mosque. Within the Khan al-Khalili itself is **Wafiq Isma'il 'Ali,** near the Coffeeshop Naguib Mahfouz, which sells fake but surprisingly vivid "papyrus" for around E£10. The bazaars are full of colorful artwork for those who think a neon pink Osiris would look great next to a velvet Elvis portrait.

BACKGAMMON. *Tawila* boards cost E£80-120, depending on the quality and your bargaining skills. Make sure the board is absolutely flat when it's opened and laid on a table, as occasionally they are warped or wobbly. Pieces are often made separately from the board. Check to see that they fit on the triangles, and that there are 15 of each color. You should pay less if the pieces are plastic. **Maka al-Mokarama,** 7 'Adly St. (☎393 89 80), next to the tourist office, has quality boards but lacks the hassle and fun of Khan al-Khalili, where scads of stores sell them.

SPICES AND PERFUME. Thousands of perfume and spice shops give some sections of Cairo a relievingly fragrant smell. Excellent Middle Eastern spices like *za'tar* are difficult or impossible to find in the West. The quality of perfumes ranges dramatically. Rub some on the back of your hand: if it's oily or shiny, oil has been added to the perfume to stretch the liquid weight. Vendors of perfume will often misquote the size of a container; they know most tourists (especially metric-shunning Americans) can't tell a milliliter from a millipede. A 30ml jar should be

---

THAT WHICH WE CALL A ROSÉ... by any other

name could be disgusting and potentially fatal. Although many tourists are familiar with **Stella**, Egypt's decent stab at beer-brewing greatness, few encounter the rest of Egypt's potent potables. Egypt produces wines such as *Reine Cléopatre* and *Cru des Ptolemées* in an attempt to evoke the wine expertise of the French and the bacchanalian ancient Greeks, but the wines (all made from imported grapes) are barely drinkable no matter how evocative their names. The vaguely suggestive wine *Obelisque* is a little kinder to the palate, but not to the wallet. Egypt's hard liquors have names that will make you tipsy just hearing them. Egyptian teetotalers must combat the harmful effects (and puns) of **Johnny Wadi's Brown Label** and **Gordon's Kin.** Before you sit down to a cool kin and tonic, be warned that these hack liquors are sometimes distilled from wood and have been linked to blindness and even death.

about the same size as a small bottle of medicine; a 60ml jar should be about the length of a middle finger. An ounce can go for as low as E£5. **Harraz Agricultural Seeds, Medicinal, and Medical Plants Co.,** 1 Bab al-Khalq St., sells every imaginable spice at reasonable prices. (Open Sa-Th 9am-9pm.) If the self-proclaimed "sheikh of spice" won't cut you a good deal, **Khodr,** next door, has similar wares, as do many vendors in the Khan al-Khalili market.

☑ NIGHTLIFE

As the sun sets on the Egyptian capital, *sheesha* smoke fills the air, strolling locals mill about the markets, and decked-out scenesters dance 'til (almost) dawn at the discotheques dotting the side-streets of the city. The free publication *Croc* is an up-to-date, hip-to-great guide to the Cairene scene available at most bars. During **Ramadan** (from Nov. 17 to Dec. 15, 2001; for further information, see p. 80), Cairenes take to the streets around al-Azhar and Hussein Sq., along the corniche, and all over the bridges spanning the Nile. Starting around 10pm, there are street performances, magic shows, and general shenanigans and tomfoolery. Most cinemas also have midnight screenings during this month. The following listings are as easy to navigate as A-B-C—**Ahwas, Bars,** and **Clubs.** Also listed are **Performing Arts** activities (dance and music) and **Other Diversions.**

AHWAS

Although you'd never guess it from the obsessive honking, city folk love to relax, meet with friends, and contemplate the sweet mysteries of life. Much of this ruminating occurs in the *ahwas* (coffeehouses) that dot many street corners and alleys east of the Nile. A typical *ahwa* has gossipers in one corner, *tawila* (backgammon) players in another, and *sheesha* smoke and Turkish coffee steam winding throughout. *Sheesha* tobacco is stronger and more delicious than cigarette shag and often comes in apple, honey, or apricot flavors. Foreign men and women are welcomed at all the *ahwas* listed below, though not at all *ahwas* in the city. For other options, try the **Cafes** listings under each region of the **Food** section (p. 99). For further info on *sheesha*-smoking, see **Puff the Magic Sheesha,** p. 71.

◪ **Fishawi's Khan al-Khalili** (☎590 67 55), four doors down from al-Hussein Hotel, just off al-Hussein Sq. Walking through the khan, you can smell the *sheesha* smoke wafting from this famous teahouse before you can see it. Ask a waiter to show you where Nobel laureate Naguib Mahfouz spent many *Arabian Nights and Days.* Nicknamed "Café des Miroirs," Fishawi's is furnished in a 19th-century Turkish style with panels of mirrors and woodwork, and brass tables that can barely hold two cups. Customers spill out into the walkway, sipping their mint tea and *karkadeh* and smoking aromatic *sheesha* (each E£2 or less). Frequented by women and men. Open 24hr.

Cafe New Sun, off Souq al-Tawfiqia in the alley left of the Sultan Hotel. This stylish *ahwa,* peopled with as many pregnant cats as customers, accompanied by the din of clacking dominoes, has been serving *sheesha* (E£1) and strong Turkish coffee (E£1.50) since 1925. Open daily until 2am.

Maroush, 64 Lubnan St., Mohandiseen (☎346 68 91), a E£5 taxi ride from downtown. A ritzy *ahwa* for a ritzy neighborhood, but relaxed, even for a coffeehouse. Outdoor patio makes for a great escape with a *sheesha* (E£5). Open daily 8am-2am.

BARS

Cairenes aren't known for beer guzzling, but considering the strict Islamic prohibition against alcohol, they have a good number of bars; the liveliest are filled with non-Muslim expats. Most of the clientele is male.

Deals, 2 al-Sa'id al-Bakry St., Zamalek (☎341 05 02), a right turn off 26 July St. at the base of the bridge to downtown. Cairo's younger set mingles and tingles in this tiny joint, attracted by the low prices and eclectic decor. Drink prices (including French wine by the glass) don't live up to the name, but the A/C and rock music pumped into the place ensure that this hangout fills up quickly. Stella E£7. Open daily 4:30pm-2am.

Cairo Jazz Club, 197 26 July St. (☎345 99 39). Groove nightly with a crowd of international scat cats who come here to grab some Ella and a Stella (E£10) or to jump, jive, and cocktail (E£16) around the clock. Restaurant serves up decent entrees (E£10-20). Shows start at 10:30pm. Cover Th-F E£30. Open daily 8pm-2am.

El Gato Negro, 32 Jeddah St., Mohandiseen (☎361 68 88). Stylish hepcats scope the Mohandiscene from this classy lair while sipping on anything from water (E£3) to top-notch scotch and whiskey (E£15). The adjacent restaurant serves up a variety of delicious foods (pizza, pasta, Levantine fare). Cover-less dance floor opens up at 10pm. Open daily noon-2am. V, MC, AmEx.

Pub 28, 28 Shagarat al-Durr St., Zamalek (☎340 92 00), kitty-corner to the Mandarin Koedar ice cream store (p. 101). Take a right off 26 July St. at the Misr Gas Station; the pub's brick facade will be on your left. The closest you'll come to Dublin in Cairo, this dimly-lit pub serves a wide selection of spirits (E£9 and up). Next thing you know, it'll be raining outside. Open daily noon-2am. V, AmEx.

Odeon Palace, 6 Dr. Abd al-Hamid Sa'id St. (☎576 79 71), off Tala'at Harb St., just northwest of Tala'at Harb Sq. A relaxing rooftop spot for insomniacs in the mood for food, *sheesha,* or a colorful nighttime view. Stella E£8. Open 24hr.

CLUBS

The Cairene club scene is smaller, tamer, and less crowded than in other Middle Eastern hotspots such as Beirut and Istanbul, but the clubs on **Pyramids Road** in Giza overflow with sweaty hipsters. Late evenings in Giza typically degenerate into pickup fests, while tight groups of young friends might hit the pricier discos at major downtown hotels. In the evenings, middle-class Egyptian couples swarm to the boat cafes (misleadingly called **casinos**) lining the Nile on Gezira Island. Some boats anchor permanently at the edge of the water. The **Casino al-Nil** and **Pasha 1901,** on the west side of Tahrir Bridge, are among the best (E£8 min.). Ranging from simple to swank, these places get packed on Thursday nights. For real **gambling,** head to the Nile Hilton, Marriott, or Sheraton. Show your passport to enter; gamblers must be at least 21. You are not permitted to game with Egyptian currency, but don't worry—they can change Egyptian pounds to US dollars faster than you can lose them (min. bet US$5). Drinks are free for all who gamble.

Jackie's Joint, Nile Hilton, Tahrir Sq. (☎578 04 44 or 578 06 66, ext. 379). One of Cairo's hotspots, with lines out the door most nights. To improve your chances of getting in, wear something sleek, black, and non-denim, and bring a date. Swing Night (M); Ladies' Night (W); Latino Night (F). Minimum charge E£35 (includes a drink). Happy Hour Sa-Su 10pm-midnight. Open daily 9pm-4am.

Crazy House Disco, Cairoland Hotel, 1 Salah Salem (☎366 10 82 or 366 10 83). Careen into other Cairenes on the dance floor at this local fave, which features a hyperactive fog machine. E£25 cover includes two beers. Open Tu-Su 8pm-3am.

Los Amigos, SemiRamis Hotel (☎578 25 37), on the corniche by Tahrir Bridge. This Egyptian version of a Mexican cantina blurs the bar/club line, featuring a smallish, but thumping dance floor (which takes requests) and a long, well-stocked bar. Latin beats vie with Arabic hits, with plenty of American pop in between. E£20 drink minimum. Open daily 7pm-3am.

NEAR CAIRO

KARDASSA

On the road from Cairo to Giza, a turnoff to the right at the second canal before the Pyramids leads to the village of **Kardassa,** where the Western Desert and the camel road to Libya commence. The village has acquired popularity among tourists owing to the variety of its local crafts (many of what appear in Cairo's tourist shops). The main products of the village are wool and cotton scarves, *galabiyyas* (E£30-70), rugs (1x1.5m rug E£50), and Bedouin weavings. The shops are in a sand lot across the canal from the village, usually in the back of the store or in the side alleys off the main drag. Also for sale among the scarves and rugs is a disturbing number of professionally stuffed animals, including gazelles, jackals, and rabbits. Despite the efforts of the Egyptian Environmental Affairs Agency, this illegal but highly profitable trade continues. Tourism is beginning to rob Kardassa of its charm, though the prices are still lower and the quality of the merchandise higher than at Khan al-Khalili. **Taxis** from Giza Sq. to Kardassa cost E£10-15. **Minibuses** run to Kardassa from Giza Sq. (40pt) as well as from the turnoff from Pyramids Rd., known as the *Mash'al* stop (35pt).

HARANIA

More interesting is the artists' school at **Harania,** 200m to the right of Maroutiya Canal Rd. (about three kilometers south of Pyramids Rd., next to the Salome Campground). Here, young children are encouraged to develop their creativity by weaving brilliantly colored carpets and making pottery. Since its inception in 1942, two generations of tapestry-weavers have studied at the school; many are still in practice as adults. Some of the most notable works are showcased in the museum at Harania and in the book *Threads of Life—A Journey Through Creativity*, available at the center. The results of this creative process are stunning but expensive (E£200-2000). Harania is best visited with the **Salah Muhammad tour** (see p. 102). Walking is the only non-taxi alternative to a guided tour. (Open daily 9am-6pm; in winter 9am-5pm. V, MC.)

BIRQASH CAMEL MARKET

Minibuses (45min., E£4 round-trip; ask for Souq al-Gamal) run to the Birqash Camel Market from the site of a closed camel market in Imbaba (near Imbaba Airport), accessible by minibus or taxi (E£5) from downtown. The Sun Hotel (☎ 578 17 86) also offers an E£20 tour (not including admission) that leaves at 6am and returns at noon; contact them two days in advance to reserve a spot. E£10. Camera privileges E£5, video E£5.

If you came to Egypt expecting camels but feel like an ass because you've seen nothing but donkeys, the Birqash Camel Market is for you. The camel market is a bumpy half-day excursion from Cairo, convening every Friday from 6am to noon in the small farming town of Birqash. Bypass the butcher shops with camel appendages on display in the windows (camel meat is supposedly low in cholesterol) and head to the market in the heart of town. Hundreds of camels stand around smiling enigmatically while Sudanese traders haggle over prices and whack the camels on the rear at the slightest hint of disobedience. If you think you know someone who could use a caning, you can buy one of the canes to take home (E£15). If you'd rather have a larger, more troublesome souvenir that is prone to biting and spitting, camels run from E£1000-3000, with strong females being the most valuable. Give a boy some *bakhsheesh* to show you to the birthing pens to see the day-old calves. The traders are happy to answer any questions you might have about their wares. One hump or two?

SAQQARA سقارة

Named after Sokar, a Memphite god of death, Saqqara is actually quite enlivening. Saqqara began as a royal necropolis in the early years of the Old Kingdom (3rd dynasty, around 2600 BCE), when nearby Memphis was the capital of Egypt. It was used as a burial site for the next 3000 years, leaving a remarkable array of tombs and pyramids that traces the evolution of funereal construction in ancient Egypt. Because it is largely free of Giza's hordes of tourists (and the hustlers who love them), Saqqara offers a wonderful opportunity to see these monuments in the stillness and stark beauty of the desert.

⚜ 🔢 ORIENTATION AND PRACTICAL INFORMATION

Saqqara consists of five archaeological finds scattered over a very large area, with nothing but sand dunes in between. The primary destination for most visitors is **North Saqqara** (see p. 132), site of the funerary complex and the famous Step Pyramid of Zoser I. The three pyramids of **Abu Sir** (see p. 136) are six kilometers north of North Saqqara, only a few kilometers from the tiny village of the same name. The two pyramids and the funerary complex of **South Saqqara** (see p. 136) are about four kilometers south of North Saqqara. The historically significant, but scanty ruins of **Memphis** (see p. 136) are even farther from Saqqara's necropolis, next to the Nile just south of the village of Mit-Rahine. The pyramids of **Dashur** (see p. 136) form the southern tip of the row.

The two easiest ways to see Saqqara and its environs are to take **Salah Muhammad's tour** (see p. 102) or to hire a driver from the Berlin Hotel (see p. 98). If you choose to go on your own, you'll want to begin at the ruins of **North Saqqara.** Public transportation to and around the area is sparse because a large swath of farms separates the ruins from Cairo. One option is to take a **taxi** from Cairo (E£20) and then try to find and share taxis at each site. However, some sites may have periods when taxis don't drive by for three or four hours. An easier and much more exciting (if expensive) option is to take a taxi to North Saqqara and then hire a **steed** at North Saqqara. This is your chance to ride through the desert on a horse with no name. A horse or camel costs about E£15 per hour, and you will probably have to pay for a guide (and his ride), as well. Another option is to take a **minibus** from Cairo to North Saqqara, but this is only for those confident in their ability to untangle the complicated minibus schedule (with route information in Arabic). Begin by taking a minibus from Giza Sq. to the village of Abu Sir (50pt). From there, the killer four-kilometer walk to the entrance takes between 30 minutes and one hour, depending on your sand-speed. Walk south (to the left as you arrive) along the canal just before the village and follow the dirt road until you reach the paved road. Turn right and it's 200m to the site entrance. You can also hire a **pick-up truck** at the canal in Abu Sir (about 50pt per person) to take a group to the site.

To get to the pyramids at **Abu Sir** from North Saqqara, ride on a steer or brave the burning sands on foot (at least 1hr.). **South Saqqara** is at least a 30-minute walk; taxis cost E£7. To get to **Memphis** on your own, take the **Metro** to Helwan (75pt) and then a microbus to the village of al-Badrasheen (25pt); after crossing the Nile in a ferry from the village, look for the **microbus** that occasionally passes by on its way to the ruins (25pt). **Minibuses** also run from Memphis to al-Badrasheen (25pt) and from al-Badrasheen to Giza (50pt). From Giza, you can take either a minibus or public bus #987 (٩٨٧) back to Tahrir Sq. or the Ramses Metro station. Have someone write your destination in Arabic to help locate your minibus. (Holding a pen and piece of paper, ask: *"Lo samaht, mumkin tiktib hinaa, min fadlik?"*)

However you get there, wear **sneakers or boots** (not sandals) as the sand is quite hot. Bring lots of **water** and a hat, and try to get an early start, since the afternoon sun can be cruel. A **flashlight** also allows you to avoid paying the *bakhsheesh* the guards will request to illuminate the poorly lit tombs. Tombs often close for preservational purposes in the summer, when there is less tourism.

🔦 SIGHTS

All sights are officially open 8am-5pm; in winter 8am-4pm. Guards lock up and go home a couple of hours early in low season and stay a bit longer in the winter. E£20, students E£10. Camera privileges E£5, video E£25. The ticket is good for all Saqqara sites; Abu Sir does not require a ticket. Some tombs also require an E£5-10 entrance fee or bakhsheesh, depending on who is on duty.

NORTH SAQQARA

Saqqara's most famous site is the **Step Pyramid of Zoser I** (Zoser-Netcherikhe), the oldest monumental tomb in the world (began in 2630 BCE) and the inspiration for

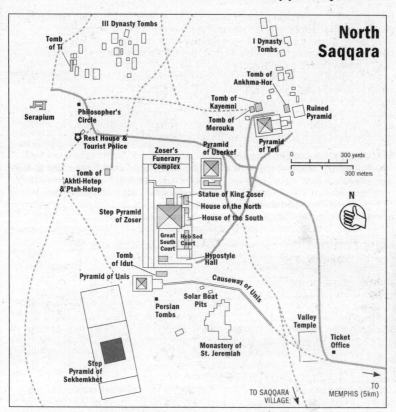

North Saqqara

(map labels:)
III Dynasty Tombs
Tomb of Ti
I Dynasty Tombs
Tomb of Ankhma-Hor.
Serapium
Philosopher's Circle
Tomb of Kayemni
Ruined Pyramid
Rest House & Tourist Police
Tomb of Merouka
Pyramid of Userkef
Pyramid of Teti
Tomb of Akhti-Hotep & Ptah-Hotep
Zoser's Funerary Complex
Statue of King Zoser
Step Pyramid of Zoser
House of the North
House of the South
Great South Court
Heb Sed Court
Tomb of Idut
Hypostyle Hall
Pyramid of Unis
Causeway of Unis
Solar Boat Pits
Persian Tombs
Valley Temple
Ticket Office
Monastery of St. Jeremiah
Step Pyramid of Sekhemkhet
0   300 yards
0   300 meters
N
TO SAQQARA VILLAGE
TO MEMPHIS (5km)

EGYPT

the pyramids and other architectural wonders in Egypt. The brilliant architect **Imhotep** initially designed the monument as a stone *mastaba*, a low, rectangular building covering a burial shaft dug into the earth. Not satisfied with a simple rectangle, he modified the original structure, greatly expanding it and stacking several layers on top of the original base. Time and weather have taken their toll on history's first monument to post-mortem egotism, but French archaeologist Jean-Philippe Lauer has made the reconstruction of the Step Pyramid a lifetime project.

STEP PYRAMID OF ZOSER I. Enter the Step Pyramid complex from the southeastern side of the limestone enclosure wall. The paneled barrier was designed to resemble the mud-brick work that graced the fortifications surrounding the cities and palaces of the period. Two fixed stone panels, carved to resemble a massive wooden doorway, open onto a 40-columned entrance colonnade. The columns are ridged to look like stylized bundles of papyrus stems, and are probably the world's first stone columns (unlike the chumps before him who used mud brick, Imhotep built for eternity). Niches between the columns once held statues of Zoser. This columned corridor culminates in the **Hypostyle Hall,** a fledgling version of the hallways found at Karnak and Abydos, which opens on to the **Great South Court.** The two weathered altars in the center of the Court symbolize Lower and Upper Egypt. The remains of a *mastaba* (Egyptian tomb) are at the base of the Step Pyramid at the northern end of the site; scholars are still debating the purpose of this superfluous *mastaba.* Some think that the tomb is the original *mastaba* onto which Imhotep added the other layers of the Step Pyramid. Others claim it is the symbolic representation of a second tomb. Earlier pharaohs had a second tomb constructed (in the south at Abydos) in addition to their tomb at Saqqara; Zoser may have been alluding to this custom by placing a small tomb at the south of his complex.

To the east, past the colonnade, the **Heb-Sed Court** runs the length of one side of the courtyard. During the Archaic Period (before the first dynasty), the pharaoh had to prove himself by performing various athletic feats at the annual Sed Festival. If he failed, he would be killed and a stronger replacement crowned. Later pharaohs turned the Sed into a rejuvenation ceremony and did away with the ritual regicide portion of the program. The Heb-Sed Court in the complex and the panels inside the pyramid that depict Zoser running a ceremonial race were meant to ensure his eternal rejuvenation. A small dais with two sets of stairs was where Zoser climbed twice to be crowned with the crowns of Lower and Upper Egypt.

STATUE OF KING ZOSER. Directly in front of the Step Pyramid's northern face stands the most haunting spectacle at Saqqara, a statue of King Zoser I. The pharaoh stares out from a slanted stone hut (known as a **sardab**) pierced by two tiny apertures. The *sardab* allowed the spirit of the pharaoh to communicate with the outside world. The striking figure here is a plaster copy of the original (which now glares at visitors in the Egyptian Museum in Cairo, see p. 122). Behind the statue is the entrance to the pyramid's locked interior.

OTHER PYRAMIDS. There are several other pyramids in the area. The only one open to the public is the small **Pyramid of Teti.** Scramble down a ramp into the underground chambers to be greeted by protruding rocks—all that remains of a pathetic attempt to deter grave robbers. A massive black sarcophagus is inside, as well as a fine example of a **pyramid text** and a ceiling decorated with stars.

On the southwest corner of Zoser's complex, up the steps to the right of the pit and over the enclosure wall, looms the massive **Pyramid of Unis.** Unis was the last pharaoh of the 5th dynasty. Inside are wall carvings known as the **Pyramid Texts,** discovered by Thomas Cook, English innovator of the conducted tour, in 1881. These writings constitute the earliest known example of decorative hieroglyph writing on the walls of a tomb chamber. Unfortunately, the Pyramid of Unis has been closed permanently for preservation.

Extending eastward from the Pyramid of Unis is the **Causeway of Unis,** a beautifully restored sunken road lined by **solar boat pits** on its southern side. Over the low ridge of dunes lie the ruins of the **Monastery of St. Jeremiah,** barely jutting out from the desert. Founded in the 5th century, it was discovered in 1907. Many of the artifacts found inside are now in the Coptic Museum in Cairo (see p. 116).

TOMBS OF THE NOBLES

The nobles constructed tombs around the pyramids, mindful of their prestige even in death. All are relatively close, and those open to the public have signs in English indicating their owners (who are always depicted in wall paintings as being bigger than their servants and companion animals). All tombs have several features in common. Most of them have narrow insets in the wall (called **spirit doors**) through which the ghosts of the deceased can pass, as well as paintings of food and entertainment for the dead to partake of in the afterlife.

TOMB OF ANKHMA-HOR. Just east of the Tomb of Teti is the Tomb of Ankhma-Hor, which contains several representations of medical operations (including toe surgery and a circumcision). One Egyptologist has asserted that the 6th-dynasty tendency to depict funerary scenes indicates a growing fixation with the afterlife as the Old Kingdom headed into its final decline.

TOMB OF KAYEMNI. To the northeast, the nearby **Tomb of Kayemni** contains reliefs depicting daily farming life along the Nile. In one hall, incredibly limber "acrobats" entertain Kayemni.

TOMB OF MEREROUKA. North from the Tomb of Teti, this tomb has separate sections for Mererouka, his son, and his wife. There are fine carvings of desert hunts, jewelry making, and officials with big sticks collecting taxes. In addition, well-preserved, colored reliefs show the slaughtering and cutting up of cattle.

HOUSES OF THE SOUTH AND NORTH. The more substantial **House of the South** stands next door to the Step Pyramid, on its eastern side. The inside walls are inscribed with ancient graffiti left by a visitor during the reign of Ramses II. The messages, expressing admiration for King Zoser, were hastily scrawled onto the walls in a late cursive style of hieroglyphics known as hieratic. The lotus columns here represent Upper Egypt—hence the name House of the South. The **House of the North** is represented by the papyrus columns, the symbol of Lower Egypt. Some scholars believe that this emphasis on North and South throughout the site at Saqqara reflects the era's desire to unify Egypt geographically and spiritually.

PERSIAN TOMBS. To the south, a humble shack covers the shaft leading to three of Egypt's deepest burial chambers, the **Persian Tombs** of Psamtik, Zenhebu, and Peleese (of the 16th dynasty). A dizzying spiral staircase drills 25m into the ground, ending in three vaulted burial chambers linked by narrow passageways. Colorful chambers make the walk worthwhile. According to the ancient inscriptions, Zenhebu was a famous admiral and Psamtik a high-ranking doctor of the pharaoh's court. Since the tombs are more isolated, some asking around and *bakhsheesh* may be necessary to gain admittance.

WESTERN NORTH SAQQARA

TOMB OF AKHTI-HOTEP AND PTAH-HOTEP. This unique tomb was built by two brothers often depicted together; their fraternal affection is conveyed across the centuries. There are many superb reliefs here, including a cow giving birth. The color in some sections of the tomb shows that men, who were often in the sun, had much darker skin than women.

TOMB OF TI. The Tomb of Ti, 300m north of the Serapium, was excavated in 1865 and has since been one of the primary sources of information about daily and ceremonial life during the 5th dynasty (25th century BCE). Serving under three pharaohs, Ti had many titles: Overseer of the Pyramids and Sun Temples at Abu Sir, Superintendent of Works, Scribe of the Court, Royal Counselor, Editrix, Royal Fluffer, Royal Tea Brewer, and even Lord of Secrets. Some scholars also believe he was a practitioner of a martial arts discipline similar to that of the Japanese ninjas. He was such a high-ranking noble that he was allowed to marry Princess Nefer-Hotep. Tomb paintings show his children wearing braided hairpieces, a sign that they were royal contenders for the throne.

SERAPIUM. The Serapium, discovered in 1854, is several hundred meters west of the Rest House at the terminus of the main road. The complex is the legacy of a bull-worshiping cult that thrived during the New Kingdom. Believers traditionally associated the Apis bulls (the sacred oxen of Ptah) with Osiris and the afterlife, but during the Roman occupation, the Apis bull cult combined with that of the Greek god Zeus (who often took the form of a bull, especially when he was fooling around with mortal women). The combined Zeus-Apis cult was especially strong around Alexandria. Work on the main portion of the underground complex was begun in the 7th century BCE by Psamtik and continued through the Ptolemaic era, though much older tombs adjoin this central set of chambers. In the oldest portion of the Serapium, two large, gold-plated sarcophagi and several canopic jars containing human heads were found, as well as the undisturbed footprints of the priests who had put the sacred animals to rest more than 3000 years earlier. Recessed tombs flank the main corridor on both sides, each containing a sarcophagus. It's difficult to imagine these mammoth coffins being transported to the confines of the cave; their average weight is 65 tons. In the final tomb stands the largest sarcophagus, hewn from a single piece of black granite.

TOMBS OF THE APIS BULLS. The mausoleum in the Serapium (a series of eerie underground tunnels with tiny lanterns) houses the **Tombs of the Apis Bulls,** where 25 sacred oxen representing Ptah's pets were embalmed and placed in enormous sarcophagi of solid granite. Only one of the bulls remains (the rest have been stolen); it now stands in Cairo's Agricultural Museum. At the end of the mausoleum tunnel metal steps ascend into one of the gigantic coffins. Go early, as the Serapium is a fair distance away from other sites and often closes around 4pm.

OTHER SIGHTS. West of the Tomb of Akhti-Hotep and Ptah-Hotep (see Western North Saqqara above) is a shady and expensive Rest House with a bathroom and a small concession stand. Farther along the highway, where the road turns sharply to the west, are several decrepit Greek statues known as the Philosophers' Circle. These statues are said to represent Homer (at the center), Pindar (to his left), Plato (to his right), and two unknowns (possibly Pythagoras and Heraclides).

ABU SIR أبو صير

The three pyramids of Abu Sir are six kilometers north of Saqqara and 2½km from the village of Abu Sir. No tour buses make it here so the site can only be reached by foot or hoof. The most imposing of the three main pyramids at Abu Sir is the **Pyramid of Neferirkare,** which towers 68m above the desert and remains one of the best-preserved monuments in the Saqqara area. It once had a stone casing like its neighbors at Giza, but suffered a similar loss of face, exposing its exterior, which bears a remarkable resemblance to a step pyramid. The **Pyramid of Niuserre** is the youngest and most dilapidated of the pyramids in the area, and the **Pyramid of Sahure** to the north completes the trio.

If you are traveling by animal between Abu Sir and Giza, have your guide stop off along the way at the 5th-dynasty **Sun Temple of Abu Sarab.** The temple is to the north, and about 1½km north of the Pyramid of Sahure. On the fringe of cultivated fields, the temple was built by King Niuserre in honor of the sun god Ra. It features an impressive altar constructed from five massive blocks of alabaster. A horse or camel ride from Zoser's Step Pyramid to the Sun Temple costs E£20. If business is slow it may be possible to bargain to as low as E£10.

SOUTH SAQQARA

South Saqqara's most interesting funerary monument is the unusual **Tomb of Shepseskaf** (popularly known as *Mastabat Fara'un*). The tomb is an enormous stone structure shaped like a sarcophagus and capped with a rounded lid. Although Shepseskaf reigned for only three years (he was the sixth king of the 4th dynasty and son of Mycerinus, whose pyramid stands at Giza), his stint on the throne was long enough to qualify him for a grand tomb—sort of. *Mastabat Fara'un* is neither a true *mastaba* nor a pyramid; scholars see it as a transitional experiment. A guard will admit you (E£1 *bakhsheesh* should suffice).

MEMPHIS ممفيس

Memphis is not worth the detour today, though it might have been in 3000 BCE. The great pyramid-building pharaohs (such as Cheops, Khufu, and Khefren) lived and ruled at Memphis, founded over five millennia ago by the legendary Menes and once populated by over half a million people. While the pyramids they built have endured, the pharaohs' city has faded away, leaving only palms, wandering goats, and the odd ruins (many closed to the public). There is a small **museum** that has a garden with well-worn statues and a large alabaster sphinx that probably stood at the south entrance of the Temple of Ptah. The most impressive statue is a 14m tall **Colossus of Ramses II,** displayed horizontally with cartouches engraved on its shoulders and waist. (E£14, students E£7. Camera privileges E£5, video E£25.) If you choose to go, you might have to take a taxi to Memphis from Saqqara or Abu Sir. Hitchhiking from here is dangerous and not recommended.

DASHUR دشور

The four unique pyramids at Dashur are worth seeing. Close to the road is the large **Pyramid of Senefru.** Senefru was the father of Khufu (whose pyramid is one of the three at Giza), and the proportions of this pyramid reveal where Khufu got his inflated post-mortem ego. You can scramble down an odd ladder into the chambers of the pyramid. A quick drive or moderate walk away from the Pyramid of

Senefru is the famous **Bent Pyramid.** This pyramid is unusual because it changes the angle of its sides halfway to the top, perhaps to keep it from collapsing under untenable weight. Much of it is still cased in limestone, showing what pyramids looked like when they were first built. A few yards behind the Bent Pyramid is the small cone of a decaying pyramid. Though not too much to look at, it has a nice view of the desert at the top and flat stones that can be used as picnic tables.

FAYYUM الفيوم ☎084

Fayyum, Egypt's largest oasis, is a vast agrarian settlement slightly over 100km from Cairo. Fayyum city's honking cars and crowded streets give little hint that open meadows lie only a few hundred meters away. The 1.8 million residents of the oasis live in 157 small villages that dot a sandy landscape swathed with chrysanthemum and sunflower fields. Lake Qarun to the north is a popular beach resort, and the local government is cultivating the rest of the area for tourism.

Fayyum was first developed through canal-building and irrigation by the rulers of ancient Egypt's 12th dynasty (20th-19th centuries BCE). The Ptolemies made the area into a rich province with its capital at Crocodopolis (near the site of modern Fayyum), the headquarters of a cult that worshiped Sebak and other reptilian deities. Roman conquerors used Crocodopolis as a vacation resort and as one of the primary granaries of the empire. An early center of Coptic Christianity, the oasis also sheltered a large population of exiled Jews in the 3rd century CE. Muslims believe the extensive canals to be the work of the biblical Joseph during his stay in Egypt; Bahr Yusef is named accordingly. Fayyum also boasts several out-of-the-way pharaonic ruins that are still under excavation and rarely touristed, making it a thoroughly enjoyable and more convenient alternative to the oases in the Western Desert. The only hassle is getting to Fayyum—buses and private taxis refuse to travel the harsh roads, so the only viable options are *service*.

▐ GETTING THERE AND GETTING AROUND

Buses and Service: The **main bus and service station** is 1km from the tourist office, tucked surreptitiously under a bridge. From the tourist office, cross the train tracks and take a right. Continue along this road for 500m and take a right before the large building on the right. Take another right after one block and you'll find the station under the bridge. Buses to **Cairo** stop at Giza Sq. and Ramses Station (2hr., every 30min. 6am-6pm, E£3.75). *Service* leave from here to Giza Sq. or Ramses Station in **Cairo** until late at night and are dangerous, but faster (E£5-6). Another **bus and service station** serves **Beni Suef** and points south. Walk to the 3rd bridge over the canal west of the tourist office, turn left, and walk 1km. Don't be misled by the local bus depot past the main crossroads—the station is 200m farther on the right.

Local Transportation: Arabic numbered *service* travel around town on different routes (25pt). *Service* to towns outside Fayyum city can be caught from these stations (50pt-E£1). You can also hire a **hantour** (horse carriage) for E£1-5 anywhere in town.

▐▌ ORIENTATION AND PRACTICAL INFORMATION

Fayyum is a roughly triangular area, stretching about 90km east to west. The eastern edge is bordered by the Nile. The saltwater **Lake Qarun** separates the northwest edge of Fayyum from the sandy plateau of the Western Desert. The city of Fayyum is almost in the center and serves as the area's transportation hub. Main hotels and offices are around the **waterwheels** in the middle of town. The city runs along the **Bahr Yusef Canal,** which flows west from the Nile. At the center of town, **Bahr Sinnuris** separates from Bahr Yusef at a right angle and flows north toward the farmlands. **Al-Gomhoriyya St.** and **al-Huriyya St.** run along the north and south banks of Bahr Yusef, respectively. There are four groaning waterwheels next to the tourist office. The inverted pyramid dominating the eastern end of Bahr Yusef is Fayyum's **Culture Palace,** housing a theater, cinema, and public library.

Tourist Office: (☎34 23 13), on al-Gomhoriyya St., next door to Cafeteria al-Medina, 50m east of the juncture of the two canals. Minimal English spoken, but the officers can provide you with outdated brochures about the region. Open daily 9am-4pm.

Currency Exchange: Misr Bank (☎35 01 62), on the same side of the canal as the Palace Hotel, just south of the tourist office on al-Gomhoriyya St. No traveler's check exchange. Also has a V/MC/Cirrus **ATM** outside. Open Su-Th 8:30am-2pm.

Tourist Police: (☎34 72 98), posted around the tourist office on al-Gomhoriyya St. Open 24hr. Minimal English.

Hospital: (☎34 22 49 or 33 35 96), on Hospital St. Pink building off Msella St. Cash only.

Telephones: Same building as the post office. International calls available. Open 24hr.

Post Office: 100m south of the first bridge east of the tourist office, on the opposite side of the river. **EMS** and **Poste Restante** available. Open Sa-Th 8am-2pm.

ACCOMMODATIONS AND FOOD

Fayyum is an easy daytrip from Cairo, which is good given that Fayyum city has few cheap beds. The 40km-long Lake Qarun and heavenly Wadi al-Ruwayan are much more peaceful roosting options (see **Near Fayyum,** p. 139). The **Palace Hotel,** on al-Huriyya St. one block west of the tourist office under a blue English sign, is the best bet within the city. Clean, breezy rooms overlook the canal and are filled with folded-down sheets, towels, and soap. Owner Ashraf Arafa speaks flawless English and is much more helpful than the tourist office. (☎35 12 22. Lunch and dinner E£10 each. Small breakfast included. Singles E£20, with shower E£30, with A/C E£45; doubles E£35, with shower E£45, with A/C E£60.) In the alley behind the Palace Hotel, the **Maka Hotel** provides simple rooms with fans. (☎35 12 23. Singles E£10; doubles E£20; extra for balcony.) The **Fayyum Youth Hostel,** at al-Hadaka, Block 7, Flat #7, is a bit distant; ask for *bayt al-shabab.* With your back to the Cairo bus stop, turn left and walk 250m to the intersection with a five-story brick building. Take a sharp left, then another left at the green "FYH" sign 50m ahead. The hostel is the second building on the right. Inside are slightly dingy rooms and a common kitchen. (☎35 00 05. Breakfast included. Dorm beds E£8, students E£7.)

Food options in Fayyum are limited to small cafeterias serving grilled meats and the usual *fuul* and *ta'amiya,* plus a few restaurants. Waltz over to the **Governorate Club,** on Governorate St. Ask your *hantour* driver for *Nadi al-Muhafzah* or take *service* #3 (٣), 6 (٦), or 9 (٩) from the Youth Hostel (#9 from the center of town). The "exclusive" club (waiters wear red jackets and bowties) makes up for its E£3 entrance fee with large, cheap meals. (Kebab E£9, full meals E£10. Open daily until 1am.) **City Cafe,** in the town center, has a pleasant view of the waterwheels, as well as outdoor seating and live Arabic music. (☎34 56 52. Basic Egyptian meals E£10.) Other than the nearby grassy meadows, the best option for vegetarians is the veggies, rice, and cucumber salad (around E£7) at the **Palace Hotel** (☎35 12 22).

SIGHTS

Fayyum city is filled with Egyptians living ordinary lives, but the real beauty is outside the city. Visitors who haven't been ossified by the Islamic architecture in Cairo should visit the **Mosque of Qaytbay,** along the canal about one kilometer west of the town center, at the very end of al-Huriyya St. The mosque is named for Mamluk Sultan al-Ashraf Seif al-Din Qaytbay, who ruled Egypt from 1468 to 1496. It was built beside a river that once flowed there, allowing worshipers to wash before prayers. The ivory on the *mihrab* was brought all the way from Somalia.

For a quick introduction to the rural life of Fayyum, head north out of town along Bahr Sinnuris. After 2km of boundless green fields, you'll reach the first of seven ancient **waterwheels,** still used in the irrigation system. Unlike Western versions, these great wooden tires are not used to power pumps but are themselves pumps, ingeniously using the flow of the stream to lift the water to a higher level.

NEAR FAYYUM

To reach any point north of Fayyum, walk north from the information stand to the railroad tracks running parallel to Bahr Yusef Canal. Turn left and walk to the 4th crossing. You'll find a "taxi" stand 300m down on the left. Trucks shuttle between Fayyum, 'Ain Sileen (50pt), and Lake Qarun (E£1). You'll need to change trucks at the village of Sanhur to reach the lake.

WADI AL-RUWAYAN

A wonderful lake and three waterfalls adorn this area, a 45-minute drive from Lake Qarun, along what becomes a pure desert passage. Sand dunes and cool cobalt waters ripple side by side, separated by no more than a few meters of greenery. The three waterfalls plunge three meters over the mossy rocks into a clear lake. Taxis run from Fayyum or Lake Qarun (7am-4pm). The earlier you set off, the better your bargaining position will be (don't pay more than E£40-60 per carload). Hitching is reportedly easy in winter, but is not recommended by *Let's Go.* Bring plenty of sunblock and insect repellent. (*Wadi* entrance E£5, cars E£5 extra.) If you find it hard to tear yourself away, lounge amid camel herds at the aptly named **Paradise Safari Camp,** owned by English-speaking Muhammad Marzuk (E£20 per person). The camp, on the lake's shore, is surrounded by golden dunes ripe for exploration. Each large tent has two crisp-sheeted beds and a nightstand with a candle (electricity is used solely for the refrigerator in the kitchen). A **snack stand** on the beach sells overpriced refreshments, but the Safari Camp's beautiful outdoor **restaurant** has meals (E£25).

LAKE QARUN

Fifteen kilometers north of Fayyum past some sunflower patches is the saltwater **Lake Qarun** (known as *al-Birka*), lined on its southern shore with expensive hotels and daytime picnic areas. In the winter, ducks escaping from the cold climes of Europe migrate to the waters of Lake Qarun. Reasonable daytrips from Cairo and Fayyum, the beaches have a tropical feel, with toasty sand, warm blue-green water, and palm frond *palapas* offering shade. The closest thing to lakeside budget accommodations is the **Waha Hotel.** In winter, the hotel rents jet skis, sailboards, and other fun toys. (Breakfast included. A/C. Singles E£35; doubles E£70.)

A bit past the west of Lake Qarun sits a deceptively simple looking Ptolemaic temple known as ▨**Qasr Qarun.** This is one place where you probably don't want to shoo away the guard offering to guide you around: a warren of secret passageways and bat-filled rooms below the main sanctuary let you live out your favorite Indiana Jones fantasy. Climb up the stairs to the roof for a beautiful view of the surrounding area. *Service* are available from Lake Qarun for 50pt. (Open daily 8am-6pm. E£16, students E£8.)

KARANIS

The mud brick houses of the Greco-Roman settlement of Karanis, 30km north of Fayyum along the road to Cairo, have not fared well over time. The town was built by the Greeks in the 3rd century and occupied by the Romans for almost 800 years. Its two stone temples are in better shape, offering an interesting contrast of architectural styles (one temple was built by the Greeks, the other by the Romans).

The infrequently visited **Museum of Kom Oshim** holds a surprisingly wide collection of statues and *stelae* found both on-site at Karanis and around Saqqara and Giza. Comb through the exhibit of Greco-Roman terra cotta figurines, displaying a survey of ancient hairstyles. The second floor of the museum, devoted to Islamic and Coptic art, houses beautifully painted wood icons. Catch a *service* or bus heading north from Fayyum and ask to be let out at Mathaf (pronounced MATT-haff) Kom Oshim. (Open daily 8am-6pm; in winter 8am-5pm. E£16, students E£8.)

'AIN SILEEN SPRINGS

'Ain Sileen Springs, 18km northwest of Fayyum, is the most easily reached but least rewarding of the area's attractions. The road to the springs winds through fields bristling with corn, palms, fruit, and vegetables, split into perfect sections by canals. The titanium-rich water is supposedly good for hypertension; drink at your own risk. The most convenient way to get there is to take a **service** or **bus** (35-50pt) from the station serving Sanhur, west of town along the railroad tracks. *Service* #7 (٧) or 8 (٨) go to the station from the center of Fayyum city, and #9 (٩) goes there from the youth hostel. The **tourist office** is 50m from the springs road, along with several small stands selling the sweetest **mangos** imaginable (E£6-9 per kg, in season in Aug.). **Restaurants** with gorgeous views of the canals serve kebab (E£12), pigeon (E£7), and salads (E£1). The springs flow into a small swimming pool packed with Egyptian children. Foreigners bathing here will create a stir; foreign women will cause widespread pandemonium.

NILE DELTA

TANTA طنطا

For most of the year, the residents of Egypt's fifth largest city live peaceful, tourist-free lives. But for one week in October, Tanta undergoes a metamorphosis from a provincial city into a tumultuous cacophony of some three million pilgrims from Egypt and the Arab world, who converge on the city for a *mawlid*, or festival, celebrating the birthday of a Coptic or Muslim saint. The **Mawlid of Sa'id Ahmed al-Bedawi** honors the founder of Egypt's largest Sufi brotherhood (as well as the cotton harvest that precedes the festival). The festival is truly a circus, with Bedawi's red-turbaned devotees mingling with lions, tigers, and near-unbearable hordes of vendors.

The main attraction in Tanta (and the center of the *mawlid* festivities) is the **Mosque of Bedawi.** Built during the Ottoman period, it has three domes and an impressively large porch. The ceiling is decorated with floral designs, while the sheikh's tomb glows eerily with green neon as devotees pay their respects. The **Sabil of Kasir,** 800m down Galna St., is a small Ottoman water dispensary. Although it is architecturally unremarkable, it has a nice garden with Islamic carvings. (Open 9am-4pm. 50pt.) Signs point to the **Tanta Museum,** which houses a drab collection of ceramics (many broken), metalwork, and coins. (Open daily 9am-4pm, closed F during prayer time. E£10, students E£5. Camera privileges E£5.)

Trains leave from the impressive station (though the clock is slow) to: Alexandria (9 per day 9am-9pm, 2nd-class E£8); Cairo (10 per day 6am-9:30pm, E£6); and Isma'ilia and Port Said (noon, 6:30pm, midnight; E£2). **Middle Delta** runs **buses** to Cairo (every 30min. 5am-11pm, E£5). The **service** depot is near the bus and train stations. **Minibuses** serve much of Tanta (25pt), and the city's **taxis** have a fixed rate of E£1 for all destinations.

The main street in Tanta is **al-Bahr St.,** which runs from one end of town to the other. Most banks and official buildings are along it, between the hospital and a collection of fast food joints about two kilometers later. Past the fast food is **Ahmed Maher St.,** which leads to the train and bus station and the **Mosque of Bedawi** after one kilometer. Most **banks** don't cash traveler's checks, but will exchange cash, and are open from 9am-2pm. Call ☎125 for the **tourist police** and ☎122 for other **emergency** services. The **hospital** (☎35 03 71 or 35 03 72), at the other end of al-Bahr St. from the fast-food restaurants, has English-speaking staff.

There are no budget accommodations in Tanta, but with so many trains and buses going to Cairo and Alexandria, there's no need to stay in the city overnight. If you get stranded, the cheapest place to bed down is the three-star **'Arafa Hotel,** the big pink building near the train station. All rooms have A/C, bath, and TV. (Singles E£120; doubles E£170; triples E£295. V, MC.) Be forewarned, though, that during the *mawlid,* even Sheikh Badawi probably couldn't get a room. Turn down the street at the CIB bank for the popular favorite **La Casa,** on al-Mu'tasem St., which serves up Italian food (E£7-15) in a Spanish interior. (Open daily 10am-1am.)

QANATIR قناطر

Bus #953 (٩٥٣) from Cairo's Abd al-Munem Riad Station in front of the Ramses Hilton runs frequently to Qanatir (45min., 40pt). On F and Su, a passenger ferry runs along the Nile from Cairo to Qanatir. The dock is on the corniche, behind the Ramses Hilton and in front of the Television Building (1½hr., 9am-4:30pm, E£2). Feluccas may be hired from the same area (3hr.). Qanatir can be a daytrip or a first stop on a journey north.

This town marks the official beginning of the Delta, where the Nile splits into the eastern (Dumyat) and western (Rashid, or Rosetta) branches 16km north of Cairo. Qanatir is also the site of the **Nile barrages,** bridges that regulate the flow of water into the Delta. Turrets and arches decorate the 19th-century structures, which were built when cotton production boomed here. The point of land where the Nile splits is home to parks, food stalls, and an arcade. Egyptian youth descend on Qanatir in a noisy cloud of Arab pop music on weekends to enjoy the fresh air and get fresh with anyone who dares stroll past them. Foreigners will be hounded into renting a bike (E£1-3 per hr.), moped, horse, or boat. The best part of the visit is the view of the Egyptian countryside on the ferry ride into town from Cairo.

ZAGAZIG AND TEL BASTA الزقازيق و تـل بستة

Trains run to Zagazig throughout the day (1½hr., every hr. 6:20am-6:30pm, E£6), as do service from the Ahmed Hilmi Sq. bus station (1¼hr., E£4.50). To reach Tel Basta, take a taxi from the Zagazig train station (10min.). You'll also have to take a taxi from the train station to the museum (10min., E£5). Orabi Museum open daily 9am-5pm. E£6, students E£3. Camera privileges E£10, video E£15.

Lower Egypt was the center of power in the Old Kingdom, and many impressive monuments were erected in the Nile Delta region throughout the pharaonic era. Unfortunately, very few of these monuments remain today, due to irrigation canals dug beneath the monuments and the natural fanning out of the river. The soil in the region is also too loose to support permanent structures (although most structures were made out of fast deteriorating mud-brick anyway). The **Orabi Museum** in Zagazig houses a small collection of local archaeological finds—all that remains of these once-great structures. Southeast of Zagazig are the ruins of Bubastis, now called **Tel Basta.** The original name means "House of Bastet" and refers to the feline goddess to whom the main temple was dedicated. Festivals held here in honor of the cat-goddess attracted over 700,000 devotees who would sing and dance, make sacrifices, and consume mass quantities of food and wine. The ancient historian Herodotus thought that Bubastis was the cat's pajamas, writing not only that "more wine is drunk at this feast than in the whole year beside," but also that the temple was the most pleasurable to gaze upon of all the Delta's pharaonic sites. Herodotus would roll over in his grave if he could see the condition of modern-day Bubastis, which looks like scattered kitty litter. Those who don't meow like mad over archaeological finds and ancient cults may want to zagazig—or just bypass—these towns.

TANIS تانس

A very long (3½hr.) drive from Cairo. Take the train or bus from Ahmed Hilmi Sq. (2½hr., E£4) to Zagazig. From there, take a service to Faqus (E£1.50) and from there to al-Housya (E£1), where a service or pickup truck taxi will take you to San al-Hagar (E£1); someone there will point you to the ruins. E£16, students E£8. Camera privileges E£5.

One of the region's most impressive sites is ancient Tanis. The remains of the city lie in the northeast corner of the Delta's fertile triangle, a 10-minute walk from the dilapidated town of **San al-Hagar.** The capital of the 21st (Tanite) dynasty, Tanis was founded in the 11th century BCE by the pharaoh Smendes.

At one time, Tanis and Bubastis were more important than Memphis and Thebes. Though the past 31 centuries have taken their toll on Tanis, the site is still impressive and slightly surreal, carelessly littered with massive broken obelisks, well-preserved carvings, and various shattered body parts from *colossi*. The tombs of Smendes and other ancient notables feature impressive hieroglyphs. Though the ruins are not as amazing as *Raiders of the Lost Ark* would have you believe, there is a structure remarkably similar to the Well of Souls. The site also has a small museum.

WADI NATRUN وادى النطرون

If the insanity of Cairo has left you aggravated, Wadi Natrun's monasteries, flowering trees, cooing doves, and friendly monks will restore you to tranquility. For 1500 years, the 50 monasteries of Wadi Natrun were the backbone of the Coptic community in Egypt. The four that stand today (forming an ill-proportioned cross in the desert landscape) are more than impressive relics; they are functional places of worship serving the spiritual needs of Egypt's Orthodox Christian population who flock here in tour buses all summer. The first Christian monastery in Egypt was established in the Eastern Desert by St. Anthony the Great (250-355 CE; see **St. Anthony's Monastery**, p. 201). In 330 CE, one of Anthony's disciples established the monastic lifestyle in Wadi Natrun. More than a millennium and a half later, during the 1980s, interest in Coptic monasticism was so great that new rooms were added to accommodate the many novice ascetics arriving in the Natrun Valley. Wadi Natrun is also home to the last surviving type of papyrus. Due to the high salinity of the water (*wadi* = valley, *natrun* = salt), it is a dwarf subspecies that does not reach over two meters (large papyrus, found in the Delta, was last seen in the mid-19th century).

■✴ 🛈 ORIENTATION AND PRACTICAL INFORMATION

A West Delta **bus** leaves from Cairo's **Turgoman station** (2½hr., every 30min. 6:30am-5pm, E£5 collected on board). Ride past the Wadi Natrun Rest House into Wadi Natrun town; the bus stop is near the gaudily painted statue of a soldier. Take a **pickup taxi** from here to the monastery Deir Anba Bishoi (10min., E£1). Coptic pilgrims are often willing to pick up travelers; this is also the best way to travel between monasteries. Start your journey early if you plan to return to Cairo or Alexandria in the evening, as there are no places to stay in Wadi Natrun town. To leave Wadi Natrun, wait at the Wadi Natrun Rest House for **service** or buses, which go to Alexandria (*service* leave about every hr., E£4) or Cairo (E£4 for frequent *service;* buses leave about every hr. until 6pm, E£4). Many travelers are offered rides by drivers passing by, but be wary of accepting rides from strangers. *Let's Go* does not recommend hitchhiking.

> **NIGHT OF THE LIVING DEAD** The monks who inhabit the four functional monasteries in Wadi Natrun live, eat, and pray as one. Few are allowed to leave, unless for medical reasons or on monastery business. When he is ordained, a monk's former self "dies," and he casts off the world of earthly desires to put on the black robe that indicates this symbolic death. The black hood symbolizes the biblical "helmet of salvation" (Ephesians 6:17); the 13 crosses embroidered upon it represent Jesus Christ (the cross on the back) and his 12 apostles (the 12 side crosses). A monk's day typically begins at 3:45am (even earlier on Sundays, when the monks of Deir Anba Bishoi rise at 12:45am for six hours of uninterrupted prayer), at which time the monks sing psalms and cantillate the Coptic liturgy amid clouds of incense, wide-eyed icons, and flickering candlelight. The service is punctuated by entrancing triangle and cymbal music (arrive before 9am to attend).

👁 SIGHTS

Deir Anba Bishoi is open every day of the year; Deir al-Suryan, Deir Anba Baramus, and Deir Abu Maqar close for various feast and fast days, particularly around Christmas and Easter. With the exception of those at Deir Abu Maqar, all monks happily receive foreign tourists and provide free tours of their monasteries. Some travelers try to arrange overnight stays, although this is primarily a privilege of religious pilgrims. For information on overnight stays, contact the Coptic Patriarch in Cairo at 22 Ramses St., Aboiyye (☎(02) 282 53 74), and see the specific monastery descriptions below for details. Non-pilgrims are often allowed to camp near the monasteries. As with most religious sites in the Middle East, wear modest attire (no shorts or sleeveless shirts) and remember to remove your shoes before entering the church. Non-flash photography is permitted.

DEIR ANBA BISHOI. The Monastery of St. Bishoi is the largest (with seven churches) and most accessible of the four monasteries. Dating from 381 CE, Deir Anba Bishoi's original limestone and silt construction is now covered in plaster. It was rebuilt in 444 after being sacked by Romans and now contains the remains of St. Bishoi, who is still believed to perform miracles for the faithful. Monks used to sleep in the desert, coming to the church only for services, but attacks by nomads in the 9th century prompted the construction of sleeping chambers and a protective wall, along with a tower connected by a drawbridge to the wall. From atop the tower you can see a white swath in the distance; it's the salt that gives Wadi Natrun its name. The second floor's **Chapel of the Virgin Mary** exhibits 1500-year-old Gothic-style arches (an Egyptian innovation brought to Europe from Byzantium by the Crusaders). Don't leave without hearing the amplified echo in the old communal dining room, along with an amazingly well-preserved set of vestments from the Islamic conquests. *(15km from the Rest House. Ask for Father Sedrak, a monk who speaks excellent English and is the designated tour guide. Open daily 8am-5pm.)*

DEIR AL-SURYAN. The "Monastery of the Syrians," named for the Syrian monks who once inhabited it, was established when a group of 4th-century monks left the Monastery of St. Bishoi following a theological dispute. With the resolution of the dispute in the 5th century, this alterna-monastery was no longer needed by the Egyptian Copts. In the beginning of the 8th century, it was purchased by a Syrian merchant for use by monks from his homeland, the first of whom arrived at the beginning of the 9th century. The monastery was prominent throughout the 10th century, and by the 11th century it housed the largest community in Wadi Natrun.

The monastery is best known for frescoes the Syrians painted over the original Egyptian work. The monks at Deir al-Suryan will be quick to tell you that they have what is widely considered the most beautiful Annunciation (when the angel Gabriel told Mary that she was pregnant) fresco in the world, in the **altar room** to the right as you enter; another lovely Annunciation fresco is at the back of the nave. Also in this room is an enormous set of ebony doors known as the **Door of Symbols,** whose leaves form the screen to the sanctuary in the Church of the Virgin Mary. The panels depict the seven epochs of the Christian era.

The **miracle tree** supposedly sprang from the staff of a Syrian saint in the 4th century. At the back of the church is a low, dark passageway leading to the private **cell of St. Bishoi.** The monks will show you an iron staple and chain dangling from the ceiling and explain how St. Bishoi would fasten it to his beard, thereby maintaining a standing position lest he fall asleep during his all-night prayer vigils. Set in the floor at the western end of the church is the **lakan** (marble basin), which is used for washing the monks' feet on holy days. *(A five-minute walk to the northwest from Deir Anba Bishoi, following the monastery walls. Open Su-F 9am-7pm, Sa 9am-5pm; in winter Su-F 9am-6pm, Sa 9am-3pm. No overnight stays.)*

DEIR ANBA BARAMUS. This structure is known as the Monastery of the Virgin Mary, but "Baramus" derives from the Coptic word "Romeos" (or Romans), in honor of Roman Emperor Valentinus's two sons, monks Maximus and Domitius.

Tradition says that a crypt under the altar holds the remains of these two holy men who worshiped here. Relics of St. Moses and St. Isadore are kept in the first section of the old church. The corpse of St. Moses once shook hands with passersby through a small aperture in his casket, but for the past 200 years, he has not been quite as cordial and the aperture has been sealed. *(4km northwest of Deir Anba Bishoi. Take a taxi from Wadi Natrun town or catch a ride from Deir Anba Bishoi. Open daily 10am-5pm.)*

DEIR ABU MAQAR. The Monastery of St. Maccarius was founded by St. Maccarius the Great (300-390 CE) and is the earliest of the Wadi Natrun monasteries. St. Maccarius remained a religious hermit throughout his life and lived in a cell connected by a tunnel to a small cave. Virtually none of that original building remains. In the beginning of the 11th century, the monastery became the refuge of monks fleeing Muslim persecution. During the Middle Ages, the monastery was famous for its library, which remained intact until Europeans discovered the treasures in the 17th century and removed them. *(8km southeast of Deir Anba Bishoi. Visitors not permitted without prior approval. If interested, send a letter to the monastery at P.O. Box 2780, Cairo. State the date and time of your visit, how long you wish to stay (no longer than 2hr.), and whether you would like to eat there. Overnight visits are granted to religious groups and students of theology or history. If invited, hire a car at the Wadi Natrun Guest House for the 15min. drive.)*

MEDITERRANEAN COAST

HIGHLIGHTS OF THE MEDITERRANEAN COAST

Many come to **Alexandria** for its **beaches** (p. 156), but the shores of **Marsa Matrouh** (p. 164) are the real treasure. The pristine waters of **'Agiba** (p. 164) and **Cleopatra's Beach** (p. 165) were a favored playground for pharaonic lovers.

A desert trek to the **Siwa Oasis** (p. 165) uncovers the unique language and culture of the Siwan community. Follow Alexander's footsteps to the **Oracle of Amun** (p. 169), famous fount of wisdom to the ancients.

The **Greco-Roman Museum** (p. 154) preserves a sense of Alexandria's glorious past, while the **Roman Amphitheater** (p. 153) and **Pompey's Pillar** (p. 155) embody it.

ALEXANDRIA الأسكندرية ☎ 03

The population of Alexandria *(al-Iskandariyya)* swells to 12 million during the summer, as Gulf Arabs, Africans, and Egyptians flock to the gentle Mediterranean breezes. Outside the immediate city center, apartment buildings cover the breadth of Alexandria's two harbors. It shares the dirt, crowds, and noise of Cairo, but a different spirit pervades Alexandria, now Egypt's second largest city. Only here can an evening meal combine Greek *souvlaki*, British ale, French pastries, and the serenade of a *muezzin's* call to prayer. Western fashions are prevalent, alcohol flows freely, and French replaces English as the second language of choice.

Besides what can be found in an intriguing museum and a large catacomb complex, only bits and pieces of classical Alexandria remain to remind the visitor of its long and vibrant history as a seaport on the Mediterranean Coast. It all started when a triumphant Alexander stumbled upon this little fishing village (then called Rhakotis) en route to the Oracle of Amun at Siwa. The conquering hero became so enamored with the spot that he ordered a grand metropolis to be built upon it, then left for Siwa and never returned. Ptolemy was just as ptempted by the Mediterranean city as his predecessor and set about pampering Alexandria with the best ancient Greece had to offer. Alexandria's *Mouseion* (including the famous 500,000-volume library) soon became the greatest center of learning in the ancient world: Euclid invented his geometry there, while Eratosthenes estimated the circumference of the earth; later Ptolemy devised a tremendously popular faith in which Zeus and the pharaonic bull-god Apis were fused into the new deity Serapis.

GIVING THEM THE FINGER

When the Apostle St. Mark the Evangelist came to Alexandria to bring Christianity to Egypt in 64 CE, he quickly won many adherents. Pagans and Gnostics, who made up the majority of the population, felt threatened by the new Bishopric of Alexandria. In 67 CE, they ambushed St. Mark while he was giving a Mass and dragged him behind some horses around the streets of the city until he was killed. Not content with his death, they tied the body to a stake and started a fire, but the corpse would not burn. Frustrated, they instead beheaded the dead saint and called it a day. His remains were gathered up by the local church where they lay until the 9th century, when zealous visitors from Venice (a city notorious across the Eastern Orthodox world for its relic-snatching) stole the body to be reinterred at the Basilica di San Marco. Meanwhile, the head remained in Egypt after being transferred to the Church of St. George in Cairo, where it would be used, like other relics, during important religious celebrations. Fast forward to 1997, when at a summit of the Sees (the regional seats of church authority), Pope John Paul II returned one of St. Mark's fingers to the Coptic Pope Shnouda III. This gesture of papal reconciliation now rests at the Coptic Orthodox Patriarchate in Alexandria.

Ptolemy's creatively named successor, Ptolemy II, fostered trade in the city, which soon became the richest commercial center of its day. To help the traffic along, Ptolemy II constructed the Lighthouse of Pharos Island, one of the seven wonders of the ancient world (now collapsed). After all the back-stabbing and booty-snatching involving Cleopatra, Marc Antony, Octavian, and others with tetrasyllabic names, the Romans took control of the city. With the return of political stability, Alexandria continued to grow in size and intellectual importance. Scholarly interests shifted to theology, and Alexandria saw the creation of the Septuagint (the first Greek translation of the Hebrew Bible) for the expatriate Jewish population after the destruction of the Temple in Jerusalem. Legend has it that this was named for the 72 scholars who each labored in isolation but produced exactly the same text. Legend also teaches that St. Mark introduced Christianity to the city in 64 CE, founding what would become the Coptic Church. With Emperor Constantine's conversion in 314 CE, the influence of the Christians grew, and they turned on their pagan neighbors with vengeful glee, burning the *Mouseion* in the process (see **A Library Long Overdue,** p. 154). It was all downhill from there: the new capital in Cairo soon eclipsed Alexandria's glory, and a series of earthquakes in the 13th century finally reduced the immense lighthouse to rubble.

The rejuvenated modern city burst forth when Muhammad 'Ali made it a port for his navy and redug the canal to the Nile. During the 19th century, Alexandria became a favorite holiday spot for expatriate Europeans, wealthy Turks, and Egyptian nationals, and the settling for several major works of literature (like *The Alexandria Quartet*). Alexandria's cosmopolitan heyday drew to a close after World War II, however, and Egyptians, for the first time in over two thousand years, finally tied Alexandria's cultural life to their own.

✈ GETTING THERE AND AWAY

Alexandria lies at the junction of lush Delta farmlands, the barren Western Desert, and the Mediterranean coast. Cairo is a three-hour drive to the southeast on either of two roads. The scenic Delta road (231km) crosses both branches of the Nile and passes through the industrial city of Tanta, while the desert road (225km) nudges Wadi Natrun and passes through Giza.

FLIGHTS. Alexandria's small **airport** is several kilometers southeast of downtown. Local bus #203 (٢٠٣) and minibus #703 (٧٠٣) run between Orabi Sq. and the airport. **EgyptAir,** 19 Sa'ad Zaghloul St., is just east of Ramleh Station Sq. (☎482 59 37. Open daily 8am-8pm.) **Lufthansa,** 6 Tala'at Harb St., flies nonstop from Alexandria to Frankfurt on Wednesdays and Sundays at 7:35am. (☎482 26 07. One-way E£2787,

EGYPT

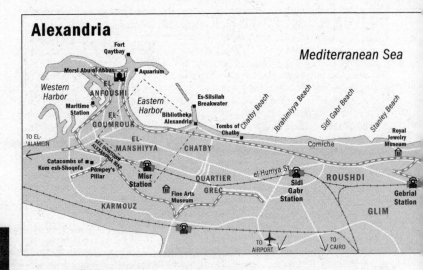

youth E£1443.) **Olympic Airlines,** on Sa'ad Zaghloul St., one block east of EgyptAir, flies from Alexandria to Athens Tuesdays and Fridays at 8:45am. (☎482 10 14 or 482 72 95; fax 482 89 01. One-way E£1304, youth E£702. Open M-F 8:30am-4:30pm, Sa 8:30am-12:30pm.)

TRAINS. All trains leave from Misr Station, in al-Attarien, and arrive at Sidi Gabr Station, near May Sq., about seven minutes later. There are two options for trains to **Cairo:** the turbocharged **Turbini** trains (2½hr.; 7, 8am, 2, 7pm; first-class E£25, 2nd-class E£20) or the slower **French** trains (3hr.; 6, 10, 11am, 3:30, 5, 8pm; first-class E£22, 2nd-class E£14). Both offer 30% student discounts. A **3rd-class A/C** train goes to Marsa Matrouh (9am, E£17).

BUSES. Find buses and tickets at the complex in 15 May Sq., behind Sidi Gabr Station. **Superjet** (☎421 90 92), offering A/C, snacks, bathrooms, and ever-endearing Egyptian movies, runs **buses** to: Cairo and stops at Giza, Tahrir Sq., al-Maza, and Cairo airport (3hr.; 9am, noon, 2, 8pm; downtown E£21, airport E£26); Hurghada (11hr., 8pm, E£75); Marsa Matrouh (6hr., 7am, E£24); Port Said (4½hr., 6:45am, E£22); and Sharm al-Sheikh (10hr., 6:30pm, E£77). **West Delta** (☎480 96 85) runs **buses** daily to: Cairo via Giza Sq., Tahrir Sq., and usually the Cairo airport (3hr., 6 per day 7am-11pm, downtown E£16-25, airport E£21-28); Hurghada (11hr., 6:30pm, E£60); Marsa Matrouh (6hr.; 7, 9, 11am, 1, 3, 6pm; E£20-23); Port Said (4½hr.; 6, 8am, 3:30, 4:30pm; E£17, with A/C E£22); Siwa (7hr., 11am, E£27); Tanta (6:45am, noon, 1:15pm; E£6); and Zagazig (8am, 2, 3pm; E£10-13).

SERVICE. *Service* are cheap but packed (sometimes 20 people per minivan). Shared vans or station wagons (mainly Peugeots) depart from **Muharram Bey Station,** a five-minute drive out of town; *service* departing from Misr Station will take you there. All prices are approximations. *Service* go to: Abu Qir (30min., 80pt); Cairo (3hr. by the desert road, E£10); Marsa Matrouh (3hr., E£10); Port Said (4hr., E£10); Tanta (1½hr., E£4); and Zagazig (4hr., E£10).

CAR RENTAL. Avis, in the Cecil Hotel on Sa'ad Zaghloul Sq., rents the Czech Skoda Filishia to those over 24. (☎483 71 73; fax 483 64 01. E£152 per day, 50pt per km over 100; includes tax and insurance. Open daily 8am-10pm.)

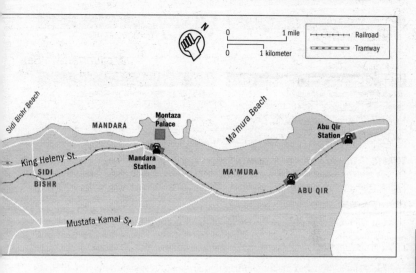

GETTING AROUND

Alexandria's main squares, transportation centers, and corniche all lie within walking distance of each other. A brisk half-hour walk will take you from Old Pharos Island to the Shooting Club along the corniche. The rest of the city is accessible by municipal tram, bus, minibus, and private microbus or taxi.

CITY BUSES. There are three terminals: one on the west side of **Sa'ad Zaghloul Sq.** (often called Ramleh Station, though the actual Ramleh Station is to the east), one in **Orabi Sq.**, and one at **Muharram Bey Station.** Buses run from approximately 5:30am to midnight or 1am (2am during Ramadan) and cost 25-35pt, or 50pt to outside beaches like al-'Agami or Montaza. Buses are marked in Arabic numerals.

FROM SA'AD ZAGHLOUL SQUARE	FROM ORABI SQUARE
#1 (١): Sidi Bishr & 15 May Station (A/C)	**#203** (٢٠٣): airport
#2 (٢): al-'Agami (A/C)	**#220** (٢٢٠): Sidi Bishr
#3 (٣): al-'Agami via Montaza (A/C)	**#231** (٢٣١): Citadel
#214 (٢١٤), **#215** (٢١٥): Maritime Station	**#251** (٢٥١): Abu Qir via al-Huriyya St.
#221 (٢٢١): Ma'mura	**#260** (٢٦٠): Abu Qir via the corniche
#403 (٤٠٣): Dakhla	
#750 (٧٥٠), **#760** (٧٦٠): Hannoville	

MINIBUSES. A more appetizing alternative to the crowded city buses, minibuses run from 5:30am to 1am (2am during Ramadan) and cost 50pt. Stand on the street and hold up the number of fingers equal to the number of passengers.

FROM SA'AD ZAGHLOUL SQUARE	FROM ORABI SQUARE
#700 (٧٠٠), **#705** (٧٠٥): Muharram Bey	**#703** (٧٠٣): Airport via Sa'ad Zaghloul
#703 (٧٠٣): Airport	**#704** (٧٠٤): Fishing club
#706 (٧٠٦): Citadel	**#724** (٧٢٤): 15 May Station
#725 (٧٢٥): Citadel via the corniche	**#736** (٧٣٦): Ma'mura
#735 (٧٣٥), **#736** (٧٣٦): Montaza	**#737** (٧٣٧): Abu Qir
#750 (٧٥٠): Bitash	**#779** (٧٧٩): Mandara

FROM SA'AD ZAGHLOUL SQUARE	FROM MONTAZA
#760 (٧٦٠): Hannoville	**#735** (٧٣٥): Sa'ad Zaghloul, Qaytbay
#781 (٧٨١): International Gardens	

FROM MISR STATION:	FROM RAS AT-TIN
#728 (٧٢٨): Montaza and Abu Qir	**#735** (٧٣٥): Montaza via the corniche
#729 (٧٢٩): Abu Qir	
#755 (٧٥٥), **#765** (٧٦٥): al-'Agami	
#770 (٧٧٠): Ma'mura	

TRAMS. Trams all start from **Ramleh Station** and come in two colors. **Blue** trams (20pt) head east and pass by the Sporting Club before ending at al-Nasser Station. **Yellow** trams (15pt) head west and pass Orabi Sq. before turning north or south. They run every few minutes until midnight, occasionally until 1am, and during Ramadan until 2am. The middle car of every three-car tram is for women only; on two-car trams, one is marked "ladies" and the other "gentlemen." Hop on at any stop or flag one down, and pay on board. Look for the route number on the front of the train, not the longer car numbers painted on the sides.

TAXIS. A local taxi ride in Alexandria is marginally less death-defying than in Cairo, and an inexpensive way to avoid the slow grind of the tram and the sardine-can squalor of the city buses. Hail one going in your direction and shout your destination into the window. The meters never run. No matter how big your group (three is the maximum), you can get away with E£3 to most places in the downtown area. Longer trips (Montaza or Abu Qir) are E£10-15, and past midnight you'll have to bargain harder. There is an E£1 minimum.

✴ ORIENTATION

Alexandria stretches from Abu Qir Bay to the western harbor. The entire 28km of coastline is crowded with glistening skyscrapers and deteriorating hotels jockeying for a spot near the Mediterranean. Alexandria's architect, Dinocrates, planned the city with broad boulevards rigidly arranged in a grid to harness sea breezes. The breezes still waft, but the order is long gone. Ancient Alexandria was built around Pharos Island (now a peninsula separating the eastern and western harbors), and the area still serves as the heart of the city. The downtown commercial district—called **al-Manshiyya**, or Midan Ramleh—is the hub of Alexandria's nightlife and tourist trade. Along the curve of the eastern harbor, west of downtown, is **al-Goumrouk,** a grandiose residential neighborhood that holds many old mosques. Immediately southeast of al-Manshiyya lies **al-Attarien,** which encompasses **Misr Station**, the city's main train depot. South of al-Manshiyya and al-Attarien, the streets of **Karmouz** overflow with students, workers, and the rest of the proletariat. Pompey's Pillar and the Catacombs of Kom al-Shoqafa are here. **Al-Anfoushi,** home to Fort Qaytbay, occupies the farthest tip of Pharos Island.

The best place to orient yourself downtown is **Sa'ad Zaghloul Sq.** on the waterfront, which showcases a massive statue of the man himself. Bordering the southeast corner of Sa'ad Zaghloul Sq. is **Ramleh Sq.** (Midan Ramleh), the main depot for the intracity tramway and a hub for intercity buses. Many municipal buses and minibuses service the busy stop in front of the square on the corniche or on the south side across from Trianon Cafe.

Heading west on the south side of Ramleh Sq. is **Sa'ad Zaghloul St.** (which does *not* border Sa'ad Zaghloul Sq.), a main shopping artery that runs to **Orabi Sq.** The two squares serve as transportation hubs. All yellow trams out of Ramleh Station pass through here, as do a number of minibuses. The southern end is also called Tahrir Sq., and the larger area al-Manshiyya Sq.

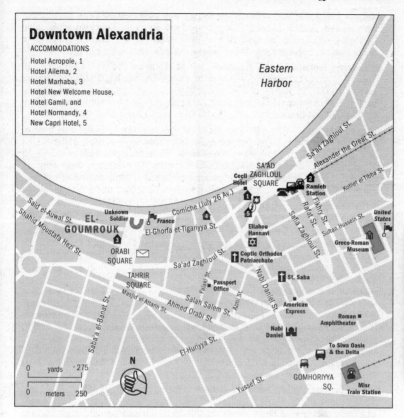

Downtown Alexandria

ACCOMMODATIONS

Hotel Acropole, 1
Hotel Ailema, 2
Hotel Marhaba, 3
Hotel New Welcome House,
Hotel Gamil, and
Hotel Normandy, 4
New Capri Hotel, 5

EGYPT

The **corniche** starts at the northern tip of al-Anfoushi and winds the length of the city to reach **Montaza Palace** and **Ma'mura Beach** (a hangout for youngsters), which demarcate the city's far eastern borders. Note that the corniche is also called **26 July Ave.** along the eastern harbor and **al-Geish Rd.** between al-Silsilah breakwater (the western promontory of the eastern harbor) and Montaza.

In addition to the corniche, two main arteries traverse the stretch from downtown to Ma'mura. The first inland is **Alexander the Great (al-Iskandar al-Akbar) St.** In Sidi Bishr, the street changes its name to Khalid ibn al-Walid St. to welcome you to *(bienvenidos a)* Miami Beach, where it ends. The second major artery is **al-Huriyya St.**, which runs all the way to Montaza. The Schultz School's *Guide Book to Alexandria* (E£25) spices up the city's plate of concrete noodles.

🛈 PRACTICAL INFORMATION

TOURIST AND FINANCIAL SERVICES

Tourist Office: Main office (☎484 33 80 or 485 15 56) on Nabi Daniel St., at the southwest corner of Sa'ad Zaghloul Sq. Fluent English speakers. Open daily 8:30am-6pm; Ramadan 9am-4pm; holidays 8am-2pm. Branch offices at **Misr Station** (☎492 59 85; same hours), **Maritime Station** (☎480 34 94; open 8am-5pm and additional hours for boat arrivals), and the **airport** (☎420 87 64 or 420 10 36). Free copies of *Alexandria by Night and Day* and *Alexandria and the Beaches*.

Passport Office: 22 Tala'at Harb St. (☎483 77 51). Walk west on Sa'ad Zaghloul Sq. from Ramleh Station Sq. and bear left on Falaky St. by the blue sign when Sa'ad Zaghloul curves toward the sea. Tala'at Harb St. is the first left. Open Sa-W 9am-2pm and 7-9pm, Th 9am-1pm and 7-9pm. Handle visa extensions in Cairo if possible.

Consulates: Israel, 207 Abd al-Salaam 'Aret St., Loran (☎586 38 74). Open Su-Th 9:30am-3:30pm. **Lebanon,** 63 al-Huriyya St. (☎482 65 89). **UK,** 3 Mena St., Rushdi (☎546 70 01), off Kafr Abdou St. about six kilometers east of downtown, several blocks south of the corniche. Open Su-Th 8am-1pm. For **US,** contact the American Center (see **Cultural Centers,** below) or the US Embassy in Cairo (see p. 94).

Currency Exchange: Better rates than banks but they only take cash. **National Bank of Egypt** in Cecil Hotel in Sa'ad Zaghloul Sq. is fast. Open Su-Th 8:30am-8:30pm, F-Sa 9am-1pm and 5:30-8:30pm. **Bank of Alexandria,** 59 Sa'ad Zaghloul St. (☎483 85 88 or 483 85 89). Open Su-Th 8:30am-2pm; Ramadan 10am-1:30pm. **Bank Misr,** on Safia Zaghloul St. between Metro Cinema and al-Huriyya St., refuses traveler's checks, but gives V and MC advances. Open Su-Th 8am-2pm. Bank Misr, on Tala'at Harb St., up the street and around the corner from the passport office, has **ATMs.**

American Express: 10 Patrice Lumumba St. (☎493 11 15; fax 495 09 17), near the Roman Amphitheater. Full service office, but doesn't hold mail. Open daily 9am-4pm.

Thomas Cook: 15 Sa'ad Zaghloul St. (☎482 51 18 or 484 78 30; fax 483 40 73), just east of Ramleh Station Sq. Full range of services. Open daily 8am-5pm.

LOCAL SERVICES

English-Language Bookstore: The best is **Al-Ma'aref,** 44 Sa'ad Zaghloul St. (☎483 33 03); another entrance is on the south side of Sa'ad Zaghloul Sq. Strange selection of textbooks, translations of Arabic works, and trashy paperbacks. Open M-Sa 10am-9:30pm. **General Egyptian Book Organization,** 49 Sa'ad Zaghloul St. (☎482 28 25), just down the street from Al-Ma'aref. Medium-sized selection ranges from *Sweet Valley High* to *The Art of Pediatrics,* with an immense collection of Agatha Christie. Open daily 10am-7:30pm. The **Used Book Market,** at the southern end of Nabi Daniel St. near Misr Station, is an entire block of obscure, inexpensive English titles.

Cultural Centers: British Council, 9 Ptolemies St. (☎482 98 90 or 481 01 99). Open Su-Th 10am-3:30pm; library open Su-W 10am-7:30pm, Sa and Th 10am-4pm. **American Cultural Center,** 3 Phara'ana St. (☎482 10 09). Turn left on al-Huriyya St. from Safia Zaghloul St., walk one block past first sign for the Greco-Roman Museum, turn left, then take first right. Book and video library. Inquire about **teaching jobs** at the English Teaching Program. Cultural events calendar posted outside. Open Su-Th 8:30am-6pm.

EMERGENCY AND COMMUNICATIONS

Emergency: Ambulance: ☎123. **Police:** ☎122. **Tourist Police:** ☎483 33 78.

Tourist Police: Montaza Palace (☎547 33 95). Main office upstairs from tourist office in **Sa'ad Zaghloul Sq.** (☎483 33 78). Both open 24hr. Other branches in **amphitheater** (☎490 62 73), **Citadel** (☎480 91 44), and **Greco-Roman Museum** (☎482 89 12).

Pharmacy: Pharmacy Strand (☎482 51 36), opposite the tram at the intersection of Sa'ad Zaghloul St. and Safia Zaghloul St. Open 9am-midnight.

Hospital: al-Mowasah (☎421 28 85 or 421 28 88), on al-Huriyya St. in al-Haddara. Open 24hr.

Telephones: Menatel phones scattered throughout downtown area. **Ramleh Station Sq.** office charges E£24 for 3min. to US; minimal phone card discount. Open 24hr. Additional offices at **Misr Station,** at west end of **Sa'ad Zaghloul St.** on Sultan Hussein St., and in post office on **Safia Zaghloul St.** Both open daily 7am-midnight. Lines are down for hours at a time, and you may be abruptly cut off. **Luxury hotels** (try the Cecil in Sa'ad Zaghloul Sq.) offer more expensive overseas connections. Rates for 3min. to: US and Canada E£32, UK E£28.50, Australia E£46. For operator **information,** dial ☎125.

Internet Access: Al-Jaber CompuComm Services, 20 Mahmoud Azmi St. (☎483 27 95; aljaber@alexcomm.net), around the block from the Coptic Patriarchate heading south. Look for the sidewalk sign mentioning "Internet." Only has one terminal, but the owner

serves tea while you're online. E£8 per 30min., E£15 per hr. Open daily 9am-11pm.
Global Net (☎487 80 51), on Nabi Daniel St. across from the French Cultural Center, after al-Huriyya St. when heading toward Misr Station. A/C room with a half-dozen computers, but slow connections. E£6 for 30min., E£10 per hr. Open Sa-Th 10am-10pm.

Post Office: All open Sa-Th 8am-3pm, and most have **EMS** (until 2pm). A branch at the tram stop at **Ramleh Station Sq.** (☎482 07 46) and two on **al-Ghorfa al-Tigariyya St.**, three blocks west of Sa'ad Zaghloul Sq. and two blocks west of Orabi Sq. Poste Restante until 1pm. Packages are held at the office of **Misr Station** (☎491 86 32), 10m south of al-Huriyya St. An office in front of the **Sidi Gabr Railroad Station** has EMS.

ACCOMMODATIONS

E.M. Forster liked Alexandria so much that he wrote a guidebook on it and named a character in *A Room with a View* after the Cecil Hotel. Nowadays, however, visitors are paying more for location than quality, although bargaining is always an option at the cheaper hotels. Steer clear of the ultra-cheap (E£10 per night) dives that line the streets running south from the corniche near Ramleh Station Sq. It's better to stay in one of the hotels listed below: all are clean, cheap, and within walking distance of the two main squares. None have fans, unless noted, as most Alexandrians depend on sea breezes for air-conditioning. In summer, look for corner rooms with cross ventilation.

Streets in **al-Manshiyya Sq.** teem with budget hotels. For a beachside retreat, head out to **Sidi Bishr** (14km) or **Montaza** (18km), where the posh amenities balance the inconvenience of staying so far from the center of town. The only **camping** possibility is the beach at Abu Qir, but police generally only give permission to large groups. Interested travelers should inquire at the tourist office. Reservations are a good idea in summer, especially on weekends.

■ **Hotel Union,** 6 Muhammad Noaman St. (☎480 73 12; fax 480 73 50), off the corniche on the second block behind the Cecil Hotel. This popular hotel has large, classy rooms with balconies and great views of the harbor. The comfortable lounge with the picture window and Mel Torme tunes can't be beat. On the pricier side, but the comfortable beds, towels, and spotless bathrooms are well worth it. Breakfast E£6. Singles E£30, with bath E£35; doubles E£40, with bath E£50.

New Hotel Welcome House, 8 Gamal al-Din Yassin St., 5th floor (☎480 64 02). On the first block off the corniche behind the Cecil Hotel. Oddly named but well-maintained hotel with old but clean rooms, great prices, and views to match. All rooms come with tiny baths. Singles E£15; doubles E£25; triples E£33.

New Capri Hotel, 23 al-Mina al-Sharaya, 8th floor (☎490 83 10 or 490 97 03). Same building as tourist office off Sa'ad Zaghloul Sq. A bit inland, but a great place to stay nonetheless. Friendly management keep the spacious rooms and bathrooms immaculate. Corner rooms offer panoramic views of the square. Breakfast and private bath E£4. Singles E£28; doubles E£42; triples E£54.

Hotel Acropole, 27 Gamal al-Din Yassin St., 4th floor (☎480 59 80), at end of the block behind the Cecil Hotel. Nice, but aging rooms and small, common bathrooms accompany lumpy, but comfy beds. Prices vary with views, which range from panoramas to brick walls. Breakfast included. Singles E£15-25; doubles E£30-35; triples E£45-55.

Hotel Ailema, 21 Amin Fikhry St., 7th floor. (☎484 70 11). East of Ramlek Station Sq., the rooms and shared bathrooms lack views but are clean and quiet. Hardwood floors are a nice touch. Singles E£27, with bath E£40; doubles E£31, with bath E£52.

Hotel Normandy, 8 Gamal al-Din Yassin St., 4th floor (☎480 68 30). Mentioned in Australian phenom Ted Simon's landmark travel narrative *Jupiter's Travels.* All rooms have three old beds, high ceilings, and shared baths. Some have a decent view of the water. Bathrooms are adequate. Prices negotiable, especially if you begin to walk out. Singles E£15; doubles E£20; triples E£25; room with a view E£5 extra.

Hotel Marhaba, 10 Ahmed Orabi Sq. (☎480 09 57 or 480 95 10), on the northwest side of Orabi Sq. These tony digs were the former summer residence of the King of Libya, and it shows: wallpapered rooms come with towels, soap, sinks, and Egyptian TV. Louis XIV sitting rooms on each floor and a rooftop breakfast buffet. Singles E£35, with shower E£45; doubles E£50, with shower E£62.

⚫ FOOD

Meat, fruit, seafood, and vegetables can be found in the **souq** in al-Mo'asker (take any blue tram six or seven stops east and walk south). The fishmongers will cook purchases on the spot for E£3-5. **Supermarkets** dot the area around Sa'ad Zaghloul Sq. Gastronomic voyeurs should sneak a peek into **Muhammad Ahmed's Falafel Workshop,** which dishes out insight into the falafel-making process; green industrial revolution-era falafel churners spin chickpeas into a heavenly mash. Go up Abd al-Fattah al-Hadari St. from Muhammad Ahmed Fuul Restaurant, listed below, and turn right down the first alley to the brick building on the left.

RESTAURANTS

The restaurants of Alexandria are a delicious reminder of the city's cosmopolitan heritage. The cheap falafel and *fuul* found throughout Egypt are readily available, but Alexandria boasts fine Italian and Greek restaurants downtown, where French pastries vie with *ba'laweh* and *kinafeh* for the affections of the strolling crowds. And of course, this "Queen of the Mediterranean" naturally has excellent seafood.

▧ **Muhammad Ahmed Fuul,** 17 Abd al-Fattah al-Hadari St. (☎483 35 76), two blocks south of Sa'ad Zaghloul Sq., 10m up on the left; no English sign. Scrumptious take-out for E£2 or less. *Fuul*-lovers rush in to this local family favorite. Open daily 6am-midnight.

▧ **Elite,** 43 Safia Zaghloul St. (☎482 35 92), one block north of al-Huriyya St. Breezy, stylin' artists' cafe and restaurant (since 1900), run by a friendly Greek matriarch. Wraparound glass windows, high-beamed ceilings, and two decks of tables give a maritime feel. DJ spins eclectic tunes. Steak E£16-23, chicken E£15-18, filling pasta E£3.50-16. Stella E£6. Open daily 8am-midnight.

Restaurant Bleik, 18 Sa'ad Zaghloul St. (☎484 08 80). Walk west on Sa'ad Zaghloul until you're two blocks from Orabi Sq. Sample such delicacies as *osso bucco*, quail, and brain. Open daily 8am-6pm.

Kadoura Restaurant, on the corniche about a block before the Tikka Grill sign, 2½km east of Sa'ad Zaghloul Sq. toward Fort Qaytbay. Delicious seafood, albeit at steep prices. Choose your prey downstairs from several varieties of fish, crab, and calamari (some still moving), then head up the slippery spiral stairs for a great view of the ocean and the corniche crowd below. Waddle out after a massive meal of seafood, salad, bread, and drink (E£30). Open daily noon-midnight.

Restaurant Denis, 1 Ibn Bassam St. (☎482 17 09), four blocks east of Sa'ad Zaghloul Sq., adjacent to the corniche. Great budget seafood. English-speaking owner Shokri will lead you into the kitchen to sea food before you eat it. Fish E£25-30 per kg, calamari E£22. Beer and wine served. Open daily 11am-11pm.

Taverna (☎482 81 89), on the southern side of Ramleh Station, across from the trams and next to KFC. Amiable, French-speaking chef grills *souvlaki* (E£16). Good bargains, like the *shawarma* special sandwich, at the ground level. Branches at Montaza Gardens (☎547 54 38) and al-Manshiyya (☎481 63 91). Open daily 7:30am-2am. V, AmEx.

Trianon (☎482 09 86), corner of Sa'ad Zaghloul and Ramleh Station Sq. A landmark from the city's *belle époque* and former hangout of illustrious literary types, the restaurant has both in and outdoor seating. Menu can get pricey (entrees E£25-40), but it does carry some bargains such as the *mousaka* (E£11) and the three-course breakfast with coffee (E£14). Open daily 7am-2am.

Asteria, 40 Safia Zaghloul St. (☎472 22 93). Casual Italian bistro serving pizza (E£7-14) and pasta (E£9-10), with tasty granitas to wash it all down. Sandwich servings, while cheap, are very small. Open daily 8am-midnight.

CAFES

Sa'ad Zaghloul Sq. is packed with coffee and pastry shops, and ice cream parlors cool off the Ramleh Station Sq. Along the corniche you'll find ritzy cafes and *sheesha* joints; cheaper, more traditional cafes *(ahwas)* await farther inland. A lively waterfront scene is at **Ma'mura**, where a youthful crowd buzzes until after midnight. Popular for grub and *sheesha* are: the **Antazza Cafe**, which serves food after 7pm (no English sign, off of Sa'ad Zaghloul St. and across from the mosque); **Minouche** (Italian food E£10-20); and **Cafino** (above Antazza, open late).

■ **Brazilian Coffee Store,** in two locations: a sit-down at 20 Salah Salem St. or a stand-up at 44 Sa'ad Zaghloul St. (☎482 50 59). Check out the ceramic tiles in the shape of coffee plants at the Salah Salem location. Home-roasted beans are ground up for great espresso (E£1.50). Croissants E£1.25. Both locations open daily 7am-11pm.

Delices (☎482 54 60), opposite the corniche in Sa'ad Zaghloul Sq. French and Middle Eastern desserts. More posh for your nosh: the sea-view terrace is a great place to enjoy savory pastries (E£2-5), ice cream (E£2.50), or coffee (E£2). Open daily 7am-midnight.

Sofianopoulo Coffee Shop (☎483 15 17), on Sa'ad Zaghloul St., near Restaurant Bleik. Classic coffee shop with the cheapest cappuccino around (E£1.50). Aspiring astronauts will appreciate Tang on tap. Open daily 8am-11pm.

Sultana (☎482 27 69), on the south side of Ramleh Station Sq., across from the trams. In the evenings, a man in a psychedelic Tweety-bird costume beckons you inside for an array of sundaes and ice cream (E£1.25 per scoop). Waffle cones made while you wait. Like an animal house at night. Open daily 8:30am-2:30am, and (boy do) they deliver.

Cafe Baudrot, 23 Sa'ad Zaghloul St. A fine retreat from the busy street. Expansive vine-trellised garden straight out of a *Town and Country* magazine. Perfect for musing over beer (E£5.05), coffee (E£2.05), or cake (E£2.25).

Samadi Patisserie, on a lush patio adjacent to Tikka Grill. It's no secret that Samadi doles out generous helpings of *ba'laweh, basbouseh, kinafeh,* and other goodehs. Fresh strawberry ice cream E£1.50. Open daily 9:30am-2am. V, MC, AmEx.

👁 SIGHTS

The modern city of Alexandria was built atop the ruins of ancient Alexandria, leaving Classical remains eight meters underground. The scattered places where ancient foundations do show through (or jut out) offer fascinating glimpses of a city with a diverse cultural and religious history.

DOWNTOWN ALEXANDRIA

■ **ROMAN AMPHITHEATER.** This dazzling white marble structure is the only Roman amphitheater in all of Egypt. Stand on the round stone in the stage, whisper *Et tu, Brute?*, and your voice will be heard by the conspirator all the way in the theater's back row. Archaeologists are currently excavating a Roman bath and villa behind the theater. *(Just northwest of Misr Station and south of Cinema 'Amir. From Sa'ad Zaghloul Sq., walk up Nabi Daniel St. past al-Huriyya St. to the next big intersection. Turn left across from a gas station and go 200m; the entrance is on the left. Open daily 9am-4pm; Ramadan 10am-3pm. E£6, students E£3.)*

ELIYAHU HANNAVI SYNAGOGUE. Guarded by a tall iron gate, this synagogue is still the center of Alexandria's Jewish community and the greatest of the few Jewish sights still standing in the city. The gracious Joe Harari in the *Communauté Israelite Grand Rabbinat* office to the right as you enter the courtyard will show you around the building, let you look at old photographs, and tell you all about Alexandrian Jews. Although Alexandria once had more than 100,000 Jews (and a synagogue in every neighborhood), this is the last one still in use for the 50 or so Jews who remain. The temple now holds an impressive collection of beautiful Torahs from the other closed synagogues. Built in 1885 by Baron Jacques L. de Menasce for the then-thriving community, the towering edifice sports five aisles, stained glass windows, pink Italian marble columns, dangling chandeliers, and wooden pews—check out the international assemblage of names on the brass seat markers. *(On Dr. Hussein Faladi St., in an alley one block south of Safia Zaghloul St. between Nabi Daniel and Abd al-Fattah al-Hadari St. Open Su-F mornings.)*

■ **GRECO-ROMAN MUSEUM.** The most interesting and unusual relics of ancient Alexandria are on display here, including a mummified crocodile, exquisitely-painted sarcophagi of Greco-Roman nobles (said to have provided inspiration for later Renaissance artists), and well-preserved statues of superstars like Caesar, Augustus, and Cleopatra. The pride of the museum is the beautiful mosaic of Alexandria as "Queen of the Ocean." A new museum devoted exclusively to mosaics found around Alexandria is scheduled to open sometime in 2001; ask at the tourist office (p. 149) for details. *(5 al-Mathaf al-Roumani St. Walk south from the corniche along Safia Zaghloul St., turn left on al-Huriyya St., then left at the museum sign. ☎ 482 58 20. Open Sa-Th 9am-4pm, F 9-11:30am and 1:30-4pm; Ramadan and holidays 10am-3pm. E£10, students E£8. Camera privileges without flash E£10, video E£15.)*

COPTIC ORTHODOX PATRIARCHATE. The Patriarchate is in a beautiful church (founded in 67 CE and rebuilt in 1950) with mosaics, stained glass, hanging ostrich eggs, and a finely painted *iconostasis*. The first 47 patriarchs of the Alexandrian See (the regional seat of church authority), starting with St. Mark (some of whose remains are in a chapel to the left of the *iconostasis*), are buried within. Their names are listed in a niche on the right side of the church. *(19 Elah 'Abad St. Open daily with services Su and F 8am, W noon.)*

MONASTERY OF ST. SABA. The 17th-century church in the Greek Orthodox Monastery of St. Saba is another testament to the historical importance of Christianity in Alexandria. Inside, there are beautiful paintings, a spectacular collection of amulets, a giant bronze bell, and a marble table on which St. Catherine was beheaded. *(Walk up Safia Zaghloul St. from Sa'ad Zaghloul Sq. to Sultan Hussein St. Turn right, then take the second left. Open daily 7:30am-12:30pm and 3:30-6pm.)*

WEST OF DOWNTOWN

MOSQUE OF MORSI ABU AL-'ABBAS. This is the city's largest mosque and Alexandria's most elaborate example of Islamic architecture. The holy Sidi Shehab al-Din Abu al-'Abbas ibn al-Khazragi came from Andalusia before the expulsion of the Moors to spread the teachings of the Qur'an in Egypt. His tomb rests in the back of the mosque, and legend has it that he rose from his tomb to catch bombs during World War II. Come nightfall, the coffin, like the exterior of the mosque, is bathed in a green neon glow. *(1km south of Fort Qaytbay along the corniche. Dress modestly. Women allowed in back room only. Open daily 5am-10pm, except prayer times.)*

A LIBRARY LONG OVERDUE Though the past is alive and kicking in Alexandria, its physical traces are few and far between. The Great Pharos lighthouse long ago gave way to earthquakes and development, and Fort Qaytbay now stands on its site. The great **Bibliotheka Alexandria,** the massive library that made Alexandria an intellectual center of the ancient world, has been destroyed entirely. Much of it allegedly burned to the ground during Rome's first attack on the city, although the exact details of who started the fire and when it occurred (or whether it even occurred at all) are unclear. The remains of the library were completely destroyed by crusading bibliophobe Bishop Theophilus in 391 CE, who led a pagan-hating mob to raze the building in the name of Christianity. In 1987, UNESCO announced a project to resurrect the building that even Cleopatra could not save. Despite numerous natural obstacles like the weather and the Mediterranean tides, construction was scheduled to be completed in time for a grand opening in January 2001. For information on the political obstacles facing the restoration team, see **In The News,** p. 68.

FORT QAYTBAY. The Islamic Fort Qaytbay was constructed on the ancient island of Pharos, on the foundations of the famous lighthouse. Fishermen and lovebirds alike congregate along the dramatic seaward walls, drawn by the waves and pleasant sunsets. Silt connected the island to the mainland, leaving the fort at the tip of a peninsula. Built in 1480 CE by Mamluk Sultan al-Ashraf Qaytbay, the citadel houses the remains of the French fleet sunk by Admiral Nelson in the battle of Abu Qir (see p. 158). There is a small mosque in the center of the tower, and the entire fortress is aligned so that the mosque's *mihrab* faces Mecca. On the road to the tramway is the **Aquarium,** which has more visiting school groups than schools of Red Sea fish. *(Take yellow tram #15 west from Ramleh Station and get off at the sharp left turn, or take any bus going to Ras al-Tin. You'll find yourself in the middle of a fish market. At the point where the tram turns left, make a right on the road between the Kuwait Airlines sign and the mosque. The fort is at the end of this road. Minibus #707 (٧٠٧) or 719 (٧١٩) from Ramleh Station Sq. takes you to the beginning of the street. ☎ 480 91 44. Fort open daily 9am-4pm. E£12, students E£6. Camera privileges E£10. Aquarium open daily 9am-4pm. E£1.)*

ANFUSHI TOMBS. The Anfushi tombs were built for Greek occupants who had adopted Egyptian customs in the first half of the 3rd century BCE. Cut into the limestone of what was once Pharos Island, they are placed in two groups around a staircase leading into an open court and may well extend farther under the palace gardens. Many of the tombs were decorated with colorful geometric designs or painted to look like marble. *(On Ras al-Tin St. Take tram #16 or minibus #735 (٧٣٥). Open daily 9am-4pm. E£12, students E£6. Camera privileges E£5.)*

SOUTH OF DOWNTOWN

CATACOMBS OF KOM AL-SHOQAFA. This massive, three-tiered complex of Roman tombs (descending some 35m below ground) is one of the best Classical sites in the city. The gate is decorated with winged serpents, Medusa heads, a pine cone (symbolizing Dionysus), and a *caduceus* (symbolizing Mercury, the *psychopompos* or leader of the dead to the Underworld). The main tombs are on the second level and are richly decorated with sculptures and reliefs of Egyptian gods with virile Roman bodies (a blend of pharaonic and Roman art). A statue of jackal-headed Anubis stands near the entrance to the innermost burial chamber. Scenes above the sarcophagi show the Egyptian gods and a mummification, along with the worship of the Apis bull. The sarcophagi are decorated in a Roman style, with garlands and bull skulls. Try to lift the lids—it's impossible, because the bodies were placed inside from passages behind. As you exit, notice two statues of Anubis, one in which he is dressed as a Roman legionnaire and one in which he has the body of a serpent. *(Take bus #309 (٣٠٩) or tram #16 from Ramleh Station Sq. and get off on Karmouz St. at Pompey's Pillar. Take a right after the entrance to the Serapium-Pillar complex's entrance on the southwest side and climb the hill. Open daily 9am-4pm; Ramadan 10am-3pm. E£12, students E£6. Camera privileges E£10.)*

POMPEY'S PILLAR. This 25m pillar of pink granite from Aswan is all that remains of the Serapium (Temple of Serapis, the bull-god), which was leveled once the Roman Empire adopted Christianity. The best finds from the ruins have been moved to the Greco-Roman Museum. Named in the Middle Ages by ignorant Crusaders with a flair for the alliterative, Pompey's Pillar actually dates from the time of Diocletian, a Roman who came to power several centuries after Pompey. One story holds that Diocletian was so incensed by an Alexandrian revolt that he swore he would massacre the rebellious people until blood stained the knees of his horse. As he entered the already defeated but mostly un-massacred town, his mount stumbled into a pool of blood, prematurely fulfilling his oath. The emperor spared the life of the city's inhabitants, and the lone pillar (once the tallest structure in Alexandria) remains as a symbol of the people's gratitude to him and his klutzy horse. Another story says that the pillar commemorates the time Diocletian gave the city free grain during a famine. *(Southwest of Misr Station. Take bus #309 (٣٠٩) or tram #16 from Ramleh Station Sq. and get off on Karmouz St. Enter on the southern side of the complex. Open daily 9am-5pm; Ramadan 10am-3pm. E£6, students E£3.)*

EGYPT

EAST OF DOWNTOWN

TOMBS OF CHATBY. The Tombs of Chatby date from the 4th century BCE and are believed to be the oldest surviving tombs in Alexandria. The postmortem trinkets that once filled the two separate chambers have been taken to the Greco-Roman Museum. *(On Port Said St., across from St. Mark's College in the Chatby beach area. Open daily 9am-4pm. E£6, students E£3. Camera privileges E£5.)*

MUSTAFA KEMAL NECROPOLIS. This necropolis consists of four tombs from the 2nd century BCE decorated in a Hellenic style. Tomb #1 has an airy courtyard with a faded fresco depicting a libation scene over the middle doorway, Doric columns, and sphinxes. *(Take tram #1 or #2 to the Rushdi tram station and walk down al-Mo'asker al-Romani St. Open daily 9am-4pm. E£12, students E£6. Camera privileges E£5.)*

ROYAL JEWELRY MUSEUM. Behind the governor's residence in Glim sits the architecturally intriguing Royal Jewelry Museum. Originally the Palace of Fatima al-Zahra'a, the museum contains gleaming baubles of the Muhammad 'Ali era. The jewelry collection is rivaled only by the lacquered interiors of the former palace. *(27 Ahmed Yahya St. Take tram #2. Look for the red sign. ☎586 83 48. Open Sa-Th 9am-4pm, F 9am-12:30pm and 2-4pm. E£20, students E£10. Camera privileges E£10.)*

🏖 BEACHES

Cairenes flood the waterfront during the summer months. For more peaceful surroundings, head to the **Sinai** (p. 181) or the calm (but expensive) waters west of Alexandria (tram #1 or 2 from Ramleh Station Sq., p. 159). The 400 acres of flora at **Montaza Palace and Gardens** were once used as the summer retreat of King Farouk. Today, they are still the jewel of Alexandria's beaches. The palace and its museum have been closed to the public, but the beach is always busy despite its steep price (especially on weekends), and the gardens and groves are still a favorite picnic spot for Alexandrians. Pizza Hut, Chicken Tikka, a supermarket, and juice and ice cream stands are all just outside the garden gates. (☎457 30 79. Gardens E£3, holidays E£4. Beach E£10. Pedal boats E£15 per hr., regular boats E£40, jet-skis E£180.) Not far from Montaza, even more expensive **Ma'mura** remains a favorite among Alexandria's ritzier youth. (Both beaches reachable by bus #221 (٢٢١), #250 (٢٥٠), or #260 (٢٦٠), or by minibus #728 (٧٢٨), #736 (٧٣٦), or #770 (٧٧٠). E£12, F E£14.) **San Stefano's Beach**, between Montaza and Sa'ad Zaghloul Sq., is much closer to the city center, as its weekday crowds and rubbish attest. Admission includes a chair and an umbrella. (Closes at 8pm. E£8. Small changing rooms on the beach E£24 per day, larger cabanas start at E£35.)

🎭 ENTERTAINMENT

CINEMAS

English-language films are shown on every corner. The **'Amir** (☎492 76 93; E£5-15) and the **Metro** (☎483 04 32; E£5-15) are both near the intersection of Safia Zaghloul St. and al-Huriyya St. Movies are occasionally subtitled in French. The **French Cultural Center** at 30 Nabi Daniel St. (☎492 08 04) shows films Tuesday through Saturday, as does the **American Cultural Center** (see **Cultural Centers**, p. 150).

PERFORMING ARTS

Every August, the outdoor **Muhammad Abd al-Wahab Theater,** on the corniche at Ramleh Station Sq., showcases traditional dancing. Al-Fir'a Rida (Rida's Troupe) and al-Fir'a al-Qawmiya (the National Troupe) both feature belly dancers and high-energy choreography representative of various areas in Egypt—including the cane dance from Upper Egypt (performances nightly at 10:30pm; reserve tickets one or two days in advance; front-row E£12, cheap seats E£5; avoid the uncomfortable box seats). The **circus** sets up camp in Alexandria during the summer. Ask the tourist office for the location of the two daily shows (E£2-7). For more high-brow entertainment, check the **Conservatoire de Musique d'Alexandrie,** 90 al-Huriyya St. (☎483 50 86), or the **Sayyid Darwish Theater,** 22 Fouad St. (☎482 51 06). In September, the **Alexandria World Festival** brings theater, dancing, and other performing arts to the city. Ask the tourist office for details.

BILLIARDS AND SPECTATOR SPORTS

Billiards tables charge by the hour throughout the city. You'll find the hippest table in town at **Cafino.** The **Marhaba Hotel,** in Orabi Sq. (E£10 per hr.; alcohol served; open nightly 10pm-2am), and **Black and White,** on the left up a side street from the lively Camp Caesar *sheesha* cafes, have three tables each. (E£15 per hr. Open 24hr.) If the sound of thundering hooves makes your pulse race, head to the **Antoniadis Palace and Gardens** in Smouha, on the wide road bordering the zoo. For over 50 years, Alexandria's working classes have gathered here on summer Sundays to watch working horses, with carriages of all kinds, race each other at breakneck speed. (Arrive by 6pm. 50pt.) Ask at the tourist office for info on the various **sporting events** in the Alexandria Municipal Stadium.

NIGHTLIFE

CLUBS AND DISCOS

The cosmopolitan days of Alexandria's Hellenistic hedonism are long gone. Nightlife in the city is now strictly a do-it-yourself affair. Alexandria's paltry nightlife is concentrated downtown between Orabi Sq. and Sa'ad Zaghloul Sq. This area has the best bars, pastry shops, and coffee houses, and hopping between them is a great way to soak up liquor or wash down desserts.

　Nightclubs can be found in most of the luxury hotels. There's no cover, but beware the stealthily levied **minimum charges.** Try the **Metropole,** one block south of Sa'ad Zaghloul Sq. Its recently renovated disco downstairs has some long lines of party-goers on the weekends waiting to hit the sleek new dance floor and beaming lights. (Open daily 11:30pm-4am. Minimum E£65.) **Lourantos** is another downtown option. (☎482 22 00. Minimum E£45.) All of the **discos** are in the major hotels as well, and play a mix of Western and Arab music. The **Ramada** rocks out on the corniche in Sidi Bishr. (Open daily 10pm-4am. Entrance on the corniche side. Minimum E£25.) The ultrafab people head to the **Sheraton** in Montaza to compare Rolexes. (Open Th-Tu 11pm-4am. Minimum E£35.) Many discos don't allow single men or women, and some relegate lone males to the bar and forbid them from dancing. These rules are usually relaxed for foreigners, especially those willing to give a small donation.

BARS

The bars in Alexandria are mostly empty. The coolest option around is the **Spitfire,** 7 Rue Bourse al-Hadema, two blocks up from the corniche between Sa'ad Zaghloul and Orabi Sq. Decals and posters cover every inch of this expat favorite, and mellow '80s music soothes rattled nerves (Stella E£6.50). A unique find is **Sheik 'Ali,** around the corner to the south from the Sofianopoulo Coffeeshop, when heading toward Sa'ad Zaghloul Sq. The long, packed marble bar is a great place to enjoy appetizers or the house specialty, rum on the rocks (E£5). The **Athineos** also has a bar with a view of the corniche, although it's often deserted (Stella E£7). To fully relive World War II memories, head to **Monty's Bar,** on the second floor of the Cecil Hotel. Prints of classic paintings are barely visible from the postmodern seats in the dim lighting. General Montgomery's former headquarters now charges five-star prices for cocktails. (Open daily 4pm-2am. Stella E£8.50.) If Monty's high prices have got you down, head up to the roof garden for a fantastic view of the square and the water, but be careful where you sit—the sharp, green seats are actually cacti (Stella E£8). The breezy **Greek Club** attracts an older clientele and is popular with English teachers. (Take the blue trams east to al-Mo'asker, go south two blocks, then take a left. Look for the "Micapaciatikoc" sign. Stella E£5.)

EAST OF ALEXANDRIA

ABU QIR ابو قير ☎03

Abu Qir, on a small peninsula five kilometers east of Alexandria, has yet to be absorbed by the relentless expansion of the "Queen of the Mediterranean." It was here in 1798 that British Admiral Nelson took the French fleet by surprise without any navigational charts to guide him. Today, all hints of a military history are gone, and Abu Qir's beach is a peaceful and convenient place to enjoy the Mediterranean and its bounty of edible denizens.

GETTING THERE AND GETTING AROUND. From Alexandria's Misr Station, take **local bus** #251 (٢٥١) or #260 (٢٦٠) or **minibus** #728 (٧٢٨) (20min., every 30min. 7am-10pm, 50pt) to Abu Qir. **Third-class trains** also leave from Misr or Sidi Gabr Station (45min., every 30min. 6am-10pm, 45pt), **local taxis** from downtown (15min., E£10-15), or **service** from Misr Station (40min., E£1). Within Abu Qir, many a **horse-drawn carriage** (hantour) start trotting from al-Bahr al-Mayyit St. (E£2-3).

ACCOMMODATIONS AND FOOD. Abu Qir Camp (☎560 14 24), on al-Bahr al-Mayyit St. about 500m south of the Zephyrion, supplies the only consistently available **camping** option in the greater Alexandrian area for E£5. Contact the tourist police or tourist office in Alexandria for permission to camp. As always, produce and the ubiquitous ta'amiyya, shawarma, and fuul stands are found in the souq near the train station. Only sharks can get seafood fresher than that found in Abu Qir's two major sit-down restaurants, both with great views along the beach. The Greek-owned, colorfully-muraled **Zephyrion**, 41 Khalid ibn al-Walid St. (☎560 13 19), is the oldest restaurant in town, founded in 1929. Blow on in for a full fish meal (E£30) and wash it down with a Stella (E£6). Nearby is the similarly priced and appropriately named **Bella Vista**. Nobel Prize-winning President Anwar Sadat was a cook here before he joined the army. Sit at his spot in the far left corner. (☎560 06 28. Open daily noon-midnight.)

BEACHES. From the train station, one of the cleanest **public beaches** in the area is a short walk down any side street on the left as you face away from the station. Most Alexandrenes go on the weekends, so weekdays are best if you want the beach to yourself. As always, women should be wary of swimming uncovered.

RASHID (ROSETTA) رشيد

*On the northern edge of the Nile Delta, about 45min. east of Abu Qir and 1hr. east of Alexandria. West Delta Bus Co. **buses** run from Muharram Bey Station in Alexandria (6 per day 8am-10pm, E£4; last return from Rashid 5pm. **Microbuses** leave from the Tikka Grill in Alexandria, one block inland from the corniche (E£3). The **train** (3rd-class only) runs from Misr Station (9 per day 6:45am-10pm, 75pt) and returns to Alexandria (9 per day 5:50am-7:45pm; Ma'mura 60pt, downtown 70pt). **Service** to Rashid are easy to catch at Muharram Bay, but the ones back to Alexandria depart infrequently (E£3-5).*

Rashid (Rosetta) is the western meeting point of the Nile and the Mediterranean (Dumyat is the eastern meeting point). Not many visitors besides aspiring Egyptologists and those with plenty of time on their hands venture here. It has received most of its fame from the Rosetta Stone, the key to unlocking the hieroglyphs discovered here in 1799 by Napoleon's soldiers. The port is dotted with provincial Ottoman mosques and houses from the 17th and 18th centuries. Unfortunately, the town center's trash-lined streets detract from Rashid's historic homes, many of which have recently been restored. A cast of the stone is on display in the museum here (the original resides in London's British Museum). It describes the coronation and numerous titles of Pharaoh Ptolemy V in three tongues: Demotic (the common language), ancient Greek (the royal language), and hieroglyphs (the holy language). Although hieroglyphs had previously been indecipherable, ancient Greek

> **IT'S ALL HIEROGLYPHS TO ME** Hieroglyphic writing was used in instances of special religious significance, such as inscriptions on a temple wall or spells designed to speed a pharaoh to a happy afterlife. Since the inscriptions are in part decorative, they are often written in mirror-image pairs; in such cases, the writings are read from different directions. To tell which direction is the beginning, look for a human character; the direction the person or god is facing is usually the beginning. Before the discovery of the **Rosetta Stone** (p. 68), the most popular theory was that each glyph represented an idea: elaborate, fanciful, and utterly incorrect translations were made from many *papyri* and inscriptions. The Rosetta Stone provided the revolutionary insight that each glyph stood for an individual sound, rather than a complex meaning. The stone became the key to the long-forgotten script because of its trilingual engraving—Greek, Demotic, and hieroglyphic. The hieroglyphic alphabet uses combinations of sounds to represent words, much like the English alphabet. To provide more exact syntax, the hieroglyphic alphabet also includes characters that clarify meaning and resolve the problem of homonyms.

certainly was not; by comparing the three translations, scholars finally created a basic dictionary of hieroglyphs (see **It's All Hieroglyphs to Me**, p. 159).

FORT OF QAYTBAY. About five kilometers from Rosetta, the recently restored **Fort of Qaytbay** (not to be confused with the one in Alexandria) guards the strategic entrance to the Nile. Built in 1479 by Sultan Ashraf Qaytbay to serve as a first line of defense against the Ottoman Turks and the Crusaders coming from the Delta, this structure used to overlook the surrounding land. Clay and silt deposits have built up around it so that the ground has risen to the level of the fort. A much more significant reconstruction took place in 1799, when the French strengthened the fortress's wall with stone imported from Upper Egypt. A soldier noticed carvings on one of the stones, and this **Rosetta Stone** enabled Jean-François Champollion to unlock the mysteries of the hieroglyphic alphabet. *(The cheapest way to get to the fort is by green-and-white local taxi (E£3-4, round-trip E£5). The romantic way is to find a willing fisherman and go by boat (20min., E£5 per person round-trip). Beautiful scenery on the way. Open daily 9am-4pm; Ramadan 9am-3pm. E£6, students E£3.)*

ROSETTA MUSEUM. On Orabi St., three blocks inland from the Nile, the Rosetta Museum features some broken ceramics, a plaster cast of the Rosetta Stone, and a small collection of artifacts from local history. It is far from worth its hefty admission charge. *(Open daily 9am-4pm. E£20, students E£10. Camera privileges E£10.)*

ZAGHLOUL MOSQUE. The badly damaged 17th-century Zaghloul Mosque is at the end of the main street running south from the train station. For a more scenic approach, walk inland from the corniche, past the museum, and south through the *souq*. Past the rancid water and refuse are some Arabic inscriptions, archways, and decorated columns.

WEST OF ALEXANDRIA   ☎03

Beach resorts stretch west from Alexandria as far as the eye can see, like an apocalyptic vision where only Club Meds are left standing. Even so, the coastline's natural beauty can do wonders for the tired body and soul. The few secluded spots left along Egypt's Mediterranean coast draw a more local contingent, mostly Egyptian families. Modesty is still the rule here; women need to cover up.

Al-'Agami, 20km from Alexandria, is popular with the Egyptian upper class and makes an easy daytrip. Continuing west, almost every inch of sand has been bought by one "vacation village" or another. Many of these cater to specific occupations: Egyptian engineers, police, and doctors hole up in separate concrete complexes near the beach. The war cemeteries of **al-'Alamein,** 99km from Alexandria, mark the site of Africa's fiercest and most significant World War II battle. **Marsa Matrouh** is a colorful resort town on a bay and features some world-class beaches.

A number of resorts along the coast let passersby use their facilities for a fee. The plush **'Aida Beach Hotel** (☎410 28 02), 72km from Alexandria, gives a choice of a low rate (E£8-12), which pays for pool use and snacks, or a high rate (E£27-35, two-person minimum), which includes lunch and use of a beach cabin. Day use at the **Atic Hotel** (☎906 07 17), 89km west of Alexandria (the domed gatehouse with red letters above it), costs E£45, but you get a splendid shoreline, two pools, a playground, and lunch. The cheapest sandy spot is the **Marina Beach Club,** 94km west of Alexandria. It'll cost you to use the beautiful beach populated by wealthy Alexandrians zipping around on jet skis (E£15 per day), but not the pools.

If you time your day right, you can bask and feast at the beach, stop to visit the al-'Alamein memorials, and make it to Marsa Matrouh by sunset. Though many coastline segments between Alexandria and Matrouh are depressingly empty of budget hotels, opportunities for free and secluded **camping** are virtually unlimited (simply check in with the nearest police station or military office). **Microbuses** and **service** cruise the Alexandria-Marsa Matrouh road all day. Just flag one down (E£3.50 from Alexandria to the Atic Hotel, another E£5-8 to get to Marsa Matrouh).

AL-'AGAMI العجمى

Upper-middle-class Alexandrian sun worshipers flock to al-'Agami to escape the bustle and character of the city, instead embracing a world of concrete villas, chain restaurants, and private beaches. During the peak summer months, crowds compete elbow-to-elbow for beach space and some women grow increasingly courageous in the quest to bare more than a knee here or a nape there. In winter, hours shorten, prices lower, hemlines drop, and the town quiets down.

To get to al-'Agami, take minibus #760 (٧٦٠) from Sa'ad Zaghloul Sq. in Alexandria. Al-'Agami is actually two towns in one—Bitash and Hannoville. In **Bitash,** villas and expensive hotels mingle with restaurants and Western-style boutiques. In **Hannoville,** the quieter, more spinsterly sister city, a few budget hotels are crammed in between rows of apartments. When Egyptians say "al-'Agami," they're generally referring only to Bitash. Each town is oriented around a two-kilometer-long main street (**Bitash St.** and **Hannoville St.,** respectively) that extends from the highway to the beach and is lined with stores and groceries.

There is no reason to stay in al-'Agami, considering that Alexandria is 30 minutes away; the pricey hotels here are a further deterrent. Most beaches, such as the belly-and-bicep baring **Fardous (Paradise) Beach,** are private and hard to gain access to. **Abu Qir** and **Montaza** are better bets. The greatest concentration of restaurants is in Bitash, where the main road forks into Bitash St. and al-Asal St. Along with various chain restaurants, **al-Omda** serves up copious quantities of meat, and **La Dolce Vita** scoops up sweet Italian-style gelato.

AL-'ALAMEIN العلمين

Al-'Alamein is a sober interruption in the giddy spree of villa construction that dominates the Mediterranean coast. Here, in November 1942, Allied forces led by British Field Marshal Sir Bernard Montgomery halted the advance of the German Afrika Korps, saving Alexandria, Egypt, and the Suez Canal and oil fields of the Middle East. The Allied victory here marked the beginning of the end for the Axis Powers in North Africa and crushed the mystique surrounding the "Desert Fox," German Field Marshal Erwin Rommel, whose force of Panzer tanks had previously seemed invincible. Nearly 10,000 soldiers lost their lives at al-'Alamein, and 70,000 were wounded.

Non-A/C **West Delta buses** traveling between Marsa Matrouh and Alexandria or Cairo pass through al-'Alamein, though you can also go to a *service* depot and name your destination. Get off at the police checkpoint, right before the road to the British War Cemetery; the museum lies to the left from the main road connecting Alexandria to Marsa Matrouh. To leave town, flag down a *service* or minibus heading to **Alexandria** (1hr., E£5) or **Marsa Matrouh** (2hr., E£5-8) on the main road (the road leading to the museum and cemetery that merges with the main road to Alexandria or Marsa Matrouh). A hired **taxi** costs E£100, for either a round-trip from Alexandria or a cross-desert run.

WAR MUSEUM. The displays of weaponry and military garb are impressive but sterile. At least there are English descriptions of Rommel, Montgomery, and other participants in the battle. A map bedecked with hundreds of tiny red and green bulbs recreates the changing landscape of the North African campaign. *(West side of the village near the bus stop and main square. Open Sa-Th 8am-5pm, F 8am-1pm and 2-5pm; in winter and Ramadan 9am-3pm. E£7. Camera privileges E£5, video E£20.)*

BRITISH WAR CEMETERY. The British War Cemetery, about 250m east down the road from the museum, is a more powerful testament to the cost of the battle. Here lie buried 7367 soldiers from all over the Commonwealth, 815 of whom have headstones bearing only the inscription "Known Unto God." Ringed by purple flowers and set against the seemingly interminable desert, the excruciatingly tidy rows are made even more poignant by the personalized epitaphs. Maintained by the British War Graves Commission, the cemetery is free and almost always open.

GERMAN AND ITALIAN CEMETERIES. The less frequently visited German and Italian Cemeteries (8km and 12km west of town, respectively) perch on a petite peninsula overlooking the sea. It is difficult to get directly to these monuments without a private car or hired taxi. Microbuses along the Alexandria-Matrouh road will let passengers off two kilometers from the monuments—lucky travelers may be able to convince *service* drivers to give them a door-to-tomb ride. Whichever way you travel, make sure you're armed with lots of water. Walking through the desert is dangerous due to old **landmines.**

MARSA MATROUH مرسى مطروح ☎046

Fanning out from a bay of pure cobalt blue, this resort city makes a pleasant stop-over for travelers in no rush to get to Siwa, and is home to the best beaches on Egypt's north coast. In summer, Egyptian families pack the mold-and-pour con-crete villas and bathe along the five-kilometer crescent of white sands and gentle waves. At night, the streets fill with horn-happy drivers, gaggles of mothers look-ing for bargains, and shouting vendors selling useless junk. Marsa Matrouh's natu-ral harbor has served travelers, merchants, and soldiers from Alexander the Great to Rommel the "Desert Fox." Now the majority of sea vessels in Marsa are rented by the hour, and the police patrolling the Libyan border comprise the only major military presence in the area.

◧ GETTING THERE AND GETTING AROUND

Flights: EgyptAir (☎ 493 43 98), on Gala'a St., 3½ blocks west of Alexandria St. Flies to and from **Cairo** (1hr.; Th, F, Su leaves Cairo 9:30am, leaves Marsa Matrouh 10:30am; E£408). Office open June-Sept. Tu-Su 9am-2pm and 6-9pm. No flights in off-season.

Trains: The train station (☎ 493 39 36), one block east of the southern end of Alexandria St., about one kilometer from the corniche, runs trains to **Alexandria** (6hr.; 7am and 3:45pm; non-A/C 2nd-class E£14, 3rd-class E£8). 30% student discount.

Buses: Book ahead for Cairo buses, especially during summer. Arrive 30 minutes early to buy your ticket and get a seat. A/C bus services drastically cut back in off-season (Nov.-May). Two **bus stations:** Superjet and Golden Arrow lines leave from the corner by the tourist office, on the corniche one block west of Alexandria St. Catch West Delta buses from the station four kilometers south of town on Alexandria St. Minibuses leave from the intersection of Shokri al-Quwatli St. and Tahrir St. (sometimes called Gamal Abd al-Nasser St.), three blocks west of Alexandria St. A/C **Superjet** buses (☎ 493 47 87) run to **Alexandria** (3hr., 8:30am and 2:30pm, E£20) and **Cairo** (5hr., 11am and 3pm, E£37). Superjet buses might not run in winter. **Golden Arrow** runs A/C buses to **Alexan-dria** (3hr.; 9, 11am, 3, 7pm; in winter 9am and 3pm; E£20) and **Cairo** (5hr.; 8:30am, noon, 3:30, 4:30pm; in winter 3:30pm; E£35). **West Delta's** non-A/C buses shuttle to: **Alexandria** (5hr.; 7, 9:30am, noon, 1, 5, 8pm; E£15); **Cairo** (7hr., 7:30am, E£28); and **Siwa** (5hr.; 7:30am, 1:30, 4:30pm; E£12).

Service: *Service* leave irregularly from the intersection of Shokri al-Quwatli St. and Tahrir St. (sometimes called Gamal Abd al-Nasser St.), three blocks west of Alexandria St. To **Alexandria** (E£12). Infrequent service to **Siwa** (E£15) and nearby beaches.

Bike Rental: On Gala'a St., one block west of Alexandria St. E£2 per hr., E£10 per day; bargain for long-term rental.

✴🛈 ORIENTATION AND PRACTICAL INFORMATION

Your feet will serve you well in Marsa Matrouh—a cross-town stroll should take no more than 15 minutes. You only need to know two streets to find your way around town: the lively **corniche**, which stretches the length of the bay, and busy **Alexandria St.**, which runs perpendicular to the corniche. Alexandria St. begins at the Marsa Matrouh Governorate and heads inland to the train station and hill, one kilometer south of town. Most of the hotels and government offices are clustered along the corniche and the streets running parallel to it. Heading inland from the corniche, the most important of these are **Gala'a St., Tahrir St.** (sometimes referred to as Gamal Abd al-Nasser), **Goul Gamal St.**, and **Allam al-Rum St.** Parallel to Alexandria St. to the east are **Port Said St.** and **Zaher Galal St.**

While Marsa Matrouh is a pleasure spot, it is also only 215km from Libya—hence the noticeable military presence in the surrounding areas. It is wise to carry your **passport** with you outside of town and on the more obscure beaches.

Tourist Office: Egyptian Tourist Authority (☎ 493 18 41), on the corniche one block west of Alexandria St., behind the Governorate building. Friendly English-speaking staff. Ask for the helpful map booklet *Alexandria and Marsa Matrouh*, which lists a few hotels and restaurants. Open daily 9am-8pm; in winter 9am-6pm.

Passport Office: (☎ 493 53 51), one block north and a half-block east of the train station, just off Alexandria St. Open for visa extensions Sa-Th 8am-3pm.

Currency Exchange: The National Bank of Egypt, four blocks west of Alexandria St. on Shokri al-Quwatli St. Changes traveler's checks. Open daily 8:30am-2pm and 6-9pm.

Police: (☎ 93 33 76), one block south of corniche, two blocks east of Alexandria St. Little English spoken. Contact them in case of a **medical emergency.** Open 24hr.

Tourist Police: (☎ 493 55 75), next door to the tourist office, on the corniche one block west of Alexandria St. Little English spoken, but the staff at the tourist office or a Superjet ticket seller can help you communicate in a crisis when they're open. Open 24hr.

Pharmacy: al-Farghaly Pharmacy, at the corner of Alexandria St. and Allam al-Rum St., three blocks south of the corniche. Open daily 8am-1am.

Hospital: Military Hospital (☎ 493 52 86 or 493 43 70), on Gala'a St., three blocks west of Alexandria St. If possible, seek treatment in Alexandria or Cairo.

Telephone Office: Opposite the post office. Crowded and unreliable for international calls. Sells phonecards. Open 24hr. **Hotel Riviera Palace,** on the northern end of Alexandria St., has pricier but more dependable phone and fax service. Open 24hr. There are **Menatel** phones along Alexandria St.

Post Office: (☎ 493 23 67), two blocks east of Alexandria St. and one block south of the corniche. No Poste Restante. Open Sa-Th 8:30am-3pm.

🏠 ACCOMMODATIONS

The high season lasts from June to October, but Marsa Matrouh sees the bulk of its tourist action during July and August. There is also a spurt of Egyptian vacationers during Ramadan. During the off-season, upscale hotels along the corniche offer surprisingly low rates. No matter what the time of year, rooms are a sure thing at budget hotels on and near Alexandria St. Because few foreigners frequent these

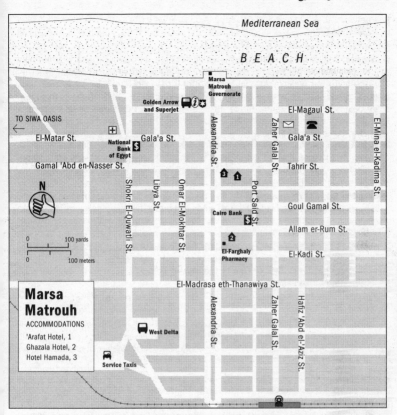

Mediterranean Sea

B E A C H

■ Marsa Matrouh Governorate

Golden Arrow and Superjet

El-Magaul St.

TO SIWA OASIS ←

El-Matar St.

Gala'a St.

Gala'a St.

National Bank of Egypt

Gamal 'Abd en-Nasser St.

Alexandria St.

Zaher Galal St.

El-Mina el-Kadima St.

Tahrir St.

N

Shokri El-Quwatli St.

Libya St.

Omar El-Mokhtar St.

Port Said St.

Cairo Bank

Goul Gamal St.

Allam er-Rum St.

0   100 yards

0   100 meters

El-Farghaly Pharmacy

El-Kadi St.

El-Madrasa eth-Thanawiya St.

Alexandria St.

Zaher Galal St.

Hafiz 'Abd el-'Aziz St.

Marsa Matrouh

ACCOMMODATIONS

'Arafat Hotel, 1
Ghazala Hotel, 2
Hotel Hamada, 3

West Delta

Service Taxis

places, many have neither English signs nor English speakers—**sign language** or Arabic experimentation (see **Phrasebook,** p. 701) may be in order.

Groups of two or more can rent one of the many flats in town. **Hotel Awam** (☎ 493 23 63), west of Alexandria St. on the corniche near the Mosque of Awam, has two-bedroom flats for up to six people with living rooms, bathrooms, and kitchens for E£55. If they don't mind sharing the beach during the day, couples can relax at **Marine Fouad** on Rommel's Peninsula, where wonderful rooms with baths, porches overlooking the sea, and three meals a day for two people cost E£120. (Open June-Sept. Reserve with the Borays in Cairo at ☎(02) 241 02 94.) **Camping** is permitted on the beach in front of the Semiramis Hotel free of charge. To pitch a tent farther out, contact the Egyptian Tourist Authority so they can inform the tourist police.

▧ **Hotel Lido** (☎ 493 33 48). Impeccable rooms with new beds, fans, TVs, and balconies. Private baths have towels and soap. Singles E£40, doubles without breakfast E£40.

Hotel Hamada (☎ 493 33 00), on the corner of Tahrir and Alexandria St. Bare-bones, reasonably clean rooms with shared baths. Avoid the din from the streets below by getting a room away from the corner. Singles, doubles, and triples E£10 per bed.

'**Arafat Hotel** (☎ 493 36 06), east of Alexandria St. on Tahrir St., past the Hotel Hamada. Large, dusty rooms with clean baths. A 3D picture of 'a(ra) fat cat watches over the reception area. Breakfast E£5. Singles E£15; doubles E£30; triples E£45.

Ghazala Hotel (☎ 493 35 19), on Allam al-Rum St., in a three-story white building just east of Alexandria St., six blocks from the corniche. Around the corner from al-Farghaly Pharmacy. Dark but well-kept rooms with firm beds and great sofas, although the dank baths don't always have hot water. Dorms E£7.50; singles E£10; doubles E£15.

FOOD AND ENTERTAINMENT

Strolling along the corniche and chilling out in *ahwas* are the major after-hours recreational sports, just as they are in most of the towns along Egypt's Mediterranean coast. **Bars** in the Rady and Beau Site Hotels serve overpriced drinks, and the Beau Site, 1½km west of Alexandria St. along the corniche, also runs a **bowling alley.** A raised outdoor patio 100m west of the end of the corniche (across from the Armed Services hotel compound) often hosts energetic **live music** in a breezy, friendly setting during the summer.

■ **Pizza Gaby,** just past the Negresco Hotel at the western end of the corniche. This A/C haven overlooking the sea is the perfect spot to admire the sunset. The hefty menu includes a variety of tasty pizzas (E£8-12), grilled meats (E£18-23), and Middle Eastern salads (E£4-7). Open daily noon-1am.

Samara Fish Restaurant (☎493 07 91), on Goul Gamal St. just east of Alexandria St., two blocks south of the corniche. This small restaurant serves up delicious grilled fish stuffed with vegetables. E£15-20 for a kilo of grilled gilled grub with salad and a heap of bread. Open daily 8am-midnight.

Abu Aly Pizza (☎494 23 04), on Alexandria St., three blocks south of the corniche. This two-story restaurant offers a wide selection of soups, sandwiches, and desserts. Take-away fresh pizza (E£6.50-14.50) or chicken *shawarma* (E£4.50) makes a long bus ride seem shorter. Open daily noon-1am.

Panayotis Greek Restaurant (☎493 24 74), on the west side of Alexandria St., two blocks south of the corniche. Also known as the one and only "Tourist Restaurant," Marsa's oldest restaurant has a simple menu including a stellar fish dinner (E£30), calamari (E£25), and Stella (E£6). Open daily 8am-1am.

BEACHES

Marsa Matrouh's glorious beaches are its *raison d'être*. However, just as in Alexandria, some women swim fully clothed, and only the most liberal beaches (designated below) allow for bikinis or revealing one-pieces. No matter how tolerant a beach may be, women should arrive well-covered and gauge the mood of the crowd once there, as the crowd's level of acceptance can vary from day to day. Since most Egyptian visitors prefer to relax on the beach, even the most crowded areas have plenty of open water for swimming.

To reach these beaches, take a shared taxi or minibus from the bus station (E£3-4 per person to 'Agiba), a shared pickup truck from the stand on the corner 300m north of the main bus station (E£2 to 'Agiba), or the open-sided *tut-tut* bus (E£1.25 to Cleopatra or 'Agiba). The *tut-tut* shuttles to and from the bus station when there are enough passengers (usually every hr. 9am-4:30pm; summer only).

■ **'AGIBA.** Surely the most spectacular of the area's sights is 'Agiba ("miracle" in Arabic), about 24km from Marsa Matrouh. Golden limestone cliffs plunge down to meet the azure waters, where waves crash over eroded rock formations and into sandy coves. Swimming is not always permitted, but a barefoot walk along the rocks is one of the best ways to spend a few hours around Marsa Matrouh. Bring food—there is only a soft-drink stand here. Along the way, hidden in the sands near Umm Araham village, stand the ruins of the tiny **Temple to Ramses II.**

BEAU SITE HOTEL BEACH. The Beau Site Hotel (on the far west end of the corniche) has, as the name suggests, one of the most beautiful beaches around. Though somewhat overrun by frolicking Egyptian children, the beach is cleaner and more liberal than most others. There is no charge for non-guests, but they ask that you rent an umbrella (E£12 per day), a chair (E£3 per day), or a sea kayak (E£10 per hr.). During the off-season, umbrellas are free. The hotel also runs a guests-only beach where security guards ensure that bathers can wear bikinis—and several do—without being bothered.

ROMMEL'S ISLE. The eastern arm of the harbor is called Rommel's Isle, but it clearly isn't an isle at all, as it can be reached by donkey cart (E£3), bike (E£10 per day), boat (E£9), or pickup truck taxi (50pt). Nestled in the peninsula is the **Rommel Museum,** housed in the caves that Rommel used as his headquarters during Germany's North African campaign. On display are Rommel's overcoat (size 41L) and various German and Italian maps showing the order of battle, yet the small faux cave is hardly worth the price. (Open daily in summer 9am-3:30pm. E£10, students E£5.) The beach outside, however, is a favorite destination of Egyptian tourists and since it is close to town, it fills up quickly.

OTHER BEACHES. To the west of the main beach, the **Beach of Love (Shati' al-Gharaam)** fondles the western horn of the bay and can be easily reached by foot or kayak. Inconsiderate visitors have begun to spoil the sand while enjoying the sun, and heaps of litter float out to sea every day. You'll encounter more wind, less trash, and the tantalizing **Cleopatra's Beach** 14km farther west, on the far right-hand side of a small cove called **Cleopatra's Bath.** Legend has it that the queen and Marc Antony would come here to bathe—as the waves crashed into the cove, the water would shoot toward the heavens and cascade back down on the lovers' entangled bodies. The peaceful but shallow **Obayyid Beach,** 18km west of Marsa Matrouh, draws Egyptian families staying at their corporation's tents on the shore, making it pretty boring unless you're there with your middle-management friends.

SIWA OASIS واحةسيوة ☎046

Emerging from 300km of barren, lifeless sand, the forest of palm trees and clear freshwater springs that make up the Siwa Oasis seem like a desert mirage. A walk among the people of this small town and its surrounding villages only deepens the sense of disbelief. Instead of Arabic, the Berber language of Siwi is spoken in homes and on the street, and the few married women who venture outside cover themselves from head to toe in blue *tarfudit* veils. Electricity only came to Siwa about 10 years ago, and the thousands of televisions in this town of mud-brick homes are only the most recent in a long history of outside invaders.

The Temple of Amun, east of the central town, housed one of the most famous oracles of the ancient world. After taking Egypt from the Persians in 331 BCE, Alexander the Great set out across the desert to learn Amun's prophecy. With the centuries that followed came more conquerors: Muhammad 'Ali brought the terri-

EGYPT

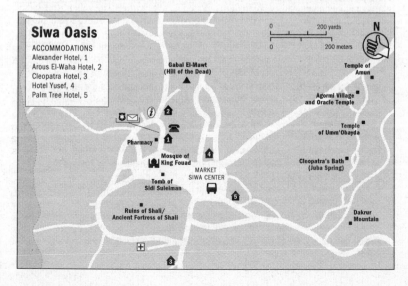

Siwa Oasis

ACCOMMODATIONS
Alexander Hotel, 1
Arous El-Waha Hotel, 2
Cleopatra Hotel, 3
Hotel Yusef, 4
Palm Tree Hotel, 5

0   200 yards
0   200 meters

N

Gabal El-Mawt
(Hill of the Dead)

Temple of
Amun

Agormi Village
and Oracle Temple

Temple
of Umm'Obayda

Pharmacy

Mosque of
King Fouad

MARKET
SIWA CENTER

Cleopatra's Bath
(Juba Spring)

Tomb of
Sidi Suleiman

Ruins of Shali/
Ancient Fortress of Shali

Dakrur
Mountain

tory under Ottoman control in 1820; the British occupied it in the early 20th century; and during World War II, the Desert Fox himself trotted into town.

Even today, Siwa feels like a culturally disputed territory. The people here are Siwans first, Egyptians second, and look with skeptical eyes on the technological changes that are making their desert buffer just a short stretch of sand. In 1984, the Egyptian government completed the road connecting Siwa to Marsa Matrouh, turning a week-long camel trek into a quick four-hour bus route. Cairo has integrated the oasis into the national economy, and Arabic has replaced Siwi as the language of instruction in schools. Today, younger Siwan women don Egyptian fashions, and local folklore is losing ground to serial soap operas. These changes have yet to become pervasive, and local tradition still regulates everyday life. Local festivals during fall and winter, especially the Feast of Siaha on the first full moon in October, are celebrated with relish and bring in droves of spectators. Older women still wear the traditional Siwan costume, with intricately braided hairdos and heavy silver jewelry around their arms, necks, and heads. Residents request that visiting women cover their arms and legs. Alcohol and open displays of affection are forbidden.

▣ GETTING THERE AND GETTING AROUND

The most practical way to reach Siwa is by **bus** from Marsa Matrouh or Alexandria, but courageous groups with a **car** can travel the 420km stretch of rough road from Bahariyya. **Taxis** can be hired to take you the other way for about E£400 per car, and one-way overnight **tours** to Bahariyya can also be arranged through any of the hotels for E£600 for up to seven people.

Buses: A/C **West Delta** buses come from **Marsa Matrouh** (5hr.; 7:30am, 1:30, 4pm; E£12) and Misr Station in **Alexandria** (10hr., 11am, E£27). Buses leave Siwa to **Alexandria** (10hr., 7am and 10pm, E£27) via **Marsa Matrouh** (another bus at 2pm; E£10).

Local Bus: The local bus crawls west from the mosque to the village of al-Maraqi, making a 60km loop to Khamisa and Bilad al-Rum (round-trip E£2). There are usually two per day (7am and 3pm; in winter 7am and 2pm).

◪ ❼ ORIENTATION AND PRACTICAL INFORMATION

The Siwa Oasis is in a desert hollow about 300km southwest of Marsa Matrouh. Its western edge comes within 50km of the closed Libyan border. The valley stretches across 82km west to east, and ranges between 3km and 30km north to south. Most visitors concern themselves only with Siwa town and nearby villages. The **bus** stops in the **market center** in the shadows of the ancient fortress of **Shali.** The **tourist office** and **police** are back up the road to Marsa Matrouh, while the **King Fouad Mosque,** the town's largest building, is nearby.

Tourist Office: (☎ 460 23 38), in the new white building across from the Arous al-Waha Hotel. Knowledgeable Mahdi Muhammad 'Ali Hweity, sociologist, fluent English-speaker, and native Siwan, arranges sightseeing expeditions, obtains camping permits, and is nearly an oracle himself on all aspects of Siwan life. Open Sa-Th 8am-2pm and 6-8pm; in winter Sa-Th 4-8pm.

English-Language Bookstore: Hassan's Handicrafts and English Bookshop, next to the telephone office. A few English books on Egyptian history and culture and some novels. Run by the fab Mr. Hweity of the tourist office. Open Sa-Th 8-11pm; in winter 3-10pm.

Pharmacy: Yusef's Pharmacy, on the road to the Cleopatra Hotel. Open daily 9am-2pm and 6pm-midnight; in winter 9am-noon.

Hospital: (☎ 460 20 19). Go south one kilometer from the town square and take a right at the first four-story building on the left. Open 24hr.

Police: (☎ 460 20 08), in the same building as the post office. Open 24hr.

SIWI MADE SIMPLE
Most Siwan children's first language is Siwi, an unwritten Berber dialect. It is incomprehensible to the rest of Egypt and sounds almost Scandinavian at times. As children grow up, parents and schools make sure they learn Arabic as well. The possible permutations of the following words should keep you occupied until the donkeys come home:

mashi	yes	**oula**	no
gaf lahk	go	**shiek**	you
oushi	give me	**ehk sehk**	I want
aksoon	meat	**aman**	want
azumur	olives	**tene**	dates

ihkseikh teswi aman   I want to drink water

tanta elhal ineik   How are you?

tanta wook   What is this?

betin ismetinik   What is your name?

sewil dede   Speak with me

Internet Access: Mohamed Ibrahem's Internet Service (☎ 460 20 49), next door to the Palm Trees Hotel. This being the middle of the desert, connections are slow, so Mohamed recommends typing messages on a word processor (E£8 per 1hr.) before going on-line (50pt per min.). Knock loudly if the lights are out. Digital camera rental available. Open 24hr.

Telephone Office: Behind the Arous al-Waha Hotel.

Post Office: Across the street from the Arous al-Waha Hotel. Open Sa-Th 8am-2pm.

▸ ACCOMMODATIONS

Most crash pads in Siwa cluster around the main square. Slow business in the summer means it is fairly easy to find a good room, but in winter Siwa has more tourists than donkeys, so make reservations or consider an outlying hotel. Unless otherwise noted, all rooms have fans. Free **camping** in shelters is available on **Dakrur Mountain,** four kilometers southeast of town, and at **Bir Wahad** (Well #1), 12km south of town (see **South of Siwa Town,** p. 170). Bring a sleeping bag and insect repellent. Check in with Mr. Hweity at the tourist office before pitching your tent.

▨ **Palm Trees Hotel** (☎ 460 23 04), 20m down a side road from the town square. Clean, comfortable rooms with fans and balconies, but the best part of this hotel is the idyllic grove filled with palm-leaf furniture out back. Laundry machine and bike rentals. Singles E£6; doubles E£12, with bath E£15; triples E£15.

▨ **Hotel Yusef** (☎ 460 21 62), in the center of town. The name is painted across the top floor. The cleanest rooms in town and a friendly owner, Salameh, who is committed to guests' satisfaction. Balconies overlook Siwa and beyond. Women can sunbathe on the roof terrace in peace. Bike rentals. Dorms E£5; private doubles E£10.

Alexander Hotel (☎ 460 50 12), across from the post office. Clean, but aging hotel with dim rooms and private baths. Dorms E£5; singles E£10; doubles E£20.

Cleopatra Hotel (☎ 460 21 48), south of the town square on the main road, past the Shali fortress. A newer and slightly pricier establishment with stuffy rooms, but great views and immaculate bathrooms. Antony and Cleo would have preferred the spacious "bungalow" doubles in the building next door (E£40). Singles E£14; doubles E£18, both with bath and balcony.

Arous al-Waha Hotel (☎ 460 21 00; fax 460 20 28), across from the tourist office in the northwestern part of town. This more upscale establishment has huge, spotless rooms and private baths. All come with soap and towels. Singles E£54.50; doubles E£72.50.

EGYPT

🍴 FOOD

Several restaurants line the two market squares and are generally open from 8 or 10am to midnight or 1am. In summertime the menus shrink. For breakfast, try pancakes with banana, honey, and yogurt (E£2.50). If asked, a local may offer you a taste of *lagbi*, a sweet palm-tree juice and local specialty served only before 10am—it ferments by noon. Siwan eateries are mainly indistinguishable from one another, but some tried-and-true places are **'Abdou's Restaurant** and **East-West,** both on the street running along the north side of the square, with an unusual quiche-style vegetarian pizza at the former and excellent couscous at the latter. The **Palm Trees Hotel** has delicious but smaller breakfasts and the best ambiance in its garden restaurant. All Siwan restaurants are vegetarian friendly, and many feature Indian-inspired meals. Local **stores** are well stocked. Because Siwans tend to be more reserved than residents of most Egyptian towns, only a few travelers receive **invitations** to eat or stay with a local family. Invitations are usually offered by children, sometimes by adult men. At dinner, your hosts may try to sell you homemade handicrafts, or they may simply want to talk. Exercise caution before accepting hospitality—solo women should decline invitations from single Siwan men.

👁 SIGHTS

Ringed by multicolored desert mesas and waves of sand dunes, all under a piercing blue sky, Siwa is Egypt's most beautiful oasis. Most of Siwa's sites are easily accessible by bike trips down smooth dirt roads lined with palm trees. The more distant surrounding villages can be reached by local bus or through one of many tours offered by hotels and restaurants. *Carettas* (donkey-drawn taxicarts) always stand ready, making for a slow, bumpy, but thoroughly Siwan trip. Mr. Hweity of the tourist office has posted new blue signs around town to mark Siwa's important buildings and roads. A **half-day tour** goes for a bargain E£15 per head.

SIWA TOWN

RUINS OF SHALI. From atop the ruins of the crumbling medieval fortress-town of Shali (which simply means "town" in Siwi), you can see the quiet streets of Siwa town wind through a cluster of mud houses and luxuriant palm gardens. Shali's encircling wall once protected the Siwans from marauding Berbers and Bedouin. There was little room to build, so houses were cramped. Although the mud-brick structures were sturdy, torrential rains washed away most buildings about twice a century. After Muhammad 'Ali conquered Siwa in 1820, there was less need for fortification, so Siwans were quick to build more spacious homes below. Several days of fierce rain in 1985 severely damaged much of Shali, and what remains today is a surreal landscape of tangled walls and eroded mud-brick that may house a donkey here, a family there, or be completely abandoned to free-range chickens. All of the walls are quite secure, and it is safe to wander through the ruins. Every Thursday night after the last call to prayer (around 9pm, in winter 6pm), some local Muslims gather for religious ceremonies outside the mud-brick **Tomb of Sidi Suleiman,** the town's patron saint, beside the King Fouad Mosque. Visitors are invited to watch.

TRADITIONAL SIWAN HOUSE. The 1985 rains motivated a visiting Canadian ambassador to try to preserve Siwan culture, so he raised funds to construct the permanent Traditional Siwan House. The house serves as a museum of Siwan garb, silver jewelry, and children's toys. *(Down the road from the tourist office, opposite the King Fouad Mosque. Open Sa-Th 10am-noon; ask tourist office for other hours. E£1.50.)*

NORTH OF SIWA TOWN

GABAL AL-MAWT (HILL OF THE DEAD). The acropolis of Gabal al-Mawt rises one kilometer to the northeast of ancient Siwa. The hill is home to several Ptolemaic-era tombs that Romans robbed and reused. These tombs went undiscovered until World War II, when Siwan families crammed into caves seeking shelter from Italian bombs. The scattered human bones and mummy wrappings that litter the site belonged to the Romans, as did the niches that mar the ancient frescoes. The first sepulchre is the **Tomb of Si-Amun.** The intact decoration shows the bearded nobleman with Osiris, and the magnificent ceiling depicts the six stages of the sun's journey across the sky, and a beautiful field of stars. The **Tomb of Mesu Isis,** five meters to the east, has damaged paintings of Osiris and Isis. The **Tomb of the Crocodile** features paintings of the scaly chomper once buried there, although his corpse has been removed. The **Tomb of Niperpathot,** the oldest in Siwa, housed the body of a nobleman of the 26th dynasty and includes paintings of his Nubian and Greek wives and their multiracial sons. *(Tombs are to the left upon entering from the access road. A custodian unlocks tombs daily 9am-3pm. Free; E£2-4 bakhsheesh appropriate.)*

EAST OF SIWA TOWN

The Temple of Amun and the Temple of Umm 'Obayda both lie only one kilometer apart on the same road. A bike trip looping around the road might take in the two temples, followed by a dip at Cleopatra's Bath, then onto Dakrur Mountain, and from there back to town. Rent a bike from town or hail a *caretta* (E£10 per load).

ORACLE OF AMUN. A 13th-century gate made of palm logs graces the entrance to the acropolis atop which this oracle is perched. Some of the massive inner chambers, all that remains upright, still carry extensive carvings. Follow the same path as Alexander the Great to reach the oracle: go through the stone temple's simple gateway into the outer court, then cross the inner court to reach the center. The Oracle of Amun is thought to date from the 26th dynasty (c. 660 BCE). It became widely celebrated in later dynasties and gained popularity even with the ancient Greeks, who constructed many shrines to Amun in their home city-states. Greek and Roman historians recorded the mystical rituals necessary to invoke an answer from the oracle: priests carried a sacred boat containing the image of Amun, while women sang and danced in procession. Alexander did all of this to seek the answer to his personal burning question: Was he a god, the son of Zeus? He also supposedly asked the oracle another question in private, but what he queried will never be known. The secret died with him, fewer than 10 years after his visit.

REVERSAL OF FORTUNES According to the ancient historian Herodotus (who was probably exaggerating a bit), **King Cambyses** of Persia "detached a body of 50,000 men with orders to attack the Ammonians [the ancient name for the Siwans], reduce them to slavery, and burn the oracle of Zeus." No one is sure *why* King Cambyses wanted to conquer Siwa, but it's a well-established fact that the Persian ruler turned his wrath on the desert oasis after invading Egypt in 525 BCE. Some have theorized that Siwa's famed **Oracle of Amun** may have predicted a short reign for the new invaders, so a threatened Cambyses decided to demonstrate his power over prophecy. Predictably, things did not go according to plan. The troops made it to Kharga, then vanished without a trace. Legend holds that the whole army was buried in a sandstorm, but explorers and archaeologists have failed to find any sign of the army among the desert's dunes. The prophecy came true as well; in 331 BCE, **Alexander the Great** ousted the Persians and ended what was indeed a short reign.

TEMPLE OF UMM 'OBAYDA. Less than one kilometer south of the Oracle of Amun, down the curving road, are the remains of the Temple of Umm 'Obayda, also dedicated to Amun. Surviving the ravages of time and an earthquake in 1877, the temple was reasonably well-preserved near the end of the 19th century, until a local government official demolished the remains in 1897 to collect stone for the construction of some new public buildings. One wall remains upright, with inscriptions dedicated to the Egyptian gods.

CLEOPATRA'S BATH. A pleasant one-kilometer bike ride through the quiet, green palm groves around Siwa leads to **Juba Springs,** renamed Cleopatra's Bath by the tourist authority. A tiled basin 15m in diameter now encircles a deep blue pool, which lightly bubbles from the large spring below. Although the pool is mostly frequented by men, fully clothed women should also feel comfortable swimming here (as comfortable as swimming fully clothed can be), and may enter via the enclosure next to the spring. If you visit these sights at sunrise or in the late evening, you may be the only person there.

HAMMAM RAMAL (SAND BATH). On **Dakrur Mountain,** one kilometer south of Cleopatra's Bath, nearly 1000 rheumatics congregate each summer for 10-day stints in the Hammam Ramal. The procedure may sound like a Siwan torture method, but it's actually painless: under the supervision of a specialist, the "bather" is buried in sand from the neck down while his head is protected from the sun's heat. After a stint in the sand, the patient stays indoors for the rest of the day, then repeats the procedure. You can try it for E£25, including room and board.

ABU SHROUF AND ENVIRONS. Abu Shrouf, 27km east of Siwa toward Bahariyya, is cooler, deeper, and cleaner than any of Siwa's pools. Local legend has it that Abu Shrouf is the only place in the oasis with female donkeys. If a male donkey escapes from Siwa, the first place his owner looks is Abu Shrouf. This myth has even influenced local slang: if a Siwan man has a pleasant night with his wife, he tells his friends, "Last night I went to Abu Shrouf!" You too can go there, either with the tour arranged by Mr. Hweity from the Siwa tourist office (4 people, E£15 each) or by private taxi from Siwa (about E£30 round-trip). A large spring called **Qurayshat,** seven kilometers west of Abu Shrouf, was a major farming area during Roman times—old olive presses still remain. A small **Bedouin village** lies five kilometers to the east. Though the government built them houses, the Bedouin preferred to live in tents. Instead, they kept their animals in the new houses. Unamused that its projects were being used as barns, the government destroyed many of the tents and forced the Bedouins to live in houses.

WEST OF SIWA TOWN

FATNAS. Plan to spend at least one sunset in idyllic Fatnas, or Fantasy Island, four kilometers west of town. Accessible by a small causeway, Fatnas Pool is smaller than Cleopatra's Bath and not as heavily frequented by locals. From the far western point of the adjoining garden, you can see across a glistening salt lake to a limitless sea of sand. The peaceful garden is owned by a small cafe so you'll have to enjoy a drink as well (tea 50pt) if you plan to stay.

BILAD AL-RUM (CITY OF THE ROMANS). The unidentified stone structure and several tombs in the hillside are known as Bilad al-Rum. Up the road behind barbed wire are the remains of a **Doric temple.** Greek archaeologist Liana Souvaltzi caused a stir in 1995 when she announced that she had discovered the tomb of Alexander the Great within the temple walls. A team of 12 archaeologists quickly flew in from Greece and determined that the tomb's inscriptions were not Alexander's, but those of an important Greek official. Although Alexander wanted to be buried in Siwa, his general, Ptolemy, swiped the corpse and buried it in his capital, Alexandria, where it lies today (somewhere underneath the modern roads and highrises). Campers can ask the tourist office for special permission to sleep here, then take the bus back to Siwa the next morning.

SOUTH OF SIWA TOWN

BIR WAHAD AND AL-ZAITOUN. Bir Wahad (Well #1), 12km south of Siwa, is surrounded by lush vegetation and sports hot water clean enough for bathing. A number of Siwan guides offer tours for around E£45. The Palm Trees Hotel runs a particularly good tour, but you should still inquire at the tourist office to find out who offers the best package. If you spend the night, bring a blanket from your

GREASED LIGHTNING Not long ago, Siwans ran a smuggling operation to carry goods on the sly from Libya into Egypt on donkeys. The nighttime treks would proceed perfectly until the beasts (unaware of the clandestine nature of the mission) would bray and alert the Border Patrol officials, thereby spoiling the whole operation. Siwans wracked their brains to figure out a way to pacify the carriers until someone somehow discovered that if the asses' asses were greased, the brutes would be unable to create the force needed to let air out of their mouths. A team of French scientists is currently researching this exciting discovery.

hotel—it gets cold in the desert, even in mid-July. About six kilometers from Siwa, a fabulous stretch of water erupts amid sand dunes one kilometer off the main road, in an area known as the **fish farm.** The farm is accessible by bicycle.

SHOPPING

You can shop for exquisite **handicrafts,** including intricately embroidered clothing, veils, and *margunahs* (large, decorated woven baskets) in Siwa. Several stores have sprung up around the town square, including **Siwa Original Handicraft,** to the left of 'Abdou Restaurant, and **Hassan's Handicrafts,** next to the telephone office. Bargaining in craft shops can be difficult, as the (mainly female) artisans set the prices and aren't around to haggle. Shawls can start at E£90 and baskets at E£30. The types of crafts sold are changing to accommodate tourist tastes. Siwa's silversmith died several decades ago without training an apprentice, so it is difficult to find jewelry here nowadays.

SINAI PENINSULA سيناء

The Sinai is the collision point of two continents—an enormous tectonic summit. A handful of small towns and a major road artery occupy the sandy shelf where the mountains meet the sea, but only the Bedouin brave the rest of the Sinai's dry, rough landscape. The greatest profusion of life in the area thrives below the sea: The Gulf of Aqaba's warm waters support a carnival of brilliantly colored coral reefs and subaquatic life. In sharp contrast to the bland browns and earthy hues of the rest of the Middle East, the underwater environs explode with color—the reds and greens of coral broken by the flashes of yellow, blue, and orange fins, set against the sparkling turquoise backdrop of the Red Sea.

The Sinai has had a surprisingly long history of war. Since the pharaohs' troops first trampled the broad plains of the northern Sinai on their march to Syria and Canaan, the favor has been returned by marauding, Egypt-bound Hyksos, Assyrians, Persians, Greeks, Arabs, and Turks. In 1903, the British drew the borders of the Sinai from Rafah to Eilat in an attempt to keep Turkey and Germany safely distanced from the Suez Canal. On the fourth day of the Six Day War of 1967, Israel regained control of the Sinai Peninsula from Egypt and began to capitalize upon the region's tourism potential. The Israelis established most of the original hotels and dive centers, including those in Dahab and Sharm al-Sheikh. The new development altered the lives of many Bedouin, who began to give camel tours and work in hotels. The profitability of the tourism industry made it possible for some to abandon their traditional nomadic lifestyle.

In the 1973 Yom Kippur War, Egyptian forces crossed the canal in a surprise offensive to recapture the Sinai. The Egyptian army broke through the Israeli defense line, but later Israeli counterattacks recaptured most of the peninsula. Israel retained the Sinai until it was returned to Egypt in two stages under the terms of the Camp David Accords: the first half in 1979, the second in 1982. The Sinai never regained its politically strategic status but has remained a highly touristed vacation spot.

EGYPT

Secluded **al-Arish** (p. 174) is the jewel of Egypt's most inviting shore, while **Sharm al-Sheikh** (p. 181) is world-renowned for the beauty beneath its waves.

Even if Dopey's not your favorite of the Seven Dwarfs, visit the Bedouin camps of **Dahab** (p. 187) and you'll put on a Happy face.

Moses made the hike up **Mount Sinai** (p. 176); now thou shalt too. Tackle some of the tougher desert hikes of the **High Sinai** (p. 180) with a Bedouin as your guide.

▣ GETTING AROUND

Travel in the Sinai Peninsula is far easier than in the rest of Egypt. Women can comfortably wear shorts and sleeveless shirts in most places, and professional con artists are rare. While many Bedouin have given up their camels for Camaros, there are still places where travelers can get a sense of their nomadic lifestyle.

BY BUS

The noble machines of the **East Delta Bus Company,** battered cruelly by the rocks, ruts, and dust of Sinai roads, heroically tread the scorched highway. With towns few and far between, buses and taxis are the only means of transportation. Timetables are really no more than an administrator's pipe dream. At bus stations, patience is more a necessity than a virtue.

BY SERVICE

Service are a reasonably priced and convenient alternative to buses. Weathered old Peugeot 504s piloted by Bedouin cabbies are ubiquitous. Hop in with other passengers or negotiate with a driver and wait while he recruits more travelers to your destination. Women should avoid riding alone with a driver. *Service* are comparable in price to the bus under ideal circumstances, but only with a full load of seven. You'll get to where you're going a lot faster, but this speed has its perils: traffic laws do not apply and the laws of physics are only grudgingly acknowledged. Consistent with the laws of supply and demand, *service* prices will drop immediately before the arrival of a bus, then skyrocket after the bus has departed.

▣ ABOVE-WATER TIPS

A number of **regulations** govern travelers to the Sinai. Unguided travel is restricted to main roads and settlements, but you may visit parts of the desert interior with a Bedouin guide. Sleeping on the beach is prohibited in some areas (notably Na'ama Bay), and the police often harass dozing backpackers. Since these areas are not always marked, ask around before settling down for the night. Nude sunbathing is illegal, as is the oft-hawked **marijuana.** You cannot bring a rented car or any four-wheel drive vehicle into the Sinai from Israel. **Prices** are higher and exchange rates poorer here than anywhere else in Egypt. If you're coming from the Nile Valley, change money before arriving. **Bug season** descends upon the Sinai in the spring and early summer. Dahab is periodically clouded by mosquitoes and flies with killer munchies. Some travelers rig mosquito nets; others advise sleeping by the beach. In summer, no one wears or carries much, and it only takes a few days before travelers begin to reexamine conventions of hygiene and appearance.

▣ UNDERWATER TIPS

Without question, the Red Sea has some of the greatest coral reefs and marine life in the world. Diving was not very big in the Middle East until Jacques-Yves Cousteau made his voyage through the Red Sea aboard *Calypso* (as chronicled in his famous book and movie *The Silent World*). Now that diving is a major part of many trips to the Sinai Peninsula, the regional administration has begun to face

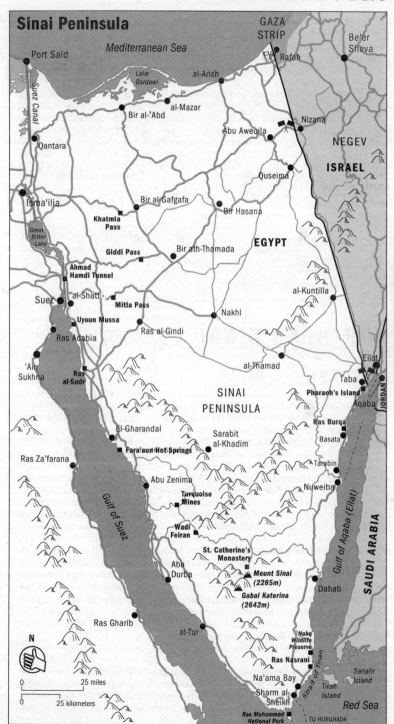

Sinai Peninsula

Mediterranean Sea

GAZA STRIP

Port Said

Lake Bardawi

al-Arish

El Rafah

Be'er Sheva

Suez Canal

al-Mazar

Bir al-'Abd

Abu Aweqila

Nizana

Qantara

NEGEV

ISRAEL

Isma'ilia

Bir al-Gafgafa

Bir Hasana

Quseima

Great Bitter Lake

Khatmia Pass

EGYPT

Giddi Pass

Bir ath-Thamada

Ahmad Hamdi Tunnel

al-Shatt

al-Kuntilla

Suez

Mitla Pass

Nakhl

Uyoun Mussa

Ras al-Gindi

Ras Adabia

al-Thamad

Eilat

'Ain Sukhna

Ras al-Sudr

Taba

Pharaoh's Island

Aqaba

JORDAN

SINAI PENINSULA

Ras Burqa

El-Gharandal

Sarabit al-Khadim

Basata

Faraun Hot Springs

Ras Za'farana

Tarabin

Abu Zenima

Nuweiba

Turquoise Mines

Gulf of Suez

Wadi Feiran

St. Catherine's Monastery

Gulf of Aqaba (Eilat)

SAUDI ARABIA

Abu Durba

▲ Mount Sinai (2285m)

▲ Gabal Katerina (2642m)

Dahab

Ras Gharib

al-Tur

Nabq Wildlife Preserve

N

Ras Nasrani

Strait of Tiran

Sanafir Island

Na'ama Bay

Tiran Island

0   25 miles

Sharm al-Sheikh

Red Sea

0   25 kilometers

Ras Muhammad National Park

TO HURGHADA

EGYPT

the serious problem of **irresponsible ecotourism.** All coral reefs from Dahab to Ras Muhammad are under the jurisdiction of the Ras Muhammad National Park. Regulations forbid the removal or defacement of any animal, plant, or shell, living or dead, from the sea. The park is fighting a difficult battle with developers waiting to exploit the region. You can do your part to preserve the reefs by observing a simple rule: look, but don't touch. Ras Muhammad, like most James Bond movies, has underwater police who will chase you out of the water if they see you breaking this rule. Even accidentally bumping the coral can damage it (and you).

Diving is very expensive, but you're paying for safety. The sites along the Gulf of Aqaba coast listed below emphasize safety above all else. **Snorkeling gear** can be rented all over, while **dive shops** are concentrated mainly in Dahab and Sharm al-Sheikh. Divers must be certified to rent equipment; most five-day courses provide certification and cost around US$300. The only decompression chamber in the area is in Sharm al-Sheikh. If you're rusty, take a check-out dive for US$35.

Beginner divers should make sure their instructors speak their language flawlessly, as small misunderstandings can have a big significance underwater ("Tanks!" "You're welcome!"). The instructor must also be certified to teach your particular course, whether it's PADI or SSI—ask to see his or her card. Some clubs are active in protecting the reefs, participating in annual clean-up dives, and making sure their operations have minimal impact on the marine ecosystems. The size of the club also matters: larger centers often have more scheduled dives and more extensive facilities, whereas smaller ones give you personal attention and will usually run a course for just one or two people rather than waiting for six to sign up. Quality of equipment and safety records are important; ask divers for advice.

NORTHERN SINAI

AL-ARISH العريش   ☎068

Al-Arish is caught in the cultural vortex between the *sheesha*-smoking Mediterranean and the who-knows-what-smoking Sinai—and manages to avoid the worst of both. Because it is only accessible through Isma'ilia, al-Arish is much less touristed than the High Sinai, and is free of the acres of concrete vacation complexes that line the Mediterranean coast near Alexandria. Al-Arish is a favorite spot for vacationing Egyptian families, and Western tourists will find themselves a bit of a curiosity, but less hassled here than in many parts of Egypt. Currently the capital of the North Sinai Governorate, al-Arish was once an important stopover on what was perhaps the oldest military route in history. It has since given up military mottos and has settled down with a more mellow one: life's a beach. The beach here is clean and inviting (some say the best on Egypt's Mediterranean coast), and the only shore in Egypt spotted with palm trees.

◪ **GETTING THERE AND GETTING AWAY.** There are two roads to know in al-Arish: **Fouad Zekry St.**, which runs along the beach, and **Tahrir St.**, perpendicular to Fouad Zekry. The **bus station** (☎34 01 08) is at the south end of Tahrir St., two kilometers from the beach. Buses run daily to **Cairo** (5hr.; 8am E£25, 4pm E£35) and **Isma'ilia** (3hr., every 30min. 7am-5pm, E£10). **Service** (E£5) run to Rafah and the Israeli border. Getting around the downtown area is easy by foot, but a walk to the beach is far—catch a *tut-tut* bus or one of the brightly colored Mercedes that serve as shared taxis (50pt). City minibuses run along the beach on Fouad Zekry St. (50pt) and a private taxi within al-Arish shouldn't cost more than E£5.

◪ **PRACTICAL INFORMATION.** The ETA **tourist office,** on Fouad Zekry St., is just off the beach. (☎34 05 69. Open daily 9am-2pm and 4-8pm.) Coming from the downtown/Tahrir St. area, bear left at the intersection with Fouad Zekry St. The **tourist office** and **tourist police** (open 24hr.) are in the same building on the right.

There are banks along Tahrir St., including the **National Bank of Egypt** (☎ 35 18 81) and the **Bank of Cairo** (☎ 35 30 32), which exchanges traveler's checks and cash or gives cash advances on credit cards. (Both open Su-Th 9am-2:30pm.) The **police station** is at the northern end of Tahrir Sq., but you're better off paying a visit to the tourist police. **Pharmacies:** in the downtown area. (Generally open daily 8am-1am.) **Government Hospital:** on al-Geish St., just off Tahrir St. (☎ 34 00 11. Open 24hr.) **Telephone office:** three blocks north and two blocks east of Tahrir Sq. (Open 24hr.) **Post office:** across the street from the telephone office. Sends **faxes** for E£5.50 plus the cost of the call. (☎ 35 15 03; fax 35 15 01. Open Sa-Th 8:30am-2:30pm.)

▐▊▐▊ ACCOMMODATIONS AND FOOD. Most of al-Arish's beachfront hotels are reasonably priced. The **Moonlight Hotel** is on the beach, just west of the tourist office, off Fouad Zekry St. Moonlit or not, the hallways are a bit dark, but the rosy-fingered (okay, bright pink) rooms with bath are like a cheerful vision of the dawn. Reservations are advised. (☎ 34 13 62. Singles E£20; doubles E£35.) The **Green Land Beach Hotel** is east of the tourist office, a little off Fouad Zekry St. Walk toward the beach on the road that angles behind William's Restaurant; the Green Land is on the beach side of the road. (☎ 34 06 01. Doubles and triples with fan, balcony, bath, breakfast, and the occasional TV E£30.) The airy **El-Salaam Hotel** is on Tahrir St., off the square and near the bus station. Ask for a room away from the street. (☎ 35 42 19. Doubles E£18.50; triples E£25; with private bath.)

Food is mostly standard Arab fare, with the exception of **William's,** on Fouad Zekry St. near the Green Land Beach Hotel. Minimalist decor doesn't detract from the fish and meat entrees, complete with french fries and salad. (Entrees E£10-20. Open daily 8am-2am.) At the western end of al-Arish is the pleasant **Basata,** roofed with palm fronds and filled with palm frond furniture. (Full meals E£10-20. Open daily 11am-1am.) In town, the best budget meal award goes to **'Aziz,** next to El-Salaam Hotel on Tahrir St., with a variety of grilled foods (E£5-15) and rice or noodle side dishes. (Sides E£1-3. ☎ 35 43 45. Open daily 9am-1am.)

▣▐▊ SIGHTS AND ENTERTAINMENT. Life in al-Arish revolves around the Mediterranean. The entire length of the **beach** is pristine and, except for brief sections in front of the Semiramis and Egoth Oberoi Hotels, there is no difference between public and private shoreline. There are a few **Bedouin craft stores** at the north end of Tahrir St. Every Thursday, Tahrir Sq. comes alive when local Bedouin sell silver, rugs, garments, and camel accessories at the weekly **souq.** A few kilometers east of town on the road to Rafah is the **Sinai Heritage Museum,** which details traditional Bedouin life on the Peninsula and has an excellent collection of clothes and jewelry. (Open Sa-Th 9:30am-2pm. E£2. Camera privileges E£5, video E£25.) In the evenings, many locals take to the *sheesha* parlors of Tahrir Sq., while the coffee shops along the promenade attract tourists. The expensive drinks (Stella E£12) outnumber the people at the **bars** of the Semiramis and Oberoi hotels.

Near al-Arish is **Zaranik Protected Area,** a nature preservation where thousands of birds migrate in the fall. The park has a bird viewing area, nature trails, and campgrounds. Get there on a *service* running between Isma'ilia and al-Arish. (US$3; camping US$5 per person.)

WESTERN SINAI

The Sinai Peninsula's west coast is a mixed blessing. The industrial wasteland of the shallow Gulf of Suez doesn't compare to the stunning beauty above and below sea level all along the Gulf of Aqaba coast. If you see the oil rigs and flame-belching smokestacks of the Suez coast out the window of the Cairo-Sharm al-Sheikh bus, you've probably seen enough. Most Western tourists avoid the Western Sinai, leaving its few memorable attractions uncrowded and peaceful.

UYOUN MUSSA. Moses buffs everywhere will be enthralled by this locale, 15km south of Suez, where Moses devised an early water purification system with the help of a tree branch. Uyoun Mussa continues Moses' work in several wells, some of which you can swim in. When Napoleon visited in 1798, he discovered a canal linking the wells to the sea, used to resupply ships with fresh water. *(Daily buses from Suez will drop you off, but finding a ride back can be dangerously unreliable. It's best to hire a taxi from Suez (E£40-50). Insist on seeing the wells—the driver may deny their existence.)*

RAS AL-GINDI. Ras al-Gindi features the ruins of Salah al-Din's 800-year-old "Fortress of the Soldier," or **Qal'at al-Gindi.** The impressive ruins stand atop a small mountain (a one-hour climb). Be careful climbing up, as the path drops off considerably on either side; one misstep and you'll wind up next to your sleeping taxi driver below. *(50km inland from Ras al-Sudr. If you take the bus to Ras al-Sudr, you must hire a taxi for E£80-100 to Ras al-Gindi, so get a group together. Taxis are at the petrol station after the turnoff for Ras al-Sudr. Getting back to Suez can be tough; know the (alleged) bus schedule, and prepare to be stranded. Bring gallons of water, a camera, and a solid pair of hiking shoes.)*

FAR'AUN HOT SPRINGS. Though the hot springs and beach at this southern spot are attractive, their location makes reaching them more trouble than they're worth. The beach at 'Ain Sukhna is infinitely more convenient. *(Just off the main highway, 80km south of Suez. Hire a taxi from Suez for E£100.)*

SARABIT AL-KHADIM. This remote spot is the site of an ancient temple that extends over 200m of desert. During the 12th Dynasty (c. 1900 BCE), a small chapel was dedicated to the goddesses Sodpu and Hathor, "Mistress of Turquoise." In the 18th dynasty, the temple was elongated and expanded. Ramses VI, the last pharaoh to visit the temple, dropped by around 1100 BCE. The stones of the ruins are decorated with religious spells and accounts of mining expeditions. Around the temple are ancient turquoise mines waiting to be explored. Your mission, should you choose to accept it, takes about three days—two for traveling, one for exploring. *(You'll have to rent or hire a four-wheel drive vehicle and get permission from the military to venture into the desert. The best place to start is the Suez tourist office (see p. 199). They can inform you of the latest regulations on travel to this seldom visited site.)*

HIGH SINAI

The central region of the Sinai Peninsula, known as the High Sinai, is worlds away from the lazy daze of Dahab. Cosmopolitan coastal life may cause you to forget that you're on the outskirts of over 60,000 square kilometers of arid desert, but savvy hikers know that high times can be had in the High Sinai. Nestled in this rugged desertscape are the biblical locales of **Mount Sinai,** the mountain on which Moses received the Ten Commandments, and **St. Catherine's Monastery,** near the Burning Bush. The **High Sinai desert** is an ideal place for unforgettable hikes.

MOUNT SINAI جبل موسى

The holy peak of Mount Sinai, or as locals call it, Mount Moses (Gabal Mussa), stands 2285m above sea level. The Bible describes a mountain engulfed in fire and smoke that Moses ascended to receive the Ten Commandments while the Israelites built a golden calf at its base. Mount Sinai is one of only two places in the Old Testament where God revealed himself to the people, making the desolate peak sacred for both Christians and Muslims (Jews have not universally identified the modern Mount Sinai as the promontory made famous by the Bible). In the Book of Exodus, God warned the people, "Take heed that you do not go up into the mountain or touch the border of it; whoever touches the mountain shall be put to death" (Exodus 19:12). This prohibition seems to have been long forgotten—busloads of tourists climb the peak each day. God should have included an 11th commandment: "Thou shalt not trash holy places;" maybe then climbers would think twice before leaving litter on the trail and the peak. Despite the Baraka bottles, the view from the summit is awe-inspiring.

▌ PRACTICAL INFORMATION

You don't necessarily need a guide, but for safety, neither men nor women should hike alone, especially at night. Most people hook up with **organized groups** from Dahab and begin their climb (via the camel path) around 2am in order to enjoy the cool night and catch the sunrise at the top. Bring a flashlight. If you're **alone,** hike in the early afternoon when it's still light, watch the sunset, and sleep on the summit. Neither hiking shoes nor sneakers are necessary for the climb, but considering the amount of camel dung you'll walk over (especially at night), you probably don't want to expose your bare feet. Socialites can stake out a spot directly on the summit platform by the refreshment stands. More secluded spots are available just beyond the boulders and human feces on the sloping shoulder to the west. Walk about 40m until you cross a ravine; the small summit ahead has several campsites protected by stone windbreaks. If you explore this area during the daylight hours, you'll discover an ancient Bedouin **cistern** where water was stored during the summers. You can also beat the crowds by sleeping in Elijah's Hollow (see **Hiking: Mount Sinai,** p. 177) or by climbing at midday (not recommended in summer).

Overnighters should bring ample **food,** and everyone should bring at least two or three bottles of **water** for the ascent. The cheapest place to buy these amenities is the supermarkets in St. Catherine's town. The monastery **rest house** also sells snacks and water at reasonable prices. There are refreshment stands on the way up, but prices increase with altitude. A stand on the summit sells tea (E£2), water (E£4), and various snacks (E£3-6). If you plan to spend the night on the mountain, bring a **sleeping bag** and **warm clothes.** Even in the summer, it's often only 8-10°C at night and the breeze makes it feel much colder. Those without the necessary gear can rent blankets (E£2.50) and mattresses (E£5) at the top. There are also "toilets" at the summit (holes in the ground with more flies than privacy). Hikers should bring a warm change of clothing—sweaty shirts quickly turn to shirtsicles.

▌ HIKING: MOUNT SINAI

The hike to the top is not that challenging, but you should still leave all but the bare essentials behind. The monks of St. Catherine's will allow you to leave your bags in a room (E£5 per piece per day). There are two paths up the mountain: the **Steps of Repentance** and a **camel path.** A nice place to take a break on the way up (or down) is **Elijah's Hollow.** To find either path, walk up the hill to the monastery, bear left at the fork, and continue to the back of the monastery. From here the camel path continues down the valley while the Steps start to the right, at the southeast corner of the monastery. There is one juncture that confuses hikers: near the top, the camel path intersects the Steps after passing through a narrow, steeply walled stone corridor. Turn left to reach the summit; the camel path stops here. Riders will have to get off their high humps and huff up the rest of the way.

HOLY MOUNT SERBAL? In some religious circles, the debate still rages over whether Mount Sinai is actually the site where Moses received the Ten Commandments. Though most believe that Mount Sinai is the real McCoy, some maintain that the actual mountain referred to in the Bible is Mount Serbal, 20 miles to the west. According to most biblical scholars, however, the Mount Serbalists are fighting a losing battle. The Bible mentions three characteristics of the mountain in question: it is surrounded by a vast plain, the summit is visible to all below, and it is accessible to all who surround it. All three describe Sinai, none Serbal. It is also doubtful that the Israelites would have chosen to camp for a year in the valley beneath Mount Serbal, the site of fierce floods, little drinking water, and hordes of mosquitoes. Besides, who wants to tell 18 generations of pilgrims they've been climbing the wrong mountain?

E G Y P T

STEPS OF REPENTANCE. Of the two paths up the mountain, this is shorter and more difficult, but you probably deserve it. It is said that the 3750 steps were built by a single monk in order to fulfill his pledge of penitence. The monk cut corners here and there and made many of the steps the height of two or three mortal ones. The steps are treacherous by night; after dark they are difficult to follow even with a flashlight. Save them for the descent in the morning. *(About 2hr.)*

CAMEL PATH. The longer route was built in the 19th century and begins directly behind the monastery. **Camel rides** up the mountain usually cost E£30 during peak hours, but if you can stand the sun and the heat, you can get a ride up in the middle of the day for the low price of E£10. Unfortunately, the camels are not always available when you need them—you may arrive at the dispatch area and find only dung. *(At night about 2½hr. by toed foot, 1½hr. by cloven.)*

ELIJAH'S HOLLOW. Turn right at the juncture about two-thirds of the way up and you'll arrive at a 500-year-old cypress tree dominating the depressional plain known as Elijah's Hollow. This is where the prophet Elijah is said to have heard the voice of God after fleeing Jezebel (I Kings 19:8-18). Two small **chapels** now occupy the site, one dedicated to Elijah and the other to his successor Elisha. Moses supposedly hid in the **cave** below when he first came face-to-face with God: "While my glory passes by, I will put you in a cleft of the rock, and I will cover you with my hand until I have passed by" (Exodus 33:22). You can still see the watering hole used by the prophet. *(The chapel is almost always closed in afternoons, but usually open immediately after sunrise for one to two hours.)*

ST. CATHERINE'S ☎069

St. Catherine's rich history of monasticism started in the 3rd century CE when Christian hermits, attracted by the tradition designating the valley below as the site of the **Burning Bush,** migrated here in a quest for holiness and freedom from Roman persecution. Living in complete poverty and isolation (except on holy days, when they gathered at the Burning Bush), these hermits often fell victim to harsh weather and raiding nomads. In 313 CE, Constantine the Great officially recognized Christianity, and soon afterward the monastery was founded by Constantine's mother, Empress Helena. The monastery thrived under the continual protection of the incumbent rulers (including Prophet Muhammad and Napoleon) during the ensuing 1600 years. As a tribute to the monks' tradition of hospitality to Christians and Muslims alike, it has never been conquered. Modern pilgrims and curious tourists of all faiths visit St. Catherine's throughout the year. Though much of the monastery is closed to the public, its beautiful architecture and mountainous setting ensure an unforgettable visit.

▐ GETTING THERE AND GETTING AROUND

Buses serving St. Catherine's are notorious for their scarcity, but they do run to Cairo (9hr., 6am, E£35) via Suez (6hr., E£25), and seasonally to Sharm al-Sheikh (3hr., 1pm, E£25). Reliable bus information is even rarer. Posted times at the tourist office and hotel owners are often wrong; ask the bus driver who brings you, but be aware that leaving St. Catherine's often takes patience and perseverance. **Taxis** are always available, but prices are entirely dependent on the number of passengers and the bus schedule. Popular destinations are Cairo (E£500), Dahab (E£120-150 per car), Nuweiba (E£200), and Sharm al-Sheikh (E£200). Taxis hover around the central square in the daytime; ask at the market if you don't see any. Lone women should avoid taxis.

✦ 🛈 ORIENTATION AND PRACTICAL INFORMATION

At an elevation of about 1600m, **St. Catherine's Monastery** is hidden away in the mountainous interior of the southern Sinai. Excellent roads run west to the Gulf of

Suez and east to the Gulf of Aqaba, both about 100km away. Tiny **St. Catherine's town** lies about three kilometers east of the monastery.

Incoming taxi drivers will drop you in St. Catherine's town, which boasts a number of modern conveniences despite its size. The **bus station** is at the main square; it's not a "station" per se, but a point in space where the bus is assumed to stop. Note that there are no more buses to or from Dahab. On one side of the square is an arcade with a **Bank Misr,** where you can exchange money or traveler's checks and withdraw cash. (☎47 04 63. Open daily 8:30am-1:30pm and 6:30-8:30pm. V only.) The local **police station** (☎47 03 13) is farther up the hill near the mosque. The **tourist police** (☎47 00 46) and the **hospital** (☎47 03 68) are opposite the bus station and open 24hr. The 24-hour **telecommunications office** (☎47 00 10) has international phone service. The nearby **post office** (☎47 03 01) is open daily 8am-3pm.

ACCOMMODATIONS AND FOOD

The cheapest and most popular choice is the free **camping** on Mount Sinai's chilly peak, though you'll have to give up the high ground and settle for a lower spot (about 100m from the top) if you want room to stretch out. The nearest budget alternative is the monastery's **St. Catherine's Auberge.** To get there, turn right at the fork just before the monastery. The clean but cramped rooms are within earshot of the monks, so keep blasphemous thoughts to yourself. The location alone is worth the price. A delectable dinner and breakfast are included. Reservations are recommended if you intend to arrive after 11pm or in August or April. (☎47 03 53. 4-5-bed dorms E£70; singles E£122; doubles E£174; triples E£231.) A cheaper option, though farther from the monastery, is the **El-Fairouz Hotel.** To reach El-Fairouz, walk out of town toward the monastery and take your first left. The hotel, encircling a giant sandy lot, is a five-minute walk away and has an incredible view of the surrounding mountains. Pitch your tent in the sand courtyard (E£5) or join the other sardines in one of the 10-bed dorms (E£12). Some rooms have private baths. (☎47 03 33 or 47 03 23. Singles E£50; doubles E£60; triples E£70.)

Gift shops, supermarkets, and **restaurants** surround the bus station. The restaurants are virtually identical, offering hearty food (usually E£5-8 dishes of spaghetti or rice and chicken) with a side order of flies. Some of them will even cook food you've purchased from a supermarket. (Markets open daily 8am-11pm.) Opposite the mosque is a brick-oven **bakery,** where the price of pita is hotly negotiated.

ST. CATHERINE'S MONASTERY

To get to the monastery from the access road, go straight past the tourist police for about 5min. until the fork in the road, then bear left; the monastery is on the right. Spend the night on the mountaintop, watch the sunrise; hike down at 7am and reach the monastery just as the doors open at 9am (to avoid crowds). Modest dress required. Open M-Th and Sa 9-11:45am, F 11am-noon; closed Orthodox holidays (Nov. 14; Jan. 6; Feb. 26-28; Apr. 7, 12, 14, 16; May 24; June 4; Aug. 28; Sept. 27; Nov. 14; Dec. 8). Free. For more information, contact Father John (☎47 03 43) or the monastery's Cairo office, 18 Midan al-Dahr, 11271 Cairo (☎(02) 482 85 13; fax 482 58 06).

St. Catherine's is believed to be the oldest example of unrestored Byzantine architecture in the world. The complex was named after the martyred Alexandrian evangelist, Catherine, whose body was found on top of Gabal Katerina to the south. About to be tortured on a wheel of knives for converting members of the Roman emperor's family, Catherine was miraculously saved by a malfunction in the wheel (but they slit her throat anyway). Her body showed up centuries later on top of the isolated mountain. Once home to hundreds of monks, the monastery now houses only a handful. These ascetics are members of one of the strictest orders; they never eat meat or drink wine, and they wake up at 4am each morning when the bell of the Church of the Transfiguration is rung 33 times.

EGYPT

ICONS. The monastery has many treasures, including over 2000 exquisite 5th-century icons. The icons with brushed gold halos have a holographic effect, an artistic style unique to the Sinai. In the 7th century, Prophet Muhammad dictated a document granting protection to the monastery and exempting it from taxes; a copy of this still hangs in the icon gallery, near a similar letter penned by Napoleon in 1798.

LIBRARY. The monastery's impressive library contains over 8000 books and manuscripts, said to be second only to the Vatican library in the number and value of religious texts. The collection is currently being copied onto microfiche to make it available to scholars everywhere.

CHURCH OF THE TRANSFIGURATION. The first permanent structure in the monastery was erected in 330 CE, when Helena built a small church and tower at the site of the Burning Bush. Around 530, Emperor Justinian ordered a splendid basilica within a walled fortress to be constructed on the top of Mount Sinai. When Justinian's trusted architect Stephanos found the mountain's peak too narrow, he built the **Church of the Transformation** next to St. Eleni's chapel instead. This structure became known as the Church of the Transfiguration, owing to its spectacular almond-shaped mosaic depicting this event in Jesus' life. The peeved emperor ordered Stephanos's execution, but the builder lived out his days in the safety of the monastery and eventually achieved sainthood (his bones are in the **ossuary**). Both St. Helena and Justinian dedicated their structures to the Virgin Mary, since Christian tradition asserts that the Burning Bush foreshadowed the Annunciation, when the archangel Gabriel heralded the birth of Christ. *(Closed F, Su, and holidays. A gift shop sells books on the area's history for E£8.)*

CHAPEL OF THE BURNING BUSH. Only the central nave of the Church of the Transfiguration is open to the public. On tiptoe you can see mosaics of a barefoot Moses in the Chapel of the Burning Bush, behind the altar. Should you manage to visit the icons back there, you'll have to remove your shoes, as the roots of the sacred shrub extend under the floor (a living descendant resides just outside). Such privileges are only accorded to true pilgrims, who are traditionally allowed to ask God for one favor. The monks themselves, with the help of the local Gabaliyya Bedouin (descended from Byzantine slaves), built a **mosque** within the fortress to convince advancing Ottoman armies that the complex was partly Muslim.

MOSES' WELL. Outside the main entrance of the Church of the Transfiguration is Moses' Well, where the savior of the Israelites reportedly freshened up after his holy ascent. The gruesome **ossuary,** a separate building outside the walls, houses the remains of former monks.

HIGH SINAI DESERT

The natural wonders of the Sinai Peninsula will make a convert of you if nothing else will. *Wadis* shrouded in misty heat lead in every direction, snaking their way around mountain ranges, lush oases, and Bedouin homesteads. Better yet, the region is fairly untouristed, meaning you'll have all the time and space you want.

▶ HIKING: SINAI DESERT

WHEN TO GO
Spring and fall are the most temperate seasons for hikes. In summer you'll spend most of the day resting in the shade with the Bedouin until the sun calms down, and in winter you'll freeze. The nights are frigid year-round. You may be able to rent blankets from the Bedouin, but don't count on it; bring a warm sleeping bag.

HOW TO GO
Organized tours can be arranged in Israel through **SPNI.** The Israeli travel outfitter **Neot Ha-Kikar** specializes in Sinai tours (offices in Tel Aviv, Jerusalem, and Eilat),

with trips beginning in Eilat and Cairo (6-day high range circuit US$360). No matter where in Israel you book your tour, however, you'll eventually end up at Sheikh Moussa's office. You'll save a lot of money by starting there, too.

To venture into any of the mountains other than Mount Sinai, you must be accompanied by a **Bedouin guide** and have a regular **Egyptian tourist visa**—the Sinai-only visa won't do. **Sheikh Moussa** (☎ (069) 47 04 57), head of Mountain Tours, has a monopoly on all the mountains, and trips must be arranged through him (reservations accepted). You are required by law to leave your passport with Mr. Moussa; he will notify the army of your whereabouts. To get to his office in St. Catherine's town, walk uphill from the town square, past the petrol station. Take the first right and walk for three minutes; Mr. Moussa will be lounging outside.

Sheikh Moussa will procure both a guide and a permit for you. The price, which includes guide, food, and camels, is US$20-30 per person per day, and fluctuates depending on the size of your party and where you go. Surplus gear can be stored in Sheikh Moussa's house. You'll leave for your hike within an hour of arriving at his office. You and your guide will camp with the Bedouin, so be prepared for long nights by the fire smoking "Bedouin tobacco," drinking tea, and learning a great deal about a little-known culture. Tell Sheikh Moussa what you want to see and how quickly, and he'll tailor an itinerary. Routes include the following possibilities (estimated length of trip in days noted in parentheses):

Gabal Banat: A mountain north of St. Catherine's town overlooking a vast desert. (2 days)

Gabal Bab: From this peak you can see west all the way to the Gulf of Suez. (2)

Gabal Katerina: The highest mountain in Egypt (2642m), 6km south of Mount Sinai. The path to the top is more difficult, secluded, and beautiful than Mount Sinai's highway. A chapel replenishes you with shade at the summit. (11hr. round-trip)

Gabal 'Abbas Pasha: A rock with a ruined palace and excellent views. (2)

Gulat al-Agrod: A deep, crystal-clear mountain pool where you can swim in the shade of overhanging trees and dive off the surrounding rocks. (3)

Wadi Talla: There are two, a big one and a small one. Go to the big *wadi* for some swimming in spring-fed pools. (3)

Wadi Nogra: A rocky valley with a natural dam (Nogra Dam). The water trickles off moss-covered boulders to form a natural shower. (3)

Sheikh Owat: A picturesque oasis with palm trees, a deep well, and a lot of goats. (3)

Farsh Romana: A campground equipped with showers on the way to Gabal Banat. (2)

Wadi Feiran: An amazingly lush oasis 50km west of St. Catherine's Monastery; Islamic tradition holds that Hagar fled there when banished from Abraham and Sarah's camp in Eltantawi. Today there is a nunnery in the center of the valley. The best way to get here is by taxi from St. Catherine's (E£70 round-trip). Although buses to and from Cairo pass by, the schedules are unpredictable, and you might get stranded.

GULF OF AQABA COAST

SHARM AL-SHEIKH شرم الشيخ ☎069

No one goes to Sharm al-Sheikh for the sights, though with its dozens of wrecking balls, cranes, and half-finished buildings, there is ample opportunity to view ruins-in-progress. Sharm, like the rest of the Sinai coast, is in the midst of a building boom. Sharm and nearby Na'ama Bay are often called twin resorts, but they're far from identical. Na'ama inherited the good looks and good-looking travelers, while Sharm got the big boats and bigger buildings. Wealthy Europeans fill Sharm's four- and five-star hotels, leaving little room for budget backpackers to enjoy the already crowded beach. The tiny bay is crammed with dive boats attracted by the calmness of the water, further adding to the congested, overtrafficked feel. For more excitement and breathing space, head north to Na'ama.

⊏ GETTING THERE AND GETTING AROUND

Flights: The **Egypt Air** office (☎ 66 10 58) is south of the bus station. Open Sa-Th 9am-2pm and 6-9pm. The airport branch (☎ 60 06 40) is far more helpful.

Ferries: The ferry to **Hurghada** (☎ 66 01 66) leaves three times weekly from the port just south of Sharm al-Sheikh (6hr.; M, W-Th 9am; E£125). From the Sharm Marina, keep walking around the harbor and over the hill at the southern end. Book tickets a day ahead, either through a hotel or at **Thomas Cook** (☎ 60 18 08), 50m south of the Pigeon House Hotel.

Buses: Buses leave daily to: **Cairo** (7-10hr., 10 per day 7:30am-midnight, E£65); **Dahab** (1½hr., 6 per day 6:30am-11:30pm, E£10); **Nuweiba** (2½hr.; 9am, 2, 5pm; E£15); **St. Catherine's** (2½hr., 7:30am, E£15); **Suez** (7hr.; 9am and 2pm; E£25); and **Taba** (3hr., 9am, E£25). Most buses leave from behind the Mobil station between Na'ama and Sharm al-Sheikh, though some leave from Sharm itself—call ahead as schedules change frequently (☎ 60 06 00 or 60 06 66).

Taxis: For taxis, call ☎ 66 03 57.

⁊ PRACTICAL INFORMATION

At the top of the hill, next to the post office, is the **Bank of Alexandria,** which allows money withdrawal with Visa and MC. (☎ 66 03 55. Open 8:30am-2pm and 6-9pm.) The **tourist police** (☎ 60 03 11 or 60 05 54; open 24hr.) and **police station** (☎ 66 04 15) are 300m from the banks. The 24-hour **hospital** (☎ 66 04 25; **ambulance** ☎ 60 05 54) is just north of the bus station. The **new hospital** (☎ 66 08 93) is halfway between Sharm al-Sheikh and Na'ama Bay. The **telephone office** is 300m from the banks, near the tourist police. (☎ 66 04 00. Open 24hr.) At the top of the hill to the right, the **post office** has **Poste Restante** and **EMS.** (☎ 66 05 18. Open Sa-Th 8am-3pm.) **Pharmacy Sharm al-Sheikh** is in the same complex. (☎ 66 03 88. Open daily 9am-1am.)

⍽⊡ ACCOMMODATIONS AND FOOD

If there is room at Na'ama Bay, there is no reason to stay in Sharm. The cheapest place is the **Youth Hostel,** at the top of the hill and to the left. From the bus station, follow the signs for the Cliff Top Hotel. Breakfast is included, and the preteen angst is free. (☎ 66 03 17. Beds E£20.) Another option is the somewhat dingy **El-Kheima Hotel,** next to the Diving World Dive Club. Be sure to tell them that you *only* want bed and breakfast, or else they'll charge double and include dinner. (☎/fax 66 01 66. Bungalow singles E£40; doubles with portable fans E£60.) A last resort (the only hotel on the beach) is **Safetyland,** at the bottom of the hill at the intersection of the road leading to Na'ama Bay and the road to the Sharm bus station. Stuffy thatched bungalows are situated in what looks like a construction site. (☎ 66 34 63. Breakfast included. Open tent sites E£20 per person; singles E£40; doubles E£80.)

The food situation in Sharm is pretty dismal. The **Sharm Express Supermarket** is next to the Pharmacy Nada'a. (☎ 60 09 24. Open daily 9am-2am.) A row of cheap **restaurants** hugging the hill south of the bus station offers an opportunity to chow down on everything from pizza to Asian food. (Most open daily 11am-midnight.)

⊂ SCUBA DIVING

The Sharm al-Sheikh and Na'ama Bay area is undoubtedly the mecca of Red Sea diving and the growth spot for most of the Sinai's tourism. Despite the large number of wealthy Germans and Italians in five-star hotels, Sharm al-Sheikh still has several undiscovered sites and unexplored gems in and around the Straits of Tiran, Ras Muhammad National Park, and the wreck of the *Thistlegorm*.

DIVE SITES

■ **RAS MUHAMMAD NATIONAL PARK.** This area encompasses most of the southern tip of the Sinai and has eclipsed almost all other dive sites in international acclaim. The most famous sites in the park are the **Shark** and **Yolanda Reefs.** The latter includes a swim through the wreckage of the freighter *Yolanda* (the actual ship has slipped off the continental shelf and lies 220m below the surface). This surreal sight is possibly the only place in the world where you can swim with sharks among broken toilets and containers. For more information, see below.

■ **THISTLEGORM.** The World War II cargo ship *Thistlegorm* was sunk in 1941 by long-range German bombers off the southern coast of the Sinai. Discovered years later by Jacques-Yves Cousteau (who kept the location secret until it was rediscovered in the early 90s), the *Thistlegorm* has become legendary among divers and is widely considered the best wreck dive in the world. Quite far off shore, the *Thistlegorm* requires at least a day and two dives to explore. The cargo bays are crammed full of tires, rifles, motorcycles, aircraft wings, tanks, trucks, and railway carriages. The commander's deck and outer shell is downright eerie. Although a more expensive dive (US$120-150), it is unforgettable.

JACKSON'S REEF. Of the four reefs extending down the center of the spectacular **Straits of Tiran,** this is the best and northernmost dive. The strong current is particularly challenging, but also encourages the growth of some of the most beautiful and plentiful coral in the entire Sinai. Not only does the current bring enough nutrients to feed the coral and schools of fish that congregate on the reef, but it also attracts a variety of sharks and turtles. Schools of hammerheads are seen frequently during July and August.

RAS GHOZLANI. In the area just north of the famous Ras Muhammad National Park lie many peaceful and often overlooked local dive sites. Many of the sites are incredibly beautiful and tranquil; Ras Ghozlani is the most superb. Divers here are less likely to see the big predators found prowling the deep at other sites, but this location is rarely crowded, uniquely preserved, and full of colorful fish.

DIVE FACILITIES

■ **Camel Dive Center,** P.O. Box 10, Na'ama Bay, Sharm al-Sheikh, South Sinai, Egypt (☎60 07 00; fax 60 06 01; email reservations1@cameldive.com; www.cameldive.com), across from the Cataract Resort. One of the oldest dive centers in the area, and probably the friendliest. Offers over six daily boats, state-of-the-art equipment, and highly trained multilingual guides, as well as inexpensive accommodations by Na'ama's standards (dorm rooms US$30). One guided dive US$30; full equipment US$20; O/W course US$360. Call for a 10% discount on all services.

Oonas Dive Club (☎60 05 81; fax 60 05 82), at the northern end of the bay. Slightly cheaper rates and much better after-hours camaraderie than the other centers. Five-day PADI course US$295-330; certification US$30. Intro dives US$65 including equipment. Full gear rental US$24. Full day with two dives US$50.

▐ DAYTRIP FROM SHARM AL-SHEIKH

RAS MUHAMMAD NATIONAL PARK

*The park is accessible by boat and taxi (E£100). Since it is beyond the jurisdiction of a Sinai-only visa, you need your passport and a full **Egyptian tourist visa.** Dive shops run trips to the park, and you may not need a full visa if you stick with their boats and hotels. Park open daily 8am-5pm (strict closing time). US$5 per person, additional US$5 per car. For information on **scuba diving** at Ras Muhammad, see **Dive Sites,** above.*

Sticking out into the Red Sea at the tip of the Sinai peninsula, **Ras Muhammad National Park** is the most famous dive site in Egypt and one of the most spectacular in the world. The tiny neck of land is bordered on the west by the Gulf of Suez and on the east by the Gulf of Aqaba. The waters of Ras Muhammad contain over 1000 species of fish, many of which are unique to the Red Sea. The aquatic wonders found here far outweigh the time and expense of the trip, making it by far the best daytrip from Sharm al-Sheikh or Na'ama Bay.

In the early 1980s, it became clear that tourist and fishing traffic was destroying the underwater treasures of Ras Muhammad, so the Egyptian government declared the area a national park in 1983. Most of the fragile underwater habitat is now closed to the public, and it is against Egyptian law to remove any material, living or dead, from the park. Diving, snorkeling, and swimming are only permitted in specified areas, mostly around the very tip of the peninsula. On rough days, snorkeling at Ras Muhammad can be difficult. For underwater advice and warnings, see **Scu-better Watch Out,** p. 186. Camping is permitted in designated sites; check with the park's Visitors Center for details. Further information about Ras Muhammad is available from the Sharm al-Sheikh info office (☎ 66 06 68 or 66 05 59).

NA'AMA BAY   ☎069

This five-star hotel nexus is the center of Egypt's anti-backpacker sentiment. The budget traveler is about as welcome in Na'ama as the narcotics agent is in Dahab; however, if you look clean-cut (and act like you own the place), you can freely roam the waterfront shops and hotels. As soon as you don your hip new tie-dye from Dahab, however, you invite stares along the promenade and may be barred from certain areas. Many budget travelers do flock here each year, drawn by the world-class diving and snorkeling as well as the most active nightlife in the Sinai. It is sometimes possible to get a job at a hotel or dive center; the pay is just enough for food and entertainment. If you work for a hotel, you usually get free accommodations; if you work at a dive club, you get free diving lessons or courses. Knowledge of Arabic is not necessary, but French and Italian are helpful.

▐ GETTING THERE AND GETTING AROUND

The **bus stop** is officially in front of the Helnan Marina Hotel, but the driver will drop you off at any hotel along the road. **Intercity buses** leave from behind the Mobil station at the southern end of town and from the Sharm al-Sheikh bus station. Southbound, open-sided **minibuses** (E£1) and **taxis** (E£10) go to Sharm al-Sheikh, and northbound minibuses (E£10) and taxis (E£20) pass Shark's Bay.

✴ ▐ ORIENTATION AND PRACTICAL INFORMATION

Na'ama Bay is a long strip of hotels on the water side of the highway, the town's only street. Most of the beach is owned by five-star resorts. Between the beach and hotels is a **promenade,** where most restaurants, bars, and diving clubs cluster.

The **National Bank of Egypt** has branches in the Marina Sharm, Gazala, and Mövenpick Hotels and usually exchanges money. (Open Sa-Th 9am-1pm and 6-9pm, F 9-11am and 6-9pm.) **Bank Misr,** at the Marriott Hotel, will give cash advances on Visa or MC. (☎ 60 16 67. Open Sa-Th 9am-2pm and 7-10pm, F 10am-12:30pm and 7-10pm.) The **Commercial International Bank** has two locations, one next to the Camel Dive Center and one across from the Mövenpick Hotel. (Both open daily 9am-2pm and 6-9pm.) There is an **ATM** that accepts Visa and MC in the Mövenpick Hotel lobby, as well as a branch of **EgyptAir.** (☎ 66 06 67; fax 66 03 37. Open daily 9:30am-2pm and 6:30-9pm.) The **tourist police** (☎ 64 03 01) are just north of the Helnan Marina Hotel. Call ☎ 60 05 54 for an **ambulance.** The **Towa Pharmacy** is in the bazaar south of the Mövenpick. (☎ 60 07 79. Open daily 10am-1am.) The **Lifeline Clinic** (☎ (012) 212 42 92), between Sharm al-Sheikh and Na'ama Bay, has American- and German-trained doctors who take drop-ins (daily 5-7pm). **Internet access** is available at **CyberDisco,** next to the Crazy Daisy nightclub. (Open daily 9pm-1am.) The **post office** is in Sharm al-Sheikh, but most hotels will drop off mail.

ACCOMMODATIONS

If there is room, opt for accommodations in Na'ama rather than in Sharm. Hotels are nicer, and you won't have to take expensive taxis to and from the beach.

Pigeon House (☎60 09 96; fax 60 09 95), at the northern end of the bay. The only relatively cheap place to roost in Na'ama. After you've flocked together with birds of a feather in the happening courtyard (*the* place for a Stella or *sheesha*), nestle down in one of their thatched huts with fans. Middle-quality rooms without A/C or the cool breeze of the huts become stifling ovens in the summer; not recommended unless you want your goose cooked. Breakfast included. Huts: singles E£38; doubles E£56. Rooms: singles E£65; doubles E£85; with A/C E£190; extra bed E£20.

Oonas Dive Club (☎60 05 81), at the northern end of the promenade. Look for the red neon sign at the top of the building. With beach access, swimming pool, A/C, and a lively bar, this dive hotel offers everything the slightly over-budget traveler could want. Singles US$40; doubles US$60.

Camel Dive Club (☎60 07 00), in the center of the small bazaar, close to the beach. This slightly pricey option is worth it for the location as well as the beautiful rooms, pool, A/C, and private bath. Breakfast included. Dorm rooms US$30; doubles US$104.

Shark's Bay Camp (☎60 09 42; fax 60 09 44), 4km north of town. A ship-shape Bedouin camp that overlooks a quiet bay. Features a breathtaking view of Tiran Island, an excellent restaurant, and a dive club, but the cost of a *service* (E£10) or taxi (E£20) to Na'ama makes these clean bungalows an expensive choice. Bedouin tent on the beach E£125. Singles E£50-60; doubles E£65-75; triples E£90-100.

FOOD

Food in Na'ama Bay is high in quality, at least along the main hotel strip. ◙**Tam Tam Oriental Corner** (☎60 01 50 or 60 01 51), on Ghazala Hotel beach next to the Hilton beach, is the cheapest place in town. An enormous bowl of *kushari* goes for E£7.70, and salads cost E£3.50. (Open daily noon-1am.) The **Pigeon House** dishes out excellent pork, meat, and fish. (Pasta E£10.50-16.75; kebab E£19.75-22.75. Open daily until 11pm.) **Viva Restaurant,** opposite the Red Sea Diving College in Kanabesh beach, serves up tasty pizzas (E£18-22. ☎60 09 64. Open daily 10am-midnight.) Live it up a little at the **Hard Rock Cafe,** around the corner from the Camel Dive Center. Indulge in the Caesar Salad for E£21 or the Club Sandwich for E£25. (☎60 26 65 or 60 26 66. Open daily 1pm-3am.)

SURF...

CORAL REEFS. Na'ama Bay itself has no spectacular reefs, but a veritable colossus of coral lies just outside the bay to the north and south. Dive centers have maps of the reefscape; pick one up and put on your flippers. The closest free site is **Near Gardens** at the northern tip of Na'ama Bay, a moderate walk down the beach. The nearby **Tower** and **Sodfa** are a decent walk south of Na'ama Bay, but both require a E£10 fee, payable at the Tower Hotel. Ask at a dive center which sites are accessible by land; some are tricky to reach.

SNORKELING. Many swear that boat-based snorkeling is the best. For US$15-25, spend a day on a boat and explore spectacular waters. Arrange trips through the dive clubs. The legendary reefs of the **Straits of Tiran** are distant and accessible by boat only. **Ras Nasrani** and **Ras Umm Sidd** are good sites a little closer to town.

AQUATIC SPORTS. Water activities are not restricted to diving. **Sun-n-Fun** booths (☎60 16 23; open 9am-11pm) at the Hilton and Aquamarine beaches rent equipment for **windsurfing** (E£50 per hr.; lessons E£65 per hr.), **water skiing** (E£40 per 15min.), **jet skiing** (one-person jet E£60 per 15min., two-person E£70), and **sailing**

EGYPT

SCU-BETTER WATCH OUT... Scu-better not die! Hidden among the crevices in the coral reefs around the Sinai Peninsula are creatures capable of inflicting serious injury and even death. If you see something that looks like an aquatic pin cushion, it's probably a **sea urchin** or a **blowfish,** both of which should be touched only in sushi form. Avoid the feathery **lionfish** as well—its harmless-looking spines can deliver a paralyzing sting. The well-named **fire coral** can bloat a leg to mammoth proportions, leaving welts the size of croquet balls. The **stonefish** is camouflaged flawlessly to resemble a mossy lump of coral or rock; if you step on one, you'll puff up and may die within hours. Reach into a hole and a two-meter-long **moray eel** may lock its jaws onto your hand. The list goes on. Before plunging in, ask at any dive shop for a look at one of the picture cards that identifies these underwater uglies.

When snorkeling, try to enter the water in a sandy area to avoid damaging underwater plants and animals. If you have no choice but to enter where sea creatures and coral may dwell, wear foot protection. **Sharks** are attracted by blood, so never enter the water with an open wound or if menstruating. Panicking and thrashing tends to excite sharks. If you see one, calmly climb out of the water and casually share the news. Most sharks, however, are not aggressive and wouldn't give you the time of day even if they could; most marine animals get aggressive only if *you* have done something threatening or irritating. If you see an animal getting defensive, simply back away slowly. *Let's Go* does not recommend dying.

(E£40 per hr.; lessons E£55). Try a **glass bottom boat** ride (every hr. 10am-4pm; E£25 per person) or the big **Discovery** (every 2hr. 11am-5pm, E£55). Frolic for free at the tiny **public beach** just south of Gafy Land Hotel.

...AND TURF

Landlubbers can strap on some plaid pants and tee off in a game of **miniature golf** at the Hilton. (E£10 per game, E£55 deposit on clubs.) **Horseback riding** is available across from the Novotel Hotel. (E£55 per hr.) **Safari Tours,** next to the Pigeon House, offers **ATV** trips out in the desert. Most leave before sunset. (US$35 per hr.)

WADI KID. Here's looking at you, Kid: this *wadi*, 40km north of Na'ama Bay, is a deep, fertile canyon where you can hike among rock formations and fruit trees. Most hotels are affiliated with a tour company that goes once a week. *(Mövenpick Hotel organizes half-day trips to Nabq and Wadi Kid for US$30, with a 4-person minimum.)*

NABQ WILDLIFE RESERVE. On the coast 20km north of Na'ama Bay, Nabq's most notable site is a strip of coastline where the largest **mangrove forest** in the Sinai flourishes, attracting herons, ospreys, foxes, and hard-to-spot gazelles. The mangroves sprout in a few feet of warm, clear water with a sandy bottom, marking ideal swimming and relaxation spots. The problem of maintaining traditional Bedouin lifestyles in the modern world is being actively addressed in Nabq: a Bedouin "reservation" attempts to preserve the culture and openly welcomes visitors. *(Most hotels organize daytrips to Nabq. Wandering off the path in the park is extremely dangerous, as there are still a number of landmines in the area.)*

LIBATIONS 'N' GYRATIONS

LIBATIONS. Nights in Na'ama are most often spent tossing back Stellas and swapping diving stories. One of the best places to do this is the **Pigeon House,** where the brew flows and the *sheesha* smoke billows. (Open daily 5:30pm-12:30am.) Slip on your eye patch and head for the **Pirate's Bar,** a popular watering hole in the Hilton. With cutlasses and rigging hanging from the wall, the bar attracts an appropriately ridiculous mix of swashbucklingly tan diving instructors and suave Europeans. They serve Stella (E£9.50), import draught beer (E£18-20), and free bar munchies.

(☎60 01 36, ext. 850. Open daily 11am-1am.) Most of the local dive masters and tourists congregate at the **Camel Dive Club,** upstairs from the dive center of the same name. The first floor is packed and often features live music; the low-key rooftop patio overlooks the main street. (Stella E£12, E£9 for divers.)

GYRATIONS. Top off the evening at the **Bus Stop Disco,** between McDonald's and the Camel Dive Club. (☎60 01 97 or 60 01 98. Open daily noon-3:30am.) Give the roulette wheel a spin at the Las Vegas-style **Casino Royale,** across from the Mövenpick Hotel. (☎60 17 31. Open daily 8pm-4am. 18+. No shorts.) The **Crazy Daisy,** next to Tam Tam, offers techno dancing. (Open daily 9pm-4am. E£10 cover after midnight.) Across the street from the Mövenpick Hotel, **Jolie Disco** spins a mix of American, Arabic, and Euro pop/disco beats. (☎60 01 00. Open daily 9pm-4am.)

DAHAB دهب ☎069

Like Goa or Amsterdam, Dahab is one of those places that has grown larger than life in the minds of travelers. For most, it conjures up images of glossy-eyed, tie-dyed hippies lounging on the shore, blissfully asphyxiating themselves in blue clouds of marijuana smoke. While this scene is still a significant part of the Dahab experience, Dahabitants no longer think of Jamaica with the reverence that Mecca inspires in the rest of the Arab world. The hippies are slowly being outnumbered by cleaner-cut travelers and dive instructors. "Bedouin" camps are the cheapest, most social places to stay, but travelers seeking more comfort can choose from a number of more expensive, middle-range hotels with air-conditioning and a family atmosphere. Dahab die-hards of yesteryear may lament its relative cleanliness, but the town is becoming more like paradise, not less. After all, its name means "gold."

▐ GETTING THERE AND GETTING AROUND

Dahab city is of almost no significance to the budget traveler, who only glimpses it between climbing off the bus and getting into a taxi headed for the Bedouin village. **Buses** leave daily from the station (☎64 02 50) in Dahab city to: Cairo (8hr.; 8:30am, 1, 10:30pm; E£55-70); Nuweiba (1½hr., 10:30am and 6:30pm, E£10); Sharm al-Sheikh (1hr.; 8:30am, 10, 1, 2:30, 5:30, 10:30pm; E£10); and Taba (3hr., 10:30am, E£20). Prices fluctuate depending on departure time—the last bus of the day is always the most expensive. If you get a group together, you can convince a **taxi** driver to go to any destination. **Service** end up being more expensive, but the rides are much faster. From the bus stop, you can catch a taxi to the **village** (E£5 per car, E£1 per person for a crowded pickup).

▐ PRACTICAL INFORMATION

The **National Bank of Egypt** is in Dahab city. (☎64 02 42. Open daily 8:30am-2pm and 6-9pm.) Other services in the city are: the **supermarket** (open daily 6am-2am); **police station** (☎64 02 15); **telephone office,** where you can make calls within Egypt or through Cairo to an international operator (open 24hr.); and **post office** with **Poste Restante.** (☎64 02 23. Open Sa-Th 8am-3pm.)

In the Bedouin village, the **Banque du Caire** allows you to withdraw money with a Visa or MC or change traveler's checks with an outrageous commission. (☎64 04 44. Open Sa-Th 9am-2pm and 6-9pm.) Above the Ghazala supermarket at the village's southern end, the **Dahab Polyclinic** treats patients. (☎64 04 44. Open 24hr.) A few supermarkets have **telephones** connecting to Cairo.

▐ ACCOMMODATIONS

There are over two dozen **camps** in the Bedouin village, and the number grows weekly. Dahab camps are an unfortunate bastardization of the thatched beach hut; someone came up with the brilliant idea of casting the huts in concrete, connecting them in rows around a central courtyard, and creating bare cells with minimal ventilation. Fortunately, the huts mostly serve as storage space for your belongings while you lounge outside in one of the restaurants. Rooms with only a mattress are cheapest (E£5-10); those with private bath are a bit pricier (E£10-30). A tangle of hotels and camps crowds the main part of the strip near the restaurants. The coolest and most comfortable are the thatched-hut quarters slightly off the main strip (the first three accommodations listed below fit into this category).

Oasis Fighting Kangaroo (☎ 64 00 11; email bedouinn@yahoo.com), down a small alleyway across from Napoleon's Restaurant (don't confuse it with the Fighting Kangaroo Camp). Generally regarded as the best place to stay in Dahab, the O.F.K. has a super-friendly atmosphere and two Bedouin-style TV rooms outside. Cell-like singles E£10; doubles E£15. Nicer rooms cost up to E£60.

Bedouin Moon Hotel (☎ 64 00 87; email reef2000@intouch.com), about 2km north of the Bedouin village. Owned and operated by 2 Bedouin brothers, the Bedouin Moon is a beautiful hotel with a sandy beach and the dive center Reef 2000. Dorm rooms E£35 (breakfast included); doubles E£110-140. Ask about 10-15% *Let's Go* discount.

Cleopatra's (email cleopatra140@hotmail.com). A Bedouin camp whose thatched huts are hot commodities in the Dahab market. Many visitors fall asleep in the lounge or on the roof as they sit on their asps waiting for huts to open up. Rooms with shower and toilet E£25-30; 2-person huts E£14; 4-person huts E£24.

Muhammad 'Ali Camp (☎ 64 02 68). Clean, cheap, and right in the middle of the action. The camp has its own supermarket, coffee shop, dive club, and laundry facilities. Breakfast E£10; dinner E£20. Doubles E£40.

Auski Camp (☎ 64 04 74), on the beach south of the Bedouin village, near the Sphinx Hotel. Friendly owner keeps rooms spic-and-span and smelling fresh. Doubles E£15.

▶ FOOD

If you find yourself with the munchies, fear not: Dahab is home to some of the best food in Egypt, but quality varies in the extreme. The local hospital has taken exception to the hygiene of many local restaurants and advises against consuming fish (except at Tarabouche's). Be wary of ordering anything slightly undercooked, especially meat. For more information on how to minimize the risks of food poisoning, see **Food- and Water-borne Diseases,** p. 22. If you want complete control over food preparation, try **Ghazala Market** at the southern end of town.

▨ **Tota** (☎ 64 92 71), next to the Crazy House. A *Let's Go* favorite for 16 years. Despite the tugboat architecture and the waiters' sailor costumes, Tota specializes in pasta (E£6.50-9.50), not seafood, but you can drink like a fish—the restaurant possesses a hard-to-come-by liquor license. Cocktails E£7.50-8.50; Stella E£7.50. Open 8am-1am.

▨ **Jay's Restaurant** (☎ 335 33 77; email julie_jays@yahoo.com), on the main street near Fantasea Dive Club. You must step out of the Dahab daze and think ahead to eat at this excellent inexpensive restaurant. Stop by before 6pm to order dinner for that night (the menu changes daily), and Jay's will have the food ready when you come back. It may test your short-term planning and memory skills, but not your math: full meals around E£10. Open for dinner 7-10:30pm; in winter 6-10pm. Open for reservations at 10am.

Tarabouche's (☎ (012) 235 63 38), on the pathway past the Banque du Caire and the Sunrise Camp, across the small parking lot. Three-course, home-cooked Egyptian meals (E£25-50) include salad, choice of fish or meat, and dessert. Food is hygienically prepared, so indulge in anything on the menu. Reservations are necessary.

Shark Club, features shakes that will leave you speechless. The owner speaks perfect English, and the dive instructors practically live here. The gigantic portions may cause feeding frenzies among patrons. Half-order pasta E£3-4; shakes E£3-5.

Crazy House Pub (☎ 64 02 81), near the southern end of the bay. The best place to go stir-crazy. Beer E£7.5; mixed drinks E£7-8. Open noon-4am.

🎵 SHAKE 'N' BAKE

SHAKE. The Helnan Hotel (20km north of town) has recently opened the **Zanzibar Disco,** which can draw quite a crowd. A free shuttle runs from town around midnight. On Monday and Wednesday nights, rock out to a live local band at the **Hilton Hotel** until dawn. Free hors d'œuvres ease the pain of pricey Stellas (E£10).

BAKE. In order to get an **alcohol license** in the Sinai, an establishment must first possess a building license (obliging the owner to keep his building above certain standards) and pay a property tax. There are six main sources of booze in Dahab: the restaurant at the Nesima Dive Club, the Crazy House Pub, Tota, the Sphinx Hotel, Green Valley, and Neptune Billiards, where pool sharks can also rack up a game. (E£10 per hr. Open 10am-2am.) This lack of liquor is one of the reasons Dahab grew notorious for its **dope scene.** Though the scene is less noticeable nowadays, marijuana is still available for those who want it. People generally do not actively advertise what type of smoke is coming out of their *sheesha*. Remember that the possession of drugs is illegal in Egypt, and Egyptian jails rate low on the Michelin system. Dealers may win an all-expenses-paid trip to the hereafter via firing squad. *Let's Go* just says no.

👁 SIGHTS

OVERLAND DAYTRIPS. Daytrips to nearby natural wonders are great ways to escape the haze of Dahab. Four-by-four trips to the **Colored Canyon** cost E£50 per person for a group of six. You can travel by camel or truck to the brackish oasis of **Wadi Gnay** (E£30 per person). A one-day camel trip to **Nabq** (E£35-50) is also an option. Hamed the Lobster Man runs **Crazy Camel Camp** (☎ 64 02 73) and organizes jeep and camel safaris. He also takes people on night **lobster hunting** trips that culminate in lobster feasts on the beach. **Blue Hole Travel** (☎ 64 02 36; email bluehole-travel@n2mail.com), across the street from the Sphinx Hotel, runs camel safaris, trips to St. Catherine's, and daily snorkeling excursions to their namesake. If you want to go anywhere nearby, ask around the Bedouin community. The Bedouin know these hills better than anyone and will often be happy to organize a trip.

SNORKELING. The snorkeling in Dahab is excellent; enter the **Blue Hole** at either end of the bay where the waves break on the reefs (just be sure to wear shoes or flippers, because if the sea urchins don't get you, the coral will). Trips to Blue Hole and **Canyon** are arranged every morning by most camps, and you can rent snorkel gear at camps or on the beach (E£5-10). Make sure the flippers fit, the mask is airtight, and the snorkel unobstructed before paying. **Paddleboats** are available for rental near the northern part of the village; use them to trek to some of the more secluded spots (E£15 per hr.).

BEDOUIN VILLAGE. The Bedouin village is no longer that. It's so loaded with tourists that the Bedouin themselves have moved north to 'Aslah. These days, the bay is lined with restaurants, camps, and gift shops that peddle the famous "Dahab pants" (E£15). Meanwhile, camels and horses trot up and down the beach road carrying Dutch women, pink-hued Brits, and intrepid adventure explorers Elizabeth White and Michael Grunwald (camels E£5, horses E£10 for 30min.). Pillowed courtyards hug the beach; at night, they are cheerfully illuminated by electric lights and Baraka bottle lanterns.

🤿 SCUBA DIVING

DIVE SITES

Dahab offers some of the best dives reachable by land. The dive sites, on the Red Sea, are all accessible by car (usually 4x4 vehicles) and cover the areas both north and south of the main lighthouse region.

E G Y P T

THE ISLANDS. The most plentiful and beautiful supply of coral and aquatic life in Dahab are here. The labyrinth of pathways, valleys, and coral peaks can make it a difficult but rewarding site to visit, as divers often navigate new and different routes while weaving through delicate cities of coral. Many guides believe that this is the best-preserved coral in the entire Sinai area.

CANYON. Most of the corals have now died due to over-tourism, but the long, narrow canyon ranging from 18m to 50m deep still thrills divers looking for deep adventure. At the end of the canyon, divers move through a man-sized crack into the "fish bowl," an enclosure almost completely filled with schools of glass fish.

BLUE HOLE. The most famous site in Dahab is well-known for all the wrong reasons. Every year, some of Dahab's best (and craziest) divers try unsuccessfully to swim through the arched passage (52m below sea level) or even touch the bottom (160m) of this Hole on Earth. The site is recognized for the incredibly blue dive, starting at The Bells and continuing along the cliff of coral to the Blue Hole.

DIVE FACILITIES

The Dahab diving scene has unfortunately turned into a cut-throat operation in which inexperienced and ill-equipped dive centers cut corners on services and prices. There are very few dive centers in Dahab aside from Reef 2000 that offer safe and first-rate services at relatively inexpensive rates.

🞖 **Reef 2000** (☎64 00 87; email reef2000@intouch.com), at the Bedouin Moon Hotel in its own bay, just north of the Bedouin village. Run by Dave and Rachelle, a British couple who offer low prices and a safe atmosphere where even the most inexperienced will feel comfortable (especially since most of the guides and instructors are English-speaking expats). One guided dive with full equipment US$40; PADI courses US$310. **Camel safaris** to Ras Abd Galum and Gabr al-Bint include full equipment, lunch, water, and two dives (US$90-95). 15% *Let's Go* discount.

Fantasea (☎64 04 83; ☎/fax 64 00 43; email fdc@intouch.com), at the northern end. Offers everything from open water dives to assistant instructor courses. The lowest prices for individual dives around.

NUWEIBA نويبع ☎069

One of Sinai's natural oases, Nuweiba lies at the mouth of an enormous *wadi* that is filled with drifting sand for 10 months of the year. About the only excitement in town occurs in winter, when sudden, rampaging walls of water 3m high charge down the *wadi*. Nuweiba resembles a younger version of Dahab: a town with no inherent appeal or style that happens to be blessed with a cheap, carefree Bedouin camp and a great beach (complete with friendly dolphin). Nuweiba's importance rests primarily on its role in interstate travel: a ferry shuttles tourists and workers to Aqaba, Jordan (see p. 454).

▐ GETTING THERE AND GETTING AROUND

Nuweiba, named after the Bedouin tribe whose territory reaches Taba, is divided into a **port** and a **city.** The city lies 10km to the north of the port; a taxi between the two costs E£10. **Ferries** to Aqaba leave from the port (for more information, see p. 74). The **bus stop** is in the port, in front of the post office. **Buses** leave daily to: Cairo (6hr., 10am and 3pm, E£50); Sharm al-Sheikh (2½hr., 6:30am and 4:30pm, E£15) via Dahab (1½hr., E£10); St. Catherine's (6:30am, E£15); Suez (7hr., 7am and 3:30pm, E£25); and Taba (1hr., 6am and noon, E£10). To get to Tarabin from the city, either walk north along the beach (1½hr.) or take a taxi (E£20).

EGYPT

⊸🔢 ORIENTATION AND PRACTICAL INFORMATION

For credit card cash advances, use the **Banque du Caire** in the Hilton Hotel. (Open Su-Th 9:30am-noon and 6-9pm.) Across the street and near the port is **Bank Misr,** with a Visa/MC **ATM.** Most stores are in either the new or the old commercial center, both in the city. The new center is near the Helnan; the old is north, closer to Tarabin. Both have **supermarkets,** but the old center keeps longer hours. A **newsstand** in the old center has English-language newspapers, international telephone service, and bus schedule information. The old center also houses a **24-hour pharmacy** (☎50 06 05). Next to the Helnan stands the **tourist police** (☎50 02 31). Farther north past the communications antenna are: the **police station** (☎50 02 42; open 24hr.); the **hospital** (☎50 03 02; open 24hr.; higher quality Israeli health care is just over the border); the **telephone office** (open 24hr.); and a **post office** with **Poste Restante** and **EMS.** (☎50 02 44. Open daily 8am-3pm.)

🏠🍴 ACCOMMODATIONS AND FOOD

Budget travelers are better off staying in nearby Tarabin. The camps are cheaper and more plentiful, the restaurants are closer to the beach, and the nightlife is livelier. The only budget accommodation in Nuweiba city is **El-Waha Village,** 500m south of the Helnan, which sports garden shed-style bungalows. (☎/fax 50 04 20 or 50 04 21. Breakfast E£10. Singles E£25; doubles E£35; triples E£45; camping E£8 per person.) The **Helnan International Hotel,** next to El-Waha Village, also offers relatively inexpensive rooms with access to a private beach and facilities. (☎50 04 01. Breakfast included. Single huts E£46; double huts E£62; triple huts E£78. Pitch your own tent for E£15.) Everything else you need lies north of El-Waha Village and the Helnan, along Nuweiba city's one road.

Dr. Shishkebab (☎50 02 73), in the old commercial center, offers sandwiches (E£3-4), meat entrees (E£15-25), and vegetarian dishes (E£3-5). **'Ali Baba,** around the corner from Dr. Shishkebab, serves up meat dishes (E£12).

👁 SIGHTS AND SAFARIS

Nuweiba's most rewarding sight is **Dolphin Beach,** named for the friendly dolphin, Uleen, who lives there (see **A Tail of Two Dolphins,** p. 192). Dolphin Beach is a 20-minute walk south of Nuweiba Port or a E£5 taxi ride. Tell your driver, "Dolphin." Bedouin will charge you E£10 to swim, and another E£10 for mask, snorkel, and fins. The beach is open until 6pm.

Nuweiba is an excellent starting point for **camel** or **jeep safaris** through the desert terrain. Ask about trips at **Explore Sinai,** in the commercial center (☎50 01 41; open 9am-4pm and 7:30-11pm), or at the slightly cheaper **Moonland Camp** in Tarabin. (☎50 06 10. Colored Canyon trips E£50 per person.) You may save E£10-15 per day by dealing directly with a guide. Look for one at Tarabin if none approach you. Guides here are generally trustworthy. Desert trips require a **permit,** achieved by some mysterious passport fermentation process at your friendly neighborhood police station (your guide will take care of it for you). Tour prices always include food, but often exclude water. The price of bottled water rises dramatically during the safari, so start off with a large supply.

🤿 SCUBA DIVING

Like all towns on the Sinai coast, Nuweiba is surrounded by beautiful coral reefs, but unlike Dahab, Na'ama Bay, and Sharm al-Sheikh, Nuweiba's shores are not teeming with dive clubs. There are only three in town. **Emperor Divers,** in the Hilton Hotel, opened in 2000. (☎52 03 20 or 52 03 21, ext. 900. Two suited dives with full equipment and transport US$70. PADI open water training and certification for around US$325. Open daily 8am-6pm.) **Diving Camp Nuweiba** is in the Helnan Hotel.

EGYPT

A TAIL OF TWO DOLPHINS Uleen is one of 12 dolphins in the world that have chosen to live and play with humans. While the exact details of her decision remain mysterious, the competing versions of this fish tale are like fatuous episodes of *Flipper*. One story is that in 1994, Awda, a Bedouin fisherman, noticed that Uleen's mother was beached on the shore. Attempting to save her, Awda pulled the dolphin back into the water; but she didn't survive the transition. The next day, Uleen followed Awda and his deaf-mute brother, Abdullah, (who could only make one sound: "Uleen") on their daily fishing trip. Abdullah jumped into the water to swim with her, forging a bond that neither would soon forget. Another version has it that Uleen's companion (who is male in this tale) was caught in a net and shot by soldiers who mistook him for a shark. Grief-stricken, the lovelorn female lay crying in the water while Abdullah stroked her silvery skin to calm her—again forging that special interspecies bond. Scientists assign more, well, scientific reasons to her behavior: she was ejected from her pod (perhaps due to some illness or weakness) and sought social interaction, which she eventually found with humans. Whatever the explanation, Uleen has not left the vicinity of the beach, where visitors swim with her every day. It became clear, however, that humans were not meeting her every need: in 1996, Uleen became the mother of a bouncing baby, whom she lost to natural causes. Though the mother entertains visitors everyday with smiles that would make any delphine dentist proud, her second calf, Ramadan, has mysteriously disappeared, leading many to ask exactly what price Uleen has had to pay for human interaction.

(☎50 04 02. Two dives with vehicular transport US$60, with boat US$65; introductory dives US$45. Open water training US$325. Open 8am-6pm.) Divers can arrange trips to Ras Abu Galum through either center. Both diving centers are open from 8am to 6pm. **Sinai Dolphin Divers,** in the Nakim Inn, offers snorkeling with the dolphin Uleen for US$20, (☎50 08 79; email sinaidolphin@yahoo.com. Full equipment dives US$40, includes transport.)

FROM NUWEIBA TO TABA

The 70km stretch between Nuweiba and Taba is undoubtedly the most magnificent part of the Sinai: mountains come down to the sea, reefs and sand turn the water a magnificent shade of turquoise, and the mountains of Saudi Arabia tower in the distance. Unfortunately, the view will soon be ruined by the five-star resorts that are popping up like weeds along this beautiful stretch. The coastline is dotted with **Bedouin camps,** which are accessible by bus or *service* from Taba or Nuweiba. East Delta buses leave from Taba for Nuweiba at 9am and 3pm, and from Nuweiba for Taba at noon (1hr., E£10). Drivers may not know the names of some camps; keep your eyes peeled for signs. The camps follow a standard layout: a couple of huts, a central lounge, and a restaurant. Most huts do not have electricity (and those that are electrified rely on shaky generators), so bring a flashlight. It's quiet out here: people spend the days reading and swimming, while nighttime brings on backgammon, stargazing, shagging like a rabbit, and all that good stuff.

TARABIN طربين ☎069

Within spitting distance of Nuweiba, Tarabin is a miniature Dahab in spirit. Unlike Dahab, however, Tarabin actually has a beach, and the water is warm and clean. There is only one road and camps, restaurants, and supermarkets line the shore. Tarabin is rumored to be the source of much of Egypt's dope; it is widely available here, but that doesn't make it legal. The quality of the huts varies little from camp to camp. Most charge E£5-15 and have their own Bedouin-style restaurant. Muhammad, who runs **Carmina Camp** at the southern end of town, will make you feel right at home. (☎50 04 77. Two-person huts E£15.) The friendly **Moonland Camp,** run by Amsalem Farrag, offers guided camel (E£85-100 per day), four-by-four (E£75 per day), trekking, and mountain bike tours (BYOB; E£45 per day), in addition to a beachfront restaurant. (☎50 06 10. Huts E£10 per person.) **Mondial Restaurant,** in the center of town, makes a great cheese omelette for E£7. (☎50 06 97. Open 24hr.) A **taxi** from Nuweiba city to Tarabin is E£10, from the port E£20.

BEACH CAMPS

Some of the most beautiful camps lie 10-15km north of Nuweiba. All camps should cost E£10-20 per person per night. Prices go down the longer you stay, the larger your party, and the fewer the number of people already staying there. Always **bargain;** it can't hurt and you may save a few pounds. All accommodations are fairly basic, with few amenities to distract you from the neighboring natural splendors—or just from your neighbor. **Magana Beach,** a Bedouin camp near colorful rock formations, has reefs and a restaurant. **Devil's Head** (Ras Shaytan), named for a rock formation three kilometers north of Magana, contains four camps. The southernmost, **Moon Island,** is the most simple and secluded. (Bamboo hut singles E£20; doubles E£40; triples E£50.) Moving north, the second and fourth camps offer more huts and consequently more people. Some of the camps occasionally let guests sleep on the beach for free. Farther north and close to the Basata camp, the ritzy **Bawaki** has a few budget-priced, non-air-conditioned sheds for US$20 (including use of pool). Between Basata and Taba is a remote and beautiful spot called the **Fjord,** where a small inlet cuts into the steep hills. The **Salima Restaurant and Camp** is right off the highway on a small ledge overlooking the sleepy bay. There are a few rooms crammed between the restaurant and the rock slope behind it (☎(069) 53 01 30; E£30 per person); **camping** is also available on the beach.

BASATA بساطة

Basata means "simplicity" in Arabic, and this environmentally conscious camp midway between Nuweiba and Taba is designed to minimize its impact on the Sinai's environment. Basata is unlike anything you will encounter in the Sinai—a gorgeous place you can enjoy without pangs of ecological guilt. Glass, metal, and plastic are all recycled; water is desalinated; organic trash is used as livestock feed; plans are underway to have electricity generated by solar panels; and perspiration collected by super-absorbent clothing is channeled into turnip and parsnip cultivation. Basata is run by German/English-educated Sharif Ghamrawi, who cultivates a family-oriented atmosphere with communal dinners, a comfy common area, and lots of rules: no nudity, no drugs or alcohol, no sleeping in the common area, and no dirty dishes. A vegetarian (E£20) or fish (E£26) meal is prepared every evening, though you can save money by cooking for yourself. The kitchen functions on trust: take what you want and write down what you take, but remember to watch the prices as you go. All prices are subject to a 10% tax. Sharif also organizes **tours** by camel (E£75 per day) and jeep (E£60). Due to recent publicity, Basata has become quite popular. Huts often sell out, but the beach is almost always available except when European, Egyptian, and Israeli holidays overlap. (☎(069) 50 04 81. Camping E£18; bamboo hut singles E£40; doubles E£56.)

PHARAOH'S ISLAND

The rocky outcrop of **Pharaoh's Island** (called Gezirat Fara'un by Egyptians, Coral Island by Israelis), eight kilometers south of the Taba border crossing, holds the ruins of a Crusader castle built around 1115 CE. Salah al-Din took the fortress in 1171 but abandoned it in 1183 after European counterattacks. The ruins have towers and passageways as well as a large water cistern. A boat ferries visitors to the island (E£14, JD24 from Aqaba); they must then buy another ticket to tour the castle (E£20, students E£10). Taxis from the ferry terminal to Taba cost E£20. En route to the island, the view of Sinai from the castle is ruined by the five-star Salah al-Din Hotel (the best view is from the mainland). The coral reef formations off the northeastern tip of the island draw divers and snorkelers, but the sites are overrated—neither the reefs nor the wildlife compares to the lower Sinai. With the number of tourist boats moored off the island, you're liable to see more fellow snorkelers than fish. Meals on the island are overpriced and often unavailable.

SUEZ CANAL قناةالسويس

The Suez Canal is the brainchild of an 18th-century idea and 19th-century engineering know-how. Napoleon Bonaparte considered digging a canal between the Mediterranean and the Red Sea, but feared that the waters of the Red Sea were higher than those of the Mediterranean. Years later, another Frenchman, Ferdinand de Lesseps, persuaded Sa'id Pasha, the *khedive* of Egypt, to try a similar plan. Excavation started on April 25, 1859, and took 10 years to complete. On August 18, 1869, the canal was opened in a grand ceremony attended by over 6000 dignitaries. A man, a plan, a canal—Suez.

Spanning 195km and reaching a maximum depth of 15m, the canal connects Port Said on the Mediterranean to Suez on the Red Sea. The average transit time for ships through the canal is 15 hours. Because it allowed for rapid travel from Europe to the Indian Ocean, the canal became a crucial element in the infrastructure of the British Empire. Nasser nationalized the canal in 1956, precipitating a British-French-Israeli invasion (to read more about the **Suez Crisis** and the rise of **Pan-Arabism,** see p. 67). During the 1967 War against Israel, Nasser blocked the canal with sunken ships. It remained closed through the 1973 War, and was cleared and reopened in 1975.

PORT SAID بورسعيد ☎ 048

Founded in 1860, Port Said (Bor Sa'id) became Africa's gateway to the Mediterranean upon completion of the Suez Canal. Since 1976, when the city was declared a tax-free zone, Port Said has developed into a shopping resort for Egyptians cashing in on duty-free deals. The town is saturated with clothing stores fronting styles unseen in the West since the 70s. However, Port Said doesn't really come alive until nighttime, when everyone takes to the streets to window shop and enjoy the cool breeze and twinkling lights of the canal. The men of Port Said are well-known for their politeness, and women here will experience noticeably less harassment than in other parts of Egypt.

▐ GETTING THERE AND GETTING AROUND

Trains: Go to the southwest end of al-Gomhoriyya St. and turn right onto Mustafa Kamal St. The jam-packed **station** is ½km down on the left. Trains run to **Cairo** (4½hr.; 5:20am, 7:15, 7:30pm; 2nd-class E£14) via **Isma'ilia** (1¾hr., 2nd-class E£6). To reach **Suez,** change at Isma'ilia.

Buses: The **West Delta** bus depot is on Salah al-Din St., on the northern side of Ferial Gardens, two blocks west of al-Gomhoriyya St. Daily buses to: **Alexandria** (7, 9am, 2:30, 4:30pm; E£15-20); **Cairo** (2hr., every hr. 6am-7pm, E£12-15); **Isma'ilia** (1½hr., every hr. 6am-7pm, E£4); and **Suez** (6, 10am, 1, 4pm; E£7.50). The **Superjet** depot is next to the train station on Mustafa Kamal St., with buses to **Alexandria** (4hr., daily 8:30pm, E£22) and **Cairo** (10 per day 7am-7pm, E£15).

Service: Near the train station and the Superjet depot (ask for *taxi ugra*).

Bike Rental: A great way to get around the city. Rent them on the south side of Hafiz Ibrahim St., between Palestine and al-Gomhoriyya St. E£3 per hr.

◀▚ ▐ ORIENTATION AND PRACTICAL INFORMATION

By road, Port Said is 343km east of Alexandria and 220km northeast of Cairo. The town is surrounded by water on three sides: the Mediterranean to the north, the Suez Canal to the east, and **Lake Manzala** to the south. The point at which the canal meets the Mediterranean is Port Said's northeastern corner. **Atef al-Sadat St.** runs along the sea, and **Palestine St.** follows the edge of the canal. **Memphis St.** and al-

Port Said

ACCOMMODATIONS
Akri Palace Hotel, 1
Hotel Delaposte, 2
Youth Hostel, 3

Mediterranean Sea

Beach

Suez Canal

PORT FOUAD

EGYPT

TO PORT FOUAD

TO CAIRO (220km)

TO ALEXANDRIA (343km)

Port Said National Museum

Es-Salaam

American Express

Thomas Cook

Palace Gardens

West Delta Bus Company

Ferial Gardens

Tourist Police

Memorial Monument

Military Museum

Saad Zaghloul Garden

Port Said Stadium

Superjet

Palestine St.

El-Gomhoriyya St.

Muhammad Mahmoud St.

Hafiz Ibrahim St.

El-Geish St.

Ramses St.

Salah ad-Din St.

Salah Salem St.

Mustafa Kamel St.

En-Nadha St.

Oraby St.

Atef es-Sadat St.

Safia Zaghloul St.

Sa'ad Zaghloul St.

En-Nasr St.

23 July St.

Muhammad es-Sayed Sirhan St.

Gomhoriyya St., one and two blocks inland, respectively, run parallel to Palestine St. Another important thoroughfare, three blocks inland, is **23 July St.,** which runs parallel to Atef al-Sadat St.

Tourist Office: 5 Palestine St. (☎23 52 89), two blocks from the southern end of the street. Open Sa-Th 9am-2pm. Another branch at the **train station** keeps similar hours.

Currency Exchange: Small offices abound. The most convenient is **Thomas Cook,** 43 al-Gomhoriyya St. (☎33 62 60; fax 23 61 11). Open daily 8am-5pm. **ATM** at Banque Misr, 30 al-Gomhoriyya St.

American Express: 83 al-Gomhoriyya St. (☎23 98 31), across from al-Salaam Mosque. Cash advances and traveler's check exchange. Open daily 10am-4pm.

Emergency: Ambulance: ☎180. **Police:** ☎122.

Tourist Police: (☎22 85 70). Stationed on the 5th floor of the abandoned post office building on al-Gomhoriyya St.

Pharmacy: Hussein Pharmacy (☎33 98 88; fax 33 97 77), on al-Gomhoriyya St., a block south of Muhammad Mahmoud St. Open daily 9am-1am. Many other pharmacies also line al-Gomhoriyya St.

Hospital: Delivrand Hospital (☎22 36 63 or 22 56 95), on al-Shaid al-Gaya St.

Telephones: (☎22 01 66; fax 32 57 05), two blocks north of the tourist office on Palestine St. Phone cards available for E£15, E£20, and E£30. Direct international dialing (E£24 per 3min. to the US). Open 24hr.

Post Office: In the southeast corner of the Ferial Gardens, at the intersection of Muhammad Mahmoud St. and al-Geish St. For **Poste Restante,** walk south from the post office, take the first left, then walk 30m. Both open Sa-Th 8am-5pm.

▛ ACCOMMODATIONS

Most accommodations in town are either on or near al-Gomhoriyya St. Super-cheap hotels are hard to come by, but there are many mid-range and luxury hotels. If you want to be able to roll out of bed and onto the beach every morning, the only budget option is the **Youth Hostel (HI),** on Muhammad al-Sayyid Sirhan St. opposite the stadium. Modern and sterile, its large bathrooms and fans are a 20-minute walk or E£1.50 taxi ride from the town center. (☎22 87 02. Breakfast included. 6-bed dorm E£12.60; nonmembers pay E£2 extra.) If you're more excited about shopping or the canal, your options are more varied. **Akri Palace Hotel,** 24 al-Gomhoriyya St. two blocks from the southern end of al-Gomhoriyya St., is owned by the friendly Greek Nicolandis brothers. A 19th-century elevator transports you to run-down but charming rooms with high ceilings, wood floors, sinks, and desks. Huge balcony doors provide a nice breeze. (☎22 10 13. Singles E£13; doubles E£26; triples E£31; add E£10 for private bath.) **Hotel Delaposte,** 42 al-Gomhoriyya St., deserves its two stars for rooms with private baths, TV, and fridge. Look for the English "Hotel" sign with Arabic underneath next to a pastry shop. (☎22 96 55 or 22 40 48. Singles E£30; doubles E£35; triples E£45; add E£10 for A/C.)

☙ FOOD

Although seafood is the main fare, most restaurants provide other options. You'll thank your sweet Lord for the sweets at ▣**Lord's Pastry** (☎23 52 02), just south of the intersection of al-Gomhoriyya and 23 July St. The friendly staff sells a wide selection of superb Western pastries, all E£1.25. Your deck may be pooped after a long day shopping or swimming, but you'll be strong to the finish after a meal at **Popeye Restaurant,** on the corner of al-Gomhoriyya and Safia Zaghloul St. There's no spinach, but it's still a good choice for zesty chicken kebabs (E£17) and banana splits (E£5.70). (☎23 94 94. Open daily 8am-midnight. V, MC.) **Galal Restaurant,** 60 al-Gomhoriyya St., serves up standard Egyptian fare at reasonable prices. Make the most of your money by sitting outside. Large, plastic crustaceans above the tables make charming dinner companions for the solitary traveler. (☎ 22 96 68. Open daily 7am-2am; closed during Ramadan. V.) A local favorite for fresh seafood, **El-Borg** sits on the beachside corniche. Resistance is futile: you will be assimilated, too, when you see that a full meal costs just E£30. (☎ 32 34 42. Open 24hr.)

SIGHTS

PORT SAID NATIONAL MUSEUM. This museum houses a fine collection of items from all periods of Egyptian history, ranging from several exquisite mummy cases to Coptic icons and Qur'anic calligraphy. See Khedive Isma'il's carriage, from which he presided over the 1869 opening of the canal. The labels alongside each of the artifacts, not to mention the building's air-conditioning, secure its status as a must-see. *(At the northern end of Palestine St. ☎ 23 74 19. Open Sa-Th 9am-5pm, F 9am-noon and 2-5pm; Ramadan 8:30am-1pm. E£12, students E£6. Camera privileges E£10, video E£20.)*

OTHER SIGHTS AND EXCURSIONS. Free **ferries** to Port Fouad leave every few minutes from the southern tip of Palestine St. The shell-covered **beach** lies along the Mediterranean shore to the north. Beach umbrellas can be rented for E£3 per day, and showers are every 100m. If the words "duty-free" make your wallet tremble, **shopping arcades** stretch three blocks inland from Palestine St. For more affordable goods, hop on a minibus (25pt) and ask to be taken to **al-Souq al-Togary** further inland. Here you'll find street after street of locals with cheap clothing, cloth, shoes, and other goods spread out on the road.

ISMA'ILIA الاسماعيلية ☎ 064

Once known as Timsah Village, Isma'ilia was renamed after Isma'il, the last independent *khedive* of Egypt, and is now the capital of the Suez Canal District. Since it sustained heavy damage during the Arab-Israeli wars of 1967 and 1973, Isma'ilia has been completely rebuilt, and today one can relax in sprawling gardens or swim at the nearby beaches. It has few tourist attractions, so Isma'ilia is blissfully free of foreigners. This might make a long stay boring, but if you're looking to get away from the hellishness of Cairo for a day or two, Isma'ilia is a nearby escape.

GETTING THERE AND GETTING AROUND

Trains: The train station is on al-Sekka al-Hadid St. in Orabi Sq. Locomotives chug to: **Cairo** (2½hr., 5 per day, 2nd-class E£11); **Port Said** (1¾hr., 5 per day, 2nd-class E£24); and **Suez** (1½hr., 6 per day, E£21).

Buses: There are two **bus stations.** The smaller one in Orabi Sq. services **Alexandria** (4½hr., 2 per day, E£14-17) and **Cairo** (2hr., 4 per day, E£26). The main bus terminal in Salam Sq., about 2km out of town, has buses to: **al-Arish** (3hr., 5 per day, E£7); **Port Said** (1½hr., 8 per day until 6pm, E£4); and **Suez** (1½hr., until 6pm, E£3).

Service: Opposite the main bus station. Offers fast and frequent service to: **al-Arish** (E£8); **Cairo** (E£5); **Port Said** (E£3.50); and **Suez** (E£3.50). For excursions within the town itself, orange taxis are available (E£2 should be enough for any distance), as well as minibuses (25pt). For both, just shout out your destination as the vehicle passes and the driver will stop if he can help.

ORIENTATION AND PRACTICAL INFORMATION

Midway along the Suez Canal, Isma'ilia is linked by road and the Isma'ilia Canal to the Delta, and by highway and railroad to Alexandria (280km) and Cairo (140km). While you can't see the canal from the center of town, Isma'ilia's two main streets, **Sultan Hussein St.** and **al-Thalatheni St.,** run roughly parallel to the waterway. **Orabi**

EGYPT

Sq. is in between the two streets, three blocks north of **Salah Salem St.,** which forms the town's southern border. Restaurants and shops line Sultan Hussein St. **Mallaha Park** stretches along Salah Salem St. toward the canal.

Currency Exchange: Bank of Alexandria (☎33 79 21), in Orabi Sq. next to Travel Misr, provides cash advances on V, MC, and AmEx. Open Su-Th 8:30am-2pm and 6-9pm; in winter 5-8pm; during Ramadan 10am-1:30pm. An ATM with V and MC links is three blocks up the first street on your left.

Emergency: Ambulance: ☎123. **Police:** ☎13. The police are one block west of the Governorate Building on Salah Salem St.

Pharmacy: Isma'ilia Pharmacy, 24 Sultan Hussein St. (☎22 93 19), is a well-stocked apothecary. Open daily 9am-5pm and 6:30-11:30pm.

Hospital: Two private clinics, **al-Shafa Hospital** (☎22 29 20) and **Karin Hospital** (☎22 75 59), serve the area.

Telephones: There is a 24hr. telephone office in Orabi Sq.

Post Office: The post office is in Orabi Sq. Open Sa-Th 8am-5pm.

▐ ACCOMMODATIONS

Centrally located in Orabi Sq., the ⬛**New Palace Hotel,** next to the Bank of Alexandria, has rooms with high ceilings, all with private bath, A/C, and TV. The kindly old manager or his son will show you to the cafeteria and kitchens. (☎32 63 27. Breakfast E£5. Singles E£30; doubles E£60.) Though a three-kilometer hike or a E£2 taxi ride from the center of town, **Isma'ilia Youth Hostel (HI),** on 'Omara Rd., is a good choice. The sandy beach and comfy common room of this spotless 266-bed hostel make it a backpacker's dream resort. Lunch and dinner are E£5 each. Don't miss the 11pm curfew. All rooms except the dorms have private bath. (☎32 28 50; fax 33 14 29. Breakfast included. 6-bed dorms E£12.60; doubles E£22.60; triples E£17.60; nonmembers E£1 extra.) With its bright purple exterior and pastel green rooms, the **Nevertary Hotel,** 41 Sultan Hussein St., three blocks north of Bank Misr, wins the Miami Vice Award for hotel color coordination. You'll want to tarry in the Nevertary's comfy rooms, with air-conditioning and private bath, complemented by a sitting area and fridge on each floor. (☎32 28 22; fax 32 11 08. Breakfast E£6. Singles E£35; doubles E£45; triples E£55; add 12% service tax.)

▐ FOOD

Vendors line the streets with cheap Egyptian fare, but for excellent seafood, try Isma'ilia's sit-down venues. **Nefertiti's,** 11 Sultan Hussein St., south of the Nevertary Hotel, is cozy and romantic. Royal portions of seafood (E£9 and up) and meat (E£15) appease the hungriest carnivore, while beer and wine satisfy the thirstiest lush. (☎22 04 94. Open daily 10am-midnight.) **George's Restaurant,** next door to Nefertiti's on Sultan Hussein St., has over 50 years of experience. Fish, meat, and pasta meals run E£10-30; the owner recommends the fried calamari. If nothing else, pull up a stool at the bar. (☎33 73 27. Open daily noon-midnight.) The **King Edward Restaurant,** at 171 Tahrir St. off Sultan Hussein St., one block south of the Nevertary Hotel and left at the obelisk, is easily identifiable with a large cutout of King Ed gracing the entrance. Clean, cool, and quiet, King Ed prides himself on seafood (E£5-45), but rice with curry is delicious. Try your luck and order "craps" if you don't have them already. (☎32 54 51. Open daily noon-2am.)

▐ ▐ SIGHTS AND ENTERTAINMENT

The **Isma'ilia Regional Museum,** on Salah Salem St., near the canal at the eastern end of town, has pharaonic, Islamic, and Roman collections. (Open W-M 9am-3pm. E£3, students E£1.50.) Near the museum, the **Garden of the Stelae** contains sphinxes from the age of Ramses II. Ask for permission to visit at the museum entrance. If you're really bored, **Mallaha Park** is worth a frolic with its 500 acres of rare flowers, trees, and benches. Just 100m south of the youth hostel, the **beach club** along Lake Timsah has two restaurants, boats for rent, and kiddie amusement park rides. (Open daily 10am-10pm. E£2.)

SUEZ السويس   ☎062

Suez (al-Suweis) sits at the junction of the Red Sea and the Suez Canal. With its open sewers and piles of burning garbage, not to mention the heavy smoke from nearby factories, you won't want to stay here longer than you have to, although Port Tawfiq provides an excellent perch from which to watch the canal at work. Most travelers pass through Suez en route from Cairo to the Sinai by way of the **Ahmed Hamdi Tunnel** (running under the canal 17km north of town), or on their way south along the Red Sea coast. Others stay a few days looking for passage on a boat at the Yacht Club. Nearby **'Ain Sukhna** is downright spectacular; its proximity to Cairo provides a convenient sun-swim-snorkel option.

GETTING THERE AND GETTING AROUND

There are two **bus stations** around al-Geish St. in the northern part of town. Buses to most destinations leave from the depot on Salah al-Din St., one block west of al-Geish St., while those heading to Upper Egypt depart up the road near the train station. Both stations are easily accessible by minibus. **Buses** shuttle to: 'Ain Sukhna (1hr.; 6:30, 10am, 2pm; E£1.75); Alexandria (5hr., 7am and 2:30pm, E£22); Cairo (2hr.; every 30min. 6am-5pm, every hr. 5-8pm; E£7); Hurghada (6hr., 8 per day until 10pm, E£22); Isma'ilia (1¼hr., every 30min. 6am-4pm, E£4); and Port Said (3hr.; 7, 9, 10:30am, 3:30pm; E£9). Reserve tickets to Hurghada and Alexandria a few days in advance. **Service** also travel these routes (except for Alexandria) at similar prices (Cairo E£5, Hurghada E£20, Isma'ilia E£3, Port Said E£7). They depart more frequently than buses, but usually aren't air-conditioned.

Suez is the main launching ground for forays into the Sinai. **East Delta** and **West Delta** buses leave every half hour from 8am to 7pm, following a route that includes Uyoun Mussa (E£6), Sharm al-Sheikh (6hr., E£20), Dahab (7hr., E£23), Nuweiba (E£25), and St. Catherine's (E£20). An East Delta bus runs to Taba (3pm, E£25). **Service** drivers charge by the trip, so the more people in the van, the less each one pays. **Private taxis** to the Sinai are generally prohibitively expensive.

For transport within the city, exit the bus station and go behind the row of food stands. **Minibus** drivers will be yelling out their destinations. To travel to and from Port Tawfiq, simply flag down a minibus on al-Geish St. (25pt).

ORIENTATION AND PRACTICAL INFORMATION

Al-Geish St. runs roughly north-south through the center of Suez, from the **bus stations** all the way down to **Port Tawfiq**, where the **tourist office** stands at the western-most end of town. The tourist office provides a complete restaurant guide for all of Egypt as well as a map of the Suez and Port Tawfiq. (☎33 11 41 or 33 11 42. Open daily 8am-8pm.) **Banque Misr**, at the intersection of 'Amr ibn al-'As and al-Geish, has an **ATM** that accepts V and MC. (☎22 05 71. Open Su-Th 9am-3pm.) **American Express** services are available for all travelers at Menatours (☎22 88 21), next to the tourist office in Port Tawfiq. The **tourist police** (☎33 11 40) share a building with the tourist office. Suez's main house of medicine is the **General Suez Hospital** (☎33 17 81), just west of the bus station. The **telecommunications office** is about three blocks west of al-Geish St., on the corner of Shohada'a St. and Sa'ad Zaghloul St. (Open 24hr.) The **post office,** on Hoda Sharawi St., one block east of al-Geish St., offers **Poste Restante.** (☎33 13 10. Open Sa-Th 8am-3pm.)

ACCOMMODATIONS AND FOOD

Star Hotel, 17 Bank Misr St., has large, clean rooms with turbo fans. The showers and balconies are stellar. (☎22 87 37. Singles or doubles E£20, with bath E£25; triples E£30, with bath E£35.) One block north of the Star, a mirrored and gilded lobby welcomes travelers into **Sina Hotel,** 21 Bank Misr St. Unsullied rooms sport fans and "hoot water." (☎33 41 81. Singles E£15; doubles E£30.) Walk three blocks east on Tahrir St., take a right, and proceed to the next street, where the **Hotel Madena** awaits on the left. Rooms are bare, but functional and decently priced. (☎22 40 56. Singles E£10, with bath E£15; doubles E£20, with bath E£25.)

The airy **Mahmoud Rawash Restaurant,** on Tahrir St. just off al-Geish St. (look for the awnings), is a typical sandwich stand, serving great food at great prices (falafel or *fuul* sandwich 25pt). The impeccable **Seaside Restaurant,** one block west of the telephone building, gives you anything from sandwiches (E£2) to grilled fish and

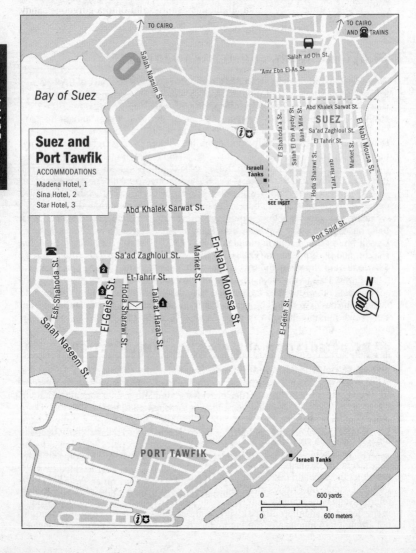

EGYPT

shrimp (E£25) in the air-conditioned interior or on the rooftop terrace. **Five Star Cafeteria,** on al-Geish in Port Tawfiq, has desserts to snack on while watching the ships roll in. Get a taste of homemade Italian goodness at **El-Eltakia** on al-Geish St., where pizzas start at E£5. (Open daily noon-midnight.)

🎦 🎵 SIGHTS AND ENTERTAINMENT

If you get stuck here for any length of time, there are few sites to keep you entertained. **Hadiqat Mubarak** on the corniche displays American-made Israeli tanks captured in 1973, as well as other military vehicles. The dirty water from the many ships at **Rex Beach,** in town near the stadium, isn't very regal, but the beach at **'Ain Sukhna** (Hot Spring), 60km south along the Red Sea, rivals those of the Sinai. **Buses** run there early in the day (1hr.; 6:30, 10am, 2pm; E£2) and return about 1½ hours later. **Service** also run down the coast from Suez to 'Ain Sukhna. The hot spring (35°C), originating in the Ataka Mountains, empties out onto a gorgeous sandy beach. Get off the bus when you see the large green-and-white sign for the **'Ain Sukhna Hotel** (☎32 84 88). Day-trippers can pay the hotel a E£15 day-use fee for chairs and umbrellas if they only plan to visually enjoy the crystal clear water, though the mouth of the hot spring is also available for prolonged soaks. The hotel offers an expensive but incredible fish, salad, and hummus meal for E£26. It's not just the best choice, it's the only choice—bring your own food if you'd rather not put your money where your mouth is.

MONASTERIES OF ST. ANTHONY AND ST. PAUL

The isolated monasteries of St. Anthony and St. Paul lie 30km apart (82km by road), near the Red Sea. These centers of faith, dating from the early Christian monastic tradition, are inhabited by monks whose austere lifestyle has changed remarkably little over the past 16 centuries. Most speak excellent English, and they warmly welcome visitors. While a few hours suffice to see the monasteries, spending the night can be transcendent. Men and women can now stay at both St. Anthony's and St. Paul's. The monks provide food and water, and although there is no formal charge, donations are welcome—even the most ascetic life requires some financing. Note that you must have a letter of recommendation from the administration office in Cairo (see below) to stay overnight at either of the two monasteries, though the monks may overlook this if they don't already have many guests. Both monasteries are open daily 9am-5pm.

Reaching the monasteries is a serious endeavor without a car (there are no organized tours to the monasteries). Plenty of patience and water are required. Travelers are completely dependent upon **pilgrims** traveling to the sight for transportation. Of the two possible options for getting to the monasteries, the less desirable is to take any form of public transportation headed for Hurghada and ask to be dropped off on the road to the monasteries. The closest stop to St. Anthony's is **Ras Za'frana,** about 33km east of the monastery. Hang out at the roadside hotel in Za'frana (spacious, clean rooms with baths run E£60-100 if you want to spend the night) until the arrival of a pilgrimage group headed for the monastery and ask to tag along. Only the fancier pilgrimages will stop at this touristy establishment, though; to improve your chances, try the intersection 100m to the south. Attempting to walk 33km can be difficult and dangerous, even at night.

The closest stop to St. Paul's from a Hurghada-bound bus is by the **St. Bola sign,** 12km from the monastery. Pilgrimage groups have been known to pick up travelers along the way and take them to the monasteries and back. This option is only remotely viable on Fridays and Sundays, and even then, it's dangerous. Although pilgrims tend to be friendly, catching a ride can be difficult. Hitchhiking, especially in the desert, is an inherently risky proposition, and women traveling alone should not attempt it. A much safer (and more hassle-free) option is to contact the **monas-**

teries' administration office in Cairo (☎ (02) 590 02 18; call daily 10am-noon and 8:30-9:30pm) and ask when local Coptic churches are planning pilgrimages to the monasteries. A group may be leaving as soon as tomorrow or as late as a month from next Sunday. Contact the churches about tagging along with their group.

ST. ANTHONY'S MONASTERY

St. Anthony, raised in the Nile Valley in the 4th century CE, became the first famous ascetic of the Christian Church when he scorned worldly concerns and retreated into the Eastern Desert. Anthony's dramatic move reflected the restlessness that overtook some Christians after Constantine made Christianity the official religion of the Roman Empire. This was a disturbing development for those who felt that the church had gained worldly security and wealth at the expense of its spiritual focus. In Egypt, some of these Christians, mostly educated middle-class men, sought to escape the secular world by retreating into the desert where they could pray in solitude and render their lives unto God rather than Caesar.

St. Anthony was paradoxically unsuccessful; his desert hermitages became popular pilgrimage sites, and crowds of the pious and the curious deprived the recluse of precious penitent isolation. Frustrated in his quest for solitude, St. Anthony came up with the comprise solution of organizing his most persistent followers into a loosely-knit group that prayed and ate together once a week, creating the model followed by many orthodox monasteries to this day. Soon after the saint's death, his disciple St. Athanasius told the story of his choice of poverty and hardship, his wild battles with demons, and his wise counsel to monks and layfolk. Athanasius's *Life of Anthony* became the prototype for much of later Christian hagiography. Around the same time, Anthony's followers settled at the present site and established the first Christian monastery. The Monastery of St. Anthony served as a refuge for some of the monks of Wadi Natrun when their own sanctuaries were attacked by Bedouin in the 6th century. During the 7th and 8th centuries, the monastery was occupied by Melkite monks, and in the 11th century it was pillaged by the army of Nasser al-Dawla. About 100 years after the sacking, it was restored and transferred to Coptic hands.

The **Church of St. Anthony** and the southern walls are the only remains predating the 16th-century construction of the present monastery. With ancient frescoes embellishing each of their sections, Anthony's church and its small chapel are the most impressive parts of the monastery. The monks are still awaiting permission from both President Mubarak and Pope Shnouda III before the church can be consecrated and opened to visitors. Inquire with the Cairo office if this fortuitous event has occurred, or else ask the monks very nicely for a peek. East of the Church of St. Anthony is the **Church of the Apostles.** During Lent, the monks cantillate the liturgy in the 18th-century **Church of St. Mark.** As in the Wadi Natrun monasteries, the **Chapel of St. Michael** is on the top floor of the tower. The extensive library contains more than 1700 manuscripts.

The major religious attraction in the vicinity of the church is the **Cave of St. Anthony,** where the ascetic himself is said to have lived. The vista from the cave, 276m above the Red Sea, rewards the requisite hour and a half of hoofing and huffing. The best time to climb the mountain is when the sun is low (before 6am or after 4pm). Try to return before dark (or light) and remember to bring oceans of water. St. Anthony's has a small snack shop with soda and cookies and a gift shop.

ST. PAUL'S MONASTERY

St. Paul (not the disciple) was born into an affluent Alexandrian family in the 3rd century CE. When his father died, he left his estate to young Paul and his brother. Naturally, this caused squabbling between the two, and when the family had heard enough, the brothers were sent off to consult with a judge. In the end, the two young men took separate routes. Paul happened to pass the funeral service of a wealthy man and, for some unexplained reason, was profoundly affected (why he wasn't so moved at his own father's funeral no one knows). Like St. Anthony, St.

A MEETING OF MINDS According to Christian lore, St. Anthony and St. Paul met in one dramatic encounter at the end of Paul's life. Wanting to reveal the holiness of St. Paul, God led St. Anthony to his cave. As the two conversed, Paul's crow dropped a *whole* loaf of bread for them (double what the bird usually brought). Paul, realizing that he was talking to another holy man, told Anthony that he was nearing death and made one final request: to wear the robe of Pope Athanasius. Anthony immediately departed to fetch the garment. On his return, he had a vision of angels carrying St. Paul's soul to heaven, and arrived at the cave to find Paul dead. While pondering what to do with the body, two lions descended from the mountain, mourned for their lifelong companion, and dug a grave. Anthony wrapped Paul in the papal robe and buried him. He then carried St. Paul's palm leaf garment back to Athanasius, who sported it every Christmas, Epiphany, and Easter.

Paul cast off all worldly concerns and, guided by an angel, headed for the hills. He lived in a cave near Mount Nemra and made his garments from palm leaves and branches. Legend has it that his strict ascetic diet of half a loaf of bread per day was dropped to him by a crow; water came from a secret source high in the mountains (which still exists today). These divine provisions enabled St. Paul to live alone for over 80 years.

The original monastery was built on the cave site not long after St. Paul's death—probably before 400 CE. St. Paul's has been attacked by Bedouin throughout its history, most notably in 1484 when the churches were burned, the library destroyed, and all of the monks killed. After the Bedouin left 80 years later, Coptic Patriarch Gabriel VII sent replacement monks to rebuild the churches, but the buildings were destroyed again before a century passed. Finally, at the end of the 16th century, Coptic Patriarch Ioannis ordered monks from St. Anthony's to reconstruct and inhabit St. Paul's. These monks were the wisest yet: they built a five-story tower with a drawbridge leading to the fourth story. The first two floors of the tower were for food and water storage and allowed the monks to endure sieges of up to three months. The monastery was most recently renovated in 1974 but, aside from the addition of electrical generators and a guesthouse, it remains the same as it has been for centuries.

The most impressive part of the monastery is the **Church of St. Paul,** built in the cave where the famed hermit dwelt. Many of the church's 4th- and 7th-century frescoes have somehow survived. Ostrich eggs symbolizing the Resurrection hang from the roof. Past the gardens, you can fill your Baraka bottles with holy water coming from the same secret source St. Paul lived on.

HURGHADA الغردقة ☎065

The Red Sea of Hurghada ("al-Ghardaqa") is dotted with small islands and chains of coral reefs where schools of tropical fish swim through the sun-dappled, tranquil cobalt waters. Since the early 1980s, when peace with Israel opened Egypt to foreign investors and tourists, scores of resorts have sprung from the sands of Hurghada. The boomtown continues to expand along the coast at a rapid pace that shows no sign of slowing down. The underwater splendors find their skewed counterparts on land in a profusion of tourist "bazaars" selling gaudy souvenir dreck to the foreign visitors who flock here for the superb diving and snorkeling.

▮ GETTING THERE AND GETTING AROUND

Flights: Hurghada Airport (☎44 75 03), 3km south of town and about 1½km inland. Served by **EgyptAir,** with flights to **Cairo** (2 per day 8:45am and 7:15pm, E£455) and **Sharm al-Sheikh** (M, F 8:10am, E£320). Tickets should be booked in advance through **Karnak Travel** (☎54 78 93), across from the mosque on northern al-Nasser Rd. Open daily 8am-8pm.

Buses: Upper Egypt Bus Co. launches from al-Nasser Rd., 300m from the southern end of town. Book seats at least one day in advance; last-minute standing room may be available. Buses to: **Alexandria** (10hr., 7pm, E£55); **Aswan** (7hr.; 4, 10pm, midnight; E£24-35); **Cairo** (6hr., 8 per day 7:30am-12:30am, E£45); **Luxor** via **Qena** (2hr.; 6am, noon, 1:30, 6:30pm, 1am; E£9); and **Suez** (5hr., 3 per day, E£18-20). **Superjet** has a different bus depot, 50m off al-Nasser St. across from the mosque at the north end of town, and jets buses to **Cairo** (noon and 2:30pm E£47; 5pm E£52).

Ferries: To **Sharm al-Sheikh** from the "New" Harbor (1½hr., variable schedule, E£115/US$33). Reserve at least one day in advance through a hotel manager, at the ferry office, or with **Eid Travel** (☎54 78 21 or 54 79 92).

Service: Run from Dahar through Saqala and south to the resorts, and vice versa (E£1). The best places to catch one are on al-Nasser Rd. or Corniche Rd.

Taxis: Congregate off al-Nasser Rd., beside the rotary just south of the telephone office. Prices are per car; form a group and you may be able to bargain lower. Taxis run to: **Cairo** (5hr., E£300); **Qena** (2hr., E£70); and **Suez** (4hr., E£200).

✷ ❷ ORIENTATION AND PRACTICAL INFORMATION

Paved highways link Hurghada with population centers, but the town itself is remote. Suez lies 410km north at the end of the Gulf of Suez and Cairo is another 130km west. Hurghada extends along the coast in a narrow strip. Downtown Hurghada (known as **Dahar**) lies two kilometers north of **Saqala,** the original fishing town out of which Hurghada grew. Buses and *service* arrive in Dahar, where budget hotels and restaurants await. Saqala has a more authentic Egyptian flavor with plenty of dive shops and cafes but few budget hotels. South of Saqala, the five-star resorts preside over private beaches.

Al-Nasser Rd. begins inland from the coastal road and connects the town and harbor. Almost everything, from the passport office in the north to the bus station in the south, lies along a two-kilometer stretch of this street. Smaller streets to the east of al-Nasser Rd. contain the budget hotels, restaurants, tourist bazaars, and **souq,** all separated from the sea by a sandy mound posing as al-Arish "mountain."

Tourist Office: (☎44 44 20 or 44 44 21), just south of the airport on Corniche Rd. Helpful advice in the poshest tourist office in Egypt. Open Sa-Th 8am-2pm.

Passport Office: (☎44 67 27), on al-Nasser Rd. at the northern edge of town, two kilometers from the bus station. Behind the Red Sea Security Dept. building. Provides visa extensions. Open daily Sa-Th 8am-2pm.

Currency Exchange: National Bank of Egypt, on al-Nasser Rd., 500m north of the bus station. Open Su-Th 8:30am-2pm and 6-9pm. Nearby **Banque Misr** has an **ATM** (V, MC, Cirrus, PLUS links). Open daily 8:30am-2pm and 3-9pm. There's also a **Thomas Cook** in Saqala. Open 8am-5pm.

Police: (☎54 67 23), on al-Nasser Rd., at a bend 900m north of the bus station. The **tourist police** (☎44 77 44) reside past the telephone building on the left.

Pharmacy: Dr. Montaser Rand (☎54 48 90), on Abd al-'Aziz Mustafa St. behind Sherry Hand Restaurant. Open 24hr.

Hospital: The best is **General Hospital of Hurghada** (☎54 67 40), on Sa'id Karin St., around the corner from Three Corners Empire Hotel and on the left. **Ambulance:** ☎54 64 90 or 54 67 40.

Telephones: Office on al-Nasser Rd., on the left after the road turns at the police station. Open 24hr. Send **faxes** (☎/fax 54 88 45) from a hut across from the phone office. To the US or Europe, E£14-20 per page. Open Sa-Th 8am-2pm and 8-10pm.

Post Office: On al-Nasser Rd., 300m north of the bus station on the right. **Poste Restante, EMS,** and orange international phones. Open Sa-Th 8am-2pm.

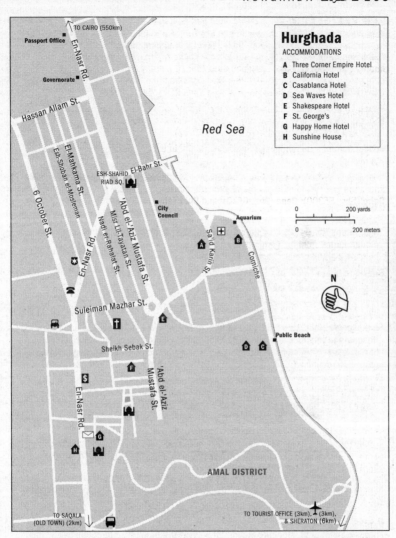

Hurghada
ACCOMMODATIONS

A Three Corner Empire Hotel
B California Hotel
C Casablanca Hotel
D Sea Waves Hotel
E Shakespeare Hotel
F St. George's
G Happy Home Hotel
H Sunshine House

ACCOMMODATIONS

Hurghada is a piaster-pincher's paradise. Watch out for spontaneous price inflation, especially during peak season. Many of the cheaper hotels work with diving
centers and get hefty commissions for the customers they bring. This either means
that you'll be strongly encouraged to dive or snorkel or that you cannot stay in the
hotel unless you book a trip with them. If you plan to dive or snorkel, check the
hotel's prices before taking a room—it is far more convenient to book through
your own hotel than through another establishment. All hotels listed below have
ceiling fans. It's a good idea to reserve a room in the summer.

NEAR THE BEACH

Sea Waves (☎ 54 50 71), across from the public beach. Take a right by the Golden Dolphin Dive Center. Clean rooms, shiny floors, and a cute cafe-style dining room. *Sprechen Sie Deutsch?* They do. Breakfast L£2. Singles E£10; doubles E£20; triples E£30. Add L£5 for private bath.

California Hotel (☎ 54 91 01). Friendly owner Abdul is justifiably proud of his hotel, where guests are livin' it up in cozy muraled rooms. Breakfast included. Singles E£10; doubles E£15; triples E£20; extra for a view or a bathroom. Find yourself California dreamin' on the roof for E£5.

Casablanca (☎ 54 82 92), on Corniche Rd. opposite public beach. Enter through side door of the Cowboy Restaurant and it'll be lookin' at you, kid. Clean, newly remodeled rooms. Guests get 20% discount at Cowboy, but some rooms hear its hee-hawing all night long. Singles E£15; Bogie-'n'-Bacall love the doubles at E£20; triples E£30.

DOWNTOWN

Happy Home Hotel (☎ 54 96 11), on Mosque St. behind the post office. In this day and age, Happy Homes are hard to find. The amiable manager makes sure that this hotel, though farther from the center of town, is where the heart is. Discounts offered at the building's diving center. Singles E£10; doubles E£20; triples E£30.

Sunshine House (☎ 54 74 63), directly across from bus station. Friendly and knowledgeable Hassan arranges snorkeling (E£45, 10% student discount) and night parties on Geftun Island. Well-maintained single-sex bathrooms in hall. Breakfast (eggs sunny-side up, of course) E£2.50. Large 3-bed dorm room E£5 per person; doubles E£15.

Shakespeare Hotel (☎ 44 62 56), at Abd al-'Aziz Mustafa St. and Sa'id Karin-General Hospital St. Tangled in a copse of weather'd trees/This taintless inn entices familys/Its fragrant garden sweetens as it blooms/As do the pink and priveat batheing rooms. Singles E£25; doubles E£35; triples E£45. To A/C or not to A/C (E£6 extra)?

St. George's (☎ 54 82 46), one-and-a-half blocks behind Banque Misr, off al-Nasser St. Charming rooms, a friendly owner, and bathrooms as clean as St. George's conscience. Singles E£15; doubles E£25; triples E£35. Add E£5 for private bath.

🍴 FOOD

In terms of grub, Hurghada is a veritable little Italy. Other than the usual street fare, it appears that the only varieties of food that have made their way to the coasts of the Red Sea are those that migrated here from a boot-shaped peninsula in the Mediterranean.

🏅 **Bella Riviera,** on Abd al-'Aziz Mustafa St., south of the Shakespeare Hotel, is one of Hurghada's best deals, with A/C to boot. Amuse yourself by watching the waiters scamper in and out of the secret door in the wall. Cheap drinks, lasagna (E£3), salads (E£1.25-2.50), and pizzas (E£7-10). Open daily noon-midnight.

Pizzeria Tarbosh (☎ 54 84 56), on Abd al-'Aziz Mustafa St. past the Shakespeare Hotel. No relation to the fez-like hat. Owner 'Amir cooked pizza in Italy and it shows in some of the best crust in Egypt. Over 20 types of pizza served in generous personal pies (E£9-20). Salads E£2.75; meat dishes (E£8). 30% student discount.

Norhan Restaurant, on Sa'id Karin-General Hospital St., between Peanut's Bar and the Shakespeare Hotel. Look for the cheerful green-and-white awning. The pungent *spaghetti basilicum* (E£4.75) is delicious. Open daily 10am-midnight.

Felfela (☎ 44 24 10), south of Saqala on Sheraton Rd., 10min. from Dahar by minibus. This installment of the national chain has the best view in town. Vegetarian-friendly *fuul* (E£2-4) and salads (E£2), as well as meats (E£25). Open daily 9am-12:30am.

◪ DRUNKEN NIGHTS

Just like the reefs, Hurghada's active nightlife attracts creatures of all shapes and sizes. The bars in town are supplemented by the resorts, which have pubs, bars, or nightclubs where you can dance like an Egyptian. **Peanut's Bar,** next to the Three Corners Empire Hotel on Sa'id Karin-General Hospital St. in Dahar, fills its patio every night. The Stellas (E£7.50) may taste good, but the grinning Black Sambo above the door isn't in the best of taste. **Scruples** pub and steak house, on al-Nasser Rd. near the center of town, buzzes and pops with neon lights and beer bottlecaps. Scruples also has a **billiard hall** near the southern end of Abd al-'Aziz Mustafa St. Jive to "world famous" Daoud and his soft-rock cover band at **The Pub,** the Sonesta Hotel's ingeniously named joint. **Kalaboush Disco** (☎ 54 50 87), at the Arabella Hotel on Corniche Rd., is a popular club with a special theme every night.

◉ SUNKEN SIGHTS

DRY AND MIGHTY. Landlubbers rejoice! Hurghada's underwater splendor can now be enjoyed without even getting your feet wet. Aspiring Captain Nemos can go a couple of leagues under in the **Sinbad Submarine** (☎ 44 46 88). US$50 buys a seat aboard a real 44-person sub for a one-hour undersea voyage. Many of the larger hotels run **glass-bottom boat tours** (E£15-20 per hr.). Make reservations for either at any luxury hotel or over the phone. Get an inkling of the subaquatic splendors at the **Hurghada Aquarium,** which features a variety of fish accompanied by remarkably informative descriptions. (Open daily 9am-11pm. E£5.)

ON YOUR MARK, GET WET, GO! There are a variety of beaches to choose from around Hurghada. **Public beaches** next to the Geisum Hotel and the port in Saqala are the smelliest and most packed. Local rumor has it that sand is buried beneath all the dirt. Women will undoubtedly feel uncomfortable here if they choose to bare anything more than toes. Head to the hotels for more liberal bathing fashions. Just north of the public beach downtown, the **Shedwan, Three Corners,** and **Sand Beach Hotels** all open their beaches and pools to non-guests for E£15; **Geisum Hotel** charges E£10. **Shellghada Beach,** just before the Sheraton, charges E£10 for a day on their soft sand and use of their showers. These beaches can be reached by minibus (E£1 from Saqala) or taxi (E£5-10).

◪ DIVING DELIGHTS

Hurghada's real attractions are silent and submerged. Red Sea creatures will astound you with their array of colors, shapes, and sizes. Buck-toothed trigger fish, iridescent parrot fish, rays with blue polka dots, sea cucumbers, giant clams, and a million others star in this briny show. The shimmering, variegated blues of Hurghada's waters have been spared the terrors of oil exploration (see **Sinai: Underwater Tips,** p. 172, for information on snorkeling and scuba diving).

GEFTUN ISLAND. There are a few reefs you can reach without a boat, including one near the Sheraton, but to reach Hurghada's most brilliant aquatic scenery you must take a barge. Hotels offer an all-day trip to Geftun Island, usually including two one-hour snorkeling stops near the island and a fish meal prepared on board. Most hotels advertise the trip at E£40, though some charge E£30-35; you may be able to bargain to as low as E£25. Some Geftun-bound boats are as crammed as cattle cars and stop only once for snorkeling.

SNORKELING. Snorkeling from a dive-boat might give you access to better underwater sights but is a bit more expensive. However, the best reefs are north of Hurghada. The northern waters aren't shielded by islands like the southern ones, so calm weather is a must in order to go. To save money, a group can make independent arrangements with a boat owner—perhaps a fisherman in Saqala—or

E G Y P T

with one of the sea-trip offices around town. One possibility is to go to Geftun and see different reefs; another is to organize an overnight trip (E£60-90 per person, including meals). Excursions to other locales can be less crowded and cheaper. For information, talk to Sayad of **Sunshine Dive Center** (☎ 54 51 13), on al-Nasser Rd., between the post office and bus station; Muhammad of **Red Sea Wonderland,** next to Happy Home Hotel; or Mahmoud of **Golden Dolphin Dive Center** (☎ 54 43 54), opposite the public beach. Rent your own gear (E£10-15 per day for mask, snorkel, and fins) at any office in town. ISIC or IYTC (GO 25) discounts are available.

SCUBA DIVING. While Hurghada may have some of the best scuba diving in Egypt, it also has some of the worst dive shops. Not all of the dive shops that have sprung up to profit on rising tourism have all that much experience. Choose your dive shop carefully, and be sure to check your instructor's or guide's certification and experience, as well as the ship's gear, especially its emergency equipment. Dive shops that are members of HEPCA, a marine protection organization, are often more environmentally conscious underwater. One well-established and professional dive center is **Subex,** between the Luxor and California Hotels. It offers open water dive certification for US$445; most smaller centers charge US$250 for the same. Choose carefully—save your life before your money.

NILE VALLEY وادى النيل

How doth the little crocodile
Improve his shining tail
And pour the waters of the Nile
On every Golden Scale.
　—Lewis Carroll

Originating at the equatorial high water marks of Lake Victoria and Lake Taru, the Nile winds north through Uganda, Ethiopia, and the Sudan, pouring into Lake Nasser and Egypt, where its banks are home to 95% of the country's millions.

Before the construction of the Aswan High Dam in 1971, the Nile overflowed its banks every year, depositing the rich silt that made the valley the most fertile region in the world. This yearly inundation was the most important time of the year for ancient Egyptians, and the reason why much ancient religion focused on the river's cycles. No major temple along the length of the Nile Valley was without a **nilometer,** a graded pit used to measure and predict the river's depth. For millions of ancient Egyptians, no oracle could have been more influential.

The region between Cairo and Luxor is known as **Middle Egypt,** home to the majority of the country's Copts. Akhenaton built his capital at Tel al-Amarna; farther south stand the temples at Abydos and Dendera. Luxor marks the northern boundary of **Upper Egypt,** stretching upstream (south) to Lake Nasser and the Sudanese border. Tourists flock here to see the underground maze of ancient architecture on Luxor's West Bank and imposing temples at Edfu and Abu Simbel.

In the summertime, temperatures average over 45°C, frequently breaking 50°C. This is *a bit* warm, but the complete lack of humidity makes it possible to continue most essential biological processes even as the sand slowly drips into beads of glass. Hoteliers, guides, and others of their ilk are desperate for business in the summer, so bargain hard. To avoid the heat, plan most of your touring for between 6 and 11am; to avoid the crowds, shoot for late afternoon. In November through May, the temperature drops and prices rise.

GETTING THERE AND AROUND

BY SERVICE, BUSES, AND TRAINS. Traveling by *service* is the cheapest and most convenient option for shuttling between the river towns at almost any time of day. The Egyptian police insist, however, that tourists travel at certain times

HIGHLIGHTS OF THE NILE VALLEY

Don't miss the massive **Luxor** (p. 217) and **Karnak** (p. 219) Temples in Luxor.

Tired of temples? Two bad: the cream of the crop are the twin **Temple of Hathor** at Dendera (p. 231) and **Temple of Horus** at Edfu (p. 235). A **felucca cruise** from Aswan lets you see them in style (for more information on *feluccas*, see p. 209).

Aswan is famous for its immense **High Dam** (p. 237), but the most stunning constructions lie south at **Abu Simbel** (p. 250).

with police convoys. *Service* drivers may refuse to take you without an official escort, fearing that they may have to turn back. Out of Aswan or Luxor, the only option may be the public bus. In any case, you'll also need nerves of steel to cope with the apparent insanity of the drivers. **Buses** are often slightly cheaper than *service*. They run more frequently, but can be horribly slow, hot, and unreliable. Most stop running at 6pm. Buses are best for transport out of Luxor or Aswan, where you can reserve the air-conditioned buses by going to the station a day or two in advance. In the smaller towns between, you may not find an empty seat, and schedule reliability plummets. **Trains** can be a hassle for short trips, but first- or second-class air-conditioned compartments are a great value for the entire Luxor-Aswan haul or for more distant sights north of Luxor. Authorities discourage tourists from taking third-class trains. See listings in **Luxor** (p. 212) and **Aswan** (p. 238) for more specific information.

OVERLAND TRAVEL ADVISORY. As of summer 2000, the Egyptian and US governments strongly discourage any surface travel through Middle Egypt. There is a massive police and military presence in the area, making visits unpleasant and ill-advised. *Let's Go* heeded the warnings of the US State Department and Egyptian Ministry of Tourism and did not send a researcher to sights or cities between Beni Suef and Sohag this year. Travel to Abydos and Dendera, though permitted, will come with a mandatory police convoy.

BY NILE CRUISER. Tough times for tourism in Egypt have opened up an option for budget travelers on a binge: the **Nile Cruiser.** Book a cabin on a triple-decker, pool-topped cruise ship and slip from Luxor to Aswan or vice versa (one-way is two nights), hobnobbing with French tourists the whole way. Travel agents can book for you at a mark-up (US$45-50 per night) or you can go to the dock yourself and chat with the boat receptionist about open cabins (as low as US$35 a night). The air-conditioned, two-room suites come complete with TVs, showers, and uniquely Egyptian bedsheet service. All meals are included, but drinks are extra pricey. A *kalish* will cart you to the temple and back at each stop. Several travel agents (including Eastmar and Misr Travel) dot the corniche south of the Winter Palace in Luxor. In Aswan, agencies can be found around the southern end of the corniche. If you find a bargain, you'll enjoy two days of pure bliss: sunning by the pool and watching the palms float by, interrupted only to for daily feedings.

BY FELUCCA. For those on tight budgets who want the experience of drifting down the Nile, a **felucca** cruise is a slow-paced way to absorb the Egyptian countryside and regain sanity after days in overcrowded *service*. *Feluccas* have been sailing the Nile for thousands of years—and *felucca* scams have been going on for at least that long. The more careful you are in navigating the crowded docks, the more carefree you can be while your captain navigates down the river.

Felucca means boat in Nubian. The typical Nile-cruising variety sleeps up to eight people, has a single tall mast with a characteristically angled boom, and is piloted by an English-speaking Arab or Nubian Egyptian. When traveling alone, gather a group of like-minded tourists (aim for six) in hotel lobbies or the many restaurants along the Nile. You can also ask at the tourist office (a good resource throughout the *felucca* planning process). As a last resort, join a group already assembled by a captain. Be sure to meet these people beforehand, or you may find yourself stuck in a horrifying Middle Eastern version of MTV's *Road Rules*.

Officially, members of a six-to-eight-person group leaving Aswan pay E£30 each to Kom Ombo (one day, one night), E£50 to Edfu (three days, two nights), E£55 to Esna (four days, three nights), and E£65 to Luxor (five days, four nights). As of August 2000, *feluccas* were not allowed in Luxor—all stopped in Edfu. Most captains add E£5 per day for food and water and a E£5 registration fee. For registration in Aswan, the captain will ask for your passport and the E£5. Have an assembled group ready, or the captain may try to keep your passports as collateral until he can corral other passengers. Prices don't vary much from captain to captain, so the most important variable is the vibe you get. The quick trip to Kom Ombo cuts the adventure short, but most find the voyage to Edfu just right.

TIPS ON TRAVELING BY FELUCCA

CHOOSE THE CAPTAIN ON YOUR OWN
From the moment you step off the train in Aswan, you will be constantly approached by *felucca* captains or, more often, middlemen sent out to round up suckers. Every hotel manager and every man in the local *ahwa* has his favorite *felucca* captain (from whom he receives a commission), so the word on the street is almost useless. Commission-charging hotels, even if they don't add to the price of the trip, will take money away from your captain who may then be inclined to cut corners on the trip to make up for his losses.

LOOK FOR EXPERIENCED CAPTAINS
Go down to the river yourself, meet and talk with several captains, inspect several boats, and take a list of potential candidates to the tourist office to make sure they aren't pirates or perverts. Ask to see comment books and talk to fellow travelers. Check for lifejackets. Be skeptical of any cute nicknames the captain uses (the "Most Inappropriate Boat Captain Nickname Award" goes to Captain Titanic)—an honest captain will tell you his real name if asked. Also be wary of captains who speak little English: these typically younger captains often lack the experience necessary to handle sailing emergencies (several capsizings in recent years have been caused by high winds and inept sailors). You're better off with a gnarled, salty old man who speaks English well (if a bit colorfully) than with some wet-behind-the-ears pollywog who is just learning the ropes. If you decide to back out of a trip or switch captains, you should receive a full refund, minus E£10-15 if your *felucca* captain has already bought food.

PRE-ARRANGE THE FINAL DESTINATION
Make sure that the captain clearly understands the final stop. For example, many *felucca* trips to Edfu actually stop at a way-station 40km from a town where pre-arranged microbuses take passengers the rest of the way. Captains are tempted to stay close to home to save themselves a time-consuming return against the current. Unscrupulous boatsmen have been known to drop their passengers off without mentioning such arrangements, claiming that it was "close enough."

CHECK YOUR PROVISIONS
Choose a captain who takes care of the cooking. An extra-special captain who cooks Nubian dishes in the *felucca* or stops at his village for a home-cooked meal is a godsend. A captain should also bring at least two cartons of bottled water; make sure it is aboard before you depart and check that the tabs are sealed, as they may be filled with tap water. In addition, bring at least three bottles of water per person per day for drinking, cooking, and brewing tea. You can also ask for a big jerry can of tap water to be brought along to be used instead of the Nile for washing dishes and faces. Those looking for more exciting libations should know that beer can be procured at the liquor store on the corniche.

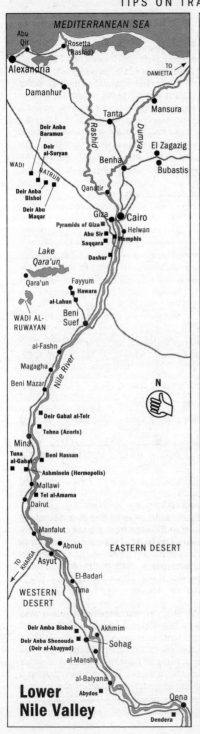

Lower Nile Valley

MEDITERRANEAN SEA

Abu Qir
Rosetta (Rashid)
TO DAMIETTA
Alexandria
Damanhur
Tanta
Mansura
Rashid
Dumyat
El Zagazig
Deir Anba Baramus
Deir al-Suryan
WADI
Benha
Bubastis
NATRUN
Deir Anba Bishoi
Qanatir
Deir Abu Maqar
Giza
Cairo
Pyramids of Giza
Abu Sir
Helwan
Saqqara
Memphis
Dashur
Lake Qara'un
Fayyum
Qara'un
Hawara
al-Lahun
WADI AL-RUWAYAN
Beni Suef
al-Fashn
Magagha
Nile River
Beni Mazar
Deir Gabal al-Teir
Tehna (Acoris)
Mina
Tuna al-Gabal
Beni Hassan
Ashmunein (Hermopolis)
Mallawi
Tel al-Amarna
Dairut
Manfalut
Abnub
EASTERN DESERT
TO KHARGA
Asyut
El-Badari
Tima
WESTERN DESERT
Deir Amba Bishoi
Akhmim
Deir Anba Shenouda (Deir al-Abayyad)
Sohag
al-Mansha
al-Balyana
Abydos
Qena
Dendera

Upper Nile Valley

0   75 miles
0   75 kilometers

N

Hurghada
al-Balyana
Qena
Dendera
Qus
Naqada
Valley of the Kings
Karnak
Deir el-Medina
Luxor
Armant
EASTERN DESERT
TO KHARGA
Esna
El-Kab
Edfu
Nile River
Gebel Es-Silsilah
Kom Ombo
Daraw
Aswan
Elephantine Island
Philae
Kalabsha
Aswan High Dam
Beit al-Wali
WESTERN DESERT
Lake Nasser
al-Sibu
Abu Simbel
EGYPT
SUDAN
Lake Nubia

EGYPT

HAVE FUN

Though *felucca* cruises can be dangerous, many captains are reputable; trips should ease your worries, not aggravate them. Choose wisely and have fun.

LUXOR الاقصر ☎095

This ancient capital of Upper and Lower Egypt still humbles visitors three millennia after the height of its power. Luxor is built on the site of *Ta Ipet* (known by its Greek name, Thebes), and flexed its influential muscles during the five-century rule of the New Kingdom (18th-20th dynasties, from 1539-1075 BCE). Egypt's ancient history is more tangible here than anywhere else in the Nile Valley, and droves of tourists come to marvel at its sandstone temples and mysterious tombs. Unfortunately, the tourism industry has spawned a society of ruthless hoteliers, greedy guides, and cunning cabdrivers; be wary of anyone who uses the word "free" in Luxor. With proper bargaining, however, only a few pounds a day can net refreshing accommodations, satisfying cuisine, and access to unforgettable sights.

⊠ GETTING THERE AND AWAY

Flights: The airport is 8km northeast of town (no bus; taxi E£10-15) and is served by **EgyptAir** (☎38 05 80), next to the Old Winter Palace Hotel. Flights to: **Aswan** (3 per day, E£190); **Cairo** (1hr.; 3-5 per day, in winter up to 11 per day; E£360); **Hurghada** (seasonal, E£265); and **Sharm al-Sheikh** (3 per week, E£347). While it is possible to purchase tickets at the EgyptAir branch at the airport (☎38 05 86 or 38 05 89), it is not recommended. Tickets to international destinations must be purchased in Luxor.

Trains: The train station (☎37 20 18) is at the head of al-Mahatta St., 750m inland from Luxor Temple. Lockers E£1.25 per day. Trains to **Aswan** are less comfortable than *service* or *feluccas* (3hr.; 7:30am and 5:30pm; first-class E£20-22, A/C 2nd-class E£12-14; students first-class E£13-15, 2nd-class E£9-11). For their protection, tourists are restricted to two express trains to **Cairo** (8-10hr.; 8:30am and 11:30pm; first-class E£51, A/C 2nd-class E£31). Cairo trains are especially crowded. Reserve sleeper cars one day in advance. Walk on for a fee; reserve a seat to be safe.

Buses: The bus station is by the exit of Karnak Temple. Buses to: **Aswan** (4½hr., 9 per day 7am-8pm, E£6.50-10); **Cairo** (11-12hr., 7pm, A/C E£51); and **Hurghada** (5 per day 6am-8pm, E£13-21). All of the above stop at **Esna** (1hr., E£3); **Edfu** (1½hr., E£7); **Kom Ombo** (3hr., E£10); **Kharga** (M, W, Sa 8:30am; E£18); and **Suez** (4 per day 6:30am-7pm, E£14-19). Hours and rates change frequently.

Service: Off al-Karnak St., one block inland from the Luxor Museum. Early morning and late afternoon *service* leave when full, usually about every 15min. Out-of-town trips must be made with police convoys. Daily convoys to points south leave from al-Baghdadi Point (3km south of the Old Winter Palace Hotel on al-Nil St.) at 7, 11am, and 3pm. Convoys to points north leave from beside the Hotel Pola, off al-Karnak St. (6, 8am, 2, 5pm). *Service* to: **Aswan** (3-4hr., E£9); **al-Balyana** (2hr., E£5); **Edfu** (2hr., E£4); **Esna** (1hr., E£2.50); **Kom Ombo** (2½hr., E£7); and **Qena** (1hr., E£3). Less frequent departures from a station on the west bank where the local ferry docks.

Bike Rental: on al-Mahatta and Television St., or ask at a hotel (E£5-7 per day). **Motorbikes** at the Sherif Hotel and Everest Hotel on Television St. (E£50-60 per day; no helmets). To visit the West Bank sites on motorbike, take a ferry in front of Luxor Temple.

✴ ORIENTATION

Luxor lies on the eastern bank of the Nile, 670km upstream from Cairo and 220km downstream from Aswan. Surrounded by a heavily cultivated floodplain, the city is an agricultural area, with a farmers' *souq* on Tuesdays. The city can be divided into three sectors: Luxor city, the village of Karnak a few kilometers north, and Thebes on the west bank. Finding your way around Luxor is easy as long as you know the main thoroughfares. **Al-Mahatta St.** (Sta-

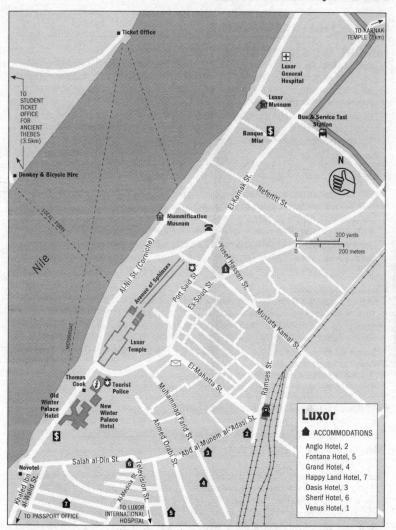

Luxor

ACCOMMODATIONS

Anglo Hotel, 2
Fontana Hotel, 5
Grand Hotel, 4
Happy Land Hotel, 7
Oasis Hotel, 3
Sherif Hotel, 6
Venus Hotel, 1

tion St.) runs perpendicular to the Nile. The **train station** is on this street, 750m inland on the eastern edge of Luxor. Exit the train station at a 45-degree angle on the left and you will eventually reach **Television St.**, where signs advertising the many budget hotels and pensions in town appear. **Al-Nil St.** (the corniche) runs southward along the river, turning into Khalid ibn al-Walid St. past the Novotel. The **service station** is at the exit of Luxor Temple. **Al-Karnak St.** begins just north of the temple and runs parallel to the corniche slightly inland. **Luxor Temple** is on the corniche at the center of town, and **Karnak Temple** is three kilometers farther, one block inland from the corniche.

You can get around Luxor by foot, though a ride to Karnak Temple can be a pleasure. **Kalishes** are good for baggage transport or a relaxing trip out to Karnak (E£5). The cheapest and quickest transportation in the city is by **minibus** (25pt). The most common route is al-Karnak St. to al-Mahatta St. to Television St.

🛈 PRACTICAL INFORMATION

TOURIST AND FINANCIAL SERVICES

Tourist Office: (☎ 37 22 15 or 37 32 94), left of the New Winter Palace Hotel. Open daily (including Ramadan) 8am-8pm. Additional branches at the **train station** (☎ 37 02 59; open daily 8am-8pm) and **airport** (☎ 37 23 06). Low on free and useful literature, but the one in the bazaar has bus and train schedules with price listings.

Passport Office: (☎ 38 08 85), on the left of Khalid ibn al-Walid St., one kilometer south of the Novotel, near the Isis Hotel. Visas extended in the foreigners' office. Open Sa-Th 8:30am-2:30pm; Ramadan 9am-2pm.

Currency Exchange: Available in most hotels on the corniche, and at the **National Bank of Egypt,** also on the corniche, 50m south of the Old Winter Palace Hotel. Offers cash advances on V, MC. Open daily 8:30am-2pm and 6-10pm.

ATM: Outside the two branches of **Banque Misr,** one on the northern terminus of Television St. and another a block inland from the corniche, a street north of the Mercure Hotel. A third **ATM** is outside the Gaddis Hotel on Khalid ibn al-Walid St., just across from the Isis Hotel. Both accept V, MC, AmEx, PLUS, and Cirrus.

American Express: (☎ 37 83 33; ☎/fax 37 28 62), on al-Nil St. in front of the Old Winter Palace Hotel, south of Luxor Temple. Holds mail, sells traveler's checks, and wires and exchanges money and checks. Open daily 8am-7pm.

LOCAL SERVICES

English-Language Bookstore: 'Aboudi Bookshop has three locations in the tourist bazaar complex on al-Nil St. Good but costly Egyptology books, countless sappy romances, and a few paperbacks in English, French, and German. Open daily 8am-10pm. Kiosks in front of tourist bazaar and in the train station sell foreign periodicals.

Swimming Pools: Beat the heat by the rooftop pool of the **Emilio Hotel,** down the street from the Venus Hotel, for E£8. Small but pleasant pools accessible for E£10 at the **St. Joseph** (on Khalid ibn al-Walid St.), the **Shady** (on Television St.), and the **Luxor Wena Hotel** (on the corniche), including unlimited rounds of billiards and backgammon.

EMERGENCY AND COMMUNICATIONS

Emergency: ☎ 123.

Police: ☎ 122. The police station is off al-Karnak St., 200m north of Luxor Temple.

Tourist Police: (☎ 38 31 11), in the tourist bazaar on al-Nil St. and train station (☎ 37 38 45). Both open 24hr.

Late-Night Pharmacy: 24hr. duty rotates—try asking a hotel employee. **Rania Pharmacy** (☎ 37 12 86), at the north end of Television St., is well-stocked with Egyptian medication and basic toiletries. Open daily 8am-midnight. **El-Manshia,** on Abd al-Munem al-Adasi St., has mostly medication. Open daily 7:30am-noon.

Hospitals: Luxor International Hospital (☎ 38 71 92), on the southern end of Television St., is a newly opened, modern facility that accepts cash, credit cards, and medical insurance. The **Luxor Public Hospital** (☎ 37 20 25 or 37 28 09), on al-Nil St. north of the museum, is a definite step down from the Luxor International. Cash only.

Telephones: Central Telephone Office, off al-Karnak St. to the west, just north of Luxor Temple. Open 24hr. Other less crowded offices are on al-Nil St. in front of the Old Winter Palace Hotel (the cheapest **fax** services in the city are here) and in the train station. Both offices open 6am-8pm. Hotels may charge twice as much as telephone offices. **Directory Assistance:** ☎ 16.

Internet Access: 'Aboudi Internet Cafe (☎ 37 23 90; email aboudi@Access.com.eg), on the 2nd floor of the 'Aboudi Bookshop on al-Nil St. just south of the Luxor Temple. E£15 per hr.; refreshments E£2. Open daily 9am-10:30pm.

Post Office: On al-Mahatta St., 100m east of Luxor Temple. Offers **Poste Restante** and **EMS** services. Open Su-Th 8am-3pm. EMS open 8am-noon. Other branches near the tourist office and in the train station. Open daily 8am-noon and 2:30-8pm. Passport required to pick up a letter or package.

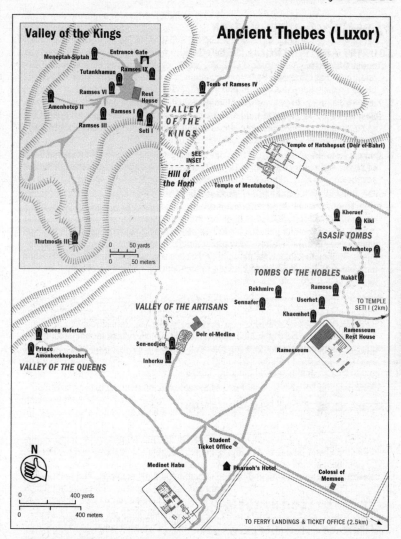

Ancient Thebes (Luxor)

Valley of the Kings

Meneptah-Siptah
Entrance Gate
Tutankhamun
Ramses IX
Ramses VI
Rest House
Amenhotep II
Ramses I
Ramses III
Seti I

VALLEY OF THE KINGS

SEE INSET

Hill of the Horn

Thutmosis III

0   50 yards
0   50 meters

Tomb of Ramses IV

Temple of Hatshepsut (Deir el-Bahri)

Temple of Mentuhotep

Kheruef
Kiki

ASASIF TOMBS

Neferhotep

TOMBS OF THE NOBLES

Nakht
Rekhmire
Ramose
Userhet
Sennafer
Khaemhet

VALLEY OF THE ARTISANS

TO TEMPLE SETI I (2km)

Queen Nefertari
Deir el-Medina
Sen-nedjem
Prince Amonherkhepeshef
Inherku

VALLEY OF THE QUEENS

Ramesseum
Ramesseum Rest House

N

0   400 yards
0   400 meters

Student Ticket Office

Medinet Habu
Pharaoh's Hotel
Colossi of Memnon

TO FERRY LANDINGS & TICKET OFFICE (2.5km)

EGYPT

ACCOMMODATIONS

EAST BANK (MODERN LUXOR)

If you come to Luxor by train, you will disembark into a writhing mass of arms waving hotel cards. Decide where you want to go and stick to your guns. Many hawkers will quote incorrect prices or tell you the hotel you have in mind is full or shut down. *Kalish* drivers may take you to a different hotel from the one you requested, assuming tourists don't know any better or are too tired to complain. Demand to be taken to your hotel or withhold payment. Women traveling alone can almost bet on sexual overtures from employees in many of the small hotels. If a refusal doesn't do the trick, complain to the manager or the tourist police.

For the most part, however, lodgings in Luxor can be a treat; air-conditioning comes quite cheap and there are ample opportunities for hard-core bargaining.

Imagine a person with a lollipop for a head—this would be an accurate depiction of someone who takes a hotelier's first price. Shop around and enjoy the wildly exaggerated accounts of just how much a breakfast costs the owner. Those traveling in groups of three or four and those with patience will be rewarded. A roof or terrace mattress may be available (E£3-4). Most budget hotels cluster around Television St. and Yusef Hassan St.

■ **Venus Hotel** (☎37 26 25), on Yusef Hassan St. Convenient but sometimes hectic, with clean, tiled rooms and large windows. "Mars Bar" on the 2nd floor features pool table, foosball, satellite TV, and cheap drinks (Stella E£6). All rooms with A/C and bath. Breakfast included. Singles E£25; doubles E£30; triples E£40.

■ **Fontana Hotel** (☎38 06 63), off Television St. Gorgeous bathrooms with towels and toilet paper and super-clean rooms (try to get one with a balcony). Breakfast included. Singles with fan E£8, with A/C E£10; doubles with fan E£10, with A/C E£15; small triples with bath and A/C E£24; prices E£10 higher in winter.

■ **Happy Land Hotel** (☎37 18 28), about 150m off al-Medina St., a few blocks past the intersection with Television St. (look for the huge sign). The owner will go to great lengths to demonstrate his establishment's nearly obsessive cleanliness, although the commission he pays *service* to dump tour groups here makes him a bit stiffer on the prices. Rooftop restaurant has polished service and a real, hearty breakfast. Books trips to Dahab for E£85. A/C dorms E£7.50; singles with fan and bath E£15; doubles with fan and bath E£20, with A/C E£25.

Anglo Hotel (☎38 16 79), in the alley directly to the left of the train station. This well-heeled hotel comes with wide beds and piped-in muzak at the touch of a button. A/C. Breakfast included. Singles E£15, with bath E£20; doubles E£25, with bath E£30.

Oasis Hotel (☎38 16 99), on Muhammad Farid St. Clean, but aging rooms are plenty big; the bathrooms could use a restoration. Sometimes pushy about tours. Breakfast included. Dorm beds with fan E£6; singles with bath and A/C E£10; doubles with bath and A/C E£15; triples with bath and A/C E£18.

Sherif Hotel (☎37 07 57; email khaeli@hotmail.com), on Badr St., first right off Television St. Bob Marley's image, music, and habits thrive in this friendly establishment. Some rooms recently renovated, but old ones still a bit dusty. Singles with bath E£9; doubles E£16, with A/C and bath E£20; triples E£22, with A/C and bath E£27.

Grand Hotel (☎38 29 05), on Muhammad Farid St. Less frequented by travelers, the dusky Grand is a bit out of the way, but quiet. Sizeable rooms have seen better days. Beware the markups on the tours lest ye be ripped off. Breakfast E£3.50. Singles with fan E£7; doubles with bath and fan E£10, with A/C E£20; extra beds E£3 each.

WEST BANK (ANCIENT THEBES)

It is generally more convenient to sleep on the East Bank in Luxor proper, but the West Bank offers quiet surroundings and the chance to roll out of bed and into the Theban necropolis at the opening bell. A taxi from the ferry docks (E£5) is the only practical way to get to hotels unless you can manage to bike it with a pack. For information on crossing the Nile, see **Sightseeing Strategy**, p. 222. The **Pharaoh's Hotel,** farther down the same unpaved road as the ticket office, is this area's best hotel, with carpeted rooms and a flowery garden. When business is slow, prices may skyrocket; insist that you know better. Rooms come with A/C, bath, and breakfast. (☎31 07 02. Singles E£40; doubles E£80; triples E£120.)

▗ FOOD

Luxor may be an archaeologist's paradise, but it's purgatory for the frugal gourmet. Two *kushari* houses stand out from the pack: **Sayyida Zeinab** (Television St.) and **Sayyida Nafisa** (Yusef Hassan St.). The **coffee shop** in the New Winter Palace has a paltry but cheap all-you-can-eat dessert buffet (E£16). A **liquor store** on Ramses St. is directly to the right as you leave the train station on al-Mahatta St. (Open daily 8am-2pm and 5-11pm.) Pension managers can also procure beer for you.

A big drawback to staying on the West Bank is its lack of decent, cheap restaurants. **Tutankhamun** and **Africa** next to the ferry landing offer the usual chicken and kebab dinners (E£15-20). Most hotels have restaurants, but they're often closed and the quality is inconsistent, especially when business is slow in the summer.

▨ **Mish Mish** (☎38 11 89), on Television St., across from El-Houda. A big hit with travelers, and with good reason. Ridiculously large pasta dishes E£3-5. Possibly the best spaghetti bolognaise this side of the Gulf of Suez. Open daily 10:30am-midnight.

Amoun Restaurant (☎37 05 47), just north of the Luxor Temple. A favorite spot among locals and tourists alike, serving a variety of western dishes. Pizza starts at E£7, entrees average E£10. Open daily 8am-midnight.

Restaurant Khased Khear (☎38 45 80), on Abd al-Moneim al-Adasi St. (al-Manshia St.), one block from the train station. The cozy and cool wood-paneled interior has a nautical feel, but there's as much seafood as there are sea chanties. Instead, the specialty (thankfully) is kebab. Take-out available. Open daily 11am-1am.

Oriental Foods, next to Chicken Hut on the intersection of al-Mahatta St. and Port Said St. Doesn't really serve "oriental" food; in fact, not really a restaurant at all, but the best place to get falafel subs or *fuul* sandwiches (E£0.50 each), bar none. Open 11am-1am.

Abu al-Hasan (☎38 53 27), on the corner of Abd al-Moneim al-Adasi St. and Muhammad Farid St., near the Oasis Hotel. This two-story behemoth serves up sizeable dishes of budget fare over this lively intersection. Two-egg omelettes (E£3.50) get the job done when hotel breakfasts fall short. Open daily 8am-midnight.

The Classic Restaurant (☎38 17 07), on Khalid ibn al-Walid St.; look for the large yellow sign near the passport office. Perfect for a well-deserved meal after conquering Thebes (especially if mild heat stroke has loosened the grip on your wallet). This classy establishment offers a delectable menu and proper service. Steaks and kebab (E£20-30) are excellent. Four-course meal E£24. Open daily 6pm-midnight. V, MC, AmEx.

El-Houda, on Television St. Friendly staff and surprisingly diverse menu. Six-course value meals are a great bargain at E£15, but you can also get pizza (E£6), chicken curry (E£6.50), *shish tawouq* (E£8), or a chicken quarter (E£6). Open daily 11am-11pm.

EAST BANK

Luxor has two major temples and two museums. **Luxor Temple** (p. 217) stands in the heart of the city adjacent to the Nile. Its lighting and late hours make it perfect for a first date. Going north along al-Nil St., the **Mummification Museum** (p. 221) and the small but excellent **Luxor Museum of Ancient Egyptian Art** (p. 221) house sculptures and artifacts unearthed at Karnak and elsewhere. **Karnak Temple** (p. 219), the Leviathan of pharaonic architecture, sprawls just a few kilometers farther north. Karnak Temple is best seen early in the morning before the sun is high, while the museums are perfect for an afternoon cool-off.

LUXOR TEMPLE

Enter on the al-Nil St. side 400m north of the New Winter Palace. The temple and its well-groomed lawns are an especially comfortable retreat at night (lights go on at 7pm year-round). Open daily 6am-10pm; in winter 6am-9pm. E£20, students E£10.

Although Karnak gets all the glory, Luxor Temple is grand in its own right and much more comprehensible to the visitor than the more northerly temple. Most of Luxor Temple was built around 1380 BCE by Amenhotep III atop a Middle Kingdom site. Significant portions were erected by famous pharaohs from Ramses II to Tutankhamun, each striving to make his mark. Luxor Temple was meant to serve as a **love nest for the Gods.** Once a year, during the Opet festival, the statues of Amun and his consort Mut would be taken from Karnak temple and loaded onto a sacred boat. Amidst much rejoicing and beer drinking, the happy couple was carried on the shoulders of priests to the Luxor Temple, where they spent 24 days and nights together in the sanctuary. During this time, the moon god Khonsu was conceived, completing the Theban triad (see **Meet the Gods,** p. 69).

Later work on the temple was done by Ramses II, who built the enormous **First Pylon,** nearly 24m tall and 65m wide. The pylon is inscribed with images of Ramses II smiting the Hittites. In front of the pylon stand three of the six original **Colossi of Ramses II,** two seated and one standing. A red granite obelisk flanks the doorway; its twin was given to France in 1831 and now graces the Place de la Concorde in Paris. The granite statues of the **Court of Ramses II,** past the pylon, originally portrayed Amenhotep, but were altered when ancient Egypt's favorite egomaniac assumed the throne. Continue through the court's papyrus columns to the **Colonnade of Amenhotep III,** where the columns have open lotus crowns. Tutankhamun had the walls of the colonnade inscribed with scenes from the festival of Opet. From here, proceed into the **Court of Amenhotep III.** Beyond this court rises the hypostyle hall, or antechamber, and its 22 gigantic columns. The Egyptian government is currently spending E£9 million restoring these columns, whose foundations crumbled when the construction of the Aswan High Dam raised the water level in the area (see **Moving a Mountain,** p. 251).

Latin inscriptions to Julius Caesar adorn an altar in a room to the left of the pillared hall. Alexander himself had the *bas-reliefs* (in which he appears in pharaonic attire before Amun and other deities) added when he built the **Sanctuary of Alexander the Great** at the end of the corridor. Fertility god Min receives disproportionate attention in the sanctuary. The Romans used the whole temple as a *castrum* (military camp) in the 4th century CE. The excavation of the temple remains incomplete because the Mosque of Abu al-Haggag, added by the Fatimids in 1077 CE and still in use today, prevents work on the left-hand gallery: only the end portions of the Avenue of the Sphinxes (the three-kilometer road connecting the Luxor and Karnak Temples), have been unearthed and restored.

MUMMIFICATION MUSEUM
North of Luxor Temple (100m) on the bank of the Nile. ☎38 15 02. Open daily 9am-1pm and 5-10pm; in winter 9am-1pm and 4-9pm. E£20. Free lectures (occasionally in English) on recent discoveries in the Luxor area (Th 7pm).

This new Nile-side museum gives an insightful view into the meticulous and often misunderstood process of mummification. The 66 artifacts on display (65 of which were taken from the Egyptian Museum in Cairo) range from sophisticated surgical instruments to a mummified menagerie consisting of a monkey, goose, and crocodile, and a cat in a Pez-dispenser-shaped coffin.

LUXOR MUSEUM OF ANCIENT EGYPTIAN ART
A 15-minute walk north of Luxor Temple on al-Nil St. Open daily 9am-1pm and 5-10pm; in winter 9am-1pm and 4-9pm. E£30, students E£15. Wheelchair accessible.

The Luxor Museum has arguably the most edifying collection of antiquities in Egypt—a testament to the fact that less is sometimes more. Unlike the heaps of objects squeezed into Cairo's Egyptian Museum (see p. 122), the treasures here have multilingual descriptions (including the original site and probable date of each subject) and the exhibits have been thoughtfully arranged with the help of the Brooklyn Museum of New York. The recreated **mural** of 283 sandstone blocks on the second floor was found within the Karnak Temple, and depicts Akhenaton and Nefertiti in adoration of the sun god Aton along with numerous artisans and peasants at work. The gallery also includes smaller artifacts such as drinking vessels, precious jewelry, bronze statuettes, and Alexandrian period coins from the 2nd century CE. The **New Hall** was built to display the cache of 16 marble and granite statues found in the 1980s beneath Luxor Temple. The most handsome statue is the red granite likeness of Amenhotep III (1405-1367 BCE).

MUMMY DEAREST The ancient Egyptians wanted to live forever, so they had to be certain their bodies were fit for the long haul of the afterlife. In pre-dynastic times, people were buried in simple pits in the sand. The heat and arid conditions dried the bodies out and prevented decay. As civilization advanced, efforts were made to provide for a person's comfort in the afterlife. Elaborate tombs served to speed decay, separating the corpse from the drying sands; the process of mummification was perfected during the New Kingdom era. Several different levels of preservation were performed before the body was wrapped in white linen bandages. The least effective and least expensive was a simple washing and cleansing of the corpse. The next level involved filling the body's orifices with a caustic, corrosive fluid, then plugging up the holes. Several days later, the plugs were removed and the putrid fluid drained. The super-deluxe preservation package required that an incision be made in the abdomen. All of the viscera, save the heart and kidneys, were removed (including the brain, either through the base of the skull or through a nostril) and preserved in canopic jars. These jars were amphora-shaped containers of alabaster with engravings on the sides and lids. The body was then packed with *natrun*, a natural salt found in Wadi Natrun. After 40 days, the salt was removed and ointments, spices, and oils such as frankincense (often imported from the Dhofar region of Oman) were applied in combination with intricate patterns of wrappings. The essences reacted over time to form a black, pitch-like substance that gives mummies their names (*moumiya* is Arabic for pitch).

KARNAK TEMPLE

*Local **minibuses** run between Karnak Temple and the train station (25pt). Ask first to make sure the driver is going as far as the temple and don't let him hike up the price at the end of the ride. You can also reach the temple by **bike, foot,** or **kalish** (E£5). The Karnak complex covers over five acres of land and is difficult to cover thoroughly, so bring water and come early in the day. Open daily 6am-5pm; in winter 6am-5:30pm. E£20, students E£10. If you seek more than a general impression of the place, a guided tour is useful, and latching onto one is easy. The sound and light show is a fascinating way to explore the temple for a first-time visit and pique your curiosity for a more in-depth visit the following morning. English shows M and Th 8pm, Tu-W and F-Su 9:15pm; in winter M 6pm, Tu 9pm, W-Su 7:30pm. Times subject to change, so check at your hotel or at the tourist office. Show E£33.*

Karnak Temple is overwhelming in its intricacy and proportions. Every major period in Egypt's ancient history since the collapse of the Middle Kingdom is represented in the additions to this complex of shrines dedicated to the sun-god Amun and his family. Karnak Temple is the product of centuries of one-upmanship. Pharaoh after pharaoh added his mark to the temple in an effort to demonstrate the greatness of Amun—and himself. It was also the center of power for Amun's high priest, whose powers often exceeded even those of the pharaoh.

The entire three-kilometer route between the temples of Luxor and Karnak was once connected by the sacred **Avenue of the Sphinxes,** built by Queen Hatshepsut (pronounced Hat-*Cheap*-Suit). The ever modest Ramses II took the liberty of adding a small statuette of himself to each sphinx. The final stretch of the avenue remains complete with two rows of sphinxes by the **Temple of Khonsu,** to the right of the main entry to Karnak Temple.

Enter the temple from the west with the Nile behind you and pass through the **Avenue of the Rams,** another double-rowed boulevard of creatures (this time, lions' bodies with rams' heads) dedicated to Ramses II. The curly-horned ram was one of Amun's sacred animals. The temple is a hodgepodge of additions and alterations spanning millennia, but because of the traditionalism of pharaonic architecture, the different pieces comprise a harmonious whole. As you push your way inside, think of each section as a layer of history built upon the original shrine at the core. The farther you proceed into the building, the farther back in time you go. The temple is oriented along two axes: a primary east-west axis following the path of the sun god Amun and a secondary axis proceeding north-south to Luxor Temple.

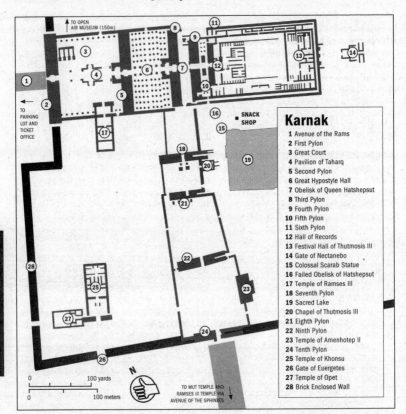

Karnak

1 Avenue of the Rams
2 First Pylon
3 Great Court
4 Pavilion of Taharq
5 Second Pylon
6 Great Hypostyle Hall
7 Obelisk of Queen Hatshepsut
8 Third Pylon
9 Fourth Pylon
10 Fifth Pylon
11 Sixth Pylon
12 Hall of Records
13 Festival Hall of Thutmosis III
14 Gate of Nectanebo
15 Colossal Scarab Statue
16 Failed Obelisk of Hatshepsut
17 Temple of Ramses III
18 Seventh Pylon
19 Sacred Lake
20 Chapel of Thutmosis III
21 Eighth Pylon
22 Ninth Pylon
23 Temple of Amenhotep II
24 Tenth Pylon
25 Temple of Khonsu
26 Gate of Euergetes
27 Temple of Opet
28 Brick Enclosed Wall

The first and largest pylon was never completed and probably dates from the 25th dynasty. Look for the ancient mud-brick scaffolding, which was used to erect the massive wall. The **Great Court,** the single largest element of the temple complex, dates from around the same time. Chambers on the left (built during the 29th dynasty) are dedicated to the Theban triad of Amun, Mut, and Khonsu. On the right is a temple built under Ramses III and lined with 20 seven-meter statues of himself. The three chapels behind the temple's inner court are also dedicated to the Theban triad. An open papyrus column in the center of the Great Court is all that remains of the 25th-dynasty (689-664 BCE) Ethiopian king Taharq's pavilion.

Pass through the recycled second pylon (Ramses II made it with blocks from one of Akhenaton's temples) into the **Great Hypostyle Hall.** With 12 central columns and 122 subsidiary columns, it's a pinnacle of pharaonic architecture. The central colonnade (from 1375 BCE) is the oldest part of the hall; Ramses II made other additions. Emerging from the forest of sandstone, find the 30m high granite **Obelisk of Queen Hatshepsut,** the tallest obelisk in Egypt, in front of the 4th pylon. Hatshepsut, who considered herself a female king, brought the stones from Aswan and inlaid them with bushels of gold. Passing through the rubble of the 5th pylon and the granite 6th pylon, enter the **Hall of Records,** containing two elegantly proportioned granite pillars, one decorated with carvings of the lotus of Upper Egypt and the other with the papyrus of Lower Egypt. Alexander the Great's brother Phillip added the **Sanctuary of the Sacred Boats,** behind the hall, around 300 BCE.

Straight ahead, the **Festival Hall of Thutmosis III** dominates the eastern edge of the Karnak complex. Built to commemorate the pharaoh's victories in the mysterious north, it contains carvings of strange plants and animals brought back from his campaigns. The star-studded ceiling survives intact, supported by 52 tapering pillars. Some of the bases were actually whittled down to make room for large processions. In the 6th century CE, the hall was converted into a church; frescoes of haloed saints still adorn the interior walls and column shafts. Beyond a low wall to the east, the **Gate of Nectanebo** marks an early entrance to the complex. South of the Festival Hall, the limpid waters of the **Sacred Lake** sizzle in the heat. Every morning, priests purified themselves in the holy waters of this rectangular pool before performing ceremonies within the temple. Note the large scarab beetle on the northwestern corner of the lake. It is said that if you run around the scarab in a clockwise direction three times, you will soon be pregnant.

KARNAK OPEN-AIR MUSEUM. This museum stands to the north of the great court; look for a small sign and return toward the entrance. It is comprised of three excavated chapels and a motley collection of well-labeled wall fragments. The **Red Chapel** of Queen Hatshepsut is displayed in rows of blocks, along with the Middle Kingdom **Alabaster Chapel.** The latter has flowing white walls streaked with brown, a welcome relief from the acres of sandstone. *(E£10, students E£5.)*

WEST BANK

When they weren't preoccupied with empire-building and invader-expelling, Thebes' rulers busied themselves preparing for eternity. As followers of the sun god Amun, the elite of the New Kingdom aspired to tombs on the West Bank, where the sun sets and the afterlife commences. Pharaonic obsession with the afterlife made the necropolis of Thebes into the world's most well-endowed graveyard. Over millennia, robbers and archaeologists have nabbed much of the treasure, but the site still features an unparalleled collection of Egyptian funerary art.

New Kingdom rulers could take no chances with the security of the afterlife. Earlier pharaohs had been too convinced of the mortality of their sacred tombs. Thieves had mastered the delicate art of pyramid pilfering at Memphis, making off with afterlife amenities of a grandeur that can now only be imagined. A radical change in burial practices was in order. The pharaohs of Thebes would not have their treasure rest anywhere but beside their mummified remains.

To conceal the location, contents, and design of the tombs, the work was done in secrecy by a team of laborers who dwelt within the necropolis. Perfecting techniques of tomb construction, decoration, and mummification, these 300 artisans devoted themselves to the City of the Dead over the course of generations, passing expertise down through familial lines. The remains of **Deir al-Medina** (the Workers' Walled City, see p. 227) have been thoroughly excavated and are among the most complete town remains in Egypt. Tomb design reflected the new emphasis on secrecy. Instead of one ostentatious pyramid, there were pairs of funerary monuments: an underground grave, lavishly outfitted with the articles demanded by the hectic afterlife and sequestered in an obscure recess of the desert; and a grandiose mortuary temple where the monarch could be worshiped for eternity. Architects incorporated dead-end passages, fake sarcophagi, hidden doorways, and deep shafts to foil the most cunning robbers. Once a pharaoh was safely stowed, workers immediately began to construct the tomb destined for his successor.

One region in particular must have seemed ideal for entombment: a narrow, winding valley walled on three sides by jagged limestone cliffs and approachable by a single rocky footpath. This isolated canyon, known as the **Valley of the Kings** (p. 222), became the burial place of New Kingdom pharaohs. Although it looked promising on papyrus, it failed to deter hoodlums, and few of the tombs escaped vandalism. Queens, favored consorts, and select offspring were accorded ceremonial burial with full honors and security precautions in a separate corner of the West Bank, the **Valley of the Queens** (p. 229). Esteemed members of the Theban aristocracy also practiced elaborate burial customs, and several of the resulting **Tombs of the Nobles** (p. 228) rival royal burial chambers in craft and design. Last but not least, the **Valley of the Artisans** (Deir al-Medina, p. 227) has two very impressive tombs of pharaonic artists. Over 400 tombs continue to decay in the necropolis, but only a handful are accessible. In addition to tombs, the West Bank hosts massive **mortuary temples** (p. 225). Most imposing are the **Colossi of Memnon**, the **Temple of Hatshepsut** (Deir al-Bahri), and the Temple of Ramses III (better known as **Medinat Habu**) near the Valley of the Queens. The ruins of the **Ramesseum** (the Temple of Ramses II), though shattered, also merit a visit.

VALLEY OF THE KINGS وادى الملوك

The Valley of the Kings lies 5km from the Nile but there's no direct path. Two possible routes to the beginning of the Valley road exist: go past the Colossi of Memnon, then 3km northeast past the necropolis sites to the start of the Valley road; or turn right (northeast) at the canal (follow the signs) and go 2km, then turn west by the Abu Qasem Hotel and go 1½km to the base of the Valley road; the road gently winds for 5km into desolate mountain valleys. Tombs open daily 6am-5pm; in winter 6am-4pm. There is a Rest House near the entrance with overpriced water and warm juice. Public toilets available.

The Valley of the Kings, no more than 400m long and 200m wide, can easily be toured on foot using the clearly marked, well-groomed gravel paths. Over 64 known and numbered tombs honeycomb the valley; the numbering is in the order of discovery. Most of them are closed to the public, but the best-known tombs are almost always accessible. Every few months the open tombs are rotated to minimize wear and tear and to add a little variety—after all, it is the spice of afterlife. Ask at the tourist office to find which are currently open.

TOMB OF RAMSES IV (#2). The first tomb on the right is the tomb of Ramses IV. Once used as a Byzantine church, the well-preserved tomb contains wall decorations excerpted from the *Book of the Dead* and the *Book of Fates*. On both sides of the tomb, 365 small statues of the pharaoh's guardian spirit were believed to facilitate his resurrection every night of the year when Amun-Ra crossed to the West Bank. The figures on the left wall facing the sun god will be resurrected, while the upside down figures on the right wall represent non-believers who won't be resurrected. A vividly colored ceiling and huge, cartouche-shaped sarcophagus make this one of the best tombs in the valley.

TOMB OF RAMSES IX (#6). The intricately detailed ceiling of the 12th-century BCE Tomb of Ramses IX (on your left once you enter the valley) features gold figures displaying their *joie de mourir* against a deep blue background. To the right of the entrance, the pharaoh is shown offering a gazelle to Amun-Ra. Farther on the right, the reliefs show him striving for the afterlife by making offerings to the god of justice (holding balance) and to Osiris, god of resurrection and by making 136 negative confessions (I never lied, I never spent time in a Turkish prison, etc.). Directly opposite these reliefs, Ramses is playing the same game with Horus to gain safe passage through the two lakes of fire. A long corridor descends to an anteroom covered with protective demons, serpents, and wild beasts. A pit beyond the long corridor in the burial chamber holds Ramses IX's sarcophagus. The ceiling of the chamber was not smoothed and the text appears in a shorthand form because Ramses IX died before his tomb was ready. Most of the painting was done during the 70 days needed for mummification.

TOMB OF RAMSES VI (#9). The third largest tomb in the valley after Ramses II and Seti I, this crypt is known for its ceiling of winged cobras, decapitated enemies, and a spectacular 18m-long depiction of the sky god, Mut. The various red disks along her body depict the daily path of the sun—she would give birth to it every morning and then swallow it in the evening. As the charred marks on its edges attest, the vast sarcophagus in the burial chamber was split by tomb robbers who heated it and doused it in water, causing the stone to expand and crack.

TOMB OF RAMSES III (#11). Named the "Tomb of the Harp Players" after the two plucky musicians depicted on one of its interior chambers, the Tomb of

SIGHTSEEING STRATEGY. Conduct your **summer** exploration of the necropolis in the early morning. In the **winter,** afternoons are sometimes less crowded than mornings. Guards at the less-visited sites tend to lock up and head home a little early, especially in the summer. All sites open at 6am and officially close at 5pm in summer and 4pm in winter; stragglers won't be kicked out as long as they get in before closing. Bring plenty of **water** and a **flashlight.** Tomb guards have been known to turn off the lights to force you to rely upon them for guidance. The cheapest way to get to the West Bank is by the local tourist **ferry,** which docks directly in front of Luxor Temple (E£1; bicycles 25pt extra). Ferries run from 6am to 4pm. **Private motorboats** take passengers across for E£7 per boat. From the local ferry landing, it is a 1km walk north to the ticket kiosk, then 3km to the Colossi of Memnon. Here are some transportation options once you're at the West Bank:

ON FOOT If you have time and stamina, the best and probably safest way to see the sights on the West Bank is to walk to them. All of the sights (except for the Valley of the Kings) are within a 3km radius of the Colossi of Memnon. Buy your tickets and start walking to the sights. Once on the main road (1km from the ticket office), catch a covered pick-up truck to the Colossi of Memnon (25pt). Special taxis travel directly from the ticket office to the Colossi of Memnon for E£5 (more in summer). The Valley of the Kings is 8km by paved road, but the walk is worth it for the chance to follow the donkey trail up and over the **Jabal al-Qurn** (Hill of the Horn). The peak was once sacred to the goddess of silence, Mirtseger, and with good reason—the serene sound of nothing at the top of the hill is matched only by the view of the ruins. A simple geographic division is **North** (Valley of the Kings, Seti Temple, Hatshepsut, Ramesseum, the Tombs of the Nobles) and **South** (Valley of the Queens, Medinat Habu, the Valley of the Artisans); this division makes for a two-day exploration.

GUIDED TOURS Guided tours in A/C coaches with English-speaking guides are most popular. All budget hotels book tours, but many charge a hefty commission. Do not under any circumstances book tours for Luxor in Cairo, as travel agents are likely to slap a hefty commission onto an already inflated price. All hotels listed in this guide schedule tours of the West Bank for as low as E£45. Book a tour with noted guide and Egyptologist Abu al-Naga Gabrail (☎37 45 94 or 38 44 20). Better known as **Moonshine,** Gabrail is cheap and of sound quality; he has led tour groups around the West Bank for over 20 years.

DONKEY Mark Twain wrote that riding a donkey in Egypt "was a fresh, new, exhilarating sensation worth a hundred worn and threadbare pleasures." The novelty of donkey travel (which wears thin as quickly as the seat of your pants) and the fantastic views afforded by the trail as it climbs its way up to the Valley of the Kings have led to a burgeoning burro-borrow market. Arrange an excursion through your hotel that includes donkey and ferry ride (E£30) or hire your own animal in the village of Gezira just inland from the ferry or at the local ferry dock. One suggested full donkey route begins at the Valley of the Kings, goes around to the Temple of Hatshepsut and the Ramesseum, and then returns home.

BIKES A bicycle ride gives you a chance to view green fields abutting sandy dunes. A few serious hills are nearly unbearable during the summer. Rent bikes in Luxor or by the local ferry landing (E£5). Many hotels, the Everest and Sherif included, rent motorbikes (E£50-60 per day).

TAXI Taxis are more expensive and lack A/C (E£30-40 for the morning is reasonable), but they allow you to cover the most ground. Hordes of drivers wait at both ferry landings. You can hire a taxi in Luxor, but the extended trip by the new bridge can drive up prices. When bargaining, ignore any nonsense about government rates and per person charges.

EGYPT

Ramses III boasts a vividly colorful portrayal of ancient chariot races on the left side of the penultimate chamber. Luckless Ramses III was killed in a palace plot, burgled post-mortem, and as a final insult, stolen and shipped in his magnificent sarcophagus to the Louvre.

TOMB OF RAMSES I (#16). The steep entrance next to the Tomb of Seti I (#17, see **Other Tombs** below) descends into the Tomb of Ramses I, a single burial chamber dominated by Ramses' pink granite sarcophagus. The tomb walls, some of the most vivid in the valley, are painted with scenes of Ramses (founder of the 19th dynasty) hobnobbing with the gods. The first corridor is the shortest in the valley, perhaps a consequence of Ramses' brief rule (1320-18 BCE).

TOMB OF MENEPTAH-SIPTAH (#18). The Tomb of Meneptah-Siptah has some splendid ceilings painted with vultures and ram-headed falcons. The rough-hewn burial chamber has suffered a good deal of damage, but the large red granite sarcophagus, carved with images of crocodiles and cobras, is still intact.

TOMB OF THUTMOSIS III (#34). The most dramatically situated burial site in the necropolis is the cliffside Tomb of Thutmosis III, reached by a long, steep staircase that ascends a precipitous ravine squeezed between towering limestone cliffs. To get to the tomb, follow the dirt road that begins next to the Tomb of Ramses III (#11) leading southeast up the hill. The tomb's location provides the ultimate example of the 18th-dynasty pharaohs' attempts to hide their tombs. Thutmosis III's is built in a fault, where it became naturally concealed by debris left from flash floods, but the ingenious design did not deter grave robbers. Queen Hatshepsut appointed her freakishly short stepson Thutmosis III as a military leader; he was so successful as a leader that he became her rival and eventually took the throne from her. His conquests reached as far as the fourth cataract of the Nile to the south, Crete and Cyprus to the north, and the Euphrates to the east. His grave is decorated with unusual hieratic text (short-hand hieroglyphic, see p. 68) and strangely beautiful stick-figure representations of Khnum and other gods. The novel cartouche-shaped burial chamber still contains his red granite sarcophagus (don't tip the guard for showing you that it's empty).

TOMB OF TUTANKHAMUN (#62). The West Bank's most renowned tourist attraction, the Tomb of Tutankhamun stands directly in front of the Rest House in the middle of the valley and requires a special ticket. (E£40, students E£20.) The real treasures are at the Egyptian Museum in Cairo (see p. 122), and the interior of this small tomb may not be worth the extra ticket. If you plan to see it, visit it first or you'll probably be disappointed after seeing the others.

GET DOWN AND DIG IT An archaeologist's work is never done, especially in Luxor. Although it would appear that most of the treasures of the old tombs and temples have been whisked away, archaeologists are still concerned with what they can learn through excavation (and finding a little new treasure never hurt anyone either). The Department of Antiquities oversees and conducts many of the ongoing projects in Egypt, from the restoration of the Ramesseum to current digs at the Karnak Temple and Valley of the Kings. A recent promising find is the discovery of the largest tomb ever found in Egypt, a vast 107-room (and counting) complex being excavated by a team led by the American archaeologist Kent Weeks. The name of Ramses II has been identified four times, giving rise to speculation that this could be the final resting place of the great pharaoh's many sons. Entry into the tomb, designated **KV5,** has been hampered by falling rocks and it is completely off-limits to the public. Other avenues of research include remote sensing, which detects irregularities beneath the surface without costly digging, and excavation within the city of Luxor itself.

The only pharaonic tomb to evade grave robbers, Tut's treasure box was discovered in 1922 by archaeologist Howard Carter and has toured the world several times before returning to its permanent home in the Egyptian Museum in Cairo. Tutankhamun's mummy was encased in the innermost of four snugly nested, superbly decorated cases, three of which can be seen in the Egyptian Museum. Fortunately, the raiding Egyptologists left behind the outermost case (a gilded wood extravagance covered in rich jewels) and Tut's exquisitely carved sarcophagus. The perfectly preserved interior walls of the burial chamber depict colorful scenes from the *Book of the Dead*, which were transcribed from the pyramid writings at Saqqara (see p. 132). Egyptologists had expected that the tomb would contain little of interest because the pharaoh reigned only two years before he died, but Carter ignored professional censure and toiled for six seasons in the Valley of the Kings. After more than 200,000 tons of rubble had been moved, Carter's patron reluctantly decided to abort the project. Before admitting failure, Carter explored one more possibility: a site in front of the tomb of Ramses VI, in an area covered with workers' huts. Confounding the critics, he chanced upon an ancient doorway beneath the shanties. The tomb had been opened by robbers, but the thieves had apparently been caught in the act by necropolis guards, because the treasures had been hastily stacked and the entrance resealed. Three mummies were found in the tomb, including that of the boy-king himself.

OTHER TOMBS. The **Tomb of Seti I (#17)**, the valley's longest tomb, honors the great 19th-dynasty military leader. The unfinished **Tomb of Thutmosis IV (#43)** was constructed in a U-shape and was the first tomb to combine all the elements displayed in tombs until the end of the 20th dynasty. The **Tomb of Ramses VII (#1)** has been open since ancient times. The **Tomb of Amenhotep II (#35)** is inscribed with the entire text of the *Book of the Dead* and contains a beautiful red sarcophagus.

MORTUARY TEMPLES

The pharaohs may have hidden their tombs, but they didn't want the living world to forget about them. In addition to its spectacular rock-hewn tombs, the west bank is peppered with **mortuary temples**, mammoth structures honoring the royal deceased. Though overshadowed by Luxor's Karnak Temple in scale and importance, the West Theban temples of Hatshepsut (Deir al-Bahri), Ramses III (Medinat Habu), Ramses II (Ramesseum), and Seti I are still fascinating. The following temples, all accessible from a road that runs parallel to the Nile, are described from south to north. From the ferry docks, head inland three kilometers past the Colossi of Memnon until you come to an intersection. A road to the left leads to Medinat Habu, 500m to the southwest.

COLOSSI OF MEMNON. All that remains of the largest mortuary temple (dedicated to Amenhotep III) on the West Bank is the statue pair known as the **Colossi of Memnon,** towering statues seated in magnificent isolation on the northern side of the entrance road to the necropolis. Looking over the plain from a height of 20m, these figures of Amenhotep were Thebes' greatest tourist attraction during the Roman era. At night, an eerie whistling sound emanated from the statues; as Memnon was the mythical son of Aurora, the goddess of the dawn, the Romans believed the sound was actually Memnon wailing in anticipation of his mother's rays. In fact, the sound was produced by a clever water device which emitted a sharp whistle when heated by the rising sun's rays. Designed by the Alexandrian engineer Heron, the device fit neatly (and secretly) into the cracked knee of the earthquake-damaged statue, and was used by priests to attract hordes of (paying) tourists. When Emperor Settimius Severus decided to restore the monument in 196 CE, the priests withdrew the device to avoid exposing their secret.

MEDINAT HABU (TEMPLE OF RAMSES III). This complex of well-preserved edifices honoring Ramses III was constructed in several stages. It stands to the left at the end of the road after the Colossi. Relatively few tourists visit this site; a tranquil hour is enough to take it in. The most impressive structure is the Mortuary

Temple of Ramses III, decorated with reliefs of the pharaoh's many successful military campaigns, including his victories over the mysterious "Sea People" (who dangle by their hair from his fist). Enter the temple through its large fortified gate. Climbing the stairs on the gate's opposite side leads to a small open chamber where Ramses III is believed to have stayed while visiting the temple. It was also likely the site of his ultimate assassination. The temple is warrior-themed throughout: the main pylon, also known as the Royal Pavilion, resembles a military fortress rather than a temple. One relief explains the importance of securing houses of worship so that peace and order could then spread elsewhere, and several reliefs show prisoners being put to death. On the back of the main pylon are savory piles of conquered hands and tongues. Beyond the gate are two relief-rich courts. In the second court on the left side is a window opening supported by statues of human heads. This "window of appearances" was used for royal speeches and was meant to show the king standing on the heads of his vanquished enemies.

RAMESSEUM (TEMPLE OF RAMSES II). Farther north, beyond the student ticket office, is the Mortuary Temple of Ramses II, or the Ramesseum. A tour of the Ramesseum may not be worth a long sidetrip and won't exceed 30 minutes. In most of the ravaged temples, visitors attempt to gather from the ruins an idea of the spectacle that once was, but at the Ramesseum, the ruins themselves are the grandest statement of all. The same pharaoh who had Abu Simbel tailor-made to his specifications built the Ramesseum to house another mammoth exercise in narcissism. The shattered remains of the **Colossus of Ramses II** (1000 ton; 17m; the forefingers are over 1m long) were the inspiration for Percy Bysshe Shelley's famous poem "Ozymandias:" "My name is Ozymandias, king of kings: / Look on my works, ye Mighty, and despair!" Their broken enormity leads many to similar sentiments. The colossus, which was transported in one piece from the pharaoh's granite quarries in Aswan to Thebes, originally overlooked the passageway leading into the second court. Even shattered, the remnants (including head, upper arms, and one foot) are imposing.

DEIR AL-BAHRI (TEMPLE OF HATSHEPSUT). Just north of the Ramesseum, a paved road leaves the main north-south thoroughfare and heads northwest, winding around to the **Temple of Hatshepsut.** If on foot, you can save some time by cutting through the village on the left side of the road (before it splits). In the center of the necropolis, this Temple is 500m north of the Tombs of the Nobles. The Temple's ancient Egyptian name, *Djeser Djesern*, means "most splendid of all," and with good reason: Hatshepsut's masterpiece rises in three broad, columned terraces from the desert floor against a dramatic backdrop of sheer limestone cliffs.

> # MUMMIES IN THE NIGHT
> In the late 1870s, members of the Antiquities Service noticed many New Kingdom funerary objects appearing on the European black market. **Charles Wilbur,** a wealthy American antiquer, was enlisted to go undercover and identify the source of the treasures. By making clear that he would pay high prices for authentic pieces, Wilbur was eventually led to Luxor. Across the river in the town of Qurna, he was shown a piece that had come from a recently opened royal burial. Wilbur secretly telegraphed Gaston Maspero, the Director General of the Antiquities Service, who rushed to Luxor and began intense questioning of all involved. Several weeks later, **Muhammad Abd al-Rasul,** the head of the most prominent antiquities-dealing family in Luxor, confessed that his family had found a tomb near the Mortuary Temple of Hatshepsut. Archaeologists were quickly summoned and found the deep shaft burial containing the mummies of the New Kingdom's greatest kings: Thutmosis III, Amosis (founder of the New Kingdom), and Ramses II, among many others. The Abd al-Rasul family had kept the shaft a secret for 10 years, quietly selling their stash. The Antiquities Service, aware of the security risk that a public disclosure would cause, employed hundreds of men to load the mummies onto ships. The bodies were hurried down the Nile at top speed and now reside in the Egyptian Museum.

After the death of her husband Thutmosis II, Hatshepsut became the ruler of the kingdom, the only woman ever to assume the title of pharaoh (see **Ancient History,** p. 64). Her temple was excavated by French and Egyptian archaeologists and is currently being restored by a joint Polish-Egyptian team with support from the US and France. No images of Hatshepsut remain intact. After her death, her stepson Thutmosis III—who had to wait 20 years before coming into his own as pharaoh because she refused to marry him—defaced virtually all of them, and placed his name on the statues of a bearded Hatshepsut that line the third level. Men—can't live with 'em...can't be reincarnated with 'em.

If you walk from the lower court up a wide ramp to the central court, you'll come upon a colonnaded back wall that contains, from left to right, the Shrine of Hathor, the Colonnade of the Expedition of Punt, the Birth Colonnade, and the Shrine to Anubis. The Punt reliefs show Egyptian expeditions to that land (today's Somalia), and the exchange of goods such as trees and animals with the locals. The Birth Colonnade details Hatshepsut's birth and childhood. Another huge ramp leads to the upper court with a rock-cut sanctuary. This court is closed to the public because it was badly ruined and sadly defaced by Christians who used the temple as a Coptic monastery in the 7th century.

TEMPLE OF SETI I. You'll have a fair amount of trouble getting to this place, and there's not that much to see once there. Go north on the main road and follow it to the end. Turn right to visit what remains of the Mortuary Temple of Seti I, father of Ramses II, a warrior who enlarged the Egyptian empire to include the island of Cyprus and parts of Mesopotamia. Seti was also one of the first men to wear earrings—archaeologists could tell this from his well-preserved mummy-lobes. Although the booty from his successful campaigns has been stolen, the relief work, ranked among the finest executed in ancient Egypt, still remains.

VALLEY OF THE ARTISANS
One ticket includes the Workers' Walled City, the Temple of Deir al-Medina, and the two tombs. E£12, students E£6.

WORKERS' WALLED CITY. To reach the plentiful though visually uninspiring remains of the Workers' Walled City, go past the Colossi of Memnon and follow the small road west. The Workers' Walled City was the only inhabited area on the West Bank during the New Kingdom, and it is the best window archaeologists have found into the nature of urban life in ancient Egypt. Since the workers and artists knew the whereabouts of the tombs they were digging, their movements were strictly controlled and observed and they lived in isolation (the entire walled city was roofed over). To prevent any leaks, the priests had many of the workers' tongues amputated when construction was over. A typical house consisted of a kitchen, a living room, and one bedroom. Some had stairways for access to the rooftops, a welcome relief from the heat and smell below.

TEMPLE OF DEIR AL-MEDINA. About 60m down the road from the Workers' Walled City stands the Temple of Deir al-Medina (Monastery of the Town), an elegant shrine from the Ptolemaic era. Dedicated to Hathor, the goddess of love, and Maat, the representation of divine order (see **Meet the Gods,** p. 69), the temple was named during Christian times when monks constructed a monastery next door.

TOMBS OF THE ARTISANS. The accessible artisans' tombs are in such excellent condition that it is hard to believe they were painted so many centuries ago. Unlike the formal decorations dictated by priests on the walls of royal tombs, these tombs contain very creative drawings of the afterlife that can be considered a form of free hand art. Some artisans spent almost 30 years building their tombs, as they could only work on their own tombs on the single rest day of the ancient 10-day week. Two amazing tombs are open to the public: the **Tomb of Sennedjen,** artist for Ramses III, and the **Tomb of Inherku,** "deputy master of the two Egypts in Truth Square" (i.e. head artist for Ramses IV).

TOMBS OF THE NOBLES

A few hundred meters southeast of the Temple of Hatshepsut is the West Bank's sardine-packed burial site, with more than 400 Tombs of the Nobles. You must buy a separate ticket for each, but it is possible to see any tomb with any ticket as long as the ticket price is the same as the entrance fee. The first two groups provide the most punch for your pound. Many villagers will volunteer their services, but a guide is unnecessary. Maps are available in bookstores on the East Bank.

Throughout the New Kingdom, Theban aristocrats had de facto control over much of the pharaoh's empire and served as advisors. The pharaoh often remained ignorant of the most crucial political developments while members of the elite fought among themselves for control of the kingdom. Some aristocrats affected pharaonic status by amply providing themselves with luxuries for the afterlife and devising well-hidden underground tombs. Unlike the pharaoh (who would assuredly live among the gods after his death), Theban aristocrats needed more assurance that a comfortable existence awaited them in the afterlife. Accordingly, every facet of their earthly lives was carefully recorded on the walls of their tombs, leaving the decoration more naturalistic and mundane than the reliefs found in pharaonic tombs. Because of the inferior limestone in this portion of the necropolis, artisans could not carve in relief. Instead, they painted murals on a whitewashed stone surface. These tombs are simpler than those of the pharaohs: they all start with a terrace leading to a decorated vestibule, followed by a corridor.

TOMBS OF REKHMIRE AND SENNOFER. The westernmost tomb belongs to Rekhmire, a governor of Thebes who advised Thutmosis III and prided himself on his administrative genius. A historian's delight and perhaps the most absorbing of the tombs in the Theban necropolis, the **Tomb of Rekhmire (#100)** is composed of biographical narratives depicting the range of activities Rekhmire oversaw.

In the first chamber, tax evaders are tried by Rekhmire, who sits with a set of rolled papyrus texts strewn at the foot of his judgment throne; the presence of the papyrus suggests that written law existed as early as 1500 BCE. On the inner, left-hand wall, processions of tribute payers arrive from Crete (top), Syria (middle), and the African kingdoms of Punt (present-day Somalia) and Nubia (bottom), the latter of whom offer a giraffe, assorted monkeys, a tiger, and an elephant tusk. Other scenes show Egyptians drinking themselves silly during what was known as, like, the "Festival of the Valley." The niche at the top of the rear wall was intended to contain a statue of Rekhmire himself.

Trek 50m up the hill west of Rekhmire's tomb to reach the **Tomb of Sennofer (#96).** This impressively vivid tomb is known as the "Tomb of the Vines" after the filigreed grapevine crawling all over the ceiling. The delightful lattice of purple and green simulates a shady arbor for Sennofer, overseer of the royal gardens of Amun under Amenhotep II. The plan of the tomb is as unusual as its decor: a curving wall leads into the first room, which in turn leads straight back into the pillared burial chamber. The big, wet eyes of **Hathor the love-cow** follow you around the tomb from the tops of the columns. The superb condition and remarkable expressiveness of the paintings of this small tomb make it worth the detour.

TOMB OF RAMOSE. The incomplete Tomb of Ramose (#55) was built during the reign of the heretic king Akhenaton (Amenhotep IV). Ramose was Governor of Thebes and Vizier under Akhenaton, and one of the first converts to Akhenaton's monotheistic religion that worshiped Aton. The tomb itself displays the stylistic contrast between the art produced in the Old Kingdom and that produced under Akhenaton. In the columned first chamber, all of Egypt pays obeisance to Aton, a blood-red disk emitting shafts of light that end in small hands holding *ankhs*, and other religious symbols. On the wall through which you enter, the images carved in unpainted relief reflect the traditional, stylized tastes of the Old Kingdom, with scenes of Ramose and his family making offerings and Egyptians cheering Ramose's conversion to the Aton cult. In contrast, the wall to the left as you enter displays the strangely distorted figures and realistic composition typical of Akhenaton's reign. These images support the intriguing and rather popular theory that the heretical Akhenaton came from another planet: the sun-disc Aton looks startlingly like a flying saucer, and the oblong heads and elongated arms of the wall figures greatly resemble common representations of aliens.

TOMB OF USERHET. Continue up from the Tomb of Ramose to the Tomb of Userhet the Scribe (#56), a few meters to the south. Although an ascetic early Christian monk who made his home within the chamber destroyed most of the female figures adorning the walls, the tomb's decor retains a certain blithe spirit because of the unusual pink tones of the interior frescoes. Userhet, Amenhotep II's royal scribe (around 1408 BCE), had his resting place painted with daily pedestrian scenes: on the right-hand wall of the first chamber men wait their turn in line for the local barber, while duck-offering scenes cover the wall of the entrance.

TOMB OF NAKHT. Slightly north of the Tomb of Ramose is a trail that leads off the main road and winds east a short distance to the Tomb of Nakht (#52). The first chamber contains a reconstruction of an exquisite statue of Nakht, scribe of the royal granaries under Thutmosis IV (the original was lost at sea on its way to the US during World War I). Also in the first chamber are photographs of some of the other removed contents and a series of well-labeled diagrams explaining the images within the second chamber. The most famous image from the Tombs of the Nobles—three musicians playing the flute, harp, and lute—is on the left wall, to remind Nakht in the afterlife that his wife was a singer.

ASASIF TOMBS. Southwest of the Temple of Hatshepsut lies Asasif, a current archaeological hot spot. Asasif became the most popular aristocratic burial area during the 25th and 26th dynasties (about the 7th century BCE), though the **Tomb of Kheruef (#192),** the finest portion of the necropolis, was constructed 700 years earlier. Enter the burial site through an outer courtyard containing other tombs, where a series of well-wrought reliefs stands against a protecting wall. Note the provocative ceremonial dance featuring a chorus line of women, a jumping bird, a noisy monkey, flutists, and drummers to the left of the doorway. On the right, 16 swooning princesses surround pharaonic heartthrob Amenhotep III.

As you enter the **Tomb of Kiki (#409),** about 10m to the north of Kheruef, the gods Thoth and Anubis discuss the readings of a giant scale. The burial chamber remains unfinished, leaving a series of faceless figures outlined in red. To get to the **Tomb of Neferhotep (#48),** walk 100m east along the dirt path from Kiki, then turn right (south) and walk 20m to the tomb, immediately in front of a village house. Most of the seated stone figures within the tomb are fairly intact.

VALLEY OF THE QUEENS وادى الملكات

During the later years of the New Kingdom, a special burial area was chosen for the wives and children of the pharaohs. Traditionally, the pharaoh's closest relatives were buried beside the monarch, but this arrangement changed during the reign of Ramses I (14th century BCE), when princes, consorts, and wives were buried in the Valley of the Queens. Directly west of the Colossi of Memnon at the end of the main road, the Valley of the Queens contains fewer than 30 royal tombs. Check at the ticket kiosks to find out which are currently open.

TOMB OF AMONHERKHEPESHEF (#55). The Tomb of Amonherkhepeshef, the son of Ramses III, is richly adorned with bas-relief carvings. In one, Ramses III introduces his nine-year-old son (wearing the groomed topknot of a pharaonic prince) to each of the major deities. Colored scenes of deities and farmers fill entire walls—a rare sight in Theban tombs. The sarcophagus that held the prince's mummy stands in the rear burial chamber. A desiccated fetus lies curled in a small glass display next to the remains of a still-born younger brother of the prince. The lively paintings make this tomb a cheaper, welcome alternative to the much more famous tomb of Queen Nefertari.

TOMB OF QUEEN NEFERTARI (#66). Touted as Egypt's finest tomb, the pricey Tomb of Queen Nefertari (#66) is open to the first 150 people who can afford a ticket (E£100, students E£50). Stay alert: the moisture on your breath damages the tomb's colors, so you'll only have 10 minutes to absorb what you can. The vivid tones of the tomb walls are breathtaking. It's good they are: it took seven winters, US$6 million, and the expertise of the Getty Institute to preserve and restore this masterpiece dedicated to the most beloved wife of Ramses II. After seeing this tomb, one can begin to imagine the grandeur of its far less-preserved neighbors. The reliefs in the first chamber include the goddess Hathor leading Nefertari by the hand, thousands of hieroglyphs, and a scarab-faced goddess. A sea-green and starry ceiling canopies the stairs down to the queen's burial chamber. Columns in the burial chamber portray green-skinned Osiris and the cow-goddess Hathor.

🎵 ENTERTAINMENT

FELUCCAS. For truly Luxorious diversion, fritter away the hours in an offhand way aboard a *felucca* on the Nile (especially if you're not planning on the *felucca* trip from Aswan to Edfu). **Banana Island,** a small, palm- and fruit-tree-studded peninsula two miles upriver, is a popular destination (E£2). Overpriced souvenir stands detract from an otherwise rustic experience. **Crocodile Island** is just as rustic, as well as touristy, but is no longer home to the thousands of crocs of yore. *Feluccas* are prohibited from sailing after sunset. (2-3hr. round-trip; E£10 per person for groups over four.)

LOCAL ENTERTAINMENT. The many **ahwas** on the streets of Luxor are filled with Egyptians smoking *sheesha*, drinking coffee, and playing dominoes and backgammon. Foreigners are usually welcome, but solo women may attract unwanted comments. The **Tikkya,** on Television St., is more comfortable and friendlier than the other shops. **Videogame** systems like Super Nintendo and Sega Playstation can be found on the sidewalks of Luxor, where outgoing local children will be more than happy to challenge you to a round or two of *Mortal Kombat* (50pt per game). Adults also enjoy meeting foreigners, so don't be surprised if you are invited to a **wedding party** while in Luxor (or at least asked to get liquor at the duty-free store "for my sister's wedding tomorrow"). Think twice before disrupting a wedding party—"guests" are often expected to pay admission.

BARS AND DISCOS. The **Mars Bar** in the Venus Hotel (Stella E£6) has a foosball table, billiards, and satellite TV. The **King's Head** on Ibn Walik St. is a popular pub with a wide drink selection (Stella E£8) and pizza (E£12). Play pool for E£10. Most discos in Luxor are not hip, not cheap, and not worth it. Dance floors are about the size of a large table, and most DJs play songs you don't like and terrible remixes of the songs you do. The **Mercure Hotel** (also called the ETAP) on al-Nil St. is a happening disco in Luxor. At 11:30pm, the music changes from Top 40 dance remixes to drum machine and synthesizer Arabic music, and the belly dancing starts. An older crowd joins the youngsters for the nightly display of undulating flesh. (Disregard E£30 minimum in summer. Stella E£10. Open daily 10pm-2am.) Most popular with local swingers is **Disco on Le Lotus** at the Novotel (intersection of Salah al-Din St. and al-Nil St.), on a boat docked beside the hotel. (E£20 minimum. Schedule changes seasonally; inquire at front desk. Usually open W-Sa 10pm-3am.)

NEAR LUXOR

After the grandeur of the Temples of Luxor and Karnak, the sites near Luxor may seem a let-down. If you're in Luxor for four or five days, however, you may want to combine both Abydos and Dendera into a full day trip, organized through the tourist office or travel agent on the corniche. Arrange your taxi and convoy meeting point and time at least 12 hours beforehand so that the driver can register at the convoy police. A taxi should cost around E£180 for both sites. A cheaper option is to take a train to the nearest city, but it may be a hassle getting back.

THE LAST OF THE ANCIENT EGYPTIANS The

sacred symbols of the ancient Egyptian religion are the stuff of souvenir shops these days, but for one woman, they were much more. After falling down the stairs of her home in England in 1907, three-year-old Dorothy Eady was declared dead. When the town doctor returned an hour later to the room where he had laid the young girl's body, he was shocked to find her contentedly playing on her bed. Alive and well, the normal (if slightly rambunctious) British lass began insisting she was an ancient Egyptian and started begging to be taken "home." She was, she later said, a former priestess-in-training at the Temple of Seti in the holy city of Abydos. After a chance meeting on the temple grounds, she fell deeply in love with the Pharaoh Seti I and found herself in a rapturous affair that contravened all the rules of the priesthood. When the temple's high priest demanded a confession, ancient Egyptian Eady-as-priestess eventually took her own life rather than betray the name of her lover.

The real life Eady devoted her life to "returning home," fulfilling her destiny at the temple, and taking her place at Seti's side in the afterlife. In 1956, after twenty years as a distinguished employee of the Egyptian Department of Antiquities (where she worked with and won the respect of some of this century's most distinguished Egyptologists), Eady transferred to the ancient site of Abydos. There, known in the village as *Omm Seti,* or *mother of Seti,* she helped to guide work at the temple, exhibiting an uncanny familiarity with the grounds. Eady treated the temple as the sacred sanctuary it once was, praying and making offerings to the gods up until her actual death in 1981. She was buried in the desert to the northwest, at last ready to take Seti's side.

E G Y P T

DENDERA دندرة

*The smoothest way to see the temple at Dendera is by **boat** from Luxor; book with a travel agent on the corniche (day cruise Tu and F-Sa E£150-180 per person, includes lunch). The cheapest options are **service** and **train** rides via Qena, which will take about an hour. Service leave Luxor in convoys from beside the Hotel Bolla at 8am and 2pm (E£3), and **trains** depart from the station. Both options will require taking a **taxi** from Qena to the temple (E£5). E£12, students E£6. Qena is only now beginning to see tourists trickle in, so your presence will probably attract considerable attention. In summer, bats inhabit the temple, so a flashlight will definitely come in handy.*

The **Temple of Hathor** at Dendera is one of the few sights in Middle Egypt that has remained accessible throughout the fundamentalist uprising. While it is a bit out of the way, those who make the effort will find a structure unique in the options it offers the exploring tourist. The temple only dates from the first century BCE, though worship of Hathor is much older. The late Ptolemies and the Romans found it politically expedient to associate themselves with the benevolent goddess. Hathor is depicted as cow-headed or with cow's ears, or shown wearing a crown of two horns cradling the sun disk. Because her specialty was love, Hathor, the "Golden One," was identified by the Greeks as Aphrodite. During an annual festival, a statue of Hathor was carried in a sacred procession down the Nile to meet Horus of Edfu (see p. 235).

Eighteen columns are topped by cow heads in the **Great Hypostyle Hall.** In the temple's inner sanctum, wall paintings portray the embalmer's art, while the ceiling is decorated with pictures of the goddess Nut. The second hypostyle hall, also called the **Hall of Appearances,** gives way to the **Hall of Offerings,** where daily rites were performed. In the artsy kiosk in the southwest corner of the roof, priests performed the ceremony of "touching the disk," in which the soul of the sun god Ra appeared in the form of light. To the right is a gently sloping staircase which leads up to the roof. Turn your flashlight off for a moment as you make your way up the stairs. The lights are dim, the smell is strange, and it is hard not to feel that you are a part of the sacred religious procession chiseled on the wall to your right.

The **Hall of the Ennead** immediately precedes the inner sanctuary. The chamber on the left is the wardrobe; opposite it, a doorway leads through a small treasury into the **Court of the New Year** where sacrifices were performed during the New Year festival. On the ceiling of the colorful portico, Nut gives birth to the sun, whose rays shine upon the head of Hathor. The **Mysterious Corridor** surrounds the **Sanctuary** on three sides, and 11 chapels, each with a distinct religious function, open off of it. A small chamber known as the **Throne of Ra** sits behind the northern-most of the three doorways behind the sanctuary. A minuscule opening in its floor leads to the crypt, a subterranean hallway embellished with reliefs, some of inlaid alabaster. Many rooms on the upper floors carry ceiling paintings of Nut swallow-ing the sun at sundown and giving birth to it at dawn. On the roof of the temple, near the edge, is graffiti left by French soldiers in 1799.

ABYDOS ابيد وس

*Although Abydos is officially open to the public, tensions in Middle Egypt will probably mean that visitors to the temple will be transported by **police convoy**. The easiest and cheapest way to visit Abydos is by taking the north-bound **train** #981 (٩٨١) to al-Balyana (2hr.) from Luxor at 8am. If you aren't able to catch a tourist bus back, you will be stranded at the train station until 2:30pm. From al-Balyana to the temple (E£7), you and a mandatory party of your closest armed friends will continue to the site. Open 6am-6pm. All sites E£12, students E£6. Bring food and water since the nearby restaurant has inflated prices and may not have any food to serve if business is slow.*

The ancient city of Abydos was the site of a necropolis and temple dedicated to the god Khenti-Amentiu. Pharaohs from the first dynasty onward chose to be bur-ied at the site and eventually corpses from all over Egypt were interred at this necropolis. **Osiris,** god of the dead, subtly co-opted Abydos and the worshipers of Khenti-Amentiu during the 6th dynasty. Legend has it that the body of Osiris him-self lies buried on these grounds. After his famed dismemberment at the hands of his brother, Seth (see **Meet the Gods,** p. 69), Osiris's head was said to have landed here. The cult of Osiris centered here ritually reenacted the battle between Osiris and Seth as a sacred annual custom. The city that was Abydos has all but vanished, but after a look at the magnificent white limestone **Temple of Seti I,** dedicated to a pharaoh of the 19th dynasty, it is not hard to imagine the wonder that drew pil-grims from all over the Kingdom to this city.

The Temple of Seti has been partially reconstructed. Three of the original seven doors remain on the **Portico of Twelve Pillars,** which guarded the entrance into the temple proper. The central doorway leads to the **First Hypostyle Hall,** lined with 24 colossal papyriform columns. This grandiose entrance gives way to the **Second Hypostyle Hall,** which contains some of the finest bas-reliefs ever carved in Egypt. At the far left corner of the Second Hypostyle Hall, a long narrow corridor known as the **Gallery of the Kings** leads toward the southeast. This simple passage houses one of Egyptology's most treasured finds, the **Kings' List,** which mentions the names of 76 Egyptian rulers from Menes of Memphis to Seti I, the temple's royal patron. Correlating this list with previous knowledge, scholars were able to map the sequence of Egyptian dynasties.

In the southern wing of the temple, beside the entrance to the Gallery of the Kings, a doorway leads to a chamber with a tiny chapel to its right. The chapel con-tains a kinky relief showing the mummy of Osiris, in the form of a falcon, impreg-nating Isis. At the temple's rear is the elaborate **Inner Sanctuary of Osiris,** painted with scenes of Osiris's life. The sanctuary is flanked by three small shrines bedecked with the temple's best-preserved reliefs. Immediately behind the temple one can find the **Osirion,** a now partially submerged tomb that Seti built for himself in the style of the Old Kingdom. Ask a tomb guard to take you to the much less well-preserved **Temple of Ramses III** through a desert of broken ceramic to the north. The temple here contains some interesting hieroglyphics as well as sugges-tions of a mixing of Coptic and Pharaonic styles.

BETWEEN LUXOR AND ASWAN

The 228km stretch of the Nile from Luxor to Aswan meanders past the heavily-touristed rural towns of the south, **Esna, Edfu,** and **Kom Ombo.** These towns make excellent daytrips—Esna and Edfu from Luxor; Edfu, Kom Ombo, and the camel market at **Daraw** from Aswan—but live like a pharaoh by taking them all in on a *felucca* trip from Luxor to Aswan. By water, the entire route (including stops in Esna, Edfu, and Kom Ombo) takes three to five hedonistic, sun-drenched days.

ESNA اسنا ☎095

Esna (58km south of Luxor) is a study in blissful obliviousness: the *doyennes* of Esna's local coffee shop calmly sip their tea and smoke their *sheeshas* as if the luxury cruiser rolling into dock were just another *felucca*. Inland, people trot through the streets of the *souq* oblivious to the extraordinary Greco-Roman temple at its center. While little here will capture the imagination for more than a few hours, the spectacle of Esna and the temple it surrounds are well worth a visit.

E GETTING THERE AND GETTING AROUND. The most Egyptian way to get to Esna is by **felucca** or **Nile cruiser** from Luxor or Aswan. Trains, buses and **service** also reach Esna from the north and south. The highway and train station are on the eastern side of the river, connected to the town by a bridge. The **bus** and *service* stations are at the town's northwestern edge beside a small canal bridge (E£1 to the temple). You can take a **kalish** from either station to the temple (don't pay more than E£1.50-2 for a ride anywhere in town), or take the two-kilometer walk.

⁊ ORIENTATION AND PRACTICAL INFORMATION. Esna has only a few main streets important to tourists. The main drag, **Nile St.,** runs along the bank of the Nile. At the **ticket booth** for the temple, which sits in a small kiosk on the river side of the street where the cruise boats dock, Nile St. is met by **Souq St.,** a 200m stretch of tourist bazaars that runs up to the temple. Follow Nile St. 200m north as it branches left away from the river for the **Bank of Alexandria.** (☎40 05 26. Open Su-Th 8:30am-2pm; Ramadan 10am-1:30pm; additional exchange hours Su-Th 6-9pm; in winter 5-8pm.) To exchange traveler's checks and foreign currency, visit the convenient **bank kiosk** opposite the ticket booth. The non-English speaking **tourist police** (☎51 06 86) are on Souq St., and the slightly more helpful **police station** is about 250m north on Nile St. as it branches away from the river. **Pharmacy Confidence** sits confidently just north of the ticket office. (☎51 05 32. Open M-Sa 9am-2pm and 5:30-11pm; in winter 5-8pm.) The local **post office** is south of the ticket booth on Souq St. (Open Su-Th 8am-2pm.) Numerous stores along the riverfront allow **international phone calls.**

⬛⬛ ACCOMMODATIONS AND FOOD. There is little incentive to remain in Esna beyond a temple visit, but the fairly clean **Hotel El-Haramein** will do in a pinch. The hotel is 1km south (through the *souq*) of the temple's eastern wall and about the same distance inland from the Nile. Pass to the right of the white wall enclosing a gray concrete building, and walk another 100m. There are no signs, but the police can help you find your way (☎40 03 40. Singles E£5; doubles E£10, with bath E£15; triples E£15-20; quads E£20-25). The *souq* provides *ta'amiyya* and produce.

⬛ SIGHTS. Although the **Temple of Khnum** was begun in the 18th dynasty, it is largely a Roman creation and in many ways a feeble imitation of inherited Egyptian technical and artistic achievements. The wall on the west side of the sight suggests original temple remains from the Greek era, but excavations have yet to begin. **Khnum** was the ram-headed creator god (he reputedly molded the first human being on a potter's wheel; see **Meet the Gods,** p. 69) who was worshiped in this region around the First Nile Cataract and at his sanctuary on Aswan's Elephantine Island (see p. 243). The Cataract was an important economic and cultural center for the area south of Luxor, and the pharaohs of the 18th dynasty dedicated this temple to the local deity to garner local support. Remains of a small Coptic church in front of the temple attest to the layered religious history of this site.

The temple's elaborate hallway (all that remains of what was once a much larger sanctuary) has managed to survive in excellent condition. In an attempt to decorate the temple in traditional Egyptian style, the Romans carved a procession of stiff, oddly deformed figures marching solemnly across the walls. The ceiling designs are among the more interesting aspects of the temple: the signs of the zodiac are portrayed just right of the last pillar on the left as you enter the hallway. Faint blue and red hues on the tops of the 24 columns hint at the interior's former brilliance. (Open daily 6am-6:30pm; in winter 6am-5:30pm. E£8, students E£4. Don't buy tickets from hawkers in the souq.)

AL-KAB الكاب

From Edfu, the cheapest way to al-Kab is a one-way service (75pt), though some will say that service don't go there. If traveling by felucca, your captain might not know where al-Kab is; give him the distances indicated below and watch for the Roman wall on the east bank of the Nile. It's best to leave early before the sun is high. To get back to Edfu, hail a pickup taxi.

Don't go out of your way to see the temples at al-Kab (20km north of Edfu and 3km south of the village of al-Mahamid) unless you have the time and energy to spare while traveling between Esna and Edfu. The temples are intriguing, but not on the order of the sites at Esna or the Valley of the Kings (see p. 222). The distance between the two will make you empathize with Moses: they are a 2½km and 4km walk from the roadside tombs and city wall. Bring several bottles of water—there's not a leaf of shade. The site was once occupied by the ancient city of Nekheb, which was dedicated to the vulture-goddess Nekhbet, protectress of the pharaohs and lady of the mouth of the desert. City remains consist of several temples and the rather unimpressive ruins of old tombs dotting the highway.

TEMPLES AND CHAPELS. Two-and-a-half kilometers along an unpaved but passable track brings you to the tiny **Chapel of Thoth** (1320-1200 BCE), built by the high priest of al-Kab for Ramses II and dedicated to Nekhbet, Thoth (Wisdom), and Horus. The much larger **Ptolemaic Temple,** built under Ptolemies IX through XI, has an impressive ramped entryway leading to a forecourt with a few nice broken capitals and a chamber with ceiling paintings and inscriptions. The stagnant pond within the compound was once considered a sacred lake. Wake up the guard in the shack across the road to open the locked gates; he'll then ride with you another 1½km to the small **Temple of Amenophis III,** with well-preserved colored paintings and carvings of Nekhbet herself coiffed with a swingin' 60's bob. Caravans going to and coming from gold mines deeper in the desert once stopped here for prayer. (All sites open daily 7am-7pm; in winter 6am-6pm. E£10, students E£5.)

TOMBS. A guard will lead you up the staircase to the four most important tombs along the highway, dating from 1570 to 1320 BCE. The most well-preserved of the tombs is the **Tomb of Paheri,** a multi-talented royal servant. Paheri was chief priest, royal tutor to Prince Wadjmose (son of Pharaoh Thutmosis I), and scribe of the accounts of corn. This tomb features brightly colored illustrations of seated lotus sniffers and Egyptians cultivating crops, fishing, shipping, and making wine. At the rear of the tomb stands a statue of a happy Paheri flanked by two female figures. The **Tomb of Setau** belonged to the powerful high priest of Amun under Ramses III through IX (20th dynasty). The **Tomb of Aahmes** is the resting place of a warship captain who suppressed a rebellion in Upper Egypt and led 18th-dynasty forces under Amenhotep I and Thutmosis I. Unfortunately, both tombs are poorly preserved. The **Tomb of Renini,** superintendent of priests under Amenhotep I, contains a geometrically painted ceiling and eyes staring out from a broken statue.

EDFU ادفو
☎ **097**

Only 50km south of Esna, Edfu is more than worth the short trip. Even the most templed-out traveler won't be able to resist the grandeur of Edfu's **Temple of Horus.** The vast, stunningly preserved temple is intricately detailed, rivaling the serenity of Kalabsha and even the awesome scale of Abu Simbel to make it one of Upper Egypt's most spectacular sights. For all its grandeur, the temple hasn't made such a big impression on the locals. When archaeologists began excavating the temple in the mid-19th century, they had more than sand and rubble to clear; the people of Edfu had also built a number of homes on the half-buried temple's roof.

🚩 **ORIENTATION AND PRACTICAL INFORMATION.** Edfu lies on the west bank of the Nile, roughly halfway between Luxor (112km south) and Aswan (121km north). The center of town, **Temple Sq.** lies about 1km inland, while a bridge crosses the Nile at the northern edge of town. The **train station** is remotely positioned on the east bank, away from town. The **service** station sits just right of the small square where the bridge reaches the west bank. Trains run north and south until 9pm, as do *service*. **Kalishes** (E£2-3) or **private taxis** (E£3-5) can take you from either station to the temple. The **bus station** is 50m up the street to the right when facing the mosque in the square. Buses run north to Luxor and south to Aswan every hour until 6pm (at the latest). Another 200m down on the right is the **Bank of Cairo.** (☎70 36 97. Open Su-Th 8:30am-2pm and 3-10pm.) Across the street from the bank is **Ezzat Pharmacy.** (☎70 38 60. Open M-Sa 7:30am-midnight.) About 100m from Temple Sq. is a tourist bazaar, the **tourist police** (☎70 01 34; open 7am-7pm; in winter 7am-4pm), and the temple. The **post office** is on Tahrir St., on the right side 50m south of Temple Sq. (Open Sa-Th 8am-2pm.) From the bridge, the riverfront road runs 100m south to the **telephone office** (☎70 17 77; open 24hr.) and another 200m to **al-Maglis St.,** which links the Nile with Temple Sq. The **telegraph office,** on the south side of Temple Sq., can help with **calling card calls** (about 90pt per 3min. to call Cairo). Several **telephone offices** line the riverfront where the cruise ships dock.

🍴 **ACCOMMODATIONS AND FOOD.** The cleanest budget hotel in town—though that's not saying much—is the musty **al-Madina Hotel,** just off Temple Sq. (☎70 13 26. Singles with breakfast E£20, less without bath; doubles E£30; triples E£40.) The cheap but run-down **Semi-Ramis Hotel** is near the bank; at E£6 per bed it's not hard on the pocketbook, but you get what you pay for. The **Tabarak Restaurant,** in the small square by the bridge, serves up large portions of chicken, beef, pigeon, and fish with side dishes (E£7-12), but space is tight, so don't plan your wedding reception here. Edfu's produce **souq** lines the streets off Temple Sq.

🏛 **SIGHTS.** The spectacular **Temple of Horus** took almost 200 years to construct and wasn't completed until 57 BCE, making it one of the last great Egyptian monuments. The Ptolemies designed this temple and the temple to Hathor at Dendera (see p. 231) as a matched set. Several important religious festivals dealing with the life of Horus were celebrated at Edfu. During the annual "Union with the Solar Disk," Horus's earthly form was brought to the roof of the temple to be rejuvenated by the sun ray. Another important ritual was the "Festival of the Happy Reunion," in which the god's icon (once held in the polished black granite shrine in the inner sanctuary of the temple) was removed from the temple in a ceremonial boat, then taken to Dendera to escort gal-pal Hathor back to his humble abode for some playtime. In a chamber behind the sanctuary, there is a modern reconstruction of the ceremonial boat used to carry the statue during festivals. *(Site open daily 7am-6pm; in winter 7am-4pm. E£20, students E£10. Bring a flashlight.)*

The path from the ticket office approaches the temple from the rear, so wind your way to the right around the complex to the front and enter through the 12 gigantic columns of the **Great Hypostyle Hall.** Proceed to the second hypostyle hall, outfitted with a similar arrangement of smaller pillars. Doorways on either side

EGYPT

lead to the **ambulatory,** a narrow exterior passageway running between the temple and its protective wall. Charred ceilings mark the time when Christians used the temple to store and burn garbage. The doorway on the right side of the second hall leads to a side **chapel** with a celestial ceiling depicting the sky-goddess, Nut, reaching around the Zodiac (for more on the mythological significance of this, see **Meet the Gods,** p. 69). Sadly, monotheists of later eras chiseled away most figures' faces, but the rest of the temple's reliefs remain untouched.

Outside the temple, directly in front of the main entrance, is a well-preserved Roman **mammisis** (birthhouse), where the birth of Horus was reenacted annually with appropriate hoopla. How many breast-feeding scenes can you count? Copts later defaced the images of the growing god on the *mammisis's* columns. Note the images of **pot-bellied pygmies,** brought to court for the royalty's entertainment, atop the exterior side columns.

GABAL AL-SILSILAH جبل السلسلة

The quarries at **Gabal al-Silsilah** are a fascinating bonus prize for *felucca* travelers who succeed in persuading their captain to stop here. Although a ramp and stairs have been built down to the water's edge in anticipation of Nile cruiser stops, the site is not yet officially open; however, *bakhsheesh* to the guard and a promise to be quick should win access. To reach the quarries by land, take a *service* from Kom Ombo to Kalabsha and ask for the **Temple of Horemheb** (a request for "Gabal al-Silsilah" will land you in the speck of a town by the same name on the east bank). *Service* should cost no more than E£3 and the boat ride over the Nile to the temple should be no more than E£2.

There are sandstone **quarries** (used from the New Kingdom in 1500 BCE to the Ptolemaic period) on both sides of the Nile, but boats only dock on the west bank. A guard can unlock the well-preserved **Temple of Horemheb,** built by General Horemheb, who seized the throne during the power struggles after King Tutankhamun's death. From the temple, a path leads 200m south along a bluff 15m above the Nile, ending in the cavernous belly of the quarry. Huge blocks of sandstone were cut from the cliff, loaded onto boats, and transported along the Nile to construction sites; notice the boat and ostrich graffiti etched into the wall's face.

KOM OMBO كوم امبو

Kom Ombo still stands in its original spot, 45km north of Aswan, and cuts the same striking figure today as it did during Ptolemaic times. Where the temples at Philae, Kalabsha, and Abu Simbel once stood, only water now remains (see **Moving a Mountain,** p. 251). The temple at Kom Ombo has been more ornery—it may have aged, but it sure hasn't budged. The beautiful temple ruins make Kom Ombo well worth the visit, but finding a parking spot may be difficult: Nile cruisers carrying an assortment of European tourists and their translators barge in on every available inch of the coastline. One look at the adjacent town will make most travelers want to make like a temple and relocate.

▣ SIGHTS. Although a temple has stood here since the time of the Middle Kingdom, the current edifice dates back only to 150 BCE. Parts of these older versions of the **Temple of Kom Ombo** now rest at the Louvre and the Egyptian Museum in Cairo. The rising waters of the Nile left the current temple almost completely buried in silt. In later years, the portion above ground was used as a quarry for construction projects; as a result, the side walls have vanished.

Nevertheless, the temple that remains provides more deity for your dollar than you will get anywhere else. **Sobek,** patron of the many crocs that lurked in the waters nearby in ancient times, came to **Horus** the elder, avenger of Osiris and the source of the pharaohs' divine power, asking for food. Horus complied, and the two gods subsequently agreed to share this temple. Kom Ombo, dedicated to the two gods, is therefore rigorously symmetrical throughout: double halls and double colonnades lead to double doorways which open onto double chambers and double sanctuaries. The right side of the temple honors Sobek, and the left Horus. (Sobek's crocodiles have since relocated to Lake Nasser). On the ceiling of the left vestibule, bright blue images of the latter still hover protectively over the chamber A tunnel in the floor of the inner sanctuary allowed clergy to climb in so they could overhear entreaties to the gods. Ask the guard to show you the reliefs of **Cleopatra II and VII,** and take it upon yourself to decipher the rather risqué hieroglyphs: can you spot the two dripping phalluses and the dismembered bodies?

Predating the Catholic tradition of confessionals by several centuries, a window in the west wall opening into the sanctuary, decorated with ears and eyes, is where the plebeians came to confess their sins to the gods and ask for forgiveness. This section of the temple also houses reliefs honoring yet another deity: Aesculapius, or the Greek god of medicine.

Adjoining the west of the temple are remains of a Roman *mammisis* (birth-house), and adjoining the northern edges of the temple are now-putrescent Roman water supply tanks, once crawling with crocodiles. The **Chapel of Hathor,** to your right as you enter the compound, has crocodile mummies which were unearthed near the road leading to the site. Cleopatra's bubble bath is also rumored to be nearby. *(Site open daily 7am-9pm; in winter 7am-7pm. E£10, students E£5.)*

DARAW CAMEL MARKET دراو

*Service careen to Daraw from Kom Ombo (8km north; 10min.) and Aswan (37km south; 1hr.). Trains and buses running between Luxor and Aswan may also stop here. The taxi stand, bus station, and train station lie along the main highway. To reach the camel market from the stations, walk 300m north, cross the tracks, and head down the road for 15min. Take a right after you pass the open fields. You've arrived when you see 200-odd people smacking the rear ends of bound, groaning camels to display their vigor. If you're gliding by on a **felucca**, have the captain stop at the Daraw ferry landing and a pickup truck will take you to the market.*

Sudanese merchants, Bishari tribespeople, and Egyptian *fellaheen* gather every Tuesday morning in Daraw for the unforgettable **camel market.** Rising very early in Aswan, you can visit the market and move on to the temple at Kom Ombo.

The Bishari (Saharan nomads with their own language and culture) purchase camels in Sudan for the equivalent of E£200, where camels are as plentiful as sand, and drive them from nearby Sudan to Daraw on what herdsmen have come to call the "40 Days Road." Look for the occasional rakehell businessman in full traditional dress: flowing pants, fighting sword and dagger, and a cloak draped over the shoulders. Typically, a Sudanese camel owner will pay a Sudanese or Bishari shepherd to drive his camels north to Egypt. The owner then flies up to oversee the selling, coming away with a 500% profit. The going rate for a big male camel is E£1200-1500, a savings of E£1000 over prices in Cairo. *(Market open Tu 7am-2pm; in winter Tu 7am-2pm, and sometimes Su-M 7am-2pm; slows down after 11am.)*

ASWAN اسوان ☎ 097

Aswan, one of the southernmost cities in Egypt, is a model of the age-old tradition of Middle Eastern hospitality. At the juncture between the Middle East and Africa, its transitory nature is most evident in its ethnic and cultural pluralism. In 1971, the completion of the Soviet-designed High Dam created nearby Lake Nasser (the world's largest reservoir) and boosted Egypt's agricultural and energy potential. The dam flooded most of Nubia, forcing massive migrations to Egypt and Sudan. Darker-skinned Nubian immigrants now thrive in Aswan, giving the city its African flavor. Its name comes from the Nubian phrase *assy wangibu*, which means, "too much water," although the high daytime temperatures will often make you wonder if there could ever be enough water. This far south, the fertile strip nourished by the Nile is not very wide, and often only a few trees separate the desert from the river. Summer temperatures average over 40°C (104°F), though the thermometer dips to a chilly 35°C (95°F) in winter. During this time, the city becomes a resort, but foreigners are welcome in any season. Restaurants, hotels, and shops are especially accommodating when there's money to be made.

Throughout the city, the gentle charm of the locals makes up for the stuffy weather. Be it the pesky street vendor stopping passersby mid-stride to hawk his wares, or the accommodating old lady giving directions in broken English, somehow tourists are coaxed into extending their stay. The cool breezes along the corniche in the evenings are also a welcome surprise for those foolish enough to stroll (and roast) during the day time. Aswan's pleasures should be experienced in groups: women traveling alone will get loads of catcalls, suggestive glances, and more-than-friendly hellos.

Aswan is a convenient base for exploring the rest of Upper Egypt. Plan on four days if you want to see the sights and stay sane. You can take *felucca* trips to Kom Ombo, Edfu, and Luxor (see **The Nile Valley: Getting Around,** p. 208). Summer, when temperatures are high and captains are desperate to capture the rare tourists, is the best time for a *felucca* trip. Not only may prices be cheaper, but drifting on the Nile provides escape from the sun-soaked sands.

▐ GETTING THERE AND GETTING AROUND

Flights: The airport (☎ 48 03 07) is 23km south of town near the High Dam. E£20 one-way by taxi, even lower if you can haggle. Served by **EgyptAir** (☎ 31 50 00; fax 31 50 05), on Corniche al-Nil, at the southern end near Ferial Gardens. Office open daily 8am-8pm. Another EgyptAir office at the airport (☎ 48 05 68), but no tickets sold there. Four flights daily to Cairo, eight during the winter (E£577 one-way). Daily flights to **Abu Simbel** leave three times per day from Apr.-Sept., 11 times Oct.-Mar. (E£288 round-trip, price will increase to E£508 if the road to Abu Simbel is re-opened). V, MC. **Airport Police:** ☎ 48 05 09.

Trains: (☎ 31 47 54), from the northern end of al-Souq St. First- and 2nd-class A/C trains depart at 5am and 8:45pm for **Luxor** (3½hr.; first-class E£20, 2nd-class E£15) and **Cairo** (14hr.; first-class E£63, 2nd-class E£40). Prices subject to the whims of the Egyptian Transportation Department. Evening trains tend to be about E£10 more. The tourist office can give the most current fares. Frequent trains run to and from the **High Dam** (30min., 6 per day, 55pt). There are often student discounts on trains.

Buses: (☎ 30 32 25), on Abtal al-Tahrir St. behind the Abu Simbel Hotel. At press time, buses and *service* were unavailable for tourists because of road closures and safety reasons, but may be available later in the year. Hours vary, but 10 A/C buses per day to: **Daraw** (45min., E£1.50); **Edfu** (2hr., E£4); **Kom Ombo** (1hr., E£1.50); and **Luxor** (4hr., E£6.50). Once the road reopens, buses to: **Abu Simbel** (4hr., 8am, 4pm, E£26 round-trip, returns to Aswan 6:30am, 2pm); **Asyut** (8hr., 7am, E£25); **Cairo** (12hr., 3:30pm, E£55); **Hurghada** (7hr.; 8am, E£20; 3:30pm with A/C, E£40); **Qena** (4hr.; 6:30, 11:30am, 12:30pm; E£10); and **Suez** (12hr.; 8am, E£28; 3:30, 5pm, E£45).

Ferries: Range from large *feluccas* to small motor boats. Ferries depart from the al-Shatii Restaurant on the southern end of the corniche, or across from the EgyptAir office even farther south (every 15-20min., 6am-6pm) to **Elephantine Island** (E£1). Hotel Oberoi's cheap ferry floats to the northern part of Elephantine Island (E£1; see **Sights,** p. 242). The **Seti** ferry (not Seti Tours) departs from the north end of the corniche across from the park to the northern part of the western bank (every 20min., 6am-6pm, E£1). Ignore captains who tell you the ferry is not running.

Service: At press time, buses and *service* were unavailable for tourists because of road closures and safety reasons, but may be available later in the year. *Service* leave from the covered station 1km south of the train station (every 15-30min., 4am-6pm depending on demand). To get there, take the overpass just left of the train station; make a left at the end of the road, then another right. To: **Daraw** or **Kom Ombo** (40min., E£1.50); **Edfu** (1¼hr., E£3); **Esna** (2-3hr., E£6); **Luxor** (3hr., E£8); **Khazan/Old Dam** (75pt); and **Qena** (4hr., E£9). *Service* occasionally depart from the corniche and Abtal al-Tahrir St.

Taxis: Found everywhere along the corniche. Not more than E£5 within the city.

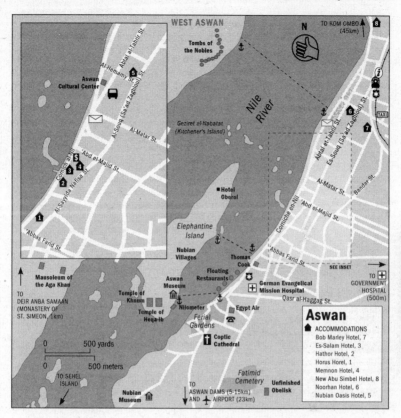

WEST ASWAN

Aswan

ACCOMMODATIONS
Bob Marley Hotel, 7
Es-Salam Hotel, 3
Hathor Hotel, 2
Horus Hotel, 1
Memnon Hotel, 4
New Abu Simbel Hotel, 8
Noorhan Hotel, 6
Nubian Oasis Hotel, 5

Bike Rental: Three locations: Abtal al-Tahrir St. next to Poste Restante office; near train station on al-Souq St.; and farther down al-Souq St. next to Nubian Oasis Hotel. E£5 per day, E£1 per hr.; in winter, prices may double. Try haggling if prices are not posted.

Kalish: After haggling, a horse-drawn *kalish* should cost E£5 for a short ride, E£10 for an extended 30-min. tour.

ORIENTATION

You're rarely more than two blocks from the river in Aswan. The northern half of the city lies along three long avenues that run parallel to the Nile. The riverfront **Corniche al-Nil** is the most picturesque, featuring several hotels, shops, banks, floating restaurants, and docks. Two blocks inland, the market-lined **Sa'ad Zaghloul St.** features everything from watermelons to water pipes. Also called **al-Souq St.**, it begins at the train station at the northeast corner of town and runs south 2km to **'Abbas Farid St.;** for the block-long stretch behind the Es-Salaam and Hathor Hotels, this path of many names is widely known as **al-Sayyida Nafisa St.** In the southern half of town, the corniche continues for another 1km and ends at the **Ferial Gardens.** The northern grid pattern falls apart at the central market. South of the *souq*, inland streets form a labyrinth of alleys. Sandwiched between the corniche and the market street, **Abtal al-Tahrir St.** begins at the youth hostel in the north and culminates in a small cluster of tourist bazaars, resuming as a narrow lane farther south. Unless you're an expert at reading signs in faded Arabic, then don't plan on being able to identify streets. Asking for directions or using maps is your best bet.

🛈 PRACTICAL INFORMATION

TOURIST AND FINANCIAL SERVICES

Tourist Office: (☎31 28 11) Domed structure on the right as you exit the train station, on the northernmost end of al-Souq St. Few brochures, but knowledgeable and multilingual staff can help in all aspects of travel. Open daily 9am-3pm and 7-9pm; in winter 9am-3pm and 6-8pm.

Tourist Police: (☎30 31 63) On the south side of the train station. Open 24hr.

Passport Office: (☎31 22 38) On Corniche al-Nil, in the police building on the 3rd floor. Registers passports and extends visas. Open Su-Th 8am-2pm.

Currency Exchange: Banque Misr, 103 Corniche al-Nil (☎31 66 92, 31 66 93, or 31 66 95; fax 31 66 94). V and MC advances. Open Su-Th 8:30am-2pm. The only **ATM** on the corniche is next to Banque Misr and takes V, MC, PLUS, and Cirrus cards.

American Express: (☎/fax 30 29 09) At the southernmost end of the corniche on the 2nd floor of the New Cataract Hotel. Arranges travel itineraries, cashes traveler's checks, and holds mail for cardholders. Open Su-Th 8am-5pm, F-Sa 9am-4pm.

Thomas Cook: 59 Corniche al-Nil (☎30 40 11; fax 30 62 09), just north of the police building. Travel and financial services and discounted rates if tours and hotels are booked through Cook. Open daily 8am-2pm and 4-8pm; in winter 8am-8pm.

LOCAL SERVICES

Bookstore: Large hotels usually have small bookstores, which carry European newspapers. Books in Arabic, English, French, and other languages can be found in shops along al-Souq St. and Corniche al-Nil.

Laundromat: Most hotels do laundry for E£1-2 per garment. Laundry service and dry-cleaning shop under the Nubian Oasis Hotel (see p. 241). Open daily 8am-2pm.

Swimming Pools: The Oberoi Hotel pool is a swanky but expensive option at E£21. The rooftop pool at the Hathor Hotel is cheaper (E£5, free if you stay at the hotel) but it is only about 4 ft. deep.

EMERGENCY AND COMMUNICATIONS

Emergency: Few places have English speakers, so call the **Tourist Police** (☎30 31 63) or **Tourist Office** (☎31 28 11) first. **Medical Emergency:** ☎123.

Pharmacy: El-Nile Pharmacy (☎30 26 74), just south of Hathor Hotel on Corniche al-Nil. Open daily 7am-1am. Other pharmacies line the corniche and *souq*.

Hospital: Mubarak Military Hospital (☎31 79 85), in the flamingo-pink building behind the Nubian Museum. Clean new facility offers everything from family planning to emergency gynecological care. Travelers pay in cash. **German Evangelical Mission Hospital** (☎30 21 76 or 31 21 76), 100m south of the police station down an alley on the left. Look for steel doors with flower symbols. The **Government Hospital** (☎32 28 55 or 24 19), on Qasr al-Hagga St., should be a last resort. These three listed in order of decreasing English proficiency. Every hotel reception can provide the name of a **doctor.**

Post Office: On Corniche al-Nil, toward the northern end of town, right before the park. Offers **EMS** and **telegraph** services. Open Sa-Th 9am-2pm. For **Poste Restante,** walk south from the main post office and turn left down Salah al-Din St., then immediately right. In the yellow building with black columns. Open Su-Th 8am-2pm.

Internet Access: Mr. Fry, general manager of the Nubian Oasis Hotel, can take you into a back room for a stable and relatively quick connection for 50pt per min. To save time and money, type letters on a word processor (free!) and then email them as attachments. Internet cafes can also be found along the corniche.

Telephones: Telephone office (☎31 38 69), two doors south of EgyptAir, on Corniche al-Nil, at the southern end near Ferial Gardens. Open 24hr. **Telegraph service, fax** available 8am-2pm and 3-9pm, E£30 for 3min. to US. **Information:** ☎16.

ACCOMMODATIONS

Prices are higher in winter and lower in summer; rates listed are approximate. If you have the energy when you arrive, you may be able to play hotel hawkers off one another to land a better price. All listed hotels have laundry service and breakfast unless otherwise stated, but none dance the credit card tango. Spend the extra money in the summer and get air-conditioning, unless you want to wake up in the morning and find half your body mass evaporated. Be sure to ask for applicable student and group discounts, but be careful of discounted group tours and *felucca* trips, which are often rip-offs. Do not agree to anything before you have checked out the competition on your own.

Nubian Oasis Hotel, 234 Sa'ad Zaghloul St. (☎31 21 23; fax 31 21 24; email nubianoasis@infinity.com.eg). From the train station, turn left onto Sa'ad Zaghloul and right two streets after Cleopatra Hotel. Simple, clean, and recently re-painted, this standout has great views from the rooftop and the cute pink breakfast room. TV lounge with cable, pool. Internet access (50pt per min.). Rooms come with fans. Check-out noon. Singles E£10; doubles E£15; E£5 each for private bathrooms and A/C.

Noorhan Hotel (☎31 60 69), on Sa'ad Zaghloul St. From train station, turn left onto Sa'ad Zaghloul and take second left at the Noorhan sign. When the sun goes down, the rooftop terrace is perfect for sipping Stellas (E£5.50). Check-out noon. Singles E£6 with fans; doubles E£12 with fans; E£1.50 more per person for a private bathroom and A/C.

Es-Salaam Hotel, 101 Corniche al-Nil (☎30 36 49; fax 30 26 51). Carpeted hallways, an elevator, and a rooftop restaurant scheduled to open in 2000 make the stay worth the extra dough. The rooms, many with wrap-around balconies, have great views of the Nile. All rooms have pristine, tiled bathrooms and A/C. Check-out noon. Singles E£35; doubles E£50; triples E£65.

Hathor Hotel (☎31 45 80), right in the middle of Corniche al-Nil, next door to Es-Salaam Hotel. New ceramic floor and wood furniture give the Hathor a relatively sophisticated air. Use of the shallow rooftop pool is free if you stay at the Hathor, E£5 if you don't. All rooms have bath and A/C. Check-out noon. Singles E£30; doubles E£45; triples E£60.

Horus Hotel, 89 Corniche al-Nil, 4th floor (☎30 33 23; fax 31 33 13). Half the rooms are marvelously renovated and tiled, complete with bathtubs and the other half are shabbier, but spacious. All include A/C and private bath. Check-out noon. Renovated singles E£35; doubles E£50; triples E£65; un-renovated rooms are E£5 cheaper.

Memnon Hotel, (☎30 04 83), Corniche al-Nil. Entrance on the street parallel to the corniche, behind the National Bank of Egypt. A homey, Nile-view throwback to the early '60s with decor somewhere between the surreal and the absurd. Rooms have A/C, private bath, red shag lamps, and 18th-century French curtains. Lunch E£12, dinner E£15. Singles E£23; doubles E£35, with view E£55; triples E£65; suites E£75.

Bob Marley Hotel (☎30 18 39). Coming out of the train station, turn left onto al-Souq St., and take a left at the sign for the hotel. Low on cash? Don't mind ergonomically challenging beds? Bob's is your place, mon. No private baths or A/C. Check-out noon. Breakfast E£1. Singles E£5.

FOOD

Aswan's **souq** carries fruits, vegetables, bread, and pigeon (a local specialty)—not to mention *ta'amiyya*, liver sandwiches, and *kushari*. **Vegetarians** may find their choices limited to a few rice dishes. For legendary legumes, a large **vegetable souq** is tucked away near the train station, on the northeast edge of al-Souq St., and another stretches between the corniche and al-Souq St. on the south end. Come in the morning for a full range of options. At the other end of the price spectrum, wallow in huge buffets and gourmet Arab and continental cuisine at luxury hotels. The Oberoi offers an elegant E£22 **breakfast buffet** (6-10:30am) in its cupola-covered ballroom restaurant. Try *karkadeh*, a sweet ambrosial purple drink made of hibiscus. Local legend says downing a glass before bedtime mellows you out.

El-Medina, take a left onto al-Souq St. from the train station. Across from the Cleopatra Hotel. Street vendors and tourists lunch here while watching a little futbol on TV. Beef, chicken, and vegetarian dishes served with rice, veggies, and salad (E£9-16) fill you up, and the speedy service won't slow you down. Open daily 1pm-midnight.

Sayyida Nafisa, turn left onto al-Souq St. after exiting the train station. As you approach, the ground in the *souq* turns rosy red from colored wood shavings. Named after a relative of Muhammad, this restaurant is centrally located and serves up the usual chicken and beef dishes (E£5-9). Refreshing juices E£1.50. Open daily noon-2am.

El-Masry (☎30 25 76). Head south from the train station and turn left onto al-Matar St. Treat yourself at this relatively upscale, tidy establishment. Although the food is almost identical to that of other restaurants, there's more of it, and the waiters are clad in slacks and white button-downs. Meals E£20-25, include main course, sides, and dessert. Open daily noon-midnight.

Darwesh Restaurant, on Sa'ad Zaghloul St., across the street from the south end of the train station. All meals come with vegetables, soup, rice, and salad (full meal E£10-12). Open daily noon-midnight.

FLOATING RESTAURANTS

More popular with locals and tourists alike, these pseudo-aquatic eateries offer decent meals and the perfect setting to watch the sun go down over the desert hills of the west bank. All serve basically the same array of meat dishes plus salads, tahini, drinks, and desserts, although you'll pay more at upscale joints. They are listed from south to north (and incidentally, from most to least expensive). They start about 100m north of the EgyptAir office, on the opposite side of the street.

Aswan Panorama (☎30 61 69). The best of floating cuisine. The delicious food and fruit trees among the tables make it well worth the walk down the corniche. Try the Bedouin coffee served on coals, filtered with dried grass, and flavored with cardamom, cinnamon, and cloves or, perhaps, the pigeon burger (E£20 total). No seating after 9pm.

Monalisa. Quite a few *feluccas* along this stretch of the Nile bear the name of Leonardo's masterpiece, but only this one has the picture to go with it. *You* may not be smiling from the overbearing heat outdoors, but turn that frown upside down with a Monalisa cocktail (E£1.50). Well-prepared meat and fish entrees (E£6-9). Open daily 8am-3am.

Emy. Everything about the only actual boat among the floating restaurants screams '80s, from the neon sign to the faded poster of Michael Jackson at the front door. Sit on the top level of the barge to sway gently as you chew (and chew and chew) on your kebab (E£11.50). They also serve smallish pizzas, as well as breakfast (E£3) and beer (E£5). The 20% student discount offsets the pain of a 15% tax and service surcharge. Open daily 8am-1:30am.

Aswan Moon Restaurant. The badly taxidermized beasts decorating the entrance watch over the *felucca* chiefs eating below. Stuffed animals watching animals stuffing! Share a meal with them for E£6-10. Omm 'Ali coconut milk bread is worth the E£3.

◼ SIGHTS

Most of Aswan's attractions can be found on the isles in the middle of the Nile. Although some of Aswan's ancient Egyptian ruins are only second-rate compared to those of Giza and Luxor, the Nubian artifacts can't be found anywhere else. Just a short train ride away, the Aswan High Dam and Lake Nasser are a token of the Egyptian people's continuing ability to outdo everyone in terms of grandeur.

To reach the sights on the west bank of the Nile, it's easiest to hire a *felucca*. The official rate for *felucca* transport in the vicinity of Aswan is E£10 per hour regardless of the number of passengers, but getting this price may take some negotiation. A complete tour of Elephantine Island, Kitchener's Island, the Aga Khan's Mausoleum, St. Simeon's Monastery, and the northern tombs goes for E£50 per group and takes about two hours. A cheap alternative is to hire a rowboat or motorboat to the west bank (E£2-3), then trek from sight to sight on foot. Trans-

KISS MY AS(WAN)

Or the top ten ways to get rid of felucca captains and other undesirables:

10. *"La, shukran" (No thank you.)*
9. *"Ultilak la" (I said no.)*
8. *"Bas" (Enough.)*
7. *"Imshee" (Go away.)*
6. *"Haram 'alayk" (Shame on you.)*
5. *"Kib nafsik" (Scram.)*
4. *"Iza arabit minni, badribak" (If you get any closer, I'll hit you.)*
3. *"La hawla wa la quwata illa billah...la" (By all the force and power of Allah...no!)*
2. *"Ya haywan" (You animal.)*
1. *"Ibn kalb" (You son of a dog.)*
Let's Go does not recommend using phrases 1 or 2.

port back to the corniche or Elephantine Island, either by ferry (E£1) or rowboat (E£8), is also relatively easy, as long as you don't get stranded late in the day, when the boatmen have you at their mercy.

ELEPHANTINE ISLAND. While historically very significant, **Elephantine Island** is not really all that exciting. The largest of Aswan's spores, got its name from the black and (you guessed it) elephant-shaped stones at its southern tip. The remains of the ancient settlement on the southeast corner of the island, directly behind the museum, have been excavated. The local ferry from the Corniche al-Nil provides the cheapest transport to Elephantine Island (E£1, see p. 238).

The **Aswan Archaeological Museum** houses a rather small collection of ancient artifacts, either hand-labeled or completely unmarked. Even the "Head of a Man Mummy," resting on a cloth sack in the museum's sarcophagus room, looks bored. An annex augments the collection with a wide array of items recently excavated from the adjacent ruins. The Nilometer near the waterfront is nothing more than a staircase with a few engravings on the banister. The most fascinating sections of the island are the **Temple of Khnum**, the **Temple of Heqa-Ib**, and the Ptolemaic temple dedicated to Alexander II. When checking out the etchings of pharaohs, scarabs, and the like, make sure to bring a ball of string to trail behind you; some of the chambers are labyrinth-like, complete with dead ends and false doors. *(Open daily 8:30am-6pm; in winter 8am-5pm. E£10, students E£5, includes the museum, adjacent ruins, and the Nilometer. Camera privileges E£15.)*

KITCHENER'S ISLAND. Behind Elephantine Island and not visible from central Aswan, **Kitchener's Island** (*Geziret al-Nabatat,* or "Island of the Plants") is a lovely botanical garden planted by the British General Kitchener, best known for crushing the Sudanese rebellion of 1898. Exotic and flamboyant birds congregate in the tropical plants from Africa and Asia that flourish here. To reach the island, hire a *felucca* to combine an island visit with stops along the west bank and Elephantine Island (a full afternoon rental runs E£10 per hour). It is also possible to hire a rowboat from the west side of Elephantine Island (about E£3 for 1-2 passengers only). Make sure boats are willing to wait for you or come back for pickup by withholding payment until the end of the trip. If you're a real cheapskate, you can still get a gorgeous bird's eye view of this miniature paradise from the south face of the Tomb of the Nobles on the west bank. *(Open daily 8am-5pm. E£5.)*

MAUSOLEUM OF THE AGA KHAN. The most placid attraction on the Nile's west bank is the **Mausoleum of the Aga Khan,** a short climb from the *felucca* dock. Aga Khans, the hereditary titles of Isma'ili Muslim *imams*, are believed to be direct descendants of Muhammad and the inheritors of his spiritual responsibilities of guidance. Aswan became the favorite winter retreat of **Sultan Muhammad Shah al-Husseini**, Aga Khan III (1877-1957). Upon his death, Begum (the Aga Khan's wife) oversaw the construction of the mausoleum, where the feisty nonagenarian still

EGYPT

spends part of her year. Unfortunately, the mausoleum has been closed by the Egyptian government since June 1, 1997, due to a dispute over entrance fees with Begum. It sports an imposing fortress-like exterior, while the interior has a quiet simplicity modeled after Cairo's Fatimid tombs. Opposite the entrance stands a beautiful marble sarcophagus inscribed with passages from the Qur'an. *(Once the mausoleum re-opens, hours will be Tu-Su 9am-4pm. Dress conservatively and remove shoes.)*

MONASTERY OF ST. SIMEON. The isolated and majestic **Deir Anba Samaan** (Monastery of St. Simeon) is a short 1km walk across the dunes from the Mausoleum of Aga Khan, heading away from shore. Built in the 6th and 7th centuries, the monastery is on a terrace carved into the steep hills and looks more like a fort than a religious sanctuary with its 6m high, turreted walls. The original walls stood 10m high, but were not strong enough to keep the 300 resident monks from being driven out by Arab conquerors in the 14th century. Upstairs, the monks' cells and stone beds (with Bible and *galabiyya* wall slots) are currently occupied by bats. The monastery had a church and accommodations sufficient for several hundred pilgrims and their camels. There are also remnants of the baptismal font and drain pipe, well-preserved paintings of Mary and Joseph, and Communion wine-making facilities in St. Simeon's chamber. Simeon's chamber has a slot in the roof for a piece of rope he tied around his beard to keep him on his feet during all-night prayer vigils.

To get there, follow the paved path that starts in front of the Mausoleum of the Aga Khan or, if you don't mind chafing your rear end a little, hire a camel near the *felucca* stop (E£20 per camel for a 20min. ride for two people). Women do not need to cling tightly to the camel driver, despite his concerns for safety, nor should the driver need to grab his passengers' legs to ensure stability. If you feel at all uncomfortable, forget the drivers' beastly manners and leave their camels behind. *(Open Tu-Su 7am-4pm. E£12, students E£6.)*

TOMBS OF THE NOBLES. The **Tombs of the Nobles** lie farther north along the west bank of the Nile, incised into the face of desert cliffs and impressively illuminated at night. These tombs of governors and dignitaries date from the 23rd to the 18th century BCE and are significantly better preserved than those at Elephantine. Climb up the 100-odd stairs to ogle the bright color and detail of the reliefs in the **Tomb of Sarenput II;** note the sacrificial stone slab with a blood drainage spout. The mummy was taken to Cairo, but there are plenty of other items on the menu to choose from. If you ask nicely, the guard will move the grating and let you peer into the enclave where baskets of yummy camel bones are stored, or you can take a moment to examine the altar where meals were offered to the gods. The interconnected 6th-dynasty **Tombs of Nikhu and Sabni,** father and son, have images of the ancients getting high on lotus blossoms. The cheapest way to visit the tombs is to take the ferry from the corniche, across the small park from the tourist office (E£1). Once across, walk uphill to the shack-like office on the left. *(Open daily 7am-4pm. E£12, students E£6. Camera privileges E£10.)*

NUBIAN MUSEUM. Nubian culture is more alive and prominent in Aswan than anywhere else in Egypt. Ten years in the making, **Aswan's Nubian Museum** is a magnificent sandstone building south of the Old Cataract Hotel. It features a vast collection of Nubian artifacts from throughout Egypt, described in Arabic and English (a rarity in Aswan). If you have a choice, the Nubian Museum, with more exhibits and labeled displays, is a better deal than the Aswan Museum on Elephantine Island. *(Open daily 9am-1pm and 5-9pm. E£20, students E£10.)*

NUBIAN VILLAGES. For a more authentic and enjoyable taste of Nubian life, step outside the museum. The central section of Elephantine Island has several **Nubian villages** where you'll find friendly residents, adoring youngsters, and brightly painted homes. The ferry to the west bank tombs (E£1) can bring you to **Gharb Aswan,** a series of Nubian villages less touristed than Elephantine Island's. A pickup truck will take you north to the villages from the ferry dock (about E£1). You may even be invited to join the celebrations and ululations of a wedding ceremony; the Nubians consider it a mark of honor to have guests from far-flung vil-

Call the USA

"feel free to call"

1-800-COLLECT

When in Ireland
Dial: 1-800-COLLECT (265 5328)

When in N. Ireland, UK & Europe
Dial: 00-800-COLLECT USA (265 5328 872)

Member of
Dublin Tourism

Australia	0011	800 265 5328 872
Finland	990	800 265 5328 872
Hong Kong	001	800 265 5328 872
Israel	014	800 265 5328 872
Japan	0061	800 265 5328 872
New Zealand	0011	800 265 5328 872

lages attend their nuptial festivities. Nubian weddings traditionally involved 15 days of partying, but the demands of modern life have trimmed the celebration down to a mere three or four. Nubians feel slighted if you reject their offers of hospitality, so be diplomatic in declining if you must. At all times, be modest in your dress and behavior. Women traveling alone will feel more comfortable amongst polite and hospitable Nubians than amongst harassing men on the east shore.

The large Nubian houses, made of Nile mud, consist of six rooms around a courtyard; each cluster of rooms has its own dome or cylindrical roof. When the High Dam threatened to destroy this traditional style, architect Hassan Fathy whipped up these reconstructed and relocated villages. Just as many Arab Muslims take pride in having made the *Hajj* (pilgrimage to Mecca) by adding the prefix "hajj" to their last name, Nubian families celebrate this accomplishment by brightly painting their huts.

ENTERTAINMENT

"Nightclubs" in Aswan feature a group of drummers and tambourinists with a loud organ player and a male singer/emcee, plus the hip-notizing gyrations of a sequin-clad belly dancer enticing men into tossing bills. Check out the scene at **Salah ad-Din Restaurant** on the water. There are often cover charges or minimums for discos and nightclubs, but they change frequently (usually E£5-10 cover or two-drink minimum). The **Oberoi Hotel** has a piano bar where you can even sit down and play (drinks E£10-35), and a mini-disco with a pounding dance mix. The bastard love child of Eastern and Western dance scenes can be found at the dank pub and disco at the **New Cataract.** (Open daily 7pm-2am, E£15 cover for disco.) The Pullman bar in the **Old Cataract** is a more legitimate alternative with no cover. For more subdued enjoyment, try the pool and snooker tables at the **Basma Hotel** on the corniche, just behind the Cataract Hotels (E£5-15 cover).

🛍 SHOPPING

If you want more authentic souvenirs than hieroglyph-emblazoned t-shirts—or even if you do want hieroglyph-emblazoned t-shirts—a stroll down **al-Sayyida Nafisa St.** provides the opportunity to buy either. Tailors measure and cut with lightning speed (pants E£10-25, shorts and simple shirts E£10-15, shirts with collars and buttons E£25-35). For traditional Egyptian clothing, there are numerous *galabiyya* (the Egyptian name for the ubiquitous Arab gown) and *qaftan* merchants in the *souq*. If you have the time, buy high-quality government cloth (at posted government prices) from one of the government shops on the corniche, then have garments made to order by the tailors on Sa'ad Zaghloul St. For authentic papyrus, head down the stairs by the waterfront to **Dr. Rayab's Papyrus Museum** on the corniche, across from the Horus Hotel. (Open daily 9am-11pm.) Papyrus ranges from E£3 to E£900, depending on whether you want a sketch of a hieroglyph or an elaborate picture of an ancient Egyptian ritual. From December through March, the **Aswan Palace of Cultures** on Corniche al-Nil, north of the post office and across from the Rowing Club, features Nubian dancing and crafts. (Open Sa-Th 9-11pm. E£5.)

To take an even more calming break from the already staid Aswani lifestyle, join locals for tea, *sheesha*, or a mean game of dominoes at the many cafes scattered throughout town. Spontaneous football (soccer) games occasionally spring up around the stadium in the northern part of town past the New Abu Simbel Hotel. For more personal relaxation, walk south along the corniche and around the Ferial Gardens to the elegant **Old and New Cataract Hotels** (☎ 30 35 28 or 30 36 28). Stroll through the gorgeous gardens, past the pool, and into the outdoor terrace cafe overlooking the river. (Open daily 9am-4pm. Drinks E£15 and up. No shorts on the terrace after 3pm.) For more expensive exertion, report to the Hotel Oberoi's health spa (☎ 30 34 55) for relaxing and rejuvenating treatments and exercises (priced individually from E£10-69).

NEAR ASWAN

In ancient times, the raging rapids of the **First Cataract** were much feared, but modern technology has transformed the surrounding area into a placid array of modern and ancient monuments. Bordered by the **quarries** and the **Unfinished Obelisk** to the south, and **Lake Nasser** to the north, the sites in between must be tackled in a series of hops, skips, and jumps. The **Old Dam,** just south of the quarries, lies 5km south of Aswan, with the **Island of Philae,** housing the Temple of Isis, just south of the dam. These structures are dwarfed by the ponderous **High Dam,** which lies another 10km upstream. On the west end of the High Dam, old and new come head-to-head with the **Temple of Kalabsha** and the **Soviet-Egyptian Friendship Monument.** Much further south, near the border with Sudan, the ruins at Abu Simbel are harder to reach, but equally impressive.

▌ TRANSPORTATION

An excellent road follows the Nile from Aswan to Khazan (a village near the Old Dam), providing access to both the dam and the motorboat launch to the Temple of Isis at Philae. The route to Khazan is serviced by **service** (50pt-E£1, depart from *service* stand) and by public **bus** (50pt-E£1). Both run frequently until about 9:30pm. Until tourists can once again use the buses and *service,* though, the only options are the **train** that runs frequently to the High Dam or a taxi which can take you by the dams and Kalabsha (E£30). Train stops are not labeled, so make sure to ask veteran-looking passengers for help identifying stations. Neither vehicles nor pedestrians are allowed to cross the dam after 6pm.

Once the road to Abu Simbel opens up again, the tourist office and most hotels in Aswan will resume arranging **minibus trips** to the ruins there. The trips generally cost E£25-35, and sometimes include the other sights south of Aswan (entrance fees not included). Arranged tours generally leave at 4am and return to Aswan by 2pm; overzealous authorities insist that tourist groups travel in a police convoy. You'll be miserable if your minibus doesn't have air-conditioning, since blowing sands may preclude opening the windows for much of the trip. A roundtrip flight to Abu Simbel booked through EgyptAir costs US$85.

SOUTH OF ASWAN

Taxi drivers returning to Aswan from the High Dam might agree to stop at the Fatimid tombs, the adjacent Unfinished Obelisk, and the nearby granite quarries. These sites are all near the camping area, 300m east of the main road at a turnoff 1km south of Aswan, and are all easily within walking or *kalish* (E£5-7) range of the city. Built during one of Islam's earliest eras, the **Fatimid Tombs** are spooky, especially when it seems as though it's just you and the ghosts wandering around the dark cemetery. By this time, the Egyptians had clearly gotten over their obsession with death, and the abandoned tombs are simply squat stone buildings with crescents on their roofs.

Surprisingly, sometimes an **Unfinished Obelisk** is more interesting than a finished obelisk. This one, across the street from the Fatimid tombs, was abandoned at its site because of a flaw in the granite; it was to have soared to a whopping 41.7m on a base 4.2m on each side. In its unadorned, supine state, the obelisk looks—well, unfinished, but it provides a rare behind-the-scenes look at the mammoth effort that went into its creation. Notice the channels along each side with curved indentations just big enough for a man to sit in and pound away with a ball made of diarite, a substance harder than granite. The earthbound side of the massive shaft would have been cut free either with copper or bronze chisels, or by pounding passages with diarite balls, inserting wooden beams, and flooding the channels so that the expanding wood would break the remaining stone. The adjacent **granite quarries,** best seen from the window of a passing train or cab, supplied ancient Egypt with the stone that was favored for temple and monument building. *(Obelisk and quarries open daily 7am-6pm, but the guard often leaves early. E£10, students E£5.)*

PHILAE فيلة

*Visited most easily by **taxi** as part of an itinerary including other sights, or take a **bus** to the Old Dam from the Aswan corniche; get off when it stops at the checkpoint on the east end of the dam. From the checkpoint, walk south along the shore to the concrete boat dock (about 2km). After paying for admission, you must hire a **motorboat** to reach the island at the official rate of E£20 per boat round-trip (price may drop in the off-season). Find a few travelers to share the expense of the boat. The captain will try to con you into paying more, but be firm. If there are serious problems, complain at the tourist office in town. The boat captain is obligated to wait for you as you tour the site, so there is no need to rush. **Service** are faster; tell the driver to let you off at the Old Dam (al-Sidd al-Qadeem). Philae also has a **sound and light show.** English performances are M, W, F-Sa 6pm, Tu 7:15pm, Su 8:30pm; in winter M, W, F-Sa 8pm, Tu 9:15pm, Su 10:30pm.*

Called "the pearl of Egypt" by one of Napoleon's soldiers, the beautiful Temple of Isis at Philae has attracted the pious and the curious since classical times. The completion of the Old Dam in 1902 partially submerged the buildings only a few years after their resurrection as a popular tourist destination. Victorian vandals then gathered around the pillars and chipped their names into the protruding columns; the graffiti now mark the earlier water level. Archaeologists feared the waters would eventually undermine the foundations of the temples and hasten their collapse, and the construction of the High Dam would indeed have utterly destroyed Philae were it not for the efforts of UNESCO and the Egyptian Antiquities Department. Between 1972 and 1980, the entire complex of temples was transferred from Philae Island to higher ground on nearby Agilkia Island. In 1980, the new site of the temples re-opened to tourism (see **Moving a Mountain,** p. 251).

TEMPLE OF ISIS. The Temple of Isis, dominating the island's northern edge, is the last bastion of ancient Egyptian religion. Isis was a goddess in the truest sense: mother of nature, protector of humans, goddess of purity and sexuality, and sister-wife of the legendary hero Osiris (see **Meet the Gods,** p. 69). It was on Philae that she supposedly found her husband's heart after he was dismembered, making the island the most sacred of Isis's homes. Her cult following continued long after the establishment of Christianity, fizzling out only in the 6th century during the reign of Justinian, who successfully replaced her with Mary. Nearly all the structures on Philae date from the Ptolemaic and Roman eras, when Egyptian artistic quality was in decline—hence the inferior quality of the decorative relief work. *(Open daily 7am-5pm. E£20, students E£10.)*

PORTICO OF NECTANEBO. From the landing at the southern tip of the island, climb the short slope up to the temple complex past Philae's oldest structure, the **Portico of Nectanebo,** which once formed the vestibule of a temple. The arrangement of Philae's courtyards corresponds to the status of the people allowed in each: the outermost courtyard was for commoners, while each successive inner courtyard was reserved for increasingly important people—the innermost for High Priests. The larger edifice has been washed away, but the eastern side of the colonnade remains. Ptolemy, Isis, and Horus are depicted on the **first pylon,** which rises 18m on either side of the temple's main entrance. Note the channels cut into the face of the pylon on either side of the doorway where brightly-painted square-cut cedar flagpoles once stood. The space on the left side of the threshold was for hinges that once supported an enormous door.

Through this entrance is the **central court,** with a Roman *mammisis* (birth-house) devoted to Horus, its columns emblazoned with the head of his consort, the cow-goddess Hathor. The walls depict the falcon god in the marshes of his birth. On the temple wall opposite the *mammisis,* Horus is transported in a boat on the shoulders of servants en route to visit another member of the divine family.

To the north is the slightly off-center **second pylon,** marking the way to the temple's inner sanctum. The *pronaos* (vestibule) was converted into a church by early Christians, who inscribed Byzantine crosses on the chamber walls and added a small altar. Farther north is the *naos,* the temple's innermost sanctuary. With a little *bakhsheesh* you can climb to the roof of the temple or enter a trap door on the interior right side leading to an inscribed crypt.

OTHER SIGHTS. Outside the temple, at left-rear, is a **Nilometer** with a stairwell and grooves used to measure the depths of the water. The stairwell is across from a French inscription from Napoleon's expedition. Because Egyptian gods supposedly liked to make house calls, to the right of the temple is **Trajan's Kiosk,** the beautifully-columned, open-air garage/divine carport (mistaken as a pharaoh's bed by the Victorians), which housed the barque of whichever god-icon came to visit Isis.

DAMS AND QUARRIES

Built by the Brits between 1898 and 1902, the **Old Dam** supplied most of Egypt's power for years. Cab-oglers can fully appreciate the impressive sheer granite wall; there are no tourist facilities here. The fertile area known as the **First Cataract** is one of the most idyllic spots in the Aswan area. Viewing what is left of the rapid waters, churning around rocky outcrops north of the Old Dam, gives some idea of the perils of early Nile expeditions (when ships were hauled past this dangerous spot with ropes). In the village of **Khazan** on the south side of the Old Dam, 90-year-old British villas (now Brit-less) sit peacefully within walled gardens.

▨ASWAN HIGH DAM (AS-SIDD AL-'ALI). The best-known attraction in the area is modern Egypt's greatest monument, the High Dam, completed in 1971. The dam is interesting intellectually as well as incredibly impressive visually. The High Dam lacks the aesthetic magnificence of ancient Egypt's colossi, but it could teach them a thing or two about size: 1km thick at the base, 3.6km long, and 100m high, the dam contains more than 17 times the material used in the Great Pyramid of Cheops. The construction of the dam created deep **Lake Nasser,** the world's largest artificial lake, and covered all of Lower Nubia in waters as deep as 200m. Because of it, thousands of Sudanese and Nubians were forced to relocate and ancient Nubia's archaeological treasures were threatened. The Egyptian government sent out an international plea for help—many countries responded, both individually and under an ambitious UNESCO plan. A rise in the Sahara's water table has been noticed as far away as Algeria, and archaeologists suspect that this effect has damaged the necropolis at Luxor and the base of Giza's Sphinx. Another danger of the dam is the possibility of sabotage. Should the dam be destroyed, the flood that would follow would wipe out 98% of Egypt's population. Nearby hills have radar installations and anti-aircraft missiles to guard against such a disaster. On the brighter side, the dam's 12 turbines doubled Egypt's electrical output, agricultural productivity has been enhanced, and the acreage of Egypt's arable soil has increased by 30%. The dam enabled Egypt to enjoy a healthy water supply during the drought of the past decade, and in August 1988 it saved Egypt from the floods suffered by Sudan when the Nile overflowed after heavy rains. For a few extra pounds or a little sweet talk, have a taxi go behind the gates to the **power plant** where itsy-bitsy people crawl around the base of the dam like industrious ants.

VISITORS' PAVILION. On the east bank (near the train station), just before the dam, the Visitors' Pavilion features plaques and sculptures blending Soviet socialist-realist motifs with Egyptian figures and symbols. At the center of the pavilion is a dusty 15m model of the High Dam and its environs, minus the water. The domed pavilion is well off the road from the dam and most taxis will not stop at it unless you insist. Ask for the *mekat. (Open daily 7am-5pm. Free.)*

SOVIET-EGYPTIAN FRIENDSHIP MONUMENT. To cross the dam you must pay E£5. The soldiers at the eastern end won't let you walk across but will stop passing vehicles and make them give you a ride. At the other end is the towering Soviet-Egyptian friendship monument, arguably premature given the alacrity with which the Egyptians spurned their Soviet benefactors once the dam was complete. A stylized lotus blossom, the monument would fit perfectly into a museum of abstract art, although amongst Egypt's ancient wonders it looks a little out of place. Due to the rise in terrorist activity, tourists are supposed to secure police permission to go to the top, either in Aswan or in the large yellow gift shop west of the monument. Some have been known to *bakhsheesh* (E£1-2) their way to the top if the dam authorities are closed. *(Open daily 6am-6pm; in winter 5am-5pm.)*

KALABSHA كلبشة

The **Temple of Kalabsha** is somewhat difficult to reach and poorly publicized, but it offers a relatively peaceful and quiet (if dimly lit) temple experience for those intrepid travelers wary of the pesky crowds at Abu Simbel. The cheapest way to reach Kalabsha is to take the **train** to the east end of the dam, ride to the west end (you'll have to pay the E£5 dam fee), then walk to the boat landing for the temple. To get to the landing from the western checkpoint, continue straight ahead for 100m, then veer left through the shipyard, following the curve of the water for about 1km. A **taxi** from Aswan to the boat landing is less of a hassle but more expensive; try bargaining down to E£25-30 (even less for large groups). Adding this stop to your taxi tour of the High Dam, Philae, and the Unfinished Obelisk should cost around E£5. Regardless of how you get to the boat landing, you only have two options for getting to the temple once there: hire either a **rowboat** (E£10 per load, which holds no more than 2-3 people) or a larger **motorboat** (E£20 for a load of 10 or so). Remember to bring lots of water, cover your head, and watch your step on the dock. *(High Dam open until 6pm.)*

The well-preserved temple at Kalabsha is considered by many Egyptologists to be second only to the treasures of Abu Simbel, but the building—situated dramatically above the placid waters of Lake Nasser—is more impressive on the outside than on the inside. Dedicated to the Nubian god Mandulis (who was renowned for his hundreds of wives and legions of children), the temple was built by Amenhotep II, augmented during the reign of Augustus, and used as a church during the Christian era. In 1962-63, the West German government paid to have the entire temple dismantled and transported in 13,000 pieces from its Nasser-flooded home to the present site, 50km north of the original (see **Moving a Mountain,** p. 251).

TEMPLE CAUSEWAY. An immense causeway of dressed stone leads from the water to the temple's main entrance. The first pylon is off-center from both the causeway and the inner gateways of the temple itself. The grand forecourt between the pylon and the vestibule is surrounded by 14 columns, each with a unique capital. This is one of the only temples in Egypt where you can legally get to the top: take the stairs to the roof from a small room just beyond the vestibule for a commanding view of the entire site.

HOLY OF HOLIES. Because the temple faces east, light flows into the Holy of Holies (innermost chamber) only in the early morning. Bring a flashlight at other times and be prepared for bats. A passageway leads north through the vestibule to an inner encircling wall; around the wall to the south is a **Nilometer.** Extraordinary carvings of Mandulis, Isis, Horus, and Osiris cover the outside walls.

NUBIAN SHRINE. Outside the huge fortress-like wall, the remains of a small shrine are visible to the southeast; the present structure is largely a reconstructed facade. The Nubian reliefs include pre-dynastic elephants, a large giraffe, and gazelles. The double-image technique, characteristic of Nubian art, is used to portray motion in some of the drawings. Carcasses of enormous desiccated fish are surrealistically scattered among the sand, as are disembodied stone heads. *(Temple open daily 7am-7pm. E£12, students E£6.)*

TEMPLE OF KERTASSI. Slightly to the southwest of the Temple of Kalabsha are the ruins of the Temple of Kertassi. Two Hathor columns remain, as well as four columns with elaborate floral capitals and a lone monolithic architrave. A stone pathway leads up the hill behind and to the right of the Temple of Kertassi to the Rock Temple, Beit al-Wali (House of the Holy Man), rescued from the encroaching waters of Lake Nasser with the aid of the US government. Ask the guard to let you in. One of many Nubian temples constructed by Ramses II, it features typically humble scenes of Ramses conquering foreigners, Ramses receiving prisoners, and a particularly understated scene of Ramses storming a castle half his size. Like a miniature Abu Simbel, this cave-temple was hewn from solid rock. Examine the bas-relief scenes closely: political and social history are portrayed in everything from chariot battles to squabbles over whose turn it is to walk the camel.

ABU SIMBEL أبو سمبل

*Abu Simbel is 50km from the Sudanese border and a treacherous 297km south of Aswan. Due to political tensions, the Sudanese border is not passable and should not be approached by tourists for any reason. **Ground transportation to the sight has been indefinitely shut down,** but when ground transportation is up and running, two buses travel between Abu Simbel and Aswan (8am and 4pm; E£10 one-way, E£26 round-trip). The morning bus gives you 2½ hours to explore the temple. Buy your ticket at the Aswan bus station a day in advance; buy the return ticket on the way back. All buses have A/C. **Airplane** fares will be discounted 50% until bus service resumes; the fare is currently US$85. Book a flight through EgyptAir (see **Getting Around,** p. 75) at least two days in advance. Airline buses meet you at Abu Simbel Airport and ferry you to and from the sight free of charge. Another option is to go by **ferry** from Aswan to Abu Simbel (3 days, 3 nights). Open 6am-5pm. E£36, students E£19.50, including admission to Temple of Hathor. Flash photographers will be escorted out.*

BIG HEADS (COLOSSI). The grandeur of the pharaonic monuments reaches its peak at Egypt's southernmost tip. Four 22m tall statues of **Ramses II**, carved out of a single slab of rock, greet the sunrise over Lake Nasser from the Great Temple of Abu Simbel. Ramses II had this grand sanctuary and the nearby Temple of Hathor built more than 3200 years ago to impress the Nubians with the power and glory of Egyptian rule; Abu Simbel still serves its purpose, leaving no visitor unmoved. For a sneak preview of the site, look at the back of the Egyptian one-pound note.

THE GREAT TEMPLE OF ABU SIMBEL. This is Ramses II's masterpiece. The temple is supposedly dedicated to the god Ra-Hurakhti, but as in all of Ramses' monuments, the focus is clearly on the great pharaoh himself. The artwork depicts Ramses first as a great king, then as a servant of the gods, next as a companion of the gods, and finally, in the inner sanctuary, as a card-carrying deity. The entrance is guarded by three-and-a-half 20m tall statues of the king wearing the Old and New Kingdom versions of the crowns of Upper and Lower Egypt. An earthquake in 27 BCE crumbled the upper portion of one of the colossi. Modern engineers were unable to reconstruct the figure (and there were debates about whether they should—if it's been broken for 2000 years, don't fix it), so they left it in its faceless state. There are (much) smaller statues of wife Nefertari and some of the kids, along with rows of **praying baboons.** Ancient Egyptians admired the baboons' habit of warming themselves in the sun's rays; they thought the beasts quite pious to pray to the sun god every dawn.

Farther into the temple are **antechambers** that once stored objects of worship. The walls show Ramses making sacrifices to the gods. In the inner sanctum, four seated statues facing the entrance depict Ramses and the gods Ra-Hurakhti, Amun, and Ptah. Originally encased in gold, the statues now wait with divine patience for February 22 and October 22, when the first rays of the sun reach 100m into the temple to bathe all except Ptah in light. February 21 was Ramses' birthday and October 21 his coronation date, but when the temple was moved, the timing of these natural feats shifted by one day (they just don't build temples like they used to). A door to the right of the temple's facade leads into the dome that supports the new and improved mountain.

TEMPLE OF HATHOR. Next door to Ramses' temple was one dedicated to his favorite wife, Nefertari, and dedicated to the young goddess Hathor. Six 10m statues of King Ramses and Queen Nefertari (as the goddess) adorn the façade. Along with the temple of Hatshepsut in West Thebes, this is one of the only temples in Egypt dedicated to a woman. Nevertheless, images of Ramses abound—scenes on

MOVING A MOUNTAIN As the water level of Lake Nasser rose in the mid-60s, Egypt realized it would lose a large piece of its heritage. The United Nations and individual governments responded by funding a US$36 million relocation effort. The international concern was not entirely selfless: any country that assisted could claim half of the antiquities it helped to rescue and receive special archaeological concessions for future research. As a result, the Temple of Dendur is now enclosed in New York's Metropolitan Museum of Art, Debed Temple can be found in Madrid, and al-Lessiya was claimed by Turin. The first tentative plan was to raise each temple, remove the surrounding mountain, and encase the structures in protective concrete boxes. The boxes would slowly be jacked up, and a thick concrete base built beneath them. Another possibility was to build a second small dam around the temples to keep the water at bay. Both of these schemes were too expensive. To the chagrin of Egyptologists, the cheapest method was chosen—cutting the temples into pieces. The mountain had to be cut away, a job that endangered the sandstone statues below. Bulldozers covered the facade of Abu Simbel with sand, and the mound of sand was penetrated with a steel tunnel so that rescue workers could set up supportive steel bars inside. It took months to saw the temple apart and move the 3000 pieces to higher ground. When it was reassembled, hollow concrete domes were engineered to support the new artificial mountain.

the walls depict his coronation with the god Horus placing the crowns of Egypt on his head. The temple was constructed in the typical three-room style: the first chamber was open to the public, the second to nobles and priests, and the inner sanctuary only to the pharaoh and the high priest.

WESTERN DESERT OASES

"The call of the desert, for thinkers of the city, has always been irresistible: I do not think they find God there, but that they hear more distinctly in the solitude, the living verb they carry within themselves."
—T.E. Lawrence

The Western Desert (known as the Libyan Desert until World War II) is the largest and driest in the world, covering two-thirds of Egypt's area but supporting only 1% of its population. It boasts some of the highest temperatures on record, despite the fact that its series of oases—**Bahariyya, Farafra, Dakhla,** and **Kharga**—marks the trail of a prehistoric branch of the cool, wet Nile. Each oasis sits in a depression surrounded by an escarpment, the top of which marks the usual level of the desert floor. Subterranean water seeps through these depressions, which lie at or near sea level. A flow of water originates as the rains of equatorial Africa replenish the wells and springs annually, taking thousands of years to journey north through underground fissures. The Romans were the first to irrigate the area by tapping deeper reserves with their waterwheels and aqueducts, known as **'Ain Romani.** The Egyptian government is following suit and spending vast amounts of resources on its **New Valley Project** to exploit underground water for the promotion of agriculture and the massive relocation of landless peasants from the Delta to the New Valley.

The desert oases are unique in that they can still be considered "off the beaten path." The few tourists in the area keep sights uncrowded and prices low. The best time to visit the oases is between October and April. It is not unusual for summer temperatures, especially at Dakhla or Kharga, to reach 52°C (126°F). Even at night, summer temperatures persist into the upper 20s (over 80°F). You won't find air-conditioning anywhere except Kharga, which makes it a good first or last stop. Kharga is also the only oasis that cashes traveler's checks, so have plenty of money on hand before you venture westward.

EGYPT

GETTING THERE AND AROUND

BY BUS. Daily buses run from the al-Azhar bus station in Cairo to the oases. Inexpensive buses run from Asyut to Kharga and Dakhla (see **Overland Travel Advisory,** p. 209). Bus travel between the oases requires more flexibility and patience than in the rest of Egypt. Published schedules are no more than rough guesses. Bus officials, locals, and passersby all peddle contradictory and inaccurate departure times. Ask as many people as possible, follow the consensus, and arrive early. The most accurate information will come from local tourist offices and bus officials.

BY TAXI OR SERVICE. Special taxis travel from Cairo to all of the oases, Asyut to Kharga, and Kharga to Luxor (but not the other way around, due to Luxor police restrictions). They sometimes offer a faster and more comfortable journey—check out what the vehicle looks like and how many people will be stuffed in. *Service* between all oases are affordable and often quicker than buses.

BY CAR. Car rental is convenient and comfortable (albeit expensive) for desert travel. A giant loop along the Great Desert Road and the Lower Nile Valley in either direction beginning in Cairo is about 1700km. Any car must be in top condition and fully outfitted for intense desert travel in order to survive the long, hot, poorly maintained roads. **Four-wheel drive** is highly recommended. Another option is a **trailer** (caravan); renting one can solve a lot of problems, including those of transporting food, water, and extra gas, and finding a comfortable place to sleep.

A NUMBER OF CAR CAVEATS. First and foremost, it is always a long way between gas stations. While every oasis has at least one fuel pump, it is essential to buy jerry cans and fill them with enough gas to cover the vast distances between towns. A trailer guzzles huge quantities of fuel, so bring extra to fill an entire tank. Foreigners are prohibited from leaving the main road; several containers of potable water, however, are vital in case you get stranded. Try to drive in the cool morning or late afternoon, but never drive at night—the chances of getting lost on unlit roads increase exponentially, and hidden potholes are especially lethal. Don't pull a Lawrence of Arabia: never drive in a sandstorm. If you do get caught in one, stop, turn the car's rear to the wind, and wait.

GETTING TO SLEEP

The best alternative to staying in hotels is **camping.** Several budget campsites are run by hotels near Bahariyya and Dakhla. Otherwise, most fertile land belongs to farmers who will usually permit you to pitch your tent. The ideal spot is just outside the main town of an oasis, where there is usually a small pool of water (ask the locals for the *'ain,* or spring) and nothing but the sound of silence. The desert itself may be more comfortable, as cool temperatures and breezes carry away the mosquitoes, and the sand makes a soft mattress. Sleeping on the dunes has its own set of dangers—you might be sharing the desert expanse with ticks, wasps, scorpions, cheetahs, foxes, mice, rats, amorous strangers, and tiny hedgehogs that roll into spiky balls when frightened. You might roll up yourself if you encounter one of the seven kinds of **poisonous snakes** in Egypt, among which is a family of lethal vipers. They rest under rocks and sand, coming out to drink at night. If you see snake tracks going in one direction, calmly go in the other. Common sense, a first aid kit, and a snake bite kit are recommended. If you prefer mosquito bites to reptile venom, each oasis has at least one cheap, clean hotel or rest house.

GETTING SOMETHING TO EAT

Oasis groundwater tastes much better than that of the other Egyptian municipalities; while safer than water near the cities, it can still ruin a trip. The main towns of all the oases have restaurants and markets where you can fill up on food, but don't expect variety or refinement. The best meals are at people's homes—with a winning smile and a little luck, you can taste for yourself.

PRACTICAL WARNINGS

WOMEN TRAVELERS. Women should follow certain guidelines when swimming in springs. In isolated ones unfrequented by locals, female travelers are unlikely to be bothered. The same goes for pools cordoned off and connected to tourist rest houses. Women should not, however, enter pools where men are already bathing. Sometimes women can bathe in a separate pool (local women bathe separately in the evening), provided they wear a *galabiyya* (loose-fitting robe). Women traveling without men should not embark on overnight desert excursions unless prearranged by a tourist official. Even then, care and common sense are key. Solo women heading for the oases should be prepared to deal with harassment. For more on what women can expect traveling in Egypt, see **Women Travelers,** p. 78.

TAXES, TOURISM, AND TRUST. Despite what out-of-date sources may tell you, you need only flash a **passport** at the numerous military checkpoints, and sometimes not even that. In Dakhla, Kharga, or Farafra, you will be asked to pay a one-time **tourism development tax** (E£5) by a tourist officer or by an employee of your hotel. Keep the receipt as proof or you may have to pay again.

The Western Desert has been attracting an increasing number of visitors with its traditional village lifestyle, stunning landscapes, and low prices. Bahariyya, in particular, is seeing an exponential increase in visitors thanks to the recently discovered Roman ruins (see **Excavators are Standing By,** p. 255) and "Valley of the Mummies" (see **Tomb Much of a Good Thing,** p. 254), as well as overnight tours to the Black and White Deserts (see p. 256). With this sudden bumper crop of tourists comes the slowly creeping disease that the smell of tourist money inevitably brings. Each oasis has people whose English is good, knowledge of the area is fair, and sense of capitalism is extraordinary. They are often friendly and helpful, but their assistance has a bloated price tag trailing behind. For the best information, head for the New Valley's **tourist officials:** 'Umar Ahmed in Dakhla, Dr. Muhammad Ra'afat Amin in Farafra, and Ibrahim M. Hassan in Kharga. They will answer your questions in excellent English for free and **arrange for fairly priced guides and transportation;** without them, you are at the mercy of the wolves.

BAHARIYYA OASIS واحة البحرية ☎018

The land turns a deep shade of red as you approach Bahariyya, thanks to the vast deposits of iron that are quarried in an immense mine just off the highway, 40km before Bawiti. This small oasis, 330km south of Cairo, has been a stopover for caravans traveling between the Nile Valley and the rest of North Africa since pharaonic times, when merchants used to load their donkeys with wine from al-Qasr (the present-day town of Bawiti). In later centuries, Bahariyya enthusiastically welcomed Mecca-bound pilgrims, who would often join the traders on their transdesert trek. Today, the only "pilgrims" in Bahariyya are the caravans of rip-roaring European adventurers gallivanting through the oasis in Land Rovers (because of its relative proximity to Cairo, Bahariyya attracts visitors who crave a few days in the desert). Factor in the opening of several Roman-era sights in 1999 in addition to growing interest in the recently unearthed "Valley of the Mummies" (see **Tomb Much of a Good Thing,** p. 254), and it's easy to see why the constant traffic has made Bahariyya far more commercial and cutthroat than the other oases. Unfortunately, many of Bahariyya's ancient ruins are scanty and inaccessible. The nearby gardens, springs, and desert offer relief, but not enough to make anyone stay longer than necessary. Food stores, a market, coffee shops, and three **gas stations** make this oasis a viable (and unavoidable) stop for those heading to Farafra.

TOMB MUCH OF A GOOD THING In June 1999, a team of archaeologists led by Dr. Zahi Hawass announced the discovery of an enormous ancient burial ground in Bawiti, the main city in Bahariyya. Fifty mummies were unearthed in four rooms of the six-mile cemetery, which probably dates back almost 2000 years. The site supposedly contains more than 10,000 mummies, making it the largest burial ever uncovered and earning it the title **"Valley of the Mummies."** Almost as remarkable as the quantity of the haul is its quality: some of the mummies (who were mostly wealthy aristocrats and rulers) wear gold masks and still have visible depictions of Egyptian deities on their chests. Others are buried in a more typically Roman style, with bodies coated in plaster or covered with linen and laid to rest in terra cotta sarcophagi marked with realistic representations of the deceased's face.

GETTING THERE AND GETTING AROUND

The Bahariyya Oasis is linked to Cairo by a decently paved road that heads past the Pyramids of Giza, then turns southwest across the desert to the town of **Bawiti.**

Buses: Touts congregate by the bus ticket and reservation office in a green shed next to the telephone office (open daily 7am-noon and 8-11pm). Buses from **Cairo** to Bahariyya leave Mahattat Turgoman by Ramses Station (4hr.; 7, 9, 11:30am, 3, 7, 11pm; E£12.50). All 11:30am and 7pm buses continue to **Farafra.** Get there early to secure a seat. There are also daily buses to **Cairo** (5hr.; 7, 11:30am, 3pm, midnight; E£12.50).

Minibuses: Minibuses run daily between Bahariyya and **Cairo's** Sayyidna Zeinab bus station (5hr., E£11). Minibuses leave when full.

ORIENTATION AND PRACTICAL INFORMATION

Tourist Office: (☎80 27 70 or 80 20 90). First floor of the government compound. The green and red sign is on the right as you walk into town from the east. Staffed by city council member Muhammad Abd al-Qader (after 2pm, look for him in the lobby of the Paradise Hotel). Open daily 8am-2pm.

Currency Exchange: The **National Bank for Development** is next to the post office. Exchanges cash only. Open Su-Th 8am-2pm.

Gas Station: One behind police station. Two more on main road out of town near Cairo.

Telephones: The office is in a driveway 10m off the main road, on the side of the building beside the government compound. They deny having international service, but try calling abroad using MCI or AT&T, both of which first require a local call. Within town, dial 0184 and the operator will connect you. Open daily 8am-midnight.

Post Office: Two buildings down from the government compound as you move toward Farafra. Limited services. Open Sa-Th 8:30am-2pm.

ACCOMMODATIONS AND FOOD

The welcoming, conical thatch huts of the ▧**Africa Home** are 17km west of Bawiti; turn off the main road near the northern end of town. Most visitors come through Hotel Alpenblick, but you can arrange your own transportation out to this clean, tranquil camp run by friendly Sudanese (E£25-30 round-trip per car). A hot spring, Bir Ghaba, is nearby. (☎80 21 84. Huts E£6 per person, with breakfast E£10.) Closer to town, **Ahmad's Safari Camp** is four kilometers south from Bawiti's center. The massive grapevine-covered veranda, clean common bathrooms, good food, and free rides to and from town sweeten the bitter taste of isolation. (☎80 27 70 or 80 20 90. Bare huts E£5 per person; concrete cabanas with breakfast E£10 per person; deluxe, white-domed gazebos with shower and breakfast E£40.) Standing with your back to the city council building and the tourist office, head down the street to the white-domed **Hotel Alpenblick,** 250m past the "cheapest shop in town" sign. Mahmoud, the general manager, organizes trips to the hot springs. Lodgings here are a bit nicer than other options in Bawiti but you don't quite get your money's worth: rooms have carpets and fans, but bathrooms are not too spectacular. (Breakfast included. Singles E£20; doubles E£35, with bath E£46; triples E£53, with bath E£69.) For those looking for a touch of class, the brand-spanking new **New Oasis Hotel** is 200m down the road leading past Bayoumi's Restaurant. Resembling something out of a honeymoon package deal, rooms sport new beds and baths, wall-to-wall carpeting, and colorful, slightly Mexican decor. (☎/fax 80 30 30. E£50 including breakfast.) The government-run **Paradise Hotel** is across from the telephone office in the main square. Shared rooms are dark and stuffy, and common bathrooms are rather grimy. (E£3.50 per person, with breakfast E£5.)

Few restaurants are in Bawiti. **Bayoumi's Popular Restaurant,** across from the police station, sits next to the government compound just off the main road to Cairo. Ask in advance about prices. (Full meal around E£8. Stella E£7.) **Paradise Restaurant, Restaurant Rashid, El-Gahsh,** and the kitchen at the **Alpenblick** offer standard meals for E£6-8. El-Gahsh also serves up morning *fuul* and falafel. Don't miss the good **falafel stands** down the main road toward Farafra.

SIGHTS

Hotel managers run group tours of all the area's springs and sights (no more than E£10 per person with a six-person group, less with a larger group). You can hire a taxi through the tourist office or on your own for E£30 for the entire day.

 EXCAVATORS ARE STANDING BY. Beginning in March 2001, travelers in the Bahariyya area will be able to visit the following sights, which are currently being excavated and prepared for visitors: the **Temple of Alexander the Great** (the only one of its kind in Egypt), the Greco-Roman spring **'Ain al-Meftela,** and the **ancient tombs** of Amenhotep I, Huy, Banntiu, and Zed Amun (E£40, students E£20). For more information on recent discoveries in Bahariyya, check Dr. Zahi Hawass's *Valley of the Mummies,* published by AUC Press.

HOT SPRINGS. Bahariyya's hot springs give you the chance to get in touch with your inner lobster and are quite clean despite the faint scent of sulphur. **'Ain Bishmu,** a local favorite between the border of the old city and Bawiti, holds steady at a lukewarm 30°C. The less crowded **Bir al-Ramla** (two kilometers out of Bawiti along a village track parallel to the road to Cairo) features a 45°C hot spring. Men can bathe here in shorts, but women must be fully clothed and may only swim later at night. The cold (25°C) and hot (48°C) springs at **Bir al-Mattar,** eight kilometers southeast of Bawiti, pour out of a viaduct into a small cement pool (taxi E£10 round-trip). Men bathe here by day, women by night. The bumpy "road" to Bir al-Mattar (really just a desert track—drivers beware) continues southeast through the desert to ☒**Bir al-Ghaba,** 17km from Bawiti, with both a hot and cold spring in another sumptuous oasis landscape. Both men and women can swim in this deserted spot (taxi E£25 round-trip). Less appealing is **Bir al-Ghilis,** a steamy, pump-activated spring only a 10-minute walk out of town (taxi E£5 round-trip).

AL-QASR. Ruined chapels, tombs, and temples from the 26th dynasty cluster in al-Qasr, Bawiti's western sibling and the capital of Bahariyya in pharaonic times. *(Inquire at the tourist office to obtain permission to visit these locked sights.)*

MUSEUMS. The **Antiquities Museum** is where some of the finds from the surrounding ruins, including pottery shards and five mummies, are kept. Ask the Inspector of Antiquities to dig up the key to the painted, subterranean tomb dating from the pharaonic era. Nature is Bahariyya's real attraction, but the **Oasis Heritage Museum** in Bawiti is also worth a visit. Talented local artist Mahmoud Eed creates life-like clay figurines to populate the dioramas depicting traditional oasis life. *(Antiquities is*

500m out of town, on a dirt road that turns right off the road toward Cairo. Ask at the tourist office to arrange a visit. Open Sa-Th 8am-1:30pm. Free. The Oasis is 900m out of town, on the left heading toward Cairo. Free; contributions welcome.)

BETWEEN THE BAHARIYYA AND FARAFRA OASES

*The best way to ensure a reasonable price for a **tour** from Bahariyya is to arrange one through Muhammad Abd al-Qader at the tourist office. Organizing overnight desert tours from Farafra may be cheaper, but call ahead for Muhammad Ra'afat Amin (see below), if possible. If you can't put together a posse, you can see the area from a public **bus** (sit on the side of the driver). Everywhere but al-Wadi Oasis can be reached by regular car, but a 4x4 is more fun. For overnight tours including food, a **pickup truck taxi** shouldn't exceed E£60-80, a more comfortable **Peugeot** E£70-90, and a **4x4** E£150-175. Summer is the cheapest time to go, but the hardest time to find riding partners. Drivers will begin by demanding E£800 for trips to Farafra, so bargain hard.*

The 183km road from Bawiti to the Farafra Oasis runs through spectacular canyons, wind-blown mesas, and rugged desertscapes from which precious gemstones were exported during the reign of Ramses II. The eastern and western escarpments of the Bahariyya depression meet at a point about 60km south of Bawiti; the road winds through this pass and onto a brief plateau before plummeting into the Farafra Oasis.

Leaving Bawiti, you'll first pass through the **Black Desert,** known for its dark mesas and crumbly flats peppered with sun-blasted rock and tufts of dry desert grass. The idyllic oasis village of **al-Hayiz** (E£60 per truckload as a daytrip from Bawiti) lies 5km off the main road to Farafra, 40km from Bawiti. Gardens and a spring make this simple village a nice spot to camp overnight and enjoy fresh watermelon or apricots for breakfast. **Crystal Mountain** (just a hill by the roadside with quartz deposits) rises about 100km from Bawiti. Farther along is **al-Sillim Pass,** revealing a view of the escarpment cascading into the distance of the desert. The palm trees and small, desolate spring of the empty **al-Wadi Oasis** (the only place that requires a 4x4) are about 140km from Bawiti. The oasis is striking amidst towering dunes and grazing gazelles. About 40km outside Farafra, the black buttes suddenly give way to the **White Desert,** known for its breathtaking views and stunning chalk formations. For more on the White Desert, see p. 257.

FARAFRA OASIS واحة الفرافرة

Farafra claims an impressive 16% of Egypt's entire territory and borders both Libya and Sudan. Three years ago, the area was home to a mere 5000 people, but immigration has swelled the population to over 14,000. Nonetheless, the main town of Farafra, Qasr al-Farafra, remains the smallest of the oases' capitals, is visited less frequently, and offers few services to travelers. Farafra makes a good starting point for overnight desert tours, but not much else. Province president Muhammad Ra'afat Amin has done much to redefine the region's image: hotels have been privatized, over 60,000 acres of land have been reclaimed through a massive irrigation effort, and an airport is in the works.

⌚ GETTING THERE. Buses and **service** arrive and depart from Titanic Cafe on the Bahariyya-Dakhla road; the owner can inform you of the latest bus schedule eccentricities. **Buses** run daily to Dakhla (5hr., 2:30 and 9:30pm, E£15) and Bahariyya (2½hr., 11am and 11pm, E£12), continuing on to Cairo (8hr., E£25). However, **minibuses** and *service* are the best way to get to Dakhla. Early morning is best; ask around the night before to secure a seat (4hr., E£15). Buses from Cairo leave Mahattat Turgoman, north of Ramses Station, en route to Farafra (8hr., 7am and 6pm, E£25) with a stop at Bahariyya. A **gas station and repair shop** is on the main road, 500m down from the bus stop. *Let's Go* does not recommend **hitchhiking.**

⛏ PRACTICAL INFORMATION. All services are on or just off the Bahariyya-Dakhla road. As you head toward Bahariyya, you'll pass the **police station** and **post office** (open Su-Th 8am-2pm) on your left, followed by the **telephone center,** which offers dubious international service. (Open daily 8am-midnight.) Next to the post office is the **city hall,** where dedicated province president Dr. Muhammad Ra'afat Amin will help you organize excursions in the area. If he's not there, find him at his massive hilltop house two kilometers from town—ask his assistant to take you, or hop in a taxi for E£2. (☎ 92 12 06. Open Sa-Th 8am-2pm.)

▚▐ ACCOMMODATIONS AND FOOD. The **Al-Bedouiya Hotel,** 750m from the bus stop in the direction of Bahariyya, has beautifully decorated, painstakingly cleaned rooms and toilets and stunning Bedouin architecture. Don't miss the roof-top terrace. (☎ 92 04 70. Singles E£10; doubles E£20; quads E£40.) The government-run **Tourist Rest House,** 1½km from the bus stop (ask to be let off there), also offers accommodations in adequately clean three-bed rooms with functional baths. (E£12 per person and up.) **Camping** in the nearby desert or at **Bir Sitta** (six kilometers from town) might make for a more organic experience, but bring plenty of insect repellent. Also check your shoes and pants before getting dressed—scorpions and huge biting ants thrive in these parts; don't let them thrive in yours. Always let Dr. Muhammad Ra'afat Amin know your travel plans. The huts of several budding gourmands are clustered around the bus station, and the **restaurant** at the Al-Bedouiya serves up filling two-course meals for E£7-10.

▨ SIGHTS. The free **art museum,** conveniently situated across from the Military Intelligence Office, displays expressive sculptures and paintings made of local materials (sand, mud, and sticks) by the talented local artist, Badr, depicting life in Farafra. (Open Su-Th 9am-2pm.) The hot **Bir Sitta** (Well #6), six kilometers west of town, is an idyllic spot to swim and camp (transportation about E£15 per carload). If you're fed up with the flatulatory scent of the sulphur wells, head to **Birkat Abu Noss,** 15km outside of town, to cool off. This lake is two kilometers off the road to Bahariyya; turn left just before the checkpoint.

NEAR FARAFRA OASIS

WHITE DESERT ‏صحراء بيضاء‎

*An average overnight trip in a **4x4** from Farafra should cost about E£350 per carload. Arrange all overnight trips through city hall; the incorrigible Mr. Saat, manager of the Al-Bedouiya Hotel, often insists on outlandish prices. More establishments in Bahariyya and Dakhla are also beginning to offer reasonable White Desert tours (see **Dakhla: Accommodations and Food,** p. 260), so inquire ahead. If you don't mind being stranded in the desert for several hours on the way back, take a **bus** to Bahariyya (11am, E£24) and ask to be let out at the White Desert (make sure the driver will do this before leaving Farafra).*

The White Desert (about 40km from Farafra) has overnight camping and breath-taking views. Spooky fungoid chalk formations stand stark white in daytime, glow shades of bashful fuchsia by dusk, and turn orange by dawn. A typical tour of the desert from Farafra (the best starting point for a trip to the White Desert) passes through both verdant **Wadi Henis** and the village of **Karaween,** which has marvelous springs and gazelles. Visiting during or near a full moon can be a particularly other worldly experience. As you leave the White Desert, you'll pass a **cold spring.** For information on **Between the Bahariyya and Farafra Oases,** see p. 256.

DAKHLA OASIS ‏الواحات الداخلة‎ ☎092

If traveling through some of the other desert oases seems like a challenge, Dakhla (also known as the "pink oasis" for the surrounding pink cliffs) is the reward. Affordable food, appealing lodgings, and picture-book Islamic sights and natural backdrops all come together unlike anywhere else in the Western Desert. The work of 75,000 Dakhlans has resulted in a widening wave of greenery, including peanuts, rice, and other crops. Yet this poster-child for the New Valley Project has not allowed itself to be urbanized in the manner of Kharga; a mix of Nubians, Sudanese, Libyans, and Berbers peacefully inhabit this laid-back oasis without abandoning their traditional way of life.

EGYPT

GETTING THERE AND GETTING AROUND

Flights: The **airport,** 10km south of Mut, is served by **EgyptAir** (☎82 20 53 or 82 20 54), which has an office in the courtyard opposite the police station in town. Open Sa-Th 8:30am-2pm and 5-9pm. Flights to **Cairo** (W at 8pm; E£560, US$161).

Buses and Service: Buses and *service* depart from **Mut Station** (☎82 15 38), in New Mosque Sq. **Local buses** go to **Balaat** and **Bashendi** (8:30am, 2:30, 5, 7, 8, 10pm; return to Mut 1hr. later; 50pt) and **al-Qasr** (6am, 2, 6pm; return to Mut 2hr. later; 50pt). **Intercity buses** are not very reliable, but supposedly travel to: **Asyut** via **Kharga** (6hr.; 6, 8am, 10pm; E£17); **Cairo** (13hr., 6am and 6pm, E£43) via **Farafra** (5hr.); **Cairo** (13hr., 6 and 8pm, E£43) via **Kharga** (2½hr.); and **Kharga** (2½hr., 5pm, E£7). Bus schedules change frequently; ask the tourist office for updates. It's more reliable to take *service* early in the morning. *Service* and **minibuses** go to **Farafra** (5hr., 6am or when it fills up, E£15) and **Kharga** (3hr., 6am or when it fills up, E£7).

Taxis: Taxis offer sightseeing tours (one day E£40, trips to eastern or western Dakhla E£8-10); ask in New Mosque Sq. Covered pickup trucks shuttle frequently between Tahrir Sq. and **al-Qasr** and between the hospital stand and **Balaat** (E£2), **Bashendi** (E£1), and **al-Qasr** (E£1). The early bird catches the truck.

Bike Rental: Next door to the Arabi Restaurant on al-Gadha St. E£10 per day.

ORIENTATION AND PRACTICAL INFORMATION

The Dakhla Oasis, 320km from Farafra and 190km from Kharga, is bounded by **West Mawhub** (80km west of Mut) on one side and the fertile **Tineida** (40km east of Mut) on the other. Cultivated regions also dot the well-paved main highway; the most appealing of these are **al-Qasr** (30km west of Mut), **Balaat** (30km east of Mut), and **Bashendi** (35km east of Mut). The capital of the Dakhla Oasis is **Mut** (pronounced "moot"), named for the Egyptian mother goddess and wife of Amun (see **Meet the Gods,** p. 69). Mut has two focal points: **Tahrir Sq.,** at the intersection of New Valley St. and the Kharga-Farafra Hwy. (southeast-northwest), and **New Mosque Sq.,** one kilometer south on New Valley St.

Tourist Office: The **new office** (☎82 16 86 or 82 16 85) is 400m away from Tahrir Sq. on the road to Farafra, across the street from Abu Muhammad Restaurant. The **old office** (☎82 04 07) is across from the mosque in New Mosque Sq., in the same building as the Tourist Rest House. The knowledgeable Omar Ahmed (☎94 07 82) speaks English and helps arrange transportation. Both open Su-Th 8am-2pm and 8-10pm.

Currency Exchange: Misr Bank (☎82 00 63), in Tahrir Sq., near the police station. Changes traveler's checks and cash. Open Su-Th 8am-2pm and 6-9pm, and sporadically Sa 8am-2pm for changing money.

Gas Station: On the outskirts of eastern Mut, on left side of the road to Kharga. Another station west of Mut, 1km from Tahrir Sq. E£1.20 per liter. Open 24hr.

Police: (☎82 15 00), in Tahrir Sq.

Pharmacy: There are seven pharmacies in Mut, three of which are on New Mosque St. Most open daily 8am-2pm and occasionally at night.

Hospital: The **main hospital** (☎82 15 55 or 82 13 32) is 1km from Tahrir Sq., toward Kharga. Smaller hospitals are in each village. Open 24hr.

Telephones: From New Mosque Sq., walk east along 23 July St. to Anwar Restaurant, then veer left toward the red-and-white tower about 30m ahead on the left. Open 24hr. For **international service,** try the two private telephone offices on Kharga Hwy. or the office by New Mosque Sq.

Post Office: One in New Mosque Sq., another on al-Ganeim St., around the corner from the telephone office. Both open Su-Th 8am-2pm.

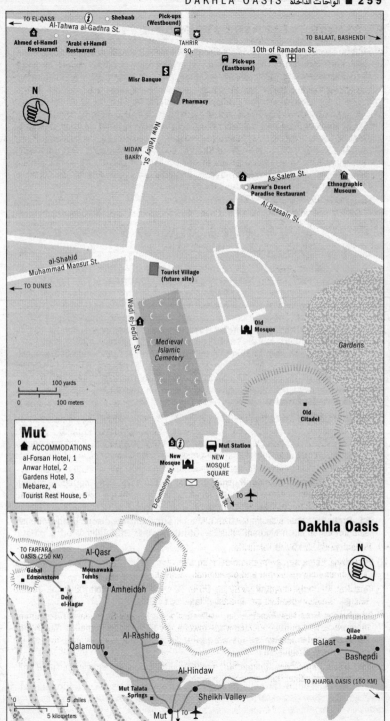

EGYPT

TO EL-QASR
Al-Tahwra al-Gadhra St.
Shehaab
Pick-ups
(Westbound)

Ahmed el-Hamdi
Restaurant
'Arabi el-Hamdi
Restaurant
TAHRIR
SQ.
TO BALAAT, BASHENDI
10th of Ramadan St.

N

Misr Banque
Pick-ups
(Eastbound)

Pharmacy

MIDAN
BAKRY
New Valley St.
As-Salem St.
Anwar's Desert
Paradise Restaurant
Al-Bassain St.
Ethnographic
Museum

al-Shahid
Muhammad Mansur St.
Tourist Village
(future site)

TO DUNES

Wadi el-Jedid St.
Old
Mosque
Gardens

Medieval
Islamic
Cemetery

0   100 yards
0   100 meters

Old
Citadel

Mut

ACCOMMODATIONS
al-Forsan Hotel, 1
Anwar Hotel, 2
Gardens Hotel, 3
Mebarez, 4
Tourist Rest House, 5

El-Gomhoriyya St.
Mut Station
New
Mosque
NEW
MOSQUE
SQUARE
Khalfa St.
TO

Dakhla Oasis

TO FARFARA
OASIS (250 KM)

N

Al-Qasr

Gabal
Edmonstone
Mousawaka
Tombs

Amheidah

Deir
el-Hagar

Al-Rashida

Qilae
al-Daba

Qalamoun

Balaat

Bashendi

Al-Hindaw

Mut Talata
Springs

TO KHARGA OASIS (150 KM)

Sheikh Valley

0   5 miles
0   5 kilometers

Mut   TO

▗▟ ACCOMMODATIONS AND FOOD

If you're not set on sleeping out in the dunes, Dakhla has the choicest lodgings of the oases, making it the place to stay should you need a couple of days' respite from the sand. **Gardens Hotel,** 20m down a dirt road from Anwar's Desert Paradise Restaurant and Hotel, has a leafy garden and very polite management. Stick to the breezy rooms with fans unless you don't mind stuffy rooftop dorms. (☎82 15 77. Dorm beds E£8; singles E£12, with bath E£15; doubles E£16, with bath E£20.) Most of the balconies and cool rooms of the **Anwar Hotel,** at the intersection of al-Salem and al-Bassain St., are built facing a breezy avenue and are a pleasant haven from the heat, though there are no private bathrooms. (☎82 00 70. Singles E£15; doubles E£30.) The four-story mustard-yellow building that calls itself **Mebarez,** 800m from Tahrir Sq. on the road to Farafra, is more upscale than the Gardens. It specializes in housing large European tour groups in winter. All rooms have fans and balconies. (☎82 15 44. Lunch E£14, dinner E£16. Singles E£28, with bath and A/C E£44; doubles E£52, with bath and A/C E£58.) The recently renovated **Tourist Rest House** (☎82 16 86) offers dusty rooms and mediocre bathrooms for E£10 per person, including kitchen access. Overlooking the road to New Mosque Sq. and abutting the old Islamic cemetery, the brand new **al-Forsan Hotel,** on Wadi al-Gadid St., wins the location and cleanliness awards, if only because it was just opened. Spacious rooms are ideal for larger groups. (☎82 13 47. Breakfast included. Singles E£23, with bath E£28; doubles E£30, with bath E£35; extra beds E£10.) If you came to the oasis for a break from the same old hotel scene, ditch Mut and head to the **Bedouin Camp,** 7km northwest of Mut on the road to al-Rashida. Clean, wooden huts with concrete floors and well-kept shared baths are E£15 with breakfast. The large common area is used for impromptu bongo performances. Inquire at the Ahmed Hamdey restaurant for availability; also inquire about tours to the **White Desert** (Farafra) from Dakhla for E£120-150 (see p. 257).

The desert oases are not known for their filling cuisine, but Dakhla's is the best going down. There are two **Hamdey Restaurants** serving chicken and meat meals for E£10, Ahmed's and Arabi's, both just before the Mebarez Hotel. Arabi serves up delicious pancakes for E£2. Around the corner from the Garden Hotel is **Anwar's Desert Paradise Restaurant,** so named, perhaps, for the aging A/C (full meal E£9). **Shehaab,** along the highway just west of New Valley St., is a local favorite (full meal E£5). The **al-Forsan Hotel** has a classy outdoor restaurant offering meals at plebeian prices (kebab meal E£15).

◉ SIGHTS

There's little of interest in **Mut,** but the oasis capital is a great jumping off point for **Western Dakhla,** which includes the village of al-Qasr and surrounding archaeological digs, and **Eastern Dakhla,** which includes the villages of Balaat and Bashendi (see **Dakhla: Practical Information,** p. 258, for more information). In the cooler months, biking to some spots is feasible, although you'll still need to bring plenty of water—and then some.

WESTERN DAKHLA

Hire a pickup for a day (E£40-50) or leapfrog on the pickup truck taxis that circle the sites. Ask the Dakhla tourist office for help on tours, itineraries, and prices.

QALAMOUN. The distinctly medieval hilltop village of Qalamoun was the capital of Dakhla in Mamluk times. In the Islamic era, Qalamoun functioned as an administrative center; its inhabitants today claim Turkish and Mamluk ancestry. The town's name has two possible translations: "Amun's pens" (*qalam* means pen), for the scribes who lived here; or "Amun's citadel" (*qala'a* means fortress), as Qalamoun's panoramic perch offers military defense. Near the center of town is an Ayyubid **mosque,** uphill through the maze of narrow passages and traditional mudbrick houses. *(5km west of Mut is the Bedouin village of al-Douhous, where the road splits for 25km before joining up again; the left fork takes you to Qalamoun.)*

AL-GEDIDA. Al-Gedida ("New Town," so named because it's only 300 years old) is known for its **arabesque factory.** In cooperation with 'Ain Shams University and the German Embassy, locals make decorated woodwork with palm tree branches. For more delicious handiwork, sample the town's sweet harvests: apricots in May, mangoes in late July, and dates in October. *(5km past Qalamoun, on the road to al-Qasr. Factory open Sa-Th 8am-2pm. Free.)*

MOUSAWAKA TOMBS. Many of the jagged rock headstones date from the first and 2nd centuries CE, while the domed tombs to the rear are slightly newer. A worker may be present to show you around, though the tombs are often deserted (except for the bats in the domes). Nowhere in Egypt can you get more up-close and personal with a mummy than here. *(3km west of al-Gedida, on the left.)*

DEIR AL-HAGAR. Half the fun of this Roman temple is the road leading up to it, which twists and turns around a small village and passes three Roman remains before leading up to a ridge from which Deir al-Hagar can be seen (the temple is still a 1½km dirt trek away). Dedicated to the Theban triad of Mut, Amun, and Khonsu, the temple was built in the first century BCE during the reign of Nero, and added to by his immediate successors. The ruins have been almost completely devoured by the sand dunes, but the government has gone to great lengths to reclaim it. Ask to see the small exhibit by the entrance. *(The ridge is 2km past the Mousawaka Tombs. Open daily 8am-5pm. E£20, students E£10.)*

AL-QASR القصر

The most edifying daytrip from Dakhla is al-Qasr, a twisty 32km from Mut on the northern fork. This charming contemporary town was built in and around the substantial remains of Dakhla's medieval Islamic capital. The older buildings, adorned with lively accounts of pilgrimages to Mecca, are a model of comfortable architecture, as their mud buildings remain cool in summer and warm in winter. The **old village** of al-Qasr lies 400m to the north of the main road through the new village. On the main road at the western edge of town, there is a large **map** of the village. Within the old village, arrows direct you to the sights. The **al-Qasr Rest House** is on the main road, at the turnoff to the old village. It serves up simple meals of rice and omelettes in summer and a more complete menu in winter (full meal E£7). Cold drinks and ice cream are available. There is also a market, 30m from the hotel on the same side of the road. A **medical clinic** is 50m toward Mut.

OLD VILLAGE SIGHTS. The **Minaret of Nasser al-Din** is the only extant part of an 11th-century Ayyubid mosque; a 19th-century mosque surrounds the old tower. Down the gnarled alleys north of the minaret stands **Qasr Madrasa,** an intact two-story mud-brick building thought to have been either an Ayyubid schoolhouse or the entertainment hall of an Ottoman palace; villagers later used the building as a courtroom. Many of the doorways of the old village are adorned with ornate wooden lintels that reveal the name of the owner, builder, and carpenter as well as the date of construction. Bits of a pharaonic arch and a Roman doorway hint at al-Qasr's pre-Islamic past. On the southern fringes of the old town you can see a waterwheel and a functioning **pottery works,** where villagers churn out everything from ashtrays to chamberpots.

EASTERN DAKHLA

BALAAT. In the crowded old section of Islamic **Balaat** (pop. 5000), long, dark passageways burst into a courtyard with palm fronds and grape vines. These pathways were built with ceilings as a defense tactic—during invasions, the enemies' camels and horses could not fit through the alleys. Balaat has a reputation for being the tidiest village in the area, as its roads are strewn with bright orange sand a few times each day. Ask to see the **mayor's house,** with its assembly courtyard, speech balcony, and ornate, Ottoman-wrought iron lamps and bedframes.

QILAE AL-DABA. Dakhla's pharaonic governors were buried in these red-brick tombs during the 6th dynasty. A team of French archaeologists has revealed several rather bizarre inverted step pyramids as well as a mummified governor. *(1km from the official bus stop, behind Balaat and just northeast of the main road. Ask locals for al-Maqabr al-Fara'oniya. Open daily 8am-5pm. E£20, with ISIC E£10.)*

BASHENDI. Though less picturesque than its younger brother Balaat, Bashendi sits atop a recently discovered temple and various Roman-era tombs that make a visit well worthwhile. The large stone **Tomb of Ketenus** contains six rooms, including one decorated with scenes of a 2nd-century Roman mingling with the gods Min and Seth. Before you can mingle with the ghosts of Romans past, you'll need to get the key from the tombkeeper. Next door to the Tomb of Ketenus is the prominent **Tomb of Bashendi,** which consists of a distinctly Bedouin domed roof atop a Roman foundation. The tomb commemorates the village's beloved namesake; you might join locals who decorate the inside of the holy man's tomb with *henna*. If the guard isn't around to open the tombs, another villager will do the honors. There are also a number of hot and cold springs to which residents can direct you, though local touts would rather lead you to the Bashendi **carpet works,** where youths weave beautiful rugs for E£100 and up. *(5km east of Qilae al-Daba, 40km from Mut. Ask locals for al-Maqabr al-Romaniya. Tomb of Ketenus E£16, students E£8.)*

KHARGA OASIS الواحة الخارجة ☎092

Kharga

⌂ ACCOMMODATIONS
Hamad Allah Hotel, 1
Tourist Office
  Rest House, 2
Waha Hotel, 3

TO ASYUT, (5km),
HIBIS TEMPLE (2km),
NECROPOLIS OF AL-BAGAWAT (2.5km)

N

■ Passport Office

Kharga Museum
Khenessa St.

Gamal 'Abd al-Nasser St.

Gas Station ■

■ Governorate

al-Adel St.

Misr Bank

al-Nada St.

TO DAKHLA

Cinema Hibis

al-Nabawi al-Mohandis St.

SHOWLA SQ.

0   200 yards
0   200 meters

TO BULAQ & BARIS

Kharga is Egypt's most effective attempt at a desert boomtown and the capital of the New Valley Province *(al-Wadi al-Gideed)*. Little is known about Kharga's early pharaonic history, although it must have been agriculturally productive—its hieroglyphic name is *hibis*, or "plow." It became prosperous during Roman times due to its proximity to trade routes, including the Darb al-Arba'een (Forty Days Road), between Egypt and Sudan. Beginning in the 4th century, Kharga became a large Christian settlement and center for monasticism, where major figures (including Bishop Nestorius, founder of the heretical Nestorian sect) were exiled by religious and political rivals. The oasis's function as a distant exile continued into the 20th century, when Nasser banished Mustafa Amin, founder of *al-Akhbar* (Egypt's largest circulating daily), to Kharga after the 1952 revolution.

When the New Valley Project began in earnest in the early 1980s, the town again prospered. The cookie-cutter apartment-filled streets of Kharga are largely lifeless and boring by Egyptian standards, but the ruins on its periphery astound. Welcome relief from Kharga's New Town can be found in the narrow alleyways of the Old Town, where locally-made ceramics and carpets are available in the *souq*. Kharga is the closest oasis to the Nile Valley, a mere 240km from Asyut.

EGYPT

A newly paved road heads south from Kharga, skirting dunes and small oases on the way to **Bulaq** (15km south), **Baris** (90km south), and **Luxor** (270km west).

GETTING THERE AND GETTING AROUND

Flights: EgyptAir (☎ 92 16 95), in the Governorate, 2 blocks north of the Misr Bank intersection on Nasser St. Open Sa-Th 8am-2pm. **Airport** turnoff is 3km north of town on Asyut Rd., then another 2km southeast. Flights directly to **Cairo** (Su 6am, E£450) or to **Cairo** via **Dakhla** (W 8:30am, E£450). Minibus or taxi to airport from Showla Sq. E£5.

Buses: Intercity buses arrive and depart from Showla Sq. to: **Asyut** (3hr., 4 per day, E£8); **Cairo** (12hr.; 7, 10am, 6, 10pm; E£37); and **Dakhla** (2½hr.; 7am, noon, 2:30pm; E£9). **Local buses** to **Baris** (3hr.; 1, 3, 7am, noon, 2:30pm; E£1.60) and **Dush** (1½hr., 6 and 11am, E£2). Schedules change, so see tourist office for updates.

Service and **Minibuses:** Catch *service* and minibuses in Showla Sq. Service to **Asyut** (3½hr., E£9); occasional service to **Dakhla** (E£8). "Special" (unshared) to Dakhla (E£56). Irregular service to **Baris** (E£1-2). With a group, a special taxi to Luxor may be feasible (4hr., E£200 per car). Hiring a *service* or minibus to Baris for the day costs E£50. Within town, **covered truck taxis** scurry along al-Nabawi St. from Showla Sq., turn up Nasser St., and head for the tourist office at the northern end (10pt).

ORIENTATION AND PRACTICAL INFORMATION

Gamal Abd al-Nasser St. runs north-south and is bisected in the middle by **al-Nada St.**, which heads west to Dakhla. At this intersection you'll find Cinema Hibis, the **Misr Bank** (traveler's check exchange, V cash advances; open Su-Th 8:30am-2pm and 6-9pm), and the **police station** (☎ 122). The main branch of the **post office** is just off al-Nasser St., behind Cinema Hibis. (**EMS** service. Open Sa-Th 8am-2pm. Smaller branch in Showla Sq.) At the northernmost end of al-Nasser St., just before it heads off to the ruins and Asyut, stand the rest house and **tourist office,** where the resourceful Mr. Ibrahim Hassan, regional director of oasis tourism, will make your stay in Kharga, or any other desert destination, the best possible by smoothing over any bumps with his excellent English. (☎ 92 12 05. Open daily 8:30am-3pm and 8pm-midnight.) The **passport office** faces the tourist office (open Sa-Th 7:30am-3:30pm), and the **tourist police** is next door. (☎ 92 13 67. Open 24hr.) Grab a **pickup taxi** (10pt) to get to this part of town.

The southern end of al-Nasser St. intersects **al-Nabawi al-Mohandis St.**, which runs east-west. This street curves slightly northeast to **Showla Sq.**, where you'll find the intercity bus, *service*, and minibus stations. The main **hospital** is off al-Mohandis St. toward Showla Sq. (☎ 122 or 92 07 77. Open 24hr.) **Aleman Pharmacy** sits one block east of Showla Sq. (Open daily 8am-3pm and 6pm-midnight.) Get connected at **Computer Technology Center,** on al-Nabawi St. (E£2 per 3min. Open Sa-Th 10am-2pm.) **Al-Dawati Telephone Central,** in Showla Sq., has the most reliable international service in town. (Open Sa-Th 8am-3pm and 5-11pm.)

ACCOMMODATIONS AND FOOD

Rooms with fans are essential in the summer, and they don't hurt in the winter. There are plenty at the **Waha Hotel,** on al-Nabawi al-Mohandis St., a 15-minute walk from Showla Sq., near grocery stores and restaurants. The rooms and balconies are simple and tidy, with crisp linen and clean baths. Common bathrooms are strictly cold water affairs. (☎ 92 03 93. Breakfast E£6. Dorm beds E£8; singles E£7, with hot water, bath, and fan E£15; doubles E£14-20.) The best thing about **al-Darel Biada Hotel** is its location. Steps away from the bus station, it's a favorite for travelers. The rooms and baths are well-cleaned but noisy due to the bustle below. (Singles E£14, with bath E£22; doubles E£20, with bath E£28.) For more peaceful surroundings, try the **Hamad Allah Hotel,** on al-'Adel St., one block from the telecom tower. Shady trees circle the quiet building, which features clean doubles with refrigerator, A/C, TV, bath, and towels. (☎92 06 38. Lunch E£15, dinner E£17. Singles E£38, with A/C E£63; doubles E£55, with A/C E£90.) The villas at **Tourist Office Rest House,** directly behind the tourist office on Gamal Abd al-Nasser St., come complete with living rooms, TV, fully equipped kitchens, and A/C—ideal for groups of four or more. (☎92 12 05. E£22 per person.)

Cuisine in Kharga is adequate on a good day, and a decent rotisserie chicken seems to be the specialty (whole bird E£8, half bird E£4). Clusters of budget eateries and coffee shops can be found on al-Nabawi al-Mohandis St. between Gamal Abd al-Nasser St. and Showla Sq. Vegetarians must make do with beans and rice. A restaurant at the entrance to the *souq* street offers *fuul* and falafel (50pt) for breakfast. If you're staying in the northern end of town, try the recently opened **al-Zubur Restaurant,** on the left fork of al-Nasser, 200m past the tourist office. Filling three-course vegetarian and meat meals are served with a smile (E£16-22).

👁 SIGHTS

MUSEUM OF AL-WADI AL-GADID. This is the *pièce de resistance* of the New Valley's tourism drive, housing a massive collection of artifacts from the New Valley oases and a few pieces from the Egyptian Museum in Cairo. A variety of pharaonic and Classical artifacts is on display, from wooden sarcophagi and sandstone sphinxes to mascara jars and Roman coins. *(Open daily 8am-5pm. E£20, with ISIC E£10.)*

TEMPLES OF HIBIS AND NADURA. The **Temple of Hibis** was begun in 588 BCE (26th dynasty) by Apnias and completed in 522 BCE by Darius I, making it one of only two Persian-built Egyptian temples. Although dedicated to the Theban triad of Amun, Mut, and Khonsu, the temple is distinguished by its depictions of Persians and Seth, the god of the Oases, with a blue body and a falcon head. First-century Roman inscriptions discuss legal issues, including women's rights. Crowning a knoll across the road from the Temple of Hibis is the **Temple of Nadura,** built in the 2nd century BCE during the reign of Roman Emperor Antonius. Little of it stands today, but the site offers an excellent view of the oasis. *(At the northern end of town, 2km north of Hotel al-Kharga and close to the road on the left. A shared covered taxi will take you to the tourist office (and possibly farther) for E£1. From there, walk or try to hop on an intertown taxi (E£2). The scaffold-covered Hibis will be closed for several years for renovation; Nadura is open to the public. Free.)*

NECROPOLIS OF AL-BAGAWAT. The 263 above-ground tombs (also called chapels) of the Christian Necropolis of al-Bagawat stand eerily at the desert's edge. From the 3rd through 8th centuries, a sizeable Christian community (including many hermits and some of the religion's first monks) inhabited Kharga. The necropolis is visible from the road, and an asphalt lane leads to the ticket booth. If you go up the hill along the marked path, you'll come to the **Chapel of Exodus,** with ceiling murals depicting the pharaoh's Roman-looking army chasing Jews fleeing Egypt, and Adam and Eve with *ankh*-like crosses. In front of the Chapel of Exodus are the interconnected frescoed chapels #23-35, the resting place of members of a wealthy local family. The interior frescoes of biblical scenes in the **Chapel of Peace** (#80) exemplify Coptic painting of the early Alexandrian style. Greek inscriptions identify Adam and Eve, Noah's Ark, and the Virgin Mary. Atop the cemetery's central hill stand the remains of a 4th-century mud-brick basilica. *(500m past the Temple of Hibis on the road to Asyut. Open daily 8am-6pm; in winter 8am-5pm. E£20, students E£10.)*

FACTORIES. A little more than 500m south of al-Nabawi St. down al-Nasser St. is the **pottery and carpet factory,** where locals make and sell handicrafts. Another 300m down al-Nasser St. is the **date factory,** where 200 women at conveyor belts take plucked, washed, steamed, blind, dried, hot, and double dates and stuff them with peanuts. *(Pottery and carpet factory open Su-Th 8am-2pm; date factory open Aug.-Feb. Sa-Th 8am-1:30pm. Both free.)*

NEAR KHARGA

Hire a pickup **taxi** for a day from Kharga (E£50-60). Plenty of shared taxis go from Kharga as far as Bulaq (50pt). Catch them at the southern end of al-Nasser St. Each day, **buses** go to Baris (1hr.; 7am, noon, 2:30pm; E£2) and back (1hr.; 6, 11am, 7:30pm; E£2). The 7:30pm bus continues on to Dush from Kharga (1½hr., E£2) and doesn't return until 6am the next morning. **Hitchhiking** is difficult and dangerous due to the extreme heat.

DARB AL-ARBA'EEN

If you've come all the way to Kharga, don't miss the road along the old camel trail south to the town of Baris, known as Darb al-Arba'een ("Forty Day Road"). This legendary caravan route extended from western Sudan to the Egyptian Nile Valley and tragically trafficked more slaves than any other land route in the world.

KHWITA TEMPLE. Vast sandscapes are all that thrive between Kharga and Khwita Temple, 17km to the south. The impressive 10m walls of the temple-fortress dominate a hill two kilometers east of the road. Dedicated to the Theban triad of Amun, Mut, and Khonsu, and built by Darius I with later Ptolemaic additions, the temple served as the center of a thriving community famous for its grape production in pharaonic times. *(Open daily 8am-5pm; in winter 8am-6pm. E£16, students E£8.)*

ZAYAN TEMPLE AND WELLS. At the 25km mark you'll come across the shaded, dirty **Nasser Wells.** Farther on, the better-developed **Bulaq Wells** offer a rest house (beds E£15) and hot springs. **Zayan Temple,** dedicated to Amun, sits five kilometers east of Nasser Wells, near the village of Araf, on a road that loops around from the north of Khwita Temple to a point north of Bulaq. Originally built in the Ptolemaic era, the site was restored by the Romans to build a fortress, of which there are still remnants. *(For transportation to Zayan Temple, hop on a pickup or public bus headed for Baris and have the driver drop you off on the way (ask for Araf). A round trip taxi should cost no more than E£20. To return to Kharga or continue on to Baris, walk the 1km to Bulaq and catch a pickup taxi, or wait by the road (bring lots of water). Let's Go does not recommend hitchhiking in this area. Open daily 8am-5pm; in winter 8am-6pm. E£16, students E£8.)*

BARIS

The secluded village of Baris (the sign at the edge of the town ironically reads "Paris") est 90km au sud de Kharga et comme l'enfer en été (over 50°C), mais il fait beau en avril. Merchants make a 40-day camel trek from here to the border of Chad to purchase an ingredient used in local soap, and each expedition reputedly brings the merchant E£20,000. Think twice before going into business for yourself, since only one family in town is privy to the location of water wells along the way.

There is a government **rest house** north of town, with no sign to mark it; look for the yellow, gray, and red buildings in a row perpendicular to the highway, about 500m north of the "Paris" sign. Arrange your stay through the tourist office in Kharga or get the groundskeeper to let you in. (Beds E£5.) Mr. Farkhat of the Kharga **tourist office** is available in Baris (Th-Su). If you walk down the central street, perpendicular to the main road, old Baris will be on your right and the gardens straight ahead. The blue structure resembling a doghouse sells kebab, *fuul*, and falafel every day except Friday.

An abandoned **public housing complex** designed by Egyptian architect Hassan Fathy stands 300m northwest of the rest house. Construction was halted and never resumed after the 1967 War, as the government correctly assumed that the villagers wouldn't want to live in buildings resembling tombs.

DUSH TEMPLE. A paved road leads 23km southeast to the Dush Temple. The building has an overabundance of heat and a shortage of visitors during the summer, but there's more to it than meets the eye. Originally built for the worship of Serapis and Isis, the temple dates back to the rule of the Roman emperors Trajan and Hadrian. The sand around the temple is slowly parting to reveal a church, pottery shards, and a well with clay pipes. These pipes tunnel down to an underground city, leading archaeologists to believe that Dush was a prosperous settlement that was abandoned when the wells ran dry. *(Baris pickup taxi drivers will make a special round-trip to Dush for E£20 (wait included), but are hard to find. Instead of tackling Baris in a day (your road time will total 7hr.), consider an overnight stay. Open daily 8:30am-5pm. E£20, students E£10.)*

ISRAEL ישראל

CURRENCY		
US$1=NIS4.13		NIS1=US$.24
CDN$1=NIS2.79		NIS1=CDN$.36
UK£1=NIS6.27		NIS1=UK£.16
IR£1=NIS4.97		NIS1=IR£.20
AUS$1=NIS2.41		NIS1=AUS$.42
NZ$1=NIS1.94		NIS1=NZ$.52
SAR1=NIS.60		NIS1=SAR1.67
E£1=NIS1.20		NIS1=E£.84
JD1=NIS5.83		NIS1=JD.17

PHONE CODES | Country Code: ☎972. Police: ☎100. Emergency: ☎101.

Halfway through its first century, Israel has yet to resolve a psychological struggle between secularism and reverence. An inevitable sense of religion and history permeates its modern cities, where pensive philosophers and microchip millionaires sit on park benches with patriotic Zionists and day-seizing disco-goers. The nation's heterogeneity is most apparent on Friday evenings, when Tel Aviv clubs and Eilat pubs explode with revelry that can almost be heard in the reverent streets of Tzfat or in Jerusalem's Jewish Quarter. Israel has been controversial since its inception. As a result of persecution culminating in the Holocaust, Jews of all cultures came together to fashion a new kind of state and to remake themselves, sometimes at the expense of Palestinian Arabs. With the country's identity and culture in constant flux, all Israelis have their own visions of what Israel could or should be. Amos Oz, Israel's leading novelist, sees his fellow Israelis as "a warm-hearted, hot-tempered Mediterranean people that is gradually learning, through great suffering and a tumult of sound and fury, to find release both from the bloodcurdling nightmares of the past and from delusions of grandeur, both ancient and modern." Ask Israelis about their bewildering national situation, and they will tell you at length how *they* see their country—there is no lack of impassioned political or apolitical opinions. But a fundamental optimism shines through; talk with them long enough, and they will eventually smile or shrug and say, *"Yihiyeh tov"* (It will be OK). For the full coverage of the sights and sounds of Israel, try *Let's Go: Israel 2001*.

LIFE AND TIMES

ANCIENT HISTORY

THE BIBLICAL AGE AND BEYOND. Want to "know" Israel in the biblical sense? The Bible begins the recorded history of the area with the story of Abraham (Avraham in Hebrew, Ibrahim in Arabic), the first of the Patriarchs. Local leaders united the Israelite tribes in the region under a single deity, **Yahweh,** and established an 11th-century BCE kingdom under **Saul** that reached its peak during the reign of Saul's successors **David** and **Solomon** (who built the Temple of Jerusalem). After Solomon's death in 922 BCE, the empire split into the northern Kingdom of Israel and the southern Kingdom of Judah.

The Assyrians conquered Phoenicia and Israel in the late 8th century BCE, forever removing the 10 tribes of northern Israel from their homeland. King **Nebuchad-**

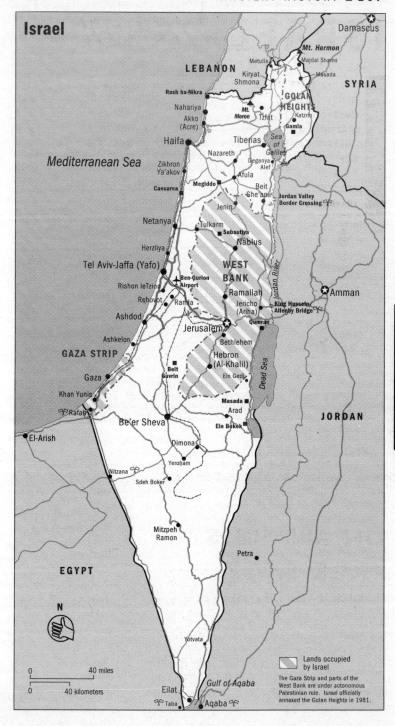

Israel

Damascus

LEBANON

Mt. Hermon

Metulla
Majdal Shams

Kiryat
Shmona
Masada

SYRIA

Rosh ha-Nikra

Nahariya

GOLAN
HEIGHTS

Akko
(Acre)

Mt.
Meron

Tzfat

Katzrin

Haifa

Tiberias

Sea
of
Galilee

Gamla

Mediterranean Sea

Zikhron
Ya'akov

Nazareth

Deganya
Alef

Caesarea

Megiddo

Afula

Beit
She'an

Jordan Valley
Border Crossing

Jenin

Netanya

Tulkarm

Sabastiya

Herzliya

Nablus

WEST
BANK

Tel Aviv-Jaffa (Yafo)

Ben-Gurion
Airport

Rishon leTzion

Ramallah

Rehovot

Ramla

Jericho
(Ariha)

King Hussein/
Allenby Bridge

Amman

Ashdod

Jerusalem

Qumran

Ashkelon

Bethlehem

GAZA STRIP

Hebron
(Al-Khalil)

Beit
Guvrin

Ein Gedi

Gaza

Dead Sea

Khan Yunis

Masada

Rafah

Arad

El-Arish

Be'er Sheva

Ein Bokek

JORDAN

Dimona

Yeroham

Witzana

Sdeh Boker

Mitzpeh
Ramon

Petra

EGYPT

N

Yotvata

0   40 miles

0   40 kilometers

Gulf of Aqaba

Eilat

Taba

Aqaba

**I
S
R
A
E
L**

Lands occupied
by Israel

The Gaza Strip and parts of the
West Bank are under autonomous
Palestinian rule. Israel officially
annexed the Golan Heights in 1981.

nezzar wreaked widespread havoc and again deported the Jews to Babylon in 587 BCE, a period known as the Babylonian Captivity. The Israelites prospered intellectually and economically under the **Persians** (who ousted the Babylonians and allowed the Jews to build the Second Temple in Jerusalem) until **Alexander the Great** rode in on a tide of Hellenism that swept through the region from 332 until 198 BCE, after which the Syrian-based **Seleucids** took over under King Antiochus IV and forbade all Jewish practices. The Jewish lower classes successfully revolted under **Judah Maccabee** (an event commemorated by the holiday Ḥanukah) and founded the strife-ridden Hasmonean dynasty.

In 44 CE, **Pompey** conquered the territory and declared it a Roman province (Judaea), leading to Jerusalem's rebellion in 65-66 CE. In 70 CE, the Roman general **Titus**, faced with the choice of sparing Jerusalem's Second Temple at great military cost or burning the city, chose the latter. The destruction of the Second Temple led to dramatic upheaval and despair among the Jewish people. Three years later, the Romans captured the last Jewish stronghold at **Masada** (see p. 402). The Romans then exiled the majority of Jerusalem's population, dispersing them throughout the empire. Perhaps to obliterate the land's historical connection with the Jews, they gave the territory the name **Palestine**, after the Philistines.

THE AGE OF EMPIRES AND SUFFIXES. With the division of the empire into Latin West and Byzantine East in 330 CE, Palestine came under the supervision of **Constantinople.** Although little changed administratively, the adoption of Christianity by the Emperor Constantine in 331 CE created increased interest in what to many was the "Holy Land." In the 10th century, Muslim Fatimids captured most of Palestine (including Jerusalem) and destroyed many Christian holy sites, such as the **Church of the Holy Sepulchre.** Enraged **Crusaders** recaptured the Holy Land in 1099, beginning the short-lived era of the Crusader States, before falling to the Kurd **Salah al-Din** and his own short-lived Ayyubid Dynasty. The age of "-uks" (Mamluks, Seljuks, etc.) nipped at the heels of the age of "-ids" (Fatimids, Ayyubids, etc.), which was followed by the lavish **Ottoman Empire.** By the end of the 17th century, however, the Ottoman ports in Palestine, Syria, and Egypt (which had once provided the sole access to the East) were rendered insignificant as Portuguese sailors steered their way around the Horn of Africa. The once-formidable Ottoman Empire became "the sick man of Europe."

MODERN HISTORY

ZIONISM AND THE BRITISH MANDATE. Although small Jewish communities were present in Palestine over the 18 centuries following the Roman exile, the vast majority were in **diaspora** communities in Europe, the Middle East, North Africa, and the Americas. These Jews hoped to someday return to and rebuild their ancient homeland. This hope became the focus of the movement of **Zionism** in the late 19th and early 20th centuries, when various writers promoted a return to Israel as a solution to the problems of the Jews; **Theodore Herzl** was the first to encourage political means to achieve Zionist ends. The first **aliya** ("going up," the term for Jewish immigration to Israel) occurred in 1882; the second, in 1904-1914, witnessed the development of **kibbutzim,** cooperative agricultural settlements.

During World War I, the British government, at war with the German-allied Ottomans, made muddled promises of sovereignty to the Arabs, Jews, and French, including the November 1917 **Balfour Declaration,** a document that declared that the British would support a Jewish homeland in Palestine if it would not affect Palestine's non-Jewish communities. After the war, however, the League of Nations handed Palestine wholesale to Great Britain, and British indecisiveness continued during their interwar control of the region, as the rise of Nazism drove tens of thousands of European Jews into Palestine. After World War II, the UN partitioned Palestine into separate Jewish and Arab states. The leaders of the former reluctantly accepted the resolution, while the leaders of the latter (and the governments of neighboring Arab states) rejected it outright, denying the UN's authority to divide and distribute territories they considered Arab patrimony.

THE 1948 WAR OF INDEPENDENCE. On May 14, 1948, the British mandate over Palestine ended and **David Ben-Gurion** declared the independence of the State of Israel. The next day, a combined army of Syrian, Iraqi, Lebanese, Saudi, Egyptian, and Jordanian troops marched in from the north, west, and south. Few observers gave the new state much chance for survival, but the war's results became clear with the signing of armistices in early 1949. Israel had secured not only its UN-allotted territory, but also land designated for Palestine in the north and in the West Bank. The Gaza Strip, which had also been designated for Palestine, was secured by Egypt, and the West Bank and half of Jerusalem by Jordan. Thousands of Palestinian refugees crowded into camps in the West Bank, Gaza, and bordering Arab states. The dispossessed Palestinians came to bitterly remember the 1948 war as **al-Naqba,** the Catastrophe.

THE SUEZ CRISIS AND THE RISE OF PAN-ARABISM. After **Colonel Gamal Abd al-Nasser** took control of Egypt in 1952, he promoted a highly emotional brand of pan-Arabism, hoping to unify the Arabic-speaking masses into one state powerful enough to resist imperial encroachments and take control of Palestine. The US and other foreign powers, who had begun to develop the oil fields of Arabia, feared their arrangements with local monarchs would collapse if Nasserism spread. In 1956, the US clumsily attempted to curtail Nasser's power by withdrawing its offer to finance the Aswan High Dam. Rather than yield to the snub, Nasser nationalized the Suez Canal to use its revenues for the dam. On October 24, 1956, Jordan, Syria, and Egypt established a joint military command, directed against Israel. Israel, Britain, and France devised a scheme to take the canal. Israel would attack Egypt, and a Franco-British "peace-keeping" force would follow. Initially, the conspiracy worked: Israel took the **Sinai Peninsula,** opened its port of Eilat to international shipping, and dealt Nasser's military a major blow. The military victors, however, had not considered world reaction to their adventure. When Israel, Britain, and France withdrew their troops to placate the furious US, Nasser was heralded as the savior of the Arab world without having won a battle.

THE SIX-DAY WAR. From bases sanctioned by the governments of Jordan, Syria, and Lebanon, the **Palestinian Liberation Organization (PLO)** raided Israel during the 1960s; in return, Israel hit Palestinian refugee camps. The cycle of raids and reprisals created tension on Israel's northern border, and a Syrian-Israeli air battle took place in April 1967. When Syria's hard-line government turned up the rhetoric, Nasser stepped in and initiated a blockade on May 22, 1967, sparking what is known as the 1967 War or **Six-Day War.** By June 9, 1967, all parties had accepted the cease-fire. To Israel went the spoils: they annexed East Jerusalem, got the Sinai and the Gaza Strip from Egypt, the Golan Heights from Syria, and the West Bank from Jordan. The defeated Palestinians decided to take things into their own hands; the extremist group FATAH, led by **Yassir Arafat,** took over the PLO in 1969, encouraging liberation through propaganda and guerilla warfare.

The stakes of the game were now higher than anyone could have imagined: with the United States behind Israel and the Soviet Union behind Nasser, any local conflict affected the world's major superpowers. **UN Resolution 242** stipulated "withdrawal of Israeli armed forces from territories occupied in the recent conflict." The intentional ambiguity of the document caused bickering immediately, while the situation along the Suez Canal degenerated into the **War of Attrition.**

The 1967 War created 400,000 more Palestinian refugees, most of whom went to Jordan, throwing the Jordanian government and the PLO into a tense relationship: Hussein wanted to hold secret peace negotiations with the Israelis, while the PLO hoped to use Jordan as a base for attacks on Israeli-held territory. In September

1970 (known to Palestinians as **Black September,** see p. 450), Hussein's frustrations and conflicts with Arafat's PLO, already at boiling point, overflowed: a brutal war was declared and martial law imposed; it was only after 3000 lives were sacrificed that the PLO reluctantly agreed to move its headquarters to Lebanon.

YOM KIPPUR WAR AND CAMP DAVID. Egyptian and Syrian forces launched a surprise assault on Israel on October 6, 1973, when most Israelis were in synagogues for Yom Kippur (the holiest day of the Jewish year); the bloody fighting of the **Yom Kippur War** and the subsequent Arab oil embargo ended only when the Arabs decided to settle matters under the supervision of the US and the Soviet Union in the Geneva Peace Conference of December 1973. Thanks to the work of US Secretary of State **Henry Kissinger,** all parties agreed to disengage forces over the next five months (one month after Israeli Prime Minister **Golda Meir** resigned amidst public uproar against the country's unpreparedness in the war). Soon after, the PLO was granted "observer" status in the UN.

Throughout the 1970s, an increasing number of Israelis began to settle in the occupied territories, an act discouraged by Prime Minister Yitzhak Rabin but encouraged by his successor, **Menahem Begin.** In 1979, Begin, Egypt's Anwar Sadat, and the US's Jimmy Carter met at Camp David in Maryland to sign the **Camp David Accords,** which returned the Sinai to Egypt but left the question of West Bank and Gaza control more muddled than before. Things cooled off in the 1980s under Sadat's successor, current Egyptian President Hosni Mubarak, but on June 6, 1982, Israel invaded **Lebanon** under "Operation Peace for Galilee," an attack most believe was aimed at wiping out PLO forces that had been attacking northern Israel. Tensions led to bloodshed, ending only when the US intervened and the Israelis withdrew in 1985, leaving a buffer zone in southern Lebanon.

THE PLO AND JORDAN. Mourning at a funeral for several Palestinians killed in an Arab-Israeli car crash in Gaza erupted into a Palestinian **intifada** (uprising, literally "throwing or shaking off") that spread to the West Bank. Palestinians in the territories began establishing networks to coordinate their hitherto sporadic acts of civil disobedience, and it soon became apparent that the *intifada* was not abating. In the summer of 1988, Jordan suddenly removed itself from the situation, and the PLO seized the opportunity to secure a role in negotiations with the rest of the world by renouncing terrorism, recognizing Israel's right to exist, and proposing an independent Palestinian state. Israeli Prime Minister Yitzhak Shamir retaliated with a proposal whose underlying tenet was that Jerusalem, whole and undivided, was Israel's eternal capital, but the PLO and Egypt refused to accept this and turned on Arafat, whom they blamed for the weakening of the strong position Palestinians had gained from the *intifada*.

THE GULF CRISIS AND OSLO ACCORD. The Gulf Crisis began when Iraqi President Saddam Hussein ordered his troops to march into Kuwait on August 2, 1990; he then slyly suggested "linkage" as a way of solving the Gulf Crisis: he would withdraw from Kuwait when Israel withdrew from the West Bank, Gaza, and Golan, and when Syria withdrew from Lebanon. SCUD missile rockets rained down on Israel (supported by Arafat) as tensions skyrocketed, but hopes were high at the 1991 Madrid peace conference because Syria entered negotiations on the side of Israel (the first time in years such a thing had happened). The year 1992 saw both the election of Palestinian autonomy-promising Prime Minister Yitzhak Rabin and increased terrorist attacks by **Hamas,** an Islamist Palestinian faction. In 1993, Israel and the PLO surprised the world by announcing a successfully negotiated, peaceful framework for solving the Israeli-Palestinian conflict. It was known as the Declaration of Principles on Interim Self-Government Arrangements (the DOP or **Oslo Accord**), which was signed on the White House lawn on September 13, 1993 with US President Bill Clinton presiding. The DOP provided mutual recognition between Israel and the PLO and the implementation of Palestinian autonomy (expanding over five years) in the Gaza Strip and Jericho area, leading to an eventual finalizing of the entire messy situation. Other agreements created the **Palestinian Authority (PA)**, a 24-member council headed by Yassir Arafat that would have some governmental control in the West Bank.

RECENT HISTORY AND THE PEACE PROCESS. On November 4, 1995, 25-year-old **Yigal Amir,** a right-wing Jewish university student, shot and killed Israeli Prime Minister Yitzḥak Rabin. Over one million mourners (50 of them world leaders) filed by the slain leader's coffin in the days following the murder. **Benjamin Netanyahu** barely scraped through elections in May 1996, in which he promised to continue Rabin's peace-oriented politics, but tensions (ignited by Hamas) over his conservative policies lead to widespread violence. Hamas suicide-bombers twice targeted Jerusalem's crowded thoroughfares in 1997, killing 20 and injuring over 10 times as many. In response, Israel cordoned off the West Bank and the Gaza Strip and arrested Palestinians.

On May 30, 1998, Israel celebrated its **50th anniversary** with widespread partying in Jerusalem. The anniversary turned grim as Palestinians mourned the 50 years since what they call "al-Nakba," the catastrophe. Violent rioting broke out in Hebron and East Jerusalem, and Israeli soldiers fired on crowds, leaving five Palestinians dead. The PA and the US set a deadline that same month for Israel to withdraw from 13% of the West Bank, but Netanyahu ignored their decision, insisting that anything over a 9% withdrawal would pose an unacceptable security risk.

IN THE NEWS

The summer of 1999 marked a tit-for-tat bombing struggle between the Israeli Army occupying South Lebanon and **Hizbullah** guerillas. In September 1999, Israeli Prime Minister Ehud Barak announced plans for a historic Israeli pullout scheduled for July 2000. Barak hoped the pullout would indicate Israeli goodwill and encourage peace talks with neighboring Syria. Escalating skirmishes through the winter, however, prompted Barak to advance the pullout first to June 1, 2000, and then to May 24, when Israel's 20-year occupation of South Lebanon came to a close. In July 2000, Arafat and Barak met for the Camp David II summit under the auspices of the US government. These talks marked the first time that Israel was willing to consider discussing the status of Jerusalem. No progress was made, however, and at press time no date had been set for future talks.

RELIGION AND ETHNICITY

Freedom of religion is safeguarded by the state under the 1948 Declaration of the Establishment of the State of Israel. Israel's population of 5.8 million is 80% Jewish and 15% Muslim; the remaining 5% includes Christians and Druze. Each community operates its own religious courts, funded by the Ministry of Religion, and controls its own holy sites. Every religion's days of rest are guaranteed by law.

About half of Israeli **Jews** are secular; 30% identify themselves as Orthodox and 18% as Ultra-Orthodox, and the religious-secular divide is something of a fault line in society. The religious establishment is quite powerful—rabbinical courts even have a state monopoly on matrimonial issues among Jews. Many Israeli Jews are either first- or second-generation immigrants, and are often divided along ethnic lines: **Sephardi** Jews come from Arab or other Mediterranean countries, while **Ashkenazi** Jews have northern or eastern European origins. The deep rift in Israeli society goes back to the 1950s, when Sephardi Jews from Morocco and Iraq were brought to an already established, Ashkenazi-dominated state. Although Sephardim comprise roughly half of the Jewish population in Israel, Ashkenazim still fill most of the positions of power in the government, military, and academia, and Sephardim are generally poorer. The last decade has brought massive immigrations from the former USSR and Ethiopia, clouded by questions concerning the religious status of immigrants claiming to be Jewish.

Among other religious and ethnic groups in Israel are the **Muslims,** who have flourished in Israel since the 7th century. After Mecca and Medina, the most important Muslim holy site—the **al-Aqsa Mosque** (see p. 303)—is in Jerusalem. A Muslim *hadith* tells of Muhammad's journey from Mecca to al-Aqsa ("The Farthest") and up through the Seven Heavens to meet God. Many **Christian** sects are also represented in Israel, including the Armenian Orthodox, Abyssinian, Anglican, Baha'i, Coptic, Greek Orthodox, Roman Catholic, and Syrian Orthodox churches. Most are Arab by language and origin. Israel's **Druze** population is divided between those living in the Galilee and in the Golan Heights. Those in the Galilee remain loyal to Israel and often serve in the army, while those in the Golan support their return to Syria. Druze generally live in separate villages and have their own communal institutions.

FESTIVALS AND HOLIDAYS

In Israel, most businesses and public facilities close Friday afternoons for **Shabbat,** the Jewish sabbath, and reopen at sundown on Saturday. They also close for Jewish holidays, which begin at sundown on the previous day. **Pesaḥ,** or Passover (Apr. 8-14, 2001), celebrates the exodus of the Jews from Egypt. Observant Jews refrain from eating bread and pastries; products made with regular flour and leavening agents may be hard to come by. **Rosh Ha-Shana** (the Jewish New Year; Sept. 18-19) is only slightly less holy than **Yom Kippur** (Sept. 27), the holiest day of the Jewish calendar; observant Jews fast in atonement for their sins, and Israel shuts down entirely. In Muslim areas, many businesses close on Friday for prayer. On holidays, they may close during the afternoon, but are generally open in the morning. For a list of religious and national holidays, see the **Appendix,** p. 699.

LANGUAGE

Hebrew and **Arabic** are the official languages of Israel. Most Israelis speak some English; many speak English with near fluency, particularly in bigger cities like Jerusalem and Tel Aviv and popular tourist destinations such as Eilat. Signs are usually written in English (sometimes Russian) as well as Hebrew and Arabic. For more information on the Hebrew language, see the **Appendix,** p. 703.

THE ARTS

LITERATURE. The compilation of the biblical narrative was followed by the age of the **Mishnah** (200 BCE-700 CE), when *halakha* (laws derived from the Bible) and *agada* (elaboration on the Bible) were compiled. The revival of Hebrew as a secular language in the 18th century brought a drastic shift in Hebrew literature. Josef Perl and Isaac Erter parodied Ḥasidic works in their writings. **Joseph Brenner** was popular at the turn of the century, thanks to his hallmark character—the tragic, uprooted settler. In the 1920s and 1930s, Nobel Laureate **Shmuel Yosef (Shai) Agnon** confronted the breakdown of cultural cohesion among modern Jews in *A Guest for the Night, The Bridal Canopy,* and *Twenty-One Stories.* In the late 1950s, writers such as **Amos Oz** began to experiment with psychological realism, allegory, and symbolism, paving the way for the skepticism of the 60s (such as *The Palace of Shattered Vessels* by David Shahar, considered the Proust of Israeli literature). *Past Continuous* by **Ya'akov Shabtai,** about Tel Aviv in the 1970s, is perhaps the best Israeli novel of the decade. The poetry of **Yehuda Amichai** will ensure that you never look at Jerusalem stone in the same way again.

Israeli literature today increasingly focuses on the Israeli-Palestinian conflict. Oz's *In the Land of Israel* is a series of interviews that documents the wide range of political sentiment. For Palestinian accounts, check out *The West Bank Story* by Rafik Halabi, an Israeli Druze television reporter, and Fawaz Turki's autobiographical *The Disinherited.* A cadre of young writers such as Etgar Keret and

Gafi Amir highlight the disaffected and cynical outlook characteristic of what has been called the **post-Zionist** era. Israel's tumultuous history has inspired a number of over-idealized, highly entertaining histories, including Ḥayim Potok's *Wanderings*, James Michener's *The Source*, and Leon Uris's *Exodus*.

MUSIC. After World War I, Jews in Palestine assembled chamber groups, a symphony orchestra, an opera company, and a choral society. With the rise of Nazism in Europe, Jewish musicians fled to Israel, and this influx also spurred the formation of several music groups. Today seasonal music activities from October to July are held in such varied settings as the historic Crusader Castle at Akko (see p. 357) and the modern, 3000-seat Mann Auditorium in Tel Aviv (see p. 330). Israeli **popular music** emerged from its folk-chant origins (often echoing Russian folk melodies) in the late 1960s. Since the 1970s, Israel has been catching up with international music fashions; local bands experiment with punk, reggae, heavy metal, grunge, and even rap. **MTV** now keeps Israeli youth abreast of the goings-on in London and New York, and they expect nothing less of their own local acts. Tel Aviv is the unequivocal hub of the cutting-edge music scene in Israel. The most popular artists perform music that's somewhere between hard rock and acoustic pop. Some native classics still on the performance circuit are Shlomo Artzi, Yehudit Ravitz, Rami Klinestein, and Gidi Gov. Achinoam Nini blends American rock with Middle Eastern sounds, while David Broza also throws in Latin American influences. Zahava Ben, a Sephardic Jew, is one of the more popular Israeli singers. She frequently tours in the Palestine Authority and has achieved a great deal of success in Egypt singing the songs of the legendary Umm Kulthum. Drag queen Dana International brought Israeli pop international fame in 1998 when she won the Eurovision Song Contest. In many places, Middle Eastern-style music (*muzika mizraḥit*, or "oriental music") blasts from car stereos and boomboxes and is very popular with Sephardim (Avihu Medina is the big name in *mizraḥi* music).

FILM. Israel has a thriving film industry with numerous festivals and award ceremonies, including an Israeli version of the Academy Awards. In the award-winning *Wedding in Galilee* (1987) by Palestinian director Michel Khleifi, a Palestinian is granted permission to waive curfew in order to hold his son's wedding, on the condition that Israeli officers be allowed to attend. Other successful films include *Clara Ha-Kedosha* (St. Clara) and *Etz Ha-Domim Tafus* (Under the Domim Tree, 1994) which deals with teenage survivors of the Holocaust in the 1950s.

FOOD AND DRINK

Some Israelis' diets are affected by **kashrut** (literally translated as "proper"), the Jewish dietary laws. Observant Jews will not eat or shop in a place that carries non-kosher goods; to keep kosher clientele coming, the big supermarket chains in Israel carry only kosher products, and many restaurants (and most hotels) serve only kosher food. Observance of *kashrut* is not necessarily the norm in Israel, and many restaurants (particularly in Haifa and Tel Aviv) are avidly non-kosher.

The typical Israeli eats a large breakfast, a big midday meal, and a light, late supper. Because of the poor quality and high cost of beef and lamb, Israelis rely largely on chicken, dairy, and vegetable products. Popular items in the Israeli diet include ever-present **hummus** (mashed chick-peas, garlic, lemon, and *taḥina*, a sesame concoction); "salad," finely chopped tomatoes and cucumbers garnished with oil and vinegar; *gvina levana*, soft white cheese; *schnitzel*, breaded and fried chicken breast; chips (french fries); and a variety of sweet dairy snacks.

You can prepare your own meals from food purchased at the *shuk* (outdoor market, like the *souqs* elsewhere in the Middle East), the *makolet* (small market), or a supermarket. *Burekas* (cheese-, potato-, spinach-, or meat-filled filo dough) are available at patisseries and some fast-food shops. Aside from the standard falafel and *shawarma*, street vendors also sell what look like hand grenades— these are only **sabras,** prickly cactus fruits with edible innards (the seeds cause indigestion). *Sabra* is also a term for a native Israeli; both the fruit and the people are said to be thorny on the outside, sweet on the inside.

Two Israeli **beers** are the decent, deep-amber Goldstar (a draft beer) and the lesser Maccabee lager. The not-strictly-enforced minimum drinking age is 18. Strong, sweet **Arabic coffee** is sometimes referred to as *turki* (Turkish); for less potent brews, ask for *hafukh* (mixed with milk) or *filter*. *Shahor* (black) or *botz* (mud) coffee is Turkish coffee brewed in a cup.

ESSENTIALS

WHEN TO GO

North Americans and students favor summer for visiting Israel and the West Bank; Europeans prefer winter. Most businesses and public facilities close Friday afternoons for Shabbat, the Jewish sabbath, and reopen at sundown on Saturdays. They also close for Jewish holy days, which begin at sunset on the previous day.

AVERAGE TEMPERATURE AND PRECIPITATION											
	JANUARY			APRIL			JULY			OCTOBER		
	°C	°F	mm	°C	°F	mm	°C	°F	mm	°C	°F	mm
Jerusalem	9	48	132	17	62	28	24	75	0	21	70	13
Tel Aviv	13	54	202	19	66	30	26	78	0	23	73	20
Haifa	14	56	13	20	67	4	28	82	0	25	76	2
Eilat	15	60	0	25	76	5	33	91	0	27	81	0

DOCUMENTS AND FORMALITIES

EMBASSIES AND CONSULATES

Most foreign embassies and consulates in Israel are in **Tel Aviv** (see **Practical Information,** p. 324), though a few countries also have consulates in Jerusalem, Haifa, and Eilat. Israeli embassies and consulates abroad include:

Australia: Embassy: 6 Turrana St., Yarralumla, Canberra ACT 2600 (☎(02) 6273 1309; fax 6273 4273). **Consulate:** 37 York St., 6th fl., **Sydney** NSW 2000 (☎(02) 9264 7933; fax 9290 2259).

Canada: Embassy: 50 O'Connor St., #1005, Ottawa, Ont. K1P 6L2 (☎(613) 567-6450, 567-6453, or 567-6455; fax 237-8865; email embisrott@cyberus.ca; www.israelca.org). **Consulates:** 180 Bloor St. W., #700, **Toronto,** Ont. M5S 2V6 (☎(416) 640-8500; fax 640-8555; email hasbara@idirect.com); 1155 boulevard Réné-Lévesque Ouest, #2620, **Montréal,** Québec, H3B 4S5 (☎(514) 940-8500; fax 940-8555; email cgisrmtl@videotron.net).

Ireland: Embassy: Carrisbrook House, 122 Pembrook House, Dublin 4 (☎(01) 668 03 03; fax 668 04 18).

New Zealand: Embassy: 13th Floor, Equinox House, 111 The Terrace, P.O. Box 2171, Wellington (☎(04) 472 23 68 or 472 23 62; fax 499 06 32; email israel-ask@israel.org.nz; www.webnz.com/israel).

South Africa: Embassy: 339 Hilda St., Pretoria 001, P.O. Box 3726 (☎(12) 342 26 93 or 342 26 97; fax 342 14 42; email cgijhb@global.co.za).

UK: Embassy: 2 Palace Green, London W8 4QB (☎(020) 7957 9500; fax 7957 9555; email info@israel-embassy.org.uk; www.israel-embassy.org.uk/london).

US: Embassy: 3514 International Drive NW, Washington, D.C. 20008 (☎(202) 364-5500; fax 364-5423; email ask@israelemb.org). **Consulates:** 800 2nd Ave., **New York,**

NY 10017 (☎(212) 499-5410; fax 499-5425; email nycon@interport.net); 6380 Wilshire Blvd., #1700, **Los Angeles,** CA 90048 (☎(323) 852-5500; fax 852-5555; email israinfo@primenet.com). Israeli consulates are also in **San Francisco, Miami, Atlanta, Chicago, Boston, Philadelphia,** and **Houston.**

ENTRY REQUIREMENTS

Visas are not required for citizens of Australia, Canada, Ireland, New Zealand, South Africa, the UK, and the US. Flights arrive at **Ben-Gurion International Airport,** between Tel Aviv and Jerusalem. Buses leave from the airport to Tel Aviv (NIS10), Jerusalem (NIS21), and other major cities. **Studying** or **working** in Israel requires a special visa and permit.

BORDER CROSSINGS

TO JORDAN. There are three border crossings into Jordan: from Jericho in the West Bank, from **Beit She'an** in northern Israel, and from **Eilat** (by far the simpler and more popular option). Crossing from Eilat to **Aqaba** (info ☎(07) 633 68 12) should take less than an hour—just pay the NIS57 exit tax and walk the one kilometer no-man's land between the two countries (there's no public transport). Get Jordanian visas valid for one month at the border (citizens of Australia JD16, Canada JD36, Ireland JD11, New Zealand JD16, South Africa free, UK JD23, US JD33). Taxis from Eilat to the border cost NIS15-20; from the border to Aqaba JD4. (Border open Su-Th 6:30am-10pm, F-Sa 8am-8pm; closed Yom Kippur and 'Eid al-Adha.) For more info, see **Border Crossings: To Israel,** p. 455.

TO EGYPT. The border crossing from **Eilat** to **Taba** is somewhat arduous. Passports must be valid for at least three months; Israeli visas must be valid for the day of travel. For travel outside Sinai, get a visa at the Egyptian consulate. The border (info ☎637 31 10) is open 24 hours, but is closed on Yom Kippur and 'Eid al-Adha. Allow at least one hour to cross. Take the #15 bus from Eilat and keep your passport handy. There are 11 exciting steps: (1) Bus drop-off. (2) Little Taba snack bar ("last beer before Sinai"). (3) Passport pre-check. (4) Passport control booth (pay NIS57 exit tax). (5) Israeli last passport check; they automatically stamp your passport at this point unless you ask them not to. (6) Stroll through no-man's land. (7) Egyptian passport control—fill out entry form, get stamp. (8) Egyptian security (X-ray machine). (9) Post-border passport check. (10) Passport check and E£17/US$6 Egyptian border tax. The Taba Hilton is the best place to **change money** (open 24hr., no commission for foreign currency converted to Egyptian pounds). (11) Welcome to Egypt! The bus station is a 10-minute walk from the border. From Taba, there are buses to: **Cairo** (7hr., E£70); **Nuweiba** (1½hr., E£12); **Dahab** (2½hr., 3pm, E£15-17); and **Sharm al-Sheikh** (3-4hr., E£25).

TO LEBANON AND SYRIA. Israel's borders with Lebanon and Syria are closed. The most common route into Syria is via Jordan. Travelers with Israeli stamps in their passports will not be granted Lebanese or Syrian visas. Ask that your passport not be stamped if you eventually plan on traveling to Lebanon or Syria.

GETTING AROUND

BUSES. Buses are the most popular and convenient means of travel in Israel. Except for the **Dan Company** (☎(03) 639 44 44) in Tel Aviv and the **Arab buses** serving the West Bank, Galilee, and Gaza, the **Egged Bus Cooperative** (www.egged.co.il) has a monopoly on intercity and most intracity buses. The modern, air-conditioned buses are direct *(yashir),* express, or local *(me'asef),* with an occasional 10% ISIC discount. Most bus stations have printed schedules, often in English. Egged has intercity **information lines** in the major cities (Tel Aviv ☎(03) 694 88 88, Haifa ☎(04) 854 95 49, Jerusalem ☎(02) 530 47 04). A *kartisia,* available from any bus driver, gives you 11 local rides for the price of 10 (NIS47); a one-month pass that

ISRAEL

includes unlimited local rides in Haifa, Jerusalem, and Tel Aviv costs NIS188. Most local bus rides cost NIS5. Buses between cities usually leave from the central bus station *(tahanah merkazit)*. Round-trip tickets may be 10% cheaper.

TAXIS AND SHERUT. Regular private taxi rides are called **special** (pronounced "spatial"). City taxis operating as *special* must use a meter *(moneh);* insist that the driver turn it on. Refuse offers of special but unspecified "discount" rates (translation: no meter and an exorbitant fare). Otherwise, set a price before you enter the taxi. **Sherut** (the equivalent of the Arab *service*) taxis hold up to seven people. Certain companies operate *sherut* seven days a week from offices in each city. Intercity *sherut* operate on loose schedules, departing when full; on Saturdays, they often whiz along the streets in search of passengers. Intracity *sherut* never follow a schedule. Most routes have set fares comparable to bus prices; ask for quotes at tourist offices or from the nearest Israeli. Always settle on a price before you depart.

TRAINS. Rail service in Israel (10% ISIC discount on tickets over NIS20.50) is useful only for travel along the northern coast. Trains are slightly cheaper than buses, but they don't run on Shabbat. Avoid traveling on Friday afternoons when trains are most crowded. See www.isarail.com for more information.

CAR RENTAL. More Israelis have been killed in car accidents than in all of the country's wars combined. Drunk driving is prevalent and the windy, hilly roads don't help. Widespread public transportation makes cars generally unnecessary, but some places (especially the Golan and Negev) are most easily reached by car. Some roads, particularly in the Negev and the Golan, have poor (or nonexistent) shoulders or few gas stations. "Scenic routes" are barely wide enough for one car, and buses often blast by in the opposite direction. The legal driving age is 17, but most agencies will only rent to credit-card holders 21 years or older (a few rent to 18-year-olds). Rentals cost about US$55-70. Deals arranged beforehand from overseas are often much cheaper. Roads are well marked and maps are available at all tourist offices. Israelis drive on the right side of the road. Car phones and cellular phones (Israelis call them "pelephones") are everywhere; most rental cars have them built in, so decide at rental time if you want the more expensive with-phone plan. Cell phones are responsible for many accidents, so laws regarding them are stringently enforced. **Sleeping in your car** is one of the most dangerous (and often illegal) ways to get your rest. If your car breaks down, wait for the police to assist you. See **Practical Information** in each city for agency addresses.

HITCHHIKING. Sexual harassment and assault related to *tremping* (as it is called in Israel) have increased in recent years. License plates carry meaning; yellow are Israeli, black with a צ are army, red are police, blue or gray are occupied territory, and white are diplomatic. Hitchers in the Negev or Golan (where sometimes the only option is a military vehicle) risk being stranded by a ride that doesn't go all the way to their destination. Hitchers flag cars by pointing to the far side of the road with the index finger. *Let's Go* does not recommend hitchhiking.

TOURIST AND TRAVEL SERVICES

MEDICAL EMERGENCIES AND HEALTH. Medical care in Israel is equivalent in quality to that in the West. For minor illnesses, go to a pharmacy (at least one pharmacy in a neighborhood is open or on-call 24 hours). Pharmacists offer medical advice and medication; most speak English. Doctors can help with more serious illnesses; almost all Israeli doctors speak fluent English. Because Israel's system of socialized medicine has only recently begun to privatize, private practices are very expensive and medical insurance is a must.

BUSINESS HOURS. Most businesses are open 8:30am-7pm, but many stay open until 10pm, particularly in shopping malls. Most have longer hours on Thursdays.

Shabbat (the Jewish day of rest) lasts from sundown on Friday to sundown on Saturday; most businesses close by 2pm on Friday and stay closed on Saturday.

USEFUL ADDRESSES. Society for the Protection of Nature in Israel (SPNI) runs expertly guided tours throughout Israel and Sinai. Tours range from half-day explorations of Jerusalem to 15-day Israel odysseys. Their main office is at 13 Heleni Ha-Malka St. in Jerusalem (☎(02) 625 23 57).

MONEY MATTERS

CURRENCY AND EXCHANGE. The primary unit of currency is the **New Israeli Shekel (NIS).** There are 100 **agorot** in a shekel. Notes come in denominations of NIS200, 100, 50, 20, and 10; coins come in NIS10, 5, 1, .50, 10 agorot and 5 agorot. It is cheaper to buy shekels in Israel than in your home country. **ATMs** in Israel are open 24 hours and accept most major American credit cards. **Post offices** usually have the best rates and charge no commission. Since you lose money with each transaction, **convert in large sums** (unless the currency is depreciating rapidly). Banks are generally open Su, Tu, and Th 8:30am-12:30pm and 4-5:30pm; M and W 8:30am-12:30pm; F and holidays 8:30am-noon. An ATM card or credit card garners the best possible rates. Traveler's checks may not be accepted in some locations.

TAXES. Israel offers a **VAT** (Value Added Tax) refund to tourists who purchase over US$50 worth of goods at a shop approved by the Ministry of Tourism. To collect the 17% refund, you must be a non-Israeli citizen, pay in foreign currency (cash or international credit card), and present a VAT invoice/receipt at your point of departure from Israel (if leaving from Ben-Gurion International Airport, go to the 24-hour Bank Leumi Counter). Eilat is a free trade zone, so there is no VAT.

TIPPING AND BARGAINING. Tipping in Israel is increasingly moving toward expensive American standards, but for the time being, a 10% tip will suffice in restaurants, bars, and hotels. Taxis are mostly metered with standardized prices; drivers do not expect tips but accept them. Bargaining in Israel is the norm, the only exceptions being department stores, drug stores, and supermarkets.

KEEPING IN TOUCH

MAIL. Post offices are usually open Su-Tu and Th 8am-12:30pm and 3:30-6pm, W 8am-2pm, F 8am-1pm, and are closed Sa and holidays. On the street, yellow mailboxes are for mail sent within the same city; red mailboxes are for all other mail. Most post offices offer international **Express Mail Service (EMS),** which supposedly takes three days. Mail can be sent through **Poste Restante** to almost every town in Israel. **American Express** offices will hold mail for up to 30 days and forward upon request, but only for cardholders. **Aerogrammes** are available at post offices for NIS1.40. Airmail from Israel averages five to nine days, although times are unpredictable from smaller towns.

TELEPHONE AND INTERNET ACCESS. To call Israel direct from home, leave off the 0 from the city code. Within Israel, major calling cards that can be used include: **AT&T** (☎(800) 949 49 49); **Sprint** (☎(800) 938 70 70); **MCI WorldPhone Direct** (☎(800) 940 27 27); **Canada Direct** (☎(800) 949 41 05); **BT Direct** (☎177 440 27 27); **Telecom New Zealand Direct** (☎177 640 27 27); and **Telkom South Africa Direct** (☎177 270 27 27). **Public telephones** are everywhere. Avoid older telephones—they devour *asimonim* (tokens) even for local calls (NIS0.50). Far more common are the beige-colored public phones (marked with yellow signs) that operate with **Telecards** (20 units NIS10.50, 50 units NIS23, 120 units NIS52; buy them at post offices). Telecards are good for long distance calls (NIS5.90 per min. to the US). International rates drop up to 50% late at night and on Saturdays and Sundays. **Bezek,** Israel's phone company, has offices with metered phones for international calls in Tel Aviv and Jerusalem. It may be more economical to call overseas from a phone office, because they charge for the exact time spent on the phone, not in calling units as telecards do. Dial ☎ 144 for the **operator** or **information.**

Israel is a highly networked country, with computer technology as one of its major industries. There are **cybercafes** in all major cities and most hostels offer inexpensive use of Internet and email.

SPECIAL CONCERNS

WOMEN TRAVELERS. Women travelers in Israel do not attract undue attention, but it's always best to take basic safety rules into account. Western women can blend in easily in Israel, as women generally dress in Western styles, but it is advisable to dress modestly (nothing sleeveless or tight, with skirts and pants well below the knees) in Orthodox Jewish and Arab sections of the country. Fashions in Tel Aviv, however, are about as liberal as they get. Persistent harassers may be dissuaded by a loud, public "*lech!*" ("Go away!"), or even an English scolding.

BGLT TRAVELERS. Tel Aviv is one of the few cities in the Middle East with a thriving gay and lesbian community. The main organization for gay and lesbian concerns in Israel is the **Society for the Protection of Personal Rights,** P.O. Box 37604, Tel Aviv 61375 (☎ (03) 629 36 81; fax 525 23 41), or P.O. Box 3592, Haifa (☎ (04) 867 26 65). A community center, library, and coffee shop are at 28 Naḥmani St., Tel Aviv. The **White Line** (*Ha-Kav Ha-Lavan;* ☎ (03) 732 55 60) is the society's gay and lesbian hotline (operates Su-Th 7:30-11:30pm).

JERUSALEM ירושלים القدس ☎ 02

There are men with hearts of stone,
and there are stones with hearts of men.
—Rav Kook

When the sun sets over the Judean hills, Jerusalem's white stone turns gold and peace seems to be within the city's grasp. The domes, spires, and minarets of three major faiths' places of worship rise over crenelated walls in quiet harmony. But Jerusalem is not always as serene as its evening breeze and rooftop view. The white stone, a requirement for all of Jerusalem's buildings, is indelibly, if invisibly, stained with the blood of centuries. During Jerusalem's 5000 years, 18 conquerors have presided over the city. David established Jerusalem as the capital of the Israelite kingdom, and his son Solomon extended it northward to the present-day Temple Mount (where the Ark of the Covenant was kept and the First Temple stood). The split of the Israelite kingdom led Judah's citizens to develop the Jewish identity in the city until 596 BCE, when King Nebuchadnezzar besieged the city and exiled the Jews to Babylon.

Jerusalem enjoyed more than a century of revival under the Persians, until Alexander the Great rode in on a tide of Hellenism that swept through the city in 332 BCE. The renaissance ended in 198 BCE, when Seleucid King Antiochus IV forbade all Jewish practices. Led by Judah Maccabee, the Jews successfully revolted and founded the Hasmonean dynasty that lasted until the Romans set up the province of Judaea. Six centuries of Roman rule began with Herod the Great, child of a Jewish father and Samaritan mother. The Jews revolted but failed, then tried once more (the 123 CE Bar Kokhba Revolt) and failed; when Hadrian razed the city after this third revolt, he divided his new *Aelia Capitolina* into quarters (that remain today) using two major roads (the Cardo and Decumanus). When Roman Emperor Constantine adopted and legalized Christianity in 331 CE, his mother Eleni visited the Holy Land in order to identify and consecrate Christian sites.

Muslim caliph Omar conquered *Aelia* in 638, beginning an era of tolerant rule; his successors built the Dome of the Rock soon after. The Fatimids and Seljuk Turks who followed were not so kind to the city and its synagogues and churches. Fired up by the rumored closing of pilgrimage routes, the Crusaders stormed and captured Jerusalem in 1099, and they subsequently begin massacring Muslims and Jews mercilessly. The year 1187 saw the city do its time (as all cities in the Middle East did) under Salah al-Din, who allowed both Muslims and Jews to resettle the city—so tolerantly that the city became a thriving center for Muslim scholarship in the Mamluk era. Ottoman rule saw restructuring and expansion until 1917, when the city fell without resistance to the British army. Both Jews and Arabs came to resent the increasing influence of the British, who promised autonomy to both during World War I but ended up keeping Palestine for themselves, heightening tension between the two sides that almost turned into a civil war in 1936 and 1939.

The next World War ignited violence that divided Palestine into separate Jewish and Arab states, but left Jerusalem an international city. In the post-evacuation war of 1948, West Jerusalem and the Jewish Quarter were besieged by Arabs, and Jordanian control of the city saw the synagogues and ancient quarters dynamited and the city divided into Jordanian and Israeli sectors for nearly two decades. In the Six-Day War of 1967, Israel captured East Jerusalem, the Old City, and the West Bank from the Jordanians. On June 29 of that year, Israel declared the newly unified Jerusalem its "eternal capital." The walls separating the Israeli and Arab sectors were torn down, and life under Israeli rule began for Jerusalem's Arabs.

The 1987 *intifada* (uprising) of Palestinians protesting Israeli occupation saw violent clashes that turned East Jerusalem and the Old City into alien territory for Jewish Israelis. Bus explosions, suicide bombings, and street fighting have fueled the fires of Jerusalem's recent history, and the future of Jerusalem is perhaps the most sensitive issue in the current Israeli-Palestinian negotiations. Israel adamantly refuses to discuss withdrawing from its capital, while Palestinians fervently oppose the idea of abandoning claims to their most important city.

HIGHLIGHTS OF JERUSALEM

Wonder anew at the glory of negative spaces in the works of Rodin and Picasso at the **Israel Museum's** sculpture garden (p. 317).

Spend a morning at the **Yad va-Shem** Holocaust memorial museum (p. 317) for a powerful reminder of the atrocities committed by Nazis in World War II Europe.

Spend the afternoon exploring the intricate Islamic architecture of the mosques of the **Dome of the Rock** (p. 303).

⌧ GETTING THERE AND AWAY

Flights: Ben-Gurion Airport (Info for all airlines ☎(03) 972 33 44. El Al English info ☎(03) 972 33 88. Automated flight reconfirmation ☎(03) 972 23 33.) is only an hour from Jerusalem and easily accessible; you do not need to go to Tel Aviv first, no matter how early your flight, thanks to the 24hr. *sherut* service offered by Nesher (see **Taxis,** below). For a hassle-free airport experience, bags for El Al flights can be checked in and inspected in advance at 7 Kanfei Nesharim St., 1st fl. (☎651 57 05; fax 651 57 03), on the corner of Jaffa Rd. near the central bus station. Open Su-Th 2-10pm for next-day flights, 2-7pm for same-night flights.

Buses: Egged Central Bus Station (☎530 47 04; www.egged.co.il), on Jaffa Rd. (see **Getting Around,** below). 10% ISIC discount on long-distance trips. Drivers often inspect ISIC cards upon boarding. Times, frequencies, and prices listed here are based on the summer 2000 schedule; call for current info (or go to the station). Info desk open Su-Th 6am-8:30pm, F 6am-3pm. To: **Arlozorov terminal** (#480; every 15-20min. Su-Th 6am-10:30pm, F 6am-4:30pm, and Sa 8:20-11pm); **Be'er Sheva** Direct (#470; 1½hr.; every 45min.-2hr. Su 6:20am-6:15pm, M-Th 6:45am-6:15pm, F 10:20am-sundown, Sa 8:20pm; NIS27) or via **Kiryat Gat** (#446; 1¾hr.; every 15min.-1hr. Su-Th 6am-9pm, F

Jerusalem Overview

JERUSALEM FOREST

MOTZA ILIT

SEE WEST JERUSALEM MAP P. 284

Sderot Ben Gurion

Kanfei Nesharim

HAR NOF

Wolfsohn

Sderot Herzl

BEIT ZAYIT

$ Bank of Israel

JERUSALEM FOREST

University Stadium

Hebrew University (Givat Ram Campus)

Givat Ram

Sderot Herzl

Mt. Herzl

Yad Vashem

Herzl's Grave

Herzl Museum

Shmuel Beyth

Jerusalem Forest Recreation Centre

Bezalel Barak

Ein Kerem

Hantke

Church of St. John

EIN KEREM

Hantke

Ha-Rav Uziel

Church of the Visitation

Russian Convent

KIRYAT HA-YOVEL

Ha-Rav Herzl

TO HADASSAH MEDICAL CENTER

Strod

KIRYAT MENAHEM

Golomb

ORA

N

Golomb

0   1000 yards

0   1 kilometer

Kenyon Yerushalayim (Shopping Mall)

Teddy Stadium

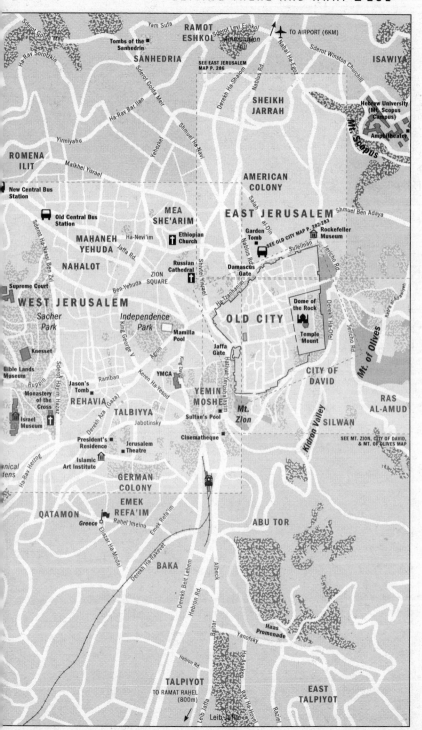

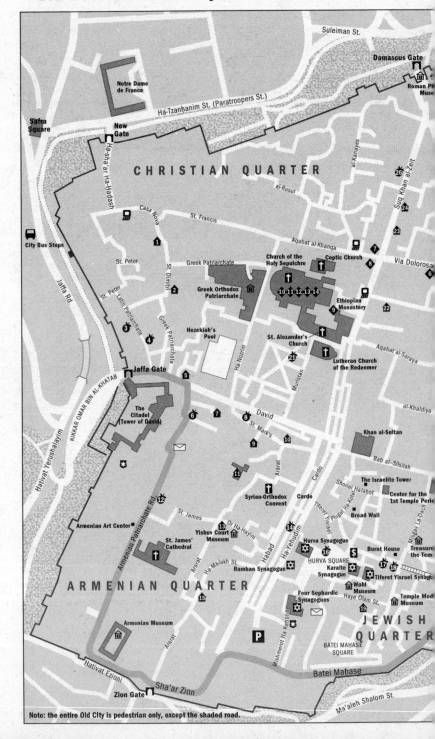

Suleiman St.

Damascus Gate

Roman Ph
Museum

Notre Dame
de France

Ha-Tzanhanim St. (Paratroopers St.)

Safra
Square

New
Gate

CHRISTIAN QUARTER

al-Kanayes

Suq Khan al-Zeit

26

al-Rusul

24

23

City Bus Stops

Casa Nova

St. Francis

Aqabat al-Khanqa

Via Dolorosa

St. Peter

Greek Patriarchate

Church of the
Holy Sepulchre

Coptic Church

7

1

6

8

St. Dimitri

2

Greek Orthodox
Patriarchate

10 11 12 13 14

Ethiopian
Monastery

22

9

St. Peter

Latin Patriarchate

3

Hezekiah's
Pool

St. Alexander's
Church

21

Aqabat al-Saraya

4

Greek Patriarchate

Ha-Nozrim

Lutheran Church
of the Redeemer

Jaffa Gate

5

al-Khaldiya

KIKKAR OMAR BIN AL-KHATAB

Jaffa Rd.

The
Citadel
(Tower of David)

6

7

David

8

St. Mark's

10

Khan al-Sultan

Hativat Yerushalayim

9

Bab al-Silsilah

JAFFA GATE

11

The Israelite Tower

Center for the
1st Temple Perio

Shonei Halahot

Syrian-Orthodox
Convent

Cardo

Cardo

Tiferet Yisrael

Broad Wall

12

Ararat

Plugat Ha-Kotel West

Misgav La-Dach

Armenian Art Center

St. James

13

Or Ha-Hayim

Yishuv Court
Museum

14

Ha-Yehudim

Hurva Synagogue

Treasure
the Tem

St. James'
Cathedral

Habad

16

Burnt House

17

18

Ararat

Ha-Malakh St.

Ramban Synagogue

HURVA SQUARE

Karaite
Synagogue

Tiferet Yisrael Synago

ARMENIAN QUARTER

Wohl
Museum

Haye Olam St.

Temple Mod
Museum

15

Four Sephardic
Synagogues

19

JEWISH

Armenian Museum

Mishmerot Ha-Kehuna

QUARTER

P

BATEI MAHASE
SQUARE

Hativat Ezioni

Batei Mahase

Zion Gate

Sha'ar Zion

Ma'aleh Shalom St.

Note: the entire Old City is pedestrian only, except the shaded road.

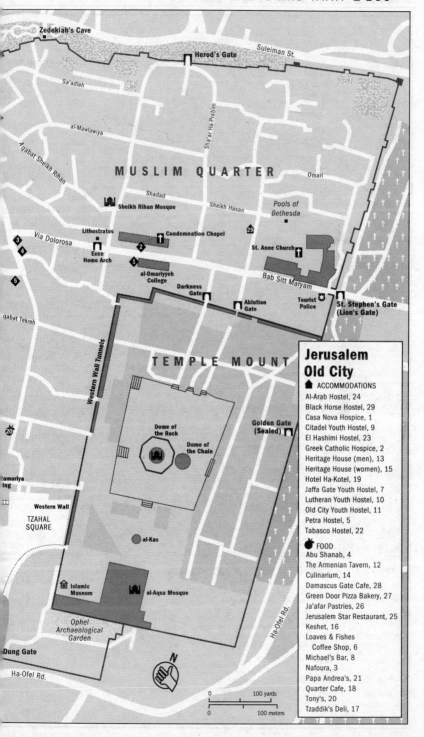

Zedekiah's Cave

Suleiman St.

Herod's Gate

Sa'adieh

al-Mawlawiya

Sha'ar Ha-Prahim

MUSLIM QUARTER

Omari

Aqabat Sheikh Rihan

Shadad

Sheikh Rihan Mosque

Sheikh Hasan

Pools of Bethesda

Via Dolorosa

Lithostratos

Condemnation Chapel

29

St. Anne Church

Ecce Homo Arch

al-Omariyyeh College

Darkness Gate

Bab Sitt Maryam

qabat Tekreh

Ablution Gate

Tourist Police

St. Stephen's Gate (Lion's Gate)

Western Wall Tunnels

TEMPLE MOUNT

Golden Gate (Sealed)

20

Dome of the Rock

Dome of the Chain

amuriya ing

Western Wall

TZAHAL SQUARE

al-Kas

Islamic Museum

al-Aqsa Mosque

Ophel Archaeological Garden

Ha-Ofel Rd.

Dung Gate

Ha-Ofel Rd.

N

0   100 yards

0   100 meters

Jerusalem Old City

🏠 ACCOMMODATIONS

Al-Arab Hostel, 24
Black Horse Hostel, 29
Casa Nova Hospice, 1
Citadel Youth Hostel, 9
El Hashimi Hostel, 23
Greek Catholic Hospice, 2
Heritage House (men), 13
Heritage House (women), 15
Hotel Ha-Kotel, 19
Jaffa Gate Youth Hostel, 7
Lutheran Youth Hostel, 10
Old City Youth Hostel, 11
Petra Hostel, 5
Tabasco Hostel, 22

🍴 FOOD

Abu Shanab, 4
The Armenian Tavern, 12
Culinarium, 14
Damascus Gate Cafe, 28
Green Door Pizza Bakery, 27
Ja'afar Pastries, 26
Jerusalem Star Restaurant, 25
Keshet, 16
Loaves & Fishes
  Coffee Shop, 6
Michael's Bar, 8
Nafoura, 3
Papa Andrea's, 21
Quarter Cafe, 18
Tony's, 20
Tzaddik's Deli, 17

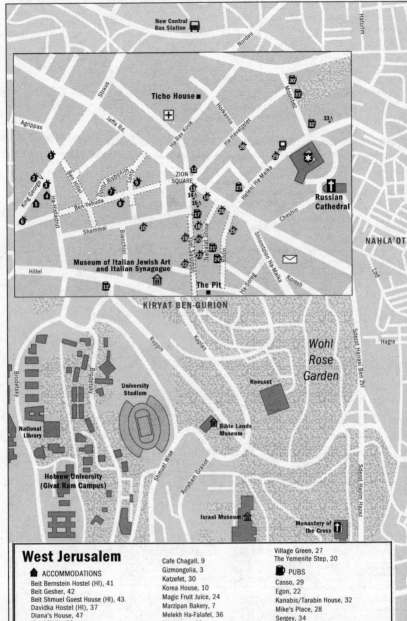

West Jerusalem

🏠 **ACCOMMODATIONS**
Beit Bernstein Hostel (HI), 41
Beit Gesher, 42
Beit Shmuel Guest House (HI), 43
Davidka Hostel (HI), 37
Diana's House, 47
Hotel Noga, 39
Jerusalem Inn Guest House, 5
The King David Hotel, 44
My Home in Jerusalem Hotel, 6
Zion Square Hostel, 13

🍴 **FOOD**
Alumah, 1
Amigos, 21
Au Sahara, 46
Babette's Party, 11

Cafe Chagall, 9
Gizmongolia, 3
Katzefet, 30
Korea House, 10
Magic Fruit Juice, 24
Marzipan Bakery, 7
Melekh Ha-Falafel, 36
Misadonet, 23
Mr. Juice, 14
Nevatim, 8
Pampa Grill, 26
The Pie Shop, 19
Pinati, 4
Shalom Falafel, 38
Spaghettim, 40
Stanley's, 29
Taco Taco, 17

Village Green, 27
The Yemenite Step, 20

🍺 **PUBS**
Casso, 29
Egon, 22
Kanabis/Tarabin House, 32
Mike's Place, 28
Sergey, 34
Shanty, 18
Strudel, 31
Syndrome, 12
The Tavern Pub, 25

🎵 **NIGHTLIFE**
Glasnost, 35
Goa, 45
Q, 15
The Underground, 16

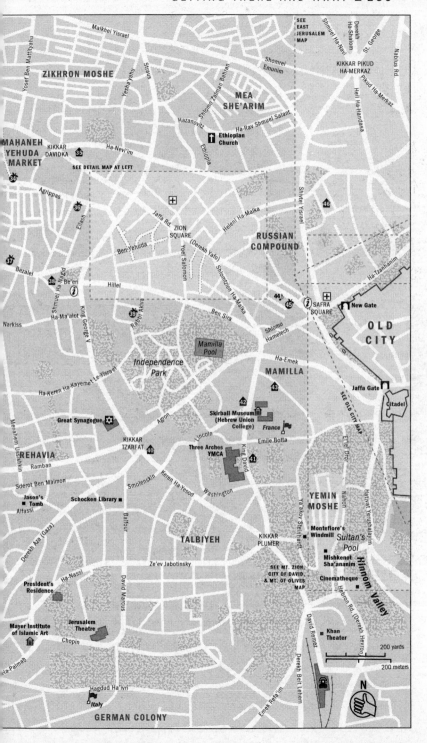

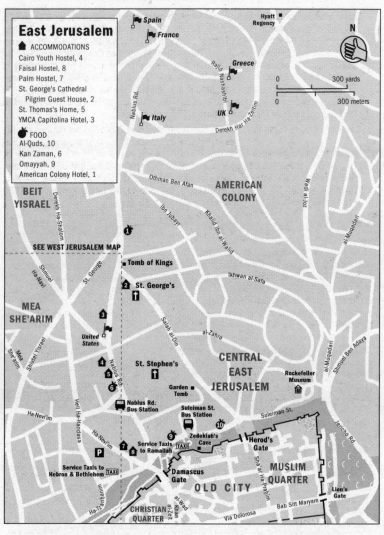

East Jerusalem

♠ ACCOMMODATIONS
Cairo Youth Hostel, 4
Faisal Hostel, 8
Palm Hostel, 7
St. George's Cathedral
   Pilgrim Guest House, 2
St. Thomas's Home, 5
YMCA Capitolina Hotel, 3

🍎 FOOD
Al-Quds, 10
Kan Zaman, 6
Omayyah, 9
American Colony Hotel, 1

6am-sundown, Sa sundown-10:35pm); **Ben-Gurion Airport** (#423, 428, 945, or 947; 1hr.; every 15-40min. Su-Th 6am-8:35pm, F 6am-sundown, Sa sundown-10pm; NIS21); **Eilat** (#444; 4½hr.; Su-Th 7, 10am, 2, 5pm; F 7, 10am, 2pm; no buses on Sa; less frequent in winter; NIS61); **Haifa** Direct (#940; 2hr.; every 15-45min. Su 6am-7:30pm, M-W 6:30am-7:30pm, Th 6:30am-8:30pm, F 6:45am-sundown, Sa sundown-10pm; NIS40) or via **Netanya** (#947; 2hr.; every 20-40min. Su-Th 6am-8:30pm, F 6am-sundown, Sa sundown-10pm); **Tiberias** (#961, 963, or 964; 3hr.; every hr. Su-Th 7am-7:30pm, F 7am-3pm, Sa 8:15-9:15pm); **Tel Aviv Central Station** (#405; 1hr.; every 10-25min. Su-Th 5:40am-midnight, F 6am-sundown, Sa sundown-midnight; NIS18). Egged buses don't go into any Palestinian towns in the West Bank; they stop only at Jewish settlements or sites. Two bus stations serve the West Bank. Suleiman Street Station, in East Jerusalem between Herod's and Damascus Gates, serves routes south while Nablus Road Station serves points north. See **West Bank: Getting There,** p. 426, for information on travel to the West Bank from Israel.

Taxis: Jerusalem is served by two main **intercity sherut taxi** companies. **Ha Bira** (☎625 45 45), at the corner of Ha-Rav Kook St. and Jaffa Rd. (near Zion Sq.) goes to **Tel Aviv** (every 20min. 6am-2am; NIS18, after 11:30pm NIS19, Shabbat NIS20.) Office open Su-Th 5:30am-11pm and F 5:30am-5:30pm. **Nesher,** 21 King George St. (☎625 72 27 or 623 12 31), provides 24hr. door-to-door service to the airport from anywhere in Jerusalem (NIS40, reserve at least 4hr. ahead). *Sherut* taxis to other locations leave from the central bus station. Split among a group they can be as cheap as buses. To West Bank towns, *service* taxis (the Arab equivalent of the *sherut*) leave from outside of Damascus Gate (see **West Bank: Getting Around,** p. 426).

Car Rental: Many companies have offices on or near King David St., not far from the Hilton and King David Hotel. Prices include full insurance. Many increase their prices during July-Sept., sometimes by as much as US$15 per day. **Budget,** 23 King David St. (☎624 89 91; fax 625 89 86; www.budget.co.il), has cars starting at US$45 per day, US$40 per day for 3-day rentals, including unlimited mileage; 23+. **Eldan,** 24 King David St. (☎625 21 51; www.eldan.co.il), has one-day rentals beginning at US$38 (100km included), US$38 per day for one week or longer with unlimited mileage.

▐ GETTING AROUND

Most distances in Jerusalem make for reasonable, pleasant walks, for those who don't mind the heat and the hills. All sections of the city are easily reachable by bus from the **central bus station** (info ☎530 47 04) on Jaffa Rd., west of city center just past the Maḥaneh Yehuda district (NIS5 per ride within Jerusalem; NIS47 *kartisia* buys 11 rides, 20 for those under 18). The current central bus station is temporary; the old one, farther west on Jaffa Rd., across from the Binyanei Ha-Umma Convention Center, is being rebuilt and will supposedly be finished sometime in 2001. A dazzling (and dizzying) **city bus map** is available at the information desk. Arab buses run irregularly every day; Egged service stops at about 4:30pm on Friday and resumes after sunset on Saturday. Taxis are widely available. Try **Reḥavia Taxi** (☎625 44 44 or 622 24 44) for 24-hour service.

COMMON BUS ROUTES:

BUS #1 To Mea She'arim and Dung Gate/Western Wall.

BUS #3 To Jaffa Gate, Shivtei Yisrael, Ha-Nevi'im, and Ma±aneh Yehuda.

BUS #4 AND 4A To Emek Refa'im, Keren Ha-Yesod, King George, Ramat Eshkol, and Mount Scopus.

BUS #6, 8, 13, 18, AND 20 To Zion Sq.; get off at the intersection of Jaffa Rd. and King George St. Buses #6 and 20 continue to Jaffa Gate; #6 goes on to the Kenyon mall.

BUS #9 AND 27 To the Knesset, the Israel Museum, the Hebrew University at Givat Ram, West Jerusalem center, and Mount Scopus.

BUS #17 To Reḥavia, Mount Herzl, and Ein Kerem.

BUS #21 To Talpiyot, Hebron Rd., King David St., and Mount Herzl.

BUS #23 To Damascus Gate, Suleiman St. bus station, East Jerusalem, and Herod's Gate.

BUS #99 (THE JERUSALINE) From Jaffa Gate or central bus station, passes 34 major tourist sights on a 2hr. loop. Su-Th at 10am, noon, 2, and 4pm; F 10am and noon. Runs less frequently in winter. One loop NIS28.

▞ ORIENTATION

Known as **Yerushalayim** in Hebrew and **al-Quds** (the holy) in Arabic, Jerusalem is a sprawling city, most of which was only developed in the last 50 years of the capital's three-millennia history.

WEST JERUSALEM. This section includes Jewish parts of Jerusalem, from French Hill in the northeast and East Talpiyot in the southeast, to Kiryat Menaḥem in the southwest and Ramot in the northwest. The main street is **Jaffa Rd.** (Derekh Yafo), running west-to-east from the central bus station to the Old City's **Jaffa Gate.** Roughly midway between the two, **Zion Sq.** (Kikkar Tzion) sits at the corner of Jerusalem's triangular *midraḥov* bounded by Jaffa Rd., **Ben-Yehuda St.,** and **King George St.** Upscale eateries line **Yoel Salomon St.** and **Rivlin St.,** off Zion Sq.

North of the city center, the **Russian Compound's** hip bar scene hugs the old-world **Mea She'arim** like spandex on a *yenta.* Northwest on Jaffa Rd. are the teeming outdoor markets of **Maḥaneh Yehuda** and, farther down, the central bus station. Southwest of the triangle are the Knesset building and the hilltop Israel Museum complex. The beautiful **Independence Park** lies south of the city center, ringed by luxury hotels; farther south are the cafes of **Emek Refa'im** and the discotheques of **Talpiyot.** The artists' district of **Yemin Moshe** huddles southeast of Zion Sq.

OLD CITY. Jerusalem's most important historical and religious sites are concentrated within the walls of the Old City, which is still divided into the four quadrants laid out by the Romans in 135 CE. To get from West Jerusalem's center to the Old City, take Jaffa Rd. past the post office to Jaffa Gate. Here you can follow the promenade along the ancient walls to most of the seven other gates. The two main roads in the Old City are the roof-covered **David St.,** an extension of which, **Bab al-Silsilah St.** (Gate of the Chain), runs up to the Temple Mount, and **Suq Khan al-Zeit,** from Damascus Gate, which enters directly into the **Muslim Quarter** and turns into the **Cardo** as it crosses David St. and enters the **Jewish Quarter.** The Jewish Quarter is also directly accessible through **Dung Gate.** The **Armenian Quarter** is to the right as you enter through Jaffa Gate and is directly accessible via **Zion Gate.** Left of Jaffa Gate is the **Christian Quarter,** which can also be reached directly from the **New Gate.**

EAST JERUSALEM. The old, invisible **Green Line** separating Jordan from pre-1967 Israel runs along **Derekh Ha-Shalom** (Peace Rd.) and is still a good general demarcation between Palestinian and Jewish areas of Jerusalem. East Jerusalem is the name normally given to the Palestinian parts of Jerusalem just outside the Old City to the north and east; it sometimes includes the Old City. **Suleiman St.,** in front of Damascus Gate, and **Salah al-Din St.,** which runs out from Herod's Gate, are the main roads in central East Jerusalem. **Ha-Nevi'im St.** (Musrada in Arabic), which runs in from Jaffa Rd. in West Jerusalem, converges with **Nablus Rd.** at Damascus Gate; the small, busy area has falafel and *shawarma* stands, fruit vendors, dry goods stores, and hostels, all cheaper than practically anywhere else in Jerusalem. Central East Jerusalem is the financial and cultural hub of the Arab community.

▞ PRACTICAL INFORMATION

OLD CITY

TOURIST AND FINANCIAL SERVICES

Tourist Office: The tourist information office in Safra Sq. in West Jerusalem is superior to those in the Old City and worth the 10min. walk from Jaffa Gate (see p. 289).

Special Interest Tourist Offices: Christian Information Center (☎627 26 92; fax 628 64 17; email cicts@netmedia.net.il; www.cits.org), inside Jaffa Gate, opposite the Tower of David. Offers information on Jerusalem's pilgrimage sights and Christian accommodations. Open M-Sa 8:30am-1pm. **The Jewish Student Information Center,** 5 Beit El St. (☎628 26 34; fax 628 83 38; e-mail jseidel@netmedia.net.il; www.geocities.com/athens/7613), in Ḥurva Sq. in the Jewish Quarter. Run by the friendly and enthusiastic Jeff Seidel, who leads tours of the Western Wall tunnels. Shabbat home hospitality available with Orthodox Jewish families.

Guided Tours: The highly recommended **Zion Walking Tours** (☎628 78 66; cell 050 305 552; www.zionwt.co.il) offers 8 inexpensive guided routes in and around the Old City. Their most popular tour is of the four quarters of the Old City (3hr.; daily 9, 11am, 2pm; US$10, students US$9, entry fees included). Their office is right inside Jaffa Gate, opposite the Tower of David. **Israel Archaeological Seminars,** 34 Habad St. (☎627 35 15; fax 627 26 60; email office@archesem.com; www.archesem.com), in the Jewish Quarter, offers walking tours in addition to day-long archaeology excursions all over Israel. A guided tour of the politically sensitive **Western Wall tunnels** requires reserving a ticket **in advance** for a 1hr. tour (NIS30-40). Individuals cannot enter the tunnels or excavations without a guide (☎627 13 33; fax 626 48 28; www.hakotel.org). Most hostels organize daily sunrise tours of the Dead Sea area (3am-3pm), run by **Alternative Palestine Tours** (NIS90 for transportation and guide).

Banks: Bank Mizrahi, 26 Tiferet Yisrael St. (☎627 31 31; fax 628 84 29), in the Jewish Quarter. Look for the blue sign in Ḥurva Sq. Hefty commission for foreign exchange. Open Su-Th 9am-2pm and 5-7pm; M, W, F 9am-noon. Has the only **ATM** and automated **currency exchange machine** in the entire Old City.

EMERGENCY AND COMMUNICATION

Police: (☎622 62 22). Inside Jaffa Gate to the right, next to the Tower of David. 24hr.

Pharmacies: Jaffa Gate Pharmacy (☎628 38 98), the first left from Jaffa Gate, immediately on the right. Open daily 9am-8pm. **Habash Pharmacy,** 104 al-Wad St. (☎627 24 27; fax 628 81 57), in the Muslim Quarter. Open daily 8:30am-8pm.

Medical assistance: Austrian-Arab Community Clinic, Qanatar Khadeir Rd. (☎627 32 46), off al-Wad St., in the Muslim Quarter, and across from the Austrian Hospice. Open Sa-W 8am-7pm and Th 8am-4pm. **Kupat Holim** (☎627 16 08), in the Jewish Quarter above the Cardo and across from Ḥurva Sq. Hours are erratic.

Internet Access: The cheapest connections are found mostly in the Muslim Quarter. **Mike's Center,** 172 Khan al-Zeit St. (☎628 24 86), at the turnoff for the 9th Station of the Cross, boasts "the fastest line in Israel." NIS12 per hr.

Post Office: (☎629 06 86), inside Jaffa Gate, across from the Tower of David, marked by a red sign. Open Su-Th 7:30am-2:30pm and F 8am-noon.

WEST JERUSALEM

TOURIST AND FINANCIAL SERVICES

Tourist Information: MTIO, 3 Safra Sq. (☎625 88 44), in the City Hall complex off Jaffa Rd. From behind the large water fountain in the municipal plaza, the entrance is on the right. Excellent computerized information. Offers pamphlets and maps, but doesn't have Carta's Map (NIS36), the best map available at Steimatzky's (see **English-Language Bookstores,** p. 290). MTIO open Su-Th 8:30am-4pm and F 8:45am-1pm.

Religious Information: See **Old City Special Interest Tourist Offices,** p. 288.

Tours: The municipality sponsors a free Shabbat **walking tour** in English (☎625 88 44) from 32 Jaffa Rd. near Zion Sq. (2½hr., Sa 10am, rotates among several routes). *This Week in Jerusalem* lists guided tours (also posted at the MTIO office). Sunrise tours to Masada and the Dead Sea (NIS90) and day tours to the Galilee (NIS120) are available through most hostels in the area, or by contacting **Alternative Tours** (☎/fax 628 32 82; email raed@jrshotel.com; www.jrshotel.com). The **Society for the Protection of Nature in Israel (SPNI),** 13 Heleni Ha-Malka St. (☎625 23 57), runs guided tours throughout Israel and Sinai. Tours range from half-day explorations of Jerusalem to 15-day Israel odysseys. Office open Su-Th 9am-6:45pm and F 9am-12:30pm.

Budget Travel: Neot Ha-Kikar, 5 Shlomtzion Ha-Malka St. (☎623 62 62; fax 623 61 61; www.neot-hakikar.com). Specializes in 1- to 6-day Sinai tours from Eilat (US$59-US$290). Open Su-Th 9am-5pm and F 9am-12:30pm. **ISSTA,** 31 Ha-Nevi'im St. (☎621 36 00). ISIC NIS40; bring photograph and proof of student status. Student discounts on airfare, car rentals, and **Eurail** passes. Open Su-Tu and Th 9am-7pm; W and F 9am-1pm. Additional offices in La-metayel camping store (☎624 31 78) and Hebrew University campuses on Mount Scopus (☎582 61 16) and Givat Ram (☎651 87 80).

Consulates: UK, 19 Nashashibi St. (☎541 41 00), in East Jerusalem near Sheikh Jarrah. Open M-F 9am-noon. **US,** 27 Nablus Rd. (☎622 72 00, after-hours emergency ☎622 72 50; www.uscongen-jerusalem.org/consular), in East Jerusalem. Open for passport renewals and other services M-F 8:30-11:30am, notary service Tu 1-3pm. Closed for Israeli and US holidays and last F of each month. Administrative offices at 18 Agron St. in West Jerusalem (☎622 72 30). Other consulates in Tel Aviv (see p. 289).

Currency Exchange: City Change, 30 Jaffa Rd. (☎625 87 58). Open Su-Th 9am-6pm, F 9am-1pm. **Money Net,** 8 Ben-Hillel St. (☎622 23 18; fax 623 27 88), on the *midraḥov*. Open Su-Th 9am-6pm, F 9am-1pm. Both give better rates than banks and charge no commission. The **post office** (see **Central Post Office**, p. 291) offers the same rates, also commission-free. **Bank Ha-Poalim** (emergency ☎(03) 567 49 99), in Zion Sq. Open Su, Tu-W 8:30am-1pm; M, Th 8:30am-1pm and 4-7pm; F 8:30am-12:30pm. **ATM** accepts Cirrus, Plus, and major credit cards.

American Express: 19 Hillel St. (☎624 69 33; fax 624 09 50), near McDonald's. Full service office with commission-free traveler's check cashing, purchasing, and replacement for cardholders. Holds mail, but not packages. For traveler's check emergencies, call 24hr. ☎(800) 943 86 94. Open Su-Th 9am-4:30pm and F 9am-noon.

LOCAL SERVICES

English-Language Bookstores: Steimatzky, 39 Jaffa St. (☎625 01 55); other locations at 7 Ben-Yehuda St. and 9 King George St. Great for maps, magazines, and travel books. Open Su-Th 8:30am-7pm (Ben-Yehuda location until 8pm) and F 8:30am-2pm. Open Su-Th 8:30am-7:30pm and F 8:30am-2pm. **SPNI Bookstore,** 13 Heleni Ha-Malka St. (☎625 23 57), often has the lowest prices on guidebooks and maps.

Cultural Centers: American Cultural Center, 19 Keren Ha-Yesod St. (☎625 57 55; fax 624 25 60; email acc-jer@usis-israel.org.il), near the Agron-King George intersection, right after King George St. turns into Keren Ha-Yesod St. Free and open to anyone. Open Su-Th 10am-4pm and F 9am-noon. Closed on all Israeli and US holidays. **Alliance Française,** 8 Agron St. (☎625 12 04), across from Supersol. French culture club for francophones of any nationality. Nominal charge for events.

Gay and Lesbian Services: Jerusalem Open House (JOH), 7 Ben-Yehuda St., 3rd fl. (☎625 31 91; email gayj@hotmail.com; www.poboxes.com/gayj), on the *midrahov*. Call or visit for a schedule of events. Office open Su, Th 4-8pm; Tu 10am-3pm; F 10am-2pm. Open house every Su and Th 8-10pm. **KLAF** (☎625 12 71; www.aquanet.co.il/vip/klaf), is an organization for lesbian feminists, with activities all over the country. On the line every W 8-10pm. **The Other 10% (Ha-Asiron Ha-Aḥer;** ☎653 54 54; www.poboxes.com/asiron), is Hebrew University's organization for gay, lesbian, bisexual, and transgendered students. Hosts activities during the school year (Oct.-June).

Ticket Agencies: Bimot, 8 Shammai St. (☎625 09 05), and **Kla'im,** 12 Shammai St. (☎625 68 69), have discount tickets for students and tourists for concerts, shows, and sporting events around Jerusalem. Both open Su-Th 9am-7pm and F 9am-1pm.

Laundry: Laundry Place, 12 Shammai St. (☎625 77 14), near the *midrahov*. Self-service NIS19 per load, includes dryer and detergent. Membership for long-term stays. Open Su-Th 8:30am-midnight, F 8:30am-sunset, and Sa sunset-midnight.

Camping Supplies: La-metayel, 5 Yoel Salomon St. (☎623 33 38; fax 623 33 52; www.lametayel.com) has the most extensive (and expensive) stock of camping gear (and an impressive array of travel books). Open Su-Th 10am-9pm and F 10am-2:30pm. **Orcha Camping,** 12 Yoel Salomon (☎624 06 55), near Cafe Kapulsky, is affiliated with SPNI (members get discounts on merchandise). Open Su-Th 8am-7pm and F 8am-3pm.

EMERGENCY AND COMMUNICATIONS

Medical Emergency: ☎101. **Magen David Adom First Aid,** 7 Ha-Memgimel St. (☎652 31 33). Turn right at the end of Jaffa Rd. (past the bus station) and take the next left. Their **Terem Clinic** (☎652 17 48) is open 24hr. and will see anyone on a walk-in basis for both emergencies and non-emergencies; most insurance plans are accepted, as is direct payment by credit card. Newspapers list hospitals on duty for emergencies.

Police: In the Russian Compound (☎539 11 11), off Jaffa Rd. in West Jerusalem. **Tourist desk** (☎675 48 11), on Cheshin St., just off Jaffa Rd., near the post office.

Help Lines: M'Lev Center for Crisis Counseling (☎654 11 11 or (800) 654 111) has a general help line and referrals for English speakers. The **Rape Crisis Center** (☎1202 from anywhere in Israel) is staffed 24hr. **Eran Emotional Health Hotline** (☎1201) assists tourists daily 8am-11pm. **Alcoholics Anonymous,** 24 Ha-Palmaḥ St. (☎563 05 24 or 583 00 92). **AIDS Hotline** (☎(03) 528 77 81), staffed M and Th 7:30-10pm. The weekly "In Jerusalem" insert in *The Jerusalem Post* lists many other support groups.

Services for the Disabled: Yad Sarah Organization, 124 Herzl Blvd. (☎644 44 25; fax 644 44 23; email info@yadsarah.org.il; www.yadsarah.org.il). Free loans of medical equipment. Offers wheelchair van for airport pick-ups (NIS150, order 2 weeks in advance) and rides anywhere within Jerusalem for fares comparable to those of taxis. Open Su-Th 9am-7pm and F 9am-12:30pm.

Pharmacy: Superpharm, 3 Ha-Histadrut (☎624 62 44; fax 624 75 75), between Ben-Yehuda and King George St. Open Su-Th 8:30am-11pm, F 8:30am-3pm, and Sa sundown-11pm. **Alba Pharmacy,** 42 Jaffa St. (☎625 37 03). Open Su-Th 7am-7pm and F 7am-2pm. Two pharmacies rotate night duty and on Shabbat; check newspaper listings.

Telephones: Solan Communications, 2 Luntz St. (☎625 89 08; fax 625 88 79), on the *midrahov*, off Ben-Yehuda St. Telegram and international fax services (NIS13 first page, NIS8 each additional page), private booths for local and international calls (NIS3 per min. to most countries). Open Su-Th 8am-11pm, F 8am-5pm, Sa 5pm-midnight. An additional branch is inside Jaffa Gate. **Global GSM,** 22 King David St. (☎625 25 85 or (800) 252 585), rents cellular phones at a reasonable rate (US$1 per day, plus US$0.49 per min. for outgoing calls within Israel; free incoming calls). Open Su-Th 9am-7pm and F 9am-1pm. **Bezeq 24hr. Information:** ☎144.

Internet Access: Cheaper in the Old City (see p. 289). **Netcafe,** 9 Heleni Ha-Malka St. (☎624 63 27), uphill from Jaffa Rd. NIS7 for 15min.; NIS25 per hr. Open Su-Tu 11am-10pm, W-Th 11am-late, F 10am-3pm, and Sa 9pm-late. **Strudel Internet Cafe and Wine Bar,** 11 Moonbaz St. (☎623 21 01; fax 622 14 45), in the Russian Compound. It doubles as a bar at night. NIS6 for 15min. Happy hour 7-9pm and midnight-12:30am (15min. computer time and a beer NIS13). Open M-F 10am-late and Sa 3pm-late.

Central Post Office: 23 Jaffa Rd. (☎629 06 47). **Poste Restante** for no fee. **Money exchange, Western Union, telegram,** and **fax** services available. Also sells phone cards. Open Su-Th 7am-7pm, F 7am-noon. For telegrams, dial 171 (24hr.). Branch post offices in most neighborhoods; look for a bright red awning.

⌐ ACCOMMODATIONS

OLD CITY

Most of Jerusalem's cheapest hostels are in the Old City, but these vary tremendously in quality and safety (neither price nor location are good barometers). Solo women should be especially discriminating about where to stay and should dress modestly: t-shirts are okay, but exposing anything more than forearms will attract undue attention in the conservative Old City. Accommodations here fall into two categories: quieter, cleaner establishments with curfews; and less clean or safe places (but sometimes more fun) with bars or lax alcohol policies. Both kinds have priceless rooftop views of the surrounding sights. Bargain for discounts on multiple-night stays or if business seems slow.

☒ El Hashimi Hostel and Hotel, 73 Suq Khan al-Zeit St. (☎628 44 10; fax 628 46 67). Take the right fork from Damascus Gate. Single-sex dorms are available. Fans in dorms; A/C and bathrooms in private rooms. Heat in winter. TV lounge. Internet access. Reception 6am-3am. Check-out 10:30am. Curfew 3am. Dorm beds NIS20; singles US$25-35; doubles US$30-45; triples US$50-70. 15% discount for stays longer than two nights (not applicable to dorm prices). Credit cards and traveler's checks accepted.

☒ Al-Arab Hostel, Khan al-Zeit St. (☎628 35 37; email alarab@netvision.net.il); take the right fork from Damascus Gate, before El Hashimi. A crowded party hostel with some of the cheapest beds in town and all the amenities: kitchen/cafe, *nargilah,* free tea and coffee, Internet service, laundry, satellite TV, luggage storage, and 24hr. reception. Roof-beds NIS14; dorms NIS18; singles and doubles NIS60; triples NIS70.

☒ Lutheran Youth Hostel (☎628 21 20; fax 628 51 07), on St. Mark's Rd., the first alley off David St., on the right when coming from Jaffa Gate. Half hostel and half guest house. The large fountained garden and overhanging dining hall are reserved for private guests, but the hostel part has its own calm garden and enormous kitchen with free tea and coffee. Breakfast included for private rooms. Reception 6am-10:45pm. Check-in noon. Check-out 10am. Lockout for hostel guests 9am-noon. Curfew 10:30pm, flexible until midnight. Guests must be under 35 (also flexible, especially when business is slow). Large single-sex dorms NIS33; singles US$40-48; doubles US$72-80; prices fluctuate according to the value of the Deutschmark. No reservations for dorms. Credit cards accepted for guest house only.

■ **Petra Hostel,** 1 David St. (☎628 66 18), just inside Jaffa Gate, on the left before the entrance to the market. Built more than 175 years ago, this is the oldest accommodation in the Old City. Mark Twain and Herman Melville stayed here. Has fantastic rooftop views (some say the best in the city) and a vast, sunny lounge. Pool table, bar, Internet, laundry, and kitchen. Full breakfast NIS14. Luggage storage NIS1 per hr., NIS5 per day. Check-out 10am. Roof mattresses NIS20, with sheets and blanket NIS25; roof-top tents (in winter only) NIS25; dorms NIS32, weekly rate (paid in advance) NIS28 per night; private rooms US$35-50. Reservations accepted only for morning arrivals.

Heritage House. Office: 90 Ḥabad St. (☎627 19 16). Men's hostel: 2 Or Ha-Ḥayim St. (☎627 22 24). Women's hostel: 7 Ha-Malakh St. (☎628 18 20). Free nightly classes (optional) at the men's hostel. Kosher dairy kitchen for guests. Lock-out 9am-5pm. Curfew midnight, 1am in the summer and on Shabbat. Dorm accommodations only; free except on Shabbat (NIS20).

Jaffa Gate Youth Hostel (☎627 64 02), in the Jaffa Gate area across from the Tower of David; a black and pink sign points down a short alley to the reception. TV lounge, patio, tiny common kitchen, and priceless rooftop view. Check-in until midnight. Check-out 10am. Curfew midnight. No smoking or alcohol. Small dorms NIS40; singles NIS60, with A/C and bath NIS80; doubles NIS100, with bath NIS160. Ask for a discount.

WEST JERUSALEM

Accommodations in West Jerusalem are generally roomier, cleaner, and safer than their Old City counterparts (and correspondingly more expensive). Hostels here are better for club-hoppers: most establishments have no curfew, and some are directly above the action. Avoid the 17% VAT by paying in non-Israeli currency.

■ **Zion Square Hostel,** 42 Jaffa Rd. (☎624 41 14; fax 623 62 45; email jrpool@inter.net.il; www.zionsquarehostel.homestead.com/opening.html), in a fantastic location. A/C, laundry service, Internet (with a web camera), cable TV, 24hr. reception and security, lockers, and luggage storage. Some rooms have balconies overlooking Zion Sq. Breakfast included. Check-out 10am. Dorms NIS60; doubles NIS190.

Hotel Noga, 4 Bezalel St. (☎625 45 90, after 2pm ☎/fax 566 18 88; ask for Mr. or Mrs. Kristal). From the city center, walk down King George, turn right onto Be'eri, left onto Shmuel Ha-Nagid, and right onto Bezalel. Comfortable walk to Maḥane Yehuda or to the area of the Knesset and Israel Museum. Feels like having a private apartment; each floor has one full bath and kitchen. Managers leave after 2pm. For longer stays, ask about the apartment down the block. Singles US$32; doubles US$40; triples US$50; small roof-top bungalow US$25 for one person, US$35 for two. 2-night min. stay. Reservations highly recommended.

Beit Gesher, 10 King David St. (☎624 10 15; fax 625 52 26), across from the Hilton Hotel. Clean and airy 39-room hostel in a beautiful, old building, frequented by youth groups in the summer but quieter the rest of the year. All rooms with private bath and A/C. No double beds. Breakfast US$7. Reception 24hr. Check-in after noon. Check-out 11am. Singles US$38; doubles US$54; add US$14 per person for 3rd and 4th people. Reservations highly recommended.

My Home in Jerusalem Hostel, 15 King George St. and 2 Ha-Histadrut St. (☎623 22 35; fax 623 22 36; email myhome@netvision.co.il; www.myhome.co.il), on the left, one block from Jaffa Rd.; a newer building with more rooms is around the corner. Take bus #8, 9, 31, or 32 from the central station. Decently clean rooms, cable TV lounge, and prime location. Shared bathrooms. The second building has more stairs, but nicer, carpeted rooms. Breakfast included. Reception and check-in 24hr. Check-out 10:30am. Dorms US$16 (more if you pay in NIS); doubles US$60. Prices vary by season.

Diana's House, 10 Hulda Ha-Neviah St. (☎628 31 31; fax 628 44 11; email dradiv@zahav.net.il). From Safra Sq., take Shivtei Yisrael past the municipality, turn right through the small park, and continue down Natan Ha-Navi; Hulda is the next left. Israel's first gay B&B ("straight-friendly"). The architect proprietor named the house for his now-departed dog. Cable TV, VCR, jacuzzi with view of the Dome of the Rock, laundry, and Internet. Breakfast included. Singles US$45; doubles US$75. Studio apartments also available. Call ahead.

EAST JERUSALEM

⊠Cairo Youth Hostel, 21 Nablus Rd. (☎627 72 16), on the left when coming from Damascus Gate; from the central bus station take bus #27. Perhaps not the most aesthetically pleasing hostel, but it wears its age well; the friendly, laid-back atmosphere will quickly overshadow the drabness of the walls. Comfortable TV sitting area, a viewlover's roof, and an immaculate kitchen. Heat in winter. Reception 24hr. Check-out 10am. Curfew 1am (flexible). Roof mattress NIS15; coed and single-sex dorm beds NIS20; private room for 1-4 people NIS90.

Faisal Hostel, 4 Ha-Nevi'im St. (☎628 75 02; email faisalsam@hotmail.com), in the parking lot opposite Damascus Gate, on the right. Crowded bunks, satellite TV lounge, cramped kitchen, and a computer with Internet access (NIS10 per hr.; a 5min. email check is free). Large but cozy bar on patio overlooking Ha-Nevi'im St., where *service* drivers can be heard yelling at almost all hours (don't expect to sleep in if your room is on that side). Reception 24hr. Check-out 11am. Curfew 1am. Coed and single-sex dorm beds NIS20; private doubles and triples NIS80.

Palm Hostel, 6 Ha-Nevi'im St. (☎627 31 89), opposite Damascus Gate, just past the Faisal Hostel. Small but comfortable; has the same noise problem as Faisal. Upper common room for eating, smoking, and watching videos. Heat in winter. Reception 24hr. Check-out 10am. Curfew midnight. Dorms NIS25, students NIS20; private rooms NIS100-120, students NIS80-100. Ask for discounts for longer stays.

SAFETY WARNING. Tensions sometimes make East Jerusalem and parts of the Old City unfriendly to Israelis and Jewish foreigners. Jewish travelers should make their tourist status as pronounced as possible. Wearing a *kippah* is a bad idea in the Arab parts of town.

FOOD

OLD CITY

Cheap restaurants crowd the narrow alleys of the Old City. The chicken restaurants on **Souq Khan al-Zeit Rd.,** inside Damascus Gate, are popular with locals. Interchangeable sit-down restaurants line al-Wad Rd. and Bab al-Silsilah St. Street vendors sell fresh, soft sesame *ka'ak* with *za'tar* in the *souq* (NIS2-3). The market also drips with honey-drenched Arab pastries for NIS12-24 per kilo. ⊠**Ja'far Sweets,** 42 Suq Khan al-Zeit St., offers the hottest, gookiest, most authentic pastries in the market, bar none. Take out or eat in with the locals. (☎628 35 82. Open daily 8am-8pm.) Small **supermarkets** can be found throughout the Old City, particularly in and near the Jewish Quarter.

⊠ Abu Shanab Pizza and Bar, 35 Latin Patriarchate Rd. (☎626 07 52), the first left from Jaffa Gate. An old favorite of natives and tourists alike. Candlelight gleams off the stone walls and intimate tables. Mini individual pizzas NIS13-18; Oriental salads NIS7-10; assortment of cocktails NIS20. Happy hour every night 6-7pm, all drinks 2-for-1. Live jazz occasionally. Open M-Sa 10am-11pm.

ISRAEL

▨ **Michael's Bar,** 3 St. Mark's St. (☎ 052 94 95 60), off David St., uphill from the Lutheran Hostel. Possibly the best falafel in Jerusalem, but the real reason to come is for Michael, one of the Old City's most charming residents. Falafel NIS8; *shishkebab* or *shawarma* NIS12. Open daily 10am-10pm.

The Green Door Pizza Bakery (☎ 627 62 71), off al-Wad St. Coming in Damascus Gate, make a sharp left when the road forks. Abu Ali has been serving his renowned Arabic-style pizza for over two decades. Filling, one-person pizzas (NIS6) are topped with cheese, egg, meat, and as many vegetables as he has. He'll also do individual orders, including vegetarian. Eat in and you get free tea and coffee. Open daily 6am-11pm.

WEST JERUSALEM

Restaurants here serve everything from *shawarma* to sushi (with a corresponding array of prices), reflecting the international make-up of its population. Chews your own meal adventure from among the many "business lunch" specials at the city center restaurants. To choose your own ingredients, head for the raucous open-air **Maḥaneh Yehuda** market between Jaffa Rd. and Agrippas St. (best time Sa-Th 7-8pm, F 1-2hr. before sundown). *Me'orav*, a mix of inner parts grilled with onions and packed in pita pockets, is a specialty of the stands on Agrippas St., behind Maḥaneh Yehuda. The stands along Etz Ha-Ḥayim St. sell the best *ḥalva* (a sesame marzipan) at NIS14 per kg. **Ma'adei Mickey** (Mickey's Deli), halfway between Jaffa and Agrippas on Etz Ha-Ḥayim St., sells excellent hummus and salads for NIS18 per kg. **Marzipan Bakery,** 44 Agrippas St. (☎ 623 26 18), at one end of the Maḥaneh Yehuda market, sells *ruggelah* to die for—eat a kilo (NIS18.40) and you just might.

RESTAURANTS

▨ **Spaghettim,** 8 Rabbi Akiva St. (☎ 623 55 47), off Hillel St. Bear left at the sign, through the gates of an Italian-style villa. Snappy and elegant restaurant serves spaghetti prepared in over 75 different methods, from "gorgonzola spinachi" (NIS38) to "vanilla and brandy" (NIS25). Beautifully lit interior and refreshing outdoor seating. Open daily noon-midnight.

▨ **Alumah,** 19 Agrippas St. (☎ 625 50 14), just between King George St. and Maḥaneh Yehuda. The one-time restaurant has turned into a factory, but still maintains a storefront and tables for the discriminating eater. The ultimate in health food: completely natural *pareve* (non-dairy) meals made using whole grains milled on location, homemade *tempeh*, purified water, rice milk, and olive oil. No margarine, sugar, yeast, aluminum, or microwaves used. Meals are served with rice, chunky veggies, and two slices of crusty, thick sourdough bread. Open Su-Th 7am-7pm and F 7am-2pm.

Nevatim, 10 Ben-Yehuda St. (☎ 625 20 07), under a large but subtle wooden sign. Unquestionably the crunchiest place on the *midraḥov;* also one of the most affordable. Impressive assortment of soups (from *miso* to *borscht;* small bowl NIS15), plus veggie burgers (NIS17), grilled tofu (NIS17), and delicious, unlimited homemade bread. Open Su-Th 10am-10pm and F 10am-before sundown.

The Yemenite Step, 10 Yoel Salomon St. (☎ 624 04 77). Grand stone building with high ceilings and outdoor seating. Try the heavenly *malaweh*, their specialty, which resembles a large, flat, flaky croissant (with honey NIS18; with meat or veggie fillings NIS38 and up). Open Su-Th noon-12:30am, F noon-4pm, and Sa after sundown-1am.

Misadonet, 12 Yoel Salomon St. (☎ 624 83 96), when coming from Zion Sq., turn right into the marked alleyway and right past Orcha Camping. Authentic Kurdish kitchen; serene atmosphere with traditional decor. Traditional specialties include *kubeh* (made from semolina and stuffed with minced meat or vegetables) and *mujadara* (rice and lentils doesn't begin to describe it). Many vegetarian options. Soups NIS18-22; entrees NIS24-58. Open Su-Th noon-11pm, F noon-sundown, and Sa sundown-11:30pm.

Taco Taco, 35 Jaffa Rd. (☎ 625 50 70), marked by a bright green sign between Yoel Salomon St. and Naḥalat Shiva. Affordable Mexican bar with fast service and fresh ingredients made to order 'round the clock. Beef or chicken taco with cheese NIS12; quesadilla NIS18. Open Su-W 11:30am-2am and Th-Sa 24hr. Happy hour daily 7-8pm.

QUICKIES

■ **Babbette's Party,** 16 Shammai St. (☎814 11 82), near the corner of Yoel Salomon. A happy addition to the sweet-tooth scene. Israelis flock just to get a whiff of Babbette's 14 amazing Belgian waffle varieties (butter and cream NIS14; Grand Marnier NIS17). Also hands-down the best hot chocolate in Israel, some would say in the world (NIS8). Open Su-Th 4pm-2:30am, F 11am-sunset, and Sa after sundown-2:30am.

■ **Melekh Ha-Falafel V'ha-Shawarma (King of Falafel and Shawarma;** ☎636 53 72), on the corner of King George and Agrippas St. Acclaimed parlor dominates the midtown scene; the tiny store is always packed, no matter what hour. Savory falafel NIS8; *shawarma* NIS12. Open Su-Th 8:30am-11pm and F 8:30am-3pm.

CAFES

■ **Tmol Shilshom,** 5 Yoel Salomon St. (☎623 27 58; www.tmol-shilshom.co.il). Enter from Naḥalat Shiva St. This bookstore-cafe, named after a Shai Agnon book, is frequented by writers and poets such as Yehuda Amiḥai; he and other local greats give occasional readings here (sometimes in English; call in advance or check the web page for dates), while aspiring writers scrawl over coffee and tea (NIS8-14). Renowned all-you-can-eat breakfast buffet every Friday morning (NIS39.50). Internet NIS7 for 15min. Gay-friendly. Open Su-Th 8am-2am, F 8am-before sunset, and Sa after sundown-2am.

Noctorno, 7 Bezalel St. (☎625 85 10), off King George St. away from the *midraḥov,* at the corner of Ha-Gidem St. Small and cozy; a quiet but funky alternative to the crowded cafes just two blocks away. Espresso NIS5; salads NIS25; sandwiches NIS20. Open Su-Th 7am-midnight. F 7am-4pm, and Sa after sundown-12:30am.

Second Cup, 4 Shammai St. (☎623 45 33), on the *midraḥov,* at the corner of Ben-Hillel St. Hugely popular with non-Israelis and others who appreciate professionally roasted coffee (they've begun to sell it by the kg). Large cafe is great for quick morning croissant and coffee (NIS10) or a cup of hot apple cider (NIS8). Students often curl up in the comfy armchairs and library-like alcoves before exams. Open Su-Th 6am-1am, F 6am-sunset, and Sa after sundown-1am.

Cafe Ta'amon, 27 King George St. (☎625 49 77), across from the old Knesset. A legendary hole-in-the-wall where older Israeli writers and intellectuals mingle with vodka lovers. Owner Mordekhai Kop's IOU book is a veritable *Who's Who in Israel.* Coffee, tea, soups (NIS15), and pastries (NIS7). Friday is *cholent* day, when regulars come for the traditional Jewish meat and potato stew (NIS20). Open Su-Th 6am-11pm, F 6am-4pm, and Sa (in winter only) after sundown-1am.

EAST JERUSALEM

■ **Kan Zaman** (☎628 32 82; www.jrshotel.com), on the patio of the Jerusalem Hotel, just behind the bus station on Nablus Rd. Glass-enclosed garden restaurant with delicate tables shaded by vines. Sandwiches NIS30-35; meat and fish meals NIS40-60. Go Sa after 8pm for their highly regarded Lebanese buffet (NIS70) with live classical Arabic music. Open daily 11am-11pm.

Omayyah Restaurant, 21 Suleiman St. (☎628 61 02), across the street and to the right from Damascus Gate. Authentic Palestinian kitchen dishes up standard *shawarma* and *shishkebab,* but also some less commercial specialties like the "upside down" rice patty (a.k.a. *maqlubeh;* NIS22). Soft drinks NIS3. Open daily 9am-midnight.

🎵 ENTERTAINMENT

Tel Avivans hate to admit it, but Jerusalem's nightlife is no longer joke-worthy. Once the city's conservative majority is tucked into bed, the bar and club scene comes to life; from Thursday to Saturday nights, the city's energy is so high it would make a rabbi's hair curl. The best weekly info in English is the "In Jerusalem" insert in Friday's *Jerusalem Post.* The tourist office in Safra Sq. (see p. 289) also has detailed monthly calendars in English.

ISRAEL

BARS

In the shadow of the stately Orthodox churches of the **Russian Compound** (Migrash Ha-Russim), two blocks down Heleni Ha-Malka St., neon beer signs lure liquor lovers like moths. After midnight, stylish bars in old stone buildings fill to capacity with a young, hip crowd jivin' to jazz, krooning along to karaoke, and doing everything in between. The **midraḥov,** just five minutes away, offers less rowdy but equally popular escapes.

RUSSIAN COMPOUND

▧ Mike's Place, 7 Heleni Ha-Malka (☎052 67 09 65), on the corner of Horkanos. Tightly packed (in a cozy way). English-speaking crowd puts away Guinness, smokes *nargilah* (NIS15), and digs excellent live music every night starting around 10:30pm. Happy hour daily 5-8pm (drinks half-price) and midnight-12:30am (cocktails and shots half-price). Serves light pub food (pizza NIS10; cheesy fries NIS20). No cover. Open daily 5pm-3am.

Kanabis, 11 Moonbaz St. (☎623 29 29), upstairs from Tarabin. Large bar-restaurant-dance floor with outdoor terrace overlooking the Moonbaz scene. Karaoke M-Tu nights beginning at 10pm. Beautiful circular bar with 3-page cocktail menu. Individual pizzas and salads NIS30-35. Cover Th-Sa NIS30; M-Tu NIS25 works as a food and drink voucher; W free. Open M-Sa 8:30pm-4am.

Sergey, 15 Heleni Ha-Malka St. (☎625 85 11), at the corner of Moonbaz St. No-frills bar packed with an intellectual twenty-something crowd of Bezalel Art Institute students so hip that they don't even wear black. Decent selection of food. Pizza NIS30; crepes NIS28; salads NIS30-36. Beer NIS16-25; mixed drinks NIS30 and up. Minimum charge on weekends NIS20. Open daily 7pm-late.

ON OR NEAR THE MIDRAḤOV

Shanty, 4 Naḥalat Shiva St. (☎624 34 34), in the alleyway between Yoel Salomon and Rivlin St., tucked in the corner. An Israeli enclave in a tourist domain; ensures an absence of teens by carding hard. Candle-lit room and outdoor tables always filled to capacity. Huge drink list with prices slightly lower than other nearby bars; buy an alcoholic drink and get a soft drink for NIS4. Excellent salads (NIS38) and house specialties (NIS21-36). Open Su-Th 7pm-late and F and Sa 8pm-even later. Kitchen closes 11pm.

Syndrome, 18 Hillel St. (☎054 805 210), on the corner of Rabbi Akiva, underneath Cafe Aroma, at the end of the row of stores. Friendly and casual atmosphere. No food, no coffee, just alcohol, chips, *nargilah* (NIS15), and music. Happy hour nightly 8-9pm (half-price draft beer). Live music performances (mostly blues and rock) on small stage almost every night 10pm-1am. Cover NIS10-30 (depending on who's playing), including a beer. Open daily 8pm-2am or later.

The Tavern Pub, 16 Rivlin St. (☎624 45 41). Supposedly Jerusalem's oldest pub—putting it at the ripe old age of 30. A magnet for all types, from European tourists and American college students to Israeli locals hoping to meet tourists and students. Eight kinds of draft beer (1 pint NIS16-20) and innumerable international beers. Cocktails NIS22 and up. Live music every other Th in winter. Open daily 3pm-5am.

CLUBS

Most clubs are clustered in the city center or on Ha-Umman St. in **Talpiot,** a southern industrial neighborhood down Hebron Rd. (taxis from the city center NIS15-20). They also open, close, and move more frequently than the city-center clubs; go to Ha-Oman 17 first and ask where to find other local hot spots.

Ha-Oman 17, 17 Ha-Oman St. (☎678 16 58; www.haoman.com), in Talpiyot. The city's largest and best dance club. Still relatively unknown among tourists (which is either good or bad, depending on who you ask). Huge after-parties on major holidays. Two huge indoor dance floors with large bar, populated mostly by scantily-clad Israeli university students. Mostly techno and pop. Th 23+ and F 19+. Cover NIS70. Open Th-F midnight-dawn (or later). Closed July-Aug.

The Underground, 1 Yoel Salomon St. (☎625 19 18), is the dance club everyone hates but goes to anyway, with a bar and batcave-like disco below. Sweaty, grinding dancers shed layers of clothing as the hours go by. Drinks NIS15 and up; buy one get one free during happy hour (daily 8-9pm). 18+. Cover Su-W after 10:30pm NIS20 and Th-Sa NIS30; includes one drink. Open nightly 7:30pm-4am.

Glasnost, 15 Heleni Ha-Malka St. (☎625 69 54), past Moonbaz when coming from Jaffa Rd. In the heart of the bar scene in the Russian Compound. Large outer courtyard overflows with toe-stepping Israelis. Live salsa every M 9pm-3am (NIS25), crash course 8-9pm (NIS35 includes both); Tu Reggae; Th house party; F-Su pub only with tables and chairs crowding out the dance floor (no cover). 21+.

MUSIC

Yellow Submarine, 13 Ha-Rekavim St. (☎656 66 11). This theater-cafe features a different kind of performance 3-4 nights a week. Frequent musical guests from unknown locals to Israeli superstars. Party for those 30+ after 11pm every other Th; for students every F (during the school year). Stand-up comedy marathon in Hebrew every other Sa. Full bar and light Mexican food. Call for a schedule of events. NIS30-60.

Pargod Theater, 94 Bezalel St. (☎623 17 65), on the corner of Nissim Bekhar St. in Naḥalot. Hip, young crowd comes for jazz and special performances. Billboard in front announces special events.

Jerusalem Symphony Orchestra (☎561 14 98; www.jso.co.il). Performs frequently at the Jerusalem Theater on David Marcus St. and the Henry Crown Symphony Hall, 5 Chopin St. A schedule of events is available on the website. NIS90-165. 30% student discount on night of show. Season runs Sept.-June.

Ein Kerem Music Center (☎641 42 50), on Ha-Ma'ayan St., opposite Mary's Well in Ein Kerem. Take bus #17 from the central bus station or Zion Sq. Features weekly classical music and operatic performances, usually on F or Sa night. Tickets cost NIS45 at the door. 25% student discount. Call for a schedule of events.

◉ SIGHTS

OLD CITY

WALLS AND GATES

RAMPARTS PROMENADE. For an amazing overview of the Old City, walk along this promenade, which tops the walls built by Suleiman the Magnificent in 1542. Begin at **Jaffa Gate** (one of the two gates from which you can access the ramparts) by climbing the hidden steps immediately on the left (just before the jewelry store). The most picturesque part of the walk stretches from here to **Damascus Gate** (20min.), where you can either descend into the market or continue on to **St. Stephen's Gate** (Lion's Gate), the beginning of the **Via Dolorosa.** To ascend the ramparts from Damascus Gate, face the gate from the plaza outside and go down the steps on the right, passing under the bridge and entering through the carriageway to the left of the plaza. *(Promenade open daily 9am-5pm. NIS14, students NIS7; combined ticket to ramparts, Temple Mount excavations (Ophel), Roman Plaza, Zedekiah's Cave, and Hezekiah's tunnel NIS35. Tickets good for five days.)*

JAFFA GATE. Jaffa Gate is the traditional entrance for pilgrims and the entrance in the western Old City wall (and thus the most convenient from West Jerusalem). A gate has stood here since 135 CE.

DAMASCUS GATE. Damascus Gate is built over the Roman entrance to the Cardo, facing East Jerusalem and providing direct access to the Muslim Quarter. Scholars recently discovered a plaza at the gate's entrance with a statue of Hadrian mounted on a huge column, explaining the Arabic name for Damascus Gate: *Bab al-Amud* ("Gate of the Column"). Also near Damascus Gate is the biblical **Zedekiah's Cave,** where stones for the Jewish Temple were hewn.

HIGHLIGHTS

EST. WALKING TIME: 1.5 to 2 hrs
INCLUDING ALL SIGHTS: 3 to 4 hrs

Walkintour!

Enter the old City in true pilgrim style through Jaffa Gate, and climb the **Tower of David** for a panoramic view of your historic surroundings.

Want to relive the times where you've felt on top of the world? Then stroll around the **ramparts** for a bird's-eye view of the entire old city.

Try not to get swept away by the commotion and clamor of the **Muslim Quarter souq**, where raw meat, textiles, and chintz abound.

The descent into the cavernous quarry of **Zedekiah's Cave** is so engulfing that it almost seems like you're being sucked into the bowels of the earth.

The Western Wall– where soldiers, Orthodox Jews, kibbutzniks, and new immigrants alike weep–is the only remaining portion of the second temple.

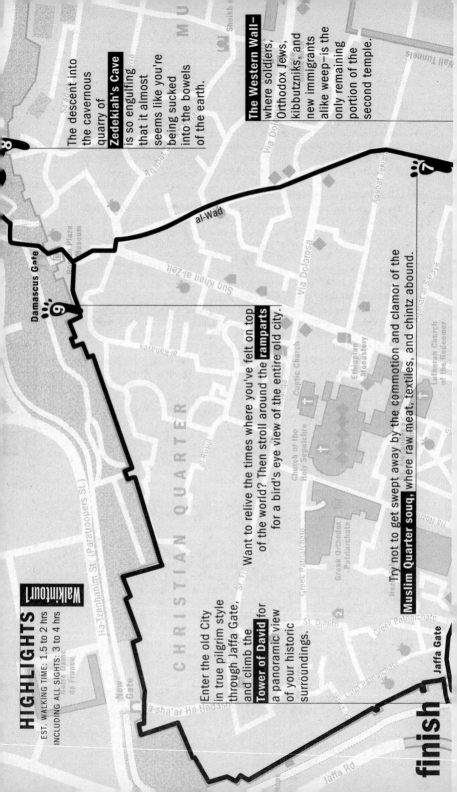

finish

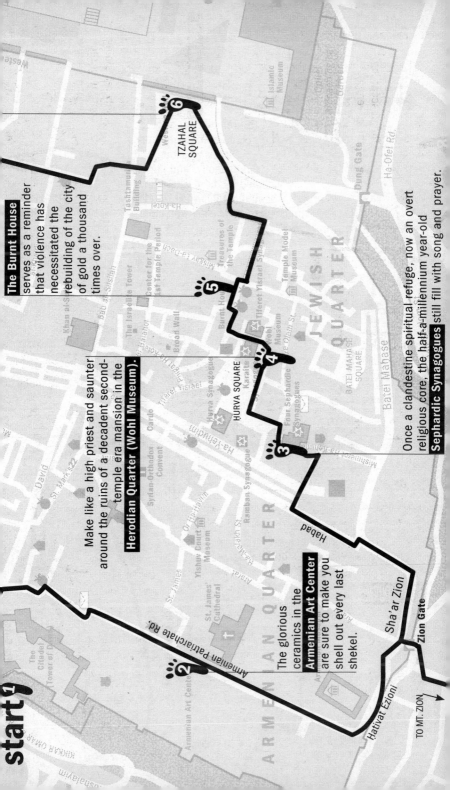

start 1

The Burnt House serves as a reminder that violence has necessitated the rebuilding of the city a thousand times over.

Make like a high priest and saunter around the ruins of a decadent second-temple era mansion in the **Herodian Quarter (Wohl Museum).**

The glorious ceramics in the **Armenian Art Center** are sure to make you shell out every last shekel.

Once a clandestine spiritual refuge, now an overt religious core, the half-a-millennium year-old **Sephardic Synagogues** still fill with song and prayer.

TZAHAL SQUARE

JEWISH QUARTER

ARMENIAN QUARTER

HURVA SQUARE

BATEI MAHASE SQUARE

Batei Mahase

Habad

Sha'ar Zion

Zion Gate

TO MT. ZION

Hativat Ezioni

Armenian Patriarchate Rd.

David

St. Mark's St.

KIKKAR OMAR

The Citadel (Tower of David)

St. James' Cathedral

Yishuv Court Museum

Or ha-Haim

Ha-Arayakh St.

Arshad

Tiferet Yisrael

Ha-Yehudim

Ramban Synagogue

Hurva Synagogue

Syrian Orthodox Convent

Cardo

Misgav La-dach

Center for the Last Temple Period

The Israelite Tower

Bab el-Silsilah

Khan al-Sheunah

Etzel Wall

Burnt House

Four Sephardic Synagogues

Karaite

Mishmerot Ha-Kehuna

Wohl Museum

Ha-Olam St.

Tiferet Yisrael Synagogue

Temple Model Museum

Treasures of the Temple

Misgav La-Dach

Islamic Museum

Dung Gate

Ha-Ofel Rd.

Western

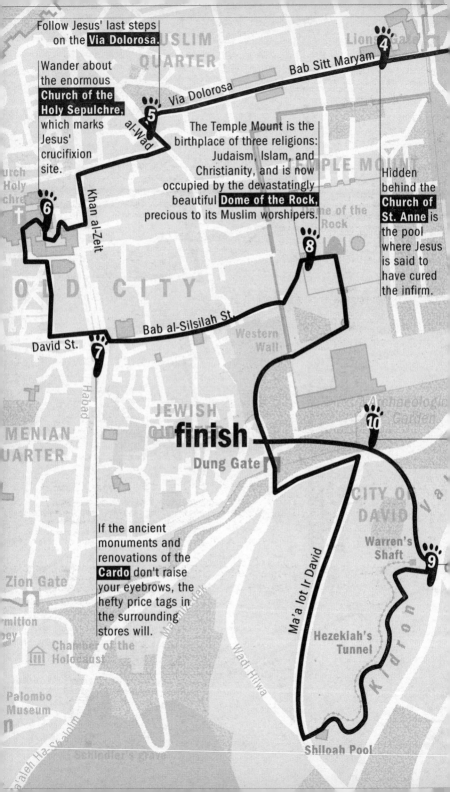

Follow Jesus' last steps on the **Via Dolorosa**.

Wander about the enormous **Church of the Holy Sepulchre**, which marks Jesus' crucifixion site.

MUSLIM QUARTER

Bab Sitt Maryam

Lion Gate

Via Dolorosa

al-Wad

The Temple Mount is the birthplace of three religions: Judaism, Islam, and Christianity, and is now occupied by the devastatingly beautiful **Dome of the Rock**, precious to its Muslim worshipers.

TEMPLE MOUNT

Dome of the Rock

Hidden behind the **Church of St. Anne** is the pool where Jesus is said to have cured the infirm.

Church Holy Sepulchre

Khan al-Zeit

OLD CITY

Bab al-Silsilah St.

Western Wall

David St.

Habad

Archaeological Garden

JEWISH QUARTER

finish

Dung Gate

ARMENIAN QUARTER

Zion Gate

If the ancient monuments and renovations of the **Cardo** don't raise your eyebrows, the hefty price tags in the surrounding stores will.

Madrel

CITY OF DAVID

Warren's Shaft

Ma'a lot Ir David

Hezekiah's Tunnel

Kidron Valley

Wadi Hilwa

Chamber of the Holocaust

Dormition Abbey

Palombo Museum

Ma'aleh Ha-Shalom

Schindler's grave

Shiloah Pool

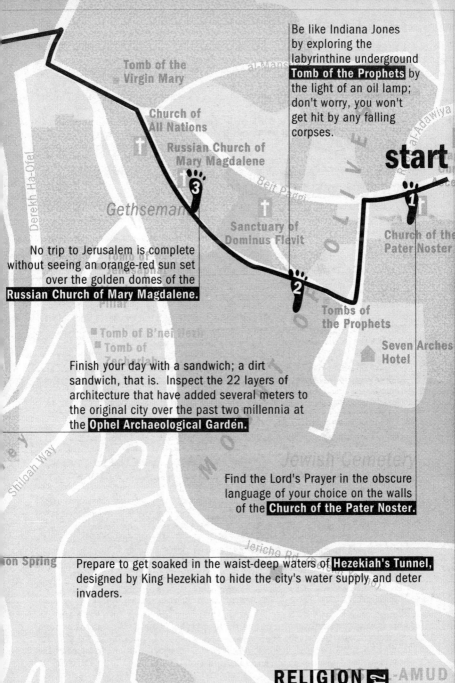

Be like Indiana Jones by exploring the labyrinthine underground **Tomb of the Prophets** by the light of an oil lamp; don't worry, you won't get hit by any falling corpses.

Tomb of the Virgin Mary

Church of All Nations

Russian Church of Mary Magdalene

start

3

Gethseman...

Sanctuary of Dominus Flevit

Church of the Pater Noster

2

No trip to Jerusalem is complete without seeing an orange-red sun set over the golden domes of the **Russian Church of Mary Magdalene.**

Tombs of the Prophets

Seven Arches Hotel

Tomb of B'nei Hezir
Tomb of Zechariah

Finish your day with a sandwich; a dirt sandwich, that is. Inspect the 22 layers of architecture that have added several meters to the original city over the past two millennia at the **Ophel Archaeological Garden.**

Jewish Cemetery

Find the Lord's Prayer in the obscure language of your choice on the walls of the **Church of the Pater Noster.**

Jericho Rd

on Spring   Prepare to get soaked in the waist-deep waters of **Hezekiah's Tunnel,** designed by King Hezekiah to hide the city's water supply and deter invaders.

SILWAN

RELIGION

EST. WALKING TIME: 2 hrs
INCLUDING ALL SIGHTS: 5 to 6 hrs

WalkInTour2

OTHER GATES. New Gate, just a few steps from Jaffa Gate, was opened in 1889 to facilitate access to the Christian Quarter. **Herod's Gate** is to the east of Damascus Gate and reaches the deeper sections of the Muslim Quarter. **St. Stephen's Gate,** also known as **Lion's Gate,** is along the eastern wall. It faces the Mount of Olives and marks the beginning of the Via Dolorosa. **Golden Gate** is blocked by Muslim graves and has been sealed since the 1600s. It is thought to lie over the Closed Gate of the First Temple, the entrance through which the Messiah will purportedly pass (Ezekiel 44:1-3). **Dung Gate,** on the southern wall, opens onto the Western Wall plaza. It was given its name in medieval times because dumping feces here was considered an especially worthy act. **Zion Gate,** on the opposite end of the Cardo from Damascus Gate, connects the Armenian Quarter with Mount Zion.

TOWER OF DAVID (THE CITADEL)

To the right inside Jaffa Gate. 24hr. info ☎ 626 53 33. Museum open Apr.-Oct. Sa-Th 9am-5pm and F 9am-2pm; Nov.-Mar. Sa-Th 10am-4pm and F 10am-2pm. NIS35, students and seniors NIS25, children 5-12 NIS15; includes tour in English Su-F 11am. Nighttime programs several nights per week. Occasional international jazz shows Oct.-June; call for dates.

The Citadel complex gives an outstanding historical introduction to the Old City. The Citadel, also called the Tower of David (*Migdal David* in Hebrew), resembles a Lego caricature of overlapping Hasmonean, Herodian, Roman, Byzantine, Muslim, Mamluk, and Ottoman ruins, but nothing from David's era (during his reign, this area was outside the city and unsettled). The tower provides a superb vantage point for surveying the Holy City. As you wind through the rooms of the fortress, listen to the high-tech museum tell the story of the city in Hebrew, Arabic, or English. Begin with the excellent 14-minute introductory movie.

TEMPLE MOUNT

The entrance to the Mount is up the ramp, just right of the Western Wall. It is also accessible from the end of Bab al-Silsilah St. Visitors may enter the Temple Mount area Sa-Th 7:30-11am and 1:30-2:30pm, though the Mount is sometimes closed to visitors without notice. Hours subject to change during Ramadan and other Islamic holidays, but it is usually open 7:30-10:30am. Tickets sold until 3pm at a booth between al-Aqsa Mosque and the museum (to the right when entering from the ramp). NIS38, students NIS25.

 SECURITY. Remember that the area is highly sensitive—incidents in the past have resulted in violence. Any conspicuous action, no matter how innocent, may result in ejection. **Modest dress** is required and wrap-around gowns are provided for those who need them. Be aware that many sections considered **off-limits** by the police are not marked as such, including the walls around al-Aqsa, the area through the door to the south between al-Aqsa and the museum, the garden walkway along the eastern wall, and the Muslim cemetery. Bags and packs are not permitted inside al-Aqsa or the Dome of the Rock and must be left outside along with your shoes; theft is not usually a problem, but you should refrain from bringing valuables when you visit. **Photography** is permitted on the Temple Mount, but not inside al-Aqsa or the Dome of the Rock.

Known as *al-Haram al-Sharif* in Arabic and *Har Ha-Bayit* in Hebrew, this 35-acre area in the southeastern corner of the Old City is one of the most venerated religious sites in the world. The **Temple Mount** is central to both Judaism and Islam and a holy site for at least 10 ancient religions. God asked Abraham to sacrifice his son Isaac here (Genesis 22:2), and King Solomon built the **First Temple** here in the middle of the 10th century BCE (2 Chronicles 3:1) before it was destroyed in 587 BCE, when the Jews were led into captivity (I Kings 5-8; II Kings 24-25). The **Second Temple** was built in 516 BCE, after the Jews' return from exile (Ezra 3-7). In 20 BCE, King Herod rebuilt the temple and enlarged the Mount, reinforcing it with four retaining walls (parts of which still stand). The Second Temple is remembered by Christians as the backdrop of Christ's Passion. Like the First Temple, the

Second Temple lasted only a few hundred years until it was sacked by Roman legions in 70 CE. Hadrian built a temple to Jupiter over the site, but the Byzantines destroyed it and used its platform as a sewage facility. After Caliph Omar arrived in 638, he ascended the Mount and began cleaning up, personally removing an armful of brown gook. According to Muslim legend, the arches on the Temple Mount will be used to hang scales for weighing people's good and bad deeds. The **Islamic Museum** is filled with fantastic relics, including elaborately decorated Qur'ans and a collection of crescent-topped spires that once crowned older domes. The museum is accesible from the ramp entrance beside the Western Wall.

DOME OF THE ROCK AND AL-AQSA MOSQUE. The Umayyad Caliphs built the two Arab shrines that still dominate the Temple Mount: the silver-domed **al-Aqsa Mosque** (first built in 715 CE), and the magnificent **Dome of the Rock** (691 CE). A stunning display of mosaics and metallic domes, the complex is the third-holiest Muslim site (after the Ka'aba in Mecca and the Mosque of the Prophet in Medina). This is where Allah took Muhammad on his mystical Night Journey (*miraj*) from the Holy Mosque at Mecca to the outer Mosque (*al-aqsa* means "the farthest") and then on to heaven. The Dome of the Rock surrounds what Muslims believe to be the makeshift altar where Abraham almost sacrificed Ishmael, his son by Sarah's maid Hagar (not Isaac, as Christians and Jews believe).

The dome, once of solid gold, was eventually melted down to pay the caliphs' debts. The domes of the mosques and shrines were plated with lead until the structures received aluminum caps during the restoration work of 1958-64. Renovations in 1993 re-coated the domes with new metal plates and a thin layer of 24-karat gold. Many of the tiles covering the walls of the Dome of the Rock were affixed during the reign of Süleyman the Magnificent, and are easily distinguishable from the ceramic tiles added with the private funds of the late King Hussein of Jordan.

Next to the Dome of the Rock is the smaller **Dome of the Chain,** the exact center of al-Haram al-Sharif, where Muslims believe a chain once hung from heaven that could be grasped only by the righteous. Between al-Aqsa and the Dome of the Rock is **al-Kas,** a fountain where Muslims perform ablutions before prayer. Built in 709 CE, it is connected to cisterns capable of holding 10 million gallons.

WESTERN WALL. Religious scholars believe the **Holy of Holies** (the most sacred spot in the temple, where the High Priest was allowed to enter only once a year) was closest to what is now the Western Wall, making this wall the holiest approachable site in Judaism. Some Jews won't ascend the Mount in the off-chance that they will walk on the Holy of Holies, which is off limits until the Messiah arrives. Most of the Western Wall stands in the Jewish Quarter (see below).

JEWISH QUARTER

Known as *Ha-Rovah* by Israelis, the picturesque Jewish Quarter is in the south-east quadrant of the Old City, on the site of the posh Upper City of the Second Temple era. After being exiled when the Second Temple was destroyed, Jews resettled here in the 15th century. Much of the Quarter was damaged in the 1948 War, and lay in ruins after two decades of Jordanian rule. The Israelis annexed the Old City after the 1967 War and began extensive restoration of the neighborhood, unearthing archaeological wonders with every lift of the shovel. They have managed to integrate the ancient remains into the new neighborhood quite gracefully. Today the Quarter is an upper-middle-class neighborhood of about 650 families (many American) who are almost exclusively Orthodox Jews.

The Jewish Quarter extends from Ha-Shalshelet St. to the southern wall, and from Ararat St. to the Western Wall. From Jaffa Gate, go down David St. and turn right at the first intersection just before it becomes Bab al-Silsilah St., or turn right past the Tower of David onto Armenian Orthodox Patriarch Rd. (in the direction of traffic) and make the first left onto St. James Rd. The high arch over the Ḥurva Synagogue marks Ḥurva Sq., a convenient reference for Jewish Quarter sights. The Quarter is home to the **One Last Day Museum** and **Wohl Archaeological Museum.**

WESTERN WALL. The 18m-tall wall (*Ha-Kotel Ha-Ma'aravi*, or just "The Kotel") is part of the retaining wall of the Temple Mount. Built around 20 BCE, the Wall was the largest section of the Temple area that remained standing after its destruction in 70 CE. Nearly 20m of Herodian wall (identifiable by its carved frames) still lie underground. Byzantines, Arabs, and Turks added the smaller stones above. The **Wailing Wall,** a dated moniker, refers to the Jewish worshipers who visited the wall in centuries past to mourn the destruction of the Temple. Today's visitors, Jewish or otherwise, often see the Wall as a direct connection with God and tuck written prayers into its crannies. Don't expect your scribble to wait there for the Messiah: all notes are periodically removed and buried in accordance with Jewish law. Pre-1948 photographs show Orthodox Jews praying at the wall in a crowded alley; after the 1967 War, the present plaza was built. Israeli paratroopers are now sworn in here to recall the Wall's capture. The prayer areas for men and women are separated by a screen, with the Torah scrolls kept on the men's side, along with recently excavated sections of the Wall. On Fridays, Yeshivat Ha-Kotel organizes dancing to usher in Shabbat. The festivities start before sundown and continue until late. Bar Mitzvahs (ceremonies marking a Jewish boy's coming of age) are held at the Wall on Monday and Thursday mornings. Photography is appropriate at these occasions, but not on Shabbat or holidays. On other nights, the Wall is brightly lit, the air cool, and the atmosphere reflective and quiet. *(The Wall can be reached by foot from Dung Gate, the Jewish Quarter, Bab al-Silsilah St., or al-Wad Rd.)*

WILSON'S ARCH. Wilson's Arch is inside a large, arched room to the left of the Wall. It was once part of a bridge that allowed Jewish priests to cross from their Upper City homes to the Temple. A peek down the illuminated shafts in the floor of this room gives a sense of the Wall's original height (women may not enter). The Wall continues from here through closed tunnels for over 500m. Women and groups can enter the passageways through an archway to the south, near the telephones. Underneath the Wall is an underground passage where Jewish radicals hid explosives in the early 1980s in a plot to destroy the Dome of the Rock. For tours of the passage, contact the MTIO, Archaeological Seminars, or the Jewish Students Information Center (see **Tours,** p. 288).

CARDO. The staircase down Or Ḥayim St. past Ḥabad St. descends to the remains of Jerusalem's main Roman and Byzantine thoroughfare, which has also been heavily excavated alongside Jewish Quarter Rd. The enormous remaining pillars suggest its original monumental proportions: it was built over a Byzantine extension of Emperor Hadrian's Cardo Maximus, which ran from Damascus Gate to David St. Archaeologists suspect that Justinian constructed an addition so the Cardo would extend as far as the Nea Church (beneath Yeshivat Ha-Kotel). Sheltered by the Cardo's vaulted roof are the best (and thus most expensive) **Judaica shops** in Jerusalem. Near the entrance to the Cardo is an enlarged mosaic reproduction of the **Map of the Holy Land,** the 6th-century plan of Jerusalem discovered in Jordan (see p. 487). *(Make a left at the bottom of the stairs on Jewish Quarter Rd. Cardo open and illuminated Su-Th until 11pm.)*

BURNT HOUSE. The Burnt House is the remains of a priest's dwelling from the Second Temple era. In 70 CE, the fourth year of the Jewish Revolt, the Romans destroyed the Second Temple and broke into Jerusalem's Upper City, burning its buildings and killing its inhabitants. Near a stairwell, the grisly bones of a severed arm reach for a carbonized spear. Sound and light shows inside the Burnt House recreate the events of its destruction. *(On Tiferet Yisrael St. From Ḥurva Sq., turn right at the Mizrahi Bank.* ☎ *628 72 11. Open Su-Th 9am-4:30pm and F 9am-12:30pm. NIS9, students NIS7. English presentations every hour on the half hour.)*

OPHEL ARCHAEOLOGICAL GARDEN. The excavations at the southern wall of the Temple Mount are known as "Ophel," though the name technically refers to the hill just outside the southern wall, at the City of David. Scholars have uncovered 22 layers from 12 periods of the city's history. A tunnel leads out to the steps of the Temple Mount. *(From the Western Wall, head out past the security point toward Dung Gate;*

the entrance to the ruins is on the left just before the gate. ☎ 625 44 03. Open daily 7am-5pm. NIS14, students NIS7. Combination tickets for Ophel, Burnt House, Herodian Quarter, and Last Ditch Battle Museum NIS26, students NIS24.)

FOUR SEPHARDIC SYNAGOGUES. Mediterranean Jews in the 16th century built the Synagogue of Rabbi Yoḥanan Ben-Zakkai, Prophet Elijah Synagogue, Middle Synagogue, and Istanbuli Synagogue in accordance with a local law that prohibited the construction of synagogues taller than the surrounding houses. To attain a semblance of loftiness, the synagogues were built in underground chambers. The renovated structures date from 1835 and remain the spiritual center of Jerusalem's Sephardic community. *(Down Mishmerot Ha-Kehuna St., near the Jewish Quarter parking lot. ☎ 628 05 92. Open Su-Th 9am-4pm and F 9am-noon. NIS7, students NIS4.)*

ḤURVA SYNAGOGUE. A single stone arch soars above the ruins of the synagogue in the square named for it, forming the center of the Jewish Quarter. Built in 1700 by followers of Rabbi Yehuda the Ḥasid, the synagogue was destroyed by Muslims, thereby earning its ominous title (*ḥurva* means "ruin"). In 1856 the building was restored as the National Ashkenazic Synagogue, only to be destroyed again during the 1948 War. In 1967, renovators opted to rebuild only the single arch as a reminder of the destruction. *(On Ha-Yehudim Rd. around the corner from Ḥurva Sq.)*

ARMENIAN QUARTER

Jerusalem's Armenian Christian population of about 1000 is cloistered in the southwestern corner of the Old City. The Quarter lives in the shadow of tragedy: the Turkish massacre of up to one-and-a-half million Armenians in 1915 (see **Turkey: Modern History,** p. 609) remains one of the century's little-noticed genocides, and persecution of those fleeing to Palestine has caused their numbers to dwindle even farther. Posters mapping out the genocide line the streets. The residential Armenian Compound is not open to the public, but the few available glimpses of Armenian culture are mesmerizing.

ST. JAMES CATHEDRAL. The massive spiritual center of the Armenian Quarter was originally constructed during the 5th century CE, Armenia's golden age, to honor two St. Jameses. St. James the Greater was beheaded in 44 CE by Herod, and his head (supposedly delivered to Mary on the wings of angels) rests under the gilded altar. St. James the Lesser, entombed in a northern chapel, was the first bishop of Jerusalem, but was run out of town by Jews who disliked his version of Judaism. Persians destroyed the cathedral in the 7th century, but Armenians rebuilt it in the 11th century, and Crusaders enlarged it in the 12th. *(The massive cathedral is on Armenian Orthodox Patriarchate Rd., the main paved road leading right from Jaffa Gate. The entrance is on the left past the tunnel, under an arch reading "Couvent Arménien St. Jacques." ☎ 628 23 31; www.armenian-patriarchate.org. Open daily 6-7:30am during the morning service and 3-3:30pm during the Vespers service. Modest dress required.)*

ARMENIAN ART CENTER. One of the few Armenian ceramic shops still producing tiles and pottery by ancient methods, this center sells items more expensive than the machine-made goods found in the *souq*, but the heavy, handmade dyes lend an unmatched richness to the colors and intricate designs. The best pieces are hidden from spying competitors; ask to see the work in the back of the store. *(On Armenian Orthodox Patriarchate Rd., across from St. James Cathedral. ☎ 628 35 67 or 628 43 05. Open M-Sa 9am-7pm. Tiles, doorhangings, plates, and other objects NIS20 and up—way, way up. Pieces available by advance order.)*

SYRIAN ORTHODOX CONVENT. Aramaic, the ancient language of the Levant, is spoken here during services and in casual conversation. Also known as St. Mark's Church, the Syrian Church believes the room in the basement to be the site of St. Mark's house and the Last Supper (most other Christians recognize the Cenacle on Mount Zion as that hallowed place). Decorated with beautiful gilded woodwork, the chapel contains a 150-year-old bible in Old Aramaic and a painting of the Virgin

Mary supposedly painted by St. Mark himself. *(Turn left from Armenian Patriarchate Rd. onto St. James Rd. and left onto Ararat St. The convent, marked by a vivid mosaic, is on the right after a sharp turn in the road. Open daily 8am-4pm. Ring the bell if the door is closed.)*

CHRISTIAN QUARTER

The Christian Quarter, in the northwest corner of the Old City, is centered around the **Church of the Holy Sepulchre,** the site traditionally believed to be the place of Jesus' crucifixion, burial, and resurrection. The alleyways of the Quarter pass small churches and chapels of various denominations, and the streets bustle with pilgrims, nuns, monks, and merchants peddling rosaries and holy water.

CHURCH OF ST. ANNE. Commemorating the birthplace of Jesus' mother Mary, the church is one of the best preserved pieces of Crusader architecture in Israel. It survived the Islamic period because Salah al-Din used it as a Muslim theological school (hence the Arabic inscription on the tympanum above the doors). Extensive excavations behind the church clearly show the layers of history; the ruins of a 5th-century basilica cover those of a 2nd- or 3rd-century chapel. The church itself has fantastic acoustics. *Let's Go* used to suggest that visitors try singing quietly in the front rows, but there's now a sign informing people that "This is a holy place for prayer and religious hymns only"—oops. The cool, beautiful crypt has a beaten-copper cross and inlaid stone floors.

Within the grounds of the church is the **Pool of Bethesda**, straight ahead and down the stairs. Crowds of the infirm used to wait beside the pool for an angel to disturb the waters since the first person in after the angel would supposedly be cured. Jesus also healed a sick man here (John 5:2-9). *(Near St. Stephen's Gate, through the large wooden doors on the right. Church and grounds open M-Sa 8am-12:45pm and 2-6pm; in winter M-Sa 8am-12:45pm and 2-5pm. NIS6, students NIS4.)*

VIA DOLOROSA (STATIONS OF THE CROSS)

The Via Dolorosa (Path of Sorrow) is the route that the cross-bearing Jesus followed from the site of his condemnation (the Praetorium) to the site of his crucifixion and grave. Each event on his walk has a chapel commemorating it; together these chapels comprise the 14 **Stations of the Cross.** The present route was mapped out during the Crusader period and passes through the Muslim and Christian Quarters, although modern New Testament scholars have suggested alternate routes based on recent archaeological and historical reconstructions. The Via Dolorosa begins at St. Stephen's Gate; most Stations are marked, but many are hard to find. On Fridays (3pm, July-Aug. 4pm), you can join the Franciscan monks who lead pilgrims along the Via Dolorosa beginning at al-Omariyyeh St.

STATION I. Just past an archway 200m from St. Stephen's Gate, a ramp with a blue railing leads back to the courtyard of **al-Omariyyeh College,** the site identified as the First Station, the **Praetorium** where Jesus was condemned. One bone of contention between sects involves the starting point of Jesus' final walk as a mortal. It is generally agreed that Jesus was brought before Pontius Pilate for judgment. Normally, Roman governors fulfilled their duties in the palace of Herod the Great, south of Jaffa Gate and the Citadel area. But on feast days such as Passover, the day of Jesus' condemnation, the governor and his soldiers presumably based themselves at the Antonia Fortress to be closer to the Temple Mount. Reflecting this holiday relocation, the **Tower of Antonia,** in the courtyard of **al-Omariyyeh College,** is considered to be the **First Station,** where Jesus was condemned. The station is not marked. For one of the best views of the Dome of the Rock plaza, walk into the courtyard of the school, turn left, and ascend the steps on the right.

STATION II. Across the Via Dolorosa from the ramp is a Franciscan monastery; inside on the left is the **Condemnation Chapel**, complete with a relief above the altar. This is the Second Station, where Jesus was sentenced to crucifixion. On the right is the **Chapel of Flagellation,** where he was first flogged by Roman soldiers. A crown of thorns adorns the dome. The Via Dolorosa passes beneath the **Ecce Homo Arch** (site of Pontius Pilate's mansion), named for Pilate's exclamation as he looked down upon Jesus (*Ecce Homo* means "Behold the Man"). The arch is actually part of the triumphal arch that commemorated Emperor Hadrian's suppression of the Bar Kokhba Revolt in the 2nd century CE. The nearby **Convent of the Sisters of Zion** sits atop a large chamber thought by some to be a judgment hall, making it yet another First Station contender. The convent is closed to the public, but the excavations are not. *(Chapels open daily Apr.-Sept. 8-11:45am and 4-6pm; Oct.-Mar. 8-11:45am and 1-5pm. Excavations: walk down the Via Dolorosa from the Second Station to the brown door on Aqabat al-Rahbat St., on the right off the Via Dolorosa. Knock to enter. Open M-Sa 8:30am-5pm. NIS6, students NIS4.)*

STATIONS III-VII. Immediately after the Via Dolorosa turns left onto al-Wad Rd., look to the left for the door to the Armenian Catholic Patriarchate. To the left of the door is the **Third Station,** where Jesus fell to his knees for the first time. A small Polish chapel inside a blue gate marks the spot; a relief above the entrance (marked "III Statio") depicts Jesus kneeling beneath the cross. At the **Fourth Station,** on the left just beyond the Armenian Orthodox Patriarchate, a small chapel commemorates the spot where Jesus saw his mother. Look for a carving above light blue iron doors, to the left of an arched alleyway. Turn right on the Via Dolorosa to reach the **Fifth Station,** where Simon the Cyrene volunteered to carry Jesus' cross (look for the brown door on the left, with the inscription "V St."). Fifty meters ahead, the remains of a small column designate the **Sixth Station** (marked with a "VI"), where Veronica wiped Jesus' face with her handkerchief. The mark of his face was left on the cloth, now on display at the Greek Orthodox Patriarchate on the street of the same name. Look for a pair of doors on the left, one green and one dark brown; the column is set into the wall between the doors. The **Seventh Station,** straight ahead at the intersection with Khan al-Zeit Rd., marks Jesus' second fall, precipitated by the sudden steepness of the road. Tradition holds that notices of Jesus' condemnation were posted on a gate at this spot.

STATIONS VIII AND IX. Crossing Khan al-Zeit Rd., ascend Aqabat al-Khanqah and look left past the Greek Orthodox Convent for the stone Latin cross that marks the **Eighth Station.** Here Jesus turned to the women who mourned him, saying "Daughters of Jerusalem, do not weep for me, weep rather for yourselves and for your children" (Luke 23:28). The small stone is part of the wall and difficult to spot; a large red-and-white sign was recently installed to mark it, but may not last long on such a narrow road. Backtrack to Khan al-Zeit Rd., take a right, walk for about 50m through the market, ascend the wide stone stairway on the right, and continue through a winding passageway to the Coptic Church. The remains of a column in its door mark the **Ninth Station,** where Jesus fell a third time.

ST. ALEXANDER'S CHURCH. Built over the Judgment Gate, the church marks the end of the Roman Cardo, through which Jesus exited the city on his way to Calvary. First-century stones line the floor, and two pillars from the original Cardo are visible. Next to the gate is a small hole in the ancient wall—this is the famed **Eye of the Needle,** through which latecomers would sneak into the city when the gates were closed. *(On the right just after turning off al-Wad St. toward the Holy Sepulchre.* ☎ *627 49 52. Open M-Sa 9am-1pm and 3-5pm. Ring bell. Prayers for Czar Alexander III Th 7am. NIS5.)*

CHURCH OF THE HOLY SEPULCHRE. Retrace your steps to the main street and continue to the next right, which leads from the marketplace to the main entrance of the Church of the Holy Sepulchre, one of the most revered structures on earth. The placement of the last five stations (X-XIV) inside the church contradicts an alternative hypothesis that Jesus was crucified at the skull-shaped Garden Tomb in East Jerusalem (see p. 316). The Church of the Holy Sepulchre marks **Golgotha,** also called **Calvary,** the site of the Crucifixion. The location was first determined by Eleni, mother of Emperor Constantine and Jerusalem's first archaeologist, during her pilgrimage in 326 CE. Eleni thought Hadrian had erected a temple to Venus and Jupiter on the site in order to divert Christians from their faith. Constantine built a small church over the site in 335, and part of the original church's foundations buttress the present Crusader structure (from 1149). The Crusader architects united all the oratories, chapels, and other sanctuaries that had cropped up around the site under one cruciform shape. By 1852, tremendous religious conflicts had developed within the Holy Sepulchre. The Ottoman rulers divided the church among the Franciscan order, the Greek Orthodox, Armenian Orthodox, Coptic, Syrian, and Ethiopian churches; the first three are the major shareholders, entitled to hold masses and processions and burn incense in the shrines and chapels.

The church is in somewhat bad shape. Restoration work in any part of the basilica implies ownership, making each sect hesitant to assist and eager to hinder the others. In 1935, the church was in such a precarious state that colonialists propped it up with girders. Since 1960, partial cooperation has allowed the supportive scaffolding to be gradually removed. To this day, the question of who gets to change a given light bulb can rage into a month-long controversy. The portions of the church not directly related to the Stations of the Cross are a dark labyrinth of small chapels through which priests, pilgrims, and chatty tourists wander. Because a denomination's ability to hang objects on the church's walls also indicates ownership, the building houses only religious paintings and spindly oil lamps. Steps lead down to two cavernous chapels commemorating the discovery of the true cross. In a small chapel on the ground floor just below Calvary, a fissure runs through the rock, supposedly caused by the earthquake following Jesus' death. According to legend, Adam (of "and Eve" fame) was buried beneath Calvary, allowing Jesus' blood to drip through this cleft and anoint him. *(Church open daily 5am-8pm, in winter 4am-7pm. Men and women must cover their knees.)*

ETHIOPIAN MONASTERY. Over part of the Church of the Holy Sepulchre is the Ethiopian Monastery; since the Ethiopians possess no part of the church itself, they have become squatters on the roof. The modest compound houses a small but spiritual church; enter through the roof and descend, exiting next to the Holy Sepulchre. Watch your head. *(Next to the Ninth Station, the first left from Khan al-Zeit Rd. when backtracking from the Holy Sepulchre. Open all day.)*

STATIONS X-XIII. The church's entrance faces the slab on which Jesus was supposedly anointed before he was buried. To continue along the Stations, go up the stairs to the right just after the entrance. The chapel at the top is divided into two naves: the right one belongs to the Franciscans, the left to the Greek Orthodox. At the entrance to the Franciscan Chapel is the **Tenth Station,** where Jesus was stripped of his clothes, and at the far end is the **Eleventh Station,** where he was nailed to the cross. The **Twelfth Station,** to the left in the Greek chapel, is a clearly marked Crucifixion site: a life-size Jesus in a metal loincloth hangs among oil lamps, flowers, and candles. Between the Eleventh and Twelfth Stations is the **Thirteenth Station,** where Mary received Jesus' body. The station is marked by an odd statue of Mary adorned with jewels, a silver dagger stuck into her breast.

STATION XIV. Jesus' tomb on the ground floor is the **Fourteenth Station.** The Holy Sepulchre, in the center of the rotunda, is a large marble structure flanked by huge candles. The first chamber in the tomb, the **Chapel of the Angel,** is dedicated to the angel who announced Jesus' resurrection to Mary Magdalene. A tiny entrance leads from the chapel into the sepulchre itself, a small chamber lit by scores of candles and guarded by priests. The walls of the tomb have been covered, but the priest in charge may be willing to reveal a small section of the original wall hidden behind a picture of the Virgin Mary. The raised marble slab in the sepulchre covers the rock on which Jesus' body was laid. Nudging the back of the Holy Sepulchre is the tiny **Coptic Chapel.** To the right of the sepulchre, the **Chapel of Mary Magdalene** marks the spot where Jesus appeared to her after his resurrection.

MUSLIM QUARTER

This sprawl of Ayyubid and Mamluk-era architecture is the largest, most heavily populated quarter in the Old City, as well as one of the most exciting. It is also the most conservative; women should dress modestly, and everyone should be particularly careful: although the Quarter is busy during the day, it becomes dark, isolated, and potentially dangerous at night.

Damascus Gate, the main entrance to the Quarter, is one of the finest examples of Islamic architecture in Jerusalem. The main thoroughfare and western border of the quarter is **Khan al-Zeit Rd.,** leading from Damascus Gate to David St., with an infinite array of booths selling spices, candy, clothing, sandals, and souvenirs in between. **Al-Wad Rd.** connects the Western Wall area to Damascus Gate. A right off al-Wad Rd. onto the Via Dolorosa leads to an array of small ceramics shops.

MUSLIM QUARTER SOUQ. The *souq* is crammed at all hours (watch for wagons and tiny tractors that charge gleefully at the crowds of shoppers) and a great place to buy Palestinian crafts such as Hebron-style wine glasses, mother-of-pearl inlaid boxes, ceramic tiles, and spherical Jerusalem candles. The *souq* is a Mamluk masterpiece of stone set within stone. Paintings of the Dome of the Rock and the Ka'aba adorn doorways; a painting of the latter signifies that a member of the family has been on the *Hajj*, the Islamic pilgrimage to Mecca and Medina.

BAB AL-SILSILAH STREET. The stretch of Bab al-Silsilah St. (Gate of the Chain St.) extending from the end of David St. to the Temple Mount is partially founded on the ancient Mamluk causeway that crossed the Tyropoeon Valley, linking the upper city to the temple platform. At the end of the first alley to the left stands the **Khan al-Sultan** (a.k.a. *al-Wakala*), a well-preserved Crusader-era *caravanserai* (an inn that provided lodging for merchants and their donkeys). Farther down Bab al-Silsilah St. on the right, just past Misgav Ladakh St., is the **Tashtamuriyya Building,** housing the tomb of its namesake (d. 1384). The multitude of Mamluk institutions in the area can be attributed to a system of succession that prevented parents from passing wealth on to their children; constructing public institutions was the best way to preserve a family's legacy. Continuing down Bab al-Silsilah St. to its intersection with Western Wall (Ha-Kotel) St. leads to the **Qilaniyya Mausoleum** and its Mamluk stalactite half-dome; the **Turba Turkan Khatun** (Tomb of Lady Turkan) is at #149. At the end of Bab al-Silsilah St., on the right and often surrounded by tour guides in training, is the **Tankiziyya Building,** built by a Mamluk slave who worked his way up to become governor of Damascus in 1312. This venerated structure, on the site of the original seat of the Sanhedrin, is currently controlled by the Israelis due to its proximity to the Western Wall and the Temple Mount.

NEAR THE OLD CITY

MOUNT ZION

Rising outside the city walls opposite Zion Gate and the Armenian Quarter is Mount Zion *(Har Tzion)*, long considered to be the site of the Tomb of David, the Last Supper, and the descent of the Holy Spirit at Pentecost. The name Zion (also applied to Israel as a whole) is derived from the Jebusite fortress of the same name, first seized by King David. During the siege of the Jewish Quarter in 1948, the area around **Zion Gate** was the scene of some of the fiercest fighting in Jerusalem; bombshell pockmarks remain. To reach the mount, exit the Old City through Zion Gate (near the Jewish Quarter parking lot) and take the path opposite the gate, bearing right at the Franciscan convent. At the next fork, a left leads to the Cenacle and David's Tomb; a right leads to the Dormition Abbey.

COENACULUM (CENACLE). The no-frills appearance of this church, identified by most as the site of the Last Supper, is due in part to an attempt by the British Mandate to avoid sectarian disputes by forbidding any change to the building. The Cenacle was converted from a mosque into a church almost four centuries ago, but the mosque's *mihrab* is still visible in the southern wall. A group in Ein Kerem, on the outskirts of Jerusalem, runs interesting Last Supper reenactment dinners in a variety of languages. *(Take the left fork after the Franciscan convent and ascend a stairway through the Diaspora Yeshiva door on the left. Open Sa-Th 8am-8pm and F 8am-2pm.)*

ISRAEL

DAVID'S TOMB. Archaeologists are skeptical of the authenticity of this site: it is written that kings (and only kings) were buried within the city proper, but Mount Zion was never encompassed by David's walls. This does little to reduce the fervor of worshipers at the tomb, many of whom whisper David's own psalms in the small, dim chamber. *(To enter, go through the Coenaculum, descend the stairs, and turn right around the corner. Open Sa-Th 8am-6pm and F 8am-2pm; in winter Su-Th 8am-5pm and F 8am-1pm. Free, although members of the yeshiva next door happily accept donations. Modest dress required; men should cover their heads with the available cardboard kippot.)*

BASILICA OF THE DORMITION ABBEY. This fortress-like edifice, commemorating the death of the Virgin Mary, was completed in 1910. Parts of the precariously situated basilica were damaged during battles in 1948 and 1967 and were never repaired. A gold mosaic rises above the apse, the floor is inlaid with symbols of the zodiac and the apostles, and the crypt holds a figure of the Virgin with all the women of the Bible above her. *(Off the right fork of the road leading to the Cenacle. ☎ 565 53 30. Open M-Th and Sa 9am-noon and 12:30-6pm; F and Su 10am-noon and 12:30-6pm. Free. Call for info on occasional classical music concerts.)*

CITY OF DAVID

As far as the archaeologists working to uncover this massive site are concerned, any exploration of Old Jerusalem must begin outside its walls, right here in the most ancient part of the city. Today's walled city dates from the Hellenic period of the Second Temple, whereas the City of David housed the throne of the biblical Kings of Israel and was included within the walls of the First Temple era. The earliest origins of biblical Jerusalem are still shrouded in mystery, but archaeologists have confirmed that the Ophel ridge, just south of the Old City walls, is the site of Jebus, the original Canaanite city King David captured and made his capital.

Recent years have seen tension in this much-disputed area. Claiming the legacy of the ancient Jewish capital, Israeli nationalists have established a Jewish presence in the midst of the almost entirely Arab **Silwan;** Arab homes were quietly purchased for large sums and Jewish families brought in. The Jewish bastion is perched precariously and conspicuously in the Arab neighborhood. Unaware tourists may find themselves walking into a potentially dangerous situation, so make your tourist status pronounced and consult tourist offices before exploring.

The excavations in the northern part of the Ophel, **Section G,** were halted in 1981 when a group of Orthodox Jews protested that the area might be the Jewish cemetery mentioned in the diaries of several medieval pilgrims. After considerable and sometimes violent political dispute, the Supreme Court of Israel ruled that the site should be closed. As a compromise, the Israeli government promised that digging would continue only under rabbinic supervision. No bones have been found.

Sights in the City of David are poorly marked and difficult to appreciate without guidance. The **City of David Visitors Center** provides an excellent three-hour tour of the excavations. The tour involves many **stairs** and **wading** through Hezekiah's Tunnel. Wear shorts and shoes that can get wet, and bring a flashlight if you can. To get to the visitors center from town, take bus #1 to Dung Gate. Facing away from the gate, make a left downhill, then the first right, downhill onto the unmarked Ma'alot Ir David St.; the center is on the left. (☎ (800) 252 423 or 626 23 41. English tours Su, Tu, and Th 10:30am, with additional days and times in summer. Book by phone at least one day in advance. Open Su-Th 9am-5pm and F 9am-2pm. NIS39, students NIS35, children NIS26.)

WATER GATE. Excavations of this site indicate that the Jebusites were confined to an area of about eight acres. The city's location above the Kidron Valley was selected for its proximity to the Giḥon Spring and its defensibility on the ridge. In times of peace, townspeople passed through a "water gate" to bring water into the city. For continued supply during times of siege, a shaft provided access to water from within the walls. This shaft played an important part in David's strategy for taking Jebus: his soldier Joab climbed its walls (II

Samuel 5:8). In 1867, archaeologist Charles Warren confirmed this biblical account when he discovered the long, sleek shaft that now bears his name. In the 1960s, Kathleen Kenyon found the 1800 BCE Jebusite city walls, which lie just above the Gihon Spring. Later, King Hezekiah devised a system to prevent David's strategy from being turned against the Israelites: he built a 500m long tunnel to bring the Gihon waters into the city walls, hiding the entrance of the spring and preventing invaders from finding water when they camped outside the wall. In 1880, a few years after the tunnel was excavated, a local boy discovered an inscription carved by Hezekiah's engineers describing the moment when the north and south construction crews met.

HEZEKIAH'S TUNNEL. Sloshing with a flashlight or candle through Hezekiah's Tunnel is one of Jerusalem's most enjoyable adventures, but it's best not to do it alone. Wading through the thigh-high water takes about 45min. Start at the Gihon Spring source on Shiloah Way and emerge at the Pool of Shiloah (Silwan in Arabic, Silo'am in Hebrew). Check in at the visitors center for a map and detailed instructions. *(Open Su-Th 9am-5pm and F 9am-2pm. NIS12, students NIS6.)*

KIDRON VALLEY AND THE MOUNT OF OLIVES

The historic Kidron Valley, which runs between the Old City and the Mount of Olives, is revered by Christians as the path of the Last Walk of Jesus. To get there, turn left from Dung Gate and walk up the narrow Ha-Ophel Rd. A newly paved sidewalk leads to an observation point for the valley, the Mount of Olives in front of it, and the four tombs directly below; a map on the floor explains the vista. Running north-to-south are the **Tomb of Jehosaphat** and **Absalom's Pillar,** allegedly the tomb of David's favored but feisty son (II Samuel 15-18). A dirt path on the left leads to the impressive rock-hewn **Tomb of B'nei Hezir** and the **Tomb of Zechariah.** The tombs are accessible from the base of the Mount of Olives or via a new staircase near the observation point just past Ma'alot Ir David St. on Ha-Ophel Rd. Women travelers are advised not to visit the Mount of Olives alone.

MOUNT OF OLIVES. The bone-dry slopes of the Mount of Olives (*Har Ha-Zeitim* in Hebrew) to the east of the Old City are dotted with churches marking the sites of Jesus' triumphant entry into Jerusalem, his teaching, his agony and betrayal in Gethsemane, and his ascension to heaven. Jews believe that the Messiah will arrive in Jerusalem from the Mount of Olives. Tradition holds that the thousands of people buried here will be the first to be resurrected upon his arrival. Ogle a monumental view of the Old City from the observation promenade outside the Seven Arches Hotel. The bell tower of the **Augusta Victoria Hospital** on Mount Scopus to the north marks the highest point in Jerusalem (903m above sea level).

CHAPEL OF CHRIST'S ASCENSION. Built in 392, this was the first church to commemorate the event for which it is named. It is the geographical (if not aesthetic) apex of the noteworthy sites in the area. In the 11th century, Crusaders adorned the chapel with columns and arches, and in the 12th century Salah al-Din constructed a domed roof. The interior contains a candle-lighting stand and sacred footprint, unidentifiable after wear and tear from generations of relic-happy pilgrims. *(Open daily 8am-5pm; ask a guard in the mosque courtyard if closed. NIS3.)*

CHURCH OF THE PATER NOSTER. St. Eleni founded this church in the 4th century as the Church of the Disciples; it is also referred to as the Church of the Eleona ("olive grove" in Greek). This was the site of the grotto where Jesus revealed the "inscrutable mysteries" to his disciples, foretelling the destruction of Jerusalem and his Second Coming. The church commemorates the first recitation of the Lord's Prayer (hence the current moniker, *Pater Noster,* Latin for "Our Father"). Polyglots can read the prayer in 78 languages (including Old Frisian) on the tiled walls. In the midst of the translations is the tomb of the Princesse de la Tour d'Auvergne, who worked here for 17 years (1857-74) and financed the excavations and renovations: she was determined to uncover the long-lost grotto where her favorite prayer was originally taught. *(Below the Chapel of Christ's ascension, under an orange sign reading "Carmelite Convent." Open: M-Sa 8:30-11:45am and 3-4:45pm.)*

TOMBS OF THE PROPHETS. This site is the supposed resting-place of the prophets Malachi and Ḥaggai. Archaeological evidence, however, suggests that the graves are far too recent—probably dating from the 4th century CE. The glass-enclosed home on the premises is the residence of the caretaker, who will show visitors around downstairs with a kerosene lamp if asked. *(With your back to the Seven Arches, turn right and go down the gray cement path to the left. Several meters down, a large green gate on the left leads to two cavernous tunnels. Open Su-F 8am-3pm.)*

To the left of the tombs is an easy-to-miss orange sign with rubbed-off black lettering marking "This Common Grave" of those who died defending the Jewish Quarter in 1948. Next to the Common Grave lies the **National Cemetery,** and farther down the path sprawls the immense **Jewish Graveyard,** the largest Jewish cemetery in the world. Take the stone staircase on the left for another small observation point and access to the Jewish graves.

SANCTUARY OF DOMINUS FLEVIT. This sanctuary was erected in 1955 to mark the spot where Jesus wept for Jerusalem (Luke 19:41), hence its Latin name ("The Lord Wept"). The chapel has a Byzantine mosaic and altar in an apse with a beautiful view of the Dome of the Rock. The glass shards of bottles cemented to the top of the walls protect the property of competing sects from trespassers. *(Downhill from the Tombs of the Prophets, on the right. Open Mar.-May 8am-5pm; June-Oct. 8am-6pm.)*

RUSSIAN CHURCH OF MARY MAGDALENE. Czar Alexander III built this church in 1885. Constructed in the lavish 17th-century Muscovite style, it is adorned with seven golden onion domes. The crypt houses the body of a Russian grand duchess, smuggled to Jerusalem via Beijing after her death in the Russian Revolution. Now a convent, the church claims a part of the Garden of Gethsemane. *(Past the Sanctuary of Dominus Flevit. ☎ 628 43 71. Ordinarily open Tu and Th 10am-noon.)*

CHURCH OF ALL NATIONS AND THE GARDEN OF GETHSEMANE. Built with contributions from many European countries, the Church of All Nations faces west toward the Old City. Among its highlights is a magnificent gold and red facade portraying Jesus bringing peace to all nations. Inside, mosaics and sculptures depict Jesus' last days, including the proverbial kiss of death, but the real highlight is the **Rock of the Agony,** where Jesus was so impassioned that he sweat blood (Luke 22:44). Although the site has been venerated since the 4th century, the present building, designed by Barluzzi, was built after World War I. The garden outside is where Jesus spent his last night in prayer and was betrayed by Judas (Mark 14:32-43). *(The church is on the left near the bottom of the main path; the entrance is on the side. Open daily Apr.-Oct. 8am-noon and 2:30-6pm; Nov.-Mar. 8am-noon and 2:30-5pm.)*

TOMB OF THE VIRGIN MARY AND GROTTO OF GETHSEMANE. The steep stairs down to Mary's tomb were built to prevent pagans from riding horses into the sacred space. To the right, the natural grotto is another candidate for the site of Jesus' betrayal and arrest. *(At the bottom of the main path, on the right. Open daily 8am-noon and 2:30-5:30pm. At the exit onto the main road are telephone booths and taxis. Damascus and St. Stephen's Gates are within walking distance. A taxi to the city center should cost NIS15.)*

WEST JERUSALEM

NEAR ZION SQ.

Zion Sq. (Kikkar Tzion) is the center of West Jerusalem and the epicenter of the pedestrian malls of Ben-Yehuda, Yoel Solomon, Naḥalat Shiva, and Rivlin St. Downhill on Ben-Yehuda St. and to the left is **King George St.,** a bustling extension of the city center. Three blocks farther downhill, the enormous and ornate **Great Synagogue of Jerusalem,** 58 King George St., is an inspiring architectural compromise between modernity and religion. (☎ 624 71 12. Open Su-Th 9am-1pm and F

9am-noon.) Services here on holidays and the first day of Jewish months feature an excellent men's choir meant to recall the Levites' choir in the ancient Temple. Across from Zion Sq. on the other side of Jaffa Rd., Ha-Rav Kook St. eventually crosses Ha-Nevi'im St. and turns into the quiet, stone-wall-lined Ethiopia St. At the end of Ethiopia St. on the right is the handsome **Ethiopian Church,** built between 1874 and 1901. Inscriptions in Ge'ez adorn the gate and doors; black-robed monks and nuns live in the surrounding compound and care for the distinctive, blue-domed church. (☎ 628 28 40. Open daily 9am-1pm and 2-6pm. Remove your shoes before entering.) Directly across from the entrance to the church, at #11, is the one-time home of the founder of the modern Hebrew language, **Eliezer Ben-Yehuda.**

MEA SHE'ARIM

Mea She'arim ("Hundredfold," an invocation of plenty), lies just north of Ethiopia St., on the other side of Ha-Nevi'im St. To get there from Zion Sq., take Jaffa Rd. and turn right onto Nathan Strauss St. (the continuation of King George St.); continue until it intersects with Ha-Nevi'im St. (Bank Ha-Poalim is on the corner). This intersection is known as Kikkar Shabbat (walk through on a Friday night around 11pm to find out why), the unofficial beginning of Mea She'arim.

 WARNING! Signs in the area caution, "Do not enter our neighborhood unless your dress and conduct conform to the standards described below," and then proceed to request that women wear at least knee-length skirts (not pants), elbow-length sleeves, and nothing tight-fitting. Men should wear below-the-knee pants. Visitors are also advised not to enter in groups. Be warned that extremists have been known to stone tourists whom they deem improperly dressed. Whether you're Jewish or not, take these warnings seriously to avoid offending local Ḥasidim and being asked to leave the area.

The neighborhood, one of Jerusalem's oldest, is among the few remaining Jewish *shtetl* communities like those that used to flourish in pre-Holocaust Eastern Europe. Several thousand Ultra-Orthodox Jews live here and in the neighboring **Geula** (Hebrew for "redemption"), preserving traditional habits, dress, customs, and beliefs with painstaking diligence. If your newfound grasp of Hebrew lets you down, it may be because you're hearing Yiddish, spoken by residents who consider Hebrew too holy for daily use. The neighborhood, just like the Orthodox suburbs to the north and northwest of the city, is largely conservative, but Mea She'arim's relatively few extremists receive a good deal of publicity for opinions and actions that do not necessarily reflect those of the entire community. The Neturei Karta ("City Keepers"), the most extreme sect of the Satmar Ḥasidim, oppose the Israeli state, arguing that Jewish law prohibits the legitimate existence of a Jewish country until the coming of the Messiah. While other Ultra-Orthodox Jews hold similar views, the Neturei Karta once went so far as to ask Yasser Arafat to accept them as a minority in the future Palestinian state.

Mea She'arim St. is probably the cheapest place in the world for Jewish books and religious items. Although the quality is not as high as in the Jewish Quarter of the Old City, the stores along Mea She'arim St. have affordable selections. The neighborhood also has some of the city's best **bakeries,** most of which are open all night on Thursdays, baking *ḥallah* and cake for Shabbat.

GIVAT RAM

ISRAELI SUPREME COURT. This building, completed in late 1992 by designers Karmi & Associates, combines Modern flair with themes from ancient Jerusalem's building traditions. This architectural masterpiece is also worth visiting for a glimpse of the justice system. Anyone may sit in on a trial—it's like Court TV, only live and in Hebrew. (☎ 675 96 12; fax 652 71 18; email marcia@supreme.court.gov.il. Open Su-Th 8:30am-2:30pm. English tour Su-Th noon; call for summer schedule. With advance notice, tours can accommodate most special needs, including touch tours for the blind.)

KNESSET. Discover why Israeli schoolteachers compare excessively rowdy pupils to members of the Knesset, Israel's Parliament. Passports are required for entrance as part of a detailed search. *(On Eliezer Kaplan St. directly across from the Israel Museum. From the central bus station or Jaffa Rd. take bus #9 or 24 and ask the driver where to get off. ☎ 675 33 33. Su and Th tours last 30min.; call to find out when the English tours begin and arrive at least 15min. early. Open sessions M and Tu 4pm, W 11am; call to make sure that the Knesset is in session.)*

OTHER SIGHTS. The **Wohl Rose Garden,** which forms a walking path between the Supreme Court and the Knesset, is a sublime picnic spot with beautifully manicured lawns and flowers. Take the path on the right when exiting the Supreme Court building, or climb up to it from anywhere on the main street. The **Ardon Window** in the **National Library,** one of the largest stained-glass windows in the world, depicts Jewish mystical symbols in rich, dark colors. *(Take bus #9, 24, or 28 from the city center. ☎ 658 50 27. Open in summer Su-Th 9am-7pm, F 9am-1pm. Free.)*

REHAVIA

South of Independence Park are some of Jerusalem's most elegant and affluent residential areas. Rehavia, the area trisected by Azza Rd. and Ramban St., was founded in the 1920s and became the refuge for the many German Jews fleeing Nazi persecution in the 30s. For years, it was famous as a German high-culture enclave, where Mozart grooved on the gramophone and libraries were lined with Goethe and Schiller. Today, the legacy lives on in the many International Style houses, designed in the best German Modernist tradition.

JASON'S TOMB. In the middle of Rehavia on Alfassi St. is Jason's Tomb, built around 100 BCE as the burial site of a wealthy Hasmonean-era Jewish family. Pottery found at the site indicates that three generations were buried there, while charcoal drawings on the plastered porch wall depict ships, suggesting that one of the deceased was involved in naval excursions. The pyramid topping the tomb is a reconstruction. *(Near 12 Alfassi St.; sign says "Rock Cut Tomb.")*

OTHER SIGHTS. Farther east past Azza Rd. is the **Prime Minister's official residence,** in the heavily guarded house at the corner of Balfour St. and Smolenskin St. Next door on Balfour St. is the **Schocken Library,** designed by renowned architect Erich Mendelssohn, who resided in Jerusalem in the late 1930s (he lived in the windmill on Ramban St. near Kikkar Tzarfat, now a ritzy shopping complex).

TALBIYYA AND QATAMUN

Farther south are the neighborhoods of **Talbiyya** (Komemiyut) and **Qatamun** (Gonen), still known by their pre-1948 Arabic names. The ornate villas, one of which was the home of renowned cultural theorist Edward Said, have become favorites of Hebrew University faculty and, more recently, well-to-do professionals. The official residence of the **Israeli President** is on Ha-Nassi (President) St., and the plush **Jerusalem Theater** is on the other side of the block, on the corner of Chopin St. and Marcus Rd.

On the other end of Jabotinsky St. from the President's House is **King David St.,** running north to the base of Shlomtzion Ha-Malka St. and Shlomo Ha-Melekh St. Just south of the intersection with Jabotinsky St. is the sprawling, green **Liberty Bell Park** (Gan Ha-Pa'amon). An amphitheater, basketball courts, climbable sculptures, and a Liberty Bell replica grace the lawns. On Saturday nights, the park hops with folk dancing festivities (take bus #14, 18, or 21 from the center). Three hundred meters up King David St. toward the city center, the **Three Arches YMCA,** built in 1933, has an imposing bell tower with fine views of the whole city. (☎ 569 26 92. NIS5.) Directly across the street, the historic **King David Hotel** retains an aura of old-world luxury, making it a favorite accommodation for international celebrities. The King David served as the British headquarters during the 1948 War of Independence and was bombed by Jewish underground forces.

YEMIN MOSHE

In the valley between King David St. and the Old City is the restored neighborhood of Yemin Moshe. It was here that Sir Moses Montefiore, a British Jew, first managed to convince a handful of residents from the Old City's overcrowded Jewish Quarter to spend occasional nights outside the city walls, thus founding West Jerusalem. To strengthen the settlers' confidence, Montefiore built **Mishkenot Sha'ananim** ("Tranquil Habitations"), a picturesque small compound with crenelated walls resembling those of the Old City. The original buildings now house an exclusive municipal guest house and a pricey French restaurant, and are at the bottom of the hill. Montefiore also erected his famous stone windmill, which now contains a tiny free **museum.** (Open Su-Th 9am-4pm and F 9am-1pm.) Yemin Moshe is crammed with artists' studios and galleries; a plaza with a fountain beneath the exclusive King David Apartments makes this a lovely spot to wander. The stepped street of Ḥutzot Ha-Yotzer leads up to Ḥativat Yerushalayim St.; at #16 is the studio of Motke Blum, whose subtle cityscapes brilliantly evoke Jerusalem in oil. The now-dry **Sultan's Pool** sits in the valley below. Named after Suleiman the Magnificent, the renovator of this Second Temple reservoir in the 16th century, the pool figures prominently in Palestinian novelist Jabra Ibrahim Jabra's *The Ship*. Today, the Sultan's Pool is most famous for its open-air concerts and annual **art fair** in July or early August (info ☎ 625 44 03).

GERMAN COLONY AND HAAS PROMENADE

The **German Colony,** a leafy neighborhood of somber European houses and spacious Arab villas, surrounds Emek Refa'im St., an upscale avenue with a lively cafe scene. Buses #4, 14, and 18 run here from the city center. To the southeast, the **Haas Promenade** is a hillside park that commands unbelievable views of the Old City and the Dead Sea. The dusk experience alone is worth the trip. On foot, walk south on Derekh Hevron, bear left onto Albeck St., and turn left onto Yanofsky St. Bus #8 runs from King George St. to the corner of Albeck St. and Yanofsky St.

NORTHERN OUTSKIRTS

TOMBS OF THE SANHEDRIN. In the heart of a park carpeted with pebbles and pine needles are the Tombs of the Sanhedrin. Composed of 70 esteemed male sages and leaders, the Sanhedrin was the ancient high court of the Jews; it ruled on legal matters and even reviewed Jesus' case. Separate burial areas were designated for the members. *(Take bus #2 from the city center to Ha-Sanhedrin St., off Yam Suf St. Open Su-F 9am-sunset. Free.)*

AMMUNITION HILL. Before the Six-Day War, this was Jordan's most fortified position in the city, from which it commanded much of northern Jerusalem. Taken by Israeli troops in a bloody battle, the hill now serves as a memorial to the Israeli soldiers who died in the Six-Day War. The architecturally striking museum, which details the 1967 battle, is housed in a reconstructed bunker. *(Buses #4, 9, 25, and 26 stop at the foot of the hill, in Ramat Eshkol, north of the Old City. ☎ 582 84 42. Open Su-Th 8am-6pm and F 8am-2pm; closes 1hr. earlier in winter. NIS10, students NIS8.)*

HEBREW UNIVERSITY OF JERUSALEM. After 1948, the Hebrew University of Jerusalem had to relocate from Mount Scopus (Har Ha-Tzofim), where it was founded in 1925, to this new campus in Givat Ram. From 1948 to 1967, Mount Scopus was a garrisoned Israeli enclave in Jordanian territory. Every week for 19 years, UN supplies were flown in to relieve the community; every week seven Israeli soldiers were let in, and seven were let out. After 1967, all but the natural and physical sciences departments moved back to the original campus. Massive reconstruction was funded largely by international donors, whose names emblazon the libraries, promenades, and pebbles that comprise modern Mount Scopus. Pick up a map from the Reception Center for an unguided stroll around Israel's top university and browse through the bookstore, library, computer labs, and botanical gardens. For a fabulous view of Jerusalem, head to the overlook point, outside

ISRAEL

the university gates along the south side of the campus. The **Hecht Synagogue** in the Humanities building overlooks the Old City and is reputed to be have the best view of Jerusalem in the entire city. Enter the synagogue via the Sherman Building. The university's gorgeous **amphitheater** faces the Palestinian Territories. *(Take bus #4a or 9 from the city center. Tours Su-Th 11am.)*

WESTERN OUTSKIRTS

CHAGALL WINDOWS. The synagogue at the Hadassah Medical Center (not to be confused with Hadassah Hospital on Mount Scopus) houses the magnificent Chagall Windows, Marc Chagall's stained-glass depictions of scenes from Genesis 49 and Deuteronomy 33. Chagall donated the windows to the hospital in 1962 and was sent an urgent cable when four of the windows were damaged in the 1967 War. Chagall replied, "You worry about the war, I'll worry about my windows." Two years later he installed replacements; three of the windows still contain bullet holes. *(From Jaffa Rd., take bus #27 or 19 to the end, about 45min. ☎ 677 62 71. Synagogue open Su-Th 8am-1:15pm and 2-3:45pm, F 8am-1pm. NIS10, students and seniors with ID NIS5. Free tours in English Su-Th every hr. 8:30am-12:30pm and 2:30pm, F every hr. 9:30-11:30am.)*

JERUSALEM FOREST AND EIN KEREM. The scenic Jerusalem Forest and the pastoral village of Ein Kerem, just west of Mount Herzl, are perfect for picnics and short hikes. Formerly an Arab village, tiny Ein Kerem (Fountain of Vines) is the traditionally recognized birthplace of **John the Baptist.** The tranquil streets of this thriving artists' colony are now lined with charming studios and craftshops. *(To get to the village, take city bus #17, west from the central bus station or Zion Sq. Every 20-30min.)*

The **Church of St. John,** with its soaring clocktower, marks the spot where John was born. The church displays several paintings, including the *Decapitation of St. John.* In the church's **Grotto of the Nativity** there is a lovely Byzantine mosaic of pheasants—the symbol of the Eucharist. Ask the guardian for a key. *(☎ 641 36 39. Open Apr.-Sept. Su-F 8am-6pm; Oct.-Mar. Su-F 8am-5pm. Free.)*

Across the valley, down Ma'ayan St. from St. John's gate, the **Church of the Visitation** recalls Mary's visit to Elizabeth and contains a rock behind which the infant St. John hid when the Romans came to kill babies. *(☎ 641 72 91. Open May-Sept. Su-F 8am-6pm; Oct.-Apr. Su-F 8am-5pm. Free.)* The newer Upper Chapel depicts the glorification of Mary. The pink tower belongs to the **Russian Monastery.** *(☎ 625 25 65 or 641 28 87; only Russian spoken. Visit by appointment only.)*

EAST JERUSALEM

ZEDEKIAH'S CAVE. Also known as King Solomon's Quarries, the cave extends far beneath the Muslim Quarter. According to tradition, stones from the quarry were used in the construction of the First Temple, but archaeological evidence suggests that the cave was used no earlier than the Second Temple period. *(Entrance is about halfway between Damascus Gate and Herod's Gate; exiting Damascus Gate, follow the wall to the right. Open Sa-Th 9am-4pm and F 9am-2pm. NIS10, students NIS8.)*

GARDEN TOMB. These skull-shaped rock formations, first noticed in 1860, have led some to believe that this quarry (and not the Church of the Holy Sepulchre) is **Golgotha** ("place of the skull"), the site of Christ's crucifixion. A nearby rock-cut tomb is that of Joseph of Arimathea, who placed Jesus' body in his own tomb after the crucifixion. *(A short distance up Nablus Rd., on the right when coming from Damascus Gate; follow the signs. ☎ 627 27 45; www.gardentomb.com. Open M-Sa 8:30am-noon and 2-5:30pm. All are invited to attend the English service Su 9am. Free, but donations encouraged.)*

ST. GEORGE'S CATHEDRAL. This cathedral, now sparkling after some months of restoration and renovation, is the Cathedral Church of the Anglican Episcopal Diocese of Jerusalem and the Middle East. The cathedral's namesake, the patron saint of England, is one of the many traces of British occupation that surround the sight. *(On the right, past the intersection and the gas stations along Nablus Rd. ☎ 628 32 61. Open daily 6:30am-6:30pm. Free. Also runs a beautiful guest house. Info ☎ 628 33 02.)*

ISRAEL

TOMBEAU DES ROIS (TOMB OF THE KINGS). Judean kings were thought to be buried here, but evidence shows that the tomb was in fact built in 45 CE by Mesopotamian Queen Helena for her family. The tombs are unlit; bring a flashlight. *(On Salah al-Din St. at the intersection with Nablus Rd. Open M-Sa 8am-1pm and 3-5pm. NIS3.)*

🏛 MUSEUMS

ISRAEL MUSEUM

The Israel Museum is the largest and most comprehensive museum in and about Israel. With extensive collections of antiquities, books, sculptures, ancient and modern art, the legendary Dead Sea Scrolls, and even a children's exhibit, the museum has nearly as many facets as the country itself. *(Take bus #9 or 17 from King George St. On foot, walk up King George, turn onto Ramban St., cross Hazaz St., and walk up Ruppin St. ☎ 670 88 11; fax 563 18 33; www.imj.org.il. Open Su-M and W-Th 10am-5pm, Tu 4-10pm, F 10am-2pm, and Sa 10am-4pm; English tours Su-M and W-F 11am, Tu 4:30pm. The Shrine of the Book is also open Tu 10am-10pm; English tours Su-M and W-Th 1:30pm, Tu 3pm, and F 12:45pm. Museum and Shrine NIS37, students NIS30, children 3-17 NIS20, family NIS108.)*

SHRINE OF THE BOOK. The display of the Dead Sea Scrolls is by far the museum's biggest attraction. Hidden for 2000 years in the Caves of **Qumran** near the Dead Sea (see **Qumran**, p. 399), the scrolls date from the 2nd century BCE to 70 CE and were written by the Essenes, an apocalyptic, monastic Jewish sect. The scrolls contain fragments of every biblical text except the Book of Esther, and are nearly identical to the modern texts, supporting claims for the dating of the Hebrew Bible. The building's white dome and black walls symbolize the struggle between the Sons of Light and Dark, an important theme to the Qumran sect, and were designed to resemble the covers of the pots in which the scrolls were hidden.

ARCHAEOLOGY AND ETHNOLOGY EXHIBITS. Rock and rust enthusiasts should go straight to the archaeology section, which has an extensive collection of tools and weapons recording 30,000 years of human habitation in the Fertile Crescent. Straight ahead from the bottom of the steps is the **ethnography** exhibit, tracing the important events of the Jewish life cycle. *(Archaeology tours in English M and Th 3pm; guided tours of the Judaica and ethnography galleries S and W 3pm.)*

ART COLLECTIONS. The museum boasts a fabulous collection of art, including the largest display of Israeli art in the world. There is a sizeable Impressionist and Post-Impressionist collection, and even a few period rooms (including a spectacular French Rococo *salon* donated by the Rothschilds). The **Weisbord Pavilion,** across from the ticket building, houses a few Rodin sculptures, early modern paintings, and rotating contemporary exhibitions. **Billy Rose Sculpture Garden** displays some incredible masterworks by Henry Moore, Auguste Rodin, and Pablo Picasso. Pick up a schedule of evening outdoor concerts at the museum, and try to visit on a Tuesday night, when the garden is illuminated.

YAD VA-SHEM

Meaning "A Memorial and a Name," Yad Va-Shem is the largest of Israel's Holocaust museums. An event as broad-sweeping and traumatic as the Holocaust cannot be memorialized by any single medium; the juxtaposition of Nazi records, victim testimony, and documentation of resistance creates a powerful and disturbing experience. It's best to start at the **Historical Museum,** which traces the origins of the Holocaust through photographs, documents, and relics. The exhibit ends with a simple, powerful memorial: symbolic tombs showing the number of Jews who were killed in each country, and a tiny shoe that belonged to one of the Holocaust's younger victims. The nearby **art museum** displays drawings and paintings created by Jews in the ghettos and concentration camps. By far the most haunting part of Yad Va-Shem is the stirring **Children's Memorial.** Mirrors are positioned to create the illusion of an infinite sea of candles while a recorded voice recites the names and ages of young victims. *(Don't plan to do too much right after a visit; the museum's several buildings deserve some time and take an emotional toll. To get to Yad Va-Shem, take bus #13, 16-18, 20-21, 23-24, 26-27, or 39 and get off at the huge, red arch just past Mount Herzl. Turn around and take a left on Ein Kerem St., then follow the signs down Ha-Zikaron St. for about 10min. Info ☎ 644 35 65 or 644 35 62; www.yad-vashem.org.il. Open Su-Th 9am-5pm, F 9am-2pm. Free. Guided tours in English available by appointment.)*

OTHER MUSEUMS

BIBLE LANDS MUSEUM. This museum records the ancient history of every geographic locale mentioned in the Bible. Ancient pottery, jewelry, seals, and figurines comprise the private collection of Dr. Elie Borowski, a Canadian antiquities collector. For an educational interlude, check out the interactive computer program on cylindrical stamps and seals. *(Across from the Israel Museum. Take bus #9 or 17 from King George St. ☎ 561 10 66; www.blmj.org. Open Su-Tu and Th 9:30am-5:30pm, W 9:30am-9:30pm, F 9:30am-2pm, Sa 11am-3pm; Nov.-Apr. W 1:30-9:30pm. English tour Su-F 10:15am, W 10:15am and 5:30pm, and Sa 11am. NIS28, students and children NIS15.)*

TICHO HOUSE. On display are watercolors and drawings by artist Anna Ticho, who lived here with her prominent oculist husband, Dr. Avraham Albert Ticho, who opened Jerusalem's first eye clinic in 1912. His collection of *menorahs* is also on display. The elegant building and well-groomed gardens are a relaxing city respite; the attached restaurant serves a classy all-you-can-eat wine, cheese and salad buffet on Tuesday nights for NIS65. *(9 Ha-Rav Kook St. About 2 blocks up the hill from Zion Sq. ☎ 624 50 68 or 624 41 86. A small library shows a videotape of Anna Ticho's life and work upon request. Open Su-Th 10am-5pm, Tu 10am-10pm and F 10am-2pm. Free.)*

WOLFSON MUSEUM. This museum houses a wonderful collection of Jewish religious and ceremonial objects. Note the texts painted on eggshells and the Samaritan Torah. The museum also has a room of detailed dioramas depicting scenes from Jewish history. *(On King George St. next door to the Great Synagogue, on the 3rd floor of the Heḥal Shlomo building. ☎ 624 79 08. Open Su-Th 9am-1pm. NIS13, students NIS10.)*

NEAR JERUSALEM

ABU GHOSH אבו גוש أبو غوش

Overlooking the Judean hills west of Jerusalem, the Arab village of Abu Ghosh is revered by Christians and Jews alike as an early site of the Ark of the Covenant, which King David later moved to Jerusalem (I Chronicles 13:5-8). In caravan days, the town was the last stop on the way to Jerusalem; its 18th-century namesake, Sheikh Abu Ghosh, required pilgrims to pay a toll here as they traveled to the Holy City. Historically, the Arabs of the village have had good relations with neighboring Jewish settlements and the State of Israel, even during the 1948 War.

Two churches grace the hills of Abu Ghosh. **Notre Dame de l'Arche d'Alliance** (Our Lady of the Ark of the Covenant), at the top of the hill (turn right across from the old police station), was built on the site of the Ark's ancient holding place. The current church was built in the 1920s on the ruins of a demolished Byzantine church; fragments of the original mosaics are integrated into the marble floor. (☎ 534 28 18. Open daily 8:30-11:30am and 2:30-6pm.)

In the beautiful garden below the sacred hill stands the magnificently preserved **Crusader Church of the Resurrection,** built in 1142 and acquired by the French government in 1873. Excavations beneath the church have uncovered remains dating back to Neolithic times; the crypt contains evidence of a Roman fortification. Today, ten monks and twelve sisters reside in the monastery and make their living from the **ceramics** hand-crafted in their small pottery studio. To reach the church, walk down the main road past the restaurants, turn right at Mahmoud Rashid Abu Ghosh St., and head for the minaret of the mosque next door. Buzz for entrance at the blue door to the right. Ask for Father Olivier, a popular monk who is known to give good advice and who has been featured in Israeli newspapers. (☎534 27 98 or 533 56 70. Open M-W and F-Sa 8:30-11am and 2:30-5:30pm. Free, but donations welcome. Regular morning mass M-Sa 11:30am, Vespers 6pm; Gregorian chant Su 10am, Vespers 5pm. Modest dress required.)

Abu Ghosh is usually a pretty quiet little village, but the excellent acoustics at both churches have attracted choirs and musicians from around the country. Twice a year, during the Jewish holidays of Sukkot (Oct. 2-9, 2001) and Shavuot (May 28, 2001), the **Abu Ghosh Vocal Music Festival** fills the town with melodious sounds and multitudes of people. *(Tickets and information ☎(03) 604 47 25 or (02) 624 08 96; during the festival (02) 534 00 66; email agfestiv@inter.net.il.)*

To get to Abu Ghosh, take Egged bus #185 or 186 (45min.; every 30min. Su-Th 6:10am-10:15pm, F 6:10am-4:45pm; NIS8.30) from the central bus station and get out at the crest of the road, just past the restaurants. *Sherut* traveling between Jerusalem and Tel Aviv will stop at the turnoff, two kilometers downhill from Abu Ghosh, for roughly the same price.

TEL AVIV-JAFFA תל אביב–יפו ☎03

Proudly secular and downright sexy, Tel Aviv pulses with cutting-edge energy. Not surprisingly, given its never-ending quest to stay current, Tel Aviv is a very political city. Despite the effort to make Jerusalem the recognized capital, most countries keep their foreign embassies here. For a brief period during the Gulf Crisis in the winter of 1991, Tel Aviv became a target for Saddam Hussein's SCUD missiles. As modern and international as the city is, CNN videos of gas masks being distributed to children demonstrated the unique tension that exists here. It was also here in November 1995 that Yigal Amir, a Jewish student, fired the bullet that killed Prime Minister Yitzhak Rabin (see **Assassination of Rabin,** p. 271). The Middle East peace process has taken its toll since then; in the last few years, Hamas bombings have claimed a number of lives in the city. However, political developments in the peace process leave residents hopeful that the recent calm will remain the norm.

Tel Aviv sprouted from Jaffa (*Yafo,* or "beautiful," in Hebrew; *Yafa* in Arabic), its neighboring city, at the end of the 19th century. Jewish settlers, unhappy with the crowded and dilapidated condition of Jaffa and its high Arab population, founded the first two exclusively Jewish neighborhoods in 1887 and 1891. In 1909, the Jewish population of Jaffa parcelled out another northern area, naming it Atuzat Bayit (Housing Property). One year later, the suburb was renamed Tel Aviv (Spring Hill) after the town Theodore Herzl had envisioned in his turn-of-the-century utopian novel, **Altneuland** (Old-New-Land; see **Zionism,** p. 268). Appealing to bourgeois Jewish immigrants from Eastern Europe, the new town quickly developed in the 1920s and 1930s and soon became the largest Jewish town in Palestine.

HIGHLIGHTS OF TEL AVIV-JAFFA

Chat with the architect-inhabitant of the Surrealist **Hermit's House** (p. 335) before strolling down to Herzliya's beautiful shoreline for a quiet afternoon of sun.

Haggle your head off at the **Shuk Ha-Pishpeshim** (p. 334) in old Jaffa.

Get up close and personal with Tel Aviv chic on **Sheinken St.** (p. 327), and disco until dawn in the myriad clubs and pubs.

⬛ GETTING THERE

Flights: Ben-Gurion Airport (English recorded info ☎972 33 44), 22km southeast of Tel Aviv in Lod. Egged bus #475 to the airport leaves from the 6th floor of the New Central Bus Station (every 30min. Su-Th 5:20am-11:40pm, F 5:20am-4:50pm, Sa 8:30-11:30pm; NIS10). Shuttle bus #222 makes a round-trip between the airport and Tel Aviv, passing most of the major hostels (every hr. Su-Th 4am-midnight, F 4am-7pm, Sa

ISRAEL

noon-midnight; NIS16; last shuttle departs from airport Sa-Th 11pm). Taxis from the airport to Tel Aviv run at a fixed tariff (about NIS70 during the day, NIS88 at night or on Shabbat; each piece of luggage NIS2).

Trains: Central Train Station (☎577 40 00), on Arlozorov St., across from Namir Rd. Take bus #10 or 18 from the city center or bus #27 from the New Central Bus Station. Open Su-F 6am-11pm. A/C trains leave every 30min. to: **Acre** (NS29); **Ashdod** (every 2hr., NIS13) via **Be'ersheva** (NIS23.50); **Hadera** (NIS16); **Haifa** (NIS21); and **Nahariya** (NIS39.50) via **Netanya** (NIS11). 10% discount with ISIC on fares NIS20.50 and above. **Lockers** NIS5-10.

Intercity Buses: Operated by **Egged** (☎694 88 88). 10% discount with ISIC on fares NIS20.50 and above.

New Central Bus Station has departures on the 6th floor to: **Be'er Sheva** (#370; every 20min. Su-Th 6am-11pm, F 6am-4:40pm, Sa 8:30-11pm; NIS20.50); **Hadera** (#852 or 872; 1hr.; every 30min. Su-Th 7am-11:30pm, F 8am-4:30pm, Sa 8:30pm-midnight; NIS17); **Haifa** #900 direct (1¼hr.; every 25min. Su-Th 7:30am-8:40pm, F 7:30am-4:35pm, Sa 8:30-10pm; NIS20.50) or late-night #901 express (1¼hr.; every 20min. Su-Th 9:15-11pm; NIS20.50); **Jerusalem** (#405; 1 hr.; every 15min. Su-Th 5:40am-midnight, F 6am-5:30pm, Sa 8:30pm-midnight; NIS18); **Netanya** (#605; 45 min.; every 25min. Su-Th 8am-9:15pm, F 8am-4:30pm, Sa 8:30am-10pm; NIS13); and **Zikhron Ya'akov** (#872; 2hr.; every 30min. Su-Th 7am-11:30pm, F 8am-4:30pm, Sa 8:30pm-midnight; NIS22.50).

Arlozorov terminal, on Arlozorov St., across from Namir Rd. To: **Be'er Sheva** (#380; 1¾ hr.; every 15min. Su-Th 6am-8:30pm, F 6am-4:30pm, Sa 8:30-10:30pm; NIS20.50); **Haifa** (#910; 1¼hr.; every 15min. Su-Th 7:45am-8:45pm, F 7:45am-4:30pm, Sa 8:30-10pm; NIS20.50); and **Jerusalem** (#480; 50min.; every 15min. Su-Th 6am-10pm, F 6am-4:30pm, Sa 8:30pm-midnight; NIS18).

Ferries: Caspi, 1 Ben-Yehuda St. (☎517 57 49), in the Migdalor Bldg. 20% discount for passengers under 24 and students under 30. Port tax NIS100/US$22. Fares drop for round-trip tickets. To: **Piraeus** (3 nights; Su and Th 8pm, NIS424/US$106; in winter Th 7pm, NIS384/US$96) via **Cyprus** (1 night; NIS232/US$58; in winter NIS192/US$48) and **Rhodes** (2 nights; NIS404/US$101; in winter NIS364/US$91).

Intercity sheruts: Across from the New Central bus station exit (platform 410), to your left (with your back to the bus station). *Sheruts* leave whenever most of the 10 seats fill up. To: **Haifa** (1hr., NIS22); **Jerusalem** (45min., NIS18); **Nazareth** (1hr., NIS25); and **Netanya** (20min., NIS10).

Car Rental: Gindy Ltd. Rent-a-Car, 132 Ha-Yarkon St. (☎527 83 44). Manual NIS200/US$50 per day; automatic NIS240/$60 per day. 200km per day limit but weekly rental discounts with unlimited mileage available. 21+; drivers under 24 have $1000 deductible in case of accident. **Avis,** 113 Ha-Yarkon St. (☎527 17 52). Manual NIS184/US$46 per day; automatic starts at NIS200/US$50 per day. 23+, 26+ for larger automatics. 250km per day limit.

▐ GETTING AROUND

Tel Aviv is mostly manageable by foot. On a hot August afternoon, though, a NIS4.70 bus ride may seem like the deal of the century. Buses in Tel Aviv are frequent, air-conditioned, and comfortable; definitely take them to sights north of the Yarkon, in the Ha-Tikva area, in the Tel Aviv University area, or in Jaffa, which are all beyond easy walking distance from the city center.

The **New Central Bus Station,** 108 Levinsky St. (☎638 40 40) can be scary and painful the first time you experience it, but the basics are easy enough. Most local buses (Dan) and local and intercity *sheruts* leave from the 4th floor; exit at platform #416 for local buses and platform #410 for *sheruts*. A few local buses with destinations outside Tel Aviv (Ramat Gan, Ramat Aviv) leave from the 1st floor. Intercity buses (Egged) leave from the 6th floor; the 4th and 6th floors have information kiosks. **Baggage check** rooms are on the 6th floor, down a small flight of stairs near the information kiosk. (NIS10 per item per day. Open Su-Th 7am-7pm and F and holiday eves 7am-3pm.)

Tel Aviv

ACCOMMODATIONS

Tel Aviv Youth Hostel (HI), 1

See Central Tel Aviv map
for further accommodations

RAMAT AVIV

Tel-Aviv University
(Beit Hatfusot)

Levi Eshkol

Namir (Haifa) Rd.

Einstein

Klausner

Reading

Brodetzky

Levanon (University)

Ayalon Hwy.

TO HERZLIYA, HAIFA

Sderot Rokakh

Ha-Yarkon Park

Eretz Yisrael
Museum

Sderot Rokakh

Bnei Dan

SHIKUN BAVLI

Yirmiyahu

Yehuda Ha-Macabi

Ha-Halakha

Bialik

Derekh Aba Hilel

Nordau

Pinkas

Weizmann

Namir

RAMAT-GAN

Sheraton
Beach

Basel

Egypt

Remez

KIKKAR
HA-MEDINA

Jordan

Hilton
Beach

Jabotinsky

Ibn Gvirol

Central
Train
Station

Jabotinsky Rd.

Ben Yehuda

Dizengoff

Arlozorov

Arlozorov

Arvey Nahal

Ayalon Hwy.

N

KIKKAR
ATARIM

SEE CENTRAL TEL AVIV MAP

Ben-Gurion

City
Hall

Bloch

Weizmann

David
Ha-Malekh

GIV'ATAYIM

Ha-Yarkon

Shelomo Ha-Melekh

KIKKAR
YITZHAK
RABIN

Australia

TO
ZOOLOGICAL
CENTER
(1.5km)

Gordon

Tel Aviv
Museum
of Art

Ha-Shalom
Station

Frischmann

KIKKAR
DIZENGOFF

Ibn Gvirol

Sha'ul Ha-Melekh

Ha-Shalom

Herbert Samuel Promenade

GTIO

Bograshov

Dizengoff

Azrieli
Center

Trumpeldor

Dizengoff
Center

Ben Zion

Kaplan

Moshe Dayan

Opera
Tower

Allenby

King George

Ha-âashmona'im

Carlebach Rd.

**KEREM
HA-TEMANIM**

Ben Yehuda

KIKKAR
MAGEN
DAVID

Sheinkin

Sderot Rothschild

Ha-Masger

Petah Tikva

**YAD
ELIYAHU**

**SHUK
HA-CARMEL**

Allenby

Nahlat Binyamin

Petah Tikva Rd.

Ahad Ha'am

Canada

Shalom
Tower

Mikve Yisrael

Old Central
Bus Station

Yad Eliyahu
Stadium

LaGuardia

**NEVE
TZEDEK**

Shomron

KIKKAR
HA-MOSHAVOT

Hedzl

Levinsky

Ha-Hagana

Suzanne
Delal
Center

Ha-Aliyah

New Central
Bus Station

Salameh Rd.

**HA-TIKVA
MARKET**

HA-TIKVA

Kaufman

Ha-Mered

Ha-Karmel

Abarbanel

FLORENTIN

Ayalon River

Ha-Tikva St.

Lehi

SEE JAFFA MAP

**JAFFA
(YAFO)**

Eilat Rd.

Salameh Rd.

Kibbutz Galuyot Rd.

Mifratz Shlomo St.

Yefet

Sderot Yerushalayim

Jaffa
Clocktower

TO
BEN-GURION
AIRPORT,
JERUSALEM

Yehuda Ha-Yamit

0   400 yards

0   400 meters

ISRAEL

Buses within Tel Aviv are operated by **Dan,** 39 Sha'ul Ha-Melekh. (☎639 33 33 or 639 44 44. Buses run Su-Th 5:30am-midnight, F 5am-5pm, and Sa 8:15pm-12:30am; do not run on Shabbat and some stop earlier. NIS4.70.) For extended stays, consider buying Dan's **monthly bus pass** (NIS176). Unlike intercity buses, local buses travel both ways, so you must be conscious of the direction. Fortunately, bus stops have clear English signs with a green marker pointing to the current stop. Decide whether you need to follow the blue or red directional path and stand on the side of the street where the appropriately colored arrow matches the flow of traffic.

SEVEN MOST FREQUENTED AND IMPORTANT ROUTES

4: From the New Central Bus Station (4th floor), runs parallel to the coastline up Allenby and Ben-Yehuda St. and back. Every 5min.

5: From the New Central Bus Station (4th floor), runs up Rothschild Blvd. and Dizengoff St. to Dizengoff Ctr., then turns right to run down the lengths of Nordau and Yehuda Ha-Maccabee before turning around. Every 5min.

10: Runs from train station along Arlozorov St., turns left to go down the coast along Ben-Yehuda St., Herbert Samuel St., and Kaufman St. to Jaffa. Weaves back up through the Florentin area along Herzl St. to Rothschild Blvd. before turning back. Every 15min.

18: Runs from the train station along Sha'ul Ha-Melekh through Dizengoff Sq. to Ben-Yehuda and then Allenby before heading down to Florentin along Ha-Aliya and Salame Rds. and turns around after reaching Bat Gam. Every 5-10min

25: Runs from Tel Aviv University down Namir Rd. then Yehuda Ha-Maccabee to Ibn Gvirol. After turning right and going for a few blocks on Arlozorov, turns left to follow Shlomo Ha-Melekh and King George down to Shuk Ha-Carmel. Until 9:30pm, continues to Bat Yam along the coast, but otherwise turns around at the *shuk.* Every 15 min.

27: From the New Central Bus Station (1st floor), runs along Petah Tikva Rd. and to Haifa Rd., Central Train Station, then along Levanon St. to Tel Aviv University, the kenyon (shopping mall) in Ramat Gan, and back. Every 10-15min.

46: From the New Central Bus Station (1st floor) to Jaffa and back along Yefet St. Every 8-10min., every 15min. at night.

Sherut taxis run along the routes of buses #4 and 5, and are numbered accordingly. At NIS4.50, they're cheaper than the bus and will stop anywhere along the route. Call a taxi anytime (☎524 90 90 or 527 19 99). **Rent-A-Scooter,** 136 Ha-Yarkon St. (☎681 57 78), provides an alternative to public transportation (NIS100/US$25 per day; 10% discounts for a week, 20% for two weeks; 18+).

❖ ORIENTATION

In the center of Israel's Mediterranean coastline, Tel Aviv is 63km northwest of Jerusalem and 95km south of Haifa. The two main points of entry into Tel Aviv are **Ben-Gurion Airport** and the **New Central Bus Station.** Frequent bus and *sherut* (minibus) service from the airport is supplemented by the vans that warring hostels send to lure potential customers.

Tel Aviv is rather easy to navigate once you learn the few main roads that run parallel to the coastline and a few big intersections. The **tayelet** (promenade) extends from Jaffa up to Gordon beach (about two-thirds of the way to the port). Parallel and one block inland is **Ha-Yarkon St. Ben-Yehuda St.** is another block inland. All three streets are lined with hotels, cafes, and restaurants—prices generally go down as you go farther from the shore. **Dizengoff St.,** home to some of Tel Aviv's trendy cafes and bars, runs parallel to Ben-Yehuda before swerving away from the coast toward **Kikkar Dizengoff,** an elevated plaza surrounded by shops and a cineplex. Dizengoff St. then continues to intersect the next big coastal-parallel street, **Ibn Gvirol St.,** with its arcades and cafes. On Ibn Gvirol, a few blocks above this intersection is **Kikkar Yitzhak Rabin,** in front of City Hall.

The third main square is **Kikkar Bath November,** where Ben-Yehuda intersects **Allenby St.** Most hostels are on or near Ben-Yehuda or Allenby. Farther down, Allenby intersects **King George St.** and **Sheinkin St.** at **Kikkar Magen David.** This is also the starting point of **Shuk Ha-Carmel** and the **midrahov** (pedestrian mall) of **Nahalat Binyamin.** Between the *shuk* and the shore are the winding alleyways of

Central Tel Aviv

ACCOMMODATIONS

Dizengoff Square Hostel, 1
Gordon Hostel, 2
Gordon Inn Guest House, 3
Ha-Yarkon 48 Hostel, 4

KIKKAR ATARIM
Ben-Gurion House
Ben-Gurion
■ ISSTA

Marina

Gordon Beach

Frishman Beach

Trumpeldor Beach

Yerushalayim Beach | Ge'ula Beach

Marina

Gordon

Ha-Yarkon
Mapu
Frishman

Supersol

France

United States

Ben Yehuda

Herbert Samuel

Ha-Tayalet (Promenade)

Frug
Dizengoff
Reines
King Solomon (Shlomo Ha-Meleh)

TO KIKKAR YITZHAK RABIN

Cameri Theatre & Mann Auditorium

Mendele Moher Sfarim
Ben-Ami
KIKKAR DIZENGOFF
Superpharm

Ha-Nevi'im

Shalom Aleichem
Hovevei Tsiyon
Bograshov

Dizengoff Center

South Africa

Shderot Ben Tsiyon

Trumpeldor

Idelson

Pinsker

Gan Me'eir

Etzel Irgun Tzva'I Le'umi Museum

Ha-Hashmona'im

United Kingdom & New Zealand

Migdalor Building
KIKKAR BETH NOVEMBER

Bialik Museum
Rashi

Bialik

King George (Ha-Melekh George)

Opera Tower   Allenby

Rubin Museum

Ge'ula

Ha-Rav Kook

Herbert Samuel

Ha-Yarkon

Ha-Kovshim

KIKKAR MAGEN DAVID

Najara

Shuk Ha-Carmel

Sheinkin

Allenby

Balfour

SHUK HA-CARMEL

YEMENITE QUARTER

Daniel

Rambam

Shefer

Maze

Yavne

Bet Ha-sho'eva

Nahalat Binyamin

Karmelit Bus Terminal

Dolphinarium

Great Synagogue

Yitzhak Elhanan

Migdal Shalom

Hagana Museum

Chlore Park

Ahad Ha-am

0   200 yards
0   200 meters

N

ISRAEL

Kerem Ha-Temanim (the Yemenite Quarter). Below the *shuk* lies the neighborhood of **Neve Tzedek,** which has profited from a recent infusion of yuppies. Allenby continues most of the way to the bus station. Below the bus station, framed by **Herzl St., Ha-Aliya St., and Salame St.,** is the bohemian **Florentin** neighborhood.

Still another parallel street, much farther from the coast, is **Namir Rd.,** a major thoroughfare that leads to Tel Aviv's northern exit; the **train station,** which has service to all major cities, is at the intersection of Namir Rd. and **Arlozorov St. Jaffa** and its waterfront lie farther south, outside the downtown area. The entrance to **Old Jaffa,** marked by a famous **clocktower,** lies at the intersection of **Eilat St.** and **Goldman St.**

◪ PRACTICAL INFORMATION

TOURIST AND FINANCIAL SERVICES

Tourist Information Office: (☎639 56 60; fax 639 56 59), in the New Central Bus Station, 6th floor, near platform 630. From the city center, take bus #4 or 5. Provides hotel and tour reservations and maps of Tel Aviv and other Israeli cities. Open Su-Th 9am-5pm, F 9am-1pm. A kiosk in the City Hall Lobby (☎521 85 00) gives out maps and information about Tel Aviv only. Open Su-Th 9am-2pm.

Tours: SPNI, 19 Ha-Sharon St. (☎638 86 74), near the intersection with Petaḥ Tikva Rd. Their English-speaking guides lead the best 1-12 day tours, year-round. Day tours NIS200/US$50-NIS300/US$75. Open Su-Th 8am-4:30pm, F 8-11am. **United Tours,** 113 Ha-Yarkon St. (☎522 20 08), offers tours around the country in English, Hebrew, French, and German. Day tours NIS232-296/US$58-74; 10% student discount with ISIC if booked directly from their office.

Budget Travel: ISSTA, 128 Ben-Yehuda St. (☎521 05 55), at Ben-Gurion St. For ISICs, bring a photograph, current student ID, and NIS40; Youth Hostel cards NIS35. Open Su-Th 9am-noon and 3-7pm and F 9am-noon. **Mona Tours,** 25 Bogorochov St. (☎621 14 33), specializes in student and charter rates. Must be under 28 to book flights; proof of age required. Open Su-Th 9am-6pm and F 9am-1pm. Both take credit cards.

Embassies and Consulates: Australia, 37 Sha'ul Ha-Melekh Blvd., Europe House, 4th fl. (☎695 04 51). Open M-Th 8am-noon. **Canada,** 3 Nirim St. (☎636 33 00), next to basketball stadium in Yad Eliyahu. Open for visas M-Th 8am-4:30pm and F 8-1:30pm. **South Africa,** Top Tower, Dizengoff Ctr., 16th fl. (☎525 25 66). Enter through gate #3. Open M-F 9-11am and W 9-11am and 2-3pm. **UK** (also serves travelers from **New Zealand**), 1 Ben-Yehuda St., Migdalor Bldg., 6th fl. (☎510 01 66 for passports and visas). Open M-Th 1:30-3:30pm and F noon-1pm. **US,** 71 Ha-Yarkon St. (☎519 75 75), just a few blocks north of Allenby St., on the left side. Open for passports M, W 8:30-11am and 2-3:30pm; Tu, Th 8:30-11am; F 8:30am-12:30pm; for visas M-F 7:30am-2:30pm. **Egypt,** 54 Basel St. (☎546 51 51 or 546 51 52), just off Ibn Gvirol. For a visa, bring a passport, photograph, and NIS75 (US citizens NIS50)—be sure to specify planned visits beyond the Sinai, or they'll automatically issue a "Sinai Only" visa. Open Sa-Th 9-11am. **Jordan,** 14 Aba Hillel (☎751 77 22), in Ramat Gan. Prearranged visas (NIS30) are required for crossing to Jordan via Allenby Bridge (see p. 425). Open Su-Th 9:30am-12:30pm.

Currency Exchange: Any post office will change money without commission. **Change Point,** 106 Ha-Yarkon St. (☎524 55 05; open Su-Th 9am-6pm, F 8:30am-1pm), and **Change Spot,** 140 Dizengoff St. (☎524 33 93; open Su-Th 9am-7pm and F 9am-2pm), also offer no-commission exchange. Banks usually exchange currency M-Th 8:30am-2pm and F 8:30am-noon for US$6 or 5% commission.

Banks: Most banks are open Su, Tu, Th 8:30am-12:30pm and 4-5:30pm; M, W, F, and holiday eves 8:30am-noon. Main bank offices: **Bank Ha-Poalim,** 104 Ha-Yarkon St. (☎520 06 12); **Israel Discount,** 16 Mapu St. (☎520 32 12); and **Bank Leumi,** 130 Ben-Yehuda St. (☎520 37 37). Branches throughout the city and suburbs.

LOCAL SERVICES

Shopping Hours: In general, 8:30am-7pm, but many stores stay open until 10pm, especially in malls. Most are open late on Th night and almost all close F by 2pm.

Camping Supplies: LaMetayel (☎528 68 94), Dizengoff Center, on the 3rd floor, near the Lev Cinema. Full range of equipment and information. Open Su-Th 10am-8:30pm, F 10am-2pm. **Steve's Packs** (☎525 99 20), next door, has a narrower selection, but may be more affordable. Open Su-Th 9:30am-8:45pm, F 9:30am-3pm, and Sa 7-10:45pm.

Ticket Agencies: Rococo, 93 Dizengoff St. (☎527 66 77). Open Su-Th 9am-7pm and F 9am-2pm. **Hadran,** 90 Ibn Gvirol St. (☎527 97 97), north of Kikkar Yitzhak Rabin. **Castel,** 153 Ibn Gvirol St. (☎604 76 78). **Le'an,** 101 Dizengoff St. (☎524 73 73). All sell tickets for concerts, plays, sporting events, and other performances. Discount student tickets sometimes available. V, MC; no checks.

EMERGENCY AND COMMUNICATIONS

24hr. Crisis Lines: Rape Crisis (☎517 61 76 for women, 517 91 79 for men). **Alcoholics Anonymous** (☎578 66 63). **Drug Counseling** (☎688 64 64). All speak English.

Pharmacy: Superpharm (☎620 37 98 or 620 09 75), on the bottom floor of Dizengoff Center. Open Su-Th 9:30am-10pm, F 9am-3:30pm, and Sa 6:30-11pm. Another location, in the London Minister building, at the intersection of Ibn Gvirol and Sha'ul Ha-Melekh St. Open 24hr. **Nayanpharm,** 75 Ben-Yehuda St. (☎522 91 21) next to the Supersol. Open Su-Th 9am-11pm, F 9am-3pm, and Sa 7:30-10:30pm.

Hospitals: Ichilov Hospital, 6 Weizmann St. (☎697 44 44). **Assuta,** 58-60 Jabotinsky St. (☎520 15 15).

Telephones: Solan Communications, 13 Frischmann St. (☎522 94 24; fax 522 94 49). Private booths for international calls (NIS7 per min). Telecards, international calling cards, fax services. Open Su-Th 10am-9pm and F 8am-3pm. **RSM Communications,** 80 Ha-Yarkon St. (☎516 83 66; fax 516 81 26; email fones@rentafone.co.il) Cellular phone rentals with voice mail NIS4/US$1 per day; local calls NIS2 per min.; international calls NIS5 per min. Open Su-Th 9am-5:30pm and F 9am-2pm.

Internet Access: Private Link, 78 Ben-Yehuda St. (☎529 98 89). Time purchased can be used over the course of one month: NIS18 per hr., NIS85 for 5hr. Open 24hr. MasloolTravelers' Equipment and Information Center, 47 Bogroshov St. (☎620 35 08). NIS8 for 30min. Open Su-Th 9am-10pm, F 9am-4pm, and Sa 7:30pm-10:30pm.

Post Office: 7 Mikveh Yisrael St. (☎564 36 51), 2 blocks east of the south end of Allenby St. **Poste Restante, fax, telegram, and telex.** Open Su-Th 8am-6pm and F 8am-noon. Other branches throughout the city.

⌂ ACCOMMODATIONS

Most hostels cluster on Ben-Yehuda and Ha-Yarkon St., with some just off Allenby Rd. or Dizengoff St. Bus #222 makes a round trip between the airport and Tel Aviv and passes most hostels. When choosing, keep in mind that drunken revelry and honking horns downtown may continue through the wee hours. Also, consider the hostels in Jaffa (see p. 332). Hostels fill up quickly in the summer, especially the private rooms, so make reservations if possible. Almost all have 24-hour reception, kitchen, safe and storage, and Internet access. A huge influx of long-term travelers and day-laborers gives a lived-in feel to some places; daily work can often be found through the hostel managers. Sleeping on the beach is illegal; theft and sexual assault are not uncommon, and the zamboni-like machines that sweep the beaches every night for bombs could crush a traveler or at least give a rude awakening.

▨ **Ha-Yarkon 48 Hostel,** 48 Ha-Yarkon St. (☎516 89 89; fax 510 31 13; email info@hayarkon48.com; www.hayarkon48.com). Take bus #4 or 16 from the central bus station. The bright rooms and showers win popularity contests, but everyone spends their time in the TV lounge playing pool for free, drinking beer in reception, or on the rooftop bar. Small breakfast included. Key deposit NIS20. Check-out 10:30am. 6-bed dorms NIS42/US$10.50, NIS120/US$30 for 3 nights, NIS142/US$38 for 4 nights, NIS252/US$63 for 7 nights. Private rooms NIS176/US$44, with fan and bath NIS208/US$52, with A/C and bath NIS228/US$57. Rooftop mattress NIS35/US$8.75 in summer if all beds are taken.

Gordon Hostel, 2 Gordon St. (☎522 98 70; fax 523 74 19; email sleepin@inter.net.il), on the corner of Ha-Yarkon St. Take bus #4 or 5 from the central bus station, and get off at Gordon St. Though the hostel is as close to the beach as you can get without getting sand in your sheets, most of the clientele sunsoaks on the rooftop lounge. Wash and dry NIS14. Check-out 10:30am. Lockout 11am-2pm. Dorms (coed or female-only) NIS36/US$9, NIS224/US$57 per week. Rooftop mattress NIS27/US$6.75. Students and repeat visitors receive 10% discount.

Gordon Inn Guest House, 17 Gordon St. (☎523 82 39; fax 523 74 19; email sleepin@inter.net.il, www.psl.co.il/gordon-inn), just off Ben-Yehuda St. From the central bus station take bus #4 to Ben-Yehuda and Gordon St. More polished and proper than most in the price range, the Guest House resides conveniently between Dizengoff Center and the beach. Breakfast included. Max stay 2 weeks, negotiable. Check-in 2pm. Check-out 11am. All rooms have A/C, some have balconies. Rooms in back are quieter. 7-8 bed dorms (coed) NIS64/US$16; singles NIS184/US$46, with bath NIS228/US$57; doubles NIS236/US$59, with bath NIS284/US$71; triples NIS288/US$72, with bath NIS340/US$85; quads NIS340/US$85, with bath NIS396/US$99. Prices 10-15% lower Nov.-June, except holidays.

Dizengoff Square Hostel, 13 Ben-Ami St. (☎522 51 84; fax 522 51 81; email dizengof@trendline.co.il; www.dizengoff-hostel.co.il), off Dizengoff Sq., across from the Chen cinema. Take bus #5 from the central bus station to Dizengoff Sq. Colorful paint, plaster sculptures in the TV/pool table room, and a breezy rooftop terrace keep the oldest hostel in Tel Aviv fresh and funky. Small breakfast included. Laundry NIS6. Check-out 10:30am. Lockout 10:30am-2:30pm. 4-8 bed dorms (coed and single sex) NIS38/US$9.50, NIS232/US$58 per week, with A/C NIS46/US$11.50. Private rooms NIS188/US$47; with A/C, bath, TV, and fridge NIS216/US$54.

Tel Aviv Youth Hostel/Guest House (HI), 36 B'nei Dan St. (☎544 17 48; fax 544 10 30, email telaviv@iyha.org.il), near Ibn Gvirol St. Take bus #5, 24, or 25 to the Weizmann St. and Yehuda Ha-Macabbe intersection and walk up one block to B'nei Dan. This spotless and shiny hostel has a large breakfast included. Check-out 10am. All rooms have A/C and private rooms have bath. 4-bed dorm NIS70/US$17.50, with bath NIS88/US$22; singles NIS148/US$38; doubles NIS224/US$56; triples NIS288/US$72. NIS6 surcharge for nonmembers. Discounts for longer stays.

No. 1 Hostel, 84 Ben-Yehuda St., 4th floor (☎523 78 07, email sleepin@internet.net.il). One block to your left as you face the sea from Gordon Inn; follow the same directions. There's a time to party and a time to relax, or so claims this middle sibling in the Gordon family. The highly social atmosphere is tempered by a midnight quiet rule. Sunny reception lounge has cable TV, pool table, and an arcade game. Breakfast included. Laundry NIS14. Check-in 2pm. Check-out 10:30am. Rooms have showers and fans. Dorms NIS39/US$10, NIS238/US$60 per week; singles NIS140/US$35; doubles NIS160/US$40; quads NIS160/US$140. Rooftop mattress in summer NIS31/US$8.

Home Hostel, 20 al-Sheikh St. (☎517 67 36). Take bus #4 from the central bus station along Allenby St. until Bialik St.; go behind Allenby 56 and turn right. As cheap as it gets, and, in terms of rooms and facilities, you get what you pay for. But, the family-like atmosphere, meals on Saturday, and a bed on your birthday are all free. Saintly owner can get discounts at local bars and clubs and find jobs for clientele. Breakfast included. Kitchen available. Dorms (coed and female-only) NIS30/US$8, students NIS27/US$7.

◪ FOOD

Come mealtime, Tel Aviv rises above and beyond the call of duty. Restaurants range from Tex-Mex to Southeast Asian, from falafel and hummus to French *haute-cuisine*, but after a brain-melting day at the beach, fast food and frozen yogurt may sound just as good. For quick, cheap belly-fillers, head for the self-service eateries on Ben-Yehuda St. (sandwich with chips or stuff-your-own falafel under NIS12). The eateries near Shuk Ha-Carmel and along Bezalel St. off Allenby and King George St. stay open the latest (1:30am or later).

Kerem Ha-Temanim (the Yemenite Quarter), south of Allenby St. between Ge'ula and Shuk Ha-Carmel, boasts cheap, spicy fried-dough, often stuffed with meat (NIS12-25). Israelis down kebab and *la'afa* in the **Shechunat Ha-Tikva** area in the southeasternmost quarter, renowned for its cheap beer and lamb, chicken, or beef skewers. Pastry stands, falafel joints, and ice cream shops line **Dizengoff Sq.** and the stretch of **Dizengoff St.** just north, where crowds of tourists and throngs of hungry young Israelis test the limits of spandex technology. **Yermiyahu St.** has a better, pricier selection (NIS20-35).

▨ **Itzik Ve' Ruthie,** 53 Sheinkin St. (☎685 27 53), serves the most scrumptious sandwiches (NIS5-15) in the city. The homemade soda (NIS2) alone is worth squeezing past all the locals crammed into this tiny shop. Open Su-Th 5am-4pm and F 5am-2pm.

▨ **Falafel 101,** 99 Dizengoff St., near the corner of Frischmann St., should be the model for all other falafel stands. For NIS10, get piping-hot falafel, a large selection of salads, and a drink. Open Su-Th 8am-midnight and F 8am-4pm.

Big Mama, 13 Najara St. (☎517 50 65). Look for the blue and red neon sign on the back right corner of the walkway behind Allenby 58. Gobble down the best pizza this side of Italy (NIS25-34), or try one of the indulgently creamy pasta dishes (NIS28-34). Open Su noon-2am, M-W and F noon-3am, and Th noon-4am.

A Taste of Life, 60 Ben-Yehuda St. (☎620 31 51). A vegan paradise run by members of the Black Hebrew community, a group whose dietary laws prohibit both milk and meat (see **Dimona,** p. 412). Entrees like wheatfurters, veggie *shawarma,* and soy barbecue twists served à la carte (NIS15) or with two sides and a salad (NIS42). Cleanse your palate on the excellent soymilk ice cream (NIS6.50) and other non-dairy, no-egg desserts. Open Su-Th 9am-11pm, F 9am-3pm, and Sa after sundown-midnight.

Hungarian Blintzes, 35 Yermiyahu St. (☎544 16 97 or 605 06 74), near the port. Turn right off Dizengoff St. and continue one block. Locals jonesing for Hungarian goulash blintzes (NIS32) flock to this intimate bistro. Sweeter jam (NIS25) and poppy seed cream (NIS30) also available. Open Su-Th 1pm-1am and Sa sundown-1am.

Yotvata B'Ir, 78 Herbert Samuel St. (☎510 79 84). There's a green and orange neon sign off the *tayelet.* Kibbutz Yotvata, renowned producers of dairy goods, ventures into the city with this well-lit oasis of fresh veggies, cheeses, and fruits. Menu highlights include salads large enough to feed a small army (NIS45-47) and pancakes masquerading as sundaes (NIS27-39). Open daily 7am-3am.

Dallas Restaurant, 68 Ezel St. (☎687 43 49), in the Ha-Tikva neighborhood, a few blocks past the *shuk.* Bus #15 and 16 go past the restaurant. Outstanding Yemenite restaurant serves every cow part, including heart (NIS13), testicles (NIS10), and udder (NIS10). Open Su-Th noon-2am, F 11am-1hr. before sundown, and Sa 8:30pm-2am.

New York Bagel, 215 Ben-Yehuda St. (☎605 35 72), above Jabotinsky St. Something from the diaspora makes a welcome return to Israel, namely bagels (NIS3), with cream cheese (NIS13) and nova lox (NIS22). Open Su-Th 7:30am-11pm and F 7am-3pm.

▐ CAFES

Crowd-gazing is an art in Tel Aviv; chairs on the sidewalk and *café-au-lait* can be found just about anywhere in the city. **Sheinken St.,** one of the hippest promenades in town, has a long tradition of artsy liberalism. Along **Ben-Yehuda, Dizengoff,** and **Ibn Gvirol,** three parallel streets, a number of cafes serve local neighborhood folk and weary shoppers alike. **Basel St.** (near its intersection with Ibn Gvirol St., a block above Jabotinsky St.) recently sprouted its own crop of chichi cafes for hipper-than-thou Sheinken expats.

ISRAEL

Tamar Cafe, 57 Sheinken St. (☎ 685 23 76), provides a quintessential Sheinken experience. Immortalized in a song by the Israeli pop trio Mango ("Living on Sheinken/drinking coffee at the Tamar Cafe/my dream is to make a short film"), the Tamar is crammed with locals arguing about who's more liberal. Open Su-Th 7am-8pm and F 7am-5pm.

Babblefish, 13 Rabbi Akiva (☎ 516 45 85), near the corner of Najara St., to the right of the *shuk* from Allenby. This adorable, cherry-pink hole-in-the-wall cafe serves a mean sangria (NIS12) and cheap salads (NIS15-20). Live percussion and funk DJ on Friday nights. Open Su-F noon-2am.

Ilan's Coffee Shop, 90 Ibn Gvirol St. (☎ 523 53 34). Tables are a prized commodity in Tel Aviv's first espresso bar. Renowned for their fantastic home brew "Angela Mia" (NIS6-16), they also just crossed the fence into the whole-leaf tea business (NIS6-14). Another location at 20 Carlebach St. Open Su-Th 6:30am-10pm and F 6:30am-3pm.

🔘 SIGHTS

ROOFTOP OBSERVATORY. When haggling, shoving, and sunning take their toll, rise above it all. Look down on the chaos of the market and the city from the observatory in **Migdal Shalom.** The tower rises 34 stories skyward and the penthouse affords a breathtaking view, although the gating does give it a somewhat caged-in feel. The mosaic walls were made by artists Naḥum Gutan and David Sharir. *(1 Herzl St. and Aḥad Ha-Am St. Enter through the Eastern Wing beneath the underpass. ☎ 517 73 04. Open Su-Th 10am-6:30pm and F 10am-2pm. NIS15, students and seniors NIS10.)*

KIKKAR YITZḤAK RABIN. Formerly Kikkar Malkhei Yisrael (Kings of Israel Sq.), the square was renamed in 1995 in memory of Prime Minister Yitzḥak Rabin. On November 4, 1995, Rabin was assassinated by Yigal Amir, a Jewish student, during a crowded peace rally. The square has since drawn mourners who have painted large portraits of Rabin and left candles, flowers, and poetry. The official memorial, surrounded by five years' worth of candlewax, is next to the City Hall. *(Just off Ibn Gvirol St., between Arlozorov St. and Ben-Gurion St.)*

GREAT SYNAGOGUE. Completed in 1926 and renovated in 1970, this huge domed building showcases arches and stained-glass windows that are replicas of those from European synagogues destroyed during the Holocaust. *(110 Allenby St., near the corner with Rothschild Blvd. ☎ 560 49 05 or 560 40 66. Open Su-F 10am-5pm and Sa 7:30-11:30am. Sa prayer open to the public; head coverings and modest dress required.)*

Near the synagogue is **Independence Hall,** where the founding of the State of Israel was proclaimed in 1948. *(16 Rothschild Blvd. ☎ 517 39 42. Open Su-Th 9am-2pm.)*

ZOOLOGICAL CENTER. This combination drive-through safari park, circus, and zoo features 250 acres of African game in a natural habitat. Stare over a *wadi* at impossibly cute gorillas and Syrian bears, or let an ostrich poke its head into your car for a bite of candy. People without picnics can have lunch at the moderately priced restaurant, and those without a car can ride the park's own vehicles through the habitat. Pedestrian tours are offered as well. *(In Ramat Gan. Take bus #30, 35, or 43 from Tel Aviv or bus #67 within Ramat Gan. From the bus stop, go ½km down Ha-Tzvi Blvd. with the park on your right; the zoo entrance is on the right. ☎ 631 21 81 or 674 49 81. Open Su-Th July-Aug. 9am-5pm, Mar.-June and Sept.-Oct. 9am-4pm, and Nov.-Feb. 9am-2:30pm; open year-round F 9am-1pm and Sa 9am-3pm. Visitors may remain on the grounds 2hr. after entrance gate closes. NIS42, students and children NIS32; with circus NIS49, students and children NIS42; extra NIS5 charge to ride on park's bus.)*

The beast-watching madness continues outside the Zoological Center in the massive **Ramat Gan National Park,** which rents boats. *(Open 24hr. Free.)*

🏛 MUSEUMS

THE ERETZ YISRAEL MUSEUM. A veritable eight-ring circus, the Eretz Yisrael museum consists of eight pavilions covering vastly different topics spread over an archaeological site that is still being excavated. The most famous attraction in the complex is the **Glass Pavilion,** with one of the finest collections of glassware in the world. The **Nehushtan Pavilion,** with its cave-like entryway, holds the discoveries of the excavations at the ancient copper mines of Timna, better known as King Solomon's Mines, just north of Eilat. Across the patio, the **Kadman Numismatic Museum** traces the history of the region through ancient coins. The **Ceramics Pavilion** contains ancient Canaanite pottery, exhibits explaining its production, and artist Moshe Shek's ceramic sculptures. Across the entrance area, past the grassy amphitheater, is the **Man and His Work Center,** an exhibition of Middle Eastern folk crafts and techniques. Follow the road to the right and go upstairs to reach the **Tel Qasile Excavations,** which have revealed a 12th-century BCE Philistine port city and ruins dating from around 1000 BCE. The area at the top of the hill contains the remains of three separate Philistine temples built on top of each other. Down the hill to the south are scattered remnants of the residential and industrial quarter of the city. Past the Philistine town is the **Folklore Pavilion,** with Jewish religious art, ceremonial objects, and ethnic clothing. The Eretz Yisrael complex also houses a library of over 30,000 books and periodicals (some in English) and the **Lasky Planetarium.** *(2 Levanon St., in Ramat Aviv, the northernmost part of the city. Buses #7, 24, 25, or 74 from the New Central Bus Station stop at the museum. ☎ 641 52 44. Open Su-Tu and Th 9am-3pm, W 9am-5pm, and F-Sa 10am-2pm. NIS28, students NIS22, children NIS20; includes access to all 8 pavilions and the Eretz Yisrael Library. Planetarium NIS20, in Hebrew.)*

TEL AVIV MUSEUM OF ART. The museum holds a sizeable collection of Israeli and international art. The handsome lobby boasts a Lichtenstein, and the museum itself runs the gamut from Impressionism (Renoir, Monet, Corot, and Pissaro) to Surrealism (including de Chirico and Magritte) to cutting-edge multimedia installations by more recent artists. Rotating thematic exhibits are exceptionally well-curated and range from "Music in Art" to "Stage Design." An English program listing special exhibits and events is available in the ticket booth or the "This Week in Tel Aviv" insert in Friday's *Jerusalem Post*. *(27 Sha'ul Ha-Melekh Blvd. Buses #7 and 18. ☎ 696 12 97 or 695 73 61; www.tamuseum.co.il. Open M and W 10am-4pm, Tu and Th 10am-10pm, F 10am-2pm, and Sa 10am-4pm. Gallery tours in English W 11:30am. NIS30, students NIS24, seniors and children NIS15.)*

◪ BEACHES AND PROMENADES

BEACHES. The beaches within the city are sandy, clean, and free, and all have showers, toilets, and changing rooms with varying degrees of cleanliness. All of Tel Aviv's beaches are rife with theft; lock up valuables before hitting the sand. The southern coastline, with fewer amenities and no luxury hotels, tends to be quieter during the day, but that is gradually changing now that the *tayelet* (promenade) has been extended all the way to Jaffa. **Gordon Beach** overflows with foreign tourists and Israelis trying to pick them up, while the **Hilton Beach** (behind the hotel) swarms with native surfers and tourists trying to pick them up. The **Sheraton Beach** is quite peaceful. From north to south, the beaches are: Sheraton, Hilton, Gordon, Frischmann, Trumpeldor, and the Jerusalem beach at the end of Allenby Rd.; the last four are almost one continuous beach. The Hebrew word for beach is *ḥof*, but it's more important to learn the **flag language** of the beach: black means swimming is forbidden, red means swimming is dangerous, white means swim on. Most beaches have lifeguards on duty 7am-5pm.

PROMENADES. If the beach doesn't sate your bare-flesh needs, perfect the Mediterranean art of nonchalant people-watching from Tel Aviv's streets and cafes (see **Cafes,** p. 327). Work that cover-girl look along the wide, high-fashion boutique-lined sidewalks of **Dizengoff St.,** no longer at the peak of their glory but still among the more crowded catwalks in town. **Dizengoff Sq.** hosts an ever-changing scene, from retirees feeding flocks of pigeons in the midday sun to late-night punks who flock to the overpass stairs.

♪ ENTERTAINMENT

PERFORMING ARTS

For the most detailed information on performance schedules and other activities in the Tel Aviv area, see *Tel Aviv Today*, *Events in Tel Aviv*, and *This Week in Tel Aviv*, all free at the tourist information office and major hotels.

The **Suzanne Delal Center**, 5 Yeḥiely St. (☎510 56 56), in Neve Tzedek, has indoor and outdoor dance, theater, and musical performances. Take bus #8, 10, 25, or 61 from downtown or #40 or 46 from the central bus station. The center is best known as the home of the Inbal and Bat Sheva dance companies, both of which perform contemporary ethnic dances. (Box office open daily 9am-5pm. Inbal: ☎517 37 11, call 8am-8pm; NIS60. Bat Sheva: ☎517 14 71; NIS45-60, 20% discount with foreign passport.) **Beit Lessin**, 34 Weizmann St. (☎694 11 11), has live jazz acts (NIS30-70). The **Tel Aviv Cameri Theater**, 101 Dizengoff St., at the corner of Frischmann St., offers simultaneous translation earphones during 8:30pm performances on Tuesday. (☎523 33 35. Tickets NIS100-125.) The **Mann Auditorium**, 2 Tarsat Blvd., (☎528 91 63) is home to the **Israeli Philharmonic Orchestra** (box office ☎525 15 02) which plays modern Israeli works as well as more internationally known pieces. Be prepared for a cough-fest like no other when the orchestra pauses—the crowd of season ticket holders is older than the auditorium.

There are also more than 40 **movie theaters** showing American and Israeli flicks. Check the *Jerusalem Post* for English listings for the artsy **Tel Aviv Cinemathèque**, 2 Sprinzak St. (☎691 71 81), at the intersection with Carlebach St., or the more mainstream **Chen Cinema** (☎528 22 88) in Dizengoff Sq.

♫ NIGHTLIFE

PUBS

After an exhausting day of suntanning at the beach, many travelers just want an evening of good company and icy Carlsbergs. Rowdy but generic bars abound around hostel-heavy **Ha-Yarkon St.** and **Allenby Rd.** Israelis—often charged cover when tourists are not because of their tendency toward smaller bar bills—head inland to bars with a little more character. Several great options are hidden away on the Ibn Gvirol sidestreets and in Florentin. As with clubs, the general closing time is "when the last customer leaves," which can be as early as midnight or 1am on weekdays, but as late as 6am on weekends.

1942, 27 Rosh Pina St. (☎688 96 92 or 052 448 516), a few blocks from the central bus station. For all your nightlife needs, this gorgeous place has a mod checkerboard dance floor, a pub with the city's cheapest (and best decorated) cocktails (NIS20-28), and an Arabian-style loft for *nargilah* (NIS20). Cover NIS40 (includes one drink), NIS60 for all you can eat and drink. Prove it's your birthday and everything is free. Open daily at 9pm, but only a dance bar Th-Sa. Also hosts an after-party at 6:30am on Sa.

Shweball at Rival 27, 27 Rival St. (☎687 43 64), off Ha-Massger St. Look for the graffiti mural reading "Rival 27." Relive your childhood, this time with alcohol. Join the friendly, young Israeli crowd for beer (NIS14-20), cocktails (NIS28, 35 for flaming versions), and games like pick-up sticks, Connect Four, and *taki,* the Israeli version of Uno. Open M-Th and Sa at 9pm and F at 10pm. Fills up at about 11pm.

End of the Night, 16 Ibn Gvirol St. (☎695 00 91), just above Dizengoff. Look for a big orange sign that reads "Mongol". Twenty-something locals pile on top of each other to jam to the well-chosen hip-hop and funk. 21+. Open Th-Sa at 11:30pm.

Florentine 5, at that address (☎682 66 34), just off Herzl St. If the candlelight, Israeli classics, and sophisticated crowd don't mellow you out, the *nargilah* (NIS15) just might do the trick. Open daily at 9pm.

He-She, 8 Ha-Shomeret St. (☎510 09 14), off Shefer St. Tel Aviv's most popular gay bar, thanks to a devoted crowd of locals and tourists. Beer NIS20. Open M-Sa at 8pm.

The Out, 45 Naḥalat Binyamin (☎560 2391), a few blocks after the pedestrian mall, on the corner of Montefiore. Two-floor cozy gay bar with red lights and wood floors that lend a mellow ambiance, especially on romantic-themed Tuesdays. Israeli rock on Mondays, but the house goes house on weekends. Beer NIS12-18, happy hour prices until 11pm. Open Sa-W at 9 and Th-F at 10.

DISCOS

Tel Aviv's dance scene is always on the move; the *only* club one year may be empty the next and a hardware store after that. To really enjoy Tel Aviv's nightlife, you may have to reset your internal clock. The music sometimes starts early, but no one arrives before midnight and places tend to peak around 3am. Friday is the hottest. Those who really want to earn their nocturnal merit badges should keep an eye out for after-party signs; different clubs take turns hosting these 6:30am (Saturday morning) bashes that tunnel on until noon.

Pacha (☎510 20 60). This sprawling club in the Dolphinarium overlooks the ocean. The hedonistic playground has two dance floors (Th house and 80s, F-Sa house), a lounge for *nargilah* (NIS15), masseuses, and more glittered and pierced navels than you can count. Th 23+ and F-Sa 18+. Cover NIS60-100. Open Th at 1am and F-Sa at midnight.

The Octopus (☎620 01 31), at the port. Turn right at the end of Yermiyahu St., near the Superpharm, and continue 300m to the cluster of clubs. After Th and F of hard-core trance, the crowd chills out at the Sa sundown party (5:30pm) then grooves up for 70s night fever (midnight). Cover Th NIS80 and F-Sa NIS60.

The Scene, 56 Allenby Rd. (☎510 85 23). A catwalk of a club, the Scene serves as the prime stomping grounds for Tel Aviv's starlets in sequins. Club goes loco for salsa on Thursday. Monday is gay night. 23+. Cover NIS50. Open M-Sa 10pm-4am.

The Second Floor, 67 Allenby Rd. Head under the blue wooden sign around back and up the stairs. Wild crowd spills out onto the balcony of this 70s-style apartment or retreats to the many chill-out rooms to enjoy pool, *nargilah,* or rooftop jazz. 20+. Cover NIS30. Open Th-F at 10pm and occasional jazz soirées on F afternoons.

Dynamo Dvash, 59 Abarbanel St. (☎683 51 59), a small street off Salame St., on your left when coming from Herzl St. DJs from all over the world craft "brain dance" electronica high above the warehouse floor. 21+. Cover NIS40-70. Open Th and F at midnight.

LIVE MUSIC

Young Israeli rock bands have appointed Tel Aviv their headquarters and play the clubs nightly. In addition, two amphitheaters at Ha-Yarkon Park hold concerts. *Ha-Ir (The City),* a weekly Hebrew magazine, has a section called "Akhbar Ha-Ir," with comprehensive listings. For listings in English, check the brochure *This Week in Tel Aviv,* produced by *The Jerusalem Post.*

Barbie, 40 Salame Rd. (☎681 67 57), halfway between Herzl St. and Marzuk Veezar. Only accessible by taxi. Look for a gray striped awning or a big crowd. Garage-like place is frequented by some of the best rock bands in Israel. Cover NIS10-50 depending on the band's fame. Shows Su-F 10pm and midnight.

Heineken Habima (☎528 21 74), on the left side of Kikkar Habima, at the top of Rothschild Blvd. Locals groove to local bands by the neon and candlelight. Beer NIS15-20. Cover NIS25, weekends NIS30. Open M-Sa at 10:30pm.

Camelot, 16 Shalom Aleichem St. (☎528 52 33). The basement echoes with live blues and R&B, while the upstairs pub stays mellow, with DJs on W, F, and Sa. Cover NIS35-80 for downstairs. Open daily 9pm-4am. Reserve at least a day before for good bands.

JAFFA (YAFO) يافا ‏יפו‎

An Israeli folk song describes Jaffa (*Yafo,* or "beautiful," in Hebrew; *Yafa* in Arabic) as possessing a "mysterious and unknown" element that allows its atmosphere "to seep like wine into the blood." Jaffa's stone houses and winding streets

DON'T ASK, DON'T TEL AVIV Today, Tel Aviv is home to Israel's most thriving gay community. From the soaring attendance at the annual gay pride day party (now held in Ha-Yarkon Park) to the large number of gay clubs, pubs, and establishments with "gay nights," the community is present, active, and powerful. The best ways to find out what's going on are by catching leaflets on Sheinkin St. and reading *Ha-Zman Ha-Varod*.

are truly intoxicating. An integral part of Tel Aviv, Jaffa has one of the oldest functioning harbors in the world, nearly 6000 years old. According to the Bible, the recalcitrant prophet Jonah shirked his divine calling and fled to Jaffa to catch a boat to Tarshish, and subsequently had his fateful encounter with the whale. The earliest archaeological finds in Jaffa date from the 18th century BCE, from which point on the city played host to a series of conquerors. In 1468 BCE, the Egyptians captured Jaffa by hiding soldiers in human-sized clay jars that were brought into the city market. King David took the city around 1000 BCE, and under Solomon it became the main port of Judea. During the 12th century CE, Jaffa was captured by the First Crusaders, Salah al-Din, Richard the Lionheart, the Muslims, and Louis IX, who built magnificent walls and towers which partly remain today. The Mamluks overpowered the city in 1267; apart from a brief stay by Napoleon around 1800 (during which much of the Jewish community vanished), Jaffa remained an important Arab stronghold until 1948. In the 1960s, the Tel Aviv municipality began a massive renovation project here, resulting in today's abundance of small museums and a thriving artists' colony amid green parks and Crusader walls.

✴ ORIENTATION

The **Jaffa Clocktower,** completed in 1906, stands by the entrance to Jaffa from Tel Aviv and is a useful landmark. A free two-hour *tour* of Old Jaffa by the Tourism Association begins here Wednesday at 9:30am, though many people line up at 9am. Bus #46 from the New Central Bus Station lets off in front of the clocktower, and bus #10 from Ben-Yehuda St. or Allenby St., near the Opera Tower, stops just a couple minutes before it. A couple blocks past the clocktower, head right and the road becomes the **Mifratz Shlomo Promenade,** which leads to the **Old City** and provides stunning views of Tel Aviv's action-packed coast and skyline. Alternatively, a left turn onto **Beit Eshel St.** will you bring you to the *shuk*.

▼ ACCOMMODATIONS

If all the beds in Tel Aviv are full, or if you just want something that feels a little less like a college dorm, the two hostels in Jaffa provide fabulous alternatives.

▨ **Old Yafo Hostel,** 8 Olei Tzion St. (☎682 23 70; fax 682 23 16; email ojhostel@shani.net). Walk one block past the clocktower on Yefet St. and turn left onto Olei Tzion St. It's rare that a hostel feels enchantingly antique without an accompanying layer of grime, but the Old Yafo manages superbly. Fully stocked bookshelves and a large rooftop garden make for delightful finishing touches. Kitchen available. Storage for non-guests NIS1. Laundry NIS10. Internet NIS10 per 15min. Reception 8am-11pm. Check-out noon. No curfew, but lights off at 11pm. Payment in any major foreign currency avoids 17% VAT. 6-bed dorms (coed or female-only) NIS40/US$8.50; singles NIS147/US$30, with TV, bath, A/C, and kitchen NIS226/US$46; doubles NIS168/US$34, with TV, bath, A/C, and kitchen NIS246/US$50.

Beit Immanuel Hostel, 8 Auerbach St. (☎682 14 59; fax 682 98 17; email beitimm@netvision.net.il; www.inisrael.com/beitimmanuel). From the clocktower, head toward Tel Aviv on Raziel St. for 5min. until it turns into Eilat St. Turn right after 12 Eilat St. onto Auerbach St. On bus #46, get off on Eilat St. near the gas stations. This family-oriented Christian hospice has a garden and playground. Breakfast included. Dinner

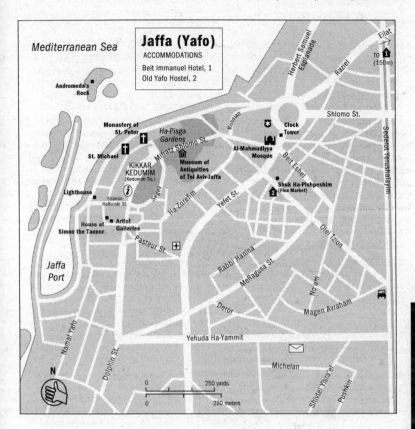

Jaffa (Yafo)

ACCOMMODATIONS
Beit Immanuel Hotel, 1
Old Yafo Hostel, 2

Mediterranean Sea

Andromeda's Rock

Monastery of St. Peter

Ha-Pisga Gardens

St. Michael

KIKKAR KEDUMIM (Kedumim Sq.)

Museum of Antiquities of Tel Aviv-Jaffa

Al-Mahmudiyya Mosque

Clock Tower

Shuk Ha-Pishpeshim (Flea Market)

Lighthouse

Shimon HaBurski St.

House of Simon the Tanner

Artist Galleries

Pasteur St.

Jaffa Port

Rabbi Hanina

Mefagusa St.

Deror

Magen Avraham

Yehuda Ha-Yammit

Michelan

Namal Yafo

Dolphin St.

Herbert Samuel Esplanade

Shlomo St.

Russian

Beit Eshel

Olei Tzion

No'am

Shivtei Yisra'el

Pushkin

Sederot Yerushalayim

Eilat TO (150m)

Raziel

Mifratz Shlomo St.

Segev

Ha-Zorefim

Yefet St.

N

0   250 yards
0   250 meters

NIS40. Shabbat NIS60. Laundry NIS10. Reception 7am-11pm. Check-in 3pm. Check-out 1pm. Lockout 10am-noon. Curfew 11pm. All rooms have A/C. Dorms NIS48/US$12; singles with bath NIS180/US$45; doubles with bath NIS280/US$70.

FOOD

The maze of narrow streets surrounding the Jaffa Clocktower is peppered with cheap falafel stands (NIS7-10), *al-ha'esh* (barbecue) meat establishments, and sweets vendors, some of which are open 24 hours. The cafes and restaurants in the Old City tend to be generic, but the surrounding gardens and views of the Mediterranean make them some of the loveliest tourist traps imaginable. For a touch of romance and a big hit to the wallet, head to Jaffa Port, off Pasteur St. on the far side of the artists' colony, where picturesque waterfront restaurants offer seafood so fresh the gills are almost moving (daily catch entrees NIS42 and up). Jaffa is also one of the best places to get a great meal on shabbat.

☒ **Said Abou Elafia and Sons,** 7 Yefet St. (☎681 23 40), one block behind the Jaffa clock-tower. Popularly known as "Aboulafia," this bakery is so famous that its name is used by Israelis to denote all stuffed-pita foods. Try the za'tar-spiced toasts, flaky Iraqi pita with cheese, or honey-drenched baklava, all for NIS3-8. Take-out only. Open 24hr. Cash only.

☒ **Parabin Yafo,** 20 Ogan St. (☎518 09 62), in the port, about 400m past the fancy fish restaurants. Feel like a sheikh, or at least incredibly chic, while lounging on pillows and puffing *nargilah* (NIS17) in this cavernous, lantern-lit hideaway. From 10pm, there's a line of large groups jonesing for their huge salads (NIS25-27), creamy hummus plates (NIS12-18), and an orgasmic chocolate cake (NIS24). Open Sa-Th 8:15pm-3am and F 10:45pm-6am. Credit cards accepted.

Shipudei Itzik Hagadol/Big Itzik's Skewers, 3 Raziel St. (☎518 18 02), a couple blocks before the clocktower. Green neon Hebrew sign. Hungry locals meet, greet, and eat skewered meat at this clean, friendly establishment. Herbivores and carnivores can achieve peaceful coexistence over a sampler platter of 18 salads (NIS14 per person), sizzling kebabs (NIS15 each), and huge, warm pita. Open Sa-Th 11am-1am.

Dr. Shakshuka, 3 Beit Eshel (☎682 28 42), corner of Yefet St. Libyan food in the heart of Old Jaffa. Eponymous dish is the *shakshuka*—a mouth watering tomato and egg concoction (NIS18). Open Su-Th 9am-1am, F 9am-sundown, and Sa sundown-midnight.

■ SIGHTS

SHUK HA-PISHPESHIM. Jaffa's large Shuk Ha-Pishpeshim is one of the livelier markets in Israel, with roofed rows of overflowing stalls offering dust-covered knick-knacks, modern hand-dyed clothing, Persian carpets, leather goods, and brassware. A vast selection of enormous *nargilahs* is also available. *(To reach the flea market, go one block past the clock tower along Yefet St., and turn left.)*

CLOCKTOWER AND ENVIRONS. Built in 1906 to celebrate the 25th anniversary of Sultan Abd al-Hamid II's ascension to power, the clocktower marks the entrance to Jaffa from Tel Aviv. Originally, the clocktower's four faces were split between Israeli and European time for the convenience of European sailors. On the right of the clocktower is the **al-Mahmudiyya Mosque,** an enormous structure erected in 1812 that only Muslims may enter. Head to the right and up the hill along the Mifratz Shlomo Promenade to the **Museum of Antiquities of Tel Aviv-Jaffa,** which contains artifacts from Neolithic to Roman times and a collection of coins found in the area. *(☎682 53 75. Open Su-Th 9am-1pm. NIS10, students and seniors NIS5.)*

KIKKAR KEDUMIM. The old city's tourist center is Kikkar Kedumim. Following signs to the visitors center, head down to the underground plaza to the excavations from 2300-year-old Tel Yafo, get a short history lesson, and pick up free maps. *(Continue along Mifratz Shlomo past the Napoleonic Cannons, pass the Church of St. Peter and go up a large staircase. Open Su-Th 9am-10pm, F 9am-2pm, and Sa 10am-10pm. Free. Church open daily 8-11:45am and 3-5pm; public masses in English Sa 8pm and Su 9am.)*

To the right of the Kikkar, just before the cafes and shops, a small alleyway leads to the colorful **Greek Orthodox Church of St. Michael,** which is worth a brief tour. *(Open daily 8-11:45am and 3-5pm.)*

The wooden footbridge from Kikkar Kedumim leads to the **Ha-Pigsa Gardens,** used by both Arab and Jewish couples to take wedding pictures. The point offers Jaffa's best view of the coast, Tel Aviv, and **Andromeda's Rock.**

JAFFA PORT. The port, past the bottom of the artists' colony to the right along Pasteur St. was the perfect depth for King Solomon when he imported rafts of cedars from Lebanon to build his temple. It was too shallow, however, for larger ships. The infamous port caused Dutch sailors to term the impossible as "entering Jaffa." Today, the port is more accessible and is an active fishermen's wharf.

NEAR TEL AVIV

HERZLIYA הרצליה   ☎03

Named after Theodore Herzl by the seven Zionist pioneers who settled the area (see **Zionism,** p. 268), Herzliya is more colloquially known as "the Bank of Israel" because of the affluent tourists and Israeli vacationers who flock to its beautiful shores. In the never-ending battle for the "best beach in Israel" title, Herzliya is a prime contender. Only 15km outside of Tel Aviv, Herzliya makes a great daytrip from the city; there are no budget accommodations.

■■ **ORIENTATION AND PRACTICAL INFORMATION.** Herzliya's **bus station** is at the corner of **Ben-Gurion St.** and **Ha-Atzma'ut Rd.** Buses #501 (35min., every 20min. 5:30am-11:30pm, NIS7) and 502 (30min., every 15min. 9am-7pm, NIS7) run between Herzliya and Tel Aviv. They stop running at around 5:30pm on Friday and start again at 8:20pm on Saturday. The town's cultural hub, the **Yad Labanim Memorial Center,** is at the corner of Ben-Gurion St. and **Ha-Banim St.;** from the bus station, head two blocks left along Ben-Gurion St. The main shopping area in Herzliya can be found by turning right from the central bus station, and making a left onto **Sokolov St.** after a few blocks. City bus #29 goes to the beaches in Herzliya's suburb, Herzliya Pituah. (10-30min. depending on traffic, NIS5.)

☐ FOOD. It's a good idea to eat in town before hitting the beach. There are refreshment stands right off the ocean, but they have high prices and little variety. Ben-Gurion has a number of cheap eats, including the falafel stand at 10 Ben-Gurion St., diagonally across from the central bus station. Tuvya, an Egyptian expat who charms his patrons in English, French, Arabic, and Hebrew, serves deliciously fresh falafel (NIS7) and a variety of salads. There is also a **supermarket** in the shopping center on the left side of Ben-Gurion St., one block before Sokolov St. (Open Su-Th 9am-7pm and F 9am-1pm.)

◪ BEACHES. The beaches in Herzliya Pituah range from the large, soft-sanded variety to the small and rocky type. The **Dabesh Beach** and **Arcadia Beach,** near the marina at the end of the bus line, belong to the former category and accordingly, charge admission (NIS12, children NIS8). While the size and sand of the **Sidna Ali** beach pales in comparison, admission is free, and it is the only beach without wall-to-wall umbrella lounge-chairs. People walking one kilometer from Sidna Ali to the pay-beaches (left as you face the sea) or those claiming to stay at one of the hotels (for example, Hotel Arcadia or Hotel Ha-Sharon) are often not required to pay. From the bus stop in Sidna Ali, the beach is up the hill and through the gate.

The Sidna Ali beach has other reasons to visit as well. The **Sidna Ali Mosque** allows modestly dressed visitors to visit when it is not prayer time. Women must cover their heads and shorts are forbidden. After the Mamluks destroyed the area during the Third Crusade, the mosque was named after one of Salah al-Din's soldiers who died in a battle on the hill on which the mosque stands.

HERMIT'S HOUSE. Herzliya's most worthwhile attraction is an inhabited sand castle known as the Hermit's House. This fantastical residence built into the side of a cliff by "hermit" **Nissim Kakhalon** is a must-see for anyone to whom "arts and crafts" is not incompatible with Surrealism. Kakhalon claims, "I make it from my love. I make it good." In other words, he spent 29 years turning other people's garbage (tires, toys, tiles, etc.) into this hallucinogenic maze of winding tunnels, flower-strewn antechambers, and plush gardens. Even more impressive, everything in the artful interior is absolutely functional, from the bathroom ceiling made entirely of Maccabee Beer bottles to the loveseat with a mirrored mosaic on one side and a huge sculpted stone face on the other. Nothing goes to waste here: Kakhalon even uses the manure from his family of goats to grow fragrant basil. Kakhalon's tours depend on the extent to which his guests are appreciative. This hermit is quite friendly, after all, and more showman than recluse. During the week, Kakhalon runs a cafe serving hummus (NIS15) and smoked fish (NIS50). (9am-sundown; hours erratic; closed for Shabbat.)

BEIT RISHONIM. Zionist history buffs may enjoy the Beit Rishonim (Founders' Museum), 8-10 Ha-Nadiv St. From Sokolov St. turn right on Ha-Nadiv St. and continue two blocks. The museum narrates the history of Herzliya, beginning with its days as a colony in 1924, using computerized presentations as well as items from the early settlement period. (☎950 42 70. Open M 8:30am-12:30pm and 4-6:30pm and Tu-Th 8:30am-12:30pm. NIS8, students and children NIS4, seniors free.)

ISRAEL

OTHER SITES. The **Yad Labanim Memorial Center** houses the diminutive and avant-garde **Herzliya Museum of Art.** The contemporary exhibits are well worth the short trip from the bus station. (☎(09) 955 10 11 or 950 23 01; www.adgo.co.il/ herzliya_museum. Open Su, Tu, and Th 4-8pm; M, W, F, and Sa 10am-2pm. Free.) An outdoor amphitheater is attached to the building and overlooks the museum's modern **Sculpture Garden,** which is the setting for concerts by the **Herzliya Chamber Orchestra** (☎(09) 950 07 61), as well as an annual theatrical festival in May.

RAMLA רמלה ☎08

Founded in 716 by the formidable Umayyad Caliph Suleiman ibn Abd al-Malik, Ramla is the only town in Israel established and developed by Arabs. Until the arrival of the Crusaders in the 11th century, Ramla was the capital of Palestine and was known for its magnificent palaces and mosques. After the 1948 War, the Arab majority was forced to flee. Today the community is predominantly composed of Jewish immigrants and a Christian Arab minority. The diversity of Ramla's history and present population, as well as its vibrant *shuk* (town market), make the town worth a visit. From **Tel Aviv,** take bus #245, 455, 450, or 451 (30min., every 20min., NIS9.50). From **Jerusalem,** take bus #401, 403, 411 (45min., every 30min., NIS14.90). Services include: **Police** 80 Herzl St. **Post office,** 4 Danny Mass St. (☎922 81 00) and **Bank Leumi** 8 Herzl St. (☎927 70 77. Open Su, Tu, W 8:30am-1pm; M, Th 8:30am-1pm, 4:30-6pm; F 8:30am-noon. Changes money with commission.) The **shuk,** on Ze'ev Zabutinsky, is open every day until dark and is especially lively on Thursdays. The street is closed to traffic until the shops close at around 7pm.

The Crusader Cathedral of St. John became the **Great Mosque** when Ramla's Muslims recaptured the town from the Crusaders. Although the mosque consequently retains little Muslim architecture, the well-preserved minaret is breathtaking, and the medieval vaulted arches are impressive. From the bus station walk right on Herzl St., turn left at the first intersection, and continue through the parking lot toward the towering minaret. The entrance is through a small green door on the side facing the parking lot. (Open Su-Th 8am-4pm.)

Ramla is supposed to be the biblical Arimathea, where one of Jesus' earliest disciples, Joseph, is said to have lived. Together with St. Nicodemus, St. Joseph Arimathea made the preparations for Jesus' burial. The large stone **Catholic Church of St. Nicodemus and St. Joseph Arimathea** was built in his honor in 1296, with money donated by European Catholics. Renovated in 1902, it now serves as a school, as well. The monks at the 18th-century monastery next door claim that Napoleon Bonaparte stayed in the upstairs chambers during his unsuccessful campaign against the Turks. The complex is past the mosque at the corner of the main Herzl St. and Bialik St. The main gate into the church is on Bialik St.

ASHKELON אשקלון ☎07

Ashkelon's strategic position along major naval and land routes made it desirable property for almost every ancient empire, from the Greeks to the Muslims. First rising to prominence as one of the Philistines' five great cities (although settlements here date back to the 3rd millennium BCE), Ashkelon reached its zenith as an independent city-state in the Roman period. Today, its main attractions are its sandy beaches, seaside national park, and well-known archaeological sites.

▟ GETTING THERE AND GETTING AROUND. The **Central Bus Station** (☎677 82 22) on Ben-Gurion Blvd., a 30-minute walk from the beach, runs **buses** to: **Be'er Sheva** (#363 and 364; 1½hr.; every 45min.-1hr. 5:45am-8:05pm; NIS23.50); **Jerusalem** (#437; 1½hr.; every 45min.-1hr. 5:50am-7:15pm; NIS22.50); and **Tel Aviv** (#300, 301, and 311; 1¼hr.; every 15-30min. 5:20am-9pm; NIS18.20-21.50). **Local bus** #5 goes to Zephania Sq. in the heart of the Afridar neighborhood and to the *midrahov* in the Migdal area, stopping at the central bus station. Catch it on the Ben-Gurion (front) side of the station for Migdal, or on the right side of the station for Afridar (every 12-20min., NIS4). **Bus** #6 (bus #13 July-Aug.) goes to the National Park and shoreline (NIS4). **Sherut** go to **Tel Aviv** (NIS16) and **Be'er Sheva** (NIS20).

⚡ PRACTICAL INFORMATION. The **Tourist Office** (☎673 24 12) is in City Hall, behind the bus station. Walk down the alley between the bus station and the Giron Mall to Ha-Gvurah St., turn left, and continue halfway down to the shopping center on the right. A Hebrew sign and flags fly in front, but the entrance is on the right. Ask about tours to local sights and activities. (Open Su-Th 8am-1pm and 4-6pm.) Change money at **Bank Ha-Poalim** (☎567 33 33), one block past the City Hall. **ATMs** accept NYCE, Cirrus, and major credit cards. (Open Su, Tu, and W 8:30am-1:15pm, M and Th 8:30am-1pm and 4-6:30pm, and F and holiday eves 8:15am-12:30pm.) The **post office** in Migdal on the *midraḥov* has good rates with no commission. For **first aid** call ☎672 33 33. The **police** (☎677 14 44) are at the corner of Ha-Nassi and Eli Cohen St. From the tourist office continue on Ha-Gvurah, and bear right. The **post office** (☎672 36 06) is behind the building with the town hall, near the *kenyon* Giron. (Open Su-Th 8am-2:30pm and F 8am-noon.)

▥ ACCOMMODATIONS AND FOOD. Cheap accommodations are lacking in Ashkelon. Free **camping** is normally available at the **Park Leumi Ashkelon** (Ashkelon National Park; ☎673 64 44). Call before your visit to see if any are available to tourists. There is no guard on duty from 8pm until 7am. Entrance to the park is free by foot, NIS15 by car. The snack bar and beach-side restaurants in the park are convenient and relatively inexpensive (steak, *shishlik*, or hamburger in a pita NIS15-25). Camping on the beach adjacent to the city is **dangerous** and not recommended.

The Herzl St. *midraḥov* in Migdal has the highest concentration of affordable eateries. Near the *midraḥov* is a lively *shuk*. From the *midraḥov*, take Ha-Kerem St. toward David Remez St.; the *shuk* is on the right. (Open M,W, Th 7am-7pm.) There are a number of outdoor, locally frequented, inexpensive restaurants on the corner of Ha-Nasi and Zephania St. at the Afridar Center, with *schnitzel*, hamburger, steak, and pizza for about NIS20. **Delilah Beach boardwalk,** a stone plaza up toward the street from the beach, showcases the city's collection of fish restaurants (meals NIS35-80). From the station, take bus #5 toward Afridar, get off at Zephania Sq., and backtrack a street to the highly visible front of the **Chinese Restaurant Furama,** 24 Ort St. Chow down on sweet and sour pork for NIS40 or wonton soup for NIS10. (☎673 84 97. Open daily noon-3pm and 7pm-midnight. Credit cards accepted.) In the middle of the *midraḥov* is **Titanic,** one of the more popular falafel joints. Get a falafel (NIS10) or satisfy your iceberg-sized hunger with a *shawarma* sandwich on delicious *lafah* bread. (NIS18. Open daily 8am-9pm.)

◉ ASHKELON NATIONAL PARK. The Ashkelon National Park was built on the site of 4000-year-old Canaanite remains, buried beneath ruins of Philistine, Greek, Roman, Byzantine, Crusader, and Muslim cities. Traces of the once-thriving Philistine city surround the picnic tables and snack bars. The **Bouleuterion,** a series of Hellenistic and Roman columns and capitals, graces the park's center. It served as the Council House Sq. when Ashkelon was an autonomous city-state under Severius in the 3rd century CE. The courtyard-like area next to the Bouleuterion is actually the inside of a Herodian assembly hall; it contains two **statues** of Nike, the winged goddess of victory, and an Italian marble statue of the goddess Isis with her god-child Horus, sculpted between 200 BCE and 100 CE. Behind the Bouleuterion lies a preserved **amphitheater.** Along the southern edge of the park are segments of a wall from the 12th-century **Crusader city.** A short hike past the amphitheater affords a close-up view of the walls and a glimpse of Ashkelon's Rothenberg Power Station. Most peculiar is the assembly of Roman columns jutting out of the ancient Byzantine sea wall on the beach. These massive marble columns were used to support the walls, which were destroyed in 1191 by Salah al-Din. Richard Lionheart partly restored them in 1192, as did Cornwall in 1240, only to have them demolished by the Sultan Baybars in 1270. *(30min. walk from the bus station. From the station, turn right onto Ben-Gurion Blvd. and follow it to the T junction at the coast, before the soldiers' recreation facility (note the striking sculpture of Samson). Turn left onto the road to the park; a small orange sign points the way. Bus #6 to the park is infrequent. ☎673 64 44. Open daily 7am-7pm; in winter closed Sa. Free, NIS15 with car. Maps at the main entrance.)*

ISRAEL

⚑🏖 BEACHES AND ENTERTAINMENT. Ashkelon's coast has four beaches where swimming is permitted; **Delilah Beach** is the most popular. Note the flag system: white flags signal safe bathing and black flags signal dangerously rough water. At Delilah Beach, breakwaters lessen the chance of black-flagging, and shady canopies and snack bars provide relief to sun-scorched bathers.

BEIT GUVRIN בית גוברין

*To reach Beit Guvrin, first travel to Kiryat Gat, which is easily accessible by **bus** from Tel Aviv (#369, 1¼hr., every 30min., NIS18); Jerusalem (#446, 1¼hr., every hr., NIS23.50) and Ashkelon (#025, 35min., every 30min, NIS11.50.) Bus #011 from Kiryat Gat goes directly to Kibbutz Beit Guvrin (25min.; Su-Th 8:05am and 5:10pm and F 8:05am and 2pm; return Su-Th 8:30am and 5:30pm and F 8:30am and 2:30pm; NIS8.50). If you miss the bus from Kiryat Gat, **Kiryat Gat Taxis** (☎ 393 60 09), in the back of the gas station to the left, takes you to Beit Guvrin (NIS60, but try haggling). Call for a taxi from Beit Guvrin back to Kiryat Gat. The park is just off Rte. 35, near Kibbutz Beit Guvrin, across from the gas station. Bring a hat or white scarf, sunglasses, sunscreen, and at least 1½L of water.*

Beit Guvrin was a flourishing Jewish metropolis in the 4th and 3rd centuries BCE and in the years between the destruction of the Second Temple and the Bar Kokhba Revolt (132-135 CE). The Arab village of Beit Jibrin stood nearby until the 1948 War, when its inhabitants were evacuated; since 1949, the modern kibbutz of Beit Guvrin has rested on its ruins. Once known as the biblical city of **Maresha,** one of the cities of Judah fortified by Rehoboam (Joshua 16:44), the area was settled by Edomites after the destruction of the First Temple, Sidonians during the 4th century BCE, and eventually Greeks, who converted it into a bustling economic center. The complicated caves and magnificent views of **Beit Guvrin National Park,** encompassing the ruins of Maresha and Beit Guvrin, are some of Israel's buried treasures. The park also contains some of the 800 glaringly white and chalky **bell-shaped caves** that characterize the Beit Guvrin region, hidden among the cacti and fig trees. Most of the caves were carved by Greeks, Byzantines, and others as they quarried for limestone. Once dug, the caves were used for storage, penning animals, and water collection, and later became sanctuaries for hermits and monks. St. John and others came here seeking solitude, and they often carved crosses and altars into the walls. The walls of the **Columbarium Cave** contain hundreds of small holes once used for storing pigeons for food, fertilizer, and cult rituals. The ruins in the lower city, near the *tel,* are worth the hot and hefty walk. Most impressive are the Hellenistic houses with their maze-like series of underground cisterns.

MEDITERRANEAN COAST

The stretch of coastline north of Tel Aviv is home to much of Israel's population and most of its agricultural output. Zionists and refugees poured onto the beaches in the beginning of the 20th century and drained the swamps of the coastal plain, clearing the path for a modern, industrial state.

HAIFA חיפה حيفا ☎ 04

Since the prophet Elijah fled the wrath of King Ahab to the caves of Mount Carmel (I Kings 18-19), Haifa has harbored religious minorities. Crusaders built the first of several monasteries above Elijah's Cave, which eventually gave shelter to the wandering Carmelite Order of Monks. German Templars established Haifa's German colony, and the Baha'i built their world headquarters here. In the 1930s, waves of European Jews seeking refuge from Nazism poured onto Haifa's beaches.

As a result, Haifa developed the philosophy, "live and let live." When the British decided to construct a port in the city, Arabs and Jews flocked to the economic opportunities and worked side-by-side in factories. Though they went home to separate neighborhoods, the municipality as a whole employed and was supported by members of both communities. Of course, the War of 1948 affected Haifa like all other areas, with thousands of Arabs abandoning the city; but today, Haifa's population of a quarter million includes a sizeable Arab minority and a small Orthodox Jewish community, who live together with little tension. Haifa University has the largest Arab population of any university in Israel and a joint community center promotes relations at the local level, especially among children. Not surprisingly, supporters of the Israeli-Palestinian peace accords often cite Haifa as the paradigm for peaceful Jewish-Arab co-existence.

✈ GETTING THERE

Trains: Central station in Bat Galim (☎856 44 44), is connected by tunnels to the central bus station. Trains to: **Akko** (30min., NIS11); **Hadera** (50min., NIS16); **Nahariya** (40min., NIS13); **Netanya** (NIS19.50) via **Binyamina** (45min., NIS16); and **Tel Aviv** (1hr., NIS21). The trip to Jerusalem requires a station change and will take longer than the bus. Trains are generally the best choice when traveling north. 10% discount with student ID. The tourist office has schedules. Credit cards accepted.

Buses: The **central bus station** (intercity info ☎851 22 08), is at Jaffa Rd. and Rothschild Blvd. Intercity buses generally run Su-Th 5:15am-11:30pm, F 5:15am-5pm, Sa 5pm-midnight. Buses to: **Ben-Gurion Airport** (#945 and 947, 2hr., every 30min., NIS28); **Jerusalem** (#940 (direct) 2hr., #945 and 947 (via Ben-Gurion) 3hr.; NIS40); **Nahariya** (#251, 271, and 272; 1¼hr.; every 15-20min.; NIS13.80) via **Akko** (50min., NIS11.50); **Nazareth** (#331 and 431, 1½hr., every 40min., NIS18.20); **Tel Aviv** (#900 (direct) and 901 (express); 1½hr.; every 20min.; NIS20.50); and **Tiberias** (#430 (direct) and 431, 1½hr., every hr. 5:30am-8pm, NIS23.50).

Ferries: Terminal (☎851 82 45) next to Merkaz train station, off Ha-Atzma'ut St. Ferries to Cyprus and mainland Greece (Th 8pm, F 7pm, and sometimes Su 8pm). Security checks are often several hours prior to departure. Check ahead. South Africans need visas to enter both countries. Tickets at **Caspi Travel**, 76 Ha-Atzma'ut St. (☎867 44 44. Open Su-Th 9am-5pm, F 9am-1pm.) Ferry tickets also available through ISSTA.

Taxis: Most taxis leave from Eliyahu St. in Paris Sq., near the Carmelit stop or from Ha-Halutz St. and Herzl St., near bus stops in Hadar. For *special* (home pick-up) taxis, call **Kavei Ha-Galil** (☎866 44 44 or 22). To: **Akko** (NIS80), **Nahariya** (NIS120), or **Lod** (NIS280). **Amal's Sherut Service** (☎866 23 24) will take you from 6 Ha-Halutz St. in Hadar to **Tel Aviv** (NIS22) and **Ben-Gurion Airport** (NIS45). Other taxi services include **Carmel Ahuza** (☎838 27 27) and **Merkaz Mitzpeh** (☎866 25 25 or 866 83 83). For 24hr. direct service to Ben-Gurion Airport, try Kavei Ha-Galil or Amal.

Car Rental: Avis, 7 Ben-Gurion Blvd. (☎851 30 50); **Budget,** 46 Ha-Histadrut Blvd. (☎842 40 04); **Hertz,** Ha-Histadrut Blvd. (☎840 21 27); **Reliable,** 140 Yafo Rd. (☎850 79 07); **Eldan,** 95 Ha-Nassi Blvd. (☎837 53 03). All open Su-Th 8am-6pm, F 8am-2pm. Most require minimum age of 24; Eldan will rent to 21-year-olds with double insurance payments.

◻ GETTING AROUND

BUSES. The **central bus station** (city line info ☎854 91 31), like the city itself, has three tiers. Intercity buses leave from the first floor, city buses depart from the second, and all buses arrive on the third. Intercity buses stop at the bus station and in Hadar along Herzl after 8pm. All urban rides cost NIS5; a 15-ride pass is NIS47.

On weekdays, buses run from about 5:30am to 11pm. On Fridays, they stop at around 4:30pm, depending on when Shabbat starts. **Saturday buses** usually begin running at 9:30am, run less frequently than on weekends, and do *not* run from the central bus station; instead they run from the Hadar area (many from Daniel St.) until about 6pm, when they switch back. **Sheruts** taper off a couple hours later than buses; many go to Hadar only (NIS4.50), while others follow specific bus routes.

Haifa's bus routes are extremely circuitous and a 20-minute walk (though uphill) may be a half-hour bus ride. To get **Downtown (Ha-Ir)** from the central bus station, take bus #17 or 41; from other parts of town, take any bus in the 70s. Almost every bus numbered 1-40 eventually stops in Hadar, but from the central bus station, #15 and 18 run most frequently. Those in the 20s go to **Carmel** and **Ahuza,** and #24 and 37 continue on to the **University of Haifa.**

SUBWAY. The best way to travel within Haifa is the Carmelit subway system, a train slanted just enough to make the ascent or descent seem flat. Though this subway has only one line, its six stops conquer steep hills and put most neighborhoods within walking distance. Starting from the bottom, the subway stops at Kikkar Paris, Solel Boneh, Ha-Nevi'im, Masada, Golomb, and Gan Ha-Eim. Yellow pavilions indicate entrances. (☎837 68 61. Every 6-7min.; Su-Th 6am-10pm, F 6am-3pm and 8pm-midnight, Sa in winter 7pm-midnight. NIS4.70 per ride for adults and children, NIS3 for seniors; 10-ride pass NIS42, NIS32.50 for seniors and those under 18. Credit cards accepted.)

CABLE CARS. A more scenic, but also more expensive alternative for getting from bottom to top and back again is to take the **Rakbal cable cars** (☎833 59 70). Colloquially known as "the Carmel's Eggs" for their ellipsoidal shape, the cable cars run down the Carmel's northwestern slope, shuttling between the orange-and-turquoise **Yotvata B'Ir** dairy restaurant on the Bat Galim Promenade and the **Stella Maris monastery** area at the mountain's peak. To Bat Galim, take bus #41 or 42; to Stella Maris take #25 or 26. (Open daily 9am-midnight, in winter 9am-7pm; NIS16, round-trip NIS22.)

⚡ ORIENTATION

Situated on a small peninsula, Haifa rises from the Mediterranean coast up the steep, northern slopes of Mount Carmel. It calls itself the "gateway of the North" for good reason; the cliffs of Rosh Ha-Nikra (and the Lebanon border) are less than 50km to the north. The Sea of Galilee is 70km to the east, and the ruins of Caesarea 40km to the south. The city itself is divided into three terraces and in this vertically oriented town, social stratification is more than just a metaphor; the rich really do live on the top, the poor at the bottom.

The **Ir Ha-Tachtit area** (downtown) fans outward from the port and **Ha-Atzma'ut Rd.** The **Old City** is one block back around **Yafo Rd.,** and it extends to the right (if facing the port) toward **Kikkar Paris,** the lowest stop of the Carmelit subway. Slightly higher up and to the left, the traditional Middle Eastern neighborhood **Wadi Nisnas** lies on and around **Khuri St.** Farther to left, **Ben-Gurion St.** runs uphill and intersects Yafo Rd. at the bottom, **Ha-Meginim Ave.** near the German Colony, **Allenby Rd.** near the **tourist office,** and **Ha-Geffen St.** at the first of the Baha'i gardens. Much farther left on the lower terrace, the **central bus station** adjoins the **train station** at the intersection of Yafo Rd. and **Rothschild Boulevard,** in the **Bat Galim** neighborhood. Yafo then becomes **Ha-Haganna Ave.,** which curves around the peninsula to the beaches.

The middle terrace, the **Hadar** district, teeters precariously on the trendy-trashy border and is home to many clothing stores, cheap hotels, bakeries, and bazaar stands. The two main streets are **Herzl St.** and **Ha-Halutz St.** Ha-Halutz runs parallel to Herzl but one block down. Buses from Herzl go up the mountain, while buses from Ha-Halutz go to the central bus station. The street parallel to and above Herzl is the quiet **Nordau midrahov** (pedestrian zone). **Balfour St.,** perpendicular to these three and bordering Nordau on the left as you face the port, leads up to **Masada St. and Hillel St.** Hadar's Carmelit stop is at the intersection of Herzl St. and **Ha-Nevi'im St.,** a few blocks past Balfour.

The highest area, known as **Carmel Center,** glitters with posh homes, five-star hotels, restaurants, and bars. This district is traversed by **Ha-Nassi Boulevard** and **Yefeh Nof St.** Both pass the Dan Panorama Hotel, next to the **Louis Promenade,** which offers a view of the lower city and the port area. One block up Ha-Nassi is **Gan Ha-Eim,** a peaceful park, near the last Carmelit stop. **Hayam Road** branches to the right off Ha-Nassi and **Wedgewood Ave.** to the left as you walk from the Carmelit

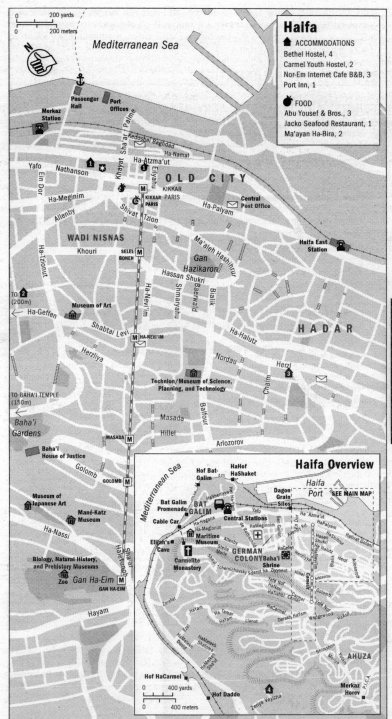

Haifa

⌂ ACCOMMODATIONS
Bethel Hostel, 4
Carmel Youth Hostel, 2
Nor-Em Internet Cafe B&B, 3
Port Inn, 1

🍎 FOOD
Abu Yousef & Bros., 3
Jacko Seafood Restaurant, 1
Ma'ayan Ha-Bira, 2

Mediterranean Sea

0 ⊢ 200 yards
0 ⊢ 200 meters

N

Passenger Hall
Port Offices
Merkaz Station

Kedoshei Baghdad
Khayat Sha'ar Palme
Ha-Namal
Ha-Atzma'ut

Yafo
Ein Dor
Nathanson
Ha-Meginim
Ha-Tzionut
Allenby

Eliyahu
KIKKAR PARIS
Shivat Tzion

OLD CITY

Central Post Office
Ha-Palyam

WADI NISNAS
Khouri
SELEL BONEH

Ma'aleh Hashihrur
Gan Hazikaron
Hassan Shukri
Baervald
Shmaryahu
Bialik

Haifa East Station

TO 2 (200m)
← Ha-Geffen
Museum of Art
Shabtai Levi
HA-NEVI'IM
Herzliya

Ha-Nevi'im

HADAR
Ha-Halutz
Nordau
Chaim
Herzl
3

TO BAHA'I TEMPLE (150m)
Baha'i Gardens

Technion/Museum of Science, Planning, and Technology
Balfour
Masada
Hillel
Arlozorov

MASADA

Baha'i House of Justice
Golomb
GOLOMB

Museum of Japanese Art
Mané-Katz Museum
Ha-Nassi

Biology, Natural History, and Prehistory Museums
Zoo **Gan Ha-Eim**
GAN HA-EIM

Halevanon
Sha'ar

Hayam

ISRAEL

Haifa Overview

Mediterranean Sea
Hof Bat-Galim
HaHof HaShaket

Dagon Grain Silos
Haifa Port
SEE MAIN MAP

Bat Galim Promenade
BAT GALIM
Central Stations
HaSheniyya Hi
Yafo
Ha-Hagana
Ha-Meginim
Allenby
Stella Maris

Cable Car
Elijah's Cave
Maritime Museum
Carmelite Monastery

HaGefen
GERMAN COLONY Baha'i Shrine

Tchernichovsky Sderot ha-Zuyonut
Yefe Nof
HaNassi
HaTishbi
Carmel
Derekh Ha'am
Wedgewood

Zarefat
HaYam
Ha-Tamar
HaYam
Llanot
HaCarmel

HaMeleeh David
HaMelech
Shlomo

AHUZA
Shimshon
Yam
Moria
PICA

Hof HaCarmel
0 ⊢ 400 yards
0 ⊢ 400 meters
Hof Daddo
4
Zeriya Veyizna

Merkaz Horev

stop. The **Cultural Center** and several cafes and bars are farther up Ha-Nassi as it curves right. From Carmel Center, it's a long walk on Moriya St. or a quick ride on bus #24 or 37 to Ahuza—a yuppie district with cafes, restaurants, and Merkaz Ḥorev, a large shopping center.

⁊ PRACTICAL INFORMATION

TOURIST AND FINANCIAL SERVICES

Tourist Information Office: 48 Ben-Gurion St. (☎853 56 06; fax 853 56 10; email haifa5@netvision.net.il). Take bus #22 to the corner of Ben-Gurion and Ha-Gefen St. or walk several blocks to the left of Kikkar Paris Carmelit along Ha-Meginim Ave. and turn left on Ben-Gurion. Distributes free maps (more detailed ones NIS3), and the bimonthly *Events in Haifa* booklet. Free short film on Haifa's highlights. Open Su-Th 8:30am-6pm, F 8:30am-2pm.

Tours: Society for the Protection of Nature in Israel (SPNI), 18 Hillel St. (☎866 41 35), on the 4th floor. Has information and maps (NIS62, in Hebrew) on hiking trips into the Carmel Mountains. Tours must be arranged with the Tel Aviv office. Open Su-Th 9am-2pm and F 8am-1pm.

Budget Travel: ISSTA, 20 Herzl St. (☎868 22 22). ISIC NIS40; HI membership NIS30. Student rates on plane and ferry tickets. Open Su-Tu and Th 9am-7pm; in winter 9am-6pm. Also at the **Technion** (☎832 67 39; fax 832 67 41), in the Student Building. Open Su-Th 9am-5pm; in summer F 9-11:30am, and **Haifa University** (☎825 39 51; fax 834 53 06), next to the #37 bus stop.

US Consulate: 26 Ben-Gurion St. (☎853 14 70; fax 853 14 76; email consage@netvision.net.il), in Hadar. Open Su-Th 9am-1pm (call first). In an emergency, call ☎(03) 519 73 70.

Currency Exchange: Any post office will exchange money without charging a commmission. Also, no-commission services cluster around Palmer Sq., by the port, and by the Gan Ha-Eim Carmelit stop. Banks generally charge a commission: min. US$6, max. 15%. **Bank Ha-Poalim,** 1 Ha-Palyam Blvd. (☎868 14 11). Currency exchange open M-Th 8:30am-2:30pm and F 8:30-11:30am.

American Express: Meditrad Ltd., 6 Ha-Yam St. (☎836 26 96). **Client Letter Service** available. Open Su-Th 8:30am-5pm and F 8:30am-12:30pm.

LOCAL SERVICES

Shopping Hours: Most shops open Su-Th 8:30am-1:30pm and 4-7pm, F 8:30am-1pm, and some open on Sa 8-11pm. Larger stores and malls usually open 8:30am-7pm.

English-Language Bookstores: Steimatzky, 16 Herzl St. (☎866 50 42), has paperbacks, magazines, and travel books. Open Su-Th 8:30am-7pm and F 8:30am-2pm.

Camping Supplies: Ha Metayel, 2 Balfour St. (☎864 42 44), next to ISSTA. Open Su-M and Th 9am-7pm, Tu 9am-6pm, W 9am-2pm, and F 9am-1pm. Also on the 2nd floor of the central bus station.

Ticket Offices: Haifa Municipal Theatre, (☎860 05 00) puts on everything from classic Neil Simon to edgy new Israeli playwrights. There are also general ticket offices for an array of plays, musicals, and concerts. **Haifa,** 11 Baerwald St. (☎866 22 44). Open Su-W 9am-1pm and 4-7pm and Th-F 9am-1pm.

Laundry: Wash and Dry, 5 Ha-Yam Rd. (☎810 78 50), in Carmel Center. NIS12 for up to 7kg; NIS1 per minute to dry. Open Su-M 8:30am-5:30pm, Tu 8:30am-3pm, W-Th 8:30am-5:30pm, and F 8:30am-2pm.

Swimming Pools: Maccabee Pool, 19 Bikurim St. (☎838 83 41), in Central Carmel. Heated and covered in winter. Open Su, Tu, and Th 6am-2pm and 4-10pm, and M and W 6am-2pm and 6:30-10pm, F 6am-2pm and 4-6pm. NIS40. The **Dan Panorama Hotel,** 107 Ha-Nassi Blvd. (☎835 22 22), has a pool open to the public Su-F 7am-5pm and Sa 7am-2pm and 4-5pm. NIS40.

EMERGENCY AND COMMUNICATIONS

Emergency: First Aid: 6 Yitzḥak Sadeh St. **Police:** 28 Jaffa St. **Emotional First Aid** (☎867 22 22). English spoken. Open 24hr.

Pharmacies: Ha-Ḥalutz, 12 Ha-Ḥalutz St. (☎862 06 29), in Hadar. Open Su-Th 8:30am-1pm and 4-7pm and F 8:30am-1pm. **Merkaz,** 130 Ha-Nassi Blvd. (☎838 19 79), in Carmel Center. Open Su-Th 8am-7pm and F 8am-2pm.

Hospitals: Rambam (☎854 31 11), in Bat Galim; **Benei Zion (Rothschild),** 47 Golomb St. (☎835 93 59); **Carmel,** 7 Michal St. (☎825 02 11); **Herzliya Medical Center** (HMC), 15 Ḥorev St. (☎830 52 22).

Post Office: Main branch at 19 Ha-Palyam Blvd. (☎830 41 82), offers **Poste Restante.** Other branches at Shabtai Levi and Ha-Nevi'im St. (☎864 09 17); 152 Jaffa Rd., on the corner of Sha'ar Palmer; 63 Herzl St. in Hadar; and 7 Wedgewood Blvd. next to #37 bus stop at Haifa University. Most open Su-Th 8am-5pm and F 8am-noon, except for the Shabtai Levi St. branch, which is open until 6pm on Su-Th.

Internet: Nor-Em Internet Cafe. See accommodations below.

▊ ACCOMMODATIONS

Options are slim, but growing in Haifa. The two *Let's Go* thumbpicks listed here have made enormously welcome contributions to the budget scene. Also, the Haifa Tourist Board (☎853 56 06) now arranges **B&B stays in private homes** (NIS25-60). Religious hostels offer immaculate premises, but strict curfews thwart nightlife revelry. Beyond these options, buyer beware and take a good look around before committing.

▩ **Nor-Em Internet Cafe Bed & Breakfast,** 27-29 Nordau St. (☎866 56 56; email info@norem.israel.net; www.norem.israel.net), off Haim St., between Herzl St. and the Nordau *midraḥov.* Brand spanking new, this B&B offers spacious rooms, all with A/C and immaculate bathrooms. Laid-back, backpacker-friendly staff serves up drinks, sandwiches, and advice on the city 24hr. a day in the posh cafe. Check-out noon. 6-bed dorms (coed) NIS80/US$20; singles NIS160/US$40; doubles NIS220/US$55. 10% discount for stays longer than 3 days; 20% discount for stays longer than a week.

▩ **Port Inn,** 34 Yafo St. (☎852 44 01; fax 852 10 03; email port_inn@yahoo.com), downtown. From the central bus station, take bus #3 or 5 to the intersection of Ha-Atzma'ut St. and Ben-Gurion. The Port Inn yearns to be your home away from home with a den-like social room, free use of the kitchen and coffee supplies, and a warm and advice-laden manager, who will even do your laundry (NIS30). Internet NIS0.50 per min. A/C in all rooms. Reception 7:30am-midnight; ring the bell anytime. Check-out 11am. 6-bed dorms (single-sex and coed) NIS45/US$11.25, with breakfast NIS55/US$13.75; singles and doubles NIS170/US$42.50, with bath NIS200/US$50.

Carmel Youth Hostel (HI) (☎853 19 44; fax 853 25 16), 4km south of the city at Ḥof Ha-Carmel (Carmel beach). Bus #43 from the central bus station and 44 *alef* from Hadar go directly past the hostel. Though extremely far from the center of town and a schlep from the beach, this simple hostel offers large rooms, cool breezes, and shaded woods. All rooms with A/C and bath. Breakfast included. Lockers NIS6. Check-in 2pm-8pm. Check-out 10am. 6-bed dorms (single-sex) NIS80/US$20; singles NIS128/US$38; doubles NIS224/US$56; triples NIS288/US$72; quads NIS352/US$88; quints NIS416/US$104. HI-card carriers get NIS5 discount.

Bethel Hostel, 40 Ha-Geffen St. (☎852 11 10). Take bus #22 from central bus station to Ben-Gurion St., walk up to Ha-Geffen, and turn right. The hostel is on the right after a couple blocks. A buzz-killer during party time, but in a quiet neighborhood close to the center of town. Christian volunteers keep the rooms sparkling. All rooms have fans. Shared bath in hall. Free dinner on Shabbat and sometimes M and Th. No smoking. Under 18 must be with an adult. Check-in Sa-Th 5-10pm and F 4-9pm. New arrivals may leave bags in locked storage and return after 5pm to register. Lockout 9am-5pm; strict 11pm curfew; wake-up 7am. 8- to 12-bed single-sex rooms NIS56/US$14.

ISRAEL

FOOD

Downtown overflows with *shawarma* and falafel shops, the best option for meals on Shabbat. There's more falafel (there's always more falafel) to be found in Hadar along Herzl and Ha-Ḥalutz St., and slightly more expensive cafes dot the **Nordau midraḥov** (pedestrian section). The lower, even-numbered end of Herzl St.—where the heady fragrance of fresh burekas and croissants wafts from a strip of baker-ies—indulges a sweet tooth, but only until early evening. The area around the Gan Ha-Eim Carmelit stop serves a late night crowd with a mix of chain restaurants, ice cream stands, and several popular cafes and bars along Natanson St.

There is an inexpensive **fruit and vegetable market** just west of the Kikkar Paris station. Another **shuk** lies one block down from Ha-Ḥalutz St., around Yehiel St., where Haifans purchase cheap clothes, groceries, and wine. Finally, Khuri St. in Wadi Nisnas can satisfy any *shuk*-cravings on Shabbat. Be stubborn and bargain.

■ **Iraqi Shishkebab,** 59 Ben-Gurion St. (☎852 75 76). The owner will put anything in a pita to make the mother of all meals. Divine kebab skewers (NIS3 for 2) set a new stan-dard for the culinary arts. Open Su-Th 12:30-10:30pm.

Ma'ayan Ha-Bira, 4 Natanson St. (☎862 31 93), in the midst of the *shuk,* look for Carls-burg signs on your left if coming from the Kikkar Paris Carmelit station. This diner's claim to fame is its home-smoked meats (NIS20-38). Eastern European delicacies like *ikra* (fish salad, NIS15) and *kisonim* (meat dumplings, NIS15) also served. Open Su-F 8am-6pm. Credit cards accepted.

Jacko Seafood Restaurant, 12 Kehilat Saloniki St. (☎866 88 13), near the Kikkar Paris Carmelit station and parallel to, but one block past, the *shuk.* Owner is a former fisher-man who still gets fresh seafood daily (entrees NIS30-60). Enjoy cheap Turkish desserts like *malaby* or semolina with coconut (NIS10). Open Su-F noon-11pm, Sa noon-6pm. Credit cards accepted.

Abu Yousef and Brothers (☎866 37 23), in Kikkar Paris across (away from the port) from the Carmelit. This spacious restaurant in the heart of downtown serves up Middle Eastern delights including kebab, *shishlik,* and *sinaya* with pine nuts (NIS30-40). All dishes come with fries, coffee, and pita on the side. A shot of licorice-flavored *'araq* (NIS7) makes a good *digestif.* Open Sa-Th 8am-midnight, F 8am-6pm.

BEACHES AND ENTERTAINMENT

The beaches surrounding Haifa may not be as large as Tel Aviv's or as beautiful as Netanya's, but they're still a great place to sun-worship or take a see-and-be-seen stroll. Although free beaches sprawl all along the northern coast, the best lie just outside of the city in **Dor** (see p. 349) and **Atlit,** both accessible by bus #921. Within Haifa, **Ḥof Ha-Carmel** and **Ḥof Dado** are most pleasant (bus #43, 44 or 45; 15min.). Hordes of Israelis pour down to these beaches on Friday and Saturday afternoons to play *matkot* (paddleball) and people-watch on the promenade; in summer, the bikini-clad and the men who love them hang out long after sunset. Near the central bus station **Ḥof Bat Galim** (bus #41, 42) has a more sedate promenade. On Tuesday evenings in summer, folk dancers kick it up at both promenades. **Ḥof Ha-Shaket** (Quiet Beach), is a true-to-name, separate-sex beach. (Women Su, Tu, Th; men M, W, F; co-ed Sa.) Lifeguards work from 8am-6pm at each of the beaches.

In the beginning of July, the nearby town of Carmiel fills with people coming to see the **Israeli Music and Dance Festival.** Carmiel is normally accessible from Haifa by buses #261 262, 361 and 501 (every 20-45min., NIS18), and Egged provides extra transportation during the festival. The artsy **Cinematheque,** 142 Ha-Nassi Blvd. (☎835 35 30), is next to the Cultural Center, a few blocks up from the Carmelit sta-tion, just after Ha-Nassi curves right. This theater shows cult classics, new Israeli films, film noir, and the latest US fare. (Su-Th shows 7, 9:30pm and occasionally 5pm; F shows 2 and 10pm; Sa shows 5, 7 and 9:30pm. NIS27).

PUBS

The Bear, 135 Ha-Nassi Blvd. (☎838 17 03), on the corner of Ha-Nassi and Wedgewood Ave., a few blocks up from the Carmel Center Carmelit stop. Everything seems sexier (even before the 4th beer) in this mellow, candlelit bar. Pleases the upper twenty-some thing crowd with indoor and outdoor seating and a monstrously large alcohol menu (beer NIS15-22; cocktails NIS27). Open daily 6pm-3am.

Little Haifa, 4 Sha'ar Ha-Levanon St. (☎838 16 58), between Ha-Nassi and Yefe Nof St., a block down from Gan Ha-Eim park. The oldest pub in the area, with a raucous decibel level matching its age. Drunk American sailors sing about home. Beer NIS10-12. Open M-Sa from 8:30pm until the ship leaves port.

Ha-Olam Hazeh (☎864 20 75), hidden away in a tiny nook on Haim St. between Herzl St. and the Nordau *midrahov*, right next to the Nor-Em Internet Cafe and B&B. This itsy-bitsy bar in Hadar teems with locals and hostel-dwellers alike on weekends and chills out with cocktails (NIS18-24) and tasty toasts (NIS22) on laid-back weeknights. Open daily 9pm-3:30am.

Camel Cafe, down the coast at Hof Ha-Carmel. Almost every customer has a delicious fruit shake (NIS18, with alcohol NIS27) and a navel ring. Skinny dipping is rumored to occur. Beer NIS15-21. Open daily 8am-sunrise.

CLUBS

Hurva (☎862 12 65), on Qedoshe Baghdad St. off Ha-Atzma'ut St. Probably best to take a cab. A veritable carnival of a club, Hurva offers one dance floor with alternative and Euro-techno downstairs and another one on the roof with MTV standards. Henna tattoos (NIS18). Beer NIS10-13; cocktails NIS18. Th 21+ and F 18+. No dress code. Cover NIS30, students with ID NIS25. Open Th-F from 12:15am.

City Hall (☎862 88 02), on Shabtai Levi St., which Herzl turns into after crossing Ha-Nevi'im St. Recently relocated from downtown to Hadar, this Haifan institution opened its doors in the 80s, and its DJ has yet to leave the decade. Beer NIS12-15, free on Th. F men 23+ and women 21+. No dress code. Beer NIS12-15. Cover Th-F NIS40 and Sa NIS35. Open Th-Sa until the dancers collapse.

👁 SIGHTS

BAHA'I SHRINE. The golden-domed Baha'i Shrine that dominates the Haifa sky-line commemorates the Persian Sayyid Ali Muhammad (the Bab), the first Baha'i prophet. In 1890, Baha'ullah, the founder of the Baha'i faith (see **The Baha'i,** p. 62), selected this spot on Mount Carmel, near where he pitched his tent following his exile from Persia to Akko, and instructed his son Abd al-Baha to bury the Bab here and build a great temple in his honor. Though the Bab was executed in 1850 for his religious teachings, devotees transferred his remains numerous times for almost 60 years to prevent them from falling into enemy hands. Finally, in 1909, the Bab was laid to rest as Baha'ullah had wished, inside the shrine, beneath the red carpet. Abd al-Baha built the preliminary structure and Shoghi Effendi, Guardian of the Baha'i religion from 1921 to 1957, embellished and expanded the structure. Modest dress is required and visitors must remove their shoes before entering the shrine. For a stunning view of the entire grounds, look up from Ben-Gurion St. or down from Yefeh Nof St., just past the Louis Promenade. *(Landscaping renovations and a project to create a pilgrim's walkway leading straight from the port all the way up to the shrine have closed the two main entrances until May 2001. Take bus #22 from the central bus station or downtown or bus #23, 25, 26, or 32 from Ha-Nevi'im and Herzl St. to Ha-Tzionut Ave., just above the shrine. Once the project is completed, visitors can ascend the stairs from Ben-Gurion at the bottom, or weave down through magnificent gardens from Yefeh Nof St. ☎835 83 58. Open daily 9am-noon; gardens open daily 9am-5pm. Free.)*

MONASTERY OF THE CARMELITE ORDER. A Latin monk named Berthold founded the Carmelite order in 1156, but the Sultan Baybars destroyed the monastery in 1291. Originally built because the monks were not allowed to live in Elijah's

Cave, the beautiful monastery, which stands on a promontory over Haifa bay, seems a more than reasonable replacement. The monks currently live in a relatively new church and monastery complex called Stella Maris (Star of the Sea), built in 1836 on the ruins of an ancient Byzantine chapel and a medieval Greek church. The monastery's small museum contains finds from the Byzantine and Crusader settlements on Mount Carmel, including toes from a large statue of Jupiter that once stood on an altar on the mount. Because of the Carmelites' affinity for Elijah (St. Elias), the Feast of St. Elias (July 20) is a great time to visit. In the days preceding the Feast, Christian Arabs set up booths with food and games, and a carnival atmosphere takes over the complex. Knees and shoulders must be covered. *(Buses #25, 26, 30 and 31 climb Mount Carmel to the monastery; get off at to the Seminar Gordon stop. A more expensive and scenic way to get to the monastery is via the Rakbal cable car from Bat Galim; see p. 340. ☎ 833 77 58. Open daily 6am-1:30pm and 3-6pm.)*

ELIJAH'S CAVE. Judaism, Christianity, and Islam all revere these grounds as sacred and even magical. According to the Bible, the caves at the base of Mount Carmel sheltered Elijah from the wrath of the evil King Ahab and Queen Jezebel. They were more than a bit peeved at the prophet's drastic attempt to win the hearts of northern Israelites from Ba'al in the 9th century BCE when he brought down a heavenly fire to consume his sacrifices and then slaughtered the 450 priests of Ba'al (I Kings 18). Muslims revere Elijah as al-Khadar, the "green prophet" of the same-colored mountains, Jews believe he will return as the harbinger of the Messiah, and Christians hold that the caves safeguarded the Holy Family upon their return from Egypt. Adherents of each religion now pray quietly in the dim light. Modest dress is required, and there is no eating or drinking inside the cave. The religious (and not so religious) worshipers offering their blessings for you expect pocket change in return. *(230 Allenby Rd. The stairs leading to the cave's entrance are just across from the National Maritime museum, but construction may force you to go around to the left as you face the cave. Just across from the monastery entrance, an inconspicuous trail leads 1km down the Stella Maris ridge to the shrine at Elijah's Cave; do not attempt in sandals. ☎ 852 74 30. Cave open Su-Th 8am-5pm and F 8:30am-12:45pm. Free.)*

TECHNION. Real nerds can check out the Technion, Israel's internationally acclaimed institute of technology. The Coler Visitors Center has English-language newsletters and computerized displays describing the institution's history and achievements from its inception in 1913 to the present. *(Take bus #17 or 19 from downtown, Hadar, or central bus stations; or, #31 from Carmel Center to Kiryat Ha-Technion. ☎ 832 06 68 or 832 06 64. Open Su-Th 8am-2pm. Free.)*

🏛 MUSEUMS

HAIFA MUSEUM

The museum consists of three separately located buildings, each on a different level of the city. All are open M, W, and Th 10am-5pm, Tu 10am-2pm and 5-8pm, F 10am-1pm, and Sa 10am-2pm. A ticket admits the bearer to all three museums for three days in a row. Adult NIS22, children under 18 and students NIS16, seniors NIS11.

MUSEUM OF ART. This avant-garde collection ranges from simplistic blank canvases to downright wacky shoebox architecture. The museum has a small permanent collection but prides itself on its ever-changing, multi-national exhibits. *(26 Shabtai Levi St. in the Hadar district. Take bus #10, 12, 21, or 28. ☎ 852 32 55.)*

TIKOTIN OF JAPANESE ART. The Japanese tradition of displaying beautiful objects in harmony with the season has been embraced by this branch of the Haifa Museum. *(89 Ha-Nassi Blvd, in Carmel Center, between the Nof Hotel and the Dan Carmel Hotel. Take bus #3, 5, 21-23, 28, or Gan Ha-Eim Carmelit. ☎ 838 35 54.)*

NATIONAL MARITIME MUSEUM. The lowest branch of the Haifa Museum (in altitude, not quality). Chronicles 5000 years of maritime history. The intricately detailed ship models, the marine mythology collection, and the Department of Marine Ethnology have the most appeal for the average landlubber. *(198 Allenby Rd., opposite Elijah's Cave. Take bus #3, 5, 44, or 45. ☎ 853 66 22.)*

OTHER MUSEUMS

REUBEN AND EDITH HECHT MUSEUM. This museum houses a permanent exhibit called *The People of Israel in the Land of Israel*, a magnificent collection of archaeological finds from excavations across the country, as well as changing exhibits in its new wings. The small art wing contains Hecht's personal collection of Impressionist paintings and a few others from the Jewish School of Paris. *(On the 1st floor in the main building of Haifa University. ☎825 77 73 or 824 05 77. Open Su-M and W-Th 10am-4pm, Tu 10am-7pm, F 10am-1pm, Sa 10am-2pm. Call for tour info. Free.)*

MA'AGAN MIKHEAL SHIP PROJECT. The main exhibit for the next several years is the reconstruction of an amazingly preserved Phoenician ship from 500 BCE. It was found off the coast of Caesarea, which didn't even have a port in 500 BCE. *(Within the Hecht museum, but affiliated with Haifa University. Hours and information number the same as the Hecht museum.)*

CLANDESTINE IMMIGRATION AND NAVAL MUSEUM. Devoted to *Ha-Apala*, the story of European Jewish immigrants smuggled into Palestine during the British mandate (see p. 268). The museum showcases impressive displays on Jewish underground movements and a recreation of a Cyprus deportation camp. Perched atop the museum is the *Af-Al-Pi-Khen* (In Spite Of Everything), a ship that once ran the British blockade in the 1940s. *(204 Allenby Rd., next to the National Maritime Museum and opposite the lower cable car station. Take bus #3, 5, 43 or 44. ☎853 62 49. Open Su-Th 9am-4pm. NIS10, children and students NIS5, free for soldiers from any country.)*

MANÉ KATZ ART MUSEUM. While the museum usually displays sculptures and canvases by Mané Katz, a member of the Paris group of Jewish Expressionists that included Modigliani, Chagall, and Cremegne, it packs everything up in storage a few times a year for special exhibits of contemporary Israeli artists. *(89 Yefe Nof St., just behind Panorama Center. ☎838 34 82. Take bus #21, 22, 23, or 28, or Gan Ha-Eim Carmelit. Open Su-M and W-Th 10am-4pm, Tu 2-6pm, F 10am-1pm, and Sa 10am-2pm. Free, except during special exhibits when the price ranges between NIS10-25.)*

NEAR HAIFA

ISFIYA AND DALIYAT AL-KARMEL   ☎04

Isfiya and Daliyat al-Karmel are all that remain of 14 Druze villages that once prospered on the Carmel. In 1830, the Egyptian *pasha* crushed a rebellion and then destroyed the area's villages. Thirty years later, the Turks welcomed Druze back to Isfiya and Daliyat, hoping that the towns would serve as buffers against Bedouin marauders and Christian missionaries. Today, some 17,000 Druze make their homes here. Religious Druze elders sport thick mustaches, baggy pants, and flowing white headdresses. Observant Druze women wear dark robes and long white shawls (for more information see **The Druze**, p. 61). A large portion of the population, however, is secular. Unlike those residing in the Golan Heights, the Druze of the Carmel acknowledge their Israeli citizenship, and young men enlist in the army. Although Daliyat is by far the more touristed and interesting of the Druze villages, a visit to Isfiya provides more authenticity.

▤ GETTING THERE. The Druze villages can be visited as a day trip from Haifa. Bus #22 (40min., departs infrequently 1-4:35pm, NIS5) leaves from the central bus station, stops in Isfiya, and then continues along the main road to Daliyat. The best option is to take a *sherut;* they leave from Kikkar Paris off Ha-Atzma'ut St. (to Isfiya NIS11, to Daliyat NIS12) and return from the Egged bus stops in Isfiya (across from the Stella Hospice) and Daliyat (at the top of the *shuk*). It is also possible to catch a bus or *sherut* to or from the University of Haifa. The last bus leaves Daliyat at 2:10pm, but *sherut* taxis run until 5pm, when stores close.

ISRAEL

⚑ ACCOMMODATIONS. Isfiya's only accommodation is the heavenly **Stella Carmel Hospice**, 18 Abu Kish St. A small, tree-shaded sign marks the hostel, which perches atop the hill on the side of the road opposite the PAZ gas station. Though run by the Anglican Church, it's open to all. A converted Arab villa, the hospice has a small, quiet library and a lounge covered in antique Persian rugs. The pleasant volunteer staff complements the serenely quiet atmosphere and provides free trail maps to the surrounding Carmel forest reserve. Reservations one month in advance are recommended, but rooms sometimes available on shorter notice. (☎ (04) 839 16 92; fax 839 02 33; email stcarmel@netvision.net.il. Hearty breakfast included. Doors locked 10:30pm, but keys available for later return. Check-out 11am. 3-4 bed single-sex dorm NIS60/US$15; doubles with bath NIS275/US$65.)

◲ SIGHTS. The scenic mountain road to the Druze villages inspires even the most agoraphobic travelers to explore the outdoors. The ridges and forests of the **Carmel Mountains** spread dramatically into the Yizre'el valley to the southeast and the Mediterranean to the west. SPNI has detailed trail maps, but ideal picnic spots are often just a few steps from the main road (see **Haifa: Practical Information**, p. 342). Down the road from the hospice, **Wadi Chiq** has well-marked forest trails.

Tourists come to Daliyat al-Karmel to shop in the small *shuk* on the main road. The bazaar is busiest on Saturdays, but weekdays make for low prices and better conversation with locals. In a back room of the bazaar's **Mifqash Ha-Akhim Restaurant** is the **Druze Heritage House** (☎ 839 31 69), full of artifacts, photographs, and explanations of all things Druze. Ask the restaurant owner, Sheikh Fadel Nasser al-Din, to let you take a peek. The house also hosts groups of 30 or more for lectures about the Druze people followed by tea and baklava (NIS12). Call ahead to ask about joining in.

The Zionist and Christian mystic **Sir Lawrence Oliphant** was one of few outsiders close to the Druze sect. In the late 19th century, he and his wife lived in Daliyat for five years, helping the Druze build their homes. **Beit Oliphant** now serves as a memorial to the scores of Druze soldiers killed in Israel's wars. A simple but eloquent memorial on the second floor displays the photographs of all the Druze slain in Israeli wars. Sir Lawrence sheltered Arab and Jewish insurgents against the British in a cave between the sculpture garden in the rear and the main house. Oliphant's secretary, the Hebrew poet **Naftali Hertz Imber**, wrote the words to "Ha-Tikva" (The Hope), Israel's national anthem, on the premises. At the far side of the football field, **Kir Ha-shalom** (Hebrew for "the wall of peace"), commemorates the Oslo Peace Accords. Turn right at the same end of the bazaar street as Mifqash Ha-Akhim restaurant and continue for 10 minutes. Beit Oliphant is the stone building across from the domed marble sculpture, shortly after the road veers to the right.

Four kilometers from Daliyat al-Karmel is the site where Elijah massacred 450 priests of Ba'al (I Kings 18:40), a weather-god who had been enjoying popularity because of a harsh drought. **Muhraqa**, the site's Arabic name, refers to the burnt sacrifice that the prophet offered to God on an altar here. Pleased with the Israelites' renewed faith, God sent life-giving rain clouds. The Carmelites later interpreted the clouds as symbols of the Virgin Mary, to whom their order is devoted. In 1886 they built a small **monastery** here. A short flight of stairs leads to rooftop views; on clear days Mount Ḥermon is visible on the horizon. *(There is no bus service to the monastery, so a car or a taxi ride is necessary (NIS20-25). If walking from Daliyat (not advisable), bear left at the only fork along the way. Monastery open M-Sa 8am-1:30pm and 2:30-5pm and Su 8am-1:30pm. NIS1.)*

EIN HOD עין הוד ☎ 04

Though perched on the western slopes of Mount Carmel, 14km south of Haifa, Ein Hod ("Spring of Grandeur") seems to reside in its own surrealist universe. Tin soldiers stand guard along winding, nameless streets, funky mobiles swing between trees, and bronze nudes recline lazily against fences in this small artists' colony. Established in 1953 by Marcel Janco (one of the founders of Dadaism), Ein Hod functions as a cooperative with about 90 members whose talents range from glassblowing to needlework.

🖪 GETTING THERE. To get to Ein Hod, take bus #921 from Haifa, which heads south along the old Haifa-Ḥadera road (20min., every 30min., NIS10). From the junction where the bus stops, the town is a two-kilometer walk uphill, but the magnificent view compensates. To get to the center of town, turn right at the colorful sign and then right again at the fork.

🖩 SIGHTS. The **Main Artists' Gallery,** one of the largest galleries in Israel, displays the work of resident artists. The fantastic exhibits change every four or five months. (☎ 984 25 48. Open Sa-Th 9:30am-5pm and F 9:30am-4pm. Free.) The **Janco-Dada Museum** (☎ 984 23 50) features paintings and *objets d'art* by contemporary Israeli Dadaist artists, a permanent display of Janco's work, a constantly changing exhibit introducing a new artist in the village, and a hilarious and informative film entitled "Excuse Me, What is Dada?" that outlines the origins of the Dada movement. (Open Sa-Th 9:30am-5pm and F 9:30am-2pm. NIS10, students NIS5.) In addition to the main gallery and the museum, residents have their own studios and shops throughout the village which are fun to browse around for window-shopping or chatting with the artist.

Workshops in glass-blowing, pottery, and other crafts are offered on Saturdays at which time no buses run and only residents can park their cars in the village (visitors park in the lot up the hill). The numerous "Pottery" signs lead to **Naomi and Zeev's Pottery Studio,** which offers 45-minute workshops in wheel-throwing for adults and hand-building for children. They also sell a wide variety of ceramics, including a large selection of clay whistles for NIS15-150. (☎ 984 11 07. Workshops offered Sa 10am until dark. NIS30, children NIS15. 50% off for *Let's Go* readers. Open 24hr. Just ring the bell outside for service anytime.)

🖫 DAYTRIPS FROM HAIFA: DOR דור

Take bus #921 from either Haifa (30min., every 30min., NIS12) or Tel Aviv (2hr., every 30min., NIS22.50), or bus #202 from Zikhron Ya'akov (20min., every 1½ hr., NIS8.50). After getting off at the Kibbutz Dor intersection, it's a 4km walk on a well-trafficked road past banana fields to the beach. Many people hitch rides from kibbutzniks going down this road. ☎ 639 09 22. Open Sa-Th 7am-5pm and F 7am-4pm. NIS15, children NIS10.

The pristine **beach** at Dor is protected by four small, rocky islands. Each has a bird sanctuary, and all can be explored at low tide. The Tel Dor archaeological site is on the hill to the right as you face the sea, just past the Kibbutz Naḥsholim beach; footwear is recommended. The site includes temples dedicated to Zeus and Astarte, as well as the ruins of a Byzantine church. Facing the sea, you can see Atlit on the right, Caesarea (or at least its power-generating towers) to the left, and Zikhron Ya'akov and the Arab village of Faradis on the hills behind you.

Next to the beach, within the boundaries of **Kibbutz Naḥsholim,** the **Center of Nautical and Regional Archaeology,** also known as Hamizgaga Museum, displays objects found at Tel Dor and underwater archaeological treasures retrieved by the center's diving team. See 4000-year-old anchors and sea-shell encrusted muskets thrown overboard by Napoleon's troops as they retreated from Acre. (☎ 639 09 50. Open daily 10:30am-3pm. Admission and English film NIS10, students and seniors NIS7.)

A few kilometers north, next to **Kibbutz Ein Karmel,** is the **Naḥal Me'arot Nature Reserve,** with prehistoric caves inhabited some 200,000 years ago. These caves are the only evidence in the world of Neanderthals and Cro-Magnons living simultaneously. Experienced guides explain the significance of the caves and can recommend or lead longer hikes in the surrounding area. English tours and film available. (☎ 984 17 50. Bus #921 goes to the site from Haifa (20min., every 30min., NIS10) and from Tel Aviv (2hr., every 30min., NIS23.20). Get off at Ein Carmel Junction and walk a few minutes south along the road until you see a sign indicating the Nature Reserve. A few hundred meters east of the main road is the entrance to the caves. Open Su-Th 8:30am-4pm and F 8:30am-3pm. NIS18, under 18 NIS9.)

ISRAEL

SOUTH OF HAIFA

NETANYA   נתניה   ☎09

Netanya celebrates laziness in all its glorious forms—baking on the beach, strolling aimlessly along the Promenade, and sipping coffee and people watching in Ha-Atzma'ut Sq. In the 1920s, the town was established itself with a citrus-farm and a few diamond factories in the 1920s, but the tantalizing call of idyllic beaches and the prime location between Tel Aviv and Haifa soon made Netanya one of the most popular hotspots in Israel. In both location and ethos, Netanya leans closer to Tel Aviv; there are even rumors among the locals of mafia infiltration, but crime is far from a glaring problem in this resort town. A significant minority of the tourists hail from landlocked parts of Israel, but there is a decidedly European, especially French, presence in Netanya. Because of the large Russian immigrant population, signs and menus are more often in French and Russian than in English. While the crowd is mostly affluent retirees and families (increasingly more of the latter), students and lone travelers are heartily welcomed into the chilled-out subculture of the young locals.

✈🛈 ORIENTATION AND PRACTICAL INFORMATION

To get to the center of town from the **central bus station** (☎860 62 02), cross the intersection to **Sha'ar Ha-Gai St.** and follow the falafel stands one block to **Herzl St.**, the town's central artery and main shopping area. Turn left and after a few blocks, just past **Dizengoff St.**, Herzl St. empties into the **midraḥov** (pedestrian zone), lined with expensive outdoor cafes and *shawarma* stands. At the end of the *midraḥov* is **Ha-Atzma'ut Sq.** (Independence Sq.), marked by a central fountain, benches and palm trees. Most Netanyans spend their days and nights milling around this area. Stairs to the beach are at the back of the square. Also at the back of the square, on your right as you face the sea, is the entrance to the **Promenade**, a walkway along the cliffs overlooking the sea with an **outdoor amphitheater** and a few playgrounds.

TOURIST AND FINANCIAL SERVICES

Buses: Central bus station, 3 Binyamin Blvd. (☎860 62 02 or 860 62 22), on the corner of Binyamin Blvd. and Ha-Halutzim St. To: **Tel Aviv** (#601 and 605; 1hr.; every 15min. 5:40am-10:30pm; NIS13); **Haifa** (#947, 45min., every 30min., NIS21.50); and **Jerusalem** (#947, 1½hr., every 30min., NIS38).

Sheruts: Across from the station on Binyamin Blvd. To Tel Aviv NIS11.

Taxis: Main services include **Ha-Shahar** (☎861 44 44), **Ha-Sharon** (☎882 23 23), **Hen** (☎833 33 33), and **Netanya** (☎834 44 43).

Car Rental: Hertz (☎882 88 90), **Avis** (☎833 16 19), and **Eldan** (☎861 69 82) have offices at Ha-Atzma'ut Sq.

Tourist Office: (☎882 72 86), at the very back corner of Ha-Atzma'ut Sq., next to the Diamond Center in a tiny brick building with an oddly angled roof. City maps, bus schedules, and event schedules. Many languages spoken. Don't be fooled by the large Foreign Resident and Tourist Center at 15 Herzl St.; it's an investment center. Open Su-Th 8am-6pm and F 9am-noon; in winter Su-Th 8am-4pm and F 9am-noon.

Currency Exchange: Global Change (☎872 47 56; fax 872 47 59), on the left of Ha-Atzma'ut Sq., changes money with no commission. Open Su-Th 8am-7pm and F 8am-1pm. **Bank Ha-Poalim,** on the right as the *midraḥov* empties into Ha-Atzma'ut Sq. Open Su-Tu and Th 8:30am-3pm, W 8:30am-1:30pm, and F 8:30am-12:30pm. **Bank Leumi** (☎860 73 33; fax 860 73 29), on the corner of Herzl and Weizmann St. Open Su and Tu-W 8:30am-1pm, M and Th 8:30am-1pm and 4:30-7pm, and F 8:30am-noon. No exchange Sun. Commission NIS25.

ISRAEL

LOCAL SERVICES

English-Language Bookstores: Steimatzky Booksellers, 4 Herzl St. (☎861 71 54), on the left of the *midraḥov*. Sells books and magazines in Hebrew, English, and a variety of other languages. Open Su-Th 8am-8pm and F 8am-2pm.

Emergency: Magen David Adom First Aid: ☎862 33 33 or 862 33 35. **Police:** ☎860 44 44. **Fire:** ☎862 22 22.

Hospital: Laniado Hospital (☎860 46 66) is the main hospital. From the central bus station, head on Binyamin Blvd. several blocks past Herzl (street will become Sderot Weizmann). Turn left on Rabbi Akiva and right on Divrei Ha-Yamim. The hospital will be on your right.

Telephones: Solan, 8 Ha-Atzma'ut Sq. (☎862 21 31). Private booths for international calls. Fax, telegrams, and cellular phone rental. Open daily 8am-11pm.

Internet Access: Solan (☎862 21 31) has private A/C booths with dial-up connections. NIS12/US$3 per 15min., NIS20 per 30min., NIS28 per hr. Open daily 8am-11pm. **Pinati Internet Cafe,** 15 Remez St. on the corner of Remez and Smilansky (☎862 46 04). In a small cafe selling ice cream (NIS6) and light meals (NIS19-35). NIS8 per 15min., NIS15 per 30min., NIS500 per 5hr. Open Su-Th 9am-9pm and F 9am-1pm.

Post Office: The central branch, 57 Herzl St. (☎862 15 77), offers **Poste Restante.** Another branch, 2 Herzl St. (☎862 77 97). Open Su-Tu and Th 8am-12:30pm and 3:30-6pm, W 8am-1:30pm, and F 8am-noon.

ACCOMMODATIONS

A cheap sleep can be hard to find in Netanya. The hotels, most of which line the beach along **Gad Machnes St.** and **David Ha-Melekh St.,** are fairly expensive (singles NIS240/US$60; doubles NIS300/US$75; add NIS110 for each additional adult). American cash can be used as a bargaining tool, hence prices in dollars don't often jive with standard conversion rates. Reservations are necessary to secure one of the few pleasant and affordable options; call at least two weeks ahead in the summer and a month in August. The most popular areas for **beach-sleeping** are near the cafes and on benches that line the promenade. Since camping on the beach is unsafe, especially for solo women, *Let's Go* does not recommend it.

Orit Hotel, 21 Ḥen Blvd. (☎/fax 861 68 18; email orith@bezenqint.net), off Dizengoff several blocks to the left of Ha-Atzma'ut Sq. This hotel provides a peaceful atmosphere and many perks, including beach towels and a library of Scandinavian and English books. The amiable Swedish management will even pick up guests from the airport (NIS140/US$35). Scrupulously clean rooms, private baths, fans, and balconies. No smoking. Breakfast included. Reception 7am-11pm, but guests can borrow keys to return after it closes. Check-out 10am. Singles NIS170/US$35; doubles NIS240/US$50; each additional bed NIS95/US$20.

Atzma'ut Hostel, 2 Usishkin St. (☎862 13 15; fax 882 25 62), at the corner of Ha-Atzma'ut Sq. and Usishkin St., on the left as you walk through the square from the *midraḥov*. Within stumbling distance of both the square and the beach. The warm and accommodating owners allow early check-ins if a room is ready and luggage storage if it is not (NIS10). To avoid late night noise, ask for a room that does not overlook the square, preferably one with a view of the sea. A/C, fridges, and private baths in all rooms. Reception 24hr. Check-out 11am. 6 and 10-bed (coed) dorms NIS50/US$10; singles NIS100/US$20; doubles NIS150/US$30.

King Koresh Hotel, 6 Ha-Rav Kook St. (☎861 35 55; fax 861 34 34). Turn right on Ha-Rav Kook St. just before Ha-Atzma'ut Sq. The princely sum is about as low as hotels in the area get. All rooms have A/C, spic-and-span bathrooms, cable TV. Daily maid service provides fresh towels and linens. Complimentary safe and luggage storage available. Reception 24hr. Check-in and check-out noon. Singles NIS200/US$50; doubles NIS280/US$70; triples NIS350/US$90. $5-15 student discount.

ISRAEL

◌ FOOD

Cheap food *is* available in Netanya. During the day, the **Shuk Ha-Ir** (the City Market) one block north of Herzl St. overflows with cheap produce and fresh pastries; Pita and hummus for NIS15 on the beach but prices go down and quality goes up closer to the central bus station. **Sha'ar Ha-Gai St.** is lined with self-service falafel stands where one can stuff just about anything into a pita. Just about any place in the square offers a Sabra breakfast—with two eggs, salad, roll and jam, coffee and juice—for NIS20. The blue-and-white **Telad Cafe,** on the right side of the square, serves particularly magnanimous portions. Stock up at the **Nitza Supermarket,** 8 Nitza Blvd. (☎862 82 16), off David Ha-Melech St.

   Mini Golf Restaurant and Pub, 21 Nitza Blvd. (☎861 77 35), perches on the edge of a cliff overlooking the sea. Ideal for a lazy lunch or snack, the restaurant serves up inner peace, a great view, and scrumptious stuffed vegetables (NIS18, with pita), but no putt-putt. Closed on Shabbat.

   Bat Ikar, 14 Sha'ar Ha-Gai St., across from the bus station, fills the tummies of weary travelers and locals alike, 24 hours a day, except on Shabbat. The house specialty, *sambusa* (delicate bread folded around your choice of stuffings, such as cheese and sauce or potatoes), is substantial enough for a light meal (NIS9-10). Pastries go for NIS1-4, any one of their 102 types of bread NIS1-3.

   Kinamon, 13 Remez St. (☎832 25 44), on the corner of Dizengoff St. This candlelit restaurant serves more than *schnitzel.* The munchies platter, a heaping basket of stuffed pastries and vegetables, serves 2-3 (NIS33, add pesto for NIS2). Open Su-Th 8:30am-12:30am, F 8:30am-4:30pm and 7:30pm-12:30am, and Sa 6pm-12:30am.

   Le Moulin, 13 Ha-Atzma'ut Sq. (☎862 77 13), on the right side at the end of the *midraḥov.* This creperie adds a little French flair to the standard fare of the square. People-watch from the outside or chill inside with the A/C while noshing on entree crepes of egg, cheese or meat (NIS17-28) or dessert crepes oozing at the seams with chocolate, fruit, or ice-cream (NIS12-25). Open daily 8am-1am; closed for Shabbat.

◪ ♫ SIGHTS AND ENTERTAINMENT

BEACHES. Netanya's **beaches** are certainly its *raison d'être.* The stunning Mediterranean coast in Netanya is clean, free, and stretches on for 11km. **Herzl Beach,** the most crowded one, just below Ha-Atzma'ut Sq., has waterslides, playing courts, and surfboards for rent. **Sironit Beach,** just to the left of Herzl as you face the sea, is the only one open year-round; the others are open from May to October. **Kiryat Sanz Beach,** farther north, caters to the religious sunsoakers with separate bathing hours for men and women (men Su, Tu, Th mornings and M, W, F afternoons; women M, W, F mornings and Su, Tu, Th afternoons).

FREE ENTERTAINMENT. The Netanya municipality organizes various forms of free entertainment almost every night during the summer and often during the winter. Stop by the tourist office for a complete listing of concerts, movies, and other activities. During the summer, you can watch the sun set over the Mediterranean while listening to classical music in the **Amphitheater** on the Promenade (check the tourist office for times). On Saturdays in summer, folk dance performers in Ha-Atzma'ut Sq. passionately incite the crowd to come join their revelry. Every Monday at noon, talented Russian musicians give classical concerts at 11 Ha-Atzama'ut Sq. (☎884 05 34. NIS18, includes food at pre-concert reception.)

ABECASSIS STUDIO. The art scene in Netanya is limited, but this small studio displays the work of Raphael Abecassis, an internationally acclaimed artist who uses brilliant colors and modern design to portray ancient Sephardic themes. (*4 Razi'el St. next to the post office; from the midraḥov, walk 1km along Herzl St. and turn left on Razi'el St. ☎862 35 28. Open Su-Th 10am-1pm and 4-8pm and F 10am-1pm).*

BARS AND PUBS

Uranus Pub, 13 Ha-Atzma'ut Sq. (☎882 99 19), on the right as you enter Ha-Atzma'ut Sq. from the *midraḥov*. Fashioned after traditional English pubs, Uranus skips the frou-frou and gets back to basics with a wide selection of beer (NIS13-17), straight-up liquor (starting at NIS26), and a laid-back twenty-something crowd. Open daily 8pm-5am.

Ropongi Pub, 9 Herzl St. (☎882 92 99), about halfway between the *midraḥov* and Bin-yamin Blvd. Packed with locals and an international crowd tossing back whatever beer and eating whatever sandwich Ropongi happens to be selling extra cheap that night (each NIS14-19).

The Place (☎844 32 11), down a flight of stairs from 11 Ha-Atzma'ut Sq. Attempts to stem the exodus to Tel Aviv dance clubs with a barrage of bouncers, a strictly enforced dress code (no jeans, but spandex and cleavage almost mandatory), and plenty of neon and blacklight. Russian locals groove to international pop music. Those who opt against the steep cover (NIS50) can still hang out in the adjacent bar. Beer NIS14-20, cocktails NIS33-38. Open Th-Sa 10:30pm-6am.

CAESAREA קיסריה ☎06

At the end of the first century BCE, **Herod the Great,** vassal king of Judaea, estab-lished *Caesarea Maritima* (Caesarea of the Sea; Kay-SAHR-ya in Hebrew). In only 12 years, he constructed a resplendent city of innovative architecture, huge entertainment complexes, and a harbor designed to bring his kingdom to the top of the pecking order of eastern Mediterranean ports. The multi-layered ruins—astonishingly resilient despite riots and rebellions, pillage and plunder, and a par-tial sinking of the coastline—now constitute one of Israel's finest archaeological sites and most popular tourist attractions. The city rapidly became a great com-mercial center and was soon the headquarters of the Roman government in Pales-tine; the procurator of Caesarea from 26 to 36 CE was Pontius Pilate, the man who ordered Jesus' crucifixion in 33 CE. The first evidence of Pilate's existence outside the accounts of the Gospels and the writings of Josephus was on an inscribed stone uncovered in the Roman theater here in 1961.

As the new commercial and cultural center of the region, Caesarea attracted a growing number of newcomers. Not only Romans, but also Samaritans and Jews flocked to the town, and ethnic conflict expanded with the population. This clash between Jews and pagans ignited the six-year **Jewish Rebellion** (the Great Revolt), which resulted in the destruction of Jerusalem's Second Temple in 70 CE (see **Ancient History,** p. 266). The Romans celebrated Jerusalem's fall by slaughtering thousands of Jews in Caesarea's amphitheater and crowning the commanding gen-eral Vespatian as Caesar. By the end of the revolt, Caesarea was the most impor-tant town in the land. Despite the widespread eradication of the Jews, Caesarea's Jewish community remained cohesive and staged a revolution 62 years later, led by **Simon Bar Kokhba.** Legend has it that **Rabbi Akiva,** one of the greatest Jewish sages, supported Bar Kokhba and was jailed in Caesarea by the Romans. They tore him apart with iron combs, and to this day some Jews of the region wear their hair unkempt to memorialize him. Jews returned to the city en masse when Judah the Prince lifted the ban on living there a few centuries later; previously, the city had been deemed impure. In the 3rd century, a school for rabbinical studies was founded, and the city's rabbis are mentioned frequently in the Talmud.

GETTING THERE AND GETTING AROUND

Getting to Caesarea can be difficult. The only practical way is via **Ḥadera,** the near-est town. Buses to Ḥadera are plentiful: from **Tel Aviv** (#852 or 872; 1 hr.; NIS17.20); **Netanya** (#706, 35min., every 30min., NIS8.30; #921, 1hr., every 40min., NIS17.2); **Haifa** (#945, 40min., every 1½hr., NIS17); and **Jerusalem** (#945, 2hr., a few times per day, NIS33). From Ḥadera, however, only bus #76 goes to the ruins (30min.,

NIS8.30) and travels only a handful of times per day. The bus stops at the three entrances to the archaeological park: next to the Roman theater, near the eastern gate of the Crusader wall, and just south of the Crusader city wall (this stop upon request only). While it is possible to get a taxi from the station in Ḥadera (NIS30), finding one for the ride back from the ruins requires advance arrangements and costs about NIS10 more.

▌ ACCOMMODATIONS

Friendly **Kibbutz Sdot Yam** (☎636 44 70 or 44; fax 636 22 11; email kef-yam@sdot-yam.org.il; www.kef-yam.co.il) feels like a ritzy summer camp. To get to the reception office, get off bus #76 at the Roman theater. The kibbutz's main gate is on the left of the theatre, next to the snack bar. Walk about 100 yards behind the tile factory, turn right at the fork in the road just after the tile factory, and follow the signposts to the "Kef Yam" office building at the end of the road. Fifteen private apartments (all with A/C, private bath, refrigerators, TV, and telephones) are ideal for families or for three- to four-person groups, while 6-bed dorms come with bath, TV, linens, and A/C. (Reception open daily 7am-5pm; in winter 7am-4pm. Check-out 10am. Safe available in office. Call at least one week in advance. 6-bed dorms Apr.-June NIS120/US$30 per person; NIS80/US$20 each additional adult; NIS72/US$18 each additional child. Prices up NIS10-20 July-Oct. and down NIS10-20 Nov.-Mar. Extra 15% weekends and holidays.) Many visitors unroll their sleeping bags on the beach, but **camping** in some places, such as Hof Shonit Beach, is forbidden. **Sleeping on the beach** is unsafe and *Let's Go* does not recommend it.

◖ FOOD

Restaurant prices in Caesarea are as high as the Crusader walls. Establishments within the ruins (right at the harbor), such as **Herod's Kosher Restaurant** (☎636 11 03) and **Charley's Restaurant** (☎636 30 50), offer great views but mostly standard fare at outrageous prices (*schnitzel* NIS40-55). The **Sdot Yam Cafeteria,** in the kibbutz, offers a taste of kibbutz life and kibbutz food like *ktsitsot*, salads, and mashed potatoes. (☎636 45 14. All-you-can-eat breakfast buffet 7-10am, NIS23; lunch noon-3pm, NIS38; dinner 6:30-8:30pm, NIS23.) Stock up on picnic supplies like fresh produce and other staples at Sdot Yam's mini-market **Markol** in the lower level of the dining hall building. (☎636 43 58. Open Su, Tu, and Th 11am-1pm and 4-6pm; M and W 11am-1pm. Non-kibbutzniks pay 20% more. Cash only.)

◉ SIGHTS

Caesarea's main sights are the Roman city, ancient port, and large Crusader fortress. A map (NIS10) sold at the three entrances to the **Caesarea National Park** provides a good history of Caesarea, and a well-illustrated booklet (NIS17, includes map) explains each well-labeled site. *(Park open Su-Th 8am-5pm and F 8am-4pm; in winter Su-Th 8am-4pm and F 8am-3pm. NIS18, students NIS15. Hold onto your ticket stub!)*

OTHER SIGHTS. A stroll through the peaceful **Kibbutz Sdot Yam** (see p. 354) provides a good antidote to the feel of the ruins. Shaded paths wind lazily through the well-manicured landscape, past kibbutzniks' cottages and a **playground** constructed from an airplane donated by the Air Force in gratitude for seven kibbutzniks who served about 25 years ago. The two museums in the kibbutz (follow the signs) are small but staffed by knowledgeable and amiable curators.

Most of the relics unearthed at Caesarea are on display at the **Sdot Yam Museum of Caesarea Antiquities** (☎636 43 67). The new archaeological garden and the museum's three rooms contain Jewish, Christian, Samaritan, and Muslim artifacts, Canaanite pottery, 3500-year-old Egyptian urns, and Roman coins and statues. Shield the eyes of any small children from the erotic oil lamps. Next to the museum is the **Hannah Senesh Memorial Centre** (☎636 43 66), built in honor of a

Sdot Yam parachutist who died while trying to save Jews from the Nazis during World War II. Admission includes a short film about Senesh's life offered in six different languages. (*Both open Su-Th and Sa 10am-4pm and F and holidays 10am-2pm. Museum and centre NIS10, students and seniors NIS9*).

☎♫ BEACHES AND ENTERTAINMENT

While the intensely blue water is cool and inviting, **swimming** within the walls of the city is not very economical (NIS25, NIS19 children). Tickets can be bought at Charley's Restaurant (see p. 354) or at the office inside the crusader fortress walls. Unless you wish to snorkel in the ancient harbor, the free public beach behind the aqueduct is a better place to swim. Diving in the harbor is an expensive but rewarding experience. The **Caesarea Diving Center** provides full scuba equipment, beginner lessons, and snorkeling gear. Those who plan to dive without a guide must bring their license, insurance, and log. (☎/fax 626 58 98. Full equipment NIS170 per day; snorkeling gear NIS58 per day; half-day lessons NIS190/US$50; full-day lessons including trip to sunken port NIS380/$US100. Open daily 9am-4pm.) The **Kef Yam Office** in the kibbutz offers glass-bottomed boat tours of the harbor (NIS32), wild tornado-boat rides off the beach (NIS45), and jeep tours to the Carmel Mountains. (☎636 44 44. Reservations required. NIS520/US$130 per 2hr. trip with up to 4 people.)

NORTH OF HAIFA

AKKO (ACRE) عكا עכו ☎04

Dominated by the emerald-domed 18th-century **Mosque of al-Jazzar,** the Old City of Akko (*Akka* in Arabic, historically written "Acre" in English) is surrounded on three sides by the Mediterranean Sea. It gazes across the bay at Haifa's crowded skyline, but the city's stone fortresses and underground Crusader City lend it a character far removed from that of its modern coastal neighbor. Visitors can stroll through the colorful maze of the *souq* or escape to the city's South Promenade and toss back a Tuborg while the waves crash against the city's white walls.

The Canaanite city-state of Akko is first mentioned in the *Book of Curses*, which records the curses of pharaohs on their enemies in the 19th century BCE. After this happy entry onto the international stage, Akko was conquered by the usual suspects: Egyptians, Persians, Greeks, Hasmoneans, Romans, and Umayyads. Crusaders came to the city in 1104 on their campaign to recapture the Holy Land for Christianity. In 1187, with the battle of the Horns of Hattim, Salah al-Din defeated the Crusader forces in Akko; three years later, Richard the Lionheart arrived from England and recaptured the city. During the next century, Crusader kings transformed Akko into the greatest port of their empire and a world-class showpiece of culture and architecture. The Mamluks ended Crusader rule in 1291, and Akko remained impoverished until the Druze prince Fakhr al-Din rebuilt it almost 500 years later. The Muslims built their city directly over the Crusader network of tunnels and basements and left the subterranean labyrinth for wide-eyed tourists. After his unsuccessful siege of the city in 1799, Napoleon claimed that had Akko fallen, "the world would have been mine." After a stint under the Egyptian Ibrahim Pasha, Akko returned to Ottoman control. When the British captured the port in 1918, it held a predominantly Arab population of about 8000.

Akkan locals are eager to share thoughts on their home and their lives while offering much-needed guidance around the dizzying network of Old City streets. However, women traveling alone are strongly advised to be cautious with many of these would-be guides, and all solo travelers are advised to avoid the alleys of Old Akko after dark; stick to the well-lit promenade by the port for a safer stroll.

☞ GETTING THERE AND GETTING AROUND

Trains: The **train station** (☎856 44 44) is on David Remez St., one street behind the central bus station. Trains are often the best way to get to and from Haifa, especially during rush hour. To: **Haifa** (40min., NIS11); **Nahariya** (10min., NIS6.50); and **Tel Aviv** (1¾hr., NIS29). Trains run every hr. Su-Th 5:30am-8:30pm and F 5:30am-3:30pm.

Buses: The **central bus station** (☎854 95 55) is on Ha-Arba'a St. in the new city. Buses go to **Haifa** (#271, 272, and 361; 45min.; every 20min.; NIS11.50; #251 makes local stops) and **Nahariya** (#271 and 272; 15min.; every 20min.; NIS7.20). Buses from platform #16 go to the **old city** until 6:30pm (NIS4).

Taxis: Sherut: off Ha-Arba'a St., across from the bus station. To: **Haifa** (NIS9); **Nahariya** (NIS7); and **Tel Aviv** (NIS25). **Special Taxis: Akko Ba'am** (☎981 66 66).

✴☞ ORIENTATION AND PRACTICAL INFORMATION

In **New Akko**, the central bus station is on **Ha-Arba'a St.** and the train station is one block behind it on **Remez St.** To get to the old city, turn left on Ha-Arba'a St. (with your back to the bus station), and after one block make a right on **Ben-Ami St.** Continue for a few blocks (past the bustling *midraḥov*) and turn left on **Weizmann St.** **Ha-Atzma'ut St.**, the new city's major thoroughfare and home to the main post office and city hall, and **Herzl St.** also run between Ha-Arba'a St. and Weizmann St. Once in **Old Akko**, visitors will likely be dismayed by the lack of street signs—locals and monuments are the best (and only) navigational tools. **Al-Jazzar St.** and **Salah al-Din St.** extend in opposite directions from slightly different points near the main entrance on Weizmann St. Most museums are on al-Jazzar St., and the **souq** begins from a plaza off the right side of Salah al-Din St. when coming from Weizmann St. **Ha-Hagana St.** runs from the far side of the peninsula to the coast of the **Pisan Harbor,** which is lined with touristy restaurants, a pleasant promenade, and sitting areas with great bay views.

Tourist Office: Municipal Tourist Information Office Booth (☎/fax 991 17 64), on al-Jazzar St. and across from the mosque, inside the same building as the post office. Open Su-Th 8:30am-6pm, F 8:30am-2:45pm, and Sa 9am-5:45pm; in winter Su-Th 8:30am-5pm, F 8:30am-2:30pm, and Sa 9am-5pm.

Currency Exchange: Mercantile Discount Bank (☎955 46 67), corner of al-Jazzar St. and Weizmann St. Open Su, Tu, W 8:30am-1pm; M, Th 8:30am-noon and 4:30-7pm; F 8:30am-1pm. **Bank Leumi** (☎995 63 33), on Ben-Ami St. near Weizmann St. Open Su, Tu, W 8:30am-1pm; M, Th 8:30am-1pm and 4:30-7pm; F 8:30am-noon. **ATMs** at both banks. **Change Spot** (☎991 68 99), at the end of al-Jazzar St., across from the post office, changes currency with no commission. Open Su-F 8am-5pm.

Emergency: Magen David Adom (☎991 23 33).

Police: 16 Ha-Hagana St. (☎987 68 68).

Pharmacy: Merkaz (☎991 47 02), at the corner of Ben-Ami and Weizmann St. Open Su-Th 8am-1pm and 4-9pm and F 8am-1pm. Pharmacies rotate 24hr. duty; schedules are posted in the windows.

Hospital: Mizra Hospital (☎955 95 95), north of new Akko.

Post Office: Central branch at 11 Ha-Atzma'ut St. (☎306 66 66) offers **Poste Restante.** Open M, Tu, Th 8am-12:30pm and 3:30-6pm, W 8am-1:30pm, and F 8am-noon. Other **branches** at 53 Ben-Ami St. and on al-Jazzar St.

☞ ACCOMMODATIONS

Dorm rooms are some of the cheapest in the area, yet remain rather empty. Quality varies greatly for even small price changes, so consider carefully before committing. All of the following will pick you up from the bus or train station; just call when you arrive. There are unofficial and unregulated rooms for rent in the old city; signs tend to cluster near the bus station, on the *midraḥov* in the new city, or around the entrance to the old city. Get an opinion from the tourist office before making a decision. **Beach camping** is forbidden and dangerous.

Lighthouse Hostel, 175 Ha-Hagana St. (☎991 19 82; fax 981 55 3), at the end of Ha-Hagana St., a few minutes before the lighthouse. This gorgeous Turkish mansion is the place to stay in Akko. The huge dorms may be plain, but they are clean. The large, airy lounge with marble pillars can make even the grimiest backpacker feel like a sultan. Bike rental NIS35 per day. Kitchen available. Breakfast NIS15. Reception 24hr. Check-out 10am. Single-sex and coed dorms NIS25/US$6.25; singles NIS105/US$26.25; doubles NIS120/US$30. Cash only.

Walied's Akko Gate Hostel (☎991 04 10; fax 981 55 30), near the eastern Nikanor Gate on Salah al-Din St., a mere stumble from the beach. Sports a rooftop bar and a pool table (NIS25 per hr.). Kitchen available. Breakfast NIS25. Check-out 10am. Single-sex and coed dorms NIS25/US$6.25; rooms NIS120/US$30, with A/C and bath NIS200/US$50. Credit cards accepted.

Paul's Hostel and Souvenir Shop (☎991 28 57 or 981 76 86). Souvenir shop doubling as reception is just across from the lighthouse at the southern end of Ha-Hagana St. under a large yellow awning. For a down-and-dirty backpacker experience, this hostel has one large room stuffed with bunkbeds and a single bathroom. Climate control, summer and winter, consists of a few ceiling fans. Reception 24hr. Check-out noon. Coed 20-bed dorms NIS20/US$5; private room with bath NIS100/US$25.

◐ FOOD

The *souq*, a tumultuous avenue of butchers, bakers, candlestick-makers, and copper, brass, and leather vendors, bustles from 6am-5pm, though supplies start to run out after noon on busier days. Food stands along the *souq* offer kebab, falafel, and sandwiches (NIS5-10) as well as cheap, fresh produce and exotic spices. There are also food stands and supermarkets on Ben-Ami St. and Yehoshafat St. in the new city. More expensive options can be found in the Pisan harbor, where standard Middle Eastern meat and fish entrees go for NIS35-65.

▨ Hummus Said's (☎991 39 45), in the midst of the *souq*, on your right when coming from the plaza off Salah al-Din St. Kick, shove, bribe: do whatever it takes to get through the hordes of locals. NIS12 buys 3 piping hot pitas, a plate of vegetables, and a deep dish of creamy hummus. If there are no tables open (and there won't be), try the take-out version, a pita stuffed with hummus, hot chickpeas, and vegetables (NIS3.50). Open M-Sa 6am until the food runs out, usually around 2pm.

Oriental Sweets, right next to Said's. Every possible combination of filo dough, nuts, and honey goes for NIS1-3. Even cheaper in large quantities. Open daily 8am-5pm.

Ptolmais Restaurant (☎991 61 12), on the left side of the marina, when facing the sea. One of the cheaper options on the marina, Ptolmais serves up lamb *shishlik* (NIS45) and various kebabs (NIS33), but herbivores just there for the great view might opt for hummus or tahini and pita (NIS13). Open daily 11am-midnight.

◐ SIGHTS

The moats and dungeons of **Old Akko** speak clearly of the city's war-filled history. Guides—a.k.a. juice bar workers, waiters, and shopkeepers in their spare time—offer tours of varying quality and for varying prices. Ballpark figures are NIS15 for a sight and NIS120 for all of Akko, but make sure to verify beforehand. Women, especially, should ascertain what is expected in return for these tours.

CRUSADER CITY. Archaeologists first thought that the rooms in the Crusader City were built underground; they have since determined that al-Jazzar simply built his city on top of once above-land buildings. Much of the Crusader city still remains buried, but excavations expose more treasures each year. Most visible structures are part of the "Hospitaller's Quarter." Decorations on the columns with images of flowers or human forms are Crusader work, while abstract embellishments and Arabic calligraphy come from Ottoman artisans. The 12th-century halls were probably part of a medical complex where the Hospitaller Order treated pilgrims. From the courtyard beyond the entrance hall, fortifications built by Fakhr al-Din and Tahir al-Omar are visible. Halfway down the stairs on the left and along the wooden path are the giant rooms of the Hospitaller Castle, called the **Knights' Halls,** built on top of 3rd-century BCE Hellenistic foundations. *(Across from the mosque on al-Jazzar St., in the same building as the tourist office. ☎ 991 17 64. Open Su-Th 8:30am-7pm and F 8:30am-3pm; in winter Su-Th 8:30am-4:45pm and F 8:30am-2pm. NIS25, children and students NIS22. For groups over 20: NIS21, children and students NIS18. Ticket includes access to all sights in the Crusader City and the Okashi Museum and comes with a hand-held audio tour in English, Hebrew, or German. Combination ticket available with Rosh Ha-Nikra.)*

MOSQUE OF AL-JAZZAR. The third-largest mosque in Israel, it dominates the city with its green dome and towering minaret. Ahmed al-Jazzar ordered its construction in 1781 on what is believed to have been the site of San Croce, the original Christian cathedral of Akko. Inside is an attractive courtyard with Roman columns taken from Caesarea. Legend has it that al-Jazzar buried a large treasure underneath the mosque to ensure that there would be plenty of money to rebuild the place if it were ever destroyed. The tower was destroyed by an earthquake in 1927, but was promptly restored; the rest of the complex is in magnificent condition. Inside, in the green cage on the right side of the balcony, is a shrine containing a hair from the beard of the prophet Muhammad. Prayers are conducted five times a day, and visitors who arrive during a prayer session may be asked to wait. *(The entrance is a short walk on al-Jazzar St., across from the post office. Open daily 8am-7pm; in winter 8am-5pm. Closed periodically for 20min. during prayer time. NIS5, NIS3 after 4pm. Modest dress required; scarves available for those not already covered.)*

To the right of the mosque is a small building containing the **sarcophagi** of al-Jazzar and son; peek through the barred windows at the marble boxes, now covered with soil and green plants. Al-Jazzar turned the buried Crusader cathedral into an underground water reservoir that received rainwater from the nearby Pasha gardens. The reservoir is accessible through a door and underground stairway at the left end of the mosque. Look for the small green sign and red arrows.

CITADEL. This stronghold, used by the British as their central prison, now houses the **Museum of Heroism,** a monument to Zionist fighters imprisoned by the British during the Mandate. The citadel, built in the late 1700s on 13th-century Crusader foundations, was used as an **Ottoman prison.** The most famous inmate during the Ottoman rule was Baha'ullah, founder of the Baha'i faith, who was imprisoned on the second floor in 1868. During the British Mandate, the prison housed about 560 inmates under the guard of about half as many British soldiers. Members of the Etzel, Ha-Ganah, and Leḥi, including Ze'ev Jabotinsky, were incarcerated here for violent anti-British activities. Nine members of the resistance were sentenced to death by hanging between 1938 and 1947. The **Gallows Room** displays the noose, along with photographs of the nine fighters. On May 4, 1947, Etzel members staged a prison break that freed 41 of their peers and enabled the escape of 214 Arab prisoners (later depicted in the movie *Exodus*, shot on location). Across from the museum looms **Burj al-Kuraim** (Fortress of the Vineyards), often referred to as the British Fortress despite its Crusader and Ottoman construction. *(The Citadel adjoins the Crusader City on Ha-Hagana St., opposite the sea wall. To reach the museum from the Old City, exit on Weizmann St. and take an immediate left on the path. At the entrance, follow the stone stairs down to the lower garden, then the metal stairs up and around the side of the prison. ☎ 991 82 64. Open Sa-Th 9am-6pm and F 9am-1pm. NIS8, students NIS4.)*

THE CITY WALLS. A stroll along the Old City's cannon-spotted perimeter yields an interesting look at Akko's seaside defenses. Akko's security in recent centuries has relied upon the **al-Jazzar Wall,** running along the northern and eastern sides of the city and surrounded by a sea water moat. The best place from which to view the wall, which originally ran the length of the harbor, is **Burj al-Kommander** (Commander's Fortress), an enormous Crusader bastion at the northeastern corner. To enter the watchtower, climb the steps beginning where Weizmann St. meets the wall. Follow the green signs, which describe Napoleon's siege in reference to the walls, despite the fact that they were built after Napoleon's retreat; the deception works because the new walls are in form, if not appearance and dimensions, the same as the old. England blew up the original walls in the siege of 1840 (almost half a century after Napoleon), when the Egyptians were using them as an ammunition dump. The **Tower of the Flies,** the site of the original lighthouse, solemnly broods in the middle of the bay. Its fortifications were toppled by a devastating earthquake in 1837. At the eastern corner near the shoreline is **Land Gate** (also known as Nikanor Gate), once the only entrance to the city. Next to the marina, locals like to leap into the water from windows in the walls.

▐ DAYTRIP FROM AKKO: LOHAMEI HA-GETA'OT

Lohamei Ha-Geta'ot lies between Akko and Nahariya. To reach the kibbutz, take bus #271 from Akko or Nahariya (10min., every 20min., NIS7) or a sherut (NIS6.50).

Lohamei Ha-Geta'ot ("Fighters of the Ghettos") is a kibbutz founded in 1949 by survivors of concentration camps and the Warsaw Ghetto uprising. It now houses an entire building dedicated to the stories of children, and is one of Israel's most powerful Holocaust museums. The **Ghetto Fighter's House** examines Jewish life in Eastern Europe during the years leading up to World War II and during the Holocaust. The exhibits on Jewish Youth resistance movements during the war and ghetto uprisings are particularly intriguing. An entire floor chronicles the Nazi invasion of Europe and more specific exhibits relate the stories of Jews in Holland and Greece. (☎995 80 80; fax 995 80 07; email mgans@gfh.org.il. Open Su-Th 9am-4pm; May-Sept., Su-Th 9am-6pm and F 9am-1pm. Free, but donation requested.) The recently constructed **Yad La-Yeled** in a nearby building is a memorial to the 1½ million children who perished in the Holocaust.

NAHARIYA נהריה   ☎04

Nahariya is literally a one-horse town—hang around Jabotinsky St. long enough, and you'll see the tired beast hauling tourists around in a white buggy. In 1935, Nahariya's first settlers tried their hands at farming, but because of stiff market competition, the relatively pleasant weather, and the beautiful coastline, they soon realized that the tourism industry was their best and only hope for survival. Most families and older people come to Nahariya to relish the slow-motion lifestyle; for travelers, it's a convenient, if expensive, base for its surrounding sites.

▐ GETTING THERE AND GETTING AROUND

Trains: Station at 1 Ha-Ga'aton Blvd. (☎856 44 46). Trains to: **Akko** (10-15min., NIS6.50); **Haifa** (40min., NIS13); and **Tel Aviv** (1¾hr.; NIS35.50, students NIS29.50). Trains depart approx. every hr. Su-Th 5:20am-8:20pm, F 6:10am-2:10pm. Sa 9:15pm-noon; in winter 7:20pm-noon.

Buses: 3 Ha-Ga'aton Blvd. (☎992 34 34). Buses #270 (express), 271, and 272 go to **Haifa** (1hr., every 20min., NIS14) and #271 and 272 go to **Akko** (20min., every 20min., NIS7).

Sherut: Or Nahariya (☎992 78 88), on the right of the central bus station when facing the street, runs to **Akko** (NIS7). *Sherut* to **Haifa** (NIS12) in front of the bus station.

Car Rental: Avis, 31 Ha-Ga'aton Blvd. (☎951 18 80), beside the Penguin Cafe. Rents automatics NIS184/US$46 per day; manual NIS168/US$42 per day. Must be 23 and have had license for 2 years.

ISRAEL

✴ 🛈 ORIENTATION AND PRACTICAL INFORMATION

Most sights and tourist resources are on **Ha-Ga'aton Blvd.** If your back is to the bus or train station on Ha-Ga'aton Blvd., **Jabotinsky Blvd.** is several blocks to the right. It has many hotels and rooms to let. The beach is another block farther along Ha-Ga'aton Blvd.; stop when you get wet.

Tourist Office: Municipal Tourist Information Office, 19 Ha-Ga'aton Blvd. (☎ 987 98 00), on the plaza of the Municipality Building, before Herzl St. Open Su-W 8am-1pm and 4-7pm and Th-F 8am-1pm.

Currency Exchange: The post office gives bank rates for no commission, as does Change Spot, 36 Ha-Ga'aton Blvd. (☎ 951 27 60). Open Su-Th 9am-7pm and F 9am-2pm.

English-Language Bookstore: Doron Books, 32 Ha-Ga'aton Blvd. (☎ 992 10 79), has newspapers and paperbacks. Open Su-Th 7:30am-1:30pm and 4-7:30pm; F 8am-2pm.

Emergency: First aid: ☎ 991 23 33. **Fire:** ☎ 982 22 22.

Police: 5 Ben-Zvi St. (☎ 992 03 44).

Pharmacy: Szabo Pharmacy, 3 Ha-Ga'aton Blvd. (☎ 992 04 54 or 992 11 97), in front of the bus station. Open Su-Th 8am-1:30pm and 4-7:30pm, F 8am-2:30pm.

Hospital: (☎ 985 05 05), Ben-Zvi St.

Post Office: 40 Ha-Ga'aton Blvd. (☎ 992 01 80), has **Poste Restante** and sells the cheapest international calling cards. Open Su-Tu and Th 8am-12:30pm and 3:30-6pm, W 8am-1:30pm, F 8am-noon.

▌ ACCOMMODATIONS

Accommodations in Nahariya are quite expensive, especially in summer. Reservations are generally a good idea. In summer, rooms are sometimes available in private homes. "Rooms to Rent" signs are common on Jabotinsky St. (NIS75 or more; polite bargaining may help). The tourist office keeps a list of officially recognized B&Bs, but not prices or descriptions; the quality range is large, check them out first. For cheaper beds, head south to **Akko** (see p. 356).

Motel Arieli, 1 Jabotinsky St. (☎ 992 10 76), on the corner of Ha-Ga'aton Blvd., and a block from the beach. Leafy paths off the patio lead to clean, if somewhat cramped, bungalows. Reception 24hr. Check-out 10am. Singles NIS100/US$25, with bath and A/C NIS150/US$37.50; doubles with bath and A/C NIS200/US$50. Cash only.

Hotel Rosenblatt, 59 Weizmann St. (☎ 992 00 69; fax 992 00 69), off Ha-Ga'aton Blvd. In furnishings and aura, this hotel vaguely resembles a 70s country club—swimming pool included (in summer). All rooms have A/C, bath, and cable TV. Breakfast included. Reception 24hr. Check-out 11am. Singles NIS160/US$40; doubles NIS240/US$60. In winter NIS20/US$5 discount. Discounts available for longer stays.

Erna Hotel, 29 Jabotinsky St. (☎ 992 98 52), a few blocks off Ha-Ga'aton Blvd. This quiet hotel rests close to the beach. Rooms have A/C, TV, and bath. Breakfast included. Singles NIS180/US$45; doubles NIS240/US$60; extra person NIS80/US$20.

🍴 FOOD

Nahariya suffers from a remarkable dearth of falafel stands (NIS10) and a glut of overpriced touristy cafes (bagel toast NIS35). The beaches and gardens make lush picnic grounds; shop at the **Co-op Tzafon supermarket,** on the corner of Ha-Ga'aton Blvd. and Herzl St. (☎ 992 72 10; open Su-Tu 7:30am-8pm, W 7:30am-8:30pm, Th 7:30am-9pm, and F 7:30am-2:30pm), or at the fruit and vegetable stores on Herzl St. between Ha-Ga'aton Blvd. and Ha-Meyasdim St. Plan ahead for shabbat.

Penguin Cafe, 31 Ha-Ga'aton Blvd. (☎ 992 00 27). Families and young couples crowd into this old-standard, established when Nahariya was a six-year-old farm town. Cakes NIS19. Open Su-Th 8:30am-midnight and F-Sa 8:30am-2am.

Penguin Gelateria, 33 Ha-Ga'aton Blvd. (☎992 42 41), neighbor of Penguin Cafe and a bit cheaper. Dozens of sundae varieties (NIS21-29) and a huge Israeli breakfast (NIS25). Open daily 7am-3am.

El Gaucho, 33 Ha-Ga'aton Blvd. (☎992 86 35), serves Argentinian fish and meat entrees (NIS45-55) in a rustic setting. Open Sa-Th noon-midnight and F noon-1am.

🔊 SIGHTS AND ENTERTAINMENT

Nahariya slowly roasts visitors along its sandy strip. **Galei Galil,** a right turn from the end of Ha-Ga'aton Blvd., has a breakwater, a lifeguard, lots of sand, and a pool. (Open end of May-Oct. 8am-6pm. NIS20.) A **free beach,** past the end of the promenade, has neither a lifeguard nor breakwater, but locals surf here anyway.

The dull but archaeologically important remains of a 4000-year-old **Canaanite Temple** dedicated to Asherah, the goddess of fertility, were discovered in 1947 on a hill next to the shore (30 Ha-Ma'apilim St., a 20min. walk to the right of the beach as you face the sea). The **Nahariya Municipal Museum,** in the Municipality Building just west of Herzl St., has exhibits on art, archaeology, malacology (the study of seashells), and the history of Nahariya. (☎987 98 63. Open Su and W 10am-noon and 4-6pm, Tu and Th 10am-noon. Free.) An ornate mosaic floor is all that remains of a 4th-century **Byzantine church** on Bielefeld St., near the Katzenelson School. (☎987 98 63; call ahead for a free visit.)

The tourist office isn't lying when they say, "Nahariya is hot, but not at night." Strolling along the Promenade is the most popular activity of all ages. Next to the beach are a couple of pubs with stupendous sunset views over the Mediterranean. Pub **Mul Ha-Yam,** a left turn after Ha-Ga'aton Blvd., meets the sand and steadfastly vends booze. (☎992 00 69. Drinks NIS14-20. Open daily 5pm until the tide comes in.) All ages participate in fun **folk dancing** at the amphitheater, near the end of Ha-Ga'aton Blvd. (Late May to early Oct. W and Sa 7:30-9:30pm.) Those determined to kick it with the 30-60 something crowd can head to the **Carlton Hotel disco,** in the middle of town on Ha-Ga'aton Blvd. (Cover NIS50. Open F 10pm.) The **Hekhal Ha-Tarbout** (☎982 99 33), on Ha-Atzma'ut Rd., screens three movies in English.

🏞 DAYTRIPS FROM NAHARIYA

ROSH HA-NIKRA ראש הנקרה

*Bus #20 and 32 depart from Nahariya to the site but only a couple times per day (NIS8). Alternately, **sheruts** to Shlomi will stop at the Misrafot Junction (NIS6); the site is a 3km uphill walk on the main road from there. ☎985 71 09. Cable car down to grottoes runs Apr.-June and Sept. Sa-Th 8:30am-6pm and F 8:30am-4pm; July-Aug. Sa-Th 8:30am-11pm and F 8:30am-4pm; Oct.-Mar. daily 8:30am-4pm. NIS34, students and seniors NIS29, children NIS27; discount ticket includes Akko sites.*

The spectacular white chalk cliffs and grottoes of Rosh Ha-Nikra occupy the northernmost point on Israel's coastline. Rosh Ha-Nikra's caves, sculpted by millennia of lashing waves, nearly make one forget the mountain of barbed wire and the Uzi-toting soldiers who guard the tense Lebanese border only a few steps from the parking lot. The British enlarged the natural chalk grottoes when they bore a tunnel through the cliffs during World War II in order to complete a railway line linking Turkey with Egypt. The nearby kibbutz, smelling the chance for a new tourist trap, blasted additional tunnels through the rock to improve access to the sea caves, topped the cliffs with an observation point and cafeteria, and connected the highway to the caves with a cable car. Don't expect arduous spelunking here, a pleasant walk through the slippery grottoes is a half-hour affair. Arrive early or be caught in the afternoon throngs of youth and tour groups.

MONTFORT AND NAHAL KEZIV

*Frequent **buses** leave Nahariya from platform #6 for the Christian Arab village of Mi'ilya (#40, 41, 43, 44, and 45; 20min.; every 30min.; NIS10). From the stop, turn left and* *climb up the steep road toward Mi'ilya for about 30min. At the wooden sign for Montfort, the road veers right to Hilla. Continue straight and follow the red-and-white markers down the rocky path to the castle (another 30min.). The set of stone steps on the right is an alternate path to the ruins. The original trail turns to the right shortly, then travels across a small bridge and up the rocks to the castle. The site is currently under renovation and officially* **closed,** *but visitors have been known to prowl around. Bus #25 (8:15pm only) goes from the park to Shlomi, where there are sherut to Nahariya (NIS7). Bus #28 from Kibbutz Eilon goes back to Nahariya (8:10am, noon, 3:15, 5:15, 7:45pm; NIS10).*

The Crusader **castle** of Montfort splendidly rewards a challenging hike; the windswept ruins overlook the western Galilee's steep Keziv Valley. The Knights Templar built the main structure early in the 12th century; Salah al-Din partially destroyed it in 1187. The Hospitaller Knights enlarged the fortress in 1230 and called it Starkenburg or Montfort ("strong mountain" in German or French). The complex's impressive 18m tower and 20m main hall stand among its remains.

Those who enjoy more strenuous pleasures can visit by way of a longer hike. The four-hour hiking loop has spectacular views and begins at the lookout point on the road to Hilla (coming from Mi'ilya, turn right at the wooden sign). It descends into the **Nahal Keziv Valley** and then circles back up to Montfort. Follow black- or blue-and-white markers down into the valley, green-and-white while along the river, and red-and-white up to the castle and back to Mi'ilya. Several other trails branch off the loop. Following the river away from Montfort, green-and-white markers lead to the **Ein Tamir** and **Ein Ziv** springs. Ascending the slope opposite Montfort leads to **Goren Park** (follow red-and-white markers), a perfect vantage point for the castle (amazing at sunset).

Just north of Montfort is the **Nahal Betzet Nature Reserve,** another fabulous stomping ground for hikers. Take a bus from Nahariya (#24; 30min.; departs 8:25am, 1, 3:30pm; NIS12) and ask the driver to stop at the path to Me'arat Keshet, or **Bow Cave.** Ascend the red-and-white marked trail for 20 minutes to reach the enormous cave, a natural arch affording dramatic views of the forested Galilean hills and cliffside caves. Descending into the cave requires ropes, and spelunkers should consult beforehand with SPNI (see **From Sea to Shining Sea,** p. 363).

YEHI'AM (JUDIN) FORTRESS מבצר יחיעם

Buses #39 and 42 from Nahariya stop at the kibbutz (20min., infrequent, NIS8). ☎(04) 985 60 04. Open Su-Th 8am-5pm and F and holidays 8am-4pm; closes 1hr. early during winter. NIS10, students NIS7, though kibbutzniks have hopped the fence during off hours.

In 1208, the Teutonic Knights inherited the **Judin Fortress,** built by the Templars in the 12th century. Mamluk Sultan Baybars destroyed the fortress in 1265, and Bedouin governor Dahr al-Omar partially restored it in the 18th century. In 1946, Jewish settlers moved back into the deserted castle and founded **Kibbutz Yehi'am.** Two years later, during the War of Independence, they became the most recent group to use it for protection. Though only half of the relief convoy reached the site, the kibbutz held out until Israeli forces took control of Western Galilee in May of 1948. The fortress still stands within the kibbutz grounds, the source of its new Hebrew name. Its nooks and crannies make for great exploration. Dancers, musicians, and artisans (in full period garb) crowd the fortress during *Sukkot* (Oct. 2-9, 2001) for the **Days of Renaissance Festival** every year.

PEKI'IN (BKE'AH) פקיעין بقيعة

Bus #44 (50min., 7 per day, NIS14) makes the round-trip to Peki'in from Nahariya and will stop just above the cave upon request. Be sure to get off at Peki'in Ha-Atika (Old Peki'in), not Peki'in Ha-Hadasha (New Peki'in). At the blue-and-white sign, turn right and descend the stairs. At the large bush with houses behind it, turn right and walk between the two large rocks; the cave is a tiny hole about 3m away. Donation requested.

Rabbi Shimon Bar-Yohai and his son Eliezer fled to Peki'in (Bke'ah in Arabic) when a Roman decree during the Bar Kokhba revolt banned the study of Torah. For 12 years, this erudite duo hid in a small hillside cave and, sustained by a nearby spring and generous carob tree, delved into their illicit book of learning. It

FROM SEA TO SHINING SEA One of Israel's most popular and challenging hikes is the three-to-four-day Yam L'Yam trek from the Mediterranean to the Sea of Galilee (or vice versa). The best place to start is at the Keziv Bridge in Akhziv, about one kilometer south of the SPNI Field School (☎ 982 37 62; also rents rooms). Contact SPNI for information and maps before attempting this hike. Cross the bridge and follow the green markers upstream along Naḥal Keziv for the first day. On the second day, the green path leads to the Druze village of Ḥurfish, a good place to restock on food. From Ḥurfish, follow the green or red markers up to the Hurbat parking lot, the next sleeping station. Black markers line the way from Hurbat to the peak of Har Meron (1½hr.). It's all downhill from here: follow the black marker down Naḥal Meron, which leads to Naḥal Amud, named for the large pillar carved out by the river. Israelis who haven't been to the Grand Canyon call it the eighth wonder of the world. The black markers on upper and lower Naḥal Amud lead to Kibbutz Hokkuk, next to the Sea of Galilee. From the kibbutz, buses #459 and 963 go to Tiberias. Plan ahead, bring a compass, and do as much walking as possible in the early morning. With proper planning, this trek can be the experience of a lifetime.

is during this period that Bar-Yoḥai is said to have composed the *Zohar*, the central text of Kabbalah (Jewish mysticism), though most evidence suggests it was composed about a millennium later. According to popular legend, Bar-Yoḥai's gaze started **angry fires** in the fields of those less worthy. When God saw this, he sent Bar-Yoḥai back into the cave to chill out for another year. In its present state, the cave does not live up to the legend surrounding it.

Peki'in is the only city in Israel claiming continuous Jewish occupation since the Second Temple period. Though now predominantly Druze, it has a Jewish presence, which endures in one remaining Jewish family and an 18th-century synagogue with Temple-era stones built into the wall. To visit the synagogue, continue down the staircase near the cave to Kikkar Ha-Ma'ayan with its oddly shaped pool. Follow the street at the far right of the square, turn left at the first intersection, and take the curving road down to the synagogue's white gate on the right. If the gate is closed, knock on the door with a blue star, around the corner and upstairs.

AKHZIV אכזיב

All buses from platform #5 in Nahariya (buses #22-25 and 28) stop at the Akhziv National Park (10min., every hr., NIS7). Sherut NIS6.

The first historical records of Akhziv are 15th-century BCE Egyptian letters found in Tel Amarna, which describe it as a fortified Canaanite port city. The city switched hands during every major conquest, and eventually the Crusaders built the large **L'Ambert Castle** to defend the coastal road. Akhziv's war days are over now, and its current claim to fame is its sunny shoreline.

Built on the site of an 8th-century BCE Phoenician port town, the sprawling lawns and sheltered beach of **Akhziv National Park** are perfect for a relaxing day. Facilities include showers, changing rooms, and a playground. (☎ (04) 982 32 63. Open daily Apr.-June and Sept.-Oct. 8am-5pm; July-Aug. 8am-7pm. NIS20, students NIS10.) Two roads lead to the **Akhziv Beach:** one along the coast, currently closed off by the military, and a noncoastal road where buses stop. Every July a **Reggae Festival** stirs it up on the beach; call for details. (Begins 4km north of Nahariya and to the left of Akhziv National Park as you face the sea. ☎ (04) 982 82 01. NIS18, children NIS9. Open Apr.-June and Sept.-Oct. 8am-5pm; July-Aug. 8am-7pm.)

The state of **Akhzibland** was founded in 1952 by the eccentric **Eli Avivi.** As the story goes, Eli was walking along the beach and saw the remnants of a village that the Israeli government had destroyed. Hopelessly in love, he claimed the land. **Eli's Museum,** housed in a deteriorated but striking Arab mansion, exhibits the benevolent dictator's extensive collection of mostly Phoenician implements and statue fragments. (☎ (04) 982 32 50. Open 24hr.) Beds in one of Eli's breezy **guest rooms**

ISRAEL

above the museum or cabins next door cost NIS100, and sleeping in the rugged **camping area** costs NIS80 per person; the beach costs NIS20 for non-guests. These prices are entirely negotiable and may be waived for those who get on Eli's good side or help him with menial chores (such as landscaping, cleaning, or passing legislation) for three hours; four hours for lodging and food.

GALILEE הגליל الجليل

When the ancient Israelites described their country as flowing with milk and honey, they must have been talking about the Galilee. This lush and fertile region, bordering the West Bank to the south, the Golan to the east, Lebanon to the north, and the Mediterranean coast to the west, is laced by cool, refreshing rivers and carpeted with rolling, green hills. The Galilee was originally a province of the ancient Israelite kingdom, called Ha-Galil (the district) in Hebrew, whose inhabitants prospered by fishing and farming. As communities in the Galilee grew, religious leaders flocked to the area. Jesus grew up in Nazareth, performed many of his first miracles near the Sea of Galilee, and gave his famous sermon atop the Mount of Beatitudes. His apostles lived and taught in nearby Capernaum. Fifty years later, when Romans destroyed the second Temple in Jerusalem, the Sanhedrin relocated to the Galilee and resided there for the next 250 years. Dozens of armies swept through the region during the following millennium.

Despite a history of almost continuous war, today Galilee is one of the most peaceful areas in Israel. Since Israel captured the strategic Golan Heights in 1967 (see p. 269), putting the Galilee out of range of Syrian rockets, the region has blossomed into a tourist mecca. Busloads of pilgrims descend a massive metal staircase into the Jordan River at the site where John is believed to have baptized Jesus, banana boats and booze cruises skim over the Sea's blue waters to deposit passengers upon the bustling Tiberias promenade, and hikers crowd the trails of the Upper Galilee where Crusader fortresses keep watch over forested valleys. Meanwhile, the ancient synagogues of Tzfat and the churches of Nazareth continue to attract the faithful.

HIGHLIGHTS OF THE GALILEE

Beat the heat in Tiberias by taking an evening swim in the lake known to Israelis as the **Kinneret** (p. 375).

See the Mount of the familiar Sermon. The **Mount of Beatitudes** (p. 377) provided the stage for the premiere of Jesus' famous oration.

Walk the winding streets of **Tzfat** (p. 378), the birthplace of Kabbalah and home to a thriving artists colony. Its mystical serenity makes for a peaceful escape.

SOUTHERN GALILEE

NAZARETH الناصرة נצרת ☎06

A vibrant center of Arab life in the Galilee, Nazareth (al-Nassra in Arabic, Natzrat in Hebrew) is a far cry from Christmas-card pictures of pastoral churches, quiet convents, and grazing sheep. Nazareth is indeed dear to Christian pilgrims as the setting of Jesus' younger years and the traditional home of Mary and Joseph, but it is also a gritty town. While devotees throng to a handful of neo-Gothic churches, drivers charge through dusty construction sites on the main road and crowds drift through the winding alleys of the hillside market.

Nazareth's population is roughly one third-Christian and two-thirds Muslim, with a small Jewish population. Unlike nationalist Palestinians in the West Bank,

Nazarean Arabs are content as Israeli citizens. Life here, however, is worlds away from the beaches of Haifa and Tel Aviv. Visitors—especially women—should dress modestly to avoid harassment on the streets and difficulty entering churches. Parts of the city may be unsafe after dark.

▐ GETTING THERE AND GETTING AROUND

Buses: The **"bus station"** consists of several stops on Paul VI St., near Casa Nova St. When taking a bus to Nazareth, make sure it goes to Natzeret Ha-Atika, not Natzrat Illit. The upper city is a 20-minute local bus ride from the old city. Buses leaving town head west on Paul VI St. The **Egged** info booth is on Paul VI St., just east of the intersection with Casa Nova. Open Su-F 7am-3pm. To: **Afula** (#355, 356, 357, 823, 824, and 953; 20min.; every 40min.-1½hr. Su-Th 5:25am-7:55pm, F 6am-3:30pm, Sa 4:15-9pm; NIS8); **Akko** (#343; 1½hr.; every 1-2hr. Su-Th 6:45am-5pm and F 6:45am-4:15pm; NIS21.50, students NIS19.50); **Haifa** (#331 and 431; 1hr.; every 1-2hr. Su-Th 5:40am-8:10pm and F 5:40am-5:10pm; NIS18); **Jerusalem** (#953, 3½hr.; 6:30am, NIS40); **Tel Aviv** (#823 and 824 go from Natzrat Illit by way of Nazareth; 2½hr.; every 30min.-1hr. Su-Th 5:10am-7:40pm, F 5:45am-3:15pm, Sa 4-8:45pm; NIS32) via **Tel Megiddo** (45min., NIS13); and **Tiberias** (#431; 1hr.; every 1-2hr. Su-Th 6:50am-9:30pm, F 7am-5:30pm, Sa 7-10pm; NIS18).

Taxis: Ma'ayan (☎ 655 51 05), **Abu al-Assal** (☎ 655 47 45), **Galil** (☎ 655 55 36), and **Saiegh** (☎ 646 35 11). Taxis can be found all along Paul VI St.

Service: *Service* taxis gather on a small side street just off of Paul VI St. and across from the central bus stop. To: **Haifa** (NIS15); **Jenin** (NIS12); **Tel Aviv** (NIS25); and **Tiberias** (NIS18). *Service* run every day.

Car Rental: Europcar (☎ 655 41 29), at casa Nova St., next to the tourist office. 24+. Cars start at US$40 per day, automatics US$60 per day; min. 3-day rental. Open M-F 8:30am-6pm and Sa 8:30am-2pm. Credit card required.

✦❧ ORIENTATION AND PRACTICAL INFORMATION

Nazareth is 40km southeast of Haifa and 30km southwest of Tiberias, on a hill north of the Jezreel Valley. All the Christian sights are in the Arab **Old Nazareth** (Natzeret Ha-Atika). Upper Nazareth (Natzrat Illit), the newer, Jewish section of town, is residential and of little interest to tourists. The Arab town's main road,

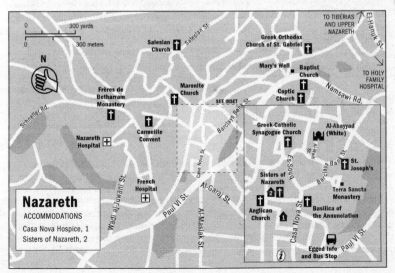

Paul VI St., lies to the east of the sights. Its intersection with **Casa Nova St.**, just below the Basilica, is the busiest part of town. Uphill from Casa Nova St., among churches, is the market area. Higher quality accommodations and panoramic views are farther up the hill toward **Salesian St.** and Mary's Well. Obtain a **map** of the city from the GTIO (see **Tourist Office**, below), as few of the streets have signs. Nazareth's Christian community shuts down on Sundays, but most establishments are open on Shabbat. Although Arabic is the major language, everybody speaks Hebrew and the proprietors of most tourist sites also speak English.

Tourist Office: Government Tourist Information Office (GTIO) (☎657 30 03; fax 657 30 78), on Casa Nova St., near the intersection with Paul VI St., next door to Israel Discount Bank. Staff distributes brochures and colorful new maps. Computerized information available. Open M-F 8:30am-5pm and Sa 8:30am-2pm.

Currency Exchange: Money Net (☎655 25 40), on the south side of Paul VI St., just west of Casa Nova St. Exchanges cash and traveler's checks with no commission. Open M-Tu and Th-F 8:30am-7pm, W, Sa 8:30am-3pm. The **post office** also exchanges cash and traveler's checks with no commission.

Banks: Israel Discount Bank (☎602 73 33), on Casa Nova St. by tourist office, has an **ATM**. Open Su, W, F 8:30am-1pm; M-Tu and Th 8:30am-12:30pm and 3:30-6pm. Bank Leumi and Arab Israeli Bank have **ATMs**, and are on Paul VI St. opposite the station.

Police (☎602 84 44), next to the post office by Mary's Well.

Pharmacy: Farah Pharmacy (☎655 40 18), next to Egged info, on Paul VI St. across from Bank Ha-Poalim. Open M and F 9am-7pm; Tu and Th 9am-1:30pm and 4-7pm; W and Sa 9am-2pm.

Hospitals: Nazareth Hospital (☎657 15 01 or 657 15 02), **Holy Family Hospital** (☎650 89 00), and **French Hospital** (☎650 90 00).

Post Office: Central branch (☎655 51 88), 2 blocks uphill from Paul VI St. from Mary's Well. Exchanges cash and traveler's checks; offers **Western Union** and **Poste Restante.** Open M-Tu and Th-F 8am-12:30pm and 3:30-6pm, W 8am-1:30pm, Sa 8am-noon.

ACCOMMODATIONS

During Christian holidays, it takes divine intervention to find a room here. At other times, hospices are crowded with tour groups but often have a bed to spare. There are very few budget accommodations in Nazareth, so call ahead if possible.

Sisters of Nazareth, P.O. Box 274 (☎655 43 04; fax 646 07 41). From Paul VI St., walk uphill on Casa Nova St. and turn left at the Basilica's entrance. This 150 year-old Catholic convent still looks brand new. The courtyard was built over ruins from the first century, which the sisters claim contain the grave of St. Joseph. They offer tours of the excavations M-Sa 8:30am. Breakfast NIS16; lunch and dinner NIS36 each. Reception 6am-9pm. Check-in 4pm. Check-out 10am (flexible). Strict 9pm curfew. Private rooms have bathrooms and great views. Single-sex dorms NIS32/US$8; singles NIS100/US$24; doubles NIS160/US$38; triples NIS240/US$57. Reservations recommended.

Galilee Hotel (☎657 13 11; fax 655 66 27), on Paul VI St., two blocks west of Casa Nova St. This modern hotel offers clean, spacious rooms with A/C, telephones, and bathrooms with tubs. Reception 24hr. Check-in 2pm. Check-out noon. Singles NIS210/US$50; doubles NIS330/US$80; triples NIS420/US$100. Credit cards accepted.

Casa Nova Hospice (☎645 66 60; fax 657 96 30), on Casa Nova St. opposite the Basilica of the Annunciation. Comfortable and clean rooms with A/C, private bath, and phones, usually full of tour groups. Breakfast included. Lunch and dinner US$8 each. Check-out 8:30am. Curfew 11pm. Singles NIS160/US$40; doubles NIS200/US$48; triples NIS290/US$72. 5% service charge. Traveler's checks accepted.

◘ FOOD

Nazareth's cuisine is not known for diversity. Dozens of falafel stands and identical "Oriental" restaurants line the downtown streets. Restaurant hours are generally 7am-9pm, and many places are closed on Sunday. Several **food kiosks** can be found along the streets, but the biggest one is directly opposite the bakery. Besides that, the only options for late-night snacks are the *shawarma* stands along Paul VI St. near Casa Nova St. These usually stay open until midnight.

La Fontana di Maria (☎ 646 04 35), on Paul VI St., to the right of Mary's Well. Inside a Turkish khan with high vaulted ceilings, this is Nazareth's only classy sit-down restaurant. House specialties include steak (NIS50), kebab (NIS40), and cornish hen (NIS50). Soups (NIS15) and salads (NIS10-25) are a bit cheaper. Open daily 11am-11pm. Credit cards accepted.

Abu Hani's Falafel and Shawarma, on Paul VI St., just west of the intersection with Casa Nova St. Look for the large sign in front advertising falafel and *shawarma* deals. This tiny place has some of the best and cheapest falafel (NIS7) and *shawarma* (NIS10) in town. Soda NIS2 extra. Open M-Sa 9am-9pm.

Fahoum Restaurant (☎ 655 33 32), on Casa Nova St., on the left, just up from Paul VI St. This modern-looking restaurant actually dates back to before the creation of the state of Israel. Delicious chicken *shishlik* NIS35; St. Peter's Fish NIS50; kebab with chips NIS40; hummus plate NIS15. Open daily 8am-9pm. Credit cards accepted.

Mahroum Sweets (☎ 656 02 14), on Paul VI St., at the intersection with Casa Nova St. Gooey, sweet pastries in a shiny, mirrored interior. *Baklavah* NIS30 per kg; cookies NIS20 per kg; coffee and tea NIS5. Open daily 8:30am-11pm.

◉ SIGHTS

Nazareth received a much-needed 60 million dollar face-lift for the millennium that included repaving many of the old city streets, constructing new promenades with scenic vistas, and putting up prominent signs to help pilgrims find their way to the numerous religious sights in town. The majority of sights are clustered around Paul VI St. and the *souq*, but the new Nazareth Village hopes to draw tourists up the hill to experience life as it was in ancient times. Nazareth's churches are all free to visitors, but they happily accept donations.

BASILICA OF THE ANNUNCIATION. Nazareth is synonymous with churches and none is more prominent than the huge basilica that dominates downtown with its faceted lantern dome. Completed in 1969, the basilica is built on the site believed to be Mary's home, where the archangel Gabriel heralded the birth of Jesus. Inside the huge, bronze doors depicting the life of Jesus is the **Grotto of the Annunciation,** the site of Mary's home. A gallery overlooking the grotto is lined with a series of artistic interpretations of the Annunciation. Outside, Madonna and Child mosaics from nearly every country in the world grace the courtyard walls. Churches have marked this spot since 356 CE; excavations of churches and ancient Nazareth lie in a garden underneath the plaza, accessible from the upper floor of the basilica. *(Walk up Casa Nova St. from Paul VI St.; the entrance is on the right. ☎ 657 25 01. Open Apr.-Sept. M-Sa 8am-5:30pm; Oct.-Mar. M-Sa 8am-4:30pm. Shorts not allowed.)*

ST. JOSEPH'S CHURCH. This church was built in 1914, on top of the cave thought to have been Joseph's house. The present structure incorporates remnants of a Byzantine church. Inside, stairs descend to caves that once stored grain and oil, as well as an early baptismal bath. Although this is usually referred to as Joseph's workshop, evidence suggests that these caves have been used since the late Stone Age. *(Next to the Basilica of the Annunciation, in the same plaza on Casa Nova St.)*

GREEK-CATHOLIC SYNAGOGUE CHURCH. Recently restored by a group of Italian archeology students, the church is built on the site of the synagogue where young Jesus is believed to have preached. Next door is the beautiful 18th-century Greek-Catholic Church of the Annunciation. Two hundred meters up from the church on street 6126, on the left in a small chapel, is the **Mensa Christi** stone where Jesus supposedly ate with his disciples after his resurrection. *(In the center of the Arab market. Enter the souq from Casa Nova St., turn left after the music shop, and follow the street to the right. Open M-Sa 8am-6pm. If closed ring the bell on the door to the left.)*

SOUQ. Nazareth's outdoor market is the best place in the city to buy olive wood camels and Bart Simpson underwear. It has been gutted and repaved in the last two years; today its white stones sparkle. Although perfectly safe in daylight, the market area is best avoided at night, when dope fiends lurk in its dark alleyways. *(Best reached via Casa Nova St. Open M-Sa 9am-5pm.)*

MARY'S WELL. Many believe that the well's water miraculously heals; recently it has begun to heal its once-ugly surroundings. Over the past few years, a new plaza, a few restaurants, and souvenir shops have sprouted nearby. The recently-built scenic promenades begin near here. From the well, continue right along Paul VI St. to the Namsawi Promenade and then up the hill to the promenades and the Salesian Church. *(The well is northeast of the bus station on Paul VI St.)*

GREEK ORTHODOX CHURCH OF ST. GABRIEL. The Church of St. Gabriel stands over the town's ancient water source. The original church was erected in 356 CE over the spring where Mary drew water and where the Greek Orthodox believe Gabriel appeared. The present structure, built in 1750, has elaborate Byzantine-style paintings and an ornate gold chandelier in the center. *(Left and uphill from Mary's Well, just off Paul VI St. Open M-Sa 7am-9pm and Su 7am-1pm and 2-9pm.)*

⚡ DAYTRIPS FROM NAZARETH

MOUNT TABOR הר תבור

From Afula, take buses to the base of the mountain (#830, 835, or 841; NIS8; tell the driver to stop at Har Tavor). Walk 2km through a Bedouin town to the spot where taxis shuttle pilgrims up to the top (NIS20 round-trip). It is worth the money to avoid the climb up the road. Church open Su-F 8am-noon and 2-5pm. Modest dress required; no visitors during services.

Mount Tabor (Har Tavor in Hebrew), the traditional site of Christ's Transfiguration, has become a standard stop on pilgrimage tours. The 588m-high hilltop is shared by Franciscan and Greek Orthodox monks. The Catholic **Basilica of the Transfiguration,** built in 1924, sits atop a 6th-century CE Byzantine church, which marks the spot where Jesus spoke with Elias and Moses and was transfigured in the presence of apostles Peter, James, and John (Luke 9:28-36). A dirt path on the left just before the stone archway that leads to the Basilica goes to the **Church of Elijah,** built atop the **Cave of Melkhizedek.** The limestone fortification, once an Arab fortress called **al-Adil,** dates from 1211. Mount Tabor is also the site where the prophetess Deborah led the Israelites to victory over Sisera's army (Judges 4-5). At the foot of the mountain is the Bedouin village of Shibli. Just down the hill from the taxi stop is the **Tent of Tavor** restaurant in an authentic Bedouin tent with a view of the Galilee countryside. Sit on mattresses and eat traditional Bedouin rice and meat for NIS45. (☎676 03 12. Open daily 9am-11pm.)

ZIPPORI צפורי

A bus to Akko (#343, every hr. 6:45am-2:25pm, NIS7) will stop at the junction, about 3km south of the site. ☎(06) 656 82 72. Open Sa-Th 8am-4pm and F 8am-3pm; in winter Sa-Th 8am-3pm and F 8am-2pm. NIS18, students NIS15, children NIS9.

About 6½km northwest of Nazareth, excavations at Zippori (Sepphoris) are uncovering a rich legacy from the Judeo-Christian, Roman, and Byzantine periods. The town was the seat of the Sanhedrin in the 3rd century CE, as well as one of the places where Rabbi Yehuda Ha-Nassi gathered the most learned rabbinic scholars to compile the *Mishnah*. Extensive finds include the remains of a 4000-seat Roman amphitheater, exquisite mosaics, a crusader fortress, and a synagogue. Archaeologists have found over 40 ancient mosaics here; the most famous is the enigmatic, gently smiling woman, now dubbed the "Mona Lisa of the Galilee." Within the crusader citadel are a variety of multimedia programs on the history of the city and an exhibit of archaeological finds. One kilometer east of the main excavations is an ancient reservoir carved into the bedrock; it was once part of the area's intricate system of 13½ kilometers of aqueducts. Christians believe Zippori was the town where Mary's parents, Anne and Joachim, lived. A Crusader Church stands over the site of their house.

TEL MEGIDDO (ARMAGEDDON) תל מגידו

Buses #823 and 824 run from Nazareth to Tel Aviv, stopping at Megiddo (45min.; every 30min.-1hr. Su-Th 5:10am-7:40pm and F 5:45am-3:15pm; NIS13). When the bus leaves Afula, remind the driver to stop at Megiddo Junction. Then walk 1km north toward Yoqneam and Haifa and turn left at the brown sign. ☎ (06) 652 21 67. Open Sa-Th 8am-5pm and F 8am-4pm; in winter Sa-Th 8am-4pm and F 8am-3pm. NIS18, students NIS15.

Bible fans and heavy metal gurus have heard of Armageddon, but few realize that the demonic battleground for the End of Days (Revelations 16:16) is actually "Ḥar Megiddo" (Mount Megiddo), an ancient *tel* just southeast of Haifa. Excavations of the site have uncovered twenty layers of ruins, ranging from the Neolithic Period (7000 BCE) to the end of the Persian Period (332 BCE).

The vision of Megiddo as an apocalyptic gathering place is derived from the city's central location. Commanding the crossroads between several ancient trading routes that linked Egypt to Syria and Mesopotamia, the fortress town was the site of many fierce battles. Megiddo was razed and rebuilt by numerous civilizations, including Canaanites, Hyksos, Egyptians, Assyrians, and Israelites. The most impressive remains include a Canaanite temple dedicated to Astarte (20th century BCE), chariot stables, and a palace from Solomon's time (10th century BCE), a public grain silo built during the reign of the Israelite king Jeroboam II (8th century BCE), and a man-made tunnel engineered by King Ahab (9th century BCE) to allow access to water during a siege. Only a few of the ruins have been reconstructed, and excavations are still underway.

From the observation point atop the *tel*, you can look out over the **Jezreel Valley** *(Emek Yizre'el)*, mostly swamp until 1920, when it was drained by Jewish immigrants. The lone mountain in the distance is Mount Tabor; also visible are the Gilboa range and the hills of Nazareth. The water tunnel terminates outside the ruins, so make sure it's your last stop at the site. When you exit, turn right and walk 500m back to the museum entrance and main road.

TIBERIAS טבריה طبرية ☎ 06

To accommodate its diverse group of visitors—vacationing Israeli families, party-seeking youths, weary backpackers, and Christian pilgrims from Hong Kong, Alabama, and everywhere in between—Tiberias has become a bizarre mix of flash and trash. Stores hawking Virgin Mary nightlights and baby Jesus key-chains shut down just when the disco ball starts to twirl in the bar next door, and cafe waiters, hostels owners, and shopkeepers stand ready to pounce on any passerby. Despite proposals to clean up the city, Tiberias remains a whiff of Israel at its rawest.

Though its central location and cheap beds make it an ideal touring base for the Galilee and the Golan, its position 200m below sea level guarantees a hot, humid, and mosquito-ridden July and August. Of course, the action in Tiberias is also hottest during those months, with increased transportation, the best parties, street fairs, and everybody's favorite—price gouging.

ISRAEL

GETTING THERE AND GETTING AROUND

Buses: Bus station (☎ 672 92 22) at the corner of Ha-Yarden St. and Ha-Shiloah St. To: **Haifa** (#430 (express) and 431; 1¾hr.; every hr. Su-Th 6am-6:30pm, F 6am-4:30pm, Sa 4:45-7pm; NIS23.50, students NIS21); **Jerusalem** (#961, 963, or 964; 3hr.; every 30-60min. Su-Th 5:50am-7pm, F 7:30am-3pm, Sa 4:30-9:45pm; NIS42, students NIS38); and **Tel Aviv** (#830, 835, 836, 840, or 841 (local); 2½-3hr.; every 30min. Su-Th 5:30am-9pm, F 6am-5pm, Sa 4-10pm; NIS35.50, students NIS32).

Taxis: *Sherut* and private cabs wait in the parking lot below the bus station and on Bibas St. To **Haifa** (NIS20) and **Tel Aviv** (NIS32). **Taxi Haemek** (☎ 672 01 31), at the corner of Ha-Shiloah St. and Ha-Yarden St.

Car Rental: Avis (☎ 672 27 66), in the parking lot below the bus station. All of the following are on Ha-Banim St. **Arad** (☎ 672 49 99). 21+, under 23 NIS90 extra. **Eldan** (☎ 679 18 22). 24+, 10% student discount. **Hertz** (☎ 672 39 39). 21+, under 23 NIS60 extra. **Budget** (☎ 672 08 64 or 672 34 96). 23+. All open Su-Th 8am-5pm and F 8am-2pm. Minimum two years driving experience required.

ORIENTATION AND PRACTICAL INFORMATION

Tiberias has three tiers: the **old city** by the water, **Kiryat Shmuel,** the new city up the hill, and **T'verya Illit** (Upper Tiberias) at the top of the hill (bus #7-10, every 10min., NIS4.10). The upper sections are residential; all boozing, boating, and beaching takes place in the old city. **Ha-Galil St.** and **Ha-Banim St.** run parallel to the water; **Ha-Yarden St.** runs perpendicular to them to the north. **Ha-Yarkon St.** and **Ha-Kishon St.** intersect Ha-Galil St. and Ha-Banim St. to the south. The central **midraḥov** (pedestrian mall) runs from Ha-Banim St. to the waterfront **promenade.**

Tourist Office: Government Tourist Information Office (☎ 672 56 66), on Ha-Banim St., in the archaeological park next to the Jordan River Hotel. Free city maps and brochures. Open Su-Th 8am-1pm and 2-5pm (until 7pm in Aug.) and F 8am-noon.

Tours: Matan Tours (☎ 672 45 74 or 054 61 61 48), offers a one-day tour from Tiberias of both Tzfat and Nazareth (NIS150).

Currency Exchange: Discount package paid in US dollars are the way of business here. The post office on Ha-Yarden St. gives top rates with no commission. **Money Net** (☎ 672 40 48), next to Bank Leumi on the corner of Ha-Banim St. and Ha-Yarden St., also charges no commission. Open Su-M and W-Th 8:30am-1pm and 4-7pm, Tu 8am-1:30pm, F 8:30am-1pm. **Bank Ha-Poalim** (☎ 679 84 11), on Ha-Banim St. between Ha-Yarden St. and Ha-Yarkon St., has a 24hr. **ATM.**

Camping Supplies: Terminal La-Metayel, 38 Ha-Yarden St. (☎ 672 39 72), between the bus station and Ha-Galil St. Open Su-F 9am-1:30pm, Su-M and W-Th 4-7:30pm.

Emergency: First Aid (☎ 679 01 11), corner of Ha-Banim St. and Ha-Kishon St. Open 24hr. **Police** ☎ 679 24 44. **Fire** ☎ 679 12 22.

Internet Access: Big Ben, at the end of the *midraḥov* on the left. NIS20 per 30min. Open daily 8:30am-late. **Immanuel Internet Cafe** (☎ 672 36 20), in the Galilee Experience gift shop. NIS10 per 15min. Open Su-Th 8am-10pm, F 8am-5pm, and Sa 5-10pm.

Post Office: Central office, 1 Kikkar Rabin (☎ 672 22 66), in parking lot off Ha-Yarden St., between Ha-Atzma'ut St. and al-Hadef St. **Poste Restante, EMS,** and **Western Union.** Open Su-Tu and Th 8am-12:30pm and 3:30-6pm, W 8am-1:30pm, F 8am-noon.

ACCOMMODATIONS

Competition is fierce in Tiberias; at peak times, hostel "runners" swoop on visitors as they get off the bus. Don't be afraid to ask to switch to a different room if there's something wrong with the first one; Tiberias is not the place to value politeness over sanity. Speaking of sanity, all rooms (dorms included) have air-conditioning.

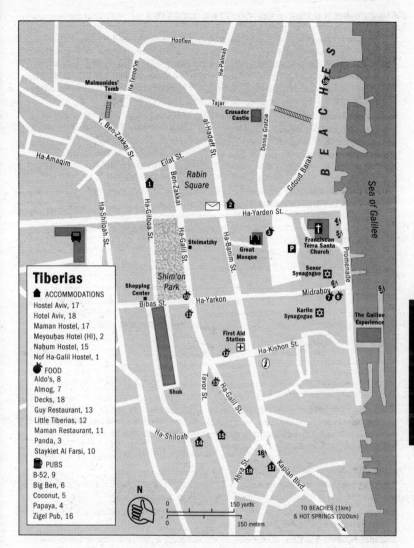

Tiberias

🏠 ACCOMMODATIONS

Hostel Aviv, 17
Hotel Aviv, 18
Maman Hostel, 17
Meyouḥas Hotel (HI), 2
Naḥum Hostel, 15
Nof Ha-Galil Hostel, 1

🍎 FOOD

Aldo's, 8
Almog, 7
Decks, 18
Guy Restaurant, 13
Little Tiberias, 12
Maman Restaurant, 11
Panda, 3
Staykiet Al Farsi, 10

🍺 PUBS

B-52, 9
Big Ben, 6
Coconut, 5
Papaya, 4
Zigel Pub, 16

ISRAEL

    Prices rise between July and September and reservations for private rooms are
recommended. The Jewish holidays of Pesaḥ, Rosh Ha-Shana, and Sukkot are mob
scenes. There are many "Room For Rent" signs throughout the city, but be aware
that private homes are unlicensed and therefore not subject to inspection. Lone
travelers should avoid sleeping in private houses.

    Maman Hostel (☎ 679 29 86), on Atzmon St. From central bus station, walk right on Ha-
Shiloah St. Bubbly international crowd keeps cool in the pool or on a stool at the tropi-
cal bar. If the atmosphere doesn't compensate for the thin dorm mattresses, at least
private rooms are tasteful. Kitchen available. Free safe and storage. Check-out 10am.
Dorms NIS25/US$6, July-Aug. NIS30/US$7.50; singles with bath NIS100/US$25,
July-Aug. NIS120/US$30; doubles NIS100/US$25, July-Aug. NIS150/US$37.50.

Hostel Aviv, 66 Ha-Galil St. (☎672 00 07 or 672 35 10), one block past the intersection with Ha-Banim St. Stomping grounds for the rough-and-rugged but oh-so-friendly backpacker crowd, Aviv has some of the cheapest (and smallest) rooms in the city. Management offers copious discounts and freebies. Kitchen available; free coffee supplies. Free safe; lockers NIS10. Internet NIS20 per 30min. Reception 24hr. Check-out 10am. Single-sex and coed dorms with bath NIS25/US$6, July-Aug. NIS30/US$7.50; singles with bath, TV, and fridge NIS60-80/US$15-20; doubles with bath, TV, and fridge NIS100-120/US$25-30. Credit cards accepted.

Meyouḥas Hostel (HI) (☎672 17 75 or 679 03 50; fax 672 03 72), at corner of Donna Gratzia St. and Ha-Yarden St., in a local black basalt rock building. Breakfast included. Free safe; lockers NIS6. Reception 24hr. Check-in 2pm. Check-out 10am. Coed dorms NIS52/US$13, July-Aug. NIS78/US$19.50; singles with bath NIS128/US$38, July-Aug. NIS172/US$43; doubles with bath NIS224/US$56, July-Aug. NIS252/US$63. NIS8 student discount; NIS7 member discount. Credit cards accepted.

Naḥum Hostel (☎672 15 05; fax 671 74 37). Head right (as you face the sea) on either Ha-Shiloah or Ha-Galil and turn onto Tavor St. Backpackers relax with a Goldstar in the rooftop bar before heading back to their huge dorms with kitchenettes, bathrooms, and thin foam mattresses. Coed and single-sex dorms NIS25/US$7; private rooms with bath NIS100/US$25. Prices rise 20% in high season. 10% discount for stays longer than three days. Credit cards accepted.

FOOD

Tiberias can easily meet all your beach and hiking picnic needs. The *shuk*, in a square block starting at Ha-Yarkon St. across from Shimron Park, sells cheap produce and baked goods every day except Shabbat. There is a **Supersol** supermarket on Ha-Banim St. (open Su-Th 8am-8:30pm, F 8am-4pm, and Sa after sundown-10pm) and a **Hafer** supermarket on the corner of Ha-Banim and Ha-Yarden St. (Open Su-Th 8am-9pm, F 8am-3pm, and Sa 9-11pm.)

The restaurant scene, plagued by too many tourists, is not nearly so ideal. Grilleries on Ha-Banim St. near the *midraḥov* serve *shishlik* with salad and pita (NIS20). Waterfront seafood restaurants offer idyllic settings complete with jet skiers and plastic bottle flotillas. A dinner of **St. Peter's fish,** a Sea of Galilee specialty, costs about NIS35-50. Ha-Galil St., Ha-Banim St., and the squares in between burgeon with culinary possibilities, but beware of menus that don't list prices.

Guy Restaurant (☎672 30 36), on Ha-Galil St., past Ha-Kishon St. when coming from the center of town. No frills and no big bills found at this fabulous Moroccan place. Stuffed veggies with rice NIS7-15, with meat NIS12-15; spicy meatballs NIS15; and some of the meanest coffee around NIS4. Open Su-Th noon-11pm and F noon-5pm.

Decks (☎672 15 38), at Lido Beach. Turn left at the end of the promenade and continue 200m down Gdoud Barak St. Cleanse your palate on the lemon and mint slushes (NIS20) and finish off with the heavenly apple crepes, drenched in sorbet and wine-soaked cherries (NIS25). Open Su-Th 6pm-midnight and Sa sundown-midnight.

Maman Restaurant (☎672 11 26), 21 Ha-Galil St. Packed with Israeli regulars. Excellent hummus with pita and olives NIS12. St. Peter's fish at the lowest price around (NIS30). Open Su-Th 11am-11pm, F 11am-4pm, and Sa sundown-11pm.

Little Tiberias (☎679 21 48 or 679 28 06), on the Ha-Kishon St. *midraḥov*. Families flock to this homey retreat from *midraḥov* mayhem. Huge salads (Greek and Caesar) NIS28; grilled meat NIS40-60; and indulgently creamy vegetarian dishes NIS34. Open daily noon-midnight. V, MC, AmEx.

SIGHTS

As the seat of Talmudic study in the 2nd and 3rd centuries CE, Tiberias hosted a number of influential scholars. Buried in the hills around Tiberias are several of the giants in Jewish thought, history, and Torah commentary. Modest dress is

The best way to keep in touch when you're traveling overseas is with **AT&T Direct**® Service. It's the easy way to call your loved ones back home from just about anywhere in the world. Just cut out the wallet guide below and use it wherever your travels take you.

For a list of AT&T Access Numbers, tear out the attached wallet guide.

Italy● 172-1011	Russia (Moscow)▶▲●755-5042
Luxembourg✦ ..800-2-0111	(St. Petersbg.)▶▲● ..325-5042
Macedonia● ..99-800-4288	Slovakia▲ ..00-42-100-101
Malta 0800-890-110	South Africa ..0800-99-0123
Monaco● 800-90-288	Spain 900-99-00-11
Morocco 002-11-0011	Sweden 020-799-111
Netherlands● ...0800-022-9111	Switzerland● 0800-89-0011
Norway 800-190-11	Turkey● 00-800-12277
Poland▲● ..00-800-111-1111	Ukraine▲ ....8✦100-11
Portugal▲ 800-800-128	U.A. Emirates● 800-121
Romania●......01-800-4288	U.K.............0800-89-0011

FOR EASY CALLING WORLDWIDE
1. Just dial the AT&T Access Number for the country you are calling from.
2. Dial the phone number you're calling.   *3.* Dial your card number.

For access numbers not listed ask any operator for **AT&T Direct**® Service.
In the U.S. call 1-800-331-1140 for a wallet guide listing all worldwide AT&T Access Numbers.
Visit our Web site at: **www.att.com/traveler**
Bold-faced countries permit country-to-country calling outside the U.S.
- ● Public phones require coin or card deposit to place call.
- ▲ May not be available from every phone/payphone.
- ✦ Public phones and select hotels.
- ◆ Await second dial tone.
- ▶ Additional charges apply when calling from outside the city.
- † Outside of Cairo, dial "02" first.
- ✖ Not available from public phones or all areas.
- ✔ Use U.K. access number in N. Ireland.

When placing an international call *from* the U.S., dial 1 800 CALL ATT.

EMEA   © 8/00 AT&T

Italy● 172-1011	Russia (Moscow)▶▲●755-5042
Luxembourg✦ ..800-2-0111	(St. Petersbg.)▶▲● ..325-5042
Macedonia● ..99-800-4288	Slovakia▲ ..00-42-100-101
Malta 0800-890-110	South Africa ..0800-99-0123
Monaco● 800-90-288	Spain 900-99-00-11
Morocco 002-11-0011	Sweden 020-799-111
Netherlands● ...0800-022-9111	Switzerland● 0800-89-0011
Norway 800-190-11	Turkey● 00-800-12277
Poland▲● ..00-800-111-1111	Ukraine▲ ....8✦100-11
Portugal▲ 800-800-128	U.A. Emirates● 800-121
Romania●......01-800-4288	U.K.............0800-89-0011

FOR EASY CALLING WORLDWIDE
1. Just dial the AT&T Access Number for the country you are calling from.
2. Dial the phone number you're calling.   *3.* Dial your card number.

For access numbers not listed ask any operator for **AT&T Direct**® Service.
In the U.S. call 1-800-331-1140 for a wallet guide listing all worldwide AT&T Access Numbers.
Visit our Web site at: **www.att.com/traveler**
Bold-faced countries permit country-to-country calling outside the U.S.
- ● Public phones require coin or card deposit to place call.
- ▲ May not be available from every phone/payphone.
- ✦ Public phones and select hotels.
- ◆ Await second dial tone.
- ▶ Additional charges apply when calling from outside the city.
- † Outside of Cairo, dial "02" first.
- ✖ Not available from public phones or all areas.
- ✔ Use U.K. access number in N. Ireland.

When placing an international call *from* the U.S., dial 1 800 CALL ATT.

EMEA   © 8/00 AT&T

required for visiting the tombs; head coverings are provided for men. All that's left of the **Old City,** shaken by earthquakes and conquerors, is a few black basalt wall fragments scattered throughout the modern town. A **free tour** leaves from the Sheraton Moriah-Plaza hotel every Saturday at 10am.

MAIMONIDES' TOMB. The best-known of the scholars laid to rest in Tiberias is Moses Maimonides, the hugely influential 12th-century physician and philosopher whose works synthesized neo-Aristotelian-Arab philosophy with Judaism. According to legend, an unguided camel carried his coffin to Tiberias. The white half-cylinder is the actual tomb; the Hebrew inscription is a Jewish saying: "From Moses [the original] until Moses [Maimonides] there was no one like Moses [Maimonides]." Ask for the tomb of "Rambam," the Hebrew acronym for his full name (Rabbi Moshe Ben-Maimon). *(Walk out Ben-Zakkai St. from Ha-Yarden St.; the tomb is two blocks up on the right, up a wide stairway. Look for the red metal sculpture above the tomb.)*

BEN-ZAKKAI'S TOMB. Rabbi Yoḥanan Ben-Zakkai snuck out of besieged Jerusalem in a coffin, popped out of the casket in front of the Roman General Vespasian, and prophetically addressed him as "Caesar." When news of the old Caesar's death arrived, Vespasian graciously granted Rabbi Yoḥanan one wish. The rabbi chose to found a house of study with his students. *(Next to Maimonides' tomb on Ben-Zakkai St.)*

RABBI AKIVA'S TOMB. Rabbi Akiva, a woodcutter who began to study only after age 40, is one of the more frequently quoted rabbis in the Talmud and was one of the students who helped carry Rabbi Yoḥanan out of Jerusalem. Believers gather to have their illnesses cured at the hillside tomb of Akiva's student, **Rabbi Meir Ba'al Ha-Nes,** above the hot springs. *(On the hillside directly above the city. See the GTIO city map for walking directions, or take bus #4, 4-aleph, 6, or 6-aleph and ask for directions.)*

FRANCISCAN TERRA SANCTA CHURCH. Also known as St. Peter's, the Terra Sancta Church was built in the 12th century to commemorate St. Peter's role in the growth of Christianity. The church is set back next to the Papaya Bar; look for the five crosses on the brown door (the symbol and color of the Franciscan church). The apse behind the altar is arched like the bow of a boat in honor of Jesus' fishing career. In the courtyard is a statue of the Virgin Mary created by Polish troops who lived in the church from 1942 to 1945. *(On the promenade in front of the Caesar Hotel. ☎672 05 16. Open daily 8:30am-6pm. Modest dress required.)*

CRUSADER CASTLE. The crumbling remains of a 12th-century **Crusader castle** overlook the Sea of Galilee. Admission includes coffee, a short historical tour, a sentinel's view of the water, and entrance to the art galleries now housed in the castle. *(A block past the Meyohaus Youth Hostel on Donna Gratzia St. ☎672 13 75. Gallery open Su-Th 9am-1pm and 3-6pm and F 9am-1pm. NIS10.)*

◢ BEACHES

For many **beaches** on the Galilee, you'll have to bring your own sand—otherwise, bring sandals for walking over the sizzling rocks. Most beaches are owned by hotels that charge hefty fees in exchange for changing rooms, showers, boat rentals, and food. The beaches just north of town are along Gdoud Barak Rd., off Ha-Yarden St.; those to the south lie off the main coastal road (Rte. 90, with which Ha-Galil merges). **Lido Kinneret,** just off Ha-Yarden St., charges NIS20 for 45-minute boat rides on the lake, but they are often only available for groups. Waterskiing is NIS200/US\$50 for 15 minutes. *(☎672 15 38. Open daily 8am-5:30pm.)* Just north of Lido, **Quiet Beach** (Ḥof Ha-Sheket), with a pool, an energetic DJ, and hordes of school kids, is anything but quiet. *(☎670 08 00. Open daily 9am-6pm. NIS25, children NIS20.)* Next in line to the north, **Blue Beach** boasts the largest swimming area and best view on the lake. *(☎672 01 05. Open daily 9am-5pm. NIS25, children NIS20; NIS5 more on Shabbat.)* A 15-minute walk from the city center or a short ride on bus #5-aleph south of Tiberias leads to **Ganim Beach.** *(☎672 07 09. Open daily 9am-6pm. NIS20.)* Next to it is **Holiday Inn Beach.** Look for the bridge connecting hotel and lakefront. Banana boats cost NIS30 for 15min. (☎672 85 36. Open daily 9am-6pm. NIS25, students NIS20.) To avoid the hefty admission prices of most beaches, circle the old city walls at the southern end of the promenade and walk 200m along the dirt path to a small **free beach.**

Those seeking a hotter and slimier time are in luck: Tiberias is home to the world's earliest-known hot mineral spring, **Ḥamei T'verya.** One legend maintains that the springs were formed in the Great Flood when the earth's insides boiled. Another holds that demons heat the water under standing orders from King Solomon. Cleanse body and wallet (NIS53, Sa NIS58; 20% student discount). The older building, **Tiberias Hot Springs,** has single-sex baths. (☎672 85 00. Open Su-F 7am-4pm.) The newer, coed building, **Tiberias Hot Springs Spa,** contains a fitness room and jacuzzis. A massage is NIS133 and a private mineral bath NIS99. (☎672 85 00. New spa open Su-M, W, and F-Sa 8am-8pm; Tu and Th until 11pm.) The springs are two kilometers south of town on the coastal road; bus #5-aleph runs from the central bus station and Ha-Galil St. (every 30min.).

♫ ENTERTAINMENT

Nightlife in Tiberias centers on the *midraḥov* and promenade area. In summer, street musicians, popcorn vendors, and occasional palm-readers set up shop. Get out the white polyester duds and thigh-highs for Lido Kinneret Beach and Kinneret Sailing's **disco cruises,** one of Tiberias' trademarks. (Daily 8-11pm. NIS15-25.) The **Sea of Galilee Festival** brings international folk troupes to Tiberias during the second week of July. Check the GTIO for info on this and other area festivals, including Ein Gev's **Passover Music Festival** and Tzemaḥ's **Tu b'Av Love Fest** (mid-Aug.), where happy young Israelis gather for some love, sweat, and rock 'n' roll.

Kibbutz Kinneret Discotheque (☎675 96 89 or (05) 195 30 36), at the Kibbutz. Volunteers from neighboring kibbutzim and Tiberias expats guzzle cheap beer (NIS10) or groove inside at what is widely considered the best discotheque in the area. Cover NIS25 not always applicable for tourists. Open W at 9:30pm and F at midnight.

Coconut (☎(05) 328 85 25). Turn left at the end of the *midraḥov* and walk to the end of the promenade. This Gilligan's Island-esque hut has a nice view of the lake and a flashy little dance floor. Dancing is hottest on F, music is worst on Sa (karaoke), and the place gets quiet and candlelit on Su. Beer NIS16-20; special tequila mixers NIS25. Open daily 8pm-late.

Zigel Pub (☎(05) 285 35 82), where Ha-Galil St. and Ha-Banim St. merge. Israeli youth headquarters. If the disco trance and strobe light in the downstairs dance bar give you a headache, head upstairs to the comfy couches and cheap *nargilah* (NIS10). F-Sa Dancebar, Tu, Th karaoke. Beer NIS16; cocktails NIS28. Open daily 10pm-late.

Big Ben, on the left near the end of the *midraḥov*. This tourist bar gets rowdy late at night with young, drunken Brits (and a healthy dose of Americans and Israelis) giving each other the time of day. Beers NIS14-17; tropical cocktails like a 'Big Ben Kiss' NIS29. Fried snacks NIS19. Open daily 8:30am-late.

☙ DAYTRIPS FROM TIBERIAS

BEIT SHE'AN בית שאן

From Tiberias, take bus #928, 961, 963, or 964 (50min., NIS19) to the Beit She'an bus stop. Walk to the main road through the mall, turn left, and make a right at the Bank Leumi, following signs to the site. ☎658 71 89. Open Sa-Th 8am-5pm and F 8am-4pm; in winter Sa-Th 8am-4pm and F 8am-3pm. NIS18, students NIS15, children NIS9.

One of the finest archaeological sites in the country, Beit She'an is a Sephardi (Jews of Middle Eastern descent) development town containing a vast complex of mostly Roman and Byzantine ruins. Excavations on and around **Tel al-**

Husn, the oldest archaeological mound, have revealed 20 layers of settlements dating back as far as the 5th millennium BCE (Neolithic period). Of particular interest is the **Roman theater,** one of the largest extant Roman constructions in Israel. Long before it became a Philistine, Jewish, Greek, Roman, and eventually Turkish city, the region was occupied by the Egyptians; the 14th-century BCE ruins of the **Ashtaroth Temple,** built on the *tel* by Ramses III for his Canaanite allies, is a remainder of that period. North of the *tel* is the **Monastery of the Noble Lady Maria,** founded in 567 CE and abandoned after the Persian invasion of 614. The best time to visit the site is in the early morning, before the sun makes climbing the *tel* unbearable.

PEACE BRIDGE BORDER CROSSING. This is one of Israel's busiest border crossing into Jordan; allow at least an hour to cross, especially Thursday through Saturday. From Beit She'an, take bus #16 (NIS8) or a taxi (☎658 84 55 or 658 64 80; NIS35) to the border. Once there, you'll pay a NIS64 **exit fee,** go through passport and customs control (where you can reclaim your VAT), and take a shuttle bus (NIS4) from in front of the Duty Free shop to the Jordanian side. A visa to enter Jordan (US$44) can be purchased on the spot. From the Jordanian border, a taxi to Amman is JD25. Coming from the Jordanian side, the exit fee is JD4; there is no entrance fee for Israel, but travelers who need a visa (see p. 275) must purchase one at the Israeli embassy in Amman; they are not available at the border. (☎658 64 44, 658 64 22, or 658 64 48; Jordanian terminal ☎(02) 655 05 23. Open Su-Th 6:30am-10pm, F, and Sa 8am-8pm. For info on crossing into Jordan, see p. 275.)

THE ROAD TO AFULA

Buses traveling between Beit She'an and Afula stop at any site upon request (#411, 412, 415, 417, 829, or 953; 45min.; every 30min. 6am-8pm, breaking for Shabbat.)

Along the beautiful valley road from Beit She'an to Afula are several sights of natural and historical interest. **Gan Ha-Shlosha,** also known as **Sahne,** is about eight kilometers west of Beit She'an and worth an afternoon excursion. Its waterfalls and swimming holes are refreshing in both summer and winter (at a constant 28°C). The springs have been popular since Roman times; the covered pool and waterslides haven't. Watch out for theft on overcrowded weekends. (☎(06) 658 62 19; fax 658 78 22. Open Sa-Th 8am-5pm and F 8am-4pm; in winter Sa-Th 8am-4pm and F 8am-3pm. NIS27, children NIS16.) A 10-minute walk along the road behind the park leads to the **Museum of Regional and Mediterranean Archaeology,** a collection of Hellenistic and Islamic art and pottery gathered from a local Canaanite temple, an Israelite community, and a Roman colony. (☎658 63 52. Open Su-Th 9am-2pm and Sa and holidays 10am-2pm. Park admission required for museum.)

Within **Kibbutz Hefziba,** another three kilometers down the road toward Afula, is the beautiful 6th-century CE **Beit Alpha Synagogue,** whose highlight is a magnificently preserved mosaic of a zodiac wheel surrounding the sun god Helios, identified with the prophet Elijah. (☎(06) 653 20 04. Open Sa-Th 8am-5pm and F 8am-4pm; in winter Sa-Th 8am-4pm and F 8am-3pm. NIS9, students NIS8, children NIS4.) Buses from Afula and Beit She'an stop at the entrance to the kibbutz. Don't be misled by the sign for Kibbutz Beit Alpha (one kilometer closer to Beit She'an).

SEA OF GALILEE (LAKE KINNERET) ☎06

Pleasant beaches, scenic trails, and historically and religiously significant sites grace the area that surrounds the Sea of Galilee. Campgrounds are available at several of the beaches around the Kinneret (contact the GTIO), or take advantage of cheap accommodations in Tiberias.

ISRAEL

GETTING AROUND

All the sights on the Sea of Galilee are in some way accessible by bus from Tiberias, but renting a mountain bike is the more convenient and scenic way to go (see **Tiberias: Practical Information,** p. 370). A complete circuit of the lake (55km) takes four to five hours. Leave as early as possible and bike clockwise around the lake to get the hilly part between Tiberias and Capernaum finished while your energy is high and the sun is low. Spring is the best time for biking; in July and August, the hills reach unbearable temperatures, but the ferries run more frequently and it's easier to catch one half-way around the lake. Bring a lot of **water.**

The **Lido Kinneret Sailing Co.** operates a ferry from Lido Beach to Capernaum, Ginnosar Beach, Mount of Beatitudes, and Tiberias. Individuals with bicycles are welcome, but schedules are at the mercy of tour groups. (☎672 15 38. 30-45min., 8am-6pm. NIS30.) The **Kinneret Sailing Company** runs cruises from Tiberias to Ein Gev on the east coast of the Sea of Galilee. Boats leave Tiberias daily (10:30am, 12:30, 3pm; return from Ein Gev 11:30am, 2:15, 5:45pm) during the second half of July and all of August. (☎665 80 08 or 665 80 09; fax 665 80 07. NIS20, children NIS15, with bicycle NIS30; round-trip NIS30, children NIS20.)

ACCOMMODATIONS

The best accommodation option in the area is **Karei Deshei,** with beautiful gardens, a serene, private beach, and wonderful views of the Sea of Galilee. (Breakfast included. Reception 7am-10pm. Check-in 3pm. Check-out 10am; noon on Shabbat. Reservations recommended. A/C 4-6 bed dorms with bath NIS90; NIS112 July-Aug., F, and holidays. Credit cards accepted.)

Camping is a good way to escape the city heat. Check out the MTIO/SPNI information office at Tzemaḥ on the southern tip of the lake, in the shopping strip across from Jordan Valley College. Their map (NIS22) shows the 25 lakeside campgrounds interspersed among the private beaches. (Take bus #26 or 28. ☎675 20 56. NIS60 per car; free without car. Open daily 8am-4pm.) Be wary of **theft.** Women should never camp alone.

SIGHTS ON THE SHORE

YIGAL ALLON CENTER. The low water level of the Galilee in 1985-86 had one serendipitous effect—the discovery of an **ancient boat** under a segment of a newly exposed lake bed off the beach of Kibbutz Ginnosar. Authorities encased its wooden frame in a fiberglass brace and hauled it to shore. The boat, dating from between 100 BCE and 100 CE, has been restored to near-pristine condition. (Take bus #840, 841, 963, or 964. NIS6.60. ☎672 14 95. Open Su-Th 8am-5pm and F-Sa 8m-4pm. NIS16, children and students NIS14.)

ḤAMMAT GADER. These hot baths, known as *al-Himmeh* in Arabic, lie in former Syrian territory. In Roman times, the town, combined with its other (Jordanian) half on the western side of the Yarmouk River, formed part of the Decapolis. At the southwest corner of the complex sits the hottest spring in the area—so hot (51°C) that the Jews call it *Ma'ayan Ha-Gehinom* (Hell's Pool) and the Arabs call it *'Ain Maqla* (Frying Pool). Ḥammat Gader also boasts an **alligator park,** where hundreds of large, sleepy gators sun themselves and slog through murky water. (30 minutes southeast of Tiberias. Bus #24; 9 and 10:30am, returns 1 and 3pm; F 8:45 and 10:30am, returns noon and 1:15pm; NIS7.20. ☎665 99 99. Open M-Sa 7am-noon and Su 7am-4pm. Weekdays NIS50, after 5pm NIS43; F-Sa NIS55.)

DEGANYA ALEF. Founded by Russian immigrants in 1909, Deganya Alef is Israel's first kibbutz and the birthplace of General Moshe Dayan. Today, the kibbutz manufactures diamond tools. A 1948 Syrian tank marks the entrance. (Near the spot *where the Jordan River flows out of the Sea of Galilee, about 8km south of Tiberias and west of Ḥammat Gader. From Tiberias take bus #22 for NIS7.)*

MOUNT ARBEL. Among the best hikes in the area, the Mount Arbel trail is to the northwest of the Sea of Galilee. The red trail leads from Moshav Arbel to the Arab village of Wadi Hamam. To start the hike, turn right and walk one kilometer. After another right turn on the next main road, walk one kilometer to Migdal Junction and take a bus back to Tiberias. The entire hike should only take three to four hours. *(To get to Mount Arbel, take bus #42 (7am, NIS7) to Moshav Arbel. Ask at the moshav for directions to Matzok Arbel. To get back to Tiberias, bus #459, 841, or 963; NIS7.)*

NAḤAL AMUD. The Naḥal Amud stream flows from Mount Meron all the way to Hukkok Beach on the lake. Along the banks are beautiful flowers and a natural pillar of rock. Serious backpackers use the trail as either the first or last leg of a multi-day **Yam Le-Yam hike** (see **From Sea to Shining Sea,** p. 363).

◉ NEW TESTAMENT SIGHTS

According to the New Testament, Jesus walked on the waters of the Sea of Galilee, and four of the most significant stories in Christian history are set in the steep hills of its northern coast. Modest dress is required for entrance to New Testament sights—no shorts above the knees or bare shoulders.

TABGHE

Take bus #459, 841, or 963 (20min., every hr., NIS11.50) to the Capernaum Junction (Tzomet Kfar Naḥum). Walk toward the sea, following the brown signs to Tabghe and Capernaum. Tabghe (Arabic), Heptapegon (Greek), or Seven Springs (English) houses two sites and lies about one kilometer down the road.

THE CHURCH OF THE BREAD AND FISH. This is the site where Jesus is said to have fed 5000 pilgrims with five loaves and two small fish (Matthew 14:13-21). The church is built around the rock upon which Jesus placed the bread, and a section of the mosaic has been removed to reveal part of the rock and the original 4th-century foundations. *(Open M-Sa 8am-6pm and Su 10am-5pm. Free.)* Around the right side of the church, past the "private" sign and down the stairs, is a small hospice for Christian pilgrims; inquire at the office inside the church for information. *(☎ 672 10 61. Singles with A/C and bath NIS140/US$35; doubles with A/C US$30/NIS120.)*

CHURCH OF THE PRIMACY OF ST. PETER. This church commemorates the miracle of the loaves and fishes and the spot where Jesus made Peter "Shepherd of his People." A Persian invasion in 614 CE destroyed the 4th-century church at this spot. Franciscans rebuilt it with black basalt in 1933. On the seaward side of the church are the steps where Jesus called out his instructions; on the shoreline are the "thrones of the Apostles," a series of six double column bases. *(50m past the parking lot of the Church of the Bread and Fishes. ☎ 672 47 67. Open daily 8am-4:30pm. Free.)*

MOUNT OF BEATITUDES. Jesus is supposed to have delivered his Sermon on the Mount (Matthew 5) and chosen his disciples at this site. A church funded by Benito Mussolini stands on the Mount; its octagonal shape recalls the eight beatitudes. Symbols surrounding the altar inside the church represent the seven virtues (justice, charity, prudence, faith, fortitude, hope, and remembrance). The gardens around the site offer a spectacular view of the Sea of Galilee, Tiberias, and the Golan Heights. *(The small path to the Mount is next to the stop for bus #16, across from the entrance to St. Peter's Church. It's a 20-minute walk uphill to the church. From the Mount, follow the road back one kilometer to catch bus #459, 841, or 963 back to Tiberias (NIS11.50). ☎ 672 67 12. Open daily 8am-noon and 2:30-5pm.)*

OUTSIDE OF TABGHE

CAPERNAUM. It was in Capernaum (Kfar Naḥum in Hebrew, Tel Num in Arabic), Peter's birthplace, that Jesus healed Simon's mother-in-law and the Roman Centurion's servant (Luke 4:31-37 and 7:1-10). A modern church arches over the ruins of a 5th-century octagonal church, marking the site believed to have held Peter's house. The ruins of a nearby **synagogue,** discernible by the black, basalt foundation, is built on top of an older, first-century CE synagogue in which Jesus may have preached. Since Capernaum did not participate in the first and second century Jewish revolts against the Romans, it survived unscathed. *(Buses #459, 841, or 963 from Tiberias pass the Capernaum junction about once an hour on the way north to Kiryat Shmona and Tzfat. Get off near the Capernaum ferry port and walk one kilometer to your left. From Tabghe, Capernaum is two kilometers farther east on the coastal road, marked by a sign. Synagogue open daily 8:30am-4pm. NIS2.)*

MIGDAL. The birthplace of Mary Magdalene lies north of Tiberias. An agricultural community founded in 1910 now accompanies the white-domed shrine and largely unexcavated ruins. *(Buses #50, 51, or 52 go to Migdal from Tiberias (10min., infrequent). Buses #459, 841, or 963 run to the Migdal Junction, "Tzomet Migdal," a short walk away.)*

KURSI. The ruins of this Christian settlement, also known as Gergessa or Gerasa, date from early Byzantine times (5th-6th centuries CE). According to the New Testament, it was at Kursi that Jesus exorcised several demons from a man's body and caused the demons to possess a herd of pigs; the pigs raced into the sea and drowned. The site harbors impressive remains of a large, Byzantine **monastery** and a small chapel, both reconstructed and with mosaic floors. *(On eastern side of the lake, 7km north of Ein Gev. Ruins 50m from the bus stop. Buses #15, 17, 18, 19, 20, or 22 run from Tiberias to Tzomet Kursi (30min., every 30min. noon-7pm, NIS14). ☎673 19 83. Open Sa-Th 8am-5pm and F 8am-4pm; in winter Sa-Th 8am-4pm and F 8am-3pm. NIS9, students NIS8.)*

KORAZIM. These ruins are on the site of the unrepentant towns chastised by Jesus (Matthew 11:21). The **synagogue** here dates from the Talmudic period, or the 3rd-4th centuries CE. *(Take bus #459, 841, or 963 (NIS11.50) and get off at Tzomet Korazim Junction. Walk east 2km on the main road, past Vered Ha-Galil and Moshav Korazim to a parking lot on the right. Signs there lead to the town. ☎693 49 82. Open Sa-Th 8am-5pm and F 8am-4pm; in winter Sa-Th 8am-4pm and F 8am-3pm. NIS14, students NIS10.50.)*

YARDENIT. The Gospels say that John baptized Jesus in the Jordan River. Today, dozens of pilgrims and tourists come to the Yardenit Baptismal Area on the banks of the Jordan. *(Right off the coastal road. Take bus #17, 19, 21, 22, 23, or 26 to Kibbutz Kinneret. ☎675 94 86. Open Su-Th 9am-6pm and F-Sa 8am-5pm.)*

NORTH OF THE SEA

TZFAT (SAFED) צפת صفد   ☎06

Situated on Mount Kenaan, the third highest peak in Israel, Tzfat is a city of mesmerizing tranquility. Streets wind through this city on a hill, raising aimless wandering to an artform. Stone buildings, spotted with turquoise-colored doorways, fall over each other. Tzfat's beauty reflects not only its physical setting, overlooking the cool, lush greenery of the Galilean hills, but also a mystical way of life. In 1777, a rabbi who had trekked to Tzfat all the way from Europe ultimately packed up and left for Tiberias, complaining that the angels had kept him up at night.

Tzfat hasn't always been a bastion of spirituality. Its Crusader-built castle was captured by Salah al-Din in 1188, reconquered by the Knights Templar in 1240, and then lost again in 1266 to the Mamluk Sultan Baybars. It wasn't until the Middle Ages that many Jews arrived in Tzfat, seeking refuge in the relatively tolerant Ottoman Empire. After the Expulsion from Spain in 1492, Jewish exiles flocked to Tzfat, bringing with them the seeds of a mystical tradition. New settlements began in the second half of the 19th century and triggered violent Arab protest. By 1948, 12,000 Arabs lived in uneasy coexistence with 1700 Jews. In May 1948, Israeli Palmaḥ troops defeated the Iraqi and Syrian forces entrenched in the fortress at the top of Mount Kenaan, and the Arab population fled with their armies.

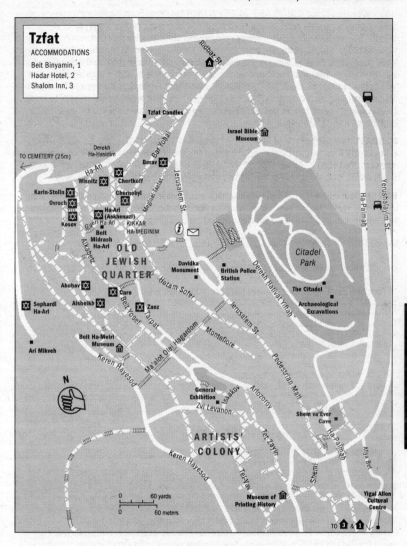

Tzfat

ACCOMMODATIONS

Beit Binyamin, 1
Hadar Hotel, 2
Shalom Inn, 3

TO CEMETERY (25m)

Tzfat Candles

Israel Bible Museum

Derekh Ha-Hasidim

Berav

Ha-Ari

Wisnitz   Chertkoff

Karlin-Stolin   Chernobyl

Ovruch   Ha-Ari (Askhenazi)

Kosov   KIKKAR HA-MEGINIM

Gverit Ha-Ari

Beit Midrash Ha-Ari

OLD JEWISH QUARTER

Davidka Monument

British Police Station

Citadel Park

Abuhav   Caro

Sephardi Ha-Ari   Aisheikh   Zanz

Ari Mikveh

Beit Ha-Meiri Museum

The Citadel

Archaeological Excavations

Keren Hayesod

Ma'alot Olei Hagardom

Montefiore

Pedestrian Mall

N

General Exhibition

Issakov

Zvi Levanon

Shem va'Ever Cave

ARTISTS' COLONY

Keren Hayesod

Ter Zayin

Arlozorov

Ha-Palmah

Atiya Bet

0   60 yards
0   60 meters

Museum of Printing History

Yigal Allon Cultural Centre

TO 3 & 1

Ridbaz St.

Baryohai

Maginei Kelat

Jerusalem St.

Alkabetz

Hatam Sofer

Beit Yosef

Tarpat

Jerusalem St.

Derekh Hativa Yiftah

Yerushalayim St.

Ha-Palmah

⬛ GETTING THERE AND GETTING AROUND

Buses: Central bus station (☎ 692 11 22). Information booth open Su-Th 6:30-8:30am and 9am-1:30pm and 2-3pm; F 6:30-8:30am and 9am-1:30pm. To: **Haifa** via **Akko** (#361 and 362; every 30min. Su-Th 6:15am-7pm, F 6:10am-3:15pm, Sa after sundown; 2hr.; NIS30); **Jerusalem** (#964, daily 7:15am, NIS47); **Kiryat Shmona** (#501 and 511; 1hr.; every hr. Su-Th 5:50am-7:30pm, F 5:50am-4pm; NIS18); **Tel Aviv** (#846, 3hr., 5:35 and 8:15am, NIS44); and **Tiberias** (#459, 1hr., every hr. 6:50am-7pm, NIS17).

Taxis: Kenaan Taxis (☎ 697 07 07), next to the bus station. *Sherut* to **Tiberias** and **Rosh Pina.** Look for white minivans.

✦☗ ORIENTATION AND PRACTICAL INFORMATION

The city can be divided into three districts: the **park area,** at the top of the mountain (ringed by Jerusalem St.), the **artists' quarter,** southwest and down the hill, and the **synagogue quarter** (Old City), immediately to the north of the artists' quarter on the other side of Ma'alot Olei Ha-Gardom St. Tzfat is arranged in curved terraces descending on the west from the castle ruins atop **Gan Ha-Metzuda** (Citadel Park). **Jerusalem (Yerushalayim) St.,** behind the central bus station, follows the lines of what was once the castle's moat and makes a complete circle around Citadel Park. Heading left from the major intersection beside the bus station, on the western side of the park, Jerusalem St. becomes the *midraḥov.* The **midraḥov** (pedestrian mall) is the strip of Jerusalem St. running southwest of the park area, up the hill from the artists' and synagogue quarters. **Ha-Palmaḥ St.** begins off Jerusalem St. near the central bus station and crosses the main street over a stone bridge. **Ha-Ari St.** also begins off Jerusalem St. near the bus station and circles around the western edge of the city, descending down to the cemetery grounds. Tzfat is a compact walking city, and getting around in the old city with a car is nearly impossible.

Tourist Information: Visitors Center (☎ 692 74 84 or 692 74 85), Kikkar Ha-Atzma'ut. At the intersection of Aliya Bet and Ha-Palmaḥ, inside the Wolfson Community Center, through the main entrance on the right. Has a small exhibit on the history of Tzfat, updated maps (NIS5), and free brochures about sights. Open Su-Th 10am-3pm.

Currency Exchange: There are several banks on Jerusalem St. on and near the *midraḥov.* **Bank Ha-Poalim** (☎ 699 48 00), on the *midraḥov,* near the Ha-Palmaḥ bridge. Hefty commission for changing cash and traveler's checks (NIS24). **ATM** outside. Open Su and Tu-W 8:30am-1:15pm, M and Th 8:30am-1pm and 4-6:30pm, F 8:15am-12:30pm.

First Aid: Magen David Adom, next to the central bus station, downhill on the side away from the main intersection.

Police: (☎ 697 84 44), outside of the main city, up the hill on the road to Rosh Pina.

Post Office: (☎ 692 04 05), on Kikkar Ha-Atzma'ut. At the intersection of Ha-Palmaḥ St. and Aliya Bet, through the parking lot on the other side of the Yigal Allon Theater and Cultural Center. **Poste Restante.** Open Su-Tu and Th 8am-12:30pm and 3:30-6pm; W 8am-1:30pm; F 8am-noon. A more convenient branch at 37 Jerusalem St., past the British Police Station at the end of the *midraḥov,* has the same hours.

▐ ACCOMMODATIONS

Rooms are plentiful, though finding quality at the right price can take a bit of planning, particularly during summer weekends (call ahead for stays over Shabbat). In high season, inexpensive **guest rooms** and flats are often available from town residents. The best way to find a rental is to walk around Jerusalem St. and the old city looking for signs. Always inspect potential quarters before paying (blankets are a plus for Tzfat's chilly nights, even in summer), and feel free to bargain.

▨ **Shalom Inn,** 3 Korchak St. (☎ 697 04 45 or 691 18 61), at the beginning of the artists' quarter. From the bus station, take a left on Jerusalem St. and a left on Aliya Bet St.; just past the cultural center take the unmarked street on the right with a small wooden sign that says "Artists' Quarter." The inn is on the left, just after the paved road curves left. Fresh and modern rooms recently redone. Views of the mountain and the artists' quarter. Private bathrooms, cable TV, A/C, and kitchen. Singles NIS75-110; doubles NIS150-200. Aug. singles NIS110-120; doubles 200-240. Credit cards accepted.

Beit Binyamin (HI), 1 Loḥamei Ha-Geta'ot St. (☎ 692 10 86; fax 697 35 14), near the Amal Trade School in South Tzfat. Take bus #6 or 7. From the bus station, take a left on Jerusalem St. and another left on Aliya Bet St. Pass the community and cultural centers and continue on to Ha-Nassi St., which curves down to the right. Stay on this street, through its curves, and look for the hostel sign on the left. Exceptionally clean, recently renovated rooms have private baths and refrigerators. Breakfast included. Check-out 9am. Wheelchair accessible. 4- to 6-bed dorms NIS78 per person; singles NIS162; doubles NIS224. Credit cards accepted.

Hotel Hadar (☎ 692 00 68), on Ridbaz St., in an alley off Jerusalem St. Take a right onto Jerusalem St. when coming from the bus station and look for the sign on the right that points down the alley. Comfortable, homey atmosphere. Rooms have bath and A/C or fans. Rooftop lounge has a great view of the city. Check-out 11am. Ring after the midnight curfew. Singles NIS100/US$25; doubles NIS200/US$50. Aug. and on Jewish holidays NIS10 more per person; in winter NIS10 less per person.

Ascent Institute of Tzfat, 2 Ha-Ari St. (☎ 692 13 64 or (800) 304 070; fax 692 19 42; email seminars@ascent.org.il; www.ascent.org.il). Take a right on Jerusalem St. from the bus station, then the first right off Jerusalem St. Run by Lubavitch Ḥasidim, many of whom are cheerful, New-Agey American expats. Reactions from secular Jews range from personal revelation to annoyance. Internet access, English library, walking tours of the city, and guided day-hikes free for guests. Breakfast, F dinner, and Sa lunch included; NIS10 rebate for each class attended on Judaism. Reception open Su-Th 9am-9pm and F 9am-4pm. Check-out 11am. Flexible midnight curfew. Call ahead for Shabbat stays. Airy 4- to 6-bed dorms with private bath NIS50; private rooms NIS150/US$32. Accepts credit cards, personal checks, traveler's checks, and cash.

🍴 FOOD

■ **Mountain View,** 70 Jerusalem St. (☎ 102 04 04), in the middle of the *midraḥov*. Specializes in vegetarian dishes. A trendy cafe with a terrific window view down the mountain. Particularly impressive at sunset. Huge salads (NIS34-38), stir-fry dishes (NIS34), pasta (NIS32-36), sandwiches (NIS20), and smoothies (NIS14-20) all fancily garnished. Open Su-Th 8am-midnight. Credit cards accepted.

■ **Pita Ha-Mama,** Jerusalem St., at the top of the Ma'alot Olei Ha-Gardom stairs. This popular bakery is a great place for a quick snack. Baked pitas stuffed with potato or spinach and onions (NIS5) are perfect for munching while strolling through the old city. Try the *lafah* bread with *za'tar* (NIS8). Open Su-Th 7am-8pm and F 7am-2pm.

Pinati (☎ 692 03 30), on the *midraḥov*, near the Ha-Palmaḥ bridge. Elvis plays the role of the Messiah here, and all await his coming. The walls are plastered with memorabilia from the tumultuous life of the swivel-hipped dreamboat. No peanut butter and banana sandwiches, but the fun keeps going. Kebabs and spaghetti NIS30-40. Open Su-Th 9am-midnight, F 9am-4pm, and Sa after sundown-midnight.

Ha-Mifgash Restaurant, 75 Jerusalem St. (☎ 692 05 10), at the lower end of the *midraḥov*. The restaurant is inside a 150-year-old stone-vaulted room that used to be part of a large underground well. Chicken soup connoisseurs must try the velvety brew (NIS12). Veggie options include stuffed pepper (NIS14) and eggplant (NIS16). Open Su-Th 8am-midnight and F 8am-4pm, Sa sundown-midnight. Credit cards accepted.

Falafel and Shawarma California (☎ 692 06 78), on Jerusalem St. just before the Ha-Palmaḥ bridge, on the left when coming from the bus station. Falafel NIS8; *shawarma* NIS13. Open Su-Th 8am-11pm and F 8am-3pm.

👁 SIGHTS

The best—and inevitably, the only—way to see Tzfat is to get lost in its circuitous sidestreets. Fortunately, there are a few **tour guides** on hand to inject some order into the chaos of navigating the city. **Aviva Minoff** gives entertaining tours starting from the Rimonim Hotel. (☎ 692 09 01, cell ☎ 050 40 91 87. 2hr. tour NIS40/US$10; M-F 10:30am; minimum 5 people; reserve in advance.) **Yosi Reis** gives good but expensive tours with advance notice. (☎ 692 28 03, cell ☎ 051 60 36 06. 2hr. tour NIS200/US$50.) Otherwise, try Yisrael Shalem's *Six Self-Guided Tours to Tzfat* (NIS25), available at the candle shop and at Ascent (see **Accommodations,** p. 381).

A WALKING TOUR OF THE SYNAGOGUE QUARTER

Navigating the gnarled synagogue quarter, also called the Old City, is a matter of luck—note landmarks carefully. Only Caro, Ha-Ari, and Abuhav are open to the public; dress modestly and don't take pictures on Shabbat. The following **walking tour** encompasses the major sights:

ASHKENAZI HA-ARI SYNAGOGUE. Across from the post office on Jerusalem St. is a small cobblestone terrace; head down the steps and turn right to reach **Ha-Meginim Sq.** ("Sq. of the Defenders"), which was the Jewish city center until the earthquake of 1837. Through the square, under the stone archway, and down the stairs by the "Synagogue Ha-Ari" sign is the Ashkenazi Ha-Ari Synagogue, built in 1580, three years after the death of its namesake, **Rabbi Isaac Luria** (*Ha-Ari* is the acronym of the Hebrew for "our master Rabbi Isaac" and also means "lion"). It was to this site that the famous mystic and founder led congregants to welcome Shabbat. He is most famous for penning the *Kabbalat Shabbat*, an arrangement of prayers in preparation for the Sabbath; Alkabetz, his student, wrote the now standard hymn, *Lekha Dodi*.

The altarpiece was modified by locals, who were concerned that it was idolatrous. They smeared the paintings, replacing the lion's head with a human face. The synagogue features two notable curiosities. One is the fertility chair, more formally used as a ceremonial circumcision chair. It is rumored to bless women who sit in it with miraculous pregnancies. The other is a small hole in the central pulpit, where visitors place notes for wishes and good luck. The hole was made during the War of Independence, when a grenade flew into the synagogue and exploded while worshipers were bowed in prayer, allowing the shrapnel to sail over their heads and leave a mark only in the pulpit's side.

ABUHAV SYNAGOGUE. Exiting the Ha-Ari synagogue, take a left down the stairs, a left at the bottom, a right on Simtat Abuhav St., and then a quick left after going down more stairs; the Abuhav Synagogue will be on the left. Rabbi Isaac Abuhav was a 15th-century Spanish mystic who never actually made it to Tzfat. His 550-year-old Torah scroll, however, is contained in the first ark to the right, inside the entrance. The second ark contains Rabbi Luria's four-century-old Torah scroll. The scroll inside the blue ark is rumored to have been the only object left intact in Tzfat following the 1837 earthquake that leveled the town. Hanging below the mural in the middle of the synagogue is a chandelier brought over from Europe as a reminder of those who suffered in the Holocaust. The chair at the back of the synagogue has been used to circumcise 8-day-old Jewish boys for 213 years, making it perhaps the single most unpleasant piece of furniture in the world.

AL-SHEIKH SYNAGOGUE. Exiting this synagogue, continue straight down the same alleyway. On the left will be the Al-Sheikh Synagogue, named for a student of Rabbi Yosef said to have been escorted to his grave by 12 doves that attended his Saturday afternoon lectures.

CARO SYNAGOGUE. Up the stairs on the left and through the door in the purple walls is the back entrance to the Caro Synagogue, one of the most famous in Tzfat. It was here that Yosef Caro, chief rabbi of Tzfat and author of the vast *Shulḥan Arukh* ("The Set Table," a standard guide to daily life according to Jewish law), studied and taught in the 16th century. Caro was well-known as a philanthropist who served simultaneously as rabbi, counselor, shelter provider, and soup kitchen coordinator. Notice the glass cabinet in the sanctuary full of Jewish books dating back to the 17th century. Caro Synagogue is also accessible by taking Ma'alot Oleh Ha-Gardom St. off Jerusalem St. and turning right at Beit Yosef St.

CHERNOBYL AND CHERTKOFF SYNAGOGUES. Back at Ha-Meginim Sq., down the narrow Bar-Yochai St., is the Chernobyl Synagogue, marked by a blue box, window grates, and a small English sign on the door. The modest Bar-Yochai St. is believed to be the alley down which the Messiah will make his way on his journey from the nearby mountains to Jerusalem. Off of Ha-Meginim Sq., on Ha-Ḥasadim St., one street above Najara St. and the Ha-Ari Synagogue, is the Chertkoff Synagogue. The chief rabbi here predicted in 1840 that the messianic redemption would begin when 600,000 Jews inhabited the Land of Israel. Both of these synagogues are closed to the public.

CEMETERIES. Three adjoining cemeteries sprawl on the western outskirts of the old city, off Ha-Ari St. at the bottom of the hill. Follow the steps all the way down, past the new stone buildings on the left. The small building on the left when the path turns into the cemetery is Ha-Ari *mikveh*, or ritual bath. This natural spring was the bathing place of Ha-Ari himself, and its vibes have attracted the interest of mystics the world over, including the Dalai Lama. The local rabbinical court has ruled that women may not enter the *mikveh*'s icy waters, but renegade females have been known to take a dip late at night while a male friend guards the door.

The oldest cemetery contains the 16th-century graves of the most famous Tzfat Kabbalists. Most prominent is Ha-Ari's blue tomb, where religious Jews come at all hours to pray, light candles, and seek inspiration. Also notice the domed tomb built by the Karaites of Damascus to mark the grave of the prophet Hosea. Legend has it that hidden under this same hill are Hannah and her seven sons, whose martyrdom at the hands of the Syrians is recorded in the Book of Maccabees. This cemetery is the domain of eighth-generation Tzfat resident Mordekhai Shebabo, who left his position as a pedicurist to single-handedly restore the graves. Every visible grave is the result of his efforts.

OTHER SIGHTS

ARTISTS' QUARTER AND GENERAL EXHIBITION. These alleys and galleries display a wide range of art inspired by the local colors. The quality varies, but a keen eye might discern a few real jewels. Gallery highlights include **microcalligraphy** (creating pictures out of verses from traditional Jewish texts) and Ruth Shany's silk artwork. A number of artists, including Avraham Loewenthal and David Friedman, create mystical art inspired by the Kabbalah. Not to be missed is Mike Leaf's studio, full of satirical paper mache sculptures. The General Exhibition is a collection of works by local artists. The art is displayed in the town's former mosque, which has been empty of worshipers since the 1948 War. *(The artists' quarter is below the Jerusalem-Arlozorov intersection. Most shops open 10am-1pm and 4-7pm. The General exhibition, well-marked by English signs, is on Arlozorov St., at the bottom of the hill south of Ma'alot Oleh Ha-Gardom St. ☎ 692 00 87. Open Su-Th 9am-6pm, F 9am-2pm, and Sa 10am-2pm.)*

SHEM VA'EVER CAVE. This site is said to be the burial grounds of Noah's son Shem and grandson Ever. Muslims call it the "Cave of Mourning" because they believe that it was here that Jacob learned of the death of his son Joseph. *(The cave is near the top of Ha-Palmaḥ bridge, at the intersection of Jerusalem and Arlozorov St. If the shrine around the cave is locked, knock at the small, domed synagogue nearby.)*

TOUCH NO EVIL Above doorways all over the old city of Tzfat, as well as on keychains, in windows, and behind picture frames throughout Israel, is the likeness of a hand. The hand has special significance in Jewish mysticism because of the Kabbalistic meaning of the numbers: a hand (generally) has five fingers, and people have two hands for a total of ten, a number that represents God in mystic texts. Some noteworthy variations on the hand symbol are the hand with an eye in its palm, which represents the evil eye, and the six-fingered hand above the doorway on the right after exiting left from Abuhav Synagogue. One of the builders had six rather than five fingers on one hand and left his mark after finishing the construction project.

MUSEUMS

BEIT HA-MEIRI MUSEUM. The 150-year-old stone building is as interesting as the exhibits on display. Its restored three floors tell Tzfat's history through colorful biographies of its elders—including the town matchmaker and the resident man-with-the-evil eye—and exhibits on how they worked and lived. *(From the midraḥov on Jerusalem St. take the Ma'alot Olei Ha-Gardom stairs all the way down to the bottom and make a right. ☎ 697 13 07. Open Su-Th 9am-2pm and F 9am-1pm. NIS10, students NIS7.)*

MEMORIAL MUSEUM OF HUNGARIAN-SPEAKING JEWRY. This small museum is dedicated to preserving the heritage of Jewish life in Hungary. Personal items on display (including prayer books, diaries, clothing, and paintings) illustrate the vibrancy of a culture that was virtually destroyed by the Holocaust. *(From Jerusalem St. walk down Aliyah Bet St. and turn left at the Wolfson center; the museum is through the parking lot on the left. ☎ 692 58 81; www.hungjewmus.org.il. Open M-F 9am-1pm. NIS10.)*

▮ CRAFTS

One of the must-see sights in the old city is the **Tzfat Candle Factory.** From Ha-Meginim Sq., head down to Najara St. and take a right past the Ha-Ari Synagogue; the factory is on the right. All of the imaginatively colored and shaped candles on display are produced by the workers at the back of the shop, busily bent over blocks and sheets of beeswax. Make your own for NIS10-40. (☎ 682 20 68. Open Apr.-Sept. Su-Th 9am-6pm and F 9am-1pm; Oct.-Mar. Su-Th 9am-6pm and F 9am-1pm. Candles start at NIS12.) In Ha-Meginim Sq. is **Torah scribe** Zalmon Bear Halevy Tornek, who can be observed hand-copying Jewish religious texts. (☎ 692 42 77. Open Su-Tu and Th noon-6pm; F 11am-2pm.)

♫ ENTERTAINMENT

Having a wild night in Tzfat takes some creative thinking. The most prominent bar is **Adios,** 73 Jerusalem St.on the *midraḥov,* in a hip, two-story seating area, which serves beer (NIS10-15) and cocktails (NIS15) to that unbelievably bluesy beat of classic American rock. (☎ 682 12 62. Open Su-Th 8am-1am, F 8am-4pm, and Sa 9pm-2am.) Movies, often in English with Hebrew subtitles, are screened at the **Yigal Allon Theater and Cultural Center** a couple nights a week. Call ahead or stop by around 8pm to see if one is showing. The cultural center is next to the main post office, near the traffic circle where Ha-Palmaḥ St. and Aliyah Bet St. meet. (☎ 697 19 90. NIS20. Movies begin around 8:30pm.)

Travelers planning a visit to Tzfat well in advance should consider arriving in time for the annual **Klezmer Festival** in late July or early August, a three-night extravaganza during which the city sways to the strains of everything from old-world Yiddish tunes to modern Ḥasidic rock. Outdoor concerts are plentiful and free, as is the spontaneous dancing that seems to erupt in front of each stage.

NEAR TZFAT

MERON AND MOUNT MERON הר מירון ☎ 06

For two days every spring, the tranquil hillside surrounding Rabbi Shimon Bar-Yoḥai's tomb at Meron transforms into the scene of a frenzied religious carnival. Some believe that the 2nd-century Talmudic scholar **Bar-Yoḥai** authored the *Zohar*, the central work of the Kabbalah. Thousands of Jews converge upon the town to commemorate the date of his death (the holiday of **Lag Ba'Omer,** May 11 in 2001). Tzfat's Visitors Center (☎ 692 74 85) has more details on the festival.

Near the tomb stand the ruins of a historically noteworthy synagogue dating from the 3rd century CE, when Meron was important in the booming olive oil trade. From Bar Yoḥai's grave, go past the *yeshiva* and follow the uphill path on the left. The **lintel**, an engraved stone slab that once decorated the entrance to the synagogue, is virtually all that remains of the edifice. Legend holds that this lintel's fall will herald the coming of the Messiah. To reach Meron from Jerusalem, take any one of hundreds of buses running all night from Malaḥi St. in Geulah.

Just west of the village is **Har Meron** (Mount Meron), the highest mountain in the Galilee (1208m). A good trail affords tremendous vistas of Tzfat and the surrounding countryside—on clear days Lebanon and Syria to the north, the Mediterranean to the west, and the Sea of Galilee to the southeast are all visible. The **information office** offers limited hiking advice. (☎ 698 00 23. Trail map NIS62. Open Sa-Th 8am-7pm and F 8am-2pm.) To reach the trail, continue past the field school turnoff, past the army base on the right, and a small parking lot on the left. The **trail** begins at the back of the lot and follows striped black-and-white, as well as orange, blue, and white trail markers. A one-hour walk uphill through sweet-smelling, wonderfully wooded surroundings leads to an observation area with striking views of the area. Continue along the red-and-white marked trail skirting the summit and follow the trail to the left when it reaches a rocky area near the army radio towers. Twenty minutes farther along the path leads to a picnic site and a traffic circle; make a quick left back into the forest to where the trail begins again. An hour-long, easy descent, again marked with black-and-white, ends at a paved road just above the village of Meron. A 15-minute walk to the right leads to the tomb of Shimon Bar-Yohai. To get to the village, turn left onto the road, follow it into the town, and take a left at the grocery store on the right. After reaching the main gate, turn right down the highway and go left and across the highway at the major intersection to reach the bus stop (#361, every 20min. 6am-8pm, NIS8).

A gorgeous 3½-hour **hike** starts from Naḥal Amud at the bottom of the Tzfat cemeteries. Interested travelers should get directions from SPNI or the tourist office or consult the rough map on file at Ascent (see **Accommodations,** p. 380).

Buses go to Kibbutz Sasa (#43 or 367; 25min.; 6:45, 9, 11:40am, 12:30, 5:30pm; NIS11.50). In summer, catch the early bus to avoid the midday heat. From the kibbutz, continue one kilometer along the main highway to the turnoff on the left marked with a green sign that indicates "Meron Field School." After one kilometer, there is a brown sign for the SPNI Field School, which is up the small hill to the right. To get to the tomb from the bus stop, walk to the intersection with a sign for Meron and follow the road up for about five minutes.

ALMA CAVE מערת עלמה ☎ 06

Legend has it that the maze-like tunnels of Alma Cave form an underground bridge between the holy cities of Tzfat and Jerusalem and contain the corpses of 900,000 "righteous men." The entrance to the cave is hidden in a gorge, behind clusters of large trees; from the green nature reserve sign on the hillside of gray stones, go right and uphill toward the metal poles—the gorge and cave entrance are just beyond this. Notice the black ropes hooked into the stone to aid in climbing down into the gorge and toward the cave entrance. Climb (or slide) down the hole, keeping to the right. At a depth of approximately 60m (one-half to three-quarters of the way down), there are two phallic rocks near the right-hand wall. Behind those lies a small hole leading to the "inner chambers" of the cave. There are markers indicating the correct path: white for the way in, red for the way out. Once inside the large room with a ridge and a steep slope, veer to the far right along the ridge instead of continuing down the slope.

A bus leaves Tzfat for Reḥania (#45; 20min.; Su-Th 8:45am and 1:30pm, F 8:45am, noon, and 3:30pm; NIS11.50). The bus goes all the way to the settlement of Alma, but get off at Reḥania. Bus #45 also makes the return trip to Reḥania to Tzfat (Su-Th 9:15am and 2pm; F 9:15am, 12:30, and 4pm). By car, drive north along the Tzfat-Meron highway and continue past the Zeition Junction to Reḥania. Across from the entrance to Reḥania village is the dirt path to Alma cave. The path is marked by red and white stripes painted on the light pole beside the main highway; from

CAVING IN. Bring water and one reliable flashlight per person as well as candles and matches for backup, and prepare to get covered with mud. Alma Cave should be tried only by those who feel they can remain up to 108m beneath the earth for several hours. Keep in mind that it is slippery in and around the cave, and large packs will not fit through the tighter spots. It is safest to go during daylight hours with a group of people and to let someone know where you're headed.

there, red-and-white trail markers are infrequent. Stay on this path for about 30 minutes, steering close to Alma (left), and away from the hilly, tree-lined area to the right (don't make any sharp turns). The walk goes past farmers' fenced off fields, to the hill covered with tree clusters and stones toward the left. The marked trail leads to the cave entrance.

TEL ḤAZOR תל חזור ☎ 06

Buses from Tzfat (#501 or 511; 35min.; NIS13) and all buses that run between Rosh Pina and Kiryat Shmona stop near the site. Don't get off at Ḥazor Ha-Gelilit; continue north to Kibbutz Ayelet Ha-Shaḥor. The kibbutz houses a small museum (☎ 693 48 55) displaying Canaanite and Israelite artifacts and explaining some of the tel's layers. From there, the site's entrance (☎ 693 72 90) is 250m up the main road. Museum and site open Sa-Th 8am-5pm and F and holidays 8am-4pm. NIS14, students NIS12, children NIS6.

Like Megiddo (see p. 369), Ḥazor was once a fortified city on the main trading route that linked Egypt to Syria and Mesopotamia. Ḥazor served as a major commercial center in the Fertile Crescent, and the Bible calls it "the head of all those [northern Canaanite] kingdoms" (Joshua 11:10). At the *tel's* northern foot lies a vast, lower city built in the 9th century BCE. The most impressive of the *tel's* ruins is the 38m-deep tunnel, engineered during Ahab's reign to bring water into the city in case of a siege. Today, archaeologists are still searching for the city's archives.

BAR'AM בר עם ☎ 06

A bus from Tzfat goes to Bar'am (#43; 6:45am, 12:30, 5pm; return 7:45am, 1:45, 5:45pm; NIS13). Ask the driver for the synagogue ruins, marked by a small brown sign that says Bar'am and points right, not the Bar'am Kibbutz a few kilometers down the road. Open Sa-Th 8am-5pm and F 8am-4pm. NIS9, students NIS8, children NIS4.

These 3rd-century ruins constitute one of the best-preserved synagogues in Israel. Archaeological evidence shows that Bar'am was home to a prosperous Jewish community in the middle centuries of the first millennium. The ruins of two synagogues have been uncovered here. Bar'am was a Maronite Christian village until the 1948 War of Independence. A few steps up the hill on the left beyond the old synagogue ruins is a beautiful stone Maronite Church that is still used by the Maronites on holidays and special occasions. In front of the church is an observation point with a view of Mount Meron to the south.

ROSH PINA ראש פינה ☎ 06

Buses go to Tzfat (#401, 459, 461, 501, or 511; every 30min.; NIS10), and buses go to Kiryat Shmona (#480, 500, 842, 845, or 909; every 30min.; NIS13).

Because many buses heading north pass through, the town serves as a gateway to the Upper Galilee and Golan. There's not much to do in quaint and quiet Rosh Pina except visit the **Rothschild Garden**, on Ha-Ḥalutzim St., a beautifully maintained park with shady poplars and dozens of varieties of roses lining its terraces or **Drora's Herb Farm**, 25 Ha-Ḥalutzim St., up the hill on the way to the hostel, one block past the post office, a sweet-smelling shop that sells everything organic. (☎ 693 43 49. Herb teas NIS5-20. Open Su-Th 10am-7pm, F 10am-6pm, and Sa 7-10pm.) The **Nature Friends Youth Hostel** has two tidy rooms with fridge, air-conditioning, and shared bath, as well as a small camping area. (☎ 693 17 64 or cell ☎ 051 57 21 41. Dorms NIS5; singles NIS15, shower and bath available. Guests must pay

ISRAEL

at the Beit Binyamin Hostel in Tzfat; call ahead.) The rest of the rooms in the hostel are occupied by **SPNI field offices** (☎693 70 86; fax 693 43 12). To reach the hostel walk straight up the hill from the main bus stop and look for a sign on the left.

KIRYAT SHMONA קרית שמונה   ☎06

Kiryat Shmona ("Town of Eight") commemorates Yosef Trumpeldor and seven others who were murdered in nearby Tel Ḥai in 1920. Situated atop the ruins of the Arab village al-Khalsa, which was destroyed in the 1948 War, the city received its new name in 1949. Due to its location on the Ḥula plain near the Lebanese border, Kiryat Shmona was the target of bombings and terrorist attacks until Israel invaded Lebanon in 1982 to create the nine-mile-wide security zone. Since then, it has been subject to shelling by the militant Islamic group Hizbullah. The town thus graduated from its grim name to an even grimmer nickname: Kiryat Katyusha, referring to the type of rockets used.

◩ GETTING THERE AND GETTING AROUND. The **Central bus station** (☎681 82 22) is on Tel Ḥai Blvd., near the north end of the city. Buses to: **Jerusalem** (#963; 3½hr.; Su every 1½hr. and M-Th every 3hr. 5:30am-4pm; NIS50); **Kfar Blum** (#31 or 32; 3 per day 6:15am-5:20pm; NIS7); **Metulla** (#20 or 21; 8 per day 6:45am-7:15pm; NIS8); **Rosh Pina** (#480, 500, 842, 845, or 969; 30min.; NIS13); **Tel Aviv** (#840, 841, 842, or 845; every 30min. 5:20am-8pm; NIS47) or (#840, 841, or 963; 1hr.; every 30min. 5:30am-8pm; NIS21.50); and **Tzfat** (#501 or 511; 45min.; every hr. 5:50am-8:40pm; NIS18). Rent cars from **Shlomo Rent-a-Car,** down Henrietta Szold St. from Tel Ḥai Blvd. Take a right into the industrial area; the office is in the first row of offices on the left under a small Thrifty sign. (☎694 16 31. 3-day minimum. Cheapest manual US$45 per day; cheapest automatic US$57 per day. Under 24 US$12 extra per day. 21+. Open Su-Th 8am-5pm and F 8am-2pm.)

▛◪ ACCOMMODATIONS AND FOOD. Kiryat Shmona is a good place to make necessary shopping excursions or to catch the bus to accommodations in outlying areas, but its **Hotel Hatira** makes it possible to use the city as an overnight base. In a castle-like building, the big rooms come with TV, air-conditioning, fridge. Also on Tel Ḥai Blvd., it's a 15-minute walk to the right out of the bus station; look for a sign for the El Gaucho restaurant. (☎694 49 44; fax 690 30 36. Singles NIS100; doubles NIS180; less for longer stays. Credit cards accepted.) There are plenty of falafel places along Tel Ḥai Blvd., as well as some fast food places in the mall. (Open Su-Th 9am-10pm, F 9am-3pm, and Sa noon-11pm.) **Club Market,** in the mall by the bus station, is well-stocked with everything from fresh produce to packaged sweets. (☎690 47 76. Open Su-Th 8am-9pm and F 7am-3pm.) On Thursday morning there is an outdoor market past the mall on Tel Ḥai Blvd.

◪ SIGHTS. The most noteworthy attraction is **Manara Cliff,** offering the longest aerial cable ride in Israel. It's just off Tel Ḥai St., at the southern end of town, on the right driving south from the bus station. Glassed-in sky gondolas carry people to two stations midway up and at the top of the 900m cliff. In addition to the birds-eye view of Galilee and the Golan, the middle station offers cliff rapelling (NIS155). From the top, the trip down can be hiked or biked (3-4km depending on the path followed), as well as traveled by gondola. (☎690 58 30; email m-cliff@inter.net.il. One-way gondola ride NIS35; round-trip NIS49. Children NIS55. Bike rental NIS67; 2½-3hr. ride down; bikes can be returned at the middle or lower station. Open daily 9:30am-6:30pm.) The big red apple on Rte. 90 at the southern edge of the city is home to the production facilities of all-natural **Galilee Cider.** Twenty-seven workers at the site fill between 120,000-150,000 cans of juice every day, and welcome visitors to see how they do it and taste the fruits of their labor. (☎694 45 54. Tour and tasting NIS15, students NIS13.50. Su-Th 9am-6:30pm, F 9am-2pm, and Sa 10am-5pm; in winter Su-Th 9am-5pm, F 9am-2pm, and Sa 10am-5pm.)

ISRAEL

NEAR KIRYAT SHMONA

HIKING

The **Ḥula Valley Nature Reserves** ranks as one of the most beautiful areas in all of Israel. At the turn of the 20th century, the entire valley was covered by a knee-deep swamp, until Jewish pioneers arrived and drained the swamps in order to farm the fertile soil beneath. Eventually, the altered land became so dry that its diverse wildlife left the Ḥula Valley and in some instances died out entirely. Out of concern for the area's ecological diversity, Israel's first nature reserve was established in the Ḥula Valley in 1964. Since then, parts of the Ḥula Valley have been refilled with water and are carefully maintained; ecologists hope to lure amphibians, water buffalo, and birds migrating between Europe and Africa to take up increased residence in the area. The five reserves of the Ḥula Valley showcase Israel's forested north, ice-cold streams, swamplands, and their inhabitants.

ḤULA NATURE RESERVE. This reserve is only really worth visiting between November and March, when it is swarming with animals and birds. The center gives details on the history of the swamp, the varieties of plant and animal wildlife it contains, and a video presentation. The the 1½km-long yellow duck-marked trail is paved except for wood-planked observation bridges and an observation tower. The visitors center rents binoculars for bird enthusiasts (NIS10; Sept.-Mar. is the best season for bird watching). Arrive early in the morning to see the wildlife and to avoid crowded family-time in the forest. *(Between Rosh Pina and Kiryat Shmona, off of Rte. 90. From the south, the turnoff is on the right, 8km north of Tel Ḥazor. Look for a brown sign on the right that says "Ha-Ḥula." Buses (#501, 511, 840, or 841; NIS13) leave Kiryat Shmona frequently and go to a junction 2½km from the entrance to the reserve. ☎ 693 70 69. Open Sa-Th 8am-4pm and F and holiday eves 8am-3pm. NIS18, students NIS15, under 18 NIS9.)*

ḤORSHAT TAL NATURE RESERVE. There are two reasons to visit this reserve: to go swimming or to go camping. The biggest draw is the ice-cold **swimming pool,** a man-made lake that is fed by the Dan river. The **Camping Ground** with a snack bar and shared bathrooms is nearby on the banks of the Dan River. (Snack bar and shared bathrooms. Tent sites NIS35 per person, children under 14 NIS25; enclosed 4-person bungalows NIS180/US$38; prices rise 50% F and holidays.) Stock up on groceries at **Alonit Market,** on Highway 99, a 15-minute walk from Ḥorshat Tal. Go west toward Kiryat Shmona; it's on the left. (☎ (06) 690 21 81. Open daily 7am-11pm.) Scattered around the grounds of the reserve are 100-year-old oak trees. According to a Muslim legend, the trees, which grow nowhere else in Israel, sprang into being because of the 10 warriors of Muhammad who once rested here. Finding no shade and not a single hitching post for their horses, they pounded their staffs into the earth to fasten their mounts, and the sticks sprouted overnight. *(Off Rt. 99, between Kiryat Shmona and Banyas. From Kiryat Shmona, buses go to Ḥorshat Tal (#36; 6:10am and 2pm, but call ahead to check times; NIS7). Ask to be let off at Ḥorshat Tal, then walk 100m down the hill on the right, toward the brown sign. ☎ 694 23 60. Park open for swimming Sa-Th 8am-5pm and F 8am-4pm. NIS27, children under 14 NIS16.)*

TEL DAN. Tel Dan contains some of the most beautiful scenery in northern Israel. Several short walks loop under a canopy of willow trees and follow the gushing Dan River, the largest tributary of the Jordan. Swimming in the river is prohibited but there is a **wading pool** where hot hikers splash around. The 45-minute circle trail is mostly paved for **wheelchair access;** the 1½-hour trail is rockier but passes by all the ancient ruins. Ongoing excavations at the *tel* have revealed the ancient Canaanite city of Laish, conquered and settled by the Israelite tribe of Dan around 1200 BCE. In 1983, archaeologists made a remarkable find at Tel Dan: a broken stele, inscribed with the words "House of David" in 9th-century BCE Aramaic. The earth-shattering piece provided the first known reference to the biblical King David and his climactic expulsion of the Philistines, aside from the Good Book itself. The **Beit Ushishkin Museum,** a stone building on the left on the way to Tel Dan, displays a replica of the stele. (*A few kilometers past Horshat Tal on Rte. 99. From the main road, take a left at the brown sign and walk a winding 1½km to the site. Take bus #36 from Kiryat Shmona (Su-F 6:10am and 2pm). Call ahead to check times. ☎(06) 695 15 79. Open Sa-Th 8am-5pm and F 8am-4pm; gates close 1hr. before closing time. NIS18, students NIS15, children NIS9; ticket includes a 25% discount at the Beit Usishkin Museum. Museum open Su-Th 8:30am-4:30pm, F 8:30am-3:30pm, and Sa 9:30am-4:30pm. NIS13, students and children NIS11.*)

METULLA מטולה

Buses #20 and 21 run between Kiryat Shmona and Metulla (15min., 5 per day 6:45am-2:10pm, NIS8). Ha-Rishonim St. runs through the center of town, with the community center and municipality building at one end and the Lebanese Border at the other. To reach the main street, walk up the steep paved road into Metulla and continue left, past the Canada Center sports complex and a small playground.

Metulla, nine kilometers north of Kiryat Shmona, is Israel's largest village on the Lebanese border. For many years its main attraction was **Ha-Gader Ha-Tova** (The Good Fence), the only opening in the border between Lebanon and Israel. Israel began passing aid and supplies through this point to Lebanese Christians in 1971, and in June 1976 the Good Fence officially opened, allowing Lebanese Christians and Druze free passage into Israel to obtain medical treatment, visit relatives, and work. When Israel withdrew from southern Lebanon in June 2000, the Good Fence finally closed and has been renamed the Fatmah Gate, its name before 1976. At press time, the future of the gate remains in doubt, and as long as Hizbullah remains a serious threat to the region's security, many southern Lebanese will be left without jobs. Curving around town is the **Iyun Nature Reserve,** full of waterfalls in the winter and early spring. Enter the park by the road that branches off of the main highway just south of the town. Just a few minutes up the trail from the parking lot is the 30m **Tanur (Oven) Waterfall,** named for the chimney-like structure it forms with the cliff. The path continues uphill for another 45 minutes past two more waterfalls. At press time, the upper entrance to the park was closed due to its proximity to the Lebanese border; the only way back to the parking lot is to retrace the path. Metulla and the bus stop to Tel Hai and Kiryat Shmona are a short walk to the right up the highway.

GOLAN HEIGHTS רמת הגולן

This formerly volcanic plateau overlooking the Hula Valley has a sparse population of 35,000 equally divided between recent Jewish settlers and longtime Druze inhabitants, many of which strongly identify with Syria and have relatives across the border. To Israelis, the region is a major source of water as well as the home of ski slopes, apple orchards, wineries, and cattle pastures. The region's natural borders include the Jordan River and Sea of Galilee to the west, Mount Hermon and the Lebanese mountains to the north, and the Syrian plains to the east.

Recent history has cast the Golan Heights into the jaws of political controversy. Throughout the 1950s and 1960s, Israeli towns in Galilee were assailed by artillery fire from Syrian gunposts atop the mountains. Israel captured the Golan in the 1967 Six-Day War but was pushed back by Syria's surprise attack in the 1973 war. Israeli forces quickly recovered and launched a counter-attack, capturing even more territory. As part of the 1974 disengagement accord, Israel returned both the newly conquered territory and part of the land captured in 1967. Israel officially annexed the remaining 768 sq. km territory in 1981, arousing international protest. Today, Jewish settlements are scattered among Israeli army bases, Druze villages, live minefields, and destroyed bunkers.

The future status of the Golan is currently under negotiation. Syria claims that the land was seized unfairly and demands its return. Israeli officials had always invoked the issue of security in their refusal to budge from the Golan Heights, until the Rabin and Peres administrations announced their willingness to cede all or part of the Golan in exchange for peace and Syrian recognition of Israel, but Syrian

ISRAEL

President Hafez al-Assad rejected the offer. The reality is that whoever commands the elevated plateau enjoys strategic views of Damascus and all of northern Israel.

The political necessity of compromise became apparent with the election of Ehud Barak in May 1999, when it was revealed that even Benyamin Netanyahu had been close to making an agreement with the Syrians. The recent death of Hafez al-Assad has added an additional twist to the story. The international community awaits to see how Assad's son, now in power, will handle negotiations with Israel. Barak's goal is to reach an agreement with Syria that will not leave Israel dependent on the US for its security, as it was during the withdrawal from Sinai. For current news on Israel, see **In the News,** p. 271.

◪ PRACTICAL INFORMATION

When wandering the Golan in summer, bring a hat, sunscreen, and water bottles. The cool pools of water often found on hikes reward weary walkers ready to take a dip, but don't drink the water. Try to avoid the cold, damp, foggy, and often snowy winter. The best time to visit the Golan is spring, when the temperature is mild, the hills are green, and the streams and waterfalls are satiated with icy-cold water from the melting snow on Mount Ḥermon. The best way to see the Golan is to **rent a car** in Tiberias or Kiryat Shmona. Those who don't plan to hike can hit the major sights in two days. Don't be afraid to lean on your horn (passing other cars in the Golan is as common as passing breathtaking views), but take care when navigating the narrow, curving roads.

Egged buses reach some sights in the Golan, but infrequent service along remote roads necessitates careful planning. Double-check schedules, and anticipate some walking. Buses to sights near the Sea of Galilee generally leave from Tiberias. The Upper Galilee, Ḥula Valley, and northern Golan are served by buses from Kiryat Shmona and Hatzor Ha-Galilit. It is nearly impossible to get to Gamla and many hiking trails by bus. Few cars traverse the Golan, and hitchhiking is not recommended. If you decide to set out alone, take a good map (see **Golan Hikes,** p. 391.)

There is a rarely-open **tourist information office** for the Golan Heights at the Maḥanayim Junction between Rosh Pina and Kiryat Shmona, where Rte. 91 branches off of Rte. 90 (look for the gas station on the right and turn right; the information office is in the strip of shops on the left). The office sells maps and has brochures, mostly in Hebrew, on activities, restaurants, and accommodations in the region. (☎693 69 45. Open F 8:30am-3:30pm and Sa 9am-2pm.) There is a **24-hour grocery** next door to the tourist office; bring several bottles of water and at least a day's worth of food on any hike.

Organized **tours** are faster, more convenient, and sometimes less expensive than other forms of transportation; they also go at a quicker pace than many would like. **Matan Tours,** in Tiberias, attracts a young backpacker crowd with one-day professionally guided tours of the Golan and Upper Galilee that include sightseeing and light hiking. (☎(06) 672 4574 or (05) 461 61 48. NIS160/US$38 per person.) **Egged** also offers professionally guided full-day tours of the region from Tel Aviv every Thursday. (☎(03) 527 12 12. NIS290/US$68; 10% ISIC discount.) **Moshe Cohen** makes military-history-oriented rounds in a van. (☎672 16 08. NIS140 per person; min. 4 people.) **SPNI** offers a three-day hiking tour of the Golan and Upper Galilee that includes kayaking on the Jordan River. (☎(03) 638 86 88. US$298. Leaves from the SPNI office in Tel Aviv.) For those who'd rather skip all the touristy kitsch and just get outside and hike, **Devorah Leah Rice** leads hikes in the Upper Galilee and Golan. (☎(06) 682 00 83. Half day NIS80, whole day NIS200.)

Jeep Plus in Moshav Ramot, on the eastern bank of the Sea of Galilee, runs guided jeep trips. (☎673 23 17. 2hr. trip for 7-8 people NIS540/US$145.) **Tractoron B'Rama,** also in Ramot, rents one-person ATVs to tourists with driver's licenses. (☎(05) 053 17 84. NIS120 per hour.) **Jimmy Jeep,** at Givat Yoav, southeast of Kursi on Rte. 789, runs 2-hour jeep trips for NIS550. (☎676 34 05. Jeep seats 8 people.)

GOLAN HIKES

The Golan offers some of the most beautiful hikes in all of Israel. Although the region gets very hot from late spring to early fall, most hikes go through streams, pools, and waterfalls, offering natural refreshment from the summer sun. Those who wish to hike in the Golan should purchase the 1:50,000 trail map available at SPNI offices and in Steimatzky's (NIS62). SPNI offices also have useful booklets with descriptions and directions for hiking routes in the area, such as the *Israeli Landscapes Vol. 1: Guide to the Golan Heights* (NIS55) and a more general map of the upper Galilee and Golan Heights, with roads and popular sights marked (NIS20). For more detailed directions and alternative trail options in the Golan, check out a copy of Joel Roskin's *A Guide to Hiking in Israel*, on sale at Steimatzky bookstores (NIS39). Consult the SPNI field schools in Katzrin or Ḥermon for up-to-date advice and information; the information desk at **Yehudiyya Reserve** (☎696 28 17) also offers helpful hiking advice. Bus service to the trails, where it exists, is very irregular; call Egged and plan carefully. Be aware that many trails do not loop back to where they started and may leave you far away from your car. Start hiking early in the morning to avoid the busloads of Israeli children and remember that it is not safe to drink water from Golan streams.

 DANGER! MINES! The Golan Heights still contain active landmine fields. they are marked off by barbed-wire fences with square yellow signs that have red triangles and say, Danger! Mines! in English, as well as in Hebrew and Arabic. In some areas the fences are marked only with red triangles. Be sure to stay on paved roads and clearly marked hiking trails. As a rule, avoid fenced-off areas whether or not you see the yellow-and-red warning signs.

YA'AR YEHUDIYYA NATURE RESERVE. The most exciting and challenging hiking in the Golan is in the Ya'ar Yehudiyya Nature Reserve, southeast of Katzrin. The highlight of the reserve, and one of the best hikes in Israel, is the action-packed **Naḥal Yehudiyya** trail, which consists of an upper and a lower section. From the Ḥenion parking lot follow the red-and-white markers across the street, past the 1800-year-old Jewish and Byzantine town ruins, and into the valley. Upon completion of the **upper trail,** ascend the green-and-white trail to return to Ḥenion (3hr. round-trip) or continue along the red-and-white marked lower trail for a longer hike (5-6hr. round-trip). The lower trail ends with an extremely difficult climb up a boulder-strewn hill (be careful: the rocks are hot during summer), a peaceful stroll through a beautiful yellow field, and a 1½km walk to the right along the highway back to the Ḥenion. Both trails feature enticing waterfalls and pools, some of which you must swim across to complete your hike (bring a bathing suit and plastic bags to protect food and valuables). Rocks are slippery when climbing from dry parts of the trail into the water, so look for the strategically placed metal foot- and hand-holds in the cliffs. Jumping off the nine-meter cliff at the second waterfall is dangerous—people have died doing this. A much safer option is to climb down the slippery ladder into the water to enjoy the swim.

The reserve also harbors the slightly drier but equally beautiful **Naḥal Zavitan;** most of its trail options also start at the Ḥenion Yehudiyya parking lot. Start on the green-and-white marked Lower Zavitan trail. A left turn on the red-and-white trail leads to the **Ein Netef** spring, which purportedly contains the only drinkable water in the reserve. From the spring, backtrack along the red-and-white trail and turn left on the black-and-white trail to reach a pleasant pool and waterfall. This trek eventually crosses the red-and-white one and returns to Ḥenion Yehudiyya (3hr.). Alternatively, turn left and continue on the red-and-white trail for 45 minutes to reach the spectacular **Brekhat Ha-Meshushim** (Hexagon Pool), where hundreds of hexagonal rock columns skirt the water's edge in a wonderful geological phenomenon. From here, backtrack to Ḥenion (total 6hr.). The **Upper Zavitan** (black-and-white trail) tends to be good for all seasons. It begins near the field school in

Katzrin and leads to less impressive hexagonal pools; after becoming a purple-and-white trail, it ends in Ḥenion Yehudiyya (3hr.). The more difficult **Lower Zavitan** should be avoided in the winter due to occasional flash floods. The dangerous **Black Canyon,** is near the Lower Zavitan trail, and can only be negotiated by rapelling. Many hikers have died here. Do not attempt to hike the Black Canyon without an experienced guide. *(By car from Tiberias, drive north along the lake, head east toward Katzrin, pass the Yehudiyya Junction, and continue along Rte. 87 until you reach the orange sign. By car from Kiryat Shmona, head toward Katzrin and the junction with Rte. 87, take a right, and look for the sign and parking lot on the right. Open Sa-Th 7am-5pm and F and holidays 7am-4pm; leave no later than 1hr. after closing time. NIS10, students NIS8, children NIS7. Most trails begin in Ḥenion Yehudiyya (☎ 696 28 17), a parking lot with an SPNI information booth, snack stand (1½L water NIS9, sandwiches NIS12), toilets, phones, and camping facilities accessible by bus from Katzrin. At the Ḥenion, bags can be stored for NIS12 per locker. Camping next to the Henion parking lot costs NIS10 per person; facilities include showers and bathrooms. Before beginning a hike, check in with the information desk and get a map.)*

NAḤAL EL-AL. This beautiful hike lies southeast of the Zavitan and Yehudiyya Rivers. In winter and spring, enough water flows through to allow swimming beneath the falls. The red-and-white trail begins at the northeast end of the kibbutz. Follow the markers to **Mapal Ha-Lavan** (white waterfall) and continue on to **Mapal Ha-Shaḥor** (black waterfall). The trail ends at Kibbutz Avnei-Eitan. From there, take a right on Rte. 98 and walk two kilometers to return to Kibbutz Eli-Al. *(By car from Tiberias, head south on Rte. 90. At Zemaḥ Junction, turn onto Rte. 98 and follow it to Kibbutz Eli-Al. The site is fairly close to Yehudiyya: turn left out of Ḥenion Yehudiyya, take Rte. 87 to Rte. 808 on the right, turn right onto Rte. 98, and look for the kibbutz sign. Without a car, this hike is impossible to do in a day, as the first bus arrives at 12:30pm and the last one leaves at 1pm.)*

NAḤAL DEVORAH AND NAḤAL GILABON. From the main parking lot, red-and-white markings lead to the left around a building and down into the canyon. Join the hundreds who have left their mark by sticking a masticated glob of gum onto the **Even Ha-Mastik** ("The Gum Rock"). The first waterfall on the trail is the Devorah Waterfall. Continuing on the red-and-white path another hour leads to the 21m Gilabon Waterfall; wonderful views of the lush Ḥula Valley await at its top. The trail continues another two hours to the Jordan River and Rte. 918, but getting back to the parking lot may be difficult if you don't have a car waiting. Otherwise just retrace your steps to return to the parking lot. *(From Tiberias, take Rte. 90 north and the turnoff for Rte. 91 east. Continue 30min. on Rte. 91; watch for a brown sign and red-and-white trail marker 3-4km after the turnoff for Road 9088. Turn left onto the dirt road and make a right farther up to reach a parking lot surrounded by destroyed Syrian bunkers.)*

NAḤAL ZAKI . Naḥal Zaki makes for a refreshing hike. In August or September, ripe grapes hang overhead and the sweltering heat makes the cool stream a godsend. Wear a bathing suit and bring plastic bags to protect valuables—half the hike is spent wading in knee-deep water. In winter, the current is strong and this trail could be dangerous. Hike in the stream following the green-and-white trail for 3km; at the pipe that stretches across the river, get out of the water on the left side and return by way of a dirt path. *(Off of Rte. 92, just south of the Yehudiyya Junction on the left. Drive along the green trail to a lot, then park and begin the hike.)*

SPIES LIKE US In the early 1960s, Israeli spy **Eli Cohen,** posing as an Arab businessman, infiltrated the Syrian government. Rising through the ranks, he virtually became the president's right-hand man. One of Cohen's suggestions was that the Syrian army plant tall eucalyptus trees to camouflage their Golan Heights bunkers; he then tipped off the IDF, and the air force began targeting the eucalyptus clusters. The Syrian government eventually caught and hanged the Israeli spy, but the destroyed Syrian bunkers sprinkled over the Golan stand as a testimony to his espionage.

KATZRIN קצרין

Katzrin is the largest Jewish settlement in the Golan. The town was founded immediately after the 1967 War with the express purpose of creating an Israeli presence in the Golan Heights. This quiet residential community of houses with orange tiled roofs has grown rapidly over the past 33 years and is now home to a successful winery and a bottled water manufacturing plant. Katzrin enjoys a high standard of living for a young settlement, but its economic growth has diminished with the possibility of an Israeli withdrawal from the Golan. A visit to the winery and museums in Katzrin takes only a few hours, but the town's central location in the Golan also makes it a convenient base for exploring the region.

▐▌ GETTING THERE AND GETTING AROUND

By car from **Tiberias,** head north on Rte. 90 and turn off on Rte. 87 toward the east. Drive 20km past Tzomet Yehudiya and turn onto Rte. 9088. From **Kiryat Shmona,** head south on Rte. 90 toward Rosh Pina and take a left on Rte. 91; a right onto Rte. 9088 leads to the town. Buses go to Katzrin from **Ḥatzor Ha-Galilit,** just north of Rosh Pina (#55, 56, or 57; 25min.; 6 per day 6:15am-7:55pm; NIS10.50); **Kiryat Shmona** (#58; 30min.; 4:40pm; NIS26); and **Tiberias** (#15, 16, or 19; 45min.; 4 per day noon-6:30pm; NIS18). **Moniot Ha-Golan** (☎696 11 11), a left out of the tourist office on the right, has *special* taxi fares to **Rosh Pina** (NIS75) and **Tiberias** (NIS120).

✴❓ ORIENTATION AND PRACTICAL INFORMATION

There are three points of entry into Katzrin on the right from the highway, all marked by brown signs. The second one leads to the main Daliyot St., at the beginning of which is a mall on the left and on the right a commercial center with the bank, tourist office, and two museums clustered together.

The **tourist information** office in Katzrin, in the shopping strip past the bank on the left, has a bus schedule and information on sights, as well as a list of bed-and-breakfasts in the Golan. (☎696 28 85. Open Su-Th 8:30am-4:30pm, F 8:30am-1pm.) **Bank Leumi,** in front of the shopping strip with the tourist office, has an **ATM** outside that takes Visa and PLUS. (☎696 16 01. Open Su and T-W 8:30am-1pm; M and Th 8:30am-1pm and 4:30-7pm; F 8:30am-noon.) Those intrigued by the *"Ha-Am Im Ha-Golan"* (the nation with the Golan) bumper stickers all around Israel may want to stop by the **Golan Residents Committee** in the shopping center across Dolyot St. from the mall. Look for the flags on the right next to the jewelery store. The committee is dedicated to keeping the Golan in Israeli hands and gives out free bumper stickers and banners and sells shirts for NIS13. (☎696 2977. Open Su-Th 8am-6pm and F 8am-3pm.)

▐◍ ACCOMMODATIONS AND FOOD

Unfortunately, Katzrin does not offer much in the way of budget accommodations. There are numerous **bed-and-breakfasts** in the town; call ☎696 28 85 or stop by the tourist office for a list. The **SPNI Golan Field School,** on Zavitan St., rents out clean 6-bed rooms with A/C and bath, when it isn't full of school groups. Go down Daliyot St. away from the shopping area, make a left at the intersection, and look for a sign for the field school on the right. (☎696 12 34. Dorm rooms NIS60 per bed; doubles with breakfast NIS305; NIS95 for each additional person; prices higher in August.) Call the central SPNI office (☎(03) 638 86 88) to book a room during Jewish holidays and in August.

For the best budget food in town head to ▧**Chicken Thai,** across from the tourist office, and order a mouth-watering chicken-veggie stir fry on a baguette for NIS16. (☎696 18 71. Open Su-Th 11am-midnight, F 11am-4pm and Sa 8:30-11pm.) For a more extensive feast **Mifgash Ha-Aish,** at the end of the parking lot farthest from Daliyot St., cooks up all sorts of meat on its flaming outdoor grill and serves it with salads, hot pita, and hummus. (Steaks NIS40-55; chicken kebab NIS35. Open Su-Th 10am-midnight, F 10am-3pm, and Sa 9pm-midnight.) Katzrin also has one of the most unique pubs in all of Israel. The ◖**Safta Pub,** inside the Ancient Katzrin Park, is inside a 1400-year-old stone building from Talmudic times. During the summer, the pub has an outdoor seating area and features theme nights. (☎696 25 21. Beer NIS12-18; cocktails NIS22-35; pizza NIS22; *malaweh* NIS12. M karaoke, Tu cocktail specials, W movie night, and Th Israeli music. Open Sa-Th 9pm-3am.)

🔍 SIGHTS

The **Field School** sells 1:50,000 maps of the Golan (NIS62), and staff members are generally helpful in suggesting hikes in the area.

ANCIENT KATZRIN PARK. The excavations at this site have unearthed a richly ornamented synagogue in use from the 4th through 8th centuries CE. Don't miss the six-screen audio-visual presentation shown in a reconstructed synagogue or the two reconstructed houses with furnishings based on finds from the excavations. *(Just outside of modern Katzrin, to the right down Rte. 9088; look for a brown sign pointing to the left. ☎696 24 12. NIS22, seniors NIS18, students and children NIS14. Save money with a combo ticket that includes the Archaeological museum as well. Ticket allows 10% discount at Gamla and the Golan Winery.)*

SHA'AR HA-GOLAN (GATE OF THE GOLAN). This newly opened information center shows on a giant screen an informative 17-minute movie that covers the history and geography of the Golan Heights. In another pavilion is an enormous, continually updated, 1:5000 three-dimensional map of the Golan that includes every house, road, stream, hill, and radio tower in the entire region. *(Next to the Ancient Katzrin Park; turn into the Ancient Katzrin parking lot and follow the road to the right. ☎696 20 96. Open Su-Th 10am-5pm, F 10am-4pm, and Sa map only 10am-5pm. Movie NIS6. 20-minute tour of map with explanations from a guide NIS10; combined ticket NIS15.)*

GOLAN HEIGHTS WINERY. For those who find Katzrin's museums and Talmudic village too sobering, the Golan Heights Winery is a great alternative. The winery produces the world-renowned Yarden, Gamla, and Golan labels. A one-hour tour includes a video explanation, a look at the production process, a souvenir glass, and a taste of grapey bliss along with a demonstration on how to taste wine. The shop sells bottles of their wine beginning at NIS25. *(From the center of Katzrin, turn right onto Rte. 9088; the winery is in an industrial area on the left. ☎696 84 09. Open Sept.-June Su-Th 8:30am-5pm; July-Aug. Su-Th 8:30am-6:30pm and F 8:30am-1:30pm. Last tour begins about 1hr. before closing. Tours NIS17, students NIS14, children NIS12. Call ahead for tours in English.)*

🔳 DAYTRIP FROM KATZRIN: GAMLA גמלא

*Take a right out of modern Katzrin, a left onto Rte. 87 at the junction, and a right onto Rte. 808. The road to Gamla is on the right, labeled with a sign. Gamla is **not accessible by public transportation;** those without cars often ask for rides from Katzrin and walk the one kilometer to the ridge overlooking the ruins. The descent to the ruins along the Roman route takes about 20min. Allot 1-2hr. for the site itself. ☎676 20 46. Open Su-Th 8am-5pm and F 8am-4pm; closes 1hr. earlier in winter. NIS18, students NIS15.*

In 67 CE, the Romans laid siege to this hilltop fortress, then a haven for 9000 Jewish refugees. As the siege wore on, Roman commanders became impatient and decided to storm down the corridor of land leading to the town from nearby hills. As the legion penetrated Gamla's walls, hordes of Jews fled to the upper part of the city, where slopes were so steep that one house's rooftop touched the floor of the house above it. The Romans followed, but so many soldiers crowded on the rooftops that the houses collapsed; the Jews quickly turned and killed their pursuers. Some weeks later, three Roman soldiers sneaked into Gamla in the middle of the night and pulled out foundation stones from the watchtower, causing it to collapse. In the ensuing confusion, the Roman army burst into the city and began to slaughter the inhabitants, many of whom hurled themselves into the deep ravine next to the citadel rather than die by enemy hands. Two women survived to tell the tale (some archaeologists take issue with Josephus's proclivity for over-dramatization and claim that Gamla's inhabitants were pushed over the cliff in the mayhem of battle). Inside the city lie remnants of what some archaeologists call the oldest synagogue ever found in Israel, dating from around the 2nd century BCE.

There are three **light hiking** trails at Gamla. The two-hour trail through the ancient city is marked in black and begins at the upper left corner of the parking lot (when facing away from the ticket booth). The climb back up from the ruins to the parking lot can be brutal on a hot summer day; there is a shuttle bus that runs every hour down to the ancient city and returns to the parking lot on the half hour (NIS15). The **Mapal Gamla,** or Gamla waterfall, is the highest in the Golan (51m). The trail to the waterfall leads past another fall, usually dry in summer, as well as ancient **Dolmens,** table-like stone graves built 4000 years ago during the middle Bronze Age. The trail is marked in red, takes about an hour, and begins out of the upper right corner of the parking lot, near the water spigots and bathrooms. The **Daliyot trail** (2hr.), marked red and white, starts out of the left corner of the parking lot nearest the ticket booth and runs through fields and along a river canyon. While hot and less interesting during the summer, it boasts a seasonal waterfall.

NORTHERN GOLAN

BANYAS בניס

Buses leave Kiryat Shmona once a day on their way through the Golan and stop by Banyas (#55 or 58; 1:30 and 4:40pm; NIS11.50). By car, Banyas lies just off Rte. 99, which runs between Kiryat Shmona and the north-south Rte. 98. ☎ 695 02 72. Park open Sa-Th 8am-5pm and F 8am-4pm. NIS18, students NIS15, children NIS9.

The most popular site in the Upper Galilee-Golan area, Banyas lies only a few minutes down the road from Dan and Ḥorshat Tal at the foot of Mount Ḥermon. The Banyas springs in the Naḥal Ḥermon Nature Reserve have witnessed an odd religious mix: Jesus gave the keys to heaven and earth to St. Peter here, Muslims built a shrine over the Prophet Elijah's (Nebi Khadar) supposed grave in the adjacent hill, and an ancient sanctuary dedicated to the Greek God Pan remains carved into the cliffside. King Herod built a temple in honor of Augustus Caesar and called the place Caesarea Philippi, after his son Philippus. Because of its ancient association with Pan, however, the area became known as *Paneas* (Pan's Place).

The first brown sign on the road that points to Banyas leads to a parking lot and the entrance closest to the 10m **Banyas waterfall,** the largest falls in the region. From the waterfall, an hour-long trail winds through woods toward the springs, which contain small pools of rare fish. Swimming is forbidden in the pool's icy-cold water, but some visitors wade in to refresh themselves anyway. From here, head toward the parking lot where the ruins of **Pan's temple** are up and to the left. Those short on time can drive from the waterfall to Pan's Temple by making a right on the main road and following the signs.

NIMROD'S FORTRESS קלעת נמרוד

*The **trail** to the fortress begins just off bus route #55 between Kiryat Shmona and Katzrin. The road to the castle sits across from the bus stop (NIS16.50). The 1hr., uphill approach leads to a view into the Druze village of Ein Qinya. The castle is accessible by a **footpath** from Banyas beginning directly above the springs and Pan's temple. This shadeless walk takes about 45 minutes each way. By **car,** continue on Rte. 99 past Banyas to Rte. 989; the fortress is up a curvy road on the left. Open daily 8am-5pm. NIS14, students NIS12, under 18 NIS6.*

Nimrod's Fortress (Qal'at Nemrud) stands 1.5km northeast of Banyas on an isolated hill. According to the biblical list of Noah's descendants, Nimrod claims the title, "the first on earth to be a mighty man" (Genesis 10:8). Legend holds that besides building the Tower of Babel, he erected this gigantic fortress high enough to shoot arrows up to God. The extensive fortress has two main sections; the one farther away from the entrance was built earlier. A look around the grounds reveals a secret passageway and game boards carved into the stone sidewalks by bored guards. The 815m-high view from the top of the fortress to the region below remains unrivaled anywhere in the Upper Galilee or Golan.

Up the road about one kilometer past Nimrod's Fortress is a Muslim tomb and hiking route at **Nebi Hazuri.** The location is marked on the left by a brown sign in Hebrew. A white gravel road begins in the parking lot and winds around picnic areas, trees, and monuments. The hiking route, marked in blue and white, heads right and downhill from beside the large wooden sign in the parking area (rocks are marked a bit farther down). After two hours, the trail ends outside the entrance to the road leading up to Nimrod's Fortress; take a left and head up the main highway to return to the Nebi Hazuri parking area.

MAS'ADA AND MAJDAL SHAMS مسعدة و مجدل شمس

The Druze of these two villages at the foot of Mount Ḥermon differ from the Galilee's Druze in one major respect: most have remained loyal to Syria and many refuse to accept Israeli citizenship. Many of them have close relatives on the other side of the Syrian border and do not want to fight against them in the event of a war. In 1982, they staged a protest against Israeli rule, and the Israeli Defense Forces were sent in to restore control. Since then, the villages have been quiet.

Mas'ada is at the foot of Mount Ḥermon, at the intersection of Rte. 99 (leading west to Kiryat Shmona) and Rte. 98 (leading south to Katzrin). Mas'ada's farmers cultivate the valley and terrace the low-lying ridges around the mountain. Two kilometers north on Rte. 98 rests the locally famous lake **Breiḥat Ram** (Hebrew for "High Lake"). The perfectly round body of water fills the crater of a volcano that has not erupted in over 1000 years. The lake is on the right, past large green gates with a big white sign in Hebrew.

Majdal Shams (Arabic for "Tower of the Sun"), the largest town in the Golan (pop. 8000), is 5km north of Mas'ada through a pleasant valley. The town abuts the border with Syria; an Israeli lookout tower that looms above the village sees eye-to-eye with its Syrian counterpart on the opposite peak, while a white UN base spans the neutral valley in between. Because the electric-fence border is closed and pocked with land mines, the lookout area on the outskirts of town provides the setting for a sad, but fascinating, daily ritual. Majdal's Druze line up on the hillside (aptly dubbed *Givat Ha-Tza'akot* or "Shouting Mountain"). Armed with bullhorns, they make small-talk with their relatives on the Syrian side; the best time to communicate seems to be Friday and Saturday afternoons.

MOUNT ḤERMON

The 2800m high peaks of the majestic Ḥermon mountain range tower over the rest of the Golan. In the wintertime there is skiing, which can be challenging; it has no trees, and steep dips in the wide expanses are easy to miss. Beginners should not fret, however—gentle runs descend from the top of each lift. On clear days, skiers can see Galilee stretch out beneath them. In summer the same chairlift brings tourists up to a panoramic lookout atop Mount Ḥermon. The mountain is particularly striking in late spring and early summer when it is covered in brightly colored wildflowers. (Call ☎ 06 698 13 37 or 03 565 60 40 for ski conditions, lodging information; in summer for chairlift.)

Ten kilometers south of Mount Ḥermon lies **Moshav Neveh Ativ** (☎ 698 13 33), founded after Israel captured the Golan. The moshav has developed an expensive resort village to take advantage of the ski slopes. Bus #55 goes from Kiryat Shmona to the moshav twice a day (1:30 and 4:40pm, NIS13). A *sherut* from Mas'ada to Kiryat Shmona in the late afternoon is usually the same price. The road from Mas'ada to Kiryat Shmona runs west along a gorge and past the hilltop village of Ein Qinya and Nimrod's Fortress. For information on outdoor activities in the area or in the Golan in general, try the **Ḥermon SPNI field school,** near Kibbutz Senir, to the right off Rte. 99 on the way from Kiryat Shmona to Banyas and just beyond Tel Dan. The field school is down a turnoff marked by a wooden sign on the right, then through the gates. In addition to patient and friendly advice, the field school has air-conditioned double rooms with private bathrooms. (☎694 10 91. NIS245/US$60; additional person NIS70; July-Aug. and holidays NIS25 extra per person. Breakfast included. Office open daily 8am-8pm.)

THE DEAD SEA ים המלח لبحر الميت

How low can you go? At 412m below sea level, this is it—the Dead Sea is the lowest point on Earth. If that factoid doesn't sound impressive, wait until you're driving on the highway, pass a "Sea Level" signpost, and then round a bend to see entire mountains whose *peaks* lie below you.

The Dead Sea is actually a large lake—65km long, 18km wide, and 412m deep. Its coasts are shared by Israel and Jordan, with the peaceful border drawn smack down the sea's middle. The sea's formation is the result of a geological phenomenon called the "Syrian-African Rift," essentially a mega-valley between shifting tectonic plates extending from southern Africa to Turkey. The resulting image of hollowness has led some to nickname the Dead Sea area "the navel of the world."

Water flows into the sea from the Jordan River and underground water sources from the surrounding desert. But with no outlet for the lake's water, the intense sun evaporates it faster than you can say "Ra." Inadequate rainfall, coupled with Israeli, Jordanian, and Syrian reliance on the sea's freshwater sources for drinking and irrigation, has begun to take its toll. The sun now evaporates more water than flows in; the sea is shrinking so severely that the southern tip has been cut off by a sand bar, and the northern part now recedes at the frightening rate of 80cm a year. Emergency measures to save the Dead Sea, driven by both ecological and economic incentives, are in the planning stages.

HIGHLIGHTS OF THE DEAD SEA

Head to **Siesta Beach** (p. 398) to dodge the tourist crowds, roll around in the black mud, and get a Thai massage after floating too hard.

Do as the Romans do when in **Masada** (p. 402): climb the mountain at sunrise via the Roman Ramp, but don't slaughter anyone.

Hike **Naḥal David** (p. 400) at Ein Gedi and glimpse some of the world's rarest wildlife.

GETTING THERE

The Egged buses that serve the rest of the country do so poorly in this region. Fares are outrageous (up to NIS10 for a 10min. ride), and the routes don't cover every destination. These difficulties, in conjunction with the nasty heat and the great distance between the main roads and sights, make renting a car an excellent idea. Most companies offer a daily rental rate of US$40-50 for single-day rentals, US$35-45 per day for longer-term rentals. Driving in the Dead Sea region provides spectacular vistas, but be careful—steep, windy roads mean nothing to speed-demon Israeli drivers. The best place to rent is Jerusalem, since cut-throat competition drives prices down (see **Car rental**, p. 287). In the Dead Sea region, try **Hertz** (☎658 44 33 or 658 45 30) in Ein Bokek.

The few Egged lines that travel along the Dead Sea coast have erratic schedules with pauses often lasting 45 to 90 minutes, so check times (Central Bus Station in Jerusalem ☎(02) 530 47 04) and plan ahead. Buses #421, 444, and 486 between Jerusalem and Eilat stop at Qumran, Ein Feshkha, Ein Gedi, and Masada. Bus #487, also from Jerusalem, runs only to Qumran, Ein Feshkha, and Ein Gedi. Buses #384 and 385 combined make about four trips per day (Su-F) between Be'er Sheva and Ein Gedi via Arad, Ein Bokek, and Masada. Buses will stop at many stations only upon request, so **confirm destinations** with the driver. Several sites listed, including Metzokei Dragot and Neot Ha-Kikkar, are **not accessible by public transportation.** On Saturdays, none of the buses head to or from the Dead Sea until the evening; to get there earlier, find a *service* across from Damascus Gate (NIS30-45 depending how far south you want to go). Locals claim hitchhiking is relatively safe in this part of the country; *Let's Go* does not recommend hitchhiking.

PRACTICAL INFORMATION

The Dead Sea coast is 65km long, and may be divided into **northern, central,** and **southern** regions. This section is organized from north to south. Remember—if the sea is on your left, you're going south, if it's on your right, you're going north.

The Dead Sea region does not have an ordinary desert climate—instead of being hot and dry, it's hot and humid. The sticky air, the very high temperatures, and 330 days a year of cloudless, steady sun are barely tolerable. While the air does have a 10% higher oxygen concentration, exertion is recommended only in the early morning. The steamroom-like weather has been known to dehydrate people simply waiting at a shaded bus stop. Keep your head covered, take a **water** bottle wherever you go, and chug liberally at the rate of about one liter per hour (more if you're hiking). Bring a large bottle with you and keep refilling at faucets to avoid getting ripped off by the 8-Shekel-a-pop street vendors once you're there. While the tap water is drinkable in most places in Israel, don't assume that shower and faucet water is safe to drink—check for "Drinking Water" signs or ask someone.

The **tourist information** hub for the entire area is in the central Dead Sea region, near Ein Gedi (see p. 400). Check in at the kibbutz reception center for information on local sights and events (☎(07) 658 44 44; fax (07) 658 43 67; email eg@mishkei.org.il; www.ein-gedi.co.il). It is possible to join the crowds on the popular one-day **tour** from Jerusalem that shuttles lemmings—er, tourists to Masada (in time for sunrise), Ein Gedi (Naḥal David and the Dead Sea beach), Qumran (jump out of the bus, take a picture, jump back in), Jericho (in time for a late lunch), and photograph stops at the Mount of Temptation, St. George Monastery, and the Mount of Olives. Tours cost NIS90 (entrance fees not included) and can be booked through most of the hostels in the Old City.

There is **no money changing office or ATM** anywhere in the Dead Sea region, so come prepared. The nearest facilities are in Arad and Be'er Sheva.

ADDING INSALT TO INJURY. Dead Sea water is powerful stuff. When it's good, it may cure arthritis, but when it's bad, it's like applying acid as aftershave. If Dead Sea water gets into your eyes, you're in for several minutes of painful blindness. Rinse your eyes immediately in the fresh-water showers, found on all beaches. Don't shave the morning before you go swimming; the water will sear minor scrapes. And, of course, resist the urge to taste it.

NORTHERN DEAD SEA   ☎02

KALYA BEACHES

This area in the northern Dead Sea region is only 25 minutes from Jerusalem (Rte. 90), and its shores are the least touristed by foreigners. Take bus #480 or 487 from Jerusalem. From Ein Bokek, take bus #421 or 966 (originating from Tel Aviv and Haifa, respectively). Remember to confirm your destination with the bus driver, and make sure you tell him you're going to the beach or else you'll end up at the Kalya kibbutz by Qumran. All of the Kalya beaches are accessible from the same turnoff and bus stop, but you'll still have to walk for one kilometer in the sun.

Farther down the road, two private beaches offer luxuries that might appeal more to the adults. **Siesta Beach** (☎994 41 11) follow a salty float with a Thai massage to calm your sunstroked bod (NIS85 for 10min.). A Jordanian/Palestinian restaurant on the beach serves "authentic" cuisine at unauthentic prices. (Falafel plate and salad NIS25. Open daily 8:30am-7:30pm; in winter 8:30am-6:30pm.) Next door, **Neve Midbar** (☎994 27 81) complements black mud with Desert's Magic holistic treatments, which include water therapy using the Dead Sea's healing properties (NIS80 for a 30min. "half-treatment"). An outdoor restaurant features pricey drinks and meals. (*Schnitzel* NIS40. Open daily 8:30am-7:30pm.)

QUMRAN קומרן قمران

About seven kilometers south of Kalya lie the ruins of Qumran, where the **Dead Sea Scrolls** were discovered. In 1947, a young Bedouin looking for a wayward sheep found a collection of earthenware jars containing 2000-year-old parchment manuscripts. Encouraged by the discovery, French archaeologists searched the caves and excavated the foot of the cliffs. By 1956, they had unearthed an entire village of the sect who wrote the Dead Sea Scrolls.

Buses #421, 444, 486, or 487 from either Ein Gedi or Jerusalem will stop upon request at the Essene Compound. A marker right outside the bus stop points toward Qumran, up the steep road on the right. Although the peak is nowhere in sight, the winding road is actually only a 100m hike. At the top is a museum, which in turn leads to the start of the path through the ruins. The cave where the scrolls were found is visible from a lookout 100 steps to the left of the site map. Humbly hidden between the water cisterns is the **scriptorium** (writing room), where archaeologists believe the scrolls were written (several desks and inkstands were found there intact and are now on display at the Rockefeller Museum in Jerusalem). The path leads through a small museum and then outside to the ruins themselves. Renovations are now underway to build a series of lookout bridges above the ruins to make them handicapped-accessible. (☎994 22 35. Open daily 8am-5pm; in winter 8am-4pm. NIS14, students NIS12, children 5-18 NIS6.)

EIN FESHKHA עין פשח'ה فشخة عين

Relief from the heat is nearby: three kilometers south is the fresh-water bathing spot at **Ein Feshkha** (also called Einot Zukim), where springs wind through the *wadi*'s reeds and tumble into small pools. Ein Feshkha is the only Dead Sea resort with fresh-water ponds adjacent to the sea area. Because of very slick mud, however, swimming is only permitted in the fresh water pools. It remains the favorite spot of nearby Jericho residents and other Palestinians. There are many more men than women, and the females who do show up don't show much. Women will probably be uncomfortable (and make others uncomfortable) without modest covering. There are showers, drinking water, a picnic area, and plenty of Dead Sea mud. (☎994 23 55. Open daily 8am-5pm. NIS22, children NIS8.)

METZOKEI DRAGOT (WADI DARJA) מצוקי דרגות

This **nature reserve,** with soaring cliffs, is for serious hikers only. About 20km south of Qumran and Ein Feshkha, a steep, winding road branches off on the right. Buses go no farther than the turnoff; the only ways to reach the reserve and the hostel are by car or a five-kilometer hike. The ascent culminates in a view of soaring cliffs and ravines on one side, the Dead Sea and not-so-distant hills of Jordan on the other. Heed the warnings on the green welcome-board—be sure to carry a trail map and a 20m security rope, both of which are usually available at the office. Climbers and rapellers with their own equipment may wish to take advantage of the excellent conditions in the reserve; unfortunately, there are no longer any organized trips or equipment rental. **You may not begin hiking in the wadi after 9am,** so it is a good idea to stay at the hostel the night before, and be on your feet at the crack of dawn. There is no place to refill water bottles; carry enough for the hike.

Owned and managed by the Mitzpeh Shalem Kibbutz a few kilometers away, the **youth hostel,** a great alternative to often-booked Ein Gedi accommodations, lies at the top of the winding road. (Check-in after 2pm; check-out Su-F 10am, and Sa noon. Dinner NIS45 with advanced notice. A/C 6-8 bed dorms NIS32; singles NIS149; bed and breakfast doubles NIS230.)

CENTRAL DEAD SEA ☎ 07

EIN GEDI עין גדי

After a hot morning hike or a muggy bus ride, the only thing better than drinking cold water is sitting in it. The Ein Gedi oasis, the epicenter of the Dead Sea region, has a long history of providing shelter and romantic getaways. The cascading waterfalls of the Ein Gedi oasis thrive just a few minutes' hike from the lifeless shores of the Dead Sea. Rare desert wildlife, including ibex, fox, and hyrax, and rare species of birds and flowers inhabit this verdant nature reserve. In 1994, the land in and around the Ein Gedi kibbutz was officially recognized as an International Botanical Garden, boasting over 800 species of trees, shrubs, and flowers from all over the world, as well as about 1000 species of cacti and desert plants. Tired hikers can relax in the afternoons at the free beach.

▐ GETTING THERE AND GETTING AROUND. From Ein Gedi, buses go to: **Be'er Sheva** (#384 and 385; 2½hr.; Su-Th 4 per day 8am-6pm, F 8am-3:30pm, Sa 3:30pm; NIS35) via **Masada** (20min.), **Ein Bokek** (30min., NIS18), and **Arad** (1½hr.); **Eilat** (#444; 3hr.; Su-Th 4 per day 7:50am-5:50pm, F 7:50am-2:50pm; NIS50); **Ein Bokek** (#486; Su-Th 4 per day 10am-2:05pm, F 9:50am and 2:05pm); and **Jerusalem** (#421, 444, 486, and 487; 1¼hr.; Su-Th 11 per day 5:45am-6pm, F 5:45am-5pm, Sa 6:25pm-10:30pm; NIS32). Students with ISICs can receive discounted fares on all bus routes. Departure times are erratic; get a schedule from the bus station in Jerusalem or check with your hostel.

▐▊ ORIENTATION AND PRACTICAL INFORMATION. Ein Gedi's 6750-acre nature reserve is the heart of this desert attraction. Around it, a kibbutz, several accommodations, a field school, a public bathing area, and a luxury spa have all been built. There are four **bus stops** in the area. The first one serves the **nature reserve** and the two youth **hostels.** Farther south is the beach stop, which is convenient for the public beach, food, a gas station, a first-aid station, and the yellow-roofed **tourist information** booth, which covers the entire Dead Sea region. (☎ 658 44 44; fax 658 43 67; email eg@kibbutz.co.il; www.ein-gedi.co.il. Open daily 9am-4pm.) The third stop, by advance request only, serves the kibbutz and its guest house. At the fourth stop are the thermal baths and spa. The hostels and public beach are a mere 10-15 minute walk apart, but the spas are six kilometers south of the beach. Food kiosks crowd the entrances to and exits from all tourist attractions, beaches, and hikes.

▐▐ ACCOMMODATIONS AND FOOD. The **Beit Sara Youth Hostel (HI),** uphill at the turnoff for Naḥal David, has clean and uncrowded rooms with A/C and private baths. Ask about discount tickets (15%) for the nature reserve, Ein Gedi Spa, and Atraktzia water park. (☎ 658 41 65; fax 658 44 44. Breakfast included; dinner US$8.50, child US$7.50. Packed lunch on request NIS22. Office open 7am-9pm; 24hr. phone reception. Check-in 3-7pm. Check-out Su-F 9am and Sa 10am. Dorms NIS72/US$17.50; doubles US$56. HI members receive US$1.50 discount on dorms. Credit cards accepted.) The **Ein Gedi Field School,** in a less touristed, more scenic spot, is a steep 10-minute climb up the road behind the more accessible youth hostel. Run by the Society for the Protection of Nature in Israel (SPNI), the field school offers free sound and light shows on the Judean Desert every night. This peak is the only place on Earth to get a glimpse of a rare species of bird called *Leilit Ha-Midbar* (Hume's Tawny Owl). A few feet from the TV room is a special bird-shrine and lookout point. Each spartan room is equipped with a coffee station and towels for the shared showers. (☎ 658 43 50; fax 658 42 57. Common kitchen and TV room. Office open Su-F 8am-7pm. Check-in 3pm. Check-out 10am. Call ahead. Dorms NIS75. Students and SPNI members 20% discount; membership available at check-in for NIS82, family NIS108. Credit cards accepted.)

Quick snacks are available at kiosks throughout Ein Gedi, including near the entrance to the nature reserve at **Kiosk Naḥal David.** (Beer NIS10. Open 8am-5pm.) A few sandwiches and some juice can provide a relatively cheap alternative to expensive tourist joints, although prices are still higher than in the cities. The cafeteria-style **Pundak Ein Gedi,** in the parking lot of the beach bus stop, serves hungry beach-goers. (☎659 47 61. Chicken with two side dishes NIS30. Open daily 10am-6pm.) The kiosk next door is open later. (Sandwiches NIS12. Open daily 7:30am-8pm.) Another dining possibility in the central Dead Sea region is **Gofrit Restaurant** at the Ein Gedi Spa. (Main course NIS20, with side dishes NIS35. ☎659 48 13. Open daily 11am-4pm.) Hostels in the area will provide an inexpensive **packed lunch** if ordered the previous night.

⚑ HIKING. Of the two entrances to the huge **Ein Gedi Nature Reserve,** only the **Naḥal David** entrance (☎658 42 85), below the youth hostels, is accessible by bus. (Open daily 8am-4pm. Several hikes end after 1:30pm. NIS18.) Naḥal Arugot (☎652 0224), three kilometers past the Naḥal David entrance, is accessible only by car.

Some sections of the Ein Gedi trails are steep, but well-placed railings and steps have been built into the rock. Once noon rolls around, high temperatures can make even inhaling strenuous, so get going by **8am.** Always bring at least one liter of water per hour of hiking (there are faucets just outside the gate), and don't forget your **swimsuit** for dipping in the occasional freshwater pool or waterfall. The names of the different pools and springs repeat frequently and are almost interchangeable (David this, Ein Gedi that), so get a free map at the entrance and pay attention to the fine print to prevent confusion. Possible hikes vary from easygoing to double diamond difficult. Some suggested trails follow:

HIKING TRAILS

1. For a short hike of 45min. each way, enter from the Naḥal David entrance and follow the path straight until **Shulamit Falls,** a delicious, slender pillar of water dropping into a shallow pool. Turning left at the falls leads to a trail that climbs up the cliffside to **Shulamit Spring** (an additional 30min. each way).

2. For a longer hike, continue from Shulamit spring along the cliff and down a ladder to **Dudaim Cave** (Lover's Cave), a mossy niche at the top of the fall (30min. from the spring). Proceed left, passing the 3000-year-old remains of a **Chalcolithic Temple** once dedicated to worship of the moon, on the way to **Ein Gedi Spring** (20min. from the Temple), whose cool water is perfect for a refreshing dip. Resist the urge to dive from the high niches into the pool—it's not deep enough in some places. Next to the spring is a sugar or flour mill from the Islamic period which was powered by water from the spring.

3. The second entrance to the reserve is at **Naḥal Arugot** (no bus; parking lot 3km inland from Rte. 90, between the beach and Naḥal David entrance). A somewhat challenging hour's hike along the river leads to a hidden waterfall and a beautiful, deep blue pool.

4. One long but highly recommended trail connects the David and Arugot entrances, with the Ein Gedi Spring smack in the middle. The trail passes the newly restored ancient **synagogue** and leads directly to the beachfront in time for an afternoon of sunbathing. The trail begins at the **SPNI Field School** and follows the "Zafit Trail" until Ein David. At Ein David, turn left and follow the main marked trail to Shulamit Falls. For a shorter hike, bear left and follow the main trail out; for the full hike, bear right and continue toward Shulamit Spring and the Chalcolithic temple. **Ein Gedi Spring** is a few hundred meters farther. Continue straight, due south, until **Tel Goren.** Turn left toward the sea, passing the ancient **synagogue** after a few hundred meters. The light blue building toward the end is the Ein Gedi mineral water bottling plant, a refreshing stop.

◪ BEACH. For good ol' Dead Sea floating and mud, Ein Gedi has its own crowded **beach.** Use of the beach and umbrellas is free, but bathrooms and lockers cost NIS1 and NIS5, respectively. **Lot's Wife,** a boat touring around the Dead Sea area, departs from the small dock to the left (when facing the water) of the Ein Gedi beach. (cell ☎054 91 50 04. Regular trips Tu and Sa at 2:30pm, but private tours arranged for groups. Call ahead. NIS40, children NIS30.) About five kilometers south of the beach is the **Ein Gedi Spa,** with indoor sulfur pools, therapeutic mud, and a restaurant. (NIS50, Sa NIS55; children NIS44. ☎659 48 13. Spa open Sa-Th 7am-6pm and F 7am-5:30pm.) Local hostels provide tickets for a 15% discount.

ISRAEL

MASADA מצדה

"Masada shall not fall again," swear members of the **Israel Defense Forces** each year at this site. Jewish Zealots' tenacious defense of Masada in the first century CE has been fashioned into a heroic symbol of the defense of modern Israel. Political significance aside, legions of tourists from around the world continue to storm this mountain fortress to catch the spectacular view of the Dead Sea, visit the extensive ruins, and envision the martyrdom of Masada's rebels.

At the outset of the Jewish rebellion against Rome in 66 CE, a small band of Zealot rebels, members of a small Jewish sect, captured the prize fortress from its unsuspecting garrison. As the Romans gradually crushed the revolt, taking Jerusalem in 70 CE and destroying the Second Temple, Masada became a refuge for surviving Zealots, and eventually the last Jewish holdout in all of Israel. With years' worth of food, water, and military supplies, the 967 men, women, and children held off 15,000 Roman legionnaires through a five-month siege. The Romans called in their best engineers to construct a wall and camps in a ring around the mount. Capitalizing on their superior strength, they built an enormous stone and gravel ramp up the side of the cliff, using Jewish slaves as laborers in order to prevent the Zealots from shooting them down as the ramp was built.

When the defenders realized that the Romans would break through their walls the next morning, the community leaders decided that it would be better to die, as their leader Eliezer Ben-Yair said, "unenslaved by enemies, and leave this world as free men in company with wives and children." Because Jewish law forbids suicide, ten men were chosen to slay the others, and one chosen to kill the other nine before falling on his own sword. Before burning the fortress and all their possessions, the Jews placed stores of wheat and water in the citadel's courtyard to prove to the Romans that they did not perish from hunger. The following morning, when the triumphant Romans burst in, they encountered only smoking ruins and deathly silence. The only survivors, two women and five children, told the story of the Zealots' last days to Josephus Flavius, a Jewish-Roman general and chronicler. Flavius, always eager to embellish a good tale, never actually visited Masada. He based his dramatic history on the survivors' accounts, later describing the two to be "of exceptional intelligence for women." Although strong corroborating evidence for the story has been found at the site, such as the murder-lottery slips Josephus describes, archaeologists have yet to unearth the Zealots' actual remains. Where the bones of almost 1000 people have gone is still a mystery.

▣ GETTING AROUND

Masada lies 20km south of Ein Gedi, a few kilometers inland from the Jerusalem-Eilat road (Rte. 90). Buses leaving Masada generally start around 8:30am; only a few leave after 4pm. Check at the Taylor Youth hostel for a current schedule, and make sure you are heading in the right direction. Buses go to: **Be'er Sheva** (#384 and 385; Su-Th 4 per day 8:15am-6:15pm, F 4 per day 8:15am-3:15pm, Sa 3:45pm; NIS35.50, students NIS31) via **Ein Bokek** (NIS11.50); **Eilat** (#444; Su-Th 4 per day 8am-6pm, F 3 per day 8am-3pm; NIS50, students NIS45); **Jerusalem** (#444 and 486; Su-Th 8 per day 8:35-7:20pm, F 5 per day 8:35am-3:20pm, Sa 6:50 and 9:20pm; NIS37.50, students NIS34) via **Ein Gedi** (NIS14); and **Tel Aviv** (#421; Su-F 2:25pm; NIS47, students NIS42). Buses #384 and 385 also go to Ein Gedi.

By car, Rte. 3199 runs from Arad to the base of the Roman Ramp, and Rte. 90 leads to the Snake Path, the eastern cable car entrance, the bus stop, and the youth hostel. The walk around the base from one path to the other is extremely arduous and time-consuming. Those who decide to do it should follow the SPNI trail, not the incline with the water pipe.

There are three ways to ascend the mountain: by either of two foot paths or by cable car. The more popular, scenic, and difficult of the two is the **Snake Path** (45min. hike), named for its tortuous bends. The **Roman Ramp,** on the western side of the mountain, is an easier hike than the Snake Path and the original path. Even

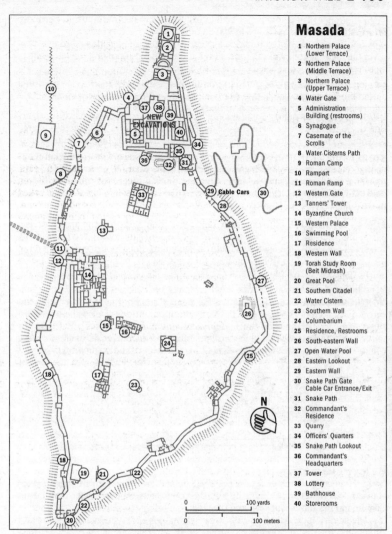

Masada

1 Northern Palace (Lower Terrace)
2 Northern Palace (Middle Terrace)
3 Northern Palace (Upper Terrace)
4 Water Gate
5 Administration Building (restrooms)
6 Synagogue
7 Casemate of the Scrolls
8 Water Cisterns Path
9 Roman Camp
10 Rampart
11 Roman Ramp
12 Western Gate
13 Tanners' Tower
14 Byzantine Church
15 Western Palace
16 Swimming Pool
17 Residence
18 Western Wall
19 Torah Study Room (Beit Midrash)
20 Great Pool
21 Southern Citadel
22 Water Cistern
23 Southern Wall
24 Columbarium
25 Residence, Restrooms
26 South-eastern Wall
27 Open Water Pool
28 Eastern Lookout
29 Eastern Wall
30 Snake Path Gate Cable Car Entrance/Exit
31 Snake Path
32 Commandant's Residence
33 Quarry
34 Officers' Quarters
35 Snake Path Lookout
36 Commandant's Headquarters
37 Tower
38 Lottery
39 Bathhouse
40 Storerooms

NEW EXCAVATIONS

Cable Cars

0   100 yards
0   100 meters

ISRAEL

the most grumpy of non-early birds will appreciate a dawn hike to catch the legendary sunrise over the Dead Sea and avoid tour group insanity and blazing heat. Today many warriors opt to take the Snake Path up and the cable car down; due to the steepness, the hike down is just as strenuous as the hike up. Another option is to take the cable car up in the afternoon and hike down when the sun is less fierce.

THE FORTRESS

The ruins at Masada were unearthed from 1963 to 1964; thousands of volunteers excavated in 11 months what would normally have taken 26 years. About one-third of the ruins is actually reconstructed—a black line indicates the extent of the original findings. The re-excavation of the Northern Palace by a group of expert Italian archaeologists has unearthed new mosaic floors and hundreds of coins near the bathhouses. The **Masada Sound and Light Show** lights up the fortress like a Las

Vegas marquee. The show is not visible from the Masada youth hostel. For more information, see **Arad,** p. 413 (☎995 93 33 or 995 89 93; fax 995 50 52).

The following suggested route covers the highlights of Masada and roughly follows the sign-posted walking tour. The numbers listed following the sites correspond to the numbers labeled on the map on p. 403.

SNAKE PATH LOOKOUT (1). This lookout offers views of the Snake Path, the earthen wall, the Roman camps, the Dead Sea, and the Mountains of Moab.

QUARRY (2). This quarry supplied much of the stone for the extensive construction throughout Masada. Between the quarry and the Western Wall, there is a large pile of large round rocks, too perfectly shaped to be anything but catapults' ammo.

STOREROOMS (3). Food, weapons, and other supplies were stored within these rooms. Though the Zealots destroyed most of their valuable possessions and the fortress, they left the storeroom containing mass amounts of food untouched. Josephus explains that the Zealots wanted to prove that their suicide was a means of escaping slavery, not famine.

ROMAN BATHHOUSE (4). Bathers would leave their clothes in the *apodyterium* (dressing room) before proceeding to the *caldarium* (hot room), recognizable by the small pillars, which used to support a secondary floor. A stove channeled hot air between these two floors. Bathers then cooled off in the *tepidarium* (lukewarm room) before a quick dip in the *frigidarium* (cold pool). Built by Herod, the bathhouse served no purpose for the austere Zealots.

NORTHERN PALACE (5-7). Go down the nearby stairwell to Herod's thrice-terraced private pad. The frescoes and fluted columns, still intact on the lower terrace, attest to the splendor Herod enjoyed even on a remote desert butte. In the bathhouse of the lowest section, the skeletons of a man, woman, and child were found, along with a *tallit* (prayer shawl), *ostraca* (lots), and arrowheads.

LOTTERY AREA (8). Climb back up from the Palace to the Lottery Area, to the left of the bathhouses as you face the Palace. The Zealots used this area as a ritual bath for cleansing and purification, but it is most notable for the dramatic discovery of 11 *ostraca*. The uniform shards of pottery inscribed with names (including one with the name Ben-Yair, Zealot commander of Masada) most likely served as lots that decided who would kill the others.

ZEALOTS' SYNAGOGUE (9). Following the western edge of the mountain leads to the Zealots' synagogue, the oldest synagogue in the world. Scrolls were found here containing texts from several books of the Torah; most are now on display at the Israel Museum in Jerusalem (see p. 317). The scrolls and other discoveries, such as a *mikveh* (ritual bath), indicate that the community followed Jewish strictures despite mountainous isolation and the siege.

CASEMATE OF THE SCROLLS (10). A number of important archaeological relics were found within the casemate, including scrolls, papyrus, silver *shekels*, a *tallit* (prayer shawl), a wooden shield, arrows, sandals, keys, and baskets.

WATER CISTERNS PATH (11). The huge cisterns can still be seen dotting the mountaintop from the western wall; they are lined with a nearly perfect water-repellent plaster that still won't absorb a single drop. Rainfall used to drain from the surrounding mountains into Masada's reservoirs, filling the entire cistern within a few hours on the one annual day of rain. The Zealots were able to store up to eight years' worth of precious water in these cavernous structures.

BYZANTINE CHURCH (12). Remote Masada, with caves and buildings for shelter, made an ideal hideout for Christian hermits in the 5th and 6th centuries. The chapel with preserved mosaic floors is the most impressive of their remains.

WESTERN PALACE (13). Farther along the edge stands the site of Herod's throne room and offices of state. A system of water cisterns underlies the western wing; the northern wing surrounds a large central courtyard; the southern wing was the royal wing, and it includes a waiting room, courtyard, dining hall, kitchen, and a throne room. Though just as sumptuous as the Northern Palace, this was Herod's "working palace." He went to his northern "country residence" to relax.

SWIMMING POOL (14). Although water was a rare commodity in the fortress, Herod insisted on maintaining a swimming pool in the backyard of the Western Palace. The Zealots used this as a ritual bath.

COLUMBARIUM (15). The small niches in the walls of this round building, farther back and slightly to the left, sparked an archaeological debate. One team contended that it was a *columbarium*, where the ashes of the non-Jewish members of Herod's garrison were placed, while others thought the niches housed pigeons. After highly scientific tests the former opinion emerged victorious; small pigeons could not fit inside the niches.

SOUTHERN CITADEL (16). At the southern tip of the mountain, the Southern Citadel looks out at the Masada *Wadi*, the Dead Sea, and Roman encampments.

SOUTHERN WALL (17). Along the southern wall lie a tower with a Zealot installation (the building might have been a bakery), a ritual bath, a dressing room (the narrow niches held clothes), and a courtyard. The path is no longer in use.

SOUTHEAST WALL (18). There is a memorial inscription for "Lucius" (possibly a soldier in the Roman Garrison) engraved in the wall of the tower. On the plaster of the southern wall, there are four impressions of the name "Justus" in Latin and Greek. There is also a lookout from which the outer wall is visible.

EASTERN WALL (19). The outer and inner walls are joined by partitions, forming casemates. The higher and thicker sections of the inner wall are the sole remains of a series of towers that lined the wall. A channel under the floor of the Zealot additions is older than the wall itself. A small grove of fir trees toward the Snake Path Gate was the site of a 1988 interpretive reenactment of the battle.

SOUTHERN DEAD SEA

EIN BOKEK עין בוקק ☎07

About 15km south of Masada, Ein Bokek, hemmed in by hordes of luxury hotels, international tour-groups, and racks upon racks of postcards, is the gaudy cubic zirconia in the tiara of Dead Sea beaches. For all the glitzy tourist-wooing of this most crowded of Dead Sea beaches, it is still a good spot for some old fashioned fun: floating and coating. Use of the beach and outdoor showers is **free** (8am-5pm); a package of mineral-rich mud from beachside vendors costs NIS10.

Farther to the right is a small **mall**, featuring a **grocery store,** Hertz office, and several restaurants, including the 24-hour **Peace and Love BBQ.** (☎658 43 71. Fruit shake NIS15; hamburger NIS12; fries NIS12.) To the left of the beach, **Me'al Hahof** (☎652 04 04), a bar on the beach, features a great view, French pop music, and a variety of beer (NIS10-16) and baguettes (NIS17). **Hertz** car rental is inside the Amiel Tours office in the mall.

Ein Bokek is 30 minutes east of Arad and 10 minutes south of Masada. **Buses** on the Masada/Dead Sea route pass through Ein Bokek and stop at each hotel along the strip. For the public beach, get off at **Ḥof Ein Bokek.** Minivans operating as *sherut* go to Arad (NIS10). **Hassan Taxi** (☎(05) 276 62 46) goes to Masada for NIS60 and Ein Gedi for NIS100. (☎658 45 30. 21+. About NIS350/US$55 per day. Open Su-Th 8:30am-4pm and F 8:30am-1:30pm.)

MOSHAV NEOT HA-KIKKAR מושב נאות הככר ☎07

About 20km south of rowdy Ein Bokek, Moshav Neot Ha-Kikkar is a desert of serenity and desolation. Take Rte. 90 toward Sodom to the Arava junction, passing the Dead Sea Works plant on the left and the southern edge of the sea. The Eilat-bound bus from Jerusalem or Tel Aviv will stop at the junction upon request. Make a left and follow the road for about 10km to the entrance to the moshav.

Taking the road to the end of the moshav leads to ▓**Fata Morgana,** an amazing oasis featuring large, clean and comfortable Bedouin-style guest-tents, a coffee-bar, and a restaurant. Fata Morgana arranges hiking tours of the region (including the famous Sodom flour caves), meeting individual requests whenever possible. It also offers **Shiatsu** massages and lessons in a special shrine tent every Friday and pick-your-own cherry-tomatoes or flowers. Work four hours in the field and sleep free. (☎655 79 92, cell ☎050 69 15 85; ask for Koreen or Ya'akov. Cold beer NIS9; hot fish meals NIS60; vegetarian meals NIS40. Free use of spotless bathrooms and showers, fridge, and BBQ grill. Tents NIS40; own tent NIS30. *Let's Go* discount.)

MOUNT SODOM AND THE FLOUR CAVE ☎07

About 74km to the southeast of Be'er Sheva, near the shores of the Dead Sea, is the glaringly white salt mountain, Ḥar Sodom. The **Flour Cave** is tucked out of direct view from Mount Sodom. The unpaved road in the site forks; go left and continue on the red-marked "Flour Cave" path that eventually leads to a parking lot (marked by a green sign) near the cave. The cave is at the end of a curving trail of high, smooth walls of light-colored sediment left behind by the lake that was a precursor to the Dead Sea. Be forewarned that these white rocks are unyieldingly bright in the sunlight and magnify the merciless daytime heat, so bring along water, sunglasses, sunscreen, and a head covering. It is a 10-minute walk through the white-walled trail to the cave itself (marked by a sign), where the dark, cool, and heavy air provides an escape from the dead-on rays of the sun. Bring a flashlight for the pitch-black cave. The short, steep ascent at the end of the cave will leave you about one mile to the right as you face the parking lot.

To reach **Sodom Mountain,** take a right onto the blue road from the first fork and another right onto the black road. It is possible to drive all the way up to the lookout point on **Sodom Mountain,** which has a captivating view of the Dead Sea Works and the seemingly frozen blue water below. Alternatively, continue past the Flour Cave entrance for about 1½hr. From the lookout point, hike the steep and winding "Stairway Trail" downward, starting at the blue-marked steps to the left.

The site can be reached only by car. From Be'er Sheva, head southeast on Rte. 25 (toward Dimona) then north (toward Jerusalem) on Rte. #90, past the industrial complex of the Dead Sea Works. From Arad, head southeast on Rte. 31 (toward Neve Zohar) then south (toward Eilat) on Rte. 90. From either direction, a small orange sign points to the Flour Cave and Sodom Mountain.

THE NEGEV הנגב

The Negev covers roughly half of Israel's territory, but for many years the region received only a small fraction of Israel's tourists. In recent years, tourism has sky-rocketed, but these 12,000 square kilometers of desert have become no more accommodating. Temperatures soar at midday—those caught without a hat and water will see vultures circling overhead in a matter of minutes. Desert outfitters recommend that hikers drink one liter of water for every hour in the sun.

It's possible to tour the desert on Egged seats; air-conditioned lines run through all major towns and past several important sites. However, buses may be infrequent and late, and some sites and trailheads are only accessible by car. Renting a car or taking a guided tour are excellent options for those who can afford it. A more exciting way to see the Negev is on a **camel** or **jeep** tour.

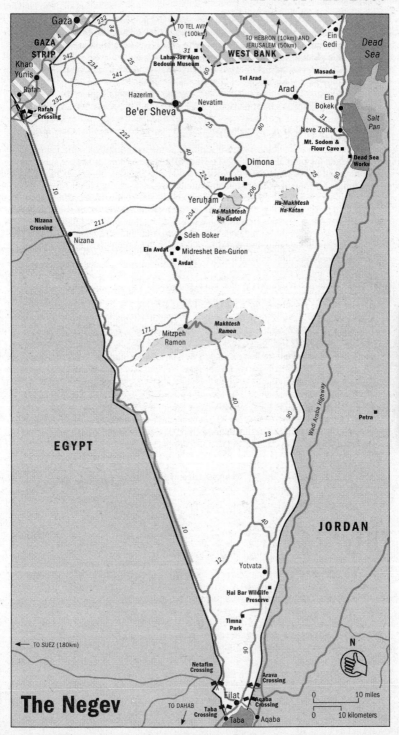

The Negev

> **HIGHLIGHTS OF THE NEGEV**
>
> Explore the pastel deserts of **Mitzpeh Ramon** (p. 416) and **Sdeh Boker** (p. 413), the country's most pristine refuges, on foot or hooves.
>
> Taste the flavor of Chicago at the Negev's dunes in the Hebrew Israelite community in **Dimona** (p. 412)—and it's vegan.
>
> Take an astounding hike through the multicolored hues of **Har Ardon** (p. 417).

BE'ER SHEVA באר שבע ☎ 07

Be'er Sheva has a long-standing tradition of serving as a point of replenishment and departure for people traversing the Negev. In recent years, however, increasing numbers of immigrants have decided to settle down in the city rather than just pass through, and the pre-fabricated apartments are as unavoidable and constricting as the spandex in Eilat discotheques. Despite the din of constant traffic and the overpowering presence of a glassed-in monster mall in the center of town, Be'er Sheva still has a few pockets of romance left, including the old city and the famous Thursday morning Bedouin market. The old city, museums in the surrounding area, and Be'er Sheva's hopping nightlife make it both a convenient base for short forays into the Negev and a destination in and of itself.

▐ GETTING THERE AND GETTING AROUND

Intercity Buses: Egged (☎ 629 43 11) to: **Dimona** (#48, 56, or 375; 45min.; every 20min. 6:30am-11pm; NIS14); **Eilat** (#392, 393, or 394; 3½hr.; every 1½hr. 7:30am-11:45pm; NIS52); **Jerusalem** (#470 (direct) or 446; 2hr.; every 40min. 6am-8pm; NIS33); and **Tel Aviv** (#369 or 370; 1½hr.; every 20min. 5:45am-9:45pm; NIS20.50).

Local Buses: Central bus station (☎ 627 73 81), on Eilat St., next to the *kenyon*. Buses #2, 3, 7, 8, 9, 11, 12, 18, 21, and 22 all go to the *shuk* and old city (5:20am-11pm), and bus #13 follows Ha-Atzma'ut St. to the Negev Museum and Beit Yatziv Youth Hostel (every 20min. 5:20am-11pm). Buses #7 and 8 go north on Yitzhak Rager Blvd., passing the hospital and Ben-Gurion University. All local rides NIS3.10.

Sherut Taxis: Moniot Ayil (☎ 623 53 33), in back of the central bus station, in the kiosk with the blue awning. *Sherut* to **Dimona** (NIS10) and **Tel Aviv** (NIS20) are slightly cheaper than buses, but don't leave until they fill up.

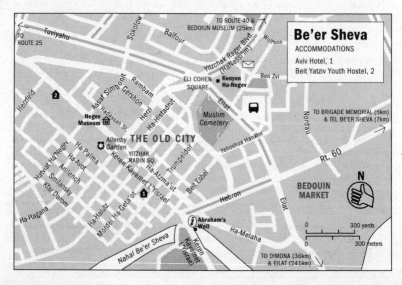

Be'er Sheva

ACCOMMODATIONS

Aviv Hotel, 1
Beit Yatziv Youth Hostel, 2

Taxis: Moniot Gan Zvi (☎623 93 32 or 623 93 33), next to the bus station, or **Moniyot Ha-Ḥalutz** (☎627 33 33 or 627 07 07), across from Bank Ha-Poalim.

Car Rental: Avis, 8 Henrietta Szold (☎627 17 77), just before the Paradise Hotel. The #5 bus passes by. From the *kenyon* walk two blocks up Yitzḥak Rager Blvd. and turn right through the parking lot behind the New York Cafe. Red Avis sign in the shopping strip across the street. 23+. Cars start at NIS195/US$42 per day. Open Su-Th 8am-6pm, F 8am-2pm. **Traffic Rent-a-Car,** 5 Ben-Zvi St. (☎627 38 78), behind the bus station, in the shopping strip on Ben-Zvi. Rents to people ages 21-23 for an additional US$12. Rates increase in July and Aug. Open Su-Th 8am-7pm and F 8am-2pm.

✳ ORIENTATION

The city's **central bus station** is on **Eilat St.**, across the road from **Kenyon Ha-Negev** (Negev shopping mall; ask for the *kenyon*), whose glass facade faces the three-way intersection of **Tuviyahu Blvd.**, Eilat St., and **Yitzḥak Rager Blvd.** The **Ben-Gurion University** Be'er Sheva campus is a few minutes from the city center.

The old **Muslim Cemetery,** sitting in a wasteland of fenced-in sand, is across Eilat St. behind the central bus station. Just on the other side of it lies the neat grid of the **old city.** This pedestrian haven holds most of the city's attractions. In the center of the Old City is **Keren Kayemet L'Yisrael St.** (**Kakal** or **KKL** for short), a pedestrian-only street between **Herzl** and **Mordei Ha-Geta'ot St.** lined with shops, kiosks, and restaurants. To reach the old city from the bus station, walk in front of the *kenyon* to Eli Cohen Sq., cross Eilat St., and take Herzl St. or Ha-Ḥalutz St.

⁊ PRACTICAL INFORMATION

Tourist Office: 1 Derekh Hevron (☎623 46 13), at Abraham's Well. From Herzl St. in the old city, walk down from the top to the end of the pedestrian KKL. The office is on the left-side corner across from the intersection. Helpful staff sells an excellent English map (NIS5). Office arranges bus tours of the city's historical sights. Call ahead for English screening of the brief movie on Be'er Sheva. Open Su-Th 8:30am-4pm.

Currency Exchange: The main **post office** (see below) exchanges cash and traveler's checks at excellent rates without commission. **Bank Ha-Poalim,** 40 Ha-Atzma'ut St. (☎629 26 62), is on the corner of Ha-Ḥalutz St. Open Su, Tu-W 8:30am-1:15pm; M, Th 8:30am-1pm and 4-6:30pm; F 8:15am-12:30pm. Minimum charge $6. **Bank Leumi** (☎623 92 22), is just past the post office on Ha-Nesi'im Blvd. Open Su, Tu-W 8:30am-1pm; M, Th 8:30am-1pm and 4:30-7pm; F 8:30am-noon. **ATM** accepts V and Diner's.

Emergency: First Aid: Magen David Adom, 40 Bialik St. (☎627 83 33). **Police:** 30 Herzl St. (☎646 27 44), at the corner of KKL St. **Fire:** (☎627 96 91).

Hospital: Soroka Medical Center (☎640 01 11), on Yitzḥak Rager Blvd., with a green walkway and a blue and green sign in Hebrew. Bus #7 or 8. Open daily 5:20am-11pm.

Internet: The **Paradise Hotel** on Henrietta Szold St. has Internet access at a computer on the mezzanine level for US$0.50 per min. Credit cards only.

Post Office: (☎629 58 32), at the corner of Yitzḥak Rager Blvd., just across from the back entrance of the mall and Ben-Zvi St. This main branch has **Poste Restante, Western Union, EMS** services, international calling, fax, phone cards, and commission-free cash and traveler's check exchange. Smaller branches on Hadassa St. and in the City Hall building. All branches open Su-Tu, Th 8am-12:30pm and 4-6:30pm; W 8am-1pm; F 8am-12:30pm.

⌂ ACCOMMODATIONS

Be'er Sheva has several options for budget accommodations, including one youth hostel and a few reasonably-priced hotels. Conveniently, the following accommodations are all within a 5-10 minute walk from the *midraḥov* in the old city.

Beit Yatziv Youth Hostel (HI), 79 Ha-Atzma'ut St. (☎627 74 44), in the old city. Three blocks up from Herzl St., on the left behind the HI sign (walk or take bus #13). Clean rooms with bath, closet, A/C, and table. Pool in back. Full breakfast. Check-out 9am. Reception 24hr. 4-bed dorms US$22; 3-bed dorms US$24. The **Guest House** next-door is run by the same reception desk. Singles US$38-42.50; doubles US$56-59. HI members NIS5/US$1.50 discount. Credit cards accepted.

Aviv Hotel, 48 Mordei Ha-Geta'ot St. (☎627 80 59 or 627 82 58). Walk down Herzl St. and turn right on KKL St. Run by a sweet Bulgarian woman. All rooms have private baths and high-powered A/C; some have balconies. Breakfast NIS20. Laundry available. Reception 24hr. Check-out 11am. Singles NIS160/US$35; doubles NIS215/US$47. 15% student discount. Cash only.

Arava Hotel, 37 Ha-Histadrut St. (☎627 87 92). Turn right off KKL from Herzl St. Close to the popular cafes at the top of KKL. Rooms are fairly comfortable, with small bathrooms and A/C. Reception 24hr. Check-in 1pm. Check-out noon. Singles NIS80/US$25; doubles NIS100/US$35. Cash only.

◖ FOOD

Lined with falafel, *shawarma*, pizza, and sandwich store fronts, the **Keren Kayemet LeYisrael St. (KKL)** *midrahov* is the best place for affordable eats. For a fast food fix, head to the food court on the lower floor of the *kenyon* across from the bus station. (Most in the *kenyon* open Su-Th 10am-midnight, F 10am-3pm, and Sa after sundown-midnight.) A **Hypershuk supermarket** exists in the supermall. There is a small grocery store in the old city on Mordei Ha-Geta'ot, just off KKL toward Ha-Palmaḥ St. (Open daily 7am-7pm.) The cheapest place to buy fresh produce, meat, and fish is the **shuk,** just south of the Muslim burial ground on Beit Eshel St. The listings below are all in the **old city** area.

▨ Sof Ha-Derekh (☎627 91 55), at the corner of Ha-Palmah and Ha-Tivat Ha-Negev. Feast on one of 22 spicy salads with homemade *lafah* bread (NIS7), or order meat from the grill. Chicken NIS15; steaks NIS55-70. Complimentary dessert of *baklava,* fresh fruit, and mint tea. Open Su-Th 11:30am-1am, F 11:30am-1hr. before sundown, and Sa after sundown-1am. Credit cards accepted.

Cafeteria Panorama (☎623 52 49), at the corner of Ha-Histadrut and KKL St., on the 2nd floor. Entrance near Rabin Sq. Francophone owner serves vegetarian blintzes, pizza, and pasta (NIS11-22) in spartan simplicity. Juice stand downstairs NIS12. Open Su-Th 10am-3pm and 6pm-1am and Sa after sundown-2am.

Beit Ha-Ful, 15 Ha-Histadrut St., at the corner of Smilansky St. Walk past the park; the restaurant's outdoor seating will be on the left. Popular with locals. *Fuul* (Egyptian beans in pita with salads) NIS11, in bowl with garnish NIS25. Eat *al fresco* or in A/C dining room. Open Su-Th 8am-midnight, F 8am-3pm, and Sa after sunset-midnight.

▣ SIGHTS

BEDOUIN MARKET. Established in 1905, the famous Thursday market is a nirvana for bargain hunters. Amid the clamor of screaming vendors are cheap Bedouin food and excellent garments. Years ago, the Bedouin hawked camels, sheep, and other wares at the end of agricultural seasons and during winter—now year-round they've added snow globes and t-shirts to the much-ballyhooed wares. Farther south, the quantity of rusty cans, scraps of paper, and dust increases, along with the smell of dung from the live animals for sale. The southern part of the market, however, houses the real gems: beaten copperware, Bedouin robes, fabrics, rugs, and ceramic items. Get there early to see the trading at its peak and to get more of a selection of genuine Bedouin goods. Many Bedouin here speak English, and some may compliment your beautiful eyes while charging six times the going rate for olive wood camels. *(The market is on the south side of the city, off Eilat St., south of the intersection with Derekh Hevron. Most local buses will stop at the market upon request. By foot, walk to Eilat St. from the central bus station and cross over to the market. Open Th all day.)*

ABRAHAM'S WELL. The well dates back to at least the 12th century CE, and many believe it to be the original well dug by Abraham. A free, five-minute tour of the site illuminates Be'er Sheva's biblical history, the well's archaeological significance, and its camel-powered hydrotechnology. From June to September, the well also serves as a nighttime entertainment venue with live music and dancing. (On the corner of Derekh Hevron and Keren Kayemet LeYisrael St. ☎ 623 46 13. Call ahead.)

JOE ALON BEDOUIN MUSEUM. At a time when approximately half of the Negev's Bedouins live in urban "settlements," this museum showcases all facets of the nomads' traditional lives, including tools, embroidery, medicine, and customary desert garb. An audio-visual presentation describes Bedouin culture and their famous hospitality. Outside the indoor exhibit are two Bedouin tents. In one, a Bedouin woman serves traditional pita and tea; in the other, Bedouin men converse with guests and serve bitter coffee. The museum also has an observation tower with a 360-degree view of the northern Negev. (Several kilometers north of the tel, on the outskirts of Kibbutz Lahav. Drive 15km north on Rte. 40 to Lahav junction or take bus #369 (20min., every 30min., NIS12) and ask to be let off there. An orange sign behind the bus stop points down the road in the direction of the kibbutz and museum, 8km away. Numbered vehicles from the kibbutz drive by often and may offer a lift. After arriving, walk along the asphalt road and follow it to where it curves to the right, up to the gate of the museum. Taxi NIS75. ☎ 991 33 22 or 991 85 97. Open Sa-Th 9am-5pm and F 9am-2pm. NIS15, students NIS13.)

PARK YOUR OWN ASS. When approaching a Bedouin tent, it is customary to cough to let your host know that he has a visitor. If you have arrived on a horse or a camel, your host will graciously take your animal and tie it to his tent. However, if you rode in on a donkey, he will refuse his tie-down services, and you must tether it yourself.

ISRAELI AIR FORCE MUSEUM. This museum displays over 100 airplanes from several generations of Israeli aerial combat, including airplanes captured from and shot down by neighboring countries. Free guided tours by Israeli soldiers relate the history behind each of the displays. (At the Haterim air force base 8km west of town on the Be'er Sheva-Haterim Rd. City bus #31 stops directly in front of the entrance. Walk up Ha-Atzma'ut St. from the youth hostel and cross over the Derekh Joe Alon Highway at the major intersection to reach the bus stop headed away from town. ☎ 990 68 55. Open Su-Th 8am-5pm and F 8am-1pm. NIS23, ages 3-13 NIS15, senior citizens NIS18. Call ahead for free tours.)

TEL BE'ER SHEVA. Five kilometers northeast of the city are the ruins of a 3000-year old planned city, recently upgraded to a national park. One pile of unearthed rubble is a 2nd-century Roman fortress, another an 8th-century BCE house, and a third a 12th-century BCE well. The view from the top of the tower in the back right corner of the site is fantastic. Fashionable Israelis flock to conduct their marriages in trendy Bedouin style at nearby marriage hall **Ohalei Kidar.** (By car, take Rte. 60 out of the city, and turn right at the set of lights after the gas stations. Taxi NIS28 each way. Buses to Arad and Omer run by the road that leads to the site: #388, every 35min. 6:45am-10:30pm, NIS6.20. The walk from the turnoff takes about 30min. There is a rotary approximately halfway down the road; keep straight to get to the ruins, which are through a parking lot on the right; an orange sign leads the way. Park open Su-Th and Sa 8am-5pm and F 8am-4pm; entrance closes 1hr. earlier. NIS9, students NIS8, children NIS4.50.)

🎵 ENTERTAINMENT

▨ **Forum,** 232 Kiryat Yehudit, in the old industrial area of town, a short drive out of Be'er Sheva's old city (taxi NIS15). Includes multiple dance floors, the largest bar in Israel, and a swimming pool. Open on Friday nights from mid-June through Aug. Call ahead to find out about theme nights like karaoke and techno. Beer NIS15-20. Cover NIS30-70. Open Tu, Th-Sa 10:15pm-5am; F after-party until noon on Sa.

Baraka, 16 Hadassah St., on the corner of B'nei Ein Harod St. This historic stone building once served as an Ottoman hospital and now serves beer (NIS15-22) outside in a desert-motif courtyard and inside to the beat of pop music. Line forms outside on weekends. No cover. Open nightly 10pm-early morning.

Punchline, 4 Smilansky St., below the Trumpeldor St. intersection. How many beers (NIS20) does it take to get a bunch of Israeli twenty-somethings drunk? Come here for the *punchline*. Salsa dancing on W and F. Cover charge for salsa nights and special performances NIS19, students NIS15. Open M-Sa 10:30pm-late.

NEAR BE'ER SHEVA

DIMONA דימונה

Since immigrating in 1969, the **Hebrew Israelite Community,** referred to as the **Black Hebrews** by non-members, has been working to combine the ideals of religious and communal living. A unique sect of English-speaking immigrants, the Hebrew Israelites trace their roots to ancient Israel. The community, which bases its religion on the revelations of spiritual leader Ben-Ami Ben Israel (formerly Ben Carter), believes that the ancestors of black slaves in antebellum America lived in Israel until they were forced to migrate to Western Africa after the Roman onslaught in 70 CE. Ben Israel's vision included a return to the Holy Land; the group's vanguard left Chicago in 1967 and spent 2½ years in Liberia before coming to Israel. Another group from Chicago followed in 1970, and a third exodus took place from Detroit in 1973. The Israeli government at first refused to grant them citizenship unless they converted to Judaism, but the Hebrew Israelites insisted they were already Jews. In 1990, the government and the sect came to an agreement on a process for normalizing the community's legal status.

Every summer, the Hebrew Israelites host the two-day **Naisik Ha-Shalom Music Festival,** which highlights community entertainment, Hebrew Israelite singers, and Israeli bands. (Call Elisheva Eli-El ☎ (05) 199 63 17 for information.) Singing groups from Dimona tour the country when they're not performing at home. Their music is a unique rendition of traditional Jewish and other religious texts in gospel and hip-hop style. Though the village welcomes solo wanderers, a tour can be much more informative. Call ahead to schedule a free tour. (☎ (07) 655 54 00, 657 32 86, or 657 32 87; donations accepted.)

Buses to Dimona leave from: **Be'er Sheva** (#48, 56, and 375; 45min.; every 20min. 6:30am-11pm; NIS13); **Eilat** (#393 and 394; 3hr.; every 1½hr. 5am-5pm; NIS43, students NIS39); and **Tel Aviv** (#375, 393, and 394; NIS30, students NIS27). To reach the village from the bus station, turn left on Herzl St., pass the tall red monument on the right, and continue for 10 minutes. The village is on the left, past a school.

MAMSHIT ממשית

The sunbleached sandstone ruins of ancient Mamshit, the only city in the Negev that was walled in on all sides, lie 15km east of Dimona. Built in the first century CE, Mamshit reached its height as a garrison town in the Roman and Byzantine periods. From Mamshit, one of the six Nabatean cities in Israel, the Nabateans ruled the Petra-Gaza spice route stretching from India to Rome. On one side is a vast desert plain; on the other, the precipitous canyon of **Nahal Mamshit** (Mamshit River). Following attacks by desert nomads in the 6th century CE, the city was destroyed and abandoned. Particularly impressive among the ruins are the Eastern Church, with its altar remains at the top of the market area, the 2nd-century CE tower which once guarded the dams of the river below, and the mansion, or "House of the Affluent." Also be sure to take a look down into the canyon from the observation point. (Open Su-Th 8am-5pm and F 8am-4pm. NIS9, student NIS8, youth NIS4; brochure of the site including small map and descriptions free.)

To view the canyon from a camel's back and with a Bedouin guide, contact the **Mamshit Camel Ranch,** one kilometer east of the ruins. (☎665 10 54; 2hr. tour NIS100.) Bedouin coffee and overnight stays available for groups of 20 or more.

Buses running between Be'er Sheva and the Dead Sea will stop one kilometer outside Mamshit, along the main highway, as will bus #394 to Eilat (1¼hr., every 1½hr., NIS19). Call **Mayam Taxi** (☎(07) 655 66 88) to get here from Dimona (10min., NIS33). Be sure to tell the bus or cab driver to stop at Atar Mamshit, the Nabatean ruins, not the new cinderblock city several kilometers to the west.

ARAD ערד ☎07

The annual **Arad Music Festival** is held every July. This popular four-day jam hosts artists and musicians from all over Israel; Egged runs all-day extra bus service to and from Arad for its duration. Contact the tourist office (☎995 44 09; fax 995 58 66) for information and dates of the 2001 festival.

Arad has only one youth hostel. Though large enough to accommodate the usual crowds, it may be packed with Israeli teens during the Arad Music Festival. Alternatively, the tourist office keeps a list of "Zimmers," or rooms to rent within Arad. The **Blau-Weiss Youth Hostel (HI)** is on 4 Atad St. From the bus stop facing Yehuda St., turn right on Palmah St. after a block. After the soccer field, make a left onto Arad St. and follow the signs. Enjoy cable TV and a free coffee bar. (☎995 71 50; fax 995 50 78. Breakfast included. Reception Su-Th 7:30am-1:30pm and 4-7:30pm, F 7:30am-noon and 4:30-7pm, and Sa 4:30-7:30pm. Check-in 4-8pm. Check-out 10am. Dorms NIS70/US$17.50; singles NIS152/US$38; doubles NIS224/US$56. On Sa NIS20/US$5 extra. Members NIS6/US$1.50 discount.)

The **Central bus station** is in a small office on Yehuda St. (☎995 73 93. Open Su-Th 5:30am-2pm and F 5:30am-1:30pm.) There is no direct service to or from Eilat or Jerusalem; in general it's easiest to go to Be'er Sheva and connect there. Buses to: **Be'er Sheva:** local #385 and 388 (40 min.; every 30min.-1hr. Su-Th 5:40am-9:30pm, F 5:40am-4:30pm, Sa 5:30pm-9:30pm; NIS18), direct #384 (9:30, 11:30am, 2, 5pm) and direct #386 (frequent 6:40am-7:45am); **Ein Bokek** (#384 or 385; 30min.; Su-Th 10:15am, 1, 3:45pm; F 10:15am and 12:45pm; Sa 2pm; NIS18) via **Masada** (50min.; NIS22.50, students NIS20); and **Ein Gedi** (1¼ hr.; NIS25, students NIS22.50); and **Tel Aviv** (#389; 2hr.; Su-Th 6, 8:30am, 2, 5pm; F 4 per day 6am-1:30pm; Sa 5 and 9pm; NIS37.50, students NIS34).

CENTRAL NEGEV

SDEH BOKER שדה בוקר ☎07

When experts advised that developing the Negev was a waste of time and money, first prime minister and Zionist visionary David Ben-Gurion insisted on searching for unconventional methods of "making the desert bloom," asking, "If the Nabateans could do it, why can't we?" When he visited the fledgling Sdeh Boker at the age of 67, he was so moved by the young pioneers that he decided to resign from office and settle on the kibbutz. Soon after, he founded the *Midresha* (institute) of Sdeh Boker, which houses laboratories and a field school devoted to the management of desert resources. Established in 1952, the kibbutz raises olives, kiwis, and other fruit, as well as wheat, corn, and livestock (though few cows).

Steeped in Ben-Gurion tributes, sights, and memorabilia, Sdeh Boker now serves as a base for desert exploration in the nearby **Ein Avdat National Park** and **Zin Valley.** There are a tremendous number of truly astounding hikes in this area, traversing jagged desert cliffs, natural springs, canyons, and monk's caves.

ISRAEL

✴❓ ORIENTATION AND PRACTICAL INFORMATION

The only public transportation to or from Sdeh Boker is Egged bus #60, which runs between **Be'er Sheva** and **Mitzpeh Ramon** (35min.; 6:35am-9:30pm; NIS19, students NIS17.50). The bus stops along the highway at three different points a few kilometers apart: the gate of Kibbutz Sdeh Boker, the turnoff to Ben-Gurion's Hut (at the edge of the kibbutz), and the roundabout outside the gate of the Ben-Gurion Institute. To reach the SPNI Field School, accommodations, Ein Avdat National Park, Ben-Gurion's grave, and the Ben-Gurion Heritage Institute, get off outside the gate. From the roundabout, the road on the right with the orange sign leads to the grave, Heritage Institute, and down the canyon to Ein Avdat. The road straight ahead leads to the SPNI office and accommodations. The institute buildings are arranged around a central square, inside of which are the restaurant, supermarket, and **post office.** (☎653 27 19. Open Su-M, W-Th 8:30am-noon and 1-2pm; Tu 8:30-11am; F 8:30-10:30am.) To reach the **SPNI Field School,** turn right at the end of the road inside the main gate and then left at the large parking lot. The helpful staff answers questions about hiking routes and desert flora, sells maps of nearby trails (NIS62), and stores bags during day hikes. (☎653 20 16; fax 653 27 21; www.boker.org.il/bet-sadeh. Open Su-Th 8am-4:30pm and F 8am-1pm and 5-7pm.)

▐⊡ ACCOMMODATIONS AND FOOD

The **SPNI Hostel** (☎653 20 16 or (05) 393 04 59; fax 653 2721; email orders@boker.org.il), on the edge of the canyon, has modern rooms with air-conditioning and private baths. The six-bed dorm rooms, Sdeh Boker's only budget lodgings, are reserved for students. (Breakfast included. Dorms NIS60; singles NIS195; doubles NIS245. Call ahead.) The field school also runs the **Hamburg Guest House** next door; the reception is in the SPNI field school's office. The rooms include air-conditioning, TV, refrigerator, and bathroom. (Singles NIS225; doubles NIS295. Prices increase during Passover, Sukkot, and Ḥanukkah. Credit cards accepted.) Both accommodations include discounted use of the community swimming pool (NIS10). Guests are entitled to **Internet** access in the field school office. Camping is free at designated locations within the Zin Valley; contact the **SPNI Field School** for information about facilities and transportation.

Food options are slim. The **Super Zin** supermarket in the institute's center is the place to stock up on food before hitting the trail. (Open Su-Th 8am-7pm and F 8am-2pm.) The **Zin Restaurant,** on the other side of the post office, serves tasty breakfasts. (NIS10-32. Open Su-Th 8am-11pm, F 8am-2pm, and Sa 10am-6pm. Credit cards accepted.) The **Sdeh Boker Inn,** next-door to Ben-Gurion's Hut, serves cafeteria-style meals, including excellent baked zucchini and goulash. (☎656 03 79. Open daily 8am-3pm. Credit cards accepted.) For Shabbat stays in Sdeh Boker, stock up before stores close on Friday night.

◺ HIKING IN SDEH BOKER AND ENVIRONS

Although many tourists come to Sdeh Boker to see its Ben-Gurion memorials, Ben-Gurion was attracted to the kibbutz because of its majestic setting. The best way to appreciate the natural beauty of the region is to try some of its spectacular hikes. These, however, require careful preparation. Trails may be poorly marked, distances deceptive, and the Negev sun unforgiving. Detailed maps and explanations for all of these hikes are available at the SPNI field office, which you should visit before attempting any hike. With advance notice, SPNI offers guided hikes across the Avdat Plateau or Zin Valley; call ahead for more information. Wear a hat, get an early start, and drink one liter of water every hour.

EIN AVDAT NATIONAL PARK. This easily accessible park is in the Zin Canyon. From the institute gate, the steep road to the park's lower, the main entrance snakes down the canyon (1hr. on foot, 15min. by car). From the entrance, the hike to **Ein Avdat** (Avdat Spring; the lower pools) is 15 minutes. Allot about one hour for the full hike to the upper gate. Getting to the upper gate requires climbing one-way ladders; unless there's a car waiting at the end of the hike, you'll either need to make a U-turn at the base of the ladders and miss the view or extend your hike a few hours by walking along the rim of the canyon after reaching the top.

Gleaming white walls tower over the green, puddled path that runs through the canyon to the lower pools of the Avdat Spring. The eerie echoes of wildlife resound through the high caves carved in the sides of the canyon, which once served as homes to **Byzantine monks.** A small dam pools water that flows down the rocks from the Avdat Spring; just before the dam an easy-to-miss small set of stairs in the rock leads up to the rest of the hike and the one-way ladders. The foliage becomes denser along the upper part of the trail, where a grove of **Mesopotamian poplar trees** sits below a series of ladders that lead to a dazzling view at the top of the canyon. From the end of the trail on the canyon's rim, a trek along the riverbed to the nearby Nabatean ruins in Avdat takes about two hours (see **Avdat,** p. 415); the trail markings are difficult to follow so consult SPNI for details before going. To either return to Sdeh Boker or head on to Avdat on wheels, exit the park through the parking lot near the upper pools and walk down the road to the highway where there are stops for bus #60 headed in both directions. (☎ 655 56 84. *Park open daily May-Sept. 8am-5pm; Oct.-Apr. 8am-4pm. Entry permitted until 1hr. before closing. NIS14, seniors and students NIS12, children NIS6. Free brochure).*

KARAKASH WADI. This magnificent three-hour hike passes an inviting pond and waterfall (water flows one-two times per year in winter). The Karakash Wadi eventually runs into the Ḥavarim Wadi. A one-hour hike along the Ḥavarim Wadi passes a Nabatean cistern and slopes of smooth, white rock that are striking (and slippery) in moonlight. The cistern is below ground, down a flight of stairs from the beginning of the Ḥavarim Wadi hike. Part of the spice traders' efforts to squeeze water out of the desert, the cistern was used to catch and hold water from rain storms. A one-hour hike along the trail leads to the bottom of the road and park entrance. The brush and rocky hills are popular spots for idling ibex. Turn right on the road to reach Ein Avdat or left to make the uphill haul back to Sdeh Boker. *(To begin the hike, turn left on the Be'er Sheva-Eilat highway from the end of the entrance road to the midresha and walk approximately one kilometer; the trailhead is to the left. For the entrance to the Havarim cistern and Wadi hike, continue along the highway past the Karakash trailhead to an orange sign on the left, a 20-minute walk from the institute. The sign points into the parking lot, where a blue-and-white marked trail descends on the left. Free.)*

EIN AKEV. This 5½-hour hike offers magnificent views from above the Zin Canyon and leads to an oasis where chilly spring water provides a refreshing respite from the desert sun. From the SPNI field school walk down the winding road toward Ein Avdat. From the bottom of the canyon, walk for 20 minutes and look on the left for a trail with green and white markers that ascends the canyon. This trail goes southeast across a desert plateau for several kilometers and reaches a green pool surrounded by lush green vegetation. After a swim in the pool head north along a trail with blue markers. Turn left at the junction and return to Sdeh Boker on the trail marked by orange, blue, and white, which leads from Lebanon to Eilat. *(This hike winds along the edge of cliffs at times. Be very careful and walk slowly in these areas. The return from Ein Akev is along the floor of the canyon and gets very hot during the middle of the day. It's best to start hiking as soon after sunrise as possible.)*

◪ DAYTRIP FROM SDEH BOKER: AVDAT עבדת

Bus #60 (40min.; 6:35am-10pm; NIS20, students NIS18) runs from Be'er Sheva to Mitzpeh Ramon, stopping in Avdat. Tell the driver you're going to the Nabatean archaeological site and not Ein Avdat (the oasis). You can also hike from Sdeh Boker via Ein Avdat (3-4hr.); consult the SPNI guides in Sdeh Boker for info. Bus #60 runs to Avdat from Sdeh Boker (NIS11) and from the highway near the end of the Ein Avdat trail (NIS5). ☎ 658 63 91; fax 655 09 54. Drinking water and bathrooms across from the ticket booth; bring water for the 20-minute uphill hike to the entrance. Open Su-Th 8am-5pm and F 8am-4pm; in winter Su-Th 8am-4pm and F 8am-3pm. NIS18, students NIS15, children NIS9.

The magnificently preserved ruins of a 4th-century BCE **Nabatean city** are perched upon a hill 11km south of Sdeh Boker. Avdat once thrived as a pit stop for caravans along the spice route from the Far East to Gaza (via Petra) that continued on to Europe. Nabateans used their strategic perch at Avdat to spy on caravans as far away as present-day Mitzpeh Ramon or Sdeh Boker. After the Romans captured the city in 106 CE, it continued to flourish, reaching its economic peak during the Byzantine period. Most of the ruins date from this time. The most important Nabatean remains are a handsome esplanade on top of the hill, a winding staircase that led to a Nabatean temple, and a potter's workshop, all dating from the first century CE. When the Nabateans converted to Christianity around 300 CE, the temple became a church. The best of the 6th-century Byzantine remains include a seven-meter surrounding wall, a monastery, two churches, and a baptistry. In this century, the site was resurrected on film as the setting for the movie *Jesus Christ Superstar*. The small grove of crops just below the ruins is irrigated through ancient Nabatean techniques.

MITZPEH RAMON מצפה רמון ☎ 07

Mitzpeh Ramon sits on the rim of **Makhtesh Ramon** (Ramon Crater), the largest natural crater in the world. At 40km long, 9km wide, and 400m deep, its sheer size is mind-boggling. Since some of the geological formations are found nowhere else in the world, hikes pass through what seem to be landscapes of desolate, far-away planets. Uphill treks wind toward phenomenal views of the desert expanse, a rainbow of multi-colored sand. Today, the crater is a 250,000-acre national park with well-marked trails through mazes of geological stunners. From campsites in the crater, the lack of artificial light offers a spectacular view of the starry sky.

◼🔊 ORIENTATION AND PRACTICAL INFORMATION. From the main stop at the Delek gas station, buses #60 and 392 run to **Be'er Sheva** (1hr.; Su-Th 5:30am-9:30pm and F 5:30am-2:15pm; NIS22.50, students NIS20). Bus #392 uses Mitzpeh Ramon as a waystation between Be'er Sheva and **Eilat;** it stops for 15 minutes at the gas station and will pick people up if there are empty seats. Drivers are instructed to take 10-minute breaks if they feel drowsy on long desert treks; don't panic if the bus is 10 to 40 minutes late. From the gas station, the tan, flat-roofed **visitors center** is visible on the left edge of the crater. Clustered around it are the **youth hostel, Bio-Ramon,** and the crater-rim **promenade.** Cross the street, turn left at the gas station, and then take a right to get to the visitors center.

A commercial center containing a **Bank Ha-Poalim** branch is a bit downhill to the right from the gas station, across **Ben-Gurion Blvd.** (Open Su and Tu-W 8:30am-12:45pm; M and Th 8:30am-12:30pm and 4-6:30pm; F 8:30am-12:30pm.) The **post office** is upstairs behind the bank and across the parking lot. It houses Western Union and offers fax services, EMS, and Poste Restante. (Emergency ☎ 630 73 30. Open Su-Tu and Th 8am-12:30pm and 4-6:30pm; W 8am-1pm; F 8am-12:30pm.) **Police** (☎ 100), **first aid** (☎ 101 or 658 83 33), and **fire** (☎ 102) offices are up the walkway through the park across from the commercial center on Ben-Gurion Blvd.

🔥 ACCOMMODATIONS. Staking out a **campsite** in the middle of the *makhtesh* is **forbidden** and environmentally destructive. Those who camp there run the risk of being awakened by an angry ranger or an even angrier **Asiatic wild ass.** There are inexpensive accommodations both in the town and in the crater, as well as interesting alternatives to hosteling and camping. There are campgrounds in town at the municipal park next to the gas station and at the SPNI field school. The **SPNI Field School** is directly on the crater's rim and has a trail leading down it. From Camel Observation Point, turn right at the Har Gamal dirt road at the crater's rim and walk along the black-marked cliffside trail toward the tall antennae. To get to the Observation Point, take bus #60 through town or turn left from the visitors center and follow the crater-rim promenade about 15min. (☎658 86 15 or 658 86 16; fax 658 83 85. A/C and private bath. No showers. Reception Su-Th 8am-6pm, F 8am-noon and Sa call ahead. Check-in 3pm. Check-out 8:30am. 6-bed student dorm NIS83; doubles NIS275/US$58; each additional person NIS110; children NIS65. Sleep outside under the bedouin tent, or pitch your own. NIS20. V, MC.) The **Mitzpeh Ramon Youth Hostel (HI)**, on the canyon's rim, is across from the visitors center and next to the promenade. (☎658 84 43; fax 658 80 74; email mitzpe@iyha.org.il. Breakfast included. Reception 24hr. Check-in 3pm. Store bags for early arrivals. Check-out 10am. 6-bed dorms NIS89/US$19.50; singles NIS190/US$43.50; doubles NIS260/$US63. HI discount US$1.50. Credit cards accepted.)

🏃 HIKING MITZPEH RAMON AND ENVIRONS.

Far-flung trailheads are best reached by car or 4x4 vehicle. For trailheads off of the main highway, bus #392 to Eilat travels through the crater and can stop at the turnoff for the Be'erot Camping Site. Locals say hitchhiking on the highway is a safe option, though the highway is not heavily trafficked. The **Park Ramon Visitors Center,** one of two hiking resources

 Makhtesh Ramon is a spectacular park, but it should not be taken lightly. Always consult with Nature Reserve or SPNI personnel before setting out. Wear a hat, hike as early as possible in the morning, and carry food and 1L of water per person per hour. Heatstroke and dehydration can be deadly in the Negev.

in Mitzpeh Ramon, is housed in the round building with the flat top overlooking the crater. Nature Reserve Authority staffers help plan hikes and provide an excellent map of the crater. If only Hebrew maps are available, ask the guides to write English names. (☎658 86 91 or 658 86 98; fax 658 86 20. Open Su-Th and Sa 8am-5pm and F 8am-4pm. NIS18, child NIS9; combo ticket with Bio-Ramon NIS21, children NIS11.) The **SPNI Field School,** near the edge of the crater, 500m southwest of Camel Observation Point, occasionally offers organized tours (call ahead to schedule). Although the trails are well marked, a pre-hike stop at the visitors center for maps is a prudent idea for an unguided expedition. Leave your route description and estimated trip duration at the field school before hiking—they have an on-site rescue team and are in direct communication with army units in the area. While hiking, keep a fix on the main highway or Be'erot Campsite. (☎658 86 15 or 658 86 16; fax 658 83 85. Open Su-Th 8am-6pm and F 8am-noon.)

HAR ARDON. Har Ardon (Mount Ardon) is a full-day hike, combining challenging terrain with unbeatable views. To climb Har Ardon, turn left out of the Be'erot campsite and follow the black markers north for three kilometers to the sign marked Mount Ardon. From here, follow the blue path on the right to a parking area, where the mountain ascent begins. The steep climb up follows a narrow trail that changes about halfway up into a smoother and wider trail. The descent from the mountain can be quite a physical feat; take it slow since the narrow, white-rock-and-sand trail is steep and slippery. Down the mountain and along the trail in the crater are the remarkable sand and hills of the **Red Valley,** which range in color from yellow to crimson. After passing the black hill of Givat Harut, turn right on the black trail and follow the signs back to the campsite to complete the hike.

WADI ARDON. South of Mount Ardon, this hike leads past unique geological formations and Nabatean ruins. From the campsite, walk along the black-marked trail for one-half kilometer, and turn right on a dirt road marked in red. After about one kilometer, take the dirt road on the left marked in black. From the parking lot, continue south through Wadi Ardon. Along the colorful borders of Wadi Ardon are a pair of vertical magma intrusions, one big and one small, known as the Father and Son Dikes. To continue on, take the blue path. It points toward **Parsat Nekarot** (the Horseshoe of Crevices), which includes **Sha'ar Ramon** (the Ramon Gate), where water exits the crater. The Parsat Nekarot river bed is flanked by soaring cliffs and cave-like enclaves that make welcome shady stops.

From Parsat Nekarot, follow the blue markings to **Ein Saharonim.** The vegetation lasts all year, but the water evaporates to mere puddles in summer. The remains of a **Nabatean caravanserai** stand at the end of the spring on the right. This is also the spot where animals are most likely to be seen wandering around in search of water sources. To return to the campsite from here, take the orange trail away from Parsat Nekarot. To start hiking from Ein Saharonim, go left from the campsite, and follow the orange trail next to a sign on the right.

SHORT HIKES FROM MITZPEH RAMON. Along the southern edge of the crater rises **Har Saharonim** (literally, Mountain of the Crescent-Shaped Ornaments). Start the climb from the western side, closest to the main road. Take a right from the campsite and turn left onto the "Oil Pipeline Route" black trail. After about 40 minutes, follow the steep incline past the green trail to Ein Saharonim and the Naḥal Gevanim turnoff. Turn left at the green markers at the top, which lead to "Mount Saharonim." The green-trail descent from Har Saharonim goes to **Ein Saharonim.** From there, follow the blue path through Parsat Nekarot in reverse.

Trailheads for the most interesting hikes are outside of town; two beautiful trails that pass by significant points of geological interest originate in Mitzpeh Ramon. An excellent three-hour hike begins at the end of the western promenade, near the mini-amphitheater, and leads to **Ha-Minsarah** (Carpentry), where piles of prism-like rocks, configured and baked by volcanic heat, resemble carpenters' supplies. Follow the promenade from the visitors center. Past two iron ball sculptures, a green-marked trail makes a rocky descent from the cliff. At the bottom of the crater, follow the green trail left to Ha-Minsarah. A dirt road leads east toward the highway. A turnoff point marked in red along the green Carpentry trail leads south to a five-hour hike along **Ramon's Tooth,** a dark rock formation of cooled magma that was exposed during the crater's creation. The hike also goes past the **Ammonite Wall,** an impressive collection of crustacean fossils embedded in rock. From the red Ammonite Wall path, a black path eventually leads off to the left and to the highway. Bus #392 from Eilat generally comes by on its way to Mitzpeh Ramon (Su-Th around 3 and 5pm).

EILAT אילת   ☎ 07

Eilat has two goals—to get you tan and to make you poor. The city is soaked with the sweat of rowdy Israelis, international backpackers, and European tourists; the air is abuzz with jet skis and cell phones. Some swear by Eilat's sun, coral, and nightlife, while others see the city as a huge tourist trap attached to a nice beach. In between the cocktails and Coppertone, stick your head in the ocean and you may notice some of the most spectacular underwater life the world's seas have to offer. Above the waves, the wildlife is bikini-clad and muscle-bound.

The busiest times of the year are Passover (Apr. 8-14 in 2001), Sukkot (Oct. 2-9 in 2001), and Israel's summer vacation (July and Aug.), when nearly 100,000 Israelis descend upon the city. Don't fool yourself into thinking that this is a good time to visit. True, there are more parties and crowded pubs, but hostels and restaurants charge double their normal rates, petty theft runs rampant, and every inch of beach crawls with human flesh.

▀ GETTING THERE AND GETTING AROUND

Flights: The **airport** (☎636 38 38) is on the corner of Ha-Tmarim Blvd. and Ha-Arava Rd. **Arkia Airlines** (☎638 48 88) flies to: **Haifa** (2 per day, NIS370); **Jerusalem** (2 per day, NIS370); and **Tel Aviv** (every hr., NIS370). **Israir Airlines** (☎634 06 66) flies to Tel Aviv (every hr., NIS268-298).

Buses: Central bus station (☎636 51 20) on Ha-Tmarim Blvd. Reserve tickets at least one day in advance, 3 days during high season. Buses to: **Haifa** (#991; 6hr.; Su, Th 8:30am, 2:30, 11:30pm; M-W 2:30 and 11:30pm; F 8:30am; Sa 5 and 11:30pm; NIS68); **Jerusalem** (#444; 4½hr.; Su-Th 7, 10am, 2, 5pm; F 7, 10am, 1pm; Sa 4:30

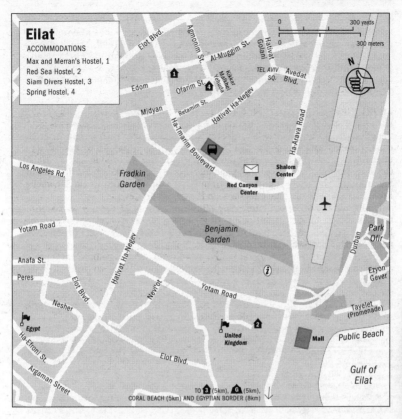

Eilat

ACCOMMODATIONS

Max and Merran's Hostel, 1
Red Sea Hostel, 2
Siam Divers Hostel, 3
Spring Hostel, 4

and 7pm; NIS58); and **Tel Aviv** (#394; 5hr.; Su-Th 10 per day, F 7 per day, Sa 8 per day; NIS58). If these are full, it is possible to take a bus to **Be'er Sheva** and transfer. ISIC discounts. Bus schedules change frequently.

City Buses: Bus #15 runs down Ha-Tmarim Blvd. and Ha-Arava Rd., through the hotel area, and past the HI hostel and Coral Beach to **Egypt** (every 20-30min. Su-Th 4:45am-8:30pm, F 4:45am-5pm, Sa 8:30am-8:30pm; NIS2.10-3.20). Buses #1 and 2 run from downtown to the hotel area (every 30min. Su-Th 7am-8pm, F 7am-2:15pm, Sa every 2hr. 10am-6pm; NIS3).

Taxis: King Solomon (☎633 33 38). City rides NIS10; to observatory NIS20; to Egyptian border NIS25-30; to Jordanian border NIS20. Taxi sharing is common. In winter, *sherut* run along the #1, 2, and 15 bus routes.

Car Rental: Hertz (☎637 50 50 or 637 66 82), in Red Canyon Center. 23+. **Budget** (☎637 41 25), in Shalom Center. **Avis** (☎637 31 64), next to the tourist office. All offer similar plans: NIS45/US$11 plus NIS1 per km. or unlimited mileage NIS160-200/US$40-50 per day. Insurance starts at NIS50/US$12 per day; NIS50/US$12 extra per day in high season. Rentals can't go into Egypt or Jordan. Open 8am-6pm.

Bike Rental: Red Sea Sports (☎633 08 66) in the marina. NIS90 per day. Open Su-Th 8am-9pm and F-Sa 8am-6pm. Rental recommended for winter only.

ORIENTATION

Eilat is a five-kilometer strip of coastline on the Negev's sandy bottom, the precarious intersection of Israel, Jordan, Egypt, and Saudi Arabia; at night the lights of all four are visible on the horizon. The city is divided into three sections: the town on the hills, the hotel area and Lagoon Beach to the east, and the port to the south.

The main entrance to the central bus station is on **Ha-Tmarim Blvd.**, which crosses the center of the city from the southeast (downhill) to the northwest (uphill). Across from the bus station is the **Commercial Center.** Uphill and to the right are most hostels and cheap restaurants. Walking downhill along the bus station side of Ha-Tmarim Blvd. leads to the **Red Canyon Center**, which resembles a futuristic Bedouin tent and houses the **post office,** supermarket, and cinema. Farther downhill is the **Shalom Center** mall. Ha-Tmarim Blvd. ends here, perpendicular to **Ha-Arava Rd.** If you turn right onto Ha-Arava Rd., you will soon find the main entrance to the Eilat airport on your left. A block past the airport, to the right of the intersection with **Yotam Rd.,** a three-level conglomeration of cheap restaurants and shops calls itself the **New Tourist Center.** On the other side of Yotam Rd. is the tourist office. Ha-Arava Rd. leads to Dolphin Reef, the Coral Beach, the Underwater Observatory, and finally Taba Beach and the Egyptian Border. Bus #15 runs this route (every 15-20min., NIS2-3). Turning left at the intersection of Ha-Arava Rd. and Yotam St. leads to the **promenade** and the **public beach.**

⁊ PRACTICAL INFORMATION

TOURIST AND FINANCIAL SERVICES

Tourist Information Center: (☎637 21 11; fax 632 58 67), at the corner of Yotam Rd. and Ha-Arava Rd. Maps and brochures. Will help find accommodations for no commission. Open Su-Th 8am-6pm and F 8am-2pm. **SPNI,** the Society for the Protection of Nature in Israel (☎637 20 21), opposite Coral Beach, has maps and info about local hiking. Open Su-Th 8am-8pm.

Consulates: Egypt, 68 Ha-Efroni St. (☎637 68 82). From the bus station, turn right on Ha-Tmarim Blvd. and left onto Ḥativat Ha-Negev. Continue 900m until Sderot Argaman St., and turn right. Ha-Efroni St. is the first street on the right; look for the flag. Submit a visa application in the morning; pick it up at noon. Visas must be paid for in NIS (US nationals NIS50; South Africans free; all others NIS70). Bring a passport photograph. Free, Sinai-only visas are available at the border. Open Su-Th 9-11am. **UK** (☎637 23 44), above the New Tourist Center (next to the Adi Hotel). By appointment only.

Currency Exchange: Bank Leumi (☎636 41 11). Open Su, Tu, Th 8:30am-noon and 5-6:30pm; M, W, F 8:30am-noon. **Bank Ha-Poalim** (☎637 61 57). Open Su, Tu, Th 8:30am-noon and 4:30-6pm; M, W, F 8:30am-noon. Both banks are across from the central bus station. The post office exchanges traveler's checks with no commission.

ATM: 24hr. machines (V, MC, Plus, Cirrus) outside Bank Ha-Poalim, next to the post office, and in the marina.

Camping Equipment: Azimut, The National Center for Hiking Equipment (☎634 11 12), on the bottom floor of the mall at the corner of Yotam Rd. and Ha-Arava Rd. Good selection of pricey gear. Open Su-Th 9:30am-midnight and F 9am-4pm.

EMERGENCY AND COMMUNICATIONS

Emergency: First Aid (☎637 23 33). **Magen David Adom** first-aid stations are on some beaches. **Police** (☎633 24 44), on Avdat Blvd. at the eastern end of Ḥativat Ha-Negev. "Lost and found" for packs stolen from the beach.

Hospital: Yoseftal Hospital (☎635 80 11), on Yotam Rd. **Maccabee Healthcare Services** (☎676 49 00; emergency ☎633 31 01), on the corner of Eilat St. and Ha-Tmarim Blvd. Modern facility that offers services for dental emergencies.

Internet Access: Internet access in Eilat is easy to find and prices are standard. **BJ's Books** (☎634 09 05; email bjsbooks@eilatcity.co.il), in the New Tourist Center. NIS30 per hr. Open Su-Th 9:30am-10pm and F 9am-6pm. **Unplugged Internet Bar** (☎632 62 99), next to the Unplugged Bar, in the New Tourist Center. Fast but oddly old-fashioned coin-operated machines accept NIS5 coins for 15min. per coin. Open 24hr.

Post Office: (☎ 637 44 40), in the Red Canyon Center. Traveler's check cashing, Western Union, **Poste Restante.** Open Su-Tu and Th 8am-12:30pm and 4-6:30pm, W 8am-1pm, and F and holidays 8am-12:30pm.

ACCOMMODATIONS

Finding a cheap room in Eilat is easy. Finding a safe, comfortable, convenient, and cheap room is another story. New arrivals to the bus station are attacked by a gaggle of apartment hawkers. Most hostels are less than three blocks from the bus station—walk up the hill on Ha-Tmarim Blvd. and take a right on Retamim St. Some of the bigger hostels are unfriendly and have been known to put out backpackers in favor of large groups or have patrons switch rooms in the middle of the night. The tourist office can assist if hostels are full. Prices for rooms rise in the summer.

There are two camping options in Eilat: expensive and legal or free and illegal. For the latest info on the former, stop by the **SPNI Field School** (☎ 637 20 21), across from Coral Beach. SPNI's campsite (NIS20 per person) offers showers and toilets; huts on the campground cost NIS300, but you have to call the Tel Aviv office (☎ (03) 638 86 88) to reserve ahead. Most hostels allow camping on their roof or in their backyard for NIS15-20. In July and August, hundreds of people ignore the "No Camping" signs on the public beach or in the park; many are victims of theft. If sleeping on the ground and taking communal showers sounds appealing, take bus #15 to **Coral Beach Campground,** the municipal campground opposite the beach of the same name. The site's small huts have only their prime location to the reefs to recommend them. (☎ 637 19 11 or 637 50 63. Breakfast included. Refrigerator NIS10 per day. Pitch-your-own-tent NIS30; huts NIS300.)

Red Sea Hostel (☎ 637 60 60), in the New Tourist Center directly above the Unplugged and Underground Bars. Location, location, location! These small, crowded rooms are just a beer bottle's throw from the rest of Eilat's hot spots on the promenade. A/C; free safe. Mattress on the roof NIS15; dorms NIS25-30; singles NIS100; doubles NIS120; triples NIS150. Prices double during high season, but bargain for multiple night stays.

Siam Divers Hostel (☎ 637 05 81), right on Coral Beach. Priority goes to divers, but the location and atmosphere make this a great pick for any traveler. Oddly shaped rooms are simple, with common bath. Only 10min. by bus from Eilat. Dorms NIS60; doubles NIS150; triples NIS180.

Villa Kibel, P.O. Box 8304 (☎/fax 637 69 11; cell ☎ 050 34 53 66; email russell@eliat.ardom.co.il). Fully furnished, upscale apartment-style rooms with TV, minifridge, fresh linen, and cooking facilities. Within 1km of the beach; some rooms have ocean view. Two are wheelchair accessible. Call for bus station pick-up. Doubles NIS150-220. Larger rooms also available. Prices negotiable, especially for longer stays.

Spring Hostel, P.O. Box 1278 (☎/fax 637 46 60), halfway down Retamim St., around the corner. Immaculate but basic rooms. Billiards, pub, a pool, and very tight security. Dorms NIS30-60; singles NIS100-160; doubles NIS120-200.

Max & Merran's Hostel, P.O. Box 83 (☎ 637 13 33; fax 637 35 13), off Almogim St. Under new ownership and in a new location next to the Home Hostel (they share a courtyard), this hostel has lost none of its friendly atmosphere. Clean and newly built rooms with kitchen and common bathrooms. Dorms NIS25.

FOOD

▓ **Pedro's Steak House,** 14 Ye'elim St. (☎ 637 95 04). Moderately expensive, but unbelievable food. A local favorite. Steak NIS63; ostrich NIS75; vegetarian options NIS38. Don't miss the freshly baked bread (NIS2) or the divine creme brulee. Open daily 5-11:30pm.

▓ **Tandoori** (☎ 633 38 79), in the Lagoon Hotel on the King's Wharf. Excellent Indian food. Very friendly waitstaff will help arrange a menu to meet a lower budget. Filling 3-course lunch special (NIS49). Great curry (NIS30-50) and *naan* (NIS5-16). Open daily noon-3:30pm and 7pm-1am.

The Spring Onion (☎637 74 34), at the marina. This popular vegetarian and dairy restaurant serves fresh salads and pasta (NIS30-40) and offers a wide selection of tea and coffee. Large breakfast NIS32; fish NIS50. Open daily 8am-3am. V, MC, AmEx.

Malibu Restaurant (☎634 19 90), adjacent to Siam Divers, near the end of Coral Beach. A great place to get a sandwich (NIS16) on the beach or dinner on the dock. Dinner specials NIS60; pizzas NIS28-35. Open daily 10am-midnight.

Mai Thai (☎637 25 17), on Yotam Rd. just uphill from the New Tourist Center, overlooking the city. A bit expensive, but a treat. Try the egg rolls (NIS15) or get a set menu for two (NIS78). Main course NIS40-47. Open daily 1-3:30pm and 6:30-11pm.

■ SIGHTS

Some say that the best of Eilat's wildlife is in the air. Avid birdwatchers flock to the salt ponds north of the lagoon mid-February through May and mid-September through November, when 30 species fly overhead on their way to or from Africa. The **International Birdwatching Center (IBC)**, P.O. Box 774, Eilat 88106, near the northern end of the airport on Eilat St., runs walking tours (US$5) and jeep tours (US$50). There's a bird watching festival in March. Contact the IBC for more information. (☎633 53 39. Open Su-Th 9am-1pm and 5-7pm and F 9am-1pm.)

Visitors pretend to be birds at the skydiving simulator **Airodium** (☎637 27 45), behind the Riviera Hotel. An air-vent contraption makes for an expensive but fun 10 minutes (NIS120). For stimulation beyond simulation, jump with **Skydive Red Sea,** P.O. Box 4139, Eilat 88150 (☎633 23 86).

■ ENTERTAINMENT

Eilat's entertainment is not exclusively limited to bars and clubs. The tourist office has information on events at the **Phillip Murray Cultural Center.** Kids of all ages like **Luna Park,** in front of the Queen of Sheba Hotel. Bumper cars and pirate ships cost NIS10; kiddie thrills are NIS5. (☎(05) 031 50 49. Open M-Sa 6pm-midnight.) The end-of-August international **Red Sea Jazz Festival,** with ten daily performances, is Eilat's most popular annual event. Ask the tourist office for information.

Unplugged (☎632 62 99), in the New Tourist Center. Loud music and big TVs. Free Sony Play Station, Sa karaoke, and foosball attract the masses. Cheap coin-operated Internet (NIS5 for 15min.). Happy hour 4-9pm: NIS7 for half-liter local beer; daiquiris NIS9. Heineken NIS12; local beers NIS7-15. Open 24hr.

Green Beach (☎637 70 32), on the promenade close to the shopping mall. A sprawling beach bar frequented by beautiful people at all hours. During the day, scantily clad waiters shoot water guns to cool the crowd, and at night they keep the liquor and coffee coming—whatever you need to stay until the sun rises over the Red Sea. Half-liter drafts NIS11 and up; cocktails NIS26 and up; coffee NIS8. Open 24hr.

Nisha (☎631 55 55), in the basement of the Neptune Hotel. This dance bar is Eilat's trendiest and craziest night spot. Reserved for the chic and beautiful. Travelers are advised to pull out their best duds for this place. Beer NIS12 and up; cocktails NIS26 and up. Cover NIS20-40. Open daily 11:30pm-4:30am.

Dolphin Reef (☎637 18 46), just before Coral Beach. The place to be on Th once the dolphins have gone to sleep. Beach parties are known as the kinkiest in Eilat. Th cover NIS50-80. Open daily until sunset and Th 11:30pm-4:30am.

Dolphin Bar (☎637 04 19), on Almogim St., across from Hard Luck Cafe, close to most hostels. Escape Eilat's exorbitant prices in this hole-in-the-wall pub. Serves the cheapest beer in town. Half-liter bottles of Tuborg NIS2.50. Billiards and Internet. Open 24hr.

◤ SCUBA DIVING

Several underwater observatories exist to help those who want to experience underwater Eilat without getting wet. The **Coral World Underwater Observatory and**

Aquarium features shark and turtle tanks and an underwater observation room. Though interesting, it is best for those who won't be snorkeling. (☎637 66 66. Open Sa-Th 8:30am-5pm and F and holiday eves 8:30am-3pm. NIS63, children NIS145.) Live a life of ease beneath the sea of green in the observatory's **Yellow Submarine,** which goes 60m below the surface. (☎637 66 66. Observatory and submarine NIS255, children NIS145.) The **Galaxy** is one of the city's many glass-bottomed boats. (☎631 63 60. 1½hr. NIS60.) The **Jules Verne Explorer** may not venture 20,000 leagues down, but glass walls make it a true underwater observatory. (☎633 36 66. 2hr. cruise to Japanese Gardens NIS80.) Both the Galaxy and the Explorer are at the marina. For an up-to-date list of dive sites and activities, try www.Eilat.net.

DIVE SITES

JAPANESE GARDENS. Arguably the finest in Eilat, this dive site gets its name from the placid, "manicured" look of the coral, which almost completely covers the sandy bottom. Sushi and *sashimi*-lovers will be glad to know that the Japanese Gardens are home to the most plentiful fish life in Eilat. *(Take bus #15; 10min. from the central bus station. Entrance is on the right by the underwater observatory. Diving available only through established dive clubs (see p. 423); snorkeling is free and open to the public.)*

CORAL BEACH NATURE RESERVE. This national reserve (which includes Moses' and Joshua's Rocks) offers a wealth of coral species and fish life, making the entry fee well worthwhile. Five water trails marked by buoys go through the reef, and two bridges into the water protect coral from human feet and vice versa. *(Take bus #15 from the central bus station toward the sea. ☎637 68 29. Open Sa-Th 9am-6pm and F 9am-5pm. NIS18, children NIS9. Lockers NIS6.)*

DOLPHIN REEF. The commercially operated scuba and snorkeling center at Dolphin Reef allows divers to observe semi-wild dolphins in a somewhat natural environment. Although the project has raised some ethical eyebrows, the dolphins are free to swim away at any time (although it would be difficult for any mammal to refuse a free feeding, as most budget travelers will agree). The dolphins perform a variety of tricks daily at the four "interaction" sessions, but observing them underwater is a more rewarding experience. The four original dolphins brought from the Black Sea have added seven new babies to the group. *(Beyond the port on bus #15. ☎637 18 46. Open daily 9am-5pm. NIS29, children NIS22. Interaction sessions every 2hr. 10am-4pm. Snorkeling NIS202, children NIS193. Beach open and free after 5pm.)*

DIVE FACILITIES

▧ **Siam Divers,** P.O. Box 1020, Eilat 88000 (☎637 05 81; fax 637 10 33; email siamdive@netvision.net.il; www.siam.co.il), at the end of Coral Beach next to the Nature Reserve. While many may initially be attracted to the high-gloss finish of the larger dive clubs, this is the friendliest, safest, and most experienced dive center in Eilat. Introductory dives (no certificate necessary) NIS160; 2 guided dives with full equipment NIS170; 5-day open water course NIS790/US$190. Extremely convenient dorms NIS60, with course NIS40. Unforgettable 3- to 5-day dive safaris to Sinai start at NIS1600/US$340. 10% student discount. For more info, email or write.

Red Sea Sports Club (☎637 65 69 or 637 00 68; fax 637 06 55; email manta1@netvision.net.il), in the Ambassador Hotel; also has an office at the King Solomon Hotel. PADI open-water courses NIS1164/US$291; dives with dolphins NIS265/US$56. Office on North Beach near the lagoon offers windsurfing (NIS68 per hr.), water-skiing (NIS120 per 15min.), and parasailing (NIS150 per 10min.). Also arranges horseback riding lessons at the nearby **Texas Ranch** (☎632 65 02. 1hr. NIS150; 2hr. NIS170; 4hr. NIS235).

Aquasport, P.O. Box 300 (☎633 44 04; fax 633 37 71; email info@aqua-sport.com; www.aqua-sport.com), on Coral Beach next to Siam Divers. This large and active beachfront houses a PADI-certified diving center (open water beginner course NIS1100/US$275) and windsurfing rentals (NIS75 per hr.).

⚠ HIKING

The beauty of the red granite mountains towering over Eilat matches that of the coral reefs thriving beneath it. The **SPNI Field School,** across from Coral Beach (bus #15), is an essential stop for independent hikers. It sells extensive trail maps and provides good advice on hikes. (☎637 20 21. Open Su-Th 8am-4pm.) Many of the sites are accessible by northbound bus #393, 394, or 397. Buses fill up fast during high season and on Sundays and Fridays—make reservations at the central bus station two days in advance.

RED CANYON. The most exciting and accessible terrain north of Eilat includes **Ein Netafim, Mount Shlomo,** and **Ha-Kanyon Ha-Adom** (Red Canyon). Buses will stop nearby upon request. From Red Canyon, hike to the lookout above **Moon Valley,** a pocked canyon in Egypt, and to the unusual **Amram's Pillars.** These hikes are not advisable in summer; October through April is the best season. Before attempting any of these hikes, consult SPNI (see **Tourist Offices,** p. 420). SPNI also runs guided hikes to Moon Valley; call its Tel Aviv office for details (☎(03) 638 86 75).

TIMNA NATIONAL PARK. Timna National Park is another hiking destination. The 6000-year-old Timna copper mines remain a fascinating destination. Some people believe the Israelites passed through here on their way out of Egypt. The park houses remains of workers' camps and cisterns dating from the 11th century BCE. The sandstone **King Solomon's Pillars** dominate the desert at a height of 50m near the 14th-century BCE Egyptian Temple of Hathor. The park's lake offers **camping** facilities (including showers) and a restaurant on its artificially created shores. *(Most buses that go to Tel Aviv or Jerusalem will stop at the sign for Alipaz. Don't get off at the Timna Mines signpost; the entrance is two kilometers away, which is too far to walk in summer.* ☎*635 62 15; fax 637 25 42. Open daily 7:30am-6pm. NIS27, ages 5-18 NIS21.)*

WEST BANK

الضفة الغربية

For the first time in history, the Palestinian flag flies over many towns in the West Bank, but the process by which self-rule was established has been long and arduous, the struggle is far from over, and the outcome is unpredictable. Daily fluctuations in Israeli-Palestinian relations and extremist actions on both sides frequently disrupt daily life, but well-informed and cautious travelers will have no problem visiting the area's major sites. Tourists may be invited into Palestinian homes, where hot spiced tea and muddily delicious coffee are accompanied by discussions of the *intifada* and occupation. Modest dress will make both men and women's experiences more enjoyable. The Israeli settlements are close to many Palestinian towns, but don't expect transportation between the two. The best way to visit a settlement is to go back to Jerusalem and catch a bus from there.

PHONE CODES	Country Code: 972. Police/Emergency: ☎ 100.

HIGHLIGHTS OF THE WEST BANK

Sip coffee at one of **Ramallah's** (p. 438) hip cafes and groove to live Arab music.

See the city of **Jericho** (p. 434), the center of Palestinian renewal and home to the ancient ruins of **Hisham's palace,** a stunning example of early Islamic architecture.

Hike near Jericho in the **Wadi Qelt** (p. 437), the closest place to Jerusalem to enjoy the striking beauty of the desert landscape.

ESSENTIALS

ENTRY

Travelers in Israel do not need any additional visas or permits to visit the West Bank; be sure to bring your passport, though. The West Bank is accessible by car, but the numerous Israeli checkpoints preclude a smooth ride. East Jerusalem is the transportation hub for the West Bank, but travel restrictions have made it impossible for Palestinians who do not live there to use Jerusalem as a transit terminal. As a result, most bus lines have been re-routed to Ramallah, in the northern West Bank; Ramallah's Manara Circle is a hub for East Jerusalem-northern West Bank connections. When possible, travel from Jerusalem into the West Bank rather than from one West Bank city to another. Direct roads from Jerusalem can often cut travel time by more than half. Check with the Israeli tourist office before going. They'll probably issue a standard governmental warning worthy of serious consideration; some may find the warning heavy-handed and decide to go anyway.

Be sure to pick up the monthly *This Week in Palestine*, available in hotel lobbies and restaurants in the West Bank and East Jerusalem, for extensive listings of events and resources throughout the Palestinian Territories.

BORDER CROSSINGS: JORDAN

Tourists crossing through Jericho's **King Hussein/Allenby Bridge** must obtain visas in advance; get them either in Tel Aviv, at the Eilat-Aqaba crossing, or from a Jordanian embassy or consulate. Allow at least an hour and a half to cross. At the bridge, your passport and belongings will be inspected (you may reclaim your VAT here). Everything remains unpredictable; get thorough, up-to-date information from your embassy or consulate before trying to cross. (NIS126. Border open Su-Th 8am-midnight, F-Sa 8am-3pm.)

SAFETY WARNING In the recent past, the West Bank has seen considerable conflict between Palestinian residents, Israeli settlers, and security forces. Carry your **passport** at all times. Be aware of the situation in each town before visiting. Avoid visiting on the anniversaries of uprisings or terrorist attacks. Do not travel if Israel has just announced a new building program or territorial acquisition. Visibly Jewish travelers may be in danger and should cover *kippot* with a baseball cap.

GETTING AROUND

TAXIS. Although shared **service** (*"service,"* pronounced ser-veece, the equivalent of Israeli *sherut*) are slightly more expensive than buses, they are faster and more reliable, and they depart more frequently (whenever they fill up). **Private taxis** (called *"special,"* pronounced SPAY-shal) are much more expensive and not usually equipped with a meter; be sure to bargain for a price before getting in. Private taxis are often the only way to reach remote sites. Drivers will take you to the site and (for a few extra shekels) wait around to make the return trip. Some West Bank cities, including Nablus and Ramallah, have color coded taxis: yellow cabs are private and orange cabs are *service*. As always, insist that the driver turn on the meter if there is one and have an idea of an appropriate price beforehand. Even for the most remote sites, do not pay more than NIS50 per hour. Most local rides average around NIS10; none should cost any more than NIS15.

BUSES. Both Arab and Egged buses serve the West Bank. Arab buses leave from two bus stations in East Jerusalem: the Suleiman St. Station, between Herod's Gate and Damascus Gate, for the south and the Nablus Rd. Station (a few steps away) for the north. Catch Egged buses at the West Jerusalem central bus station on Jaffa Rd. Egged buses cost more and often stop only at the outskirts of Palestinian towns, but they are convenient for traveling to the Jewish settlements. Arab bus schedules to the West Bank are unpredictable; the intervals listed in this book are approximate. Transportation to Nablus and Jericho is erratic. For the former, take a *service* to Ramallah and continue to Nablus from there. For Jericho, go first to Abu Dis or al-Izariyyeh (Bethany) and connect from there. Buses run from Jerusalem to: **Bethlehem** (every 15min., NIS2); **al-Izariyyeh** (every hr., NIS2); **Abu Dis** (every hr., NIS2); **Ramallah** (every 30min., NIS3); and **Nablus** (Tamini Bus Co., every hr., NIS6).

CARS. A system of colored license plates differentiates vehicles. Those registered in Israel, Jerusalem, and Jewish settlements have yellow plates. White plates with green numbers belong to vehicles registered with the Palestinian Authority. Blue plates are a remnant from the days when the Palestinian territories were the Occupied Territories; they signify Arab cars not registered with Israel. Others are black-on-white (UN or diplomatic), red (police), and black (army). It's probably safer to travel with white or blue plates, but many Arab-owned cars that are registered in Israel (with yellow plates) travel hassle-free in the West Bank.

TOURS. An easy way to see the West Bank is to hire a Palestinian guide for the day. **Alternative Tourism Group** (see **Bethlehem Tours**, p. 430) is a reliable company with excellent guides. Alternatively, look for a taxi driver who speaks decent English (there are many) and ask whether he can drive by the major sights. Specify how many hours you wish to spend and agree on a price in advance; something in the range of NIS45 per hour is reasonable for transportation and waiting time.

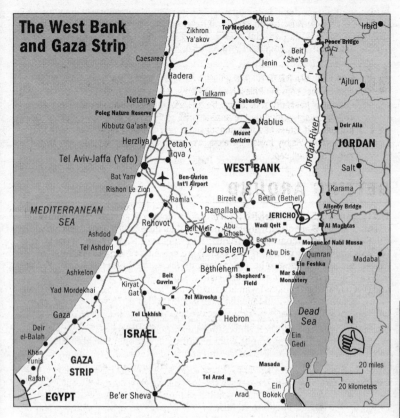

The West Bank and Gaza Strip

MONEY

The **New Israeli Shekel (NIS)** is the currency most frequently used in the West Bank and Gaza, although **Jordanian dinars (JD)** and **US dollars (US$)** are also sometimes accepted. Expect prices to increase by a significant margin when paying in foreign currency. **ATMs** are not nearly as common as in Israel, though most cities have at least one equipped bank. **Traveler's checks** and **credit cards** are not always recognized, so carry enough cash. Keep in mind that many of the banks and money exchange services may be closed on Fridays in Muslim areas.

KEEPING IN TOUCH

The **postal service** in the West Bank is, for now at least, part of the Israeli mail system. All major towns in the West Bank have at least one post office with Poste Restante. The Palestinian Authority in Jericho has its own postal system, with stamps that are currently good only for sending mail between Jericho and Gaza. The **telephone system** is also part of the Israeli network. All services, including collect and calling-card calls, are available from any private or public phone. Shekel-operated phones are available in the West Bank, but can be difficult to find. Blue-colored Telecard-operated phones are conveniently located in most post offices, where cards can also be purchased, but these phones do not accept Israeli Bezeq cards.

DRESS AND ETIQUETTE

Modest dress will make both men and women's experiences more enjoyable. Tourists may be invited into Palestinian homes, where hot spiced tea and coffee are accompanied by discussions of the *intifada* and occupation. Try to refrain from expressing strong political opinions. Jewish travelers should weigh out the situation before openly revealing their religion. Visitors should make their tourist (i.e. non-Israeli) status apparent.

HISTORY

The West Bank represents the most complex facet of the Arab-Israeli conflict, due to its relevance to three major groups: Palestinian Arabs, Israelis, and Jordanians. Palestinian Arabs form the region's largest indigenous group and have resided throughout Israel and the West Bank for hundreds of years. Jews lived in the West Bank long before the 1967 and even the 1948 wars. For the most part, Jews were drawn to the holy city of Hebron, but in 1929 they fled after an Arab massacre claimed 80 Jewish lives. Over 70% of Jordanians are of Palestinian origin.

The political region now called the West Bank was created in the 1948 Arab-Israeli War, when Jordan conquered the "west bank" of the Jordan River (see p. 269). The Jordanian government subsequently did little to develop the West Bank and discriminated against its Palestinian residents. Overall, Palestinians in the West Bank fared slightly better than those in the Egyptian-occupied Gaza Strip, since the fertile West Bank was economically vital to Jordan. In the 1967 Six-Day War (see p. 269), Israel captured the West Bank, placing the area under temporary military administration (except for East Jerusalem, which was annexed). Arab mayors and police kept their offices, Jordanian school curricula continued to be taught, public welfare programs were established, National Social Security payments made, and Israeli medical treatment instituted. Israeli occupation was not all benevolent, however. Because the area was administered under martial law, basic rights granted to Jews and Israeli Arabs were denied the Palestinians, who suffered curfews and mass arrests. Houses were destroyed in retaliation for the terrorist actions of one family member. There was no freedom of assembly—Palestinians could not have weddings without permits from Israeli authorities. Flying the Palestinian flag was illegal, and the infrastructure, schools, and public works of the West Bank were neglected in comparison with those of Israel proper. Palestinian attempts at establishing economic independence were thwarted. **Birzeit University** (see p. 440) was denied a building permit for years and shut down frequently. Israeli settlements in the West Bank were, and continue to be, a source of constant controversy. Some 160,000 Israeli Jews have settled in the West Bank since 1967. Launched by Labor governments eager to establish an Israeli presence in areas of strategic importance such as the Jordan Valley, the settlement project has been an ideological cornerstone of right-wing Likud governments since 1977. The settlements are motivated primarily by strategic considerations, but also by the desire to maintain the historical boundaries of *Eretz Yisrael* (the biblical land of Israel), an area including Israel, the West Bank, the Gaza Strip, and a bit beyond. Often strategically situated on hilltops overlooking Palestinian towns, some settlements resemble military installations more than housing developments.

In December 1987, a traffic accident in the Gaza Strip sparked the Palestinians of the occupied territories to begin the **intifada;** two decades of occupation, economic stagnation, and increasing Israeli settlement erupted into stone-throwing, demonstrations, the unfurling of the Palestinian flag, and other expressions of nationalism. The *intifada* (see p. 270) led to major changes in the nature of the Palestinian-Israeli conflict. The populist nature of the uprising and the televised suppression by the Israeli army managed to draw more international attention than decades of PLO terrorism. The *intifada* had stopped making headlines by the time of the 1991 **Gulf War,** when the PLO and most Palestinians supported Iraq, rather than supporting the US-led movement, like most Arab governments.

In the aftermath of the Gulf War, Middle Eastern governments became convinced that it was high time for a regional peace conference. Since the historic Madrid conference in October 1991, negotiations have gone on intermittently. Most recently, Israel's 20-year occupation of southern Lebanon came to a close. Current prime minister Ehud Barak hoped the pullout would indicate Israeli good will and encourage peace-talks with Syria (see **Recent History,** p. 271).

LITERATURE

Much recent Palestinian literature concerns the agony of foreign occupation and exile, touching also on the themes of reconciliation with the Israelis. **Ghassan Kanafani,** perhaps the greatest contemporary Palestinian fiction writer, recreates the desperation and aimlessness of the refugee in his short stories *All That Remains: Palestine's Children* and *Men in the Sun and Other Palestinian Stories.* His *Return to Haifa* is an electrifying account of a face-to-face encounter between an exiled Palestinian family and an elderly Jewish couple who are Holocaust survivors. The poetry of **Mahmoud Darwish** depicts Palestinians' attachment to the land. The poems of **Fouzi al-Asmar,** collected in *The Wind-Driven Reed and Other Poems,* share the longing for a homeland. **Jabra Ibrahim Jabra's** novel *The Ship* is engrossing, as is his autobiography *The First Well,* an idyllic account of his Christian upbringing in Bethlehem. In his *Wild Thorns,* **Sahar Khalifeh** describes an expatriate's return to Palestine and his conversion from an intellectual to an ideologically committed terrorist. Israeli Arab **Anton Shammas's** *Arabesques* documents Palestinian identity crises; Fawaz Turki's autobiographical tomes discuss life in exile. The works of **Liyana Badr, Raymonda Tawil,** and **Samih al-Qassem** all deserve note; most of these authors and others are translated in **Salma Khadra Jayyusi's** behemoth *Modern Palestinian Literature.*

BETHLEHEM   בית לחם   بيت لحم   ☎02

Bethlehem and its environs were the backdrop for some of history's quieter religious moments: Rachel's death, the love between Ruth and Boaz, the discovery of the shepherd-poet-king David, and of course, the pastoral birth of Jesus. Bethlehem, which is almost entirely Christian, and the surrounding villages of Beit Sahour and Beit Jala are home to most of the Palestinian Christian minority. The glow-in-the-dark Virgin Marys and plastic crowns of thorns may take crass commercialism to a new level, but some visitors still manage to see past the blinding flashbulbs to a site of true religious significance.

Besides being home to one of Christianity's most important sites, Bethlehem is a prime example of what independence can achieve. In 1995, Bethlehem celebrated Christmas for the first time under Palestinian rule. The changing of the guard has breathed new life into this town; grants from other countries have been pouring in. The most crowded and interesting time to visit Bethlehem is during a Christian holiday, especially Easter 2001, for which you should make hotel reservations well in advance (i.e. it might already be too late). Other times allow more personal space to explore and a more accurate portrait of life in Bethlehem.

✷🛈 ORIENTATION AND PRACTICAL INFORMATION

The three Wise Men followed a star to a peaceful manger; today's pilgrims can follow **Star St.** to bustling **Manger Sq.,** where most of the Christian sights are clustered. **Rachel's Tomb,** on the northern outskirts of Bethlehem, is a 30-minute walk (or NIS2 *service*) from there. Manger St. forks into Star St.; **Paul VI Rd.** branches off this, and a right turn leads into Manger Sq. Alternatively, take a *service* from Rachel's Tomb to **Bab al-Zaqaq,** the transportation hub for the region, at **Hebron Rd.** and Paul VI Rd. The walk from Bab al-Zaqaq to Manger Sq. takes 15 minutes. Star St. and **Najajreh St.** are home to the town's shopping district and open-air market.

Buses: Buses make the 8km trip from the Suleiman St. Station in East Jerusalem, right outside Damascus Gate to **Bab al-Zaqaq** (30min., daily every 15-30min. until 5pm, NIS2.50). Buses stop running after dark.

Taxis: Taxis are the only local transportation; you can find them on Beit Sahour Rd. behind the Peace Center. To get back to Jerusalem, take a taxi to Bab al-Zaqaq or Rachel's Tomb (NIS1.50) and flag down a Jerusalem-bound *service*. A private taxi from the checkpoint to Jerusalem is NIS25-30; set a price before you leave.

Tourist Office: PA Ministry of Tourism (☎276 66 77; fax 274 10 57), in the Peace Center in Manger Sq. Distributes a free PA **town map** with a glossy pamphlet of major sights, details about special events during Christmas and Easter, and transportation information. Open M-Sa 8am-6pm.

Tours: Alternative Tourism Group (ATG; ☎277 21 51; fax 277 22 11; email atg@p-ol.com; www.patg.org), in Beit Sahour, runs inexpensive tours of Palestinian cities and refugee camps throughout the West Bank. Prices are in the vicinity of $16 per day.

Currency Exchange: Mercantile Discount Bank (☎274 25 95), in Manger Sq. Open M-Th and Sa 8:30am-12:30pm, F 8:30am-noon. There are **no ATMs** for foreign bank cards in Bethlehem. Most services accept US dollars and many take credit cards as well.

Police Station: (☎274 49 35), but first try the **tourist police** (☎277 07 50 or 277 07 51), in Manger Sq. beneath the Andalus Hotel; another branch in the new bus station.

Hospital: Beit Jala Government Hospital (☎274 11 61), on Main St. (the continuation of Paul VI Rd.) on the Beit Jala side of Hebron Rd.

Internet Access: ICC Internet Center (☎276 58 48), on Manger St. just past the new bus station, has the fastest connection in the Manger Sq. area. NIS7 per 30min. Open M-Sa 9am-10:30pm, Su 10am-1pm. Further up Manger St., **Speed Net** (☎276 48 47), in the Middle East Building opposite Moradeh St., complements speedy computers with an espresso and cappucino maker. Open daily 10am-10pm.

Post Office: (☎274 27 92), in Manger Sq., beneath the Municipality Building. Open Sa-Th 8am-2:30pm. Send and receive mail via Israel and buy PA telecards and stamps.

▞ ACCOMMODATIONS

There's no problem finding a place to stay during the off-season, but at Christmas there's no room unless you reserve a year in advance. One attractive addition to Bethlehem's options is a **bed and breakfast** program intended to give individuals a taste of Palestinian family life at a reasonable cost.

Franciscan Convent Pension (Franciscaines de Marie; ☎274 24 41), on Milk Grotto St., on the left past the Grotto. Look for a set-back gray gate with small "White Sisters" plaque. Welcoming French nuns rent 3 sparkling flower- and Bible-bedecked rooms. Breakfast NIS20. Check-out 9am. Curfew 9pm; in winter 8:30pm. Reservations recommended. "Dorms" (for 2-3 people) NIS50; singles NIS100. No credit cards.

Azzaitune Guest House (☎/fax 274 20 16; cell ☎052 36 07 69), a 20min. walk from Manger Sq. Follow Paul VI Rd. away from Manger Sq. until it becomes Main St. on the other side of Hebron Rd.; after the intersection take the 2nd right. The closest thing Bethlehem has to a youth hostel, complete with clean, carpeted rooms and a kitchen for guests. Dorms NIS50/US$12; singles US$22; doubles US$35. No credit cards.

Casa Nova (☎274 39 80; fax 274 35 40), off Manger Sq., in a corner to the left of the basilica entrance. Modern rooms and plenty of hot water. Heated in winter. Reception 24hr. Check-out 8am. Flexible midnight curfew. Faxed reservations recommended. Bed and breakfast US$22 per person; half-board US$27; full board US$33; single supplement US$15. 5% service charge.

Al-Andalus Guest House (☎274 35 19; fax 276 56 74; email andalus@p-ol.com), in Manger Sq. across from the Peace Center. Basic rooms, all with fans, private baths, and views of Jerusalem or Manger Sq. Guests can use the kitchen. Bed and breakfast rooms US$25 per person, US$30 during peak times.

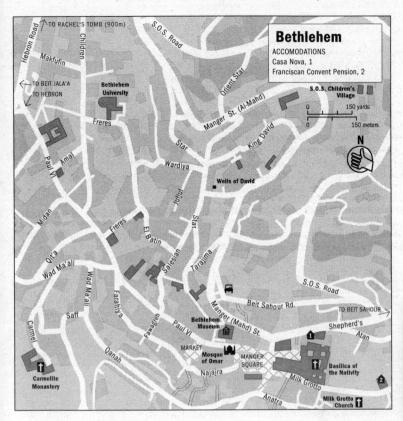

Bethlehem

ACCOMODATIONS
Casa Nova, 1
Franciscan Convent Pension, 2

Bethlehem Hotel (☎277 07 02; fax 277 07 06; email bhotel@p-ol.com; www.bethlehem-hotel.com), at the corner of Manger St. and S.O.S. Rd. Halfway between Rachel's Tomb and Manger Sq.; main entrance is downhill on S.O.S Rd. A modern hotel built especially for heavy 2000 tourism. Nice but antiseptic rooms, all with carpeting, TV, and A/C; some are handicapped accessible. Breakfast included; other meals US$10. Check-out noon. Singles US$50; doubles US$75; triples US$90. Children ages 2-6 50% discount, age 7-12 30% discount.

Tourist Bedouin Village (☎277 38 75; fax 277 38 76), in Beit Sahour's Shepherd's Valley, has tent accommodations with modern bath facilities and breakfast (US$12 per person). Occasional storytelling and Bedouin dinners. Open Apr.-Oct.

Alternative Tourism Group (ATG; ☎277 21 51; fax 277 22 11; www.patg.com). This B&B program overseen by ATG has 27 double rooms in private homes, all with clean private baths and some with telephones. NIS95 per person with breakfast. Lunch or dinner NIS25. Contact George Rishmawi at ATG in Beit Sahour.

🗂 FOOD

Cheap falafel and *shawarma* stands in Manger Sq. and on Manger St. provide *fuul* for church-hopping excursions. Bethlehem's one-and-only nightspot, **Balloons,** on Hebron Rd. near Rachel's Tomb, dishes up renowned pizza. They only serve soft drinks, but don't let that burst your balloon—the alcohol pours at **Memories,** the pub upstairs. (☎274 10 36. Open Sa-Th 1pm-1am.) **St. George,** in Manger Sq. next door to the post office, gets most of the tourist traffic from the basilica with its impressive bar and extensive menu. (☎274 37 80. Salads NIS18; omelettes NIS20; meat plates NIS35-50. Open daily 8am-6pm.) One of Bethlehem's nicer lunch options is **Sababa,** on Manger St., near the junction of Star St. Their set daily menu includes a salad, traditional main dishes, coffee, and dessert for NIS55. (☎274 40 06. Open daily 11am-4pm.) At **Al-Andalus Restaurant,** just off Manger Sq., around the corner from the affiliated guest house, affordable meals are disguised as "snacks." Hot dogs and hamburgers (NIS12-20) come with salad and fries. They offer a large variety of Middle Eastern foods for NIS28-45. Ask for a free, excellent map of Bethlehem, edited by the owner. (☎274 35 19; fax 276 56 74. Open daily 8am-midnight.) **Al-Atlal (The Ruins) Restaurant,** one block from Manger Sq. on Milk Grotto St., provides needed respite from the hordes. (☎274 11 04. Lamb *me'orav* (mixed grill) NIS35; cheese toast NIS16. Open daily noon-4pm and 8pm-midnight.)

◉ SIGHTS

There are two ways to "do" Bethlehem. Traditionally, tourists arrive from Israel, hop from one Christian holy place to another in several hours, and return to Jerusalem before dinner. Because no reliable public transportation is available, the best way to see the sights is to hire a guide with a vehicle for an afternoon. Guides gather in Manger Sq.; be sure to choose someone wearing a PA-issued ID tag. Tours should cost no more than US$10-12 per hour, including transportation. Guides will ask for double that, so be sure to bargain. To explore the villages and other West Bank cities from Bethlehem, contact ATG (see **Tours,** p. 430).

BASILICA OF THE NATIVITY

Manger Sq. is dominated by the Basilica of the Nativity, a massive basilica honoring the spot generally considered to be Jesus' birthplace and the oldest continuously used church in the world. Erected in 326 CE by Queen Helena, mother of Constantine, it was spared the Persian invasion (when virtually every other Christian shrine in the Holy Land was demolished) because of its mosaic of the three (Persian) wise men. The church lapsed into disrepair after the Crusader kingdom fell, but its importance as a holy shrine never waned; during the ensuing centuries, struggle for its control repeatedly led to bloodshed. In the 1840s, the church was restored to its former dignity, but squabbles between the various sects continue. An elaborate system of worship schedules, established in 1751, has worked through competing claims, but the confusion resulting from the Greek Orthodox Church's rejection of summer daylight savings time demonstrates the teetering balance of this arrangement. As of summer 2000, Catholic mass was held M-Sa at 6am, Armenian at 1:30pm, and Greek Orthodox at 4pm; Su has a schedule of its own. Check at the entrance to St. Catherine's Church for the exact times.

DOOR OF HUMILITY. Despite its impressive history, the Basilica of the Nativity is not particularly attractive from the outside. The main entrance and windows were blocked up as a safety precaution during medieval times. To enter, assume a kneeling position and step through the narrow Door of Humility—a remnant of Christian attempts to prevent Muslims from entering on horseback. Fragments of beautiful mosaic floors are all that remain of Queen Helena's original church. View them beneath the huge wooden trap doors in the center of the marble Crusader floor. England's King Edward IV offered the oak ceiling as a gift. The Russian royal family bequeathed the handsome icons adorning the altar in 1764.

GROTTO OF THE NATIVITY. The sanctuary beneath the church is the Grotto of the Nativity. Crosses are etched into the columns on both sides of the cramped doorway—religious graffiti from centuries of pilgrims. The focus of the hubbub is a silver star bearing the Latin inscription: *Hic De Virgine Maria Jesus Christus Natus Est* (Here, of the Virgin Mary, Jesus Christ was born). The 14 points represent the 14 stations of the Via Dolorosa (see p. 306). The star, added by Catholics in 1717, was removed by Greeks in 1847 and restored by the Turkish government in 1853. Quarrels over the star are said to have contributed to the outbreak of the Crimean War. *(In Manger Sq.,Tour guides often roam the square and nave; a reasonable fee is NIS15 for an hour-long tour with a licensed guide. Basilica complex open daily 5:30am-7pm; in winter 5am-5pm. Free, though donations are encouraged. Modest dress required.)*

OTHER SIGHTS

ST. CATHERINE'S CHURCH. Built by the Franciscans in 1881, this simple and airy church is a welcome contrast to the grim interior of the adjacent basilica. Superbly detailed wood carvings of the 14 stations of the cross line the walls. The first of the downstairs crypt rooms, the **Chapel of St. Joseph,** commemorates the carpenter's vision of an angel who advised him to flee with his family to Egypt. The burial cave of children slaughtered by King Herod (Matthew 2:6) lies below the altar and through the grille in the **Chapel of the Innocents.** Beyond the altar, a narrow hallway leads to the Grotto of the Nativity, although it is blocked by a thick wood door pierced by a peephole. During times of greater hostility between Christian sects, this glimpse was as close as Catholics could get to the Greek Orthodox shrine. To the right of the altar, a series of rooms contains celebrity sepulchres including the **Tomb of St. Jerome,** as well as those of St. Paula and her daughter Eustochia. These lead to the spartan cell where St. Jerome produced the **Vulgate,** the 4th-century translation of the Hebrew Bible into Latin. The Franciscan fathers conduct a solemn procession to the basilica and underground chapels every day. To join in the 20 minutes of Gregorian cantillation and Latin prayer, arrive at St. Catherine's by noon. St. Catherine's also broadcasts a **midnight mass** to a worldwide audience every Christmas Eve. *(Adjoins the basilica. Use the separate entrance to the left of the basilica entrance, or face the altar in the basilica and pass through one of the doorways in the wall on the left. Open daily 6:30am-8pm.)*

MILK GROTTO CHURCH. The cellar of this church is thought to be the cave in which the Holy Family hid when fleeing from Herod into Egypt. The cave and church take their names from the original milky white color of the rocks, most of which have now either been blackened by candle smoke or painted blue. According to legend, some of Mary's milk fell while she was nursing the infant Jesus, whitewashing the rocks. Today, women with fertility problems can request small packets of white dust as a charm. Male visitors may be slightly uncomfortable amid the women who come here to pray for fertility and the photo-diorama of suckling babies born to those whose prayers were rewarded. *(A 5-minute walk down Milk Grotto St. from the Basilica of the Nativity. Facing the line of stores in Manger Sq., turn left and take the narrow alleyway to the Franciscan flag; the grotto is on the right. ☎ 274 38 67. Open daily 8am-6pm; in winter 8am-5pm. If the door is locked, ring the bell.)*

MUSEUMS. The two adjacent stores that comprise the **Palestinian Heritage Center** display and sell traditional crafts. The small but interesting exhibit features a "traditional Palestinian sitting room" complete with handwoven carpets and teapots. The stores sell inexpensive needlework and other crafts, most of which are made by women from the Bethlehem area and nearby refugee camps. The **Bethlehem Museum** showcases Palestinian crafts, traditional costumes, and a 19th-century Palestinian home. *(Heritage Museum: on Manger St. near the intersection with Hebron Rd. ☎ 274 23 81. Open M-Sa 9am-7pm. Bethlehem Museum: off Star St., between the market and Manger Sq. ☎ 274 25 89. Open M-W and F-Sa 8am-5pm, Th 8am-noon. NIS8.)*

⚑ DAYTRIPS FROM BETHLEHEM

TOMB OF RACHEL. *Kever Raḥel* is a sacred site for Jews, a spot where synagogues have been built and destroyed throughout history. When Rachel died giving birth to Benjamin, Jacob is said to have erected a pillar upon her grave (Genesis 35:19-20). On one side are fervently praying Ḥasidic men, and on the other, weeping Yemenite women. The tomb, a timeless symbol of maternal devotion and suffering, is now revered as a place to pray for a child or a safe delivery.

There are separate entries for women and men. Women should dress modestly; men must don a paper *kippah*, available at the entrance. While the IDF has left Bethlehem, the Israeli government retains control of the Tomb of Rachel. The PA insists that the tomb is the property of the Islamic *waqf*, though the status quo leaves the tomb in the hands of the IDF. *(The tomb is on the northern edge of town on the road to Jerusalem, at the intersection of Manger St. and Hebron Rd., a 30min. walk from the Basilica of the Nativity. All buses between Jerusalem and Bethlehem or Hebron pass the tomb. ☎ 654 11 42. Open Su-Th 7:30am-4pm, F 7:30am-1:30pm.)*

BEIT SAHOUR. Beit Sahour, on the eastern edge of Bethlehem, is believed to be the setting for the biblical Book of Ruth, in which a wealthy local farmer falls in love with a poor young widow, a new convert to Judaism. Home to some 15,000 inhabitants, the town contains vast open stretches of grazing land, including the **Fields of Ruth.** The name of the village means "House of the Shepherds" in Hebrew, and Christian tradition holds that this is **Shepherd's Field,** where those tending their flocks were greeted by the angel who pronounced the birth of Jesus (Luke 2:8-12). A sign points left toward an alternate Shepherd's Field, promoted as the real thing by the Franciscans. The site includes a tiny chapel, monastery, and excavated Byzantine church. *(Most of the time, buses from the parking lot below Manger Sq. run to Beit Sahour (NIS1); from the drop-off, it's a 20min. walk to the site. You can also walk the 1½km from Bethlehem. A taxi costs NIS15.)*

HERODION. Herodion is one of the world's finest examples of well-preserved early Roman architecture. Eleven kilometers east of Bethlehem, the man-made, flat-topped mountain of Herodion arrests the eye with its startling silhouette. Much of the road between Herodion and Bethlehem crosses over the "Valley of Fire," where fathers sacrificed their first-born sons by fire in biblical times. It was also the site of the suicide of Judas, betrayer of Jesus. Built as a summer palace by King Herod, Herodion contained swimming pools and bathhouses, all of which have been carefully dug up. Herod's body is believed to be buried here, and although it has not yet been found, excavators have unearthed bones dating back to 2000 BCE (some of the oldest ever discovered) inside Kroutoon Cave.

There are two ways to ascend the mountain: the excruciating outdoor steps or the naturally air-conditioned 200 steps inside the mountain, carved into the cisterns and leading directly into the palace's central courtyard. At the top, the western defense tower is directly above the Kroutoon Cave. The red roofs below are those of the Jewish settlements of **Teqoa, Noqedim,** and **Ma'ale Amos,** where the prophet Amos is buried. Take the outside steps to get back down. The bridge was recently built directly over what used to be the palace's main gate. *(From Jerusalem, take Egged bus #166, which stops at the bottom of the hill, a 5-10min. walk from the entrance. A round-trip private taxi from Bethlehem should cost NIS30, including waiting time. Although located in the West Bank, Herodion is an Israeli National Park. cell ☎ 050 50 50 07. Open daily 8am-5pm; in winter 8am-4pm. NIS18, with ISIC NIS15.)*

JERICHO יריחו أريــحا ☎ 02

The first city to fly the Palestinian flag and the headquarters of the Palestinian Authority, Jericho vibrates with ground-breaking activity. Streets strewn with banners, flags, and portraits of Yassir Arafat convey Palestinian pride and optimism, which shines through in the hospitality and openness of the city's residents. Settled 10,000 years ago, Jericho is believed to be the world's oldest city. At 250m below sea level, it's also the world's lowest. Its location in the middle of the Judean Desert leaves Jericho brutally hot in the summer and pleasantly hot in the winter, making it a winter resort for vacationers as far back as the 8th century, when Syrian King Hisham built a magnificent winter palace here. Excavations at several sites around Jericho have been extensive, but besides several beautiful mosaic floors, the ruins themselves aren't that spectacular—after all, the city walls are famous for having tumbled down.

After Joshua destroyed the city with a blast of his trumpet (Joshua 6:20), Jericho remained in shambles for centuries. The oasis town was partially rebuilt in the days of King Ahab in the early 9th century BCE (I Kings 16:34), embellished by King Herod during the Hasmonean Dynasty, and further strengthened under Roman, Crusader, and Mamluk rule. The population skyrocketed after 1967, when thousands of Palestinian refugees fled here from Israel. Free from Jordanian control, the refugee camps were replaced by apartment buildings, and the standard of living drastically improved. Today Jericho is the site of several noteworthy million-dollar investment projects, including a new luxury resort popular with wealthy Palestinians, a cable-car/hotel complex at the foot of the Mount of Temptation, and the Oasis Casino, the region's very own mini-yet-majestic sin city. Jericho is under the custodianship of the Palestinian Authority and can be visited without difficulty. All travelers should dress modestly, and women travelers may feel safer with a male companion.

✳🛈 ORIENTATION AND PRACTICAL INFORMATION

Forty kilometers east of Jerusalem, Jericho is on the road to Amman, at the junction of the highway to Galilee (for information on crossing to **Jordan**, see p. 425). The quickest and most reliable way to get to Jericho is by **service** taxi. Direct transportation from Jerusalem (across the street from Damascus Gate) is possible, but expensive (NIS15) and infrequent. Take a *service* to Abu Dis instead (NIS2.50; coming out of Damascus Gate turn right and head toward the end of the line of taxis), get out at the gas station, and switch to a Jericho-bound *service* (NIS6), which will stop in the central square or at the Oasis Casino. There is no schedule—*service* taxis leave when full, and they fill most quickly during morning and afternoon rush hours. Repeat this process backwards to return to Jerusalem; from the casino, however, you might be better off going into Jericho first because *service* taxis usually only depart for Abu Dis or Jerusalem when full.

There is no public transportation within the city, but there are a multitude of yellow taxis. Hiring a taxi for several hours is the recommended way of seeing the sights, since the blistering heat most of the year makes even walkable distances unbearable. Pay no more than NIS30-40 per hour. A great way to see the sights on cooler days is by bike. **Zaki Sale and Rent Bicycle,** in the main square by the corner of al-Kastal, rents 21-speed mountain bikes with locks. Bring water and watch out for cars. (☎232 40 70. NIS3 per hr. or NIS12 per day. Open daily 8am-10pm.)

There's no official tourist office, but you can get free maps and information at the municipality building in the main square or at the **Elisha's Spring complex** (☎232 24 17; email info@jericho-city.org), across the parking lot from the old city. Exchange currency at the **Cairo Amman Bank,** in the main square (☎232 36 27. Open Sa-Th 8:30am-12:30pm.) The **police** are in the main square, next to the bank. (☎232 21 00 or 232 14 26. Open 24hr.) The **tourist police** are across from Elisha's Spring. (☎232 40 11. Open daily 8am-6pm.) **Arabi Pharmacy,** 74 Ein al-Sultan St., by Hisham's Palace Hotel, has the latest bedtime in town. (☎232 23 25. Open Sa-Th 8am-11pm.) If it turns out to be more serious, go to the **Palestinian National Authority Ministry of Health Clinic,** 51 Jerusalem Rd. just off the square. (☎232 24 06. Open Sa-Th 8am-2:30pm.) The **New Jericho Hospital** (☎232 19 66), farther down Jerusalem Rd., is open 24hr. Head down Amman St. from the police station to get to the **post office.** (☎232 25 74; fax 232 36 09. Open Sa-Th 8am-2pm.)

▮🍴 ACCOMMODATIONS AND FOOD

With only a few sights to see and a relatively easy commute to Jerusalem, there isn't much reason to sleep here. **Jerusalem Hotel** (also known as al-Quds Hotel), is down Amman St., about 1½km east of the city center, on the right. Its "dorms" (no more than 4 beds per room) are airy (fan, no A/C) and have shared baths. Upstairs, medium-sized rooms have A/C, satellite TV, and phone; most have balconies. (☎232 24 44; fax 232 13 29. Breakfast included. Check-out noon. Dorms US$25 per person. Singles US$60; doubles US$80; triples US$100.) **Jericho Resort Village,** off Qasr Hisham St. near Hisham's Palace, is a full-fledged resort complex with swimming pools, restaurants, cafes, bars, and luxurious lounge areas—a magnet for wealthy Palestinian families. (☎232 12 55; fax 232 21 89; email reservation@jericho-resort.com; www.jericho-resort.com. Breakfast included. Check-out noon. Singles US$100-120; doubles US$120-140. 4-person bungalows including kitchenette and sitting room US$140-150.) **Hisham's Palace Hotel,** on Ein al-Sultan St., close to the city center, isn't quite palace-like anymore. Rooms, hallways, and bathrooms are time-ravaged to the extreme and only borderline clean. Rooms have either A/C or fans; some have balconies and private baths. (cell ☎052 48 38 08. Flexible check-in and check-out. NIS30-80 per person, depending on season, type of room, and bargaining skills. No credit cards.)

Many cheap and tasty restaurants cluster around the city center. Falafel should be about NIS3, *shawarma* NIS6. Cheap fruit and vegetable bins are crowded in the southeastern corner of the square (near al-Kastal St.). The city's best restaurant, catering to native tastes and pockets, is **Abu Nabil,** under the red awning in the main square. A full lunch or dinner includes grilled meat, salad, pita, and hummus for NIS25. (☎232 21 60. Open daily 6am-midnight.) **Green Valley,** on Ein al-Sultan St., on the way to Hisham's Palace, has excellent local specialties in a well-touristed and spacious indoor-outdoor restaurant. (☎232 23 49. Live music on F and Sa nights in winter. Open daily 8am-midnight.)

◉ SIGHTS

Hire a taxi for several hours from the city center and beat the heat (NIS30-40 per hour; set a price in advance). Visit Hisham's Palace first, as a cluster of restaurants and a cooling spring near the ancient city provide a pleasant post-tour rest stop.

HISHAM'S PALACE. Begun in 724 CE and completed in 743, Hisham's Palace was ravaged only four years later by an earthquake. Known as Khirbet al-Mafjar in Arabic, the palace was designed for the Umayyad Caliph Hisham as a winter retreat from Damascus—although there is no evidence that the caliph ever actually spent any time here. The most renowned feature is a courtyard window in the shape of the six-pointed Umayyad star. In the "guesthouse," a beautifully preserved mosaic depicts a sinister tableau in which a lion devours a gazelle as its naive playmates frolic beneath the Tree of Life. Get a guide from the entrance to show you around (tip NIS5-10). *(To reach the palace from the square, head three kilometers north from Qasr Hisham St., following the signs to the turnoff at a guard post. Coming from ancient Jericho, head east on Jiftlik Rd., past the synagogue and the Ein al-Sultan refugee camp. After 1½km, turn right on the road back to Jericho; the turnoff to Hisham's Palace appears on the left. ☎232 25 22. Open daily 8am-6pm. NIS10, students NIS7, children NIS5.)*

ANCIENT JERICHO. Thought to be the oldest city in the world (as opposed to Damascus, the oldest continually inhabited city), ancient Jericho is now a heap of ruined walls. Called **Tel al-Sultan,** the mound contains layer upon layer of garbage from ancient (and modern) cities. Some of the finds date from the early Neolithic period, leading archaeologists to suspect that Jericho was inhabited as early as the 8th millennium BCE. The oldest fortifications are 7000 years old. A limited amount of excavation has exposed many levels of ancient walls, some of them 3½m thick and 5½m high. Imagination will have to substitute for visible splendor at this site, which is distinctly unimpressive. *(To get to ancient Jericho from the city center, follow Ein al-Sultan St. to its end. The entrance is through a parking lot around the corner, opposite the Elisha's Spring complex. From Hisham's Palace, two kilometers away, turn right onto the road that runs past the Palace (away from the city center), cross a narrow bridge, then take a left at the next junction, following the "Tel Jericho" signs. ☎232 29 35. Open daily 8am-6pm; in winter 8am-5pm. NIS10, students with ISIC NIS7, children NIS5.)*

MOSQUE OF NABI MUSSA. About eight kilometers from Jericho on the road to Jerusalem, the huge Mosque of Nabi Mussa stands in a sea of sand on a hill a short distance from the road, topped with a complex of white domes. The mosque was built in 1269 CE on a spot revered throughout the Muslim world as the grave of the prophet Moses. Islamic tradition holds that Salah al-Din had a dream about the location of the place where God carried the bones of Moses. The tomb is said to have special powers—run your hands over the velvet cloth of Moses' Tomb while making a wish and see for yourself. Across from the tomb, stairs lead upward into a minaret with incredible views of the surrounding Judean desert. Ask the souvenir vendors to unlock the gate if it is wired shut. *(The only way to visit is by car or taxi (NIS40 from Jericho). To get to the mosque, head toward Jerusalem about five kilometers, then turn left at the sign, and follow the road for another five kilometers. Open daily 8am-sunset. Free but donations welcome.)*

MONASTERY. An imposing Greek Orthodox monastery stands on the edge of a cliff among the mountains west of Jericho; the peak is believed to be the New Testament's **Mount of Temptation,** where the Devil tried to tempt Jesus. The complex of buildings stands before a grotto, said to be the spot where Jesus fasted for 40 days and 40 nights at the end of his ministry (Matthew 4:1-11). Three Greek monks now live in the monastery, built in 1895. The summit of the mountain, named **Qarantal** after the Latin word for "forty," is also a pedestal for the Maccabean **Castle of Dok,** beside which lie the remains of a 4th-century Christian chapel. *(The monastery can be reached by climbing up the mountain from the base, not far from the ancient city; the hike takes under an hour, but bring plenty of water. A much easier way up is to take the téléphérique (see below), which still requires a short hike to reach the monastery. Open M-F 9am-1pm and 2-5pm, Sa 9am-2pm, Su 10am-2pm. Modest dress required.)*

SULTAN TOURIST CENTER AND ELISHA'S SPRING. Papayas, grapes, oranges, bananas, and mint thrive behind the spring. A new US$10 million project for attracting tourism includes a hotel (not yet completed as of summer 2000), souvenir shops, restaurants, and a **cable car** ("téléphérique") that saves tourists the difficult, albeit scenic, 45-minute hike up the Mount of Temptation. The 5-minute ride goes over the old city ruins and provides stunning views of the valley and mountains; the view can be further enjoyed from the **Sultan Coffee Shop** at the top. *(Opposite the entrance to Ancient Jericho. ☎ 232 15 90. Open daily 8am-7pm. Cable car round-trip ticket US$8, students US$6, children US$5; one-way ticket US$5.)*

🎵 ENTERTAINMENT

The beautiful public **Spanish Garden,** on Amman St., near the center of town, was built recently through the contributions of the Spanish government. Reminiscent of a medieval Andalusian *hadeeqa*, the garden livens up after 6pm, when families, small children, and teenagers show up to enjoy Arabic music, coffee, and *argeileh.* A small cafe serves inexpensive snacks next to an game-room. (☎ 232 39 31 or cell ☎ 050 51 55 18. Open daily sunset-1am; in winter sunset-9pm. NIS2, children NIS1.) Few visitors to this city of temptation can resist the **Oasis Casino Hotel,** several kilometers before the city center. This state-of-the art casino, with the full array of slot machines, blackjack, poker, and other tables, would hold its head high even in Las Vegas. All gambling is in US dollars, which can be exchanged from any currency at the door. (☎ 231 11 11. Min. bids at most tables US$10-25, though some are US$5. No T-shirts. Passports required for entrance. Open 24hr.)

🏃 DAYTRIP FROM JERICHO: WADI QELT

Threading 28km between imperious limestone cliffs and undulating ridges of bone-white chalk, the three fresh-water springs of Wadi Qelt nourish wildlife and lush greenery, 20 minutes outside of Jerusalem. A string of murders, presumably political, took place here in the mid-90s, but fortunately the last few years have been peaceful and problem-free; nevertheless, it's not a good idea to hike in the *wadi* alone or after dark. **SPNI** offers one-day tours focusing on both natural and artificial attractions in the *wadi.* (☎ (03) 638 86 36 or (02) 624 46 05. Departs Monday from Tel Aviv at 8am, Jerusalem at 9am; US$59.) Bring 4-5L of water per person. The most interesting and accessible section of the *wadi* extends from the spring of Ein Qelt, past the 6th-century St. George's Monastery, and down into Jericho, 10km east. The trek takes about four hours. The best place to start is at the turnoff from the Jerusalem-Jericho highway about nine kilometers west of Jericho, marked by the orange sign for "St. George's Monastery." *Service* taxis to Jericho, Ein Gedi, and Allenby Bridge stop here on request. By car, it is possible to skip the hike and drive most of the way to St. George's Monastery.

St. George's Monastery dates from the 5th or 6th century CE. Byzantine mosaics decorate the floor of the church; look for the likeness of a two-headed eagle, the Byzantine symbol of power. According to tradition, the monastery occupies the site of the cave where St. Joachim took refuge to lament the infertility of his wife Hannah. An angel told him to return to Hannah, who then gave birth to the Virgin Mary. The neighboring **St. John's Church** houses a spooky collection of skulls and bones of monks slaughtered when the Persians swept through in 614 CE. The Greek Orthodox monks who maintain the monastery can refill canteens for a journey into Jericho. (Open M-Sa 8am-1pm and 3-5pm; in winter 8am-1pm and 3-4pm. Modest dress required; modest donation desired.) On the way to Jericho from St. George's, the ruins of **Tel Abu Alaya** (also called **Herodian Jericho**) are on the right. The palaces here, used by the Hasmoneans and later by King Herod, boast decorated walls, nearby bath houses, and pools.

RAMALLAH رام الله ☎02

Perched 900m above sea level, Ramallah, along with its smaller sister city al-Bireh, is famous for its cool, pleasant mountain air. Before 1967, the then-prosperous town was a summer haven for Arabs from Jordan, Lebanon, and the Gulf region. With vacationers long gone by the time of the *intifada*, Ramallah and the energetic young intellectuals at nearby Birzeit University joined Nablus as leaders of West Bank resistance. Now under PA control, the city has become a transportation hub and will replace Gaza as the administrative hub of the PA when Palestinian self-rule expands. It already houses several important Palestinian Authority offices, including the Ministries of Transportation and Education.

Ramallah is known for its religiously relaxed atmosphere (alcohol flows freely and movie theaters are well attended) and the cafes along its main streets. It is, without question, the cultural capital of the West Bank, with a highly educated and fashionable population. It is also the hub of Palestinian feminist activity; the city's women frequently attend university rather than marry early, and several women-run cafes are used to fund local feminist organizations.

🛈 PRACTICAL INFORMATION

Due to its location 16km north of Jerusalem and the frequent closures of East Jerusalem roads, Ramallah has become a transportation hub. It is possible to get from Ramallah to most northern West Bank towns by direct *service*. From **Jerusalem**, take a *service* from outside Damascus Gate (20min., NIS3.50) or an Arab bus from the station on Nablus Rd. (40min., NIS2). Buses and *service* to Jerusalem leave from the second floor of the bus station on al-Nahda St., just off **Manara Circle** ("al-Manara"), the town's epicenter. The last bus leaves at about 5pm.

Tours: The Palestinian Association for Cultural Exchange (PACE; ☎295 88 25; fax 298 68 54; email pace@palnet.edu), on Nablus Rd. in al-Bireh, organizes full- and half-day tours throughout the West Bank and Gaza Strip. Full day in Ramallah and vicinity NIS120. Also serves as an unofficial tourist office.

Currency exchange: Money changers and banks can be found on all major streets and at Manara Circle. The only bank that accepts foreign ATM cards is **HSBC,** at the corner of Jaffa St. and al-Rashid St., downhill from al-Bardouni's Restaurant.

Police: (☎295 70 20), on al-Nahda St., past the al-Wehdeh Hotel from Manara Circle.

Hospital: The **Ramallah General Hospital** (☎995 65 61 or 995 65 62) is more accessible than Ramallah's **pharmacies,** which close at 8pm or earlier.

Internet Access: Carma Cyber Club (☎298 48 54), on the 6th floor of the Lo'lo'at al-Manara building, near Manara Circle on Main St. NIS4 per hr. Open Sa-Th 8am-1am, F 3pm-1am. **Leader Net** (☎296 52 31), on the 6th floor of the Burj al-Sa'a Building in Mughtarbin Sq. NIS5 per hr. Open Sa-Th 9am-midnight, F noon-midnight.

Post office: (☎295 66 04), on Park St., off Main St., downhill from Rukab's Ice Cream, sells beautiful Palestinian stamps and serves the rest of the world with Israeli stamps. Open Sa-Th 8am-2:30pm.

ACCOMMODATIONS

Although a night in Ramallah is very worthwhile, accommodations are expensive compared with nearby Jerusalem. There are no true hostels in Ramallah.

Panorama Inn (☎/fax 295 68 08), on Jaffa St., downhill from Al-Bardouni Restaurant near the Faisal St. intersection. Not too far from the center of town but surprisingly quiet with a sunny patio. Rooms with private bath, TV, and phone. Some with balcony and/or small fridge; large balcony in the hall on both floors. Knowledgeable and helpful staff. Breakfast included. Check-out noon. Singles NIS120; doubles NIS150.

Al-Wehdeh Hotel (☎298 04 12; fax 295 48 72), on al-Nahdah St. one block from Manara Circle. Ramallah's cheapest accommodation and also the most central, if you don't mind the noise from the street (it does quiet down eventually). Recently renovated. Rooms with TV, fans, and private bath; some with balconies. Breakfast included. Check-out flexible. Singles NIS100; doubles NIS150; long-term discounts available.

Al-Hajal Hotel (☎/fax 298 67 59), off Jaffa Rd. opposite the Ramallah park. Spacious rooms with satellite TV, fan, phone, and private bath, but not worth the price for just one person. Breakfast included. Check-out noon. Singles US$40; doubles US$55.

Royal Court Suite Hotel (☎296 40 40; fax 296 40 47; email rcshotel@rcshotel.com; www.rcshotel.com), on the corner of Jaffa St. and Faisal St., next to the Panorama Inn. Snazzy new luxury hotel. All rooms have kitchenettes, balconies, A/C, cable TV, phones, Internet access lines (you supply the laptop), minibars, safe boxes, and even hair dryers. Breakfast included. 24hr. reception. Single US$69; double US$99.

FOOD

Ramallah's streets are lined with falafel and *shawarma* stands. Good, inexpensive restaurants look down on the city from the tops of the buildings all around Manara Circle, especially along Main St. Most restaurants serve international dishes as well as traditional Palestinian cuisine. Ramallah's hip cafes attract Arabs from all over the West Bank and even Israelis from across the green line.

Rukab's Ice Cream (☎295 64 67), at the corner of Main St. and al-Exhibition St., one block from Manara Circle. Possibly the best ice cream in the hemisphere; their gum-thickened, gooey goodness comes in a rainbow of blissful flavors. Try the popular pistachio. Tiny cones NIS3; large, multi-flavored cones NIS9. Open daily 8am-1am.

Angelo's (☎295 64 08), a left turn off Main St. one block after Rukab's; the restaurant is on the corner. Flings pizza (small cheese NIS20; large "Angelo's Supreme" NIS55) into the air and onto the plates of plucky budget travelers. The garlic bread (NIS8 per basket) is a local favorite. Open daily 11am-midnight.

Al-Bardouni (☎295 14 10), on Jaffa St., several blocks from Manara Circle. A stone's throw from the city center, but in a quiet part of town. Especially beautiful (and packed) on sunny afternoons. Salads NIS8-12; BBQ dishes NIS38-50; *musakhan* (traditional dish with half a chicken) NIS35. Open daily 11am-midnight.

Tal Al-Qamar (☎298 79 05), on the 5th floor of the Nasser Building on Main St., on the right, one block past Rukab's. Beautiful Arab cafe with a terrific view serves well-priced sandwiches (NIS15) and grilled meats (NIS25-50). Su-W live *oud* after 9pm. Th nights live Arabic singing. Open daily noon-1am.

👁 🎵 SIGHTS AND ENTERTAINMENT

The main attraction is the city itself; on Saturdays, Manara Circle is a crammed jungle. For a more historical view, the **Palestinian Folklore Museum,** in the town of al-Bireh a few blocks away, exhibits traditional costumes, handicrafts, and rooms of a Palestinian house. (☎240 28 76. Open Sa-Th 9am-2:30pm.) The **al-Siraj Theatre** (☎995 70 37) near Clock Circle, the **Ashtar Theatre** (☎82 72 18) on Radio St., and the **Popular Arts Cinema** (☎995 38 91) on al-Bireh St. produce performing arts and dance: call or ask around town for details. **Al-Walid Cinema,** on al-Nahda St., screens three films daily and caters to a predominantly male clientele. There's a **swimming pool** at Ramallah First Sarriyeh. It is in lower Ramallah; walk about 25 minutes along Main St. or take a taxi. (☎995 20 91. Tu women only. NIS15.)

▤ NIGHTLIFE

On weekends, many restaurants offer live music (in particular the *oud,* a bassy Middle Eastern stringed instrument). As comparatively liberal as Ramallah may be, local single women rarely congregate in the evenings unchaperoned; nevertheless, it is perfectly acceptable for foreign women to go out.

> **Rumours** (☎295 37 70), in the basement of a building on Main St., on the left, one block past Rukab's. Stylish cafe/bar/restaurant, with an extensive alcohol menu. Sex on the Beach NIS18. International cuisine NIS25-60. Tables are cleared Saturday nights for one of Ramallah's only weekly dance parties; DJ mixes European and Arabic pop. Occasional live performances. Open Su-F noon-midnight, Sa noon-3am.

> **Mocha Rena** (☎298 14 60), on Mafad St., off Main St., to the right before Rukab's. The funky, modern atmosphere in this French-Italian cafe attracts a suave, young crowd. One of the few places in Ramallah where you can get a breakfast that doesn't involve salad (pancakes NIS10-18; omelettes NIS18). Lunches and dinners run about NIS15-35; a slice of delicious NY-style cheesecake is NIS15. Open daily 9am-midnight.

> **Cafe Ole** (☎298 41 35), on the second floor of a building on al-Anbyara St., off Main St., a block from Manara Circle. There is no food here. One of Ramallah's most popular bars, with Thursday night disco parties (cover NIS25, includes 1 beer) and drunken revelry all other nights (no cover). Open daily 4pm-midnight, Th until 2am or later.

▶ DAYTRIP FROM RAMALLAH: BIRZEIT بيرزيت

Twelve kilometers northwest of Ramallah is the extensive campus of **Birzeit University,** the largest university in the West Bank. Birzeit's 2500 students have a history of vocal opposition to the Israeli occupation; the university was often shut down by the Israeli Army during the 1980s and was closed altogether from the first years of the *intifada* until April 1992. Today, Birzeit remains a vital presence. The university takes pride in its history and its strong leadership position in the West Bank, and it has even developed an Internet training program and an extensive website (www.birzeit.edu). Foreign students can study at the university through the Palestinian and Arab Studies (PAS) Program. For details, see **Alternatives to Tourism,** p. 42. *(From Ramallah, take a Birzeit-bound service from Manara Circle for NIS3.)*

AL-IZARIYYEH (BETHANY) العزرية

Between Jerusalem and Jericho, near Abu Dis. Take a service from Jerusalem's Damascus Gate (NIS2.50) or from Jericho's central square (NIS7); ask for al-Izariyyeh (ih-zar-EE-yeh). Service stop at the gas station next to the road to al-Quds University. The sites are east, along the main road. Women should dress modestly and travel in groups.

A relatively prosperous Palestinian village, Bethany is sacred to Christians as the home of Lazarus and his sisters Mary Magdalene and Martha. Jesus performed one of his best-known miracles here, raising Lazarus from the dead (John 11:1-44). Signs and souvenir vendors point tourists left up a small road to the Franciscan

New Church of St. Lazarus. Built in 1954, it marks a spot where Jesus was supposed to have slept. Excavations near the church have unearthed shrines dating back to the 4th century. The excavations are unlit—bring a light. (☎ 674 92 91. Church and excavations open daily Apr.-Sept. 8-11:30am and 2-6pm; Oct.-Mar. 8-11:30am and 2-5pm. Donations accepted.)

Signs from the Franciscan Church point uphill to the first-century **Tomb of Lazarus.** When the Crusaders arrived, they built a church over Lazarus's tomb, a monastery over Mary and Martha's house, and a tower over Simon the Leper's abode. In the 16th century, Muslims erected a mosque over the shrine, and in the following century, Christians dug another entrance to the tomb so they too could worship there. The tomb does not contain Lazarus's body—although some believe that he was re-buried in the same spot when he died again 30 years later. Descend the steps and stoop down to observe. (Tomb open daily 8am-7pm. Someone will ask you for a donation; NIS2 is appropriate.)

HEBRON חברון الخليل

Service leave frequently from the parking lot across the street from Damascus Gate in Jerusalem (45min., NIS7). From Bethlehem, service leave from Bab al-Zaqaq, at the corner of Hebron Rd. and Paul VI Rd. (30min., NIS6). To find a service back to Jerusalem or Bethlehem, take the right fork uphill from the center of town. Security has been very tight since the shootings several years ago by a Jewish extremist. All Jews are officially barred from entering the mosque portion of the building, and all entrants are required to present a passport (without a Jewish-sounding last name) and pass through several metal detectors. Modest dress required. Mosque closed F; synagogue open M-F, Jews only Sa.

Today, Hebron is the most important industrial center in the West Bank. While promised security as part of the redeployment agreements, the enclave of about 500 Israelis who live here engenders strong feelings of resentment from the Palestinian population. As of summer 2000, relations were relatively peaceful; nevertheless, all visitors to Hebron should make their tourist status as obvious as possible.

While the city lags behind other West Bank destinations in terms of Western influences and infrastructure, it is not without tourist appeal. For the intrepid traveler, this is *terra incognita* waiting to be explored. Tour agencies that offer full- or half-day trips to Hebron (sometimes combined with Bethlehem) include **Alternative Tours** (☎ 628 32 82 or cell ☎ 052 86 42 05; 6hr., NIS70), leaving from the Jerusalem Hotel in East Jerusalem; **PACE** (☎ 298 68 54; 10hr., NIS170), leaving from their office in Ramallah; and **ATG** (☎ 277 22 11; full- or half day, price and length depend on group size and length of trip), leaving from Beit Sahour. Call for schedules.

The primary tourist site in Hebron, the half-synagogue, half-mosque **Tomb of the Patriarchs** is thought to lie directly above the underground tombs of Abraham, Isaac, Rebecca, Jacob, and Leah. The tomb of Abraham is visible through bars from both sides; the tombs of Isaac and Rebecca, however, are entirely within the mosque. The cave itself may not be visited but can be seen through an opening in the floor of the mosque, in front of Abraham's tomb. While in the same room, note the huge, oak lectern from which the *imam* delivers the Friday sermon. Added by Salah al-Din in the 12th century, it is one of the few in the world carved from a single block of wood. In the same room, the longest Herodian cut stone ever discovered forms part of the walls. More than 4m in length, it lies in the southeast corner of the room. Lift the carpet to get a glimpse or ask someone to point it out.

GAZA غزة

The distance separating Israel from the Gaza Strip is covered in a one-minute car ride from one side of the border checkpoint to the other. Once in Gaza City, however, it becomes apparent that the short distance from Israel's booming industrial centers to Gaza City's Palestine Square sets the two regions worlds apart. A 46km long and 6-10km wide sliver along the Mediterranean coast, the Gaza Strip contains some of the most densely populated areas of the world. Population has increased dramatically in recent years, swelling to more than one-million people with an influx of over 570,000 Palestinian refugees since 1951.

Gaza's history stretches back to 3000 BCE, when it was inhabited by Arab Canaanites. It grew as a stopping point for traders traveling from Africa and the Sinai to the southwest and from parts of the Middle East and Asia to the east. The Prophet Muhammad's grandfather, Hashem ibn Abd Manaf, is said to have been one such trader. He died when passing through Gaza City and is purportedly buried in one of the city's mosques (see p. 446). Gaza is perhaps most well-known for its history of occupation and uprising under Israel. The region was administered by Egypt from 1948 until the 1967 Six-Day War. Refugees flooded the area after the Israeli occupation of that year, and of the 770,000 refugees living in Gaza today, over 420,000 continue to live in the overcrowded UN-sponsored camps. The *intifada* (see p. 270) began in 1987 in Gaza in the Jabalya camp near Gaza City. The peace process intensified with the onset of the *intifada*, and the Oslo and Cairo agreements of 1994 placed the Palestine Authority in control of the Gaza Strip.

Gaza now seeks to reinvigorate its long history as an intercontinental crossroads, as evidenced by widespread construction and the growing numbers of international trade and investment signs that line Gaza City's streets. Renewed attempts are being made to rehabilitate refugee camps with the help of the UN, the European Union, and other international resources. Tourist officials hope that the sea and beaches will entice crowds of visitors. However, it is the disorderly everyday life of Gaza's present—the mosques, churches, and unearthed archaeological finds that blend haphazardly into side-streets and vending stalls—that makes for the most fascinating and affordable random wandering for travelers. Gaza throbs with the activity of its capital's outdoor markets, chokes in the dust and cramped quarters of the refugee camps, and embraces its visitors with hospitality and an eagerness to communicate the experience of life in the strip.

 SAFETY WARNING. Since 1994, the Gaza Strip has been governed by the autonomous Palestine Authority (PA). While Israeli citizens cannot travel into Gaza without special permission, foreign tourists can generally visit without problems. Travel in the Gaza Strip is usually perfectly **safe,** though tourists should register with their respective consulates in Israel before going and should keep abreast of current events in the region so as to avoid visiting during times of unrest or tension. Women must dress modestly—long sleeves and a long skirt—and men should not wear shorts. Have your **passport** on hand at all times.

BORDER CROSSINGS

At press time, **Erez** was the only border checkpoint open for crossing from Israel into Gaza. Passing through the checkpoint is relatively easy for foreign tourists. From **Jerusalem,** *service* taxis meet across from Damascus Gate and go directly to the checkpoint (1hr.; infrequent, depart when full; NIS30). Though it is not possible to enter Gaza by car, it is helpful to understand the system of colored **license plates** that differentiates vehicles (see **West Bank: Getting Around: Cars,** p. 426, for an explanation of the various plates).

Crossing the checkpoint takes three steps. First, Israeli soldiers will inspect your passport and record the reason for and proposed length of your stay in Gaza. They will then give you a slip of paper for presentation when entering Gaza. Taxis cross the border for NIS10, but the walk is very short. After crossing into Gaza, your information will once again be entered into a ledger. On the Gaza side of the checkpoint, taxis heading into Gaza City abound. A *service* taxi should cost NIS5 to Palestine Square on the main street, **Omar al-Mukhtar.** A *special* taxi can cost anywhere from NIS20-50.

GETTING AROUND

The bus system in Gaza Strip tends to be erratic, slow, and uncomfortably warm. Taxis are far more convenient and almost as cheap. Within Gaza City, where there is no intracity bus service, seemingly half of all cars serve as taxis. *Special* taxis are more expensive than *service* (group) taxis. Rides anywhere along Omar al-Mukhtar St., which runs from the Palestine Sq. market to the hotel strip along the beach, cost NIS1. Destinations off the main road will cost more; pay NIS1 and negotiate an additional fare upon entering the taxi. Buses and taxis to destinations in the Gaza Strip outside of Gaza City, such as Khan Yunis and Rafah, leave from a parking lot in Palestine Square, just beyond the Gaza City municipality building. Long yellow *service* taxis depart whenever they fill with passengers.

LANGUAGE AND KEEPING IN TOUCH

Do not exercise any newly-gained knowledge of Hebrew during your stay; counter any taunting *"shalom"* with an Arabic *"marhaba."* Many people, especially children, are eager to practice their English on a native speaker. For some basic Arabic words and phrases, see the **Arabic Phrasebook,** p. 700.

The blue public phones in the Gaza Strip operate on phone cards that can be purchased in small shops and groceries throughout Gaza (NIS15-60). Phone calls can be made from hotels as well, but are more expensive.

GAZA CITY ☎ 07

Despite an initial assault on the senses by the bustle, noise, sights, and smells of the city, visitors soon settle into the remarkably laid-back rhythm of urban life. Roaming around the centers of activity brings a glimpse of present-day life but also offers encounters with the city's architectural and cultural treasures.

■✦🛈 ORIENTATION AND PRACTICAL INFORMATION

Taxis from the Erez checkpoint let off in **Palestine Sq.** *(Midan Filisteen)*, the site of the main market, the Gaza City municipality building, taxis and buses to other destinations in the Gaza Strip, and many of the historical sights of the city. The main street, **Omar al-Mukhtar St.,** runs from Palestine Sq. to the coast. Almost all hotels are in the **Remal** (beach) district of the city, lined up along the coastal road **Ahmed Orabi,** which forms a T-junction at the end of Omar al-Mukhtar St. Another commercial center is built around the **Unknown Soldier Garden,** a grassy and flowered walkway median that divides the lanes of Omar al-Mukhtar St. Only major streets have both English and Arabic street signs and establishments are rarely numbered. Taxis along Omar al-Mukhtar St. cost NIS1.

Flights: Gaza Airport (☎ 213 5696 or 213 4228), near Rafah. **EgyptAir** (☎ 282 51 80) is on Jala'a St. at the corner with al-Wihda St. Flights to **Cairo** (NIS240/US$80 one-way, NIS668/US$167 round-trip). Cash only. **Royal Jordanian** (☎ 282 54 03) flies to Amman (US$120 one-way, US$190 round-trip). **Palestinian Airlines** (☎ 282 28 00) also flies to Cairo (US$142 one-way) and other destinations.

Buses: In Palestine Sq., in front of where the taxis leave. **Gaza Bus Company** (☎ 282 26 16) sends non-A/C buses to **Rafah** (1½hr., NIS2.50).

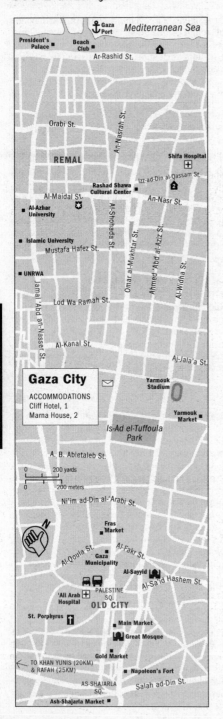

Gaza City

Mediterranean Sea

President's Palace

Beach Club

Gaza Port

Ar-Rashid St.

Orabi St.

REMAL

Ar-Nasrah St.

Shifa Hospital

Rashad Shawa Cultural Center

Izz-ad-Din al-Qassam St.

Al-Maidal St.

An-Nasr St.

Al-Azhar University

Islamic University

Mustafa Hafez St.

Al-Shohada St.

Omar al-Mukhtar St.

Ahmed 'Abd al-Aziz St.

Al-Widha St.

UNRWA

Lod Wa Ramah St.

Jamal 'Abd an-Nasser St.

Al-Kanal St.

Aj-Jala'a St.

Gaza City

ACCOMMODATIONS
Cliff Hotel, 1
Marna House, 2

Yarmouk Stadium

Yarmouk Market

Is-Ad el-Tuffoula Park

A. B. Abietaleb St.

0   200 yards
0   200 meters

Ni'im ad-Din al-'Arabi St.

Fras Market

Al-Fakr St.

Al-Qoula St.

Gaza Municipality

Al-Sayyid

Al-Sa'id Hashem St.

'Ali Arab Hospital

PALESTINE SQ.

OLD CITY

St. Porphyrus

TO KHAN YUNIS (20KM)
& RAFAH (25KM)

Main Market

Great Mosque

Gold Market

Napoleon's Fort

AS SHAJARLA SQ.

Salah ad-Din St.

Ash-Shajarla Market

GAZA

Taxis: *Service* taxis (NIS1 for trips along Omar al-Mukhtar St.) depart when full to **Rafah** (45min., NIS4.50). **Imad** (☎286 40 00) will pick up passengers.

Car Rental: Yafa Rent-a-Car (☎282 51 27), on Omar al-Mukhtar St. one block toward Palestine Sq. from Ahmed Orabi St. Look for the blue sign on the left side of the street. One day car rentals NIS120-200/ US$30-50. Min. age 24. Open Sa-Th 8am-10pm.

Tourist Office: Gaza City's **Public Relations and Information Office** (☎282 47 00), beginning of Palestine Sq., near the Arab Bank and under an English sign. Enter from Omar al-Mukhtar St. through the gate for the Municipality Building and walk through the parking lot and under the overhang to the door on the left. Open Su-Th 8am-2:30pm.

Human Rights Organizations: UNRWA (☎677 74 88), on Gamal Abd al-Nasser St. Take a taxi to the "UN." Once there, go to the public information office. Offers tours to **Jabalya refugee camp,** a 15-minute ride from the city. Call in advance to arrange a tour—the office has limited finances. Donations requested. Open Su-Th 7:30am-3pm.

Currency Exchange: Private agencies on Omar al-Mukhtar St. and near Palestine Sq. change money for no commission: look for dollar signs. Open Sa-Th 9am-9pm. **Western Union** (☎282 10 77), on Omar al-Mukhtar St., 20m past the Bank of Palestine toward Palestine Sq. Open Sa-W 8:30am-12:30pm and 2-4pm, Th 8:30am-12:30pm.

Pharmacy: Masoud (☎286 18 79), at the corner of Charles de Gaulle St. and Omar al-Mukhtar St. Open daily 7:30am-midnight. Call 24hr. for emergency.

Hospitals: Ahli Arab Hospital (☎282 03 25), on the first street to the right just beyond the bus and taxi stand in Palestine Sq. **Shifa Hospital** (☎286 55 20), on Ez al-Din al-Qassam St. From the beach, turn left on Omar al-Mukhtar St. just before the Rashad Shawwa Cultural Center.

Telephones: El-Baz (☎286 01 20), on Omar al-Mukhtar St. just after Canal St., on the left, coming from the beach. International calls NIS4 per min. Open Sa-Th 9am-10pm.

Post Office: 183 Omar al-Mukhtar St., next to the Municipal garden, halfway between the Unknown Soldiers' Park and Palestine Sq. Palestinian (not Israeli) stamps are issued here. Open Su-Th 8am-2:30pm.

ACCOMMODATIONS

Gaza City has the only accommodations in the Gaza Strip, along the coastal Ar-Rashid road in the Remal district, a short walk from the end of Omar al-Mukhtar St. Proprietors generally speak English and are eager to offer suggestions of sights and places to eat. ■**Marna House,** on Ahmed Abd al-'Aziz St. From Palestine Sq., walk along Omar al-Mukhtar St. and turn right on Ez al-Din al-Qassam St., just past the Rashad Shawwa Cultural Center. Ahmed Abd is on the right and the hotel is on the left. The lounge downstairs has English books on Gaza, maps of Gaza City, and the infamous talking bird. Rooms are tastefully decorated, with bath, satellite TV, and A/C. (☎282 26 24 or 282 33 22. Singles NIS200/US$50; doubles NIS240/US$60. Traveler's checks accepted.) **Adam Hotel,** on Ahmed Orabi St., 120m past Cliff Hotel, has small rooms with red decor, abundant mirrors, private bath, TV, and A/C. (☎286 69 76. Reception 24hr. Singles NIS160/US$40; doubles NIS220/US$55. NIS20/US$5 student discount. Cash only.) At **Palestine Hotel,** on Ahmed Orabi St., 100m past the Cliff Hotel, all rooms behind the glitzy facade have balconies with a seaside view, as well as satellite TV, fridge, bath, and A/C. Beds are especially large. (☎282 33 55; fax 282 68 13. Check-out noon. Singles NIS220/US$55; doubles NIS260/US$65. Additional person NIS60/US$15. 15% student discount. V, MC, and traveler's checks accepted.)

FOOD

Gaza City's speciality is its seafood, served up in restaurants along the coastal road that offer the most after-dark activity in the city. Drinking water is of inconsistent quality: for bottled water, as well as other basics, try the **Yazji Supermarket** on Omar al-Mukhtar St. When coming from the beach, look for the red awning on the right side of the street, one block past Charles De Gaulle St. (Open daily 8am-11pm. MC.) Keep in mind that the Islamic prohibition of alcohol makes asking for or consuming alcohol in Gaza a bad idea.

■ **Palestine Restaurant** (☎284 85 83), on Omar al-Mukhtar St. Look for the large sign on the building overlooking Palestine Sq. Offers affordable food high above the city. Extensive menu includes hamburgers (NIS10), kebabs (NIS20), and pizza (NIS20-45). Relax with a *sheesha* (NIS5-6). Open Sa-Th 8am-1am and F noon-midnight.

El Samak Restaurant (☎286 43 85), on Ahmed Orabi St., on the corner of Omar al-Mukhtar St. Inviting seafood restaurant with a beautiful ocean view. Wide variety of fish and shrimp dishes (NIS40-60) are complemented by a large salad (NIS30) and soup (NIS10) selection. Open daily 9am-midnight. Cash only.

Loveboat Restaurant, through the courtyard in the Cliff Hotel on Ahmed Orabi St. Full meat (NIS40) or fish (NIS50) meal includes salad and coffee or tea, served in room shaped like the hull of a boat. Come aboard daily 7am-10pm.

Pizza Inn (☎284 04 25), on Omar al-Mukhtar St., in the middle of the Unknown Soldier Garden. Specialty pizzas (small NIS25, medium NIS35, large NIS48), all-you-can-eat salad bar (NIS15), hamburgers (NIS10), and spicy chicken wings (NIS12) served in this monolithic glass building. Open daily 9:30am-midnight.

Arafat Sweets (☎286 37 14). From the beach on Omar al-Mukhtar St., take a left on al-Nasser St., walk 3 long blocks to al-Wihda St., and take another left. On the right, with a large sign in English. The Arafats have been churning out pastries since 1912. Ask to see the factory in back where workers grind out and hand-mold loads of cookies (NIS18 for ½kg), cakes, and traditional Palestinian desserts (NIS10-36 per kg). Another location on Famey Buuk St., next to Palestine Sq. Open M-Sa 7:30am-11:30pm.

👁 SIGHTS

GREEK ORTHODOX CHURCH OF ST. PORPHYRUS. Gaza's major historical church abuts the minaret of a small mosque to the right. The church was first built on the site in the beginning of the 5th century and was named after Saint Porphyrus of northern Greece, who was charged with spreading Christendom in Gaza. When he predicted the birth of the empress's child, St. Porphyrus won a mandate for the city's temples to be torn down and for a Christian church to be built. March 10, the day of the saint's death, is still celebrated by Gazan Christians. The church has a remarkable, sky-blue arched ceiling dotted with white stars. There also is an impressive collection of dark Orthodox icons along the walls of the church. *(Across Palestine Sq., on the 2nd street that curves down to the right beyond the bus station. To see the inside of the chapel go to the 2nd floor of the modern church building to the left and ask to see the church. ☎ 282 68 06. Open daily 9am-1:30pm).*

AL-REDWAN CASTLE. This 17th-century fortress was built from the remains of a 13th-century Mamluk Palace. Napoleon spent three nights here in 1799 while waging a war against Egypt and Syria. During Ottoman rule, the building served as the governor's residence, and during the British mandate, it was a prison. Today, the dilapidated fort is hidden behind an overgrown garden on the grounds of a girls' school. *(Streets branching off to the left from the souq and the gold market lead to al-Wihda St. and the fort. Look for an opening in the gate. Caretakers usually let visitors see the fort 7am-7pm.)*

AL-SAYYID HASHEM MOSQUE. The great-grandfather of the Prophet Muhammad, a merchant who died while traveling through Gaza City, is said to be buried under one of the four porticos of the courtyard, built in 1850 by an Ottoman Sultan. *(From Palestine Sq. take the side street on the right when facing the Palestine Restaurant. At the intersection bear left, and the minaret and mosque walls will come into view.)*

🎫 DAYTRIP FROM GAZA CITY: RAFAH

From Gaza City, take a bus (1½hr., NIS2.50) or service taxi (45min., NIS5). From Khan Yunis, backtrack along the main street from the khan toward the fruit and vegetable market, until reaching the corner with two-way traffic. Take a taxi from the khan (NIS2).

Rafah, the strip's third-largest town and its border crossing point with Egypt, is 45 minutes south of Gaza City and a mere 15-minute drive from Khan Yunis. Rafah has been on the lips of ancient Egyptians, Assyrians, Greeks, Romans, and Arabs in the region for thousands of years. Today, it is known as the town that was divided between Egypt and Gaza in 1979. Part of its population remained in Egypt, while the remaining Palestinians fell under Israeli and ultimately PA jurisdiction. To see the border with Egypt where Palestinians stand on boxes to talk to their relatives on the other side of the fence, walk on the main street with the market on your right for half a kilometer, then turn left.

JORDAN الأردن

CURRENCY		
US$1=0.71 JORDANIAN DINAR (JD)	JD1=US$1.41
CDN$1=JD0.48	JD1=CDN$2.09
UK£1=JD1.07	JD1=UK£0.94
AUS$1=JD0.41	JD1=AUS$2.45
SAR1=JD0.1	JD1=SAR9.78
EUR1=JD0.66	JD1=EUR1.51
E£1 (EGYPTIAN POUND) =JD0.21	JD1=E£4.83
NIS1 (NEW ISRAELI SHEKEL) =JD0.17	JD1=NIS5.83
S£100 (SYRIAN POUNDS) =JD1.58	JD1=S£86.41
L£100 (LEBANESE POUND)=JD0.5	JD1=L£2,135.75
TL100,000 (TURKISH LIRA) =JD0.12	JD1=TL869,040

PHONE FACTS | Country Code: 962. **International dialing prefix:** 00.

Take it from the late King Hussein, the longest-ruling head of state in the world: "Jordan is a beautiful country: wild, with limitless deserts where the Bedouin roam....The mountains of the north are clothed in green forests, and where the Jordan River flows it is fertile and warm in winter. Jordan has a strange, haunting beauty and a sense of timelessness. Dotted with the ruins of empires once great, it is the last resort of yesterday in the world of tomorrow."

In ancient times, the Hashemite Kingdom of Jordan was where John the Baptist baptized Jesus, desert trade routes flourished during the Roman Empire, and the mysterious Nabatean people carved an entire city into red rock at Petra—all in the course of a few decades. Modern Jordan *(al-Urdun)* is now sandwiched between some of the roughest players in a rough neighborhood: Saudi Arabia, Israel, Syria, and Iraq. The memory of Black September, 1970 (a brutal suppression of Palestinian political activity by Jordanian authorities), has not disappeared, nor has the trauma of the Gulf War, in which Jordan supported Saddam Hussein. However, Jordan's former King Hussein (and his ever-gracious wife, US-born and educated Queen Noor) did much to raise morale within its borders and raise support from without. A growing tourism industry has been the key to opening Jordan to the hearts (and pockets) of outsiders, but despite this growth, most of the country and its sites of interest are largely untouched by the sticky fingers of gross commercialism. Close your eyes as you wander through Jordan's many natural and human-made wonders—you could be in any century.

HIGHLIGHTS OF JORDAN

Hit spectacular **Azraq and the Desert Castles** (p. 481) en route to the lost Nabatean city of **Petra** (p. 491).

The only thing better than the desert beauty of **Wadi Rum** (p. 503) is the hospitality of its Bedouin community (no wonder Lawrence of Arabia stayed here for so long).

Be sure to visit the impressive Roman ruins at **Jerash** (p. 473), which is also home to the **Jerash Festival,** a summertime musical and cultural extravaganza.

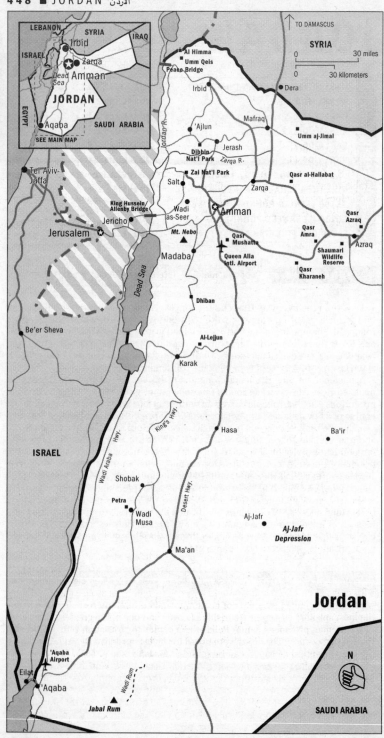

TO DAMASCUS

SYRIA

0   30 miles

0   30 kilometers

LEBANON

SYRIA

IRAQ

Irbid

ISRAEL

Zarqa

Dead
Sea

Amman

JORDAN

EGYPT

Aqaba

SAUDI ARABIA

SEE MAIN MAP

Al Himma

Umm Qeis

Peace Bridge

Irbid

Dera

'Ajlun

Mafraq

Umm aj-Jimal

Jerash

Dibbin
Nat'l Park

Zarqa R.

Qasr al-Hallabat

Zai Nat'l Park

Salt

Zarqa

Jordan R.

Tel Aviv-
Jaffa

King Hussein/
Allenby Bridge

Wadi
as-Seer

Amman

Qasr
Azraq

Qasr
Amra

Azraq

Jericho

Jerusalem

Mt. Nebo

Qasr
Mushatta

Shaumari
Wildlife
Reserve

Madaba

Queen Alia
Intl. Airport

Qasr
Kharaneh

Dead Sea

Dhiban

Be'er Sheva

Al-Lejjun

Karak

King's Hwy.

Hasa

Ba'ir

ISRAEL

Wadi Araba Hwy.

Shobak

Desert Hwy.

Petra

Wadi
Musa

Aj-Jafr

Aj-Jafr
Depression

Ma'an

Jordan

'Aqaba
Airport

Wadi Rum

Eilat

N

'Aqaba

SAUDI ARABIA

Jabal Rum

LIFE AND TIMES

Though not quite as chock-full of sights as its neighbors, Lebanon and Syria, Jordan needs only two things to recommend it: Petra and the unparalleled hospitality of the Jordanian people. With its sights, cheap and delicious food, and hospitable people, Jordan is the perfect place to enjoy Arab culture at its best.

ANCIENT HISTORY (1800 BCE-614 CE)

THE HYKSOS. Sometime in the Middle Bronze Age (around the 18th century BCE), a mysterious martial people known as the Hyksos (a Greek bastardization of the Egyptian *hkaw haswt*, "rulers of foreign lands") descended on Egypt and Arabia from the north. Their newfangled horse-drawn chariots and bronze weapons helped them easily conquer the area and permanently change military practices in the region. The identity of these strangers is still up for debate, but most archaeologists agree that they came from the region that is modern-day Jordan.

THE CANAANITES AND THE PERSIANS. For all their innovative power, the Hyksos' rule was short-lived; the Egyptian pharaohs eventually took over and ruled Jordan (along with Palestine and Syria) as one empire called Canaan. During the Iron Age, small city-states that initially developed along trade routes rose into three major kingdoms in Jordan. These kingdoms bickered constantly, both with their Israelite neighbors and among themselves. The arrival of Macedonian superstar **Alexander the Great** in 332 BCE ushered in an age of social and artistic development heavily influenced by Greek culture. The Greeks founded new cities (such as **Gadara**, see p. 480) and renamed others (Jerash became Antioch, see p. 473, and Amman became Philadelphia, see p. 458). Hellenistic influence lasted through the reign of Alexander's successor Ptolemy, invasion by the Seleucids, and conquest of the area by the Romans under Pompey in 63 BCE.

THE NABATEANS. Before Alexander's conquest, a thriving new civilization had emerged when a nomadic tribe from Arabia known as the **Nabateans** settled in southern Jordan during the 6th century BCE. The Roman scholar Strabo wrote that their capital was at **Petra** (see p. 491), where they carved buildings, temples, and tombs out of solid sandstone rock. As desert dwellers, the Nabateans were also skilled water engineers who irrigated their land using an extensive system of dams, canals, and reservoirs. Petra became a center of trade routes between Assyria, China, India, Egypt, Syria, Greece, and Rome, and the dialect of Arabic spoken by its inhabitants (versus the Aramaic that most tribes in the area spoke) helped spread that language around the region. Sometime during the 4th century CE, the Nabateans left their capital at Petra without explanation. Everything from localized famine to alien invasion has been cited as the cause for their exodus.

THE ROMANS. The departure of the Nabateans inaugurated a period of Roman control that would last four centuries. In northern Jordan, the Greek cities of Philadelphia (Amman), Antioch (Jerash), Gadara (Umm Qeis), Pella, and Irbid joined with cities in Palestine and southern Syria to form the **Decapolis League**, a fabled confederation linked by bonds of economic and cultural interest. Jerash became the most splendid city in the flourishing League and one of the greatest cities in all of the Roman provinces, while Pella was a center for Christian refugees fleeing Roman persecution. The cities were noted for their impressive Byzantine mosaics, the most beautiful of which can be found at **Madaba** (see p. 485)—including the intricately detailed 6th century **Map of the Holy Land**. At the same time the Map was being created, however, Jordan experienced severe depopulation: the plague of 542 CE took the lives of many inhabitants, while many more were wiped out by the Sassanian invasion of 614 CE. The invading Sassanians paved the way for the invading Ottomans, who would rule the area until the outbreak of World War I.

MODERN HISTORY (1916-PRESENT)

JORDANIAN INDEPENDENCE. Once the Ottoman Empire breathed its last at the end of World War I (in part because of Arab revolts led by **Lawrence of Arabia**), the League of Nations gave Western European powers control over the Levant in order to prepare these territories for independence. Great Britain was put in charge of Iraq and Palestine (which included modern-day Israel, the West Bank, the Gaza Strip, and Jordan), and in 1921 established the area east of the Jordan River as the **Emirate of Transjordan.** A 40th-generation direct descendant of the Prophet Muhammad, **Abdullah**, was set up as emir, and the British-controlled emirate spent most of the period until the end of World War II keeping the peace between local Arabs and immigrant Jews fleeing to Palestine from Europe. Shortly after the end of World War II, Great Britain handed the Palestine problem over to the newly-formed United Nations, which granted Jordan independence. After Israel became a state in May 1948, Jordan offered refugees full citizenship (the only Arab country to do so), much to the chagrin of most Arab leaders.

KING HUSSEIN. Unification efforts with the Palestinians were cut short in 1951, when Abdullah was assassinated by a Palestinian youth while praying at Al-Aqsa Mosque in Jerusalem. Abdullah's eldest son, Talal, ruled for six months before resigning, and Talal's son **Hussein** (who had also been shot but survived thanks to a well-placed medal) took over the throne just before his 18th birthday. King Hussein ruled for 48 years until his death on February 7, 1999—the longest serving executive head of state in the world. Hussein's moderate political stance (a result of his British education) and two (of four) gracious Western wives (including his widow, **Queen Noor**, who was born and educated in the US) made him a favorite of Western leaders. Even domestically he was known as *Al-Malik al-Insani* ("The Humane King"), particularly for his reception of Palestinian and (more recently) Kuwaiti refugees. Hussein opened his powerful cabinet to Palestinians and Bedouin, who form the bedrock of the monarchy's support.

JORDAN AND THE PALESTINIANS. The aftermath of the 1967 war with Israel did not shine favorably upon Hussein. Over 400,000 Palestinians fled to Jordan, throwing the Jordanian government and the Palestine Liberation Organization (PLO) into a tense relationship: King Hussein wanted to hold peace negotiations with the Israelis, while the PLO hoped to use Jordan as a base for attacks on Israeli-held territory. In September 1970 (known as **Black September**), King Hussein declared war on the PLO after it hijacked several commercial airlines, and imposed martial law. Clashes between Jordanian and PLO troops took over 3000 lives. After Arab League mediation and Egyptian president Nasser's personal intervention, an agreement was forged requiring the PLO to move its headquarters to Lebanon.

THE GULF WAR. The **Gulf War** of 1990-1991 brought its own problems. A tide of pan-Arabism and resentment of Western power led many Jordanians to support Saddam Hussein. Jordan's refusal to join the US-led anti-Iraq coalition devastated both the nation's economy and its international political clout after the war. Most foreign aid was suspended, and the annual per capita income fell from US$2000 (1990) to US$1400 (where it stands today). Unlike its neighbors, Jordan has neither oil reserves nor abundant natural resources, and is dependent upon Arab and American financial aid to augment its income, which consists largely of the export of phosphates and vegetables grown in the Jordan Valley. The country's main source of income had been money sent home from Jordanians working in the Gulf States, but after the war they were largely replaced by Egyptian workers (whose country was considered more acceptable by the anti-Iraq coalition).

PEACE WITH ISRAEL. Hussein improved international relations in August 1994, when he and Israeli Prime Minister Yitzhak Rabin signed the **Washington Declaration**, ending the state of war between the two countries and opening the border between Aqaba and Eilat. The monetary umbilical cord from the West was reconnected, and the US and Great Britain relieved millions of dollars of Jordan's foreign debt. An increase in tourism, heartily encouraged by Hussein and his successor, has given the country a much-needed economic boost.

KING ABDULLAH II. On February 7, 1999, **King Hussein** died of cancer-related health complications. The King's brother, former **Crown Prince Hassan**, was to inherit the throne from Hussein; just days before his death, however, Hussein announced that his eldest son, 37-year-old **Abdullah**, would succeed him. Hussein criticized Hassan for jumping the gun when the king went abroad, running the country as though Hussein would never return. Though Hassan did dismiss the King's loyalists in the army and altered some of Jordan's domestic policies, many have speculated that Hussein acted out of fear that if Hassan became king, it would be his sons and not Hussein's who would ascend to the throne in later years. Many have also questioned whether the young and relatively inexperienced Abdullah is capable of being king. However, Abdullah is in an ideal position to encourage the peace process in the Middle East: he is boarding one of the most politically troubled ships of state carrying no political baggage. The Palestinian heritage of his wife, **Queen Rania**, has also made the couple popular with the dueling sectors of Jordan's population.

IN THE NEWS

Since his ascension to the throne, Abdullah has visited Syria three times to discuss the peace process. Relations between the two countries have improved dramatically since the late Syrian President Hafez al-Assad's surprise attendance of the late King Hussein's funeral. Abdullah is set to go to Teheran in the summer of 2001 in an attempt to improve Jordan's relationship with Iran. Ties with Iran, severed after the Islamic Revolution there in 1979, were renewed in 1991. Abdullah has also invited Iranian President Muhammad Khatami to Jordan.

In economic news, the government convinced the International Monetary Fund that the proceeds from the privatization of state-owned companies could not go toward paying off Jordan's US$7 billion foreign debt.

RELIGION AND ETHNICITY

The vast majority of Jordanians are **Sunni Muslims**, though pockets of Shi'ite Muslims exist as well. Centuries of Byzantine rule and Crusader occupation have left their mark; Jordan has a sizeable community of **Christians** (roughly 8% of the population). Most Jordanians are ethnic Arabs (including many Palestinian expats and refugees), but about 2% of the population are Armenian, Circassian, or Druze.

LANGUAGE

The official language of Jordan is **Arabic**, but the spoken dialect differs from classical Arabic and the variations spoken in Egypt, the Gulf States, and North Africa. Due to decades of British colonial rule, **English** is Jordan's second language, taught at both public and private schools. Most signs are written in both Arabic and English, and Jordan Television's second channel broadcasts subtitled British and American programs as well as some French programs after 8:30pm.

THE ARTS

LITERATURE. The Jordanian region itself has a long tradition of prose: the oldest example of a Semitic script, the 9th century BCE relic known as the **Mesha Stele**, was found in Karak. Jordanian literature does not exist as its own genre as Egyptian or Lebanese literature does, although many Jordanian writers publish frequently. **Diana Abu-Jaber** recently achieved prominence for her first novel, *Arabian Jazz*, which was a finalist for the national PEN/Hemingway award. Many exiled Palestinian authors have written from Jordan, the most famous of whom is **Mahmoud Darwish**. Of Western non-natives writing in and about Jordan, the most famous is the British rabble-rouser T.E. Lawrence, also known as **Lawrence of Arabia**. His *Seven Pillars of Wisdom* contains vivid descriptions of the battles fought and the territory explored during the Arab Revolt of 1916. Even if you don't reach Lawrence's old haunts at Wadi Rum, don't miss David Lean's swooning and romanticized movie Lawrence of Arabia. **Gertrude Bell**, one of the first female Western travelers in the region, writes of her journeys through Jordan and Syria in The Desert and the Sown (for more info on Bell's life, see **An Englishwoman in Arabia**, p. 489). The last word in desert mystery is **Agatha Christie's** *Argument with Death*, which introduces readers to the mesmerizing power of Petra (see p. 409).

VISUAL AND PERFORMING ARTS. Both the Jordanian government and private groups are taking measures to promote and foster the **visual arts**, and Jordan's architecture, painting, and sculpture have all developed substantially in this century. Skillful **weavers** use techniques developed over countless centuries to make traditional Jordanian rugs and tapestries out of wool and goat hair. Leather handicrafts, pottery, ceramics, and coral curios are also very common, but **wood-carving** is the Jordanian specialty. Jordanian art is often an expression of Arab and Muslim identity, but the country's mix of cultures also results in themes relating to traditional Bedouin life or a desire to return to the Palestinian homeland. **Dabke** is a traditional line dance performed to the rhythmic beat of feet pounding on the floor. Two decades ago, Queen Noor founded the annual Jerash Festival. The summer festival features diverse international offerings, from Romanian choirs to Indian dance troupes. Traditional Arab and Bedouin arts are displayed, and music and theater features prominently in the celebration. For more information on the **Jerash Festival**, see p. 474. Jordan's film industry has been at a standstill since the 60s and 70s when it produced mostly films dealing with the Palestinian-Israeli conflict. Today, Jordan mainly produces television sitcoms. In 1999, the World Bank announced it would help fund a film on Jordan's Hijaz railway, the first feature film made in Jordan since the 70's.

MUSIC. Jordanians have a strong oral tradition of storytelling and ballad singing. Eavesdrop on a wedding for a taste of traditional folk music and for the women's salutatory shouts and ululations (*ha-WEEE-ha!*), known as **zaghroutah**.

FOOD AND DRINK

Jordanian cuisine has evolved through centuries of Bedouin and Palestinian cooking. The national dish is **mensaf**, and its main ingredients appear in most other Jordanian dishes. *Mensaf* consists of rice on a large tray of flat bread, topped with pine nuts, an entire lamb or goat, and a tangy yogurt-based sauce known as *jamid*. It is eaten from a communal dish while standing: the right hand is used to ball the rice while the left hand holds the flat bread which is used to pull off chunks of meat and dip them into the warm sauce. The Bedouin serve the head of the lamb on top, reserving the prize delicacies (tongue and eyes) for speechless guests.

A combination of hummus, cheese, honey, jam, bread, and sometimes *fuul* (beans) form a standard breakfast. Traditional dinners are served around 2 or 3pm; popular dishes include *musakhan* (chicken baked with olive oil, onions, and spices, served on bread) and *mahshi* (a tray of vine leaves, squash, or eggplant stuffed with mincemeat, rice, and onions). Supper is usually smaller and lighter. A staple at any time of the day is *za'tar*, a sauce of thyme mixed with sesame seeds and spices, eaten either by dipping the bread into olive oil and then into the mix, or pizza-style (*mana'eesh*).

Drink bottled water (300fils, more at restaurants and tourist haunts) or use iodine tablets. **Coffee** and **tea** are expressions of Jordanian hospitality, and tourists are likely to be offered refreshment many times a day. If a hot drink doesn't tickle

SUGAR AND SPICE Jordan has long been a safe haven and cultural breeding ground for Syrian and Palestinian refugees. Nevertheless, immigrant kitchens compulsively guarded their native dessert recipes—that is, until the **Jabri** and **Habiba** pastry chains came onto the scene around 1950. Jabri introduced Damascene **ba'laweh**, while Habiba hooked the country on **kinafeh** from the Palestinian villages of Nablus. Half a century later, the Jordanian sweet tooth can only be satisfied by the honey-coated, nut-filled pockets of filo-dough joy that have become an inseparable part of the country's more established traditions.

your fancy, ask for *barid* (Arabic for "cold"). Jordanians drink tremendous amounts of tea (*shay*), almost always made with mint (*na'na'*). Stereotypes hold that bumpkin fellaheen (country people) drink their tea syrupy sweet; restaurants will assume you do too unless you prove your gentility by asking for *sukkar aleel* (just a little sugar). A cup of the thick, black, bittersweet Arabic coffee (ahwa) is stronger than espresso. Drinking **alcohol** is prohibited by Islam, so imbibing in Jordan is subject to some restrictions and conventions. Anyone who looks older than 16 may buy at a liquor store (usually owned by Christians). Locally-brewed Amstel is the most popular alcoholic drink (600fils); imports are also available. '*Araq* is a popular aniseed hard alcohol (similar to the Greek ouzo and Turkish raki) that is mixed with water until it turns cloudy and white.

FACTS AND FIGURES

OFFICIAL NAME: Hashemite Kingdom of Jordan

GOVERNMENT: Constitutional monarchy

CAPITAL: Amman

LAND AREA: 91,860 sq. km.

GEOGRAPHY: Arid plateau; the Great Rift Valley (Jordan Valley and Dead Sea) runs to the West

CLIMATE: Dry and hot summers with occasional dust storms; wet and cool winters; hottest in Aug., coolest in Jan.

MAJOR CITIES: Amman, Jerash, Aqaba, Karak

POPULATION: 4.5 million; 0-14 yrs 43%, 15-over 57%

LANGUAGE: Arabic

RELIGIONS: Muslim (92%), Christian (8%)

GNP PER CAPITA: US$1650

MAJOR EXPORTS: Phosphates, fertilizers, potash, agricultural products

ESSENTIALS
WHEN TO GO

It's best to visit Jordan during the relatively mild spring and autumn seasons. Most attractions in Jordan are in the mountain region, where summer days could melt a cheap wig but evenings are deliciously cool. Winters are cold, with frequent rain. Aqaba enjoys balmy winter weather.

AVERAGE TEMPERATURE AND PRECIPITATION

	JANUARY			APRIL			JULY			OCTOBER		
	°C	°F	mm	°C	°F	mm	°C	°F	mm	°C	°F	mm
Amman	7.9	46.2	63	15.8	60.4	17	25.1	77.2	0	20.2	68.4	6
Aqaba	14.5	58.1	0	24.3	75.7	0	32.5	90.0	0	26.2	79.2	0
Petra	7.5	45.5	6.4	16.6	61.9	3.6	25.4	77.7	0	19.4	66.9	3.4

DOCUMENTS AND FORMALITIES

CONSULAR SERVICES ABROAD

Jordanian embassies and consulates abroad include:

Australia Embassy: 20 Roebuck St., Red Hill ACT 2603, Canberra (☎(02) 295 99 51, 2950 5663; fax 239 7236).

Canada Embassy: 100 Bronson Ave. #701, Ottawa, ON K1R 6G8 (☎(613) 238 80 90; fax 232 33 41).

South Africa Embassy: 209 Festival Street, Hatfield, P.O.Box 14730, Hatfield, 0028, Pretoria (☎(12) 342 80 26 or 342 80 27; fax (12) 342 78 47; email embjord@embjord.co.za).

UK Embassy: 6 Upper Philimore Gardens, London W8 7HB (☎(171) 937 36 85; fax 937 87 95).

US Embassy: 3504 International Dr. NW, Washington, D.C. 20008 (☎(202) 966-2664; fax 966-3110; email HKJEmbassyDC@aol.com). **Consulate:** 866 2nd Ave., 4th Floor, New York, NY 10017 (☎(212) 832-0119; fax 832-5346).

CONSULAR SERVICES IN JORDAN

Embassies and consulates of other countries in Jordan include:

Australian Embassy: (☎(06) 593 02 46, visa info ☎593 27 80), on Jabal Amman between 4th and 5th Circles, Amman.

Canadian Embassy: (☎(06) 566 61 24; fax 568 92 27), in Shmeisani behind Jabri Restaurant, near the Petra Bank, Amman.

New Zealand Consulate: 4th floor, Khalaf Building, 99 al-Malek al-Hussein St. (☎(06) 462 51 49), Amman.

UK Embassy: (☎(06) 592 31 00; fax 592 37 59; www.britain.org.jo) on Damascus St. in Abdoun, Amman.

US Embassy: (☎(06) 592 01 01, visa info ☎592 32 93; fax 592 41 02; www.usembassy-amman.org.jo), P.O. Box 354, Abdoun, Amman.

ENTRY REQUIREMENTS

Visas can be obtained at Amman's Queen Alia International Airport and are valid for one month but renewable at any police station (US$44). Visas may also be obtained in person or by mail from any Jordanian embassy or consulate (takes up to five days). Requirements include a passport (valid for at least six months), a completed application form with one photo, and a self-addressed, stamped envelope. A group visa can be issued for tours of five or more.

BORDER CROSSINGS

Getting a visa to enter Jordan is a breeze, as the government issues visas at all international border crossings (except King Hussein/Allenby Bridge). There are three separate **departure taxes:** JD4 for departure by land (except for travel to the West Bank); JD6 by sea (from Aqaba); and JD10 by air (does not apply to transit travelers in Jordan under 72 hours).

TO EGYPT. A ferry shuttles between Aqaba and Nuweiba. There is a slow ferry (3½hr. or more, noon, JD6), and a faster, less crowded, and more punctual **speedboat** (1hr., noon, JD20 plus JD4 departure tax). Tickets can be purchased at any travel agency in Aqaba; be sure to show up a few hours before departure. You can get a free **Sinai-only visa** if you only plan to visit the Sinai; otherwise, you'll need an **Egyptian visa** (2-week or 1-month), which can be obtained in one day at the Egyptian Consulate in Aqaba for JD12 (see p. 500). Visas can also be obtained on board the ferry for an extra charge, or you can risk it and wait to obtain a tourist visa upon arrival in Nuweiba.

TO IRAQ. There are two JETT buses from Amman to Baghdad (14hr., 8:30am and 2pm, JD12). Citizens of Western countries are unlikely to be granted Iraqi visas.

TO ISRAEL. There are three border crossing points between Israel and Jordan. There is no entrance fee into Israel and **free visas** are given at the border, though most Western citizens do not need visas (see **Israel: Entry,** p. 275). However, a **departure tax** is required if crossing in either direction. The simple crossing between **Aqaba** and **Eilat** should take less than an hour; take a taxi from Aqaba to the border (JD4), then walk the one kilometer no-man's land between the two countries (there's no transport). Once over the border, the Israeli authorities will call you a taxi into Eilat (NIS15-20). There is no bus service on either side of the border. Though it is much more of a hassle, travelers coming from Amman can cross the **Sheikh Hussein Bridge** (*Jisr Sheikh Hussein;* called Allenby Bridge on the Israeli side) to just outside of Jericho, from which buses and *service* frequently depart for Jerusalem. There is a third border crossing in northern Jordan, at the **Peace Bridge,** which goes to the Israeli town of Beit She'an in Galilee.

TO SAUDI ARABIA. The official crossing points between Jordan and Saudi Arabia are on the coast of the Gulf of Aqaba at al-Durra and farther east at al-Mudawwara. JETT and SAPTCO buses (JD31) run from Amman to: **Jeddah** (10am), **Dammam** (11am), and **Riyadh** (11:30am). The hardest part about traveling to Saudi Arabia from Jordan is getting a **visa;** tourists can only register for transit visas, which sometimes let you travel along the Trans-Arabia Pipeline but usually only allows for one day in Riyadh.

TO SYRIA. The official road crossing into Syria runs through the town of **Dera.** Daily buses and *service* run from Amman to **Damascus** and **Aleppo.** Although *service* are faster (and more expensive) than the buses (2-3hr., JD5), they are usually detained longer at the border, meaning *service* travelers may end up spending more money for a trip that takes just as long as the cheaper bus route. The painfully slow **Hijazi** railway chugs between Amman's Abdali Bus Station and Damascus. The train (US$3.50) departs Amman at 8am every Monday, arriving at Damascus at 5pm; it departs Damascus every Sunday at 7:30am to arrive in Amman at 5pm.

TO THE WEST BANK. The King Hussein/Allenby Bridge between Amman and the West Bank is a very popular (and crowded) option (border open Su-Th 8am-10:30pm, F-Sa 8am-1pm). Visas are not issued at this border, but most Western citizens do not need a visa to enter the West Bank. Take a JETT bus (45min., 6:30am, JD6) from either station in Amman or a minibus or *service* (45min., JD1.5) from Abdali Bus Station.

GETTING AROUND

BY PLANE. There are three airports in Jordan: Queen Alia International Airport and Amman-Marka International Airport in Amman, and Aqaba International Airport. Flights between Amman and Aqaba take 50 minutes and cost approximately $84 round-trip.

BY LOCAL TRANSPORTATION. Camel caravan trips can be arranged in Wadi Rum. Horse and camel rides through Petra are also available.

BY TAXI. Private taxis are yellow and have "taxi" written on them. They are most useful (and crowded) in Amman. Insist that drivers use the meter; the starting fare is 150fils. Women should always sit in the back seat, whether or not there are other passengers; men should always sit in the front when alone. It's rude to give exact change; drivers expect you to round up from the meter fare. Public taxis or **service** (ser-VEES) are usually white or gray Mercedes with a white sign written in Arabic on the roof (سرۈۑ). The front doors display the fixed route and number (in Arabic numerals only). Service travel set routes in Amman and between the central terminals of larger cities. Schedules are unpredictable—*service* leave when full, but can be hailed en route.

BY BUS. The government owns a monopoly on intercity bus service, so the **Jordan Express Tourist Transport (JETT)** is the only option. However infrequently, these buses cover the most popular routes, including daily trips from Amman to Aqaba, Petra, Ma'an, the King Hussein/Allenby Bridge, Damascus, and Cairo via Aqaba. Bus fares are slightly lower than *service* rates, but buses are slower and their routes sometimes confusing. The air-conditioned JETT luxury coaches cost 20% more than regular buses; those from Amman to Aqaba come with hosts, professional wrestling videos, and screeching Egyptian movies. Booking ahead is often necessary. In Amman, most buses follow the pattern of *service*, with traffic to the north leaving from Abdali Station and buses to the south from Wahdat Station.

BY CAR. For groups of four to six, renting a car can be an affordable and efficient way to reach less accessible sights. The beautiful King's Highway route, barely served by other modes of transportation, can be seen by private car in a full day. Desert heat and police regulations require fire extinguishers in cars. **Four-wheel drives** are only needed to reach Wadi Rum. The law requires **seatbelts** (JD5 fine for those flying unfettered).

BY THUMB. Hitchhiking is very difficult during the major holidays. At other times, it is possible, though groups of females will never pick up male hitchhikers. You should offer a small amount of money to the driver, but less than the cost of bus fare. Hitchhiking is dangerous, however, and *Let's Go* does not recommend it.

TOURIST SERVICES AND MONEY

TOURIST OFFICES. In Amman, try the Ministry of Tourism and Antiquities (☎ (06) 464 23 11 or (06) 464 23 14) to collect a map, some glossy pamphlets, and fact sheets about the country. There's also a branch at Amman's Queen Alia Airport (☎ (06) 445 12 56). In Jerash, the office is near South Gate (☎ (04) 45 12 72); in Petra, it's at the entrance of the site (☎ (03) 33 60 20).

CURRENCY AND EXCHANGE. The Jordanian dinar (JD) is a decimal currency, divided into 1000 fils. Notes come in denominations of JD20, 10, 5, and 1, and 500 fils. Coins are in denominations of 500, 250, 100, 50, 25, 20, 10, 5 and 1 fils. Prices are always labeled in fils, but the usual spoken practice is to call 10fils a piaster (pt, also called a *qirsh*). Prices are written in Arabic numerals, although the currency itself is marked with Western-friendly numbers.

Bank exchange hours are regularly 8:30am to 12:30pm, with some banks opening from 3:30pm to 5:30pm as well. Hours during Ramadan are 8:30am to 10am, although some banks open in the afternoon. All banks are closed on Friday. There are many branches of the national **Housing Bank** *(Bank al-Iskan)* outside Amman; there are also exchange offices in many of the *souqs*. Queen Alia International Airport has exchange facilities for incoming passengers. A passport is required to change traveler's checks. Traveler's checks may be exchanged for a hefty commission at most banks and exchange offices. **Credit cards** are only accepted in expensive hotels. **ATMs** work for local and international bank cards.

PRICES. Jordanian prices are generally very low; JD20 (US$28) should easily cover a day's budget travel.

TIPPING. A tip of 10% is expected in restaurants, unless "service included" appears on the menu; servers at fancier establishments expect a little something even if service is included. Taxi drivers do not expect tips, but will round off fares to their advantage. Members of large sightseeing groups tip the bus driver about 500fils. A small tip (500fils) to room cleaners and porters in hotels is appropriate.

BUSINESS HOURS. All businesses close on Friday. Most stores and offices are open from 8 or 9am until 1pm, then reopen around 3 or 4pm. In the larger cities, the stores may remain open all afternoon. In Amman, retail stores close at 8 or 9pm. Banks and government offices retain only a skeleton crew in the afternoon.

HEALTH AND SAFETY

EMERGENCY   **Police:** ☎ 191 or 192. **Ambulance:** ☎ 193.

MEDICAL EMERGENCIES AND HEALTH. Health care is quite good in Jordan, and the World Health Organization's figures show that even in the mid-1980s, safe water and adequate sanitary facilities were accessible to 100% of the urban population and 95% of the rural population. Most doctors speak English and pharmacies have a wide selection of medicines and other pharmaceutical products, including condoms. No vaccinations are necessary for entry into Jordan, except for those arriving from countries infected with yellow fever or cholera, but consider getting vaccinated for hepatitis, tetanus, and typhoid. Drink bottled water rather than tap water for the first few days until your system adjusts. Top-class hotels often have their own filtering systems so their tap water is safe for drinking. Remember to wash all fruits and vegetables before eating them and be wary of food that has been sitting out, especially in the summer.

WOMEN TRAVELERS. Jordan is a modernized country and women will generally feel quite comfortable, although harassment is not uncommon (just ignore it). Women should dress conservatively, as those dressed inappropriately will be punished with higher prices from offended merchants and possibly even pinches. For more tips, see Women Travelers, p. 38.

MINORITY TRAVELERS. No matter what color you are, if you're clearly not Jordanian, you can expect some staring. Jordanians tend to think that all black people are Sudanese and therefore assume that they speak Arabic. Likewise, it is assumed that all Asians are Japanese tourists. Latinos usually blend in and will probably be left alone.

BGLT TRAVELERS. Jordan does not condone homosexual behavior. Be careful how you act in public.

ACCOMMODATIONS AND CAMPING

HOTELS. Regulated tourist hotels charge prices as high as Jordan's mid-summer temperatures. Bargaining is difficult, but hotel owners may be more flexible in the off-season winter months. Fall and spring are the busiest times, though sunny Aqaba sees the most activity during the winter and spring. Single women may feel uncomfortable at cheaper hotels and may not be admitted. Jordanian law bars unmarried couples from sharing a room; for foreign travelers, a "don't ask, don't tell" policy seems to be the norm. Most budget hotels do not abide by government prices; "official" prices are listed in Arabic and cheaper ones in English. Most hotels add a 10% service charge; ask whether it's included in the price. Hotel owners may ask to hold your passport for the length of your stay, but they will return it after a night if you need to change money.

CAMPING. Camping is an option at government-approved sites, though facilities are virtually nonexistent. Approved areas include the beach north of Aqaba, Dibbin National Park, and the Dana Wildlands Campsite. Camping is allowed next to most government **Rest Houses** (free or JD1-2 per person per night, plus 10% tax). You'll need a sleeping bag or blanket for cool summer nights; winter evenings can bring freezing temperatures. You can also spend the night in a **Bedouin camp** on the outskirts of most towns and scattered around the desert. Tea, Arabic coffee, and meals are always included in an invitation, though showers and toilets are rare. While the Bedouin won't accept money, a pack of cigarettes is always appreciated.

KEEPING IN TOUCH

MAIL. Most post offices have Poste Restante. American Express offices (Amman and Aqaba) also hold mail. **Airmail letters** to North America cost 400fils, aerogrammes or postcards 300fils (to Europe 300fils, 150fils). Mail from Jordan to North America and Europe takes one to two weeks, if you're lucky. Post office opening hours are 8am to 6pm Saturday to Thursday, closed on Friday, except for the downtown post office on Prince Muhammad St. in Amman. International **Express Mail Service (EMS)** is available in major post offices and costs less than Western companies like DHL and FedEx.

TELEGRAMS. Telegrams may be sent from the Central Telegraph Office at the Post Office in 1st Circle, Jabal Amman or from major hotels and post offices.

TELEPHONE AND INTERNET ACCESS. Although the telephone system was recently revamped, international lines are often overloaded, especially around holidays. **Phonecards** have made a welcome appearance, and are probably the easiest way to make both local and international calls; **no collect calls** can be made except from a private phone. **Calling card** calls can only be placed from private phones. You can make **international calls** from telephone offices (JD6.6 per 3min. to the US) or luxury hotels (fast but expensive). Use a private phone and reimburse the owner (to US, Europe, or Australia JD1.83-2.2 per min.; 30% less 10pm-8am). **International operator:** ☎0132. **Information:** ☎121. In most major cities, almost every place—from the hostel to the supermarket—is wired to the Internet, often at a cheaper rate (JD1-1.5) than cybercafes.

CUSTOMS AND ETIQUETTE

Jordan is socially conservative by Western standards, making modest dress a necessity for both sexes. Neither sex can wear shorts (except in hedonistic Aqaba), and women's skirts must be at least ankle-length. Shirts should cover the shoulders and upper arms. Sandals that expose feet are acceptable. Amman slackens its dress code at night and by the pool.

Jordanians have a very strong hospitality ethic. Bedouin invitations to coffee or tea should be strongly considered, as declining an invitation is often interpreted as a direct insult. If you choose to reject an offer, be calm and firm and repeat yourself until the point sinks in. Lone women should never accept an invitation from a single man. Most people who offer to help you, feed you, or take you somewhere are probably not con artists; they often represent the best of a culture that is serious about kindness to visitors.

AMMAN عمان ☎06

Noisy, crowded, and cosmopolitan, Amman thrives on its mix of modern business and traditional culture. The sidewalks in Amman are as packed with people as its streets are with cars, and the entire frenetic scene grooves to the beat of the popular Arabic music pouring out from downtown storefronts. When the sun goes down and the lights come up, the jasmine-scented streets provide the perfect setting for lazy summertime strolls through the city's seven hills. Hospitality is also a way of life in Amman; the greetings you hear are quite sincere, and chances are a "welcome" will lead to a cup of tea and a conversation. Seasoned globetrotters agree—travelers are welcome in Amman as in few places on earth.

Though it was the Ammonite capital in Biblical times, modern-day Amman was a mere village in the decades preceding 1948, when its population of 6000 could have easily fit inside the city's Roman Theater (see p. 469). Following the Arab-Israeli wars of 1948 and 1967, however, many Palestinians took refuge here, and Amman expanded exponentially. Descendants of these Palestinians now make up about 70% of Jordan's population. Some Palestinians are highly successful doctors, businessmen, bankers, and politicians, but many still live in Amman's huge refugee camps much like their fathers and grandfathers did in Palestine. Egyptian and Southeast Asian workers also make up a large part of the city's population, and after the Gulf War in 1991, they were joined by immigrants from Iraq and Kuwait. Today, Amman's more than 1.5 million inhabitants make up roughly one-third of Jordan's total population.

Amman's central location makes it the country's principal transportation hub and the base for exploring Jordan's other sights. The ruins at Jerash and Ajloun are just over an hour north, the Dead Sea is an hour west, and Petra is three hours south; there's nothing at all to the east.

✈ GETTING THERE AND AWAY

Flights: Queen Alia International Airport (☎ 445 32 00, Royal Jordanian ☎ 445 33 33), 35km south of Amman. **24hr. buses** connect Abdali Bus Station and the airport (45min.; every 30min. 6am-10pm, every 2hr. 10pm-6am; JD1). Private **taxi** to the airport JD10, at night JD15; two pieces of luggage free, additional pieces 200fils. **Service** do not run to the airport. Housing Bank and Jordan Bank (both open 24hr.) and a tourist office (open daily 9am-2pm) are in the airport. JD10 **exit fee** when leaving Jordan.

Intercity Buses:

Abdali Bus Station, on King Hussein St. at Jabal al-Weibdeh. Minibuses to the north central and northwestern parts of Jordan (including Jordan Valley) leave to: **Ajloun** (450fils); **Irbid** (825fils); **Jerash** (300fils); **King Hussein/Allenby Bridge** (open Su-Th 8am-7pm, F 8am-noon; JD1.5); and **Salt** (175fils). **Hashemi St. Station** (also called **Raghadban Station** or **Interchange**), near the Roman Theater, launches northeast traffic to: **Mafraq, Zarqa,** and points east of Irbid.

Wahdat Station, several kilometers from downtown Amman between the Abu Darwish Mosque and the Wahdat Refugee Camp, controls traffic to and from the south, sending buses to: **Aqaba, Karak, Ma'an, Madaba, Musa, Petra,** and **Wadi.**

JETT Bus Station (☎ 566 41 46, international routes 569 61 51 or 569 61 52) has two offices on King Hussein St., past Abdali Bus Station and opposite Army Headquarters. Both open daily 6am-9pm. A/C buses to: **Aqaba** (4hr., 8 per day, JD4); **Beirut** (6hr., M and Th 9am, JD15); **Cairo** (20-24hr., Tu and Sa 6:30am, JD35); **Damascus** (4-5hr., 2am and 4pm, JD4.5; visa required); **King Hussein/Allenby Bridge** (1hr., 6:30am, JD6); and **Petra** (3½hr.; Su, Tu, and F 6:30am; JD5.5, round-trip JD11, round-trip including admission to Petra JD33). Reserve one day in advance.

Intercity Service: Intercity *service* leave from the same stations as buses and go to the same regions, but tend to be 40-50% more expensive. From **Abdali Bus Station,** *service* to: **Ajloun** (775fils); **Irbid** (900fils); **Jerash** (500fils); **King Hussein/Allenby Bridge** (JD1.5); and **Salt** (375fils). From **Wahdat Bus Station,** *service* to: **Aqaba** (JD6); **Karak** down the King's Highway (JD1.5); **Ma'an** via the newer Desert Highway (JD3.5); **Madaba** (500fils); and **Petra** (JD4). All prices, bus and *service* alike, are government-regulated, but government regulations are not always observed.

Car Rental: Local agencies have fewer restrictions. **Reliable Rent-a-Car** (☎ 592 96 76) offers insurance, unlimited mileage, and 24hr. breakdown service for a 1998 Nissan at JD25-35 per day. The manager will send someone to pick you up at your hotel and bring you out to their office in Abdoun. If you prefer name recognition, try **Avis** (☎ 569 94 20; fax 469 48 83) or **Budget** (☎ 569 81 31; fax 567 33 12), both around JD40 per day. For a real cheapie, check out **Firas** (☎ 560 20 82; fax 461 68 74), at 1st Circle and Shmeisani, with small cars and a 200km limit for JD18. **Valid driver's license** and **passport** required by all agencies. Reserve in advance. Drivers under 21 may have more luck with local agencies than with corporate heavyweights.

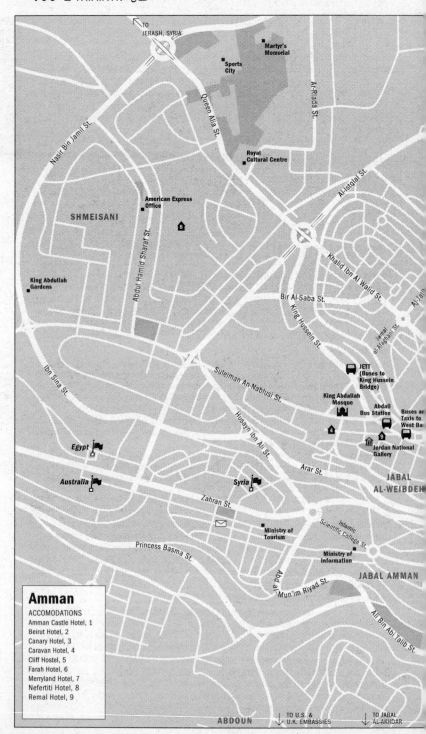

TO
JERASH, SYRIA

Martyr's
Memorial

Sports
City

Queen Alia St.

Ar-Riada St.

Royal
Cultural Centre

American Express
Office

Al-Istqlal St.

SHMEISANI

8

Khalid Ibn Al Walid St.

Al-Fath

King Abdullah
Gardens

Bir Al-Saba St.

King Hussein St.

Jamal
al-Alagiani St.

Abdul Hamid Sharaf St.

Ibn Sina St.

Suleiman An-Nablusi St.

JETT
(Buses to
King Hussein
Bridge)

King Abdallah
Mosque

Abdali
Bus Station

Buses and
Taxis to
West Ba

Husayn Ibn Ali St.

4

9

Jordan National
Gallery

Egypt

Arar St.

JABAL
AL-WEIBDEH

Australia

Syria

Zahran St.

Islamic
Scientific College St.

Ministry of
Tourism

Princess Basma St.

Ministry of
Information

JABAL AMMAN

Abd al-Mun'im Riyad St.

Ali Bin Abi Talib St.

Amman

ACCOMODATIONS

Amman Castle Hotel, 1
Beirut Hotel, 2
Canary Hotel, 3
Caravan Hotel, 4
Cliff Hostel, 5
Farah Hotel, 6
Merryland Hotel, 7
Nefertiti Hotel, 8
Remal Hotel, 9

ABDOUN

TO U.S. &
U.K. EMBASSIES

TO JABAL
AL-AKHDAR

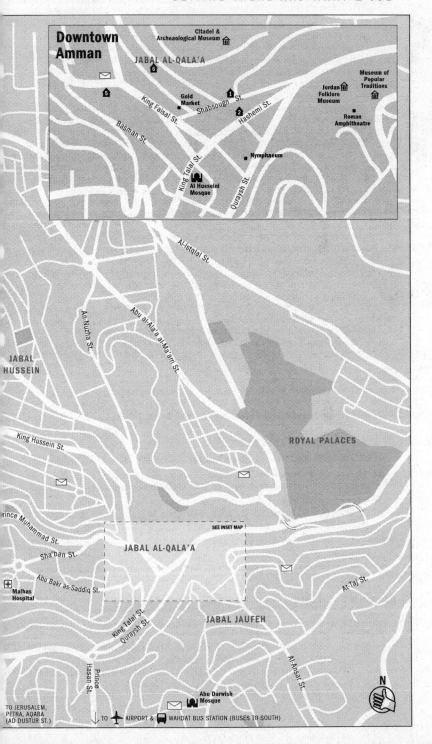

Downtown Amman

JABAL AL-QALA'A

Citadel & Archaeological Museum

King Faisal St.

Gold Market

Shabsough St.

Hashemi St.

Jordan Folklore Museum

Museum of Popular Traditions

Roman Amphitheatre

Basman St.

King Talal St.

Nymphaeum

Al Husseini Mosque

Quraysh St.

Al-Istqlal St.

Abu al-Ala'a al-Ma'arri St.

An-Nuzha St.

JABAL HUSSEIN

King Hussein St.

ROYAL PALACES

Prince Muhammad St.

Sha'ban St.

Abu Bakr as-Saddiq St.

Malhas Hospital

SEE INSET MAP

JABAL AL-QALA'A

At-Taj St.

King Talal St.

Quraysh St.

JABAL JAUFEH

Prince Hasan St.

Al-Ansar St.

Abu Darwish Mosque

N

TO JERUSALEM, PETRA, AQABA (AD DUSTUR ST.)

TO ✈ AIRPORT & 🚌 WAHDAT BUS STATION (BUSES TO SOUTH)

⊏ GETTING AROUND

To reach locations within the city or to find the departure point for **buses** and **service**, ask a downtown shopkeeper. You can flag buses and *service* anywhere along their routes, but *service* are often full (they take five passengers) from the beginning to the end of their prescribed courses. Public transportation stops at 8 or 9pm, and a couple of hours earlier on Fridays. Walking is a safe alternative. Metered **taxis** prowl the streets and honk their horns at potential passengers. After 11pm, taxi drivers expect about double the daytime fare; make sure you bargain before getting in. 500fils is about right for a trip from downtown to 3rd Circle or from 3rd to 6th Circle; 350fils is usual for the downtown-Abdali route. A taxi between the two bus/*service* stations should cost 800fils. The trip along Jabal Amman from 1st to 8th Circle should cost no more than JD1.1; check to make sure the meter is running (see **Getting Around,** p. 455). It is an Arab custom for men to ride in the front seat of taxis. Women should always ride in the back seat.

BUSES. Buses traveling within Amman cost about 100fils; it's a little more if heading for the suburbs. Flag any bus traveling in your direction and ask the driver if it stops where you want to go, or find out at any bus station. Pay the fare after the ride has begun. Drivers and their assistants don't like making change, so carry 100fils in change with you. Most buses have the name of their destination written in Arabic on the front, sides, or both. Some have numbers, but since buses going on different routes may display the same number, what worked one time may not the next. Asking around is the best way to find a bus.

SERVICE. Although it may cost a bit more, transportation by *service* or white taxi is much easier on the nerves than bus travel and offers frequent opportunities to meet Jordanians. *Service* routes are clear and comprehensive, with their numbers and the names of their routes listed on the doors in Arabic. All routes within the city originate downtown. Stopping a *service* en route is difficult—many drive at breakneck speed, so make yourself visible without stepping into the street, and then stick out your arm with the palm down. Popular routes include:

#1 (١): On Jabal Amman, from Center City through 1st–3rd Circles (100fils).

#2 (٢): From Basman St. (behind Cliff Hostel) along Jabal Amman to Malik 'Abd Ribiya St. and between 2nd and 3rd Circles (90fils).

#3 (٣): From Basman St. along Jabal Amman to 3rd and 4th Circles (100fils).

#4 (٤): From Omar al-Khayyam St. (the street running alongside and behind downtown post office) to al-Amaneh Circle and gardens, passing near all points of interest on Jabal al-Weibdeh (90fils).

#6 (٦): From Cinema al-Hussein St. (a.k.a. Malik Ghazi St.), along King Faisal and King Hussein St. to Ministry of Interior Circle, passing Abdali and JETT bus stations (100fils).

#6a (٦ء): From Cinema al-Hussein St. to Shmeisani near the Ambassador Hotel (110fils).

#7 (٧): From Cinema al-Hussein St. past Abdali to Shmeisani near Arab Bank (70fils).

Service and **minibuses** to Wahdat Bus Station start at Kureisha St. (or *Sakfi Seil*) near Petra Bank and pass near Abu Darwish Mosque on Jabal Ashrafiyyeh. *Service* directly to Wahdat Bus Station from Abdali cost 120fils. Another route starts at Shabsough St. near the gold *souq* downtown, passing Abdali Bus Station and Jabal Hussein to Ministry of Interior Circle (90fils). Some prices are higher or lower than those listed, but drivers rarely cheat passengers, even tourists. Be wary of *service* drivers who "misinterpret" your directions to mean you want to hire the *service* as a private taxi. This usually only happens if you catch the *service* at the beginning of the route, but you can prevent it by insisting on waiting for other passengers, or by simply handing the correct fare (generally 100fils) to the driver.

⚜ ORIENTATION

Take advantage of Amman's summits to get a perspective on this roller-coaster city. Rocky **Jabal al-Qala'a** ("Fortress Hill"; also called the Citadel), where the Archaeological Museum sits amid Roman and Umayyad ruins, provides a panoramic view of tall buildings, mosques, and ruins, all of which serve as useful landmarks. The government has installed some street signs in downtown Amman; most have English translations. Although most people know **King Faisal St.** and **Hashimi St.**, other inquiries are likely to produce blank stares. Successful navigation of Amman means knowing its landmarks. Try to find out which numbered circle your destination is near and you'll have an easier time finding your way.

Amman's downtown district, **al-Balad,** is neatly framed by the city's seven hills and is the best location from which to orient yourself. Al-Balad has three major landmarks: the **al-Husseini Mosque (Masjid Malik Hussein),** the **Roman Theater,** and the **Central Post Office** *(maktab al-bareed).* Amman's eight **numbered traffic circles** follow a line leading westward out of town and through **Jabal Amman** on Zahran St. Beyond 3rd Circle (Amman's diplomatic center and home of most embassies), traffic circles have been replaced by busy intersections. Although the city is earnestly attempting to rename these intersections "squares," each is still fondly called a "circle," or *duwwar.* Following King Hussein St. northwest from the city center leads to **Jabal al-Weibdeh,** a tree-lined middle-class neighborhood perched on a hill. The **JETT** and **Abdali Bus Stations** are in this neighborhood. The blue dome and octagonal minaret of the Jabal's enormous **King Abdullah Mosque (Masjid Malik Abdullah)** are visible from all surrounding heights. To the north of the city lies **Jabal Hussein,** a largely residential district. This area is bordered to the northwest by the Ministry of Interior Circle *(Duwwar al-Dakhiliyyeh)* and the modern suburb of **Shmeisani,** complete with luxury hotels and American-style fast food restaurants. **Abdoun** and **Sweifiyyeh,** Amman's two other hotbeds of Western-style decadence, lie west of al-Balad. To the southeast of the city, in the direction of the airport, rises **Jabal al-Ashrafiyyeh.** Its ornate **Abu Darwish Mosque** can be seen above the **Wahdat Bus Station** and the Wahdat Palestinian Refugee Camp.

❷ PRACTICAL INFORMATION

TOURIST AND FINANCIAL SERVICES

Tourist Office: (☎464 23 11), adjacent to the Roman Theater. Recently renovated, the tourist office boasts maps and brochures.

Ministry of Tourism: P.O. Box 224 (☎464 23 11; fax 464 84 65). From 3rd Circle on Jabal Amman, walk down Abdul Muneim Riyad, then take the first right onto al-Mutanabbi St. to reach the imposing building on the right. Helpful office staff will do its best to answer questions with a limited inventory of brochures. Open Su-Th 8am-3pm.

Embassies and Consulates:

Australia (☎593 02 46, visa info 593 27 80), on Jabal Amman between 4th and 5th Circles, across from a large grassy knoll. Helpful with foreign visas. Open Su-Th 7:30am-3pm, consular services M-W 9am-noon.

Canada (☎566 61 24; fax 568 92 27), in Shmeisani behind Jabri Restaurant, near Petra Bank. Open Su-W 8am-4:30pm, Th 8am-1:30pm; consular services Su-Th 9-11am.

Egypt (☎560 51 75, visa info 560 52 03; fax 560 40 82), on Jabal Amman between 4th and 5th Circles, next to the Dove Hotel (Best Western). Take a right off Zahran St. after the grassy space and it's 50m down on the right. Bring photo and JD12 before noon; pick up visa that afternoon. Open Sa-Th 9am-3pm; consular services 9am-noon.

Israel (☎552 54 07, visa info 552 61 57 or 552 61 58; fax 552 19 71, visa fax 552 51 76), in 4th Circle on Jabal Amman. Far from *service* routes so take a yellow taxi. Visas issued Su-Th 9am-1pm (JD13). Open Su-Th 8am-4pm.

Lebanon (☎/fax 592 91 11), in Abdoun, behind UK Embassy. Bring photo and passport without any evidence of a trip to the West Bank or Israel, and get the visa in 24hr. UK and US citizens can also obtain visas upon arrival in Lebanon. One-month visa JD26; 3-month visa JD52. Open Su-Th 8am-2pm; consular services 8am-11am.

Syria (☎464 19 35 or 464 19 45), on Jabal Amman up from 3rd Circle toward the reflecting building. Take a left at the intersection and head up the hill. Look for the Syrian flag (red, white, and black stripes with two green stars). Only issues work visas; apply for tourist visas before arriving in Jordan. In theory, a visa costs JD43.5, but they are difficult to obtain—you must have a Jordanian entry stamp and no evidence of visits to the West Bank or Israel. Open Sa-Th 8:30am-2pm; consular services 9-10:30am.

UK (☎592 31 00; fax 592 37 59), in Abdoun on Damascus St. Instead of turning right to the US Embassy, continue on the road until reaching the Orthodox Club (the walled-in playground with the red jungle-gym protruding above the walls). The embassy is behind, with a blue iron fence. Open daily 8:30am-3pm; consular services Su-Th 8:30am-noon.

US (☎592 01 01, visa info 592 32 93; fax 592 41 02), in Abdoun, head north on Jabal Amman (Zahran St.), make a left at 5th Circle and continue to the first intersection. Make a left on Cairo St. and take the 3rd right. The fortress-like complex is 500m down that road. Open Su-Th 8am-4:30pm; consular services 1:30-4pm.

Currency Exchange: Banks are generally open Su-Th 8:30am-3:00pm and closed Friday and Saturday. Many authorized **money changers** (found downtown between the al-Husseini Mosque and the post office) are open daily, usually late into the evening. They offer roughly the same exchange rates as banks but will not ask for a bank's commission. Passport sometimes required. Most **ATMs**, including the one next to the Arab Bank on King Faisal St., can give **cash advances** on V and MC and many bank cards on international networks (Cirrus, PLUS).

American Express: P.O. Box 408 (☎560 70 14, emergency 79 58 44 64 or 79 52 05 76; fax 566 99 05; email guest@traders.com.jo), on Abdul Hamid Sharaf St. opposite Shmeisani's Ambassador Hotel. Holds mail. Open daily 8:30am-6pm.

LOCAL SERVICES

English-Language Bookstores: Gibraltar Bookshop (☎462 37 99), next to Hashem Restaurant, sells up-to-date American, French, and British magazines, stationery and postcards. Open daily 9:30am-8pm. **Al-'Ulama Bookshop** (☎463 61 92; fax 465 60 17), just uphill from the post office, has travel guides, dictionaries, and maps. Fax and photocopier (50fils per copy) available. Open Su-Th 8am-8pm, F 11am-8pm. **Istiqlal Library** has three locations in Amman: downtown, opposite the post office (☎462 24 75; open daily 7:30am-6pm); Shmeisani, downhill from Kentucky Fried Chicken (☎566 31 30; open Sa-Th 9am-1pm and 3-6:30pm); and Sweifiyyeh, around the corner from Turino Hotel (☎582 11 69). All have helpful English-speaking staffs. **Amman Bookshop** (☎464 40 13), at 3rd Circle down Prince Muhammad St. on the left, across from the large Kodak sign, is a huge store replete with trashy novels, esoteric art history books, CDs, and oodles of stationery. Open Su-Th 8:30am-2pm and 3:30-6:30pm. V, AmEx.

Local Press: *Your Guide to Amman*, published monthly and available free at larger hotels, bookstores, and travel agencies, is helpful. The *Jordan Times* (200fils), a daily newspaper with excellent coverage of the Middle East and Africa, lists useful telephone numbers, 24hr. pharmacies, and cultural events in Amman. *Jordan Today*, published monthly and available at larger hotels, has invaluable information on tourism, culture, and entertainment. The *International Herald Tribune* arrives after 3pm one day late at newsstands; *Time*, *Newsweek*, and *The Economist* are sporadically available. The weekly *Jerusalem Star* (350fils) lists cultural events and all the piddling details about the lives of the royals. The *New York Times* is sometimes available one day late at the gift shop in the Marriott and Inter-Continental Hotels.

Cultural Centers: American Cultural Center (☎592 01 01, ext. 2052; fax 585 91 01), in Abdoun, inside the American Embassy Complex. Free American films every Th and lectures by scholars and visiting politicians. Library has American periodicals, comfy couches, a video library, and a good selection of mostly-nonfiction books. Center and library open Su-Th 8am-5pm. **British Council** (☎463 61 47 or 463 61 48; fax 465 64 13), on Rainbow St. Facing uphill at 1st Circle, go left. The British Council is past the Saudi Embassy on the right. Sponsors films, lectures, and various other activities. Language Center Su-Th 11am-8:30pm; A/C library Su-Th 10am-7pm.

Laundromat: Laundromats are sparsely scattered throughout Amman, but many hotels and hostels provide laundry service (350fils per piece). **Dry Clean** (☎464 19 55), 3rd Circle in Jabal Amman and 50m down the street from the Ministry of Tourism, charges 500fils for shirts and 750fils for pants. **Aj-Jami'a Laundry** (☎534 78 57), on the first right heading away from the city past the main gate of Jordan University, is a do-it-yourself joint. Wash and dry JD2.

EMERGENCY AND COMMUNICATIONS

Emergency: Ambulance: ☎193 **Police:** ☎192. **Fire:** ☎462 200 90 or 462 200 93.

Late-Night Pharmacies: *Jordan Times* and *Your Guide to Amman* list weekly rotating late-night pharmacies and doctors. Pharmacies open Sa-Th 8am-9:30pm. The **Rawhi Pharmacy** (☎464 44 54), between 3rd and 4th Circles has an English-speaking staff. For non-prescription medicine, try **Safeway** (☎568 53 11), on the edge of Nasser ibn Jamil St. near the northwestern edge of Shmeisani, or in 7th Circle. (☎365 37 33. Open 24hr.)

Hospitals: The *Jordan Times, Jordan Star,* and *Your Guide to Amman* list doctors and hospitals. The **Shmeisani Hospital** (☎560 74 31) is reputable; others include the **Jordan Hospital** (☎560 75 50) in 4th Circle, and the **Arab Heart Surgical Hospital** (☎592 11 99), an ultramodern research institute in 5th Circle.

Telephones: Overseas calls can be made from hotels, but it's cheapest to use payphones around Amman, which accept phonecards but not cash. **Alo** and **JPP** cards available at most newsstands and some restaurants in denominations of JD1, JD5, and JD15; good for both local and international calls. Private phone offices on Omar al-Khayyam St. To get there, take a left out of the post office and make the first left up the street across from the Cliff Hotel.

Directory Information: ☎121 (Amman). ☎131 (Jordan). ☎0132 (international).

Internet Access: The **JAI Internet Cafe** (☎461 77 46 or 461 02 05), on the 3rd circle in Jabal Amman (4th floor of a building on the circle; look for signs) allows you to set up an account for larger discounts (500fils for 30min., JD1 per hr.). Eight slow pentium computers with Win95 and telnet, and one scanner. English-speaking staff.

Post Office: Generally open Sa-Th 7am-5pm, F 7am-1pm. The main post office is at the base of Prince Muhammad St., just before it joins King Faisal St. downtown. Stamps and Poste Restante. **Faxes** (JD2 per page to US) can be sent from this office. Open Sa-Th 8:30am-7pm, F 8am-noon. **EMS** (☎568 81 90) is on Lifta St., a dead end behind Qawar Arthroscopy Center. From downtown, go up King Hussein St. past the Abdali and JETT Bus Stations. Take a right on Bir al-Sab'a St. and look left. Open daily 8am-8pm; holidays 8am-2pm.

⌐ ACCOMMODATIONS

Most backpackers are **downtown,** which is overgrown with small, seedy hotels conveniently located near the main post office, several telephone offices, a large market, and many affordable restaurants. Many clean and reputable (and more expensive) hotels are near the **Abdali Bus Station** in Jabal al-Weibdeh, an area close to the city center and convenient for transport out of Amman. Just beyond Jabal al-Weibdeh is the upscale **Shmeisani** district, with a few reasonably priced accommodations worth the hunt. Rooms have private baths unless otherwise noted. Prices come down during the ambiguously defined off-season; basically, you pay more if the hotel is close to full, so always ask for discounts and try to bargain.

DOWNTOWN/AL-HUSSEINI MOSQUE AREA

Farah Hotel (☎465 14 43 or 465 14 38; fax 465 14 37), on Cinema al-Hussein St. Follow red and yellow signs at the intersection of King Hussein and King Faisal St. through an alley and across a street to this six-story behemoth. Each floor has four smallish rooms with TVs, two bathrooms (free showers, no toilet paper), and a large fridge. International phone office with high rates downstairs. Laundry 350fils per piece. Internet JD1 per hr. Breakfast JD1. Rooftop mattresses JD2.5; shared rooms JD4 per person; singles JD7; doubles JD9.

Bdeiwi Hotel, P.O. Box 182462 (☎464 33 94; fax 464 33 93), on Khayyam St. uphill from post office. Brightly painted, immaculate rooms and clean, shared bathrooms on quiet sidestreet downtown. Fans in all rooms and international telephone service at the front desk. Comfortable for lone women. Singles JD6; doubles JD8.

Al-Harmin Hotel (☎465 58 90; fax 465 58 45), on al-Hashimi St. across from the Roman Theater. English-speaking manager welcomes visitors to this clean, 2nd-floor hotel, accessible via an outdoor staircase. Singles JD5; doubles JD6.

Cliff Hostel, P.O. Box 184381 (☎462 42 73), on Prince Muhammad St. Facing away from the post office, cross to the left-most of the two streets ahead (toward the blue "Citizen" sign). Take a left and walk half a block to an alley beneath a Coca-Cola-postered terrace. Clean, high-ceilinged rooms with fans. Showers 500fils. Lockout at midnight, but a knock will get you in later. Reserve in advance during busy season. Terrace mattress JD2; singles JD5; doubles JD8; triples JD10.5; slightly lower prices in summer.

Beirut Hotel (☎463 69 86 or 463 80 99; fax 465 09 16), al-Hashimi St. between the al-Husseini Mosque and the Roman Theater. Walking from the mosque, look for the blue sign with white English letters on the left side of the street after about 90m. Eager-to-please manager caters to Arab and Western clientele. Carpeted rooms are small and somewhat dirty. Private telephones and common bath. Almost exclusively male clientele. Singles JD5; doubles JD8; triples JD15.

Amman Castle Hotel (☎/fax 464 68 09), on Shabsuq St. between al-Husseini Mosque and the Roman Theater, 90m down on the right-hand side of the mosque. "HOTEL" in red letters on yellow background. Few foreigners. Proprietors speak minimal English, but small rooms are comfortable and clean. 3rd-floor common kitchen. JD4.5 per person.

NEAR ABDALI STATION

◪ **Caravan Hotel,** P.O. Box 9062 (☎566 11 95 or 566 11 97; fax 566 11 96; email caravan@go.com.jo; www.myfreeoffice.com/caravan-hotel//amman.html), on the corner of al-Ma'moun St. and Khalil Toutah in Jabal al-Weibdeh. Only 100m southwest of Abdali Bus Station, immediately south of King Abdullah Mosque. Entrance is a short walk down the street directly opposite the mosque, across from an Orthodox church. Spacious, spotless rooms have carpeting and soft beds. Ask for a balcony. Fans and satellite TV in every room. Free local calls. Internet JD2 per 30min. Singles JD24; doubles JD27; triples JD32 (tax, service, and breakfast included). 15% *Let's Go* discount or off-season and extended stay discounts, but no double discounts. V, MC.

Canary Hotel, P.O. Box 9062 (☎463 83 53 or 463 83 62; fax 465 43 53; email canary_h@hotmail.com), Karmali St. in Jabal al-Weibdeh near Terra Sancta College. From Abdali Station, walk 1½ blocks downhill along the right side of King Hussein St. When the main road forks downhill to the left, continue straight and uphill on al-Ba'oniyah St. Take the first right on al-Karmali St. and try to survive the final 1½-block climb. Owned by the same family as the Caravan, this hotel offers the same quality facilities, at slightly lower prices. Singles JD22; doubles JD25; triples JD28.

Merryland Hotel, P.O. Box 9122 (☎464 37 39 or 465 42 39; telefax 463 03 70 or 463 03 72; email merrylandhotel@hotmail.com), on King Hussein St. Walk downhill on the right-hand side of King Hussein St.; Merryland is approximately 90m past Abdali Station, on the right. The hotel-restaurant features glass chandeliers, a small bar, and a sleazy disco downstairs (open daily 11pm-3am). Almost exclusively male clientele.Huge rooms have springy mattresses, color satellite TV, electric fans or A/C, and refrigerators. Check-out noon. Dry cleaning 250fils per shirt. Singles JD12; doubles JD15; triples JD18; quads JD21; quints JD25. V, MC, AmEx.

Remal Hotel, P.O. Box 910477 (☎463 06 70, ☎/fax 465 57 51), on Sa'id ibn al-Harith St. Look downhill from the Abdali Bus Station for the police station on the right; the hotel is 100m up the small street that runs up the right side of the station. Rooms have large and comfy beds with fluffy feather pillows. Attached restaurant offers traditional

Arab fare for breakfast. Some rooms have balconies. TVs, fans, and phones (free local calls). Singles JD14; doubles JD18; triples JD24; add 13% tax, 10% service charge.

Al-Monzer Hotel, P.O. Box 926595 (☎463 94 69; fax 465 73 28; email mfj@nol.com.jo), on King Hussein St. across from Abdali Station. Reasonably priced rooms with fans and phones. Some rooms come with in-room bath. Singles JD7-9; doubles JD8-11; triples JD19. Student discounts. V, MC.

SHMEISANI

Nefertiti Hotel, 26 al-Jahed St. (☎560 38 65 or 560 35 53), two streets downhill from and directly in line with the Ambassador Hotel. All rooms are quite large. Some have gigantic glass-enclosed terraces, delightful places to enjoy the quiet neighborhood. Others have glass-enclosed bathrooms that afford spectacular toilet-seat views of Amman without compromising your privacy. Be sure to check out several rooms before committing; they differ enough that one may suit your taste more than another. Some with private bath, others without. Singles JD11.5; doubles JD14.5; triples JD18. Cash only.

◌ FOOD

RESTAURANTS

The better sit-down restaurants in Amman cluster near 3rd Circle, in Shmeisani, and along Mecca St. These places usually add a 10% service charge to the bill. The jewels of the city's offerings are the street foods. If the listings are in Arabic, ask the vendor to translate. The **souq** is near the al-Husseini Mosque (with your back to the mosque turn left and walk about four blocks); prices are steady and bargaining unnecessary. (Open Su-Th 8:30am-sundown.) For some cool treats after these cheap eats, try **Crema Creme** or **Frosti** on Paris St.

Westerners and wealthy Ammanites swear by the **Safeway** stores on the edge of Shmeisani and at 7th Circle, where dry cleaning, shoe repair, a hardware store, Internet access, and a branch of the American sandwich shop, **Subway** (open 24hr.), stand. American grease-to-go has also invaded Jordan: **McDonald's, Pizza Hut, Arby's,** and **Kentucky Fried Chicken** draw locals and tourists—the neon signs in Shmeisani burn brightly and taxis know the route well. For a real taste of Americana, head to **Cheers Elite Cafe** in Sweifiyyeh's Turino Hotel, where everybody knows your name. There is now a **Planet Hollywood** in Abdoun.

▨ **New Orient Restaurant (Abu Ahmad)** (☎ 464 18 79), 3rd Circle in Jabal Amman behind the Amman Surgical Hospital. Follow signs marked "City Center" from 3rd Circle to al-Amir Muhammad St.; take a right onto al-Sharq St. and the restaurant will be on the right. Splurge at this luxurious restaurant among vines, green tablecloths, and a hyper-attentive staff. Award-winning *nouvelle* Arabic cuisine. Appetizers 600fils-JD2; entrees JD2-6.5. Open daily noon-4pm and 7pm-midnight. Traveler's checks, V, MC.

▨ **Hashem Restaurant** (☎463 64 40), on Prince Muhammad St. in the alley directly across from the Cliff Hotel. Arabic fast food at its best. Almost on top of the intersection of King Faisal St., Prince Muhammad St., and King Hussein St., Hashem is a great place to see, hear, and taste Amman. Hummus and *fuul* served with an amazing pickled pepper concoction and fresh bread. Tea, hummus, and an evening's conversation with locals totals well under 650fils. Take-out makes good packed lunches for daytrips. Open 24hr.

Cairo Restaurant (☎462 45 27). Facing away from the al-Husseini mosque, head left past the clothing shops, turn left at the second street, and look for the big red and white sign. Often crowded, the Cairo offers an extensive Arabic menu, including Jordanian *maglouba*, an "upside-down" dish of rice, chicken, and vegetables. *Maglouba* JD1, kebab JD1.3, hummus 300fils. Open daily 5am-midnight.

Al-Quds Restaurant (Jerusalem Restaurant) (☎463 01 68), on King Hussein St. around the corner from the post office. Exiting the Hashem Restaurant, make a left and cross the street before the greenish al-Quds awning on the right. Although it looks like an

American pancake house, al-Quds serves authentic Arabic food in a wonderfully clean setting. Try their variation on *mensaf,* made with chicken instead of lamb (JD2), or sample their kebab (JD1.9) and hummus (500fils). Open daily 8am-10pm.

Salam Restaurant (☎ 462 26 26), on King Faisal St. half a block up from the al-Husseini Mosque on the left-hand side of the street, next to the Bata shoe store. Very small English sign; look for spitted chickens in the window. Come for the colorful crowd, tasty food, and enticing aroma; stay for the pastries. JD2.5 buys bread, bird, and fries at the tables upstairs. Friendly service and English menu. Open daily 8am-10pm.

Romero (☎ 464 42 27 or 464 42 28), 3rd Circle, Jabal Amman. Walking toward 2nd Circle from 3rd, take the second right; it's across from the Ambassador Hotel. Take the hottie from the hostel to this romantic outdoor cafe for the best Italian food in Amman. Pasta JD3-4.5, meat and seafood JD4-9. Open daily 1-3:30pm and 8-11:30pm. Reserve in advance. V, MC, AmEx.

Abu Khamis and Abu Saleh Restaurant (☎ 462 27 82), on King Faisal St. one alley over from the Cliff Hostel in the direction of the al-Husseini Mosque. A small facade masks a spacious, smoky interior. Half-chicken and kebab JD1.4 each. Open daily 7am-10pm.

L'Olivier Garden (☎ 592 95 64), in Abdoun. Serves tasty French cuisine on a pleasant patio. The restaurant offers a bizarre "Car Park" buffet, in which take-out food is served from the backs of cars (JD8). Appetizers JD3-5; entrees JD4-7.

Rasetelbab Restaurant (☎ 962 12 53). Walking from the Cliff Hostel toward the al-Husseini mosque on the left side of King Faisal St., turn left up the alley next to the green Abu Sara Cousins store. Rasetelbab does not have an English sign, but it's the only restaurant in the alley. Look for the brightly colored straw stools and take a seat. Pleases patrons with omelettes and meat with tomatoes (300-350fils).

CAFES

Jordanian cafes are mostly frequented by men. Anyone who is anyone mingles at the **Caffe Moka** on al-Qahirah St. in Abdoun, which serves tarts, sundaes, and various types of coffee, all for JD1-3. (☎ 592 62 85; fax 593 24 09; email moka@go.com.jo. Open daily 7:30am-midnight.) Also try **Ma'atouk's** in 3rd Circle (coffee 300fils), or the absurdly named **Eco-Tourism Cafe** on King Faisal St., where a friendly mix of young and old Jordanian men shoot the breeze over *ahwa* and *argeileh*. (☎ 465 29 94. Open daily 9am-midnight.) Women may feel more comfortable (bring a male friend) at such places as **Reem al-Badawy,** Tla' al-'Ali, al-Ubeel Circle, which offers *argeileh* for smoking in traditional Bedouin camel-hair tents. **Babiche Cafe** and **Geneva** in Shmeisani serve coffee, drinks, and pastries to a chichi coed crowd. The popular **al-Sultan Coffee Shop,** along the main drag in Shmeisani, provides Turkish coffee (JD1) worthy of a sultan and a lively after-dinner atmosphere for couples and their children. Live music nightly. (☎ 560 59 29. Open 24hr.) A slightly younger crowd mixes on the sprawling rooftop patio at **Books@Cafe** (☎ 465 04 57), on Mango St. in Jabal Amman. The cafe serves tasty crepes (JD2) and pasta dishes (JD3), and the bookstore below offers Internet access and sells English-language books and magazines.

⚫ SIGHTS

CITADEL HILL. From the Roman theater or any other downtown locale, climb the steep steps and streets to the flat top of Citadel Hill. A trip to the top of Citadel Hill is a good idea for the first day in Amman, as the view gives the best perspective on the city's labyrinthine ups and downs. The trip is best taken with a companion (especially true for women). The citadel is the site of ancient Amman, called Rabbath-Ammon or "The Great City of the Ammonites"—an ancient people who make several cameos in the Bible. Try wandering around the extensive ruins alone, since guides charge an outrageous JD5 to decipher the site's historical wealth, more of which Spanish and American archaeological teams are constantly uncovering.

Tours lead visitors from the three remaining columns of the Roman **Temple of Hercules** to the much later and recently renovated **Umayyad Palace.** (*Accessible by taxi from downtown for 500fils. Open daily 8am-5pm.*)

ANCIENT ROMAN RUINS. Amman's best-preserved and most intriguing ruins lie behind the Archaeological Museum. Vaulted chambers tower 10m over a spacious courtyard where elaborate floral decorations can still be seen in the stonework. A 7th-century structure once supported a huge stone dome and was used as a mosque, audience hall, and residence. Below the Roman walls, directly to the north, an open pit leads into the underground passageway that connected the fortified city to a hidden water supply. With fancy footwork and a flashlight you can enter the cavernous rock-hewn cistern by this route (the more conventional approach is from the gate on the street below). Avoid the grassy area across from the Temple of Hercules: despite its location, it's not part of the ruins but a youthful 40-year-old cemetery. A path between the two leads to a hard-to-see shortcut down the steep steps and backyards of the hillside neighborhood. The route is safe and offers local color, but *Let's Go* does not recommend it to lone women.

AL-HUSSEINI MOSQUE AND ENVIRONS. The Citadel was the heart of ancient Amman, but today Amman's pulse emanates from downtown, in and around this noted mosque (also called *Masjid Malik Hussein*). The Ottoman-style structure was built in 1924 on the site of an ancient mosque built by Umar, the second caliph of Islam. The nearby **Nymphaeum** was a sacred fountain and bathing ground for the ancient city. At the center of the triangle formed by the Roman Theater, the mosque, and the post office is Amman's **gold souq,** featuring shop upon shop of gold jewelry and a few shops selling antique Bedouin silver jewelry. Although bargaining is a way of life in much of Amman, prices in the gold market are fixed at JD5.5 per gram. (*Open Sa and M-Th 9am-9pm, Su 9am-1pm.*)

KING ABDULLAH AND ABU DARWISH MOSQUES. Barely out of a *muezzin*'s range from al-Husseini Mosque stands Abdali's own place of worship, the *Masjid Malik Abdullah.* Constructed over seven years in memory of the late king (the current Abdullah's great-grandfather), King Abdullah Mosque's blue mosaic dome can shelter 3000 Muslims kneeling in prayer. The black-and-white checkered dome of the nearby Abu Darwish Mosque *(Masjid Abu Darwish)* peeks over Jabal Ashrafiyyeh. In the 1940s, Circassians built this mosque, one of the most unusual religious structures in the Middle East, entirely from white rock and black basalt, brought from quarries in the northern part of the country. The two colors were also used for the mosque's decoration and ornamentation.

SWEIFIYYEH MOSAIC. Amman's finest Byzantine artifact was found during construction at the western edge of the city in 1970. The mosaic illustrates the passing of the seasons and once belonged to a 6th-century church. Ask the caretaker to hose down the floor for a better look at the bizarre creatures: leaf-bearded men, eagles with ears, and eel-men. The most worthwhile site north of Madaba. (*Follow the signs from the first left west of 6th Circle. Open Sa-Th 9am-4pm, F 9am-1:30pm. Free.*)

ROMAN THEATER. The Roman Theater, on Jabal al-Qala'a downtown, is the most renowned of Amman's historical sights. Built by Roman Emperor Antonius Pius (138-161 CE), the Roman Theater could once accommodate all 6000 of Amman's inhabitants. (*Open daily 8am-9pm. Free.*)

🏛 MUSEUMS

HERITAGE MUSEUMS. Two museums are built into the foundations of the theater on either side of the enclosed stage area. On the right, the **Folklore Museum** has dioramas on the diverse heritages of the Jordanian people—from Circassian military weaponry to Palestinian embroideries and Bedouin encampments. The **Traditional Jewels and Costumes Museum** shows off attire and accessories from the country's past. The gallery to the right of the entrance displays 6th-century mosaics from Madaba and Jerash. (*Folklore Museum* ☎ *465 17 42. Open daily 8am-5pm. Museum of Popular Traditions* ☎ *465 17 60. Open daily 9am-5pm. Both JD1. Students can try begging for free admission.*)

ARCHAEOLOGICAL MUSEUM. This museum on Citadel Hill contains a chronologically organized series of finds from ancient sites throughout Jordan. Fragments of the **Dead Sea Scrolls** and 200,000-year-old rhinoceros teeth share the limelight with Iron Age anthropomorphic sarcophagi, minimalist Nabatean portraits, and sublime Roman marble statuary. In front of the museum are the foundations of a 2nd-century Roman temple that housed a 10m statue of Hercules, to whom the temple was likely dedicated. Three of the statue's giant marble fingers hint at the shrine's former glory. (☎ *463 87 95. Open daily 8am-5pm. JD2.*)

JORDAN NATIONAL GALLERY. This gallery displays a vast amount of contemporary artwork representing the cultural output of the entire Middle East and the Islamic world. Many of the works are surprisingly critical of daily life. Shift gears to this day and age to take a break from the ancient ruins. (*On Jabal al-Weibdeh at Muntazah Park.* ☎ *463 01 28. Open W-M 10am-1:30pm and 3:30-6pm. JD1.*)

🎵 🍸 ENTERTAINMENT AND NIGHTLIFE

Though there's plenty of action **downtown**, the two hippest neighborhoods are **Shmeisani** and **Abdoun**, suburbs on the western side of the city. Shmeisani is the older of the two, and its restaurants and cafes are frequented by families and couples. Abdoun is so young that new streets are laid nightly (literally), and here you will find the most recent movies in town, trendy nightclubs (open until 2am), and young, hip, and wealthy crowds. There are no bargain beer joints in these neighborhoods (or anywhere in Amman, for that matter), but a night in Shmeisani or Abdoun affords a glimpse of the new, modern, and Western-influenced Middle East. Women (alone or in mixed groups), gays, and lesbians will feel more comfortable going out in these two neighborhoods than anywhere else in Amman. *Service* run during the day to Shmeisani from downtown (150fils), but not yet to Abdoun, so take a taxi (JD1.5).

CINEMA AND THEATER

Four **cinemas** show English-language films: the **Philadelphia** (☎ 463 41 44), 100m down Prince Muhammad St. from 3rd Circle; **Concord** (☎ 567 74 20), Abdali; **Plaza** (☎ 569 92 38), at the Forte Grande in Shmeisani; and the luxurious **Galery 1 and 2** in Abdoun. A few scattered theaters show B-grade action movies from India and the US, as well as 1970s soft porn. The word on the street says the censors have cut these to ribbons by the time they hit the screens, so buyers beware. **Cinema al-Hussein,** downhill from the Farah Hotel is a good spot for such titillating fare. The **Nabil & Hisham's Theater** (☎ 462 51 55), on Rainbow St. in 1st Circle, sometimes produces Arabic-language plays.

AL-VEGAS

Lone men and progressive couples interested in a more authentic (if slightly seedier) experience should explore the nightlife on Prince Muhammad St., about 300m downhill from the 3rd Circle. **Arizona** and her neighbor down the hill, **Kinz,** boast live Arabic music and belly dancers in a restaurant-style setting. No nudity, no cover. At JD5 for a beer, though, don't expect an excursion into Amman's slightly sketchier underbelly to be cheap. **Caesar's Palace Restaurant,** on Jabal al-Weibdeh, offers more traditional Jordanian music and dancing, including belly dancing on Thursday nights. For traditional Arab singing and music, brave the hefty cover at the **Roof Garden,** near Salute and Gengiskhan Restaurant. Waitresses in red body suits with shiny chest ornaments will bring large Amstels to you and your 18+ companions. (☎ 465 88 51. Drinks JD2-2.5; cover JD5-6, includes first drink).

BARS

For less trendy elitism and more good old-fashioned drinking, try the canned Guinness at the **Irish Pub** in the basement of the Dove Hotel (Best Western), between 4th and 5th Circles, next door to the Egyptian Embassy. (☎ 569 76 01 or 569 76 02. Beer JD3-4; happy hour M 7-9pm. Open daily 6:30pm-2am.) You can also find a wide selection of beer in Abdoun at the newer Irish pub, **The Big Fellow,** part of the Sheraton Entertainment Center on al-Kaldera St. A favorite among Westerners for watching live soccer matches, its glitzy atmosphere and pool tables draw sleek young locals as well. (Cocktails JD3-5, Guinness JD3.2, Amstel JD2.8. Open daily 1pm-2am.) Around the corner on Abdoun Circle, the **TCHE TCHE Cafe** (☎ 593 20 20) is a another popular hangout. Cocktails, milkshakes, and sandwiches all go for around JD2. There are also a variety of grimy dives downtown; one is as good as another, and the **Jordan Bar,** buried in the left-most alleyway off Prince Muhammad St., facing away from Hashem Restaurant, serves tall beers at low prices (JD2).

CLUBS

Amman has its fair share of nightclubs. The scene picks up noticeably in the summer, when the sweltering days give way to cool evenings. Thursdays rage by all accounts, Sundays and Mondays also produce a fair-to-middling crowd, but the rest of the week is dead. Many of the hippest discos have members-only policies. One consistently popular hotspot is **Salute,** between 1st and 2nd Circles, under the Villa d'Angelo Italian restaurant. If you can squeeze yourself onto their breezy patio, consider yourself a member of the "in" crowd. Unaccompanied men are not admitted. (☎ 465 14 58. Drinks JD2-5. No cover. Happy Hour Th 11:45pm-12:45am.) Chic clothing and a silver tongue will get you into **Yesterday's** (☎ 565 42 01), in 4th Circle. In Abdoun, **Ciro's Pizza Pomodoro of Knightsbridge,** on an alley off al-Kaldera St., converts into a bar and club at night. The DJ spins Top 40 American tunes for a good-looking twenty-something crowd. (Drinks JD2-5. Cover JD3).

🞐 DAYTRIPS FROM AMMAN

WADI AL-SEER AND ENVIRONS

The easiest path begins from the al-Husseini Mosque in Amman. Walk left past the screeching taxis to a fork in the road (10min.). Head left at the fork; the lines of **minibuses** *off to the right will stop at Wadi al-Seer (150fils). From Wadi al-Seer, catch a minibus headed down the valley road (150fils). The whole trip takes 45min.-1½hr., depending on your driver's skill at avoiding stray chickens; buses leave when full. Bring plenty of water and patience—you may have a bit of a wait for the return trip.*

Burgeoning Amman has begun spreading westward into the quiet valley of Wadi al-Seer, a region first settled by the fair-skinned Circassians. Its high desert plateau suddenly gives way to the Jordan Valley, where a little stream (*"wadi,"* hence the name) snakes through the countryside on its way to the Dead Sea. The narrow asphalt road that follows this valley out of town is ideal for daytripping motorists and tramping backpackers, even on scorching summer days. Groups of friendly children wander through the verdant pomegranate plants and olive trees that line the 12km road that runs southwest to the remains of Qasr al-Abd.

Soon after leaving Wadi al-Seer, you'll pass **al-Bassa Springs,** the source of the valley's fertility and the site of a local swimming pool. Carved into the face of the cliff above the left bank of the *wadi* is **al-Deir,** the monastery. This extraordinary building merits the 20-minute climb, even if you don't find any of the Roman gold that villagers claim is buried under the floor. Each of the ossuary's thousands of triangular wall-niches once cradled a monk's skull.

QASR AL-ABD (CASTLE OF THE SLAVE) قصر العبد

Qasr al-Abd is the last stop at the end of the road from Amman through Wadi al-Seer. The guard or his son should let you in for free; a donation of 100-200fils is appreciated.

The story behind the creation of this impressive rock palace is almost as fascinating as the monolithic carvings on its walls. Local legend holds that a love-smitten slave named Tobiah built **Qasr al-Abd** (Castle of the Slave) to win the hand of his master's daughter. Tobiah carved lions, panthers, and eagles into its walls while his master was away. Unfortunately, the master returned before Tobiah could finish, and the slave's efforts went unrewarded save the Aramaic inscription "Tobiah" carved near the entrance of one of the 11 hand-dug **caves,** 500m back up the valley road. Kill-joy historians, however, explain the inscription and the castle remains with references to Tobiah the Ammonite Servant (of God), a rich priest in Jerusalem. Ancient historian Josephus records yet another story about a wealthy Tobiah family and the exploits of the young son Hyrcanus, who built a strong fortress constructed entirely of white marble and enclosed by a wide, deep moat.

Regardless of who actually built the palace, two red stone lions remain intact, though there is no roof. The most impressive is the lioness (without a mane) on the northwest corner, but both lions have a unique twist: the male (with the flowing mane) is breast-feeding a baby with its female nipples, and the female lioness, prowling the corner alone, has male genitals.

NORTH OF AMMAN

SALT السلط ☎ 05

Salt (pronounced SULT) thrived as an administrative center during Ottoman rule, making it a likely choice for the capital of the new mandate of Transjordan when it was formed in 1921 (see **Modern History,** p. 450). The more centrally located village of Amman won that honor, however, and Salt's main connection to governmental administration today is that the swanky preparatory school there can claim almost all of Jordan's high officials as alumni.

Nevertheless, Salt's position as a regional Ottoman stronghold is still very evident: whole sections of archways from a church destroyed during the reign of the Ottomans snuggle up beside older local homes. The Ottoman barracks (built over a 13th-century fortress destroyed to prevent its capture by Crusaders) also remain intact, and Salt's large Christian community has peppered the hillsides with church towers. In the second half of the 19th century, Salt again became the center of regional society when industrious Saltis built Jordan's first hospital, modern church, and secondary school. Downhill from the bus station in Salt lies **Wadi She'ib.** Natural streams bubble out of the ground and break through the pavement of the main road. Unexplored caves, abandoned stone houses, and numerous dirt paths wrap around the *wadi*, lush terraced farmlands, and eucalyptus groves, making a minibus ride up Wadi She'ib the most dramatic approach to Salt.

GETTING THERE AND PRACTICAL INFORMATION. From Amman, corner an Abdali Station bus driver to find the **minibus** going to Salt (30min., 175fils). Minibuses depart when full; be prepared to wait. Return minibuses run until early evening. The **post office** (☎ 554 96 85) is uphill on the main road, a good 10min. walk from the bus station. (Open Sa-Th 7:30am-7pm, F 7:30am-1:30pm.)

ACCOMMODATIONS AND FOOD. Although Salt has no hotels, Saltis are proud to uphold the Bedouin tradition of *khuttar*, whereby prominent (and not-so-prominent) local families take it upon themselves to host any visitors that cross their paths or knock on their doors.

For the best kebab north of Amman, head to **Al-Amad's** (☎ 355 07 65), established in 1927 by Radi al-Amad and inherited by his son, who runs it today. Amad's is uphill and to the left from the bus station, but it is hard to find—ask a local. (Chicken JD2. Open daily 7am-midnight.) Finish up with freshly-baked pastries at the chain-patisserie **Al-Habiba,** up the road from Canam and across from the Archaeological Museum (the *warbaht* is especially good).

SIGHTS. To get to the free Salt Archaeological and Folklore Museums, walk 300m uphill from the bus station, veering right. It's the cream stone building on the right with green wrought-iron balconies and a big black sign. The **Archaeological Museum** (☎355 65 51) consists of two rooms with lots of coins, pottery, and jewelry dating from the Chalcolithic period (4000 BCE) to the Islamic period (1516 CE). The **Folklore Museum** (☎355 36 53) is one flight up from the Archaeology Museum. (Both open Sa-Th 8am-6pm, F 9am-5:30pm.) The highest point in Salt is the 1000-year old mosque on **Jabal Yushah,** which, according to Muslim legend, houses the tomb of the Prophet Hosea, or Yushah, the grandson of Moses. Since tradition holds that Yushah was 12m tall, his tomb is quite impressive. Moreover, the awe-inspiring view of the West Bank will make the trip up the hill worth your while: in the morning, it is possible to see from the Dead Sea to Lake Tiberias. (A round-trip taxi from downtown Salt costs JD2.)

JERASH جرش ☎02

Buried by sand for many centuries, much of the ancient city of Jerash remains remarkably intact. Its main road, which still bears evidence of chariot traffic, extends several hundred meters through a magnificent series of columns, shops, temples, theaters, and arches. Stumbled upon by German traveler Ulrich Seetzen in 1806, Jerash is one of the most extensive provincial Roman cities still in existence. In ancient times it was dubbed Gerasa and was an important member of the Decapolis League, a loose association of trading cities allied with Rome (see **Ancient History,** p. 449). Because of Jerash's isolation in a remote valley, it survived long after the other nine cities were destroyed.

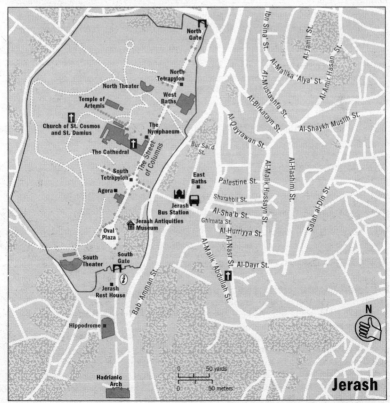

Jerash

Jerash is typically Roman in design. The city's builders trampled over earlier settlements, so little evidence of pre-Roman days remains. Inscriptions calling the town **Antioch** reveal that the Seleucid king of that name had a prominent outpost here, but Jerash entered its golden age only after Roman general Pompey conquered it in 64 BCE. Over the following three centuries, Jerash experienced a period of prosperity rivaled only by the city's recent tourist boom. Granite was brought from as far away as Aswan and old temples were razed and rebuilt according to the latest architectural trends. In 106 CE, the Emperor Trajan annexed the surrounding Nabatean lands and built a highway from Damascus to Aqaba that passed through Jerash. The impressive Triumphal Arch built for Emperor Hadrian's visit in 129 still stands. The town was later converted to Christianity and housed a bishop by the mid-4th century.

Following the destruction of the Syrian trading center at Palmyra (see p. 580) and the decline of the Nabatean kingdom, trade routes shifted from the desert to the sea. Frantic construction continued through the 6th century, but without their former wealth, the citizens of Jerash could only replace the older monuments with inferior structures subsequently plundered by invading Persians in 635. The great earthquake of 749 destroyed much of the area and few remnants of the ancient city were left by the time the Muslim Arabs came to control the city. The Crusaders described Jerash as uninhabited, and it remained abandoned until its rediscovery in the 19th century. After the invasion of the Ottomans, Circassians built the modern town in what was once the main residential area.

▐ GETTING THERE AND GETTING AROUND

Getting to Jerash is gleefully easy. **Minibuses** (275fils) and air-conditioned **buses** (300fils) leaving from Amman's Abdali Station make the one-hour journey routinely throughout the day. **Service** are a bit pricier, somewhat faster, and also leave from Abdali. Ask the driver to stop at the Hadrianic Arch; otherwise he'll stop across the river, next to the Eastern baths.

Buses and *service* leave town from the Jerash Bus Station. **Buses** serve Abdali Station in Amman (1hr.; 275fils, A/C 300fils), Ajloun (300fils), and Irbid (300fils). *Service* generally cost 50% more than buses. Public transportation shuts down around 5pm. Hitchers to Amman, Dibbin, or Ajloun are known to walk south about one kilometer from the Visitors Center to the intersection with Highway 20. Turning right (west) leads to Ajloun and Dibbin National Park. Going straight leads to Amman. Buses pass frequently toward Amman and are easy to flag. Stand back from the road as you signal the bus—drivers seem to consider time and speed infinitely more important than toes.

JERASH FESTIVAL The immensely popular Jerash Festival was instituted in 1981 by the ever-gracious Queen Noor and takes place every summer in the second half of July. The South Theater and Artemis Steps provide a dramatic setting for musical, theatrical, and dance groups who come from all over the world to perform in celebration of past and present Jordanian and international culture. Performers have ranged from superstar Umm Kulthum to the Royal Jordanian Orchestra, and from Spanish flamenco dancers to the Royal Shakespeare Company. The festival has become very popular in recent years thanks to the presence of beloved Arab pop star Majdah al-Roumi (a Lebanese Celine Dion). The festival lasts two weeks, and spectators can buy one day passes (JD1) for most events, but must buy separate tickets in advance for the top acts (JD5-10). Tickets are sold all over Amman (and usually sell out) in the weeks beforehand. Transport to and from Jerash is chaotic. Your best bet is to get a group together and share a private taxi. For details and line-up, check with the Jerash Festival Office, P.O. Box 910 582, Amman (☎(06) 567 51 99), look on the web at www.jerashfestival.com.jo, or read the *Jordan Times*. Also see **Jerash Festival**, p. 452.

🎯 ORIENTATION AND PRACTICAL INFORMATION

Pass through the Hadrianic Arch and walk five minutes along the main road, past the Hippodrome, to reach the **Visitors Information Center,** which will appear on the right. (☎ 635 12 72. Open daily 8am-7pm; in winter 8am-5pm.) The **Jerash Bus Station** is on the western edge of the new city, across the river from the Visitors Center. The **post office** is behind the bus station. (Open daily 8am-5pm.) The **tourist police** station stands across the street.

Jerash dazzles along the one-kilometer walk from the South Gate down the Street of Columns to the North Gate. The tiny Chrysoras (Golden) River separates the ancient ruins on the western bank from the new town on the eastern bank. Groups can hire **guides** (JD5; tip JD1 also expected). Booklets including maps and explanations of the sights invite leisurely exploration (JD1-6).

🏠 ACCOMMODATIONS AND FOOD

An easy daytrip from Amman, Jerash has few accommodations in town. The luxurious **Olive Branch Resort,** P.O. Box 2314, Amman 11181, is five kilometers uphill from the ancient ruins. A minibus runs about every 30 minutes from the Jerash Bus Station to a spot 800m below the resort (60fils; walk the final stretch) and taxis cost JD2 from downtown. The resort offers sparkling clean rooms and breakfast at high prices, but budget travelers can enjoy the mountaintop views, swimming pool, barbecue grills, billiard tables, and hot showers by camping on the grounds. (☎ (07) 952 35 46 or 956 57 38; fax (06) 582 60 34; email olivekh@go.com.jo. Own tent JD5; resort's tent JD6; singles JD25; doubles JD38.) You might consider taking a taxi (JD3) or bus (500fils) to **camp** out at Dibbin National Park, about eight kilometers away, or stay at the Dibbin Rest House (see p. 476). The **Al-Khayyam Restaurant,** just past the Visitors Center on the right, serves bread, salad, and grilled meat (JD4). Escape the scorching sun on their open-air patio, complete with fountain and ceiling fans. (☎ 635 10 18. Open daily 8am-9pm.) The **Jerash Paradise Restaurant** (☎ 635 13 25), next door to Al-Khayyam, offers similar fare at slightly lower prices; mixed grill and kebab cost JD1.8 each. Street stands surrounding the bus station sell cheap falafel and *fuul* (100-200fils). Walking into town saves money and brings you to the lively streets of untouristed Jerash.

👁 SIGHTS

Jerash's claim to fame is its ruins; nevertheless, over 75% of ancient Jerash still awaits excavation. *(Unless otherwise stated, all sights open daily 7am-7pm. JD5.)*

TRIUMPHAL (HADRIANIC) ARCH AND ENVIRONS. This arch, 400m south of the ancient walls, honors Emperor Hadrian's arrival in the winter of 129 CE. Spare parts strewn about the arch suggest how big the structure once was. Passing through it leads to the remaining stables and spectator seats of the **Hippodrome.** This arena hosted chariot races and other contests of skill for the amusement of up to 15,000 spectators. Continuing north, you'll see the Visitors Center and enter the site proper at the **South Gate,** followed by the **Forum** or Oval Plaza, the most photographed part of the city. The Ionic columns encircling the plaza have been reconstructed to first-century CE form. A statue once topped the central podium.

SOUTH THEATER. A footpath to the left of the Forum leads to this theater, where Greek doodles reveal that 4000 of Jerash's wealthiest citizens reserved seats for their bloodthirsty viewing pleasure. The two-story backstage was once furnished with curtains and marble statues. Try to find "the spot," a groove in the floor of the lower stage where voices carry and magnify to several times their regular volume. The circular niches below the first row of seats are ancient telephones—speak into any one and have a friend listen at any other "receiver." The top row of theater seats offers the best view of the ruined Temple of Zeus, which lies between the theater and the South Gate.

THE CARDO. Otherwise known as the **Street of Columns,** the Cardo runs from the Forum to the **North Gate.** Its 260 pairs of columns are Corinthian replacements for earlier Ionic columns once capped by aqueducts carrying water throughout the city. The holes in the floor drained rainwater into a sophisticated sewer system. Massive sidewalk coverings protected pedestrians from the sun, but only traces of these metropolitan parasols remain. The main avenue's first intersection is named the **South Tetrapylon** after its four huge slabs of stone, once accompanied by pillars and a large statue. Going west (left) at the cross street leads to the remains of a 7th-century Umayyad building. Back on the Cardo to the left, frescoes depicting lizards, cats, and turtles decorate the floor of the 4th-century **Cathedral,** built from and on top of the remains of a 2nd-century temple to Dionysus. Next along the avenue of arches is the **Nymphaeum,** built in 191 CE. Intricate stone carvings and the incorporation of marble and gypsum indicate that this two-story fountain was assembled at the height of Jerash's fortune, later used in an annual reenactment of the Miracle at Cana where Jesus changed water into wine (John 2:1-11). The gigantic bowl in front of the fountain was not the water dish of an oversized canine but a pool that caught water as it cascaded over the Nymphaeum's facade.

JERASH ANTIQUITIES MUSEUM. Well hidden to the right, this museum lies a short way down the pillared promenade. Tall display cases mounted along the walls show neatly arranged artifacts from the Neolithic Age to the Ottoman period. Theater "tickets" made of stone, a three-dimensional model of the ruins, coins, and jewelry highlight the museum's small collection. Opposite the museum and across the Cardo is the city's **Agora,** a newly-restored meeting place with a central fountain. This small area served as the city's meat and fish market. *(Museum open daily 8am-6pm; in winter 8am-5pm. Free.)*

TEMPLE OF ARTEMIS. A short jaunt farther down the Cardo leads to the impressive Artemis Temple Stairway. Two flights up, the ominous columned structure at the top of the hill to the left of the Cardo is the Temple of Artemis. The patron goddess of Jerash, daughter of Zeus, and sister of Apollo, Artemis held special significance throughout the Decapolis, once the territory of similar goddesses Ishtar and Anat. Her temple consisted of a Great Gate, a shrine-topped podium, and a courtyard surrounded by giant pillars. Descend Artemis's staircase and continue on the Cardo to the **West Baths,** including a 2nd-century cold bath *(frigidarium)*, warm bath *(tepidarium)*, hot bath *(caldarium)*, and changing rooms. The **East Baths,** across the *wadi* by the bus station, are even larger and more majestic. Taking a left at the **North Tetrapylon** leads to the **North Theater.**

CHURCH OF ST. COSMOS AND ST. DAMIUS. A good 200m to the left (facing the temple), behind Artemis's monument, lie a series of Byzantine churches built in the 6th century CE. Especially worth the walk is the Church of St. Cosmos and St. Damius, dedicated to a twin-brother team of doctors who treated their patients for free. Though barbed wire bars entrance to the church, peering over the edge from above affords a great view of its mosaic floor. Depicting the doctors surrounded by animals, the floor is one of the few pieces of art to survive the attempt of Umayyad Caliph Yazid II to destroy all images of God's creations in 720 CE. Try the archaeologist's trade while walking into the adjoining Church of St. John—hidden mosaics emerge with a gentle shuffle of the feet.

■ DAYTRIP FROM JERASH: DIBBIN NATIONAL PARK

The access road about 2km south of Jerash off the Amman-Jerash Highway leads to the park; look for the signs. Take a car or hire a taxi (round-trip JD5), as neither buses nor service travel to the park. Another option is taking the bus from Jerash to the nearby village of Dibbin and then hiking 2km uphill from the village to the park.

The pines and oaks of this fertile woodland are a sight for sore eyes in the middle of the desert wasteland. In the hills 10km southwest of Jerash and 65km north of Amman, the Dibbin National Park (pronounced dib-EEN) encompasses some

20km of forest stretching south from the town of the same name. On the old road to Jerash near Dibbin village is the **Dibbin Rest House,** offering private "bungalows" that come with refrigerators, TVs, and porches. (☎ (02) 633 97 10; fax 635 11 46. Doubles JD25; camping JD5.)

AJLOUN عجلون   ☎ 02

Atop the highest peak of the Ajloun region lies the ancient **Qal'at al-Rabad** (Ajloun Castle), an imposing fortress built in 1184 to thwart the efforts of the Crusaders. Its name loosely translates as "the castle that straddles a hill." Izz al-Din Usama, Salah al-Din's nephew, built the fortress in order to outdo the Castle of Belvoir on Lake Tiberias, but with its four corner towers and seven floors, Qal'at al-Rabadh more closely resembles Karak Castle, south of Amman (see **Karak,** p. 488). Filled with secret passages, dark corridors, and winding, crumbly staircases, the castle makes any gumshoe feel like Indiana Jones.

░ GETTING THERE. Ajloun lies a mountainous 24km west of Jerash, an easy bus ride from Amman (1½hr., 450fils; last returns 5pm, in winter 3pm) or Irbid (45min., 250fils). The **bus** from Abdali Station in Amman stops a few streets down from the main circle. Follow the sound of honking cars and the smell of roasting *shawarma* a few blocks uphill until you reach the traffic circle at the center of town. From the circle, the castle is a strenuous, but not impossible, four-kilometer hike up a mountain road (1hr.). Catch a **taxi** for 500fils-JD1 (be sure to negotiate before getting in) or see if the oft-broken **minibus** is running (60fils). Especially on Fridays, public transportation can be slow—start walking uphill and flag the bus or a taxi on the way. Generous passersby may also give you a lift if you're looking tired.

░ PRACTICAL INFORMATION. Ajloun's **Directorate of Tourism,** about 200m downhill from the castle, gives out free maps and brochures and can arrange for a guided tour of the castle. (☎ 642 01 15. JD4, tip JD1.) Exchange money on the center circle at the **Housing Bank** (V/PLUS ATM) or at the **Bank of Jordan.** (Open Su-Th 8:30am-3:00pm.) The **post office** is on Amman St. to the right as you enter the town, a few hundred yards from the circle. (Open Su-Th 8am-5pm.)

░░ ACCOMMODATIONS AND FOOD. Both hotels in Ajloun are within walking distance of the castle along the road to town. At the **Al-Rabad Castle Hotel,** new rooms come with TV, phone, balcony with sunset view, and immaculate bathrooms. (☎ 642 02 02. Singles JD24; doubles JD32; with breakfast, add 10% service charge. Student discounts.) The **Ajloun Hotel,** closer to the castle, offers clean, bright rooms, built-in closets, therapeutically hard mattresses, a swimming pool, and awesome views. (☎/fax 642 05 24; mobile (07) 965 62 33; email ajloun@firstnet.com.jo. Singles JD24; doubles JD32. Student discounts if vacancy.) The restaurants of both hotels offer lunch with a view for a hefty JD4-6.

Those who prefer to fill their bellies rather than their eyes should stop in at the **Green Mountain Restaurant,** just off Ajloun's center circle. A half-chicken goes for JD1.25, a kebab sandwich is 300fils, and 850fils buys a complete meal. (☎ 642 09 05. Open daily 6:30am-9:30pm; in winter 6:30am-8pm.) The **Abu al-Izz Restaurant** (☎ 642 20 32), on the main circle in front of the Green Mountain, is a sprawling outdoor cafe that offers the usual Middle Eastern food for higher prices than the Green Mountain, but with leafy trellises and nicer ambiance. Buy half of a chicken for JD2, and complement with hummus for 500fils. The **Bonita Ajloun Restaurant,** adjacent to the Directorate of Tourism office, has a magnificent view of the castle with an expensive Middle Eastern buffet (JD6; salad JD4). As always, street vendors provide economical and delicious alternatives.

░ SIGHTS. The **Ajloun Castle** once controlled a long stretch of Jordan's northern valley and protected lines between Jordan and Syria. Crusaders spent decades trying to capture the castle and nearby village. After the Crusader threat dissipated,

Salah al-Din used the castle as a base to control nearby iron mines and transmit messages by beacon and pigeon; from Baghdad to Cairo, the relay could be made in 12 hours. During the Ottoman period, 50 soldiers were stationed in the castle at all times. After that, the castle was mostly uninhabited until 1812, when the Swiss explorer J.L. Burkhardt (better known for discovering Petra the same year; see **Petra**, p. 491) found 40 members of the Barakat family living there. Two major earthquakes in 1837 and 1927 inflicted damage the Crusades never could. While the castle is in quite good condition today, parts of it are still under restoration by the Department of Antiquities. Hiring a guide is cheap, but it's more fun just to poke around with a flashlight. *(Open daily 8am-7pm; in winter 8am-5pm. JD1.)*

IRBID اربد ☎02

The streets that were once crowded with the residents of ancient Dion (a city in the Decapolis League) are now a fluorescent maze of Internet cafes and pool halls catering to the students of Yarmouk University, one of the biggest institutions of higher learning in Jordan. The cosmopolitan bustle that Yarmouk's students lend to Irbid makes the city an enjoyable base from which to plan trips to Umm Qeis, al-Himmeh, Israel, or Syria. The university's **Museum of Jordanian Heritage** (☎724 56 13 or 750 00 71), near the campus's North Gate, offers the nation's best and most comprehensive narrative of Jordan's history from prehistoric times to the present.

▐ GETTING THERE AND GETTING AROUND

Arab travelers may hitch to Irbid via Jerash, but the quickest and safest way to the city from Amman is with the A/C **Hijazi Bus Co.** (1½hr., 825fils). **Minibuses** to Irbid from Amman, Jerash, and Ajloun are slightly cheaper (500-600fils), but slower. Both the Hijazi **buses** and the **minibuses** will drop you off at **al-Janoubi Station,** from which you can take a **service** downtown (80fils). **Taxis** from al-Janoubi to downtown cost approximately 500fils, as do taxis from downtown to Yarmouk. The latter may cost JD1 after midnight. *Service* from downtown to Yarmouk (120fils) leave from Abu Bakr al-Siddiqa St., at its intersection with Jama St. (also known as University St., but "Shafeeq Rshaidat St." on street signs). From King Abdullah Sq., walk down Arar St. to the obelisk monument. Continue south to Jama St. and walk two blocks until you reach Abu Bakr al-Siddiqa St. The line of white *service* will be on the left. **Minibuses** to Umm Qeis and al-Himmeh leave often from **Shamali Station.** Between al-Janoubi and Shamali Station, taxis cost 750fils.

Go to **New South Station** (ask for "Mujma Amman Jadeed") to travel to Ajloun or Amman. **Minibuses** run regularly to Ajloun (250fils) and to Amman's **Abdali Station** (825fils). The last **buses** depart for Amman at about 8pm (in winter 6pm). *Service* also leave New South Station for **Damascus** (3-4hrs. depending on border crossings, JD4). Bring your **visa** and JD5 exit fee; it should be painless as long as there is no evidence of a trip to Israel in your passport and you carefully follow your *service* driver's instructions (for details, see **Border Crossings**, p. 454). You'll first pass through Jordanian customs and then Syrian customs a mile later.

Irbid is a convenient departure place for **Israel.** Take a *service* from **East Station** (Aghwar) to the al-Sheikh Hussein Bridge (bring passport and JD5 exit fee). **Al-Thinkah Company** buses (☎725 09 78) travel directly from East Station to Tel Aviv.

▐ ORIENTATION AND PRACTICAL INFORMATION

Irbid has two town centers: the older **city center,** and the younger, more modern one around Yarmouk University. The northern and southern boundaries of the old city center are Hashimi St. and King Hussein St. (also known as Baghdad St.), with **King Abdullah Sq.** (a traffic triangle with a fountain) at the focal point. The town **mosque** and **market** are about one block downhill from King Abdullah Sq., to the right. The **Housing Bank,** with V/PLUS **ATMs,** has branches at Hashimi St. and King Hussein St. To get to the **post office,** walk past the fountain in King Abdullah Sq.

and make a left onto King Hussein St. Walk about 200m and the post office is on the right. (☎ 724 47 19. Open Sa-Th 7:30am-7pm, F and holidays 7:30am-12:30pm.)

Yarmouk University is across town to the south, just a *service* ride away. Backtrack to the circle and turn left to reach **University St.**, the main drag of the Yarmouk region packed with restaurants and **Internet providers** (500fils per hr.). Travelers should note that inhabitants of Irbid often call streets by names that are not written on street signs. No tourist office exists in Irbid and maps of the town are nearly impossible to come by, so be assertive and ask locals for directions.

▌ ACCOMMODATIONS

It is wise to stay around the older city center, as hotels in happening Yarmouk cost more. If you're up for the splurge, have about JD30 ready per night.

Al-Amin Al-Kabir Hotel (☎ 724 23 84 or 727 18 79; email al_ameen_hotel@hotmail.com.), on Orouba St., approximately one block south of King Abdullah Sq. Bright and breezy rooms, clean communal baths, courteous management, electric fans, and a small kitchen for guest use. Street-side rooms with balconies have private baths. Manager Ahmad al-Wazani speaks English well and is probably the best guide to the city. Hot shower 500fils. Singles JD5; doubles JD8.

Omayed Hotel (☎/fax 724 59 55), above Irbid Supermarket on Baghdad St. Rooms have phones, fans, private baths (some with bidet), and curious three-window television nooks. Upstairs restaurant boasts a magnificent view of the city and serves specials for JD2-3.5. English-speaking receptionist Ahmad Mansour can tell you how to get where you want to go. Singles JD14; doubles JD18. Add 10% tax.

Hotel Al-Wehdeh Al-Arabiah (☎ 724 20 83), sits atop Arar St. Prepare to be plied with tea, coffee, and exotic fruit in the "Bedouin tent" just past the entrance on the right. Some rooms have balconies, and the gregarious Egyptian management is eager to bargain. Dorms JD2; singles JD6; doubles JD8, with bath JD10.

Abu Bakr Hotel (☎ 724 26 95), around the corner from the Al-Amin on Wasfi al-Tal St., in same building as the Bank of Jordan. Stuffy rooms combatted by ceiling fans and free showers. Almost exclusively male clientele. Singles JD3; doubles JD6; triples JD6.

◔ FOOD

Streets around Yarmouk University are lined with sprawling restaurants packed with everyone from procrastinating students to local families. Restaurants serve filling regional dishes at low prices (JD1-4). Popeye's Fried Chicken, Subway, and Pizza Hut are on University St. near Yarmouk, but even if you've been unimpressed with falafel and *shawarma* so far, give the food stands around the university a chance. The cheapest food in Irbid is some of Jordan's best (falafel 150fils; *shawarma* 250-300fils). The local market is held downtown, around the mosque.

Andalusia Restaurant (☎ 724 15 86), across from post office, on the 6th floor of the building above Grindlay's Bank. This four-star dining experience is far nicer on the palate and far harder on the wallet than most Irbid fare. Hummus or *baba ghanoush* 400fils; salad 600fils-JD1.1; mixed grill JD2.5. Open daily 10am-10pm.

Palestine Restaurant, east of Andalusia on King Hussein St. Known throughout Irbid for its chips, french fries, falafel, and hummus for 350-550fils. Open daily F-W 6am-9pm.

Ish Al-Hana Restaurant, uphill from the circle on University St. Keeps kebabs coming past Irbid's 9pm bedtime. Mixed grill JD1.8; hummus 400fils. Open 7:30am-midnight.

♫ ▣ ENTERTAINMENT AND NIGHTLIFE

Nightlife in Irbid exists primarily on University St. near Yarmouk University, where Internet cafes share space with pool halls and music stores. Cruising the main drag is enough for a night's entertainment, but those seeking a more mellow atmosphere should check out the **News Cafe,** in the basement of the Al-Joude Hotel, for drinks (beer JD2.25), pool tables, and Internet access. (☎ 727 55 15 or 727 55 16. Open daily 10am-midnight.) Step right up to thrills and spills (for a mere 200fils) at the **Yarmouk Amusement Park,** north of the University (look for the ferris wheel). Irbid residents scream and sing on the Pirate's Ship, while kids of all ages get belligerent on the bumper cars for 500fils. (Open daily until midnight.)

UMM QEIS أم قيس ☎ 02

Umm Qeis was the Biblical **Gadara,** where Jesus turned a sinner's demons into a herd of pigs that drowned in the Sea of Galilee. This thriving town was one of the ten cities of the Decapolis League, founded by Pompey after his conquest of Syria and Palestine in 64 BCE. Its name comes from a Semitic word meaning "stronghold," reflecting the city's role as a fortified border town guarding the crucial land routes between southern Syria and northern Palestine. Once a resort for Romans vacationing at al-Himmeh's therapeutic hot springs, Umm Qeis was renowned for its arts and orgiastic extravagances. Earthquakes and plagues in the 7th and 8th centuries CE, however, left Umm Qeis nothing more than a hamlet.

◪ PRACTICAL INFORMATION. The bus from Irbid's North Station will stop at the base of the ruins if you tell the driver where you are headed. To get to the **post office** (☎ 750 00 05), just off the main road through modern Umm Qeis, walk away from the ruins toward town, then take the first street to your right. The post office is about 50m down the hill. (Open daily 8am-2pm.) Stock up on water and postcards at the **Ziad Store** and the **Jadara Gift Shop,** both in the building to the left of the road leading to the Umm Qeis ruins. (Both open daily 7am-7pm.)

▐░ ACCOMMODATIONS AND FOOD. The value-packed ◪**Umm Qeis Hotel** is about 100m from the ruins. Walk away from the ruins on the main road toward town and look for signs on the left. The hotel is up a pink alley. Its brightly painted rooms have large windows that may overlook the street. The best view is from the roof, where you can dine in sight of the ruins and the Golan Heights. Ideal for solo women travelers. (☎ 750 00 80. Breakfast JD2.5; dinner JD3-4. JD6 per person, with bath JD8.) The beautiful **Umm Qeis Rest House,** next to the museum, is an offshoot of Amman's glitzy Romero restaurant and serves up refreshments at reasonable prices. Chow down on soup, salad, or pasta for JD2-3 while taking in a spectacular view of the Sea of Galilee. (☎ 750 05 55. Open 9am-10pm.) Middle Eastern food is also available at a few relatively inexpensive places along the main road.

▣ SIGHTS. Visitors to the **Umm Qeis Ruins** will wander among a mix of Greco-Roman, Byzantine, and Ottoman architecture, strategically located atop a mountain in northwest Jordan. (Open daily 8am-5pm. JD1.) The two-room **Umm Qeis Museum** (two-story white building flying the Jordanian flag) is a good starting point for wandering around the ruins. Check out **Tyche,** the patron goddess of Gadara who lacks a few important appendages, but still holds onto her fruit-filled cornucopia, a symbol of fertility. Journey back in time through the **Roman ruins.** The foundation of the **North Theater,** once able to accommodate 5000, is barely visible just outside the museum. The Ottomans took the actual stones of the structure to build the village on the hill; German archaeologists are now attempting to reconstruct parts of it. West of the North Theater is the **Basilica Terrace,** on which black basalt Corinthian columns surround octagonally arranged white limestone ones (once a Byzantine church). The Roman-built **Main Road** traverses the ancient village, running from the North Theater to the **Roman Bathhouse,** which lies at the northwest corner of the ruins. Alongside the road, you may see a series of barrel-vaulted rooms that functioned as street-front **shops.** Near the shops are the weed-entangled ruins of the **East Baths** and **Nymphaeum.** Looking downhill, you can see the **Roman Aqueduct,** which brought water to Umm Qeis from present-day Syria.

⏏ DAYTRIP FROM UMM QEIS: AL-HIMMEH الحمة

*A mere 10km from Umm Qeis, al-Himmeh is accessible by bus (150fils) or taxi (JD2); you may also take a bus from North Station in Irbid (300fils). To catch the bus from Umm Qeis, stand outside the Umm Qeis Hotel and flag down buses until you find one going to al-Himmeh. Get off the bus in front of the Al-Himmeh Hotel and Restaurant immediately after passing the post office on the right. To return to Umm Qeis or Irbid from al-Himmeh, follow the same protocol outside the Al-Himmeh Hotel and Restaurant (last bus 5:30pm). Bring a **passport** along for the ride to al-Himmeh—there is a checkpoint along the way.*

The therapeutic hot springs and lush vegetation of al-Himmeh seduce visitors from all over the Arab world. The few westerners who make it to this town, which straddles Jordan's borders with Israel and Syria, find al-Himmeh to be one of the most hospitable villages in Jordan. Covered with banana, guava, and lemon farms, al-Himmeh is an ideal place to swim, camp, and unwind in the shade.

The hotel and restaurant complexes are perfect if you're staying longer than a day in al-Himmeh. The **Sah Al-Noun Hotel,** tucked among the banana farms at the base of the Golan Heights, boasts a hot springs canal in its garden restaurant. To get there, follow the road to the left as it forks after the Al-Himmeh Hotel and Restaurant. Sah Al-Noun is about 100m down the road. The hospitable English-speaking manager, Samara Samara, will take guests for a swim in the Roman-style hot springs pool next door (JD1-3), arrange hunting tours, and talk about his farm over tea. (☎ 750 05 10, 727 31 58, or (07) 953 96 77. Breakfast included. JD6.5 per person. Foreign currency and traveler's checks accepted; ask about camping options.) The **Al-Himmeh Hotel and Restaurant** is a resort-style establishment that offers standard food and clean hotel rooms at reasonable prices. Swim in the central 40m pool of hot spring water for JD1. For a swankier stay, check out Al-Himmeh's "chalet" rooms. (Doubles JD10; triples JD11, chalet JD29; chalet quints JD40.)

EAST OF AMMAN

AZRAQ AND THE DESERT CASTLES ☎06
الازرق و القصور الصحراوية

The springs at Azraq were once the only permanent bodies of water in more than 2500 square kilometers of sun-scorched, sand-and-scorpion desert. So much water is now pumped into Amman, however, that the area has dried up significantly. As recently as four years ago, the palm trees were green, the animals abundant, and the sky was colored with hundreds of species of exotic birds. Now, no evidence of the vast springs remains: what used to be green is a parched brown, and the only movement is that of trucks passing through. Water isn't the only thing to have disappeared from Azraq. The most remarkable records of human habitation are the scattered Umayyad castles (*qusur*; singular *qasr*), a group of structures that originally formed a chain from the north of Damascus to Khirbat al-Mafjar, near Jericho. Built in the 7th and 8th centuries CE by the Umayyads, the castles were mysteriously abandoned a century later. The imposing stonework of Qasr Kharaneh and strategic location of Qasr Azraq support speculation that the castles sheltered caravans along the trade route between Syria, Arabia, and the Far East. The baths near Qasr al-Hallabat and the magnificent frescoes at Qasr Amra provided respite from the vast, unforgiving desert. Still relatively tourist-free, these quietly majestic ruins will awe you with the strength of their standing arches.

◪ **GETTING THERE AND GETTING AROUND.** A trip to the Azraq Oasis and the Desert Castles is fraught with uncertainty and difficult to arrange, but it's worth every annoyance. Only three options for transportation to the castles exist. You can start by trying to bargain for a **taxi** from Amman, which should include a half-day's wheels and someone who knows the route (half-day JD25, full-day JD30). If you're over 18 and have a few friends, renting a **car** for the day is the most enjoyable way to do the desert loop. You can rent one in Amman with unlimited mileage and the option to return it in Aqaba or at the airport. **Reliable Rent-a-Car** offers the best deals. (☎/fax 592 96 76. JD25-35 per day. See **Car Rentals,** p. 459.) The third and easiest way to get to the desert castles, in terms of both your pocketbook and your peace of mind, is to arrange a daytrip through the **Cliff Hostel** (JD15; see p. 466). This tour offers less mobility and typically skips the least spectacular castle, Qasr al-Hallabat, but it will likely bring you in contact with the charismatic Fouad, a five-year veteran of the castle route whose close relationship with the Bedouin makes for a memorable journey. Arrange a few days in advance. At least four people must sign up before the trip will leave.

As always, **hitchhiking** in the desert is discouraged and potentially suicidal. Hitchhikers should beware the intense sun and vast, desolate spaces involved in the desert loop. Travelers report that ever-friendly Jordanians are quick to pick up hitchers, but vehicles can be few and far between in these parts. Those who decide to try their luck by thumb (or downward turned palm, as tradition has it here) should bring a head covering and much more water than they think they will need, and tell their hostel where they have gone and when they expect to return. *Let's Go* does not recommend hitchhiking as a viable means of transport, though many travelers have and will continue to travel this way.

NAVIGATING THE DESERT CASTLES. The following description details a three-part, clockwise road trip that allows a traveler to take in all the castles and Azraq: (1) north from Amman to Zarqa (30km); (2) east from Zarqa to Azraq (87km), passing the unimpressive Qasr al-Hallabat (30km from Zarqa); and (3) returning west along the southern highway from Azraq back to Amman, passing Qasr Amra (25km from Azraq), Qasr Kharaneh (40km from Azraq), and Qasr Mushatta (about 90km from Azraq and 40km from Amman). Going the other way (Amman-Azraq-Zarqa) is deadly for hitchhikers, since cars come as frequently as snowstorms in the desert. *Service* from Abdali Station in Amman can take you to Zarqa quickly and cheaply (300fils). Accepting rides from the army is illegal, and will take you only as far as some lonely desert depot anyway.

QASR AL-HALLABAT قصر الحلابات

Qasr al-Hallabat's ruined arches appear in the desert approximately 30km east of Zarqa. Angle off at the right, turn onto the paved road, and turn left up the track to the gate. The gatekeeper's tent is to the right of the main gate, far from the crumbling castle. You're free to roam around whatever is left, but keep in mind that any gatekeeper who gives you information will expect a few hundred fils in return. Originally constructed as a Roman fort by the bath-obsessed emperor Caracalla (198-217 CE), Qasr al-Hallabat was later used by the Byzantines as a monastery. The Umayyads rebuilt it as a residential palace in the 8th century and added a mosque just meters away from the main defense structure. Look for the Byzantine carvings on the remaining walls and fallen slabs of stone.

Back on the main highway, the sand and limestone desert to the south contrasts sharply with the gray volcanic desert to the north. Just off the road to the south is **Hammam al-Sarh,** the ruined bathhouse modeled after Qasr Amra. A 1000-year-old well covered by a rusty metal grating lurks to the left of the bathhouse. Though some daredevils have been known to climb onto the grating and peer into the abyss below, *Let's Go* does not recommend taking the risk.

AZRAQ الازرق

On the long and grinding road east of Zarqa, you'll hear nothing but the entreaties of your overheating engine until, after ages of drab desert, the formerly lush gardens of the **Azraq Oasis** appear. Once Jordan's only permanent body of fresh water, the oasis is quickly drying up, though **Azraq Junction** remains a place to relax and reassemble your bearings. The junction is where the northeastern highway leads to Iraq and the southeastern road to the southern castles and Saudi Arabia.

About 13km north of Azraq Junction on the highway to Iraq stands **Qasr Azraq**, in excellent condition thanks to extensive restoration. The black basalt fort was built by the Romans in 300 CE and rebuilt by the Ayyubids in 1237. Of its three levels, only parts of the second level survived a 1926 earthquake, including a ceiling that exposes a web of basalt beams. The Druze gatekeeper will haul open the remarkable three-ton stone portal of the castle. He might also show you his photocopied **Lawrence of Arabia** photograph collection (many of the photographs look suspiciously like the gatekeeper's grandfather). The most interesting attractions lie within a few meters of the entrance. Looking up from the main door, you'll see the *machicoulis* (holes) through which boiling oil and molten lead were poured on invaders. Carved into the pavement behind the main gate is a Roman board game—ask the gatekeeper to show you how to play. In the center of the courtyard lies a small cube of a mosque, originally built as a Roman church. Just above the entrance was the living space of Lawrence of Arabia, who used the fort as his headquarters during the height of the Arab revolt against Ottoman rule in 1917.

Keep an eye out for the desert wildlife making a comeback ever since Jordan started protecting its fragile habitat. In the **Shaumari Wildlife Preserve,** near Qasr Amra, the government is reintroducing armadillos, Himalayan dwarf hamsters, ostriches, Syrian wild asses, and Arabian oryxes. (500fils, students 300fils.) Cheetah and desert wolves roam regions to the northeast and southwest of Azraq.

Many small markets and stands in town provide cheap nourishment. Azraq does have a **post office** (☎383 50 01; open Sa-Th 8am-2pm) and a **Housing Bank.** (Open for exchange Sa-W 9am-1pm and 4-5pm, Th 9am-1pm.) For a true oasis experience, stay at the slightly run-down **Sayad Hotel,** visible from the Azraq castle, graced with an olive grove, a rose garden, and paintings of the owner. (☎383 40 94. Singles JD24; doubles JD32; breakfast included.) On the north side of Azraq, down a tree-lined road, is the government-run **Azraq Resthouse.** Rooms include bath, A/C, color TV, minibar, and a view of the pool, which non-guests can use (JD3). The overpriced restaurant in the Resthouse serves meals for JD4.5. (☎383 40 06; fax 383 52 15. Singles JD17; doubles JD24.) The **Azraq Palace Restaurant,** right at the junction to Qasr Azraq, offers a large buffet (JD6), but the only real reason to suffer through this tourist buffet is to use the ▨**best bathrooms** in all of Jordan, in the rear of the restaurant. (☎/fax 439 71 44. Restaurant and bathrooms open daily 7am-11pm.)

QASR AMRA قصر عمرة

For a sneak preview of Qasr Amra, simply look at any *half-dinar* bill. Constructed under the auspices of Umayyad Caliph al-Walid ibn Abd al-Malik, the hunting lodge and bath complex of Qasr Amra impress visitors with the elegant simplicity of their designs. The interior is also the best preserved of the desert palaces: its vaulted stucco ceilings are splashed with lively frescoes, and mosaics cover two of the floors. As you walk in, look to the right at the **mural** depicting the enemies of Islam—among them are the emperors of Byzantium, Persia, and China as well as Roderique, then King of Spain. Their faces appear similar to traditional depictions of Jesus, so many believe that the artist was Roman rather than Muslim. Moreover, the frescoes throughout the castle ignore the Muslim tradition forbidding the pictorial representation of human beings, making them all the more riveting. Especially surprising are the many portrayals of nude women, which somehow escaped the decree of Umayyad Caliph Yazid II (720-24 CE), a weekend visitor of the castle who ordered all human images and likenesses destroyed. An early portrayal of the zodiac covers the domed ceiling of the *caldarium*, or hot room. *(Reach Qasr Amra on the road heading southwest of Azraq Junction, 28km from Qasr Azraq. The very hospitable gatekeeper expects a small bakhsheesh of 250-500fils per person.)*

QASR KHARANEH قصر الخرانة

Qasr Kharaneh is named for the small black stones that blanket the area. Some experts believe Kharaneh was a defensive fort; they point to the four corner towers and the square plan of a Roman fortress, and to the enigmatic arrow slits in the walls. Others think the slits were part of an elaborate ventilation system and argue that Kharaneh served as a retreat for Umayyad leaders to discuss state matters. Most historians, however, believe it was the first *khan* (inn) of the Islamic world, evinced by the architectural style of the castle that later typified Umayyad inns. A painted Arabic dedication in a 2nd-story room dates the building's construction to 710-11 CE. Greek inscriptions on the doorjambs imply that the Umayyads built upon an earlier structure. For a good view of the courtyard and the barren landscape stretching to Saudi Arabia and Iraq, climb the staircase to the left of the entrance. The neighboring military base and the maneuverings of Jordanian troops are also visible. When you've finished exploring, the gatekeeper will let you ride his camel (500fils *bakhsheesh* should do). As he leads you around the castle, listen carefully: he insists that the ghosts of horses, camels, and people roam the ruins.

QASR MUSHATTA قصر مشتة

This final castle is a hassle to get to and a downer after sights past. Those determined to find it can take any turnoff to Queen Alia International Airport. Hitchhikers often hire *service* from the village of **Muwaqaar** in the north to reach the castle. The castle is on the left as you approach the airport from the north, but the public access road turns off to the right and loops about 4km around the airport. If walking from the airport, don't take this marked turnoff. Continue to the left of the airport, past the Alia cargo terminal, until Mushatta appears on the left (30min. walk). Soldiers at checkpoints will ask to see your **passport,** may take it temporarily, and possibly turn you away. Catch a taxi or bus back to Amman via the airport.

The entrance to the 8th-century castle once beckoned travelers with wonderfully carved floral designs, but most of these stones were delivered to Kaiser Wilhelm II as a gift from Ottoman Sultan Abdulhamid II and only fragments remain. A piece of the wall now resides in the Berlin Museum. Although the size of the ruins attest to the ambition of the construction, the castle was never completed. Indeed, Mushatta was constructed with smaller, weaker bricks than the other castles.

SOUTH OF AMMAN

Three roads link Amman and Aqaba: the **Wadi Araba Highway** (a.k.a. Jordan Valley), the **Desert Highway,** and the **King's Highway.** Of these routes, the King's Highway (Wadi Mujib Rd.) is the best way to travel the length of Jordan. This ancient route journeys through spectacular canyons, passing Biblical sites, Crusader castles, and Byzantine churches along the way. Supposedly traveled by the Israelites during their exodus from Egypt, this road later became a popular spice route. Amman to Petra is 226km along the King's Highway, but the distances between sights along the way are more manageable: Amman to Madaba 32km, Madaba to Karak 86km, and Karak to Petra 108km. The only indoor accommodations are in Karak and Madaba (most camp in the *wadis* north of Karak or between Karak and Petra). The easiest route is to see Madaba before heading to Karak for the night. If you leave early from Karak, the trip to Petra can be done comfortably in a day, stopping in Shobak and at the Dana Nature Reserve along the way.

Service and **minibuses** run most of the way from Amman to Petra, but generally in the mornings only. **Hitchhiking** south of Amman is possible (hitchers stick their right arm out), but is risky and difficult along the deserted King's Highway. It is illegal to hitchhike on the Wadi Araba, which runs along the Israeli border. To get to the Desert Highway from downtown Amman, hitchhikers head south on Jerusalem St. (in Jabal Nadhif across Wadi Abdoun), which becomes Rt. 15 (the Desert Highway). To get to the King's Highway, hitchers take a *service* from Amman's

Wahdat Station to Madaba, then try their luck on the road to Karak, which passes out of Madaba by the Apostles' Church. Small groups of hitchers stand by the mini-obelisk marking the intersection of the King's Highway and the Desert Highway, 18km south of Amman. To reach the intersection, take a Madaba-bound *service* from Wahdat Station or hitch south from 7th Circle.

DEAD SEA البحر الميت

More than 400m below sea level, the Dead Sea is the lowest point on earth. Now a serenely quiet shore, the Dead Sea region is thought by many to be the site of five biblical cities: Sodom, Gomorrah, Admah, Zeboin, and Zowr. Indeed, a dried pillar of salt nearby is believed to be the remains of Lot's wife, who, upon fleeing the damned city of Sodom, disobeyed God's command to not look back. Four times as salty as regular sea water, the peculiar buoyancy of this briny liquid forces even the densest swimmer into a back float, and the wealth of salts and minerals gives it renowned curative powers (recognized for over 2000 years). Be warned that the awful tasting salt water makes a tiny paper cut feel like an amputation; don't get any in your eyes, or you'll have to beg to use one of the eye-flushing plastic water bottles that those in the know tote along to the beach. The Dead Sea is easier to reach by public transport and cheaper if visited from Israel (see **Israel: Dead Sea,** p. 397). Its northeastern shore, about an hour from Amman or Deir Alla, hosts the only stretch of sand open to visitors on the Jordanian side.

▐ GETTING THERE

Buses connect to the Dead Sea from Amman's Muhajereen Station, on al-Quds (Jerusalem) St. Take a taxi there and indicate that your destination is the Dead Sea, as it is possible the driver will not understand the station name. Don a Panama hat, bring plenty of water, and don't forget your passport—several military roadblocks along the way may demand identification. Buses generally leave every 30 minutes but schedules can be precarious, so set aside plenty of time. Some buses go to **Shouna** (1hr., 400fils), where you can catch a second bus to the **rest house** (30min., 200fils). Arrange group daytrips with one of many Amman hotels (Farah Hotel charges JD15 per person). **Taxis** to the Dead Sea from Amman can be found for as little as JD8, but most will demand JD25; try bargaining.

▐▐ ACCOMMODATIONS AND FOOD

The **Dead Sea Rest House** offers free showers until sundown to relieve you of Lot's wife's encrusted fate (☎(05) 546 110; JD2.5). The rest house proper has bungalows with A/C, bathroom, and TV. Singles JD25; doubles JD35; quads JD50. An over-priced restaurant completes the complex. (Hummus 650fils; salad bar JD3; soft drinks JD1; water JD1. Open daily 7am-midnight.) Skip the resort prices by going to the **free beach**, 200m to the right of the rest house. To get there from the bus stop at the rest house, backtrack along the road until you reach a junction, then take a left. The entrance to the free beach is next to the Ministry of Tourism Information building. The beach includes a muddy shore, spartan changing rooms, grungy showers, and seaside **camping.** The rocky walk into the water can be tough so consider foot protection. Shelters are available to ward off the sun. The last bus leaves at 6pm, but if you get stranded, the sunset over the West Bank almost makes it worthwhile. About 12km south of the resthouse, the natural spring of **Zara** nestles between the colorful Jordan Valley cliffs. Less than 30km south on the highway to Aqaba (Rte. 35) lies **Zarqa Ma'in,** a cascading hot spring.

MADABA مادبا ☎05

Perched atop a plateau of orange groves overlooking the Jordan Valley, Madaba lures visitors with its magnificent scenery, craft shops, and Byzantine mosaics.

While the Roman columns scattered about town only hint at the flourishing trade center that Madaba once was, archaeologists at work in the impressive downtown "Archaeological Park" have recently uncovered some of the city's past glories. A Roman road, a burnt palace, and several churches have been discovered only meters away from the Church of St. George (home of the famous **Map of the Holy Land**, see p. 487). The elaborate masterpieces scattered throughout this "City of Mosaics" attest to Madaba's importance as a Byzantine ecclesiastical center. The town received its own bishop as early as the 5th century CE. Persians attacked Madaba in 614 CE, slaughtering the residents and damaging many Roman and Byzantine artifacts; an 8th-century earthquake finished off the job. Madaba remained a ghost town for the next 1100 years until Christian clans from Karak reinhabited the city in the late 1800s. Now a peaceful, rural town that relies heavily upon tourism, Madaba serves as a home base from which to take daytrips to **Mt. Nebo** (p. 488), **Jerash** (p. 473), or **Amman** (p. 458). Women report that Madaba is particularly high on the nuisance list—expect to be talked to and stared at from the moment you arrive. Look out for tourist traps, but don't miss the carpet shops, if only to watch the fascinating process of loom weaving.

GETTING THERE AND GETTING AROUND

Minibuses shuttle between Madaba and Amman's **Wahdat** (180fils), **Raghadan** (220fils), and **Abdali Stations** (1hr., last bus 7pm; in winter last bus 5pm; 275fils). **Service** don't run this route. **Hitchhiking** doesn't get any easier than on this road, though *Let's Go* does not recommend hitchhiking. To reach the city center from Madaba's bus station, take a *service* (70fils), **taxi** (500fils), or hike 20 minutes uphill toward the Church of St. George.

ORIENTATION AND PRACTICAL INFORMATION

The **tourist office** is around the corner from the Church of St. George. (☎324 55 27. Open Sa-Th 8am-2pm.) The **Housing Bank** (open Su-Th 8:30am-5pm) and the **Arab Bank** (☎324 55 36; open Su-Th 8:30am-3pm) have international **ATMs** at their branches on King Abdullah St., around the corner from the tourist office. In a general **emergency** dial ☎191; for the **police** dial ☎192; in a **medical emergency** dial ☎193. The nearest public hospital is **Nadim Hospital** (☎324 17 00), one kilometer from town. The new, private **Mahabba Hospital** stands near the entrance to town. Access the **Internet** at **TourDotNet**, on King Talal St. near the Church of St. George, where high prices are justified with fast connections. (☎325 15 23. JD2 per hr. Open daily 10am-midnight.) The central **post office** is next to the banks on King Abdullah St., around the corner from the tourist office. (☎324 40 05. Open Su-Th 7:30am-7pm, F-Sa 7:30am-1:30pm; in winter Su-Th 7:30am-5pm, F-Sa 7:30am-1:30pm.)

ACCOMMODATIONS

Blessed with high-quality budget hotels, Madaba offers a sweet countryside relief to hostel-weary travelers.

Lulu's Pension (☎324 36 78), has clean bathrooms and guest kitchen. The remodeled rooms on the 2nd floor are among the nicest in Jordan. Ring the bell if the door is locked. Royal room with king-sized bed and private bath JD25, with shared bath JD20.

Black Iris Hotel (☎324 19 59), a few blocks from Lulu's, just off the main street near al-Mouhafada Circle, has spacious rooms and a congenial family atmosphere. Just wait until you see the size of their breakfast. Rooftop mattresses JD1; singles JD18; doubles JD25; triples JD35; cheaper with shared bath; camping JD1. 10% *Let's Go* discount.

Queen Ayola Hotel (☎/fax 324 40 87; email queenayola@yahoo.com), on King Talal St., one block south of the Church of St. George. This cozy hotel offers multilingual management and spotless rooms that come with fans, towels, and shampoo. Doubles JD18-22; breakfast included. 10% student discount. V.

Madaba Hotel (☎324 06 43). The cheapest hotel in town rivals its competitors with clean rooms, extremely hospitable management, and a mosaic-friendly location. Recommended for solo women travelers. JD7 per person. Breakfast JD1.

FOOD

■ **Haret Jdoudna** (☎324 86 50), on King Talal St. across from the Queen Ayola Hotel. Easily the best restaurant in Madaba, if not all of northern Jordan. An extensive menu ranges from Arabic specialties like *siwani* (JD2.5-3.75) to excellent thin-crust pizza (JD2-4). The pita is so fresh that it comes still-inflated from the heat of the brick oven. For the best place to hang out after dinner, sit down at the coffee shop and listen to the live music. The labyrinthine building houses over 20 craft shops. Open daily 9am-1am.

Dana Restaurant (☎324 57 49), on al-Nuzha St. near the Apostles' Church, is excellent with prices slightly lower than most. Serves Arabic, Indian, Chinese, and American food. Lamb-burger, fries, and coke JD1.75; pasta JD2. Open daily 8am-10pm.

El-Cardo (☎325 10 06; ☎/fax 325 10 07), across from the Archaeological Park. Prices evoke the words "highway robbery." Buffet JD6. Open 8am-midnight.

Resthouse (☎324 40 69), across from the Church of St. George. Similar fare and prices to El-Cardo. Drinks JD1. Open 8am-midnight.

Shaheen's Restaurant, off Palestine St. next to the pharmacy. Best falafel in town for 250fils and generally cheap chow. Open daily 7am-midnight.

Ayola Coffee Shop, on Palestine St. Serves deli-style sandwiches (JD1) in a pleasant Bedouin restaurant full of Madaba's young hipsters. Open daily 8am-11pm.

SIGHTS

CHURCH OF ST. GEORGE. Built in 1896 atop the foundation of a Byzantine church, the prominent Greek Orthodox Church of St. George stands in the center of town, right off the square. Parts of the 6th-century CE **Map of the Holy Land** (originally composed of 2.3 million tiles) are housed within the church's yellow brick walls. The Map is the oldest preserved and most detailed ancient map of this region, and once depicted the entire Middle East (as shown by the few remaining tiles of Turkey, Lebanon, and Egypt). Now only the Palestinian cities of Byzantium, Nablus, Hebron, and Jericho remain. The most well-known section of the map is the inset map of Jerusalem at its center, with representations of the buildings that existed in the 6th century (including the Church of the Holy Sepulchre, see p. 307). According to some devout local Christians and Muslims, the church hosted the Virgin Mary in 1978. A small shrine in the crypt contains an icon of Mary with a third arm and a blue "healing hand" supernaturally imprinted on the icon during the Madonna's visit. *(Open M-Th and Sa 7am-6pm, F and Su 10:30am-6pm. Free.)*

MADABA MUSEUM. Madaba's museum, tucked in an alley down the hill from the Apostles' Church off Prince Abdullah St., is divided into three sections: the Old House of Madaba, the Folklore Museum, and the Archaeological Museum. The complexes feature an extensive collection of mosaics, including a depiction of the Garden of Eden, traditional Jordanian dresses, and pottery dating as far back as 4500 BCE. *(Open W-M 9am-5pm. JD2; ticket also good for Archaeological Park.)*

ARCHAEOLOGICAL PARK. The Archaeological Park, around the corner from the Church of St. George, is a playground of ancient finds, featuring the **Church of the Virgin Mary** and **Hippolytus Hall.** Along with a recently uncovered **Roman road,** the park is home to mosaics from the days of Herod the Great (first century BCE) to the Umayyad period (8th century CE). Madaba's largest mosaic from 758 CE lies within the remains of the **Apostles' Church,** on the southern edge of town. *(Open W-M 8am-7pm; in winter 8am-5pm. JD2; ticket also good for Madaba Museum.)*

▪ DAYTRIPS FROM MADABA

MOUNT NEBO

No buses go to Mt. Nebo. Take a **taxi** *(round-trip JD5, including 30min. wait at the site)* or a **service** *from Madaba to Feisaliyyeh (150fils). At Feisaliyyeh, walk to Mt. Nebo or bargain with the driver to take you there once other passengers get off (JD2.50 for the extra 3km up, 30min. wait, and trip back to Madaba). Without a prearranged ride, the only way off Mt. Nebo is to walk back to Feisaliyyeh. Buildings and Siyagha Peak are open daily 7am-7pm; in winter 7am-5pm. 500fils; pay the guard an extra 500fils to see the sunset.*

The view from Mt. Nebo is so spectacular that Moses' last request to God was for a view of the promised land from its heights. Although the Bible says that "no man knows the place of his burial to this day" (Deuteronomy 34:6), Moses' grave is rumored to be in a cave somewhere along 'Ain Musa. On Nebo's **Siyagha Peak,** the Christians of Madaba built a three-nave **Memorial Church,** next to which looms an imposing serpentine cross. Archaeological work has revealed a complete mosaic floor in the church dating from 531 CE, as well as foundations of monasteries from the 3rd century CE. In the 7th century, the **Chapel of the Theotokos** (or Mary, Mother of God) was added, with lavish decorations adorning the walls.

Just beyond Feisaliyyeh, a marked turnoff leads to **Khirbet al-Mukheiyat,** once known as the ancient village of **Nebo,** on the southern base of the mountain. A one-hour hike (round-trip) will allow you to see the secular scenes of fishing, hunting, and wine-making that decorate another finely preserved Byzantine church floor. Despite repeated warnings by the Surgeon General, cigarettes are the preferred *bakhsheesh* for the Bedouin gatekeeper who lives on the hill at the end of the paved road. (Church open until dusk, or whenever the gatekeeper leaves.) The trip out here is worth it—the mosaic is astounding and the views are, well, enough to make it onto a dying prophet's wish list. If the opportunity arises, head out to the waterfall **'Ain Musa** (Spring of Moses) to cool off. To get there, take a right before the Mt. Nebo sign and follow the road down into the valley; walk around the old pump buildings and follow the path down to the right.

KARAK الكرك ☎ 03

Once the ancient capital of Moab, Karak now humbles itself in the shadow of **Karak Castle,** the largest of the mountaintop Crusader castles that stretch from Turkey to the Sinai. Home to some of Jordan's most influential clans, the prosperous modern town of Karak extends away from the castle on its northern and eastern slopes and serves as an ideal resting place for travelers on the King's Highway.

▪ **GETTING THERE AND GETTING AROUND.** Travel to Karak from Amman's **Wahdat Station** by **minibus** (2hr., 750fils) or **service** (JD1.2) along the Desert Highway. A **taxi** along the King's Highway from Madaba costs around JD15. The most reliable way to reach Petra from Karak is to first take a **minibus** from the **Karak Bus Station** to Ma'an (2hr., JD1) and then take another **bus** from Ma'an to Petra (45min., 500fils). To get to the Karak station, you may also **walk** 20 minutes east of the castle. A slightly less direct route involves taking a **bus** from the Karak station to Tafilah (30min., 500fils), from there to Shobak (1hr., JD1), and finally from Shobak to Petra (30min., 250fils). *Service* rarely run along these routes. During the high season, **buses** may directly travel from Karak to Petra, depending on tourist traffic (2hr., 9am). Again, *service* don't usually run from Karak to Petra, but **private taxis** charge a hefty JD40. Those who hitch the route along the King's Highway say it's easy, though *Let's Go* does not recommend hitchhiking. If traveling in the late afternoon, don't expect to see cars or stay in anything more than homes of hospitable locals or the grounds of Shobak Castle. The desert mountains can get cold and lonely at night—try warming up in Karak and leaving on a morning bus.

AN ENGLISHWOMAN IN ARABIA

Wrapped in a heavy sun hood, with her skirts and petticoats whipping up the dry sands, **Gertrude Bell** traveled throughout the Arabian desert advising sheikhs, documenting archaeological sites, and hosting proper teas on her Wedgwood china. In the 1880s, Bell was one of the first women to study at Oxford University, where she gained high honors but shocked professors with her brazenness. Her family sent her to Bucharest, Romania, to be schooled in the ways of Victorian femininity, but Bell's insatiable wanderlust would have none of it. Soon Bell was traveling farther East and in 1909, with a bevy of male servants in caravan, she set out for "Mesopotamia." Dubbed an "honorary man" by the Arabs she met, Bell befriended graduate student T.E. Lawrence (later to be known as **Lawrence of Arabia**) and became the only woman to be drafted to Cairo's Arab Bureau as an intelligence agent at the break of World War I. She ignited controversy during the war with her support of Arabic self-determination and her indisputable femininity. After the war, she published an official report on the administration of Mesopotamia—no small task during that particularly tumultuous period. When Iraq rebelled in 1920, she helped carve out the nascent state of Iraq and served as one of King Faisal's closest aides. Nevertheless, Bell took her own life in 1926. The next day, Baghdad's crowds filed past to pay respects to this "uncrowned queen of Iraq."

7 PRACTICAL INFORMATION. The two main landmarks in town are the castle and the center circle, which has a statue of a horse-and-rider. The former is at the top of the hill, while the latter is at the bottom. Karak's renovated **tourist office** is next to the Peace-Ram Restaurant on al-Hadar St. (Open Sa-Th 8am-2pm.) Banks and international **ATMs** cluster downhill from the castle, on the sidestreet across from the Jordan National Bank. Karak's **Italian Hospital** (☎235 11 45 or 235 10 45) is downhill from the road leading to the castle, in the direction of the manic horseman's dagger. The **police station** is down the street and on the right of the tourist office, next to the huge radio tower. Karak's **post and telephone office** is across the street from the tourist office and the Tower Hotel. (Open Sa-Th 8am-2pm.)

☎◘ ACCOMMODATIONS AND FOOD. The best domicile for your dinar is the **Rum Cottage Hotel,** on al-Hadar St. around the corner from the Rest House. It's spotless, and prices are negotiable, especially in the off-season. (☎235 13 51 or 235 37 89; fax 235 11 05. Singles JD10; doubles JD15, in the off-season JD10.) The **Karak Rest House,** next to the entrance to Karak Castle, offers the nicest rooms and the best views in town. (☎235 11 48 or 235 17 17; fax 235 31 48. Singles JD25; doubles JD35; triples JD45; breakfast included. Slow business brings discounts of JD10-15. V, MC, AmEx.) The Rest House restaurant offers full meals including salad, main dish, dessert, and coffee for JD6. (Open daily 7-9:30am, 12:30-4pm, and 8-10pm.) The management of the Rest House also runs the **Karak Guest House,** downhill from the castle on Castle St. It offers similar services and facilities at slightly lower prices than its competitors. (Singles JD20; doubles JD30; triples JD40; breakfast included.) The **Towers Castle Hotel,** between the Rest and the Guest, offers spacious rooms. (☎235 24 89; ☎/fax 235 42 93. Singles JD12; doubles JD16; triples JD22.) Despite its noisy, stuffy rooms, the **New Karak Hotel,** downhill from the castle on Italy St., has hot showers and low prices. (☎235 19 42. JD3 per bed.)

The restaurants in Karak serve similar dishes. The **Kir Heres Restaurant,** adjacent to the Towers Castle Hotel, cooks kebabs and grills to castle-climbing tourists (JD4-5). The **Rum Cottage Restaurant,** across the street from the police station and the radio tower, offers oven-warmed frozen pizza or *mensaf* with salad starting at JD1.5-3. (☎235 37 89. Open daily 8am-10pm.) Popular with tourist groups, the **Fida Restaurant,** down the street from the Ram Hotel, serves an open buffet luncheon for JD5. (☎235 26 77. Open daily 8am-10pm.)

◙ **SIGHTS.** Built into and on top of the hill overlooking its sleepy hamlet, **Karak Castle** is full of secret passageways and hidden rooms. Bring a flashlight for easier exploration and allow at least two hours. In 1142 CE, Baldwin I of Jerusalem built the castle midway between his capital and Shobak, on the site of an Iron Age citadel mentioned in the Mesha Stele of 850 BCE. The castle was renovated in 1188 under Salah al-Din, and although the fortress's walls have mostly collapsed since then, its building blocks remain large enough to inspire starry-eyed wonder. The bolt holes for mammoth stone doors that have since turned to dust are still visible. To the west across the dry moat are battlements from which the charming Renauld de Chatillon cast prisoners 40m to their deaths (with wooden boxes fastened around their heads so that they would not lose consciousness too quickly). When Salah al-Din took the castle after the 1187 Battle of Hittim, he personally saw to it that Chatillon's head was removed. Below, a 50m tunnel leads out of town through an arched gateway. Ask the museum guard to unlock the underground chamber opposite the museum entrance—the 150m long vaulted room used to be the main entrance to the castle. Steep, jagged walls atop an even steeper hill turn a tour of the windblown ruins into a challenge. To the right of the castle entrance is a stone staircase that descends to the **Archaeological Museum.** A copy of the Mesha Stele rests alongside original Nabatean, Roman, and Mamluk artifacts. (Open daily 8am-5pm. Castle and museum JD1.)

NEAR KARAK: MAZRA'A

Hitchers report that little traffic exists between Mazra'a and Karak. For help, visit the ***Mazra'a Police Post,*** *5km north of the junction. Heading out of Mazra'a is the Wadi Araba Highway, where hitchhiking is prohibited. In towns surrounding Karak, tourist services are nonexistent. If you are lost or need a ride or a place to stay, approach a friendly looking store owner or businessperson and ask for help (offer 500fils-JD1 in return). Solo women should refuse hospitality from single men.*

West of Karak, Highway 49/80 (some call it Highway 50) drops over 20m from the King's Highway to the Dead Sea "port" of **Mazra'a** and the al-Lisan ("Tongue") Peninsula. Five kilometers before reaching Mazra'a and the Wadi Araba Highway to Aqaba, Highway 49/80 passes **Bab al-Dhira.** The cemeteries here contain 20,000 shaft tombs enshrining 500,000 bodies (an unfortunate 25-to-1 body-to-tomb ratio) and over three million pottery vessels. The length of the bones indicates that the average height in Bab al-Dhira was a sturdy 2m (over 6½ ft.), which explains why the Bible describes its inhabitants as giants. Reaching this site may be more trouble than it's worth for all but the most morbidly curious.

The mosques at **Mu'tah** and at the nearby village of **Mazar** (bus 150fils) commemorate the Muslim generals who died in the first great battles between the forces of Islam and Byzantium in 632 CE. The green-domed mosque in Mazar houses a small **Islamic museum** on the first floor. (Usually open daily 9am-4pm.)

SOUTH OF KARAK

SHOBAK شوبك

Amman-bound minibuses (500fils) reach Shobak from Wadi Musa (the modern town next to Petra), departing from Wadi Musa gate in the early morning. Around the same time of day, minibuses make the trip from Karak to Tafilah (30min., 250fils), where you can catch a connection to Shobak (JD1). If you hire a taxi (at most JD10 from Karak, JD5 from Wadi Musa), make sure the driver waits while you explore.

The first castle of King Baldwin I of Jerusalem pales in comparison to his later creation at Karak. **Shobak Castle,** known to locals as "Mons Realis" or "Montréal," is 4km from the marked turnoff at the northern edge of Shobak town. The castle first fell to Salah al-Din in 1189, just 74 years after it was built. In 1260, the Mamluks gained possession of the castle, restored it, and inscribed records of their work on its main walls and towers. Most of the castle is gone today, but the view from the approaching road across the natural moat is inspiring: colossal white stones silhouetted against desert brush and a cobalt sky. Villagers who lived inside the castle walls depended upon the water from the rock-hewn well, 375 steps deep. They have long since abandoned the area, leaving a secluded spot for free **camping.**

DANA NATURE RESERVE

Buses between Tafilah and Shobak (JD1) will drop you off along the King's Highway, but they are rare and you'll have to hitch or hike the last few kilometers to the reserve. As always, taxis are a more efficient option (around JD7 from Karak).

Fifty kilometers south of Karak and just west of the King's Highway, the Dana Nature Reserve harbors an impressive array of ibex, mountain gazelles, jackals, and the occasional red fox. Founded in 1990, Dana is Jordan's newest national reserve, but the site has an incredibly long history. Archaeological evidence of Paleolithic, Edomite, Nabatean, and Roman settlements have been found within the reserve's borders. **Hike** the several well-marked trails and take rest at the expensive **campground,** whose prices seem to fluctuate depending upon how much the caretaker likes you. For more information on Dana, call the Dana Visitors Center (☎(03) 227 04 97 or 227 04 98; fax 227 04 99) or contact the Royal Society for the Conservation of Nature (☎(06) 533 79 31).

PETRA البتـراء ☎03

Match me such marvel save in Eastern clime,
a rose-red city 'half as old as Time'!
 —Dean Burgon, *Petra*

As one approaches the once-lost city of Petra, towering sculptures peek out from the walls of a natural three-meter-wide fissure to reveal raw mountains that were fashioned by human hands into impossibly delicate structures. Petra ("stone" in Ancient Greek) is perhaps the most astounding ancient city left to the modern world, and certainly a must-see for visitors to the Middle East.

For decades after Petra's rediscovery, the Bedouin adapted to the influx of tourists by providing them with food and accommodations inside Petra, a practice outlawed from 1984-85 out of concern for Petra's monuments. While many Bedouin have been relocated to a housing project near Wadi Musa, a large portion still make their homes in the more remote caves and hills of the city (spanning 50km, most of which tourists never see). Some Bedouin sell souvenirs and drinks amidst the ruins, and others tend goats—don't be surprised if you smell a barnyard stench emanating from inside an ancient tomb. If you venture on paths that go beyond the standard one-day itinerary, you will notice stones piled into neat columns; as long as these cairn markers are in sight, you're near a trail, and Bedouin will pass by.

HISTORY

For 700 years, Petra was lost to all but the few hundred members of a Bedouin tribe who guarded their treasure from outsiders. In the 19th century, Swiss explorer Johann Burkhardt heard Bedouin speaking of a "lost city" and vowed to find it. Though initially unable to find a guide willing to disclose the city's location, he guessed that the city he sought was the Petra of legend, the biblical Sela, which should have been near Mt. Hor, the site of Aaron's tomb. Impersonating a Christian pilgrim, Burkhardt hired a guide, and on August 22, 1812, he became the first non-Bedouin in thousands of years to have walked between the cliffs of Petra's *siq* (the mile-long rift that was the only entrance to Petra). In the nearly two centuries since Burkhardt's discovery, Petra has become a feature tourist attraction, admired by visitors from all over the world, including the film crew of *Indiana Jones and the Last Crusade.* Petra has its own camel corps to protect the blushing ruins from the many overzealous pilgrims who follow in Burkhardt's footsteps.

Humans first set foot in the area back in the 8th millennium BCE. By the 6th century BCE, the Nabateans, a nomadic Arab tribe, had quietly moved onto land controlled by the Edomites and had begun to profit from the trade between lower Arabia and the Fertile Crescent. Over the next three centuries, the Nabatean kingdom flourished, secure in its easily defended capital. The Nabateans carved their temples out of the mountains, looking to Egyptian, Greek, and Roman styles for inspiration. Unique to the Nabateans are the crow-step patterns that grace the crowns of many of the memorials. The crow-steps so resemble inverted stairways that the people of Meda'in Salih (in Saudi Arabia) claimed that God threw Petra upside down and turned it to stone to punish its people for their wickedness.

More historically verifiable evidence suggests that the Nabatean King Aretes defeated Pompey's Roman legions in 63 BCE. The Romans controlled the entire area around Nabatea, however, prompting the later King Rabel III to strike a deal: as long as the Romans did not attack during his lifetime, they would be permitted to move in after he died. In 106 CE, the Romans claimed the Nabatean Kingdom and inhabited this city of rosy Nubian sandstone. In its heyday, Petra housed as many as 30,000 people, but after the earthquake in 363 CE, a shift in trade routes to Palmyra (see p. 580), expansion of the sea trade around Arabia, and another earthquake in 747, much of Petra had deteriorated to rubble.

▐ GETTING THERE AND GETTING AROUND

Petra lies in the rocky wilderness near the southern extreme of the King's Highway, about 282km from Amman (262km via the Desert Highway). **JETT buses** leave Amman daily and drop off passengers at the Petra Visitors Center (3½hr.; Su, Tu, F 6:30am; JD5.5, including entry to Petra JD33). Make reservations in person well in advance (especially in fall and spring) at JETT stations; questions can be handled by phone (☎66 41 46). More than one day is needed to do longer hikes, but the JETT tour will cover the most impressive (and frequented) sights. **Service** also travel to Petra from Wahdat Station in Amman, but there is a wait in Ma'an (5hr., JD2). *Service* drivers will stop at the **Al-Anbat** or **Musa Spring Hotel**; from Wadi Musa, walk 3km or take a **private taxi** to Petra (JD1). From Aqaba, take a **minibus** (2hr., JD3). Start early in the morning to make any of these connections.

To reach Petra from the King's Highway, take the well-marked turnoff and head west into the colorful, steep-sided town of **Wadi Musa.** Halfway through Wadi Musa on the way to Petra, you'll pass the main traffic circle and travel through the main market area. A tortuous one kilometer from the traffic circle, the spur road leaves town and ends at the entrance to Petra. The cluster of buildings here includes the Visitors Center, the Government rest house, a group of five-star hotels, and the gatehouse to the valley that leads to the *siq* and Petra proper.

To leave Petra, catch a **minibus** or **service** to Aqaba (JD3), Amman (JD3), or Wadi Rum (JD3) at the center of Wadi Musa near the post office or at the Musa Spring Hotel. Buses leave early in the morning (6-8am); ask your hotel to reserve you a spot on the morning bus, and the bus will pick you up from the hotel (even budget hotels offer this service). A local **bus** to Ma'an also leaves early in the morning (500fils); ask at your hotel for exact information.

▐ ▐ ORIENTATION AND PRACTICAL INFORMATION

The **Petra Visitors Center** offers a variety of services. (☎215 60 20. Open daily 7am-6pm.) For a "low-tour" of the city center, hire an official guide (2½hr., JD8). More comprehensive tours go to al-Madbah (JD8), al-Deir (JD15), and Jabal Harun (JD35-60). For remoter areas, arrange trips directly with a guide (full-day tour JD35). You can rent a horse (JD7), but are responsible for renting the guide's horse as well. It's more interesting, however, to remain on foot. Without much effort, you can tag along with a guided group or form your own. Various guidebooks are available at the Visitors Center, but there's no substitute for the expertise of an official guide, especially for the remoter sites of al-Barid or al-Madras.

Next to the Visitors Center are the rest house and the swinging gate that mark the beginning of the trail down to the *siq*. There are almost as many banks and

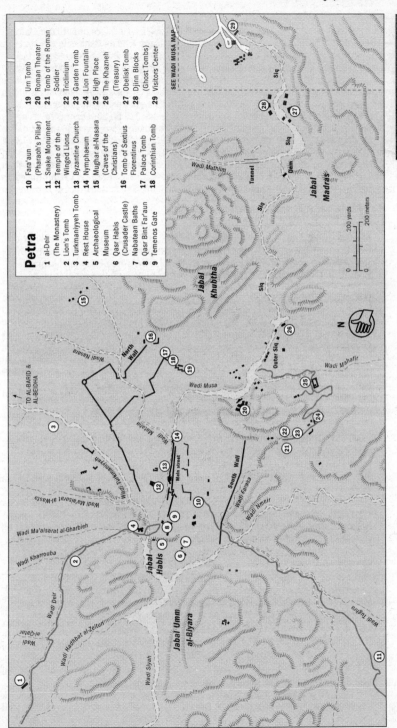

Petra

1 al-Deir (The Monastery)
2 Lion's Tomb
3 Turkmaniyyeh Tomb
4 Rest House
5 Archaeological Museum
6 Qasr Habis (Crusader Castle)
7 Nabatean Baths
8 Qasr Bint Far'aun
9 Temenos Gate
10 Fara'aun (Pharaoh's Pillar)
11 Snake Monument
12 Temple of the Winged Lions
13 Byzantine Church
14 Nymphaeum
15 Mughar al-Nasara (Caves of the Christians)
16 Tomb of Sextius Florentinus
17 Palace Tomb
18 Corinthian Tomb
19 Urn Tomb
20 Roman Theater
21 Tomb of the Roman Soldier
22 Triclinium
23 Garden Tomb
24 Lion Fountain
25 High Place
26 The Khazneh (Treasury)
27 Obelisk Tomb
28 Djinn Blocks (Ghost Tombs)
29 Visitors Center

SEE WADI MUSA MAP

money exchanges in Wadi Musa as there were Nabateans in Petra. The two largest, the **Arab Bank** (☎ 215 68 02) and the **Housing Bank** (☎ 215 60 82), are next to the main traffic circle. (Both open Sa-Th 8:30am-12:30pm.) **Cairo Amman Bank** is in the Mövenpick Hotel, just outside the entrance to Petra. (Open daily 8:30am-3pm.) All banks extract exorbitant commissions. Visa **cash advances** are available from any bank. If you need to contact the **tourist police** (☎ 215 64 41), they can be found munching on cigar ends outside the Visitors Center. The **Wadi Musa Pharmacy** is on the main traffic circle. (☎ 215 64 44. Open 24hr.) The **government health center** is a 15-minute walk uphill from the main traffic circle. (☎ 215 60 25. Open 24hr.) The **Petra Polyclinic** (☎ 215 66 94), at the traffic circle, costs more but has modern equipment. Plug in at the **Rum Internet Cafe** just downhill from the main circle. (☎ 215 72 64. JD3 per hr.) Of the many **post offices** in Wadi Musa, one with **Poste Restante** service lies next to the Musa Spring Hotel. (☎ 215 62 24. Open Sa-Th 7:30am-7pm, F 7:30am-12:30pm.) A second branch is behind the Visitors Center, by the entrance to the *siq*. (☎ 215 66 94. Open daily 8am-7pm.)

▌ ACCOMMODATIONS

Since Jordan and Israel signed a peace treaty, visitors from all over the world have flooded the Jordanian hillside, and construction has boomed in Wadi Musa. Most of the development revolves around luxury resorts, but there are plenty of cheapies to go around, and budget travelers should have little trouble finding a suitable place to sleep (prices also become negotiable in the off-season, May-July and Dec.-Feb.). **Camping** inside Petra is illegal, but lingering explorers (especially women) may receive invitations for overnight stays from Bedouin. Others pick off-the-beaten-path caves for the night. Camping is available in Wadi Musa at some of the hotels.

▨ **Al-Anbat 1 Hotel** (☎ 215 62 65 or 215 79 65; fax 215 68 88). Follow the trough down from the spring. Has the best views around. Free and frequent buses to Petra. Witness the most beautiful sunset in Wadi Musa from mattresses in the "greenhouse" (JD2). Buffet dinner JD4; breakfast JD2. Camping facilities (tents, communal baths; JD2). The basement of this two-star hotel (soon to be three-star, after the addition of a swimming pool and Turkish bath) offers cavernous student rooms with private baths. Student rooms JD4 per bed; singles JD9; doubles JD15; triples JD18.

Petra Gate Hotel, P.O. Box 120, Wadi Musa (☎ 215 69 08; email petra-gate-hotel@hotmail.com). 40m up the hill from the main circle in Wadi Musa, on the right, overlooking the valley. A homey atmosphere with smallish rooms and home-cooked dinners. Cordial, helpful employees live up to the "funky and friendly staff" slogan. Free billiards, so you can bet all the money you're saving by staying here. Breakfast JD1.5. Rooftop mattresses JD1; dorm beds JD2; singles JD5; doubles JD8; triples JD10.5.

Orient Gate Hotel and Restaurant, P.O. Box 185, Wadi Musa (☎/fax 215 70 20). Left of traffic circle, facing downhill. Small, cozy rooms, some with downhill view and balcony, house backpacker clientele. Two neighboring mosques and their competing *muezzins* create an interesting aural experience. Breakfast JD1-2; dinner buffet JD2.5-3. Rooftop mattresses JD2; singles JD6, with bath JD8; doubles JD8-10; triples JD15.

Sunset Hotel, P.O. Box 59 (☎ 215 65 79; fax 215 69 50), 200m uphill from Visitors Center. If your feet are sore and your bottom hurts from a Petra camel ride, this is the place for you—the first inexpensive and clean option outside the mega-hotel complex. Breakfast JD2. Singles JD7, with bath JD15; doubles JD10, with bath JD18. V.

Cleopetra Hotel, P.O. Box 125 (☎/fax 215 70 90), 50m uphill from the main traffic circle, on the left. Colorful rooms with relatively clean private baths. Friendly manager gives maps and info. Breakfast included. Rooftop mattresses JD3; singles JD10; doubles JD15; triples JD18-21.

Musa Spring Hotel and Restaurant, Wadi Musa Gate (☎ 215 63 10; fax 215 69 10). The first hotel as you enter from Amman, but a trek from Petra proper. Plenty of budget traveler companionship. Free shuttle to Petra (leaves 7, 8am; returns 6pm). Free use of kitchen. Breakfast JD1.5; salad lunch 500fils per salad; all-you-can-eat dinner buffet JD3. Rooftop mattresses with hot showers JD2; dorm beds JD4; singles JD7, with bath JD10; doubles JD10, with bath JD12; triples JD15.

Araba Hotel (☎/fax 215 61 07), 200m uphill from the main circle in Wadi Musa. Pastel-hued rooms have soft, colorful mattresses. Some rooms come with private bath. Breakfast JD2. Rooftop mattresses JD2; rooms JD6 per person.

FOOD

The farther you go from the ruins, the less you'll pay for falafel. Wadi Musa boasts the best bargains, especially in the streets to the right of its main circle as you approach from Petra. Many hotels have all-you-can-eat buffets at reasonable prices; others offer filling meals with pasta, rice, chicken, salad, and bread (JD2-3; open 6-9pm). The **Star Supermarket,** on the left and uphill from the traffic circle, has the cheapest water (300fils) and the most reasonably priced basics for bagged lunches. **Pizza Hut** and **Papazzi** (☎215 70 87), next to each other uphill from the Visitors Center, can satisfy your post-Petra pizza cravings (medium pizza at both JD5-7). Even if you can't afford to eat there, the **Mövenpick** offers affordable ice cream (JD1 per scoop), an excellent salad lunch buffet (JD4.5), and a deliciously air-conditioned interior. The Mövenpick and its rival, the **Petra Forum Hotel,** also house the most pleasant bars in town. The former rests in a tea garden on the roof of the hotel, and the latter sits on a lobby-level terrace at the base of the Petra hills, offering the best (and closest) view of the sunset over Petra (drinks JD3-5).

Al-Wadi Restaurant (☎215 71 63), in the city center on the main circle. Climb the steep staircase for delectable omelettes (JD1.5) and filling *mezze*. Soups and salads 500fils; main meals JD1-3. Ask about student deals. Open daily 6:30am-midnight.

Al-Janoub Restaurant (☎215 75 65), on the first street on the right before reaching the main circle from Petra. Modest kebabs are the cheapest in town (JD1). Hummus 500fils; falafel 500fils; soda bottles 200fils. Open daily 6am-1am.

Cleopetra Restaurant, to the left of the main circle when facing downhill. Friendly Egyptian cooks serve rice, salad, bird, and bread (JD2.5). Arabic breakfast JD1.5; kebab or mixed grill JD2.5; buffet JD4; soda 75fils. Open daily 5am-midnight.

Rose City Restaurant (☎215 73 40), just uphill from the site. Pick up a sandwich lunch for the park at this diner-cum-souvenir shop. Hummus 600fils; sandwiches 400fils-JD1; grills JD3; soda 300fils. Open daily 6:30am-1pm and 6:30-11pm.

Red Cave Restaurant (☎215 77 99; fax 215 69 31), up the street from Petra. Well-decorated and bamboo-covered restaurant. Delicious food matches elegant setting. Daily specials and *mensaf* (JD5). Pasta JD3-3.5; appetizers JD1. Open daily 11am-midnight.

The Petra Pearl (☎215 50 60), across the street and 10m uphill from Cleopetra. Serves up a chicken buffet (JD3) and *ad hoc* Arabic lessons. Open daily 6am-midnight.

SIGHTS

Many spectacular monuments are close enough to be viewed in a day, but a few require multi-day expeditions. Guides are expensive, but recommended for four of the remoter hikes. Bring water bottles from outside; Bedouin sell water throughout the park, but at JD1-1.5 per bottle, you'll need to empty the Treasury to stay hydrated. Open daily 6am-6pm; in winter 6am-5pm, but hours loosely enforced. If you stay to see the sunset, you should have no problem getting out. One day JD20; two days JD25, children JD12.5; three days JD30, children JD15.

Although the Nabateans worshiped only two deities—Dushara, the god of strength, and al-Uzza (Atargatis), the goddess of water and fertility—the number of temples and tombs in Petra seems infinite. Climbing will allow you to escape the tour groups crowding the inner valley.

OBELISK TOMB. If you head toward the canyon-like *siq*, large *djinn* monuments (ghost tombs) and caves will stare down at you from distant mountain faces. The Obelisk Tomb is built high into the cliff on the left. Closer to the entrance of the *siq*, rock-cut channels once cradled the ceramic pipes that brought 'Ain Musa's waters to the city and the surrounding country. A nearby dam burst in 1963, and the resulting flood killed 28 tourists in the *siq*. While designing the new dam, the Nabateans' ancient dam was uncovered and used as a model.

■**KHAZNEH.** As you enter the *siq*, 200m walls on either side begin to block out the sunlight, casting enormous shadows on the niches that once held icons meant to hex unwelcome visitors (you should be safe if you've paid the admission fee). The *siq* winds around for 1½km, then slowly emits a faint pink glow at the first peek of the Khazneh (Treasury). At 90m wide and 130m tall, the Khazneh is the best preserved of Petra's monuments, though bullet holes are clearly visible on the upper urn. Believing the urn to be hollow and filled with ancient pharaonic treasures, Bedouin periodically fired at it, hoping to burst this petrified *piñata*. Actually, the Treasury is a royal tomb and quite solid. The Khazneh's rock face changes color as the day progresses: in the morning, the sun's rays give the monument a rich peach hue; in late afternoon it glistens rose; and by sunset it drips blood red.

ROMAN THEATER. Down the road to the right as you face the Khazneh, Wadi Musa opens up to the 7000-seat Roman Theater. The long row of Royal Tombs on the face of Jabal Khubtha stands to the right. The Romans built their theater under the red stone Nabatean necropolis, and the ancient carved caves still yawn above it. The theater has been restored to its 2nd-century appearance, and audiences are returning after a 1500-year intermission. A marble Hercules (now in the museum) was discovered just a few years ago in the curtained chambers beneath the stage.

ROYAL TOMBS. Across the Wadi are the Royal Tombs. The **Urn Tomb,** with its unmistakable recessed facade, commands a soul-scorching view of the still-widening valley. The two-tiered vault beneath the pillared facade is known as the **prison,** or *sijin*. A Greek inscription on an inner wall describes how the tomb, originally dedicated to the Nabatean King Malichus II in the first century CE, was converted to a church 400 years later. Nearby sits the **Corinthian Tomb** (allegedly a replica of Nero's Golden Palace in Rome) and the **Palace Tomb** (or the Tomb in Two Stories), which juts out from the mountainside. Laborers completed the tomb by attaching preassembled stones to its upper left-hand corner. Around the corner to the right is the **Tomb of Sextus Florentinus,** who was so enamored of these hewn heights that he asked his son to bury him in this ultimate outpost of the Roman Empire.

MAIN STREET. Around the bend to the left, a few restored columns are all that remain of the paved Roman main street. Two thousand years ago, columns lined the full length of the street, shielding markets and residences. At the beginning of the street on the right, the **Nymphaeum** ruins outline the ancient public fountain near its base. On a rise to the right, before the triple-arched gate, recent excavations have uncovered the Temple of al-Uzza (Atargatis), also called the **Temple of the Winged Lions.** In the spring you can watch the progress of US-sponsored excavations that have already uncovered several workshops and some cracked crocks.

BYZANTINE CHURCH. A joint Jordanian-American team has recently excavated an immense Byzantine church with a wealth of mosaics. The site lies several hundred meters to the right of the Roman street, near the Temple of the Winged Lions, from which some of the church's column bases and capitals were probably lifted. Each of the church's side aisles is paved with 70 square meters of remarkably preserved mosaic, depicting humans of various professions, representations of the four seasons, and indigenous, exotic, and even mythological animals. Recent studies attest that the church was the seat of an important Byzantine bishopric in the 5th and 6th centuries, an assertion that challenges the belief that Petra was in decline by 600 CE. The archaeologists on the site constantly dig, scrape, and sniff. They also protect their site quite zealously—entrance may require charm and luck.

SOUTHERN TEMPLE AND ENVIRONS. A team from Brown University in the US is in the process of unearthing the Southern Temple. White hexagonal paving stones cover an extensive tunnel system that marks the importance of this holy site. Farther along, the triple-arched **Temenos Gate** was once the front gate of the **Qasr Bint Fara'un** (Palace of the Pharaoh's Daughter), a Nabatean temple built to honor the god Dushara. On the left before the gate are the **Nabatean Baths.** On a trail leading behind the temple to the left, a single standing column, **Amud Fara'un** (Pharaoh's Pillar), gloats beside its two fallen comrades.

MUSEUMS. To the right of the Nabatean temple, a rock-hewn staircase leads to a small **archaeological museum** holding the spoils of the Winged Lions dig as well as carved stone figures from elsewhere in Petra. On the way to the monastery, the **Nabatean Museum** has good artifacts and air-conditioned restrooms with what is probably the ▨**world's best toilet seat view.** *(Both museums open daily 9am-4pm. Free.)*

▨ HIKES: AROUND PETRA

Many people rave about Petra's most accessible ten percent, content with what they can see in one day. The Bedouin say, however, that in order to appreciate Petra, you must stay long enough to watch your nails grow long. The following seven treks fill two days, but you can easily spend a week wandering, especially if you venture beyond the ancient city limits. Four of these seven hikes require a guide (officially JD35, but good luck finding one who charges less than JD50): **Jabal Harun,** the **Snake Monument, al-Madras,** and **al-Barid.** It's unwise to hike the remote hills alone. If you feel lost, keep a sharp eye out for remnants of donkey visits, which can serve as a trail of crumbs.

WADI TURKMANIYYEH وادى تركمانية

The shortest and easiest of the hikes leads down the *wadi* to the left of and behind the Temple of the Winged Lions. Fifteen minutes of strolling down the road running through the rich green gardens of Wadi Turkmaniyyeh leads to the only tomb at Petra with a Nabatean inscription. The lengthy invocation above the entrance beseeches the god Dushara to protect the tomb from violation. Unfortunately, Dushara took a permanent sabbatical and the chamber has been stripped bare.

AL-HABIS الحابيس

A second, more interesting climb begins at the end of the road that descends from the Pharaoh's Pillar to the cliff face, a few hundred meters left of the museum. The trail dribbles up to al-Habis, the prison. While the steps have been restored recently, they do not lead up to much. A path winds all the way around the mountain, however, revealing gorgeous canyons and (you guessed it) more tombs on the western side. The climb to the top and back takes less than an hour.

JABAL HARUN جبل هارون

This climb begins just to the right of Jabal Habis, below the museum. A sign points to **al-Deir** (the Monastery) and leads northwest across Wadi Siyah, past the Forum Restaurant and on to Wadi Deir and its fragrant oleander. Squeeze through the narrowing canyon along an endless, twisting stairway to confront a human-shaped hole in the facade of the **Lion's Tomb.** A hidden tomb awaits daredevils who try to climb the cleft to the right; less intrepid wanderers can backtrack to the right and spot the tomb a few minutes later.

Back on the path, veer left to reach Petra's largest monument. Larger (50m wide and 45m tall) but less ornate than the Khazneh, al-Deir has a single inner chamber that dates back to the first century CE. Most scholars believe that al-Deir was originally either a Nabatean temple or an unfinished tomb dedicated to one of the later Nabatean kings. It picked up its orthodox appellation in the Byzantine period. On the left, a lone tree popping through a crack in the rock marks more ancient steps, which continue all the way up to the rim of the urn atop the monastery. Those with more courage than caution may actually step out onto the ancient urn. Straight across the *wadi* looms the highest peak in the area, **Jabal Harun** (Aaron's Mountain or Mt. Hor). On top of the mountain, a white church reportedly houses the **Tomb of Aaron.** The hike straight up to al-Deir (no side trips) takes 30 minutes, but the whole trip takes a few hours. Expect to spend a couple more hours if you detour into **Wadi Siyah** and visit its seasonal waterfall on the way back.

JABAL UMM AL-BIYARA جبـل أم البيارة

It takes a grueling three-hour hike to ascend **Jabal Umm al-Biyara** (Mother of Cisterns Mountain), which towers over the Crusader castle on Jabal Habis. Follow the trail from the left of the Nabatean temple past the Pharaoh's Pillar and down into the *wadi* to the right. A 50m scramble up the rock chute to the left of the blue sign leads to the beginning of a stone ramp, which leads to the top. Exercise caution on the ramp, as the footing is fickle. It was here, at the site of Petra's original acropolis and the biblical city of Sela, that a Judean king supposedly hurled thousands of Edomites over the cliff's edge. The gigantic piles of shards, over 8000 years old, are the only remnants of the mountain's first inhabitants.

If you continue south along Wadi Tughra (which runs by its base) instead of climbing Umm al-Biyara, you'll eventually reach the **Snake Monument,** one of the earliest Nabatean religious shrines. From here it's about two hours to the Tomb of Aaron on Jabal Harun. The path meanders around Jabal Harun before ascending it from the south. When it disappears on the rocks, follow the donkey droppings. As you start to climb Jabal Harun you'll see a lone tent. Inside, a Bedouin, the official holder of the keys, will escort you the rest of the way and open the building for you to explore. The entire trek takes five or six hours.

THE HIGH PLACE OF SACRIFICE المكان العالى

One of the most popular hikes is the circular route to the **High Place of Sacrifice** on **Jabal al-Madhbah,** a site of sacrifice with a full view of Petra—even the tourist police come here to watch the sunset. A staircase sliced into the rock leads to the left just as the Roman Theater comes into view. Follow the right prong when the trail levels and forks at the top of the stairs. On the left, **Obelisk Ridge** presents one obelisk to Dushara and another to al-Uzza. On the peak to the right, the High Place supports a string of grisly sights: two altars, an ablution cistern, gutters for draining away sacrificial blood, and cliff-hewn bleachers for an unobstructed view of animal sacrifices. Head downhill past the Pepsi stand, leaving the obelisks behind you, and backtrack under the western face of the High Place. A hard-to-find staircase leads down to a sculptured **Lion Fountain.** The first grotto complex beyond it is the **Garden Tomb.** Below it is the **Tomb of the Roman Soldier** (named for the tough guy carved in the facade) and across from it a rock **triclinium** (feast hall), which has the only decorated interior in Petra. The trail then leads into Wadi Farasa and ends near the Pillar. The circle, followed either way, takes about 1.5 hours.

AL-MADRAS AND AL-BARID المدرس و البارد

Beyond Petra, tourist groups and commercialism disappear. Bedouin here remain unaltered by modernity and wildlife roam free. The isolated antiquities can only be reached by donkey or foot. All roads lead back to the King's Highway.

A trail branching to the left just past the Obelisk Tomb and before the entrance to the *siq* leads to **al-Madras,** an ancient Petran suburb with almost as many monuments as Petra. On the way, watch for the short-eared desert hare and a full spectrum of long, lanky, white lizards in dazzling purple, fuchsia, and iridescent blue. Come with water, a snack, and a guide. The round-trip takes four to eight hours.

Past the Tomb of Sextus Florentinus and the **Mughar al-Nasara** (Caves of the Christians), a trail chisels into the rock that leads to the northern suburb of **al-Barid.** A road passing the new hotel in Wadi Musa also approaches this archaeological site. Al-Barid is a curious miniature of Petra, complete with a short *siq,* several carved tombs, and caves. If you don't feel like hoofing it, a Wadi Musa **taxi** will take you there and wait at the entrance for an hour (JD7). Also off the new road past the hotel is **al-Beidha.** Excitement runs high among the members of the excavating expedition here—they've uncovered traces of a pre-pottery Neolithic village, a sedentary society dating from the 8th millennium BCE. Conclusive evidence of this site's age would make al-Beidha one of the oldest known farming communities in the world (along with Jericho). A Bedouin guide can lead you here via a painless trail (about 3hr. each way). Bring an extra JD2-3 or some of your own native trinkets (such as cigarettes) to trade.

AQABA ‏العقبة‎ ☎ 03

Set in a natural theater beneath a crescent of rugged hills, Aqaba is Jordan's sole link to the sea. Beneath the water, legions of brilliantly colored fish flit through a universe of coral. Aqaba's reefs are in better condition than the damaged reefs of Eilat, but they aren't quite on par with the spectacular snorkeling spots that circle the southern Sinai. Above the water, Aqaba serves as an important trade and military center and has become the darling of an Arab elite in need of periodic respite from dry cityscapes. At the tip of the gulf of the same name, Aqaba's strategic setting has been apparent since biblical times, when King Solomon's copper-laden ships embarked from here. The Romans stationed their famous Tenth Legion at this point, and the Crusaders fortified the port and Pharaoh's Island, 7km off the coast (now in Egyptian territory). During the 1917 Arab Revolt, Faisal Ibn Hussein and T.E. Lawrence staged a desert raid on the Ottoman fortifications and captured the port. In 1965, King Hussein not-so-shrewdly traded the Saudis 6000km of southeastern desert (before he knew there was oil beneath the sand) for 13km of coastline, and started developing the city. The reopening of the Suez Canal in 1957 and the Iran-Iraq War in the 80s boosted Aqaba's importance as a regional port. During the 1991 Gulf War, Aqaba was Iraq's chief outlet for illicit exports, but a blockade slowed traffic considerably. Recently, Aqaba has bounced back—trade has resumed and the open border with Israel has exposed the city to tourism.

▐ GETTING THERE AND GETTING AROUND

Flights: Royal Jordanian (☎201 24 03), a 10-min. walk northeast of town on al-Sharif al-Hussein Ibn 'Ali St., just past the rotary. One regular flight daily to and from **Amman** (1hr., JD30). More flights during high season. Some hotels run buses from Aqaba International Airport to the center of city. Taxis to airport JD2-3 per person.

Buses and minibuses: The **minibus station** (☎201 63 78) is uphill past the post office; turn right onto King Talal St. and walk two blocks. **JETT buses** (☎201 52 22), just north of the Miramar Hotel, go to **Amman** (4hr.; 7, 9, 10:30am, noon, 2, 3:30, 5pm; JD4). Daily minibuses to **Petra** leave when full (2hr.; 8:30, 10:30am, noon; JD3); sometimes another bus departs in early afternoon. Another way to Petra is to take a minibus to **Ma'an** (1½hr., JD1) and catch a Petra bus from there (1½hr., JD1). There is normally only one minibus to **Wadi Rum** (1½hr., 7:30am, JD1.50), but during busy season others sometimes leave during the afternoon. Check times in advance.

Taxis: Talal (☎201 24 77) offers groups (max. 4 people) quick transport to: **Aqaba ferry terminal** (10km, JD3); **Petra** (3hr., JD30); and **Wadi Rum** (1¼hr., JD20).

Car Rental: Government-controlled prices are JD18-57 per day, plus JD0.31-0.57 per km. Rental agencies include **Avis** (☎202 28 83), downhill from the Jordan National Bank; **Hertz** (☎201 62 06), in front of the Aquamarina II Hotel; and **Rum** (☎201 35 81), across from the post office, which is perhaps the cheapest.

▐▪▮ ORIENTATION AND PRACTICAL INFORMATION

Aqaba is essentially one elongated beach extending from the royal villa on the Israeli border to the huge, fenced-in port facilities four kilometers southeast down the arching corniche. Luxury hotels and military complexes have gobbled up a good part of the beach near town. Four countries come together in the small northern tip of the Gulf of Aqaba: Egypt meets Israel near the conspicuous resort hotels at Taba, Israel's Eilat faces Jordan's Aqaba across the border, and Saudi Arabia looms to the southeast (for information on **border crossings,** see p. 454).

Shops line the streets of central Aqaba, branching around the post office and behind the **Hussein Ibn 'Ali Mosque.** South of the port and 10km from central Aqaba, the **ferry dock** handles the thousands of Egyptian workers and occasional foreign travelers who cross the Gulf of Aqaba to Nuweiba in Egypt. The **Marine Research Center** is about one kilometer past the ferry port. Past that lie Aqaba's finest coral reefs and a sandy beach that stretches south to the Saudi border.

Visitors Center: (☎201 33 63 or 201 37 31). Worthwhile stop on grounds of Aqaba Museum, about halfway to the port from the town center. Short walk or 500fils taxi ride. Maps, brochures, and information on travel to nearby cities. Open Sa-Th 7:30am-2pm.

Consulate: Egypt (☎201 61 71), on al-Istiqlal St. Turn right along curve 800m northwest of the Aquamarina II; look for guard booth. Same-day **Egyptian visas.** Bring passport, photo, and JD12. Apply for visa 9am-1pm, pick-up 2pm. Open Sa-Th 9am-2pm.

Currency Exchange: Arab Bank (☎201 35 45), just north of the park in the main square. **ATM** accepts V and MC. Open Su-Th 8:30am-3pm. **Jordan National Bank** (☎202 23 51), 10m downhill from the post office on the first right. Allows MC withdrawal. Hefty JD3 commission on traveler's checks. Open Su-Th 8:30am-3:30pm.

American Express: International Traders Travel Agency Office (☎201 37 57). Walk downhill from the post office, take the first left, and continue for 30m. The office is just before the 'Ali Baba. Holds mail for anyone. Open daily 8:30am-1pm and 4-7pm.

English Bookstore: Yamani Bookshop (☎201 22 21), opposite the post office. Good newspaper, magazine, and travel guide selection. Sells film, snorkeling gear, sunscreen, and other odds and ends. Open daily 9am-2:30pm and 6-9:30pm. V, MC.

Laundromat: Most hotels provide expensive laundry service. **Al-Abbi Dry Cleaning** (☎201 57 22), one block down from the minibus and *service* station on King Talal St., is cheaper. Shirts 500fils, pants JD1. Open Sa-Th 8am-9pm.

Police: (☎192 or 201 35 03), uphill past the post office. Turn right onto King Talal St. and walk two blocks; it's across from the minibus station. **Tourist Police** (☎201 97 17), at the Israeli border. **Ambulance** (☎198 or 199).

Pharmacies: Aqaba Pharmacy (☎201 22 37), next to Jordan Flower Hotel. Open Sa-Th 8am-1am, F 8pm-1am. V, MC. **Jerusalem Pharmacy** (☎201 47 47), on Tunisiyya St. next to the al-Zeitouna Hotel. Open Sa-Th 7:30am-midnight.

Hospital: Princess Haya al-Hussein (☎201 41 11), 10-min. walk northeast of town on al-Sharif al-Hussein Ibn 'Ali St., just past rotary near Royal Jordanian Office. One of the best, with decompression chambers and staff who deal with diving accidents.

Telephones: Turn left out of the bus station and take the next left. Next to post office. Cheaper on F or after 8pm. Open daily 7:30am-10pm.

Post Office: (☎201 39 39). Turn left out of bus station and take next left. Next to the large radio tower. **Poste Restante** and **EMS.** Open Sa-Th 7am-7pm, F 7:30am-2pm.

ACCOMMODATIONS

Aqaba has some of the highest prices in Jordan (after Petra), but several good values exist. Keep in mind, however, that many hotels add a 10% tax to prices. **Camping** is free, legal, and common south of the port; the only legal camping north of the port is on the lots beside some of the larger hotels. The Aqaba Hotel also has a small site and the JD6 fee includes access to the private beach and showers.

■ **Nairoukh Hotel 1,** P.O. Box 1138 (☎201 92 84; fax 201 92 85). From the traffic circle joining al-Hashimi St. and al-Sharif al-Hussein Ibn Ali St., walk 50m up al-Sharif away from the beach. Turn right and walk toward Hani 'Ali, but then turn left on the alley running between 'Ali Baba and Hani 'Ali. Amira Hotel will be in front of you and Nairoukh 1

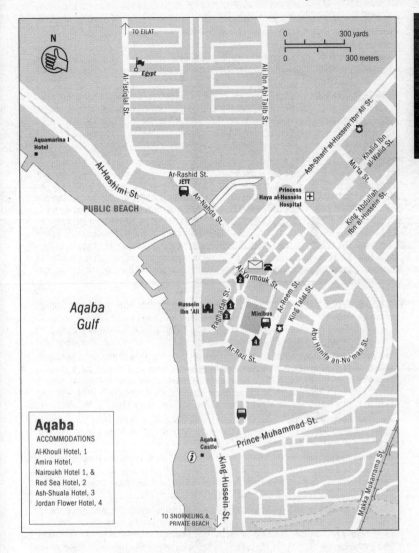

N

TO EILAT

Egypt

Al-Istiqlal St.

Ali Ibn Abi Talib St.

0   300 yards

0   300 meters

Aquamarina I Hotel

Al-Hashimi St.

Ar-Rashid St.
JETT

An-Nahda St.

Ash-Sharf al-Hussein Ibn Ali St.

Khalid Ibn al-Walid St.

Mu'ta St.

Princess Haya al-Hussein Hospital

PUBLIC BEACH

King 'Abdullah Ibn al-Hussein St.

Aqaba Gulf

Al-Yarmouk St.

Raghadan St.

Ar-Reem St.

King Talal St.

Hussein Ibn 'Ali

Minibus

Ar-Razi St.

Abu Hanifa an-Nu'man St.

Prince Muhammad St.

Aqaba Castle

King Hussein St.

Makka Mukarrama St.

TO SNORKELING & PRIVATE BEACH

Aqaba

ACCOMMODATIONS

Al-Khouli Hotel, 1
Amira Hotel,
Nairoukh Hotel 1, &
Red Sea Hotel, 2
Ash-Shuala Hotel, 3
Jordan Flower Hotel, 4

will be off the first alley to the right that runs behind the 'Ali restaurant. There are two different Nairoukhs. Staff cleans incessantly and the place sparkles. Spacious rooms have A/C, TV, fridge, towels, and phone. Breakfast JD1.5. Singles JD14; doubles JD18; triples JD25. 10% tax.

Red Sea Hotel, P.O Box 65 (☎201 21 56 or (07) 956 68 96; fax 201 57 89), next door to Nairoukh 1. Somewhat dark and dingy with basic rooms and bathrooms. Helpful manager 'Amer can arrange snorkeling with lunch for JD18. Dorms JD6; singles with bath JD6; doubles JD12; triples JD15. Western toilet, A/C, TV, and fridge JD6-9 extra.

Al-Shuala Hotel, P.O. Box 211 (☎201 51 53 or 201 51 54; fax 201 51 60), on Raghadan St., behind Hussein Ibn 'Ali Mosque. Luxury hotel with low prices. Some rooms have bidets, balconies, and a charming view of Eilat. Singles JD16-18; doubles JD28-34. 10% tax.

Al-Khouli Hotel (☎/fax 203 01 52), in the square behind Al-Shuala Hotel. Small entrance with bigger rooms. A/C, fan, and phone. Breakfast JD2. Be sure to bargain. Singles JD14; doubles JD18.

Amira Hotel, P.O. Box 383 (☎201 88 40; fax 201 25 59), next to Nairoukh 1. Clean rooms come with TV, towels, fridge, private bath, and A/C. Singles JD14; doubles JD18; triples JD20-25. 10% tax and 13% service.

Jordan Flower Hotel, P.O. Box 681 (☎201 43 77; fax 201 43 78), in the commercial area across the park from the Arab Bank. Dreary entrance with comfortable rooms. Some with balcony seaview, ceiling fans, and shared bathrooms. Breakfast JD1. Singles JD4-5; doubles JD7; triples JD10. A/C JD2.

🍴 FOOD

Fresh fish is surprisingly hard to find in Aqaba, despite its seaside location. The low plankton count in the northern waters of the Gulf of Aqaba forces hungry sea creatures to forage elsewhere. Jordanians are not permitted to fish the richer Saudi waters, and the Egyptian export tax is outlandish. A **market** sprawls behind the Al-Shuala Hotel. (Open daily 7am-11pm.) Shops around the square sell everything from ice cream to **fried sloth.** Many restaurants cluster around the Aquamarina II Hotel and lamb, beef, and falafel are everywhere around the Hussein Ibn 'Ali Mosque. **Gelato Uno,** a popular chain serving frozen treats throughout Aqaba, has one franchise near Tikka Chicken. (Open 10am-midnight.)

🖼 **Al-Shami Restaurant** (☎201 61 07), on Raghadan St., across from the Hussein Ibn 'Ali Mosque and next to Al-Shuala Hotel. The best food for your fils in the main district. Go in a group and get mixed appetizers (JD3) and a mixed grill (JD2.5) while shooting the breeze in the A/C. Salads 500fils, chicken dishes JD2, fish JD5. Open 10am-midnight.

'Ali Baba Restaurant (☎201 39 01; fax 201 48 55). From the traffic circle joining al-Hashimi St. and al-Sharif al-Hussein Ibn Ali St., walk 50m up al-Sharif, away from the beach. It's on the right-hand side near Nairoukh Hotel 1, next door to Hani 'Ali Restaurant. Top-notch french onion soup and grape leaves. *Baba ghanoush* 500fils, hamburgers JD1.75, and a huge variety of steaks JD7. Open daily 9am-11pm. V, MC, AmEx.

Hani 'Ali Restaurant (☎201 52 00), next to 'Ali Baba Restaurant. Hani 'Ali is always crowded with customers noisily munch, munch, munching on its reasonably priced, world-class pastries. Open daily 8am-11pm.

Captain's Restaurant (☎201 69 05), on al-Nahda St., by Aquamarina II Hotel. Look for the blue and white veranda. One of Aqaba's best, but it goes overboard on the naval decor. Fish flown in fresh from Egypt and Yemen. Spaghetti with fresh cheese JD2, meat dishes JD3-6.25, seafood JD6-8, and simple omelettes 600fils. Open daily 9am-11pm.

China Restaurant (☎201 44 15), on 3rd floor of building behind the post office. Gaudy red interior and varied menu of quality food (entrees JD2-4). Hits the spot for those with a hankering for Chinese. The King eats here. Open daily 10:30am-3pm and 6:30-11pm.

Tikka Chicken (☎201 95 16), on al-Nahda St., west of the Aquamarina II Hotel on the right. Seven different chicken entrees with various side dishes JD1.75-2.5. Herbivores will enjoy the veggie salad (500fils) and hummus (500fils). Open daily noon-midnight.

👁 SIGHTS

Aqaba should thank its lucky starfish for its aquatic splendors, because the sights above sea level are all washed up.

RUINS OF AILA. The recently discovered ruins of Aila ("god" in Aramaic) are a minor exception. In a plain beachside lot across from the Miramar Hotel, archaeologists have uncovered the original 120m by 160m city. From the 7th to 10th centuries CE, Aila was an Islamic port, trading as far away as China. Visitors are free to wander amid signs explaining the paltry ruins. Items recovered in the excavations, including Greek and Arabic inscriptions and pottery shards, are displayed in the recently completed **Aqaba Museum,** in the same building as the Visitors Center between the castle and the southern waterfront. *(Open daily 8am-7pm; in winter 8am-5pm. Ruins free, museum JD1.)*

PHARAOH'S ISLAND. An accord between Jordan and Egypt has recently opened the Egyptian **Pharaoh's Island** (known as **Gezirat Fara'un;** see p. 193), seven kilometers off shore, to tourists from Jordan. The **Aquamarina II Hotel** (☎201 62 50) runs full-day trips to the island for JD24 (reserve at least 24hr. ahead). The Aquamarina also runs day-long snorkeling jaunts (JD10) and daytrips to **Wadi Rum** (JD40).

🅰 UNDERWATER ADVENTURES

BEACHES. The majority of Aqaba's cleaner, emptier, and more scenic public beaches are quite far away, but a free and relatively clean **public beach** awaits near the Miramar Hotel. Southeast of downtown, a free **pebble beach** hides behind a "Restricted Area—No Camping" sign. Both public beaches are mostly male scenes and women may become the focus of unwanted attention. The **Aquamarina Hotel** has a gorgeous white sand beach, but will gouge you JD2.5 for the privilege of burning your feet (shade and lounge chairs are reserved for guests). The beaches south of the port, off the road leading to Saudi Arabia, are more remote but have beautiful views and great snorkeling.

SNORKELING. Yemeniyyeh Reef, just south of the Marine Research Center beyond the port, ranks among the world's best snorkeling spots for scoping fish. The **Royal Diving Center** (☎201 70 35; fax 201 70 97) in the Yemeniyyeh area can help you get into the water. They rent snorkeling gear (JD3) and conduct beach dives (JD10, for two JD17). Novices can enroll in a six-day dive course (JD300). Entrance to the center costs JD2, which includes use of the private beach and saltwater swimming pool. A bus runs to and from major hotels in Aqaba (to diving center 9am, back to Aqaba 4-5pm) for 500fils. Otherwise, it is a 15min. taxi ride south of the city. Most luxury hotels also rent out equipment and organize outings. Armed with a mask, snorkel, and pair of fins, aquatic adventurers can wander off alone to more isolated spots near the Saudi border, where the fish run on super-octane. For important information on snorkeling and scuba diving, see **Scu-better Watch Out,** p. 186.

SCUBA DIVING. The **Seastar Watersports Center,** in the Al-Cazar Hotel, conducts dives daily at 9am and 2pm; arrive 30min. early. Snorkeling gear costs JD7 per day. Beginners can take a test dive for JD34; a full PADI scuba course costs JD280. All prices include transportation. (☎201 41 31 or 201 41 32; fax 201 41 33. One dive JD24; two JD38; discounts for multiple dives.) The **Yamani Bookshop,** oddly enough, has a good selection of masks and fins (see **English Bookstore,** p. 500). The **Aquamarina Club** (☎201 62 50), at the Aquamarina Hotel, offers a number of **water sports,** including waterskiing (JD4.3), wind surfing (JD5 per hr.), and tubing (JD2).

NEAR PETRA AND AQABA: WADI RUM وادي رام

Taxis constantly run to Wadi Rum (1hr. from Aqaba, 2hr. from Petra; JD20-25). *Buses and service* along the Desert Highway can drop passengers off 25km north of Aqaba at the turnoff marked "Rum 30km." From there it is possible to hitch a ride to the government rest house at Wadi Rum; hitching, though always risky, is feasible in the summer. Another option is to rent a *car* in Aqaba (see p. 499). Four-wheel drive vehicles are unnecessary unless you plan on exploring the desert alone. The Aquamarina Hotel in Aqaba arranges daytrips to Wadi Rum. *Buses* leave Wadi Rum in the morning for Petra (2hr., 8:30am, JD3) and Aqaba (1½hr., 7am, JD1.5)—inquire about exact times. JD1, includes a complimentary cup of tea or coffee; JD5 extra if you bring your own car.

Two tectonic plates split to create the sublime desert valley of Rum. At the northern end of the *wadi* lies the village of Rum, home to hundreds of Bedouin, the Desert Police, and a government rest house. At the southern end of the valley

JORDAN

A ROCKIN' GOOD TIME Rock climbing is a fabulous but little-known way to enjoy Wadi Rum. Many Europeans (especially the French) arrive each year, and suit up for sheer-face scaling in this spectacular region. Experienced climbers will take thrillseekers on trips and their prices generally won't put you between a rock and a hard place. One recommended guide to seek out is Sabbah Atieeq. Inquire at the rest house for the rock climbing book, which contains descriptions of a number of different climbing routes and visitors' accounts of their adventures. If you want to climb but don't have equipment, you can rent some from a Bedouin guide. One day of climbing, including equipment rental and a guide, costs around JD35.

stands the fort of the **Desert Camel Corps,** the descendants of the British-trained Arab Legion. The members of the Desert Patrol proudly pose for photographs in their green robes and red *kefyehs.* When not posing for visitors, they chase smugglers and renegade Bedouin or offer desert jaunts to beautiful star-gazing areas.

Just beyond the village of Rum, a vast wilderness of sand and rock begins. Massive, rust-colored cliffs tower over the desert floor, some shooting up to heights of 1700m. Although there is little escape from the sun during the day, the evening brings fantastic shadows, transforming the desert into a vast jigsaw puzzle of light and dark. The whopping slabs of granite and sandstone erupted from beneath the desert floor millions of years ago and it's easy to imagine that Wadi Rum has not changed a bit since then. In *Seven Pillars of Wisdom,* **T.E. Lawrence** (better known as Lawrence of Arabia) wrote that when he passed between these rusty crags, his "little caravan fell quiet, ashamed to flaunt itself in the presence of such stupendous hills." The hills and dunes provide a magnificent setting for a few days of desert exploration and camping.

With its otherworldly lavender mountains set against an empty sky, Wadi Rum deserves the name **Valley of the Moon.** For JD5, a Bedouin will lead you by camel to a crack in the rocks, the origin of the springs that support all of the *wadi*'s life. Dark stains point out the conduits carved by the ancient Nabateans to conserve the precious water. Try to see **Lawrence's Well,** a small spring next to which T.E. Lawrence once napped. A large concrete cistern now holds the spring's water. The Bedouin may also point out mammoth boulders inscribed with millennia-old graffiti. Other sights include the **Rock Bridge,** a massive rock with an arch through the middle, and the elusive **moving sand dune,** an enormous red mountain of sand.

The only place to stay in the village is the **government rest house.** (☎201 88 67. Breakfast JD3, other meals up to JD6. Rooftop JD2; tents JD3.) A half dozen supermarkets provide pricey provisions. A large tent beside the rest house is often the site of **traditional Bedouin music and singing** in the evenings. You can arrange an **overnight** in the desert for the official rest house price of JD30-40.

The village is the base for desert explorations. Check out the list in the rest house for possible destinations. While a camel ride certainly sets the tone (2hr. to the Well JD7; overnight JD30), jeeps cover more ground. For jeep trips, it is cheapest to join a group of six or fewer at the rest house. A full-day jeep itinerary (4-5hr. trip that visits a number of sights, JD40) allows tourists to climb through narrow *siqs* and hikes up sand dunes. Plan to visit at dusk, when the *wadi* explodes with color. Though the easiest way to arrange a trip is through the **tourist police** (☎201 82 15; in the rest house), several travelers report problems, such as sudden extra charges for the ride back to Rum once your guide has taken you to the middle of the valley. Those in Aqaba and Petra suggest arranging a trip with one of the burgeoning Aqaba-based guide companies, who will pick you up at the rest house or on the highway leading into the valley (JD30-40, but prices vary). The effort to find a good guide is well worth it because a night in the desert is truly unforgettable. Ask your hotel owner to recommended someone before you leave for Wadi Rum. One reputable operator is Atallah Faraj (P.O. Box 2354, Aqaba. ☎(07) 951 34 71; fax 215 69 10; email aa@index.com.jo).

LEBANON لبنان

CURRENCY		
US$1=1507.39 LEBANESE POUNDS (L£)	L£1000=US$0.66
CDN$1=L£1006.78	L£1000=CDN$0.99
UK£1=L£2252.03	L£1000=UK£0.44
IR£1=L£1780.39	L£1000=IR£0.56
AUS$1=L£863.28	L£1000=AUS$1.16
NZ$1=L£691.89	L£1000=NZ$1.45
SAR1=L£215.56	L£1000=SAR4.64
EUR1=L£1402.17	L£1000=EUR0.71
JD1 (JORDANIAN DINAR) =L£2123.15	L£1000=JD0.47
S£100 (SYRIAN POUNDS) =L£3350	L£1000=S£29.85
TL10,000 (TURKISH LIRA) =L£24.45	L£1000=TL409,068.41

PHONE CODES | **Country Code: 961. International dialing prefix: 00.**

Lebanon has long enjoyed its privileged position at the crossroads of three continents, proving its resilience over millennia of razings by foreign invaders and natural disasters. Before the recent 15-year civil war, Lebanon was the multi-faceted "jewel of the Middle East," with *souqs*, ritzy hotels, and cutting-edge fashions. The self-proclaimed Lebanese sophistication is a blend of Mediterranean and Arab elements with a healthy dose of panache from the French, whose 1918-1943 occupation of the area left a lasting impression on the cuisine, language, and culture. In the political sphere, four major religious groups—Sunni and Shi'ite Muslims, Druze, and Christians of different denominations—vie for power and influence. In times of peace, this diversity adds flavor to the famed sights and natural splendor of the country. Tension can make it explosive.

The country has emerged from the civil war with its spirit (if not its structures) intact. A wave of reconstruction allowed Lebanon to reclaim its cosmopolitan air, and Lebanon now welcomes back a growing number of tourists. Beirut in particular is rising from the ashes of its internal strife more alive than ever. Large areas of the capital are being rebuilt and rejuvenated. Ba'albeck's international festival, world famous in the 1960s, is once again a hot ticket. Ancient cities, pristine mountains, hot springs, and other historical and natural monuments make Lebanon a worthwhile destination, and the ambitious and worldly spirit of its people distinguish it within the Middle East.

HIGHLIGHTS OF LEBANON

Shop, Rock 'n' Roll: sample the international flavor of **Beirut** (p. 516), best known for its cheap-cheap, chichi shopping and party-til-dawn nightclubs.

The stellar Roman ruins and world-famous cultural festival at **Ba'albeck** (p. 540) will make you long for the days of pagan abandon.

The Umayyad ruins at **Anjar** (p. 544) are some of the best in the Middle East.

LIFE AND TIMES

In the Middle East, Lebanon stands out as a study of contrasts. As Europe's gateway to the Middle East, Lebanon is home to numerous factions of Christians and Muslims. Its geography, complete with coastal beaches and interior mountain ranges, permits both skiing and swimming. Islamic cultural rhythms combine with

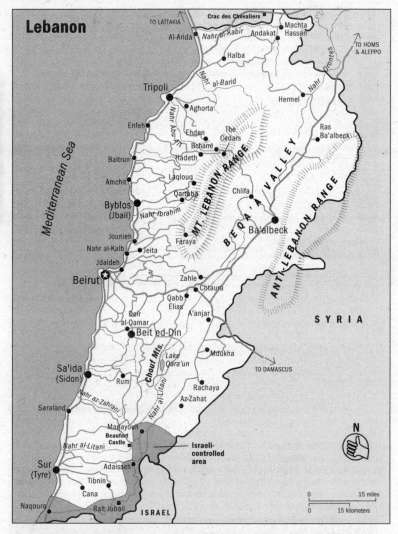

Lebanon

TO LATTAKIA | Crac des Chevaliers
Al-Arida | Nahr al-Kabir | Andakat | Machta Hassan
TO HOMS & ALEPPO
Halba
Tripoli
Nahr al-Barid
Aghorta | Hermel
Enfeh | Ehden | The Cedars | Ras Ba'albeck
Baltrun | Boharré | Hadeth
Amchit | Laqlouq | Qartaba | Chlifa
Byblos (Jbail) | Nahr Ibrahim
Jounieh | Faraya | Ba'albeck
Nahr al-Kalb | Jeita
Jdaideh
Beirut | Zahle | Chtaura
Qabb Elias | A'anjar
Deir al-Qamar | Beit ed-Din
Chouf Mts. | Mdukha
Sa'ida (Sidon) | Lake Qara'un
Rum | Rachaya | TO DAMASCUS
Nahr az-Zahrani | Az-Zahat
Sarafand | Nahr al-Litani
Marjayoun | Beaufort Castle | Israeli-controlled area
Sur (Tyre) | Adaisseh | Nahr al-Litani
Tibnin | Cana
Naqoura | Bait Jubail | ISRAEL

Mediterranean Sea

MT. LEBANON RANGE
BEQA-A VALLEY
ANTI-LEBANON RANGE
Orontes
Nahr

SYRIA

N

0   15 miles
0   15 kilometers

an ever-rising Western beat, as upscale restaurants and discotheques share commercial space with old-time street vendors.

Combinations do not come without conflict and Lebanon has had more than its fair share. Civil war, Syrian influence, and Israeli occupation have disrupted Lebanese life over the past twenty years. Nevertheless, the Lebanese drive to modernization remains indomitable. Alongside Crusader castles, Beirut remains the most cosmopolitan city in the Middle East. Its nightlife ensures some rollicking fun.

HISTORY

ANCIENT HISTORY (3500 BCE-1516 CE)

The earliest settlers of Lebanon were the **Phoenicians** from the Arabian Peninsula who spread their 22-letter alphabet wherever they went and established Beirut,

Ba'albeck, and the important port cities of Byblos, Sidon, and Tyre. The people of **Tyre** were particularly resourceful, building one of the first business empires in history nearly 3000 years ago. The sailing-savvy Phoenicians from Tyre also founded the city of **Carthage** in the 9th century BCE and left it under the rule of **Queen Dido,** who eventually went mad with love and hurled herself atop a sword. The remaining Tyrian settlers cut their own swathe through the heart of the Mediterranean, colonizing parts of Cyprus, Rhodes, and the Aegean Islands before sailing around Africa and discovering the Straits of Gibraltar.

Egyptian domination of the Phoenician cities began in 1500 BCE and was long-lived but fairly ineffective, like any modern-day Egyptian bureaucracy. Life under the invading **Assyrians** was downright brutal. The relative prosperity of the age of city-states only returned once Phoenicia became part of the **Persian Empire** under King Cyprus in 538 BCE. **Alexander the Great** overthrew the Persians in 332 BCE, marking the beginning of the Greco-Macedonian cultural domination of the Middle East during the following centuries. Phoenicia was thoroughly Greek when the Romans (themselves a belligerent carbon copy of the Greeks) made Phoenicia a part of the province of Syria under **Pompey** in 64 BCE. Phoenicia was a rather safe and uneventful place throughout the Roman and Byzantine era, and its geographical inaccessibility made it a refuge for minorities fleeing persecution during those religiously volatile times. In the 7th century CE, the Christian sect that later became the **Maronite Church** settled in the northern districts of the Lebanese mountains to avoid conversion to Islam by the Arabs that controlled the area until the arrival of the Christian Crusaders in the 11th century. Shi'ite Muslims also sought refuge there during the 9th century, and the Druze followed suit two centuries later. This situation would have serious repercussions in modern times.

MODERN HISTORY (1516-1998 CE)

THE FRENCH MANDATE. Muslim Druze and Christian Maronites coexisted peacefully under Ottoman rule, but once the Turks's power began to decline, the two sects began fighting ruthlessly until the end of World War I, when the League of Nations authorized the French government to pick through the ruins of faction-ravaged Lebanon and institute reforms from politics to health care. Educational reforms formalized the study of the Arabic language, which fed into the rising tide of Pan-Arabism washing over much of the Middle East in the postwar era.

INDEPENDENCE BREEDS CONFLICT. In 1926, Lebanon became a republic in name only. The French did not grant independence until November 22, 1943. The infant government that came to power was militantly nationalistic and tried to cut itself off from France immediately and completely. Riots erupted when the French refused to comply and strong-armed their way back into the Lebanese government. The country reeked so much of anti-French sentiment, however, that they finally departed after World War II. The US has been the most important Western influence on Lebanese society since—an interesting cultural clash evidenced by modern-day Beirut's many McDonald's-lined *rues* and *boulevards*.

Postwar Western leanings concentrated governmental power in the hands of Lebanon's Christian population, to the exclusion of the Muslim citizenry. But when Yassir Arafat moved the headquarters of the **Palestinian Liberation Organization (PLO)** to Beirut from Amman, Jordan in 1970, the stormy political climate in Lebanon turned torrential. The PLO added their numbers to the growing Muslim population, making Christians the minority. Fearing PLO guerilla activity, the Christian government (with the help of the Lebanese National Army) retaliated as a "defense" measure—an act of outright aggression in the eyes of many Lebanese Muslims. Many soldiers defected and joined anti-Christian opposition factions, leaving the National Army weakened by 1980.

In the 1970s, Israel began attacking the southern half of the country, where PLO forces were stationed. Much of the predominantly Shi'ite Muslim population in the area migrated to Beirut to escape these attacks, cinching the western half of the capital with an impoverished **"Belt of Misery"** that barely contained the overflowing gut of Maronite wealth in the eastern half of Beirut. On June 6, 1982, Israel initiated **Operation Peace for Galilee,** a cheerful-sounding plan that actually involved surrounding and shelling Beirut at an immense civilian cost. This attack led to a public outcry against the ruthless Israeli military tactics, which in turn led to the formation of the fundamentalist Muslim group **Hizbullah** ("Party of God"), determined to act with more immediacy and extremity than the PLO had.

CIVIL WAR. The Lebanese civil war came to the global forefront in 1982 (although it had officially begun in 1975), after Islamic fundamentalists started taking hostages. The target for kidnappings were Westerners who lived and worked in Beirut, particularly those who lived in the expat Hamra district. In July, David Dodge, president of the American University of Beirut, became the first foreign hostage; such tactics persisted until the last hostage was released in June 1992. By then, 50 foreigners had been taken, some kept chained and blindfolded for five years. The US government instituted a ban on American citizens' travel to Lebanon that lasted until 1997, though Europeans visited the country for several years before the US ban was lifted. The US government still advises that travelers exercise extreme caution when traveling in Lebanon.

POLITICAL AND ECONOMIC RESHUFFLING. Part of the rebuilding of the country has required restructuring the government. Until 1990, an unwritten agreement called the **National Pact** required that the President be a Maronite Christian, the Prime Minister a Sunni Muslim, the speaker of Parliament a Shi'ite Muslim, and the Chief of the Armed Forces a Maronite, and this arrangement had contributed to the civil war. Because of high Muslim birth rates and Christian emigration, Muslims began to outnumber Christians and became discontent with Christian minority rule. Under the reforms of the peace accord that ended the civil war in 1990, many of the powers of the Christian president were shifted to a half-Christian, half-Muslim cabinet, and the Muslim Prime Minister was required to countersign presidential decrees.

Parliamentary elections were held in 1992, with Hizbullah winning the largest number of seats. Current Lebanese President **Emile Lahoud** was elected in October 1998 with the hope that his work reforming the Lebanese National Army in the aftermath of the civil war would meet with similar success in the political world. Lahoud assumed the Presidency over a country in a politically uncertain but eager position. Political apathy is discouraged by law. Voting is optional for both males and females 21 years and over.

Lebanon has few natural resources, so the economy is dependent on banking, commerce, and tourism. Before the war, the country was the "gateway to the Mediterranean," where backpackers and jet-setters frolicked side by side. It was also the banking capital of the Middle East, holding half the wealth of the Arab world in secret bank accounts. Wartime inflation forced the economy to adopt a more stable currency than the Lebanese pound. The invisible hand chose the US dollar.

IN THE NEWS

The summer of 1999 marked a tit-for-tat bombing struggle between the Israeli Army occupying South Lebanon and **Hizbullah** guerillas. In September 1999, Israeli Prime Minister Ehud Barak announced plans for a historic Israeli pullout scheduled for July 2000. Barak hoped the pullout would indicate Israeli goodwill and encourage peace talks with neighboring Syria. Escalating skirmishes through the winter, however, prompted Barak to advance the pullout to June 1, 2000. When Hizbullah attacks intensified, Barak realized that holding out an extra six days would lead to increased conflict. On May 24, Israeli forces executed a preemptive withdrawal from South Lebanon, and with them fled 2000 refugees from the Israeli-backed South Lebanese Army. Israel's twenty-year occupation of South Lebanon came to a close.

As Hizbullah's flag waves over South Lebanon, many questions remain regarding the Lebanese government's future. South Lebanese, finally returning to their homes, see Hizbullah as their leaders and Hizbullah has since acquired additional seats in the Lebanese Parliament. How Hizbullah, older-stock politicians such as Lebanese President Emile Lahoud, and the Syrian government reconcile political differences will determine Lebanon's future.

CULTURE

RELIGION AND ETHNICITY

Lebanon's religious composition differs greatly from that of the rest of the Arab world. The country has more **Shi'ite** than Sunni Muslims (who are the Muslim majority most everywhere else in the world) and also has a sizeable **Druze** population of about 300,000. **Maronite Christians** are rare in most of the world, but in Lebanon (the birthplace of their sect), they are the most prevalent Christian denomination. The beginnings of Maronite Christianity are unclear. The sect is named after St. Maron, a 5th-century hermit from Syria, and St. John Maron, a monk who later preached St. Maron's theology. For the most part, religious groups have remained geographically separate. Before the start of the war, Shi'ite Muslim communities dominated southern Lebanon (including Sur) and the northeast region along the Syrian border. The Maronite Christian population held the majority in central Lebanon, including Eastern Beirut, and the northwestern coastline approaching Tripoli. Tripoli, northern Lebanon, and western Beirut were populated primarily by Sunni Muslims.

FESTIVALS AND HOLIDAYS

Although the practice is officially discouraged, Shi'ite Muslims beat themselves with a variety of instruments as a sign of devotion on **Ashura,** a religious holiday recalling the martyrdom of **Imam Hussein.** This grandson of **Prophet Muhammad** was slain in a doomed battle against a rival Muslim force more than 1300 years ago.

On a livelier note, the **Tyre Festival** boasts performances of Lebanese heritage, culture, and artistic activities through national music and folk dances in the ancient **Roman Hippodrome** every summer. A more international show, the **Beit al-Din Festival** entertains thousands with books, music, photo exhibits, and ballet by artists from around the world, like Barbara Hendricks, Sebastio Salgado, Mounir Bashir, along with the Moscow Ballet and Korean Dance Troupe.

In addition to the perpetual rustle and bustle inherent to Lebanon, the world-renowned **Ba'albeck Festival** further enlivens the country each summer. The festival began in 1955 and continued until 1974, drawing performers like Ella Fitzgerald, Rudolf Nureyev, and Margot Fonteyn. Over the last couple of years, the festival has been revived and has been wildly successful.

LANGUAGE

The official language of Lebanon is **Arabic,** but it is unique among its neighbors in the degree of **French** that is spoken. Many people speak **English** as well (English is the most widely spoken language in most of Beirut). Street signs throughout Lebanon are written in Arabic and French. Radio programming airs in French, English, and Arabic. French is taught in predominantly Christian areas, while English is more common as a second language among Muslims. There is also a minority of Armenian speakers. There is no local English daily newspaper, but newsstands carry an assortment of British and American dailies and weekly magazines. A local English-language weekly, *Monday Morning,* reviews local news and social events. The local French newspaper is *L'Orient le Jour.*

THE ARTS

LITERATURE. Largely because of its liberal political history, Lebanon has one of the richest and most diverse literary traditions in the Arab world. In the 19th century, Beirut led a broad Arab cultural renaissance. Mystic, metaphysical poet, novelist, and artist **Khalil Gibran** (1883-1931) is most famous for his work *The Prophet.* A museum in his hometown, Bcharré (p. 538), is devoted to his life and works. **Amin Ma'alouf** has published four historical novels in French that have established his presence as a Lebanese writer. He made history when his novel *The Rock of Tanios,* about a 19th-century Lebanese village, won the distinguished French *Prix de Goncourt* in 1993. **Amin Rihani** (1876-1940) is a 20th-century poet whose work is classified as *Adab al-Mahjar,* or "Literature of the Migration." Influenced by American poet Walt Whitman, Rihani introduced free verse into Arabic poetry. These writers and many modern Lebanese authors often wrote from abroad. What makes their work "Lebanese" is its enduring fascination with and love of Beirut, its interest in the problems of war and strife, and its form. Lebanese **poetry** has developed a distinctive form, the *zajal,* where verses are sung rather than recited. World literature has also contemplated the civil war. Kamal Salibi's *A House of Many Mansions—The History of Lebanon Reconsidered* recounts events of the war. Robert Fisk's *Pity the Nation: Lebanon at War* gives a first-hand account of the conflict and its major players. Italian journalist Oriana Fallaci's *Insh'allah* also tackles the topic of the civil war through a personal account of her time in the capital city, and the book has been translated into numerous languages.

VISUAL AND PERFORMING ARTS. Lebanon's cities and villages come alive with annual festivals that feature traditional folk dancing and music. The largest of these is in Ba'albeck (see **Ba'albeck,** p. 540). **Belly dancing** is a popular form of entertainment at nightclubs and even at private parties. A type of provincial dance is the **dakle,** in which dancers wearing traditional mountain garb enact themes from village life. The national dance is the **dabke,** a line dance performed to the rhythmic beat of feet pounding on the floor.

Modern **theater** in Lebanon took off in the 1950s and 60s, and was featured in many of the annual festivals around the country. The luxurious Hotel al-Bustan in Beit Meri, a suburb of Beirut, hosts Lebanon's main dramatic and musical festival, the **International Festival of the Performing Arts,** for five weeks in February and March. The war has colored theatrical themes—most contemporary theater ponders the effects of conflict. **Cinema** has undergone a similar evolution. The Lebanese film industry now revolves around documentaries somehow incorporating the civil war. Popular movie theaters play mainly American and European films.

MUSIC. Female artists dominate Lebanese music culture. **Laure Daccache** is a master of introducing melodies of classical repertoire into her music. She has composed over 120 songs and invented a new Arabic rhythm, accomplishments that have secured her the respect of her male counterparts. Nouhad Haddad, more popularly known as **Fairouz,** is more than just a singer's name—she is a woman whose connotations are ethnic and nationalistic as well as musical and poetic. During most of her singing career, Fairouz was part of a three-member team including the two Rahbani brothers, whose poetic and musical genius aided in the success of her songs. **Nour al-Houdda,** whose name means "light of guidance," sang more than 100 songs during a career that spanned more than 60 years. She earned the respect of conservative Arabs and was given medals by the Russian and Eastern Orthodox churches not only because she was thought to be the "girl with the golden voice," but also because she refused to kiss or wear revealing clothing on screen or in performance.

FOOD AND DRINK

Lebanese food is known all over the Middle East for its variety, flavor, and quality. Vegetarian dishes are common. **Tabbouleh** is the national dish, made with parsley, *burghul* (cracked wheat), onions, tomatoes, lemon juice, and spices. **Fattoush** is a salad of lettuce, tomato, and cucumber with small pieces of toasted pita mixed in to soak up the dressing. Lebanese *mezze* (appetizers) include any combination of green peppers, cucumbers, radishes, scallions, olives, pickles, hummus, *baba ghanoush*, eggplant, and fuzzy raw almonds. *Mujeddra* is a lentil stew cooked with sauteed onions and spices. *Kibbeh naye* is raw beef and spices, whipped into a dip and eaten with pita. There are different varieties of **pita** as well: *marqooq* is a paper-thin bread cooked on a metal dome in a wood fire, common both in the mountains and at stands in Beirut; *ka'ak* is a sesame bread, molded either into little round balls or breadsticks. These are customarily dipped into coffee.

Lebanese meals often finish with cornucopias of fresh fruit, but sweets are also popular. The best are made with secret recipes closely guarded by those who possess them (mostly Sunni Muslims). Tripoli is especially famous for sweets like *halawat al-jibn* (unsalted cheese kept in a warm place for a few days and then rolled out with semolina into long sheets with sugar, syrup, and sweet cream). Lebanon is most famous for its **'araq,** an aniseed liquor similar to Greek *ouzo*, produced in small villages by families that have passed on techniques for years. The non-alcoholic specialty is *jellab*, a raisin syrup served with pine nuts.

FACTS AND FIGURES

OFFICIAL NAME: Republic of Lebanon

GOVERNMENT: Republic

CAPITAL: Beirut

LAND AREA: 10,452 sq. km.

GEOGRAPHY: Narrow coastal plane bounded by two mountain ranges on the north and south; bordered by the Mediterranean Sea on the west

CLIMATE: Rain and cool season with snow in the mountains from Dec.-Mar.; hot season with little rain from Apr.-Dec.

MAJOR CITIES: Tripoli, Zahle, Byblos, Sa'ida, Sur, Ba'albeck

POPULATION: 3,111,828; urban 88%, rural 12%

LANGUAGE: Arabic, French, English

RELIGIONS: Muslim (70%), Christian (30%)

AVERAGE INCOME PER CAPITA: US$2700

MAJOR EXPORTS: Foodstuffs and tobacco (20%), textiles (12%), chemicals (11%)

ESSENTIALS

WHEN TO GO

Lebanon's climate is moderate and Mediterranean. Along the coast, winters are mild and summers are hot, while in the mountains, winters are snowy and summers are mild. Snow falls during the winter months, and small mountain villages become burgeoning ski-towns (see **Bcharré,** p. 538). Non-skiers should travel during summer months to avoid crowds in the mountainous regions. Rainy season extends from December through March. It's best to travel during the summer, unless you like soggy clothing.

AVERAGE TEMPERATURE AND PRECIPITATION

	JANUARY			APRIL			JULY			OCTOBER		
	°C	°F	mm	°C	°F	mm	°C	°F	mm	°C	°F	mm
Beirut	13.5	56.3	195	18.5	65.3	48	27.1	80.8	1.0	23.8	74.8	35
Tripoli	12.3	54.1	184	17.0	62.6	55	25.1	77.2	0	22.1	71.8	12
Ksara	11.0	52.0	122	21.0	70.0	43	31.0	88.0	0	24.0	75.0	18
Zahle	7.0	44.6	0	13.0	55.4	0	24.0	75.2	0	19.0	66.2	0

DOCUMENTS AND FORMALITIES

LEBANON'S CONSULAR SERVICES ABROAD

Lebanon's embassies and consulates abroad include:

Australia Embassy: 27 Endeavour St., Red Hill ACT 2603, Canberra (☎(02) 62 95 73 78; fax 62 39 70 24). **Consulate:** Level 5, 70 William St., Sydney NSW 2000 (☎(02) 93 61 54 49 or 93 61 08 43; fax 93 60 76 57). **Consulate:** 117 Wellington St., Windsor, Victoria 3181 (☎(03) 95 29 45 88 or 95 29 44 98; fax 95 29 31 60).

Canada Embassy: 640 Lyon St., Ottawa, Ontario, K1S 3Z5 (☎(613) 236-5825 or 236-5855; fax 232-1609; email emblebanon@synapse.net; www.synapse.net/~emblebanon). **Consulate:** 40 Chemin Cote St., Catherine Outremont, Montreal, Quebec H2V 2A2 (☎(514) 276-2638 or 276-2639; fax 276-0090).

South Africa Embassy: 7 16th Ave., Lower Houghton, Johannesburg 2198 (☎(11) 483 11 07; fax 483 18 10).

UK Embassy: 21 Kensington Palace Gardens, London W8 4QN (☎(020) 7229 7265; fax 7243 1699; email emb.leb@btinternet.com). **Consulate:** 15 Kensington Palace Gardens, London W8 4RA (☎(020) 7727 6696).

US Embassy: 2560 28th St. NW, Washington, D.C. 20008 (☎(202) 939-6300; fax 939-6324; email embLebanon@aol.com; www.emofleb.org). **Consulate:** 9 E. 76th St., New York, NY 10021 (☎(212) 744-7905, 744-7906, or 744-7985; fax 794-1510; email lebconsny@aol.com).

CONSULAR SERVICES IN LEBANON

Embassies and consulates of other countries in Lebanon include:

Australian Embassy: Farra Building, Rue Bliss, Beirut (☎(01) 37 47 01, 37 47 21, or 37 47 13; fax 37 47 09, 37 47 14, or 37 47 16; email austemle@cyberia.net.lb).

Canadian Embassy: 434 Autostrade Jal al-Dib, Coolrite Building, Jal al-Dib (☎(04) 52 11 63, 52 11 64, 52 11 65; fax 52 11 67; email beirut@paris03.x400.gc.ca).

Ireland Embassy: The embassy with jurisdiction over Lebanon is located in Egypt: 3 Abu al-Fada St., Zamalek, Cairo (☎(02) 340 82 64; fax 341 28 63; email irishembassy@rite.com). **Honorary Consulate:** Rue de Chilie, Kollelat Building, P.O. Box 11-746, Beirut (☎(01) 86 30 40 or 86 32 39; fax (01) 86 00 76).

UK Embassy: 8th St., Rabieh, P.O. Box 60180, Beirut (☎(04) 41 70 07, 40 36 40, or 40 50 70; fax 40 00 32; email britishemb@britishembassy.org.lb; www.britishembassy.org.lb). **Consulate:** Daher al-Ein, Tripoli (☎(01) 43 13 20).

US Embassy and Consulate: P.O. Box 70-840, Awkar, Lebanon (☎(04) 54 26 00 or 54 36 00; fax 54 41 36; email usvisas@inco.com.lb; www.usembassy.com.lb).

ENTRY REQUIREMENTS

PASSPORT. Passports are required of all visitors to Lebanon. If you visit **Israel** before a trip to Syria, insist that Israeli customs place **no stamp** in your passport, or more practically, have them stamp a piece of paper inserted in your passport that can be removed. Be warned that Syrian border officials may still refuse entry into the country if they see that you have no Jordanian stamp or have an Egyptian exit stamp from Taba. They realize that you exited through Israel.

VISA AND PERMIT INFO. All nationalities require a visa to enter Lebanon, and most need to arrange for one well in advance. Citizens of **Canada, Ireland, New Zealand,** the **UK,** the **US,** and most of the **EU** can obtain a visa upon arrival at Beirut International Airport or at any official surface-entry border post with a valid passport. Single entry visas cost US$35 and are valid for three months; multiple entry visas cost US$70. If you need to obtain a visa in advance, print out an application online at www.embofleb.org/visas.htm#Tourist%20Visa. You can also send a letter of request to the nearest embassy or consulate, specifying length of stay and the reason for your trip. Applications require a completed application (not photocopied), passport (without evidence of a trip to Israel), one passport-sized photograph, a contact address in Lebanon (any Beirut hotel is fine), a money order for the type of visa you are requesting, and a self-addressed stamped envelope.

INOCULATIONS AND MEDICATIONS. There are no inoculation requirements for entry into Lebanon. Vaccinations are recommended for polio, typhoid, and tetanus. Malaria pills, while not necessary, may foil them nasty mosquitoes.

BORDER CROSSINGS

TO SYRIA. Crossing into Syria may take a long time due to hyper-security at the border. Daily buses run from Tripoli or Beirut to Damascus, and from Beirut north to Aleppo and Lattakia. Though costly, it's possible to hire a *service* to Damascus. UK, US, and most European citizens must obtain a Syrian visa before embarking on the border crossing. Visas should be procured from one's home country in advance, as there is no Syrian representation in Lebanon and it is difficult to get a visa at the Syrian embassy in Amman. In a pinch, go to the Immigration Office in Marseh Sq. in Damascus and request an **exit visa** that entitles you to another visa at the Syrian border. This unusual request will require much bureaucratic dilly-dallying and is to be avoided if possible.

TO ISRAEL. Though Lebanon borders Israel, direct travel between the two countries is impossible at this time. Most travelers go to Syria, then into Jordan, where the Israeli border is open (see **Border Crossings: To Israel,** p. 455).

GETTING AROUND

BY BUS. Most **buses** are privately owned and efficient. Some are luxury Pullmans, while others are older vehicles with vinyl seats, no air-conditioning, and tacky interiors. The only way to find out schedules is to ask locals.

BY PUBLIC TRANSPORTATION AND TAXIS. Taxis and **service** are indistinguishable. Most *service* cast aside their plebeian airs and become ultra-expensive private taxis the minute they see a newly arrived foreigner. Be firm when approaching a taxi and have a landmark or region of the city in mind. When the taxi slows down, shout the name of your destination through the window. If the taxi driver already has passengers, he will either invite you inside or quickly drive off. If the cab is empty, say *"service"* and the taxi should stop. *Service* stop around 11pm or midnight. Taxi drivers set their own schedules.

BY CAR. Renting a **car** is possible in Beirut, but not advisable. There are few universally understood or respected traffic signals in Lebanon, and most drivers are graduates of the bat-out-of-hell school of driving.

BY THUMB. While **hitchhiking** is common in some rural areas, it is dangerous and not recommended by *Let's Go* due to the tense political situation in the mountains of southern Lebanon. Most places are accessible by *service* or bus.

TOURIST SERVICES AND MONEY

TOURIST OFFICES. The National Council of Tourism in Lebanon is on 550 Central Bank St. in Beirut. Mail to P.O. Box 11-5344. The best of its kind in the Middle East. Fluent English speakers provide helpful information and brochures. Other tourist offices are in major cities throughout Lebanon.

CURRENCY AND EXCHANGE. The basic unit of currency is the **Lebanese pound** (LₓS), sometimes known locally as the **lira.** Bills are in denominations of LₓS100, 250, 500, 1000, 5000, 10,000, 50,000, and 100,000, while coins of LₓS100, 250, and 500 are now in circulation. US dollars are widely accepted, especially at restaurants and hotels. **ATMs** give cash advances on major credit cards; many are plugged into the **Cirrus** and **PLUS** network. Only major banks accept **traveler's checks.**

BUSINESS HOURS. Government offices are open M-F 8am-2pm and Sa 8-noon. Banks hold hours M-F 8am-12:30pm and Sa 8am-noon, and businesses M-Sa 8am-5pm. Muslim-owned shops close Fridays. The Lebanese week ends on Sunday.

PRICES. Because of Lebanon's westernization, prices are higher than in neighboring Jordan, Syria, Egypt, and Turkey, but still lower than in Israel. L£40,000 (US$25) should easily cover a day's budget travel.

TIPPING AND BAKHSHEESH. *Bakhsheesh* (see p. 14) may be necessary in far-out places, but is not as widespread as in Egypt, Jordan, and Syria. Since prices are higher and travelers tend to be wealthier than those in other countries, spoiled guards and officials may expect more palm-greasing than their counterparts in other countries. Liberal tipping at restaurants is expected. *Service* drivers do not expect tips, but taxi drivers should get a little something extra (especially for long rides or ones that include many military checkpoints).

USEFUL INFORMATION. For a comprehensive links page dealing with Lebanese politics, culture, and tourism, as well as hard facts about visas, customs, and international embassies, visit www.lebanonlinks.com or www.lebanon-online.com. Find additional hard facts at the **World Travel Guide's** Lebanon site at www.wtgonline.com/data/leb. You may also contact one of the **Lebanon Tourist Offices** abroad: **Egypt,** 1 Talaat Harb St., Maidan al-Tahrir, Cairo (☎/fax (20) 2 393 75 29); **France,** Office du Tourisme Libanais, 124, Rue du Faubourg, St. Honoré, 75008 Paris (☎(33) 143 59 10 36, 143 59 12 13; fax 143 59 11 99); and the **UK,** Lebanon Tourist and Information Office, 90 Piccadilly St., London W1V 9HB (☎(44) 20 7409 2031; fax 7493 4929; email abdallah@lebanon.demon.co.uk).

HEALTH AND SAFETY

EMERGENCY   Police: ☎160. Ambulance: ☎140. Fire: ☎175.

MEDICAL EMERGENCIES. In a medical emergency, dial ☎140 for an **ambulance** or ☎86 55 61 for the **Red Cross.** In Beirut, head to the **American University Hospital** in Hamra (see p. 521). **Pharmacies** generally have someone on hand who can prescribe medication for those who know what they need.

HEALTH. Take standard precautions for developing world nations when traveling in Lebanon. While no **vaccinations** are necessary for entry, hepatitis B, typhoid, and immunoglobulin are all recommended. When on the ground, follow the colonial adage: boil it, cook it, peel it, or forget it. Only eat thoroughly cooked meat, poultry, fish, and eggs. Fruits and vegetables should be personally peeled. Stay away from unpasteurized dairy products. Wash your hands often with soap and water.

WOMEN TRAVELERS. Women traveling alone should not have much trouble. Gender relations in Lebanon are arguably the most comfortable in the Middle East, thanks mostly to the influence of the French. Women should be aware that Lebanese men may give them unwanted attention, which may be nothing more than leers and catcalls, but many women report unsavory offers ranging from a night on the town to proposals of marriage. There is little violent crime. For more tips, see **Women Travelers,** p. 38.

MINORITY TRAVELERS. Lebanese are often noted as hospitable people, and this is reflected in their good treatment of visitors from ethnic backgrounds other than their own. Discrimination against people who do not appear to be native is mostly limited to price-gouging in taxis and sandwich shops. An easy solution to this problem is to know how much items should cost and negotiate. In less expensive hotels and pensions, Arabs may feel uncomfortable, because some proprietors think that the presence of Arabs drives off Western visitors. Asian travelers will find that they are assumed to be Japanese, while black visitors will be treated as a novelty by locals. Though annoying, this treatment is generally free of animosity.

BGLT TRAVELERS. Homosexuality is illegal in Lebanon, but attitudes toward gays are more relaxed than in other parts of the Middle East, especially along the urbanized coast. Visible gay populations live in Beirut and Tripoli. Travelers, however, should take note: many Lebanese see no problem in mocking or making offensive comments about gays, and fundamentalist groups may severely harass them.

ACCOMMODATIONS AND CAMPING

HOSTELS AND HOTELS. Wartime inflation caused prices to skyrocket, and lodging prices are particularly astronomical. Availability varies based on location. Accommodations fall under four unofficial categories: uninhabitable but very cheap, cheap but surprisingly nice, "middle range" establishments that start at around US$20 per night, and luxury resort havens patronized mostly by vacationing Arabs from the Gulf States. Along the coast and in Beirut, accommodations are plentiful and expensive. Places to stay in all but the ski villages tend to be more reasonably priced (and negotiable when less crowded), but many medium-sized towns (especially in formerly-occupied South Lebanon) lack lodging of any kind.

CAMPING. It is hard to learn about camping sites, as they are not well publicized. The two commercially-run campgrounds in the country are Camping Amchit and La Reserve, near Afqa grotto.

KEEPING IN TOUCH

MAIL. **Poste Restante** is not the reliable service it was before the war—mail sent to the main post office in Beirut has been known to disappear. A one pound package to Lebanon costs US$8.48 or AUS$21.00 and takes approximately one week for delivery. Mail from Lebanon takes four to seven days to reach the US, and two to four days to reach Europe. Lebanon also sports **DHL** offices, but no Federal Express service. Packages take up to four days for international express delivery.

TELEPHONES. International calls can be placed from public telephone offices. There is one in every Beirut district, though not in every Lebanese city. Phonecards are becoming increasingly common. The **MCI World Phone** access code is ☎ (01) 42 76 27. Access **AT&T USADirect** operators from any phone by dialing ☎ 42 68 01 in Beirut; add 01 outside Beirut (charged as a call to Beirut). Do not try to make a collect call from telephone offices. The attendant will likely figure out what you're doing and scream at you to hang up. Cellular phones are available for rental. Telex and fax services are also available, though mostly in Beirut.

INTERNET ACCESS. It's easy to find Internet access in all urban centers. In major cities like Beirut and Tripoli, Internet access might be easier to find than a phone with a reliable long-distance connection. Rural villages lag behind in this respect, but everything in Lebanon is only a daytrip from Beirut.

CUSTOMS AND ETIQUETTE

Lebanon's Westernization is reflected in its liberal attitudes toward dress and demeanor. In the big cities and along the coast, tank tops and shorts are perfectly acceptable for men and women. Both sexes should dress modestly when touring the country's rural areas and when visiting monasteries and other religious sites. Men should wear loose-fitting pants and shirts. Women should wear long skirts and loose-fitting shirts with sleeves below the elbow and cover their hair.

HOLIDAYS

Lebanon observes all Muslim holidays (see **Appendix** for a complete listing, p. 699). Christian holidays are also national holidays. The most important non-religious holidays are Labor Day (May 1) and Independence Day (November 22). Government offices and businesses are closed on religious and national holidays.

BEIRUT بيروت   ☎01

In the 1960s, Beirut was the gateway to the Mediterranean, the meeting point of East and West. Europeans could sample the flavors of the Orient while lounging in western comfort, and wealthy Arabs could sneak away to a hedonistic haven of social pleasures condemned by their conservative nations. A tightly knit group of international jet-setters, journalists, and socialites unwound at seaside cafes, casinos, and resorts. During its golden years, Beirut was home to people of many religions and ethnicities. The reality, however, was that a growing underclass of disaffected refugees was living in squalor on the edges of the city; exiled Palestinians and Shi'ites were silently witnessing the extravagant lifestyle of the expats and chic crowds.

The civil war blew away the illusion of Beirut as a content, multicultural melting pot, but an overriding sense of nationalism has survived the class and ethnic conflict. Beirut has been dubbed "The City That Would Not Die" by the Ministry of Tourism, and the epithet is, for the most part, well-earned. Some parts of the city, most famously the city center and its landmark Place des Martyres, were ravaged more than others, but 15 years of constant conflict took its physical and psychological toll on every district. Archaeological evidence confirms that Beirut has actually been destroyed seven times—by a tidal wave, fire, several earthquakes, and war—since first gaining fame as the site of a Roman law school in the 3rd century BCE. In spite of present efforts to improve and standardize the city's dishevelled, inconsistent appearance, Beirut remains a town of patchworked visual contrast. At opposite ends of the spectrum lie glittering high-rises and the remains of shellshocked neighborhoods, battered into an eerie silence by years of sniper attacks. Rather than fading into obscurity, though, Beirut continues to blossom. Buildings spring up at a staggering pace, as the city restakes its claim as the Arab world's most cosmopolitan city. For those who can afford the Western-style prices, Beirut is as hedonistic and forward-thinking as any European metropolis. The city's dedication to the capitalist credo is in full effect in its many Internet cafes, jazz clubs, and opulent shopping districts, and its future in the global marketplace seems assured. Arab tourists are returning in force, and even Europeans (and to a lesser extent, Americans) are exploring this erstwhile Paris of the East.

✈ GETTING THERE AND AWAY

There are three main transport hubs for **buses** and **service**: Cola Bridge, Charles Helou Bus Terminal, and Dawra. Buses and *service* to all points south of Beirut and the Beqa'a Valley (including Ba'albeck) congregate at **Cola Bridge** in southern Beirut, accessible by any intracity bus heading to the National Museum. Buses heading north of Beirut or to Damascus and Amman depart from the brand-new **Charles Helou Bus Terminal** near the port in western Beirut. Shorter journeys to the north (e.g. Jounieh and Byblos) and intercity *service* all leave from **Dawra** in western Beirut, across the river. Both Dawra and Charles Helou are easily accessible by the intracity buses that terminate at Dawra. For more general information about transportation, see **Getting Around**, p. 513.

FLIGHTS. Beirut International Airport (☎ 62 90 65 or 62 90 66), five kilometers south of downtown, has regular flights to Damascus, Amman, and London. **Taxis** to the airport should cost no more than L£10,000.

BUSES AND SERVICE. Buses depart when full, so schedules are unpredictable. **Lebanese Commuting Company** buses service Sur and Sa'ida for L£500 from Cola. Buses leave from Charles Helou to Tripoli (2hr.; A/C Pullman bus L£2000, less comfy coaches L£1000). **Beirut Pullman Terminal Company** serves as a ticket agent and sometimes bus operator for international routes; there should be an English speaker at their ticket window. **Buses** go to: Aleppo (8hr., L£11,000); Amman (8hr., L£27,000); and Damascus (3½hr., L£10,000). Buses from Dawra depart to Byblos (1½hr., L£500) via Jounieh (45min.). All buses stop running at 8 or 9pm. Like buses, **service** depart when full. Cola Bridge to: Ba'albeck (3hr., L£7000); Beit al-Din (1½hr., L£5000); and Sur (3½hr., L£5000) via Sa'ida (2hr., L£1000).

CAR RENTAL. There are many car rental companies in Beirut, but by driving you risk life and limb. **Europcar** (☎48 04 80 or 50 22 00) has an office in the Sa'arti building on Hayek Ave. in Sin al-Fil, and another in 'Ain Mreisse (☎60 22 23). **Budget Rent-a-Car** (☎74 17 40 or 74 17 41) is in the Minkara building on Rue Clemenceau.

⌐ GETTING AROUND

The best way to get around Beirut is on foot. Almost all listings are centrally located in Hamra, and even the walk from 'Ain Mreisse to the Pigeon Rocks takes no more than a pleasant 30 minutes.

BUSES. Intracity buses all cost L£500 and are surprisingly easy to use. Over 20 different lines criss-cross the city, and are ideal for going to well-traveled destinations such as Cola Bridge, the National Museum, Dawra, or the Pigeon Rocks (Raouche). Rather than trying to memorize the schedule that the Ministry of Tourism hands out, treat them like *service*. Stand on the proper side of busy streets and shout your destination as the bus slows down. Intracity buses finish their runs around 7 or 8pm; after that *service* or private taxis fill all transportation needs.

SERVICE AND PRIVATE TAXIS. *Service* within Beirut should cost L£1000-2000, and you should rarely pay more than L£5000 for a private taxi except for trips late at night or all the way across town. *Service* stop running around 11pm or midnight. Private taxis can be called 24 hours and can be identified by their red licence plates. **Radio Taxi** (☎35 22 50) and **Lebanon Taxi** (☎34 07 17, 34 07 18, 35 31 52, or 35 31 53) are among the cheapest and most reliable.

⊞ ORIENTATION

Situated on a promontory jutting into the Mediterranean, Beirut is bounded on the north and west by the sea and in all other directions by a mass of closely packed commercial and residential areas. The tourist office and the vast majority of budget accommodations, restaurants, and shops congregate in the **Hamra** district, a roughly rectangular area marked by Rue Bliss to the north, Rue de Rome to the east, Rue Emile Edde to the south, and Rue Sadat to the west. This area has also become home to many administrative buildings that used to be downtown until they were destroyed in the war. Just north of Rue Bliss is the beautiful **American University of Beirut (AUB).** The quieter streets of **'Ain Mreisse** are home to cheap hotels. To get there, follow Rue John Kennedy away from AUB and turn left on Rue Graham toward the sea. The area in front of the Hard Rock Cafe marks the start of the **corniche,** a nice place to see Beirutis at play.

Avenue de Paris runs parallel to the sea. Following it west for several kilometers leads to the wealthy district of **Raouche** (RA-oo-sheh), home to many of Beirut's finest restaurants and the famed **Pigeon Rocks.** Heading south, the street becomes Avenue du Général de Gaulle and passes the fishing harbor before becoming Boulevard Sa'ed Salam, which heads inland. Passing first **Cola Bridge,** then the horse-racing **Hippodrome,** this road finally arrives at the **National Museum.** Just seaward lies the elegant district of **Ashrafieh,** centered around **Place Sassine.** Farther north

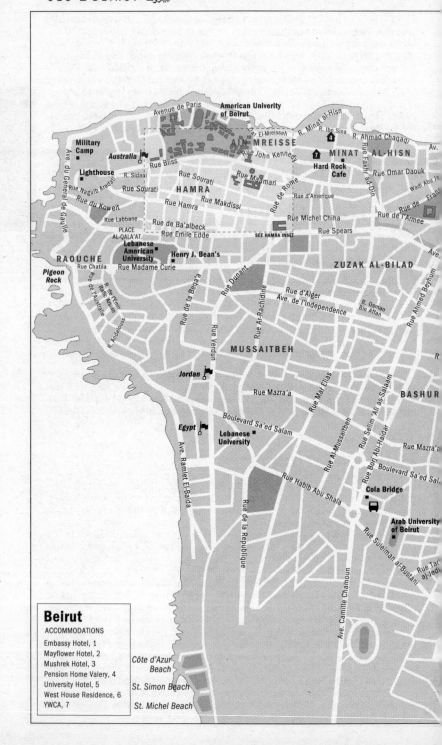

Military Camp

Australia

Lighthouse

R. Naguib Aradati

Ave. du General de Gaulle

Rue du Koweit

Rue Labbane

PLACE AL-QALA'AT

RAOUCHE

Pigeon Rock

Rue Chatila

R. de l'Australie

R. de Henri Rafic Abas

R. Andaous

Avenue de Paris

R. Sidani

Rue Bliss

Rue Sourati

Rue Sourati

HAMRA

Rue Hamra

Rue Makdissi

Rue de Ba'albeck

Rue Emile Edde

Lebanese American University

Rue Madame Curie

Henry J. Bean's

American Univerity of Beirut

R. Der El-Mreisseh

AIN MREISSE

Rue John Kennedy

Rue Maamari

Rue de Rome

R. Minat al-Hisn

R. Ibn Sina

Hard Rock Cafe

MINAT AL-HISN

R. Ahmad Chaqaqi

Rue Fakhr ad-Din

Rue Omar Daouk

Wadi Abu Jn

Rue de l'Armee

Rue de Fran

Ave.

'Rue d'Amerique

Rue Michel Chiha

Rue Spears

SEE HAMRA INSET

ZUZAK AL-BILAD

Ave.

Rue de la Bekaa

Rue Dunant

Rue Al-Rachidine

Rue d'Alger

Ave. de l'Independence

R. Osman Bin Affan

Rue Ahmed Beyhum

Rue Verdun

MUSSAITBEH

Jordan

Rue Mazra'a

Rue Mar Elias

BASHUR

Rue Selim Ali as-Salaam

Rue Al-Mussaitbeh

Egypt

Boulevard Sa'ed Salam

Lebanese University

Rue Borj Abi-Haidar

Boulevard Sa'ed Sal.

Rue Mazra'a

Ave. Ramlet El-Balda

Rue Habib Abu Shala

Cola Bridge

Arab University of Beirut

Rue de la Republique

Rue Suleiman al-Bustani

Rue Tar al-Jedi

Ave. Camille Chamoun

Côte d'Azur Beach

St. Simon Beach

St. Michel Beach

Beirut

ACCOMMODATIONS

Embassy Hotel, 1
Mayflower Hotel, 2
Mushrek Hotel, 3
Pension Home Valery, 4
University Hotel, 5
West House Residence, 6
YWCA, 7

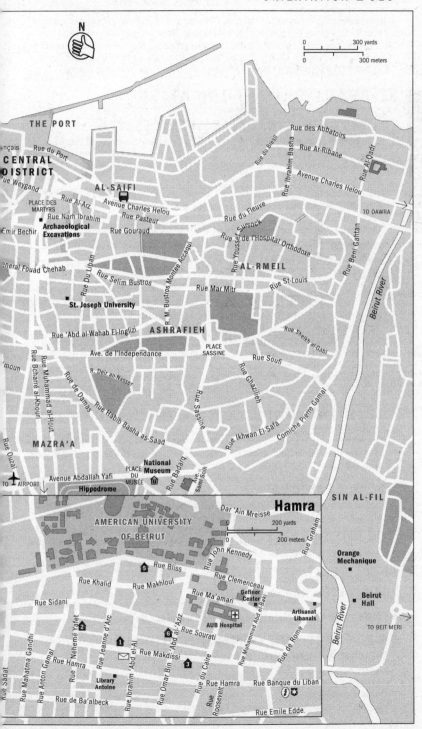

is **Downtown,** once the heart of the city. Construction has been completed on many new buildings in western downtown, near the **Place d'Etoile** and its clock tower, but eastern downtown and **Place des Martyres** remain a big construction site. Continuing east on Avenue Charles Helou, first leads to the **Charles Helou Bus Terminal** (shar la-LOO) and, several kilometers later, to the transport hub of **Dawra.**

⁊ PRACTICAL INFORMATION

TOURIST AND FINANCIAL SERVICES

Tourist Office: Ministry of Tourism (☎34 30 73), at the intersection of Rue de Rome and Central Bank St. in Hamra, to the left of Pizza Hut. Fluent English speakers distribute sleek, up-to-date maps and brochures for every region of the country. Open M-F 8am-4pm, Sa 8am-1pm.

Tours: Nakhal Tour Company (☎(01) 38 93 89; fax 38 92 82) offers six-day tours of Lebanon leaving from Beirut for L£52,500-82,500 per day (lunch included), one-day tours to Ba'albeck, Anjar, and other sights, and week-long tours to Syria, Jordan, Cyprus, Egypt, Turkey, and Greece. The **Ministry of Tourism** also arranges tours.

Embassies:

Australia (☎37 47 01; fax 37 47 09), on Rue Bliss in Ras Beirut.

Canada, 434 Autostrade Jal al-Dib (☎52 11 63 or 52 11 64; fax 52 11 67).

Egypt (☎86 79 17, 86 29 32, or 80 27 34; fax 86 37 51), on Rue Thomas Edison in Ramlet Baida.

Jordan (☎(01) 80 36 13, 92 25 00, or 92 25 01; fax 92 25 02), on Rue Verdun.

UK (☎41 70 07, 40 36 40, or 40 50 70), in Rabieh. Another branch in Raouche (☎80 58 98 or 81 28 49; fax 86 64 37).

US (☎(04) 54 26 00 or 54 36 00; fax 54 41 36), in Awkar. Take a *service* headed anywhere north of Beirut, like Byblos or Tripoli, and ask to be dropped off at Dbayye. From Dbayye, take a taxi (L£5000) to the embassy.

Currency Exchange: Exchange foreign currency at any bank or currency exchange shop. US dollars are universally accepted at shops, on buses, and in hotels. **ATMs** give cash advances on V or MC; many are plugged into the Cirrus network. **Fransabank** (☎34 01 80 or 34 01 88) is across from the tourist office in Hamra. Open M-F 8:15am-2:30pm, Sa 8:15am-noon.

American Express: (☎34 18 25 or 34 18 56), in the Gefinor Center on Rue Clemenceau in western Hamra. Will hold mail for card members, frequently for non-members, too (just ask nicely). Open M-F 9am-4pm, Sa 8:30am-1:30pm.

LOCAL SERVICES

English Bookstores: Naufal Booksellers (☎35 48 98), on Rue Sourati, across from the Idriss Market. One of the best English-language magazine and travel guide selections in the Middle East. *Time, Newsweek, Financial Times,* and a wide selection of English novels and Penguin classics. Open M-F 9:30am-6pm, Sa 9:30am-2pm. V, MC. **Librairie Antoine,** (☎34 14 70 or 34 14 71), Rue Hamra near Rue Jeanne d'Arc. Mostly French, with a smaller selection of English books and dailies. Open M-F 8:30am-6pm, Sa 8:30am-1:30pm.

Laundromat: Five Star Cleaners (☎74 28 56), on Rue Nehme Yafet just off Rue Sidani. Laundry and dry cleaning services. Shirts (L£3000), trousers (L£4000), and socks (L£1000) all cleaned to perfection. Open M-F 8am-6pm, Sa 8am-4pm.

EMERGENCY AND COMMUNICATIONS

Emergency: Ambulance: ☎140. **Police:** ☎160 **Fire:** ☎175.

Tourist Police: (☎34 32 86), in the same building as the Tourist Office. Much to the chagrin of the Ministry of Tourism, there is not always an English speaker on duty, although there is sure to be someone to translate for you when the tourist office is open. If you find the language barrier insurmountable and can't wait for the tourist office to be open, just call the city police. Start here with minor complaints or if you're the victim of petty crimes. More serious issues should be directed to the city police. Open 24hr.

Pharmacy: Pharmacie Rishani (☎34 28 31), on Rue Sourati opposite Naufal Booksellers in Hamra. English, French, and Arabic spoken. Open daily 8am-8pm. **Mazen Pharmacy** (☎313 362), in Mazra'a. Open 24hr., but English speaker not always on duty.

Hospital: American University of Beirut Hospital (☎34 04 60 or 35 00 00), in Hamra, at the intersection of Rue Ma'amari and Rue Claire. The best in Beirut, so if you find yourself in an ambulance ask to be taken here.

Telephones: The **telephone office** (☎34 89 03) in Hamra is in a small, glassy room in the same building as the Ministry of Tourism. 3min. minimum. Open daily 8am-11pm.

Internet Access: The best value in Beirut is **Virus: The Cyber Infection** (☎37 37 94), on 2nd floor of the office building on the southeast corner of Rue Abd al-Aziz and Rue Bliss, facing the AUB medical gate. Dark, well-decorated operation with TVs playing music videos and one of the only no smoking sections in the country. Internet L£3000 per hr. Delicious crepes L£2500. Open 24hr. You can have your web and eat it too at **Web Cafe,** on Rue Makhloul next to Flying Pizza in Hamra. L£5000 per hr. Open daily noon-midnight. **PC Club** (☎74 53 38), on Rue Mahatma Gandhi; walk along Rue Bliss keeping AUB to your right, and take a left at Popeye's Chicken. Play network games (L£3000 per hr.), use the Internet (L£5000 per hr.), or rack it up on the pool table (L£1000). Open 24hr.

Post Office: On Rue Makdissi, nearly opposite Embassy Hotel, on the 2nd floor of a non-descript, hard-to-find building with few signs. With the Embassy Hotel on your left, turn right into the doorway next to the sign that reads "Amin A. Faris, MD, Neurology." **Poste Restante** is unreliable. Open M-Th 8:15am-2pm, F 8:15-11am, Sa 8:15am-1pm. **DHL** (☎98 33 97) is in the Lazaristes building, on the corner of Rue Emir Barchir and Rue Bechara al-Khoury, facing Place des Martyres. Open M-F 8am-5pm, Sa 8am-3pm.

▐. ACCOMMODATIONS

Finding decent budget lodging can be difficult, as most of it was destroyed in the war. There are a few "hostels" that are barely habitable and a full host of luxury resorts, but little in the middle range. The cheapest options are in 'Ain Mreisse, a short walk from Hamra.

▨ **Pension Home Valéry** (☎36 21 69 for 2nd fl.; 36 49 06 for 3rd fl.), in 'Ain Mreisse. Keeping the Hard Rock Cafe on your left, walk 100m down the street and take a right; enter just after the Wash Me Carwash. Beirut's rock bottom; offers clean but boxy rooms with fans, sofas, and tile floors. The 3rd floor, with an A/C common room and a convenience-store style fridge stuffed with drinks, is nicer and the people are friendlier. Hot showers free on 2nd floor, L£2000 on 3rd. 2- to 4-bed dorms L£7500.

▨ **The Lord's Hotel** (☎74 03 85; fax 74 03 85), on Rue du Koweit, near the intersection with Avenue Général de Gaulle. The best value for sea-view rooms. A/C, private bath, maid service, satellite TV, and minibar make it stand out. July-Aug. singles L£60,000, doubles L£75,000; Sept.-June singles L£52,500.

Mayflower Hotel (☎34 06 80 or 34 70 80), on Rue Nehme Yafet, two blocks off Rue Hamra. A splurge, but like a Pilgrim in search of a new world, the Mayflower is the first to reach the realm of excellence. TV, A/C, private bath, maid service, and the cleanest rooms in town. Singles L£97,500, plus 16% tax; budget rooms L£52,500. 5% service charge added to all rooms.

University Hotel (☎36 53 91), just off Rue Bliss in Hamra across from AUB. Private bathrooms, A/C and excellent location in the heart of budget Beirut help compensate for smallish rooms. Singles L£30,000; doubles L£45,000; triples L£52,500. Student rates for monthly stays L£225,000 per month.

Mushrek Hotel (☎34 57 73 or 34 57 72), on Rue Makdissi, two blocks down from the post office in Hamra. Green checkered floor, huge wardrobes, refrigerators, fans, and large balconies. Communal bathrooms with peeling paint fall somewhere between nasty and tolerable, depending on when they were last cleaned. Singles L£25,000; doubles L£35,000; triples L£40,000; suites with kitchenette, private bath, and A/C L£50,000.

Y.W.C.A. (☎36 77 50 or 36 77 51) in 'Ain Mreisse, around the corner from Pension Home Valéry. Keeping the Hard Rock Cafe on your left, walk 100m down the street and take a right. This international center is usually populated by students and is **open to women only.** Comfortable rooms with bath and fridge. Laundry service available. Curfew 1am. Dorm beds L£22,500; singles L£37,500; doubles and triples L£45,000.

West House Residence (☎35 04 50), near the corner of Rue Sourati and Rue Abd al-Aziz. Oh my brothers, these ultra-funky 70s apartments out of *A Clockwork Orange* are the cheapest "furnished apartments" in town. Viddy the fully-equipped suites with A/C, private bath, TV, and kitchenette. Streetside rooms are noisy, but worth it for the pretty polly you'll save. Don't go by the board—the 'official' rates mean nothing. Singles and doubles L£48,000, L£300,000 per week, L£975,000 per month. 5% tax added. V.

Embassy Hotel (☎34 08 14; fax 34 08 15), on Rue Makdissi, across from the post office. Pleasant lobby and clean rooms with A/C, TV, mini-fridge, private bath, and springy mattresses. Plant-filled indoor and outdoor restaurant and Beirut's only hotel garden present a bucolic escape from the urban jungle outside. Breakfast L£5250. Laundry service. Free welcome drink for *Let's Go* readers. Singles L£50,000; doubles L£70,000; triples L£82,000; 14% service charge. Student discount.

☐ FOOD

European pub grub, Western fast food, glitzy and exotic foreign cuisine, cafe fare, and Lebanese favorites are all part of Beirut's food scene. "Snacks" are sandwich shops with little ambiance but good value. The Hamra district, especially around AUB, is packed with small, affordable eateries. Raouche is home to many of Lebanon's most renowned restaurants, some with sunset views of the Pigeon Rocks.

Flying Pizza (☎35 19 04 or 35 39 75), on Rue Makhloul at Rue Jeanne d'Arc, next door to Web Cafe in Hamra. Sushi bar feel with a checklist instead of a menu. Create your own Italian-Lebanese pizza. Small pizza L£5500, toppings L£1000 each. Open daily 11am-midnight. Delivery free in Hamra.

Web Cafe (☎34 88 81 or 34 88 80), on Rue Makhloul in Hamra, adjacent to Flying Pizza. For caffeine and **Internet** addicts. A slick, polished joint where slick, polished AUB students hang out to rack up their trend points. Gourmet sandwiches L£6000-9500. Espresso drinks L£2000-3000. Beer L£3500-4500. Open daily noon-midnight.

Hamadeh Snack (☎34 26 70), at the corner of Rue de Rome and Central Bank St. in Hamra, across the street from the Ministry of Tourism. Popular morning stop for commuting Beirutis like Rita seeking traditional Lebanese chow. Nothing beats a "beetza" with olives (L£3500). Delicious *mana'eesh* with *za'tar*, lamb, and cheese L£1000-2500. Open daily 6am-5pm.

Al-Amadouli (☎34 05 52), on the corner of Rue Makdissi and Rue Nehme Yafet, diagonal from the White Tower Hotel. Downstairs is a take-away bar, upstairs is a sit-down restaurant whose interior design is a fight to the death between gold and pastel, fake greenery, oversized chandeliers, and Christmas decorations. Tasty dishes (L£6000-8000) and live lute player (performances W-Su evenings; cover L£1000). Beer L£2000. Open daily noon-midnight.

Tiger Restaurant (☎(04) 87 05 64). In Beit Marie, about a one-kilometer walk uphill from the main traffic circle (just ask a local). Take bus #7 (L£500) from the National Museum. This cat's been roaring for about a century. The best deal with a mountain view of Beirut. Entree and selection of *mezze* L£15,000. Open daily 10am-midnight.

Restaurant Mashawi Assaf (☎37 23 64). From Wash Me Carwash in 'Ain Mreisse, walk past Holiday Inn; the restaurant will be on your left. The favorite stop for Pension Home Valéry guests seeking cheap, filling, and appetizing Lebanese sandwiches. Craving steak? Try the 'Brochettes Grillées' (grilled steak kebab with onions) sandwich (L£3000). Open daily 6am-3am.

◉ SIGHTS

For a city with a 5000-year heritage, Beirut is a bit slim on sights of archaeological importance. Since the war ended in 1991, the reconstruction effort and urban digging initiatives have peeled back otherwise inaccessible layers of destroyed cityscape. Although archaeological teams have uncovered ancient ruins, most are not currently available for public viewing. Some are in the process of being catalogued and taken apart to be deposited in city parks, although the redevelopment of commercial areas seems to have taken precedence over the creation of permanent homes for these remains of times past.

▨NATIONAL MUSEUM. The civil war forced the national museum to close its doors (see **Ars Longa, Bellum Breve,** p. 524), but extensive restoration and renovation was completed a few years ago, and today visitors can again walk through the halls of the most glorious museum in the Middle East. Especially impressive are the intricately carved Roman sarcophagi, the mosaics from Ba'albeck, and the set of 27 eerily lit, anthropomorphic coffins in the basement. *(Ave. Abdullah Yafi near the race track. Open Tu-Su 9am-5pm. L£5000, students and those under 18 L£1000.)*

PIGEON ROCKS. Ministry of Tourism pamphlets proclaiming these Rocks Beirut's major natural landmark neglect to describe the neon signs and fast food-riddled landscape that make the scene more discouraging than uplifting. Still, the rocks' mere geological uniqueness merits a brief visit, and it's worth scrambling down to the rocks for the cliff views. Created by an earthquake eons ago, the two rocks are huge formations just off the coast; one has a hole in the center through which small boats pass. Today home to daredevil divers, the shores near Pigeon Rocks have yielded the oldest evidence of human existence in Beirut. The flints and tools that were found here are now displayed in the AUB Archaeological Museum. *(Off the coast of Raouche. Take a minibus or #15 city bus along the corniche from 'Ain Mreisse or Hamra (L£500) or walk away from the port and central Beirut along the corniche.)*

SURSOCK MUSEUM. Donated in 1912 by Lebanese philanthropist Nicholas Ibrahim Sursock, the museum is housed in a mansion whose *fin de siècle* Lebanese-Italian architectural style is a spectacle in and of itself. The temporary exhibits revolve around Lebanese themes and culminate in an annual Salon d'Automne, which showcases the best in modern Lebanese art. *(On Rue Sursock in Ashrafieh. Open daily 8am-2pm and 4-8pm during exhibits only. Free.)*

AUB ARCHAEOLOGICAL MUSEUM. This museum is small, but full of local history, excellent glazed work, and sublime ivory carvings. The campus is also a nice place for a picnic or a stroll: runners or walkers can use their track, carved into the hillside and offering great views over the valley. *(On the AUB campus on Rue Bliss, in Hamra. ☎ 35 00 30, ext. 2662. Museum open M-F 9am-2:30pm; in winter M-F 9am-4pm. Free.)*

ANCIENT AND MODERN RUINS. Behind Central Bank St. near the port are the remains of a large **Roman bath.** Originally discovered in 1968, it has undergone a thorough excavation and cleaning over the past two years. Now, you can sit on the patio of one of several western-style cafes, eat western-style avocado, sip western-style latte, and listen to western-style yuppie talk interrupted only by the call to prayer at a nearby mosque as you ponder the ongoing struggle between east and west. For a living testament to the ravages of contemporary warfare and the modern ruins it has created, the best place to go is *not* downtown. Though this area was the epicenter of the fighting, it has been completely razed and is now the site of a massive **reconstruction project** supervised by the Solidere Company (which offers tours of the rebuilding sites upon request; ☎ 64 61 29). Instead, walk up from downtown on Rue de Damas toward the National Museum: nearly every building in the area is pocked with bullet holes, and many are barely standing.

ARS LONGA, BELLUM BREVE When the officials at Beirut's National Museum realized that civil war was about to break out, they moved quickly to save the thousands of pieces of precious artwork in their care. The Roman sarcophagi and statuary (arguably the most impressive works) could not be moved due to their massive weight, so they were entombed in nearly three feet of concrete. Many of the smaller pieces were sent to Germany or stored in National Bank vaults. Space and time were limited, however, and much of the pottery could only be unceremoniously dumped in cardboard boxes and stored in the basement to wait out the hostilities. Unfortunately, the intense humidity in the flooded basement caused the cardboard boxes to disintegrate, damaging many of the ceramics and other pottery pieces. The war itself caused inevitable damage: snipers poked holes through priceless mosaics, the museum's majestic columns were so badly bullet-pocked that they were left barely standing, and giant exhibit halls brimmed with debris. Nevertheless, a remarkable percentage of the art was preserved. Since the war ended, the museum's facade has received a facelift, the bank vaults have been emptied, the oil and grime staining the pottery have been removed, and most gloriously, the cement cases have been opened. Today's National Museum is as much a monument to the resilience and ingenuity of the modern Lebanese people as it is to their fascinating and varied history.

 SHOPPING (AND OTHER SPORTS)

Beirut is known for its cheap, high-quality luxury goods: gold-leaf calligraphy and filigree, silver jewelry, traditional crafts, perfume, and intricate embroidery are all dirt cheap. The **Artisanat Libanais,** on Rue Clemenceau, sells beautiful and affordable Lebanese crafts. Walk east on Rue Bliss past AUB; Rue Bliss becomes Rue Clemenceau at Rue John Kennedy. The market is on the right just over a block past the Gefinor Center and at the branch next to the St. Georges Hotel downtown. Les Artisans, as cooperative craft unions are called, are non-profit—all revenue goes to the artists themselves. There are jewelry shops on every corner in Beirut, but it is a good idea to ask a trustworthy local for directions to an honest shop. Bargaining for gold and silver is usually acceptable, but prices are fixed at the Artisanat. Beirut's traditional *souqs*, which were once world renowned, were destroyed during the war. Many of the *souqs* have been restored, but purists will be disappointed that they are too wide and the shops too upscale to be considered true *souqs*. Outdoor shopping mall would perhaps be a better term, as the architecture looks more like the neo-mediterranean facade of a newly completed western shopping complex than anything that might actually be found in the region. For a real live *souq*, try the ones in Sa'ida or Tripoli.

Virile sporting urges may be quenched at the **Beirut Racetrack (Hippodrome)** (☎63 25 30), where purebred Arabian horses run every Sunday (Saturday in summer). But be warned that there are a limited number of horses and it is not uncommon for races to be canceled because a few horses have become ill. Beirut's posh **Golf Club** (☎82 24 70) is open to foreigners, who can use the eighteen-hole course, swimming pool, and squash and tennis courts for a fee (around L£20,000). The club has survived some difficult times: in 1982 the Israeli army bulldozed the gold club pavilion, and in 1989 alone 360 shells landed on the course. But an extensive re-landscaping effort has restored the course's appeal, an appeal that is sure to increase with time as the new flora reaches maturity. The **Mediterranean** is quite polluted around Beirut, but locals don't seem to mind. There are also several **swimming pools** open to visitors. The cleanest and best is at the St. Georges Hotel downtown (L£20,000 per day for use of pool and facilities).

◪ NIGHTLIFE

Beirutis who can afford it support a thriving dance and party scene. During the war, clubs in the northern suburbs of Jounieh and Kaslik helped people forget about life for a while. When the darkest years of conflict ended, discos and bars filled with optimistic youth re-energized by the end of sniper threats and car bombings. Ras Beirut now throbs with a new beat after years of boarded-up silence, rivaling the club meccas of the suburbs. An added incentive to shake it on down to downtown Beirut is that after-hours public transportation to and from suburbia is limited to expensive private taxis. All places listed below are accessible from Beirut by bus or *service* before midnight and should cost no more than L£8000 for return taxi fare to Beirut.

A word to the wise: so-called super night clubs are common in Lebanon. Many visitors wrongly assume that "super" means "very good." Those in the know simply call these clubs "brothels." So unless your planet is lonely, avoid this scene.

CLUB-HOPPING

▩ B018, (☎(03) 80 00 18). Right next door to the forum de Beyrouth in Karantina. This spawn of Orange Méchanique is a jazzy hip-hop joint equipped with Star Trek control deck seats and a retractable roof with a great view of starry Beirut nights. Beer L£10,000; mixed drinks L£15,000. Open daily 7pm-dawn, but the superstars don't really come out until after 10pm. V, MC, AmEx.

Orange Méchanique, on Sin al-Fil, 300m up from Beirut Hall along the river. The most popular and notorious discotheque in Beirut. Follow the eclectic crowds and professional dancers for a melange of New York techno, acid jazz, and rave. Drinks L£10,500. No cover. Open Th-Sa and holidays 10pm on.

Indiana (☎36 26 66), off Rue Monot in Ashrafieh. Formerly the teeny-bopper central Monkey Rose, Indiana has a more adult feel than its predecessor. Rock standards dominate the playlist and a desert-hued interior rife with images of American Indians evokes the Old West. A good place to go if you want something a little more laid back than the funky dance clubs. Drinks L£8000-12,000. No cover. Open daily 8pm-late.

Oliver's, in Ma'ameltein, on the main seaside drag. The first disco to open in the area has seen better days, leading some to say "thank you sir, but may I have some more (disco)?" Nevertheless, this mirrored *boite* is often crowded to capacity. Usually no cover for foreigners, who bounce around to commercial hip-hop and dance music. Beer L£5000; mixed drinks L£8000-14,000. Open daily 9:30pm-4am.

Caracas, Inc. (☎74 31 05). The highlight of the reborn Ras Beirut club scene, in the Jana building on Caracas Street. Arrive after 1am, when the crowd gets crazy and disco is at its funkiest. One of the better spots in Beirut for meeting unattached girls (unattached guys are abundant most everywhere). V, MC, AmEx.

Amor y Libertad (☎(03) 64 08 81), in Kaslik, in the Debs Center on the main road. Move to a Latin beat with the beautiful offspring of Lebanon's elite. Drinks L£8,000-11,000. Open daily 8pm-4am. Usually no cover. V, MC, AmEx.

Club 70 (☎36 97 29). This techno-driven dance haven has become one of the hippest spots in Beirut. Deep leather chairs allow you to relax when you need to, but a kickin' system and rad DJ should keep you bopping around this sleekly furnished party space. Manages to sooth and hype all at once. Drink prices could be much worse (Almaza L£4500, cocktails L£10,000). No cover. Open Th-Su 10:30pm-4:30am.

BAR-HOPPING

▩ The Smugglers (☎(03) 619 382), on Rue Makhloul in Hamra, on the left as you walk from Rue Abd al-Aziz. Mainly a bar with a few tables, but by midnight customers dance in the lava lamp-lit aisles. Unlike in many places in Beirut, the music, though loud, does not stifle conversation. The beer is the best deal in town. Almaza L£3000, L£2000 during happy hour (7pm-9:30pm). Open daily 6pm-3am.

Henry J. Bean's, "but his friends call him Hank." Just east of the Lebanese American University on the north side of Rue Madame Curry. The bar and its English-speaking staff hold 'Crazy Hour' daily (4-8pm), when you can satisfy your hankering for anything on the menu at half-price (normally L£5000-6500). The place keeps hopping thanks to everyone's favorite heavily-hopped brew: Guinness. Open daily noon-1am.

L'Escroc (Cheap Shots), on Rue al-Inglisi in Ashrafieh. With your back to Circuite Empire in Place Sassine, walk 100m down the large street leaving the Chase on your right. Although this local favorite's name means "crook" in French, you won't be swindled, only wasted (cheap shots L£2500). Very crowded on weekend nights. Many people seem to just stop in for a cheap drink before heading out to more glamorous pastures. If you'd rather inhale smoke than alcohol, have an *argeileh*. Open daily noon-1am.

Pacifico, off Rue Monot in Ashrafieh. "The goddess made me a cup of tea with a spot of rum, but she herself drank only the rum." Heine's words on the menu may inspire you to imitate the goddess with the L£6500-10,500 shooters. Alternately, you can worship her with cigars (L£9500-33,500), fancy meals (L£14,500-24,500), Almaza (L£4000), and even Corona (L£6000). Happy hour M-Sa 6:30-8pm.

Janneh, (☎(04) 87 31 20), in Beit Marie. A pain to reach—take the #7 bus from the National Museum to Beit Marie. Patrons heading home after 7:30pm will have to grab a private taxi to get home. This tropical food and drink complex nearly lives up to its name ("heaven"). Waterfall, pond, and crossbridge flow through two restaurants serving Middle Eastern (L£37,500, all you can eat) and French (prix fixe, L£33,000) cuisine. Pub features drinks for L£4000-10,000. Open daily 9am-5am.

Blue Note, on Rue Makhloul in Hamra. An excessively ambient jazz joint, serving pasta lunches (L£22,500-30,000) and pricey dinners (L£30,000-37,500). A budget-friendlier option is to fill up on the *mezze*. Live music F and Sa nights. Beer L£3900-5200. 20% tax added. Cover L£6000. Open M-Th noon-1am, F-Sa noon-2am.

Pickwick Pub, (☎346 260), at the Marble Tower Hotel, NE corner of Rue Makdissi and Rue Nehme Yafet in Hamra. Beirut's own 'ye olde pub' will transport you to where the men are men and the sheep run—wait, that's Wales... Almaza L£4000. Open daily 3pm-midnight.

NEAR BEIRUT

JOUNIEH جونية ☎01

Take a service to Dawra (L£500) and hop another service (L£500). Some go directly to Jounieh, but those headed for Byblos or Tripoli can also drop you off at Jounieh.

High-stakes risktakers gamble and bikini-clad women gambol at the casinos, clubs, and luxurious beach resorts of Jounieh, Lebanon's capital of hedonism. Wealthy Beirutis and well-heeled visitors jaunt 21km north of Beirut to frolic at the three coastal towns—Kaslik, Jounieh, and Ma'ameltein—that compose the area collectively referred to as Jounieh. Though it undoubtedly possesses as ancient a history as neighboring Beirut and Byblos, Jounieh today betrays no hint of antiquity to taint its many disco floors (see **Beirut: Club-Hopping,** p. 525), Western-style steakhouses, pizza factories, and falafel stands.

Most boutiques and clubs are in **Kaslik,** just off the Beirut-Tripoli freeway, southeast of the seaside road. This area is often referred to as the "Rodeo Drive of Lebanon," perhaps not the best spot to purchase that extra pair of underwear you need. For window-shopping and people-watching, however, Kaslik is hard to beat.

Food in Jounieh is fairly expensive, but don't overlook the budget options. Cheap Arab eats are on the main street parallel to the sea. **Sailor's Snack** serves up munchies like *shish tawouq* and kebab sandwiches for L£2500. (☎(09) 63 57 00. Open 24hr.) If you ride the téléférique, enjoy a meal with a view of Jounieh and the sea (unfortunately, through layers of pollution) at the **Téléférique Restaurant.** The menu runs the gamut from budget to bank-breaking; grab a sandwich for L£3500. (Open daily 10am-midnight.)

SWIMMING. Jounieh's primary attraction during hot summer days is its swimming. Beach resorts along the city's coast typically charge L£10,000-15,000 for use of pool facilities. A cheaper option is the **ocean,** thankfully devoid of the floating debris which plagues much of the Lebanese and Syrian coast. Free surf, sand, and sun are everywhere—just walk toward that big, blue thing on the left.

HARISSA MOUNTAIN. Check out the stunning views from the heights of Harissa Mountain. The preferred mode of ascension is via **téléférique,** a nine-minute gondola skyride that provides spectacular views of the heavily developed coastline. When it gets too steep for the cable cars, a funicular takes over the ascent to the pinnacle. *(Entrance left of Hospital St. Louis, just off the main seaside drag. ☎91 43 24. Open daily July-Sept. 10am-10:30pm; Oct.-June 10am-midnight. L£7500, ages 4-10 L£3500.)*

CASINO DU LIBAN. The world-famous Casino du Liban towers over Ma'ameltein to the north. In its heyday, the casino dueled with Monte Carlo for Mediterranean gaming supremacy and was filled with celebrities, international jet-setters, and suave British spies sipping martinis. War shut down the funhouse, but it has recently reopened to tourists from all over the world. The opulent excess of the three gaming rooms, five restaurants, two auditoriums, and eight bars will shake, but not stir you. The doorman may sneer at dirty backpackers, and those in sandals will be turned away. Signs say no shorts, but shorts-clad gamblers abound. *(☎83 20 97. 21+ admitted. Open daily 8pm-4am.)*

CHURCHES. Perched atop Harissa Mountain is the **Church of the Virgin of Lebanon.** The interior sports tacky electric candles and a statue of questionable aesthetic value, but the exterior spiral staircase leads to unmatched vistas from the base of the huge **Statue of the Virgin Mary.** Gamblers can also pray for big bucks at the modernist **Maronite Cathedral,** a magnificent glimmering glass building. *(Open daily 10am-9pm. Services M-Sa 7:30am, 5, 6pm; Su and holidays every hr. 7am-noon and 4-7pm.)*

JEITA GROTTO مغارة جيتا

Getting to Jeita (20km north of Beirut) without shelling out a lot of cash for a private taxi can be difficult. Try hopping a bus at Dawra to Jounieh or Byblos (L£500) and asking to be let off at "Mafra' Jeita" or walking uphill for 5min. into the modern town. From there, hail a service to "Mafra' maghaarat Jeita." Get out at the turnoff to the caverns (L£1000); the grotto is 2km downhill. The parking attendant specializes in hooking carless visitors up with rides, but some must brave the uphill climb on the return journey. Open Tu-Su 9am-5pm, May-Sept. Tu-Su 9am-6pm; lower grotto closed for 20 days or so in Jan. and Feb. when water level is too high for tour boats to pass through the cave. L£16,500, under 12 L£9250, under 4 free. No photography.

The Jeita Grotto formed where the Nahr al-Kalb (Dog River) hollowed out the insides of a wooded mountain off the coastal highway near Beirut, creating one of the largest and most intricately carved caverns in the world. The caverns house the river's source and a soaring cathedral of latticed stalactites and stalagmites. Humans have appreciated the Jeita Grotto since the Paleolithic Age, but credit for the most recent and well-publicized discovery goes to Reverend William Thomson, an American missionary who ventured 50m into the cave in 1836. Once he reached the underground river, he fired his gun, and the gunshot echoes revealed the subterranean immensity. In his honor, the still water in the cavern's lower gallery is named **Thomson's Pool.**

The Lebanese Minister of Tourism, Nicolas Fattouche (no relation to the salad), was responsible for reopening the grotto after the war. He hired the German company, Mapas, to overhaul the attraction and make it tourist-friendly. After paying a high (but worthwhile) admission fee, visitors are whizzed to the entrance of the **upper cave** in one of four "Austrian" cable cars. Discovered years after Thomson's gunshot, the upper cave is now entered through a 100m tunnel drilled into the mountain. A snack bar stands next to the tunnel, along with a theater showing a film detailing the caves' history (23min.). In the summer, when the cave is full of water, a little replica of a steamboat tugs visitors 100m to the entrance of the **lower cave.** In the winter, the water level is sometimes too high to be navigable. The upper caverns are more spectacular than the lower caverns and contain remarkable mineral formations.

FAQRA AND FARAYA فقرة وفـرايـة ☎09

Venture just east of Beirut into the Mount Lebanon area, and Lebanon's nickname, "Little Switzerland," suddenly makes sense. The ski resorts of this alpine interior are very close to the beaches of the coast, yet the opulence that also characterizes this region puts Faqra and Faraya high among the nation's best resorts. At 1600m above sea level, the reason for their superiority is eminently clear.

▣ GETTING THERE. Faqra (45km from Beirut) and Faraya (50km from Beirut) are difficult to reach. Neither *service* nor white minivans trek up to this area, and private taxis cost a prohibitive L£30,000-45,000 each way, making a daytrip difficult without a private car.

▟▛ ACCOMMODATIONS AND FOOD. Hotel prices in "Little Ritzerland" are as steep, fast, and out of control as you'll be on the slopes. One reasonable option in Faqra is the **Faqra Club,** where comfortable, spotless quarters are rented as single rooms. All rooms feature private bath and satellite TV. Junior suites include a sitting area and executive suites a kitchenette. (☎30 05 01 or 30 05 02. Doubles L£226,000-340,000; triples L£283,000-415,000; junior suites L£354,000, weekends L£490,000; executive suites L£384,000, weekends L£550,000. Prices negotiable.)

The hotels in Faraya are more accommodating to the wallet. Near the main traffic circle is the **Old Bridge Hotel and Restaurant** (Arabic sign only, الجسر القديم). Rooms are large, well-maintained two-bed suites with kitchenettes. (Singles L£38,000; doubles L£60,000; triples L£68,000.) The in-house restaurant features *mezze* (L£2000-2500) and grills (L£15,000-25,000). With the Old Bridge Hotel on the left, walk down the main street to reach the family-run **Coin Vert Hotel and Restaurant,** a relatively inexpensive place to crash. Clean rooms (some with balconies) come with private baths. (☎72 08 12. Singles L£45,000; doubles L£60,000; triples L£75,000. Up to 15% summer or student discounts. Ski rental L£7500 per day. V, MC.) Dollar-for-dollar, the best deal in town is **The Grand Hotel.** With Coin Vert on the left, walk downhill, bearing left at the intersection; the hotel will be on the left. Rooms (some featuring balconies) with private bathrooms fit one to three people, though they are small and have hard beds (L£30,000 per person).

Food in Faqra and Faraya ranges from Middle Eastern standard *mezze* to Western standard pizza. For leafy outdoor seating and an equally wholesome meal in Faqra, head to **An-Nahr al-Hawi Restaurant** (Arabic sign only, النهر الهوى), just past the main traffic circle. (☎72 02 60. *Mezze* L£3500 per dish; entrees L£4000-7000. V, MC.) In Faraya, try the large, outdoor **Restaurant Jisr al-Kamer.** A babbling brook runs by as you chomp on your L£18,000 *mezze*. (☎(03) 87 79 93. Open daily 7am-7pm. V, MC.) For something cheaper and more western, walk uphill with Coin Vert on the right. After a few minutes, the **Snowman Restaurant** appears on the right, where an Italian-style pizza for two goes for about L£8000. (☎32 10 78. Open Su-F 11am-midnight, Sa 11am-1am.)

◪ SIGHTS. Over 3000 years of continuous settlement in this region have left their mark in the form of several interesting ruins: the **Archaeological Site** in Faqra contains ruins of buildings believed to have been built by the Romans in the first century CE. The **main temple,** about 50m northwest of the tower, features columns restored during the 20th century and the remains of an altar. Near the main temple stand a small temple and several free-standing altars. (Open W-M 8:30am-dusk; foreigners L£2000, Lebanese nationals L£1000.)

The nearby town of Hrajel contains a few places of interest. Fifteen minutes on a harrowing one-lane mountain road will take you to the 200-year-old **Church of St.**

Mary, on a cliff overlooking the town. As several large carved stones attest, St. Mary's was built on the site of a Roman temple dedicated to the god Dionysus. Between this outpost and the center of town lie the remains of **Phoenician tombs,** now visible as deep rectangular depressions carved into the rocks. You may also have time to visit Hrajel's two **grottoes.** Part of one cave, **al-Karkouf,** collapsed in 1307 CE trapping a group of Maronites who were hiding from their enemies. As of July 2000, the other cave, **Nabeh al-Maghara,** was only open to experts, but the ongoing installation of lights and walkways will soon make it tourist-friendly. Bring your own spelunking equipment, like lights and helmets.

The main reason people visit these villages is **skiing.** Faqra has four slopes, ranging from beginner to advanced levels, while Faraya boasts 13. Locals say Mzaar provides the best thrills. (Solipro, ☎ (01) 25 72 20, offers information on Faqra; Mr. Christien Rizk, ☎ (09) 34 10 34 or (03) 77 12 11, provides information on Faraya. Open Dec.-Apr. daily 8am-4pm. Lift tickets and equipment rental each L£30,000.)

NORTH OF BEIRUT

BYBLOS (JBAIL) جبيل ☎09

Byblos is still duking it out with Jericho, Damascus, and Aleppo for the title of oldest city in the world. According to ancient myth, the handsome youth Adonis was killed by a boar in the nearby Afqa Grotto, only to emerge from Hades every summer to frolic in Byblos with Aphrodite. Better substantiated is the 7000-year-old city's historical origin as a small fishing village. Even the ancients considered Byblos historical—in the beginning of the 3rd millennium BCE, it was the main source of timber (from the famed Cedars of Lebanon) for Egyptian pharaohs. Byblos also supplied others with papyrus, a legacy that survives in the etymology of words like "Bible" and "bibliography." The city finally evolved into modern-day Jbail, leaving Roman, Muslim, and Turkish rulers behind. It only suffered minimal damage during the Civil War and now welcomes back international hep-cats.

▐ GETTING THERE AND GETTING AROUND

Buses from Dawra in western Beirut (L£500) stop along Rue Jbail near the modern Diab Brothers building. **Service** to Amchit bunch up on Rue Jbail in front of the Mobil station (L£1000). Returning to Beirut is easy until about 9pm—walk up toward the highway past Diab Brothers where a battalion of buses await passengers for the return trip to Dawra (L£500).

■❖❷ ORIENTATION AND PRACTICAL INFORMATION

Byblos's layout is straightforward and simple to master. The main drag of the modern town is **Rue Jbail,** where buses stop to let off passengers and *service* congregate before departure. Walk up toward the highway past the Diab Brothers building and bear right without getting on the highway to reach the entrance to the sandy **Tam Tam Beach.** Across the street from the police station on Rue Jbail, **Byblos Bank** exchanges traveler's checks. (Open M-F 8am-5:30pm, Sa 8am-1pm.) Rue Jbail soon turns 90 degrees to the right at the Kentucky Fried Chicken (KFC). Taking a left just before this curve leads to the **Old City Souqs,** the **Wax Museum,** the entrance to the archaeological site, and the small **Ministry of Tourism.** (Ministry: ☎ 54 03 25. Open M-Sa 9am-4:30pm, Su 10am-1pm; in winter M-Sa 9am-4:30pm, Su 10am-2pm.) The street directly across from KFC leads to **Byblos Harbor.** Continuing on Rue Jbail toward Amchit, look to the right for the **Central Telephone Office.** (Open daily 8am-midnight. Three-minute

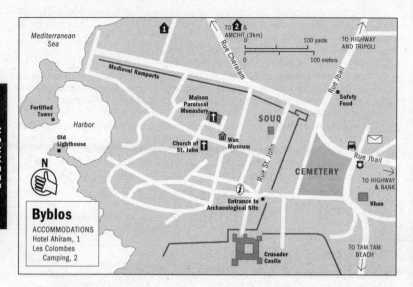

minimum; L£300 per min. discount 10pm-midnight.) A right just past Diab Brothers leads to the nondescript **post office**. (☎54 00 03. Open M-Th and Sa 8am-2pm, F 8-11am.) Farther along Rue Jbail on the left is the **police station** (☎94 58 53). For an **ambulance**, call the **Red Cross** (☎125).

▌ ACCOMMODATIONS

Finding a place to stay in Byblos itself is nearly impossible without shelling out of a small fortune. Staying in nearby areas may be easier on your wallet.

▨ **Les Colombes Camping** (☎54 03 22), in Amchit, just a short *service* ride (L£1000) or a 3km northward walk away from Byblos. One of the best budget options in all of Lebanon. Sits atop a beautifully lush cliffside, from which a path leads down to the sea (ideal for swimming). Aside from tents, tangalows may be of interest (but come with noisy neighbors): edifice-shaped tents that feature bungalow-like bathrooms. Chalets are homes away from home, for they come equipped with dining rooms and kitchenettes. Make sure to bring insect repellent or else you will leave looking like Scarface. Tents L£1500; campsites L£4500 per person, on weekends L£7500; tangalow singles L£23,000, doubles L£30,000; chalet singles L£30,000, doubles L£45,000.)

   Hotel Ahiram (☎54 04 40 or 54 15 40; fax 94 47 26; email ahiram@inconet.com.lb.), the last right before the sea on the harbor road. The cheapest downtown option with two restaurants. Modern rooms with A/C, TV, refrigerator, private bath, and windswept balconies with sea views. Breakfast included. Singles L£63,000; doubles L£100,000; triples L£120,000. Bargain if staying longer than two nights. V, MC, AmEx.

▌ FOOD

The food options in Byblos run the gamut from imported grease-to-go (KFC, Pizza Hut) to ultra chic snack machines lining the port.

▨ **Byblos Fishing Club** (☎94 37 58). Once the most glamorous restaurant in the Middle East, the Fishing Club and its eccentric owner, Pepe "the Pirate" Abed, prompted a French critic to remark, "Visiter le Liban sans connaitre Pepe...c'est passer sa lune de miel avec un eunuque!" Or, "to visit Lebanon without knowing Pepe...that is like spending your honeymoon with a eunuch!" Check out the pictures of Pepe with Marlon Brando, Charles de Gaulle, and David Rockefeller. The prix-fixe menu with meat (L£26,000) or fish (L£30,000) may be too pricey, but this is *the* place for a sunset drink. Open daily 10am-1am; in winter 10am-11pm. V, MC, AmEx.

Seven Seas Restaurant, on Rue St. John's next to Pizza Hut, a short walk toward the harbor from the Wax Museum. For an upscale meal, rig up the HMS Pancreas and weigh anchor at this newly relocated establishment. Features lunch of salad and fish or *shish tawouq* (L£8500). Cap it off with a bottle of local wine from their extensive list. V, MC.

Al-Kadroun (☎94 68 06), on the left of Rue Jbail, just past the divided highway as you walk away from the old city. Sign in Arabic. Ice cream (L£2000) and fruit cocktails (L£5000) melt in your mouth, or in your hands if you're slow. Open daily 10am-2am.

Mafrak Amchit Farhat. Head up to the two-lane artery just east of the campground, make a right, and walk straight for about 100m. It is on the right, just past the intersection with a road crossing the freeway to the east. A splendid *shish tawouq* sandwich for L£3000. Open 6am-11pm.

🔍 SIGHTS

ARCHAEOLOGICAL DIG. Remnants spanning nearly all of Byblos's 7000 odd years of continuous inhabitation can be found at the archaeological site. Enter the site through the largest and best preserved of the ruins, the **Crusader Castle.** Franks built the castle in the 12th century out of stones pillaged from Roman buildings and newer stones cut to replicate the Roman style. The castle towers afford panoramic views that serve as a useful orientation to the rest of the ruins. To the west are columns from an ancient **Roman Colonnade** in front of a small **Roman Theater,** reconstructed after its 20th century excavation to only half its original size. Walking toward the boarded-up modern building, be careful not to fall into the **King's Well,** a remarkably deep depression that remained in use until Hellenistic times. Nearby lie the crushed limestone floors of Byblos's earliest settlements. Dating from the Neolithic (5th millennium BCE) and Chalcolithic (4th millennium BCE) eras, these settlements are among the earliest human remains in the world. Walking to the east away from the sea, you'll soon come to the **Obelisk Temple,** comprising a forecourt and a slightly raised sanctuary. Originally built on the site of the 5000-year-old Temple of Resheph, the obelisks were moved to the new site to facilitate further excavation. Only one of the 26 sandstone obelisks carries an inscription: a hieroglyphic dedication to an Egyptian god. Those who want a closer look at the inscriptions will be disappointed, however, as the Lebanese government has erected a fence around them to prevent vandalism. A **necropolis,** filled with nine underground tombs of Byblos kings, dates to the 2nd century BCE and lies near the railroad tracks. Conquer your fears and descend the spooky steps leading into the Tomb of King Chemou. *(Open daily 8am-sunset. L£6000.)*

OTHER SIGHTS. Save some time for the Maronite cathedral of **St. John Mark** between the harbor and the wax museum. Originally the crusader church of St. John the Baptist, it was destroyed, rebuilt, and eventually expanded. A small **Wax Museum** displays scenes from ancient and modern Lebanese history (the portrayal of the martyrs facing Ottoman soldiers is particularly striking). But it is questionable whether this 15-minute excursion into the histoire du Liban is worth L£5000. Even if you don't want a drink at the **Byblos Fishing Club,** check out Pepe's free museum, featuring antiquities he recovered during diving expeditions. The museum structure dates back 800 years; UNESCO has declared it a world heritage site. Gaze longingly at the gleaming water of **Tam Tam Beach** while broiling at the top of the Crusader Castle. An easy 20-minute walk from town, it buzzes with youth who listen to Bob Marley and drink too much beer. Avoid weekend crowds.

BATROUN بترون ☎06

Unlike Byblos, Batroun is happy to admit that it is one of the oldest cities in the world. Before succumbing to the Greeks and Romans (who called it Botrys), Batroun was occupied by Phoenicians. For many years, the people of Batroun used the natural resources around them for profit: they developed the peculiar industry of sponge-diving. Today, this quaint, predominantly Christian town claims one superlative that only the most exacting connoisseurs would dispute: the world's best lemonade, available at shops all over town.

☰ GETTING THERE. Catch a *service* just south of the Allah sign on Rue Fouad Chebab in Tripoli (L£4000). From Byblos, your best bet is to stand alongside the freeway and catch one of the many passing *service* (L£2000) or white minibuses (L£1000).

🛈 PRACTICAL INFORMATION. The two-lane coastal highway is the main street of Batroun. All major shops flank this highway and historical sites tend to lie just off of it. An English-language tourist map, free at most shops, simplifies navigation. If unavailable, walk to the large statue of a diver on the north side of town, a reminder of the town's past as a sponge-diving center, and follow the site-specific arrows. West of the main street lies the **Old City** with its authentic **souq.**

🖿🗋 ACCOMMODATIONS AND FOOD. The cheapest accommodation, a seaside resort-o-tel called **Aqualand,** is just south of town on the main drag. Don't be misled by the name—it will keep you dry—but it comes at quite a price. Weary travelers with enough money can enjoy the sauna, jacuzzi, and hot tub. (☎74 27 41. Singles L£75,000; doubles L£90,000. V, MC.)

　 ▧Chez Hilmi, on the east side of the main street near the center of town, has been owned by the Rahim family for more than 85 years. These guys originated Batroun's lemonade craze. Their home-brewed, tangy lemonade comes in three sizes (20oz., L£2000). Their homemade sweets are so good that they ship them around the world via their website: www.chezhilmi.com. (Open daily 7am-11pm. V, MC, AmEx.) A cheaper choice with sandwiches and lemonade is **Hannouch Restaurant,** on the main street a few blocks south of the diver statue. The English menu simplifies ordering and the *tawouq* sandwich is a bargain at L£3000. (☎74 04 38. Open daily 8am-midnight.)

🖸🗋 SIGHTS AND ENTERTAINMENT. Perhaps the staunchest holdover from Batroun's days of yore, **▧Musheilla Castle** is just over 2½km north of town on a turnoff from the freeway, east of the coastal highway. Built in the 16th century, the castle stands on a 25m stone outcrop. Reach it by hailing one of the taxis that periodically pass through town (L£4000 round-trip). Although the rubbish-strewn field surrounding the outcrop detracts from the area's charm, you'll forget this blemish upon ascending the stone stairway to explore the castle's interior. Wear sturdy shoes and be careful: it is full of uneven steps and unmarked ledges, and it's a long, long fall. At the south end of the old city stands the **Church of Mary, Lady of the Sea,** originally a Roman temple. East of the main drag, now serving as a wall of a photography studio's courtyard, are the remains of a **Roman Amphitheater.**

　 Taiga Pub, Batroun's lone nightclub, sits on the east side of main street near the center of town. During the week, sparse crowds sip brewskies (L£2000), but come Friday and Saturday nights, clubbers from Tripoli pack the place, jamming to Middle Eastern and European techno. (☎(03) 49 94 08. L£5000 cover on F and Sa. Open Tu-Th and Su 6pm-midnight, F-Sa 6pm-5am.)

TRIPOLI طرابلس ☎06

Tripoli (*Trablos*) is known as the "capital of the North," with a character distinct from any other region in Lebanon. While the general flavor of Tripoli is that of

Here's your ticket to freedom, baby!

NAME YOUR OWN PRICE!

Wherever you want to go...
priceline.com can get you there for less.

- Save up to 40% or more off the lowest published airfares every day!

- Major airlines serving virtually every corner of the globe.

- Special fares to Europe!

If you haven't already tried priceline.com, you're missing out on the best way to save. **Visit us online today at www.priceline.com.**

priceline.com ℠
Name Your Own Price ℠

Mashriq (Eastern) Arab culture—with mosques, *souqs*, and *hammams*—the al-Mina district has a subtle Mediterranean flavor.

Tripoli's rich history began when the Phoenicians established a small port in the al-Mina area in the 9th century BCE. Before the turn of the millennium, it was taken over by the Persians, the Macedonians, and then the Romans before an earthquake and resulting tidal wave utterly destroyed the city in 551 CE. The Mamluks resettled the area a century later. Under the Mamluks, Tripoli flourished as an intellectual center complete with an extensive library. Crusading Europeans arrived in the 1090s; the first batch was staved off with bribery and persuasion, but in 1099 Tripoli succumbed to Raymond Saint-Gilles. The Crusaders' occupation lasted 180 years, and the Mamluks had their revenge in 1289: years of scheming and minor skirmishes paid off when they were finally able to send the Crusaders packing, and they set to work fortifying the peninsula against future attacks. Mamluk Sultan Qalaoun even razed the old Crusader city to the ground, building a new one (now known as al-Madina) at the foot of the hill near the castle. The city's second great Mamluk age lasted until 1516, and the *khans*, *hammams*, mosques, and *madrasas* that dot the city today date from that period. When the Ottomans came to power, Sultan Suleiman I, who ruled from 1520 to 1566, maintain Tripoli's architecture and even restored many of its treasures.

Tripoli's history is matched in variety only by the city's cultural diversity. The Tripolitanians shuffling along the sea-side corniche dress in fashions ranging from miniskirts to *hijabs*. As the lazy Mediterranean sun lingers on the horizon, cars zip past each other in a chaotic race home, and Tripoli's fishermen call it a day and begin their cafe-side lounging.

▐ GETTING THERE AND GETTING AROUND

Buses: From the **Ahdab Bus Station,** just west of al-Nasser Sq. Smoking and non-smoking buses to **Beirut** (every 15min.; 5am-7pm; L£2000, students L£1500). **Karnak Office,** on Rue Fouad Chehab around the right-hand corner from Ahdab, houses Karnak buses departing to: **Aleppo** (5hr., L£7500); **Damascus** (4½hr.; Tu, Th, and Sa 4:30am; L£4500); **Hama** (3hr., L£4500); **Homs** (2½hr., every hr. 8:30am-midnight, L£6000); and **Lattakia** (3½hr., 3:30pm, L£4500) via **Tartus** (2hr., L£4500).

Service: Depart from the south side of al-Nasser Sq. To **Beirut** (L£4000) and nearly every other destination in Syria and Lebanon. *Service* to **Bcharré** (L£3500) and the mountains leave from the south side of al-Nasser Sq. and outside the Ministry of Tourism office. No regular *service* go to Ba'albeck.

✳ ORIENTATION

The major north-south road of Tripoli is **Rue Fouad Chehab.** Approaching from Beirut on this road arrives at **al-Karami** roundabout with its distinctive "Allah" (الله) sign in the middle. The next major intersection sends **Rue Jemayzat** off to the left and Rue 'Abd al-Hamid Karami, popularly known as **Rue Tell,** off to the right—**Big Bite Restaurant** marks this intersection. On the left of Rue Tell is the landmark **al-Tal clocktower,** and across the street is the dusty **Jamal 'Abd al-Nasser Sq.** This area forms the heart of modern Tripoli and is filled with *service* drivers boisterously plying their trade. Taking the first right after al-Nasser Sq. leads to **Koura Sq.,** and a left at Koura Sq. leads to **al-Nejmeh Sq.** From here the towering citadel is visible, and almost all of the sights are a short walk away. To find your way to the sights, however, either ask a local or go to the Ministry of Tourism Office (on al-Karami roundabout) to pick up their excellent map, as the streets around here mock all attempts at city planning. **Al-Mina** is 2km from the city center toward the sea. *Service* taxis (L£500), which leave directly across the street from the clocktower, will get you to the main seaside drag, **Rue Ibn Sina,** also known as the **corniche.**

⚡ PRACTICAL INFORMATION

Tourist Office: (☎ 43 35 90), in al-Karami Sq. near the "Allah" sign. Provides an enormous historical map and pamphlets on all major tourist destinations in Lebanon. The multilingual staff is an excellent resource for honest information about hotels across the country. Open M-Sa 8am-6pm, Su 8am-1pm.

Banks: Banque Libano-Française (☎ 44 18 74), from tourist office, walk counter-clockwise around rotary at al-Karami Sq. and cross one street. ATM, multilingual. Open M-F 8:15am-4pm, Sa 8:15am-noon. **Société Générale Libano Européenne** (☎ 43 24 03). Near DHL on Rue Fouad Chehab. ATM, multilingual. Open M-Sa 8am-1:30pm.

Laundromat: Express Laundry (☎ 62 58 25), around the corner from the City Complex mall on Rue Riyad Assoulh. With the Big Bite on your right, walk away from the clocktower until you reach the first traffic roundabout. Take a right and the mall follows on the left, past the Hallab Brothers Patisserie. Opposite Krameh Palace. Shirts L£2500, pants L£4000. Open M-Th and Sa 7:30am-6pm, F 7:30am-3pm; in winter M-Th and Sa 7:30am-4:30pm, F 7:30am-3pm.

Emergency: Police: ☎ 17. **Red Cross:** ☎ 140; also dispatches ambulances. **Hospital: Hospital Mazloum:** (☎ 43 03 25, 43 03 26, 62 83 03, 62 83 34; fax 62 83 05) Emergency room, x-ray. Will airlift the most seriously ill or injured patients to Beirut.

Pharmacy: Ayoub Pharmacy (☎ 62 42 95), in al-Nasser Sq., directly across from the clocktower. Multilingual staff. Open M-F 8am-5pm, Sa 8am-2pm. **Assaray Pharmacy** (☎ 44 46 57), facing the post office. Open M-F 8am-9pm, Sa 8am-2pm.

Telephones: ☏ Funet. Walk away from the clocktower on Riyad Assoulh St., make the first right after City Complex. Make the first left, walk about 20m; Funet will be on your right. Internet phone service is one of the best deals in Tripoli. Although sound quality varies, you can call any number in the US, UK, Canada, and sometimes Australia for L£4000 per hr. **EasyNet** (☎ 44 70 41 or (03) 91 73 62), off al-Koura Sq., facing the al-Zahree Building. Very friendly English-speaking staff will place international calls to the US, Western Europe, Australia, and Canada (L£1000 per min). Open daily 9am-midnight. To reach the **Central Telephone Office,** walk toward the "Allah" sign on Rue Fouad Chehab for one block, turn left, and walk one more block. The telephone office is in the shabby white concrete building on your right. Clerks speak little English and rates are posted only in Arabic. Open 24hr.

Internet Access: Easily accessible in Tripoli. **Funet** offers access for L£3500 per hr. Open daily 10am-midnight. **Compugames,** in the City Complex on Riyad Assoulh St., around the corner from the laundromat. Charges slightly more (L£4000 per hr.) but is a shorter walk. Open daily 9am-2am. **EasyNet** also charges L£4000 per hr. and is closer to the clocktower area.

Post Office: (☎ 43 21 01), on Fouad Chehab St., 100m south of the "Allah" sign. First right after municipal building; walk 20m down on the right. Open M-Th and Sa 8am-1:30pm, F 8-11am. **DHL office** (☎ 43 32 05), off Rue Fouad Chehab in Helou Plaza, about 500m north of Big Bite. Documents up to ½kg L£38,000-68,000; add L£23,000 for parcels, L£38,000 for each additional ½kg (students L£38,000, add L£7500 for parcels and L£7500 per additional ½kg). Open M-F 8am-5pm, Sa 8am-3pm. Major credit cards accepted.

⚡ ACCOMMODATIONS

Tripoli's accommodations are generally much cheaper and less crowded than those in Beirut. Many tourists make Tripoli a long daytrip from Beirut, but a few nights' stay allows more leisurely exploration of the northern half of the country. Most budget hotels in Tripoli accept both Lebanese pounds and US dollars, but credit cards tend not to be accepted.

☒ **Pension Haddad** (☎ (06) 62 43 92, (03) 50 77 09; email haddadpension@hotmail.com), situated in an alley to the right off Rue Tell, just past al-Nasser Sq. Perhaps

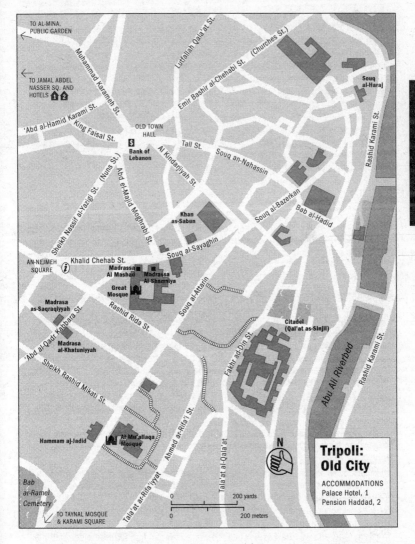

Tripoli: Old City

ACCOMMODATIONS
Palace Hotel, 1
Pension Haddad, 2

the best value in Tripoli, it's like staying at your Lebanese grandma's house. Immaculate, well-furnished shared bedrooms and bathrooms and brilliant three-nozzled shower. Breakfast L£5000. Tea and Coffee included with the room. Fans. Laundry service. Singles L£15,000; doubles L£24,000; triples L£33,000.

Palace Hotel (☎ 43 22 57), on Rue Tell, stands just past al-Nasser Sq. and the watch salesmen on Haddad Alley. The regal reception area with lovely ceiling seems to have earned the hotel its name, and stained-glass windows abound. On-duty manager will call the English-speaking owner. A/C units do not work, but a pleasant breeze blows into rooms facing Rue Tell. Laundry service. Singles L£15,000, with bath L£22,600; doubles L£30,000, with bath L£37,700; triples L£45,000, with bath L£68,000.

Al-Koura Hotel (☎ (03) 32 68 03) lies down an alley named Rue Ez al-Din, the 2nd right-hand turn past the outdoor cafe on al-Nasser Sq. Though somewhat pricier, al-Koura's cedar rafter ceilings and original Ottoman-era brickwork are worth the extra cash. Breakfast included. A/C. Laundry service. English-speaking staff. Singles L£30,000, L£15,000 for sparsely furnished singles; doubles L£45,000; triples L£68,000; less well-maintained 3-bed dorms L£7500.

Hotel Central (☎44 15 44). From tourist office, walk counter-clockwise around rotary. Make first right, walk two blocks. The hotel is on the left of the street—look for its sign. Perhaps comes the closest to a western floorplan, with numbered rooms off of corridors and a large rack o' keys in the lobby. Large shared balcony provide a great view of downtown Tripoli. All rooms have sinks and fans. L£12,000 per person.

Hotel Hayek (☎60 13 11). On Rue Ibn Sina, just off the corniche near the small boat docks in al-Mina. Although not directly on the sea, sea-side rooms provide a view of the Mediterranean and a refreshing sea breeze. Breakfast included. Singles L£27,000; double L£36,200; triples L£53,000.

FOOD

Tripoli is famous for sweets containing a special kind of cream called *'ashta* (see **Food and Drink,** p. 510). Some of the best sweets in town are at **Hallab Brothers,** on the right side of Rue Tell. close to the center of town. Tripoli's well-dressed elite mix with the proletariat, enjoying some syrupy goodness. Try the baklava (L£3750 per ¼kg) or Tripoli's specialty, *halawat al-jibn* for L£3000. (☎44 44 33 or 44 44 45. Open daily 5am-10pm.) Otherwise, traditional Middle Eastern cuisine abounds.

Big Bite (☎43 01 56 or 44 09 65), on the corner of Rue Tell and Rue Fouad Chehab. Falafel and french fry—together at last! Garnish your burger (L£3000) with a side of hummus (L£1000) or go for straight almost-Americana with a respectable vegetarian pizza (L£4500). Open daily 4am-10pm.

Continental Rest (☎44 54 75), on Rue Tell under the green awning, on the left as you climb the steps facing the building with the "ABC" sign. Provides a pleasant and affordable sit-down meal. Kebab and hummus can be yours for under L£6500, but the menu is in Arabic and the staff only speaks Franglish. Open daily 8am-10:30pm.

Captain Fish Restaurant (☎61 30 31), off Rue Ibn Sina and the corniche in al-Mina. Air- conditioned interior and pick-a-fish meals. For those with a fishy craving, they'll cook it however you like it. ½kg of fish is enough for two (L£45,000 per kg). The beautiful mirrored ceiling and a breezy view of the sea give it an ambience any aspiring sea-dog will appreciate. Open daily noon-midnight.

Restaurant Rivoli (☎62 42 27), will be on your left as you approach al-Koura Sq. from the clocktower and make the first left. The relaxed atmosphere of this sit-down establishment provides a welcome break from the action outdoors. Offers a different Middle Eastern special each day for L£5000. Open daily 6am-9pm.

Tasty (☎61 29 09). Walk south on the corniche from the boat docks. It faces the sea just past the *"Le tourbillon,"* a monument created with the carcasses of old computers. Western-style and Middle Eastern fast-food in an air-conditioned and clean setting. Food lives up to the restaurant's name. Open daily 10am-midnight.

SIGHTS

The Old City features a maze-like array of narrow alleys, *souqs,* and several fascinating but dilapidated baths. A random assortment of street vendors who speak little English or French have keys, so hiring a guide is the best option. ◙**Ali Khawaja,** son of a late community leader, will show you every nook and cranny of the Old City for free (yet most visitors give him L£4000-L£7000, which he donates to poor families). Ask for him at the tourist office or look for him in front of Taynal Mosque. If Ali is not around, the tourism office can recommend someone else.

TAYNAL MOSQUE. Tripoli is divided into two sections: **al-Mina,** the old, run-down area, and **al-Madina,** the new section built by Sultan Qalaoun in 1289 CE.

To start your sightseeing tour, take the 2nd left off the "Allah" roundabout as you approach it from downtown Tripoli; you'll soon approach the green-domed **Taynal Mosque.** The most beautiful mosque in Tripoli, it was built in 1336 according to some scholars, by Saif al-Din Taynal on the site of a ruined Carmelite church. This location was outside the limits of the Mamluk city and was originally a Roman Temple to Zeus, then a Byzantine church, and finally the Carmelite structure. Visitors are sometimes allowed to climb the minaret, but entry depends on the presence of the guard. *(Women must wear a full-length cloak available at the entrance. Visitors requested not to enter during prayer times, normally between 11:30am and 1pm. Free.)*

BAB AL-HADEED. Al-Hammam al-Jadeed is the largest bathhouse in Tripoli, built in 1740 but non-functional since the 1970s, when militia used it as a base. It's still worthwhile to take a look at the faded grandeur of the interior. *(Take the 2nd left off the "Allah" roundabout as you approach it from downtown. Pass the mosque, turn right and then left into the neighborhood of Bab al-Hadeed. Free. The keymaster hangs out in a local shop, and will ask for a L£2000 "donation.")*

Through the arch in the same direction is the **Silyagheen Souq.** Replete with over-flowing stalls and smells of rotting organic matter underfoot, the *souq* is one of the oldest and best-maintained *souqs.* Ambitious bargainers can haggle gold jewelry prices to less than half of what it would cost in the Western world. A street running perpendicular to the *souq* leads to two *madrasas,* **Madrasa al-Khatuniyyah** and **Madrasa al-Saqraqiyyah,** built in 1373 and 1359, respectively. The inscriptions above the door of Khatuniyyah list the details of the *waqf,* or endowment left by the founder for students and the poor. On the other wall is the image of a cup, a symbol that recalls the Mamluks' days as slaves. Saqraqiyyah was founded by a soldier, and its dome stands over a former Mamluk tomb.

THE GREAT MOSQUE (AL-MANSOURI AL-KABIR). This mosque was built from 1294 to 1315 on the remains of a ruined 12th-century Crusader cathedral. Remains of Western architecture from the old church have been incorporated into the mosque structure; most notably, a Lombard-style bell tower was transformed into the minaret. Attached to the mosque facing Rue Khalid Chebab are two *madrasas* from the same period, **Madrasa al-Shamsiya** and **Madrasa al-Mashad.** *(Along a street running perpendicular to the souq. Pass the madrasas and continue to the right. Modest dress required. Women must cover themselves with a full-length cloak available at the entrance and are requested not to enter during prayer hour. No shoes. Free.)*

CITADEL (QAL'AT SINJIL). A visit to the Citadel takes you to the heart of al-Madina. The Citadel, towering over the *souqs, hammams,* mosques, and *madrasas,* is known as Qal'at Sinjil (Citadel of St.-Gilles), after Raymond St.-Gilles, the Crusading tough guy who took the city from the Mamluks in 1099 CE. Layers of Mamluk and Ottoman additions are visible. Stroll to the top of the building for an impressive view of Tripoli. *(Open daily 8am-6:30pm; in winter 8am-5pm. L£5000.)*

HAMMAMS AND SOAP FACTORIES. Unused since the 70s until it recently reopened, the soap factory Khan al-Sabun looks like it needs a good wash. During the Middle Ages it was used as a hotel by camel-riding travelers. The first left down the long alley after the soap factory leads to the **Hammam al-'Abd** (Bath of the Slave), Tripoli's only functional hammam. *(Along a street running perpendicular to the souq. Pass the madrasas and continue on to the right. Beyond the Great Mosque, the road forks on the left to reach the Khan al-Sabun.* ☎ *44 65 83. Open daily 7am-midnight. L£15,000; for a look around, the doorman may expect L£1000-2000. Men only.)*

Retracing your steps to the soap factory, a right and then a left leads back to the main north-south *souq.* At the end of the main street is the brass *souq.* A right turn after that takes you to the large **Hammam Izz al-Din,** the oldest Turkish bath in the city (completed in 1298 CE).

LEBANON

🎵 ENTERTAINMENT

After a long day dodging traffic in al-Mina, Tripoli's nighthawks usually converge around two activities: walking and smoking (which are sometimes combined).

Corniche Walk. A splendid place to sit on the sea-side rocks and watch the sun set. Cross a footbridge to nearby islands and look down into the water to see remains of buildings destroyed by past earthquakes.

Boats. A more scenic option is touring the nearby islands on one of the many boats that dock along the waterfront. Tours L£3000-5000. Touring the more distant **Palm Islands** is more expensive and requires a permit from the tourist office. Boats usually run between 9am and 6pm, docking at sundown to serve as cafes during the evenings.

Al-Badi Cafe. With the sea to the left, stroll to the end of the corniche walk. The only place on the corniche directly on the water, and the atmosphere's not badi at all. A bit pricey (*argeileh* and Turkish coffee for L£6000), but worth it. Open daily 9am-1am.

Daccour Cafe. Make a left off the corniche at Captain Fish Restaurant and make the first left. The blue-shuttered cafe is 25m on the left. Tripoli's elder statesmen sit beneath a vaulted ceiling smoking *argeilehs* and drinking Turkish Joe. Chase down a waiter for hot and cold beverages at L£1000. *Argeileh* rental L£3000. Open daily 6am-8pm.

Ahwa Moussa. Second left off the "Allah" roundabout as you approach from downtown. Pass the mosque, turn right and then left. Boasts fountainside seating across the street, where men sit smoking and drinking as they have for 100 years at this establishment. Turkish coffee L£750; soft drinks L£1000; *argeilehs* L£500. Open daily 4am-11pm.

Clou Club (☎(03) 25 46 22). In the City Complex mall on Riyad Assoulh St., around the corner from the Laundromat. Tripoli's club scene is limited, but local hipsters swear by this newly opened joint. Friendly bartender suggests drinks from a variety of beers and liquors (try Almaza), and foreign visitors get royal treatment. If he offers you green liqueur *gratis*, do not decline. Open Tu-Th 7:30pm-1:30am, F and Sa 7:30pm-3am.

🧭 DAYTRIPS FROM TRIPOLI

If you find the bus schedules confining or wish to visit sites between Tripoli and Bcharré, hire a private taxi for about L£50,000. It is usually possible to share the fare with fellow budget-minded travelers (groups up to five), making a fully-loaded taxi more affordable than any other option. Make sure the driver knows where you want to go before you depart. It might be a good idea to have a local write your itinerary in Arabic to avoid any miscommunication. If you can't find anyone, check with the Pension Haddad, well-known for stuffing as many people as they can find into a cab.

FROM TRIPOLI TO BCHARRÉ

Heading through the olive groves east of Tripoli, the roadside is packed with increasing numbers of crosses, a sign of the predominantly Christian Mount Lebanon Range ahead. After passing through **Zgharta,** the road enters the resort town of **Ehden.** According to locals, Jesus visited the town on a donkey. If traveling by private taxi, ask the driver to take you to the memorial to Sayyid David Maoda for a beautiful view of the coast. Adjacent to the memorial is the Chapel of Our Lady of the Castle, which is believed to have originally served as a Roman look-out post.

BCHARRÉ بشرى

A bus (L£2500) sometimes runs from near the tourist office in Tripoli. Buses depart at 10am and noon and return at 5pm. Schedules vary during the winter, so it is best to ask the tourist office. Bcharré is most reliably reached by service from al-Koura Sq., across from the Ahram Hotel (L£3500). Service traffic back to Tripoli becomes thin later in the day, so it makes sense to start your trip early. Another more expensive option is a private taxi.

The largest city in the region, Bcharré sits about 1400m above the Kadisha Valley. The clean, quiet mountain atmosphere provides a refreshing break from the noise and pollution of Lebanon's bigger cities, and the red-roofed Christian village in the valley is among the most scenic spots in the country.

The **Khalil Gibran Museum** in itself is worth the trip to Bcharré. It houses the author's personal library and many of his drawings, manuscripts, and letters. A guidebook costs L₤7500, but copies can be borrowed from the museum for free. The guide contains informative tidbits reflecting the sentiments that inspired Gibran's works. Gibran was a romantic, fascinated by the interplay of humans with each other and with God. Born here in 1883, he immigrated to Boston, Massachusetts, at a young age. In 1898, he returned to Lebanon to spend the summer with his father before enrolling at the Sagesse College in Beirut, where he studied Arabic and French. From Beirut, Gibran went to Paris to start his career. A certain Auguste Rodin, who called Gibran the William Blake of the twentieth century, arranged to have Gibran's painting, *The Autumn*, entered in a prestigious art show. Gibran soon proved that he had more than a big-name connection, winning the silver medal for the piece and establishing himself as an artist. Among his best-known paintings displayed here is *The Divine World (#12)*. Gibran later returned to Boston where he wrote his English masterpiece, *The Prophet*. By the time he died in 1931, he had published 17 works in Arabic and English. His body was returned to the Bcharré hermitage for burial. In the last room of the museum, it provides a haunting epilogue to Gibran's life and work. *(L₤3000, students L₤2000. Open daily 9am-5pm; in winter Tu-Su 9am-5pm.)*

Since Bcharré's two budget hotels recently closed down, the least expensive accommodation is the **Palace Hotel,** 100m past the imposing St. Saba Church on the left. It offers fluffy carpeting, private baths, and a cavernous downstairs restaurant with a well-apportioned bar to complement its superb mountain views. (☎(03) 67 10 05; fax 67 14 60. Singles L₤38,000-45,000, doubles L₤53,000-68,000, triples L₤68,000-90,000.) The **Shallal Rest,** next to the waterfall on the road that leads from Bcharré to the Gibran Museum, is a better deal. The owner of Shallal, Farid Geoga, speaks fluent English and visitors get a suite replete with private bathroom and use of his swimming pool. One-person suites cost L₤30,000 and two-person suites L₤53,000. Shallal Rest also serves affordable food (L₤1500-3000) and beer (L₤2000). For a drink with a kick, try some of Farid's homemade Arak (L₤4000); just be sure to add water. (☎(03) 69 84 71. Open daily 9am-9pm.)

THE CEDARS OF LEBANON أرز الرب

Getting to the Cedars from Tripoli is difficult by any method other than private taxi. If traveling alone, take a service from Bcharré and hire a private taxi to the Cedars from there (negotiate fare down to L₤10,000). A L₤2000 donation is requested at the entrance to the cedar grove.

The **Cedars of Lebanon** (*Arz al-Rab*, "Cedars of God"), perched in the mountains about 5km from Bcharré, are more than just a grove of gigantic, rare trees. Cedars are a revered symbol of the modern Lebanese nation and one appears on the national flag. The grove is also the backdrop of some of the most beautiful ski slopes on the Mediterranean Coast. Most of the woods were decimated for timber trade with Egypt (where the resin was used for mummification), Phoenician shipbuilding, and Roman temple and tomb construction. The few remaining patches have been protected since 1876. A dead tree, skinned and varnished, creates a curious monument near the end of the roped path through the grove. Next to the tree, a stone stairway provides a view of the grove.

The grove is especially elegant when cloaked with snow. The tourist office in Beirut (see **Beirut: Practical Information,** p. 520) has detailed information on winter skiing and snowboarding in the area. Accommodations in the area are generally expensive resorts that rely on the high season (Dec.-Mar.) for survival. Among the more affordable options close to the Cedars is the **Centre Tony Arida.** Tony Arida operates a full-service complex for skiers, including rooms, ski area, restaurant, and nightclub. Clean, modern rooms with comfortable beds, soft pillows, and private toilets, come with breakfast. (Doubles L£38,000, L£53,000 during ski season.) Tony also rents skis for L£30,000 per day with a free ride to the resort and gives skiing lessons (L£23,000 per hr.). If Arida's not arounda, a smile and a few thousand Lebanese pounds should win you a lift with the next group that departs. The Resort boasts a **sports-bar restaurant** (open 24hr.) and a retro-70's **nightclub.** (Open Sa 10:30pm until the cows come home.) The **Hotel Mon Refuge** has cheaper singles for L£30,000 (L£45,000 with breakfast during ski season). But for those traveling en masse, the best deal at Mon Refuge is the **Chalet,** which sleeps 8-10 people for only L£150,700 (L£226,000 during ski season).

A restaurant stands across the street from the entrance to the grove. The staff speaks French and serves decent Lebanese fare for L£2000-4000. For those craving a quick bite, a well-stocked convenience store, **Nano Snack,** sits next door to the restaurant (non-alcoholic beverages, candy, and snacks L£1000; beer L£1500).

BEQA'A VALLEY بقعة

The Beqa'a Valley is situated between the snow-capped Mount Lebanon range and its arid counterpart, the Anti-Lebanon range. Its location between these two ranges minimizes rainfall; northern Beqa'a is quite dry. Several rivers, fed by mountain and valley springs, along with a vast man-made irrigation system, provide the water which makes central and southern Beqa'a Lebanon's breadbasket.

BA'ALBECK بعلبك   ☎08

Ba'albeck, 86km from Beirut, is the site of Lebanon's greatest Roman treasure—a majestic temple complex towering over the fertile Beqa'a plain. To the founding Phoenicians, the city was the center of worship for their leading deity, Ba'al. But when Alexander the Great and his band of merry Macedonians conquered the city in the 4th century BCE, they saw fit to make a few alterations. The city was redubbed **Heliopolis** (City of the Sun) and the names of the leading Phoenician gods were changed to honor three Roman deities: Jupiter (the Roman version of Ba'al), Venus (a Roman correlate to Ba'al's consort, Astarte), and Mercury (the messenger of the gods with no known Phoenician equivalent). When Christianity became the official religion of the Roman Empire in 325 CE, Emperor Constantine closed Ba'albeck's temples. Not to be outdone by polytheism's remains, Emperor Theodosius tore down Jupiter's altars in the Great Court of the complex and used the stones to build a basilica. The remains of the three apses of this basilica, originally oriented to the west, can still be seen in the upper part of the stairway in the Temple of Jupiter. After the Arab conquest in 636 CE, the temples were transformed into a fortress (*qala'a*) and the original Phoenician city's name was restored. Over the next millennium or so, the litany of conquerors common to Middle Eastern towns (Umayyads, Abbasids, Fatimids, Ayyubids, Mamluks, Ottomans) had their way with Ba'albeck. The ruins were first restored in the late 19th century by Germany's Kaiser Wilhelm II and later by the French after World War II.

Today Ba'albeck is perhaps best known as home to the headquarters of **Hizbullah** (see **Modern History,** p. 507). As a result, it was a virtual no-go for tourists until 1993. Ever-present pictures of **Ayatollah Khomeini,** gun-wielding Hizbullah fighters, and even the occasional **Qadaffi** might give tourists pause, but in the interests of local (and undoubtedly its own) prosperity, Hizbullah is making tourists feel welcome. Shopkeepers go out of their way to explain that their quarrel is with the US government, not US citizens. Though Ba'albeck beckons to Western tourists today, visitors should respect local customs, avoid tight or revealing clothing, and keep abreast of potential conflict in the area.

▐ GETTING THERE AND GETTING AROUND

The most common way to get to Ba'albeck is by **service** from Cola Bridge in Beirut (L£7000-8000). You may have to change cars in Shtawra, Beqa'a Valley's transport hub, but only pay once. **Buses** also run from Cola Bridge (L£3000). Leaving Ba'albeck, *service* can be hired to Shtawra (1hr., L£2000) and from there to most destinations including Homs and Sa'ida (30min., L£7500).

▐ ORIENTATION AND PRACTICAL INFORMATION

The approach to Ba'albeck from Beirut is via **Rue 'Abd al-Halim Hajar,** one of two main streets and home to two of Ba'albeck's three hotels. The other main drag is **Ras al-'Ain Boulevard,** intersecting Rue Hajar just past al-Shams Hotel. A left at the intersection leads to the temples; a right takes you along the river, past a park in Ba'albeck's most attractive area. On the other side of the park are the **Hizbullah Headquarters.** Following the boulevard east for about five kilometers leads to pleasant **Ras al-'Ain** (a spring), remains of a Mamluk shrine dating to 1277 CE, and bits and pieces of a Roman *nymphaeum* and shrine. Off Rue Hajar on Sheikh 'Abdullah Hill, about one kilometer before the intersection with Ras al-'Ain Blvd., a **quarry** is home to the world's largest stone.

Fransabank, along Ras al-'Ain Blvd., does not exchange traveler's checks. (☎37 18 70. Open M-F 8:15am-2:30pm, Sa 8:15am-noon.) Use one of the **exchange booths** along Rue Hajar. For the **police,** dial ☎112. The **tourist police** can also help. (☎37 11 77. Open 24hr.) Employees of **Pharmacy Ghassan,** on Rue Hajar, across the street and up from the al-Shams Hotel, speak a little English and French. (☎37 03 20. Open M-Sa 8am-10pm.) The **Central Telephone Office** is off to the left of Ras al-'Ain Blvd., about 150m from the main intersection. If you can't find it, ask locals for directions to the *"Markaz Telephone Centrale."* (Australia L£2400 per min. daily, L£2100 10pm-8am; US and Europe L£2100, L£1800.) The **post office** is several kilometers out of town along Ras al-'Ain Blvd. (Open M-F 8-11am, Sa 8am-2pm.)

▐ ACCOMMODATIONS AND FOOD

Old beds, some rock-hard, some squishy-soft, and one or two just right, come with a spectacular temple view at **Pension Shuman,** in front of the temples on Ras al-'Ain Blvd. European-style toilets are included. (☎37 01 60. L£10,500 per person.) Lunar-surfaced beds and clean bedrooms and bathrooms accompany slightly obstructed views at **Al-Shams Hotel,** on Rue Hajar just before the intersection. The owner is a friendly dentist who provides tooth-talk free of charge. (☎37 32 84. Dorms L£9000; doubles L£22,500.) For a step back into the heyday of Victorian tourism, powder your nose at the **Palmyra Hotel,** familiar to all in Ba'albeck. Built in 1874, its guest-book includes Kaiser Wilhelm II, Kemal Atatürk, and Charles de Gaulle. Many of the rooms have views of the temple (some even have balconies) and are cooled by a crisp valley breeze and somewhat noisy fans. If you are one of just a few guests, be sure to remind the management to turn on the hot water. The vine-lined cafe serves dinner on temple fragments, preserving a bygone era of European decadence. (☎37 02 30. Singles L£57,000; doubles L£79,500; triples L£94,500.)

Cheap Middle Eastern sandwich shops line Rue Hajar. The best of the lot is **Sindibad** (☎37 02 71), where the friendly owner wraps up flavorsome vegetables or meat for immediate consumption (L£1500-2500). Quality outdoor restaurants serving large portions of traditional Lebanese *mezze* line Ras al-'Ain Blvd. Peruse the bill carefully, as some restaurants specialize in ripping off tourists. Try **Jawhari Restaurant,** a nice outdoor setting across the park from Ras al-'Ain Blvd., a few doors down from Hizbullah headquarters. Snackers can get a small ice cream cone for just L£500, but more ambitious eaters can spend several thousand pounds on *mezze.* (☎37 39 43. Open daily 9am-2pm.)

👁 🎵 SIGHTS AND ENTERTAINMENT

⊠ TEMPLE COMPLEX. The **Temple of Jupiter** is easily recognized by its six remaining Corinthian columns, each towering 22 meters high. It is still a mystery as to how the massive stones were so precisely placed. The columns hint at the immensity of the original standing structure, which was completed around 60 BCE. Jupiter's **Propylaea** and **Hexagonal Court,** the first structures encountered, were added in the 3rd century CE. The circular **Temple of Venus,** facing the present-day entrance, dates from the same century. It is much smaller than the site's other temples and a fence prevents visitors from getting too close. The **Temple of Bacchus,** parallel to the much larger Temple of Jupiter and Great Court, is the best-preserved building in the complex; its size and the intricate detail of its adornments make it one of the greatest Roman temples in the world. The temple, completed in the 2nd century CE, was dedicated to Venus, but exquisite reliefs of grapes and poppies on the main door indicate that it was consecrated to the small cult of Bacchus, whose members were infamous for drinking wine and smoking opium during rituals. *(Open daily 8:30am to 30min. before sunset. L£12,000, Lebanese citizens L£7000, students with ID L£2500, free with a letter from the Beirut Ministry of Tourism saying you're a student. Free brochures at the entrance to the site in English, German, Spanish, French, and Arabic.)*

THE GREAT MOSQUE. The ruins of the Great Mosque face the entrance to the temple complex. Originally built as a Byzantine church dedicated to St. John, the edifice became a mosque around the year 700 CE.

BA'ALBECK FESTIVAL. The temple complex, and more specifically, the **Great Court,** is the site of the world-famous Ba'albeck Festival (see **The Arts,** p. 510). The festival began in 1955 and continued until 1974, drawing performers like Ella Fitzgerald, Rudolf Nureyev, and Margot Fonteyn. Over the last couple of years, the festival has been revived and has proved wildly successful. Get tickets in advance for next year's July through August bash—almost the entire country attends. *(☎(01) 37 31 50; email baalbeck@inco.com.lb. During festival, buses available round-trip from Beirut for around L£9000, and service available from both the Cola and Barbir bridges in Beirut for L£10,000. Festival tickets L£30,000-200,000; more if you buy from scalpers at the gate.)*

🏛 DAYTRIPS FROM BA'ALBECK

RAS BA'ALBECK رأس بعلبك
To get to Ras Ba'albeck, take minibus north from Ba'albeck (L£1000) or south from Hermel or Nahr al-Assi (L£500). Drivers will drop off at a turnoff, 1km from the town's center.

Ras Ba'albeck (the head of Ba'albeck) acquired its name because it provides a vantage point on all of northern Beqa'a, scrunched against the base of the Anti-Lebanon range. Romans used it as an outpost to identify attacking armies. Today, it is one of the few Christian pockets in the heavily Muslim northern Beqa'a.

The **Melkite (Greek Catholic) Monastery,** along the main street on the east side of town, is Ras Ba'albeck's main attraction. Ancient stonework on the bottom of the southern wall betrays its Roman builders. In 1759 CE, an earthquake destroyed most of the original structure, leaving only the small chapel built in 1111. The monastery was rebuilt soon after the earthquake and took its final form during reconstruction in 1943. Apart from the chapel, a museum features various artifacts from the Romans, early Christians, Byzantines, and Melkites. A small garden behind the monastery shelters remains of various Roman structures. (☎21 04 84. No official hours. Call ahead or arrive from 10am-4pm to guarantee admission.)

The ruins of a **Roman Temple** rest on the left side of the road into town. Little preservation work has been done, but the altar area is in decent shape and the rest of the site is worth a walk-through. Don't miss the few **old houses** still standing proudly amidst the drab concrete of the main street.

Several small sandwich shops dot the main drag near the center of town despite Ras Ba'albeck's few accommodations. On the northwest corner of the highway and main road intersection into town, **Restaurant Abou-Khalaf's** multilingual staff assembles relishing sandwiches for L£2000-3000. (☎21 00 62. Open 24hr.)

HERMEL حرمل

*To get to Hermel, take a **minibus** north from Ba'albeck (L£3000) or the hotel complex at Nahr al-Assi (L£500). To get to Deir al-Maroun, take a southbound minibus from Hermel or Nahr al-Assi (L£500). Walk several hundred meters down the road, under the powerlines, and turn left down the steep gravel road leading to a noisy water-pumping plant. Hang a left at the river and follow the trails along its bank until you reach the trail that leads to the cliffside gravel road, providing vehicular access to the monastery.*

Once a Hizbullah stronghold, Hermel grew rapidly during Lebanon's civil war as a safe haven for Shi'ites fleeing the fighting. After the war, Hermel became a hub for drug and counterfeit currency trade. Since 1998, the town has been under the firm control of Syrian and Lebanese authorities pledging funds to provide economic support. Though Hermel itself is nothing special, its ruins are quite captivating.

Deir al-Maroun, on a cliff overlooking Nahr al-Assi a few kilometers south of town, is intimately linked to the early days of Maronite Catholicism (see **Culture,** p. 509). St. Maron (founder of the Maronite order) established the monastery in the 5th century CE. The Maronites fled to Mount Lebanon and the monastery as a result of Byzantine emperor Justinian's persecution. In later centuries, Muslims utilized the structure as a fortress. The monastery has fallen into disrepair, but its remains hint at its former glory. The lower chamber is easily accessible, though the upper chamber requires a tricky climb up a well-creviced rock face. Ambitious explorers can ascend still farther, to the upper chamber's second (but not third) level via a spiral staircase. Be sure to use a flashlight and be careful of the well inside the upper chamber—the ground is 100m below. It's a good idea not to go alone, as it is a challenging walk.

Continue down a gravel road, visible from the road at the monastery's base, to reach the **Ain al-Zerga,** a well-shaded pool emerging from a spring in the rocks. To cool down further, gulp down a refreshing drink at the small snack bar.

Just south of Hermel and visible for miles around is a large boxlike stone structure capped by a pyramid. The structure, estimated to be over 2000 years old, is known as **Amor** (or **The Hermel Pyramid**). Decorated with hunting scenes, it is believed to be a tomb marker for a Syrian king. *(To get to the pyramid, ask the minibus driver for 'Amor' or 'the pyramid.' If he does not understand, gesture when the pyramid becomes visible, south from Nahr al-Assi bridge or Hermel (L£500), or north from the access road to Deir al-Maroun (L£250). It is a 500m uphill walk along an access road from the highway to the pyramid.)*

SOUTHERN BEQA'A VALLEY

ZAHLE زحلة   ☎08

Zahle is accessible by service from Cola Bridge in Beirut (L£7000). Minivans travel to Shtawra (L£2000), from which service go to Zahle (L£1000). You may also ask the driver to stop at Zahle. Private taxis from Beirut L£35,000-40,000; Shtawra L£5000-10,000.

Zahle is an enchanting red-roofed city renowned for the quality of its wine and the quantity of poetry its wine-imbibing poets have produced. Founded about three centuries ago, Zahle's first 150 years were tragic: the town was destroyed three times, each time by fire. Ever unflappable, Zahle rose like a phoenix and by 1885 a newly constructed railroad made the town a vital internal port used by Beirut, Damascus, Mosul, and even Baghdad.

Today, dozens of restaurants, most with outdoor seating, line the northern bank of the **Bardouni River.** It's easier to find excellent, economical accommodations here than to drink the well-priced *'araq.* Situated on Rue Brazil, directly across from the Khowry Hospital, **Hotel Akl** is set in an old house with high ceilings and fans. The rooms are spotless, the management friendly and trilingual, and the communal areas sunlit and inviting. Get a room facing away from the street to avoid the loud traffic. (☎82 07 01. L£25,000 per person, with private bath L£30,000. Tea or coffee L£1500.) Next door, the similarly set **Hotel Traboulsi,** is run by the friendly Umm George (George's mom). Be wary of the unpainted furniture (it may scratch), but take advantage of the tidy rooms, big beds, and patio sitting areas. (☎81 26 61. L£20,000 with private bath.)

Fine restaurants abound in Zahle. **Restaurant Le Coin,** at the end of Rue Brazil, hits the middle ground between fine dining and sandwich shop but the staff can be less than amiable to shaggy-looking, smelly backpackers. (☎32 01 44. *Mezze* L£11,000, *burak* L£7500 per dozen, local wine L£30,000 per bottle, *'araq* L£3000 per glass. Open daily 10am-1am.) Continuing north along the river into the casino area, you will encounter two of the grandes dames of Lebanese dining, the **Casino Arabi** and the **Casino Mhabba,** 80 and 100 years old, respectively. They are similar in character: both serve meals for L£30,000-60,000 per person. The Arabi is on the left as you walk upstream. (☎80 01 44. Open May-Oct. 6:30am-1:30am. V, MC, AmEx.) The Mhabba is across the stream from the Arabi on the side of the main walkway—you can't miss the lady making bread. (Open 12:30pm-2:30am. V, MC, AmEx.) If you want something cheaper, grab a sandwich for about L£2500 with some freshly squeezed juice or a fruit cocktail at **Adonis Cocktails and Sandwiches,** on the left side of the main street facing uphill after the taxi stand. A cool, clean interior with an selection of snacks and an English-speaking owner. (☎82 03 29. Open M-Sa 6:30am-10:30pm, Su 6:30am-noon and 5-10:30pm.)

▨ KSARA WINERY   ☎08

To get to the Ksara Winery, take a service from Zahle or Shtawra (L£1000-2000). Get out when you see the large 'Caves de Ksara' sign on a slanted-roofed building to the left.

The village of Ksara lies just south of Zahle. Although there are several wineries in the village, the oldest is the **Ksara Winery** (its sign says, **Caves de Ksara**). The site of a Crusader fortress, Ksara was already famed for its wine when the Jesuit order purchased it in 1856. The Jesuits then sold the estate in 1973, when the second Vatican council ordered that the church no longer participate in commercial activities. Ksara offers free, three-part tours with English, French, or Arabic speaking guides. You will first visit the tunnels in which wine is aged. Discovered and enlarged by Romans, these tunnels form an underground network totalling nearly two kilometers and remain between 11 to 13 degrees Celsius all year (ideal for storing wine). Bottles of wine dating back to 1918 and cognac dating back to 1910 are stored in the tunnels. The tour ends with a video and wine tasting. (☎81 34 95. Open daily 9am-7pm; in winter M-Sa 9am-4pm.)

ANJAR عنجر   ☎08

Service from Shtawra run to Mafra' Anjar (L£1000-2000); signs direct you down the 500m road to the site. To get to Shtawra, catch a service from Beirut's Cola Bridge (L£6000) or from Ba'albeck (L£3000). Alternatively, take minivans from Beirut bound for Zahle or Ba'albeck and ask to be dropped off at Shtawra (1½hr., L£2000). Open daily 7am-7pm. L£6000.

This amazing locale dating from the Umayyad dynasty is the largest and best preserved Umayyad site in all of Lebanon and perhaps the Middle East. Originally occupied by the Romans, Anjar was rebuilt by Caliph Walid ibn 'Abd al-Malik as a prosperous trade hub. Anjar covers a staggering 114,000 square meters constructed in an almost perfect square. Like most Roman towns, Anjar is oriented around the north-south **Cardo Maximus** and the east-west **Decumanus Maximus,** both lined with the remains of a columned arcade. The first building after the entrance on the left side is the **public bath,** complete with a vestiary (where bathers undressed and relaxed) and three separate rooms for cold *(frigidarium)*, warm *(tepidarium)*, and hot *(caldarium)* baths. The **Little Palace,** about 20m down the Cardo Maximus, is the best place to examine the intricate details that once adorned each building in the site.

The **Tetrapylon,** at the intersection of the Cardo Maximus and the Decumanus Maximus, shows Greek influence with Greek lettering on the bases and acanthus leaves on the Corinthian columns. On the same side of the Cardo Maximus is a mosque and the monumental **Great Palace.**

SOUTH OF BEIRUT

BEIT AL-DIN بيت الدين

17km down the coastal highway and 26km inland. Accessible by service (1hr., L£4000) or A/C bus (1 hr., L£3000) from Cola Bridge in Beirut. The Beirut tourist office has an informative floor plan and site map. Palace and museums open Tu-Su 9am-6pm. L£7500, Lebanese nationals L£5000, students studying in Lebanon L£2,000.

The ▧Beit al-Din ("House of Religion") Palace is a breathtaking example of early 19th-century Lebanese and Italian Baroque architecture. Built over a 30-year period by the dashing Emir Bechir al-Shehab II, ruler of Mount Lebanon for over half a century, it bears triumphant testimony to his long reign. The ground floor houses a less-than-inspiring **museum** dedicated to the life of Druze leader Kamal Jumblatt, a member of Parliament and cabinet minister. The collection of correspondence with world leaders and mementos of the successful political leader's life merit a visit. To the right upon entrance to the outer courtyard (Dar al-Baraniyya, where courtiers once mingled), is **al-Madafa,** a two-story structure originally used for receiving guests and now home to two museums. On the ground level is an exhibit of photographs by well-known Lebanese and European shutterbugs. Upstairs, the long corridors of the **Rashid Karami Archaeological and Ethnographic Museum** house an impressive model of the palace complex, Bronze and Iron Age pottery, and Roman glass. The middle section of the palace (directly ahead, with al-Madafa on the right) leads to a large courtyard complete with fountain and countryside view. Surrounding the courtyard are the well-appointed reception rooms used by the emir's secretaries. Notice the soldiers guarding the building in front of you. They are better dressed and taller than the average Lebanese soldier—they guard the president's summer house. Named **Dar al-Harim,** it once housed the private apartments of the emir. To the right of the presidential pad is the palace's hammam, and beyond the baths lies the tomb of Sitt Chams, the emir's first wife, to which they added his ashes in 1947. Stands in the palace complex sell soft drinks, snacks, and grilled sandwiches.

Emir Bechir built three palaces, one for each of his sons—Qassim, Khalil, and Amine. Qassim's is now in ruins and Khalil's is used as Beit al-Din's seat of local government, but Amine's estate has proved to be Bechir's greatest investment. The **Emir Amine Palace** perches just up the hill to the right of Beit al-Din. The facade of the central courtyard (Dar al-Wusta) is among the palace's most beautiful features. It is now a fully restored luxury hotel with 24 large, seemingly perfect rooms, many with private terraces. It may be hard to justify spending L£185,000 for a single or L£220,000 for a double during high season, but the prices are slashed by 50% come low season (Oct.-May) on top of the 15-20% student discount offered when the hotel is empty. (☎ (05) 50 13 15. V, AmEx.) The hotel's terrace restaurant, **Al-Diwan Terrace,** has a great view of the valley, but the high prices for food (sandwiches L£8100-11,600) probably rule out anything more than an overpriced soft drink (L£3500) or Almaza (L£5800). The **Al-Hatemia Restaurant,** near the main square, is more affordable. (☎ 50 05 26. Grilled sandwiches L£2500. Beer L£2000 at table, L£1000 to go. Open daily 7:30am-4am.) The **Beit al-Din Festival,** held every July and August in the palace's outdoor courtyard, draws thousands of visitors and features internationally renowned musicians. Last year's show featured the Budapest Concert Orchestra, Joe Cocker, and Lebanese superstar Fairouz. Tickets for individual shows usually run from L£25,000 to L£225,000, depending on the seats and artists. Ask at the tourist office for details.

SA'IDA (SIDON) صيدا ☎ 07

Sa'ida, known as Sidon to the Phoenicians, is 48km south of Beirut and was one of the three great Phoenician city-states, along with Byblos and Tyre. Many of Sa'ida's ancient artifacts were plundered and sold by treasure hunters in the 19th century—some have recently turned up on the black market. Lebanon's third largest city has a rich history, with evidence of habitation dating from 4000 BCE. The port flourished in the Phoenician era (12th-10th centuries BCE) and peaked during the occupation of the Achaemenid Persians (550-330 BCE). Although glass was its biggest industry, Sidon achieved fame primarily for its purple dye, made from the small shell of the Murex snail (see **To Dye For,** p. 547). Like other Phoenician city-states, Sidon suffered under a succession of conquerors, including Alexander the Great, the Romans, the Crusaders, and Salah al-Din. Skirmishes continued until 1291 CE, when the city capitulated to the Mamluks. It fell into obscurity during the French Mandate, but revived as an urban center over the past century. Modern Sa'ida is not as fun-filled as its ancient incarnation was; mediocre places to stay and eat, nonexistent nightlife, and the ugly cement architecture characterize Sa'ida today. The Phoenician and Crusader ruins, and a lively *souq*, however, make Sa'ida a worthwhile daytrip.

▣ GETTING THERE AND GETTING AROUND

Buses from Beirut's Cola Bridge should cost L£750, while **service** cost around L£2500. Both buses (L£500) and *service* (L£3000) depart regularly from Sahet al-Nejmeh on **Rue Riad al-Solh** for **Sur.** It's also possible to catch a *service* to **Shtawra** (L£7500) in the Beqa'a Valley.

▧ ▨ ORIENTATION AND PRACTICAL INFORMATION

Though Sa'ida is large, almost all sights (and the only hotel) fall within a concentrated area. Buses and *service* arrive and depart from **Sahet al-Nejmeh,** a bustling roundabout filled with patisseries on **Rue Riad al-Solh,** the main north-south street. Buses from Beirut follow this road past the beach and fairgrounds. The street continues past Sahet al-Nejmeh to the Castle of St. Louis, where it becomes **Rue Fakhr al-Din.** A right turn off Riad al-Solh leads to the parallel **Rue Shakrieh,** home to the only hotel in Sa'ida. Follow Rue Shakrieh north toward the sea to reach the entrance to the Sea Castle.

Just south of Sahet al-Nejmeh, on the left of Rue Riad al-Solh, next to Grand Stores, is **Kotob Exchange,** one of the few places that exchanges traveler's checks. (☎ 72 03 22. L£3000 charge per check. Open M-Sa 8:30am-2pm, F 8:30am-noon.) In an emergency, call the **police** (☎ 112) or an **ambulance** (☎ 140). Just across the street from the Kotob Exchange is **Pharmacy Atef Bissat,** an extensive drugstore with the longest hours in town and a staff that speaks English and French. (☎ 72 18 21. Open daily 8am-10:30pm.) **Hamond Hospital** (☎ 72 31 11 or 72 10 21) is the best in Sa'ida. The **post office** is about 200m north of Sahet al-Nejmeh (toward Beirut) on the left of Rue Riad al-Solh. (Open M-Th 8am-2pm, F 8am-1pm.)

▥ ▢ ACCOMMODATIONS AND FOOD

The only hotel in Sa'ida proper is **Hotel d'Orient** on Rue Shakrieh, 200m south of the Sea Castle (Arabic sign: نازل الشرق, *Nazel al-Sharq*). Dorm-style rooms have grimy floors, miserable mattresses, and a smelly communal bathroom. Upstairs rooms are cleaner with TVs and fans. (☎ 72 03 64. Dorms L£20,000 per person; singles and doubles L£25,000; triples L£30,000.) The four-star **Mounes Hotel,** halfway between Sa'ida and Sur in Sarafand, is a splurge, but comes with a saltwater pool, dock for ocean swimming, outdoor restaurant, private baths, old refrigerators, and A/C. Hop a bus or *service* bound for Sur and ask to get out at the Mounes. (☎ (03) 66 66

TO DYE FOR Since antiquity, the royal wardrobes of the world have been made from fabrics of the deepest purple hue. The color's regal associations originated off the coast of Sa'ida, where two species of **mollusk**, *Murex* and *Buccinum*, live in great numbers. Legend has it that the intense purple ink within their shells was discovered when the lovesick god **Melkart** was wooing the nymph **Tyrus**. One day Melkart's dog playfully bit into a shell and his muzzle turned purple. Tyrus then demanded that Melkart make her a purple garment from the shell in exchange for the consummation of his passion. Melkart quickly pulled some strings, establishing a powerful precedent for the dye's importance in trade and romance. The Phoenicians' production of purple dye was considerably more complex and messy, and probably less rewarding. Narrow-necked baskets baited with frog or mussel meat were placed in the sea; when a quantity of mollusks were gathered, they were brought to the factories. The yellowish sacs, which turn purple when exposed to light, were removed and boiled in lead pots. The Phoenicians did not like to clean up after themselves—snail shell refuse now forms the 50m high Murex Hill.

57; fax (07) 39 06 07; email fakihco@cyberia.net.lb. Singles L£45,000; doubles L£60,000; triples L£75,000. Pool L£5000 for non-guests, kids L£3000.)

Food options in Sa'ida are as unspectacular as the accommodations. The **government rest house** provides outdoor patio seating amid palm trees and views of the Sea Castle. Factor in the 20% tax when choosing *à la carte* among salads (L£3000-7500) and meat or fish entrees (L£5500-17,000), or get the palatable tourist menu (L£18,000, tax included), reserved for groups of six or more. (☎72 24 69. Open daily 11am-midnight. V, MC.) **Al-'Arabi** is the first restaurant you pass when coming from Beirut, about 2km north of central Sa'ida on the right side of Rue Riad al-Solh. *Mezze* and entree should run about L£15,000 person, plus drinks: Almaza is L£3000, cocktails average L£7500. (☎72 03 42. Open daily noon-midnight. V, MC, AmEx.) Out in Sarafand, try the **'Aroosat Kheyzaran,** 350m up the main road toward Sa'ida on the left side; there is no English sign. This restaurant specializes in weddings, but you'll betroth yourself to its free pool and deck. Fish and *mezze* for two cost L£15,000-20,000. (☎(03) 24 92 31. Open daily noon-midnight.) Pastries are Sa'ida's specialty and easy to find. **Patisserie Kanaan,** on the right just south of Sahet al-Nejmeh, has a secret recipe for their famous ice cream. (☎72 02 71. L£3000 for a large bowl. Open daily 5am-midnight.)

👁 SIGHTS

The **Old City** developed at the end of the Crusader period and contains *souqs, khans,* and other medieval remnants. The most interesting site in Sa'ida proper is the **Sea Castle,** a Crusader fortress built in 1228 on a small island, connected to the shore by a stone walkway. While the southwestern tower combines Crusader and Mamluk influences, a small Ottoman-era mosque sits atop the northeastern Crusader tower. Fishermen mend their nets on the foul-smelling and polluted beach by the entrance. Impressive *souqs* lie between the Sea Castle and the **Castle of St. Louis,** a ruined 13th-century structure erected on top of a Fatimid fortress during a crusade led by French King Louis IX. Locals call it al-Muizz citadel, as it was restored by al-Muizz li-Din, a Fatimid Caliph. Unfortunately, there is no regular public access and the gates surrounding it are usually locked. The **Great Mosque** is south of the *souq* on the way to the Castle of St. Louis. It was built during the Crusades, then converted into a mosque by the Mamluks. Most of the current structure is new, as it was rebuilt after being destroyed during the Israeli invasion of 1982. **Murex Hill** (see **To Dye For,** above) is just south of the Castle of St. Louis. *(Open daily 8am-6pm. L£2000, children under 10 L£1000.)*

The 🏛**Temple of Echmoun** (known locally as *Bustan al-Sheikh*), about 2½km out of town along the fast flowing Nahr al-Awali, is impressive. Built in the 7th century

BCE to commemorate Echmoun, Sidon's favorite god, the temple is the most complete Phoenician site remaining today. This god of healing and medicine, represented by a snake coiled around a staff, lives on in the medical symbol known as a *caduceus.* Most healing happened in the **sacred basin,** to the left of the main temple as seen from downhill. A canal system and nearby spring fed the 5th- century basin. The large, pyramidal temple is the oldest part of the complex, while the colonnade, surrounded on both sides by mosaics, is a later Roman addition. Climb to the top of the temple for a good view. Don't miss the **Throne of Astarte,** carved out of granite and flanked by two sphinxes. It was Astarte who made Echmoun a god. *(With the beach on the left, follow Rue Riad al-Solh north. After the fairgrounds, take a right and then bear left following the bank of the river. The temple is on the left. Taxis cost about LÉ4000; ask for Bustan al-Sheikh. Open daily 8am-6pm. Free.)*

SUR (TYRE) صور   ☎07

The modern city of Sur sits alongside and atop the remains of the ancient Phoenician city-state of Tyre, 79km south of Beirut. When Herodotus, the "Father of History," visited Tyre's Temple of Hercules in the 5th century BCE, the city had already been in existence for over 3000 years. The original settlement consisted of two islets, later connected by a landfill by King Hiram in the 10th century BCE. The next two centuries witnessed a golden age under the Phoenicians. Its most famous citizen was the doomed princess Dido, who found herself on the losing end of a power-struggle and set sail for the ruined north African city of Kambeh, later founding Carthage. At the time, Tyre was so important that it lent its name to the Mediterranean, then known as the Tyrean Sea. During the 6th century BCE, the Babylonian Nebuchadnezzar besieged the city, but the headstrong Tyreans resisted for 13 years. The 4th century BCE brought Alexander the Great, cutting his bloody swath to Persia. For seven months the Tyreans held the city, frustrating the great Macedonian so much that he destroyed half of Sur and massacred or enslaved 30,000 of its residents. The Romans arrived in 64 BCE, the Umayyads in 634 CE, the Crusaders in 1124, the Mamluks in 1291, and the Ottomans in the 16th century.

Modern-day Sur has amazing Roman ruins, including one of history's largest hippodromes. Though the city stands 20km north of the Israeli border, Tyre was safe at press time. Check the news and ask locals about the situation before visiting.

█ GETTING THERE AND GETTING AROUND

White **vans** (LS500) and A/C Pullman **buses** (LS1500) connect Sur to Sa'ida. From Beirut, change at Sa'ida by **microbus** (full trip LS1000-1250) or Pullman bus (full trip LS2500-3000). Direct **service** run from Beirut's Cola Bridge (LS5000-6000).

✴ ▮ ORIENTATION AND PRACTICAL INFORMATION

Modern Sur rests on a promontory that was once an island but has long since been silted over. The two harbors are named according to what they face, with the **Sidonian harbor** to the north and the **Egyptian harbor** to the south. The **taxi stand** and **bus station** are in the center of town, a few meters from the Sidonian port. Walk south, toward the Egyptian harbor, and take the first left to reach **Rue Abu Dib,** Sur's main shopping thoroughfare. The first right off this street leads to the impressive ruins, **Area One** (locals call it **Assar Ja'fariyya**). A 25-minute walk farther along Abu Dib leads to Sur's highlight, the **Roman Ruins,** known as **Assar Romaniyya.** The **rest house** lies 150m toward the sea from the entrance to the ruins.

The **telephone office** is 200m east of the taxi stand across from the UN building on Rue Bawaba (Open 24hr.) The same building also serves as the **post office.** (☎ 74 00 18. Open M-F 7am-5pm, Sa-Su 8-11am.) With the post office on the right, the first pharmacy down the street is **Saed Pharmacy,** which has a helpful English- and French-speaking staff. (Open M-Sa 7:30am-6pm, Su 7:30am-2pm.) In an emergency, call the **police** (☎74 00 09) or an **ambulance** (☎140).

ACCOMMODATIONS AND FOOD

Sur's accommodations are limited to two pricey options. The nicer (and more expensive) of the set is the **rest house.** Its air-conditioned bedrooms with large, comfortable beds and great bathrooms provide a nice rest, as do the pool, jacuzzi, sauna, and nearby beach. For the more active visitors, a workout room awaits. (☎ 74 06 77; fax 34 51 63; www.resthouse-tyr.com.lb. Singles L£147,000, in winter L£75,000; doubles L£147,000, in winter L£90,000. V, MC, AmEx.) The **Murex Hotel,** about 200m north along the coast from Area One, is directly across the street from the beach and less demanding on the pocketbook. (☎34 71 11. Singles L£105,000, in winter L£67,500; doubles L£127,500, in winter L£82,500. 10% student discount. V, MC, AmEx.)

Cheap eateries cluster around the taxi stand. For a somewhat authentic taste of Italy, try **Pizzeria Italia** on Rue Abu Dib across from Restaurant Abu Dib. (☎74 25 62. Pizzas L£1500-L£9000. Open daily 9am-11pm.) For a cheap, more authentic meal, try **Ali Restaurant,** along the seacoast about 250m southeast of Area One. Sandwiches (L£2000-3000) and full meals (L£10,000) are available. Refresh yourself with a tall glass of freshly-squeezed fruit juice for L£1000. (☎74 13 05. Open daily 7am-11pm.) **Le Phénecien,** one of the last buildings along the harborside toward the sea, has a star-studded past. Once owned by Pepe the Pirate, it was frequented by some of the same jet-setters who chilled at his Byblos Fishing Club (see p. 530). A Lebanese feast costs L£20,000—cap it off with Almaza for L£2000 per bottle. Note the inscription by Bridget Bardot above the bar. (☎74 05 64. Open daily 8am-5pm.) For the only nightlife in town, visit the **Tenit Pub and Restaurant,** between the port and the taxi stand. UN peacekeepers quaff pints of Guinness and Almaza (L£4000-5000) while devouring grilled seafood. (☎74 09 87. Meals with drinks L£19,500. Open daily 10am-3:30pm and 6pm-midnight; closed during Ramadan.)

SIGHTS

ROMAN RUINS. From the entrance to the site, bear right, crossing from the entrance road to the Roman road that leads to the monumental **archway.** Pass through the large **necropolis,** which holds hundreds of marble sarcophagi. Some tombs are blocked by makeshift barriers, while others are open to visitors. Once reaching the archway, a large **cardo** comes into view. To the left is the former **aqueduct,** along with Sur's **hippodrome** (once buried under six meters of sand). One of the world's largest and best preserved, the hippodrome can hold over 20,000 spectators. Check out the stonework underneath the bleachers before climbing the stairs for stellar views. (☎75 05 30. Open daily 7am-7pm. L£5000, students L£2500.)

AREA ONE. The small ruins at **Assar Ja'fariyya,** also called Area One, are filled with swirled colonnades, intricate mosaic floors, remarkably well-preserved living quarters, and the remains of Roman temples and sarcophagi. What appear to be islands are actually the remains of Phoenician breakwaters. (Open daily 8am-8pm. L£5000, students L£2500.)

DAYTRIPS FROM SUR

TOMB OF HIRAM

On the right hand side of the Sur-Qana road as you approach Qana. Service (L£1500-2000) run from Sur as do private taxis (L£5000 to the tomb, L£7000-8000 to Qana). Service continue to Qana (L£500-1000).

The **Tomb of Hiram** is commonly believed to be that of the famous king of Tyre, dating back to 1200-800 BCE. The area around the tomb is littered with rubbish and the tomb itself has been defaced with graffiti. Still, its age, sheer immensity, and accompanying **sarcophagus** make it worth a look. The sarcophagus for Penymer, architect of many (now lost) Phoenician monuments, is in the same style as that of King Ahiram of Jbail, but is now on display at the National Museum in Beirut.

QANA قانا

Take a service from Sur (30min., L£2000-3000). Do not stay late, as service are virtually non-existent at night. On the weekends, hire a private taxi (L£7000-8000).

According to the Bible, Jesus performed his first miracle—changing water into wine—in a cave near a place called Cana of Galilee. Many biblical scholars have identified modern Qana as that town and Qana's two adjacent caves as the actual site of this miracle. A system of steps leads down the valley wall to the caves. The first contains a carving of a woman believed to be the bride of Qana and is aptly named **Woman's Cave.** Step inside to see carvings of the last supper adorning the cave's right-side walls. Continue down the steps to reach the cave where the miracle itself is said to have occurred, a conclusion first reached in 1976 by Professor of Archeology, Dr. Yusef Hourani (Lebanon University).

After spelunking, head back toward town to see the ancient **wine presses,** which also date back to nearly biblical times. The presses are difficult to locate (they lie behind a valley-side home near the city center), so it might be a good idea to ask a local for help. Unfortunately, Qana's recent history has not been trouble-free. In response to Hizbullah shellings in 1996, Israel accidently struck a UN hospital and refugee center nearby, killing 102 Lebanese civilians. A **monument** to these victims resembling three large sails now rises high above the main street.

SOUTH LEBANON

For twenty years South Lebanon was the site of constant warfare between Israeli-backed Christian militias and Hizbullah-backed Muslim militias. This came to an end in May of 2000 when the Israelis withdrew from the 60km strip of land along the Israeli border that they had been occupying since 1985. Today, the area is becoming increasingly popular with tourists, Lebanese or otherwise.

CAUTION! Since May 2000, when Israel pulled out of South Lebanon, the area has been open to visitors. Travelers should exercise extreme caution, however, and keep abreast of current events in the region to avoid going during times of unrest. It is safest to go with an **organized tour** such as the one offered by Concord Travel and Tourism (see below). Never leave visibly traveled roads without a guide as there are still **landmines** in the area. A knowledgeable guide will be willing to walk directly in front of you. Bring your **passport.**

▐ GETTING THERE

Nabatiyyeh is the transport hub for South Lebanon. **Microbuses** leave from Beirut's Cola Bridge (3hr., L£3000) and from Sa'ida (2hr., L£1500); **service** charge twice as much. At press time, transportation within South Lebanon was not reliable and accommodations were limited. The best way to visit the area is through an organized tour. **Concord Travel and Tourism** operates a one-day English-language tour, which leaves from its office in the Saroulla Building on Rue Hamra in Beirut. The tour includes the Beaufort Castle, the al-Khiyam prison, Marjayoun, and the Fatima Gate. Transportation is on an air-conditioned coach. Reserve three days ahead of time. (☎ (1) 34 06 44. Lunch included. Tours F-Su. L£25,000.)

Before heading on, stop at Nabatiyyeh's **Souq al-Itnein,** or Monday market. During this all-day budget traveler's paradise, local traders line the main streets of Nabatiyyeh, selling everything from produce to clothing and music.

BEAUFORT CASTLE قلعة الشقيف

The Beaufort Castle is difficult to reach without an organized tour. There are no guides at the castle. Hiring a private taxi from Nabatiyyeh is expensive (L£22,700-30,300).

The imposing ▨Beaufort Castle (*Qal'at al-Shaqif* in Arabic) stands on a hilltop and provides an excellent vantage point for viewing the surrounding region. The castle was built by French Crusaders in 1179 CE and later reinforced by Muslims, who used it as a lookout point over the strategic road from Damascus and the Beqa'a Valley. Facing the castle from the western side, you'll see ruins dating from Crusader times to your right and early Muslim times to your left. Although time and conflict (the castle was one of the last outposts abandoned by the Israelis in May 2000) have taken their toll on the exterior, many of the interior chambers remain in good condition. For more recent history, ask your guide to show you the Hizbullah lookout post, and stop for a look at Israel. Be warned that some climbs are steep and difficult; hiking boots are recommended. The area surrounding the castle is heavily **mined**—do not wander off into the countryside.

MARJAYOUN مرجعيون   ☎07

Microbuses run to Marjayoun from Nabatiyyeh (L£2000). Service are hard to find (L£5000).

Founded in 1139 CE, Marjayoun ("meadow of springs") was known for its prosperity before the conflict with Israel began. Today, this small town near the Israeli border is an excellent starting point from which to visit the Fatima Gate or the al-Khiyam prison.

Uphill from the main square is **St. Georges,** a beautiful Greek Orthodox church. The paintings and chandeliers inside are stunning, but electric candle mania has unfortunately hit this church, marring the overall aura of the place. There are no set hours. To be let in, ask a townsperson to take you to Father John Dib.

The **post office** is just off the main square. (Open M-Sa 8am-2pm.) Currently, the only establishment approaching budget accommodation lies outside of town. The **Racha Hotel,** a few kilometers before Marjayoun on the left side of the road from Nabatiyyeh, has clean, recently renovated doubles with fridge, private bath, and air-conditioning. (☎(03) 75 24 26. Breakfast L£7500; lunch L£15000. Doubles L£53,000.) For a quick bite to eat, try **Falafel Imad,** 300m from the main square, on the right when walking toward Nabatiyyeh; look for the sign with red Arabic writing on a white background. A falafel sandwich costs L£1500. Several hundred meters south is the **Rajed Restaurant,** which features delicious steak sandwiches for L£2000. (☎(03) 70 56 53. Open daily 8am-9pm.)

FATIMA GATE باب فاطمة

Take a service from Marjayoun (L£3000-4000). Private taxis (L£12,000-15,000 round-trip) may occasionally have trouble getting through the checkpoints on the way to the gate.

This border crossing point for Lebanese working in Israel during the occupation became a prime tourist attraction and star of international television news during and following the Israeli withdrawal. Buy some roast corn or a Hizbullah keychain from one of the vendors and glance across the border at the well-fortified military posts flying the Israeli flag and the settlement beyond.

AL-KHIYAM PRISON سجن الخيم

Take a service (L£3000) or private taxi (L£5000) from Marjayoun. Bring a flashlight as some rooms are quite dark. Tours in English. Open daily 9am-5pm. Free.

Originally constructed in 1932 as a camp for French forces, the al-Khiyam prison is one of the more depressing sights in Lebanon. Lebanese traveling through the South make a point of visiting this detainment camp where the South Lebanese Army (SLA) held their political enemies. Soon after the Israeli withdrawal, the prison was opened to tourists. It is now in the process of being turned into a museum; all rooms have signs in Arabic and English. Many tours are led by former prisoners, who describe the torture they endured and the 40 day wait between abbreviated showers.

HASBAYA حسبايا   ☎03

Hasbaya can be reached by service from Marjayoun (L£7000) or Nabatiyyeh (L£10,000), by microbus (L£10,000) from Nabatiyyeh, or by private taxi from Marjayoun (L£15,000).

Hasbaya's **citadel** dates to the Crusader period and was turned into a palace by the Shehab princes in the 12th century. There is an extensive system of cellars to your right as you enter; you'll need a flashlight to explore them. As you walk farther into the main courtyard, you'll notice the residences still occupied by the Shehab family, descendants of the princes. In fact, there remains one prince, Talal Irslan, who serves in the national parliament. Beyond the courtyard are the upper levels of the compound. Though old furniture lies about in disarray, spiral staircases, stunning arches, and impressive stonework make this a worthwhile stop. Ask the family's permission to enter. (Open daily 8am-8pm.) Across the street is the Hasbaya **mosque,** built in the 13th century, with thick walls similar to those of the citadel. It has been well-preserved—its intricate stonework was not, as in many other mosques, plastered over and painted puke green during the 1930s. (Women welcome, but must cover their heads. Closed during prayer times.)

El Amana Restaurant has sandwiches for around L£1500, as well as the occasional spare room. Ask Asad if he can arrange a room for the night. (☎26 70 11, ext. 2054. Restaurant open daily 6:30am-11pm. Rooms US$7-10 per person per night.)

JEZZINE جزين   ☎07

Accessible by service from Sa'ida (L£3000).

The area now called Jezzine has been inhabited since Roman times, but the modern town was founded in the 18th century. Today, this Maronite Christian town is a picturesque valleyside home to craftsmen and well-priced (but not cheap) hotels. A 40m waterfall, said to be the highest in Lebanon, drops from the edge of town into the deep valley. In 1635, Prince Fakhr al-Din hid from the Ottomans in a cave in this valley. He was eventually captured and taken to Istanbul after Ottoman soldiers used smoke to drive him out. The Israelis controlled the hills surrounding Jezzine from 1982 to 1999 and frequently entered the town, which was controlled by the SLA. Now that the Israelis have left, Jezzine is flooded with tourists. Visitors are advised to arrive early if they hope to find a seat at one of the town's many cafes.

Among the town's sights are the imposing **municipal buildings,** on the right as you enter town from Sa'ida, constructed in 1898. Next to the Jezzine Pharmacy is the **Bsharn Rhuyyen Factory,** where local men craft the cutlery for which Jezzine is known. The workers don't mind visitors watching them work. (Usually open for viewing M-Sa 8am-1pm.) Nearby shops sell these wares, often at half the price they would fetch in Beirut. Single utensils and letter openers can be had for less than L£7600, but for a flashy sword you'll have to fork out nearly L£3,000,000. Jezzine also has a few **churches** dating from the 18th century.

There are no hostels or pensions in Jezzine, but the **Wehbi Hotel** provides a lot of bang for your buck, with large, well-appointed rooms and private baths. Although there is no air-conditioning or fans, large windows let in a nice breeze which keeps the room temperature pleasant even in the height of summer. (☎78 02 17. Singles L£37,800; doubles L£53,000; triples L£68,000. 10% student discount with ID.) The best restaurant in town, the **Rock of the Waterfall,** just off the main drag and next to the waterfall, overlooks the valley. Traditional Lebanese fare will set you back about L£22,700, but the view is priceless. (☎(03) 42 55 25. Almaza L£3000. Pepsi L£1500. Open daily 9am-midnight.)

The **police** can be reached at ☎78 00 89. There is a **hospital** (☎78 01 06) on the main road on the way in from Sa'ida. The **Jezzine Pharmacy** lies on the main commercial street, one street over from the road to Sa'ida, to the right when facing the town from Sa'ida and the valley. It is large and well-stocked, and its staff speaks English and French. (☎78 03 05. Open M-Sa 8am-1pm and 3-9pm, Su 8am-noon.)

RASHAYA رشاية   ☎03

*The red-roofed town is reachable by minibus from Chtura and Zahle (45min.-1hr.,
L£1000). Rashaya is the closest you can get to Mount Hermon without hiring a private
taxi or renting a car, so it is frequently used as a starting point for treks up the mountain.*

Rashaya is located at the southern end of the Beqa'a Valley in the shadow of
Mount Hermon, the highest peak in the Anti-Lebanon range. Most of the town was
destroyed by Druze rebels in the 1920s and has been rebuilt since.

   The **citadel** is currently used as a base by the army; the soldiers tend to be very
friendly and accommodating to visitors, and it is very likely that there will be an
English or (even more likely) French speaker handy to serve as a tour guide. As
always, ask before photographing anything that might be military-related. Originally built in 1800 for use by the Shehab princes, it was reconstructed by the
French in 1923 to serve with the Suweida and Hasbaya citadels as a bulwark
against rebellious Druze. On October 23, 1925, British-backed Druze rebels
besieged the citadel. A plaque just inside commemorates the imprisonment of the
prime minister, foreign minister, and other officials of the nascent Lebanese
republic here on November 22, 1943. (Open daily 8am-8pm. Free.) The reconstructed **souq** lies just off the town square. Various stores sell crafts and jewelry
(some locally made) at generally reasonable prices. One of the shops even features a workshop where visitors can watch the production of gold and silver jewelry. (Most shops open daily 8:30am-7:30pm.)

   If visiting the citadel makes you hungry, head over to the **Castle Restaurant,** at
the entrance to the castle, for a sandwich (L£1000-2000). It affords a great view of
the citadel and the countryside downhill. (☎87 21 42. Open daily 8am-11:30pm.)
The staff at the **al-Kalaa Pharmacy** in the *souq* speaks French and a little English.
(Open M-Sa 8am-9pm, Su 9am-7pm.)

MOUNT HERMON جبل الشيخ   ☎03

Nearby Mount Hermon is often called the holy mountain. Phoenician and Roman
temples were usually built to face it, and it is considered holy by Druze, Muslims,
and Christians. In fact, this is where the Bible says Jesus advised his followers to
"turn the other cheek" (Matthew 5:39). Many travelers say the best way to ascend
the mountain is by donkey. **Mehdi Fayek** (☎96 46 05), a local guide, provides donkeys and leads treks up the mountain. For one person, an overnight trek will cost
L£45,400, for groups of four or more the price drops to L£15,150-22,700 per person.
The journey takes you to a monastery on the mountainside and to the summit.
Most travelers spend the night in a cave. Be warned, however, that the summit is
technically in **Syrian territory.** *Let's Go* does not recommend illegal border crossings (especially for those who do not hold a valid Syrian visa), but the Syrian side
of the mountain and the surrounding areas are currently a UN-occupied security
zone, and travelers report that friendly Swedish peacekeepers permit trekkers
from the Lebanese side of the border to reach the summit.

LEBANON

SYRIA سوريا

US$1=45 SYRIAN POUNDS (S£)	S£100=US$2.22
CDN$1=S£30.06	S£100=CDN$3.33
UK£1=S£67.23	S£100=UK£1.49
IR£1=S£53.15	S£100=IR£1.88
AUS$1=S£25.77	S£100=AUS$3.88
NZ$1=S£20.66	S£100=NZ$4.84
SAR1=S£6.44	S£100=SAR15.54
EUR1=S£41.86	S£100=EUR2.39
JD1 (JORDANIAN DINAR) =S£63.38	S£100=JD1.58
L£100 (LEBANESE POUNDS) =S£2.99	S£100=L£3349.75
TL100,000 (TURKISH LIRA) =L£7.30	S£100=TL1370.28

CURRENCY

PHONE CODES | **Country Code: 963. International dialing prefix: 00.**

Syria's unique position at the crossroads of Asia, Africa, and Europe has made it a bastion of civilization. Encapsulated by the Caspian Sea, the Indian Ocean, the Black Sea, the Nile River, and the trade-routes connecting them, Syria has been home to at least seven great empires. The silk route, linking China with the Mediterranean, made Doura Europos an ancient center of trade. The kingdom of Ugarit (Ras Shamra) on the Mediterranean coast developed the first alphabet in history and a royal palace at Ebla (see p. 601) contains one of the largest documentary archives of the ancient world. It was in Syria that copper was made pliable and bronze invented.

After a recent history of closed regimes and enmity with Israel, Syria is now open to travelers. From the sparsely populated Syrian Desert in the east to the west's balmy seashore, the country's natural beauty remains unmolested by masses of tourists, as backpackers and tourist groups are only beginning to discover Syria's treasures. Get there before they do and discover magnificent Roman ruins, medieval castles, and prices that haven't changed since the dawn of time. Syria is one of the last frontiers of budget adventure in the Eastern Mediterranean.

HIGHLIGHTS OF SYRIA

Splendid stronghold of a city of rebels, the ruins of **Palmyra** (p. 580) defy the tug of time with the same flourish with which its queen once resisted the Romans.

This ain't just a castle—it's a castle on Crac. See **Crac des Chevaliers** (p. 586), the Crusader fortress that even Salah al-Din couldn't conquer.

LIFE AND TIMES

For years, Egypt and Israel garnered the glitz and glamour of the Middle East while Syria played the ugly second cousin. But in the last decade, travelers have begun to discover what Syrians knew all along—Syria is the hidden jewel of the Middle East. The ruins rival Semitic sites anywhere and the developing economy keeps prices low enough to soothe budget travelers' pockets. Syria's authentic air has been preserved, thanks partially to former President Hafez al-Assad's efforts. Its inhabitants, nevertheless, are pleasantly helpful and accommodating to tourists. Just walk to the nearest *souq* to see what Syria has to offer: authentic Middle Eastern culture uninterrupted by the outside world.

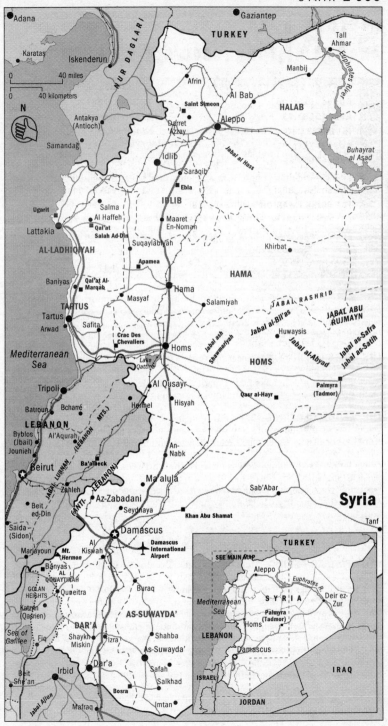

HISTORY

ANCIENT HISTORY (8000 BCE-1516 CE)

EARLY HISTORY. Andrea Pavrot, a former director of the Louvre Museum in Paris, once said, "Each person has two homelands: his own and Syria." Her words are not far from the truth. The oldest alphabet in the world, and the precursor to most ancient and modern alphabets, was discovered at **Ugarit,** a site near Lattakia (p. 590). Excavations at **Mureybet** have revealed a settlement where inhabitants made pottery and cultivated *einkorn,* a single-grained wheat, as early as the 9th millennium BCE. The production of bronze, an alloy of copper and tin, appeared after the mid-4th millennium BCE. **Ebla,** one of the oldest civilizations in the world founded in the 3rd millennium BCE, was unearthed near present-day Aleppo. Last but not least, the city of Damascus is the world's oldest continually inhabited city.

Greater Syria, a land area incorporating present-day Lebanon, Israel, Jordan, and Syria, has been the locus of countless land squabbles since ancient times and continues to be fought over today. The list of conquerors and rulers of the region reads like a who's-who of ancient history. After the rise and fall of Ebla around 2500 BCE, the Assyrian king **Shamshi-A'adad I** established his capital at Shubat Enlil around 1800 BCE (known today as Tel Leilan, in northeast Syria). The **Hittites** moved in 200 years later and ruled until their rivals, the Egyptians, wrenched control of the area two centuries later. The **Aramaeans** migrated into Syria around 1200 BCE and established several minor kingdoms, the most important being Aram near present-day Damascus. An endless array of ancient conquerors had their way with Syria in the years that followed: the Assyrians returned, quickly succeeded by the Babylonians, the Persians, and the Seleucids (who gave Syria its name).

THE ROMAN PERIOD. Alexander the Great added Syria to his empire during his massive land campaign in 333 BCE, establishing the city of **Antioch** as its capital. Next up were the Romans under Pompey, who made the entire region one of its many provinces in 64 BCE. It remained a Roman province for several centuries.

THE MEDIEVAL PERIOD. The Arabs conquered Syria in 636 CE and established Damascus as the capital of the powerful **Umayyad** caliphate. The Abbasid caliphs were less drawn by Damascus's many charms and moved the capital to Baghdad when they took over in 750 CE. Muslim rule ended in the 11th century when the Crusaders arrived and made Syria part of the Christian Kingdom of Jerusalem. Syria, along with the rest of the Arab world, was freed from Christian control when the great liberator **Salah al-Din** overthrew the Kingdom of Jerusalem at the end of the 12th century. The Mamluks moved in from Egypt around 1300 and ruled until the coming of the Ottomans.

MODERN HISTORY (1516-2000 CE)

THE OTTOMAN PERIOD. Most of the coastal region of modern-day Syria officially became part of the **Ottoman Empire** in 1516 CE, and Syria's economy thrived over the following four centuries. The market towns of **Damascus** and **Aleppo** were successful because of their locations along the trade routes between Persia and Europe. Come World War I, a decisive battle was fought between German-backed Turks and Suez-based British. **Emir Faisal** and his Arab nationalist army backed the British, who promised pan-Arab independence. After emerging victorious, however, the British betrayed Faisal by carving up the Levant and placing Syria under the control of the French. In response, Faisal and British colonel T.E. Lawrence (better known as **Lawrence of Arabia**) conquered Damascus in October 1918.

MANDATE AND INDEPENDENCE. A bit peeved, the French strong-armed their way back into control with the help of the 1920 mandate from the League of

Nations. They battled nationalist rebels in and around Damascus until falling to the Germans in 1940. British and French forces liberated the territory in July 1941. Syria finally gained **independence** when foreign troops withdrew in April 1946.

SYRIA AFTER INDEPENDENCE. The first few decades of independence were anything but peaceful. In March 1949, the country came under the first of a series of military dictatorships. **Pan-Arabism** became a major political force in Syria (and the rest of the Middle East) during the 1950s, heralded mainly by the rise of the **Ba'ath Party** (the Arab Socialist Resurrection Party). The Ba'ath Party has been the strongest political force in Syria since rising to power in the 1963 **March Revolution.** The party was dealt a major blow by the **Six-Day War** against Israel in June 1967, which cost Syria the **Golan Heights.** Syria suffered further casualties, both in terms of lives and morale, when Jordanian forces defeated Syrian-backed Palestinian guerillas in the **Black September** hostilities of 1970 (see **Jordan: Modern History,** p. 450). After frantic finger-pointing among government officials, **Hafez al-Assad,** the Ba'ath's fair-haired boy and commander of the Syrian Air Force, seized control of the country and was sworn in as president on March 14, 1971.

THE AMARANTHINE ASSAD REGIME. From 1971 through June 10th, 2000, the late-President Assad ran the supposedly "democratic" nation of Syria as a tight-fisted dictatorship, though two events in the early years of his rule challenged his supremacy. In 1973, Assad and Egypt's President Anwar Sadat launched a surprise attack on Israel known as the **Yom Kippur War** (see **Egypt: Modern History,** p. 66). After early Arab gains, the Israelis surged forward and came within 35km of Damascus, forcing Assad to cease fire and sign an armistice. In February 1982, the militant **Muslim Brotherhood** launched a rebellion from Hama. Most estimate that Assad's forces retaliated by killing between 5000 and 25,000 people. Assad's political skills proved more successful in the mid-1980s. When Israel invaded Lebanon in 1982, Assad responded by backing the main Lebanese Muslim militias, Amal and Hizbullah. Over the next few years, Israel and Syria clashed; by 1985, Israel withdrew from Lebanon, but Syria did not. Though formally an independent nation, Lebanon continues to take its major political cues from Damascus.

The money gained from **oil sales** in the 1970s allowed Assad to pursue a program of capital formation, but industries were haphazardly chosen and poorly run, leaving Syria with nothing but inefficient factories. The Syrian economy today suffers from the two-headed monster of rapid **population growth** and massive **inflation** (which reached 300% in late 1991, but has since dropped to a less stratospheric 22%). Unemployment stalled at 35% in the 70s and 80s, and the colossal bureaucracy (20% of workers are government-employed) is matched only by its colossal inefficiency. Western economic aid has been scarce due to Syria's connections with terrorist groups, support of Iran, and skirmishes with Western favorite Jordan. However, in exchange for support of the US-led coalition against Iraq in the 1991 **Gulf War,** Syria received financial concessions and a free hand in Lebanon. In more recent times, Assad had actively sought Western aid to revitalize Syria's plodding economy: the loosening of travel restrictions for Syrian Jews and talks with Israel have curried favor with Western governments and investors.

In 1999, Assad was elected to his fifth term with 99% of the vote. Assad's policies stabilized and even improved Syrian politics, for he diluted the Ba'ath's centralized power by mandating the election of local councils (of which at least 51% were required to be workers or peasants). His political longevity, however, could also be attributed to the aggressive suppression of his enemies. The omnipresent internal security forces, known as the **Mukhabarat,** quelled all anti-Assad sentiment. The government also had an abysmal human rights record, and has repeatedly been accused of harboring terrorists. Today, all political parties are associated with the **National Progressive Front (NPF),** a coalition dominated by the Ba'ath Party. The **People's Council** is a 250-member legislative body, but since it is controlled by the NPF, Ba'ath policies pass with minimal opposition.

IN THE NEWS

With Israeli Prime Minister Ehud Barak's pledge to begin talks regarding the **Golan Heights,** which has been under Israeli control since 1967, Syria and Israel seemed closer than ever to peace. Motivated by expedient economic reforms and his own uncertain health, Assad dropped all preconditions to peace-talks, and in December 1999, the two nations approached the bargaining table. Each side, however, maintained decidedly different interpretations of the new border: Syria wanted a return to the 1967 borders while Israel sought the 1948 UN-approved border, and talks became bogged down by April. On May 24, 2000, Israel pulled its troops out of Lebanon as a unilateral gesture designed to restart the peace talks.

On June 10, 2000, President Assad passed away, leaving the country in his son Bashar's hands. World leaders now look upon Bashar, Syria's first Western-educated leader, to take new strides in Syria's quest for peace.

CULTURE

RELIGION AND ETHNICITY

Islam is the dominant religion of Syria, the faith of 88% of the country's 17 million inhabitants. Of these, about 74% are Sunni and 14% are Shi'ite. The Shi'ite branch is split into several sects, two of the most popular being the Alawis (12%) and the Isma'ilis (2%). The former group counts President Bashar Assad as one of its adherents. About 10% of Syrians belong to the Catholic or Eastern Orthodox churches. Two percent are Druze.

About 85% of Syria's population are ethnic Arabs. The rest is a mix of Kurds, Turks, Armenians, and Circassians. Part of the Kurdish minority has long since vowed to create an independent state, which would also include Kurds in Turkey, Iran, and Iraq. Their grievances have not yet been accompanied by constructive action; pamphlets distributed in 1992 brought about the arrest of 200 Kurdish activists. For more on the struggle for Kurdish independence, see **Turkey: Religion and Ethnicity,** p. 610.

LANGUAGE

The official state language of Syria is **Arabic,** with **French** coming in as a close second. English is becoming more prevalent, though not quite as widespread as Arabic or French. Minority groups, such as the Kurds in the east and the Armenians in Aleppo, continue to use their respective languages. In some villages, you may encounter Turkish or even Aramaic, the language spoken during Jesus' time. For some handy Arabic phrases, consult the **Phrasebook,** p. 701.

THE ARTS

LITERATURE. Although the alphabet was first discovered in Syria, only recently has the world discovered anything noteworthy in Syrian letters. One of the greatest poets in contemporary Syrian literature is the iconoclast **Adonis** (Ali Ahmad Sa'id). Adonis's experiments in modernism have earned him international fame; some claim he transformed Islamic culture as radically as Dante influenced Christianity. Adonis was the central figure of the **New Poets,** a group of Arabs who used poetry to challenge language, religion, and authority in the 1960s and 1970s. The first of Adonis's seven poetry collections, *Aghani Mihyar al-Dimashqi* (*Songs of Mihyar the Damascene,* 1961), is readily available in English translation.

Possibly the most popular Syrian poet, **Nizar Qabbani** was born in Damascus. He had a special passion for Beirut: he believed in a "Lady of the Universe" so beautiful that Arabs tried to destroy her out of envy. Such lover's passion characterized Qabbani's early works, mainly poems scandalizing traditional Arab society. His poems were so popular that they were set to music by famous singers including Umm Kulthum (see **Umm Kulthum**, p. 71). After serving as Syrian ambassador, Qabbani abandoned the practice of politics and began writing about it. His strong nationalism led him to pen poems and essays ridiculing Arab dictators for their military failures, social backwardness, and human rights abuses. When Jordan and the Palestinians signed peace accords with Israel, Qabbani provoked fierce debate with the poem, "When will they announce the death of the Arabs?" Newspapers and magazines that printed his writings were banned in several countries. Other poems treat the oppression of women as a metaphor for Arab political problems.

VISUAL AND PERFORMING ARTS. Native to Syria is 2000-year old **glassblowing**, the art of forming unique glass formations by blowing molten glass. Areas of Sidon, Hama, and Palmyra show evidence for glass molds as early as the first century BCE, which bear the signatures of Syrian masters. These blown vessels for everyday and luxury use were produced commercially and exported to all parts of the Roman Empire. Other art forms, like **calligraphy** and **photography** can be found at the **Free Art** exhibit in the Russian Cultural Center, as can **Rabi al-Aleras's** surrealistic and expressionist sculptures. The **Attasi Fine Arts Gallery** presents the work of artists like **Nizar Sabour,** whose creations of icons describe saints as ordinary people eager to express their sadness and love for life. Don't miss the aromatic **Damascus International Flower Festival** held every May in Tishreen Park.

If theatre is more enticing, make sure to visit the town of Hussein al-Bahr, the birthplace of Syrian playwright, **Sa'adullah Wannous.** On June 2, the date of his death anniversary, fans attend the performance of a variety of his plays. Syrians continue their artistic activities year-round: June hosts the **Syrian Theatre Festival;** September uniquely presents the **Bosra Folklore Festival;** and October is time for the **Damascus Film Festival** and the **Theatre Arts Festival.** Do not count on watching much television, though; only three channels exist, one in Arabic, the second in English and French, and the third by satellite.

MUSIC. Though individual artists claim national pride and usually identify with one country or another, the music of the Middle East transcends disputed boundaries and diverse religions. Syrians do listen to outsiders, like Fairouz, but they have their prized possession, **Farid al-Atrash,** the artist known as the "sad singer." As a child, he was unable to express his feelings while singing, so his instructor advised him to cry as he sang, and this advice worked and remained a theme that lasted throughout his career. Farid is also known to Arab musicians as the best *oud* player of his time. In an effort to create a niche during the age of established giants like Muhammad Abd al-Wahab and Umm Kulthum, Farid adopted themes from flamenco and tango in his compositions to mix Arabic and European styles. Singers respect him as a man so talented that he is often unashamedly imitated.

MARY ATE A LITTLE LAMB Anyone with knowledge of Middle Eastern cooking knows that Syrian cuisine is one of the region's best. Such a claim should not be put forth sheepishly; it is supported by the large numbers of high-quality patisseries and Arab eateries that dot the streets of most major cities. The uninitiated should note, however, that some dishes require an acquired taste. Notorious "sheep eggs," which are actually testicles, are the most famous example. Sheep also get special treatment in a Damascene favorite, *ma'adim,* which consists of sheep hooves drenched in a hummus-like dressing and served over bread. Moving up the sheep anatomy, we arrive at *mukh,* sheep brains: these are normally mixed with lettuce and lemon to create the intriguing "brain salad." If such a mix proves to be a gastrointestinal disaster, consider washing it down with a soothing cup of *zghourat,* a tea made from "useful plants in the ground" that tastes curiously close to its rough English translation.

SYRIA

FOOD AND DRINK

Syrian meals feature the typical Levantine staples: hummus, falafel, *sha-warma*, shish kebab, and *shish tawouq*, among others. A particularly common dish is **farooj**, roasted chicken served with chilis and onions. Syrian desserts are delicious: **ba'laweh** is pistachio- or almond-filled filo dough; **burma** is shredded, fried dough with pistachios; and **basbouseh** is wheat pastry with syrup. Don't leave without trying the desert banana **bybil** for desert; its short growing season (culminating in a harvest around October 1) makes it one of the most prized fruits in the world. Other fruits are available in abundance; the **aseer** (fruit juice) available at stands is a sweet way to rehydrate. Arabic coffee is a potent and bittersweet brew known as **ahwa.** Be careful when adding milk, though—Syrian milk is not always pasteurized. **Mandarin** is a Syrian-brewed soft drink. Liquor ranges from locally brewed beers such as Sharq and Barada (as well as Amstel smuggled from Lebanon) to **'araq,** an anise-flavored liqueur mixed with water and consumed from shot glasses. Ask for **booza** and you'll get ice cream, not alcohol.

SYRIA

FACTS AND FIGURES

OFFICIAL NAME: Syrian Arab Republic

GOVERNMENT: Republic under military regime

CAPITAL: Damascus

LAND AREA: 184,050 sq. km.

GEOGRAPHY: Narrow coastal plane with semi-arid desert conditions and mountains in the east

CLIMATE: Hot, dry summers from June-Aug. and mild, wet winters from Dec.-Feb.; desert-like in the east

MAJOR CITIES: Damascus, Aleppo, Lattakia, Palmyra

POPULATION: 17,213,871; urban 53%, rural 47%

LANGUAGE: Arabic, some French

RELIGIONS: Muslim (90%), Christian (10%)

AVERAGE INCOME PER CAPITA: US$2500

MAJOR EXPORTS: Petroleum (65%), textiles (16%), food and livestock (13%), other (6%)

ESSENTIALS

WHEN TO GO

The best time to go to Syria is either during the spring or autumn, when rain is infrequent and temperatures are mild. During the summer, Syria becomes less traveler-friendly, as temperatures climb as high as 45°C/113°F. In the winter, colder temperatures and periodic rains can put a damper on travel.

AVERAGE TEMPERATURE PRECIPITATION

	JANUARY			APRIL			JULY			OCTOBER		
	°C	°F	mm	°C	°F	mm	°C	°F	mm	°C	°F	mm
Damascus	6.5	43.7	39	15.8	60.4	13	26.7	80.1	0	18.9	66.0	9
Aleppo	5.77.1	42.3	61	15.6	60.1	34	28.4	83.1	0	19.5	67.1	21
Lattakia	11.6	52.9	162	17.6	63.7	44	26.2	79.2	1	22.1	71.8	61
Palmyra	6.9	44.4	20	17.8	64.0	19	29.3	84.7	0	20.5	68.9	8

DOCUMENTS AND FORMALITIES

SYRIA'S CONSULAR SERVICES ABROAD

Syria's embassies and consulates abroad include:

Canada Embassy: 151 Slater St., Suite 1000, Ottawa, Ontario, K1P5H3 (☎(613) 569 55 56; fax 569 38 00).

South Africa Embassy: 772 Government Ave., East Clyff/Arcadia, Pretoria, South Africa (☎(12) 342 47 01; fax 342 47 02).

UK Embassy: 8 Belgrave Sq., London SW1X 8PH (☎(171) 245 90 12; fax 235 46 21 or 235 89 76).

US Embassy: 2215 Wyoming Ave NW, Washington, D.C. 20008 (☎(202) 232-6313; fax 265-4585). **Consulate:** 820 2nd Ave., New York, NY 10017 (☎(212) 661-9313).

CONSULAR SERVICES IN SYRIA

Embassies and consulates of other countries in Syria include:

Australian Embassy: 128 al-Farabi St., E. Villas, Damascus (☎(11) 613 23 23; fax 613 24 78; email austdmas@go.com.jo).

Canadian Embassy: Block 12 al-Mezzah, Damascus (☎(11) 611 68 51; fax 611 40 00).

UK Embassy: 11 Muhammad Kurd Ali St., Malki, Damascus (☎(11) 371 25 61 or 371 25 62; fax 373 16 00). **Consulate:** Aleppo (☎(21) 268 05 02 or 268 05 03; fax 268 05 01).

US Embassy: 2 al-Mansour St., Abu Roumaneh, Damascus (☎333 13 42, emergency ☎333 13 42; fax 224 79 38).

ENTRY REQUIREMENTS

PASSPORT. Passports are required of all visitors, except for citizens of Lebanon who hold national ID cards.

TRAVEL TO ISRAEL. If you visit **Israel** before a trip to Syria, insist that Israeli customs place **no stamp** in your passport, or more practically, have them stamp a piece of paper inserted in your passport that can be removed. Be warned that Syrian border officials may still refuse entry if they see that you have no Jordanian entry stamp or have an Egyptian exit stamp from Taba.

VISA AND PERMIT INFO. Visas are required to enter Syria. Australian citizens may obtain visas at the border. All other applicants must apply for a visa before entering Syria. Applications are available from any Syrian embassy. Send two completed applications (no photocopies), passport (without evidence of a trip to Israel), two signed photographs, a self-addressed stamped envelope (US$2), and money order to a Syrian embassy (3-month double-entry visas US$61). All visitors staying in Syria for more than two weeks (even those with six-month visas) must apply for a **visa extension** on the 13th day of their stay. It makes sense to do this in a smaller city where the lines will be shorter.

BORDER CROSSINGS

Hard currency is needed to cross the Jordanian and Lebanese borders to Syria. Fees vary according to nationality and duration of stay, but ideally you should carry US$100 in cash (you will not need the full amount). This is the best way to avoid extremely poor exchange rates at the borders.

TO LEBANON. Crossing into Lebanon may take a long time due to security at the border, but the path is well-trodden and simple. Daily buses run from Damascus to Tripoli or Beirut, Aleppo and Lattakia to Beirut, and Homs to Tripoli. Though costly, it's possible to hire a *service* to drive across the border from Damascus. Citizens of Canada, Ireland, the UK, the US, and most European countries can obtain a Lebanese visa at the border (L₤20,000 for US citizens), though prices depend on your nationality and are subject to change. Syrian visas, however, are not available if crossing from Lebanon to Syria. If you have a single-entry visa, you may reenter Syria within 48 hours after departure for US$10. After this time, the price and difficulty to return will increase. The word on the street is that a Syrian single-entry visa is good for two entries from Lebanon before the visa expires. It is also possible to return to Syria with a **multiple-entry Syrian visa,** though it is more expensive and hard to obtain (there is no Syrian representation in Lebanon and it is difficult to get a visa of any kind at the Syrian embassy in Amman).

TO JORDAN. The official road crossing into Jordan runs through the town of Dera. Daily buses run from Damascus or Aleppo to Amman. *Service* from Damascus are faster, but also more expensive. Jordanian visas are available at the border. Bring US dollars or use the bank next door. They charge according to nationality; US citizens must pay about US$50. For true penny-pinchers, the painfully slow Hijaz railway chugs (and chugs, and chugs) between Damascus and Amman. The train departs Amman at 8am every Monday, arriving at Damascus at 5pm, and leaves Damascus every Sunday at 7:30am to arrive in Amman at 5pm.

TO TURKEY. Of the four official land crossings between Syria and Turkey, the Bab al-Hawa post on the Aleppo-Antakya road is the most popular, and often gets so congested that it takes a few hours to cross. Buses run from Damascus, Aleppo, and Lattakia to a number of Turkish destinations, most commonly Istanbul and the travel hubs of Antakya and Iskenderun near the border. Buy a Turkish visa at the border for US$20.

TO ISRAEL AND IRAQ. Syria's borders with Israel and Iraq are closed; neither situation is likely to change soon. The most common route between Syria and Israel is via Jordan and the West Bank. In the past few years, a few trade delegations have been permitted to travel by road between Baghdad and Damascus, but it remains to be seen whether a loosening of border restrictions will follow.

GETTING AROUND

BY PLANE. Syrian Arab Airlines fly from Damascus to Aleppo, Palmyra, Deir al-Zur, and Lattakia. Fares tend to be very inexpensive.

BY TRAIN. Strictly speaking, trains connect some cities in Syria; frankly speaking, roller skates would serve you better. Trains are slow, crowded, and dirty, and in most places they drop you off about 30km out of town. Use the buses.

BY BUS. Karnak, the government-run bus company, has extensive routes and low fares on orange-and-white, air-conditioned buses. Buses occasionally depart on schedule, and reservations are required. **Pullman** buses are a step below Karnak. Over 50 **private bus companies** now operate in Syria; they have ship-shape coaches and competitive prices. Reservations are a good idea for these buses too. Karnak, Pullman, and private buses usually leave from different stops—make sure you're at the right one. All tickets must be bought at the stations, as drivers do not handle money. **Microbuses** (MEEK-ro-bus) are easy, cheap, and relatively hassle-free. They are white minivans that drive on set routes within Damascus and to outlying areas. Like most *service*, they usually depart only when full. Untangling their confusing schedules may be difficult at first (destinations are often written in Arabic on the side of the vehicle), but they are cheaper than taxis for long rides. Fees in

Damascus are set, but vary everywhere else depending on where you get off; ask the person next to you (not the driver) how much to pay or wait to see what other people are paying. Microbuses differ from clattery old **minibuses,** which are becoming less frequent on the roads.

BY TAXI. Yellow private taxis, also known as *service* (ser-VEES), are 50-70% more expensive than buses. But *service* are more user-friendly and still relatively cheap. To hail one, hold out your hand with the palm down. Taxis have meters, but drivers rarely use them; negotiate a price before getting in. If a driver refuses to bargain, just point to the meter to get a fair rate. Beware and be firm—many drivers specialize in cheating newly arrived travelers.

BY CAR. Very few people in Syria own private cars, which is why public transportation is good. If you want to risk your life driving one, cars can be rented at a few places in Damascus (see **Damascus: Car Rental,** p. 567). Cars are generally not worth the expense, as all the sights you could possibly want to see are easily accessible via cheap public transportation. For negotiable prices, some *service* drivers will be your private chauffeur for the day—a cheaper option than renting a car if you want the freedom to visit out-of-the-way places and don't want to risk your life on the way.

BY THUMB. There is no need to hitchhike in Syria. If you stand by the side of a road, an ultra-cheap microbus will eventually stop. It is not unusual, however, for truck drivers to pick up passengers in order to subsidize their trips (they usually expect S£1-2 per km). Hitchers caught by the police may be hauled in for questioning or given a stern warning. *Let's Go* does not recommend hitchhiking.

TOURIST SERVICES AND MONEY

TOURIST OFFICES. The **Ministry of Tourism** runs an office in Damascus on Abu Firas al-Hamandi St. (☎(11) 223 74 90 or 224 28 52; fax 224 26 36; email min-tourism@syriatel.net; www.syriatourism.org), as well as a **Tourist Information Center** on 29 May Street (☎(11) 232 39 53).

CURRENCY AND EXCHANGE. The basic unit of currency is the Syrian pound (S£). Each pound is divided into 100 **piasters** (pt), or *qirsh.* Bills are in denominations of S£5, 10, 25, 50, 100, 500, 1000, while coins are in denominations of S£1, 2, 5, 10, 25. You may bring as much foreign currency into the country as you like, but may not leave with more than you brought in. Amounts up to US$5000 do not need to be declared. The Commercial Bank of Syria has exchange desks at its many branches, as well as in major hotels. US dollars are the preferred currency for exchange.

Credit cards cannot be used to obtain cash advances, though major credit cards are increasingly accepted at large hotels and stores for purchases (V, MC, AmEx are the most widely accepted). It is illegal to cash traveler's checks anywhere besides the bank, but the AmEx office will do it in an emergency. If you are in a bind, some shopkeepers in the Damascus *souq* will disguise a cash advance as a purchase, although the exchange rate will be lower than the official bank rate. **Black market** exchange is not the flourishing industry it once was, as secret service agents have begun to clamp down upon illicit dealings. Still, it is common in *souqs* or near al-Marjeh Sq. in Damascus, where some trading takes place beneath the thumb of secret service agents on the lookout for offenders. Some hotels will unofficially change money for you at the black market rate, usually up to S£8 per US$1 more than the bank rate. The best rate you can hope for is S£50 per US$1 using cash or traveler's checks. Transactions using US dollars are illegal (except to pay hotel bills); in 1986, a law was passed making illegal exchange or possession of hard currency punishable by up to three years in prison.

It used to be the case that nothing would get done in Syria without a bit of **palm-greasing.** Now, increased contact with the world market is changing the general

SYRIA

attitude toward *bakhsheesh*. While bribes are no longer necessary to accomplish the smallest task (and are inappropriate when dealing with high government officials and police officers), tipping makes everything run a little smoother. Taxi drivers, waiters, and movie theater employees should be given at least a 10% tip. If you stay multiple nights at a hotel that cleans its rooms daily, a small thank you (S$20-40 per day) to the person responsible is appropriate.

PRICES. Due to its struggling economy, Syria's prices are among the lowest in the Middle East. S$900 (US$20) should easily cover a day's budget travel.

 SIGHT SAVVY. Admission to sights in Syria is literally 20 times more expensive (usually S£300 instead of S£15) without an ISIC card. At all costs, get an ISIC card in your home country before departure.

BUSINESS HOURS. The work week begins on Saturday and ends on Thursday. Friday is the official day off. Stores are generally open 8:30am-2pm, then again from 4:30-8pm. Some stores stay open all day in the winter. Government offices are open 9am-2pm; banks 8:30am-1pm. Museums always close on Tuesdays, and are generally open November to March from 9am-6pm and April to October from 9am-5pm. Restaurant hours vary. Most establishments serve food from 11am until the last few patrons leave (often after midnight).

USEFUL ADDRESSES. For a comprehensive bibliography of Syrian politics, culture, and tourism, as well as hard facts about visas, customs, and embassies, visit www.cafe-syria.com. Find additional hard facts at the **World Travel Guide's** Syria site (www.wtgonline.com/data/syr/). In **Syria, A Photographic Journey** (www.man-hal.com/), professional photographs of Palmyra, Aleppo, and Damascus are accompanied by quotes from famous English authors who traveled in the region.

HEALTH AND SAFETY

EMERGENCY Police: ☎ 112. Ambulance: ☎ 110. Fire: ☎ 113.

MEDICAL EMERGENCIES. The Syrian government runs several hospitals and clinics, and there are also many private practices. Syrian facilities, however, are not state-of-the-art, and in cases of serious emergency, travelers should consider traveling to Lebanon or Jordan (or, ideally, Israel), or returning to their home countries. In case of **medical emergency,** dial ☎ 110.

HEALTH. While no **vaccinations** are necessary for entry, those for hepatitis B, typhoid, immunoglobulin, and malaria are recommended. Syria is a clean and healthy country, and water in cities is normally chlorinated and safe to drink. Outside of the main cities, however, most tap water is likely to be unsterilized. Bottled water is readily available and advised in small towns. Make sure milk is pasteurized. Eat only well-cooked meat, fish, and peeled vegetables and fruits. There are numerous pharmacies in Syria and no shortage of Western medicine. Quality and prices are regulated by the Ministry of Health.

WOMEN TRAVELERS. Common sense is the best companion for women traveling in Syria. Men may make comments, but remember that ignorance is bliss; the best way to deal with harassers is simply to ignore them. If they prove persistent, raise your voice and threaten to call the police. If things get out of hand, alert the tourist police. Many female travelers have found that wearing a wedding band wards off many unwanted advances. Females traveling alone should know their destination ahead of time so that they do not appear bewildered on the street. Women should not venture out alone at night. For more tips, see **Women Travelers,** p. 38.

MINORITY TRAVELERS. Unlike other Middle Eastern countries, Syria surprises Western travelers with its lack of outward hostility toward those who are obviously not Syrian. Blacks and whites exist in Syrian society; those from East Asia will stand out, but not to a dangerous degree. All travelers should avoid discussing Israeli politics, unless they are equally informed about the countering Arab side.

BGLT TRAVELERS. Homosexuality can land you in jail, which doesn't mean that it doesn't occur. The *souq* in Aleppo is known for its gay pick-up scene. You may want to read Robert Tewdwr Moss's *Cleopatra's Wedding Present*, an account of a gay journalist's travels in Syria (Duckworth, UK). As in other Middle Eastern countries, it is best to be discreet.

ACCOMMODATIONS AND CAMPING

HOTELS. Two hotel options span opposite ends of price and quality: expensive international chain resorts or basic hole-in-the-wall, bed-and-a-roof crash sites. The higher the room quality, the more likely owners will require payment in US dollars; all hotels two-star or higher carry this requirement. In most places, there is an even split between hotels that charge Syrian pounds and those that demand US dollars, but in heavily touristed towns like Palmyra, prepare to part with dollars. Different employees from the same establishment often quote contradictory rates; bargaining can save some money. Damascus and Aleppo hotels are less likely to respond to haggling, but if they look empty, give it a shot. Even posted rates can sometimes be brought down, if only by a few pounds. Unmarried couples may have a difficult time getting a room together; this is less of a problem in more expensive hotels. There are no hostels in Syria.

OTHER LOCAL ACCOMMODATIONS. Guest houses are available in Damascus, Aleppo, Zabadani, Idlib, and Bosra. *Cités Universitaires* also offer summer accommodations.

CAMPING. Syria has official campsites in Aleppo, Lattakia, Palmyra, and Tartus. Camping is also permitted near resorts.

KEEPING IN TOUCH

MAIL. Poste Restante service is available in Damascus's main post office; bring your passport and enough money to cover customs charges on parcels (letters carry no charge). The **American Express** office in Damascus (see **Practical Information,** p. 571) also holds mail. A one-pound package to Syria costs US$8.48 from the US and AU$21 from Australia. Mail from Syria is inexpensive but slow. Parcels to Europe take one week to arrive, while parcels to the US can take up to three weeks. Overseas letters cost about S£18; postcards cost S£11. Take packages to a post office for inspection before wrapping them up.

TELEPHONES. Damascus has a 24-hour telephone office where you can place international calls, but you'll need your passport, lots of money, and patience (at least an hour's worth). Some other cities have offices as well. Most hotels have direct-dial international capabilities, but rates from Syria are exorbitant (US$12 per 3min. to the US), and hotels charge at least double the phone office rates. It's much cheaper to have your party call you back or to call collect. The access code for **MCI's World Phone** program is 0800, **AT&T's USADirect** 0801, and **Sprint** 0888 (only to the US). You can now use phonecards to make local calls; they are available at most post offices. Inside Syria, you need to dial 0 before the city code.

INTERNET ACCESS. The Internet is not a viable means of communication in Syria. Cyber access is in its most rudimentary stage, and Internet cafes are not open to the public. There are Internet terminals in the National Library in Damascus, but you must be supervised by an official. The process is also difficult and expensive. Internet access, without hotmail, is available in two Damascus offices at S£5 per minute. If you're dying to check your email, go to Lebanon.

CUSTOMS AND ETIQUETTE

Conservative dress is the norm for both sexes. Shorts, tank tops, and short skirts will invite stares, comments, and possibly sexual advances. Pants and skirts should fall to at least mid-calf and shirts should cover the shoulders and upper arms. It is considered impolite to point directly at someone or to point the sole of your shoe at someone (as when sitting down and placing an ankle on one knee). When Syrians tip their heads up and make a clucking noise, this means "no"—Westerners have been known to mistake it for a sign of acknowledgment or a "get in the back seat" gesture by a taxi driver.

HOLIDAYS

Syria observes all Muslim holidays (see p. 699 for a complete listing). Christian holidays are also national holidays. March 8 is Revolution Day, May 1 is Labor Day, May 6 is Martyrs' Day, and October 6 is October Liberation War Day.

DAMASCUS دمشق ☎ 11

Pre-Islamic Arabs looked upon the site of present-day Damascus and named it *Balad al-Sham*, a phrase denoting green hills, plentiful soil, and an otherwise blessed *Jannat al-Dounia* ("Heaven on Earth"). In the intervening centuries, other colors—Roman red, *service* taxi yellow, the French tricolor—have refracted through the prism of history to create a city as unique as the Syrian presidency is long.

Though Aleppans disagree, the Damascus area has been continuously inhabited longer than any other place in the world. Early historical references to the city include 3000 BCE Ebla tablets, as well as 15th-century BCE pharaonic inscriptions and records of the city as the capital of the Aramaic Kingdom. Centuries later, Roman invaders left their mark, most notably in the form of the Temple of Jupiter, built by Apolodor the Damascene (see p. 574). During the Byzantine era, Christians converted the temple into a church and built other monuments that stand today. In 636 CE, Khalid ibn al-Walid, also known as the "Sword of God," conquered Damascus in the name of Islam. The city served as the Umayyad Empire's capital for close to a century, at a time of enormous growth for the Islamic community. Damascus began to suffer when the Abbasids replaced the Umayyads and moved their capital to Baghdad. In the ensuing centuries, Damascus fell under the thumb of various Muslim dynasties and empires, including the Ottoman Turks, whose influence remains quite visible in existing Damascene architecture. During World War I, German and Turkish armies used Damascus as a base. After Syria came under French control, resistance raged hardest in Damascus; in 1925, the French crushed a popular revolt in the unruly city. Syria won its independence in 1946, with Damascus appointed the capital of a modern nation-state.

Today, the pulse, physical appearance, and odors of the city reflect contemporary realities rather than historical splendor. Damascus is a city of many faces: large fountains, parks, and wide avenues grace the newer part of town, while the winding cobblestone streets of the Old City house Damascus's Christian population and a plethora of small craft shops and bakeries. Downtown, pedestrians and cars thrust and parry in an everyday street-level duel. Meanwhile, fruit stand owners and pastry makers pull chairs up to the curbs and look on, passing the day at a safe distance from the frenetic pace of bustling Damascus.

✈ GETTING THERE AND AWAY

Flights: Damascus International Airport, southeast of Damascus. Buses to the airport leave from Victoria Bridge on al-Quwatli St. (S£10 per piece of luggage, free if no luggage). Taxis to the airport cost S£300-500. Regular flights to European and Arab capitals and domestic one-way flights daily to: **Aleppo** (S£900); **Deir al-Zur** (S£900); and **Lattakia** (S£500). Air travelers to **Beirut** must pay in US dollars (US$60, 21-day round-trip ticket US$100). Flights may be arbitrarily canceled up to 24 hours before departure. There is an **exit fee** (S£100) if you leave Syria by air. The **SyrianAir** office (☎222 07 00) on Sa'ad al-Jabri St., is across from the post office. Open daily 8:30am-7pm.

Buses: For **intercity transportation** north of Damascus, 30 private bus companies with competitive rates operate out of **Karajat Harasta,** on the eastern edge of the city. Arrive at any time and chances are a bus will be leaving for your destination within 30 minutes. Among the most reliable operators are the **Damas Tour Co.** (☎511 90 67) and **Qadmoos** (☎512 22 60). Buses depart daily to: **Aleppo** (4½hr.; 11:30am, 1:30, 3pm; S£150); **Hama** (3hr., noon, S£85); **Lattakia** (4hr., every hr., S£150); and **Suweida** (1½hr., S£50). The government-run **Karnak Bus Co.** (☎231 14 93 or 231 61 36) is a 15-minute walk west of al-Marjeh Sq. Run-down buses serve: **Amman** (4hr., 7am and 3pm, S£270); **Beirut** (3-3½hr.; 7:30, 8:30am, 3:30pm; S£175); and **Bosra** (30min.; 11am, 2:30, 5, 7:30pm; S£50). Similarly decrepit Karnak buses depart from Karajat Harasta to: **Aleppo** (4-4½hr., 7:30am and 4:30pm, S£130); **Homs** (2hr., every hr. 7:30am-6:30pm, S£60); **Lattakia** (4-4½hr.; 7:30, 8:30am, 1:30, 2:30pm; S£125); **Palmyra** (3hr.; 10, 11am, 1, 2:30, 6pm; S£100); and **Tartus** (5hr., 2pm, S£100).

Service: Minibuses and **service** are fairly cheap and have the dubious advantage of leaving when full. Shout your destination to the driver—if he's going there, he'll motion you in. *Service* travel to: **Aleppo** (3hr., S£300); **Amman** (4hr., S£400); **Beirut** (3hr., S£400-500); **Sidon** (4hr., S£500); and **Tripoli** (5hr., S£500). Domestic *service* leave from Abbaseen Stadium; international *service* leave from Barumkeh.

⬅ GETTING AROUND

Microbuses: These white minivans (also called *service*) have predetermined routes and pick up passengers along the way. If one is going your way, flag it down and jump in. *Service* run to Mezzeh from the beginning of al-Thawra St. and to Muhajereen and Abu Roumaneh from under the President's Bridge (Jisr al-Rais). A *service* also connects Baramkeh Station with Karaj Halab. As rides only cost S£3-10, even a short ride is usually worth it. Rap on the window when you want out.

Taxis: Private or **service taxis** (yellow cars) have meters and drivers are required by law to use them. If the meter isn't turned on (starting fare S£3), either demand that the driver use it or negotiate a fair price before getting in. Longer trips, like the one from Hijaz Station to Karajat Harasta, shouldn't cost more than S£80. If you think that the driver is cheating you, point to the side of the road and indicate that you are getting out; if this doesn't attract his attention, try opening the door. Although drivers are likely to get mad, they will usually concede a fairer price if you remain firm. Most drivers, however, will give you an honest rate and appreciate a small tip (S£5-10).

Car Rental: Rental cars are remarkably expensive. A few places around the post office rent, but not much English is spoken. For helpful driving information in English, try **Hertz** (☎221 66 15; fax 222 61 81) at the Cham Palace Hotel. Rent with unlimited mileage for a day (S£2700 per day) or on a weekly basis (S£2500 per day).

⊞ ORIENTATION

With the help of a few landmarks, Damascus is easy to navigate on foot. The impressive **Hijaz Railway Station** is at the intersection of **al-Nasser St.** and **Sa'ad al-Jabri St.,** with an old railway car on display in front of its stone steps and an extra-

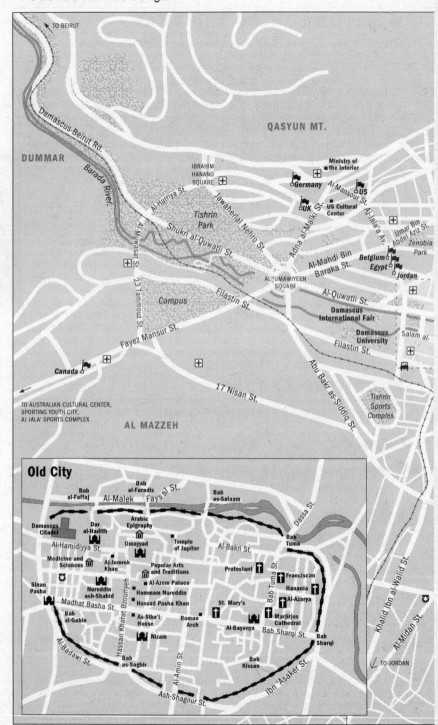

TO BEIRUT

DUMMAR

Damascus-Beirut Rd.

Barada River.

QASYUN MT.

Ministry of
the Interior

IBRAHIM
HANANO
SQUARE

Germany

US

Al-Mansour St.

UK

US Cultural
Center

Al-Hurriya St.

Jawaherial Nehro St.

*Tishrin
Park*

Shukri al-Quwatli St.

Adna al-Malki St.

Al-Muwasat St.

Umar Bin
Abdel Aziz St.

*Zenobia
Park*

Al-Mahdi Bin
Baraka St.

Belgium
Egypt

Jordan

AL-UMAWIYEEN
SQUARE

23 Tammouz St.

Campus

Filastin St.

Al-Quwatli St.

**Damascus
International Fair**

**Damascus
University**

Salam al-

Fayez Mansur St.

Canada

17 Nisan St.

Abu Bakr as-Siddiq St.

Filastin St.

*Tishrin
Sports
Complex*

TO AUSTRALIAN CULTURAL CENTER,
SPORTING YOUTH CITY,
AJ JALA' SPORTS COMPLEX

AL MAZZEH

Old City

Bab
al-Faffaj

Bab
al-Faradis

Al-Malek Faysal St.

Bab
as-Salaam

Dassa St.

**Damascus
Citadel**

Dar
Al-Hadith

Arabic
Epigraphy

Al-Hamidiyya St.

Umayyad

Temple
of Jupiter

Al-Bakri St.

Bab
Tuma

Medicine and
Sciences

Aj-Jumrok
Khan

Popular Arts
and Traditions

Protestant

Franciscan

Hanania

Bab Tuma St.

**Sinan
Pasha**

Nureddin
ash-Shahid

Al-Azem Palace

Al-Azarya

Madhat Basha St.

Hammam Nureddin

St. Mary's

Marjirjos
Cathedral

Hassad Pasha Khan

Bab
al-Gabia

Hassan Kharat Bzouriyeh

As-Siba'i
House

Roman
Arch

Al-Bayanya

Bab Sharqi St.

Bab
Sharqi

Nizam

Al-Badawi St.

Bab
as-Saghir

Al-Amin St.

Bab
Kissan

Ibn 'Asaker St.

Khalid Ibn al-Walid St.

Al-Midan St.

Ash-Shagour St.

TO JORDAN

N

0   750 yards
0   750 meters

TO HOMS

TO KARAJAT
HARASTA

Al'-Askari
Sports Complex

Al-Fayha
Sports
Complex

As-Salaam
Park

Al-Malek al-'Adel St.

Al-Arsouzi
Park

Al-Pakistan St.

As-Sades min Tishrin St.

AL-QABOUN

Ath-Thawra St.

AL-'ABBASIYEEN
SQUARE

Baghdad St.

AL-YARMUK
SQUARE

Al-'Abbasiyeen
Stadium

SEE DOWNTOWN INSET

AT-TAHRIR
SQUARE

An-Nasra St.

YOUSEF
AL-AZMEH
SQUARE

SEE OLD CITY INSET

Al-Manama St.

Baroudi St.

Al Malek Faysal St.

JOBAR

An-Nasr St.

Hijaz
Railway
Station

Madhat Basha St.

Bab Sharqi St.

Ibn 'Asaker St.

Damascus

🏠 ACCOMMODATIONS

Al-Afamia Hotel, 8
Al-Hamra Hotel, 9
Al-Haramain Hotel, 3
Al-Mahaba & Al-Salan Hotel, 1
Ar-Rabi' Hotel, 2
At-tal Hotel, 4
Barada Hotel, 7
Hotel Basman, 6
Imad Hotel, 5
Sultan Hotel, 11

Al-Badawi St.

Al-Amin St.

Ash-Shagour St.

HASAN
AL-KHARRAT
SQUARE

Al-Mujtahid St.

Ibn 'Asaker St.

AL-YARMUK
SQUARE

International
Airport Rd.

TO
AIRPORT

Downtown

Al-Majles Al-Nabi St.

29 Mai Av.

Al-Azmeh St.

Al-Jala'a Av.

Al-Brazil St.

Hafez al-Assad Rd.

National
Museum

Maysaloun St.

YOUSEF
AL-'AZMEH
SQUARE

Takiyyeh
as-Sulaymaniyyeh

Jumhuriyyah Av.

Az-Zahira St.

Salam al-Barudi St.

Port Said Ave.

AL-MARJEH
SQUARE

Ramy St.

Hijaz
Railway
Station

An-Nasr St.

Ath-Thajura Av.

Al-Quds St.

Filastin St.

large picture of the late Assad. Facing away from the station, Sa'ad al-Jabri St. stretches directly away from the railway station. Walking down this street, the **post office** and **exchange bank** are on your left. Across the well-traveled footbridge crossing **al-Quwatli St.**, Sa'ad al-Jabri St. becomes **Port Said St.** Continuing on Port Said St. leads to **Yusef al-'Azmeh Sq.** Radiating to the right of this landmark is **29 Mai Ave.** (called **29 Ayyar Ave.** in Arabic) and the **Tourist Information Center.** To the left is **Maysaloun St.** and the five-star **Cham Palace Hotel** (pronounced "sham"). Continuing past the Cham Palace brings you to **Abu Roumaneh St.** (officially named **al-Jala'a Ave.**), a nicer residential area and home to several embassies and cultural centers.

For those seeking cheap eats and hotels, pistachio desserts, or money changing, find **al-Marjeh Sq.** (also named, but never called, al-Shuhada or Martyr's Sq.), two blocks off al-Nasser St. in line with the post office. Al-Marjeh Sq. has developed something of an ill reputation, as Russian prostitutes frequent many of the cheaper hotels. In the center of the square, the **Barada River** surfaces from its underground lair in the form of a big fountain. Just up from al-Marjeh Sq., across al-Quwatli St., and to the right of al-'Azmeh Sq. is the **Bahsa** district, home to some of the nicest budget hotels in the Middle East. Continue right on al-Nasser St. from the Hijaz Station to enter the **Souq al-Hamidiyyeh** and the **Old City.** A walk through the covered *souq* to the end brings you to the **Umayyad Mosque.**

A left turn from the Hijaz Station onto **al-Baroudi St.** eventually leads to the site of the annual international exposition: **Foire Internationale de Damas,** where the Barada River flows and fountains shoot high in the air. The **Taqiyyeh al-Suleimaniyyeh Mosque** and the **Military Museum** are on the right as you walk away from the station. The **National Museum** borders the river. The local **bus** and **service station** can be found under the **President Hafez al-Assad Bridge** on al-Quwatli St.

⃞ PRACTICAL INFORMATION

TOURIST AND FINANCIAL SERVICES

Tourist Office: 29 Mai Ave. (☎ 232 39 53). From Yusef al-'Azmeh Sq., walk to the right of the white modern building; the clearly-marked office will be on the left. Free maps and info in English. Open 24hr.

Tours: Nawafir Travel and Tours (☎ 231 93 27; fax 231 94 57; www.nawafir-tours.com), in basement of al-Assima Hotel in Bahsa. More helpful than the disorganized official office, Nawafir serves as the *de facto* tourism office for Damascus and greater Syria. Ask 'Adnan Habbab and Martin about "Marhaba Service," which arranges transportation from the airport and a one-night stay at a two-star hotel for newly arrived travelers (S£2025). Open daily 9:30am-2pm and 5-9pm; in winter 9:30am-2pm and 4-8pm.

Embassies: Canada, Block 12, al-Mezzeh (☎ 611 68 51; fax 611 40 00). Open Su-W 8:30-11:30am and 2-4pm, Th 8:30-11:30am. **Egypt** (☎ 333 35 61), on al-Jala'a Ave. in Abu Roumaneh. Open daily 9am-3pm. **Jordan** (☎ 333 93 13), on Ibkila St. in Abu Roumaneh. Open Sa-Th 9-11am. **Turkey,** 48 Ziad ibn Abi Sufyan St. (☎ 333 14 11; fax 333 42 53). Open Su-Th 8:30-11am. **UK** (☎ 371 25 61 or 371 25 62; fax 373 16 00), on Malki Kurd Ali St. Open M-Th 8:30-10:30am. **US,** 2 al-Mansour St. (☎ 333 13 42, emergencies 333 13 42; fax 224 79 38). Take al-Jala'a Ave. (in Abu Roumaneh) away from al-Quwatli to Rawdat Abilalan Sq. The stars and stripes are flying to the left. Consular section open Su-Th 8-11am; observes all US and most Syrian holidays.

Visa Extension Office: Head to the Barumkeh station and cross the street. Next to the news agency is the large, brown **Immigration Office.** Travelers staying in Syria for longer than two weeks must register with the police and apply for a visa extension. Know this: it will take all morning, so plan for lunch in the area. Bring four photographs and a copy of your passport. Start at the 3rd floor and follow instructions. Go early!

Currency Exchange: Always a chore. Even though it's illegal, many shop owners and travel agents in Damascus discreetly offer to change foreign currency at higher rates than banks. Many now claim that this practice is in decline and that the rewards of the black market outweigh the possibility of getting caught. Talk to locals and other travelers for advice on the current climate. Banking hours are Sa-Th 8am-2pm; many are also open 4-8pm. The **Commercial Bank of Syria,** at Yusef al-'Azmeh Sq., has a foreign cash exchange window, but does not exchange traveler's checks. Open Sa-Th 9am-1:30pm. The branch in front of the Hijaz Station exchanges cash and traveler's checks. To change traveler's checks, have passport, purchase record, and S£25 per check ready. Open Sa-Th 10am-6pm, F 10:30am-3pm.

American Express: (☎ 221 78 13; fax 221 79 38), to the right of the Sudan Airways office on al-Mutanabbi St. Heading away from Hijaz Station toward Yusef al-'Azmeh Sq., take a left on Fardous St. and al-Mutanabbi is the first left; go up the stairs. Holds mail for AmEx clients and exchanges traveler's checks in case of emergency. Staff is among the most well-informed in Damascus. Open Sa-Th 9am-1:30pm and 5-8pm.

LOCAL SERVICES

English-Language Bookstores: The **Librarie Universelle** (☎ 223 23 00, ask to be transferred), in the Cham Palace Hotel near Yusef al-'Azmeh Sq., has two big shelves full of paperbacks in various languages. Yesterday's *International Herald Tribune* and last week's *Time* and *Newsweek* available. Open daily 9am-9pm. The **Sheraton** and **Meridien Hotels** have smaller selections.

Cultural Centers: American Cultural Center, 87 Ata Ayoubi St. (☎ 333 18 78). Frequent film screenings and concerts. Open Su-Th 8am-4:30pm. **British Council** (☎ 333 84 36), at Rawdah Sq. on the left side of al-Jala'a Ave. in Abu Roumaneh. A/C reading room. Open Sa-Th 9am-9pm.

Laundromat: Al-Akrami, next to Al-Haramein Hotel in Bahsa, off al-Marjeh Sq. Pants S£25, shirts S£25, socks S£10, underwear S£10. Open Sa-Th 7am-7pm.

EMERGENCY AND COMMUNICATIONS

Emergency: Police: ☎ 112. **Ambulance:** ☎ 110. US citizens can call the embassy (☎ 333 32 32). For medical problems call the **Red Crescent** (☎ 442 16 00) or **al-Assad al-Jami'i Hospital** (☎ 212 65 00).

Tourist Police: (☎ 222 00 00). Take al-Quwatli St. past the National Museum; the office will be directly under the Hafez al-Assad Bridge, on the left side of the street. English-speaking. Open 24hr.

Late-Night Pharmacies: Hours are generally Sa-Th 9am-1:30pm and 5-9:30pm. Try **Kassar** (☎ 222 73 47), across from the post office on Sa'ad al-Jabri St. Pharmacies rotate late hours; if you can't read the posted Arabic lists, inquire at a larger hotel. The all-night **Central Pharmacy,** on Saba 'Abhar Sq., closes for lunch 1-5pm.

Telephones: The telephone office is on al-Nasser Ave., one block to the right of the Hijaz Station toward the Old City. Open daily 8am-10pm. For international calls, bring your passport, lots of cash, and a good supply of patience—placing calls can take up to an hour. A far easier way to place both domestic and international calls is to buy an **Easycomm phonecard** from the post office. Cards come in various denominations and can be used at any of the many Easycomm phone booths that dot the city. You cannot, however, dial toll-free Syrian numbers with these cards; your only hope of using a foreign phone card is at a hotel.

Internet Access: ▓**Zoni Internet Service** (☎ 232 46 70), behind Al-Haramein Hotel toward the big parking lot. No hotmail or telnet. Open a USNet or yahoo! account before you go. S£500 per 5hr., S£150 per hr., S£5 per min.

Post Office: (☎ 221 90 00), on the left of Sa'ad al-Jabri St. as you head down the street directly in front of the Hijaz Railway Station. Open Sa-Th 8am-7pm, F 9am-noon. **Poste Restante** service charges for parcels. Rates depend on Syrian customs. The **EMS** (☎ 223 69 00) office is directly behind the post office, in a little building in the parking lot. Delivery to North America or Europe normally takes three days and is more expensive than at the post office, but certainly worth it. Open Sa-Th 8am-6pm.

■ ACCOMMODATIONS

In two-star or better hotels, prices for foreigners are listed in US dollars, though other Western currencies are often accepted. The Syrian government, eager to grab greenbacks, charges "wealthy" tourists two to three times what Syrians and those with residence permits pay. To avoid this problem, use Syrian pounds whenever possible. Most hotels accept traveler's checks and will give change in dollars, but it's a good idea to have small bills on hand to simplify exchange and avoid horrible hotel exchange rates. Most two-star hotels are near Hijaz Station and the post office, but al-Marjeh Sq. has cheaper, equally comfortable options. Many "hotels" in this area moonlight as brothels and may turn you away if you're not paying extra for a bedmate, but don't let the sleazy places keep you from finding jewels—inexpensive hotels with high ceilings, tidy bathrooms, and bug-free beds. Many one-star hotels are both cheaper and cleaner than the "superior" two-star joints. The Bahsa district has more character and is a safer location, so try there first. Never forget to bargain, especially in the off-season or if a place looks empty.

BAHSA

■ **Al-Haramein Hotel** (☎ 231 94 89 or 231 42 99), on Bahsa St. With your back to the Cham Palace in Yusef al-'Azmeh Sq., walk down the windy road next to a big parking lot until you come to a sharp right. On the right, on a shady, ivy-laced street. This old Damascene house with an open courtyard and fish-filled fountain has a super-friendly staff you'll want to take home with you. Breakfast S£75. Hot showers included (S£35 for non-guests). Communal bathrooms. Reserve 3-4 days in advance, even longer during high season. Singles S£235; doubles S£395; triples S£495. V, MC.

■ **Ar-Rabi' Hotel** (☎ 231 83 74; fax 231 18 75), on Bahsa St. next door to the Al-Haramein Hotel. With your back to the Cham Palace in Yusef al-'Azmeh Sq., walk down the windy road next to a big parking lot until you come to a sharp right. Similar in style to the Al-Haramein with a larger courtyard, though not as well maintained. International phone service, airport transport, aid with hotel reservations. Breakfast S£75. Staff recommends reservations up to 10 days in advance during summer. 3-bed dorms S£175; singles S£250; doubles S£375; triples with bath S£525.

Al-Mahabba & Al-Salaam Hotel (☎ 231 65 84), on Bahsa St., toward Yusef al-'Azmeh Sq. This "peace and love hotel" offers just that to weary travelers. Famed for filling up when Al-Haramein is full. Tidy and comfortable rooms, with spotless and luxurious bathrooms. Bargain away—they take pity on students. Singles S£990; doubles S£1620.

AL-MARJEH SQ.

Hotel Basman (☎ 221 80 03; fax 224 66 89), one block uphill from al-Marjeh Sq. on the right corner of Rami St. Pleasant, pink rooms with mini-fridge, TV, fans, and bathrooms that could be cleaner. Staff speaks Persian and enough English to help. Singles S£315; doubles S£945; triples S£1125.

Imad Hotel (☎ 231 42 25), next to the At-Tal Hotel. Walk toward Bahsa on the bridge in al-Marjeh Sq; al-Shuhada St. is the second right near the live animal souq. A nice option in al-Marjeh, with refrigerators, fans, A/C, and satellite TV. Some rooms have breezy balconies with great views. Singles S£990; doubles S£1350; triples S£1710.

At-Tal Hotel (☎ 231 55 82 or 231 55 83). Walk toward Bahsa on the bridge in al-Marjeh Sq.; al-Shuhada St. is the second right near the live animal souq. Look for yellow and green sign. Rooms sunny and large, with A/C, but bathrooms could use some scrubbing. Extras: TV/VCR (S£45), fridge (S£45), bed (S£360), and breakfast (S£135). Laundry service available. Singles S£1080; doubles S£1395; triples S£1620.

NEAR HIJAZ STATION

Barada Hotel (☎ 221 25 46 or 224 14 45), directly across from post office on Sa'ad al-Jabri. Sparkling, sunny rooms, new furniture, friendly staff, and a family atmosphere make this family-owned hotel ideal for single women. Singles S£540; doubles S£810; triples S£1035; quads S£1215; private bath S£135 extra.

Sultan Hotel (☎222 57 68 or 221 69 10; fax 224 03 72), on al-Baroudi St. With your back to the station, turn left. The homey, tourist-friendly Sultan is a block down across the street. Colorful rooms with red and green carpets. Small, multi-language library in the lobby. Recommended for single women. Breakfast S£135. Singles with bath S£855; doubles S£990; triples S£1350. Rooms with A/C S£45 extra.

Al-Afamia Hotel (☎222 91 52 or 222 89 63; fax 221 46 83), off Jomhoriyyah St. directly behind the post office; take the first left after the massive building. Ask for one of the rooms on the top floor, which are brand-new with art-deco furniture. Less than ideal for single women. Singles S£1125; doubles S£1260; triples S£1485.

Al-Hamra Hotel (☎21 07 17 or 23 73 49), on Furat St. Go to the Al-Afamia Hotel on Jomhoriyyah St. directly behind the post office; take the first left. Spacious hallways, which could use extra scrubbing and more light, lead to rooms with hard mattresses. Singles S£765; doubles S£1035; triples S£1260.

◘ FOOD

There are as many food stands around al-Marjeh Sq. as portraits of Assad—hummus, falafel, and *shawarma* are Damascene staples. Fresh fruit stands serve juices that are meals unto themselves. Prices are fairly low (hummus S£30, falafel S£15, *shawarma* S£25, large juice S£40-50). The best pastry shops are around al-Marjeh Sq.—don't miss *ba'laweh*, sinfully honey-glazed pistachio treats.

Maysaloun St., just off Yusef al-'Azmeh Sq. past the Cham Palace Hotel, is home to numerous sit-down restaurants and ice cream parlors. In the evenings, the street fills with cologne-scented sweet-lovers, strolling with a sundae or large juice in hand. **Damer Patisserie** is the best ice cream parlor in Damascus. (Open Sa-Th 9am-12:30am.) If you've had enough hummus, good pizzerias line Abu Roumaneh St., one block down from Damer Patisserie. The **Christian Quarter** in the Old City (Bab Touma Sq.) has both good atmosphere and falafel, and a fast-food pizza joint. Christians have been known to flaunt their freedom from alcohol restrictions here.

▨ **Ash-Shamiat** (☎222 72 70), off Abu Roumaneh St. in al-Nijma Sq. Beaded lamps, tables with hand-sewn embroidery, fresh flowers, and hanging baskets create a kitsch conspiracy. This local favorite caters to an eclectic crowd of expats and Damascene intellectuals. Appetizers S£10-30; entrees S£60-100; drinks S£15-25. Open 24hr.

▨ **Scheherazade Palace Restaurant** (☎544 59 00). Walk down Souq al-Hamidiyyeh to the Umayyad Mosque; Scheherzade is directly behind the mosque on the right. This gorgeous restaurant is relatively inexpensive and its delectable dishes take Syrian cuisine to a new level. Outdoor seating available. Appetizers S£20; main courses S£140. Open daily 10am-1am.

Nadi al-'Ummal (☎231 87 69). Turn right off 29 Ayyar Ave. at Cinema al-Sufara and follow the lamp-lined path to the end of the street. You won't find many proletarians at this "Workers' Club," but you will find excellent appetizers (S£50-70) and grills (S£85-100) while relaxing in the *argeileh*-scented breezes of an old Damascene courtyard. Barada beer S£60. *Argeileh* S£80. Open Sa-Th 5pm-midnight.

(ALMOST) FINGER-LICKIN' GOOD Slower than its neighbors Lebanon and Jordan to import grease-to-go Western fast food chains, Syria may seem to be catching up based on the plethora of KFC advertisements that have recently sprung up. Contrary to the signs and to popular belief, though, there is no Kentucky Fried Chicken in Damascus. The Colonel and his artery-clogging fare opened for just one day before the government shut him down for being too Western. The unlucky but enterprising owner soon hit upon an ingenious solution: he made a few alterations on his sign and quickly reopened shop as the Kuwaiti Food Company. Plans to garb the Colonel in traditional Arab headgear have been put on hold.

Abu al-Ezz (☎221 81 74 or 224 60 05). With your back to the Umayyad Mosque, walk through the arch of the Temple of Jupiter and take the first right; it's on the left. One of the best places in Damascus to soak up Syrian atmosphere and food. Try the *bas bash-kat* (S£85). Lunch and dinner S£350-400. Reservations required for dinner. Live music and whirling dervishes in the Bedouin tent after 9:30pm. Open daily 8am-1am.

Pizza Roma (☎331 64 34), off Maysaloun St., on the right just past the Cham Palace. A modern and authentic pizza joint with a rare (but rather feeble) salad bar (e.g., no lettuce). Create your own pizza with thick or crispy crust and a variety of swineless toppings. Pizzas S£50-150. Open daily 11am-1am.

Abu Kamal (☎222 42 65), in Yusef al-'Azmeh Sq, upstairs in the Ministry of Labor building on the corner of Fardous St. Devastating Syrian fare at foreign prices. Bow-tied waiters bring succulent entrees (S£90-200) while you gaze through large windows onto the square. Delicious *kebbeh* (breaded lamb fried with onions). Appetizers S£35-100; desserts S£50. Open daily 7am-2am. V, MC.

'Ali Baba (☎222 54 34), in Yusef al-'Azmeh Sq. A monumental achievement in Arab aesthetics, the basement is a womb of Arab decoration and decorum. Appetizers S£40-90; entrees S£100-200. Whirling dervishes (and dervishettes) entrap happy eaters in summer Th and Sa 8:30-11pm. Open daily 9am-midnight. V, MC, AmEx.

📷 SIGHTS

CITADEL. Built by the Seljuks in 1078 CE, the Citadel once housed elaborate baths, mosques, and schools. During the crusader invasions, it functioned as headquarters for Egyptian and Syrian sultans, including Salah al-Din. The Ayyubid Sultan Malik al-'Adil demolished and rebuilt the Citadel in 1202 CE because he felt it was no longer suitable for contemporary warfare. The new fortress has 300 arrow slits and was once surrounded by a deep moat, now filled in to serve as the *souq* floor. As of August 2000, it was closed for renovations, but you can still get a peek through the wrought iron gate. *(Next to the entrance of Souq al-Hamidiyyeh in the Old City.)*

SOUQ AL-HAMIDIYYEH. A rich and colorful trail of desserts, spices, nuts, sequined gems, raw meat, men selling corn out of boiling pots for pennies, and a large bath (see **Hammam Nour al-Din**, p. 577), Souq al-Hamidiyyeh assails all your senses as you whisk through seemingly endless tunnels. *(Beginning next to the Citadel and stretching to the Temple of Jupiter and the Umayyad Mosque.)*

UMAYYAD MOSQUE. Caliph Walid ibn Abd al-Malik supervised the building of the Umayyad Mosque, one of the oldest and grandest mosques in the world. Originally the site of an ancient temple dedicated to Hadad (an Aramaean god revered around 1000 BCE), it was later the temple of Jupiter the Damascene. In the 4th century, a Byzantine church dedicated to St. John the Baptist was erected on this site. The church was destroyed to make room for the grand mosque; the only relic that survived was the head of St. John (known to Muslims as the Prophet Yahya), now resting in its own shrine in the mosque's prayer hall. The shrine is a site of veneration for both Christians and Muslims. Today, the mosque is an energetic, if crowded, center of socializing, business transaction, gossip, and worship. The mosque's three minarets were built in different styles, reflecting the changes of different empires. Intricate mosaics decorate the walls of the mosque, and on the central dome are the names of some of the most significant figures in early Muslim history. *(Follow Souq al-Hamidiyyeh to the end. Open daily 9:30am-9pm, closed for prayer F 12:30-2pm. S£10 includes entrance to Salah al-Din's Tomb; S£50 may occasionally be charged in summer. Use the visitors' entrance to the left of the main entrance. Robes S£15, but conservatively dressed women with head scarves can avoid this fee.)*

SALAH AL-DIN'S TOMB. The famed fighter's body lies under a red dome in a peaceful garden mausoleum. Built in 1193 CE and later restored by Kaiser Wilhelm II of Germany in the 19th century, the building contains both a wooden and a marble tomb in the place of honor. The marble was a gift from the Kaiser; Salah al-Din chose to stay in the wooden one. Before the Umayyad Mosque at the end of Souq al-Hamidiyyeh stand the remains of the 3rd-century CE **Temple of Jupiter,** now a source of shade for magazine and Qur'an sellers. *(Follow Souq al-Hamidiyyeh down to the end. The tomb is to the left of the Umayyad Mosque, on the way to its visitors' entrance. Open daily 9am-5pm; in winter 10am-4pm. Free with paid admission to the Umayyad Mosque.)*

■**IRANIAN MOSQUE (SAYYIDA RAQAI'YA'S MOSQUE).** Financed by Iranians, this mausoleum and mosque was built for Lady Raqai'ya, the daughter of Imam Hussein. Beautiful blues and yellows of mosaics surround her golden, chandelier-lit shrine. *(Near the Umayyad Mosque, but farther north toward the Barada River. Open daily 4am-2am. Conservative dress and headscarf required (provided free). All faiths welcome.)*

AL-AZEM PALACE. First built under the Ottomans in 1749 for As'ad Basha al-Azem, the governor of Damascus, this palace also briefly housed King Faisal after the Ottomans' fall in World War I. Surrounding the courtyard are various rooms with reenacted Ottomanesque scenes, including a *madrasa* and a bridal room complete with mother-in-law, unwed daughters, and maids. Inside, the **Museum of Popular Traditions** has the usual stone-faced mannequins in anatomically impossible poses, with French-only labels. *(On the right side of the Umayyad Mosque when approaching from Souq al-Hamidiyyeh. Palace and museum open W-M 9am-5:30pm; in winter 9am-3:30pm. S£300, students S£15.)*

CHRISTIAN QUARTER. The **Chapel of Ananias,** dedicated to the Christian disciple who restored sight to St. Paul, is here. *(Follow Souq al-Hamidiyyeh to the Umayyad Mosque. Circle to the right around the mosque and continue farther down any road; you're in the Christian Quarter when mosques turn to churches. Cross Bab Touma St. and the chapel is ahead. Open daily 9am-1pm and 4-7pm. Free.)* Across Midhat Basha St. stands **St. Paul's Chapel,** the Armenian Orthodox church from which that same saint was lowered out of a window to escape arrest by his Jewish enemies. You may have to knock at the gate for entrance; the friendly multilingual staff will be happy to let you in and give you a religious history lesson. *(Open daily 8am-1:30pm. Free.)*

TAQIYYEH AL-SULEIMANIYYEH MOSQUE. While this mosque, in downtown Damascus, is open only to Muslims, its simple yet striking exterior is a compelling expression of Ottoman architecture. Built in 1554 CE by the famed architect Sinan, its two lofty minarets frame an imposing dome reflected in a courtyard fountain. The surrounding *madrasa* was converted into the **Artisanat,** an Ottoman market offering silver jewelry, oil paintings, and mother-of-pearl inlaid backgammon boards. *(From Yusef al-'Azmeh Sq., walk down Port Said St. to Salam al-Baroudi St. Take a right; the mosque and market are down on the right. Most shops open daily 9am-9pm. V, MC.)*

▥ MUSEUMS

■**NATIONAL MUSEUM.** Admire the collection of writings in Ugarit (the first alphabet dating from the 14th century BCE), Aramaic (the language that Jesus spoke), and Arabic amidst the shady green courtyard. The permanent collection contains Syrian sculpture, a Qur'an collection, Palmyran textiles from the first three centuries CE, original scientific writings of Ibn Sina, and an entire reconstructed underground tomb from Palmyra. Beyond the door at the end of the last hall stand the frescoed walls of a synagogue excavated from the 3rd-century CE town of Doura Europos. *(One street over from the Taqiyyeh al-Suleimaniyyeh mosque. Open M-W 9am-6pm. S£300, students S£15. Ask the guard to let you in.)*

MILITARY MUSEUM. This museum stands at attention, displaying both ancient and modern weapons and photographs that pay homage to those who have perished for their country. *(Across the street from the cafe of the National Museum, next door to the Taqiyyeh al-Suleimaniyyeh mosque. Open W-M 8am-1:30pm. S£200, students S£5.)*

> ### WHY YOU GOTTA (FORE)PLAY ME LIKE
> **THAT?** No self-respecting Damascene movie theater lacks eye-catching adver-
> tisements. Go to any of these movie houses and you will likely encounter posters
> depicting couples in titillating positions, captured *in flagrante delicto*, adding a bit of
> erotic flair to the already frenzied Damascene streets. A striking example of this is two
> healthy maidens clad in black bikinis, captured by the camera as they jump off a boat
> into the sea and expose just the requisite amount of flesh to set those raging hormones
> aflame. Anyone hoping that the promises made outside the theater will come to frui-
> tion inside will be disappointed: Syrian censorship laws require that sexually explicit
> material be deleted from films. Laws say nothing about advertisements, however, and
> Damascene movie house managers accordingly exploit the loophole.

◪ NIGHTLIFE

When it comes to nightlife, Damascenes know how to sit back and relax. Soak in a
hammam before heading off to a cafe or bar for the night. If you'd rather catch a
movie, the high-quality **Cham Palace Theater** has regular showings of American
films (every 3hr. 12:30-9:30pm, S£100.)

CAFES

As the evenings cool, Damascenes of all stripes take to the streets. Outdoor
cafes pepper the area behind the Umayyad Mosque. By the end of the evening,
the place grows into a big street party as people pull up chairs to drink or
smoke *argeileh*. Try one of the best Old City cafes, **An-Nawafara,** which features nightly Arabic storytelling (9pm; in winter 6:30pm). Take Souq al-Hamidiyyeh to the Umayyad Mosque. Turn right at the mosque and proceed around
the mosque wall. Take the first right; the cafe is on the immediate right. Unlike
most cafes, this one welcomes single women. (☎543 68 13. *Argeileh* S£35;
Turkish coffee S£25. Open daily 8am-midnight.) Younger people line **Maysaloun
St.** in downtown Damascus at night. This street sits at the crossroads of Yusef
al-'Azmeh St. and Port Said St.

BARS

Much late-night and early-morning activity in Damascus takes place in bars of
large hotels and in the Christian quarter around Bab Touma, where alcohol restrictions are thrown by the wayside. Women will not be received warmly at most local
bars, though hotels and nicer bars in Bab Touma are exceptions. It is wise for
women to find trustworthy male companions. Many embassies rotate hosting parties on Thursday nights; call the American or British embassies for details.

Mar Mar (☎541 00 41), in Bab Touma near Hammam Bakree, across from the Al-Issar
Restaurant. The closest approximation to a mellow Western bar. Its lovely decor and setting in an old Damascene mansion explain its popularity. Young, wealthy jet-setters
drink beer (S£100) and eat steak (S£275) while listening to the fresh tunes of local
groups. Open Th-Su until 2am. Reservations recommended Th and Sa nights.

Le Piano (☎543 03 75), on the last left off of Hanamia St. before Bab Sharqi in the Old
City. Serves cold beer (S£120) and plays karaoke amid a musically themed decor. No
cover. Reservations necessary. Only singles admitted.

Casa Blanca, on the last left off of Hanamia St. before Bab Sharqi in the Old City, down
the street from Le Piano. Classy decor with beautiful roofed courtyard and open-air fountained terrace. Great place for lap-of-luxury drinks. Beer S£100-150; wine S£450-900.

POOLS AND BATHS

You can take a dip for S£200 in the numerous **swimming pools** in Damascus (many at larger hotels). True decadence, however, is most closely approximated at the *hammams* (Turkish baths) that gurgle around the *souq*.

Hammam Nour al-Din (☎222 95 13), in the covered street between the Umayyad Mosque and Midhat Basha St. The most luxurious *hammam* in Damascus, but caters to men only. Full massage, bath, soap, and sauna S£240. Open daily 9am-midnight.

Hammam al-Ward (☎231 43 07), near the black and white al-Ward Mosque in Bahsa, two streets behind the Al-Haramein Hotel. This is for women who want to experience a Damascene *hammam*. Make a special appointment for any time or day, but the fee will be exorbitant (and you'll be lonely unless you've formed a private female brigade). The works S£200. Open for women Tu-W 11am-11pm, for men Th-M 11am-11pm.

ⓘ DAYTRIPS FROM DAMASCUS

BOSRA بصرى

Luxury buses from Damascus leave for Bosra from Karajat Barumkeh (1¾hr., every 2hr. 8am-8pm, S£50). Ask upon arrival what time they return (the last bus usually departs at 8:30pm). These buses are very punctual, so arrive at least 10 minutes before departure time. Luxury buses are probably the best option for traveling to Bosra, since they are quick and cheap. Microbuses from Karaj Dara'a on the southern edge of Damascus go to Dar'a (2hr., S£45), but it's another 30 minutes and S£15 to Bosra. The Citadel is open daily 8am-7pm. S£300, students S£15.

For an under-touristed piece of Syria and solitude amongst Roman ruins, make your way to Bosra (only 20km from Jordan). Nineteen centuries ago, Bosra was the northern capital of the Nabatean kingdom, best known for building and abandoning the castles at Petra, Jordan (see p. 491). The Romans annexed the city in 106 CE, renamed it *Neatrajana Bustra*, and made it the capital of the Province of Arabia. Muslim control began in 634 CE, and the 6000-seat theater (with standing room for 3000 more) was converted into a citadel over the next six centuries: fortifications were added, a second outer wall was constructed, and more rooms were built to accommodate increasing numbers of horses and soldiers.

Enter Bosra through the stark **City Gate,** constructed around 200 BCE and known to former inhabitants as *Bab al-Hawa* (Gate of the Wind). At the entrance, several Roman columns will greet you. Straight ahead is the **Cryptoportic,** once a great market constructed in the first half of the 2nd century. The well-preserved 3rd-century **Central Arch,** known to locals as *Bab al-Qandil* (Gate of the Lantern), stands to the right. Continue to the right to reach the splendid **Roman Baths.** For a little extra money, the guard will open a back gate to the actual bathing and washing area. To see the most impressive structure in Bosra, the **Roman Theater-Arab Citadel** complex, retrace your steps to the Central Arch and turn left. Second only to Palmyra in terms of Roman remains in Syria, the Roman Theater is one of the best preserved in the world, with secret stairways and an undamaged stage.

Bosra boasts historically significant Muslim sights as well. The 7th- (some say 8th-) century **Mosque of 'Umar** is purportedly the third oldest mosque in the Islamic world, yet still maintains some of its original form as a pagan temple. The **Mabrak Mosque** also rests in Bosra, to which (according to legend) a camel brought the first copy of the Qur'an in Syria. The 3rd-century **basilica** is where Prophet Muhammad allegedly met Nestorian monk Bahira, who was the first to predict the Prophet's future greatness. South of the City Gate is *Birkat al-Hajj* (Pool of Pilgrimage), a huge reservoir dug by the Romans. A branch of Wadi Zeid supposedly fed by a conduit system flowed down from the hills and emptied itself into this reservoir. For a moment of peace, walk east toward Suweida to the **Cistern.**

If the afternoon of sightseeing makes your tummy grumble, face away from the reservoir gate and look for the biggest restaurant in the right-hand corner of the tourist courtyard. **Al-Tarajana** provides food on the spot (salad, hummus, french fries), as well as freshly prepared dinners if you call ahead. Try the *mishawi*, or mutton or veal fried with onions and spices. (☎ (015) 97 02 95 or 790 02 95. Entrees S£350. Open daily 8am-midnight. 20% ISIC discount.)

MA'ALULA معلولا

Ma'alula is an easy daytrip from Damascus, with frequent minibuses from Karaj Ma'alula on the east side of town (1hr., S£20). To get to the karaj, take a service to Abbaseyeen Sq.; it's down al-Nasra St. on the left. Alternatively, take a taxi (S£30).

The tiny town of Ma'alula (56km northeast of Damascus) is tucked quietly into the al-Qalamoun Mountains. Ancient churches and old mosques drowse among blue houses, precipitously clinging to steep slopes beneath staggering cliffs. Ma'alula is worlds away from the rapid developments of nearby Damascus—townspeople still speak **Aramaic,** the language in which both Jesus preached and the Lord's Prayer was authored. Aramaic remained the vernacular of Syria until replaced by Arabic after the Islamic conquests of the 7th century. The language only survived among the few Christians who lived in isolated villages in the mountains.

The **Monastery of St. Taqla** was carved into the face of a nearby barren cliff in the 4th century to hold the remains of the young saint. The daughter of a Seleucid prince, Taqla was a disciple of St. John and a convert to Christianity before such behavior became popular. She ran away from home when a servant revealed that her father had plans to kill her. While being pursued on the night she was to be burned, she was led by an angel toward safety: a mountain opened up for her and then quickly closed, crushing her father's soldiers.

The road around to the left of the town and the cliffs leads to the mountaintop chapel of **Mar Sarkis,** named after a Syrian horseman during the reign of King Maximus (3rd century CE). If you continue along the road past the Safir Hotel, you'll see the entrance to the mountain path at the bridge on the left. This takes you to St. Taqla's Monastery; a right turn leads to cliffs and spectacular views.

SAYIDNAYA صيدنايا

To get to Sayidnaya, take a bus from Karaj Ma'alula on the east side of town (40 min., S£15). To get to the karaj, take a service to Abbaseyeen Sq.; it's down al-Nasra St. on the left. Alternatively, take a taxi (S£30). Though infrequent minibuses connect Sayidnaya and Ma'alula, you'll likely have to backtrack to Damascus to do it all in one day.

Sayidnaya (Arabic for "Our Lady"), a sandstone town of small shops, beautiful views, and a glowing hilltop chapel, rests 29km between both Damascus and Ma'alula. The **Chapel of the Virgin** in the center of town was built in 547 CE to honor the spot where the Virgin Mary appeared before a wealthy hunter. Today, it serves as both a small orphanage and school, demonstrating the communal interplay between religion and education. Within a maze of stone stairways, a shrine to the Virgin contains an **icon** (said to have been painted by St. Luke), to which miracles throughout the ages have been attributed. To the right of the church is the entrance to a small, underground **sanctuary** where Mary supposedly stood. It may be necessary to get the security guard to ask one of the nuns to open the mirrored doors protecting the icon and sanctuary. The inscription outside the entrance echoes the commandment Moses was given before the Burning Bush (Exodus 3:5): "Take off your shoes, for the ground you are treading upon is sacred." In the time of the Crusaders, Sayidnaya was second only to Jerusalem as a place of pilgrimage, and was called (redundantly) Notre Dame de Sayidnaya. Pilgrims and respectful visitors may be allowed to spend one night in the clean, spacious rooms of the convent for free.

QUNEITRA قنيطرة

*Visitors must obtain permission from the Syrian Tourist Police before going to Quneitra. The free permit can be obtained at the office behind Palace Adnan al-Malki. Go up the stairs from the white monument and look for men with rifles out front. Bring your **passport** (which will often be checked on the way to Quneitra). Permit office open Su-Th 8am-2pm; permit valid for that day or the next. **Buses** leave every 10 minutes (or when full) from Baramkeh Station for Khan Arnabeh (1½hr., S£20), then from Khan Arnabeh to Quneitra (15min., S£5). More expensive buses go straight from Damascus to Quneitra. Pick up your mandatory guide/security officer between Khan Arnabeh and Quneitra. Don't take pictures of anything vaguely official-looking: your whole roll of film could be confiscated.*

The war-ravaged town of Quneitra (a diminished form of *qantara*, "bridge") owes its misfortune to its location beside the Golan Heights at an intersection of roads leading to four countries. Quneitra was destroyed during the Syrian-Israeli conflict in 1967 (see **Modern History,** p. 556) and has recently been opened by the Syrian government as a "museum." The incident on the Golan was a major factor in the political destabilization that allowed the still-governing Ba'ath Party to seize control in November 1970. Quneitra is a fair distance from Damascus, but a visit to the town is worthwhile: although unimpressive as a memorial to those who perished during the bombings, the town does offer a firsthand look at the aftermath of military conflicts that have long plagued the Middle East. Visitors are given a guided tour of the modern ruins, including a walk through the crumbled main street, now overgrown with weeds. The partially destroyed mosque, church, and hospital have been stripped bare and are riddled with bullet holes. On some days, especially Fridays, you can see families yelling at each other by megaphone between the Golan and the Syrian UN border (only 2km), adding a human face to a conflict plaguing the Middle East. Binoculars are provided at the Quneitra Restaurant to gaze out over the UN Military Security Zone at Israel, just 500m away.

SUWEIDA سويدة

Buses from Damascus to Suweida (130km southeast) leave from Karaj Suweida, which is actually the same place as Karaj Dara'a (1½hr., S£30). Service from Damascus to Suweida leave Karaj Suweida rather frequently (1½ hr., S£30). Damas Tours also offers regular service to Suweida (1½hr., S£50). To get to Suweida from Bosra, take a service from the town to Karaj Suweida in Damascus (30min., S£10).

In the 3rd century, the Romans considered Suweida (then known as Dionysis) one of the most important towns in the Province of Arabia. Late in the Nabatean period, the area was called Suwada ("little black town") because it was constructed with black volcanic rock. In recent decades, however, this provincial town has been bulldozed to make way for new houses built to accommodate the growing population. Suweida has little to offer travelers as a daytrip from Damascus, and is best visited in order to see Qanawat. Don't leave, however, without appreciating the well-organized and informative **Suweida Museum,** one kilometer up the hill from the bus station. Many of Suweida's ruins have been preserved in this museum, built and organized in 1991 with the aid of the French. It contains artifacts dating from the Stone Age to the Roman Empire, including many well-preserved basalt statues. The highlights are the mosaics from Shaba in the main room, especially the beautiful "Artemis surprised while bathing" from the mid-3rd century CE. (Open daily 9am-6pm; in winter 9am-4pm. S£300, students S£15.)

If you're hungry, Suweida has several restaurants in the city center *(wust al-balad)*. For a unique East-meets-West experience, turn your back to the bus station and admire the gaudy, mirrored **al-Luts Restaurant** in Basil Hafez al-Azem Sq. Bounce to 80's tunes while eating hamburgers and cheese pie. (Appetizers S£20-50; entrees S£50-100. ☎23 01 59. Open daily 9am-midnight. Western style toilets.)

QANAWAT قنوات

Buses to Qanawat leave frequently from the main bus station in Suweida (S£2-5). Buses from Damascus to Suweida leave from Karaj Suweida, which is the same place as Karaj Dara'a (1½hr., S£30). Service from Damascus to Suweida leave Karaj Suweida rather frequently (1½ hr., S£30).

Once a member of the Decapolis League of merchant cities, ancient ▧Qanawat flourished under Ghassanid rule in the first century BCE. Apart from the monuments at Bosra, those at Qanawat are the most impressive and richly decorated in the region around Damascus. Cracked yet superb, ancient stones dot the ground, hide themselves in present-day dwellings, or soar up as haughty columns. Qanawat also prides itself as a pilgrimage site for the **Druze,** a sect derived from the Ismai'ili branch of Shi'ite Islam. They have been living in the area of Mount al-Duruz since the 11th century CE.

Qanawat stretches from the crest of a hill to the side of a valley, framed by trees, gardens, and meadows. Coming from Suweida, a cluster of columns belonging to a 2nd-century temple rises at the entrance to the present village. The village square of Qanawat currently takes the place of the ancient forum. Old paving-stones still cover parts of the ground. The street up the hillside leads to the **Temple of Zeus,** which boasts a view over the entire valley, and "the serail," a group of monuments at the highest point in Qanawat. A clump of trees marks the monuments and a little wall surrounds them. Ask the gatekeeper to let you in.

Roman and Christian buildings diversify the ruins in Qanawat. Columns of an ancient temple, used to support a basilica in the 4th and 5th centuries CE, can still be seen. A characteristic floral pattern marks the walls of this building as well as the many fragments lying on the ground. The right slope of the valley is home to a few steps of a small theatre, the remains of a nymphaeum and an aqueduct, and the foundations of a both a round and square tower. For a more reflective visit, grab something to drink at the only cafe in town, where you can also browse the Arabic and French guidebook for more maps and photographs of Qanawat.

CENTRAL SYRIA

PALMYRA تدمر ☎31

The desert oasis of Palmyra ("City of Palms," also known locally as Tadmor, "City of Dates") first offered travelers shade in the first century BCE, when it was a stopover for caravans passing from the Persian Gulf to the Mediterranean. Palmyrenes prospered from tax revenues collected from tired, thirsty traders and grew even wealthier after their city became a Roman colony in 129 CE. Palmyra became the keystone of a thriving trade between the Roman Empire, the Middle East, and India, and most of the city's surviving ruins date from this period of prosperity.

During the middle of the 2nd century CE, reduced trade and increased distaste for Persian rule inspired Palmyran resident **Odenathus** to overthrow the city's senate and declare himself king. Odenathus and his son were assassinated in 267 CE after defeating the encroaching Persians, but Odenathus's multilingual and strikingly beautiful second wife **Zenobia** took control of the city on behalf of her young son. Possessing "manly understanding" according to 18th-century historian Edward Gibbon, this Greek-Arab woman not only secured Palmyra's full independence from Rome, but also attacked the Roman territories and took possession of lower Egypt and much of Asia Minor. The minting of coins emblazoned with her image was the last straw: infuriated Roman emperor Aurelian successfully attacked Palmyra and carted Zenobia off to Rome.

In succeeding years, Palmyra served as a Roman border fortress until Muslims conquered it in the 7th century CE. Local emir Fakhr al-Din built the castle overlooking the site in the early 1600s, but the ruined city was only sporadically inhabited. By mid-century, no one knew the once-proud city existed. In 1678, two English merchants rediscovered the city, but excavations did not begin until 1924. First centered in the courtyard of the Temple of Bel, the modern town was relocated northeast of the ruins between 1929 and 1932. Today, Palmyra maintains much of the grandeur from its days as a Roman province: its column-lined avenues stand proudly in a lush oasis surrounded by miles of uninhabited desert. Palmyra's ruins, though weathered by centuries of war and sandstorms, rank among the most spectacular in the Middle East. As a result of its well-deserved fame, Palmyra has fallen prey to the clutches of tourism. Nevertheless, Palmyra's sunsets over majestic ruins endure.

▐▛ GETTING THERE AND GETTING AROUND

Buses: The **Karnak Station** (☎91 02 88) is near the circle by the post office. From Karnak, buses run to: **Damascus** (3hr.; 10:15am, 12:30, 1:45, 5pm; S£100); **Deir al-Zur** (2hr.; 11:30am, 1:30, 3:15, 5:30, 7, 9pm; S£75); and **Homs** (2hr., 7am and 2:30pm, S£65). **Qadmoos,** a more luxurious option, runs to: **Damascus** (3hr., every hr., S£110); **Deir al-Zur** (2hr., every 30min., S£85); and **Tartus** and **Lattakia** via **Homs** (2:30, 3:30am, 4:30pm; S£145). **Damas Tours** are among the most luxurious of the numerous private buses that travel to **Damascus, Homs,** and several smaller towns. Schedules are unpredictable; ask New Afqa Hotel owner Mahran for updated info.

Service and public buses: To **Homs** (2hr., S£50) from the *service* station, a 5-minute walk down the main street past the post office. *Service* to Damascus leave just across the street, starting at 6am (S£75).

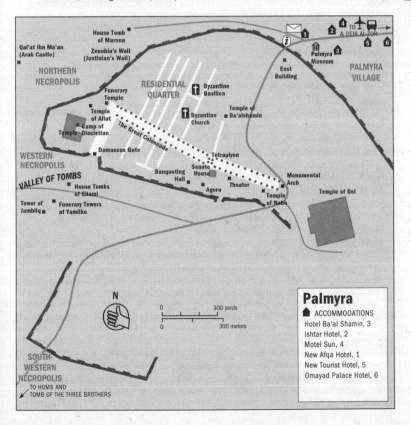

Palmyra

⌂ ACCOMMODATIONS

Hotel Ba'al Shamin, 3
Ishtar Hotel, 2
Motel Sun, 4
New Afqa Hotel, 1
New Tourist Hotel, 5
Omayad Palace Hotel, 6

SYRIA

▶ PRACTICAL INFORMATION

Tourist Office: (☎91 05 74). On the highway between the ruins and the new city. This new, bilingual office provides maps, brochures, and a few backgammon hints. Open Sa-W 8am-2pm and 5-8pm, F morning only. Get more helpful books and guides at the entrance to the Museum of the Temple of Bel.

Currency exchange: Best done before coming to Palmyra, though some hotels change money. The Cham Palace does it most legally, but at the worst rates.

Police: An English-speaking representative of the **tourist police** can be reached at the Temple of Bel (☎91 05 17), while the **police station** (☎91 01 58) is on the main street off the highway as you reach the first hotels in the new town.

Pharmacy: (☎91 04 55). Just down from the Spring Restaurant on the right of the main street. Open Sa-Th 9am-1pm, F 9am-noon.

Hospital: ☎91 05 51.

Telephones: Outside the post office, inside the Temple of Bel, and outside the museum. Purchase a phonecard in the post office.

Post Office: Near the circle on the highway. Open daily 8am-2pm.

▶ ACCOMMODATIONS

The town of Palmyra has been steadily encroaching upon the outlying ruins of Palmyra for years. Despite the renovation of hotels and the continual rise of prices, a number of friendly and inexpensive options remain. Most hotels and restaurants are on the main street starting at the highway. Hotels that charge in dollars are more comfortable, though about six times more expensive.

New Afqa Hotel (☎91 03 86), near the post office and the new tourist office, before the Karnak station. The best budget deal in town, if not in all of Syria. Gregarious manager Mahran goes to great lengths to keep patrons happy. Pleasant, well-kept rooms come with clean sheets. Breakfast S£50. Singles S£200; doubles S£400.

Ishtar Hotel (☎91 30 73; fax 91 32 60), on the left at the beginning of the main street, is one of the first hotels you'll see upon entering the city. Warren Beatty never had service this good. Doubles with bath and breakfast US$20. V, MC, AmEx.

Omayad Palace Hotel (☎91 07 55), 250m down the main street to the right of the fountain. Rest like an Umayyad caliph in the pastel-hued lobby and spacious, shaded courtyard of this former Palmyrene house. Spartan, but pleasant rooms come at a good price. Breakfast S£50. Singles S£200; doubles S£300; triples S£450.

Hotel Ba'al Shamin (☎91 05 37), one block south of the main street and a block down from the museum. Boasts spacious rooms and the cheapest inhabitable singles in Palmyra. Check out the oblong, private baths bent L-shaped around the bedrooms. Singles S£150; doubles S£300; triples S£600.

Motel Sun (☎91 11 33). Walk away from the ruins and take the first left after the Ishtar Hotel. It's more like a homey bed-and-breakfast than a hotel, but prices are fair for well-maintained rooms. Singles S£200-300; doubles S£350; triples S£450.

New Tourist Hotel (☎91 03 33), on the right side of the main street, is actually the oldest in Palmyra. The effusive comments in the guestbook confirm that this is a backpackers' haven. Summer rooftop mattresses S£100; 3-bed dorms S£125, with bath S£150; singles S£200; doubles S£325.

▶ FOOD

Palmyra's main street abounds with restaurants catering to tourists' every desire. Meals are universally decent, but prices vary depending on tourist traffic. Some hostels serve local beer (S£75) until 11pm. Local diners are also ready and eager to feed you, but don't let them rip you off. The best option is to get invited for some down-home Syrian cookin'. Be sure to sample the traditional Levantine dish *mensaf* (see **Jordan: Food and Drink,** p. 452).

Palmyra Tourist Restaurant (☎91 03 46) dazzles with fountains, canopies, an in-house boutique, and reasonably priced meals. *Mezze* chicken, mineral water, and salad S£200; hummus with meat S£75; soup S£30. Beer, wine, and *'araq* also served. Open daily 7:30am-midnight.

Spring Restaurant (☎91 03 07), on the right of the main street. Offers tasty *mensaf,* served with a choice of chicken or lamb and yogurt on the side (S£200-250). Get meat entrees (S£125) in the relaxing upstairs Bedouin tent. A breakfast of omelettes and cheese goes for S£50. Open daily 7am until the *shawarma* runs out.

Oasis Restaurant (☎91 14 39). A male haven next to the tourist office. Offers a large group buffet at the ruins with music and dancing in tents. Open daily 7pm-midnight.

👁 SIGHTS

Palmyra takes a full day to explore. The best way to see the ruins is to follow the sun: wake up at dawn, catch the spectacular sunrise, and begin exploring before the sun is directly overhead. In the summer, take necessary precautions because it is **hot.** Bring about 2L of water and finish exploring no later than noon.

TEMPLE OF BEL. This mammoth building, enclosed in a high, largely reconstructed wall, is a good place to begin exploring Palmyra. The gatehouse has books on Syria and Palmyra, and the guides who gather here are useful for a more in-depth appreciation of the ruins (they may charge up to S£1000 per day, though bargaining can cut prices in half). The existing Temple of Bel was constructed in 32 CE over an older Hellenistic site. Bel is a Babylonian pronunciation of the Semitic word *Ba'al* ("master"), the name for the supreme deity who was identified with the Greek god Zeus (Jupiter in Rome). The **altar** in the middle of the temple was used for animal sacrifices; blood ran into the drain in the floor and was emptied into a sophisticated plumbing system (only a large stone pipe sitting beside the drainage hole remains). The impressive **cella** ("shrine")—the free-standing building in the center of the temple—was built from 17 to 32 CE. Small shrines to the right and left reflect the multitude of deities that constituted the godhead of the mighty Bel. Several intricate carvings of grapes and pineapples, hinting at Palmyra's rich agricultural past, can be found outside the entrance and at the bottom of the stone slab. *(Gatehouse open daily 8am-1pm and 4-6pm; in winter 8am-4pm. S£300, students S£15.)*

MONUMENTAL ARCH. The Great Colonnade once led from the Temple of Bel to the Monumental Arch and the rest of the city. Constructed in 200 CE, the oft-photographed structure is richly decorated with rows of pears, acorns, and palm trunks, as well as acanthus, oak, and grape leaves. On the left, just past the arch, stands the **Temple of Nabo,** raised two meters off the ground. Dedicated to the Babylonian god of writing (later identified with Apollo), this first-century CE construction (along with **Zenobia's Baths** to the right) is largely in ruins. Up the colonnade and to the left is a newly renovated **theater.** More than half of it was reconstructed in the past two decades. The stage, the semi-circular pit where the chorus performed, and the foundations of the actors' dressing rooms remain visible. *(S£300, students S£15.)*

AGORA AND ENVIRONS. Farther down the street to the left are the not-so-distinct remains of the **Agora** (public market) and the **Senate House.** Social position determined one's placement in the Agora: Palmyran and Roman officials sat in the northern portico, senators in the eastern portico, soldiers in the western portico, and merchants and caravan leaders in the southern portico. Next door is the **Banqueting Hall,** where religious fraternities congregated to celebrate deity-inspired holidays. The prominent Tetrapylon consists of four groups of poorly rebuilt columns. The pedestals in the center of each group of columns once supported statues, including ones of the great Zenobia and her husband, Odenathus. To the right of the Tetrapylon, near the Zenobia Hotel, is the **Temple of Ba'alshamin,** dedicated to Zeus Ba'alshamin, whose name means "Master of the Heavens." Ba'alshamin was the god of storms and fertilizing rains. The locked vestibule of the temple has six columns with platforms as bases for statues. To the right, the ruins partially covered by the Zenobia Hotel used to be a colonnaded courtyard surrounded by rooms and a chapel. This complex's role within the temple remains unknown.

QAL'AT IBN MA'AN. The imposing Qal'at Ibn Ma'an, or Arab Castle, is attributed to Fakhr al-Din, who once ruled the area between Mount Lebanon and the Syrian desert. This fortress, built in the 12th or 13th century to protect Palmyra from Crusader attacks, is *the* place to be at sunset, though busloads of photo-snapping tourists can mar the experience during the high season (Mar.-May). Climb the 150m slope for free (30-45min.) or bargain for a ride from town; S£200 with a two-hour wait is reasonable. *(Open daily until just after sunset. S£150, students S£15.)*

FUNERARY TOWERS. To the left of Qal'at Ibn Ma'an are funerary towers, known as "eternal houses" in Palmyra. Each of the most important families had its own mausoleum, though there are also individual sepulchres. The tombs are a 30-minute walk from the main city. As always, there's a catch—the keymaster won't move a muscle until you've arranged transportation. If you haven't rented a car, this means getting a taxi (S£200 after bargaining), many of which prowl outside the museum around tour time. You can hire a guide to the tombs for around S£300, but once at the towers most guides will let you latch on to their group for a small fee. *(Tombs unlocked W-M 8:30, 10, 11:30am, 4:30pm; Tu 8:30, 9, 10, 11, 11:30am, 4:30pm; Oct.-Mar. last opening 2pm. Trips leave from the Palmyra Museum, where tickets can be purchased. S£300, students S£15.)*

VALLEY OF THE TOMBS. The **Tomb of Elahbel,** which belonged to a rich Palmyran family, has stairs to its roof for a good view of the Valley of the Tombs. The impressive underground **Tomb of the Three Brothers** is southwest of the city. The center panel of the colorful wall frescoes in this tomb depicts Achilles hiding in feminine dress among the daughters of Lycomedes. He has done so upon hearing the Delphic oracle foretell his death, which would come only after the cross-dressing hero suited up for war and was shot in his now-famous left heel.

MUSEUMS. The **Palmyra Museum,** at the entrance to the new town, is larger and more interesting than most Syrian museums. Statues from family tombs, coins with godly depictions, and a tacky model of an ancient Palmyran cave and its seminaked inhabitants highlight the collection. The **Ethnographic Museum** won't have Madame Tussaud melting with envy: the mildly interesting displays attempt to catalogue different aspects of Bedouin life with wax statues. *(Palmyra Museum open Apr.-Sept. daily 8am-1pm and 4-6pm; Nov.-Mar. W-M 8am-1pm and 2-4pm. S£300, students S£15. Ethnographic Museum open daily 8am-2:30pm. S£150, students S£20.)*

HOMS حمص ☎ 31

Any Syrian will tell you that oil is the most refined thing in Homs. All over the Levant, "Homsies" are the butt of jokes ridiculing their supposed stupidity, but they thrive under the abuse and are some of the most genuine people in Syria. Now an industrial wasteland strewn with bent telephone poles, hanging electrical wires, and rank streets, Homs has seen better days. In ancient Roman times (when it was known as Emesa), Homs was an important metropolis along the trade route that passed through Palmyra. Most buildings of historical interest have been destroyed by wars and earthquakes, however, and the city is now little more than Palmyra's destitute older brother. As much as travelers try to avoid the smoke-belching city, Homs often serves as a default transportation hub; roads from Hama, Palmyra, Damascus, and Tartus converge here, and Crac des Chevaliers is only a short bus ride away. Be it ever so humble, there's no place like Homs.

▐ GETTING THERE AND GETTING AROUND

The **Karnak Station,** next to the public bus station, sends **buses** daily to: Damascus (2hr., 10 per day 6:30am-7pm, S£75); Hama (45min., 10 per day 5am-6:30pm, S£25); and Tartus (1hr., 3:30pm, S£40). **Minibuses** go to Crac des Chevaliers (1hr., every hr. 8am-5pm, S£25). **Microbuses** make frequent runs to: Aleppo (2½hr., 2 and 8pm, S£75); Damascus (2hr.; 6, 6:30, 9, 9:30, 10:30am, 2:30, 4:30, 6, 7pm, midnight; S£60); Hama (45min., every 30min., S£17); Tartus (1hr., 10:30am and 4pm, S£25).

❈ ▐ ORIENTATION AND PRACTICAL INFORMATION

The **bus station** sits at the intersection of **al-Corniche St.** and **Hama St.** A right turn out of the station leads to the Hama St. intersection, where you'll find food vendors and small, cheap restaurants. Hama St. intersects **Quwatli St.,** past the Khalid ibn al-Walid Mosque, at a bus stop and fountain. A right onto Quwatli St. brings you to a clocktower and most of Homs's accommodations. The public **bus station** is past the small clocktower circle on Hama St., near Khalid ibn al-Walid Mosque.

Don't expect much more than a smile from the **tourist booth** (☎47 38 98) on Quwatli St., in the middle of a small park past the hotels. Instead, speak with Ahmed at the Nasser al-Jadid Hotel, who speaks near-flawless English. For visas and renewals, take a right after the Turkish Airlines Office to get to the **passport office,** on the right side of Ibn Khaldoun St. at the Quwatli St. intersection. You'll need four passport-sized photographs, available from the photo office to the left of the passport office. (Open for visa extensions Sa-Th 9am-1pm.) An **exchange booth** set up by the Commercial Bank of Syria changes money at the usual rates. Facing away from the entrance of Hotel Nasser al-Jadid, it's 50m up the street, on the left. (Open Sa-Th 8:30am-noon.) The **police** (☎112) are headquartered in the government building on Hashem al-Atasi St., a sharp left from the clocktower on Quwatli St. Across from the mosque on Hama St. is the 24hr. **Umaliyya Pharmacy** (☎46 62 49). The government **hospital** (☎110 for an ambulance) is on al-Corniche St. at the intersection with al-Salamiyeh St. The tourist office at the clocktower circle also serves as the **telephone office.** (Open daily 8am-2pm and 7-10pm.) To reach the **post office** on Riad St., head away from the clocktower circle and the Army Club on the right. The post office immediately follows on the left. **Poste Restante** is available.

▐ ACCOMMODATIONS AND FOOD

Hotel options in Homs border on awful, especially if you're traveling alone. Most rooms are in large, old buildings in various states of disrepair on Quwatli St. The best of slim pickings is **Hotel Nasser al-Jadid,** on Quwatli St. about 50m past the park. Amiable, English-speaking manager Ahmed will show you to tidy, well-worn rooms sporting powerful fans and dirty bathrooms. (☎22 74 23. Cold showers S£25; hot showers S£50, for hot water give manager 2hr. notice in winter and 30-40 min. in summer. Singles S£200; doubles S£300; triples S£450; quads S£500.) **Ghazi Hotel** sits on Quwatli St., one block from the Nasser al-Jadid toward the park where an English sign says "HOTEL." The pretty tile floors and the curtains' leafy print fail to compensate for the overall gloominess and rock-hard mattresses. (☎22 21 60. Warm showers S£35. Singles S£160; doubles S£275; triples S£375.) **Basman Grand Hotel,** on Abu Ala'a St. off Quwatli St. before the park, has cute checkered floors and relatively tidy private baths. (☎22 50 09 or 22 57 00. Singles S£765; doubles S£990; triples S£1215.)

Falafel, *shawarma,* and pastry shops line Hama St. between the bus station and Quwatli St. Most stay open until midnight. Roving merchants hawk fresh-roasted corn on the cob, fruits, vegetables, and nuts. Myriad juice and snack shops squeeze onto the street parallel to Quwatli, behind Hotel Nasser al-Jadid. Most are open until midnight and offer affordable sandwiches (S£15) and cocktails (S£25-50). For a sit-down meal and a glass of beer (S£36-50), try the yellow and blue **City Cafe.**

Steak, filet, pizza, kebab, and *shish tawouq* can be yours in an oh-so-hip setting. (☎22 40 85. Open 24hr.) The nearby **Nile Restaurant's** special is what locals call *sha'abi*, or "of the people." The people eat *fatteh*, a huge bowl of hummus with pita, lemon juice, and olive oil (S£17)—real Homstyle cooking. The **Rawda Cafe,** across Quwatli St. from the Nile Restaurant, provides welcome relief from the industrial decay. Homsboys calmly smoke *argeilehs*, sip tea (S£30-40), and play backgammon around a tree-lined fountain.

◉ SIGHTS

KHALID IBN AL-WALID MOSQUE. This silver-domed mosque-turned-community center should be your first (and perhaps last) sightseeing stop in Homs. It is dedicated to the Arab commander known as "the Sword of God," who brought Islam to Syria in 636 CE; his alms-laden tomb lies inside. The mosque mixes Byzantine, Ottoman, and Arab styles. Ask the attendant in the office for a guided tour. *(On Hama St. between city center and bus station. Robes provided. Free.)*

GREAT AL-NOURI MOSQUE AND ENVIRONS. Built in 1162 CE by Ayyubid commander Nour al-Din Zanki (Nuraddin), this mosque is famous for its square minaret and wooden pulpit. The nearby *souqs* date from the Ayyubid, Mamluk, and Ottoman periods. *(On the left when walking toward the souq from Khalid Ibn al-Walid Mosque.)*

UMM AL-ZUNNAR CHURCH. Built in 59 CE, Umm al-Zunnar served as the holy house for Homs's earliest Christians. They worshiped here secretly, fearing persecution by their pagan rulers. The church was expanded during the Christian era and now holds the so-called Belt of the Virgin Mary, found under the altar in 1953. *(In the Old City, take a left at the souq and make a right at the first major street. Then take the first major left and the church is on the right.)*

▣ DAYTRIP FROM HOMS

QAL'AT AL-HISN (CRAC DES CHEVALIERS) قلعة الحصن

Buses and service leave Homs station for Qal'at al-Hisn daily (1hr., every hr. 7am-5pm, S£25). Officially, the last bus returns to Homs around 5pm. In low season, however, shark-like service drivers may claim to be private taxis after 3pm and charge an outrageous S£300 for the return trip. Walk 10min. down the hill (through the village) to catch a local service at the restaurant. Start the trip in early morning to avoid the heat and allow ample time to explore. Open June-Nov. W-M 9am-6pm; Oct.-Apr. W-M 9am-4pm, Tu 9am-3am. S£300, students S£15. Guided tours S£200, groups S£500.

This must-see mountaintop Crusader castle, also known as *Qal'at al-Hisn*, ranks among the best sights in Syria. Those who proclaim it the Greatest Castle in the World are not far off the mark. Crac des Chevaliers is really a castle within a castle, separated by a moat, with a larger moat surrounding the entire structure. The governor of Homs built the original structure in 1031 CE, leaving a Kurdish garrison to defend the castle against enemy attacks on the Tripoli-Homs-Hama road. In 1110, Crusaders nearly destroyed the fortress while capturing it. They built a new castle on the ruins of the old and used it to control the "Homs Gap," a narrow pass linking the coast to the Orontes Valley. Possession of this pass, the only gap in a 250km stretch of mountainous terrain, guaranteed control over inland Syria. The Crusaders held the medieval fortress for 161 years; Salah al-Din supposedly withdrew his troops upon viewing the imposing castle. The stronghold finally fell to the Mamluk army under the command of Sultan Baybars in 1271, after a month of intense fighting. The Crusaders were allowed to leave the country peacefully. Perched on a hill 750m above sea level and spreading over 30,000 square meters, the castle's high towers afford panoramic views of the Mediterranean, the Port of Tripoli, and Homs Lake on a clear day.

Upon entering through the main door, continue up the ramp past the **guard rooms** and **stables.** Straight ahead, through the door of the first tower, are the moat and the outer wall. To get to the **main courtyard,** take a sharp right. In front of the courtyard, the **seven-arched facade** is the castle's most aesthetically impressive feature. Behind it is the **main assembly room,** where Crusader kings were received by the knights of the castle under a vaulted Gothic roof. The long room against the castle's back wall contains a huge **oven,** 5m in diameter. To the right is a **cathedral** that was converted into a mosque in 1271. The intriguing nooks in the rest of the castle lend themselves to impromptu exploration; a map might cramp your style, but a **flashlight** makes a great companion. Be sure to trek up to the southern towers for an inspiring view of the Syrian countryside with Lebanon in the distance. Those accustomed to warmer climates should bring a sweater.

At the **Roundtable Restaurant and Hotel,** 150m to the left and up the hill from the castle entrance, passable beds and baths await for S₤500; meals cost S₤200. The **Restaurant Des Chevaliers,** in front of the main entrance, has slightly higher prices and similar food. (☎74 04 11. Meals S₤150, beers S₤100, hummus S₤25, coffee or tea S₤25.) If you get hungry or thirsty exploring the castle, visit the **Restaurant Princess Tower,** Rapunzel-style on the top level of the castle toward the northern end. Lovely, if foggy, views and a helpful, English-speaking manager accompany the *mezze* for S₤150. (☎74 00 07. Open daily 7am-8pm.) **Camping** (☎74 02 80) for S₤125 a head, including shower, is also an option.

HAMA حماة ☎33

Although the city of Hama was once an important trade center, the only remaining monuments to its former glory are the **norias** (Aramaic for "waterwheels") scattered throughout the city. The low-pitched groaning, produced by wood rubbing wood, has echoed through Hama since the *norias'* construction in the Middle Ages. The graceful turning of these irrigation devices, matched by the smooth flow of the nearby Orontes River, has long set the pace for this town. Hama's serenity makes it difficult to remember that the city was ground zero for the government's bloody quelling of the Muslim Brotherhood uprising of 1982. Nevertheless, Hama's numerous shoreside parks and high-quality budget accommodations make it an ideal locale to spend a relaxing couple of days. The best way to see Hama's sights is to make like a *noria* and roll along the banks of the river.

▐ GETTING THERE AND GETTING AROUND

Al-Ahliah Bus Station (☎52 25 51) has luxury service to all major Syrian cities. Walking toward the post office, go past the Basman Grand Hotel, and take a left after the large, white government building. The station is on the left around the corner. Frequent service to: Aleppo (2hr., every hr., S₤65); Damascus (3hr., every hr., S₤90); Homs (40min.; 5:30, 6, 7am, 12:15, 2, 6:15pm; S₤20); Lattakia (3hr.; 6am, 12:15, 5, 7:15pm; S₤70); Raqqa (4hr.; 6:45am, 3:30, 4:30, 5:30, 6:30, 8:30pm; S₤125); Tartus (2hr.; 6am, 12:15, 5, 7:15pm; S₤70). The **Karnak Bus Station** (☎22 99 85), on the corniche in the middle of town (doubling as the Afamia Restaurant and pastry shop), has frequent service to: Aleppo (S₤60); Damascus (S₤75); and Homs (S₤25). **Al-Rayyan Bus Company** (☎22 55 81 or 22 79 77), a high-quality third option, runs to: Aleppo (S₤65); Damascus (S₤90); and Homs (S₤20). The **minibus station** is a left turn away from the river at the intersection of Murabet and Quwatli. Conquer the hill by foot (20min.) or take a city bus (S₤2). **Minibuses** depart when full to: Aleppo (2hr., S₤25); Damascus (3hr., S₤35); Homs (45min., S₤11); and Suqelbia (1hr., S₤20). Impractical and hugely expensive **service** (of the gas-guzzling, boat-sized sort) leave from the station across the street to: Aleppo (S₤150); Damascus (S₤200); and Homs (S₤40).

🛈 ORIENTATION AND PRACTICAL INFORMATION

Navigating the small city of Hama is easy and can be done almost entirely on foot. The intersection of **Quwatli St.** and **Sadiq Ave.** marks the city center. Most budget hotels and restaurants are on Quwatli St., facing the bank and the post office across the intersection. Continuing in this direction leads to **Murabet St.** and the city's second major intersection. Walking toward the grinding sound will bring you to the river. The **tourist office** is on Sadiq Ave., across the river from the central intersection. (☎51 10 33. Open daily 8am-2pm.) They do have maps on hand, but as holds true for most of Syria, you're better off finding a knowledgeable, English-speaking hotel manager to introduce you to the city. In Hama, the best person to contact is Anas, manager of the **Cairo Hotel.** He can provide information on everything from the transportation to visa requirements for almost any nationality. For the remarkably efficient **passport office** take a right at the intersection of Murabet and Quwatli; it's on the left. Bring four passport-sized photographs and S£50 to renew visas. (Open Sa-Th 9am-1pm.) The **Commercial Bank of Syria,** next to the post office, exchanges cash and traveler's checks. (Open daily 9am-2pm and 5-8pm.) In an emergency, call the **police** (☎112), an **ambulance** (☎110), or go to **Medical Center Hospital** (☎51 58 01, 51 58 02, or 51 58 03), just uphill from the al-Ahliah Bus Station. **Ummalia Pharmacy,** 8 March St. (☎225 097), is open 24 hours. Contact your hotel manager first about getting medicine; he will probably know where to procure necessary items at the best prices. The **post office,** on Quwatli St. just past the Sadiq Ave. intersection, has minimal services, but is very efficient. (Open daily 8am-2pm.) The **EMS** office is in the post office. A phonecard from the post office is less expensive than placing calls from your hotel.

📷 ACCOMMODATIONS AND FOOD

Hama's hotels outshine those in almost any other Syrian city. Amenities abound, floors sparkle, and managers practically tap dance to keep visitors happy. Prices vary drastically between high season (summer) and low season (winter). It never hurts to ask for a discount. ■**Cairo Hotel,** on Quwatli St. near the intersection with Gamal Abd al-Nasser St., is a two-star hotel with one-star prices. Some travelers have dubbed Anas, the helpful manager, a Syrian National Treasure. Well-maintained rooms have fridges, beautiful bathrooms, and color TVs. (☎22 22 80; fax 23 72 06. Breakfast S£75. Roof mattresses S£100; dorm beds S£150; singles S£250-300; doubles S£400; triples S£525-600; June-Aug. S£50-150 more; A/C S£100. V, MC, AmEx.) Cairo's rival and next-door neighbor, the ■**Riad Hotel,** with its young, hip manager, is a worthy match. Clean rooms have fridges and speakers connected to a central sound system. The hotel sells beer out of the lobby cooler. (☎23 95 12 or 23 55 40, fax 51 77 76. Breakfast S£75. Full bath or shower S£45. Rooftop mattresses and facilities S£75-100; singles S£280; doubles S£405; triples S£505; quads S£605. V, MC, AmEx.) Across the street, the luxurious and welcoming **Noria Hotel** is under the

TOTALITARIAN TISSUE No traveler in Syria can fail to notice that a box of tissues, complete with fancy borders, floral designs, and sophisticated lettering, accompanies almost every meal in Syria. After a few meals, inquiring minds want to know why this peculiar form of advertising (name, address, and phone number on the thin little boxes) is so popular. Back in the economic recession of the 1980s, Syria's nominally socialist regime branded tissues a frivolous bourgeois luxury. Many speculate that the government's blowing the horn on tissues was due less to the tissues' inherent extravagance than to the lack of Syrian-based tissue factories. Today, tissues have become a sizzling item in Syrian society, a fact easily observed by their omnipresence in restaurants. Thankfully, though, Syrians now make their own.

same impeccable management as the Cairo. One of the only two-star hotels to justify its prices, all rooms come with A/C, continental breakfast, and a bevy of four-star services. Magnificent suites (for 2-5 people) have a kitchen, a taste-fully decorated living room, and views of the *norias*. (☎51 24 14; fax 51 17 15. Singles US$18; doubles US$28; triples US$33; suites US$40-60. Fax summer reservations a month in advance. V, MC, AmEx.)

Most of Hama's restaurants are of the standard chicken, meat, and falafel variety. A full meal shouldn't cost more than S£100. The diners scattered along Quwatli St. have plumper chickens and larger portions; more expensive restau-rants line the waterfront. **Sultan Restaurant,** behind the Hama Museum, pro-vides a memorable riverside meal in an Ottoman insane asylum. If the grinding noise from the neighboring *noria* doesn't drive you mad, Hama's fit-inducing specialty, *batirsh*, surely will: layered eggplant, mincemeat, and *tahini* eaten with bread for S£55. (☎23 51 04. Entrees S£15-20.) **Dream House,** off Medina Sq. near the Grand Mosque, offers spring rolls (S£45), excellent pizzas (S£90-110), and genuine banana splits (S£70). Barada beer (S£75) and a variety of liquors and imported wines (S£90-750) help ensure happy dreams. (☎41 16 87. Open daily 10am-1pm.) A 15-minute walk from the center of town (with the river to the left) leads to **Four Norias** (☎22 10 13), an upscale riverfront restaurant with views of its namesakes. Try Hama's specialty, *sajaia*, lamb cooked with pista-chios in yogurt for S£100. 'Araq and Sharq beer (S£36) also available. Yes, those creatures flying along the water are bats. (☎22 10 13. Full meal S£200-250. Open daily 9am-2am).

👁 SIGHTS

OLD CITY AND OTTOMAN BATH. When facing the Orontes from the center of town, walk left along the bank and enter the cobblestone-paved Old City. The nar-row, winding streets were built to provide protection from the sun at all hours. A small sign above an old door on the left that reads "Automan Public Bath" marks the Hammam Othmania, a Turkish bath from the Ottoman era. A bath with soap and a massage is only S£100. *(Open for men 7am-noon and 7-11pm; women noon-5pm. Women seldom use the baths in summer.)*

HAMA MUSEUM. The Hama Museum, directly across from the Ottoman Bath in the Old al-Azem Palace, was built as a residence for As'ad Pasha al-Azem, gover-nor of Hama from 1700 to 1742. After al-Azem was promoted to a Damascus post, he built an even grander structure of the same name. The palace's men's section (the *Salamlek*) and women's section (the *Haramlek*) conveniently join at the baths. The museum also houses the remarkable Maryameen Mosaic, which cap-tures the lovely ladies of the house jamming on 18th-century lutes and other funk machines. *(Open W-M 9am-4pm. S£300, students S£15.)*

AL-NOURI MOSQUE AND CITADEL. After passing the al-Jabariyya waterwheel (home to daredevil child divers in the late afternoon), the road opens up at the al-Nouri Mosque. Built in 1162 by Ayyubid commander Nour al-Din Zanki (Nurad-din), the mosque thrusts a square minaret into the Syrian sky, mirroring its cousin in Homs. A left turn at the mosque leads to the citadel, the center of the old city and a popular spot for evening strolls. Supposedly, relics from the 6th millennium BCE were unearthed beneath this hill. Today, the only digging is done by kids play-ing in the huge park planted on top. *(You may be asked to pay a S£10 entrance fee.)*

GRAND MOSQUE. The citadel once hid Hama's Grand Mosque, which contains the tombs of two Ayyubid kings, Muhammad II (d. 1284 CE) and al-Muzaffar III (d. 1298 CE). The 1982 uprising struck this Umayyad structure, along with the tombs inside, and it has yet to be fully reconstructed. Greek writing from a previous edi-fice marks some of the fallen stones. *(Free. All faiths welcome; males only.)*

NEAR HAMA: APAMEA أفاميا

To reach Apamea, take a microbus from Hama to Suqelbia (S£20), then a service to Qasr al-Mudiq (S£10). The Colonnade is 2km farther up. Leave early in the day, when transportation is more frequent. Open W-M 8am-2:30pm. Ruins S£150, students S£10; combination ruins and museum S£350, students S£25.

Apamea lies on a hill overlooking the lush Ghab Valley and the Orontes River (Nahr al-Assi), 55km north of Hama. The Macedonians knew the city as Barnakeh, but a smitten King Sahicos renamed the military stronghold after his beloved wife Afamia in 310 BCE. After Apamea fell in 64 BCE, the victorious Romans supplied the city with an impressive rock-hewn water canal and ornate stone **colonnades** (the longest of which is 1850m)—still the city's most impressive features. They also built an **amphitheater** and a **public bath** (about 500m downhill and to the left of the colonnade), which have weathered the years much less gracefully. While in Apamea, you will likely encounter several moped-riding sharks selling "antiques" supposedly found in nearby graves. Beware—chances are these "antiques" were manufactured in nearby shops just hours before your arrival.

The **cathedral,** to the left when facing the modern cafeteria, harbors a selection of mosaic floors. While even the best of these floors have suffered centuries of erosion from weather and warfare, the cathedral still houses a cross and a set of jewels given to the King of Persia in 540 CE. The Persians nonetheless invaded and razed the city 33 years later, enslaving almost 300,000 Apameans. Muslim Arabs entered the city on peaceful terms under the leadership of Abu Obeida ibn Jarrah. Between 1137 and 1170, inhabitants likely abandoned Hama as a result of a series of earthquakes. One of the more impressive structures is the circular **al-Mudiq Castle,** about two kilometers from the colonnade, near modern Apamea. The Ottoman Stan Pasha built a great *khan* (courtyard inn) inside the castle that contained an inn, a stable, and a market. Now a museum, the *khan* is worth checking out. The museum **cafeteria** has standard Syrian fare at slightly inflated prices.

MEDITERRANEAN COAST

LATTAKIA اللاذقية ☎41

Lattakia is a decidedly practical city. Its aesthetically pleasing buildings, crowded streets, and fashionable student population give it a cosmopolitan feel. Plenty of cheap eats and budget accommodations make Lattakia a good base for exploring the ruins at Ugarit and the castle of Salah al-Din. Founded in the 2nd century BCE by the Seleucids, Lattakia once welcomed St. Peter and Marc Antony to its shores, but the only remaining witnesses to its glorious past are a few columns, a Roman arch, and some Ugaritic artifacts, all housed in the overpriced museum inside the Ottoman Khan al-Dukhan. As Syria's largest seaport and the country's major import-export center, Lattakia donates much of its coastline to industry, but leaves beaches for swimming. For Lattakia beachbum style, take a Ugarit-bound microbus (S£5) to the Cham Côte d'Azur or Meridien Hotel (ask to be let out).

▐▀ GETTING THERE AND GETTING AROUND

From **Karnak Bus Station** (☎47 20 96), at the corner of Baghdad Ave. and Haria St. (turn left off Baghdad Ave. after it intersects al-Quds St.), **buses** run daily to: Aleppo (3hr., 3pm, S£65); Beirut (4-5hr., 6am, S£175); and Damascus (4hr., every ½hr., S£100) via Homs (2hr., S£65). The **Pullman Bus Station,** at al-Yaman Place roundabout, the first right facing away from the train station, sends **buses** to Baniyas (45min., S£15), which is not accessible by microbus. From **al-Shati' Transport Co.,** 14 Ramadan St. (☎46 71 49), **buses** run daily to Antakya (2½hr., 6am, S£400), and then to various cities in Turkey. Bring your passport and US$45 to get a **Turkish**

visa at the border. Within the city, travel by **taxi** (refuse to pay more than S£25) or *service* (white minivans). To get to the **microbus station,** with regular departures to neighboring areas, walk down Ramadan St. toward the tourist office, break left on al-Maghreb al-Arabi St. at the big traffic circle, take the first right, and walk 500m.

ORIENTATION AND PRACTICAL INFORMATION

The main thoroughfare is **14 Ramadan St.,** running northeast from the harbor and ending at the **tourist office.** (☎41 69 26. Open daily 9am-8pm.) Farther inland, running north-south from the beginning of 14 Ramadan St., is **8 Azar St.,** which turns into **Baghdad Ave.** at the al-Quds St. intersection. Heading east on al-Quds St. (which soon morphs into al-Ghafiqi St.) leads to the large **al-Yaman Pl.** roundabout.

The **Commercial Bank of Syria** faces the sea on 8 Azar St. before the traffic circle; it does not exchange traveler's checks after 2pm. (Open daily 8am-2pm and 5-8pm.) At the intersection of 14 Ramadan St. with Ibrahim Hanano St., Hanano Pl. is home to the **Assad statue,** the **police station** (☎112), and many budget hotels. **Sani Daker Pharmacy,** on 8 Azar St. before the Karnak office, has excellent, multilingual service. (☎47 69 79. Open Sa-W 9am-1:30pm and 5-8:30pm.) In a medical emergency, call the **Assad Hospital** (☎48 77 82), on 8 Azar St. To reach the surprisingly efficient **telephone office,** turn right onto Haria St., from Baghdad Ave. (Open daily 8am-8pm.) To get to the **post office,** face away from the train station and take the second right off the circle; it's 50m down on the left. (Open daily 8am-6pm.) **Mail service** is across the street. (Open daily 8am-7pm.)

ACCOMMODATIONS AND FOOD

To get to the homey **Hotel Lattakia,** walk a direct line from Assad's much admired backside until you reach a sprawling outdoor coffeeshop; look for the flashing yellow sign in the alley to the right. The intensely friendly management provides spacious rooms with comfy beds, fans, balconies, and bottomless cups of tea. (☎41 95 27. Rooftop mattress S£75; singles S£100, with bath £150; doubles S£200-50; triples S£300-75.) To reach the **Dounia Hotel,** face away from the Assad statue and outdoor cafe, and take the second right after the gas station; the small hotel is on the left. The Dounia is another good deal, though its less-than-central location, lack of private baths, and occasionally stained floors make it a runner-up. An exceedingly comfortable bed with a pair of exceedingly comfortable slippers awaits. (☎42 12 96. Singles S£100; doubles S£200; triples £300; quads £400.)

Dining is more central to the Lattakian experience than to the average Syrian town. Budget foodstops line the area around the Assad statue, while more upscale restaurants sit pretty on and around America St. For mouth-watering kebabs, visit **Spiros,** on Gamal Abd al-Nasser St. in front of the harbor. Fish is pricey at S£1000, but there are savory Syrian delicacies to devour for S£75-300. (Open 10am-1am.) To reach the **Italian Corner Restaurant and Bar,** near America St., follow Ramadan St. toward the sea and take a right at the end. The staff serves up several noble attempts at Western meat dishes (filet mignon S£160), a wide array of pizzas (S£85-120), and cocktails (S£90-115). Beer goes for S£75. (☎47 72 07. Open daily 1pm-12:30am.) **Sindbad Restaurant and Cafe,** in a tiny man-made cave with chairs that resemble Elvis's hair, is a bit reminiscent of an opium den. Take a right at Italian Corner and follow America St. for two blocks. A left at the al-Atlal Hotel leads to Sindbad's doorstep. This is a place for strong coffee, booze (beer S£50; drinks S£130), and serious conversation. (Closes at 10:30pm.)

DAYTRIPS FROM LATTAKIA

UGARIT (RAS SHAMRA) راس شمرة

To get to Ugarit, take the last left before reaching the rear of the Assad statue and walk to the first intersection on the right. Hop on a service (S£5) heading to Ras Shamra and ask to be dropped off at the ruins. To get back, hail a service on the main road; they come more frequently earlier in the day. Open daily 8am-6pm; in winter 8:30am-4pm. S£300, students S£15. Guidebook S£50.

The historic Kingdom of Ugarit once stood upon the site of this tiny town, 16km north of Lattakia. Ugarit's greatest gift to our time is its 28-letter **alphabet,** preserved in a stone tablet from the 14th century BCE that now sits in the National Museum in Damascus (see p. 575). The oldest phonetic alphabet in the world, Ugaritic is the probable ancestor of both the Phoenician and Hebrew alphabets (though not the languages), as well as those of Latin and Greek. In 1928, a peasant farmer discovered this site when he unearthed a few slabs of stone marking a spot originally settled in the 7th millennium BCE. Since the Kingdom of Ugarit built its structures of stone, it left an architectural legacy better preserved than almost all other Bronze Age cities, which typically consisted of mud-brick houses. Nevertheless, snail-covered weeds are winning the war against the ruins. Professional guides can help decipher the fascinating remains and explain the elaborate system of waterworks. English- and French-speaking guides hang out at the entrance and will show you around for S£250 or your best offer, depending on demand. As you enter, the **royal palace** (where the alphabet was found) is to the right; the **residential quarters** and **acropolis** are farther down.

QAL'AT SALAH AL-DIN قلعة صلاح الدين

*Take a **microbus** from the main microbus station to al-Haffeh (45min., S£10) to get to Qal'at Salah al-Din. For easy thrills, hire the services of one of the Honda **motorcycles** across the street, though women should be extra careful about jumping on a high-powered bike with a stranger (possible 1hr. wait; round-trip S£25-100). **Taxis** ask for S£100 one way—they know how few cars drive along the seven-kilometer road to the castle (hitchers should think twice). Open W-M 9am-6pm; in winter 9am-4pm. S£300, students S£15.*

This fortress, 35km east of Lattakia, is named for the exalted warrior who took the "impregnable" castle from the Crusaders in 1188 CE. Perched on a plateau flanked by two deep gorges, the site's most impressive feature is the 156km long, 18m wide, and 28m deep trench that laborers cut by hand to completely isolate the fortress from the adjacent land—perhaps the pinnacle of the Crusaders' architectural achievements. The lone column of rock that stands in the gorge once supported a drawbridge. Inside the walls, you'll find the arched entry to a stable on your right and a **dungeon** in the drawbridge tower. Holes in the dungeon walls mark where prisoners' chains were drilled into the stone. Up the path and inside the next tower, a hollow column conceals a secret staircase that soldiers on the roof descended to attack the enemy from behind. Across from the entrance sits a huge **cistern** that collected rain water for 4000 soldiers' tea. To the left are remains of Byzantine and Crusader **churches,** and directly in front is the **mosque.** Views from the tops of many of the buildings take in the surrounding valley. Though no warriors remain to guard it, the castle's highest point is virtually impenetrable due to the thick tangle of prickly briars.

JABLEH جبلة

Buses leave for Jableh every 30 min. from Lattakia (S£25). Taxis are a costlier option.

A small coastal town near Lattakia, Jableh's slow pace and sparsely-touristed streets make it a nice place to spend the afternoon. Strolling from the main bus station toward the sea, take notice of Jableh's past. The **Roman amphitheater** seems of little interest to locals, but its austere hallways deserve a quick look. (Open W-M 9am-2pm. S£100, students S£15.) Behind the amphitheater sits the **local mosque,** built on the site of a former Byzantine Church, which is home to the shrine of a Muslim saint, Ibrahim ibn Adham, as well as a house for daily worship.

If sightseeing gives you a bear of an appetite, stop off by the sea at the ▧**Zoo-zoo Restaurant and Cafe** (☎ 83 38 15). Famed locally for its breakfasts, Zoo-zoo's proprietors also sell kebab for an affordable S£200. Take a break before returning to the bustle of the city by snoozing on the rocks while your stomach does the work.

KASSAB كساب

Buses leave Lattakia for Kassab frequently until 8pm or until the demand dies down (S£25). In the off-season, be prepared to pay S£50 or wait endless hours until the microbus fills up. Though Lattakia is the wisest departure point for Kassab, microbuses leave Kassab for Aleppo and depart from Aleppo to Kassab at noon and 3pm (S£125).

Crisp air, lush spruce forests, stone settlements, and stunning vistas surround the traveler all the way to Kassab, while the town itself equally impresses visitors. Sharing a dense, forested border with Turkey, Kassab is home to Armenians who fled the genocide in Turkey in 1915. Kassab's shops and churches bear signs in Armenian as well as Arabic. Locals will tell you about their Armenian dialect, which is spoken only in Kassab. Brave bathers should catch the bus to Ras al-Bassit to take advantage of its black-sandy beaches (30min., 10am). When you get there, use a luxury hotel's private beach—locals frown on public skin-bearing.

Kassab is a wonderful place to spend the day. If more time is desired, try **Hotel al-Rawdah.** (☎71 10 08 or 71 11 39; fax 71 14 00. Singles S$810; doubles S$945; triples S$1125. Prices negotiable.)

TARTUS طرطوس ☎43

Syria's second major seaport is Tartus, the charming older sister to buck-toothed Lattakia 90km to the south. The Phoenicians called this Mediterranean town Antardus, reflecting its secondary importance to the more secure island of Arwad ("Anti-Arwadus" means "the town opposite Arwad"). The Crusaders called it Tortosa and not only fortified the town's seaport, but also built its **Cathedral Church of Our Lady of Tortosa,** which many consider the premier piece of Crusader religious architecture standing outside Jerusalem. Salah al-Din made short work of the fortifications in 1188 CE, while the Templar garrison cowered in the dungeon. Nonetheless, Tartus served as the last Crusader stronghold on the mainland, remaining secure until August of 1291, when the Crusaders retreated to Arwad for a decade of ineffectual revolt. Modern-day Tartus offers relaxation: bare-armed beauties cruise along the corniche arm-in-arm with their partners, stopping at designer clothing stores and ice cream parlors. Don't let the showy face of Tartus trick you—Tartusians still inhabit the narrow lanes and arched buildings of the old town, while their calls to prayer echo off the water.

▐ GETTING THERE AND GETTING AROUND

The **Kadmous Transportation Co.** (☎31 67 30 or 31 28 29), at the intersection of Ibn al-Walid St. and al-Thawra Ave., sends **buses** to: Aleppo (3½ hr.; 6, 11:30am, 4:30, 9pm; S$115); Baniyas (30min., every 30min., S$12); Damascus (3½hr., every 2hr. 2:30am-9:30pm, S$110); Hama (1½hr.; 6am, 4:30, 9pm; S$65) via Homs (1hr., S$40); and Lattakia (1hr., every 15min., S$30). The **microbus station,** a 15-minute walk from the town center, services nearby destinations. Take either Wahda St. or Ibn al-Walid St. away from the sea, pass al-Thawra Ave., and turn right on Tichrin Ave. To get to **Lebanon,** either hop on a bus bound for Homs and transfer to another bus there, or hire a **service** from either the clocktower or a sidestreet about 50m before the microbus station (Tripoli S$200, Beirut S$300). Remember to have a **Lebanese visa** and a **multiple-entry Syrian visa** (or exit visa) for reentry into the country, and carry some hard currency just in case.

▐ ORIENTATION AND PRACTICAL INFORMATION

Three main streets and the corniche bind the downtown area of Tartus into a rectangle. **Wahda St.** and **Ibn al-Walid St.** run from the sea to **al-Thawra Ave.** Walking downhill toward the sea on Ibn al-Walid St. takes you past the **tourist office** on the right. (☎22 34 48. Open Sa-Th 8am-2pm.) The **Commercial Bank of Syria,** which changes traveler's checks for those wary of the black market, is on the left. (Open Sa-Th 8am-2pm.) Most of Tartus's reasonably priced hotels and restaurants line

Wahda St., running east from the corniche at the **Arwad dock.** From the **clocktower circle,** walk away from the sea and take a left on al-Thawra Ave. to get to the **police station.** A right at **Basil Park,** across from the police station, onto Gamal Abd al-Nasser St. leads to the **immigration and passport office** two blocks later. The **telephone office** is a block farther from the police station and to the right of al-Thawra Ave. (Calls S£90-115 per min. Open daily 8am-midnight.) Across from the Daniel Hotel is the friendly and efficient **al-Iman Pharmacy.** (Open Sa-W 8:30am-1:30pm and 5-8pm, Th 8:30am-1:30pm.) Backtracking to the clocktower circle and hanging a left on Ibn al-Walid St., a 150m uphill walk across another traffic circle, leads to the **post office.** (Open Sa-Th 7:30am-7pm.) Ibn al-Walid St. ends back on the corniche in front of the **Old City.**

■◌ ACCOMMODATIONS AND FOOD

Tartus houses enough budget hotels and restaurants to make any brief stay pleasant. ◼**Daniel Hotel,** one of Syria's premier budget hotels, sits a block and a half up from the beach on Wahda St. Large, spic-and-span rooms have fans and private baths; some even come with balconies. The hotel rents mountain bikes and runs trips to beaches along the Syrian coast. (☎22 05 81; fax 31 65 55. Breakfast S£75. Singles S£350; doubles S£600; triples S£800.) Two and a half blocks up the beach on Wahda St. to the right of the next intersection is the **Republic Hotel.** Reasonably clean rooms come with sink and phone. There is a communal refrigerator. (☎22 25 80. Hot showers £35. Singles S£175; doubles S£275; triples S£375.) A step down in quality, the **Hotel Seyaha (Tourism)** sits farther up Wahda St. on the left and offers habitable rooms for the lowest prices in town, but without private bathrooms. (☎22 17 63. Hot showers S£25. Singles S£200; doubles S£250; triples S£350.) Perhaps the best quality and highest priced of the bunch is the **Blue Beach Hotel,** on the corner of Wahda St. and the corniche. Sunny rooms come with balconies near the big blue sea. Fans, heat, and phones are also included. (☎22 06 50 or 32 63 75. Singles S£585; doubles S£765; triples S£900. Discount for groups of six or more.)

For luxurious dining, explore **The Cave,** 300m from the dock on the waterfront by the Old City, where the view and decor are worth the splurge. Chef Ahmed spent 18 years as a cook on a Greek ship and brews his own *'araq* (S£15). The calamari is a tasty, hefty treat for S£350. (Open daily 9am-10:30pm.) For a cheaper, bass-ic fish experience, try **Al-Nabil Restaurant.** On the right of Wahda St. as you approach the sea, al-Nabil offers choose-your-own seafood, with quality red fish (S£100), white fish (S£225), and shrimp (S£300). Meat dishes (S£100-150) and beer (S£50) round off the menu. (☎22 09 59. Open daily 6am-12:30am.) At the **Venicia Restaurant,** near the corner of the corniche and Wahda St., the fresh fish is a catch at S£1600 per kilo. Despite what the sign on the street says, there is no pizza. Tables for two on the balcony overlook the sea. For Westernized dining, check out **Tic Tac Restaurant,** across from Port Arwad. Chow down on cheeseburgers for S£150 and shrimp pizzas for S£160. (Open daily 8am-10pm.)

◉ SIGHTS

Almost entirely unrenovated, the sturdy walls of the medieval **Old City** enclose a hive of activity and chronologically jumbled architecture. With your back to **The Cave** on the waterfront, walk left until you reach a large, white mosque. Walk up the hill to the mosque's right to reach the fortified, 12th-century **cathedral,** which claims to house the world's oldest altar dedicated to the Virgin Mary. Now a **museum,** it displays an eclectic collection of artifacts from all over coastal Syria. (Open W-M 9am-2pm, students S£15.) Take a break at **Basil (al-Assad) Park,** on the corner of al-Thawra Ave. and Ibn al-Walid St. With its rare collection of rose-bushes, this fountained beauty is perfect for a picnic or quiet read.

█ DAYTRIPS FROM TARTUS

ARWAD ارواد

Ferries run about every 15 minutes from Port Arwad in Tartus. (20min.; round-trip S£20; pay before returning; last boat leaves 8:30pm.) The choppy ride can be nauseating for those weak of stomach—prepare yourself. There are no formal lodgings available on the island, so don't get stranded. Crusader fort open W-M 9am-4pm. S£200, students S£15.

Arwad, Syria's sole island, floats just three kilometers from the coast of Tartus. In ancient times, Arwad served as a sanctuary for those seeking protection from foreign invaders. As such, it was the last Crusader stronghold to return to Muslim hands. More recently, the French used it as a prison for Syrian nationalists. The Phoenician kingdom of Aradus was centered on the island and though its defensive walls no longer stand, two grand medieval forts remain; one of them now calls itself a museum. Wandering Arwad's narrow lanes and enjoying a sea-side cup of tea are equally popular activities. Alternatively, take a 30-minute empathy walk around the island for a more realistic view of Syria's current economic plight. The environmental police would have a heart attack over the litter scattered liberally over Arwad's backside.

CASTLE LE BLANC

*To get to Castle le Blanc, take a **microbus** from Tartus to Safita (40min., S£10). From Safita center, hop on a service to the base of a cobblestone side road (ask for al-Burg). On foot from Safita center, walk up the steepest street and look for the cobblestone side road on the right leading up to the tower. It may seem like a good idea to continue from Castle le Blanc to Crac des Chevaliers, but be warned that the return trip to Tartus becomes overly complicated. Site officially open daily 9am-7pm. Free, but a tip (S£10) may be expected on the way out.*

Of the once majestic Castle le Blanc, only one remaining tower stands guard over the tiled roofed houses and olive trees of the small mountain town of Safita. A beautiful chapel graces the tower's entrance level. Never deconsecrated, it continues to serve as a place of worship today. Upstairs are spacious living quarters, which represent one of the finest examples of Romanesque architecture in Syria. Another flight of stairs leads to the roof, which offers panoramic views of Lebanon and, on a clear day, Crac des Chevaliers (see p. 586).

NORTHERN SYRIA

ALEPPO حلب   ☎ 21

Aleppo (*Halab* in Arabic), the "second capital of Syria" 350km north of Damascus, has flourished since the 3rd millennium BCE. Abraham is said to have milked his gray cow on the acropolis here—hence the name *Halab al-Shahba*, or "he milked the gray." Situated at the crossroads of several vital trade routes, ancient Aleppo controlled the "Great Syrian Passage" connecting Mesopotamia and Persia with the Mediterranean Sea. Though previously occupied by the Romans, Persians, and Byzantines (whose Christian influence is still felt), Aleppo reached its cultural peak in the days of the Arab Hamadanis; Sayf al-Dawla, who established the Hamadani state in 944 CE, built the city's towering Citadel, hosted great poets al-Mutanabbi and Abu al-Firas, and filled the city with splendid mosques, schools, and tombs. The city's *khans* were built later to accommodate the many traders passing through; several still stand. Construction continued during Ottoman rule, when the majority of the ancient city's covered *souqs* were built.

Along with the city's Arabo-Muslim population, today's Aleppans include Armenians, Russians, and Greek Orthodox Christians. The cafes and outdoor restaurants that crowd its wide, tree-lined streets make contemporary Aleppo a sophisticated metropolis, with some of the best shopping available along the Eastern Mediterranean. The downside of Aleppo's modernity is that it lacks some of the moral uprightness of which Syrians are proud and can be a challenge for women traveling alone. Some tourists may also be disappointed by Aleppo's pollution and hunkering socialist architecture, but more and more flock here not just as a stop en route to other sights, but as an end in itself.

▐ GETTING THERE AND GETTING AROUND

Flights: Aleppo International Airport (☎478 69 00), 30km east of the city center. Buses leave for the airport across from the tourist office, but *service* are more flexible (not more than S£200).

Buses: To ride local buses, purchase a card valid for 4 rides (S£10). Intercity **microbuses** depart from the Pullman Station to: **Damascus** (S£90-150); **Hama** (S£35-60); **Homs** (S£45-75); **Lattakia** (S£90-125); and **Tartus** (S£90-150). Prices depend on the quality of buses. **Private bus companies** have offices on Ibrahim Hanano St. (a short walk to the right if facing the Amir Palace) and across the street from the Baron Hotel. The **Pan Bus Company** (☎222 42 76) has daily service to **Antakya, TUR** (3hr.; 5am, 12:30, 1:30, 6:30pm; S£250), and from there to many destinations in Turkey, including **Iskenderun** (4hr., S£300) and **Istanbul** (22hr., S£1200). US$20 buys a visa at the border. The **Karnak** station (☎221 02 48), facing the Baron Hotel, sends buses to: **Amman** (10pm, S£450); **Beirut** (10am and noon; S£250); **Homs** (2½hr., 10am-1pm, S£75) via **Hama** (2hr., S£60); and **Lattakia** (4hr., 7am, S£65).

Taxis: Service stop next to the **Pullman Station,** behind the Amir Palace Hotel (S£2-5). Drivers of **private taxis** dislike the meter; few journeys should cost more than S£25.

▐ ◪ ORIENTATION AND PRACTICAL INFORMATION

Mastering Aleppo's square layout is simple. Almost all budget accommodations and some restaurants are in the area bounded by **al-Ma'ari St.** and **Quwatli St.** (running east-west), and **Baron St.** and **Bab al-Faraj St.** (running north-south). Be careful if walking in the vicinity of the latter set of streets at night, especially when Kung Fu and porn movies let out. The National Museum, tourist office, private bus services, travel agents, and a few expensive restaurants lie on al-Ma'ari St. A sharp right onto **al-Walid St.,** which turns into **Sa'adullah al-Jabri St.,** leads to the **Christian Quarter,** where the wealthy strut their stuff around the restaurants and cafes. It is pleasant to stroll through the enormous **Public Garden** opposite the Christian Quarter, but it is not recommended at night or if alone. South of Bab al-Faraj St. is the congested **al-Mutanabbi St.,** which eventually leads to the **Citadel.** Any right turn will lead to the bustling **souqs.** The easiest way to gain perspective on Syria's second-largest city is to hike up the Citadel's bridge and climb the western wall.

Tourist Office: (☎222 12 00), on al-Ma'ari St. at the intersection with Baron St., across from the National Museum. Pick up the map with bus and transportation information. Open Sa-Th 9am-2pm.

Currency Exchange: Changing anything but cash is a hassle. The **Commercial Bank of Syria,** on Baron St. just past the Ugaritic theater, accepts traveler's checks for a small commission; bring your passport. Other branches on al-Mutanabbi St. only change cash. All branches open daily 8am-noon. An **exchange booth** at the intersection of Quwatli St. and Bab al-Faraj St. changes cash only. Open Th-Sa 8am-8pm, F 9am-7pm. Some areas of the *souq* specialize in black market exchange at good rates.

English-Language Bookstore: Kussa Library, Homsi St. Go down Baron St. away from the tourist office and pass the Kung Fu theaters. Take a right after Ma'had al-Mahabba School (bombed-out building on right); it's on the immediate left. Carries 3- to 4-day-old copies of the *International Herald Tribune*, *Wall Street Journal*, and English versions of the Lebanese *Daily Star* and Egyptian *al-Ahram*. Open daily 8am-2pm and 5-9pm.

Emergency: Police and Medical: ☎112. **Hospital:** ☎110.

WORLDWIDE CALLING MADE EASY

The MCI WorldCom Card, designed specifically to keep you in touch with the people that matter the most to you.

MCI WORLDCOM   WORLDPHONE.

1·800·888·8000

J. L. SMITH

www.wcom.com/worldphone

Please tear off this card and keep it in your wallet as a reference guide for convenient U.S. and worldwide calling with the MCI WorldCom Card.

HOW TO MAKE CALLS USING YOUR MCI WORLDCOM CARD

> **When calling from the U.S., Puerto Rico, the U.S. Virgin Islands or Canada** to virtually anywhere in the world:

1. Dial 1-800-888-8000
2. Enter your card number + PIN, listen for the dial tone
3. Dial the number you are calling :
   Domestic Calls: Area Code + Phone number
   International Calls:
   011+ Country Code + City Code + Phone Number

> **When calling from outside the U.S.,** use WorldPhone from over 125 countries and places worldwide:

1. Dial the WorldPhone toll-free access number of the country you are calling from.
2. Follow the voice instructions or hold for a WorldPhone operator to complete the call.

> **For calls from your hotel:**

1. Obtain an outside line.
2. Follow the instructions above on how to place a call.
   Note: If your hotel blocks the use of your MCI WorldCom Card, you may have to use an alternative location to place your call.

RECEIVING INTERNATIONAL COLLECT CALLS*

Have family and friends call you collect at home using WorldPhone Service and pay the same low rate as if you called them.

1. Provide them with the WorldPhone access number for the country they are calling from (In the U.S., 1-800-888-8000; for international access numbers see reverse side).
2. Have them dial that access number, wait for an operator, and ask to call you collect at your home number.

*For U.S. based customers only.

START USING YOUR MCI WORLDCOM CARD TODAY. MCI WORLDCOM STEPSAVERS℠

Get the same low rate per country as on calls from home, when you:

1. **Receive international collect calls to your home** using WorldPhone access numbers
2. **Make international calls with your MCI WorldCom Card** from the U.S.*
3. **Call back to anywhere in the U.S. from Abroad** using your MCI WorldCom Card and WorldPhone access numbers.

* An additional charge applies to calls from U.S. pay phones.

WorldPhone Overseas Laptop Connection Tips —
Visit our website, www.wcom.com/worldphone, to learn how to access the Internet and email via your laptop when traveling abroad using the MCI WorldCom Card and WorldPhone access numbers.

Travelers Assist® — When you are overseas, get emergency interpretation assistance and local medical, legal, and entertainment referrals. Simply dial the country's toll-free access number.

Planning a Trip?—Call the WorldPhone customer service hotline at 1-800-736-1828 for new and updated country access availability or visit our website:

www.wcom.com/worldphone

MCI WorldCom Worldphone Access Numbers

Easy Worldwide Calling

MCI WORLDCOM.

The MCI WorldCom Card.

The easy way to call when traveling worldwide.

MCI WORLDCOM   WORLDPHONE.

1·800·888·8000

J. L. SMITH

The MCI WorldCom Card gives you...

- Access to the US and other countries worldwide.
- Customer Service 24 hours a day
- Operators who speak your language
- Great MCI WorldCom rates and no sign-up fees

For more information or to apply for a Card call:
1-800-955-0925

Outside the U.S., call MCI WorldCom collect (reverse charge) at:
1-712-943-6839

✂

COUNTRY	WORLDPHONE TOLL-FREE ACCESS #
Argentina (CC)	
Using Telefonica	0800-222-6249
Using Telecom	0800-555-1002
Australia (CC) ♦	
Using OPTUS	1-800-551-111
Using TELSTRA	1-800-881-100
Austria (CC) ♦	0800-200-235
Bahamas (CC) +	1-800-888-8000
Belgium (CC) ♦	0800-10012
Bermuda (CC) +	1-800-888-8000
Bolivia (CC) ♦	0-800-2222
Brazil (CC)	000-8012
British Virgin Islands +	1-800-888-8000
Canada (CC)	1-800-888-8000
Cayman Islands +	1-800-888-8000
Chile (CC)	
Using CTC	800-207-300
Using ENTEL	800-360-180
China +	108-12
Mandarin Speaking Operator	108-17
Colombia (CC)	980-9-16-0001
Collect Access in Spanish	980-9-16-1111
Costa Rica ♦	0800-012-2222
Czech Republic (CC) ♦	00-42-000112
Denmark (CC) ♦	8001-0022
Dominica+	1-800-888-8000
Dominican Republic (CC) +	
Collect Access	1-800-888-8000
Collect Access in Spanish	1121

COUNTRY	ACCESS #
Ecuador (CC) +	999-170
El Salvador (CC)	800-1767
Finland (CC) ♦	08001-102-80
France (CC) ♦	0-800-99-0019
French Guiana (CC)	0-800-99-0019
Germany (CC)	0800-888-8000
Greece (CC) ♦	00-800-1211
Guam (CC)	1-800-888-8000
Guatemala (CC) ♦	99-99-189
Haiti +	
Collect Access	193
Collect access in Creole	190
Honduras +	8000-122
Hong Kong (CC)	800-96-1121
Hungary (CC) ♦	06*-800-01411
India (CC)	000-127
Collect access	000-126
Ireland (CC)	1-800-55-1001
Israel (CC)	1-800-920-2727
Italy (CC) ♦	172-1022
Jamaica +	
Collect Access	1-800-888-8000
From pay phones	#2
Japan (CC) ♦	
Using KDD	00539-121 ▶
Using IDC	0066-55-121
Using JT	0044-11-121

COUNTRY	ACCESS #
Korea (CC)	
To call using KT	00729-14
Using DACOM	00309-12
Phone Booths +	
Press red button ,03,then*	
Military Bases	550-2255
Luxembourg (CC)	8002-0112
Malaysia (CC) ♦	1-800-80-0012
Mexico (CC)	01-800-021-8000
Monaco (CC) ♦	800-90-019
Netherlands (CC) ♦	0800-022-91-22
New Zealand (CC)	000-912
Nicaragua (CC)	166
Norway (CC) ♦	800-19912
Panama	00800-001-0108
Philippines (CC) ♦	
Using PLDT	105-14
Filipino speaking operator	105-15
Using Bayantel	1237-14
Using Bayantel (Filipino)	1237-77
Poland (CC) +	800-111-21-22
Portugal (CC) +	800-800-123
Romania (CC) +	01-800-1800
Russia (CC) +	
Russian speaking operator	
	747-3320
Using Rostelcom	747-3322
Using Sovintel	960-2222
Saudi Arabia (CC)	1-800-11

COUNTRY	WORLDPHONE TOLL-FREE ACCESS #
Singapore (CC)	8000-112-112
Slovak Republic (CC)	08000-00112
South Africa (CC)	0800-99-0011
Spain (CC)	900-99-0014
St. Lucia +	1-800-888-8000
Sweden (CC) ♦	020-795-922
Switzerland (CC) ♦	0800-89-0222
Taiwan (CC) ♦	0080-13-4567
Thailand (CC)	001-999-1-2001
Turkey (CC) ♦	00-8001-1177
United Kingdom (CC)	
Using BT	0800-89-0222
Using C& W	0500-89-0222
Venezuela (CC) + ♦	800-1114-0
Vietnam + ♦	1201-1022

KEY
Note: Automation available from most locations. Countries where automation is not yet available are shown in *Italic*

(CC) Country-to-country calling available.

+ Limited availability.

✳ Not available from public pay phones.

● Public phones may require deposit of coin or phone card for dial tone.

● Local service fee in U.S. currency required to complete call.

▶ Regulation does not permit Intra-Japan Calls.

✳ Wait for second dial tone.

■ Local surcharge may apply.

Hint: For Puerto Rico and Caribbean Islands not listed above, you can use 1-800-888-8000 as the WorldPhone access number.

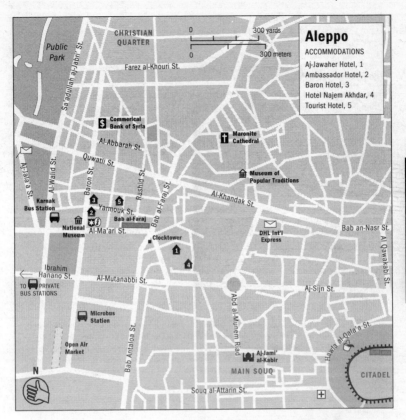

Aleppo

ACCOMMODATIONS

Aj-Jawaher Hotel, 1
Ambassador Hotel, 2
Baron Hotel, 3
Hotel Najem Akhdar, 4
Tourist Hotel, 5

SYRIA

Tourist Police: (☎ 222 12 00), on al-Ma'ari St. at the intersection with Baron St., across from the National Museum. The same number and building as the tourist office; ask to be transferred.

Late-Night Pharmacy: Pharmacies rotate late-night duties. The **Ummal al-Naji Pharmacy** (☎ 225 14 78) is next to the entrance of Baghdad Station. Open 24hr. Other pharmacies open 9:30am-2pm and 5-9:30pm.

Medical Assistance: Dr. Faher (☎ 225 52 52) offers medical assistance in English.

Telephones: In the post office on al-Jala'a St. just before the park, under a giant radio tower. Bring your calling card and pay at the desk after your call. S£120 per minute to the US, UK, Canada, or Australia. Open daily 8am-10pm. Check hotel phone services and consider buying a Syrian phonecard.

Post Office: (☎ 144), on al-Jala'a St. just before the park, under a giant radio tower. Open daily 8am-8pm. **EMS** open Sa-Th 8am-2pm. Bring your passport. **DHL** (☎ 224 09 88); after Bab al-Faraj St., take the first right off Quwatli St.; it's in a small alley to the left. Open Sa-Th 9am-2pm and 4-8pm.

▌ ACCOMMODATIONS

Hotels in Aleppo range from the seat of sleaze to the lap of luxury. Higher-priced options cluster on Baron St. in the center of town; more affordable places are scattered among the car parts and hole-in-the-wall eateries near the Bab al-Faraj clocktower. Those searching for the very cheapest should be warned that some are frequented by Russian prostitutes. Look carefully before parting with your cash.

Tourist Hotel (☎221 65 83), off Yarmouk St. across from the museum. Walking away from the clocktower on al-Ma'ari St., take a right just before the Syria Hotel; it's 75m down on the left past an intersection. Spotless rooms, all with comfy beds and some with huge, beautiful balconies, are second only to common areas with antique furniture and multi-colored flowerpots. The distinguished owner, Madame Olga, gives good deals. Singles S£350, with bath S£400; doubles with bath S£700; triples with bath S£1050.

Baron Hotel (☎221 08 80; fax 221 81 64), on Baron St. When Aleppo was the end of the line on the Orient Express, the Baron was a stopover for illustrious guests like T.E. Lawrence, Agatha Christie, and Kemal Ataturk. These days, its prices are the most grandiose thing about it. The bar is the best place in Syria to drink local and German beer and the rare stiff cocktail (gin and tonic S£150) with other blasé expats, tourists, and writers. Breakfast S£135-180. Reserve in advance. Singles S£1350; doubles S£1800; stunning suites S£3600.

Al-Gawaher Hotel (☎/fax 223 95 54), on Bab al-Faraj St. With your back to the clocktower, walk toward the Cultural Center (keeping it on your left), and take the first left. New, freshly painted rooms have gleaming bathrooms with tubs. Nice communal eating room and quiet neighborhood are bonuses. Breakfast S£100. Laundry service available: shirt S£30, pants S£40. Singles S£350; doubles S£700; triples S£950.

Hotel Najem Akhdar (☎223 91 57). Facing the library from the clocktower, take a left and then a right around the mosque; the hotel is on the right. Full of life with a cat, birds, and ultra-friendly management. Even better, ice cream awaits in the lobby. Decent rooms, but "showers" resemble meat lockers. Rooftop restaurant with excellent Aleppan views makes up for rooms and showers. Breakfast S£75. Rooftop mattresses S£150; dorm beds S£200; singles S£300; doubles S£450-500; triples S£600-700.

Ambassador Hotel (☎221 02 31), on Baron St. next to the Baron Hotel. Rooms cheerfully decorated with blue curtains, bedspreads, tablecloths, and Impressionist-style paintings. Less pricey than the Baron Hotel for the same location, but lacks ambiance. All rooms have wardrobes and nice blue bathrooms, and some have balconies. Breakfast S£90. Singles S£765; doubles S£1035; triples S£1260. More for A/C and fridge. Payment in US dollars or European currencies preferred. V.

⬛ FOOD

For great inexpensive restaurants and cafes, turn around the corner from the exchange booth on Quwatli St. onto Bab al-Faraj St. Take a right at the **fruit shake stands** and you'll see six or seven places on the right. Baron St. is lined with rooftop restaurants. The Christian Quarter, near the park off Sa'adullah al-Jabri St., is home to true Middle Eastern opulence.

▨ **Beit Wakil** (☎221 71 69 or 224 70 83), in the Christian Quarter. Head down Khayali St. toward al-Hatab Sq. and take a right onto a small alley (Sirsi St.) The sweetest splurge in Syria is on the left, near the Maronite church. Munch on traditional Aleppan fare as a belly dancer cuts a rug. Ottoman architecture and design provide an authentic backdrop, and the congenial manager offers to cater to "all budgets." Huge entrees S£300-500. 10% charge for V, MC, Diners. Discounts for groups over 7-8 people.

Abu Nouwas (☎221 03 88). From Bab al-Faraj clocktower, go up al-Ma'ari St. and take the first right; it's two blocks uphill on the left. This A/C diner with its distinctive orange sign looks like a former bureaucratic center that has made a change for the better. There are no menus: the manager gives tours of the kitchen where you'll find outstanding lentil soup (S£50) and tasty kebab with warm pita, veggies, soup, salad, and drink (S£200). Breakfast S£75. Open daily 7am-midnight.

Al-Kindi (☎223 11 54 or 221 08 89). Walking uphill on Bab al-Faraj St. from the clocktower, take the second left; al-Kindi is on the right. Synchronize your mastication with the whacking of a distant meat mallet in this cheap, local favorite. Lightning-quick service. Extensive English (but not-so-vegetarian-friendly) menu featuring well-prepared kebab (S£80), *shish tawouq* (S£70), and lamb eggs (S£70). Open daily 7am-2am.

Ali Baba Restaurant (☎ 221 50 24). From the clocktower, head up Bab al-Faraj St. and take the first left at the fruit shake stands. This rooftop restaurant's specialty is the kebab *halabi* (S£100). All-male crowd sips copious amounts of Sharq beer (S£50) and 'araq (S£25). Open daily 8am-3am.

Patisserie Mousattat (☎ 21 27 47), the third left up from the clocktower, just off Bab al-Faraj St., next to the exchange booth. A classic *ba'laweh* bakery. Can't stomach *shawarma* before noon? Bring your morning munchies here and ask for *ma'mouniyya:* a cream-of-wheat-like starch drenched in warm syrup, doused with cinnamon, and eaten with pita bread (S£25). Open daily 5am-midnight.

■ ♫ SIGHTS AND ENTERTAINMENT

CITADEL. Begin your sightseeing tour with an outstanding view of Aleppo from the Citadel. Built in the 10th century CE by Sayf al-Dawla, the Citadel stands 50m above the city on a hill *(tel)*, heightened by the remains of prior civilizations. In times of war, Aleppans equipped themselves with provisions and took refuge in this fortress. Its enormous entrance gate is fortified with three sets of steel doors, and the 12th-century **moat** (20m deep by 30m wide) is lined with smooth stones to make climbing difficult (some of the tiles are still in place today). The watery defense is now full of refuse, and not for the first time. Historical accounts describe in gruesome hyperbole how in 1400, Timor's Central Asian forces couldn't penetrate the Citadel until the moat brimmed with fallen soldiers' bodies.

Inside and to the immediate left of the main path lies a **bath** that was once used as a metal-working studio and is assumed to be part of an Ayyubid palace. Beyond that is the **small mosque** (with a well in the middle of its courtyard), the **great mosque** (bigger, but with a fountain rather than a well), and a cafeteria that serves overpriced food and drinks (soda S£35). Connected to the cafeteria are the **barracks,** now a museum displaying objects found during the Citadel's excavation. Below the barracks is a modern **amphitheater** that stages occasional performances. To the right of the main path are **storage rooms,** followed by stairs that lead to the **Royal Palace.** One of the most interesting sections of the Citadel, this area has its own baths and a courtyard paved with black and white marble. From the palace, a passage leads to the opulent, graffiti-covered **Throne Room,** which sits directly above the main entrance. *(Open W-M 9am-6pm, in winter 9am-4pm. S£300, students S£15. Museum S£150, students S£15.)*

HAMMAM YALBOAGHA AL-NASIRI. Outside the Citadel, the **Hammam Yalboagha al-Nasiri** awaits to steam, wash, and massage the sweat and grime off dirty, sore bodies. This beautifully restored 14th-century bath is heavily marketed by the Ministry of Tourism. *(Take a left with your back to the Citadel entrance. Open for women Su, Tu-W, and F 10am-1:30pm; in winter Sa, M, and Th 9am-1:30pm. Open for men Su, Tu-W, and F 5pm-2am; in winter daily 5pm-1:30am. Soaping, massage, and cup of coffee or tea S£415; unassisted bath with own soap S£200.)*

MAIN SOUQ. Between the Hammam-Citadel area and the hotel district is the **best souq in the eastern Mediterranean.** All nine kilometers of ancient, winding passageways burst with leather goods, backgammon boards, carpets, Qur'ans, *argeilehs*, brass goods, gold and silver jewelry, and even lingerie. Several **khans** (courtyard inns) in the *souq* housed international traders during the Mamluk and Ottoman periods. On Friday evenings, the dark and deserted *souq* invites leisurely exploration on foot. *(Walking around the souq should be safe even during less busy hours; women travelers are advised not to walk alone in the evenings. Open Sa-Th early morning until 7-8pm.)*

AL-JAMI' AL-KABIR. Appropriately situated just behind the gold market, **al-Jami' al-Kabir,** the Great Mosque of the Umayyads (also called **Zacharias's Mosque,** after the father of John the Baptist), is a real gem. Built on top of a Byzantine cathedral in the 8th century, its square minaret with five levels of arches is a remarkable piece of architecture. To the left of the main entrance stands an empty 600-year-old **insane asylum** in good condition. A fragrant smell emanates from two **soap factories** around the corner. Aleppo's high-quality soap (made of olive or laurel oil) is known throughout the Middle East. Both factories have been in the same unsullied families for generations.

NATIONAL MUSEUM. Aleppo's National Museum is second only to that in Damascus in the quality of its exhibits. Several 100,000-year-old Ugaritic flint axes, a 3rd-millennium BCE basalt altar from Ebla, and a stone lion from an 18th-century BCE temple will leave you reeling with the knowledge of your own temporal existence. The third floor includes a terrific modern art wing offering a rare look into the experience and psyche of the Syrian artist; insist that a guard open it for you. *(Across from the tourist office on Baron St. Open Sa-M and W-Th 9am-6pm, F 9am-12:30pm and 2-6pm; in winter Sa-M and W-Th 9am-4pm, F 9-11:30am and 2-6pm. S£300; students S£15.)*

CHRISTIAN QUARTER. Fabulous 17th- and 18th-century homes line the narrow streets of the Christian Quarter. Within a few blocks, churches from four different denominations attract worshipers. Walk down Quwatli St. past Bab al-Faraj St. and take a left at the fascist-style stone gate onto an airy, tiled street. Take the first right to get to the 19th-century **Maronite Cathedral.** On the right is a gorgeous **Greek Catholic Church.** At the store with underwear in the window, take a right to the **Greek Orthodox Church** and the **Armenian Church of the Forty Martyrs.** These buildings feature 3rd-century artwork, engraved marble altars, and antique chandeliers.

⚡ DAYTRIPS FROM ALEPPO

BASILICA OF ST. SIMEON قلعة سمان

To reach St. Simeon from Aleppo, take a microbus to Darret 'Azzay (1hr., S£10). From this small town, negotiate with locals for the 8km ride to the cathedral. Service minivans will ask for S£100 one-way, but locals in brightly-colored Suzuki 3-wheelers might do a round trip for S£150-200. Open daily 9am-6pm; in winter 9am-4pm. S£300, students S£15.

Born in 392 CE, **St. Simeon of Stylites** acquired the first and last parts of his name by spending almost 40 years preaching from atop a stylite (from the Greek *stylos*, meaning "pillar"). Simeon's popularity with locals and his ability to starve himself made his superiors jealous, so they banished him to a nearby cave. Peasants began to hound the local legend for advice, and the game of "Simon Says" was born. As his disenchantment with humanity grew, so did the pillar; at the time of his death in 459 CE he was sitting 15 meters in the air. While he would gladly answer male pilgrims' spiritual questions, Simple Simeon refused to talk to women.

Simeon's death did not stop pilgrims from visiting his pillar, and the emperor Zenon had a **cathedral** built around his home, which is considered a masterpiece of pre-Islamic architecture. A large dome covered the octagonal courtyard where the pillar stood, surrounded by four basilicas that formed a giant cross. One basilica was a chapel; the other three housed pilgrims. The rear wall of the chapel was decorated with delicate acanthus leaves and Byzantine crosses. An earthquake destroyed the structure less than 50 years after its completion, causing pilgrims to question the site's holiness and deterring pious investors from rebuilding the cathedral. The 5th-century remains are still impressive, but years of souvenir seekers chipping away at the pillar have reduced it to a large boulder. In the 10th century, the site was converted to a Byzantine fort with 27 towers along an enclosing wall. The fortifications are easily distinguishable from the cathedral ruins and afford excellent panoramic views of the rocky terrain leading up to Turkey.

If your taxi driver refuses to lower his price, insist on a side trip to **Qatura** to better justify the expense. This Roman tomb, the resting place of the warrior Titus Flavius Julianus, is carved into rock about one kilometer off the road to St. Simeon. Above the entrance to the main tomb, an eagle—identical to one in Palmyra's Temple of Bel (see p. 583)—poses with spread wings, a symbol of the soul.

EBLA أبلا

From the Aleppo station, take a microbus headed to Ma'arat al-Nu'man (S£25) and ask to get off at the road to Ebla. It's a 30-minute walk to the site, and there is no food or water available, but able will you be, ere you see Ebla. Back on the highway, it's easy to catch a bus back to Aleppo; they come frequently from both Ma'arat al-Nu'man and Hama. Open daily 6am-6pm. S£200, students S£15, if the guy is there to collect it.

This *tel*, 60km south of Aleppo, was discovered in 1964, and excavations are still in progress. Ebla is thought to have been the oldest city in Syria, dating back to the 3rd millennium BCE. Over 17,000 **cuneiform tablets** have been recovered in an ancient **palace library**, revealing much about Syria's early history. Apparently, Ebla was the center of an important north Syrian empire during the 3rd millennium BCE, but as fate would have it, the city was to prove itself a rather irritating obstacle to the expansion of empires. Both Sargon of Akkad (in about 2300 BCE) and the Hittites (around 1600 BCE) razed Ebla almost completely. Today, signs insist that you remain on the edges of the site—this shouldn't come as too much of a disappointment unless you have a strong interest in archaeology.

MA'ARAT AL-NU'MAN معارة النعمن

To get to Ma'arat al-Nu'man, take a service or minibus from Aleppo or Hama (S£20). From town, hire a local or private taxi to take you around the Dead Cities (S£600, but bargain).

Journeying to Ma'arat al-Nu'man will give you very few hints as to the splendor of its main attraction, the neighboring **Dead Cities**. Despite its bustling populace and *souq*, this peripheral, dusty town has only one minor point of interest. Two hundred meters left of the bus terminal and directly next to the *souq* stands an old Ottoman Khan that has been converted into a **museum**. Its Byzantine mosaic collection, restored from surrounding churches and old houses hints at the past majesty of the Dead Cities. (Open Sa-M and W-Th. S£200, students S£15.)

AL-BARA. Ten kilometers west of town and five kilometers to the north lies the least inspiring of the Dead Cities. This 5th-century site was one of Syria's major wine-producers, as well as an important religious site. Al-Bara's main attractions are two well-preserved **pyramid tombs** that house Christian carvings. Today, al-Bara is home to wandering sheep, green orchards, and a modern Bedouin village.

SERJILLA. Seven kilometers east on a lonely road from Bara is Serjilla, perhaps the grandest of the Dead Cities. Built on a plateau, the town once housed 11,000 people; its baths, olive oil mills, and Roman and Byzantine churches have remarkably withstood the test of time. Townspeople spoke Syriac and Greek until the Muslims, led by Nour al-Din, conquered Serjilla in 1148. Hire a **guide** (Sa-M and W-Th 9am-4pm; S£150, students S£15, tips appreciated) to learn about Serjilla's complex water-heating system and its hidden **underground caverns** and **cisterns.**

RUWEIHA. Twelve kilometers north of Ma'arat al-Nu'man, Ruweiha sports your standard Dead City sights (churches, baths, mills, and villas). Bedouins have settled into many of the ruins. The highlight of Ruweiha is the grandiose columned **basilica** from the 5th century.

EASTERN SYRIA

DEIR AL-ZUR ضيرالزور ☎51

Tourists may consider Deir al-Zur remote, but its location has always been its greatest asset. The city first flourished due to its strategic position next to the Euphrates River, at the crossroads of two major communication routes. During the 1980s, oil was discovered beneath the city's sands, fueling a massive growth spurt. Fortunately, the Turkish dams harnessing the river's hydraulic force have not stripped Deir al-Zur of its splendor. Enjoy its troubled waters from a safe distance on the **suspension bridge** built by the French. Aside from one decent museum and magnificent views of the river, dry and distant Deir al-Zur offers travelers little more than a hub for visiting the nearby ruins at Rasafeh, Halabiyyeh, and Zalabiyyeh, and a glimpse into the life of the nomadic desert people of eastern Syria.

▐ GETTING THERE AND GETTING AROUND

The **bus/micro station** is about one kilometer out of town on 8 Azar St. Hourly **microbuses** go to Mari (2hr., S$50), Raqqa (2hr., S$60), and other southern areas. Old **buses** leave less frequently to: Aleppo (S$70); Damascus via Palmyra (S$110); and Homs (S$75). The **luxury bus station** is about 2km out of town past the bus/micro station. **Karnak Bus Co.** (☎22 18 85) runs to Damascus (6hr.; 8, 10, 11am, noon, 3, 10pm; S$160) and Palmyra (2hr.; 8, 10, 11am, noon, 3, 10pm; S$75). **Qadmoos** (☎21 29 20) runs buses to: Aleppo (6hr.; 1, 6:30, 9am, 2:30, 8pm; S$135); Damascus (6hr.; 1, 8, 10:15, 11:15am, 4pm; S$150) via Palmyra (2hr., S$75); Homs (4hr.; 2, 11, 11:45pm, 1:15am; S$150); Lattakia (5½ hr.; 2, 11, 11:45pm, 1:15am); Palmyra (2hr., S$85); Raqqa (2hr.; 5, 10:30am, 5pm; S$75); and Tartus (5hr.; 2, 11, 11:45pm, 1:15am). **Furat Tours** (☎22 39 34) sends buses to: Damascus (6hr.; 9:30, 11pm, 1am; S$175); Palmyra (4hr., 12:45pm, S$135); and Raqqa (2hr., 9:30am and 1pm, S$75).

▐ ORIENTATION AND PRACTICAL INFORMATION

Deir al-Zur is easy to navigate. Hotels, restaurants, and shopping areas are centered around the main intersection of **8 Azar** and **al-Iman St.** The statue of President Assad on a horse is a handy landmark—nearly everything is a five-minute walk away. Few signs are written in English or French—rely on maps and landmarks.

The **tourist office** is east of the square, one block south of Khalid ibn al-Walid St. English skills are tenuous and maps are rarely available. (☎22 61 50. Open sporadically Sa-Th 9am-2pm.) Exchange cash at the **Commercial Bank of Syria,** a 10-minute walk along al-Iman Ali St. (Open Sa-Th 8am-4pm.) The **police** (☎112) are around the corner from the museum on 6 Ayyar St., across from the river. Call ☎110 for an **ambulance.** Al-Shifa'a Pharmacy (☎22 12 41) is next to al-Jamia'a Hotel, east of the main square. There are two **post offices:** the new one is near the bus/micro station on 8 Azar St.; the old one is a five-minute walk west of the square on al-Iman Ali St. (Both open 8am-2pm and 6:30-8pm.) The only **public phones** are around the corner from the old post office; get expensive **phonecards** inside (S$500).

▐ ACCOMMODATIONS AND FOOD

Lodgings in Deir al-Zur are limited to dingy-looking buildings in disrepair. Don't count on hot showers and be prepared for some not-so-clean beds. **Hotel Damas,** across the street from the Euphrates on 8 Azar St., is the best of slim pickings. Rooms overlooking the main street are breezy, but loud at night. (☎22 14 81. Singles S$200; doubles S$325; triples S$425.) **Hotel al-Jamia'a al-'Arabia** jams on Grande St., about two blocks away from the central square. A cool sitting room with a TV and balconies makes this hotel somewhat cheery, but rumors of bedbugs abound. (☎22 13 71. Singles S$200; doubles S$400; triples S$500.) **Hotel al-'Arabi al-Kabir,** east of the square on Khalid ibn Walid St., is brighter and cleaner than other options in town, but the unpleasant setting is a drawback. (☎22 20 70. Singles S$200; doubles S$400; triples S$600.)

Don't expect fine dining—most culinary options come from the small falafel, *shawarma,* and pastry shops and the fresh produce **souq** around 8 Azar Sq. If the stand-up routine grows tiresome, there are a few sit-down places around the square and on the river. **Lucost** is a beautiful restaurant along the main branch of the Euphrates. Grab a decent meal (S$200) or just sit with a beer (S$100) and enjoy the view. (Open daily late.) **Sahara Restaurant,** a short walk west of the square, provides cheap, filling meals for S$65-75.

ZENOBIA, WARRIOR PRINCESS Previously called **Zenobia** (after the Palmyrene queen under whose auspices it was built), the 3rd-century CE town of **Halabiyyeh** once guarded trade routes along the Euphrates and the desert. The Romans took Halabiyyeh after destroying Palmyra. In the following years, the town was a stronghold against the encroaching Sassanian Persians. Its citadel was once heralded as the greatest Byzantine fortification outside Constantinople. The city was destroyed and eventually abandoned after sieges in 540 and 610. Nevertheless, Halabiyyeh's outer walls and upper fortifications remain relatively intact and it is still possible to make out the foundations of some churches and baths. What isn't difficult at all to discern is the incredible view of the Euphrates. The twin fortress town of **Zalabiyyeh**, 3km downstream on the opposite bank, once defended the approaches to Halabiyyeh. With the exception of the main gateway, the site is almost completely destroyed. Getting to these towns is an arduous process. From Deir al-Zur, take a **microbus** to Tibne (S£15, every hr., 30min.). From this turnoff, you'll have to hitch or suffer the two-hour walk to Halabiyyeh. Getting to Zalabiyyeh is much harder and probably not worth it. From Halabiyyeh, cross the bridge just beyond town, walk for three hours along the main road, pass through the tunnel under the railway (just after the station), and proceed up the hill.

🞛 SIGHTS

Deir al-Zur's **National Museum**, considered one of the best in Syria, was opened in response to growing archaeological discoveries in the area. It was established in 1996 as a joint venture between the Syrian Antiquities Department and the Frei Universität of Berlin, Germany. The museum presents the region's history starting with the biblical era, moving through Arab-Islamic culture, and ending in the present day. Especially interesting are the life-sized models and artifacts. The museum pays particular attention to the region's delicate environmental situation. *(Open W-M 9am-6pm. S£300, students S£15.)*

RAQQA رقة ☎22

Looking around modern Raqqa, one would hardly guess that this bustling market town possesses a glorious past. On the left bank of the Euphrates between Aleppo and Deir al-Zur, Raqqa was founded in the 4th century BCE by Alexander the Great and rebuilt by many empires through the ages, though few ruins remain to attest to its former splendor. In 662 CE, Abbasid Caliph Mansour built a new city atop Raqqa's ruins, with a semicircular plan inspired by Baghdad. The southern, straight side of this horseshoe-shaped city was determined by the course of the Euphrates. Raqqa reached its apex in the beginning of the 9th century under notorious Abbasid Caliph Harun al-Rashid, but virtually ceased to exist after Mongol invasions in 1260. It was not until the end of World War II that Syrians revitalized the city as a Euphrates basin commercial hub, once again built over its own ruins.

📧 GETTING THERE. The **microbus station** is about 200m south of the clocktower past the Assad statue. Microbuses leave regularly to al-Mansoura (30min., S£15) and Aleppo (3hr., S£75). The main **bus station** is across the street. The cheapest of the luxury bus lines is **Karnak** (☎22 40 97), with **buses** to Aleppo (2hr.; 1, 7, 8, 11am; S£85) and Damascus (7hr., 12:30am, S£150) via Homs (5hr.). The nicer **Qadmoos** (☎22 16 28) runs to: Aleppo (2hr.; 7:15am, 12:15, 7:15pm; S£85); Damascus (7hr.; 8am, 2:30, 8, 11pm; S£190) via Homs (5hr., S£125); and Deir al-Zur (2hr.; 9:30am, 2pm, 1am; S£60). **Al-'Aliah,** another luxury bus line, services Aleppo (2hr.; 7, 8, 9, 11am, 1, 3:30, 6:30, 9pm; S£85).

📧🞅 ORIENTATION AND PRACTICAL INFORMATION. Orientation around Raqqa is easy from the **clocktower** in the central square and the **Assad statue** down the hill to the south. Don't expect much help from the **tourist office.** (☎24 44 45. Open Sa-Th 8:30am-2pm.) In contrast, the **hospital** (☎22 23 40), just west of the clocktower on al-Shahid Bassel al-Assad St., is clean, economical, and friendly. The **post office** (☎23 58 99), south of the clocktower on the east side of the street, is the only place to make **international phone calls.** You must buy an S£1000 **phonecard,** available outside. Very little English and an unhealthy suspicion of foreigners mean that it's hard to get any information. Even placing simple calls can be trying.

█ ▒ ACCOMMODATIONS AND FOOD. Hotel Tourism, on the main street just east of the clocktower, is the best bet in town, with a pleasant sitting room and perks like showers, fridges, and TVs. Ask the manager to turn on the hot water or you'll be in for a frigid shock. (☎22 07 25. Doubles S£450; triples S£600.) The non-descript rooms at **'Ammar Hotel,** on a side street one block north of the clocktower, are a little cheaper, with sinks but no showers in the rooms. (☎22 26 12. Singles S£200; doubles S£400; students S£150.) **Hotel Karnak** is a five-minute hike west of the Assad statue along the winding al-Shahid Bassel al-Assad St. The receptionist is helpful even to non-guests and big rooms come with clean baths, A/C, and fridges. Ask for a top-floor room with a balcony and tremendous views. (☎23 22 66. Singles S£765; doubles S£1350; triples S£1575. Traveler's checks accepted.)

Many falafel and *shawarma* stands cluster around the main square, and delightful pastry shops beckon the hungry north of the clocktower. Finding a sit-down is often as rewarding as it is difficult. **Ar-Rashid Restaurant** (☎24 19 19) is about a block west of the clocktower through a small park. Enjoy a splendid Syrian meal (S£250) with beer (S£100) in the comfort of its air-conditioned dining room with views onto the garden. The **Hotel Karnak Restaurant** also serves cheap eats (S£200) that can be enjoyed on the patio overlooking the main street and lawn.

▣ SIGHTS. Most of Raqqa's former splendor has been lost over time, but there are a few exceptions. To the east and northeast of the clocktower, parts of the Abbasid wall remain. Raqqa's 12th-century **city gate** is a 10-minute walk east of the clocktower. To the northwest lie the remains of the old **Grand Mosque,** built during the reign of the Abbasid caliph al-Mansour in the 8th century CE. Only parts of the wall and the arcade of the sanctuary wall still stand. Syrian and French archaeologists have uncovered parts of the Abbasid palace, known as the **Palace of the Maidens,** to the north of the mosque. A small **museum** a few blocks to the east of the clocktower provides a two-tiered analysis of the region; the first floor details the archaeology from the province of Raqqa, and the second floor contains items from the city of Raqqa proper. A new museum is scheduled to open on the banks of the Euphrates in late 2000. *(Open F-W 8am-4pm. S£150, students S£35.)*

NEAR RAQQA: RASAFEH رسافة

> **Service** depart from Raqqa to al-Mansoura (30min., S£15), where local taxi drivers circle like sharks in search of tourists. **Taxi** rides to Rasafeh and back cost S£200. Hitchhiking is a popular option, though Let's Go does not recommend it. Hitchers first walk the short distance to al-Mansoura's main road to look for a lift. It may take about an hour and possibly require a few different rides, so bring water, small bills to offer your driver(s), and plenty of patience. Women should not travel alone to Rasafeh; bring a male companion.

The towering walls of Rasafeh (30km south of Raqqa and the Euphrates), one of the most extraordinary desert cities in the Middle East, appear suddenly from the vast, flat desert expanse. Around 303 CE, **Sergius,** a Christian officer in the Roman army, was brutally tortured for refusing to worship the Roman god Jupiter. His death sent shockwaves though Syria's Christian community and Sergius became the patron saint of Rasafeh, where his shrine became a major pilgrimage site. The city was renamed Sergiopolis in the 5th century and fell to Persian Muslims in the 7th century. The Umayyads eventually depopulated and then deserted the area. Rasafeh's relative inaccessibility means that few tourists crowd the town.

Enter Rasafeh through the Byzantine **North Gate,** often called one of the loveliest city entrances in Syria. Three Corinthian columns support the richly decorated triple entrance and serve as a graceful frame for the city beyond. Climb the ramparts for a better view of the whole fortress. The bulk of the site has not been excavated, so the interior looks somewhat like a lunar landscape, with high ground where walls once stood and depressions where roofs collapsed. In front of the gate is a run-of-the-mill Roman **basilica** and about 100m farther lies the **khan.** To the west, the arched openings of the enormous **cisterns** lead to vast underground caverns, supplied by aqueducts connected to a huge open reservoir. These caverns were capable of holding enough water to supply the entire city for two to three years. To the east stands the early 6th-century **Basilica of St. Sergius,** the best preserved building in Rasafeh and one of the most ornate cathedrals in the region.

TURKEY (TÜRKİYE)

CURRENCY		
US$1 = 650,670 TL	100,000 TL = US$0.15
CDN$1 = 438,874 TL	100,000 TL = CDN$0.23
EUR€1 = 586,248 TL	100,000 TL = EUR€0.17
UK£1 = 956,966 TL	100,000 TL = UK£0.10
IR£1 = 744,382 TL	100,000 TL = IR£0.13
AUS$1 = 372,053 TL	100,000 TL = AUS$0.27
NZ$1 = 281,391 TL	100,000 TL = NZ$0.35
SAR1=93,756 TL	100,000 TL = SAR1.07

Ten thousand years of stunning historical riches, overflowing modern cities, and exquisite natural wonders grace the modern Republic of Turkey. From the Ancient Greeks to the Romans, the Byzantines and the Ottomans, Asia Minor has hosted the advance and retreat of numerous great civilizations and their cultural traffic. Humanity's influences on the region are retained in its diverse religions, languages, and architectural wonders, among them İstanbul's majestic mosques and Eastern Anatolia's Armenian churches. Mother Nature has done her part too, from the glittering Aegean and Mediterranean beaches to northern *yayla* plateaus, central deserts, and Mount Ararat towering in the East. Well-trodden tourist paths grace İstanbul's Sultanahmet district, the coasts, and Cappadocia. The rest of Anatolia remains a purist backpacker's paradise: pristine alpine meadows, cliffside monasteries, medieval churches, tiny fishing villages, and countless cups of *çay* offered by people who take pride in their tradition of hospitality.

LIFE AND TIMES

HISTORY

Humanity has been mixing Asian and Western influences in what is now Central Turkey (known as "Anatolia" or "Asia Minor") since the 8th millennium BCE, making it one of the world's oldest continuously inhabited areas. Since the first human settlements appeared, Turkey has hosted the greatest of civilizations, each waxing with exuberance and then fading with despair.

ANCIENT HISTORY. By the start of the 2nd millennium BCE, the iron-forging **Hittites** had migrated from the Caucasus into central Anatolia to establish a millennium-long feudal empire headquartered at Hattuşaş (modern **Boğazkale,** p. 668). Despite Hittite dominance in central Anatolia (and beyond—the Hittites even managed to acquire Syria), other groups established themselves in the area of present-day Turkey, the most notable among them being the Phrygians (sometimes called the Trojans). **Troy** sprung up at the mouth of the Dardanelles, and archaeological excavations suggest that the Trojans unsheathed their swords for the Trojan War around 1250 BCE. After the collapse of the Hittites came the Persians, who used Turkey as a base for forays into Greece. Next in line was **Alexander the Great,** who invaded the region and took it from the Persians in less than a year. The Mediterranean coast's importance in the Roman province of Asia Minor paved the way for the creation of the East Roman Empire, centered in the city of **Constantinople** (now İstanbul). Founded by Emperor Constantine in 324 CE over the Greek city of Byzantium, Constantinople became the center of Greek Orthodox culture and the capital of a renewed empire stretching from the Balkans through Greece to the Levant and Egypt.

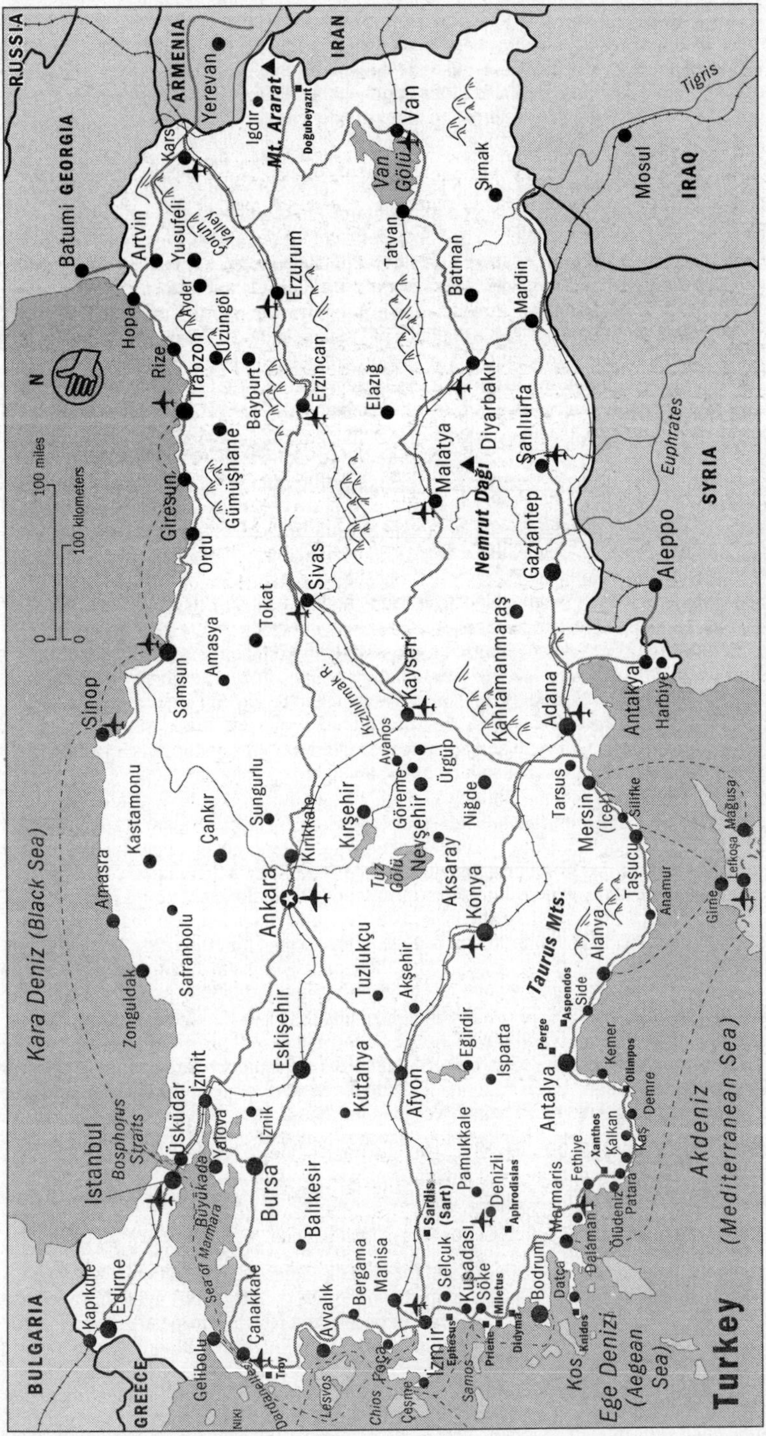
Turkey
Kara Deniz (Black Sea)
Akdeniz (Mediterranean Sea)
Ege Denizi (Aegean Sea)
Sea of Marmara
Bosphorus Straits
Dardanelles
BULGARIA
GREECE
GEORGIA
RUSSIA
ARMENIA
IRAN
IRAQ
SYRIA
Istanbul
Üsküdar
Izmit
Edirne
Kapikule
Gelibolu
Çanakkale
Troy
Büyükada
Yalova
Iznik
Bursa
Balıkesir
Ayvalık
Bergama
Manisa
Foça
Izmir
Çeşme
Ephesus
Selçuk (Sart)
Sardis
Kuşadası
Söke
Priene
Miletus
Didyma
Bodrum
Datça
Knidos
Marmaris
Dalaman
Ölüdeniz
Fethiye
Patara
Xanthos
Kalkan
Kaş
Demre
Olimpos
Kemer
Antalya
Perge
Aspendos
Side
Alanya
Anamur
Taşucu
Silifke
Mersin (Içel)
Tarsus
Adana
Antakya
Harbiye
Girne
Lefkoşa
Mağusa
Kos
Samos
Chios
Lesvos
Denizli
Aphrodisias
Pamukkale
Afyon
Kütahya
Eskişehir
Eğirdir
Isparta
Akşehir
Tuzlukçu
Konya
Taurus Mts.
Aksaray
Niğde
Nevşehir
Göreme
Ürgüp
Avanos
Tuz Gölü
Kırşehir
Kırıkkale
Ankara
Zonguldak
Safranbolu
Amasra
Kastamonu
Çankır
Sungurlu
Sinop
Samsun
Amasya
Tokat
Kızılırmak R.
Kayseri
Sivas
Kahramanmaraş
Gaziantep
Nemrut Dağı
Malatya
Şanlıurfa
Diyarbakır
Elazığ
Erzincan
Bayburt
Mardin
Batman
Tatvan
Van Gölü
Van
Şırnak
Erzurum
Gümüşhane
Ordu
Giresun
Trabzon
Rize
Uzungöl
Ayder
Hopa
Artvin
Yusufeli
Çoruh Valley
Kars
Iğdır
Doğubeyazıt
Mt. Ararat
Yerevan
Batumi
Aleppo
Mosul
Tigris
Euphrates
N
0 100 miles
0 100 kilometers

TURKEY

By the 9th century, the ancestors of the Turks had begun to migrate from Central Asia and resettle everywhere from Iran to India. In the 11th century, **Selçuk Turks** from inner Mongolia established states in Persia (today's Iran) and Anatolia. Great Selçuk Sultans from this latter state—namely Tughril-Beg and Alp Arslan—led raids into the Byzantine realm they bordered, and the Selçuks in Anatolia became increasingly independent of the Great Selçuk Sultanate, centered in Persia. The Turks gained a foothold in Anatolia in 1075, when **Süleyman** (the son of Alp Arslan) captured Nicaea from the Byzantines, renamed it İznik, and set it up as the capital of the newly reorganized **Sultanate of Rum,** which declared its independence from the Great Selçuks in Persia a decade later. By its heyday in the 13th century, the Sultanate of Rum had developed into one of the most important Islamic states of its time, with thriving trade, agriculture, and arts.

When Selçuk rule broke down in the 14th century, separate Turkish principalities picked up the pieces. A general named **Osman** claimed the northwest corner of Anatolia and united several fiefdoms against the Byzantines, laying the religious and cultural foundations for one of the largest and most enduring empires in the history of civilization: the *Osmanlı,* or **Ottoman,** Empire. From the mid-14th to the mid-15th century, Ottoman rulers slowly gnawed away at the Byzantine Empire. In 1453, after a 54-day siege, Constantinople fell to **Mehmet the Conqueror,** who went directly to the great Byzantine basilica Aya Sofia and prayed to Allah (thus converting it into a mosque). The city came to be called **İstanbul** and became the capital of his new and vigorous empire, which included Greece, Cyprus, and the Balkans as far as Belgrade. **Selim I** (1512-20) added Syria, Palestine, Egypt, and the Arabian Peninsula to the Empire, making the Ottoman Sultan the guardian of the three holy places of Islam—Mecca, Medina, and Jerusalem—in one fell swoop.

Such a vast and heterogeneous empire was necessarily politically decentralized. The hinterland regions developed almost entirely independently; this eventually led to the Ottomans' downfall. Non-Muslims were left to practice their religions freely, but in accordance with Islamic law they had to pay the **cizye,** a special head tax. Many of the empire's minorities, including Greeks and Jews, were peacefully incorporated into Ottoman society, and many fared better under Muslim authority than they had under the Crusaders and Spanish Monarchs.

When **Süleyman** became Sultan (1520-66), the Ottoman Empire grew further. He doubled its size, securing borders that stretched from the Balkans and Greece north to the Black Sea (and even knocked on the gates of Vienna), west to Iraq, and south into the Arabian Peninsula and Africa. Süleyman's military conquests and lavish lifestyle earned him the sobriquet of "Magnificent" among Europeans. Süleyman's administrative, artistic, literary, and architectural legacies were equally dramatic. His commitment to legislation earned him the title of **Kanuni** (the Lawgiver), and his patronage of Mimar Sinan, the great Ottoman architect, resulted in some of the greatest of Ottoman monuments. Süleyman the Magnificent appointed his son Selim the not-so-magnificent (a.k.a. **Selim the Sot**), who transferred all his political power to the Grand Vizier and presided over an era of palace infighting (before he drowned in his tub in a drunken stupor in 1574). This period is sometimes referred to as the **"rule of the women,"** as mothers of potential sultans vied for power and had rivals' sons knocked off.

THE OTTOMAN PERIOD. By 1812, the Ottomans had lost all of their territories north of the Black Sea, and the government was growing weaker as it went deeper into debt. A series of administrative reforms known as the **Tanzimat** ("Reorganization") were instituted, beginning in 1839 with the Noble Edict of the Rose Chamber that declared all Ottoman citizens equal regardless of ethnicity, race, or religion. Despite major reforms, European and Russian diplomats feared that time was up for the **"sick man of Europe"** (as the empire was known), and feared even more what would happen to the European balance of power as a result. European powers intervened in the 1821 Greek War of Independence and fought the bloody **Crimean War** (1853-56). The 19th century saw one rebellion after another in the Ottoman domains (including uprisings among the Albanians, Serbs, Bulgarians, and Armenians). In response to an impending sense of doom, a group of bourgeois intellectuals that included the poet Namık Kemal (see **Literature,** p. 611) formed a group known as the **Young Turks.** They sought to draft a Western-style constitution providing for an elected parliament—a wish that was fulfilled in 1876 upon the ascension of **Sultan Abdülhamid II** (1876-1909), though he suddenly suspended the constitution and all democratic reforms two years later. In 1908, the **Young Turk Revolution** ended Abdülhamid's stranglehold on power and restored the 1876 constitution. The new leaders, known as the **Committee for Union of Progress (CUP)**, embarked on a reform program designed to increase centralization and promote industrialization. CUP leaders continued with reforms, but these were far overshadowed by such bloodbaths as the Albanian uprisings and the **Balkan Wars** (1912-13). Bloody disaster was all the Ottoman Empire saw in World War I, when they sided with Germany and were completely humiliated save at the **Battle of Gallipoli** (1916), when the Turks defended the Dardanelles against the Allies. Festering internal strife erupted in the 1915 Armenian genocide, when approximately 1.5 million Armenians were killed. The Unionists were not gone or forgotten, and under Ottoman general **Mustafa Kemal** they plunged head-long into the **Turkish War of Independence** (1920-22) against the Allies, who were looking to partition Anatolia amongst themselves. An armistice was signed on October 11, 1922. The new Grand National Assembly (under President Kemal) abolished the sultanate on November 1, 1922 and set up the Turkish Republic by 1923.

MODERN HISTORY. As part of his obsessive campaign to westernize Turkey (and forge a distinctly Turkish identity), Kemal required that all Turks adopt surnames, taking **Atatürk,** or "father of the Turks," for himself (many place names also changed, such as Angora, which became Ankara). Atatürk oversaw the adoption of a western-style constitution, abolished (Islam-sanctioned) polygamy, prohibited the use of the *fez* (traditional Islamic headwear), instituted secular law codes, adopted the Gregorian calendar, and closed religious schools and courts. By 1928, Islam was no longer the official state religion. As Alexander the Great had purged the country of Persians before, Atatürk purged Turkish of all Arabic and Persian influences, replacing the Arabic alphabet with a Latin version, and declaring that the *adhan* (call to prayer) be recited in Turkish instead of Arabic.

Shortly before World War II, the increasingly auto(tür)kratic Atatürk died and was replaced by his associate **İsmet İnönü.** The government remained neutral until the Turkey joined the Allies at the very end of the war. During the Cold War, the country's position within firing range of the Soviet Union and its control over the Bosphorus made it strategically vital to both Soviet and US interests. Even today, Turkey remains one of the largest recipients of US economic and military aid. Politics became increasingly polarized during the turbulent 1970s, reaching a fever pitch when **Abdüllah Öcalan** formed the **Workers' Party of Kurdistan (PKK)** for Kurdish sovereignty. Turkey's foreign relations were no calmer than its domestic affairs. Fearing that Cyprus would be annexed by Greece, Turkey invaded the island in 1974; economic and arms embargoes soon followed, and Turkey responded by closing foreign military installations. The "Turkish Republic of Northern Cyprus" is still only officially recognized by the Republic of Turkey itself.

In September 1980, General **Kenan Evren** led a bloodless coup against the government and instituted brutally-enforced martial law throughout the country until 1983. Elections that year brought the **Motherland Party** (ANAP) of **Turgut Özal** to power. Özal encouraged positive principles such as free-market and foreign trade, but the worldwide recession of the following years sent Turkey into massive inflation, deficit, and unemployment. Based in Syria and Iraq and filled with ranks of disaffected young people, the PKK waged guerilla warfare against the government, catching civilians in the crossfire. The government in turn banned the use of the Kurdish language and outlawed expressions of sympathy for the Kurds.

While discussion of the Kurdish issue has been forcibly silenced, the secularist tenets of the Turkish state have been the subject of increasing debate. In May 1993, the True Path Party elected **Tansu Çiller** the first female prime minister. Controversy arose around Turkey's secular **dress code,** which attempted to curb religious attire such as head scarves in schools and universities. Religious female students have protested and circumvented this rule by holding street demonstrations and wearing showy blond wigs over their head scarves (since the code dictates that the women's hair must be showing).

In early 1995, Turkey was accepted into the European Customs Union (after being rejected in 1989) on the condition that the Turkish Parliament make hundreds of new laws and changes to the constitution. The European Union again denied Turkey candidacy for membership in December 1997. The EU's simultaneous selection of Cyprus as a potential candidate greatly incensed Turkey, who threatened in late March 1998 to begin a new war with Cyprus.

IN THE NEWS. Nature has not been kind to Turkey in the last two years. On August 17, 1999, an **earthquake** hit İzmit, killing 18,000 people, injuring tens of thousands more, destroying 60,000 buildings, and leaving 200,000 homeless. A series of aftershocks plagued the area for weeks afterward, followed by a **second major quake** in mid-November, not far from the first epicenter. While neighboring countries and international relief groups aided the rescue, the Turkish government was criticized for slowness and disorganization. In December 1999, the Helsinki European Council nominated Turkey as a full candidate for membership to the EU. However, the Turkish government protested prerequisites, including peace with Greece (though relations had warmed since their aid in the quake relief), and the relinquishment of Northern Cyprus. Tensions in the southeast have decreased since the spring 1999 capture, arrest and death sentence of PKK leader **Abdüllah Öcalan.** His capture was a cause for joy in many of Turkey's cities, and Kurdish outrage throughout Europe and in Turkey. In June 2000, Parliament voted to lift the state of emergency for certain predominantly Kurdish southeastern provinces, including Van, which had been in place since 1987. In early May 2000, the Turkish Grand National Assembly elected **Ahmet Necdet Sezer** the 10th president of the Turkish Republic. A career judge, Sezer stated in his May 16 inaugural speech that he would focus on higher standards for democracy, secularism, and rule of law.

RELIGION AND ETHNICITY

Though Atatürk set modern Turkey on a secular course, Islam has played a key role in the country's evolution. About 99% of Turks are **Muslim,** while about 26,000 are **Jews,** concentrated mainly in İstanbul with large communities in İzmir and Ankara. **Orthodox Christians** of Greek, Armenian, and Syrian backgrounds compose the other religious minority. The **Alevi** are Shi'ites who follow simple moral norms rather than the *sharia* (Islamic law) and the traditional pillars of Islam. "Alevi" has also come to refer to the numerous heterodox communities that make up 15-25% of the population. Roughly 12 to 15 million **Kurds** make up a quarter of Turkey's population, making them the largest ethnic group in the world without its own nation. Kurdish nationalist movements have existed since before the fall of the Ottoman Empire, but the most famous and extremist of these, the **Workers' Party of Kurdistan** (or **PKK**) was founded by Abdüllah Öcalan in 1978 (see **Modern History** and **In The News,** above). Until the early 20th century, ethnic **Armenians** comprised approximately 10% of the Anatolian population, but after the deportation and slaughter of about 1.5 million Armenians in 1915, almost none are left in Eastern Anatolia today. In the past few decades, Armenians and their supporters have demanded that Turkey officially recognize the genocide and provide some form of apology or compensation. The **Laz, Hemşin,** and **Circassian** people are Caucasian minorities that live in Eastern Turkey and the northern Caucasus region.

LANGUAGE

English is widely spoken wherever tourism is big (mostly in the major coastal resorts). In the rest of Anatolia, only university students know English. French and German are also widely spoken in cities. For pronunciation tips and handy phrases, see the **Phrasebook,** p. 705.

THE ARTS

LITERATURE. The Sufi poetry of **Celaleddin-i-Rumi** and **Yunuş Emre** survived the Ottoman centuries, as did *The Book of Dede Korkut*, a collection of 12 legends of the noble Oğuz Turks, the ancestors of modern Turks. Among these folk tales, those of **Nasrettin Hoca**—a friendly, anti-authoritarian, religious man—are particularly popular, plastered on *ayran* cups and well known by children.

Satire has always been important in Turkish literature. Poet **Namık Kemal** is particularly famous for his satire of the Ottoman Empire during its final years. A fervent republican and free-speech advocate, **Aziz Nesin** was a provocative Alevi writer. **Yaşar Kemal**, author of *Memed, My Hawk*, has been nominated several times for the Nobel Prize for Literature. He has been charged with anti-Turkish activities by the government for his *corpus* of work that consistently criticizes Turkish society and government. The magical realism of **Orhan Pamuk** has made him the best-selling author in Turkish history. He is internationally known for his three major novels, *The White Castle*, *The New Life*, and *The Black Book*.

VISUAL ARTS. Long before Atatürk's revolution, Ottoman painting had gradually begun to adopt Western forms. In 1883, the **Academy of Fine Arts** was founded by the Ottoman artist, museum curator, and archaeologist **Osman Hamdi Bey.** In 1914, the Ottoman government opened an Academy of Fine Arts for Women headed by the painter **Mihri Müşfil Hanım**, whose work blended the world of veiled ladies in İstanbul with the Parisian flair for Levantine fashions. The two eventually merged, and the Academy (as the combined institution is known) has had an unparalleled influence on the artistic movements of modern Turkey: the **Çallı group** of the 1920s, the **'D' Group** of the 1930s, and the **New Group** of the 1940s, 1950s, and 1960s.

FOOD AND DRINK

Turkish cuisine reflects its Ottoman heritage. The ubiquitous **kebap** (kebab) and **pilav** (rice) are flavored by the cuisine of the nomadic Central Asian tribes of Asia Minor. Fans of Greek, Armenian, and Levantine food will recognize their favorites on Turkish menus. Lunch and dinner often begin with **mezze**, which ranges from simple *beyaz peynir* (feta cheese) to more complicated vegetable dishes. Meals often involve meat (usually lamb), and especially **köfte** (small, spiced meatballs) or **mantı** (tiny meat-filled ravioli). Dessert highlights include **baklava** (a flaky nut pastry with pistachio), *kadayif* (shredded pastry dough filled with nuts, in syrup), *tavukgöğsu* (creamy, made of chicken fibers), and *helva* (sesame paste).

Turkey's national drink must be the strong, black tea known as **çay**, served everywhere in small, hourglass-shaped glasses. *Elma çayı* (apple tea), which tastes like warmed cider, is a good alternative to conventional Turkish tea's strong brew. A demitasse-full of pure caffeine, **kahve (Turkish coffee)** can be ordered *sade* (black), *orta* (medium sweet), or *şekerli* (very sweet). When you finish your *kahve*, read your fortune in the goop remaining in the bottom of your cup.

Alcohol is widely available but frowned upon in the more conservative parts of the country. Restaurants that post *içkisiz* have no alcohol, while those with *içkili* posted do have it. **Bira** (beer) is ever-popular: *Efes Pilsen* and *Tüborg* are the leading brands. The best domestic white wines are *Çankaya*, *Villa Doluca*, and *Kavaklıdere*, made in Cappadocia. The best red wines are *Yakut* and *Kavaklıdere*. Ice-cold **rakı**, a clear anise-seed liquor with the taste of licorice, is Turkey's national alcohol. Customarily mixed in equal parts with water, *rakı* is similar to Greek *ouzo* or Levantine *'araq*, but even stronger. İstanbul's local specialty is *balyoz* ("sledge hammer" or "wrecking ball"). It's easy to get wrecked with this combination of *rakı*, whiskey, vodka, and gin mixed with orange juice.

ESSENTIALS

DOCUMENTS AND FORMALITIES

EMBASSIES

Embassies and consulates within Turkey are in **Ankara** (p. 665) and **İstanbul** (p. 622); British and American consulates are in smaller cities. Turkish embassies abroad include: **Australia,** 60 Mugga Way, Red Hill, Canberra ACT 2603 (☎(02) 6295 0227 or 6295 0228; fax 6239 6592; email turkembs@ozemail.com.au); **Canada,** 197 Wurtemburg St., Ottawa, ON, K1N 8L9 (☎(613) 789-4044 or 789-3440; fax 789-3442; email turkish@magma.ca); **Ireland,** 11 Clyde Rd., Ballsbridge, Dublin 4 (☎(01) 668 5240 or 660 1623; fax 668 5014; email turkemb@iol.ie); **New Zealand,** 15-17 Murphy St., Level 8, Wellington (☎(04) 472 1290 or 472 1292; fax 472 1277; email turkem@xtra.co.nz); **South Africa,** 1067 Church St., Hatfield, Pretoria 0181 (☎(012) 342 6053 or 342 6057; fax 342 6052; email pretbe@global.co.za) and 6 Sandown Valley Crescent 2nd fl., Sandown-Sandton, Johannesburg 2001 (☎(011) 884 9060 or 884 9061/2/3; fax 884 9064); **UK,** 43 Belgrave Sq., London, SWIX 8PA (☎(020) 7393 0202; fax 7393 0066; email turkish.embassy@virgin.net); **US,** 2525 Mass. Ave. NW, Washington, D.C. 20008 (☎(202) 612-6706; fax 612-6744; email info@turkey.org).

ENTRY REQUIREMENTS

Citizens of Canada, New Zealand, and South Africa do not need **visas** to enter Turkey. Canadians and New Zealanders can stay in Turkey for three months; South Africans are permitted to stay for one month. Citizens of Australia, Ireland, the UK, and the US need visas to enter Turkey. Though visas can be obtained from any Turkish embassy or consulate, it is most convenient to get one upon arrival in Turkey. Three-month, multiple entry sticker visas are available for cash at all official points of entry (AUS$30 for Australians, £10 for British citizens, £5 for Irish citizens, US$45 for Americans). Visitors on a tourist visa need a **work permit** to hold a job in Turkey. Exchange students must obtain a **student visa.**

BORDER CROSSINGS

TO SYRIA. Daily buses connect **Antakya** (p. 663) to **Aleppo** (4-5hr., including formalities). The border crossing is hassle-free, but you must get a visa beforehand in **Ankara** (p. 665), **İstanbul** (p. 616) or another Syrian embassy or consulate. Ideally, obtain the visa in your home country; it is not always easy, or even possible, to get one from an embassy or consulate in Turkey.

TO GREECE AND EUROPE. Buses leave from İstanbul's **Esenler Otobüs Terminal** and trains from İstanbul's **Sirkeci Gar** station (p. 616) to various European cities, including Athens, Sofia, Vienna, Munich, Bucharest, and Moscow. **Ferries** also leave from many cities on the Aegean close to the Greek islands, which are in turn connected by boat to Athens. Citizens of the US, Canada, Australia, New Zealand, and EU countries do not need a visa to enter Greece. South Africans must obtain a visa beforehand from any Greek embassy or consulate.

TO NORTHERN CYPRUS. The best place to catch **ferries** from mainland Turkey is Taşucu, which sends seabuses (2½hr.) and ferries (5hr.) daily to **Girne,** in Northern Cyprus. Less frequent ferries also travel to Girne from Alanya and Anamur, and three night ferries per week embark from Mersin to Mağusa. Turkish air carriers are the only ones that fly into Northern Cyprus; flights run between Lefkoşa's Ercan airport (☎231 46 39) and most major airports in Turkey.

TO GEORGIA. The border is open 24 hours. Turkish procedures are straightforward and free, while Georgia accounts for any hard currency entering and leaving the country and charges US$3 each way, providing a receipt. Georgian officials may try to extract an additional US$5 on the Georgian side of their offices. Georgian taxis to **Batumi** are US$5-10 for 15km, while US$1 minibuses are slow to fill. This process is exactly reversed when returning to Turkey from Georgia.

GETTING AROUND

BY AIR. Turkish Airlines (THY) flies to over 30 cities in Turkey. **İstanbul** and **Ankara** are the hubs for domestic flights. Domestic flights are about US$90 one-way (some discounts for ages 12-24). It is often cheaper to purchase tickets for domestic flights while in Turkey. In some cities, an airport shuttle bus leaves from the downtown ticket office 30 to 90 minutes before flights (for an extra charge). There are reduced fares for passengers who book an international flight with THY.

BY BUS. Frequent, modern, and cheap **buses** run between all sizeable cities. In large cities, the *otogar* (bus station) is often a distance from the city center, but many bus companies have branch offices downtown. Buy tickets in advance (10% ISIC discount on some lines). Fares go up during summer and religious holidays.

Because road safety is a serious concern in Turkey, *Let's Go* strongly recommends that you only travel on reputable bus lines (such as **Varan, Ulusoy,** and **Kamıl Koç**), particularly for long trips. Although these are the most expensive tickets, the extra money allows companies to take additional safety precautions.

Fez Travel, 15 Akbıyık Cad., Sultanahmet, İstanbul (☎ (212) 516 90 24; fax 638 87 64; email feztravel@escortnet.com; www.feztravel.com), Turkey's flexible "backpacker bus" service, runs around a long loop encompassing İstanbul, Çanakkale, Gallipoli, the Aegean and Mediterranean coasts (including Ephesus, Troy, Kuşadası, Bodrum, Marmaris, Pamukkale, Antalya, and Side), Konya, Cappadocia, Ankara, and Bursa. A season pass (June-Oct. US$175, under 26 US$165) allows you to get on and off along the route at your own whim. There are also various scheduling alternatives, including cheaper passes that cover smaller portions of the route. Buses have English-speaking staff full of information on accommodations and activities. Tickets can also be purchased through **STA Travel** (p. 30).

BY DOLMUŞ. Extensive *dolmuş* (shared taxi) service follows fixed routes within larger cities and between small towns. *Dolmuş* post their final destinations in their front windows, but if you're headed to an intermediate destination, you'll probably need to ask locals which is the right one for you: *"Bu dolmuş X gidiyor mu?"* (Does this *dolmuş* go to X?). To ask your neighbor or the driver how much it costs to go to your destination: *"X kadar ne kadar?"* (How much is it to X?). The driver may remember your stated destination and stop there without any reminder. Otherwise, clearly say *"inecek var"* (getting off).

BY TRAIN. Despite low fares, trains within Turkey are no bargain, as they are slow and follow circuitous routes. First class gets you a slightly more padded seat, but most Turks travel second class. Since couchettes are available, overnight train trips are preferable to overnight bus trips. Lock your compartment door and keep your valuables on your person. Reserve at least a few hours ahead at the station.

BY BOAT. Ferries do not serve the west coast, but a **Turkish Maritime Lines** (TML) cruise ship sails between İstanbul and İzmir (21hr., one per week). A weekly boat connects İstanbul with destinations on the Black Sea Coast. İstanbul has frequent service to Bandırma and Yalova. Larger ports have ship offices; otherwise, just get on the boat and find the purser. Most Turkish ferries are comfortable and well-equipped, though ferry food is outrageously pricey; bring your own provisions. Fares jump sharply in July and August. Student discounts are often available.

BY MOPED AND MOTORCYCLE. Motorized bikes are a good way to tour coastal areas and countryside. Exercise extreme caution—they're uncomfortable for long distances, dangerous in the rain, and unpredictable on rough roads and gravel. Always wear a helmet and never ride with a backpack. Expect to pay about US$20-35 per day; remember to bargain. Motorcycles normally require a license. Ask if the quoted price includes tax and insurance, or you may be hit with an additional fee. Avoid handing your passport over as a deposit; if you have an accident or mechanical failure, you may not get it back until you cover all repairs.

TOURIST AND TRAVEL SERVICES

MEDICAL EMERGENCIES AND HEALTH. Serious medical problems should be taken to the *klinik* or **hospital** *(hastane)*. Private hospitals, located in urban areas, provide much better care than state-run institutions *(devlet hastanesi)* and are not much more expensive for foreigners. Most doctors speak some English, and cash payments are expected. **Pharmacies** *(eczane)* in each town stay open all night on a rotating basis; signs in their windows and local newspapers tell which is on duty *(nöbetçi)*. For **medical emergencies,** dial ☎112 (ambulance) or call your consulate; they can provide a list of English-speaking doctors.

USEFUL ADDRESSES. Turkish cities and popular tourist towns have tourist offices with maps and lists of accommodations in the area. Turkish tourist offices abroad include: **UK,** First Floor, 170-173 Piccadilly, London W1V 9DD (☎(0171) 629 777, brochure request line ☎(0891) 887 755; fax ☎(0171) 491 0773; email tto@turkishtourism.demon.co.uk) and **US,** 821 UN Plaza, 4th floor, New York, NY, 10017 (☎(212) 687-2194; fax 599-7658; email tourny@idt.net; www.turkey.org/turkey). Surf on over to **Türkiye on the Web** (www.columbia.edu/Isss31/Turkiye) or **All About Turkey** (web.syr.edu/~obalsoy/Turkiye).

MONEY MATTERS

If you stay in hostels and prepare your own food, expect to spend anywhere from US$15-30 per day. Carrying cash with you, even in a money belt, is risky but necessary; though banks will exchange traveler's checks, most establishments in Turkey do not accept them. The **Turkish lira (TL)** is the main unit of currency in Turkey. Western currency, particularly US dollars and German marks, will sometimes be accepted. Credit cards are generally accepted by larger businesses. Because of constantly fluctuating exchange rates and Turkey's high inflation, prices are quoted in US dollars to minimize increases.

The high inflation rate means that it's best to convert small amounts of money on a regular basis despite the commission charges. Using an ATM or a credit card will often get you the best possible rates. **ATMs** are widespread throughout the country; larger banks usually accept Cirrus and PLUS, and major credit cards—particularly Mastercard and Visa—can also be used for cash advances. Most stores and offices are open Monday to Friday 8:30am-12:30pm and 1:30-5:30pm. Unlike in the rest of the Islamic world, the official weekend is on Saturday and Sunday.

Tipping is widely expected and accepted, and leaving a bit of small change at your table after a meal or with a taxi driver or hotel porter is appreciated as a friendly gesture and a sign of gratitude. Only luxury restaurants require a 15-20% service charge *(servis dahil)*, usually included in the bill; an additional small tip is customary. Turkey has a 10-20% **value-added tax,** known as the *katma değer vergisi* or **KDV,** which is included in the prices of most goods and services (including meals, lodging, and car rentals). Before you pay, check whether the KDV is included in the price to avoid paying it twice. Theoretically, it can be reclaimed at most points of departure, but this requires much persistence.

ACCOMMODATIONS

There are very few accredited International Youth Hostels in Turkey, and if you ask for a hostel *(yurt)*, you'll probably be directed to **university dormitories.** Many colleges and universities open their residence halls to travelers when school is not in session—some do so even during term-time. **Pensions** that call themselves **aile** (family-style) try to maintain a wholesome atmosphere, and may be the preferred choice for women traveling alone in remote parts of Turkey, particularly the East and the Black Sea coast. In the more touristed areas along the Aegean and Mediterranean coasts, Turks are accustomed to **unmarried couples** staying together, but such relations are often culturally unacceptable in rural and conservative regions, including the Black Sea coast and southeastern Turkey. It is generally a good idea to wear rings to help gain admittance. Men may be turned away from pensions if there are no other men staying in the house.

KEEPING IN TOUCH

Airmail from Turkey averages one to two weeks for each destination. If regular airmail is too slow, there are faster, more expensive, options such as *Acele Posta Servisi* (APS). **Poste Restante** is available at the **PTT** (post, telegraph, and telephone office) in most towns. For phone calls, a **calling card** is your best bet. Deposit a **prepaid card (telekart)** or a token-like **jeton** (buy both at the PTT) to activate the phone. To call home with a calling card, dial the appropriate access numbers for Turkey: **AT&T** (☎(888) 288-4685); **Sprint** (☎(800) 877-4646); **MCI** (☎(800) 444-4141); **Australia Direct** (☎13 22 00); **Canada Direct** (☎(800) 565-4708); Telecom Éireann **Ireland Direct** (☎(800) 250 250); **Telecom New Zealand** (☎(0800) 00 00 00); **Telkom South Africa** (☎09 03); British Telecom **BT Direct** (☎(800) 34 51 44). To place a **collect call,** dial ☎115 for an international Türk Telekom operator. You can reach an English-speaking operator through the appropriate service provider listed above, and they should place a collect call even if you don't have a phone card.

    Internet access is available in most regions of the country for US$1-2 per hour. Access is widespread in areas of İstanbul, Cappadocia, and the Aegean and Mediterranean coasts, but thins out a bit along the Black Sea and in Eastern Turkey.

WOMEN TRAVELERS

Foreign women, especially those traveling alone, attract significant attention in Turkey. Because Western movies and TV often depict women as seductive sex symbols, female travelers are frequently perceived as likely sexual partners; however, although verbal harassment is common, physical harassment is rare. If harassed, women can attract attention by making a scene and using the expression *"ayıp!"* ("shame!") or *"haydi git"* ("go away"). If a situation becomes threatening, holler *"imdat"* (eem-DAHT, "help") or *"polis"* (PO-lees, "police"). More touristed parts of Turkey—İstanbul, the Northwest, the Aegean and Mediterranean coasts, Cappadocia and Ankara—may be more comfortable for women. Only confident, experienced female travelers should venture into Central and Eastern Anatolia and along the Black Sea coast. For more tips, see **Women Travelers,** (p. 38).

DRESS AND ETIQUETTE

Shorts scream "I am a tourist." Women will find a head scarf handy (even essential) in more conservative areas. Long skirts and loose pants are most acceptable (and practical), but t-shirts are fine (though it's a good idea to cover your arms in more religious parts of the country). While topless bathing is common around the resorts, it is a bad idea elsewhere. Nude sunbathing is officially illegal.

    Turks value hospitality and will go out of their way to offer travelers a meal or a cup of *çay* (tea). If you are invited as a guest, it is customary to bring a small gift

TURKEY

such as flowers or chocolates and to remove your shoes before entering. When making conversation, do not speak with disrespect or skepticism about Atatürk, the founder of modern Turkey, and avoid other sensitive subjects such as the Kurdish issue, Northern Cyprus, Armenia, and Turkey's human rights record.

İSTANBUL ☎ 212/216

Straddling two continents and almost three millennia of history, İstanbul exists on an incomprehensible scale. The city unfolds against a densely historic landscape of Ottoman mosques, Byzantine mosaics, and Roman masonry. In its current incarnation, İstanbul is the most crowded and cosmopolitan city in the Turkish Republic. This urban supernova explodes out into the surrounding countryside behind an ever-expanding front of new construction sites, but no crane or cement truck could possibly hope to keep up with the pace of İstanbulian life.

Legend has it that in the 7th century BCE, **Byzas,** a Greek speculator looking for prime real estate, consulted the infallible Oracle at Delphi, who told him to settle "opposite the Land of the Blind." Byzas and his crew settled here in 667 BCE, and the city was named **Byzantium** in his honor. Roman infighting at the beginning of the 4th century CE determined the city's fate for the next millennium. The victorious Constantine declared Byzantium **"New Rome"** and renamed it **Constantinople,** the capital of what came to be the Byzantine Empire. Justinian, the most famous Byzantine emperor, doubled the city's glory with the Aya Sofia and other architectural monuments, only to have many of them destroyed centuries later by marauding Crusaders. Why did Constantinople get the works? That's nobody's business but the Ottoman Turks, whose rise was paralleled by the decline of the Byzantine Empire. Constantinople fell to the Ottomans on May 29, 1453, and the new sultan, **Mehmet II,** transformed the city into the exalted administrative, cultural, and commercial center of his empire. Under Ottoman rule, the city, which came to be called İstanbul (a Turkish corruption of the Greek phrase *"steen poli,"* or "to the city"), remained one of the world's major cosmopolitan centers and an architectural treasure trove, best known for its collection of Imperial mosques.

Ankara is now the governmental capital of the Republic of Turkey, but İstanbul remains its cultural heart. Between 1960 and today, the city's population has increased tenfold to over 13 million inhabitants. Even as İstanbul's centuries-long expansion has engulfed entire towns, each neighborhood of the city retains a distinct character: the poverty of İstanbul's *gecekondus* (shanty towns) coexists with an ambitious commercialism as audacious and ostentatious as any to be found in New York or London. The challenge is to see beyond the Ottoman palaces, carpet salesmen, and backpacker bars, and venture out into neighborhood produce markets, back-alley tea shops, and Byzantine fortifications.

■ ORIENTATION

Waterways divide İstanbul into three sections. The **Bosphorus Strait** (Boğaz) separates Asia **(Asya)** from Europe **(Avrupa).** The **Golden Horn,** a sizeable river originating just outside the city, splits Avrupa into northern and southern parts. Directions in İstanbul are usually further specified by neighborhood. **Sultanahmet, Taksim** (both on the European side), and **Kadıköy** (on the Asian side) are the most relevant for sightseers. The other half of "Europe" is focused on commercial **Taksim Sq.** The Asian side of İstanbul is primarily residential.

▐ GETTING THERE AND AROUND

Flights: İstanbul's airport, **Atatürk Havaalanı,** is 30km from the city. Domestic and international terminals connected by a **bus** (every 20min. 6am-10pm). To get to **Sultanahmet,** take a Havaş shuttle bus from either terminal to Aksaray (every 30 min. 6am-9pm,

US$7). From there, take an Eminönü-bound **tram** to Sultanahmet (walk uphill along the overpass to the Lâleli tram stop). You can also take a **taxi** (US$4) to the Yeşilköy train station and take the commuter rail *(tren)* to the end of the line in Sirkeci. A direct taxi to Sultanahmet costs US$17-20. To **Taksim,** take the Havaş shuttle bus to the end of the line (every 30min. 6am-9pm, US$6). To get to the airport, have a private service such as **Karasu** (☎638 66 01) or **Zorlu** pick you up from your hostel (US$5.50), or take the Havaş shuttle from the Taksim McDonald's (45min., every 30min., US$6).

Public Transportation: AKBİL is an electronic ticket system that lets you save 15-50% on fares for municipal ferries, buses, trams, seabuses, and the subway (but not *dolmuş*). After an initial deposit of US$5, add money in 1,000,000TL increments from any of the white IETT public bus booths that have the sign "AKBİL satılır."

Trains: It's quicker and cheaper to take the bus. **Haydarpaşa Garı** (☎(216) 336 04 75 or 336 20 63), on the Asian side, sends trains to Anatolia. Take the ferry from Karaköy pier #7 (every 20min. 6am-midnight, US$.65), halfway between Galata Bridge and the Karaköy tourist office, where rail tickets for Anatolia can be bought in advance at the **TCDD** office upstairs. To **Ankara** (6½-9hr., 6 per day, US$6-12) and **Kars** (11-13½hr.; daily 8:35am; M, W, F, 9am; US$10-15). **Sirkeci Garı** (☎(212) 527 00 50 or 527 00 51), in Eminönü sends trains to Europe via: **Athens** (24hr., 1 per day, US$60); **Bucharest** (17½hr., 1 per day, US$30); and **Budapest** (40hr., 1 per day, US$90).

Intercity Buses: Esenler Otobüs Terminal (☎658 00 36). Take the tram to Yusufpaşa (US$.50), walk to the Aksaray Metro, and take it to the *otogar* (15min., US$.50). Most companies have courtesy buses, called *servis,* that run to the *otogar* from Eminönü, Taksim, and other city points (free with bus ticket purchase). From İstanbul, buses travel to every city in Turkey. **Ulusoy** (☎658 30 00; fax 658 30 10) runs to: **Ankara** (6hr.; 9 per day; US$25, students US$22); **Bodrum** (13hr.; 3 per day; US$31, students US$27); and **İzmir** (9hr.; 4 per day; US$28, students US$24). **Varan** (☎658 02 74 or 658 02 77) runs to **Ankara** (6hr.; 7 per day; US$25, students US$23) and **Bodrum** (14hr.; 2 per day; US$31, students US$28.50). **Kamil Koç** (☎658 20 00 or 658 20 02) runs to **Ankara** (6hr.; every hr.; US$22, students US$20). **Pamukkale** runs to **Pamukkale** (10hr.; 7 per day; US$21, students US$19). Unlicensed **international** companies have been known to offer discounts on trips to Western European destinations and then ditch their passengers in Eastern Europe.

Ferries: Turkish Maritime Lines (☎249 92 22), near pier #7 at Karaköy, to the left of the **Haydarpaşa** ferry terminal (blue awning marked *Denizcilik İşletmeleri*), ferries travelers to **İzmir** (combo ticket US$10-25) via **Bandırma.** Buy the schedule *(feribot tarifesi)* for US$.60 at any pier, or call **Seabus Information** (☎(216) 362 04 44).

Local Buses: Run 5am-midnight, less frequently after 10:30pm, arriving every 10min. to most stops. Hubs are **Eminönü, Aksaray** (Yusuf Paşa tram stop), **Beyazıt, Taksim, Beşiktaş,** and **Üsküdar.** Signs on the front indicate destination, and signs on the right-hand side list major stops. **Dolmuş** are more comfortable but less frequent than buses. Most *dolmuş* gather on the side streets north of Taksim Sq.

Trams: The **tramvay** runs from Eminönü to Zeytinburnu (US$.50 per ride). A ramshackle **commuter rail** (known locally as *tren*) runs between Sirkeci Gar and the far western suburbs. A two-stop **metro** runs from the Karaköy side of Galata Bridge to Tünel, where an old-fashioned trolley car continues along İstiklâl Cad. to Taksim.

Taxis: Little. Yellow. Fiats. Better? Not really; taxi drivers are even more reckless and speed-crazed than other İstanbul drivers. One light on the meter means day rate; two mean night rate. Rides within the city shouldn't cost more than US$5.

🛂 PRACTICAL INFORMATION

Tourist Office: 3 Divan Yolu (☎/fax 518 87 54), at the north end of the Hippodrome in Sultanahmet. Open daily 9am-5pm. Branches in Taksim's **Hilton Hotel Arcade** on Cumhuriyet Cad., **Sirkeci train station, Atatürk Airport,** and **Karaköy Maritime Station.**

Tram and Cable Car **T**

Metro and Tünel **M**

BALAT

Arda

Ibadullah S.

Haskoy Sok.

Kırkambel Cad.

Demirhisar Cad.

Malta Şakir So.

Çırçınlı Çeşme Sok.

St. Stephen of the Bulgars

Kamış Sok.

Rifat Ef. Sok.

Çilinger Sok.

Haci İsa Bostan Sok.

Müselpaşa Cad.

FENER

HALİÇ
(GOLDEN HORN)

Old City Walls

Topkapı Edirnekapı Cad.

Savaklar Cad.

Karlye Camli (Chora Church)

Neşter Sok.

Kesmeyaka Cad.

Fethiye Museum

Orthodox Patriarchate

Kiremit Cad.

Draman Cad.

Paşa Hamam Sok.

Kutüçeşme Sok.

Kahpeçeşme Sok.

Kiremit Cad.

Niyazi Mısri Sok.

Naci Sezeri Sok.

Salmatomruk Cad.

KARAGÜMRÜK

Fethiye Cad.

Manyasa

İsmailağa Cad.

Mercimek Sok.

Tabak Yunus

Selimiye Camii

Abdülezel Paşa Cad.

Sarmaşık Sok.

Baston Sok.

Sofar Çeşme Sok.

Dökümciler Cad.

Keskek Sok.

Keçeci Sok.

Fevzipaşa Cad.

Uzunyol Sok.

Dimac Sok.

Zade Cad.

Darüşşafaka Cad.

Haliç Cad.

Karasarki

Nafinc Cemal Cad.

Bıçaki Hamam

Salhpaşa Cad.

ÇARŞAMBA

İspanarcı Çeş.

Çıratıç Çeş.

Kadıçeşme Sok.

Müftü Hamam Sok.

Karadeniz Cad.

Cibali Cad.

Ali Tekin Sok.

Melektoca Cad.

Eski

Altay Sok.

Alişannettine Cad.

Yavuz Selim Cad.

Yusuf Ziyapaşa Sok.

Bağhoca Cad.

Sinancamil Sok.

ZEYREK

Sofar Keçeciler Cad.

Adembaba Sok.

Zambak Sok.

Aksemsetin Cad.

Şemsetin Sami Sok.

Fevzipaşa Cad.

Tevhimmeler Cad.

Haydar Cad.

Zeyrek Mehmet P. Sok.

KÜÇÜKPAZAR

Adnan Menderes Bulvarı

Hasan Fehmi Paşa Cad.

Sayar Ağaç Sok.

Fatih Camil

FATİH

Faith Türbesi Sok.

İtfaiye Sok.

Zeyrek Sok.

Hacıkadın Cad.

SÜLEYMANİYE

Atatürk Bul.

ÇAPA

Guraba Hastanesi Cad.

EMNİYET **M**

Akdeniz Cad.

Müteferl Sok.

Ocak Sok.

Kumsal Sok.

Koremanl Sok.

Kiracımescit Sok.

T ÇAPA

Millet Cad.

Oğuzhan Cad.

Adnan Menderes Bul.

Açıklar Sok.

Dolap Cad.

Macar Kardeşler Cad.

SARAÇHANE

Cemal Yener Toynal Cad.

Himmet Sok.

Bededcadeci

16 Mart Seh.

Darülfunun Ca.

FINDIKZADE **T**

HASEKİ

YUSUFPAŞA **T**

Yeşilfrenk Cad.

S. Baş Yezneciler Cad.

Belediye (City Hall)

Kızılelma Cad.

AKSARAY **M**

AKSARAY

Rampoey Sok.

Molla Husrev Toprak Sok.

Atatürk Bul.

Yeşiltulumba Sok.

Fevzibey Cad.

Fethbey Sok.

H. Zedder Sok.

Reşitpaşa Cad.

LALELİ **T**

ÜNİVERSİTE **T**

Ordu Cad.

Yeniçeri

Haseki Cad.

Hekimoğlu Alipaşa

Cerrahpaşa Cad.

İnkılap Cad.

Tir. Hasan P. Sok.

Küçük Langa Cad.

Langabastoni Sok.

Mesih Paşa Cad.

Azimkar Sok.

Hayriye Tüccar Cad.

Koca Regip Sok.

Kurban Nişancabostan S.

Pehli

Katlik

Türkeli Cad.

Eserkapı Sok.

Koca Mustafa Paşa Cad.

Güvenlik Cad.

Hacımedar Cad.

Sepetçi

Selim Sok.

Mallatas Cad.

Sinnolü Sinan Sok.

Balaban

Kemanbey Sok.

Kızıltaş Cad.

Namık Kemal Cad.

Mustafa Kemal Cad.

YENİKAPİ

A. Nafiz Gürman Cad.

Küçük Langa Cad.

Kennedy Cad.

Arapze

K. Mustafa Paşa Tren. İst.

Yenikapi Seabus Pier

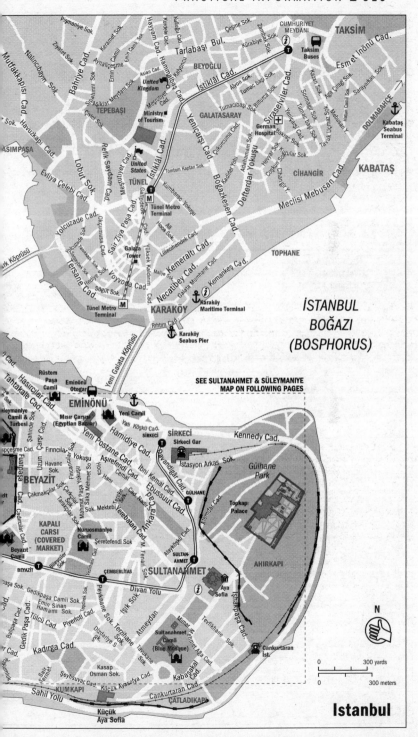

Istanbul

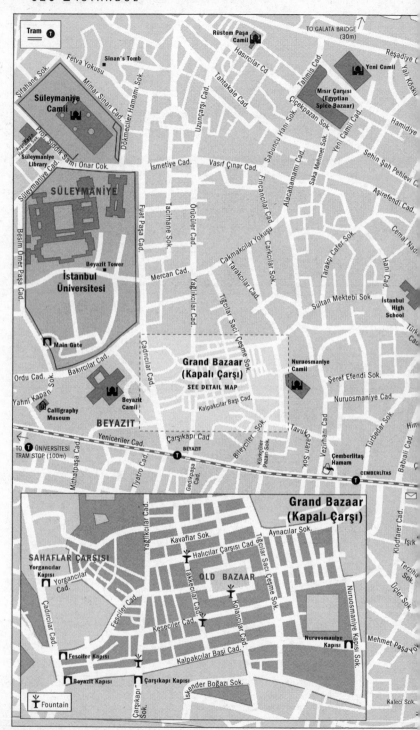

Tram T

TO GALATA BRIDGE (30m)

Fetva Yokuşu

Sinan's Tomb

Rüstem Paşa Camii

Hasırcılar Cd

Reşadiye C

Yeni Camii

Yalı Köşku

Mısır Çarşısı (Egyptian Spice Bazaar)

Tahmis Cad.

Çiçekpazarı Sok.

Yeni Camii Cad.

Hamidiye

Süleymaniye Camii

Mimar Sinan Cad.

Tahtakale Cad.

Sıfahane Sok.

Dökmeciler Hamamı Sok.

Prof. Sıddık Sami Onar Cok.

Ayşekadın Hamamı Sok.

Süleymaniye Library

Süleymaniye Cad.

Uzunçarşı Cad.

Sabuncu Hanı Sok.

Saka Mehmet Sok.

Alacahamamı Cad.

Şehin Şah Pehlevi C.

Aşirefendi Cad.

İsmetiye Cad.

Vasıf Çınar Cad.

Fincancılar Cad.

SÜLEYMANIYE

Cemal Nadir

Besim Ömer Paşa Cad.

Beyazıt Tower

İstanbul Üniversitesi

Fuat Paşa Cad.

Tacirhane Sok.

Örücüler Cad.

Mercan Cad.

Yağlıkçılar Cad.

Cakmakcılar Yokuşu

Çarıkçılar Sok.

Tarakçılar Cad.

Tarakçı Cafer Sok.

Hanı Cad.

Sultan Mektebi Sok.

İstanbul High School

Türk Cad.

Main Gate

Tığcılar Saçı Çeşme Sok.

Çadırcılar Cad.

Grand Bazaar (Kapalı Çarşı)

SEE DETAIL MAP

Nuruosmaniye Camii

Şeref Efendi Sok.

Ordu Cad.

Bakırcılar Cad.

Kalpakçılar Başı Cad.

Nuruosmaniye Cad.

Yahni Kapan Sok.

Beyazıt Camii

Türbedar Sok.

Babıali Cad.

Calligraphy Museum

BEYAZIT

Yeniceriler Cad.

Çarşıkapı Cad

Bileyciler Sok.

Kürkçüler Pazarı Sok.

Tavukpazarı Sok.

Vezirhanı Cad

Hin

TO T ÜNİVERSİTESİ TRAM STOP (100m)

Mithatpaşa Cad.

BEYAZIT

Tiyatro Cad.

Gedipaşa Cad.

Çemberlitaş Hamam

ÇEMBERLİTAŞ

Ç

Işık

Grand Bazaar (Kapalı Çarşı)

Yağlıkçılar Cad.

Kavaflar Sok.

Aynacılar Sok.

Halıcılar Çarşısı Cad.

Tığcılar Saçı Çeşme Sok.

SAHAFLAR ÇARŞISI

Yorgancılar Kapısı

Yorgancılar Cad.

OLD BAZAAR

Kılofarer Cad.

Terzihâ Sok.

Üçler Sok.

Çadırcılar Cad.

Fesçiler Cad.

Takkeciler Cad.

Kolancılar Cad.

Keseciler Cad.

Nuruosmaniye Cad.

Nuruosmaniye Kapısı

Mehmet Paşa Yo

Fesçiler Kapısı

Kalpakçılar Başı Cad.

Nuruosmaniye Kapısı Sok.

Beyazıt Kapısı

Çarşıkapı Kapısı

İskender Boğazı Sok.

Çarşıkapı Sok.

Kaleci Sok.

Fountain

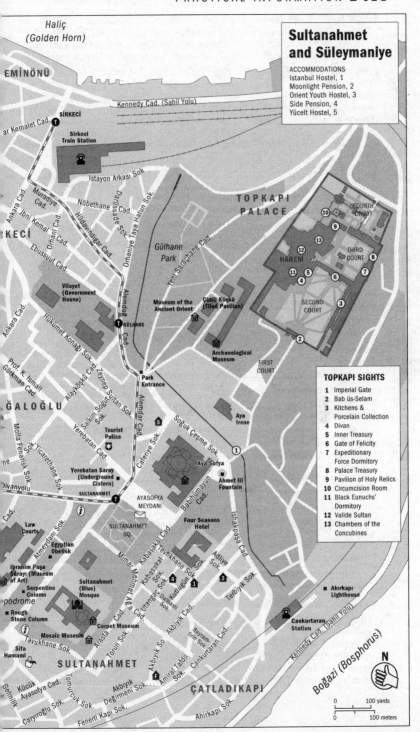

Sultanahmet and Süleymaniye

ACCOMMODATIONS
Istanbul Hostel, 1
Moonlight Pension, 2
Orient Youth Hostel, 3
Side Pension, 4
Yücelt Hostel, 5

Haliç (Golden Horn)

EMINÖNÜ

Kennedy Cad. (Sahil Yolu)

SIRKECI

ar Kemalet Cad.

Sirkeci Train Station

Istayon Arkası Sok.

Muradiye Cad.
Ankara Cad.
Ibni Kemal Cad.
Nöbethane Cad.
Darüssade Sok.
Hüdavindigar Cad.
Osmani Cad.
Ebussut Cad.
Umaniye Taya Hatun Sok.

KECI

TOPKAPI PALACE

FOURTH COURT

Gülhane Park

Yeni Saraçhane Cad.

Vilayet (Government House)

Alemdag Cad.

HAREM

THIRD COURT

SECOND COURT

Museum of the Ancient Orient

Çinili Köşkü (Tiled Pavilion)

Archaeological Museum

GÜLHANE

Hukümet Konağı Sok.
Ankara Cad.
Prof. K. İsmail Gürkman Cad.

Park Entrance

FIRST COURT

Aya Irene

GALOĞLU

Alayköşkü Cad.
Zeynep Sultan Sok.
Salkim Söğütlü Sok.
Alemdar Cad.
Caterive Sok.
Soğuk Çeşme Sok.

Yerebatan Cad.

Tourist Police

Aya Sofya

Aya Sofya

Molla Fenariski Sok.
Ticarethane Sok.

Yerebatan Saray (Underground Cistern)

Ahmet III Fountain

Divanyolu Cad.

SULTANAHMET

AYASOFYA MEYDANI

Babıhümayun Cad.

Ishakpaşa Cad.

Law Courts

Egyptian Obelisk

SULTANAHMET SQ.

Four Seasons Hotel

Ibrahim Paşa Sarayı (Museum of Art)

Serpentine Column

podrome

Rough Stone Column

Sultanahmet (Blue) Mosque

Mimar Mehmet Ağa Cad.
Kabasakal Cad.
Tevfikhane Sok.
Utrangır Sok.
Dalbasti Sok.
Adliye Sok.
Terbıyık Sok.

Ahırkapı Lighthouse

Carpet Museum

Mosaic Museum

Sifa Hamamı

Arasta Sok.
Torun Sok.
Akbıyık Cad.
Amiral Tafdıl Sok.
Cankurtaran Cad.
bayram fırn Sok.

Cankurtaran Station

Tavukhane Sok.

SULTANAHMET

Küçük Ayasofya Cad.
Tomurcuk Sok.
Caryıroğlu Sok.
Gelmilk
Fenerli Kapı Sok.
Akbıyık Degirmeni Sok.

ÇATLADIKAPI

Ahirkapı Sok.

Boğazi (Bosphorus)

Kennedy Cad. (Sahil Yolu)

N

0   100 yards
0   100 meters

TOPKAPI SIGHTS

1   Imperial Gate
2   Bab üs-Selam
3   Kitchens & Porcelain Collection
4   Divan
5   Inner Treasury
6   Gate of Felicity
7   Expeditionary Force Dormitory
8   Palace Treasury
9   Pavilion of Holy Relics
10 Circumcision Room
11 Black Eunuchs' Dormitory
12 Valide Sultan
13 Chambers of the Concubines

Budget Travel: Indigo Tourism and Travel Agency, 24 Akbıyık Cad. (☎517 72 66; fax 518 53 33; email indigo-tour.com), in Sultanahmet's hotel cluster. GO25 cards US$10. Sells bus, plane, and ferry tickets, arranges airport shuttle service and tours, and holds mail. Email US$1.50 per hr. Open daily 8:30am-7:30pm; in winter M-Sa 9:30am-6pm.

Consulates: Australia, 58 Tepecik Yolu, Etiler (☎257 70 52; fax 257 70 54). Visas 10am-noon. **Canada,** 107/3 Büyükdere Cad., Gayrettepe (☎272 51 74; fax 272 34 27). **Ireland** (honorary), 25/A Cumhuriyet Cad., Mobil Altı, Elmadağ (☎246 60 25); visas 9:30-11:30am. **New Zealand,** 100-102 Maya Akar Center, Büyükdere Cad., Esentepe (☎211 11 14; fax 211 04 73). **South Africa,** 106/15 Büyükdere Cad., Esentepe (☎275 47 93; fax 288 76 42). Open M-F 9am-noon. **UK,** 34 Meşrutiyet Cad., Beyoğlu/Tepebaşı (☎293 75 40; fax 245 49 89). Open M-F 8:30am-noon. **US,** 104-108 Meşrutiyet Cad., Tepebaşı (☎251 36 02; fax 251 32 18). Open M-F 8:30-11am.

Currency Exchange: *Bureaux de change* around the city open M-F 8:30am-noon and 1:30-5pm. Most don't charge commission. **ATMs** generally accept all international cards. Most banks exchange **traveler's checks.** Exchanges in Sultanahmet have poor rates and a 2% commission, but are open late and on the weekends.

American Express: Türk Express, 47/1 Cumhuriyet Cad., 3rd fl. (☎235 95 00), uphill from Taksim Sq. Open M-F 9am-6pm. Branch in Hilton Hotel, Cumhuriyet Cad. (☎241 02 48). Open daily 8:30am-8pm. Neither gives cash advances or accepts wired money.

English Bookstores: In Sultanahmet, *köşk* (kiosks) at the Blue Mosque, on Aya Sofia Meydanı, and on Divan Yolu, sell international papers. **Galeri Kayseri,** 58 Divan Yolu (☎512 04 56), caters to thinking tourists with books on Turkish, Islamic, and Byzantine history, as well as a host of guidebooks in multiple languages.

Laundromat: Star Laundry, 18 Akbıyık Cad. (☎638 23 02), below Star Pension in Sultanahmet. Wash and dry US$1.50 per kg; 2kg min. Open daily 8am-8pm.

Tourist Police: In Sultanahmet, at the beginning of Yerebatan Cad. (24hr. hotline ☎527 45 03 or 528 53 69). Speak excellent English, and their mere presence causes hawkers and postcard-selling kids to scatter. In an **emergency,** dial from any phone.

Hospitals: American Hospital, Admiral Bristol Hastanesi, 20 Güzelbahçe Sok., Nişantaşı (☎231 40 50), applauded by İstanbul natives and tourists. Has many English-speaking doctors. **German Hospital,** 119 Sıraselviler Cad., Taksim (☎251 71 00), also has a multilingual staff and is conveniently located for Sultanahmet hostelers.

Internet Access: In low-rent corners and ambitious hostels all over Sultanahmet and Taksim. **The Antique Internet Cafe,** 51 Kutlugün Sok., offers a fast connection and serves tasty meals. US$1.50 per hr. Open 24hr. **Sinem Internet Cafe,** 16 Dr. Emin Paşa Sok. (☎513 62 77), in an alley off Divan Yolu by the Metro stop. Waits are rare at this cafe with cushions and full drink service. US$1.80 per hr. Open daily 9am-10pm.

PTT: All PTTs accept packages. **Main branch** in Sirkeci, 25 Büyük Postane Sok. Stamp and currency exchange services open daily 8:30am-7pm. 24hr. phones. The branch off Taksim Sq. at the mouth of Cumhuriyet Cad. is convenient for mailing packages or making calls. 24hr. international phone office. No collect calls allowed. Open M-F 8am-8pm, Sa 8am-6pm. Phonecards available in increments of 30, 60, or 100 *kontür* (credits). **Sirkeci postal code:** 5270050 and 5270051.

Telephone Code: ☎212 for the European side, ☎216 for the Asian side.

☛ ACCOMMODATIONS

Budget accommodations are concentrated in **Sultanahmet** (a.k.a. Türist Şeğntral), bounded by Aya Sofia, the Blue Mosque, and the walls of the Topkapı Palace. The side streets around **Sirkeci** railway station and **Aksaray** have dozens of dirt-cheap and pretty dirty hotels. Hotels in **Lâleli** are the center of prostitution in İstanbul and should be avoided. Rates sometimes rise by 20% in July and August. All accommodations below are in Sultanahmet.

■ **İstanbul Hostel,** 35 Kutlugün Sok. (☎516 93 80; fax 516 93 84; email info@valide.com), down the hill from the Four Seasons Hotel. Cleanest bathrooms in town, with major amenities. Internet US$2 per hr. Happy hour 6:30-9:30pm. Breakfast US$2. Dorms US$7; doubles US$16. Traveler's checks and cash only.

■ **Orient Youth Hostel,** 13 Akbıyık Cad. (☎517 94 93; fax 518 38 94; email orienthostel@superonline.com; www.hostels.com/orienthostel), 2 blocks south of Aya Sofia, on the backpacker strip. At night, the fun moves to the bar (see **Entertainment,** p. 629). Belly dancing M,W,F at 10pm. Breakfast included. Dorms US$5; doubles US$17; deluxe with TV and bath US$35; quads US$28 per person.

■ **Moonlight Pension,** 87 Akbıyık Cad. (☎517 54 29 or 518 85 36; fax 516 24 80). Far from the backpacker scene. Rooftop views. Kitchen. Moonlights as a laundromat and Internet cafe. Breakfast US$2. Dorms US$5; doubles US$16; triples US$21. V, MC.

Yücelt Hostel/Interyouth Hostel, 6/1 Caferiye Cad. (☎513 61 50 or 513 61 51; fax 512 76 28; email info@backpackersturkey.com; www.yucelthostel.com). Lots of amenities and friendly staff make this a backpacker favorite. Breakfast US$3. Dinner US$3. Dorms US$7-9; singles US$18; doubles US$18; triples US$27. V, MC.

Side Pension/Hotel Side, 20 Utangaç Sok. (☎/fax 517 65 90), near the entrance of the Four Seasons Hotel. Look for the giant bearded heads on the street. This hotel/pension occupies the 2 buildings by the corner of Tevfikhane Sok. and Utangaç Sok. Pension singles US$20; doubles US$25; triples US$35. Add US$10 for clean, modern bath. Hotel singles US$40; doubles US$50; triples US$60. Prices 20% less in winter. V, MC.

Poem Hotel, Akbıyık Cad., 12 Terbıyık Sok. (☎/fax 517 68 36; email hotelpoem@superonline.com). Luxury rooms marked with poems instead of numbers. Female owned, female friendly. Free Internet. TV, safe, A/C, bath. Breakfast included. Singles US$55; doubles US$70-95; triples US$90-115. Subtract 25% in winter. V, MC.

◪ FOOD

İstanbul's restaurants, like its clubs and bars, often stick by the golden rule that if it's well advertised or easy to find, it's not worth doing. Sultanahmet's heavily advertised "Turkish" restaurants aren't difficult to find, but much better meals can be found on İstiklâl Cad. and around Taksim. Small Bosphorus suburbs such as **Arnavutköy** and **Sariyer** (on the European side) and **Çengelköy** (on the Asian side) are the best places for fresh fish. *Vişne suyu* (sour cherry juice) is sold by vendors in Ottoman costume wearing big steel teapots on their backs (US$.20-.30). The best open-air market is the daily one in **Beşiktaş,** near Barbaros Cad.

■ **Doy-Doy,** 13 Şifa Hamamı Sok. (☎517 15 88). From the south end of the Hippodrome, walk down the hill around the edge of the Blue Mosque and look for the blue and yellow sign in the trees. The best-best and cheapest-cheapest of Sultanahmet's cheap eats, the 3-story Doy-Doy keeps locals and backpackers coming back for more-more. Tasty *kebap* and salads (US$3.50 and under). Open daily 8:30am-late.

■ **Naregatsi Cafe,** upstairs at the mouth of Sakezağacı Cad., across from the Ağa Camii. Perhaps the weirdest spot in the Taksim area, Naregatsi serves gourmet cafe fare in the midst of a galactic, high-speed collision of kitsch and concept art. Warhol would feel right at home. Cappuccino (4 flavors) US$3.50. Open daily noon-11:30pm.

Dârüzziyâfe (☎511 84 14; fax 526 18 91), behind the Sultanahmet Camii on the Hippodrome. Mellow atmosphere and attentive service. The specialty, *Süleymaniye çorbası* (meat and veggie soup, US$2) is a must, as is the *çilek keşkül* (strawberry pudding, US$1.50). No alcohol—they serve rosehip nectar instead. Open daily noon-11pm.

Cennet, 90 Divan Yolu Cad. (☎513 14 16), on the right side of the road as you walk from Sultanahmet toward Aksaray. Watch women make *gözleme* (Anatolian pancakes) (US$1). Live Turkish music and dancing nightly. Open daily 10am-midnight. US$1 service charge added per person.

Haci Baba, 49 İstiklâl Cad. (☎ 244 18 86 or 245 43 77), has perfected a wide range of Turkish standards in its 78 years. Stylish dining room and terrace overlooking the courtyard of Aya Triada. Vegetarian friendly. Entrees about US$7. Open daily 10am-10pm.

Pudding Shop, 6 Divan Yolu Cad. (☎ 522 29 70; fax 512 44 58). A major pitstop on the Hippie Trail to the Far and Middle East during the 70s. The setting for the drug deal scene in *Midnight Express* is now clean and tasty. A/C upstairs.

👁 SIGHTS

İstanbul's incomparable array of world-famous churches, mosques, palaces, and museums can keep an ardent tourist busy for weeks. Most budget travelers spend a lot of time in **Sultanahmet,** the area around the **Aya Sofia,** south of and up the hill from Sirkeci. Merchants crowd the district between the **Grand Bazaar,** east of the university, and the less touristy **Egyptian Bazaar,** just southeast of Eminönü.

SULTANAHMET AND ENVIRONS

AYA SOFİA (HAGIA SOPHIA)

Museum open Tu-Su 9:30am-4:30pm. Gallery open Tu-Su 9:30am-4pm. US$6.50

Aya Sofia was built by Justinian in 537 CE, and at that time its area (7570 square meters) and height (55.6m) made it the grandest building in the world. Upon entering the church, which was even larger than King Solomon's temple in Jerusalem, Emperor Justinian exclaimed, "Solomon, I have outdone you!" Twenty years later, an earthquake brought the dome crashing to the ground, and in 1453 the entire building fell to the Ottomans and was converted into a mosque (as it remained until 1932, when Atatürk declared it a museum).

Aya Sofia's austere interior amplifies its awesome size. The nave is overshadowed by the massive, gold-leaf mosaic dome lined with hundreds of circular windows that make it seem as though the dome is floating on a bed of luminescent pearls. The **mihrab,** the calligraphy-adorned portal pointing toward Mecca, stands in the **apse,** the space that housed the altar during the mosque's Orthodox incarnation. The marble square on the floor marks the spot where Byzantine emperors were once crowned. The **minbar,** the platform used to address the crowd at prayer time, is the stairway right of the *mihrab.* The **gallery** contains Byzantine mosaics uncovered from beneath a thick layer of Ottoman plaster as well as the famed **sweating pillar,** sheathed in bronze. The pillar has a hole where you can insert your finger to collect the odd drop of water, believed to possess healing powers.

⛪ BLUE MOSQUE (SULTANAHMET CAMİİ)

Open Tu-Sa 8:30am-12:30pm, 1:45-3:45pm, and 5:30-6:30pm. The Blue Mosque is a working religious facility. Dress modestly, remove your shoes, and women should cover their heads. On your way out, expect to make a small donation. Tomb open Tu-Su 9:30am-4:30pm. Tomb US$1, students free.

The mosque between the Hippodrome and Aya Sofia is the ⛪**Blue Mosque** (Sultanahmet Camii), so named for the beautiful blue İznik tiles that decorate the interior. Completed in 1617, it was Sultan Ahmet's "size doesn't matter" response to Justinian's larger Aya Sofia. The mosque has several "modern" constructions: the internal framework of iron bars across its domes allows the entire structure to bend in earthquakes (it's withstood 20 so far), and an underground pool moderates the mosque's interior temperature (heating in winter and cooling in summer). Numerology is the name of the game at the Blue Mosque: Sultan Ahmet was the 16th sultan of the Ottoman state and the 6th since the Turkish conquest of Constantinople; consequently, the mosque has 16 balconies and six **minarets.** These minarets are the primary source of the mosque's fame. Only the mosque at Mecca had six minarets at the time of the Blue Mosque's construction, and the thought of equalling that sacred edifice was considered heretical. Sultan Ahmet got around this difficulty by financing the construction of a 7th minaret at Mecca. The mosque copies the "floating light" motif of the Aya Sofia; the interior was originally lit with candles, the chandelier structure intended to create the illusion that tiny starlights floated freely in the air. A small stone from the **Ka'aba** at Mecca is almost invisible from the tourists' area. The small, square, single-domed structure in front of the Blue Mosque is **Sultanahmet'in Türbesi,** or Sultan Ahmet's Tomb, which contains the sultan's remains and his family's; it also has İznik tiles. The reliquary in the back contains strands of the prophet Muhammad's beard.

HIPPODROME (AT MEYDANI)

Though all of the major Sultanahmet sites provide insight into pre-Ottoman and Ottoman history, few conjure images of the glory of Byzantine Constantinople like the **Hippodrome,** behind the Blue Mosque. Built by the Roman Emperor Septimus Severus in 200 CE, it served as a place for chariot races and public executions. The politically opposed **Hippodrome Factions** arose out of the Hippodrome's seating plan, which was determined by social standing. The "blues" were wealthy citizens seated in the front rows and the "greens" urban plebeians in cheap seats. In 532 CE, a tax protest turned into the full-out Nika Revolt. The city was ravaged in the ensuing melee, and Justinian's post-revolt reconstruction efforts culminated in the building of the Aya Sofia. The tall, northernmost column with hieroglyphics is the **Dikili Taş,** an Egyptian obelisk erected by the Pharaoh Thutmosis III in 1500 BCE and brought to Constantinople in the 4th century by Emperor Theodosius I. Farther south, the subterranean bronze stump is all that remains of the **Serpentine Column,** originally placed at the Oracle of Delphi. The southernmost column is the **Column of Constantine,** whose original gold-plated bronze tiling was looted by Crusaders during the sack of Constantinople.

MUSEUMS

MUSEUM OF TURKISH AND ISLAMIC ART. This superb museum (also known as İbrahim Paşa Sarayı) features a large Islamic art collection organized by period. The museum's main wing consists of a long hall with carpet and silver displays, off of which the rooms contain works from specific periods. The Selçuk displays and the Ottoman calligraphy with tuğras (seals) of sultans are particularly impressive. *(Museum and cafe open Tu-Su 9:30am-4:30pm. US$2, students US$1.20.)*

UNDERGROUND CISTERN (YEREBATAN SARAYI). This underground "palace" is actually a vast cavern whose shallow water eerily reflects the images of its 336 supporting columns, all illuminated by colored ambient lighting. The echoing sounds of continuously dripping water and the muted strains of classical tunes will accompany your stroll across the elevated wooden walkways. Underground walkways originally linked the cistern to Topkapı Palace, but were blocked to curb rampant trafficking in stolen goods and abducted women. *(As you stand with your back to Aya Sofia, the entrance lies 175m from the mosque in the small stone kiosk on the left hand side of Yerebatan Cad. Open daily 9:30am-5:30pm. US$4, students US$3.25.)*

TOPKAPI PALACE AND ENVIRONS

TOPKAPI PALACE (TOPKAPI SARAYI)

Open Tu-Su 9am-4:30pm. Each day's open galleries are posted next to the ticket window. Palace US$6.50. Harem closes at 4pm. Mandatory tours of the Harem leave every 30min. 9:30am-3:30pm. Harem US$4.

Towering from the high ground at the tip of the old city and hidden behind walls up to 12m high, Topkapı Palace (Topkapı Sarayı) was the nerve center of the Ottoman Empire. Topkapı offers unparalleled insights into the wealth, excess, cruelty, and artistic vitality that characterized the Ottoman Empire at its peak. Built by Mehmet the Conqueror between 1458 and 1465, the palace became an imperial residence during the reign of Süleyman the Magnificent. The palace is divided into a series of courts, all surrounded by the palace walls.

FIRST AND SECOND COURTYARD. The **first courtyard,** through the **Imperial Gate,** was the popular center of the Palace. The general public was permitted entrance to watch executions, trade, and view the nexus of the Empire's glory. At the end of the first courtyard, the capped conical towers of the **Gate of Greeting** (Bab üs-Selam) mark the entrance to the **second court.** To the right beyond the colonnade, the **Imperial kitchens,** with their distinctive conical and vaulted chimneys, house three collections of porcelain and silver. The last set of doors on the left of the narrow alley open into the palace's deservedly world-famous Chinese and Japanese **porcelain collections.** Across the courtyard, where ostriches and eunuchs once roamed, lies the divine **Divan** (also known as Kubbealtı), with its window grilles, awnings, walls, and ceilings slathered in gold leaf. The **Council Chamber,** the room closest to the Harem, retains its original classical Ottoman *faience* decor. The plush Rococo-style room abutting the Council Chamber was where the Grand Vizier would receive foreign dignitaries. Next door and to the right is the **Inner Treasury,** where various instruments of cutting, bludgeoning, and hacking are kept.

THIRD COURTYARD. The **third court,** officially known as **Enderun** (inside), is accessible through the **Gate of Felicity.** In the **Expeditionary Force Dormitory** is a costume collection that traces the evolution of imperial costumes. Moving along down the colonnade brings you to the awesome **Palace Treasury.** One of the highlights is the legendary **Topkapı dagger** (essentially three giant emeralds with a knife sprouting out of them), a gift Sultan Mahmut I intended to present to Shah Nadir of Iran in return for the solid-gold throne displayed elsewhere in the treasury. Wrestle your way to the front of the line leading up to all 86 karats of the Pigot Diamond, better known as the **Spoonmaker's Diamond** because it was traded to a spoonmaker in exchange for three spoons. A nearby glass compartment reportedly contains some of John the Baptist's bones. This display is excellent preparation for the **Pavilion of Holy Relics,** just on the other side of the courtyard and leagues ahead in beauty and elegance. Even the most İzniked-out traveler will be amazed by the calligraphied tiles of this holy site. The pavilion holds the booty taken from Egypt by Selim the Grim as well as relics from Mecca, including the **staff of Moses,** hairs from **Muhammad's beard,** and some of the Prophet's personal effects (including his bow and mantle, a handwritten letter, and two swords).

FOURTH COURTYARD. Three passages lead into the **fourth courtyard.** If Topkapı was the nerve center of the Ottoman Empire, then the fourth courtyard certainly qualifies as its pleasure center, as it was amongst these pavilions, gardens, and fountains that they really got their mojo working in the Ottoman age. Uninterrupted vistas of the Sea of Marmara and the Bosphorus extend from the broad marble terrace at the west end. At one end of the portico is the **Circumcision Room,** a chamber hanging over the edge of the pavilion, built by Ibrahim the Mad.

HAREM. The harem's 400-plus rooms housed the sultan, his immediate family, and an entourage of servants, eunuchs and general assistants. The mandatory tour begins at the **Black Eunuchs' Dormitory,** which is just what its name says it is. Next up is the women's section of the harem, the center of which are the lavish chambers of the **Valide Sultan,** the sultan's mother and the most powerful woman in the Harem. Surrounding the room of the queen mum are the chambers of the **concubines,** the women who put the slut back in sultanate. If a particular woman attracted the sultan's affections or if the sultan spent a night with her, she would be promoted to coveted "odalisque" status (immortalized in Ingres' nudes), which meant she had to stay in İstanbul (concubines were allowed to leave after nine years) but got nicer quarters in exchange for her undying ministrations.

ARCHAEOLOGICAL MUSEUM COMPLEX

150m downhill from the Topkapı Palace's first courtyard. When the palace is closed, enter the museums through Gülhane Park, where a separate road next to the park ticket booths leads to the museum complex. A single ticket theoretically gets you into all 3 museums, although one or another is often closed. Museum complex open Tu-Su 9:30am-5pm. US$5.

TILED PAVILION AND ANCIENT ORIENT MUSEUM. The **Tiled Pavilion** *(Çinli Köşk)* exposes more than you ever wanted to know about the omnipresent İznik tiles. The once fully-tiled pavilion was built in 1472 by Mehmet to view the athletic competitions below, but fires and earthquakes have destroyed much of the original *faience*. The displays cover the full spectrum of Ottoman tilemaking, including some rare early İznik tiles. The smaller cement building adjacent to the Tiled Pavilion is the **Ancient Orient Museum,** which houses treasures so rare that the curator seems reluctant to let anyone see them. If you catch this place when it's open, don't miss the excellent collection of 2nd millennium BCE stone artifacts from the ancient Middle East (including Anatolia, Mesopotamia, and Egypt). The pride of this museum is the **Treaty of Kadesh,** the world's oldest-known written treaty, drafted after a battle between Ramses II of Egypt and the Hittite King Muvatellish (a copy graces the entrance to the United Nations).

ARCHAEOLOGY MUSEUM. The 19th-century Archaeology Museum has one of the world's great collections of Classical and Hellenistic art. The first portion of the building is a walking tour through Classical sculpture. The highlight is the misnamed **Alexander Sarcophagus,** modeled on a Greek temple and covered with intricate carvings; it actually holding the remains of the Sidonese king Abdalonymus. Other exhibits include "İstanbul Through the Ages" and "Ancient Turkey."

GRAND BAZAAR

From Sultanahmet, follow the tram tracks toward Aksaray for 5min. until you see the Nuruosmaniye Camii on the right. Walk down Vezirhanı Cad. for one block, keeping the mosque on your left. Follow the crowds left into the bazaar (www.grand-bazaar.com). Open M-Sa 9am-7pm. A small number of stores close 1-2hr. before the rest of the bazaar.

Consisting of over 4000 shops, several banks, mosques, police stations, and restaurants, the enormous **Grand Bazaar** *(Kapalı Çarşısı,* "covered bazaar") could be a city in itself. Now the largest covered bazaar in the world, the Grand Bazaar began in 1461 as a modest affair during the reign of Mehmet the Conqueror. Today, the enormous Kapalı Çarşısı forms the entrance to the massive mercantile sprawl that starts at Çemberlitaş and covers the hill down to Eminönü, ending at the **Egyptian Spice Bazaar** *(Mısır Çarşısı)* and the Golden Horn waterfront. This colorful, chaotic, labyrinthine world combines all the best and worst of shopping in Turkey. Though the bazaar is loosely organized according to specific themes, much of it is a jumble of shops selling hookah pipes *(nargiles),* bright baubles, copper filigree shovels, Byzantine-style icons on red velvet, Turkish daggers, rugs, embroidered pillows, amber jewelry, silver flintlock guns with mother-of-pearl handles, musical instruments, chess sets, ornaments, and the ubiquitous evil-eye bedecked keychains. Through banter, barter, and hassle, a day spent at the Kapalı Çarşısı is bound to tempt and tantalize on a scale unmatched by even the most frenetic of *souqs* elsewhere in the Middle East. You'll surely get lost, so enjoy the ride.

SÜLEYMANİYE COMPLEX

From the university, head out the northwest gate and take a right on to Besim Omar Paşa Cad. Follow that past the painted walls of the grammar school and take another right when the street ends onto Süleymaniye Cad. Walk straight. From Sultanahmet, either walk along the tramvay (15min.) or take the tramvay to the "Üniversite" stop, walk across the square, and take Besim Ömer Paşa Cad. past the walls of the university to Süleymaniye Cad. Open Tu-Su 9:30am-4:30pm, except during prayers.

TURKEY

To the north of İstanbul University stands the massive, elegant **Süleymaniye Camii**, one of Ottoman architect Sinan's great masterpieces. This mosque is part of a larger *külliye* (complex), which includes **tombs**, an **imaret** (soup kitchen), and several **madreses** (Islamic schools). Prof. Sıddık Sami Onar Sok. is the major street running between the university and the mosque. Passing through the graveyard brings you to the similarly decorated **royal tombs** of Süleyman I and his wife, Haseki Hürrem. Walk along the Süleymaniye Camii's southwest side to the large arch just below the dome and enter the mosque's central courtyard through the smaller tourist entrance to the left of the main door. After removing your shoes and covering your head, proceed inside the vast and perfectly proportioned mosque—the height of the dome, 53m, is exactly twice the measurement of each side of the square base. The **stained-glass windows** are the sobering work of the master Sarhoş İbrahim (İbrahim the Drunkard). The İznik tile İnzanity all started here: the area around the *mihrab* showcases Sinan's first experiment in blue tiles.

🎭 ENTERTAINMENT

HAMMAMS (TURKISH BATHS)

Most baths have separate women's sections or women's hours, but not all have designated female attendants. For details of the *hammam* experience, see **Hammam-o-rama**, below.

🛁 **Çemberlitaş Hamamı,** 8 Verzirhan Cad. (☎522 79 74), just a soap-slide away from the Çemberlitaş tram stop. One of the cleanest and most beautiful *hammams* in İstanbul, built by Sinan in 1584. Vigorous "towel service" after the bath requires a tip of US$1.50-3. Bath US$14, with massage US$18; students US$8, with massage US$12. Open daily 6am-midnight.

🛁 **Çinli Hamamı,** in Fatih, near the butcher shops at the end of Itfaiye Cad. Built for the pirate Barbarossa, this excellent authentic bath still has a few of its original İznik and Kütahya tiles. Bath US$5; massage US$6. Both sections open daily 8am-8pm.

Mihrimah Hamamı (☎523 04 87), right next to Mihrimah Mosque on Fevzi Paşa Cad., about 50m from Edirnekapı. large, quiet, clean, cheap, and hot. Bath US$4; massage US$3.50. Men's section open daily 7am-midnight; women's section 8am-7pm.

HAMMAM-O-RAMA *Hammams* can be intimidating for first-timers,
but they're well worth the effort. Pay the entrance fee plus massage and *kese* (see below). Bring your own shampoo, soap, and towel, or pay to use the bath's. Some *hammams* have cubicles *(camekan)* for personal storage. You will be given a large towel *(peştemal)*. Men generally strip and wrap the *peştemal* around their waists, but don't drop that sucker! Turkish women frequently strip naked (in the *hammam*).

Some *hammams* have a hot, sauna-like room. After you've worked up a sweat, proceed to the warm main room with its large, heated stone *(göbek taşı)*. Mix hot and cold water and pour it over yourself with the bowl provided.

A wash and **massage** on the large, heated marble stone costs a little more. Usually, the masseuse is your gender; female visitors may request a female masseuse. The massage is often very vigorous; try the phrase *"lütfen daha yumuşak"* (gentler please) if need be. The *kese* (abrasive mitt) used can also be purchased at pharmacies. Following the massage and *kese,* you will usually be sponged gently and shampooed. When you're clean as a whistle, rehydrate with water and have a nap.

NIGHTLIFE

Turkish nightlife generally falls into one of three categories. The first includes male-only *çay* houses, backgammon parlors, and dancing shows. Women are not prohibited but are unwelcome and should avoid these places. The second category includes **cafe-bars, rock bars,** and **backpacker bars.** Cafe-bars are smaller and more relaxed than the sometimes cavernous rock bars. Backpacker bars are concentrated in the Sultanahmet area. **Clubs** and **discos** comprise the third nightlife category. The hippest İstanbul clubs often move from unlisted locations in Taksim in the winter to unlisted open-air summer locations throughout the city. Even taxi drivers can't keep up with the scene. Nightlife is centered around **Taksim** and **İstiklâl Cad.** In **Sultanahmet,** all pubs are within 100m of each other and have standardized beer prices (US$1-1.25). The Beşiktaş end of **Ortaköy** is a maze of upscale hangouts; along the coastal road toward Arnavutköy are a string of open-air clubs. Cover charges are high (US$18-45), and bouncers highly selective, but wander between **Ortaköy** and **Bebek** and try your luck.

▨ **Mordi Cafe Bar,** 47 Akbıyık Cad., down the street from the Orient Hostel in **Sultanahmet.** Leagues above the other backpacker bars in cleanliness and ambiance, this spot was formerly a private residence. Extraordinarily friendly staff. Happy hour until 10pm.

▨ **Jazz Stop,** at the end of Büyük Parmakkapı Sok. in **Taksim.** Live bands lay the funk and jazz on thick as a mixed group of music lovers look on. Live music nightly from 11pm. Beer US$3; liquor from US$6. Sept.-May F-Sa cover US$10. Open daily 11am-4am.

Peyote, İmam Adnan Sok. (☎ 293 32 62), next to Leman Kültür, in **Taksim.** This humble spot is one of the area's cheapest venues for live music, popular with artists. Live music Tu-Sa at 11:30pm. F-Sa cover US$7.50; 1 drink included. Open M-Sa 6pm-4am.

Riddim, 6 Büyük Parmakkapı Sok. If you are looking for Jah, he is here, in the only bar in **Taksim** that spins reggae all night long. Crowd is a mixed group that likes to dance. Men need a date on weekends. Beer US$2.50. Open F-Sa 8pm-4am, Su-Th 8pm-2am.

Madrid Bar, İpek Sok., off Küçük Parmakkapı Sok., which is off İstiklâl Cad. in **Taksim.** Small, mellow spot is popular with Turkish students and young foreigners. Play spot-the-*madrileno* as you sip the cheapest brew in Taksim (US$1). Open 2pm-2am.

Orient Bar, 13 Akbıyık Sok. (☎ 517 94 93), in the Orient Youth Hostel in **Sultanahmet.** Revelry abounds in this boisterous basement bar. *Nargile* (water pipe) nights (Th, Su at 9pm) attract international types, while evening belly dancing shows (M, W, F at 10pm) are inauthentic but entertaining. A/C. Open daily 8pm-2am; happy hour until 10pm.

NORTHWESTERN TURKEY

The cradle of the Ottoman Empire, Northwestern Turkey wraps around the Sea of Marmara with a diverse collection of cities and towns—fantastic quick escapes from İstanbul's urban sprawl. The terra-cotta hue of the soil, silvery olive groves, and fields of peach trees take over like the countryside's own city blocks. This is the region that nourished the young Ottoman Empire, and it has two Ottoman capitals, **Bursa** (p. 631) and **Edirne** (p. 629) to show for it. The region's artistic achievements, including Edirne's masterful architecture and Bursa's silk, are world-famous. The **Gallipoli Battlefields** (p. 634) remain a major pilgrimage site for those commemorating the bloody World War I battle for the Dardanelles.

EDİRNE   ☎ 284

Edirne has worn many masks throughout its almost 2000 years of historical prominence: founded as the Roman outpost Hadrianopolis by the humble Emperor Hadrian, Edirne has been an Ottoman capital (and is still home to the Turkey's greatest Ottoman mosque, *Selimiye Camii)* and a modern Greek military possession. In the 19th century, Edirne was still the 7th-largest city in Europe; now, though, it has a frontier town feel, removed from the rest of Turkey. Trakya University, which serves European Turkey, keeps Edirne young. Not coincidentally, the finest brand of *rakı* is produced nearby.

⚡🔢 ORIENTATION AND PRACTICAL INFORMATION. At the heart of Edirne is the triangular **Hürriyet Meydanı,** bounded on three sides by **Hükümet Cad., Talat Paşa Cad.,** and **Üç Şerefeli Camii.** *Dolmuş* from the bus station stop here. **Buses** depart from the **otogar,** 2km from the city center, to: **Ankara** (9hr., 1 per night, US$20); **Antalya** (17hr., 1 per night, US$23); **Bursa** (7hr., 5pm, US$16.50); **Çanakkale** (4hr., 7:45pm, US$8.25); **İstanbul** (3½hr.; 5:30, 7am, then every 30min. until 6:30pm; US$5); and **İzmir** (9hr., 7:45pm, US$15.50). **Dolmuş** leave from the dusty gravel lot behind the Rüstem Paşa Kervansaray Hotel (US$.25-.45). The **tourist office,** 17 Talat Paşa Cad. (☎213 92 08), 300m down the road from the center of town, hands out free maps (open M-F 8:30am-5:30pm). **Türkiye İş Bankası** and **Vakıfbank,** both on Saraçlar Cad., exchange **traveler's checks** and have **ATMs** (both open M-F 9am-12:30pm and 1:30-5:30pm). Take *dolmuş* #1 to the Mega Park stop (10min., US$.25) to reach the **police** (☎213 92 40). For pharmaceutical fancies, go to **Şifa Eczanesi,** on Talat Paşa Cad. (☎225 46 36. Open M-F 8:30am-7:30pm.) There are two **hospitals** in town: the private **Özel Trakya Hastanesi** (☎213 92 00) and the public **Edirne Devlet Hastanesi** (☎225 46 03). The **PTT** is at 17 Saraçlar Cad. (Open daily 8:30am-5pm; phones open daily 8:30am-10pm.) **Postal code:** 22100.

📷🏠 ACCOMMODATIONS AND FOOD. Cheapies cluster around Maarif Cad. Call ahead when visiting Edirne in July, when the town is home to the Kırkpınar Grease Wrestling Festival (see **Sights,** below). **📷Hotel Kervansaray** (☎225 21 95; fax 225 04 62), also known as Rüstempaşa, runs the length of Hürriyet Meydanı on Eski Camii Altı. Built in the 1550s, but its courtyard and stone hallways complement modern facilities (bath, TV, phone) and a billiards/Internet parlor. (Breakfast included. Singles US$30; doubles US$60; triples US$90.) **Hotel Aksaray** (☎225 39 01), at the intersection of Maarif Cad. and Ali Paşa Ortakapı Cad., has small rooms, most without bath. (Singles US$8.25; doubles US$15, with bath US$16.50; triples US$20, with bath US$21.50.)

Saray Restaurant (☎212 13 92), behind the PTT (look for a red awning), serves daily lunch specials at US$.50-1 per serving (open for lunch only). **Yudum Tava Ciğer Salonu** (☎212 43 52), on the road stretching down from the Bedesten, serves Edirne's beefy specialty, *Tava Ciğer* (US$1. Open daily 4am-10pm.) The **teahouses** of Edirne are world-famous; try **Şera Park Cafe,** on Selimiye Meydanı (*çay* US$.25).

🔲 SIGHTS. Every July, competitors from all over Turkey travel to Edirne, don giant leather breeches, slather themselves in oil, and hit the mats. The champions of the **📷Kırkpınar Grease Wrestling Festival** are assured lasting fame and a portrait in the wrestling room of the Islamic Art Museum (see below). Despite the infamy of the festival, Edirne is *really* famed for its magnificent mosque architecture.

📷Selimiye Camii is considered the finest mosque in all of Turkey, surpassing İstanbul's Aya Sofia (Hagia Sophia) in size, structural stability, and aesthetic unity. Construction of the famous Ottoman architect Sinan's self-proclaimed masterpiece did not actually begin until 1567, the year after Sinan died. The interior fills with light from 999 windows, illuminating the colorful lace patterns and calligraphic inscriptions on the 32m interior dome (as well as the *minbar* and *mihrab).* The former *madrasa* of the mosque houses the **Turkish and Islamic Art Museum,** which has a multitude of Islamic artwork and a special room recounting the history of the Kırkpınar Wrestling Festival.

Edirne's two other mosques (both on Hürriyet Meydanı) trace the architectural transition from the Selçuk style of Konya and Bursa to the distinctly Ottoman style of Selimiye Camii. The nine-domed **Eski Camii** ("Old Mosque") and its marble *mihrab* are an excellent example of pre-conquest Ottoman architecture. The limestone **Üç Şerefeli Camii** ("Three Balconies Mosque") replaced Eski Camii as the main mosque for Friday prayers upon its completion in 1447. The mosque is known for its 23m dome, the largest Ottoman dome of its time.

BURSA ☎224

Surrounded by fertile plains and blessed with vast gardens and parks, the city has earned the moniker "Green Bursa"—a name with double significance, as Bursa is one of Turkey's holiest cities (green is the color of Islam). While the city's 14th-century mosques and tombs still receive visitors, Bursa's rapid economic growth has spawned a wealthy resort area, including one of Turkey's most popular skiing spots. Silk trade remains a major industry here, as attested by the silkworm cocoon harvests held every June and September. The town also claims a number of culinary triumphs: the *İskender kebap* and *İnegöl Köfte* (a type of meatball) were both invented in Bursa's kitchens. Anticipating the gastric distress such tasty victuals would conjure, Sultan Süleyman's Grand Vizier had several mineral baths (said to cure everything from heart trouble to athlete's foot) constructed here.

◆🔁 ORIENTATION AND PRACTICAL INFORMATION

Bursa's sights are along a three-kilometer stretch of **Atatürk Cad.,** and most of the hotels and restaurants are within a block of Atatürk Cad. in an area called **Heykel.** Bursa's **terminal,** 20km outside the city center, is reached by local bus #90/A (every 30min. 6:20am-midnight, US$.45). **Buses** go to: **Ankara** (5½hr., every hr. 6am-3am, US$9.25); **İstanbul** (3½hr., US$8.25); and **İzmir** (5hr., every hr., US$8.25), among other cities. Small **dolmuş** (US$.40-.60 per person) leave from Atatürk Cad., behind the *Adliye,* and from the Atatürk statue in Heykel. The **tourist office,** is on Atatürk Cad. near the Atatürk statue, down the stairs and to the left. (☎220 18 48. Open daily May-Sept. 8:30am-6pm; Oct.-Apr. 8am-5pm.) **Police** can be reached at ☎221 35 12. Hospitals come in private (**Vatan Hastanesi;** ☎220 10 40; on İnönü Cad.) and public (**Devlet Hastanesi;** ☎220 00 20) varieties. Get yourself connected at **Elite Internet Cafe,** 37 Yeşil Cad., before the overpass leading to Emir Sultan Camii. (☎327 03 34. US$1.20 per hr. Open daily 10am-1am). The **PTT** is opposite Ulu Cami (open daily 8am-11pm; airmail and currency exchange until 5:30pm).

◤◎ ACCOMMODATIONS AND FOOD

Bursa's budget hotels are off Atatürk Cad., south of the PTT. Clean, quiet **Otel Güneş,** 75 İnebey Cad. also has shared baths. (☎222 14 04. Singles US$10; doubles US$16.50; triples US$21.50; quads US$24.) **Otel Deniz,** 19 Tahtakale Veziri Cad., is left off Atatürk Cad. after the Sümerbank. (☎222 92 38. Singles US$8; doubles US$14.) The birthplace of *İskender kebap* has many restaurants claiming maternity. █**Kebapçı İskender** is the tastiest of the claimants, with two locations (7 Ünlü Cad. and on Atatürk Bul. by the cultural center) serving the same *İskender kebap* since 1867. (☎221 46 15. Open daily 11am-9pm.) **Çiçek Izgara,** 15 Belediye Cad., behind the town hall on Atatürk Cad., serves delicious *köfte* and *kasarlı köfte* (meatballs and cheese) for US$4. (☎221 65 26. Open daily 11am-4pm, 6-9:30pm.)

👁 SIGHTS

ULU CAMI. The unique layout and domed splendor of the immense Ulu Cami, in the heart of town on Atatürk Cad., was a compromise between Sultan Beyazıt I and Allah. Beyazıt promised he would build 20 mosques in exchange for victory, but when he squashed his enemy, he built one mosque with 20 domes. The interior columns and walls are bedecked with Selçuk calligraphic excerpts from the Qur'an. The *mihrab* contains an astronomical guide with pictures of the planets.

YEŞİL TÜRBE AND YEŞİL CAMII. The gorgeous **Yeşil Türbe** (Green Tomb) stands atop a hill, its blue-green, tile-sheathed octagonal form rising out of the surrounding foliage (right off Atatürk Cad., along Yeşil Cad.). Inside, everything is covered with beautiful İznik tiles, even the sarcophagus of Ottoman hero Sul-

tan Mehmet I (who is best known as the patron of the Harem of the Topkapı
Palace in İstanbul; see p. 616). Across the street stands the 15th-century **Yeşil
Camii** mosque, whose Selçuk influence is apparent in its brick-and-stone construction and its almost onion-shaped minarets. The mosque's real beauty lies
within, where intricately stenciled İznik tiles adorn the walls. The balcony that
hangs low above the entrance is where the sultan could enter and pray unob-
served, while keeping his eyes peeled for potential assassins. The large, central dome is one of the first used in Ottoman architecture. *(Tomb open daily
8:30am-noon and 1-5:30pm.)*

MURADIYE. *Şehade* (royal sons) are buried in the tombs around the Muradiye
Camii, a testament to the early Ottoman practice of fratricide. In order to
ensure a smooth succession, the eldest son would execute his younger or
weaker brothers. The complex includes 12 tombs, but at the time of publication, only four were open to the public. Cem Sultan's tomb, covered in İznik
tiles, is particularly spectacular. Adjacent to the tomb is the Muradiye or **Murat
II Camii,** built in the same style as the Yeşil Camii. *(Catch one of the frequent
"Muradiye" dolmuş or buses from the Atatürk Cad./Heykel area. Open daily 8:30am-noon and 1-
5:30pm. US$.60.)*

🎵 ENTERTAINMENT

Entertainment in Bursa means winding down at a mineral bath. The bars and clubs
of **Arap Şükrü** district, near Altıparmak Cad., are as close to nightlife as Bursa gets.

MINERAL BATHS. Bursa's fabled mineral baths are in the Çekirge ("Grasshop-
per") area west of the city. The three-bath complex **Yeni Kaplıca** ("New Baths") was
constructed by Süleyman the Magnificent's Grand Vizier atop the remains of
another built by Justinian. (Men only; bath US$3-5.25, massage US$3.50, *kese*
US$2; open daily 5am-11pm.) The **Kaynarca** is a women's bath. (US$3, massage
US$3.50, *kese US$2*; open daily 7am-10:30pm.) Soak in a tub of smooth, pasty mud
at **Karamustafa.** (US$4. Open for men 7am-5pm, for women 8am-4pm.) One of the
finest in the country, ◪**Eski Kaplıca** ("Old Bath") features a hot pool, a hotter pool,
and a great massage room. (Open daily 7am-11pm. Men US$7.50, women US$6.)
*(Take bus #40 from Heykel or any dolmuş with a "Çekirge" sign (US$.60). Get off on Çekirge Cad.
by the Atatürk Museum. For Eski Kaplıca, walk west and bear right at the fork onto Yeni Kaplıca
Cad. Signs point down the stairs.)*

MARKETS. The **Koza and Emir Hans** have been the centers of the city's silk *(ipek)*
trade for the past 500 years. Restored by the Ağa Khan, the **Koza Han** draws silk
cocoon dealers every July and September. The rest of the year, the *han* is home to
a slew of silk fabric shops. The **Emir Han** is concerned only with the sale of the finished product. Both *hans* open into the 14th-century **bedesten** (covered market),
architecturally like İstanbul's Grand Bazaar. *(On Atatürk Cad. behind the Ulu Camii.)*

ÇANAKKALE   ☎ 286

Modern Çanakkale presides over the mythic and eternally strategic Dardanelles,
straits that have seen poets and soldiers come and go for centuries. With its inexpensive accommodations and frequent bus connections, Çanakkale is an easy
base from which to explore Gallipoli and Troy. Though not the most scenic locale,
it appears to be improving as the central Cumhuriyet Meydanı is refurbished and
local tourist establishments are expanded. If you intend to visit only Gallipoli and
not Troy, Eceabat is a more peaceful and less frantic base. Nevertheless,
Çanakkale is particularly hospitable to the thousands of Australians and New
Zealanders who make the pilgrimage to Gallipoli around ANZAC Day (Apr. 25th),
when every hotel in town is sure to be overbooked.

⚡️ ORIENTATION AND PRACTICAL INFORMATION. Most things related to the mechanics of budget travel are within one-block of the ferry dock and the clocktower. From the *otogar*, turn left along **Atatürk Cad.**, make a quick right onto **Demircioğlu Cad.**, and follow the signs marked "Feribot." **Buses** run to: **Ankara** (11hr., 10 per day 7am-1pm, US$15); **Bursa** (4½hr., 5 per day 6:15am-5pm, US$6.50); **Edirne** (5hr., 4 per day 1-10pm, US$7.50); **İstanbul** (5hr.; every hr. until 7pm, every 2hr. afterward; US$10); and **İzmir** (5hr., 16 per day 6:45-2:30am, US$8); and **Selçuk** (6hr., 16 per day 6:45am-2:30am, US$8.75). *Dolmuş* (US$.50-US$1) leave from near the small bridge over the Sarı Çay inlet. To **Troy** (25min., leaves when full).

The English-speaking staff at the **tourist office**, 67 İskele Meydanı, distributes free maps and helps find rooms. (☎/fax 217 11 87. Open M-F 8am-7pm and Sa-Su 10am-6am.) Several **banks** with Cirrus/PLUS **ATMs** stand in a secluded part of the city. Walk up Demircioğlou Cad. and take the fourth right from Anzac House; follow this street to a four-way intersection. (Banks open M-F 9am-12:30pm and 1:30-5:30pm.) The **police** (☎212 14 66) are off İnönü Cad., next to the PTT. A pharmacy, **Pelini Eczanesi** (☎217 12 60), is on Demircioğlou Cad. just down from Anzac House. Hospitals include **Devlet Hastanesi** (public; ☎217 10 98), off İnönü Cad. across from the PTT, and **Özel Hastanesi** (private; ☎217 74 61), one kilometer from the tourist office. The **PTT** is on İnönü Cad. (Open daily 8:30am-5pm.) **Postal code:** 17100.

🛏 ACCOMMODATIONS. Budget accommodations cluster around the clocktower, with good restaurants and bars only a few steps away. Many feature a nightly screening of *Gallipoli*, starring Mel "Kanga" Gibson, and can arrange Gallipoli and Troy tours. To reach **Efes Hotel**, 5 Aralık Sok., walk to the left of the clock tower, then turn left onto Aralık Sok. Completely tiled, this spotless hotel has relatively spacious rooms, each with bath. (☎217 3256. Breakfast US$2.50. Singles US$10; doubles US$13; triples US$15. 25% discount for *Let's Go* readers.) **Anzac House,** 61 Cumhuriyet Meydanı, across from the taxi stand, is a popular spot for Aussies and Kiwis, with refurbished rooms and clean communal baths with hot showers. Perks include laundry service, Internet access (US$4 per hr.), and a barbecue every evening. (☎217 01 56; fax 217 29 06. Breakfast US$1.50. Dorms US$5; singles US$9.75; doubles US$14.50; triples US$18; quads US$24.) Another backpacker hangout, **Yellow Rose Pension,** 5 Yeni Sok., is around the corner, 50m from the clocktower, with a garden, moderately clean single-sex dorms, laundry facilities, Internet access (US$2 per hr.), and international phone and fax services. (☎/fax 217 33 43. Dorms US$4; singles US$7; 2 twin beds US$6; double bed US$5.)

🍴 FOOD AND ENTERTAINMENT. Çanakkale's restaurants serve the catch of the day along the waterfront, and its bars and clubs are close by on the streets behind. Excellent *İskender kebap* (US$2.50) and *lahmacun* (US$.45), combined with local popularity, have forced the expansion of **Doyum Pide ve Kebap Salonu** (☎217 46 87), on the right side of Demircioğlu Cad., up from Anzac House. The buffet-style **Boğaz 2000,** 4 Saat Kulesi Meydanı, is on your left when facing the clock tower. Step inside, choose small portions, and the waiter will bring you your meal. Specialties include *döner kebap* (US$2.50) and *Kemal Paşa Tatlısı.* (☎214 08 88. Dessert with cheese inside US$.75. Open daily for lunch and dinner.) The best of the bars is the explosive **TNT Bar/Garden,** on Saat Kulesi Meydanı, which draws in hostelers to play pool (US$4 per hr.) in a big wooden house. The garden serves drinks and quality fare (meals US$4-6), and an acoustic guitarist croons nightly at 10pm. (☎217 07 74. Open daily until late.)

NEAR ÇANAKKALE

Several agencies provide group tours of Troy and the Gallipoli Battlefields, which generally include round-trip transportation, breakfast or lunch, an English-speaking guide, and admission. **The Hassle Free Travel Agency,** 61 Cumhuriyet Meydanı provides daily Gallipoli tours. (☎213 59 69; email hasslefree@anzachouse.com. Apr.-Nov. 11:45am, Dec.-Mar. 10:45am; US$19) and almost-daily Troy tours (Apr.-

TURKEY

Nov. 8:45am, Dec.-Mar. 7:45am; US$14) that depart from Anzac House. ▨ **TJ's Tours** (☎814 29 40; fax 814 29 41; email TJs_TOURS@excite.com) provides daily Gallipoli tours (12:30pm, US$19) and Troy tours (8:45am, US$14) when sufficient demand. Call ahead to reserve a space.

BATTLEFIELDS OF GALLIPOLI (GELIBOLU)

Gallipoli's battle sights and memorials are spread out, so your best bet is to take an organized tour, many of which provide lunch, excellent English-speaking guides, and transportation. Bring along your swimsuit, since tours often make a short stop for a swim. If you want to visit the area on your own, take a dolmuş to the Kabatepe Müzesi (☎814 12 97) from Eceabat. The museum has a good collection of memorabilia including two bullets that collided in midair. Museum open daily 8:30am-noon and 1-5:30pm. US$1.20.

The strategic position of the Gallipoli Peninsula on the Dardanelles made it the site of one of the most catastrophic Allied offensives in World War I. According to a plan proposed by Britain's young First Lord of the Admiralty, **Winston Churchill**, the Allies could conquer Constantinople, drive Turkey out of the war, and open communications with Russia attacking at this spot. Eighty thousand Turks and more than 200,000 soldiers of the British Empire—including a disproportionate sacrifice by the Australian-New Zealand Army Corps (ANZAC)—lost their lives in the hideous, entrenched stalemate in December 1915. This battle launched its hero, **Atatürk**, on a rapid rise toward his status as Turkey's founding father. Each year, thousands of Aussies and Kiwis make pilgrimages to Gallipoli's war cemeteries, and April 25, the date of the Allied landing, is an important day of remembrance Down Under. The battle sights and accompanying memorials are spread out, so your best bet is to take an organized tour.

TRUVA (TROY)

32km south of Çanakkale. In summer, Troy-bound dolmuş leave from the Çanakkale lot M-Sa every 30min. until dark (US$.80). On Su, evenings, and in winter, take the Ezine minibus from the otogar or Atatürk Cad. to the intersection with the Troy road (20km; US$.50). From there, it's a relatively flat 5km walk. Site and Excavation House open daily in summer 8:30am-7:30pm; otherwise 8am-5pm. Admission to both US$2.50.

For the casual visitor with no romantic attachment to Homer, Troy's jumbled, partially excavated ruins may well prove a disappointment. People raised on stories of the Trojan War should not expect imposing ruins—the city Homer wrote about came tumbling down 3000 years ago. When Heinrich Schliemann rediscovered Troy in the 1880s, it had been a ghost town for at least 13 centuries. The site is confusing and not immediately striking to the imagination, a situation hardly improved by the hokey wooden horse and academic dryness of the displays in the excavation house. The site's presentation focuses more on what people ate or how they made pottery than on the quasi-historical legacy of Homer, who was quite a storyteller but not exactly a stickler for details. Troy offers extensive ruins of unmatched significance; nine distinct strata contain the remains of different cities that stood here, dubbed Troy I (from 3200 BCE) through Troy IX. The city of Homer's *Iliad* is now believed to be Troy VI, not Troy II, the city Schliemann excavated. An illustrated explanation of each stratum is available in the **Excavation House** (on your right after passing the horse). Look out for house foundations, city walls, a temple, and a theater.

BOZCAADA (TENEDOS)

Ferries run from Geyikli (Yükyeri dock) to Bozcaada (daily in summer 10am, 2, 7pm, midnight) and back to Geyikli (daily in summer 7:30am, noon, 5:30, 11pm). Minibuses run from the Çanakkale otogar (1hr., every hr., US$1.50) and arrive in Geyikli near, but not at, the ferry dock. To get to the dock, take a dolmuş from the bus stop to the Yükyeri dock (5min., US$.35). Dolmuş wait for ferries coming back from the island before heading to Çanakkale (20min., US$.60) and other local destinations.

Sandy coves, rolling hills, a perpetual cool breeze, and plentiful wine make Bozcaada a natural paradise. The charm of the white-washed, pastel-trimmed houses of the island's only town provides a distinctively Greek feel. Though the island is short on residents (pop. 2500), even the summer arrivals aren't enough to crowd the place. And there's no lack of beach. And there's enough wine to go around; this tiny island supplies more than 10% of Turkey's wine. In antiquity, Tenedos's wine was considered some of the finest in the world. Today's product standard has dropped a bit, but it's cheap and available everywhere except (maybe) the post office.

The well-preserved **castle** dominates the area around the harbor. The edifice was constructed in the Byzantine period and renovated by the Venetians, Genoese, and Ottomans. (Castle open daily 10am-1pm, 2-7pm. US$1.20, students US$.40.) The island's main attractions, however, are its beaches and cliffs, from which you can gaze out over the cobalt sea. The best way to check it all out is by bike. **Ada Cafe,** in the main square, rents bikes and provides maps and an Anglophone staffer. (☎697 87 95. US$1.30 per hr., US$6.50 per day. Open daily 8:30-2am.) The beautiful beaches of **Ayana, Ayazma, Solubahçe,** and **Habbele** are the best on the island and the most popular, though they are rarely crowded.

AEGEAN COAST

Fabulous classical ruins and a sinuous coastline concealing sublime beaches have helped transform Turkey's once-tranquil Aegean coast into an increasingly popular destination. Framed by 5000-year-old mythology and history, the region's intensely rich culture is an eyeful for photographers, archaeologists, nature-lovers, and hedonistic nomads alike. Hellenistic ruins—especially extensive at Pergamon, Ephesus, Aphrodisias, and Pamukkale—stand as weathered testaments to the coast's glorious heritage.

İZMİR ☎232

İzmir, formerly ancient **Smyrna** (reputed to be the birthplace of Homer), has risen from the rubble of the 1922 Turkish War of Independence to become Turkey's third-largest city. Due to İzmir's sheer size, many travelers find themselves here for a bus transfer or even an overnight stay en route to the Aegean coast's more impressive sights. The city is only worth a more extended visit between June and August, when it hosts the **International İzmir Festival,** attracting world-renowned musical, dance, and theater performers.

◪▤ ORIENTATION AND PRACTICAL INFORMATION. Cumhuriyet Meydanı, on the waterfront, is the city's financial center. Many budget hotels and inexpensive restaurants, along with several bus company offices and the **Basmane train station,** are located around **9 Eylül Meydanı,** the center of the Basmane district. To get to the city center and to Basmane from the **Yeni Garaj,** İzmir's new intercity bus station, take bus #601 to its end on **Sehit Fethibey Bulvarı** in museum-laden **Konak** or bus #605 to Basmane. Alternatively, walk from Konak to Basmane. **Airport Adnan Menderes,** 20km south of İzmir, connects Turkey to major European cities and other Turkish cities. Take the Havaş bus from the tourist office (30min., 1½hr., US$2.50). **Turkish Airlines,** 1/F Gazi Osman Paşa (airport office ☎274 24 24 or 274 28 00, ticket office ☎484 12 20, reservations ☎455 53 63), just up from the tourist office, runs flights to **İstanbul** and **Ankara** (both US$85, students US$58; open daily 8am-7pm). Intercity bus destinations include: **Ankara** (8hr., every hr. 9am-1am, US$13.75); **Antalya** (8hr., every hr., US$13); **Bodrum** (4hr., every hr. 7am-1am, US$10); **Bursa** (5hr., every hr. 9am-1am, US$8); **İstanbul** (9hr., every hr. 9am-1am, US$18); **Kuşadası** (1hr., every 1½hr., US$3.25); and **Marmaris** (5hr., every hr. 7am-1am, US$10). For **Selçuk,** take a Bodrum or Kuşadası bus and tell the driver where you're going (1hr., US$4). Many **banks** have offices along the waterfront.

▛▜ ACCOMMODATIONS AND FOOD. Head for 9 Eylül Meydanı and don't look back. ▨**Hotel Oba,** 1369 Sok. No. 27, four blocks west of 9 Eylül Meydanı (away from the train station), has a rare combination of cheap, clean lodgings and great amenities, including a lobby bar. Each room has a private bath, TV, and air conditioning. (☎441 96 05 or 441 96 06; fax 483 81 98. Breakfast included. Singles US$12; doubles US$16.) To reach the **Lâleli Otel,** 1368 Sok. No. 5-6, walk 1 block from 9 Eylül Meydanı on 1369 Sok. and turn left. All rooms have showers and ceiling fans and an English-speaking staff member is always available. (☎484 09 01 or 484 09 02. Breakfast US$1.60. Singles US$10; doubles US$17.85; triples US$24.50. Beds US$12, in dorm-style quads US$10. V, MC, AmEx.) A display case at the front of **Basmane Kebap Salonu,** 157/A Fevzipaşa Bul., on the dead-end leading to the train station, holds the meats from which you create a fantasy *şiş* mix (US$2.80-3.50). Ask for the specialty, *içli köfte* (meatballs with deep-fried batter, US$.75 each. ☎425 50 19. Open daily 9am-midnight. V.) All sorts of *börek* (cheese, potato, spinach, meat; US$1) and *pide* are on display at the **Çankaya Börek ve Pide Salonu,** 8 Mimar Kemalettin Cad. No. 130/B.

PERGAMON (BERGAMA)

Pergamon gazes across the river at the modern town of Bergama. It can be visited as a daytrip from Çanakkale, İzmir, Bursa, or Kuşadası. Buses run to: **Ankara** *(10hr.; 9:30am, 8:45pm; US$18);* **İstanbul** *(10hr., 9:30am and 9:25pm, US$20); and* **İzmir** *(2hr., 2 per hr. 6am-7:30pm, US$3.25). Acropolis and Asclepion open daily 8:30am-5:30pm. Acropolis US$3.50, students with ISIC card free. Asclepion US$2.50, students US$1.25.*

Once a dazzling center of cultural activity, Pergamon was for a time the capital of the Roman province of Asia and had one of the two largest libraries in the ancient world. The ruins of this great Hellenistic and Roman city dominate the top of the hill, while buildings from later eras, when the city's stature and importance declined, cling lower down at the hill's feet. Pergamon traces its roots back to the Aeolian Greeks, who built a settlement here in the 9th century BCE. The city was beautified by Philataeros, a successor of Alexander the Great, but all his work was undone by an earthquake in the 2nd century CE and subsequent kicks to the proverbial stomach from various ancient conquerors.

From the river (near the Pension Athena), cross the bridge and head up the hill through the old town. Follow the paved road until you come upon a gate, and take the path to the right of the gate (which eventually turns into a stone-paved road) up to the temples and marble ruins of the **Acropolis** looming over the city. On your way up, take in the breathtaking view of the Hellenistic **theater** that once seated 10,000. Farther up, try to land three coins on top of the column inside the **wishing well** for good luck. Follow the yellow signs from Atatürk Meydanı on the west side of town to reach the famed **Asclepion,** an ancient healing center where the foremost doctor of the ancient world, Galen (born in Pergamon), once worked. A marble colonnade, theater, and healing rooms remain visible today. Near the river and the old part of Bergama stand the remnants of **Kızıl Avlu,** a pagan temple that became one of the Seven Churches of the Apocalypse mentioned in the Book of Revelations—"this is where Satan has his altar" (Rev. 2:3).

KUŞADASI   ☎256

Named for the pigeons that make their home in the town's 14th-century Genoese castle, Kuşadası ("Bird Island") transformed a few decades ago from a quiet town to a grand resort, thanks to its picturesque setting on sea-sloping hills and excellent sandy beaches, as well as its proximity to the magnificent archaeological wonders at Ephesus and Selçuk. Kuşadası's broad tourist apparatus accommodates every group: backpackers arrive by ferry from the Greek island of Samos and by bus from the north, while wealthy Americans and Europeans flood the carpet shops whenever their luxury cruise liners dock in the small harbor. Excellent budget hotels and towering luxury palaces are surrounded by myriad high-end jewelry and carpet shops, and over 100 pubs, which reputedly dot the city.

TURKEY

Kuşadası

ACCOMMODATIONS

Golden Bed Pension, 1
Hotel Sammy's Palace, 2

TO
SELÇUK &
İZMİR

TO
AYDIN

Atatürk Yolu

Cemali Dağyaran Sok.

M. Akgöl Sok.

Okul Sok.

Topallı Sok.

Minare Sok.

Turizm Sok.

Ergene Sok.

**Friday
Market**

Gençlik Cad.

Leylak Sok.

Emginler Sok.

Sevinç Sok.

Bahçearası Sok.

Unlu Sok.

50 yıl Cad.

Mustafa Yaran Sok.

Zeki Aydını Sok.

Yıldıray Sok.

Arslı Sok.

Kıratalı Sok.

Burç Sok.

Adnan Menderes Bul.

Tarhan Bul.

Dağılgan Sok.

Özgür Sokağı

Öztürk Sok.

Kalender M. Sok.

Candan Sok.

Taksim Sok.

Çevre Yolu

TO
(350m)

Avcı Sok.

İsmet İnönü Bul.

**Bus
Ticket
Office**

**Hacı Hatice
Hanım Camii**

Sağlık Cad.

Kışla Sok.

Bozkurt Sok.

Castle

Sabuca Sok.

Kahramanlar Cad.

Zafer Sok.

Sönmez Sok.

Barlar Sok.

San Sok.

Güneş Sok.

Kaynak Gök Sok.

Public Beach

K. Arıkan Cad.

Atatürk Bul.

**Kale
Hamamı**

**Town
Hall**

Barbaros Hayrettin Bul.

Aslanlar Cad.

**Belediye
Hamamı**

Altın Sok.

Yıldırım Cad.

Sabri Mumcu Cad.

TO
SÖKE

Fisherman Harbor

Harbor

**Passport
Police**

Customs

Liman Cad.

Kıbrıs Cad.

2

Anıt Sok.

Güzel Sok.

İmam Sok.

Aydınlık Sok.

İteri Sok.

Soysa Sok.

Güvercinada Cad.

Bezirgan Sok.

Tepe Sok.

Güvercin Sok.

Doğan Sok.

Sülün Sok.

Sülün Sok.

Şahin Sok.

Kartal Sok.

Kuğu Sok.

Saire Sok.

Evrim Sok.

**Genoese
Castle**

Güvercinada

Mehmet Işık Cad.

Botanik İzci Sok.

Ali Basın Sok.

Küçük Bey Ramazan Sok.

TO KADINLAR PLAJI
(LADIES BEACH, 2km)

Aegean Sea

Public Beach

Public Beach

200 yards

200 meters

N

> **BLACK, WHITE, AND READ WITH ENVY** In
> ancient times, only the **Great Library of Alexandria** (see p. 154) surpassed Perga-
> mon's, which contained over 200,000 volumes in repositories all over the city. So
> great was Alexandria's jealousy of the Pergamenes' literary hoard that they made what
> they thought was a brilliant strategic move: they limited the flow of Egyptian papyrus to
> Pergamon. The Pergamenes countered by writing all subsequent volumes on parch-
> ment pages made from goat hide, an exponentially more durable, manageable
> medium. The scheming Alexandrians were foiled only temporarily. After the Alexandrian
> library burned down, **Marc Antony** and his boys plundered Pergamon's shelves and
> presented the pilfered publications to Cleopatra, as a token of his love to replace the
> charred editions. In 640 CE, the ill-fated collection was put to the torch by the **Caliph
> Omar.** If the books agreed with the Qur'an, Omar argued, they were superfluous, and if
> they disagreed with the Qur'an, they were heretical and fit for combustion.

✴🛈 ORIENTATION AND PRACTICAL INFORMATION

The duty-free shop, tourist office, and customs office are all in the port area.
Dolmuş depart from a separate *dolmuş* stop on **Adnan Menderes Bulvarı,** about
1½km southeast of the intersection of **Atatürk Bulvarı** and **İnönü Bulvarı,** two of the
main streets. **Kıbrıs Cad.** runs uphill and inland from the tourist office, passing an
ancient **caravanserai** and a covered bazaar. On the other side of the caravanserai
the broad, pedestrian-only **Barbaros Hayrettin Paşa Bulvarı** is home to the PTT,
travel agencies, and several banks.

Buses: The *garaj* is on Kahramanlar Sok., about 2km from the center of town. Most
hotels will either provide or pay for transportation from the *garaj*. To: **Ankara** (9hr., 3
per day 8:30am-9:30pm, US$21); **Antalya** (7hr., 9:30am and 11pm, US$18); **Bodrum**
(2½hr., 9:30am and 4:30pm, US$9); **Fethiye** (5½hr., 10:30am, US$13); **İstanbul** (9hr.,
6 per day 10:45am-11:45pm, US$22.75); **İzmir** (1½hr., every 20min. 6am-10pm,
US$4); **Konya** (8hr., 6pm, US$16); **Marmaris** (4hr., 9:15am, US$11.50); **Nevşehir**
(11hr., 6pm, US$24.50); **Pamukkale** (3½hr.; 9am, returns 5pm; US$9). Pamukkale
can also be reached by *dolmuş* via **Denizli.** Take the İzmir bus to the İzmir **airport.** Call
ahead for bus tickets F-Su.

Dolmuş: City *dolmuş* run between the *dolmuş* stop on Adnan Menderes Bul. and the lot
adjacent to the *garaj* (US$.50). Inter-city *dolmuş* head to **Selçuk** (30min., every 20min.
7am-11:30pm, US$1.20) via Ephesus (ask to be let off) and **Söke** (30min., every 30
min. 7am-11:30pm, US$1.20).

Ferries: Ekol Travel beats the official rate. Youth and student 10% discount; flash *Let's
Go* for an additional 15% discount. To **Samos** (1½hr.; in summer daily 8:30am,
4:30pm; in winter 2 per week; US$30, including port tax).

Tourist Office: 13 Liman Cad. (☎614 11 03; fax 614 62 95), corner of Liman Cad. and
Güvercin Ada Sok. Open May-Oct. daily 8am-5:30pm; Nov.-Apr. M-F 8am-5:30pm.

Travel Agencies: Ekol Travel with **WorldSpan,** Kıbrıs Cad., 9/1 Buyral Sok. (☎614 92 55
or 614 55 91; fax 614 26 44). Cheap flights, ferry tickets, temporary baggage storage,
room search, message board, car rentals, and emergency help finding English-speaking
doctors. 15% *Let's Go* discount on ferry tickets. Open daily May-Nov. 8:30am-10pm;
Dec.-Apr. 8:30am-5:30pm.

Banks: Several dot the waterfront area. **Türkiye İş Bankası,** on the corner of Atatürk Bul.
and Liman Cad., offers a 24hr. V/MC/Cirrus **ATM.** Open M-F 9am-12:30pm and 1:30-
5pm. **Koç Bank,** by the police station on Atatürk Bul., has a V/MC **ATM.** Open M-F
8:45am-5:30pm. Both offer **currency** and **traveler's check exchange.** Koç doesn't
charge for changing cash, but both banks charge hefty fees for traveler's checks.

Hammam: Kaleiçi Hamamı (☎614 12 92). Follow signs behind the PTT. Bath and massage US$16.25. Both sexes bathe together. Open daily 7am-10pm.

Police: Headquarters, 6 Atatürk Bul. (☎614 13 82), and **Tourist Police** (☎614 10 22) are in the same building, past the caravanserai walking with the sea on your left.

Hospital: Kuşadası Devlet Hastanesi, 30 Atatürk Bul. (☎614 10 26 or 614 16 14), on the waterfront, past the police station, with the sea on the left. Little English spoken.

PTT: (☎614 33 11 or 614 15 79), across from the *kervansaray*, on Barbaros Hayrettin Paşa Bul. Open daily 7am-11pm. **Phones** available 24hr. **Currency** and **traveler's check exchange** open daily 8:30am-midnight. **Postal code:** 09400.

■ ACCOMMODATIONS

▩**The Golden Bed Pansiyon,** 4 Aslanlar Cad. (☎614 87 08; fax 612 66 67; email goldenbed_anzac@hotmail.com; www.kusadasihotels.com/goldenbed). Off Yıldırım Cad. Turn right onto Uğurlu Sokak as you walk up the hill away from the harbor. Owned by a Turkish-Australian couple, this newly renovated pension offers marvelous views of Kuşadası harbor from the balconies and rooftop terrace. Rooms are light and refreshing. Free transportation to and from Ephesus; taxi from *garaj* paid. Laundry US$2 per kg. *Hammam* 25% off. Internet US$1.50 per hr. Nightly chicken and fish BBQs US$5. Breakfast US$2. US$5 per person; US$6 per person with balcony.

▩**Hotel Sammy's Palace,** 14 Kıbrıs Cad. (☎612 25 88; cell ☎(532) 274 21 29; fax 612 99 91; email sammy@superonline.com). Ideal for the fun-loving, group-loving backpackers always up for a rip-roaring late night complete with belly dancing in the hotel common room/bar/dance hall (free in summer). 32 well-furnished, peaceful rooms, all with bath and most with balcony, make recuperating from the festivities enjoyable as well. Satellite TV and free movie showings. Free transportation to and from Ephesus. Cab fares from *garaj* paid by the manager. Internet US$4 per hr. Laundry US$2 per kg. Breakfast US$3.25. Dinner and breakfast on rooftop US$6.50. Roof US$2.50; dorms US$5; singles US$11.50; doubles US$16. 10% *Let's Go* discount.

Liman Otel, Kibris Cad. Buyral Sok. No. 4 (☎614 77 70; fax 614 69 13). On the waterfront, past the tourist office, with the sea on your right. Entrance in rear. Owner "Mr. Happy," provides a dorm room on the roof for his most frugal guests, inexpensive rooms with no view for those travelers who sacrifice scenery for savings, and beautiful seaside rooms for vacationers who want it all. Terrific location. A/C in all rooms except dorm. 10% discount on any bus ticket. Free transport to and from bus station and Ephesus. Internet US$1.50 per hr. Laundry US$2 per kg. Breakfast US$1.50. Dorm US$4; interior room US$5; rear room US$16; harbor-side room US$19.50.

◖ FOOD

Yuvam Ev Yemekleri ve Mantı Evi, Camikebir Mah., 7 Kaleiçi (☎614 94 60). Behind the post office. Turn left at Yapı Kredi as you walk away from the sea, and take the first right. Similar to Avlu Restaurant, but slightly smaller with more atmosphere. Thursday is homemade *mantı* night US$2. Meat dishes US$2. Open daily 8am-10pm.

Avlu Restaurant, 15 Cephane Sok. (☎614 79 95). The first left off Barbaros Hayrettin Paşa Bul. as you walk away from the sea. A standard *lokanta* with no menu, just a display of the day's dishes to choose from. Decor isn't fancy, but food is fresh and prices are low. Meat dishes US$1.25-1.60 per serving. Large selection of vegetarian dishes US$1.20 per serving. *Tatlı* (dessert) US$.80. Open daily 8am-11pm.

Seyhan Restaurant, 63 Sağlık Cad. (☎614 79 85). A slightly higher-end restaurant with wicker chairs, tablecloths, and a location great for people-watching. Huge selection and menu in 4 languages. English or Turkish breakfast US$4; shrimp cocktail US$2.50; excellent *sebzeli güveç* (vegetable stew) US$5.75. Open Apr.-Sept. daily 9am-midnight.

♫ ENTERTAINMENT

The nighttime music and madness of the appropriately named **Barlar Sokak** ("bars street") gushes out for blocks, drizzling onto side streets like **Tuna Sokak,** where

TURKEY

roofless bars with live European and Turkish bands are the norm. The killer combination of dozens of discos and no weekday cover charge makes club hopping easier than standing still.

Heaven, 13 Sakarya Sok. (☎613 24 56). Behind the PTT, is one of the largest, most popular music clubs. Decorated in a mock Roman style with vines, a columns, and a few authentic remains. Live Turkish pop in its inner open-air courtyard every night 1-4am. Beer US$4; cocktails US$7.25. US$8 cover only on Sa (one domestic drink included). Open June-Sept. daily 9pm-4am.

Adı Meydanı, 18 Kaleiçi Bahar Sok. (☎614 34 96). Behind the PTT. A romantic night-time spot, including open-air courtyard with lamp-lighting, fireplaces, and attractive stone walls. Live traditional Turkish music every night (9pm-2am). The most popular dish is Brain Salad (US$1.60), but there are plenty of more standard options too. Mixed grill US$5.50. Beer US$1.50-2.50. Open daily 7pm-2am.

The Green Bar, 33 Tuna Sok. (☎612 45 62). Behind the PTT. Mammoth banana trees adorn this small roofless bar. Live Irish music nightly at 11pm. Cocktails US$5. Beer US$1.50-2.50. Wine US$1.60 per glass. Open daily 4pm-4am.

◆ SIGHTS

Kuşadası's best known sights are its shopping areas and its clean (but crowded) beaches. Contrary to the claims of the carpet and jewelry store owners, the **Grand Bazaar** and **Barbaros Hayrettin Paşa Bul.** are expensive places to shop, but browsing's always free. Kuşadası also hosts the **Kuşadası Music Festival,** an annual contest during which Turkish pop bands vie for bubble-gum glory. For tourists, this means free concerts in the last week of June.

BEACHES AND ISLANDS. Kuşadası's beaches are clean and sandy, but everyone this side of the Aegean knows it. Head to the Mediterranean coast for more secluded sunbathing. **Kadınlar Plajı** (Ladies Beach), 3km from the city, is easily accessible by a US$.50 *dolmuş* ride (beach chairs US$2, with umbrella US$3). **Balcı Pension** (☎614 14 10; fax 614 17 30) offers **scuba** courses (US$40). A trip to Kuşadası would be incomplete without a visit to **Güvercinada (Pigeon Island),** the jutting peninsula that Kuşadası's namesake birds call home. Roam around the 14th-century Genoese castle, which the Ottomans turned into a military outpost, and enjoy a glass of *çay* at the tea houses along the old lookout point.

DILEK NATIONAL PARK. Dilek National Park, 26km from Kuşadası, contains four beaches and over 30 animal species. While overnight camping is not permitted, Dilek offers daytime canyon hiking (6km from entrance gate), sandy beaches (**İçmeler Beach,** one kilometer from the gate), and sand-and-pebble shores (**Aydınlık Beach,** 5km from the gate; **Karvakı Beach,** 7km from the gate). Don't leave without seeing **Zeus Mağarası** (Zeus's Cave), a small cavern opposite the sea, 100m outside the park entrance. Once rumored as the site of hidden treasure, the cave is filled with water bubbling up from the ground. *(Open daily in peak season 8am-8pm; extended hours July-Aug.; off-season 8am-5pm. Canyon open Oct.-June. US$1.20 per person, US$1.60 per motorcycle, US$8 per car.)*

EFES (EPHESUS) ΕΦΕΣΟΣ   ☎232

Stretching from early archaic times to the 6th century CE, Ephesus's glorious prosperity has not gone the way of other notable ancient cities. To this day, Ephesus boasts a concentration of Classical art and architecture surpassed only by Rome and Athens. As both the capital of Roman Asia and the site of a large, wealthy port, Ephesus accumulated almost unparalleled wealth and splendor, the marble specter of which still leaves visitors in awe. The ruins, with their extensive marble roadways and columned avenues, rank first among Turkey's ancient sites in terms of sheer size and state of preservation.

HISTORY

Fiery and intense, Ephesus's history has all the makings of an ancient tragedy. Out of devotion to its patron goddess Artemis, it stayed close to her colossal temple near modern Selçuk. When the harbor silted up, deteriorating into a mosquito-infested wasteland and resulting in a massive malaria epidemic, this decision proved disastrous, sealing the city's fate by the 6th century.

Ephesus' origins are equally romantic. The Delphic Oracle had prophesied that a fish and a wild boar would determine the ideal site for the city. Soon after, Androclus was passing through a seaside village where fish were being roasted along the shore. One fish, covered in burning wood, fell from the fire, igniting a nearby bush and upsetting a wild boar, who tore out from the foliage. Androclus slew the boar, and heeding the oracle, he founded the city on the site, now 10km inland.

The ancient traveler Pausanias deemed Ephesus the "most wondrous of the Seven Ancient Wonders" and "the most beautiful work ever created by mankind." The first major structure built entirely of marble and the largest edifice in the ancient Greek world, the **Temple of Artemis** was four times as big as the Parthenon. Remarkably, the Temple of Artemis was actually built twice. It was set afire during the reign of Mad King Hesostratos in 356 BCE on the night of Alexander the Great's birth. According to legend, the pyro-king succeeded only because Artemis—watching over Alexander's birth at the time—was absent. Fittingly, Alexander himself offered to restore the temple when he passed through the city. The Ephesians, however, declined his offer and rebuilt the temple even more splendidly with their own resources and the offerings made by hundreds of thousands of pilgrims. Today, little remains of the magnificent structure. Goths sacked the sanctuary in the 3rd century, and the Byzantines followed suit.

Ephesus reached its zenith after 129 BCE, when the Romans established the province of Asia with Ephesus as the capital. After Rome, it was second only to Alexandria in population, with more than 250,000 inhabitants. St. Paul, recognizing the significance of the metropolis, arrived in 50 CE and converted a small group of Ephesians to Christianity. Not surprisingly, many perceived the development of the new religion as a threat to Artemis and Cybele (mother goddess of Anatolia) and forced St. Paul and his followers to depart. Eventually, however, Ephesus became a center of Christianity in the Roman Empire, so much so that the Ecumenical Council met here in 431. Pope Paul VI visited the site in 1967 and prayed with a congregation in the ruins of Ephesus's 4th century church to the Virgin.

▐▌ GETTING AROUND AND PRACTICAL INFORMATION

Ephesus lies 2-3km outside of Selçuk along the main Kuşadası-Selçuk road called **Dr. Sabri Yayla Bulvarı.** The easiest way to get to Ephesus from Kuşadası or Selçuk is to take advantage of the free **shuttle** service offered by practically every hotel and *pansiyon*. Otherwise, to get to Ephesus from the Kuşadası *otogar*, take a **dolmuş** to Selçuk and tell the driver to stop at Efes (30min., US$1). From the Selçuk *otogar*, take a Pamucak-bound *dolmuş* toward Kuşadası (5min.; May-Oct. every 30min., Nov.-Apr. every hr.; US$.50). **Taxis** also run from Selçuk to Ephesus (US$4) and to the House of the Virgin Mary (9km, US$21 round-trip including 45min. to visit the house). The site is also an easy walk (25min.) from Selçuk along a fig tree-shaded path (beside Dr. Sabri Yayla Bulvarı) that passes by the spectacular Ephesus Museum (see **Selçuk: Sights,** p. 645) and the Temple of Artemis. The lower entrance, to which you arrive by *dolmuş* or on foot, has **toilets** (US$.40) and a **PTT.**

🏛 EXPLORING EPHESUS

☎ 892 64 02. Site open daily 8am-6pm. US$6.50. Bring a water bottle and sunscreen.

VEDIUS GYMNASIUM AND STADIUM. On the left as you walk down the road from Dr. Sabri Yayla Bulvarı to the lower entrance is the Vedius Gymnasium, built in 150 CE in honor of then-emperor Antonius Pius and Artemis, the city's patron goddess. Beyond the vegetation lie the horseshoe-shaped remains of the city's stadium, originally constructed by the Greek architect Lysimachus and then expanded during the reign of Nero. The dual construction highlights the fundamental differences between Hellenic and Roman public entertainment. The original Greek structure would have been a semi-circular theater whose shape followed the contours of the land to add a natural emphasis to the staged dramas. The Roman stadium was built atop the old theater for the viewing of such martial spectacles as bloody gladiator games, wild beast hunts, and public executions.

ON THE WAY TO THE ARCADIANE. Of the three holy Christian sites in the Efes vicinity, only the very long, skinny building of the **Church of the Seven Councils** is in the Ephesus site itself. Just inside the lower entrance, a dirt path leads to the right; follow this path and turn right where it splits to the ruins of the Church. Here, the Ecumenical Council met in 431 CE to iron out the **Nestorian Heresy,** in which the bishop Nestor called into question the humanity of Christ. This was also the site of Pope Paul VI's visit in 1967. Beside the Church of the Seven Councils is the **Archbishop's Place,** which was destroyed by Arabs in the 6th century CE.

ALONG THE ARCADIANE. Back at the main entrance gate, a tree-lined path leads straight ahead to the Arcadiane, Ephesus' main drag. Running from the Grand Theater to what was once the harbor, the magnificent, colonnaded marble avenue would have been thronging with stevedores (men who unload ships' cargoes) and carts bringing wares to sell in the *agora*. The street eventually liquefied into a small marsh, and only a few marble stumps remain of the covered arcade which ran along the sides of the main road. The large expanse of column stones laid out in tidy rows to the left as you face the theater are the remnants of the **Theater Baths and Gymnasium.** This area, used in the Roman Period for training actors, is currently a focus of excavation. The **Grand Theater,** at the end of the Arcadiane, is a stunning 30m by 145m heavily restored beast. Its *cavea* (seating area), carved into the side of Mount Pion, had a capacity of 25,000 people. (Archaeologists have used this number to estimate the population of this and other Hellenistic cities.) The hard marble and the sound-catching colonnade across the top gave the theater excellent acoustics. The *skene* (where the scenery and props stand in a modern theater) is a forest of columns, stelae, and statues dating mostly from the reigns of Claudius and Trajan. Denizens of Ephesus placed 89 golden idols of Artemis here to celebrate the goddess's annual festival each April. St. Paul railed against these same false gods. Today, the **International Efes Festival** is held here in September.

THE MARBLE ROAD. From the Grand Theater, approach the Street of Curetes by walking along the Marble Road. To your right as you walk along the Marble Road is the **agora,** which is currently off-limits, but was once a large commercial area built during the reign of Nero. A square stone in the center marks all that remains of the city's **horologium,** a sundial and water clock that kept accurate time. At the southern end of the *agora* is the **Gate of Maxeus and Mithridates,** two wealthy freedmen who had the gate built and dedicated to the first Roman emperor, Augustus. About halfway to the Street of Curetes, on the right-hand edge of the Marble Road, stands a small metal barrier surrounding and protecting a rough-hewn inscription thought to be the world's first advertisement. The inscription consists of a picture of a foot, a cross, a woman, and a heart-shaped blob. The ad-wizards of the day intended this to designate the **brothel** down the road. The foot indicated the viewer's position as well as the need to walk to the crossroads ahead, represented by the cross. The heart above and to the left of the cross showed the house's position at the intersection, and the woman depicted is just that, a woman.

THE STREET OF CURETES. A slight incline signals the beginning of the Street of Curetes, which connected the city to the Temple of Artemis, now in Selçuk. Ruts in the road are evidence of the enormous concentration of traffic between the temple and the city, and gaps between the slabs reveal glimpses of the city's **sewer system.** At the very bottom of the Street of Curetes is the **Library of Celsus,** which was restored by Austrian archaeologists. A memorial to Gaius Julius Celsus and a general fount of knowledge, the library was covered with inscriptions recording important events and once contained 12,000 scrolls. The facade's frontal curvature and the slight thinness of the peripheral columns serve to create an impression of greater width. This tempers the minimizing effect of being sandwiched between the broad *agora* and another building. Scholars suspect that the large building behind the library is the **Temple of Sarapis,** an Egyptian god associated with grain.

Walking up the Street of Curetes from the library, the **brothel** is on your left. Romantic commerce took place by oil light in the windowless side rooms, where archaeologists unearthed the infamous statue of **Priapus,** the god of fertility, now in Selçuk's Efes Müzesi (see p. 645). Adjacent to the brothel are the **Baths of Scholastica,** built in the 5th century at the behest of a wealthy woman. You will find a **public restroom** just beyond the brothel.

Farther up the Street of Curetes are the imposing ruins of the **Temple of Hadrian** on the left. It is marked by its double-layered column construction, several friezes depicting the creation of Ephesus, and a bust of the goddess Cybele that adorns the keystone. The temple was built in 118 CE during Hadrian's rule, atypical for Romans, who usually preferred to deify their emperors only after death. Covering the hillside on the right are the famous stephouses, home to the local bourgeoisie. Since they are currently under excavation, most are off limits to tourists. A little further up the hill on the left are the ruins of the exquisite **Fountain of Trajan.** A statue of the **Emperor Trajan,** who extended the Roman Empire's borders as far as the Indian Ocean, once stood before the fountain. Today only its base remains.

Two pillars in the middle of the road mark the location of the **Gate of Hercules.** Farther uphill and to the left is the **Prytaneion.** Dedicated to the worship of **Vesta** (Hestia to the Greeks), goddess of the hearth and home, the Prytaneion contained an eternal flame that was tended by the **Vestal Virgins,** a small group of priestesses who served Vesta. Worship of Vesta was of such great significance to Romans that the Vestal Virgins were afforded social standing close to that of men.

Adjacent and in fine repair is the **odeon** (bouleterion), a small theater that seated approximately 1500 people. It was used as both a theater and a meeting place. The **state agora** on the right was the heart of political activity from the first century BCE until the city's final demise. On the left after the odeon lie the upper **baths.**

OTHER SITES. The road that runs by the top entrance of Efes leads to the **House of the Virgin Mary** (8km, 1-1½hr. walking), where, according to a legend supported by some archaeological and literary evidence, she lived with the Apostle John and later by herself after leaving Jerusalem (see **Selçuk: Sights,** p. 646). Much closer to the Ephesus site are the **Caves of the Seven Sleepers,** easily reached by leaving Ephesus through the bottom gate, turning right at the "Seven Sleepers" sign, and walking for 10 to 15 minutes. Legend has it that seven youths fleeing religious persecution under Emperor Decius slept in the cave for what they thought to be a night. Upon waking up, they discovered that they had slept for 112 years, during which time Christianity had become the official religion of the Empire. Amazed by their story, Emperor Theodosius II built a church atop the caves and decreed that the sleepers' remains be buried there. All that remains of the church is a fence in front of the cave. It is covered with tiny napkins representing wishes. The youths' tombs are at the top of the hill, abutting the fence. *(Always open. Free.)*

SELÇUK ☎ 232

Selçuk serves as the most convenient base from which to explore nearby Ephesus, and offers several notable archaeological sites of its own. The Selçuk castle dominates the city's skyline, and the Basilica of St. John, where the apostle John is buried, the İsa Bay Camii, and the ruins of the Temple of Artemis lie just below. The House of the Virgin Mary *(Meryemana)* can also be reached from Selçuk. Selçuk is also home to the famous Camel Wrestling Festival, held annually during the third weekend of January near Pamucak Beach, a short *dolmuş* ride away (contact the tourist office for more information).

✦ 🛈 ORIENTATION AND PRACTICAL INFORMATION

The İzmir-Aydın road, **Atatürk Cad,** is one of Selçuk's main drags. **Dr. Sabri Yayla Bulvarı,** also called **Kuşadası Cad.,** meets Atatürk Cad. from the west, and **Şahabettin Dede Cad.** meets Atatürk Cad. from the east to form the town's main crossroads.

Buses: The **otogar** is at the intersection of Şahabettin Dede Cad. and Atatürk Cad. To: **Ankara** (9hr., 9:30pm, US$18); **Bodrum** (3hr., every hr. 7:30am-8:30pm, 10:30pm, 12:30am; US$9); **Fethiye** (6hr., every 2hr. 8am-9:30pm, US$12); **İstanbul** (10hr.; May-Sept. 7 per day 9:45am-midnight, Oct.-Apr. 3 per day; US$19.50); **İzmir** (1hr., every 20min. 6:30am-8:30pm, US$3.25); **Marmaris** (4hr., every 2hr. 8am-9pm, US$8). **Minibuses** run to **Kuşadası** (20min.; every 20min. May-Sept. 6:30am-midnight, Oct.-Apr. 6:30am-8:30pm; US$1.20). To get to **Pamukkale** go first to **Denizli** (3hr., every 30min. 8am-8pm, US$5.75) and then catch a *dolmuş* (20min.). From May-Sept., you can take a bus directly to **Pamukkale** (3hr.; 9:30am, return 5pm; US$7.30).

Tourist Office: 35 Agora Çarşısı, Atatürk Mah. (☎892 63 28; fax 892 69 45; email info@selcukephesus.gen.tr; www.selcuk.gov.tr or www.selcukephesus.gen.tr), at the intersection of Kuşadası Cad. and Atatürk Cad. Free city maps. English spoken. Open M-F 8:30am-noon, 1-5:30pm; Apr.-Dec. also open Sa-Su 9am-5pm.

Banks: Türkiye İş Bankası, İsabey Mah., 17 Namık Kemal Cad. (☎892 61 09 or 892 65 14), under the aqueduct. Exit the PTT, turn left, and walk 1 block. **Currency** and **traveler's check exchange** and a V/MC/Cirrus/Plus **ATM.** Open M-F 8:30am-5:30pm.

Police: (☎892 60 16), office beside Türkiye İş Bankası, and a booth at the corner of the *otogar* on Atatürk Cad.

Hospital: (☎892 70 36), across Kuşadası Cad. from the tourist office.

Internet Access: Australian New Zealand Pension (see below). US$1 per hr.

PTT: 1006 Sok. No. 9 (☎892 90 65 or 892 64 25), 1 block west of All Blacks Pension (walk away from train tracks) on Cengiz Topel Cad. Full service 8:30am-12:30pm, 1:30-5:30pm. **Currency, traveler's check exchange,** and **phone** open daily 8am-11pm. **Postal code:** 35920.

▌ ACCOMMODATIONS

▧**Artemis Guest House,** Atatürk Mah., 1012 Sok. No. 2 (☎892 61 91; email jimmy@egenet.com.tr; www.artemisguesthouse.com). Guests are greeted with a refreshment, shown to a carpeted room complete with bath and towels, invited to join the BBQ in the garden (every other night, US$5), and finally, welcomed to retire either to a cushion in the tree-house lounge to smoke fruit tobacco in the water-pipe, or to watch one of Jimmy's 100 movies. One of the few gay-friendly establishments in Turkey. Arranges group excursions to the *hammam* for women. Free transportation to Ephesus, and to Pamucak and Tusan beaches in the morning. Internet US$1.50 per hr. Laundry US$5. Breakfast US$2. US$5 per person. 2 hotel-style rooms with A/C US$30 per night. V.

▧**All Blacks Hotel and Pension,** Atatürk Mah., 1011 Sok. No. 1 (☎892 36 57; email abnomads@egenet.com.tr; www.allblacks.8m.com). Named after the famous Kiwi rugby squad. Ultra-clean floors and bathrooms. Rooftop terrace with views of the fortress and the Roman aqueducts. Free transportation to and from Ephesus, Pamucak Beach, and Kuşadası harbor. Ring the bell to enter. Guest kitchen. Laundry US$4 per load. Internet US$2.50 per hr. Breakfast US$1.60. Singles US$6; doubles US$12; triples US$18.

Australian New Zealand Pension, 7 Prof. Miltner Sok. (☎892 60 50; www.anzturkishguesthouse.com), behind the museum. Nightly BBQs and Turkish dinners (vegetarian options available). Free service to Ephesus and the beach. Trips to

Mary's House and Şirince for groups of 3 or more. Boat tickets to Samos (Apr.-Nov., US$30) and winter trekking packages available. 20% discounts for trekking groups larger than 7. Laundry US$5 per load. Internet US$1 per hr. Breakfast included. Dorms $3; $5 per person, with bath US$6.50. 15% discount for *Let's Go* readers.

Diana Pension, Zafer Mah., 3004 Sok. No. 30 (☎892 12 65; jesseakin@hotmail.com), beyond the railroad tracks. After crossing the bridge, walk 50m with the track on your left, turn right onto 3008 Sok, walk 3 blocks, and turn left onto 3004 Sok. Immaculate rooms and bathrooms. All-you-can-eat BBQ ($5). Free transport to Ephesus. Guest kitchen. 24hr. hot water. Laundry $5. Breakfast $3.25. $6.50 per person with bath.

🍴 FOOD

🍴 **Karameşe Restaurant** (☎892 04 66), Tarihi İsabey Camii Önü, beside İsa Bey Camii. A maze of stone paths wind through miniature waterfalls, fountains, and gazebos. Bench seating or low tables surrounded by cushions available. In the rear, a miniature zoo is home to swans, monkeys, and even camels. All *ayran* and yogurt made with milk from on-site cows. *Gözleme* US$1-2; *çop şiş* US$3.25; *ayran* US$.50. Open daily 9am-1am.

Özdamar Restaurant, Atatürk Mah., 33 Cengiz Topel Cad. (☎892 00 97). Outdoor seating with a view of the castle. Dine on just about any Turkish dish imaginable. Choose from pizza (Italian or Turkish), fish *kebaps, döner kebap* (US$2.40), cold dishes (US$1), or mixed grill (US$3.25). Open daily 8am-midnight. V, MC, AmEx.

Eski Ev (Old House) Restaurant and Cafe, Atatürk Mah., 1005 Sok. No. 1/A (☎892 93 57), around the block from the PTT. Quiet dining in the garden of a century-old home. Mixed *mezze* plate US$1.60; *gözleme* US$1.25-1.50; lamb *şiş kebap* US$2.80; bottle of Pamukkale wine US$6.50. Open daily 8am-1am.

👁 SIGHTS

Selçuk's archaeological sights have always been overshadowed by the towering majesty of neighboring Ephesus. However, they should not be overlooked.

BASILICA OF ST. JOHN. The colossal and unadvertised Basilica of St. John lies on the site of St. John's grave. The Byzantine church's entrance is inaccurately called the **Gate of Persecution;** believed to depict a Christian being thrown to a lion, it in fact shows Achilles slaying a lion. If it were reconstructed today, it would be the 7th-largest cathedral in the world. *(Open daily 8am-6:30pm. US$2.50.)*

İSA BEY CAMİİ. This stunning Selçuk mosque, built in 1375 on the order of Aydınoğlu İsa Bey, it features columns taken from Ephesus, which the Ephesians had pilfered from Aswan, Egypt. Inside the courtyard is an enormous collection of well-preserved Ottoman and Selçuk tombstones and inscriptions. The façade features Persian-influenced geometric black and white stone inlay. *(Open daily 10min. before and 10min. after times of prayer.)*

EFES MÜSEZİ. Back in town, directly across from the town's tourist office, Selçuk's **Efes Müzesi (Ephesus Museum)** houses a world-class collection of recent Hellenistic and Roman finds from Ephesus. Most of the earlier finds are in Vienna. The collection includes the infamous statue of **Beş** (Priapus) that graces postcards throughout Turkey, rather tastelessly displayed in peep-show setting: push the button for a 10-second glimpse. While this particular piece was found in the vicinity of the Ephesian brothels, the image of the erect, and generously endowed, demi-god was not a smutty novelty, but rather a fairly common piece of iconographic currency in the ancient world. The museum also houses an excellent collection of statuary. *(Open daily 8:30am-noon, 1-5:30pm. US$5.)*

TEMPLE OF ARTEMIS. A few hundred meters down Dr. Sabri Yayla Bul., walking away from town with the tourist office on your right, are the sad remains of the

Temple of Artemis. Once the largest temple in the ancient world, it's now a reconstructed column twisting upward from a bog that approximates the area of the temple's foundation. *(Open daily 8:30am-5:30pm. Free.)*

HOUSE OF THE VIRGIN MARY. Nearer to Selçuk than to any other town, but still a US$21 round-trip cab ride away, the tranquil House of the Virgin Mary lies 100m off the road from Ephesus to Bülbüldağı (Nightingale Mountain). About five years after the death of Christ, St. John is said to have accompanied the Virgin Mary to Ephesus, where they lived in a small house on the slopes of Bülbüldağı. It is a popular pilgrimage destination for both Christians and Muslims, who leave wishes and prayers in the form of tissue tied to chain-link screens.

PAMUKKALE (HIERAPOLIS) ☎258

Whether as modern Pamukkale ("Cotton Castle") or ancient Hierapolis ("Holy City"), this village has been drawing the weary and the curious to its thermal springs for more than 23 centuries. The Turkish name refers to the extraordinary surface of the shimmering, snow-white limestone, shaped over millennia by calcium-rich springs. Legend has it that the formations are actually solidified cotton (the area's principal crop) that giants left out to dry. Most of the terraces are currently under restoration. In any case, the site remains impressive, even if it is not open for bathing. Overshadowed by natural wonders, Pamukkale's well-preserved Roman ruins and museum have gone unadvertised by travel agencies.

ORIENTATION AND PRACTICAL INFORMATION

Pamukkale is roughly divided into two areas: **Pamukkale Köyü**, or village, is home to hotels and restaurants; the **Pamukkale site** contains the pools and the ruins of Hierapolis. The road to the tourist complex begins from the central square, curves around to the left (past bus company offices), and heads uphill to the site, tracing the course of an ancient road. It's also possible to ascend to the top of the deposits by climbing up the calcium mountain face starting from the main square.

Buses to Pamukkale stop in Cumhuriyet Meydanı in the center of **Pamukkale Köyü**. Most direct buses come from Kuşadası and pass through Selçuk (3½hr.; daily May-Aug. 9:15, 9:30, 9:45am; return 5pm; US$5), but the more common route is through Denizli. **Dolmuş** run between Denizli and the beginning of the Pamukkale walking path, where Atatürk Cad. meets Mehmet Akif Ersoy Bul. (25min., every 15min. 6:45am-11pm, US$.50). Otherwise, a pension can arrange free pick-up from the Denizli *otogar*. At the top of the hill within the site gates are: the **tourist office** (☎272 20 77; fax 272 28 82; open May-Sept. 8am-noon and 1:30-6:45pm; in winter M-F 8:30am-noon and 1-5pm); **tourist police** (☎272 29 09; open 24hr.); and the **PTT** (☎ 272 21 21; open daily 8:30am-7pm). **Pharmacies** can be found in the village.

ACCOMMODATIONS AND FOOD

Both hotels listed have swimming pools filled with Pamukkale thermal water and offer free pickup from the Denizli bus station. ▓**Koray Hotel,** 27 Fevzi Çakmak Cad., has carpeted rooms around an inner courtyard, where guests can relax and eat their meals by the pool. It also offers TV, a bar, Internet access, laundry, and a restaurant for winter dining. Unlimited dinner buffet US$5. (☎272 23 00; fax 272 20 95. Breakfast buffet included. Singles US$12; doubles US$18.) With a warm welcome to backpackers, ▓**Meltem Motel,** 9 Kuzey Sok., just outside Cumhuriyet Meydanı, offers satellite TV with stereo sound for nightly movie showings. Owner Ali Baba takes guests on daily trips to the red springs, his "secret waterfall," and a nearby mud bath for a "magic massage" (US$12). Blue tiled rooms all have bath. Enjoy the view of Pamukkale mountain from the top-floor restaurant/lounge. (☎272 24 13; fax 272 24 14; email meltemmotel@superonline.com.tr. Internet US$1.60 per hr. Laundry US$4. Breakfast US$2. US$5 per person; dorm US$4.)

Most of the pensions serve better dinners than those available in town. The large buffet at the **Koray Hotel** is the best option. **Konak Sade**, on Atatürk Cad., has a traditional Turkish salon and pool-side terrace seating with a view of cornfields and the Pamukkale mountain. (☎272 20 02. Chicken US$2.50; *kebap* US$3.65; ice cream US$2. Free swimming for diners. Open daily 7:30am-2am.) **Pamukkale Cafe-Bar-Restaurant**, 13 Cumhuriyet Meydanı, features 5 fixed menus: 2 vegetarian (US$3.25); 3 including wine and either fish, chicken, or *kebap* (US$5-6). A la carte dining also available. (☎272 21 90. Open daily 9am-midnight.) Although Pamukkale's nightlife doesn't rage like the coast's, there are still some spots for drinking and dancing. Try **Paşa Disco and Bar**, where Atatürk Cad. meets Mehmet Akif Ersoy Bul. (Beer US$1.60. Open daily 9pm-2am.)

👁 SIGHTS

BATHS. A favorite getaway for vacationing Romans almost two millennia ago, the warm baths at Pamukkale still bubble away. Elegant, shallow pools at the top of the hill gradually deepen farther down the slope, while the center of the formation is graced with intricately shaped terraces. All pools are now off-limits to public bathing due to overuse, but small walkways leading down the slope still allow barefoot visitors to touch the thermal waters. Don't leave Pamukkale without a savory dip in the **Sacred Spring** at the Pamukkale Motel, the only place where you can still swim in the warm, fizzy waters. On the pool's floor rest remains of Roman columns, toppled by the earthquake that created the spring. *(Site open 24hr. US$5.50. Spring open daily 8am-8pm, until 6pm in winter. US$5 for 2hr.)*

RUINS OF HIERAPOLIS. Carved into the side of the mountain, the enormous **Grand Theater** is one of the best-preserved in Turkey; many carved stage decorations and much of the 25,000-person seating area remain intact. In front of the theater are the lesser preserved remains of the 3rd-century **Temple of Apollo** and the **nymphaeum,** a fountain temple dedicated to those frisky nymphs. Ancient priests performed rituals at the nearby **Plutonium** (a.k.a. *Cin Deliği* or "Devil's Hole"), a pit emitting toxic carbonic acid gas. After demonstrating the hole's potency by killing off a couple birds, the priests would duck inside while holding their breath, then reemerge having supposedly made a trip to the underworld. Down the road to Karahayıt are the north **city gate,** the ruins of a 5th-century Christian **basilica** dedicated to St. Philip (martyred here 1000 years ago), and a **necropolis,** holding some 1200 tombs and sarcophagi. These plots were prime real estate; it was believed that proximity to the hot springs and vapor-emitting cracks would ease one's trip to the underworld. *(Behind the Pamukkale Motel.)*

NEAR PAMUKKALE: GEYRE (APHRODISIAS)

Perfect for a daytrip from Pamukkale. Buses leave daily (2hr.; depart 10am, return 5pm; round-trip US$10). Site open daily in summer 8:30am-7:30pm; in winter 8:30am-5pm. Museum open daily 9am-6:30pm; in winter 8am-5pm. Site US$4; museum US$4.

The ruins of Aphrodisias are still very much under excavation, but some archaeologists predict that they will eclipse Ephesus in grandeur after another 50 to 60 years. Ancient Greeks came here to pay respects to the goddess of love, **Aphrodite,** and ask for her blessing. Aphrodisias was well-known as a center for astronomy, medicine, and mathematics, but above all as a showcase for sculpture chiseled from the famed white and bluish-gray marble quarried in the nearby foothills. The highlights of a visit to Aphrodisias are the three magnificent structures at the back of the site. The soaring Ionic columns of the **Temple of Aphrodite** mark the original home of a famous statue of the goddess. Sculpted nearly 2000 years ago, the statue was similar in appearance to the many-breasted Artemis of Ephesus. So far, only copies of the original have been unearthed. The grand **tetrapylon,** the gateway into the ancient city, has elegant spiral-fluted Corinthian columns and floral reliefs on its pediment. Its name, which means "four gateways" in Greek, refers to the four rows of four columns that comprise the structure. The ancient 30,000-seat **stadium** is one of the most intact ever excavated. Even the marble blocks that once marked the starting line for foot races remain in the central arena. The new **museum,** near the site entrance, displays an impressive collection of Roman-era sculpture. Among the highlights are the large statues of Aphrodite, her priests, and a satyr carrying the child Dionysus.

BODRUM ☎252

Before it became the "Bedroom of the Mediterranean," the ancient city of Halicarnassus was known for Herodotus, the "father of history," and the 4th-century BCE Mausoleum of Halicarnassus. The latter's tomb was so magnificent that it was declared one of the Seven Wonders of the Ancient World, and the king's memory lives on in the word "mausoleum." While Bodrum's night scene is the most notorious in Turkey, the surrounding Acadian Peninsula is famous for its silica beaches, lush forests, secluded swimming coves, and ancient ruins. As multitudes of Turkish jetsetters, international yachtsmen, backpackers, and package tourists attest, it's easy to get sucked into Bodrum's daily rhythm of sun, shopping, sight-seeing, and water sports—but all of these relatively innocent activities are a mere prelude to the bacchanalian delights that begin once night falls.

✦🛈 ORIENTATION AND PRACTICAL INFORMATION

Bodrum's most prominent landmark is the central **Castle of St. Peter** (*kale*), from which several streets radiate. From the castle, **Cumhuriyet Cad.,** the main commercial drag, runs along the beach, twisting slightly inland to allow room for a small beach before returning to the sea. Ferries and yacht cruises depart from the breakwater and **Kale Cad.,** which runs from the left side of the castle and ends at a mosque. The ever-popular **Atatürk Cad.** stems to the right off **Cevat Şakir Cad.**

Flights: The **Bodrum Airport** is about 30min. out of town. Buses to the airport depart from the *otogar* (US$5). **Turkish Airlines,** 208 Neyzen Tevfik Cad. (☎313 31 72). Open daily 9am-5pm. International flights go through İstanbul. To **İstanbul** and **Ankara** (both 1hr., 4 per day 6:10am-9:15am, US$90).

Buses: The *otogar* is on Cevat Şakir Cad. To: **Antalya** (8hr., 9:45am and 10:15pm, US$12); **İstanbul** (12hr., 6 per day, US$19-26); **İzmir** (4hr., 2am-6pm, US$7); **Kuşadası** (2½hr., 2am-6pm, US$6); **Pamukkale** (5hr.; 8:30, 10:30am, 3:30pm; US$7); and **Selçuk** (3hr., 2am-6pm, US$8).

Dolmuş: Depart from the *otogar* to **Marmaris** (3hr., every hr. 7am-8pm, US$6).

Ferries and Hydrofoils: Bodrum Express Lines (☎316 40 67; fax 313 00 77) has offices in the *otogar* and near the castle. All ferries and hydrofoils run from the end of the jetty May-Sept. To **Marmaris** (2hr.; Th and Su 8am, return 5:30pm; US$24, round-trip US$29, open return US$39) and Greek islands such as **Kos** and **Rhodes.** Arrive at the jetty 30min. early for passport check. Call for schedule; it changes depending on the season.

Car and Moped Rentals: Botur Agency (☎313 90 52), on Cevat Şakir Cad. Cars US$36-96 per day, mopeds US$14-72 per day.

Tourist Office: 48 Barış Meydanı (☎316 10 91; fax 316 76 94), at the foot of the castle. Pension information and room listings. Free brochures with maps. Open Apr.-Oct. daily 8:30am-5:30pm; Nov.-Mar. M-F 8am-noon and 1-5pm.

Travel Agencies: Botur, 24/A Cevat Şakir Cad. (☎316 90 52). Open daily 9am-10:30pm. Organizes bus trips to: **Pamukkale** and **Ephesus** (2 days; W and Sa 7:30am, return Th and Su 8pm; US$45 includes overnight stay in a 4-star hotel); **Dalyan and Kaunos** (12½ hr.; Th and Su 7:30am, return 8pm; US$20). **Village tour** (11am, return 4pm; US$8).

TO
MILAS

N

Dervis Görgün Cad.

Mümtaz Ataman Sok.

Onurça Dere Sok.

Artemis Cad.

Üçkuluyar Cad.

Cevat Şakir Cad.

MARKETS

Huseyin Özsoy Nafiz Cad.

Kulcüoğlu Sok.

Stadium

Türkkuyusu Cad.

Atatürk Cad.

Cumhuriyet Cad.

Halikarnas Disco

BEACH

Kumbahçe Bay

Dr. Alim Bey Cad.

Kale Cad.

Belediye
Meyd Cad.

Gerence Sok.

Turgut Reis Cad.

Hamam Sok.

Mausoleum

Kanlıdere Sok.

Turkish
Airlines

Neyzen Tevfik Cad.

Fırkateyn Sok.

Afer Paşa
Cad.

Antique
Theatre

Kıbrıs Şehitleri Cad.

TO
PENINSULAR BEACHES
AND GÜMBET

West Harbor

Fortress

Ferry
Dock

Aegean Sea

TURKEY

Bodrum
ACCOMMODATIONS
Aşkin Pansiyon, 1
Emiko Pansiyon, 2
Sevin Pansiyon, 3"
Uslu Pension, 4

Consulate: UK, Kıbrıs Şehitleri Ca. no. 421 1B (☎317 00 93/4), in Konacik. A 15min. bus ride from Bodrum. M-Th 9am-12:30pm, 2:30-4:30pm.

Currency Exchange: At the PTT from 8:30am-midnight. Most exchange booths along the harbor on Kale Cad. and along Cumhuriyet Cad. do not charge commission.

ATMs: Cirrus/Plus/MC/V ATMs throughout the shopping areas. **Türkiye İş Bankası** (☎316 10 12), on Cevat Şakır Cad., is about halfway between the bus station and the castle. Open M-F 9am-12:30pm and 1:30-5:30pm.

Laundromats: Mainly on Türkkuyusu Cad., Cevat Şakir Cad., and Atatürk Cad. US$4 per load. Most open daily 8am-10pm.

Hammam: A new *hammam* has recently been built in a convenient location across from the *otogar*. Open M-Sa 8:30am-midnight.

Police: 50 Barış Meydanı (☎316 10 04). At the foot of the castle, next to the tourist office. Open 24hr. **Emergency Police:** (☎316 12 15).

Pharmacies: Especially prevalent on Cumhuriyet Cad., Cevat Şakir Cad., and Atatürk Cad. All open daily 8:30am-8pm. All post the nighttime on-duty pharmacy; call ☎118 to find out which one is open 24hr. for that day.

Hospital: Bodrum Devlet Hastanesi (☎313 14 20 or 313 21 27), Kıbrıs Şehitleri Cad., uphill from the amphitheater. Public. Open 24hr. **Private Bodrum Hospital** (☎313 65 66). Walk inland on Cevat Şakir Cad., take a left onto Artemis Sok., turn left onto Kulcuoğlu Sok., take the 3rd right, and then make the first right. English spoken. Open 24hr. Or try the brand spanking new **Universal Hospital** (☎317 15 15) in Konacik.

Internet Access: Palmiye Internet Cafe (☎313 91 84; fax 313 91 81; email palmiye1@efes.net.tr), on Neyzen Tevfik Cad. From the mosque in front of the castle, walk along Neyzen Tevfik Cad. for 300m; the cafe will be on the right. 9 computers with Internet access (US$3 per hr.), frozen yogurt (US$1-2), and fruit juice bars (US$1-2). Open M-Sa 10am-midnight, Su noon-midnight. Other Internet cafes can be found throughout Bodrum. Prices range from US$1.50-3 per hr.

PTT: (☎316 12 12), on Cevat Şakir Cad., 4 blocks from the *otogar* (when heading toward the castle). *Poste restante,* international phone, and faxes. Open daily 8:30am-midnight. **Postal code:** 48400.

■ ACCOMMODATIONS

Finding a bedroom in the "Bedroom of the Mediterranean" is easy (pensions are plentiful) but requires advance planning. Single travelers should call ahead in the summer. Cheap pensions cluster behind the bank right of the castle as you face inland. There are also some finds off Türkkuyusu Sok. and on Atatürk Cad.

NATAŞAS The world's oldest profession is legal in Turkey, and trafficking in **prostitutes** from the former Soviet Union (hence their Turkish name, *Nataşas,* from the common Russian name Natasha) has increased dramatically since 1989. Turkish brothels are supposed to be officially licensed and regulated by health and social service authorities. Aspiring prostitutes must attain a certificate and agree to regular AIDS and venereal disease check-ups, and a 1990 law set the penalty for abducting or raping a prostitute to be equal to that for crimes against any other woman (rather than two-thirds of the penalty, as it had been previously). According to officials, there are 56 brothels in Turkey and 2376 prostitutes, but a more realistic estimate would be close to 100,000 *Nataşas.* Many of these women are the victims of what has grown into a billion-dollar trafficking business. **Pimps** lure desperate former-Soviet-bloc women to Turkey under the pretense of employment offers, marriage, or modeling. These women are frequently abused, threatened, drugged, and raped by pimps who hold their passports and demand that they work to repay the "debt" they have accrued for being taken abroad. As illegal immigrants, they are often left with no political recourse, and their life expectancy averages a grim 35 years.

TURKEY

■ **Otel Kilavuz,** No. 50 Atatürk Cad. (☎316 38 92; fax 316 2852). From the *otogar* follow Cevat Şakir Cad. toward the castle, turning left onto Atatürk Cad. Walk 3 blocks and turn left onto Adliye Sok. This modern hotel has a garden, a pool, and a bar. Each of the 12 rooms has a large bathroom, phone, and art on the walls. Singles US$12; doubles US$16. Prices drop in off-season.

Emiko Pansiyon, Atatürk Cad., 11 Uslu Sok. (☎/fax 316 55 60; email emiko@turk.net). From the *otogar*, follow Cevat Şakir Cad. toward the water, turning left onto Atatürk Cad. After 50m, turn right down the alley marked with a sign for the Emiko Pansiyon; it's the 2nd building on your left. Run by the Anglophone Emiko, this *pansiyon* offers 8 simple rooms with hardwood floors and bath. Breakfast under the shade of grape leaves on the patio. Guest kitchen. Breakfast US$2. Laundry US$3. Singles US$15; doubles US$20.

Dönen Pansiyon (☎316 40 17). Walk inland from the taxi station on Türkkuyusu Cad.; the *pansiyon* is 3 blocks down on the left. Run by a friendly family, it has 14 lovely rooms, some with bath. Breakfast included. Laundry available. Singles US$10; doubles US$12; triples US$15.

Aşkin Pansiyon (☎313 31 67). Following Cevat Şakir Cad. from the *otogar* toward the castle, turn left onto Atatürk Cad., right down a passageway about 20m past the sign for Emiko, and then left down a corridor with the *pansiyon*'s yellow sign. The rooftop terrace has a splendid view of the sea. 10 basic rooms, some with bath. Discos nearby, so ask for a room at the back if you crave quiet. US$8 per person.

◖ FOOD

Cheap eats in Bodrum consist of the usual *kebap* stands (*kebap* and chips US$3) and the small cafeteria-style joints on Cevat Şakir Cad. (meals US$2). Corn on the cob (US$.50) is sold from small carts along the main streets, and wherever you turn, the doughy beginnings of fresh pizzas (US$6-8) are being tossed in the air.

■ **Tarçin** (☎313 87 50). Turn onto Atatürk Cad. from Cevat Şakir Cad. and turn left into the 2nd alleyway. Tarçin is 30m down, at the back of a grape-filled courtyard. Serves sumptuous homemade dishes that make use of the Bodrum market's colorful selection of fresh fruits and vegetables (US$4-9). Open M-F 8am-6pm.

■ **Sandal** (☎316 35 59). Turn onto Atatürk Cad. from Cevat Şakir Cad. and walk 5 blocks. Go straight at the Babil center spice exchange. For those craving the taste of the east, Sandal offers authentic Thai food *al fresco*. Munch on *pad thai* under the thatched roof while listening to sultry jazz tunes. Dinner around US$9. Open M-F 10am-1am.

Paradise Garden. Turn onto Atatürk Cad. from Cevat Şakir Cad. and walk until you see the large white spice exchange. Turn right. The restaurant is on your left. Eat pizza and grilled meat (US$3-5) under the shade of large cyprus and cedar trees. Glass of freshly squeezed orange juice (US$2.50). Open daily 8am-midnight.

◐ SIGHTS

RUINS OF HALICARNASSUS. Despite what everyone says about the nightlife, the ruins of ancient Halicarnassus are Bodrum's most noteworthy attraction. Unfortunately, most of the remains were either destroyed, buried beneath the modern town, or shipped to London's British Museum. The old city walls and the large but uninspiring remains of the theater are still partly visible. The Mausoleum, one of the seven wonders of the ancient world, once rose to a height of 50m, but Crusaders demolished the structure to fortify the Castle of St. Peter (see below). Covered with a pyramidal roof, the mausoleum was crowned by a statue of Mausolus driving a chariot drawn by four horses. Today the mausoleum site houses a small porch with reconstructions of the mausoleum's friezes and an open-air museum with columnar fragments. *(To reach the theater, head toward Gümbet on Kıbrıs Şehitler Cad. To reach the mausoleum, turn onto Kirkateyn Sok. from Neyzen Tevfik Cad. Theater and "mausoleum" open Tu-Su 8am-noon and 1-5:30pm; until 5pm in the off-season. US$2, students US$1.)*

TURKEY

CASTLE OF ST. PETER. Crusaders from the Knights of St. John decimated the nearby Mausoleum of Halicarnassus to construct Bodrum's formidable castle over the ruins of an ancient acropolis during the 15th and 16th centuries. Decorated with 249 coats-of-arms, the castle towers have been dubbed the English, French, German, and Italian Towers after the nations responsible for their construction. Despite their extensive fortifications, the Crusaders' towers were no match for Süleyman the Magnificent's forces, who overpowered the knights in 1523. Under Ottoman rule, the castle's importance waned, and in 1895 it was converted into a prison. The fortress now houses a museum with maritime and cultural exhibits. *(The most central landmark in Bodrum, the castle is right on the harbor. ☎316 25 16. Open Tu-Su 8am-noon and 1-5pm. US$4.80, students US$2.40.)*

🎵 ENTERTAINMENT

Bodrum, a.k.a. the "Bedroom," is a wild flesh-pot whose excesses seem to bring out everyone's extremes. All of the following except for Halikarnas Disco are on Cumhuriyet Cad. For a taste of England, hop over the western ridge of Bodrum to Gümbet, where more discos and bars can be found glittering in the night (30min. walk or 10min. *dolmuş* ride; *dolmuş* leave the *otogar* every 10 min.; US$.40).

🔳 **Halikarnas Disco**, Z. Müren Cad. At the end of Cumhuriyet Cad., one kilometer from the center of town. This famed open-air disco juts out into the ocean, where its strobe lights reflect off the sails of nearby yachts. The dressed-to-be-seen clientele dances under the gaze of spectators who pay to sit in the VIP seats. Daily shows featuring 25 performers, great music, and a celebrity-style entrance tunnel make this club the definitive Bodrum experience. US$18 cover charge includes 1 local drink. Beer US$3; cocktails US$6.

🔳 **Hadi Gari** (☎313 80 97). Next to the castle, the oldest disco in Bodrum fuses elegance and funkiness. Stylish customers get down on the large outdoor dance floor. Offers an unbeatable view of Bodrum's colorful nightlife. Beer US$3; *rakı* US$3.60; cocktails US$4-8. Restaurant open daily 6pm-midnight, dance club midnight-4am.

Karşı (☎(532) 256 44 17). Sexy bartenders and an enticing and diverse crowd make for a sultry evening of intrigue and alluring glances. The bar loudly dispenses underground, jazz, blues, and pop. Beer US$3; *rakı* US$3; cocktails US$4-8. Open daily 10am-5am.

Sensi (☎316 68 45). For a riotous ride in bar craziness, join the mostly-British crowd at Sensi, where table dancing, karaoke, and wig-wearing 70s nights keep this joint shaking. For those who dare, drown your cares in an alcoholic fishbowl (US$18). Beer US$1.80; *rakı* US$2; cocktails US$3.60-5. Open daily 5pm-5am.

MEDITERRANEAN COAST

Alternately chic, garish, and remote, the Mediterranean coast stretches along lush national parks, sunsoaked beaches, and pine forests. Natural beauty and ancient ruins have made the western Mediterranean one of Turkey's most touristed regions. Though increasingly overrun with pushy touts, Armani sportswear, and mega-hotels, the western coast also caters to those on the backpacker circuit. By day, travelers take tranquil boat trips, hike among waterfalls, and explore submerged ruins; by night, they exchange stories over Efes, dance under the stars, and fall asleep in seaside *pansiyons* and treehouses.

MARMARİS ☎252

Marmaris contains all the beach-town necessities: eclectic tourist shops, seaside restaurants, expensive yachts, a boisterous beach front, and decadent after-hours festivities. Rumor has it that Marmaris derived its name from Süleyman the Magnificent's order to "hang the architect" *(mimarı as)* of the local fortress. Exactly what was so distasteful about this understated castle is hard to say, as throngs of appreciative international tourists swarm to the landmark each summer. Some claim that the best part of Marmaris is getting away from it: boats set off from Marmaris for spectacular nearby coves and the Greek island of Rhodes.

ORIENTATION AND PRACTICAL INFORMATION

From the bus station, outside of town on Mustafa Münir Elgin Bul., take a *dolmuş* (US$.40) or taxi (US$3) to the town center on **Ulusal Egemenlik Bulvarı,** where the **Tansaş Shopping Center,** bus offices, and the *dolmuş* hub can be found. Located at the intersection of Ulusal Egemenlik Bul. and the sea, the **Atatürk Statue** is a good reference point. Facing the water at the monument, turn left down **Kordon Cad.** to reach the tourist office and harbor. **Barlar Sokak** (Bar St.) and the **castle** are also to the left. **Atatürk Cad.** and **Uzunyalı Cad.** run from the right of the statue. Atatürk Cad. leads to the popular waterfront walkway and public beach before veering right and becoming **Kemal Seyfettin Elgin Bulvarı.**

Buses: To reach the *otogar*, go down Ulusal Egemenlik Bul. from the statue and make a right onto Mustafa Münir Elgin Bul. The station is around the corner from the shopping center. Buses run to: **Ankara** (11hr.; 9:45am, 9, 10pm; US$25); **Antalya** (7hr., 11pm, US$10); **Bodrum** (3¾hr.; summer 8:30am-5:30pm, winter 8:30am-2:30pm; US$4); **Eskişehir** (10hr., 7:30pm, US$14); **Göreme** (14hr., 10:30am, US$16); **İstanbul** (12½hr.; 9am, 6, 9pm; US$20-23); **İzmir** (4½hr., 5:15am-3am; US$9); **Konya** (10hr., 7pm, US$14); **Kuşadası** (5hr., June 15-Sept. 15 10:45am, US$9); and **Pamukkale** (4½hr., 8:15am-5:15pm, US$6).

Dolmuş: Inter-city dolmuş: From the hub at the Tansaş Shopping Center to: **Bozburun** (1½hr.; high season noon, 2, 5pm; low season noon; US$2.40); **Dalaman** (2hr., 7:30am-10pm, US$3); **Fethiye** (4hr., 7:30am-10pm, US$6); **İçmeler** (10min., 7am-1am, US$.50); **Köyceğiz** (1hr., 7:30am-10pm, US$2); **Milas** (2½hr., 9am-5pm, US$6); **Muğla** (1hr., 9am-5pm, US$1.80); **Ortaca** (1½hr., 7:30am-10pm, US$2.40). **Kalkan** and **Kaş** can be reached from Fethiye, and **Dalyan** can be reached from Ortaca. **Local Dolmuş:** Two main inner-city *dolmuş* routes both start at Tansaş Shopping Center.

Tourist Office: (☎412 72 77 or 412 10 35), 250m along Kordon Cad. English-speaking and very helpful. Open daily 9am-6pm; in winter M-F 8am-5:30pm.

Budget Travel: Interyouth Hostel, Tepe Mah., 42 Sok No. 45 (☎412 36 87; fax 412 78 25), can help find cheap airline, bus, and boat tickets. Jeep and moped rentals. Extraordinary Backpacker's Cruise on the hostel's beautiful yachts (US$200 for 5 days).

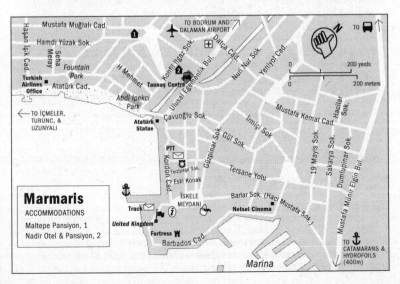

Marmaris
ACCOMMODATIONS
Maltepe Pansiyon, 1
Nadir Otel & Pansiyon, 2

Consulates: UK (☎ 412 64 86; fax 412 50 77), in Yeşil Marmaris office building on the harbor, around corner from tourist office. Open M-F 7:30am-noon and 2:30-5pm.

Police: (☎ 412 14 94), on 49 Sok., 3 blocks from the tourist office, close to the PTT.

Hospital: Esen Sağlık Medical Center (office ☎/fax 413 13 16), on Kemal Seyfettin Elgin Bul. English-speaking doctors and nurses. Open 24hr.

PTT: (☎ 412 12 12), on Fevzipaşa Cad., off Kordon Cad. **Currency exchange** 9am-10pm; **phone service** 8am-midnight; **direct money transfer** 8:30am-12:30pm and 1:30-5:30pm. **Postal truck** outside the tourist office. Open daily 8am-11pm.

ACCOMMODATIONS

Interyouth Hostel, Tepe Mah., 42 Sok. No. 45 (☎ 412 36 87; fax 412 78 23; email interyouth@turk.net). Deep within the bazaar. Hospitable managers take care of guests and non-guests alike. Not to be confused with the Interyouth Hostel at Kemeraltı Mah., 14 İyilikataş Mevkii. Book exchange, Internet access (US$4 per hr.), international phone, laundry (US$6). Sunset cruises (US$10). Can arrange cheap packages. Breakfast in the terrace bar and nightly spaghetti dinners (7:30pm, free for guests). 5-night cruises US$200. Dorms US$5; private room US$13. US$1 ISIC, HI, IYTC discount.

Nadir Otel and Pansiyon, Kemeraltı Mah., 56 Sok. (☎ 412 11 67 or 412 18 06), behind the Tansaş Shopping Center. All rooms with TV and balcony. Ask for the side away from the shopping center. The *pansiyon* has 20 rooms, some with bath. Laundry US$.60 per item. Breakfast included. Singles US$12; doubles US$17; *pansiyon* US$5 per person.

Maltepe Pansiyon, 64 Sok. No. 7 (☎ 412 16 29 or 412 84 56). Walk 400m down Ulusal Egemenlik Bul. from the Atatürk statue, turn left on G. Mustafa Muğlalı Cad., and turn left 25m from Eet Cafe. Friendly management. 18 simple rooms with bath. Breakfast US$1.80. Free use of washer and kitchen. 1- to 4- person rooms US$6 per person.

Özcan Pansiyon, Kemeraltı Mah., 3 Çam Sok. (☎ 412 77 61), next to Maltepe. 17 tidy rooms with balconies, most with bath. Communal kitchen. Colorful outside patio/bar. German spoken. Owner runs 2 boat trips to sites around Marmaris. Laundry and international phone. Breakfast US$1.80. US$6-7 per person; off-season US$5 per person.

FOOD

Kervansaray Restaurant (☎ 412 64 84). From the statue, head straight on Ulusal Egemenlik Bul., turn left on Datça Yolu, and left again on Yunus Nadi Cad.; the restaurant is on the right. For US$12, feast on a large meal with wine or beer and enjoy live Turkish music, wrestling, folk dances, and the most famous male belly dancer in Marmaris.

Marmaris Turkish Kitchen (☎ 412 40 60). In the bazaar on the left, 1 block past the PTT. Simple Turkish cooking served *al fresco*. Salads US$1.80; omelettes US$3; meat US$3-7. Everything comes with a huge piece of delicious Turkish flat bread.

Eet Cafe Mozart, Org. Muğlalı Cad. #1-2-4 (☎ 413 87 64). Head straight down Ulusal Egemenlik Bul. and turn left on the street after Tansaş Shopping Center; this charming Dutch cafe/patisserie/restaurant is on the right. Serves European fare (fish and chips wrapped in newspaper US$8.50). Turkish and English breakfasts US$2-3; apple tart US$3; croissants US$1. Open daily 8:30am-12:30am.

Internet Cafe (☎ 413 72 37), Yat Limanı. Breezy patio and colorful antique-filled interior. Turkish dishes and vegetarian options US$2-5; moist homemade cakes and cookies US$1.50. Open daily 9am-2am.

ENTERTAINMENT

It is hard to tell which is hotter in Marmaris: the burning sun or the blazing nightlife. 11pm is showtime for Barlar Sok., Uzunyalı Cad., and Barbados Cad. (the harbor), when bars and clubs kick into high gear. Loud, bright, contagious music and neon lights spill onto the street.

TURKEY

To reach **Barlar Sok.** (Bar St.), take the left road next to the tourist office (when facing the office), turn left into the bazaar at the next corner, and walk straight. Let the music and lights be your guide. **Uzunyalı** is on the opposite side of Marmaris, right on the waterfront. **Barbados Cad.** is the pavement along the harbor. Most bars and clubs have no cover. Unless otherwise noted, all are open daily year-round. At bars with both indoor and outdoor seating, drinks are usually cheaper outside.

Backstreet (☎412 40 48). On Bar St. An open-air tropical oasis. Ultra-hip dancers groove to international rock and pop, while onlookers chill under palm trees along a tiny creek. Beer US$3; *rakı* US$3.50; cocktails US$4-8. Open May-Sept. daily 9am-4am.

Greenhouse (☎412 50 71). Halfway down Bar St. Known for its excellent cutting-edge music and comfortable setting, this bright turquoise A/C dance club and bar is a Marmaris favorite. Beer US$2; *rakı* US$3.50; cocktails US$5-10. Open daily 9pm-5am.

Cheers (☎412 67 22). On the beach at the far end of Uzunyalı. An outrageously fun disco "theme park" featuring *Grease* and *Saturday Night Fever*. A mega sound system blasts 60s and 70s music. Beer US$1.80; *rakı* US$3.60; cocktails US$4-6 (try the special "fishbowls" and you'll be swimming home US$20). Open Apr.-Oct. daily 8am-4am.

Mavi Bar (☎412 01 97). On Barbados Cad. This simple yet elegant bar with small candlelit tables hosts live Turkish and Mediterranean folk music for a mostly Turkish crowd. Beer US$1.20; *rakı* US$1.80; cocktails US$4. Open daily 9am-1am.

SAND AND SURF

BEACHES. Only 1500m away, **Günlücek National Park** offers a small, quiet beach and picnic tables set against a lush forest with fragrant frankincense trees. Follow the harbor road past the marina and across the wooden footbridge, or catch a *dolmuş* from in front of the Tansaş Shopping Center (US.40). While the crowded beach in Marmaris proper is lively, quieter and prettier beaches in the area are accessible only by boat. Pleasant **İçmeler beach** is an easily reached exception. *Dolmuş* from the front of Tansaş Shopping Center or anywhere along Atatürk Cad go to İçmeler (10min., every 5min. 8am-1am, US.50), or take the water *dolmuş* to İçmeler from the waterfront next to the tourist office (20min., in summer 7am-7pm, US$4).

BOAT TRIPS. Water *dolmuş* going to **Turunç Beach** depart from the waterfront behind the Atatürk statue (45min., in summer every hr. 7am-7pm, US$1). Full-day boat tours stop at **Paradise Island Beach**, the **Akvaryum** (aquarium), some phosphorous caves, and the popular **Turunç Beach.** Others go to **Dalyan** and **Kaunos**, including **Turtle Beach** and **mud baths** (US$18). Most continue to the **Gölenye Springs**, whose waters reputedly cure intestinal ills; the less crowded **Kumlu Buk Beach**, near the remains of a fortress; and the tiny village of **Keçi**, in the heavily-wooded Nimara Peninsula (US$10-15 per person; lunch included). Legends say that Marc Antony imported the white sand from the Red Sea some 2100 years ago in an attempt to get Cleopatra into the sack. Those less romantically-inclined suspect that fossilized plankton make the sand so white. Take a boat to Kleopatra's Island through an organized tour (45min., in summer 17 per day from 10:30am, return 7pm.) Book through a travel agency.

FETHİYE
☎252

Fethiye rests peacefully on a harbor surrounded by pine forests and mountains. Most visitors take daytrips to Ölüdeniz and the Butterfly Valley by day and enjoy Fethiye's winding streets and low-key nightlife come sundown.

GETTING THERE AND GETTING AROUND. Ulusoy (☎612 37 37), **Kamil Koç** (☎612 06 36 or 614 19 73), and **Pamukkale** bus companies serve Fethiye. **Buses** run to **Ankara** (9hr.; 10, 10:30, 11pm; US$19); **Antalya** (4hr., 2:30pm and 2:30am, US$7); **Bodrum** (5hr., 5 per day 8:30am-4pm, US$8); **Bursa** (10hr.; 5, 9:30, 10:30pm;

US$14.50); **Çanakkale** (12hr., 12:15pm, US$17); **Cappadocia** (13hr., 6pm, US$14.50); **Eskişehir** (7hr., 9:30 and 10:30pm, US$12), **İstanbul** (13hr., 7 per day 5pm-11:30pm, US$24); **İzmir** (6½hr., 5:30am-12:30am, US$10.80); **Kaş** (2hr., 4am-5:30pm, US$3.60); **Marmaris** (2½hr., 12:30-6:30pm, US$4.80); **Pamukkale** (4½hr.; 9:30am, noon, 3:15, 4:30pm; US$6); **Selçuk** (6hr., 6:15am-12:30am, US$10.80). **Dolmuş** run from the *dolmuş* stop near the intersection of Hastane and Atatürk Cad. to **Çalış Beach** (5min., every 5min. 7am-1am, US$.40); **Ölüdeniz** (20-25min., every 10min. 7am-9pm, US$1); **Saklıkent** (45min., every 30min. 7am-7pm, US$2). *Dolmuş* run to **Kayaköy** from the main *dolmuş* station on Atatürk Cad. (40min., every hr. 7am-7pm, US$1.20). **Dolmuş boats** to **Çalış Beach** leave from the waterfront to the right of the main harbor (every 20min. 9:30am-8pm, every 30min. 10pm-midnight; US$2). On Atatürk Cad., across from the Atatürk head, there is a 24hr. taxi service. (☎614 44 77.) **Abalı Rent,** between the antique theater and the entrance to the old town, rents mopeds. (☎614 95 36. US$20 per day. Open daily 8am-midnight.)

■🖉 **ORIENTATION AND PRACTICAL INFORMATION.** The *otogar* is 2km from the center of town, on the way to Ölüdeniz. If there are no *servis* shuttles to the town center, leave the terminal, cross the street, and wait for a *dolmuş* heading to Fethiye (10min., frequent, US$.40). The *dolmuş* runs on the main street, **Atatürk Cad.,** past a mosque, PTT, and the Atatürk head. **Çalış Beach** is to the right along **Sedir Sok.,** which becomes **Akdeniz Cad.** The anglophone **Tourist Office,** 1/A İskele Meydanı, past the PTT, offers map and lodging info. (☎/fax 614 15 27. Open daily 8:30am-5pm; in winter M-F 8am-5pm.) **Fetur,** past the tourist office on Fevzi Çakmak Cad., arranges flights and tours. (☎614 20 34; fax 614 38 45; www.fethiye-net.com. Open daily 9am-5:30pm.) **Garfield Tourism and Travel Agency,** on Fevzi Çakmak Cad., offers 3-day cruises (US$119 in high season; B.Y.O.B.) (☎614 93 12; fax 614 25 93.) The **European Diving Center** (☎614 97 71; fax 614 97 72) offers beginning and advanced scuba dives (US$60). Several banks with 24hr. **ATMs** line Atatürk Cad. **Money exchange** open daily 8:30am-5:30pm. The **Police** (☎614 10 40) are around the corner from the tourist office, near the ancient theater. A larger branch (☎614 13 09) is on Atatürk Cad., across from the PTT. **Kestepli Eczanesi Pharmacy** is across from the mosque. The 🖾**Letoon Hospital,** on Patlanak Mahaller Cad., has English-speaking doctors. (☎612 54 84. Open 24hr.) The public **Devlet Hastanesi** (☎614 40 17 or 614 40 18) is near the PTT at the intersection of Atatürk and Hastane Cad. **Internet Cafe,** on Atatürk Cad. next to Imagine Bookstore, has Internet access. (US$1.80 per hr. Open daily 9am-midnight.) The Ferah Pansiyon also offers Internet access to guests. The **PTT,** on Atatürk Cad., offers *poste restante,* international phone calls, money exchange, and fax. **Postal code:** 48300.

🛏🍴 **ACCOMMODATIONS AND FOOD.** Cheap *pansiyons* cluster around Hastane Cad. and Fevzi Çakmak Cad. 🖾**Ferah Pansiyon,** 2 Karagözler Ordu Cad. No. 21, is one of the best hostels in Turkey, with spacious rooms (most with bath) and a free pool. (☎/fax 614 28 16; call for free pickup from the *otogar.* Laundry US$3. Dinner US$5. Breakfast included. Dorms US$3.60; rooms US$10-12.) Down the street from the Ferah Pansiyon, the 🖾**Artemis Pansiyon** offers 14 bright rooms with balconies and bath. It also has a beautiful terrace and a gourmet chef. (☎612 49 80; fax 612 50 13. Breakfast included. Singles US$8; doubles US$14.) 🖾**Meğri Lokantası,** Cumhuriyet Mah. 13/A Çarşı Cad., off Atatürk Cad. by the harbor, features an enormous selection of sumptuous Turkish fare. (☎614 40 74; fax 612 04 46. *Mezze* US$1.40, *şiş* US$3.60. Open 24hr.) **Yörükoğlu,** on Çarşı Cad., serves huge "Turkish burritos." (☎612 20 64. US$2. Open daily 8am-1am.) The large, outdoor **Meğri Restaurant,** in the main square of the bazaar, specializes in fresh fish. (☎614 40 47. Fish US$4-7; *mezze* US$2. Open daily 9am-1am.)

🎭 **ENTERTAINMENT.** **Ottoman Bar,** on the right, before Maman Sok. runs into Çarşı Cad., is fit for a pasha: fragrant smoke drifts from the large selection of water pipes as the crowd lounges outdoors or dances. (☎612 11 48. Water pipe US$3.60; beer US$1.80; *rakı* US$2. Open daily noon-3am.) **Car Cemetery Bar,** 33 Hamam

Sok., across from the old *hammam* in the old city, offers beer amidst deceased car parts. Cocktail names like "orgasm" and "slippery nipple" will be sure to spice up your evening. (☎614 11 81. Beer US$1.80; *rakı* US$2; cocktails US$4-6. Open daily 10am-4am.) Everybody dance now at tourist favorite **The Music Factory,** on Hamam Sok., a pumping metallic cage with two levels of flashing dance floors. (☎617 51 72. Beer US$1.80; *rakı* US$2; cocktails US$2-6. Open daily 5pm-5am.)

NEAR FETHİYE: ÖLÜDENİZ AND THE BUTTERFLY VALLEY Dolmuş
boats to Butterfly Valley leave from Ölüdeniz (45min.; 11am, 2, 6pm; return 8am, 1, 5pm; US$3). Blue Lagoon is a 20min. walk or US$6 taxi ride from the dolmuş station. Park and lagoon open daily 6:30am-9pm. US$1.20, students US$.60. Butterfly Valley US$1, students US$.50.

The town of Ölüdeniz's main attraction is the **Blue Lagoon,** an idyllic peninsula cradled in wooded hills and lapped by shining clear water. Enter from Tabiat Park, on the right of the road from Fethiye, where potable water, bathrooms, and showers are available. The next best thing to swimming in the Blue Lagoon is seeing it from above by tandem **paragliding,** available through **Sky Sports Paragliding** (☎617 05 11). Passengers are driven to the top of Baba Dağı and given take-off and landing instructions (2hr., US$130; book in advance). The tiny turquoise bay known as ▓**Butterfly Valley** near Ölüdeniz is home to waterfalls and several species of butterfly, including the nocturnal orange and black Jersey Tiger. From the entrance to the valley, follow the blue dots up the rocky path to the two **waterfalls.** Spending the night means camping on the beach (US$1.60 per tent), renting a mattress in the treehouse (US$3 per person), or bedding down in **The Greek Home** (US$3 per person). All accommodations have toilets and showers. Food is readily available at the local eatery (US$4 per plate). It isn't hard to find **The Rock Cafe,** built into the sides of the cliffs (juices and stronger drinks US$1.50).

KAŞ   ☎242
Sandwiched between the depths of the sea and the stunning heights of the mountains, cosmopolitan Kaş is refreshingly hassle-free. Its streets are lined with inexpensive, hospitable places to stay, excellent restaurants, and laid-back bars. Kaş is a great base for exploring the sunken city of **Kevova** and the beautiful beaches of the Blue Caves nearby.

▐ ⁊ GETTING AROUND AND PRACTICAL INFORMATION. Buses run from the *otogar*, uphill on Atatürk Cad., to **Ankara** (11hr., 8:30pm, US$19); **Antalya** via **Olimpos** (3hr., every 30min. 8am-10pm, US$5.40); **Bodrum** (7hr., 9am, US$10.80); **Fethiye** (2hr., 6 per day 9:30am-10pm, US$3.60); and **İstanbul** (15hr., 4 per day 6-8pm, US$24). Most of the activity centers around the small harbor along the main street, **Cumhuriyet Cad.** At its west end near the mosque, Cumhuriyet Cad. intersects **Hastane Cad.** before becoming **Atatürk Cad.** At its east end near the Atatürk statue, Cumhuriyet Cad. intersects **Çukurbağlı Cad.** (also known as Şübe Sok.), which leads to the PTT. From the Atatürk statue, **Hükümet Cad.** passes above the harbor to the two beaches. The street going uphill behind the tourist office—the one with most of the souvenir shops—is **Uzun Çarşı Cad.** The **tourist office,** 5 Cumhuriyet Meydanı, is to the left of the Atatürk statue. (☎836 12 38. English spoken. Open daily 8am-noon and 1-7pm; in winter M-F 8am-5pm.) Nearly all **travel agencies** have tours to **Kevova. Bougainville Travel,** 10 Çukurbağlı Cad., offers diving courses, **kayaking** trips to Kekova (US$35), and **Jeep Safaris.** (☎836 37 37; fax 836 16 05. Open daily 8:30am-10pm.) **Simena Tours,** 1 Elmalı Cad. (☎836 14 16), near the *otogar*, books airline tickets and popular daytrips to **Kevova.** For emergencies, try the **police** (☎836 10 24), across the entrance to Küçük Çalık Plaj (Little Pebble Beach). The **hospital** (☎836 11 85) is on Hastane Cad., 500m past the mosque by the tourist office. **Munise Ozan** (☎836 41 42), offers free public health services and has a certified tourism doctor. The **PTT,** on Çukurbağlı Cad., does **currency exchange** until 5pm. (☎836 14 50 or 836 14 78. Open daily 8:30am-midnight.)

TURKEY

◨◪ ACCOMMODATIONS AND FOOD. There are many *pansiyons* on the side streets to the right of Atatürk Bul. **Motel Korsan Karakedi,** 17 Yenicami Sok., is east along Hastane Cad. toward the theater, on Yenicami Cad., and left after the mosque. The motel features sea-view rooms with bath, fan, and balcony. (☎836 18 87; fax 836 30 86. Pool. English spoken. Breakfast included. US$12 per room.) **Hermes Pension,** 2 İmdi Cad., 1 block from Atatürk Cad., has clean, airy rooms with bath and balcony. (☎836 32 22. Singles US$9; doubles US$14; triples US$16.) To reach the **Spaghetti House,** turn left at the tourist office, walk 25m and take another left. (Salads US$1.20; pasta US$2-4; dessert US$2. Open daily 10am-1am.) **Don Quixote,** in the main square, is a great place to relax and people-watch. (Large salads US$1.20; pizzas US$2-4; burgers US$3. Open daily 8am-1am.)

◪ BEACHES. Kaş's two main beaches rock—both are tucked in rocky coves surrounded by rocky cliffs—and have names to prove it. The entrance to **Küçük Çalık Plajı** (Little Pebble Beach) is at the top of the hill on Hükümet Cad., while the less crowded **Büyük Çalık Plajı** (Big Pebble Beach) is 15 minutes down the road to the left of the tourist office. Most travelers who pass through Kaş take a dip in the **Blue Caves,** 15km from Kaş and home to the Mediterranean's only **seal colony.**

NEAR KAŞ

KEKOVA. The Lycian city of Kekova lies submerged beneath the clear Mediterranean waters as a result of an earthquake that struck in 25 CE. During the Hellenistic and Arab eras, the city served as a lookout post and refuge from marauding pirates. From craggy Kekova Island, it is possible to see through calm water to the underwater walls and staircases (calm seas afford views sharp enough to discern details on amphoras). Above sea level, a motley assortment of doors and walls still bear evidence of long-gone floors and ceilings. The highlight of the trip is the partially submerged Lycian sarcophagus near the village of Kale. **Swimming or snorkeling among the ruins is forbidden.** *(Trips from Kaş, often on glass-bottom boats, cost around US$30. Kayaking (US$35) allows for the best views of the ruins and some hearty exercise. Inquire at Bougainville Travel in Kaş for more details. In the morning it is less crowded, and the sea is calmer and clearer. Kekova is also reachable from Demre.)*

DEMRE AND MYRA. The ancient ruins of Myra, a mixture of Lycian rock tombs, sculptures, and a Roman theater are truly awe-inspiring. St. Paul is said to have stopped here in Demre in 61 CE on his way to Rome. Demre was the diocese of St. Nicholas, better known as **Santa Claus.** The kind-hearted saint, born in Patara (60km west of Demre), became the Bishop of Myra in the early 4th century. In addition to Santa, the town has a nearby beach and cold springs accessible by car.

Myra was one of the most important cities in the Lycian League, a federation that included 70 cities, including Xanthos, Patara, Olimpos, and Tlos. Myra is divided into three areas: the **sea necropolis** in the southwest part of the site, the **acropolis** area and its surrounding walls, and the **river necropolis.** The **rock tombs** built into the sea and the river necropolis are of particularly high quality. The site also has a **theater** with 35 consecutive rows of seats and a still-intact stage. (Open daily in summer 8am-7:30pm; in winter 8am-5:30pm. US$1.15, students US$.70.)

Demre's other major attraction is the **Church of St. Nicholas,** thought to be built on the site of the saint's tomb. An Orthodox service takes place in the theater on December 6, the anniversary of St. Nicholas's death. The 8th-century structure, which suffered centuries of neglect, was repaired by the Russian Tsar in the 19th century, only to be covered with sand and mud years later. Excavations since 1989 have uncovered new rooms and treasures, and scholars generally agree that the tomb of St. Nicholas is in the southern nave of the church. His remains were stolen in 1087 by Italian merchants and taken to Bari, Italy, leaving behind only those that appear in the **Antalya Museum** (see p. 662; open daily 8am-7:30pm; in winter 8am-5pm; US$2.80, students US$1.85). **İpek Restaurant,** near St. Nicholas Church, dishes out Turkish specialties. (☎871 54 48. Hot *mezze* US$1.60-1.80; *pide* US$1.60. Open daily 6am-1am.) To satisfy a sweet tooth, **İnci Pastanesi**, across from the İpek restaurant, sells pastries. (Open daily 8am-11pm.)

From the *otogar*, **buses** run to: **Antalya** (3hr., every 20min. 6:45am-7:45pm, US$3); **Fethiye** (3¼hr., every hr. 9am-10pm, US$4.65); **Kaş** (1hr., every 30min. 8:30am-10pm, US$1.40). **Myra Otogar Taksi** has taxis (☎871 43 43) at the *otogar*. Other services include: **banks** and an **ATM** on Noel Baba Cad., including a Türkiye İş Bankaşı on the way to St. Nicholas Church (open daily 11am-5:30pm); a **police station** (☎871 42 21), near the *otogar*; and a **PTT** (☎871 55 19), 200m to the right of the T-junction (open daily 8:30am-6pm). **Postal code:** 07570.

OLİMPOS ☎242

Enchanting Olimpos is a true backpacker's town, one of the few budget spots along the Turkish Riviera. Olimpos brings travelers closer to the heavens by giving them the chance to make a nighttime ascent of the Chimaera, where a naturally occurring flame has burned since ancient times, and sleep in **treehouses**, charming *pansiyons* that perch in the trees along the dirt road to the beach and ruins.

⌐▊ GETTING AROUND AND PRACTICAL INFORMATION

To get to Olimpos from Antalya, take a Kaş- or Demre-bound bus and ask to be let off at Olimpos. From Kaş, take an Antalya-bound bus. **Buses** stop at a rest station on the main road. From there, **dolmuş** run down the 10km dirt road that leads to the treehouses (15min., every hr. 9:30am-6:30pm, US$1.15), dropping passengers off at the pensions of their choice. Olimpos has **no PTT, pharmacy, bank,** or **police station.** Many pension owners accept US dollars, offer international phone calls, and arrange tours that include trekking or rafting. **Postal code:** 07350.

▊ ACCOMMODATIONS

All prices for treehouses include breakfast and dinner. **Şaban Pansiyon** is a welcoming family-run pension with tasty dinners and 24hr. service to Antalya airport for US$42. (☎892 12 65. US$7 per person; doubles US$20; camping US$6.) **Carreta Carreta,** across the road from Şaban, has some of the largest, best-quality, and sturdiest treehouses in town. (US$7 per person.) More like a sprawling Ewok village than a pension, **Kadir's Yörük Treehouses** is a post-adolescent summer camp: volleyball and ping-pong included. (☎892 12 50; fax 892 11 10. Dorm beds US$6; doubles US$14; bungalows US$13 per person.) Kadir's hits puberty after dark, though, when it becomes the focus of Olimpos nightlife (beer US$1.15; cocktails US$2.35).

▨ SIGHTS

▨**CHIMAERA.** Olimpos's proximity to this perpetual natural flame in the mountainside (once so bright that ships navigated by it) inspired the residents of the city to worship Hephaestos, god of fire and the forge. Today's Olimpians are less reverent: most bring marshmallows to toast. The ancients believed the flame was the breath of the Chimaera, a mythical beast that was part lion, part goat, part serpent—and pure evil. Geologists have not produced a better explanation, but they suspect natural gas plays a role. (*Best seen at night. Ask pension owners about bus tours (2½hr., 9:30pm, US$2.80). Bring a flashlight for the tricky 20min. uphill trek to the flame.*)

RUINS. The ruins at Olimpos are a jumbled pastiche of everything from ancient temples to crumbling walls of medieval castles. Follow the road from the pensions to the beach. The ruins tend to be overgrown with vines and dry bushes, and inhabited by **snakes** and **scorpions,** so be cautious when exploring. About 10m beyond the entrance booth, you can cross the dry riverbed to a row of tombs and one of the crumbling arches. If you continue on the main path about 40m farther, a small path leads off to the left, climbing uphill to a rather large but unimpressive archway. Beyond the archway it is easy to get lost in overgrown orange groves and reeds. The sign at the beginning of the pathway reads simply "temple."

On the other side of the road across the stream are the decrepit **theater** and **medieval walls.** Though it is not unusual to see locals at the stream swimming and drinking, tourists should avoid doing so. If you continue along the main path once more, you will reach the beautiful beach, where the best-preserved group of ruins looms over the water on a rocky cliff to the right. *(Open when staffed. US$2.80, students US$1.85. Hold onto your ticket stub, as it will be good for multiple entry to the beach and site.)*

ANTALYA ☎242

Capital of the so-called Turquoise Riviera and linked by air with Munich, Moscow, and Amsterdam, Antalya has spawned modern white buildings along its shoreline cliffs. Contemporary Antalya encircles Kaleiçi ("inside the fortress"), the crescent-shaped old city that brims with cobblestone streets, Ottoman houses, pensions, restaurants, boutiques, and carpet dealers. At Kaleiçi's heart, pricey eateries and cutting-edge nightclubs line the ancient walled harbor that once sheltered Roman ships. Tourism has made Antalya *très* chic and *très* Western (from its Burger King head to its Benetton toes)—so much so that it even has its own cinema celebration, the Antalya Altın Portakal ("Golden Orange") Film Festival, held every fall.

✴🔢 ORIENTATION AND PRACTICAL INFORMATION

In 1997, Antalya gave birth to a gargantuan orange **otogar,** replete with fountains, several **ATMs,** cafes, A/C, and labyrinthine bathrooms with seat toilets. Unfortunately, this wonderland is 4km out of town at **Anadolu Kavşağı,** the intersection of Namık Kemal Cad. and Dumlupınar Bul. Gray buses (US$.40) run from outside the *otogar* to the city center, near **Kaleiçi,** the old city. **Işıklar Cad.,** at the intersection of **Kazım Özalp Cad.** and **Cumhuriyet Cad.,** is marked by a brick-red fluted minaret and a stone clock tower. Hostels, restaurants, and historically important ruins and buildings, are in this area. The two beaches are on the outskirts of town.

Flights: Antalya International Airport (domestic info ☎330 30 30; international info ☎330 36 00), 15km from town. **THY** (☎243 43 81/2), has an office on Cumhuriyet Cad. next to the tourist office. Open M-F 8:30am-8pm, Sa-Su 8:30am-5:30pm. Buses run between THY and the airport in summer (10 per day 4:45am-2:30am, US$3). Flights to **İstanbul** (US$61, students US$47; round-trip US$79, students US$61) and many foreign cities.

Buses: To: **Ankara** (8hr., 7am-midnight, US$9.50); **Fethiye** (5hr., every hr. 8am-11pm, US$6); **Cappadocia** (10hr., 8:30 and 10pm, US$14); **İstanbul** (12hr., 6:30am-11pm, US$17); **İzmir** (8hr., 9am-midnight, US$10); and **Kaş** (3hr., every 30min. 8am-10pm, US$4).

Dolmuş: Antalya has 2 *dolmuş* hubs. **Doğu Garaj** sends *dolmuş* to **Lale** and **Lara Beaches.** To get here from Atatürk Cad., turn right on Ali Çetinkaya Cad., walk 1 block, and turn right at the Start Hotel. The **Meydan Garajı,** at the intersection of Mevlâna Cad., Aspendos Bul., and Ali Çetinkaya Cad., 1½km from the city center, has *dolmuş* to **Perge** and **Aspendos.** *Dolmuş* to the **museum** and **Konyaaltı Beach** run along Antalya's main roads, Konyaaltı Bul. or Işıklar Cad. Most *dolmuş* trips cost around US$.30.

Trams: A new tram system runs from the Antalya Museum along Cumhuriyet Cad., then down Atatürk Cad. to the stadium (every 20min., US$.25). Blue signs mark tram stops.

Tourist Office: (☎241 17 47), on Cumhuriyet Cad., to the left of the red fluted minaret and past the military complex. Helpful, English-speaking staff distributes free maps. Open M-F 8am-7pm, Sa-Su 9am-7pm; in winter M-F 8am-5pm, Sa-Su 10am-5pm.

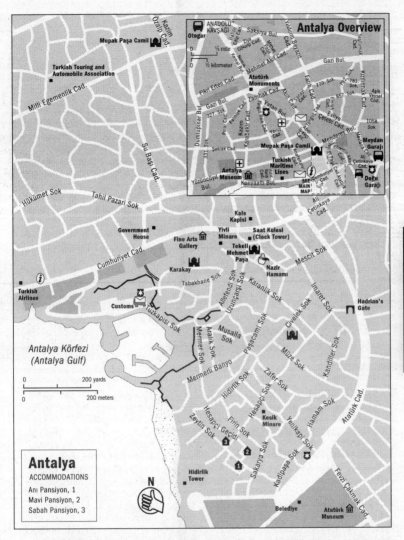

Antalya

ACCOMMODATIONS

Anı Pansiyon, 1
Mavi Pansiyon, 2
Sabah Pansiyon, 3

Consulates: UK, Dolaplıdere Cad. Pırıltı Sitesi, first fl. (☎247 70 00; fax 824 67 03). **The Turkish Republic of Northern Cyprus (TRNC),** Kışla Mah. 35th Sok. Dörteldemir Apt. 11 PK 633 (☎248 98 47).

Tourist Police: (☎/fax 243 10 61). Face the water and turn left on a little street left of the Atatürk bust at the harbor. Little English spoken.

Hospital: The closest hospital to Kaleiçi is the private **Akdeniz Sağlık Vakfı Hastanesi,** 17 Ali Çetinkaya Cad. (☎247 90 01 or 247 90 02; fax 247 90 03), on the left side of Cumhuriyet Cad., 400m past the intersection with Atatürk Cad. There is also the **Özel Interhospital,** Kiziloprak Mn 933 Sok. Medyan PTT Arkasi (☎311 50 00).

Internet Access: Natural Internet Cafe (☎243 87 63; fax 243 87 64), in the shopping area on Cumhuriyet Cad., downstairs and west from the Atatürk statue. US$1 per hr.

PTT: To get to the **main branch** (☎243 45 79), head west on Cumhuriyet Cad. and take the first major right onto Anafartalar Cad. Open daily 8:30am-5:30pm for stamps, *poste restante,* and **currency exchange. Telephones** and **Internet** also available.

Postal code: 07100. Mail sent *poste restante* should be addressed 07000.

ACCOMMODATIONS AND FOOD

The best place to stay is within the ancient walls of **Kaleiçi,** which contain over 200 pensions and hotels. Unless otherwise stated, all include private shower and breakfast. **La Paloma Pansiyon,** Kılıçarslan Mah., 60 Hesapçı Sok., a beautiful new *pansiyon,* offers gorgeous rooms with spotless tile showers, air conditioning, and comfortable beds. Guests eat a poolside breakfast in the courtyard. Worth the splurge. (☎244 79 24; fax 244 79 25. Singles US$20; doubles US$35.) **Sabah Pansiyon,** Kaleiçi, 60 Hesapçı Sok., is a popular backpackers' hangout with a pleasant courtyard area. (☎247 53 45; fax 247 53 47. Vegetarian and regular dinners US$3.50; beer US$.80. Laundry US$4. Vehicle rental US$20-24 per day. Singles US$6; doubles US$8, with bath US$13, with A/C US$18; roof, couch, or floor US$3; camping US$2.50-3.) The understated and luxurious **Anı Pansiyon,** 26 Tabakhane Sok., Hesapçı Sok., has large windows, high ceilings, and wooden furniture in a converted Ottoman home setting. (☎247 00 56. Singles US$12; doubles US$19.) Facing away from the water, turn left off of Atatürk Cad. onto Mescit Cad.; **Taşob Restaurant** is on the right, serving the best *kebaps* in Antalya sizzling with fresh, warm flatbread (US$2.50). The Turkish clientele attests to the quality. *Mezze* US$1.20. If you're tired of *kebaps,* head to **Shang Hai Chinese Restaurant,** which offers cheap, high-quality Chinese food. Try the homemade noodles.

SIGHTS

■**ANTALYA MUSEUM.** This museum is one of Turkey's best and a winner of the 1988 European Museum of the Year Award. The exhibits chronicle the history of Turkey from prehistoric times to the founding of the Turkish Republic. One of the museum's highlights is the **Salon of the Gods,** with large 2nd-century BCE statues of Nemesis, Zeus, Aphrodite, Tyche, Athena, Artemis, Hermes, and Dionysus, and their Egyptian sidekicks Serapis, Isis, and Horus. The **Salon of Small Objects and Underwater Remains,** to the right, houses several gorgeous silver and ivory Phrygian statuettes; the gem of the collection is a magnificently painted Grecian urn, mysteriously labeled "Tibet Crater." The adjoining **Icon Hall** is home to a small collection of Orthodox Christian icons, among them a portrait and bones of St. Nicholas. The **Hall of Money and Jewelry** contains a few of the world's first coins, minted between 640 and 630 BCE by the Lydians from white gold or electrium. *(2 Konyaaltı Cad., about 2½km from town along Cumhuriyet Cad., which changes its name to Konyaaltı Bul. Dolmuş labeled "Konyaaltı/Liman" head along this street, stopping at the large "D" signs (US$.30). Ask to be let off when you see the yellow museum signs. The train also runs to the museum (US$.25). ☎241 45 28. Open Tu-Su 9am-6pm; in winter Tu-Su 8am-5pm. US$3.50, students US$2.35.)*

OTHER SIGHTS. Near the entrance to Kaleiçi, at the intersection of Cumhuriyet Cad., stands the symbol of Antalya, the unique red-tinted **Yivli Minare** (fluted minaret). Dating from the 13th century, this minaret was constructed by the Selçuk Sultan Alaeddin Keykubad. Down Atatürk Cad., on the right, stands the three-arched **Hadrian's Gate,** built in 130 CE to commemorate the visit of the emperor Hadrian. Through this gate to the old city, about halfway down Hesapçı Sok., is the **Kesik Minare** (Broken Minaret). The ruined mosque traces Antalya's history: it was once a Roman temple, then a three-nave basilica, and finally a Selçuk mosque. At the far end of Hesapçı Sok. is the **Hıdırlık Tower,** which resembles a Roman-era mausoleum but is believed to have been built as a lighthouse in the 2nd century.

♫ ENTERTAINMENT

Whether you're looking for an elegant dance club or a more rowdy bar, there's no shortage of nightlife in Antalya. **Cinemas** generally show English-language films with Turkish subtitles. **Oscar**, Zafer Sok., along Atatürk Cad., shows Hollywood blockbusters and other foreign films (US$3.50). **Club Alley**, above the harbor, is the be all and end all of nightlife for Antalya's young and affluent. Eight independently-owned bars encircle a central bar in this spacious outdoor establishment. The evening begins with mellow hip-hop, while bass-heavy dance beats pick up the pace as the night wears on. (Beer and *rakı* US$6; cocktails US$10. Cover Su-Th US$8.15, F-Sa US$11.65. Open daily 8pm-4am.) **Yelken Cafe Bar** sells the cheapest beer on the harbor. For a low-key drink with friends, this place should do you good. (Beer US$1.15.) The fortress-like **Tequila Mexico Bar**, 24 Yat Limanı, near the bazaar, looms over Antalya's quiet harbor. Festively decorated, it has nightly music, with live Latin tunes on Wednesday and on the weekend. (☎243 41 15. Beer and *rakı* US$3.50. Corona US$7; tequila US$5. Open daily 7pm-3:30am.)

Antalya's two beaches, **Lara** and **Konyaaltı**, are both accessible by *dolmuş* (from the Doğu Garaj to Lara, from Konyaaltı Bul. to Konyaaltı; US$.30). On the way to Lara, you might want to stop at the **Lower Düden Waterfall**, a cascade that tumbles 20m into the sea. The spectacular **Upper Düden Falls**, about 10km from Antalya, are included in most half-day tours of Termessos.

ANTAKYA (HATAY)　　　　☎326

In Antakya, site of the ancient city of Antioch, the throngs of tourists thin out and the Mediterranean resort atmosphere subsides to give way to sprawling markets, manicured tea gardens, and the world-famous Hatay Museum. It was in Antioch that "the disciples were called Christians for the first time," and nearby St. Peter's Grotto is where Peter is said to have "christened" the religion in 40 CE (and rechristened the city Theopolis, "City of God") in an attempt to curb the city's excesses. The original sin was committed by Seleucus I Nicator, one of Alexander the Great's chief generals, who founded Antioch as the capital of his Asian empire in 300 BCE. Antioch fell from grace when it became a vice-ridden stop along the silk road and a comparable sin city under the Romans. Thanks to St. Peter's work, the city cleaned up its act and became a thriving theological and cultural capital. An earthquake in the 6th century was the cause of its present state of disrepair, although crumbling ruins around this city of 150,000 hint at its former glory.

✦ 🛈 ORIENTATION AND PRACTICAL INFORMATION

The **Asi River** divides Antakya into two parts. At the center of town in the western half of the city, a theater, the PTT, a government office, and the museum snuggle up to the Atatürk statue rotunda. The eastern half has the budget hotels, restaurants, markets, *otogar*, and old neighborhoods. To reach the center of town, turn left at the exit of the *otogar*, make another left onto **İstiklâl Cad.**, and continue 700m to the river. Cross the second bridge into the square with the Atatürk statue, without which everyone would be lost.

The *otogar* runs buses to: **Ankara** (10hr., 6 per day 10am-10pm, US$13.50); **İstanbul** (16hr., 8 per day 2:30-6pm, US$19); **Aleppo, Syria** (3-4hr., 4 per day 9am-6pm, US$8); and **Damascus, Syria** (9hr., 9:30am and noon, US$15). *Dolmuş* leave opposite the station to **İskenderun** (30min., every 15min., US$1.25), a popular border crossing town. For more information on crossing the border into Syria, see p. 612. The **tourist office**, 47 Atatürk Cad. (☎216 06 10), is an inconvenient 15-minute walk down Atatürk Cad. (Open M-F 8am-noon and 1:30-5:30pm). **Türkiye İş Bankası** has branches on İstiklâl Cad. and on Hürriyet Cad. down from the Saray Hotel, both with **currency exchange** and 24-hour **ATMs**. The *otogar* and the exchange office on İstiklâl Cad. change Syrian pounds at better rates. **Devlet Hastanesi** (☎214 54 30), 4km from town, is the best **hospital** in Antakya (taxi US$3-4). The **PTT**, in the center of town, has 24-hour phone service (mail service daily 8:30am-6pm).

ACCOMMODATIONS AND FOOD

Most accommodations are not well suited to the budget traveler. ■ **Jasmine Hotel,** 14 İstiklâl Cad., has shared bathrooms, a rooftop patio, and lawn furniture. Rooms open into a central atrium. (☎212 71 71. Singles US$5; doubles US$8; triples US$10.) ■ **Hotel Saray,** 3 Hürriyet Cad., the best of the mid-range choices, offers a pleasant breakfast salon and new rooms with bath. (☎/fax 214 90 01. Breakfast included. Singles US$14; doubles US$17; triples US$25.) Culinary enthusiasts will swoon over Antakya's specialty, *içli köfte* (a.k.a. *oruk*), a spicy bulgur wheat and red pepper stuffed with seasoned lamb and pine nuts. *Ekşi aşı,* a variation on *oruk,* is covered in tomato sauce. For dessert, *künefe* (or *peynirli kadayıf*) is a baklava-style pastry stuffed with white cheese. Much of this Syrian-influenced Turkish cuisine is unavailable in the rest of Turkey. ■ **Sultan Sofrasi,** 18 İstiklâl Cad., has no peer in town. Sample *mumbar, aşur,* and *sultan sarma* in air-conditioned comfort. (☎213 87 59. Open daily 7am-10pm.) ■ **Anadolu Restaurant,** 50/C Hürriyet Cad., down the street from the Saray Hotel, serves vegetarian *mezze* and excellent hummus, with the option of outdoor seating. (☎215 15 41. Full meal US$5-6; open daily 10am-midnight.) **'46 Edem Dondurma** (☎214 53 36), on Atatürk Cad., 100m from the center of town, scoops up your favorite fruit flavors and three varieties of *dövme* ("pounded," thick ice cream; US$1).

◉ SIGHTS

HATAY MUSEUM. The famous Hatay Museum is all that is left of ancient Antioch's magnificence, displaying possibly the world's best collection of **Roman mosaics.** The museum is divided into six numbered rooms. In **Salon I,** fated lovers Atalanta and Meleager hunt down a well-rendered boar in a panel from the 2nd-century mosaic. **Salon II** is not as well-preserved, but **Salon III** makes up for it with its small, priapic hunchback (*The Happy Hunchback*) that bears the Greek superscript *kai su* ("and you?"). Salon III also contains the *Evil Eye*, with a scantily clad man running in horror from an enormous levitating eye radiating farm implements. **Salon IV** has a giant 5th-century floor mosaic. *(Open Tu-Su 8:30am-noon and 1:30-5pm. US$3.50, students US$2.)*

ST. PETER'S CHURCH (SEN PİYER KİLİSESİ). Founded by the apostle Peter and carved into a cave so that services could be conducted in secret, this is the cave where the congregation coined the term "Christianity" to describe their new religion. A delegate of the French Commissary in Syria donated the nearby statuette of St. Peter. The hillside above the church, riddled with the remains of carved tunnels, natural caves, and bits of Antioch's city walls, has been a holy place since pagan times. A path zigzags 200m to a high relief of an obscure veiled figure, alternately described as a wind-blown Mary and the Syrian goddess of Hierapolis, flanked by Charon, boatman of Hades. *(Turn left from the otogar and make an immediate right onto İstiklâl Cad. After one block, turn right at the twin gas stations and continue 1.2km to a sign on the right. The church is 250m uphill. Take bus #6 or a taxi from town (US$2.20). Church open Tu-Su 8am-noon, 1:30-4:30pm. US$1.25.)*

CENTRAL ANATOLIA

Central Anatolia fosters the traditional spirit of Turkish culture. The astonishing landscapes and improbable natural formations of Cappadocia are some of the most fascinating in the world. The proximity of Cappadocia, an ancient Christian stronghold, to Konya, Turkey's most conservative Islamic city, hints at the area's diversity. A vibrant culture, welcoming atmosphere, and inspiring landscape characterize these windswept plains of Turkey's heartland.

ANKARA ☎312

The capital of the Turkish Republic and once the domain of King Midas, Ankara hides its ancient roots of gold beneath the modern veneer of an administrative metropolis of parks, tree-lined boulevards, and embassies; it is also the nation's premier college town, which contributes to a vibrant nightlife. In 1923, Atatürk built this planned city overnight from a few goat pastures and swampland that were dredged to make way for the garish Gençlik Park. The Museum of Anatolian Civilizations may well be Turkey's best museum, and one can begin to understand Atatürk's pivotal place in the national consciousness after visiting his mausoleum. Ankara is also a convenient base for securing visas to the rest of the Middle East.

✈❷ ORIENTATION AND PRACTICAL INFORMATION

The city's main street, **Atatürk Bulvarı**, runs north-south. At its north end is the **Ulus** precinct, centered around an Atatürk statue. The traditional village of **Hisar** (Citadel) is east of Ulus and crowned by the 9th-century **Ankara Fortress** *(Ankara kale).* Ulus and Hisar comprise **Eskişehir** (Old City). Farther south along Atatürk Bul. is **Kızılay,** the center of **Yenişehir** (New City). West of Kızılay is **Maltepe,** a district full of grim nightclubs and cheap student dorms. **Kavaklıdere, Çankaya,** and **Gaziosmanpaşa,** south of Kızılay, have lush residential areas, embassies, and nightclubs. Bus #413 runs the length of Atatürk Bul., from the Atakule tower to the equestrian statue in Ulus. The **Ankaray suburban railway line** is the subway system in Ankara, running east-west from its center in Kızılay.

Flights: *Havaş* buses (every 30min. 4am-11:30pm, US$5) to Esenboğa Airport (☎398 00 00) depart Hipodrom Cad. (next to train station). **Turkish Airlines (THY),** 154 Atatürk Bul., Kavaklıdere (info and reservations ☎419 28 00; sales ☎468 73 40 or 468 73 41) has flights to: **Antalya** (1hr., 3 per day, US$70); **İstanbul** (1hr., 15 per day, US$82); **İzmir** (1¼hr., 12 per day, US$82); **Sivas** (1hr.; M, Th; US$59); and **Trabzon** (1¼hr., 3 per day, US$68). Open M-F 8:30am-8pm, Sa-Su 8:30am-5:30pm.

Buses: The *otogar* is the westernmost stop on the Ankaray subway line (take any train to Kızılay). To get to Ulus, take a *dolmuş* (US$.60), city bus (US$.50), or taxi (US$6.25), or ride the metro 2 stops north to Cumhuriyet Cad. Buses to **Boğazkale** via **Sungurlu** (3hr., 20 per day 6am-1am, US$5). **Varan,** 34/1 İzmir Cad., Kızılay (☎418 27 06 or 224 00 43), and **Ulusoy,** 18/A İnkılâp Sok., Kızılay (☎419 40 80 or 224 01 72 or 286 53 30) offer safer, comfortable, faster service for trips to major cities.

Local Dolmuş: Hubs near Hacı Bayram Camii and at the intersection of Denizciler-Adnan Saygun Cad. US$.35-.60, depending on distance. Student fare available.

Subway: The east-west Ankaray line (stations marked by a white "A" on a green background) connects the bus station to Dikimevi, with stops in Tandoğan, Maltepe, Kızılay, and the Colleges (Kolej). The north-south Metro line (white "M" on red background) also stops in Kızılay, running north from there to Sıhhiye, Ulus, and the northwestern suburbs. 5-ride passes US$2.50, students US$1.50. Open daily 6:15am-midnight.

Tourist Offices: 121 Gazi Mustafa Kemal Bul. (☎231 55 72), at Maltepe stop on Ankaray (from Kızılay, take the train headed toward AŞTİ). English-speaking staff can serve as your interpreter to the tourist police (☎303 63 53). Open daily 9am-5pm. A 24hr. airport tourist office (☎398 03 48) offers similar services.

Embassies: Australia, 83 Nenehatun Cad., Gaziosmanpaşa (☎446 11 80 or 446 11 87; fax 446 11 88); **Canada,** 75 Nenehatun Cad., Gaziosmanpaşa (☎436 12 75; fax 447 21 73); **Greece,** 9-11 Ziaürrahman Cad., Gaziosmanpaşa (☎436 88 60; fax 446 31 91); visas M-F 9:30am-noon; **Iran,** 10 Tahran Cad., Kavaklıdere (☎427 43 20; fax 468 28 23); visas M-F 3-5pm; **Ireland,** Ugur Mumcu Cad. MNG Binasi, B Bloc, Kat 3, Gaziosmanpaşa (☎(312) 446 61 72; fax (312) 446 80 61); **New Zealand,** 13/4 İran Cad., Kavaklıdere (☎(312) 467 90 56; fax 467 90 13); **Northern Cyprus,** 20 Rabat Sok., Gaziosmanpaşa (☎437 60 31; fax 446 52 38); **Russia,** 5 Karyağdı Sok., Çankaya (☎439 21 22; fax 438 39 52); **South Africa,** 27 Filistin Sok., Gaziosmanpaşa

(☎446 40 56; fax 446 64 34; email saemb@ada.net.tr); **Syria,** 40 Sedat Simavi Sok., Çankaya (☎440 96 57; visa department ☎440 17 21; fax 438 56 09); visas M-F 8:30-9:30am; **UK,** 46/A Şehit Ersan Cad., Çankaya (☎468 62 30/42; fax 468 66 43; email britembank@ankara.mail.fco.gov.uk); and **US,** 110 Atatürk Bul., Kavaklıdere, Ankara 06100 (☎468 61 10; fax 768 61 31).

Banks: All large banks offer **currency exchange,** but only major banks such as **Akbank** (no commission) and **Garanti** will cash **traveler's checks.** 24hr. **Türkiye İş Bankası, Yapı ve Kredi, Pamukbank,** and **Garanti Bankası** accept V/MC/Cirrus/Plus; Vakıfbank and Akbank also accept AmEx. AmEx cardholders can send and receive moneygrams at Koçbank by the statue in Ulus Meydanı. **ATMs** lurk on virtually every street corner.

Hospital: Bayındır Tıp Merkezi, Kızılırmak Mah. #3-3A, 28th Sok., Söğütözü (☎287 90 00), is Ankara's best private hospital. Centrally located, brand-new **Bayındar Klinik,** 201 Atatürk Bul. (☎428 08 08), Kavaklıdere, is smaller but offers all services.

Internet Access: **Internet Center Cafe,** 107 Atatürk Bul. (☎419 27 54; fax 425 79 27), on the 3rd floor of the Engürü İş Hanı. Fast connection. Color printing, photocopying, scanning. US$1.25 per hr. Open daily 9am-11pm.

PTT: In **Ulus,** on Atatürk Bul., just south of the equestrian statue. Open 24hr. In **Kızılay,** on Atatürk Bul. just off Kızılay Sq. Open M-Sa 8am-8pm; Su 8:30am-12:30pm, 1:30-5:30pm. In **Kavaklıdere,** on Cinnah Cad. just off the Kavaklıdere roundabout. Open daily 8:30am-12:30pm, 1:30-5pm. In the **train station** on Talat Paşa Cad. Open daily 7am-11pm. All offer full services. **Postal code:** 06443.

✳🛌 ACCOMMODATIONS AND FOOD

The lively, student-oriented **Kızılay** is more expensive but more pleasant than the dustier, noisier **Ulus** (which is nearer the sights). To get to ▓ **Hotel Kale,** Anafartalar Cad., 13 Alataş Sok., Ulus, from the statue, follow Anafartalar Cad. toward the Citadel; bear right before it becomes Hisarparkı Cad., and take the 3rd left onto Şan Sok. Hotel Kale is about 150m ahead at the intersection of Şan Sok. and Alataş Sok. All the rooms have baths; most have TVs. (☎311 33 93 or 310 35 21. Singles US$14; doubles US$24; triples US$34.) Rooms at Kızılay's **Otel Ertan,** 70 Selânik Cad., have shower, toilet, and TV. (☎418 40 84 or 425 15 06. Singles US$15.50; doubles US$24.50.) **Hotel Ergen,** 48 Karanfil Sok., Kızılay, the first right off Meşrutiyet Cad., is an elegant two-star hotel with private showers, baths, and TVs. (☎417 59 06 or 417 59 07; fax 425 78 19. Singles US$28, students US$24; doubles US$40, students US$30.)

The main food hotspots are Gençlik Park (cheap), Kızılay (mid-range), and Hisar and Kavaklıdere (embassy worker-filled upscale). **Hoşdere Cad.,** southeast of Atakule Tower, lays claim to many good restaurants. The supermarket **Gima** has branches on Atatürk Bul. in Kızılay and on Anafartalar Cad. in Ulus. ▓ **Göksu Restaurant,** 22/A Bayındır Sok., one of the classier places in Kızılay, offers excellent Turkish and European food. (☎431 22 19. Filet mignon US$4.50. Open daily noon-midnight.) ▓ **Daily News Cafe,** 1 Arjantin Cad., Kavaklıdere, lets patrons peruse a free copy of the English-language *Turkish Daily News* or just pore over the newspaper decor. (☎468 45 13. Fusilli with porcini mushrooms US$6. Open daily 9am-midnight.) **Uludağ Lokantası,** 54 Denizciler Cad., Ulus (☎309 04 00; fax 312 18 19; www.uludagkebap.com.tr), is possibly the best restaurant in Ankara, serving wonderful, reasonably priced food (*Özel Uludağ kebap* US$3.50). There's nothing rotten at the Danish **Kristiansen,** 24 Arjantin Cad., Kavaklıdere. Escape cafe fare with salads (US$6), *smørrebrød* (sandwiches, US$6), and, of course, danishes. (☎466 13 46. Open daily 8am-11:30pm.)

🎵 ENTERTAINMENT

Ankara's low-key, sit-a-spell nightlife is centered around Kızılay. Pub life thrives on **İnkilâp Sok.** and **Bayındır Sok.,** east of Kızılay Sq. Bar prices are fairly uniform: a pint of *Efes*, the local favorite, goes for US$1.10-1.50; mixed drinks are US$3-4. In

Ankara

ACCOMMODATIONS
Hotel Kale, 1
Otel Ergen, 2
Otel Ertan, 3

Kazım Karabekir Cad.

Demir Cad.

Çelik Cad.

Çankırı Cad.

Tunç Cad.

Roman Baths

Maliye Meslek Sok.

Ulu Çınar Sok.

Bentderesi Cad.

Hükümet Cad.

Hacı Bayram Camii

ULUS

Column of Julian

Temple of Augustus & Rome

Ağaç Efendi Sok.

War of Independence Museum

Equestrian Statue

Çamlıca Sok.

Anafartalar Cad.

Hisarparkı Cad.

Bentderesi Cad.

HİSAR

İstanbul Cad.

Museum of the Republic

M ULUS

İstiklál Cad.

Sanayi Cad.

Teğmen Kalmaz Sok.

Kevgirli Sok.

Hisar (Citadel)

Konra Işıklar Cad.

Çıkrıkçılar Sok.

Gençlik Park

Atatürk Bul.

Main PTT

Museum of Anatolian Civilizations

Aslanhane Camii

Cumhuriyet Bul.

Marmaris Hamamı

Antalılar Cad.

Ahi Elvan Camii

Saraçlar Cad.

Can Sok.

Opera House

Kosova Sok.

Denizciler Cad.

Şengul Hamamı

Ulucanlar Cad.

Talat Paşa Cad.

Dermar Sok.

Concert Hali

Kacabey Hamamı

Talat Paşa Cad.

Celâl Bayar Bul.

Painting and Sculpture Museum

Türk Ocağı Sok.

Adnan Saygun Cad.

Ali Suavi Sok.

Ethnographic Museum

Hacettepe Hospital

Gazi Mustafa Kemal Bul.

Kızılay Sok.

Gevher Nesibe Yolu

TO TOURIST OFFICE (500m)

ANKARA UNIVERSITY

Cemal Gürsel Cad.

Cemal Gürsel Cad.

M SIHHİYE

Abdi İpekçi Park

M KURTULUŞ

Toros Sok.

Onur Sok.

Akıncılar Sok.

DEMİRTEPE

Strazburg Cad.

Sezenler Sok.

Hatti Monument

Tuna Cad.

Kurtuluş Park

M

Cinah Sok.

Ziya Gökalp Cad.

Süleyman Bey Sok.

Maltepe Camii

Hanımeli Cad.

SIHHİYE

Libya Cad.

Umit Sok.

Şehit Güreş Cad.

Necatibey Cad.

Mithat Paşa Cad.

M KOLEJ

Veyzen Tevfik Sok.

Bayındır Sok.

Ziya Gökalp Cad.

Mahmut Esat Bozkurt Cad.

Hasan Ali Yücel Cad.

TO ANIT KABIR (ATATÜRK'S TOMB, 1km)

Kumrular Sok.

Menkşe 2 Sok.

İzmir Cad.

Sakarya Cad.

İnkılâb Sok.

Selanik Cad.

Yahya Galip Cad.

Müdafaa Cad.

KIZILAY

M KIZILAY

Yüksel Cad.

Mesrutiyet Cad.

Gençlik Cad.

Güven Park

Konur Sok.

Karanfil Sok.

Kızılırmak Cad.

Libya Cad.

Başparuş Sok.

3

Vekáletler Cad.

2

Kocatepe Camii

Olgunlar Sok.

TO EMBASSIES AND KAVAKLIDERE

Olgunlar Sok.

N

0 — 400 yards
0 — 400 meters

Kızılay, at **Brothers Bar,** 61 Selânik Cad., just past the Ertan Hotel, enjoy acoustic renditions of Turkish tunes while collegiates sing along. (☎419 41 26. Open daily 11am-midnight.) **Zx Bar Disco,** 14/A Bayındır Sok., Kızılay, packs a 3-floor Turkish pop punch: disco downstairs, live music upstairs, and a bar in the middle of it all. (☎431 35 35. Beer US$1.50. Open daily noon-12:30am.) At Kavaklıdere's **Süleyman Nazif Club,** 97 Güvenlik Cad., a young, mostly Turkish crowd lets loose. (☎468 57 83. Open W-Sa 10pm-2am.) Also in Kavaklıdere, **Marilyn Monroe,** 54/A Büklüm Sok., serves the Anglo-American expat crowd. (☎467 12 12. Open daily 10am-midnight.) **Metropol Sanat Merkezi Movie House,** 76 Selanik Cad., Kızılay, offers six screens of artsy and pop films, mostly American. (☎425 74 78. US$3.75, students US$2.50.)

◉ SIGHTS

▩MUSEUM OF ANATOLIAN CIVILIZATIONS. This restored 15th-century Ottoman building won Europe's Museum of the Year Award in 1997. It houses a collection of astoundingly old artifacts tracing the history of Anatolia from the 6th millennium BCE onward. Some of the greatest hits include artifacts from Çatalhöyük, which vies with Jericho (see p. 434) for the title of Oldest City in the World; perfectly preserved Hittite bull vessels; a life-sized reproduction of King Midas's tomb; and a room of 3300-year-old hieroglyphic tablets. (2 Gözcü Sok. Walk to the top of Hisarparkı Cad., turn right at the Citadel steps—without climbing them—and follow the Citadel boundaries to a set of steps leading up to the entrance. ☎324 31 60; fax 311 28 39. Open daily 8:30am-5:30pm. US$3, students US$2; M US$6.50, students US$5.)

ATATÜRK'S MAUSOLEUM (ANIT KABİR). Upon Atatürk's death, Turkey held an international contest to select a plan for his mausoleum; the winner, Emin Onat, designed the Hittite-influenced Anıt Kabir. Now covering 750,000 sq. meters near Tandoğan Sq., the building took nine years to complete and is simple in execution but monumental in scope (like Atatürk himself). Six unhappy statues at the mausoleum's entrance represent Turkey's grief for its father's death. Across the courtyard is the tomb of **İsmet İnönü,** first prime minister of the Republic. The mausoleum complex has such Atatürkana as his 1936 Lincoln sedan and even photographs taken after his death showing cloud formations shaped like his profile. (Anıt Cad. Take the Ankaray line to Tandoğan and follow the Anıt Kabir signs along Anıt Cad. The unmarked entrance is guarded by two soldiers. It's a 10min. uphill walk from the gate to the mausoleum entrance. ☎231 79 75. Open M 1:30-5pm, Tu-Su 9am-5pm. Free.)

MOSQUES. Completed in 1987, **▩Kocatepe Mosque** is a 20th-century take on 16th-century piety, complete with electric chandeliers, digital clocks blipping away prayer times, and an underground shopping strip. Inside is a model of the mosque at Medina (the second holiest Muslim site in the world), a gift from Saudi Arabia's King Fahd. Amid the nearby Roman ruins is one of Ankara's most important mosques, the **Haci Bayram Camii,** built alongside the tomb of dervish saint Haci Bayram Veli. The mosque first did time as the Roman Temple of Augustus. (Kocatepe: east of Kızılay on Mithat Paşa Cad. Haci Bayram: east of Ulus' equestrian statue on Anafartalar Cad.; take a left at Gima supermarket.)

NEAR ANKARA: SUNGURLU AND BOĞAZKALE   ☎364

Nowhere is the former glory of the 4000-year-old Hittite civilization more evident than at its ruined capital, Hattuşaş, on the outskirts of present-day Boğazkale (just over 200km east of Ankara and 30km off the Samsun highway). Beginning in 1600 BCE, the great Hittite kings occupied Hattuşaş for four centuries, competing with the Egyptians for control of the fertile lands and trade routes of Mesopotamia. The 8km loop passing through the site makes for a beautiful hike through a wild landscape of cliffs and valleys. Two kilometers northeast of the site is Yazılıkaya, an open air temple with bas-reliefs of 100 of the 1000 or so Hittite gods. On the main road, Boğazkale's museum maintains a collection of the site's artifacts.

⊞⊡ GETTING AROUND AND PRACTICAL INFORMATION. Sungurlu is nothing more than a jumping off point for Boğazkale. Buses to Sungurlu stop on the main highway or at the *otogar*, just off the highway across from a Petrol Ofisi gas station. **Buses** leave the *otogar* for: **Ankara** (3hr., 13 per day 7:15am-9pm, US$3.75); **Bodrum** (10hr., 6:30pm, US$15); **Fethiye** (10hr., 7pm, US$16.25); and **İstanbul** (9hr., 8:30pm, US$12.50). **Türkiye İş Bankası,** within sight of the Hotel Fatih, cashes traveler's checks and has an **ATM.** The local hospital is **Devlet Hastanesi** (☎311 80 07).

▐▒ ACCOMMODATIONS AND FOOD

If you're stuck in Sungurlu, crash at the **Hotel Fatih,** 23 Cengiztopel Cad. (☎311 34 88; singles US$8, with shower US$12; doubles US$16, with shower US$22; triples US$24). Hit the **Hitit Motel,** one kilometer farther along the highway away from Ankara, for bungalow-style rooms with TV and bath. (☎311 84 09. Breakfast US$4, dinner US$9. Singles US$17; doubles US$25.) Decent meals await at **Birand Restaurant,** inside Özel İdare İşhanı; follow Lise Cad. past the intersection with Cengiztopel Cad. and take the next right onto Çorum Cad.; the restaurant is 100m down on the right. (☎311 99 16. *Dolma* US$1.50, cold *mezzes* US$1.25. Open daily 6am-11pm). Crunchy *leblebi* (roasted chickpeas), a regional specialty, are available at dozens of shops throughout town.

▥ BOĞAZKALE

Both sites open daily 8am-7pm; in winter 8am-6:30pm. US$2. The ticket is valid for both Hattuşaş and Yazılıkaya. Hattuşaş isn't near any restaurants; pack a lunch.

HATTUŞAŞ. Hattuşaş is where many of the Hittite artifacts housed at the Museum of Anatolian Civilizations in Ankara (see p. 668) were unearthed. Walking the loop around Hattuşaş in a counter-clockwise direction, you'll first pass the **Büyük Mabet,** a temple dedicated to the storm god Teshub and the sun goddess Hepatu in which everything is in groups of three (the Hittite holy number). The green Egyptian stones inside the entrance were the altar for animal sacrifices. Farther in are attendants' quarters and the temple's **warehouses,** where thousands of cuneiform tablets were found in 1907. Downhill from the temple were the offices of Assyrian merchants, where the "Rosetta Stone" of Hittite was found: a text translated into Akkadian and Hittite hieroglyphs allowed scholars to translate the elusive Hittite language. On the right of the forked road is the *Aslanlıkapı,* or **Lion's Gate,** outfitted with special grooves for the hubs of entering chariot wheels to pass through unscratched. A photographic computer reproduction posted nearby shows what the gate might have looked like in the 13th century BCE. Follow the restored city walls running atop the embankment to the *Sfenksli Kapı,* or **Sphinx Gate,** once guarded by four sphinxes (only one remains). The plum tree to the left of the gate marks the point where the inscribed Boğazkale tablets at Ankara's Museum of Anatolian Civilizations were found. Eastward and downhill along the wall are two hieroglyphic chambers, 50m apart on the right side of the road. **Chamber 2** was commissioned around 1200 BCE by King Shuppiluliuma II, the last king of Hattuşaş, and has a relief of the king holding a symbol with an inscription mentioning a "divine earth road," the symbolic entrance to the underworld. Last on the tour is the **Büyük Kale,** a ruined complex of archives, offices, and royal apartments linked by courtyards and containing over 8000 cuneiform tablets (including a treaty between Hattuziliz II and the pharaoh Ramses II).

YAZILIKAYA. The nearby holy shrine of Yazılıkaya was originally a series of narrow ravines in the rock (*Yazılıkaya* means "inscribed rock" in Turkish) with reliefs of gods and goddesses on parade. Goddesses appear in profile, wearing long, trailing robes; gods face forward, and their rank can be inferred by the number of horns on their hats. Archaeologists believe that **Chamber A** was used to celebrate the Hittite New Year every spring. Here, reliefs of 42 male gods face half as many goddesses. On the far wall, the sculpture culminates in the marriage of the Hittite's most powerful deities, **Teshub,** the storm god, and **Hepatu,** the sun goddess. Facing the procession of deities is the famous 2.6m high relief representing **King Tudhaliya IV** (c. 1250-1220 BCE), who stands astride two mountains and under a winged sun disk. **Chamber B,** accessible via a passage to the right of the entrance, was the site of animal sacrifice and contains a relief of 12 sword-carrying gods that are believed to represent the months of the year.

CAPPADOCIA

No other place on earth looks quite like Cappadocia. The unique landscape began to take shape 10 million years ago, when volcanic lava and ash hardened into a layer of soft rock called *tufa*. Rain, wind, and flooding from the Kızılırmak River shaped the *tufa* into a striking landscape of cone-shaped monoliths called *peribaca* ("fairy chimneys"), which are grouped in cave-riddled valleys and along gorge ridges. Throughout Cappadocia's other-worldly moonscapes, stairs, windows, and sentry holes have been carved into the already eerily-eroded rock.

⊡ GETTING AROUND

During high season, a *dolmuş* follows the Ürgüp-Göreme-Çavuşin-Zelve-Avanos circuit (June-Sept. leaves Ürgüp M-F every other hr. 10am-6pm; returns from Avanos M-F every other hr. 9am-5pm). *Dolmuş* also run frequently between Ürgüp and Mustafapaşa, and Ürgüp and Ortahisar. In winter, most connections within Cappadocia must be made via Nevşehir, from which buses depart every 30min. for all major Cappadocian towns. Transportation within this region costs US$.60-2.50. Most visits to southern Cappadocia must be made through Aksaray. Buses from Nevşehir to Ankara stop in Aksaray (every hr., US$2.50 to Aksaray).

Car rentals start at about US$30 per day, though prices skyrocket to about US$50 for automatics. **Europcar** (☎341 34 88 or 341 43 15) in Ürgüp rents automatics with air-conditioning for US$90 per day. Rental agencies in Göreme and Ürgüp rent **bicycles** (US$3 per hr. or US$14 per day); **mopeds** (US$8 per hr. or US$20 per day); and **motorcycles** (US$50 per day).

Guided tours of Cappadocia's major sites are run through agencies in Göreme (see **Tours,** p. 671) and Ürgüp (see **Practical Information,** p. 674). These agencies typically provide a day-long tour of the region including bus, lunch, and admission to all the sights (US$30). Multiple-day tours are planned for outdoors enthusiasts.

GÖREME   ☎384

The village of Göreme is indisputably the capital of Cappadocia's backpacker scene. Surrounded by picturesque fairy chimneys, Göreme offers tourists no fewer than 50 pensions, mostly cave dwellings carved into the soft *tufa*. Its central location really makes it the best base for exploring Cappadocia, and the glorious Open-Air Museum is only a short walk away. A local adage says, "once you've tasted Göreme's water, you're bound to come back." The staggering number of foreign brides (locals say around 200) who've settled here suggests a different allure...

◪◪ ORIENTATION AND PRACTICAL INFORMATION

Göreme main road heads out west toward Nevşehir and northeast toward Çavuşin. The *otogar,* just off the main road, is at the eastern end of the town center. At the eastern end of town, a road to the Open-Air Museum breaks off from the main road, uphill. Restaurants are mostly near the main road, and *pansiyon*s are everywhere.

Buses: From the *otogar,* buses travel via **Nevşehir** to: **Ankara** (4hr., 14 per day 7am-8:30pm, US$8); **Bodrum** (14hr.; 7:30, 9, 10pm; $20); **Bursa** (10hr.; 5:30, 7:30pm;

$16); **İstanbul** (11hr., 8 per day 6:30-8:30pm, US$16); **İzmir** (11hr.; 6:30, 7:30, 8pm; US$15); **Marmaris** (14hr., 5 per day, US$20); **Olimpos** (12hr., 4 per day 7:30am-9pm, US$19); and **Pamukkale** (10hr., 4 per day 7-9pm, US$14).

Tourist Office: (☎ 271 25 58; www.wec-net.com.tr/belediye/göreme). In the *otogar*. Provides info on Göreme's lodgings. **Backpacker Information** (on your left as you exit the *otogar*; ☎ 271 27 36) can help "the independent traveler" organize an itinerary, and offers US$10 per day (for lodging and transportation) hostel-based tours.

Tours: Zemi Tours (☎271 25 76; fax 271 25 77), on the left side of the road leading from the *otogar* to the Open-Air Museum, and **Neşe Tours** (☎ 271 25 25 or 271 26 43; fax 271 25 24; www.prizma.net.tr/~nesecafe), next to the Internet Cafe, are reputable and affordable. Zemi, in addition to full and multi-day tours (US$30-150), offers a unique 2-day Ihlara Gorge Camping Trip (US$50 per person) with tents, beds and meals provided. **Kapadokya Balloons** (☎271 24 42; fax 271 25 86; www.kapadokya-balloons.com), with an office next door to Cafe Doci@, offers breathtaking 90min. balloon tours, a.k.a. "aerial nature walks," through the Cappadocian landscape. Professional and multilingual pilots fly as high as 700m and low enough to pick flowers. Balloons fly for 1½hr. with 8-12 passengers Apr.-Oct. daily at dawn, weather permitting. US$230 per person; book at least 2 days before.

Banks: Two are next to the Open-Air Museum. Open daily 9am-5:30pm. There is an **ATM** in the center of Göreme, across from the *otogar* and to the left.

Laundromat: (☎271 25 79), behind the *otogar*, across from the Göreme Belediye Handicrafts Market. Wash and dry US$7, ironing US$6. Open daily 9am-8pm.

Pharmacy: Kapadokya Pharmacy (☎271 21 37), on the main road near the hospital. Open daily 8am-8pm.

Medical Assistance: Göreme Sağlık Ocağı Hospital (☎271 21 26), near the PTT.

Internet Access: Cafe Doci@ (see p. 672) and Internet C@fe. **Internet Cafe** (☎271 25 25). Next door to Neşe Tours, across from the bus terminal. Offers a printer, non-alcoholic drinks, daily newspapers and weekly magazines. English-style keyboard to preserve your sanity. US$4 per hr. Open daily 8am-10:30pm.

PTT: On the main road after the turnoff for the Open-Air Museum. Has the best exchange rates in town. Open daily 8:30am-12:30pm and 1:30-5:30pm. **Postal code:** 50180.

ACCOMMODATIONS

Under Göreme's government, all pensions have fixed minimum prices for non-dormitory rooms: US$5 per person, with bath US$7, and up to US$10 for a single. Starred hotels may charge higher rates. Hit the tourist office (see above) for more accommodations information. Most pensions will pick you up if you call ahead.

Köse Pansiyon (☎271 22 94; fax 271 25 77). Just behind the PTT. Makeshift Ottoman divans, swimming pool, and helpful Scottish-Turkish owners make Köse the backpacker's mecca. Breakfast US$2. Vegetarian and 4-course dinners US$4. Two dorm rooms with mattresses on the floor (US$4 per person; bring your own sleeping bag, if possible) and 13 rooms, some with private bath.

Peri Pansiyon (☎271 21 36; fax 271 27 30). On the right walking east on the road to the Open-Air Museum. Lounge on the sunny, floral courtyard. Tame atmosphere, but close to the action at **Flinstone's**. Four-course dinner (US$5) on the wood-panelled *kilim*-ed terrace. Cave and non-*tufa* rooms available. Singles US$7, with bath US$10; doubles US$20. Cave rooms: singles US$10, luxury caves US$25.

Kookaburra Pansiyon (☎271 25 49). Take a left on the first dirt road behind Orta Mah. and fork left to reach Kookaburra. 10 attractive rooms, some with private showers and stunning views. Charming decor adds old Turkish flair. US$3 breakfasts and a cave bar.

Paradise Pension (☎/fax 271 22 48). An excellent pension on the road to the Open-Air Museum. Two fairy chimney rooms, each with 5 beds and shared bath. Nine smaller rooms. Turkish breakfast $1.60. Special meals offered most nights. Laundry $6.

Göreme Dilek Camping (☎271 23 96). Across from Peri Pansiyon. Vast, floral campsite and pool snuggle among phallic rocks. Campsite US$4.50 per site; tents US$3 per person, tent rentals US$8; caravans US$10.

FOOD AND ENTERTAINMENT

Orient (☎/fax 271 23 46). A highly-recommended local favorite opposite the Yüksel Motel and Cafe Doci@ featuring delicious Turkish food and atmosphere. Charming furniture complements the wood floors and cave atmosphere of this restaurant and bar. The sizzling *sac tava* is a must-try house specialty (US$4). Entrees and vegetarian dishes US$3-4. Five-course daily special US$5. Open daily 7:30am until crowds leave, usually 1am.

Cafe Doci@ (☎271 29 03; www.indigoturizm.com.tr/cafedoci@). To the left as you exit the *otogar* on the road toward Nevşehir. Run by young entrepreneurs Arman and Haluk, whose flawless English has an Australian twang. Mammoth burgers (US$3), beer (US$3-US$5), and good times make this a backpacker's hotspot. Blaring Ameri/Euro pop draws nightly crowds. A big-screen TV offers American channels and movies during the day. Internet US$2 per hr. Open daily 8am for breakfast. Closes when the partying ends (around 2am).

Flinstones Bar (☎271 22 48). A revamped cave at the turnoff for the Open-Air Museum. "*Rakı* is the answer; I don't remember the question." Partiers at this "Backpacker's Underground Pub" can hit the stocked bar or sprawl out on the *kilims* with a few friends and a hookah. Fans of Britpop will delight in the DJ's discerning taste. Beer US$2. Open daily until the party ends around 3am.

SIGHTS

GÖREME OPEN-AIR MUSEUM. With seven Byzantine churches, a convent, and a kitchen/refectory, the Open-Air Museum is a delight to history, art, and religion buffs. In the 4th century, St. Basil founded one of the first Christian monasteries here, setting down religious tenets that influenced the entire Western monastic tradition, which was put to a halt in the 15th century under Turkish rule. From then until the 1923 Population Exchange, the Greeks and Turks used the old churches to store goods. Today, the remains offer tourists some of Cappadocia's most spectacular frescoes. A close look at the 10th-century frescoes in the **St. Basil Church,** an early Christian monastery, reveal the artist's fingerprints. The **Çarıklı Kilise (Sandal Church)** earns its name from the footprints, supposed molds of Jesus' feet, inside. The church itself dates back to the 11th century, rendering the holy footprints but a popular myth.

Yilinlik Kilise (Dragon Church), marked by frescoes of St. George slaying the dragon, and another of a hermaphroditic figure, is also known as St. Onuphrius church. One popular legend claims that the Egyptian girl Onophirios was so beautiful that she could not drive away all the men seeking to ravish her. She prayed for assistance and was granted a long white beard and moustache, which solved all her problems. Another tale tells of St. Onuphrius, who belonged to a 4th-century commune of Egyptian hermits. **Karanlik Kilise (Dark Church)** houses the most impressive artwork in the museum. The dome also houses a rare fresco of a teenage Jesus. *(US$10. Watch your head walking in. From Göreme village, follow the Open-Air Museum Way about 2km east, walking uphill. Open year-round 8am-5pm. US$5.25.)*

A ticket to the Open-Air Museum will also admit you to a number of nearby churches. The first, the **Tokalı Church,** is right outside the museum's entrance and contains three smaller churches and a chapel. About 250m from the entrance are the **Church of Mother Mary** and the 10th-century **Church of St. Eustathios.**

◤ HIKING: NEAR GÖREME

When good Christians die, they go to heaven; when good hikers die, they go to Cappadocia. Mountain ranges with spectacular views and eerie rock formations are all within throwing distance of Göreme. Follow the road leading to the Open-Air Museum one kilometer past the museum, take a left on the dirt road by Kaya Camping, turn left again at the next paved road, and walk three kilometers to reach **Sunset Point** (US$.60, students US$.40). From there, you can descend into the **Rose Valley,** where bizarre, multi-colored rock formations make for one of the area's better hikes. After getting lost a few times, you'll eventually end up in Çavuşin; take the Avanos-Nevşehir **bus** or the Avanos-Zelve-Göreme-Ürgüp minibus back to Göreme (every 30min. until 6pm, weekends every hr.), or take a **taxi** instead (US$5). Follow the canal west of the bus terminal to reach **Pigeon Valley,** whose namesakes have unfortunately been hunted almost to extinction. This hike is also somewhat confusing, but ultimately you'll end up in Uçhisar. To the north of Göreme is **Love Valley,** affectionately known as "Penis Valley" because of the ▧ phallic rock formations that would give even Dirk Diggler a complex. If you're short on time, consider a **guided tour** of the nearby terrain. Tour companies all peddle similar trips, typically departing at 9:30am and returning around sunset (US$25, students US$23).

UNDERGROUND CITIES: KAYMAKLI AND DERİNKUYU

By dolmuş, Kaymaklı and Derinkuyu are about 30min. and 45min. from Göreme, respectively, with a connection in Nevşehir. From Göreme, dolmuş run to Nevşehir (every 30min. 6:30am-7pm, US$.50) and then go to Kaymaklı (US$.60) and Derinkuyu (US$.80). Both sites open daily 8am-5pm. Each site US$3.75.

Although Cappadocia contains almost 30 **underground cities** carved from *tufa*, Kaymaklı and Derinkuyu are the largest. Some think the cities began as cave dwellings that were later used by the Hittites for storage and ambushes. Between the 5th and 10th centuries, the Byzantines expanded them into full-fledged cities that shielded people from Iconoclast and Sassanid raids.

Low and narrow passages, easily blocked off by massive millstones, hindered prospective invaders. It was forbidden for anyone to leave while the cities were occupied, lest their departure give away the hideouts. Strangely enough, no evidence of a permanent settlement has been conclusively found in either Derinkuyu or Kaymaklı.

Derinkuyu, 45m deep with a 55m well, is slightly more impressive than Kaymaklı. With eight levels open to the public, Derinkuyu has sizeable rooms and halls, good lighting, and relatively easy access. Kaymaklı, smaller than Derinkuyu, boasts a more complex structure. The village has been built around the underground city, so residents could enter storage areas through tunnels in their courtyards.

In both sites, red arrows lead down, blue arrows up. Although all explorable areas are lit, a flashlight may come in handy. Stick to the marked and lighted areas, and you'll be safe. If you wish to stray from the herd, just remember that these cities were designed to foil potential trespassers, who would fall to their deaths from sudden drops hidden behind corners.

ÜRGÜP ☎384

Ürgüp emerges from a pastiche of rock formations, early Christian dwellings, and old Greek mansions. With fewer *pansiyons* and neo-hippies than Göreme, Ürgüp appeals to independent travelers fleeing the commotion of tourism.

⌘ GETTING AROUND. English-speaking Aydın Altan of **Nevtur** (☎341 43 02) answers bus-related questions. **Buses** run to: **Ankara** (5hr., 5 per day 7am-5:30pm, US$8); **Bodrum** (14hr., 7pm, US$19); **Fethiye** (15hr., 3 per day 6-8pm, US$19); **İstanbul** (12hr., 4 per day 6-8pm, US$16); **İzmir** (12hr., 6:30pm, US$16); **Konya** (4hr., 6 per day 8am-7pm, US$6); **Kuşadası** (13hr.; 6:30 and 7:30pm; US$18); **Marmaris** (15hr., 7pm, US$19); **Pamukkale** (10hr., 7pm, US$15); and **Selçuk** (13hr., 6:30pm, US$18). Several **vehicle rental agencies** are near the *otogar*. You can rent: bikes US$5-10 per day; mopeds US$15-20 per day; cars from US$30 per day. Roads are reasonably organized in this area, though only skilled stick-handlers may conquer the hills.

⌘⌘ ORIENTATION AND PRACTICAL INFORMATION. The main square, marked by a bath house and an Atatürk statue, is 20m down **Güllüce Cad.** from the *otogar*. This road forks uphill into two smaller roads, both near accommodations. Intersecting Güllüce Cad. in the main square is **Kayseri Cad.** The **Tourist Office** is inside the garden on Kayseri Cad. English- and German-speaking Zeki Güzel offers maps and brochures. (☎341 40 59. Open daily Apr.-Oct. 8am-7pm; Nov.-Mar. 8am-5pm.) Alternatively, fork left at the *hammam* and walk up to the **Turkish Airlines Office,** which doubles as a classier tourist office. Arrange plane tickets, get info, or simply cool off in the stone building that was once Ürgüp's prison. (Open daily 8am-5pm.) The reliable and affordable **Erko Tours** (☎341 32 52; fax 341 37 85; www.erkotours.com.tr) in the *otogar*, gladly organizes tours of Cappadocia. Upscale and professional **Argeus Tours** also operates out of the Turkish Airlines Office. (☎341 46 88; www.argeus.com.tr. US$70 for all-inclusive day tours.) Be forewarned: the **Tarihi Şehir Hamamı,** in the main square is co-ed, and there is only a male masseur. (Open daily 7am-11pm.) The **hospital,** off Kayseri Cad. just behind Tourist Information, can be reached at ☎341 40 31. The **Cappadocia Health Center,** 28 Dumlupınar Cad. (☎341 54 27 or 341 54 28; fax 341 34 92), offers more private, out-patient clinical care. For **Internet Access,** see **Asia Teras** (see **Food,** p. 675). To reach the **PTT,** turn right out of the tourist office and take the first right uphill. It offers telephone services, stamps, fax, and currency exchange. (☎341 80 12. Open daily 8:30am-7pm; in winter 8am-5pm. Currency exchange closed noon-1:30pm.) Postal code: 50400.

▛▟ ACCOMMODATIONS AND FOOD. Its *kilim*-ed lounge and bar, parking space, cave restaurant, and ping-pong table make ▨ **Hotel Surban** ideal for groups, and lots of fun. Rooms have private bath and towels. (☎341 47 61 or 341 46 03; fax 341 32 23. Singles US$10; doubles US$20; triples US$30.) The **Bahçe Hostel** across the street and uphill from the *hammam*, was once known as Ürgüp's only backpacker hostel. Less bohemian than it once was, but its inviting cave bar/disco remains. Rooms are spacious but unspectacular. A buck more will get you a private bath. (☎341 33 14; fax 341 48 78. Singles US$7; doubles US$10; triples US$15.) At the **Hotel Elvan,** İstiklâl Cad., 11 Barbaros Hayrettin Sok., downhill from Hotel Akuzun, to the left off the *hammam*, Maternal Fatma Hanım will boil medicinal teas for her diarrheal guests. Rooms are tidy and have private bath. (☎341 41 91; fax 341 34 55. Singles US$15; doubles US$20; triples US$30. V, MC.) Fork right at the mosque, climb up the hill and steer left at the next fork to reach the **Türkerler Otel, Camping and Swimming Pool** (☎341 33 54). Pitch a tent for a couple of bucks on the environs of this tiny pension. Call ahead to check if the swimming pool is in fact filled, and cut a price with the laid-back owners (Turkish business at its best). If camping's lost its novelty, patrons can check into the on-grounds hotel or pension.

Heavy with Turkish spirit, **Han Çırağan** (☎341 25 66) is in a 300-year-old caravanserai whose rooms are still used by traveling merchants. The bar and winery next door specialize in all-you-can-drink "Turkish nights," where the din of *kanun, saz,* and merriment echo through the cave (US$12 per person). Did we mention all-you-can-drink? The **Şömine Cafe** (☎341 84 42; fax 341 84 43), across from the Atatürk statue, caters largely to the tourist scene with a multilingual menu and professional service. Entrees cost US$2-4. **Asia Teras,** 20m to the left when exiting the tourist office offers billiards (US$2 per hr.) and Internet access (US$2.50 per hr.), along with mediocre American food (burgers US$1-1.50). (☎341 38 39; email asiateras@hotmail.com. Beer US$1; *rakı* US$2. Open daily 10am-midnight.) A local favorite, **Mikro Restaurant** (☎341 20 68; fax 341 32 39) serves unbeatable Turkish food. Main courses run about US$4.

⬕ ENTERTAINMENT. Cappadocia is one of Turkey's major viticultural regions, with its center in Ürgüp. Uphill to the right behind the Atatürk statue, the renowned **Turasan Winery,** supplier of 60% of Cappadocia's wines, offers free tours and tastings in its rock-carved wine cellar. (Open daily 8am-8pm. Tours available until 5pm.) Several wine shops around the main square also offer free tastings. In late September, the Ürgüp **wine festival** brings eager competitors from France, Italy, Argentina, and the US, among others.

If you find yourself still energized after a day of boozing and trooping through Ürgüp's narrow cobblestone streets, put on your dancing shoes. The ▨**Prokopi Pub Bar,** right in the town square is popular with tourists. This hip bar plays an excellent selection of electronica, dance beats, and American and Brit pop. For the inspired or intoxicated there is a dance floor. (☎341 64 98. Beer US$2.50; *rakı* US$3; mixed drinks US$4-6. Open until the party dies, usually around 3am.) **Bar Barium** features funky mirrored walls and a solid mélange of Turkish and American pop. (Beer and *rakı* US$2.50. Open until 4am.) At the **Harem Disco,** at the foot of the road to the winery, Turkish and European techno blast in a candlelit cave complete with a fireplace and disco ball. (Open daily until 4am.)

BLACK SEA COAST

Along the shores of the Black Sea, the heat of Anatolia gives way to sea breezes and tall fir forests. Where forests thin out, fields of tobacco and cherries alternate with sloping pastures spotted with grazing cattle. Traveling between towns often requires hours of transit in a crowded *dolmuş* careening treacherously around narrow mountain roads. The relative brevity and regular afternoon rain showers of the summer season on the Black Sea coast may have left the area untouched by international tourism, but its allures are no secret to Turks. The beaches of

Amasra and Sinop teem with vacationing Turkish college students. First settled by Phoenician and Greek colonists, the ancient trading posts of Sinop, Trabzon, and Amissos (now Samsun) were once pivotal links on the Byzantine Silk Road. Until recently, NATO naval bases dotted the coast, staring down Soviet fleets on the horizon. Of late, commerce with Georgia and other former Soviet republics has brought prosperity, but has also led to a marked increase in prostitution in urban areas like Trabzon.

SAFRANBOLU ☎370

The entire 19th-century Ottoman town of Safranbolu has been preserved, with development relegated to the new city three kilometers away. The restoration effort began in 1975, and today many of the refurbished houses have been converted to hotels or *gezi evleri* (open houses). Safranbolu remains one of the best places in Turkey to laze like a pasha and soak in Ottoman culinary traditions.

ORIENTATION AND PRACTICAL INFORMATION. Safranbolu has two distinct sections: the beautiful old town, called **Çarşı**, and the dusty, uninteresting new one, called **Yeni Safranbolu** or Kıranköy. While direct **buses** do travel to Safranbolu, you may have to take a *dolmuş* from **Karabük**, a less-than-lovely steel manufacturing town 10km away (15min., frequent 7am-7pm, US$.45). Avoid Karabük entirely by getting off on the road to Safranbolu and waiting for the Karabük-Safranbolu *dolmuş* there. Buses and *dolmuş* will most likely stop in the new town. To get to Çarşı from there, catch any *dolmuş* running along the broad boulevard (5min., frequent 7:10am-11pm, US$.25). To return to Karabük, which has more bus options, take a *dolmuş* from Çarşı. Buses from new Safranbolu go to: **Amasra** (2hr., 8:15am, US$4); **Ankara** (3hr., 15 per day 5am-6pm, US$9); **Antakya** (15hr., 6:30pm, US$20); **Bursa** (9hr., 7pm, US$15); **İstanbul** (7hr., 17 per day 7am-11:30pm, US$14); **İzmir** (12½hr., 8:30pm, US$18); and **Trabzon** (13hr., 6pm, US$20). **Taxis** between the old and new town cost about US$3.

The **tourist office**, 5 Arasta Sok., offers maps. (☎/fax 712 38 63. Open daily 8:30am-6pm.) **TC Ziraat Bankası**, behind Cinci Han, has an **ATM.** (Open M-F 8:30am-noon and 1-5pm; **currency** and **traveler's check exchange** until 4:30pm). The **hospital** (☎712 11 87) is in the new town, near Kaya Erdem Cad., behind the Kız Sağlık

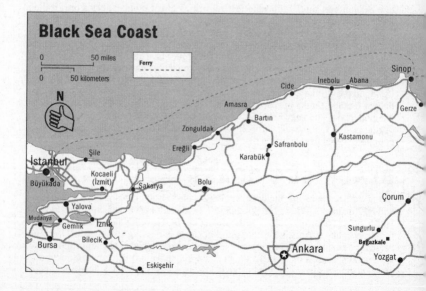

Black Sea Coast

Meslek Lisesi. The **PTT** is on Hamamönü Sok., near the Çarşı Pansiyon. (Open M-Sa 8:30am-12:30pm and 1:30-5:30pm.)

▓▓▓ ACCOMMODATIONS, FOOD, AND ENTERTAINMENT. Since Safranbolu is popular year-round, try to make reservations a few days in advance. Off the main square in a magnificent Ottoman house, ▓ **Otel Teras,** Çarşı Meydanı, 4 Mescit Sok., offers rooms with bath and TV. (☎725 17 48. Singles US$16; doubles US$24; triples US$32.) From the square, signs lead to **Çarşı Pansiyon,** 1 Bozkurt Sok. (☎725 10 79.) Çarşı gives the choice of standard rooms with shared bath or rooms with private bath and floor mattresses. (Breakfast included. Singles US$14; doubles US$24; triples US$32.) In the new town, **Otel Gülen,** 2 Utku Sok., Ulu Camii Karşısı (☎725 10 82), is the ultimate bargain in an authentic Ottoman house. Walk from the roundabout in new Safranbolu toward Çarşı and take the second right onto Cumhuriyet Cad.; the hotel is about 200m ahead. (Singles US$3; doubles US$6.50; triples US$9.50.)

   Safran Ocakbaşı, Çarsı Meydanı, Hamamönü Sok., serves good grub. (☎712 10 76. *Kanat* (wing) *şiş* US$1.30. Free *ayran.*) At **Karaüzümler Gezi Kafeterya,** Hacı Halil Mah., Mescit Sok. No. 20 (☎715 14 49), up the road from Otel Teras, enjoy five kinds of *gözleme* (US$1) in the garden or in the Ottoman salon.

   Most nightspots are clustered together around the Cinci Han. ▓ **Beyaz Ev Pub,** 18-20 Pazar Yeri, has a friendly environment, great live music, and US$1.50 draft beer. (☎712 52 53. Live guitar and *saz* music W, F-Sa. Open daily 11am-2am.) **Arasna Bar,** Arasta Arkası Sok. No. 4, is on the ground floor of the Aransa Hotel. Live music from 10pm on F-Sa. (☎712 41 70. Beer US$1.75.) Try your moves on at **Hangar Disco,** next to the Beyaz Ev in Pazar Yeri. (☎712 67 27. Beer US$2. Cover US$3 from 1-6pm, US$4 from 7pm-3am; first drink included. Open daily 1pm-2am.)

▓ SIGHTS. The highlight of Safranbolu is unquestionably its Ottoman architecture. The traditional wooden mansions are characterized by an overhanging second floor and highly ornate ceiling decorations. The complex and contradictory floor plans were designed to maximize comfort and to keep men and women separated. To see the architecture up close, take a peek inside the fancier hotels or visit the *gezi evleri*, restored houses that accept visitors for a small fee. The best place to start is **Kaymakamlar Evi (Governor's Residence),** the local museum. From the square,

TURKEY

walk along Akın Sok. to the Cinci Han; Kaymakamlar is on the little street past the TC Ziraat Bankası and behind the Cinci Han. (☎712 66 78. US$.80, students US$.40. Open daily 9am-9pm; in winter 9am-5pm.) Other *gezi evleri* include the **Karaüzümler Gezi Evi**, on Mescit Sok. past the Otel Teras. (US$.70, students US$.30. Open daily 9am-10pm). Walk up the narrow broken street past Kaymakamlar Evi to reach **Hıdırlık Tepesi**, a lookout point with fantastic views of Safranbolu in all its antiqued glory. Hıdırlık Tepesi houses the **tomb of Hasan Paşa**, an Ottoman notable exiled to Safranbolu in 1843. On Manifaturacılar Sok. past the Cinci Han, the **İzzet Paşa Camii**, built in 1796, verges on Baroque excess with its decorative squiggles.

AMASRA ☎378

Over 3000 years of trade and fishing have left Amasra the same lovely, quiet beach getaway that Queen Amastris was looking for in the 4th century BCE, when she founded the town on the site of Sesamos, an ancient Miletian port. With its stunning coast, excellent seafood, and unforgettable sunsets, Amasra is one of the Black Sea's best places to kick back and catch your breath.

GETTING AROUND AND PRACTICAL INFORMATION. Amasra sits on a peninsula that juts out into the Black Sea, forming two harbors, **Küçük Liman** and **Büyük Liman.** The main transport hub closest to Amasra is **Bartın,** 16km south, accessible by *dolmuş* (every ½hr. 7:30am-9pm; US$.80, students US$.60). Buses run directly to **Ankara** (4½hr., 8 per day 5:30am-1am, US$9.50) and **İstanbul** (8hr., 7 per day 6:30am-11:30pm, US$13). Minibuses run to **Bartin** and **Cide** (2½hr.; 7, 11am, 2:30, 7pm; US$3, students US$2.50). In the square, the **Türkiye İş Bankası** has an **ATM** and exchanges cash and traveler's checks. (Open M-F 9am-12:30pm and 1:30-5:30pm.) The **PTT**, on the square by the western harbor, also has a currency exchange. (Open daily in summer 8am-11pm; rest of year 8am-5pm.) For information in English, visit the **Aydın Eczanesi** (☎315 23 23), a pharmacy next door to the PTT. Friendly chemist Aydın Söğüt and family help with currency exchange and offer medical assistance.

ACCOMMODATIONS AND FOOD. Since Amasra swells with Turkish tourists in the summer, small household *pansiyon*s pick up the hotels' slack. Toward the center of town, the **Otel Belvü Palas**, 20 Küçük Liman Cad. has 15 rooms with views and bath. (☎315 12 37. Singles US$13; doubles US$25.50; triples US$38.50; quads US$51.) The **Nur Turistik Pansiyon**, Küçük Liman Mah., 3 Çamlık Sok., along the waterfront road, offers 17 rooms, eight with waterfront views. (☎315 10 15. Singles US$7; doubles US$14.50; triples US$21.50.)

The restaurants along Amasra's western harbor dish out the port's predictable specialty, fish. The large and luxurious **Canlıbalık Restaurant**, 8 Küçük Liman Cad., recognized as the town's best, provides an open-air setting with harbor views (☎315 26 06. *Barbun* fish US$3; *mezgit* fish US$2.50; *rakı* US$1.25. Open daily noon-midnight.) Overlooking the fishing boats in the eastern harbor, the **Çeşm-i Cihan Restaurant,** 21 Büyük Liman Cad., serves a wide variety of tasty fish (from US$3) and *Efes* (US$1.25) on an outdoor terrace. (☎315 10 62. Open daily 11am-midnight.) There is a small village **market** in the square.

SIGHTS. Amasra is above all a place to relax, a sleepy resort draped in Byzantine ramparts. Although the town was fortified as far back as the 3rd century BCE, the **citadel** that stands today dates from the 9th century CE. Walk uphill from the bridge to the **Fatih Camii**, a ruined 9th-century Byzantine church, converted into a mosque when Sultan Mehmet II conquered Amasra in 1460. The town's **museum** has items from the Hellenic through Ottoman eras, including a collection of Ottoman pistols. (☎315 10 06. Open Tu-Su 8:30am-5:30pm. US$1.50, students US$1.25.) The local **woodworking market** on Çekiciler Cad. features local crafts and fine traditional musical instruments. (☎315 22 64. Open daily in summer 9am-9pm.) *Dolmu@* from Amasra run east to pristine beaches in **Bozköy** and **Çakraz.**

SİNOP
☎382

Sinop takes its name from Sinope, a nymph who spurned the advances of the thunderbolt-hurling god Zeus. Hoping to lure her into his Olympian sack, he offered to grant her a single wish; slyly, she asked for eternal virginity. Bound to his promise, Zeus isolated her on the tiny mountainous peninsula where modern Sinop now slumbers, a town yet to be deflowered by tourists. College students in town for a beach holiday and old-timers nostalgic for friends from the recently closed NATO base warmly welcome the few foreign travelers who straggle into town.

■🖪 **ORIENTATION AND PRACTICAL INFORMATION.** The Sinop peninsula juts northeast into the Black Sea. The town's main street, **Sakarya Cad.**, runs from the city center southwest past the **otogar** toward the mainland. In the center of town at a large roundabout, Sakarya Cad. intersects **Atatürk Cad.**, which runs south toward the harbor and a large square, **Uğur Mumcu Meydan₵. Buses** from the *otogar* run to: **Ankara** (9hr.; 9pm; US$16; students US$14.50); **Bursa** (10hr.; 2:30pm; US$12, students US$11); **İstanbul** (11hr.; 9am and 7pm; US$28, students US$24); **İzmir** (18hr.; 2:30pm; US$28, students US$24); **Kastamonu** (3hr.; 6 per day 10am-7pm; US$8, students US$6.50); **Ordu** (6hr., 8pm, US$9.50); **Samsun** (3hr., 10 per day 7am-8pm; US$8, students US$6.50); **Trabzon** (8hr.; 8pm; US$13, students US$11); and **Unye** (5hr.; 8pm; US$9.50, students US$8). The larger bus companies don't serve the treacherous road from Sinop west to **Amasya;** local companies pick up the slack. **Atatürk Hastanesi** (hospital; ☎261 45 10) is open 24 hours, and there are many pharmacies on Sakarya Cad. **FVT Internet Cafe,** Aşıklar Cad. No. 31, is on the main coastal road. (US$.80 per hr. Open daily 9am-midnight.) The **PTT** is in Uğur Mumcu Meydanı. (Open daily 8:30am-11pm, full services until 5pm.)

🖪🖪🖪 **ACCOMMODATIONS, FOOD, AND ENTERTAINMENT.** A popular spot for young Turks on vacation, Sinop has plenty of reasonably priced rooms, mostly next to the fortifications along the quiet waterfront. 🖪 **Otel Meral,** 19 Kurtuluş Cad., has large, sunny rooms and solar-powered hot water. (☎261 31 00. Singles US$6.50, students US$5, with bath US$9.50; doubles US$12, students US$9.50, with bath US$19; triples US$16, students US$14.50; quads with bath US$24.) **Uğur Aile Pansiyon,** 4 İskele Cad., along the waterfront, is a budget-friendly place with large rooms, common baths, kitchen, and free laundry. The **restaurant** on the harbor offers good fish. (☎261 59 47. Singles US$8, students US$6.50; doubles US$13, students US$9.50; triples US$14.50, students US$13; quads US$19, students US$16.) **Gazi Piknik ve Mesire Yeri** campsite is in a forest by the beach. Turn right from the *otogar* on Sakarya Cad. and walk 100m; the campsite is on the left. (☎260 23 87. US$4 per tent or caravan. Electricity US$.50. Student discount.)

Try the fresh crabs at 🖪 **Balık Restaurant,** 1/B İskele Cad., near the port next to the fortress. (US$.50 per crab. *Rakı* US$1.25. Open daily 9am-4am; in winter 9am-midnight.) Following the waterfront past the tourist office brings you to the ultra-cheap *mantı* and *gözleme* restaurants. After a day at the beach, Sinop vacationers play backgammon at the waterfront cafes on Kıbrıs Cad. **Burç Cafe,** atop the citadel's tower, is a great place to drink a beer and enjoy the view. (☎260 32 19. Live *saz* performances nightly at 9pm; open Apr.-Oct. 8am-midnight.) Stay out 'til almost dawn at **Teleskop Disco,** on Karakum beach, where DJs spin Turkish and foreign dance music (beer US$1.20 open daily 6pm-4am), or at **Diogenes Bar,** 5 İskele Cad., across from Uğur Restaurant, the most vibrant bar in Sinop. (☎261 57 21. Beer US$1.40; open daily 8pm-4am; in winter 5pm-midnight.)

🖪 **SIGHTS.** Sinop's **fortifications** date from 770 BCE, when the port was settled by Miletian colonists. What stands today is a mish-mash of Pontic and Ottoman renovations. Most notable for a large Hellenistic sculpture of a deer strangely unconcerned about being devoured by lions, Sinop's **museum,** at the eastern end of Sakarya Cad., also houses a sizeable collection of Greek, Roman, and Ottoman coins, early Bronze Age pottery, and various amphorae. In the back of the museum lie the remains of the **Temple of Serapis,** dating to the 4th century BCE. Serapis is closely associated with Asclepius, god of medicine, healing, and dreaming. *(Open Tu-F 8am-noon and 1:30-5:30pm, Sa-Su 9am-noon and 1:30pm-5:30pm. US$1.50.)* Sinop's two oldest Islamic monuments are the 13th-century Selçuk **Alaaddin Camii** and **Pervane Medresesi,** next to each other on the north side of Sakarya Cad. Abandoned and deteriorating rapidly, **Balatlar Kilisesi,** a 7th-century Byzantine church near the intersection of Radar Yolu and Kemalettin Sami Paşa Cad., one kilometer northeast of the museum, retains some beautiful frescoes.

◸ **BEACHES.** Beach-goers have a number of options in Sinop. The best bet is beautiful, uncrowded **Akliman Halk Plajı,** 12km from town on the western coast. *Dolmuş* leave from Uğur Mumcu Meydanı (20min.; every 30min. M-F 8am-6pm, Sa-Su 8am-10pm; US$.50). Nearby **Yuvam Belediye Plajı** and over-developed **Karakum Plajı** are crowded with sun-seeking college students (a 30min. walk or brief *dolmuş* ride (US$.35) northeast from Uğur Mumcu Meydanı along Kıbrıs Cad.).

AMASYA ☎358

A fortuitous meeting of human and natural architecture, Amasya suggests a Turkish Venice, framed by towering cliffs, a quiet river, carved rock tombs, ornate Selçuk *hammams* and mosques, and stately Ottoman houses. The birthplace of the geographer Strabo, Amasya was the capital of Pontus, a kingdom of Greek-speaking Persians that arose after the death of Alexander the Great. Under the Ottomans, who arrived in 1391, Amasya became an important theological and cultural center with 18 *madrasas* (Islamic theological schools) by the 18th century.

✳🛈 ORIENTATION AND PRACTICAL INFORMATION

Amasya is divided by the **Yeşilırmak (Green River),** which runs roughly east-west. The **north bank,** home to Ottoman houses and the Pontic cliff tombs, is the older part of town. The tourist office and most restaurants and hotels lie on the **south bank,** either on **Mehmet Paşa Cad.,** the road running immediately along the river, or the more substantial **Atatürk Cad.,** one block south. Arriving buses stop either at the city center or at the **otogar,** three kilometers northeast of town. To get to the center, take any of the city buses ($.20, students $.15) or *dolmuş* ($.25, students $.20) that stop across the street from the *otogar.* A taxi costs US$2.50. Alternatively, turn left at the exit of the *otogar* and follow the road to the city center. Buses run from the *otogar* to: **Ankara** (5½hr.; 7 per day 8:30am-12:30am; US$9.50, students US$8); **Antalya** (12hr.; 3pm; US$22, students US$19); **Bursa** (11hr.; 3 per day 6:30-8pm; US$19, students US$16); **İstanbul** (10hr.; 9 per day 9:30am-11:15pm; US$19, students US$16); **İzmir** (14hr.; 5pm; US$22.50, students US$21); **Marmaris** (15hr.; 4pm; US$22.50, students US$19); and **Trabzon** (8hr.; 5 per day 5-10pm; US$13, students US$11). The **tourist office** is in a kiosk on the river's south bank. (☎218 74 28. Open Apr. 15-Sept. 15 M-F 10am-noon and 2-6pm; Sa-Su 1-6pm.) Many **banks** with **ATMs** line the south bank of the river. **Yapi ve Kredi,** across the street from the PTT, cashes **traveler's checks.** (Open M-F 9am-12:30pm and 1:30-5pm.) The local hospital is **Devlet Hastanesi** (☎218 40 00). The **PTT** is on Mehmet Paşa Cad., 100m west of the main square. (Open daily 8:30am-12:30pm and 1:30-5pm. Phone card sales and services 8am-11pm.) **Postal code:** 05100.

🏠🍽 ACCOMMODATIONS AND FOOD

Though the Ottoman houses along the river are more expensive than most lodgings in Turkey, their beautiful views and traditional decor make them worth the extra expense. The 180-year-old ◼ **İlk Pension,** Gümüşlu Mah., 1 Hitit Sok., down a small side street off Mehmet Paşa Cad. facing the tourist office, offers large rooms of an authentic ilk with private baths. (☎218 16 89. Breakfast US$3. Singles US$17-34; doubles US$25-45. 10% student discount.) Each sparkling new room at **Yalıbolu Otel**, 19/D Ziyapaşa Bul., offers TV and private bath. The excellent rooftop restaurant serves *Amasya kebap* for US$2.50 and *Efes* beer for US$1.50. (☎218 70 29. Singles US$16, students US$13; doubles US$29, students US$25; triples US$40, students US$37.) If you're in more of a do-it-yourself mood, stock up at **Yimpaş**, a supermarket just across from the tourist office. (Open daily 8am-10pm.) **Ocakbaşı Restaurant**, 5 Ziya Paşa Cad., on the river, serves Turkish dishes in an outdoor plaza. (*Lahmacun* US$.75; *pide* US$2. ☎218 56 92. Open daily 6am-10:30pm.)

🔍 SIGHTS

PONTIC RUINS. Carved out of the cliffs north of the city are the **Kralkaya mezarları**, the tombs of the Pontic kings. Though the graffiti-covered tombs are less impressive up close than from below, a climb up offers beautiful panoramic views of the valley and city. Dating to the 3rd century BCE, an ancient **fortress** *(kale)* looms high above Amasya. It was renovated first by the Ottomans and again in the 1980s. The extensive ruins and spectacular views of the entire gorge are worth the long, steep hike. *(From the south bank, follow Mehmet Paşa Cad. east past the tourist office, then cross the river at the next bridge, and follow Zubeyde Hanım Cad. to a large roundabout with signs to the tomb. Alternatively take a US$4 round-trip taxi from town.)*

MUSEUMS. The **Ottoman House Museum (Hazeranlar Konağ)** on the north side of the river is one of Amasya's best preserved Ottoman houses, along with the İlk and Emin Efendi *pansiyons*. The **Archaeological Museum** has an impressive collection of artifacts spanning the history of the region, including the grisly mummified remains of Mongol rulers and their children, on display in the old Selçuk *türbe*. *(Just past the Sultan Beyazıt Mosque on Atatürk Cad. Open Tu-Su 8:30am-noon and 1:30-5:30pm. US$1, students US$.50.)*

SELÇUK AND OTTOMAN SIGHTS. Follow the river a short way west from the PTT to the **Sultan Beyazıt II Camii.** Amasya's largest Islamic monument, the mosque was completed in 1486 by Sultan Beyazıt II's eldest son and heir apparent Ahmet, who lost the throne in 1513 to his younger brother. From here, continue west on Atatürk Cad., past the Archaeological Museum, to the Selçuk **Gökmedrese Camii** (Blue Seminary Mosque). The blue tiles that gave the mosque its name (*"gök"* means "sky") are now mostly gone, and the spectacular carved door is in the museum. Across the street is the Ottoman ▓ **Yörgüç Paşa Camii,** with striking sections of red stone and frescoes. East along the river, past the tourist office, is the early Ottoman **Mehmet Paşa Camii,** a sprawling complex that now houses a girls' Qur'anic school. **Yıldız Hatun Medresesi,** 20m east of the tourist office, was an insane asylum built in 1308 by the Mongol Sultan Olcaytuas. The carved doorway and other features of the building look remarkably Selçuk and remarkably crazy.

TRABZON   ☎462

Since the collapse of the Soviet Union and the re-opening of Turkey's northeastern borders, Trabzon has resumed its role as the button on the Black Sea's underbelly—a sieve for trade into Georgia, Armenia, Azerbaijan, and Iran. The cell phones, thick traffic, concrete edifices, and visible prostitutes that emerged after the region's most recent boom are merely another incarnation of a city that for three millennia has sheltered smugglers, pimps, and dethroned emperors. Battered by marauding Crusaders, the Comnenus dynasty took refuge here until 1461, when they ran out of daughters to marry off to appease the usurping Ottomans. Despite its seedy central square, Russian bazaar, and frenzied pace, Trabzon is a good stop to organize trekking tours in the Kaçkar Mountains to the south.

✈ 🛈 ORIENTATION AND PRACTICAL INFORMATION

All of the city's hotels, restaurants, and services are concentrated around **Atatürk Alanı**, the main square, just uphill and west of the city's central port. **Kahraman-maraş (Maraş) Cad.** runs west out of Atatürk Alanı, leading past banks, the PTT, and a few historical sites before ending just below the ancient **Aya Sofia. Gazipaşa Cad.** is the short main road between Atatürk Alanı's western edge and the coastal highway, **Sahil Yolu**, which leads to the intercity **otogar**, three kilometers east.

Flights: *Dolmuş* leave from Atatürk Alanı and the coastal highway. **THY** (☎321 16 80), at the SW corner of Atatürk Alanı, flies to **Ankara** (1½hr.; 5:50, 10:05am, 7:30pm; US$68, students US$54) and **İstanbul** (2hr.; 5:40, 9:40am, 7:20pm; US$85, students US$63).

Buses: 3km east of the main square. **Ulusoy** (☎325 22 01) and **Metro** (☎325 72 86) run to: **Ankara** (12hr., 7 per day 7:30am-8pm, US$25); **Bursa** (17hr., 4 per day noon-2pm, US$33); **İstanbul** (18hr., 10 per day 11am-7:30pm, US$33). Sinop, Amasya, Amasra, Safranbolu, and all points west can be reached via **Samsun.**

Ferries: Turkish Maritime Lines, inside the gate at the base of İskele Cad., runs between Trabzon, Samsun, and İstanbul (June 15-Sept. 15). Open M-F 8am-5pm.

Tourist Office: Opposite the southeast corner of Atatürk Alanı, adjacent to the Hotel Nur. New and well-equipped government tourist office; some English. Open daily 8am-5:30pm; in winter closed on weekends.

Travel Agencies: Afacan Tour, 40/C İskele Cad. (☎321 44 39 or 321 58 04; fax 321 70 01), 100m from Usta, has tours of **Sumela** (daily 10am-4pm, US$4.50); **Uzungöl** (Sa-Su 9am-7pm, US$12); **Karaca Cave and Zigana** (Sa 9am-6:30pm, US$12 with lunch). Open daily 9am-7pm. **Usta Tour,** 4 İskele Cad. (☎326 18 70; fax 326 18 71), across from the northeast corner of Atatürk Alanı and adjacent to the Usta Hotel complex. Tours of **Sumela** (Tu and Th 11am-6:30pm; US$6.50, students US$5.50); **Uzungöl** (W and Sa 9am-6:30pm; US$8, students US$7); **Ayder Yayla** (Su 9am-7pm; US$11, students US$10). Open in season daily 8:30am-5:30pm.

Banks: Most of Trabzon's larger banks are lined up on Maraş Cad., just west of Atatürk Alanı. Cash is easy to exchange, but **traveler's checks** may require some persistence.

Police: Trabzon is split into 6 police districts, each with its own telephone number. The best option is to call ☎155. The tourist police can be reached at ☎326 30 77.

Hospital: K.T.U. Farabı Hastanesi (Karadeniz Teknik Üniversitesi Tıp Fakultesi; ☎325 30 11 or 377 50 00). Take any *dolmuş* marked K.T.U.

Internet Access: In Atatürk Alanı, try **World Internet Cafe** (☎323 11 34), on the 2nd floor of the building adjacent to McDonald's. Open daily 9:30am-1am.

PTT: West down Maraş Cad. Open daily 8:30am-5:30pm. Telephone services open 24hr. **Postal Code:** 61020 (downtown only).

⌂🗋 ACCOMMODATIONS AND FOOD

It's difficult to find a sinless and silent hotel in Trabzon. ▨ **Otel Anıl,** Güzelhisar Cad. No. 10. Adjacent to Otel Yuvan, 50m off İskele Cad., is a welcoming oasis of peace and cleanliness in 36 big rooms with hot water baths, and TV. (☎326 72 82 or 326 72 83. Breakfast included. Singles US$13; doubles US$21; triples US$30.) **Hotel Nur,** Meydan Camii Sok. No. 10. Off Atatürk Alanı, opposite the İskender Paşa Camii, next to the tourist office, has a friendly management and 15 large, clean rooms, all with shower, toilet, and TV. (☎323 04 45 or 323 04 46; fax 323 04 47. Singles US$13; doubles US$22.50; triples US$35.) **Hotel Yuvan,** Güzelhisar Cad. No. 10, is adjacent to the Otel Anıl, 50m off İskele Cad. This simple, good-value hotel has shower, toilet, and TV in every room. (☎/fax 326 68 23 or 326 68 24. Singles US$10; doubles US$16; triples US$20.)

Trabzon's cuisine is a melange of standard Turkish fare, fresh Black Sea fish, and corn, potatoes, and peas from the fertile highlands south of the city. The dense foot traffic around Atatürk Alanı supports a dazzling array of restaurants, including *Chez McDonald's*. Grocery stores are at the northeast corner of Atatürk Alanı. **Kebabistan,** Maraş Cad. No. 30, opposite the Zorlu Grand Hotel, is among the cleanest and best restaurants in Trabzon. (☎321 86 51. *Vali kebap* (US$4); *ayran* (US$.40). Open daily 11am-11pm.) **Güloğlu Restaurant,** Atatürk Alanı No. 4/E, is a recently-renovated *kebap* and *lahmacun* salon. Enjoy the A/C while you indulge in the *Sarma Beyti Kebap* (US$2) and finish with a 6-piece portion of delicious baklava (US$1). (☎321 53 32. Open daily 6am-11pm.)

■ SIGHTS

Aya Sofia and its peaceful garden have done time as a temple of Apollo, a basilica, an Orthodox church under Comnenian Emperor Manual I (who commissioned the construction of the present edifice), and a mosque. A 1960s restoration project uncovered some of Turkey's best frescoes, many about the life of Jesus. Carvings of sailboats on the eastern wall were made by Genoans and Venetians pining for their distant homelands. *(To reach the Aya Sofia, either take a dolmuş from Atatürk Alanı, or, from the old city, take a dolmuş along the coastal highway; ask the driver for Aya Sofia and walk 2 blocks uphill. Museum open Tu-Su 9am-5pm. US$1.50, students free.)* The 7th-century **St. Anne's Church,** in an alley of Maraş Cad., is the oldest extant Christian structure in town, but is currently closed for restoration. **Gülbaharhatun Camii** (the Mosque of the Spring Rose), on Uzun Cad. past Atapark, holds the remains of Ottoman Sultan Selim I's mother. Up the road on Amasya Sok., Selim I's wife gave birth to Süleyman the Magnificent. Farther down Maraş Cad., within the walls of the old city, is **Fatih Camii,** once the cathedral of the *Panagia Chrysokephelos*, the Golden-Headed Virgin. In 1461, Sultan Mehmet covered the Virgin in plaster, but a portion of the original is intact on the east side.

♫ VIVALAS TRABZONSPOR! (AND OTHER ENTERTAINMENT)

Trabzon is a **football** town, and **Trabzonspor,** the adored local team, plays regularly from late August to late May (with half-length matches in Jan. and Feb.). The stadium is about 5km east of downtown, on the seaside Spor Cad. (sheltered seats US$4, open seats US$1). After the game, head to **English Pub,** Zorlu Grand Hotel, Maraş Cad. No. 9, 2nd fl., to unwind in plush armchairs in Trabzon's best hotel. (*Rakı* US$2. Open daily 5pm-2am.) The **High Life Disco** is on Gazipaşa Cad.; head toward the sea, and the disco is on the right 20m before the bridge. A favorite among area students and free of *Nataşas*. If you'd rather a massage, head 2km out to **Sekiz Direkli Hamam** (☎322 10 12), Pazarkapı Mah. Follow the signs along Maraş Cad. until it turns downhill, or take a US$2 taxi. (Open daily 4:30am-11pm. Th 8am-5pm reserved for women only. Bath US$4.50, *kese* US$5.50.)

NEAR TRABZON: SUMELA MONASTERY

The monastery and adjoining national park are accessible by dolmuş or private tours, which run from June through September. Dolmuş start loading up by Trabzon's Russian Bazaar about 8am, leaving as they fill. It's tough to find one after 11am. The ride to the park from Trabzon takes one hour. Tours tend to rush; they'll generally consist of a ½hr. hike through the park to the monastery (park admission US$1.50, students US$1) and a lunch of fresh trout (US$3) at the Sumela Restaurant. If you bypass the tour option, there are two trails up to Sumela, so ask locals at the top for directions down the alternate route via the ruins of the Santa Barbara Chapel.

Nowhere else in northwestern Anatolia is the region's Byzantine legacy so breathtakingly combined with the jagged, forested landscape than at Sumela Monastery, which is built into a cliffside cave to provide natural protection from the elements. Approximately 45km southwest of Trabzon, high in the mountains, Sumela was founded in 385 CE by two Athenian monks who were allegedly visited by the Holy Virgin. The monastery's inner chapel is a spectacular display of three layers of secular, Old Testament, and New Testament frescoes (all of which are partially exposed) covering the chapel's interior and exterior, which is shielded from harsh weather by the overhanging cave. The cave couldn't save the monastery from a recent fire, though. Turkish authorities are currently restoring it, but to see Sumela in all its pre-conflagration flagrante, check out the postcards (2 for US$1) in the gift shop of the adjacent park.

YUSUFELİ   ☎466

Yusufeli is cradled in the gorgeous, undeveloped **Çoruh Nehri** (Çoruh Valley). The Çoruh River narrows as the valley walls steepen into dry, crumbling spires and cliffs. Yet at the confluence of the Çoruh and its Barhal tributary is a corridor of lush greenery that defies the barren slopes above. If arriving from the south, you'll drop down from rolling grasslands and the huge Tatum Reservoir into a canyon system utterly unlike Anatolia's hilly steppe. Yusufeli, Turkey's **white-water rafting** capital, was home to a 1993 rafting championship. Tekkale (6km up the valley) also makes a relaxing base for walks, hikes, and treks in the upper Çoruh Valley or the Kaçkars. Even a day or two is enough to explore the Georgian churches.

🖅🚹 GETTING AROUND AND PRACTICAL INFORMATION. The tourist center of Yusufeli is the rectangular area enclosed by four streets named after Turkish politicians: **Enver Paşa Cad., Fevzi Çakmak Cad., Mustafa Kemal Cad.,** and **İnönü Cad.** Most hotels occupy the upstream end of İnönü Cad., the central street that passes the *otogar* lot, **pharmacies,** and some decent dry restaurants. **Artvin Express,** in the *otogar* lot, runs to: **Ankara** (18hr., noon, US$19); **Artvin** (2hr., 10 per day 6am-5pm, US$2.50); **Bursa** (22hr., 9am, US$24); **Erzurum** (3hr., 2 per day 9-11am, US$3.50); **Hopa** (2½hr., 9am, US$5); **İstanbul** (20hr., 10am, US$24); **Rize** (4½hr., 9am, US$6); **Trabzon** (6hr., 9am, US$7). *Dolmuş* head from the *otogar* up the Çoruh and Barhal valleys, with prices set according to distance (US$1.50 to Tekkale; US$2.50 to Sarigol). A small **hospital** (☎811 20 15) and **police** station are also centrally located. **Akin Cafe** on Ersis Cad. has Internet access. The **PTT** is on İnönü Cad. at the downstream end of town. **Postal code:** 08800.

🖪🍴 FOOD AND ACCOMMODATIONS. Yusufeli's better hotels are all close to each other on İnönü Cad. All establishments listed are clean and quiet. The **Hotel Çiçek Palas** (☎811 21 02) and the **Hacıoğlu Oteli** (☎811 35 66), both just off İnönü Cad., offer basic, peaceful rooms. (Singles US$6; doubles US$10.) While the more homely Hacıoğlu has hot showers, **Çiçek Palas** has a common stove. The **Barhal Hotel** (☎811 31 51), overlooking the Bahol River from a courtyard about 20m upstream on İnönü Cad, offers sterile rooms with river views. (Singles US$6; doubles US$10; triples US$15.) The owner, Sırali Aydur, runs the Mountain Sports Club. To reach **Greenpeace Camping,** cross the bridge by the Barhal Hotel, turn right, take another right at the T-intersection, and turn left. The grounds offer secluded campsites in a garden, cold shower, and light meals. (US$1-2 per night. Open mid-June-mid-Sept.) *Dolmuş* are infrequent; many travelers hitchhike. The 🖼 **Mavi Köşk Restorant** (☎811 23 29), off İnönü Cad., has delicious food and a well-stocked bar. (Full meal about US$3.50. Open daily 8am-1am.) One of the more popular meeting places is **Çınar Lokantası** (☎811 23 65), which overlooks the river beneath the Barhal Hotel. Its menu includes grilled meat, fresh trout, *rakı*, and vegetarian *mezze* (Full meal with beer US$3.50. Open daily 9am-midnight.) Also popular with the locals is **Mahsen Restaurant** (☎811 20 08).

🔼 HIKING: THE ÇORUH VALLEY

As the Çoruh River winds its way through a stunning, arid valley toward Yusufeli, it leaves a line of small farms, lush trees, and sleepy hamlets in its wake. The village of **Tekkale,** about 6km up the paved road from Yusufeli, makes an excellent base for hikes up tributary streams to the area's numerous abandoned **Georgian** churches and *yayla* (high-altitude meadow villages). Longer hikes lead up past the spring snow line to the peaks and freezing lakes of the southeastern Kaçkars. Infrequent *dolmuş* run to Tekkale only in the afternoon (US$1.50); many travelers hitchhike. Taxis runs about US$5.

From Tekkale, a rough side road climbs up toward **Barhal** (also accessible by a separate road from Yusufeli). This slightly remoter village is popularly known as a base camp for treks. *Dolmuş* head to Barhal at sporadic times in the late afternoon and early evening. At the south of town, the **Barhal Pension** has new wooden rooms occupying the second floor of a house. (☎ (466) 826 20 31. Dinner and breakfast included. US$10 per person.) At the town center, the road splits right 4km to the **Karahan Pension**, 50m uphill from the Barhal Kilise (ask locals for directions). Run by Mehmet Karahan, the Karahan offers great lodging for the Kaçkars-bound, including an airy deck where meals are served. (Dinner and breakfast included. US$12 per night) From the center of Barhal, the road splits left to various *yayla*, and right to **Barhal Kilise**, 4km away, a well preserved 10th-century Georgian church that now serves as the town's mosque. From Tekkale, follow the road to Yusufeli for 7km to **Dörtkilise** ("Four Churches"), now home to only one of the original four. The remaining Georgian church is a hauntingly beautiful place to spend the evening, and the grounds outside make a prime campsite.

EASTERN ANATOLIA

Welcome to Eastern Turkey, where sheep outnumber people, where you can search in vain for an English speaker for days on end, and where police identification checks are more common than Efes Pilsen. Almost no Turks raised in the western part of the country have been to Eastern Anatolia, having been taught that the region is war-torn, remote, and impoverished. The Armenian slaughter of 1915 occurred largely within Turkey's eastern border territory, and intermittent fighting persists between the PKK and the Turkish army. This negative image of Turkey's frontier land has permeated its global reputation, leaving the area untouched by all but the most intrepid of travelers. However, the region offers some of Turkey's most astonishing beauty, both natural and man-made.

TRAVEL WARNING Travel in Eastern Turkey should be approached with caution. Travelers should be updated on all consular advisories and warnings, and should be careful to follow all relevant rules and laws. That said, tensions in the region have decreased significantly over the past two years, and tourists should not avoid Eastern Turkey solely on safety grounds. Cooperation with police and military personnel is imperative. The unpredictable nature of travel in Eastern Anatolia requires that travel schedules be flexible. *Let's Go* does not recommend that **women** travel alone to Eastern Turkey. Even with a head scarf and long, concealing clothes, females may be mistaken for *Nataşas* (prostitutes). To avoid unwanted advances, dress very conservatively, memorize some key phrases, and stay in the more expensive hotels.

ŞANLIURFA ☎ 414

Though known as Şanlıurfa (Glorious Urfa) to the Turkish state, Muslims refer to the city as *Peygamberler Şehri*, the City of Prophets. Urfa is said to be the birthplace of the prophet Abraham and dwelling place of the prophet Job, making it a popular pilgrimage destination. It's also the best base from which to visit the spectacular 2000-year-old funerary ruins at **Nemrut Dağı** (see p. 687).

🔼 PRACTICAL INFORMATION. Urfa's **otogar** is 1½km from the town cente Some buses have free shuttle service to the *otogar*, or you can take a taxi (US$ 5). Buses run to: **Ankara** (12hr., 8 per day, US$17); **Doğubayazıt** (16hr., 4 per da

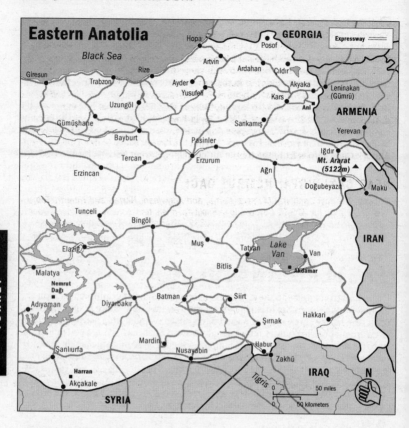

Eastern Anatolia

Black Sea

GEORGIA
Expressway

Hopa
Posof
Artvin
Ardahan
Çıldır
Rize
Giresun
Trabzon
Ayder
Yusufeli
Akyaka
Leninakan
(Gümrü)
Uzungöl
Kars
Ani
ARMENIA
Gümüşhane
Bayburt
Sarıkamış
Yerevan
Pasinler
Tercan
Erzurum
Iğdır
Mt. Ararat
(5122m)
Erzincan
Ağrı
Doğubeyazıt
Maku
Tunceli
Bingöl
IRAN
Muş
Lake
Van
Elazığ
Tatvan
Van
Bitlis
Akdamar
Malatya
Nemrut
Dağı
Adıyaman
Diyarbakır
Batman
Siirt
Hakkari
Şırnak
Şanlıurfa
Mardin
Nusaybin
Habur
Harran
Akçakale
Zakhū
IRAQ
Tigris
SYRIA
N
0   50 miles
0   50 kilometers

US$22); **İstanbul** (17hr., 9 per day, US$20); **İzmir** (17hr., 2 per day, US$20); **Kars** (20hr., 1 per day, US$24); **Trabzon** (15hr., 4 per day, US$22); and **Van** (12hr., 4 per night, US$13). *Dolmuş* and minibuses leave from the same parking lot. The **tourist office** is 23m from the doors of the Hotel Edessa (opposite Hasan Paşa Camii), in the marble complex. (☎215 24 67. Open M-F 8am-noon and 1:30-5:30pm.)

■☐ ACCOMMODATIONS AND FOOD. Urfa's heat persists through the night, so consider splurging on rooms with air-conditioning. ⊠**Hotel Ugur Palas,** Koprubasi Cad., is a budget dream. The rooms are clean with shared bath. (US$4 per person.) ⊠**Valiligi Konuk Evi,** on Vali Fuat Bey Cad., in an exquisitely restored mansion with only six rooms, fills up quickly. (Singles US$22; doubles US$40; suite US$40.) Clean and quiet **Hotel İpek Palas,** 4 Şanmed Hastanesi Arkası, behind the Şan-Med Hospital on Atatürk Cad. at the town center, has air-conditioning, private hot showers, and TVs. (☎215 93 77. Singles US$12; doubles US$18; triples US$24.)

Urfa is renowned for its culinary wonders, but its kitchens have a downside: many foods (especially meats) become infested with bacteria in the sweltering heat, and visitors often leave with stomach problems. To reach ⊠**Sultan Sarayi Restaurant** (☎316 37 50), three kilometers north along Atatürk Cad., catch the *dolmuş* marked 'Karakopru' (US$.20), and get on at the university. Those with kebap-
rder *lebeni* (yogurt and wheat), spicy *bostona* salad, and chicken with drinks) before 10:30pm. ⊠**Gulizar Konuk Evi** is by the Ulu Camii. aniye Sok. from Sarayonu Cad. (☎215 05 05. Open until 10pm.)

⊡ SIGHTS. Though Urfa contains some ancient ruins, the real marvels are at Nemrut Dağı to the north. Religious pilgrims, however, flock to Urfa's Old Testament holy sites. Behind the first mosque on Göl Cad. lies the large **Mevlid Halil Camii,** which houses the believed **birth cave** of the prophet Abraham. Women are able to forge all the way back into the sacred cave, while men may only look through a barred fence, praying in the proper direction. (Dress respectably.) The entrance to the city's **citadel** is marked by Corinthian columns constructed in 242 BCE, from which, according to legend, Nemrut shot firebrands at Abraham. (Open daily 8am-6pm. US$2, students US$1.) **Eyyüp Peygamber,** 3km south of the bazaar, contains the cave where the prophet Job lived for seven years while his body was being consumed by worms. Take an "Eyyübe" *dolmuş* (every 5min., US$.20) from Atatürk Cad., across from the tourist office. (Open during daylight hours. US$1.)

NEAR ŞANLIURFA: NEMRUT DAĞI

*Accessible from Şanlıurfa, Malatya, Kahta, and Adıyaman. **Harran and Nemrut Tours** (☎ 215 15 75; fax 215 11 56), based in Şanlıurfa, offers transportation and tours. Open during daylight hours. US$3.50, students US$2. Allow at least 2hr. to explore the site, including the walk up. The monument is at the base of a cone-shaped pile of rocks, at the bottom of which are 3 terraces on the north, west, and east. Rough winds can cause chills and dehydration: bring layers and water.*

Upon the highest peak in the region (2150m), Commagene King **Antiochus I** ordered the construction of a 75m pyramid of rubble, flanked by massive statues, their heads long since decapitated by earthquakes (most recently 1938) and time. At dawn and dusk, solitude and silence prevails on this impressive funerary monument, the calm broken only by the whipping of a constant wind. Antiochus broke away from the Seleucids in the wake of Alexander the Great's death. He created specific plans for the construction of this egomaniacal monument, made up of nine towering figures of the king surrounded by deities and animals on east and west terraces. Careful observation can match fallen heads to the torsos above. The figures mirror each other from north to south: Lion, Eagle, Apollo, Tyche (Fortuna), Zeus, Antiochus, Hercules, Eagle, and Lion. This juxtaposition of man and god was arranged to demonstrate the king's relation to these deities.

VAN ☎432

For 3000 years, Van and the surrounding area has been Eastern Turkey's most vibrant cultural center. The natural beauty is a backdrop for the area's unique blend of Urartian, Armenian, and Kurdish influences. In the past century, however, the Van area has been the stage on which Turkey's most dramatic conflicts have unfolded. The first organized Kurdish rebellion occurred here during the 1880s, and World War I brought on the forced exile and slaughter of 600,000 to 800,000 Armenians. Today, the focus of conflict in Van is militant Kurdish separatism. Over one million people are estimated to live in the greater Van area, and the population is almost entirely made up of ethnic Kurds.

⌷ GETTING THERE. Travelers arrive at the **airport** (5km south) or the **bus station** (1½km north of the city). Frequent *dolmuş* marked "İskele-Otogar" go to town (US$.30). An airline bus usually meets flights at the airport. Otherwise, walk 300m to the main road for a US$.40 *dolmuş* to avoid the US$10 taxi. Most companies have free transport to the bus station 30 minutes before departure. Buses run to: **Ankara** (18hr., 8 per day, US$25); **Antakya** (18hr., 1 per day, US$20); **İstanbul** (25hr., 8am and 1pm, US$36); **İzmir** (25hr., 3 per day, US$37); **Şanlıurfa** (10hr., 2 per day, US$13); and **Trabzon** (12hr., 1 per day, US$20). *Dolmuş* leave for **Doğubeyazıt** 200m west of Beş Yol (4 per morning, US$4).

⧈▨ ORIENTATION AND PRACTICAL INFORMATION. Cumhuriyet Cad. runs the length of downtown, between the Atatürk statue (north) and the tourist information center (south). The **tourist office,** across from the Asur Otel in a yellow building marked "Turizm Müdürlügü," offers brochures and a photocopied map, but the staff speaks little English. (☎216 20 18 or 216 36 75. Open M-F 8am-noon and 1:30-5:30pm.) If you have more complicated needs, someone from the **Buyuk Asur Otel** (☎216 37 53, ask for Remzi Bozbay) can translate. **Türkiye İş Bankası** and **Vakıf Bank,** on Cumhuriyet Cad. near the PTT, exchange traveler's checks. (Both open daily 8am-noon and 1:30-5:30pm.) **ATMs** line the main avenue. The **Devlet Hastanesi** (state hospital) is 300m south of Beş Yol on İskele Cad. Access the Internet at **Cafe Net,** upstairs at No. 71/1 Cumhuriyet Cad. (US$1 per hr. Open daily 8:30am-midnight.) The large **PTT,** on Cumhuriyet Cad. near Sok. 6, has Poste Restante service and a row of 15 Türk Telekom phones. (☎214 34 90. Mail service open daily 6am-11pm; phone service 24hr.) **Postal code:** 65100.

⏏♨ ACCOMMODATIONS AND FOOD. Van's 1990s tourist boom created many now-empty hotels, most of which charge surprisingly low rates as a result. The cheap hotels stand together, 200m south of the Atatürk statue, tucked into Eski Sümerbank Sok., off Cumhuriyet Cad. ◪**Ada Palas** is the best of these. (☎216 22 34. US$1.60 per person.) **Hotel Ipek,** Cumhuriyet Cad., Sok. 1, #3, is in the heart of the market district. Some rooms have showers, but share a bath. (☎216 30 33. Singles US$2.50; doubles US$5; triples US$7.50; with shower add US$3.) **Hotel Büyük Asur,** Cumhuriyet Cad. and Turizm Sok. #5, is a traveler's hub, and a major step up in quality. All rooms have large beds and are equipped with 24-hour hot water showers. The lobby boasts a breezy deck and a traditional *kilim*-pillow lounge. (☎216 87 92. Singles US$12; doubles US$16; triples US$24.) **Camping** along the lake shore is possible; check all available resources for the latest news in safety.

Kurdish cuisine has sadly disappeared from restaurant menus, leaving behind standard Turkish fare. ◪**Merkez Et Lokantasi,** on the busy corner of İskele Cad. and İpec Yolu, is Van's best, and worth the one-kilometer trip from town. (☎216 97 01. Meal and soft drink US$4. Open daily 8am-11pm.) ◪**Cinar Restaurant,** behind the Bayram Hotel, has a broad menu, a pleasant upstairs location, and the best food on the street. (☎214 66 06. Open daily until 9pm.) **Erol Kardeşler Kahvaltı Salonu,** Sok. 8 on Cumhuriyet Cad., is the best breakfast house in town, serving thoroughly fresh *oltu peynir*, honey and butter, omelettes, hot sweet milk, tomatoes, and yogurt. (☎214 66 06. Open daily from 5am.)

⚑☷ SIGHTS AND ENTERTAINMENT. After the Russians destroyed the old city of Tuşba, local Kurds and their Turkish rulers built the new city of Van 5km to the south. Consequently, Van's center offers nothing of historical importance aside from the **Van Museum.** The ground floor contains prehistoric finds from Tilkitepe as well as Urartian helmets, textile tools, bronze belts, and cremation bowls. The inner courtyard has large stone carvings of lions and Urartian inscriptions. Upstairs is a *kilim* collection and a gallery called the "Genocide section," which presents a misleading portrayal of the slaughter of Turks by Armenians and omits any mention of the Armenian genocide. (Open daily 8am-noon and 1:30-5:30pm. US$1.50, students US$1.)

Carpet and **kilim** sellers here are the primary distributors for western Turkish dealers, and thus they are in a position to offer the same quality found in tourist areas for up to 70% less. Here, **Sene Kilim,** crafted by Kurdish villagers in Northern Iran and Southeastern Turkey, are easy to find. As always, do not purchase carpets at high prices unless claims of age and rarity can be authenticated.

NEAR VAN

ÇAVUŞTEPE AND ENVIRONS

Çavuştepe must be visited in the morning, as the road closes at 3pm. Dolmuş (US$4) heading for Hoşap Castle via Çavuştepe depart 200m west of the İstanbul Airlines office on Cumhuriyet Cad. (open daily 7am-1pm). Cavuştepe open daily 8am-6pm. US$1.50. Hoşap open daily 8am-5pm. US$1.50, students US$1.

The Urartian peoples dominated the entire Van region from the 9th through the 6th centuries BCE, with an architecturally sophisticated kingdom featuring towering fortresses, extensive tunnels, highways, canals, and piers. The Urartians built shrines and temples around the holy Van "Sea," believed to purify their weapons and fulfill their desires. Three of their major fortresses still stand a short distance from Van. Closest to town lies the fortress constructed by King Sarduri I (840-830 BCE), known today as the Rock of Van, or **Van Kale.** Called Tuşba by the Urartians, it was the center of their vast kingdom, which extended from the Mediterranean to Iran. Of the three fortresses, this is the only one that visitors can explore extensively. **Toprakkale,** 4km southeast of Van, was built in 735 BCE to defend Urartu from invaders. Access to Toprakkale is prohibited, as it lies in a military zone. **Mehir Kapısı's rock niche,** a Urartian site between the bluff and the castle, may be open to visitors. In 764 BCE, Sarduri II (764-735 BCE) built a sprawling, three-sectioned castle 25km south of Van. Once more than 850m long and 80m high, the remains of **Çavuştepe** are today not as impressive as those of the other Urartian sights. Archaeologists are currently excavating the little-known fortress of **Ayanis,** 33km northeast of Van.

Built in 1643, **Hoşap Castle** is one of Turkey's greatest Kurdish castles. After the erection of his magnificent complex, which included a bridge over the Hoşap River, Kurdish feudal lord San Süleyman chopped off the hands of the architect to prevent him from building another of equal beauty. The walls are made of a mixture of dirt and pigeon eggs, and the entrance gate has two reliefs of lions with chains around their necks, denoting the gladiator matches between animals and men that occurred within the castle walls. The upper level contains royal rooms, the harem, and a *hammam,* all with a view of the valley and the village below.

AKDAMAR CHURCH

50km west of Van on an island, 5km off the coast. Dolmuş headed for Gevaş will go the additional 9km to the dock if you clear it with the driver before boarding. Dolmuş depart from Van, 400m north of Cumhuriyet Cad. on K. Karabekir Cad. (every hr. when full 6am-5pm., US$1.50.). Ferries run 6am-sundown (daily every 30min. or when full; US$3, students US$2). M-F boats fill slowly. Commission an entire boat for US$30.

Armenians flourished in the Van region for more than two millennia. The remaining Armenian churches are fascinating, especially in light of the fact that the majority have been destroyed or converted into mosques. One such marvel is the the **Church of the Holy Cross** at Akdamar Island (Akdamar Church). A major architectural and artistic feat, the sandstone church stands on a plateau at the center of the island, along with a monastery that remained active until it burned down in the 20th century. The surviving reliefs on the outside of the church tell the story of human evolution, Armenian history, and Christian religious history. Those familiar with the Bible will quickly recognize many of the engraved stories: Adam and Eve, Samson and Delilah, David and Goliath, Mary holding a baby Jesus. The jewels originally placed in every figurine's eye sockets have long since been stolen.

DOĞUBEYAZIT   ☎472

Turkey's portion of the Silk Road ends at Doğubeyazıt. This is a frontier town, a bit rough around the edges, that worries little about its looks. Having long outgrown its tiny main street, Doğubeyazit pulses with the roar of traffic to Iran. On either side, the town is flanked by marvels that ensure its place on the map: **Ağrı Dağ** (Mount Ararat) and the **Işak Paşa Palace.**

▐ GETTING THERE. Visitors arrive either at the **otogar,** at the east end of town, or the **dolmuş stop,** at the other end of the same street. **Buses** depart from the *otogar* for western locations including **Ankara** (18hr., 2 per day, US$25) and **İstanbul** (22hr., 2 per day, US$25). However, service is limited and indirect. At the far west end of Belediye Cad., near the *dolmuş* stop and above the *çay* house, stands the **THY office,** 5 Meyramane Cad. (☎312 67 72. Open daily 7am-8pm.) **Dolmuş** leave for **Van** (3hr., US$5) via **Çaldiran** (US$3) and **Kars** (4hr., US$6) via **Iğdir** (US$2).

■ **ORIENTATION AND PRACTICAL INFORMATION.** Belediye Cad. has all the necessities. **Turan Demirhan** (☎311 39 74; email turandemirhan@hotmail.com) offers free tourist information in English, and organizes all tours from his travel agency at Büyük Agri Cad., 2nd fl., near the BP sign. Cheap hotels are clustered near the east end of town, and the **PTT** and **banks** are near the middle. **Currency exchange** is available at **Turkiye İş Bankası.** (Open daily 8am-12:30pm and 1:30-5:30pm.) V/MC/ Cirrus **ATMs** are prevalent throughout town. Three **Internet cafes** line Çarşi Cad., including **Omega** (☎312 75 48) and **Klas** (☎312 49 18), the latter doubling as a *biliardo salonu* (pool hall). The **PTT** is open daily from 8:30am to 5pm, with 24-hour phones (note: Türk Telekom cards will not function). **Postal code:** 04400.

■ **ACCOMMODATIONS AND FOOD.** The tourist boom of the 1990s brought a plethora of hotels to Doğubeyazıt, most of which are now empty. A cluster of very cheap hotels lies around the far east end of Belediye Cad. Of these, the best value are ▧ **Hotel Tahran,** on Küçük Agri Cad., and ▧ **Hotel Kenan** (☎312 78 69), on Emniyet Cad. (Breakfast included. Doubles US$15.) The cheapest options include **Hotel Saruhan** (☎311 30 97), **Hotel Yayla,** and **Hotel Erzurum** (☎312 50 80), all along Çarşi Cad. (Singles US$5; doubles US$9.) Near the hotels, three restaurants, serving *lokanta*-style food, receive local acclaim. The **Dorya Restaurant** is opposite the PTT. (☎311 53 09. US$3 per meal.) Equally good is **Tad Lokantası,** 134 Carsi Cad. (☎312 44 30), serving *kebap* and *asure* (regional Turkish pudding; US$.60).

■ **SIGHTS.** Aside from the spectacular view of Mount Ararat, most visitors come to Doğubeyazıt to see the ▧**Işak Paşa Palace,** built in 1685 by a local Kurdish chief. The intricacy and beauty of the structure are most apparent in the ornate entranceway, covered in relief work and *muqarnas* (stalactite ornamentation). The large entrance with lion reliefs leads to the **harem,** the **master's chamber,** and the **kitchen.** A nearby hole in the ground is the archetypal "loo with a view," a squatting toilet that allowed the ruler to gaze at the kingdom. Starting again at the outer courtyard, the northwest corner has an eight-sided **türbet,** a **mosque,** and a **sarcophagus.** Up the hill and beyond the mosque is an earlier mosque and Urartian fortress. *(Take the road east from the Hotel Saruhan past an army checkpoint and up 6km up to the palace, a 1-1½hr. walk or a US$6 taxi ride. Open daily 6am-5:30pm. US$2, students US$1.)*

▧ **MOUNT ARARAT.** "...and in the seventh month, on the seventeenth day of the month, the ark came to rest upon the mountains of Ararat" (Genesis 8:4). Movement on **Mount Ararat** is subject to military restrictions, given the current tensions with Armenia. The first **permits** are now being offered to foreign climbers. At present, climbers require a military clearance from *Genel Kurmay Baskanligi* military headquarters in Ankara. Though a formality, regional approval in Ağri and local military permission cause delay. With the correct papers, climbers pass the two military road blocks and climb to 4200m on day one, then reach the summit early the next morning. Equipment can be rented in Doğubeyazıt. Upon invitation of a local, tourists without a permit can be escorted as high as 2500m.

BORDER CROSSING: TURKEY TO IRAN In both directions, the Iranian border crossing is far easier than it has been in previous years. A letter of invitation must be processed through Teheran, which takes at least a week. The border is 35km east of Doğubeyazit. There is an Iranian consulate four hours west, in Erzurum. Alcohol, drugs, playing cards, and pornographic material are likely to complicate matters with Iranian officials.

KARS ☎474

The poverty of Kars contrasts sharply with the haunting beauty of the rugged steppe that envelops it. Yet this contrast and that of the brutal winters and dusty summers only add to Kars's old-world charm. Horse-drawn carts drive alongside automobiles, and vendors set out their varied wares on poorly paved streets. In the town center, a few stately 19th-century buildings founder, submerged under smog, dust, and other hastily built dwellings. Recent public works (fountains, malls, and manicured lawns) promise better times ahead for Kars. Unfortunately, because the key commercial routes to the east bypass the city, those opportunities are limited. Kars has numerous interesting historical relics, all dwarfed by the magnificence of the Armenian ruins at **Ani,** just 48km to the west.

⚆ PRACTICAL INFORMATION. The new **otogar** is 7km east of town and the airport 6km east. **THY,** 80 Atatürk Cad. (☎212 38 38), flies to **İstanbul** (11am, US$68) via **Ankara** (US$50). Buses go to: **Ankara** (9, 10, 11am, noon, 5pm; US$16) via Sivas (US$12); **İstanbul** (9:30, 11:30am, 1pm; US$25); and **İzmir** (11am, US$25). **Eski Otogar,** the old bus station two blocks east of the town center, has become the *dolmuş* lot to local destinations. A minibus or two leave daily for **Trabzon** (US$12) and **Yusufeli** (US$6). Doğubayazıt cannot be reached directly. Get a permit to visit Ani at the **tourist office** (☎212 68 17), in a gray building on the corner of Karadağ Cad. and Atatürk Cad. in the downtown business district. Many **banks** downtown exchange cash and have 24-hour **ATMs.**

▛▟ ACCOMMODATIONS AND FOOD. Most hotels in Kars are clean, comfortable, and noisy. **Hotel Kervansaray,** 204 Faık Bey Cad. (☎223 19 90), and neighboring **Hotel Nursuray** (☎223 13 64), are super budget options, centrally located with basic rooms, clean sheets, and shared baths. Back rooms are quieter. (Showers US$1. US$4 per person.) Another good bet is **Hotel Yilmaz,** 146 Küçük Cad., perhaps the quietest hotel in town. Here rooms are well maintained, with TVs and phones. (☎212 51 74. Singles US$11; doubles US$20.) Kars is known for its *kaşar* (meaning "kosher"), a yellow cheese. The upbeat **Salon Sema Piknik,** 9 Faık Bey Cad., one block east of the Hotel Kervansaray, satisfies vegetarians with its *Kaşarli pide,* a cheese-*pide*-pizza with vegetables and egg. (☎223 21 18. Full meal US$3. Open daily 8am-10pm.) Crowds gather at **Cafe Kristal,** 181 Atatürk Cad., for the tasty *döner kebap.* (☎223 22 67. Full meal US$3.50. Open daily 8am-10pm.)

NEAR KARS: ANİ

All visitors to Ani must obtain a permit from the Kars tourist office before setting out (see Practical Information above). No public transportation runs between Kars and Ani. Taxis carry up to 4 for $33. Larger groups can negotiate a minibus or take a dolmuş ($8 per person) organized through the tourist office. Dolmuş drivers usually take passengers through the permit process and to the Ani museum, where tickets are sold. US$2, students US$1. Çelil Ersözoğlu (☎223 63 23) is the main tour guide and usually the dolmuş driver. Otherwise, Ani Tour (☎223 99 90), in the old bus station, offers a similar package deal. Cameras and camping at Ani are illegal.

Situated 45km east of Kars on the present-day Armenian border, the ancient Armenian capital of Ani is a tremendous site. A strategic point on a lucrative trade route, Ani prospered and grew to a population that (at over 100,000) rivaled Constantinople (İstanbul). Ani sits on a triangular plateau wedged between the Alaçay and Arpaçay Rivers, accessible through the **Aslan Kapısı (Lion's Gate),** the only remaining entrance of the original seven gates. After dealing with the preliminary security, most tourists are set free to roam in Ani. Heading left from the entrance will enable you to make a wide circle, touching all the ruins.

The ruins of the **Church of the Holy Redeemer,** built in 1034, is the first step along the southeast path. Head downhill to find one of the three **Churches of St. Gregory (Tigorn Honents).** On the east wall, realistic frescoes depict the life and times of

St. Gregory the Illuminator, who brought Christianity to Armenia. Soon after King Titridates tortured St. Gregory, he realized his sins and converted himself and soon his state to Christianity. Down in the valley stand the remains of the **Covenant of the Virgins,** from which you can see over the border into Armenia. Head up the plateau to the largest building in Ani, the **Cathedral of Virgin Mary,** designed by Titridates in 939 CE, who also collaborated in the restoration of İstanbul's Aya Sofia. A passage to the left of the altar leads up to a private room; bring a flashlight for safe exploration. Farther southwest lies the **Menüçehir Camii,** built in 1072 and said to be the first mosque in Anatolia. Its climbable minaret bears the uniquely non-Selçuk inscription of Allah's name. From the rotunda-style **Church of St. Gregory (Abighamrets),** northwest of the citadel, the view of the Alaçay River shows carved caves in the canyon gorge, where Armenian and Georgian frescoes are said to be painted. In the center of the plateau is the **Church of the Holy Apostles,** once converted into a *kervansaray,* but now mostly a lot of rubble. Note the variety of Islamic geometric designs and *muqarnas* (stalactite ornamentations). To the northwest is the third **Church of St. Gregory,** built by the Armenian king Gegik I, and the **Selçuk Palace.**

CYPRUS ΚΥΠΡΟΣ

CURRENCY		
US$1 = £0.60		£1 = US$1.68
CDN$1 = £0.41		£1 = CDN$2.45
UK£1 = £0.91		£1 = UK£1.10
IR£1 = £0.73		£1 = IR£1.37
AUS$1 = £0.36		£1 = AUS$2.78
NZ$1 = £0.28		£1 = NZ$3.52
SAR1 = £0.09		£1 = SAR11.68
100DR = £0.17		£1 = 583.38DR

PHONE FACTS   Country Code: 357. Police/Emergency: ☎ 199.

The ancient playwright Euripides once wrote that Cyprus is "where the Loves who soothe mortal hearts dwell." The lovely port cities of Limassol and Paphos (easy ferry trips from Haifa) will surely soothe you with their sunny beaches, breezy ruins, and friendly locals, who have grown accustomed to the growing number of tourists that pass through their hometowns. For coverage of the sights and sounds of all of Cyprus, check out *Let's Go: Greece (including Cyprus) 2001.*

 Ferries from **Haifa, Israel** (p. 339) leave frequently for Limassol and Paphos. Residents of Australia, Canada, New Zealand, the UK, and the US need only present a valid **passport** for entry into Cyprus (good for 90 days). Residents of South Africa will need a **visa** to enter (NIS32), available from the South African consulate in **Tel Aviv** (see p. 324).

CYPRUS

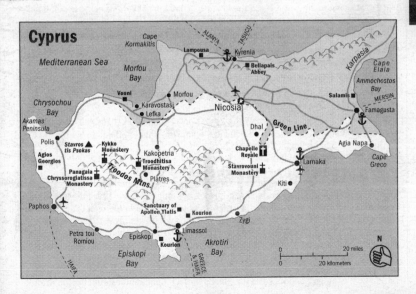

LIMASSOL Λεμεσος
☎ 05

Equal parts fast-paced industrial hub and laid-back resort town, Limassol is a cordial introduction to Cyprus. A barrage of cultural festivities entertains visitors and natives year-round, while the city's elegant restaurants, designer stores, and architecture add an air of sophistication lacking in most other Cypriot cities.

✈🛈 ORIENTATION AND PRACTICAL INFORMATION

Passenger boats arrive at the **new port,** 5km southwest of the town center. Bus #1 runs to the port from the station near Anexartisias Market, and bus #30 runs from the new port to downtown (every 30min., Sa every hr.; £0.35). Buses wait near the customs building or outside the port gates. Taxis to town cost £2.50. The blocks neighboring the town hall house tourist services. A number of dining and entertainment venues are on **Ag. Andreou,** parallel to the waterfront two blocks inland.

Buses: KEMEK (☎747 532), 400m north of the castle at Irinis and Enosis, serves **Lefkosia** (M-F 5 per day, Sa 3 per day; £1.50) and **Paphos** (M-Sa 6-10 per week, £1.50). **Kallenos** (☎(04) 654 850) picks up by the old port and heads for **Larnaka** (M-Sa 3-4 per day, £1.70). The **Episkopi Village** and the **Kourion archaeological site** bus stops in front of Limassol Castle (every hr. 9am-1pm; returns June-Sept. 11:50am, 2:50, and 4:50pm; £0.60).

Ferries: Poseidon Lines (☎745 666; fax 745 577) and **Salamis Tours** (☎355 555; fax 364 410) run to: **Haifa, Israel** (11hr., 2 per week, £50); **Rhodes** (18hr., 2 per week, £44); and **Piraeus** via **Rhodes** (45hr., 2 per week, £47).

Cruises: Salamis Tours (☎355 555; fax 364 410), **Louis Tourist Agency** (☎363 161; fax 363 174), and **Paradise Island Tours** (☎357 604; fax 370 298) stop at **Haifa, Israel,** and **Port Said, Egypt.**

Service Taxis: Taxis run 6am-6:30pm to **Lefkosia** (£3.45), **Larnaka** (£3), and **Paphos** (£2.50). Contact **Makris** (☎365 550) or **Kyriakos** (☎362 061). Free port pickup.

Bike and Moped Rentals: Allipsos rentals along the Promenade (☎376 1650), with 24hr. service. Motorbikes £6.50 per day.

Tourist Office: CTO, Spiro Araouzos 15 (☎362 756), on the waterfront one block east of the castle. Open M-Tu and Th-F 8:15am-2:30pm and 4-6:30pm, W 8:15am-2:30pm, Sa 8:15am-1:15pm. Office at the **new port** (☎343 868) open following arrivals.

Police: (☎330 411), on Gladstone and Leondios next to the hospital. Open 24hr.

Hospital: Government General Hospital, outside Limassol near the village Polemidia; take the #15 bus. There are many private doctors and clinics.

Telephones: CYTA on the corner of Markos Botsaris and Athinon.

Internet Access: Cybernet Café, Eleftherias 79 (☎745 093). £1.50 for 1hr., £1 per additional hr. Open daily 1pm-2am.

Post Office: (☎330 190), next to the central police station on Gladstone. Open May-Sept. M-Tu and Th-F 7:30am-1:30pm and 4-6pm, W 7:30am-1:30pm, Sa 9-11am; Oct.-June Th-Tu 3-5pm. **Postal Code:** 3900.

🏠🍴 ACCOMMODATIONS AND FOOD

Quirky downtown guest houses are Limassol's budget best, but solo travelers (especially women) may prefer the upscale hotels on the waterfront. The **■Guest House Ikaros,** Eleftherias 61, may make you giddy with its tapestries, fish tanks, animal skins, and chandeliers, but you'll come to your senses once you settle down in the spacious rooms with shared bath. (☎354 348. Singles £5; doubles £10; 1st daily shower free, 2nd £0.50.) **Luxor Guest House,** Ag. Andreou 101, has an understated decor that lends a simple elegance to this well-located guest house. (☎362 265. Singles £5; doubles £10; shared baths). **Continental Hotel,** Spiro Araou-

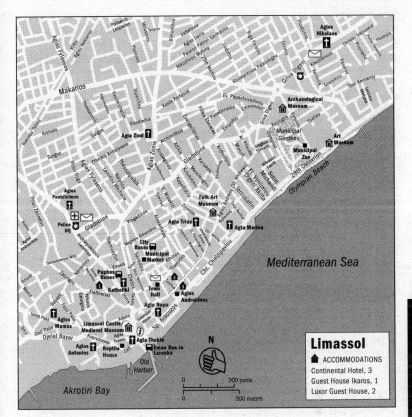

Limassol

🏠 ACCOMMODATIONS
Continental Hotel, 3
Guest House Ikaros, 1
Luxor Guest House, 2

zos 137, offers privacy and convenience. All guests get private baths, phones, and a free breakfast. (☎362 530. Singles ₤15; doubles ₤25; triples ₤35; A/C ₤2 extra.)

You'd be crazy to pass up a meal at ☒**Cuckoo's Nest,** Ag. Andreou 228. (☎362 768. Village wine ₤2.25 per bottle. *Mezze* ₤4; entrees ₤1.25-3.) **Mikri Maria,** Ankara 3 serves exquisite food cooked over hot coals. Try the grilled *lountza* and *halloumi* or the refreshing *tzatziki*. Live guitar music entertains in winter. (☎357 676. Entrees ₤3-5.50. Open M-Sa until 10:30pm.) **Sidon,** Saripolou 71-73, next to Municipal Market, is an upscale restaurant with a Lebanese twist. (☎342 065. Vegetarian *mezze* ₤5.50, entrees ₤4-12.) **Ta Kokkalakia,** Ag. Andreou 239, has an exotic garden and bar to match its exotic African menu. (☎340 015. Ostrich steak and South African sausage entrees ₤5-11. Open M-Th 6pm-11pm, F and Sa 6pm-midnight.)

👁 SIGHTS

KOURION. The ruins at Kourion were colonized by wandering Achaeans in the 14th and 13th centuries BCE. The **Sanctuary of Apollo Hylates** (8th century BCE) and the **stadium** (2nd century CE) have been reconstructed to their former glory. The earliest structure on the site is a 2nd-century BCE Roman **amphitheater** used for dramas, animal fights, and professional wrestling. Across the road from the main site are a group of ruins under excavation. In the northwest corner are the remains of the **House of Gladiators** and its mosaic gladiator pin-ups. The **House of Achilles,** next to the ancient theater, has beautiful mosaic floors. The nearby **Museum of Kourion** provides clear explanations of the artifacts. (*12km west of Limassol. Buses leave*

Limassol Castle (every hr. on the hr. 9am-1pm; return 11:50am, 2:50, and 4:50pm, £0.70). Open June-Sept. 8am-7:15pm; Oct.-May 8am-5pm. £1. The museum is in Episkopi village and is open M and W-F 7:30am-2:30pm, Th 3-6pm. £1.)

LIMASSOL CASTLE. The Limassol castle, where Cyprus's King Richard married Queen Berengaria in 1191, was destroyed by earthquakes and Genoese assaults. The castle is best known as a prison: the Knights of St. John converted the chapel into a series of jail cells, and the West Hall was used as a prison under the British until 1940. Now the castle houses the **Cyprus Medieval Museum,** which has medieval armor and religious objects. (☎305 419. Open M-F 9am-5pm, Sa-Su 10am-1pm. £1.)

SPECIAL EVENTS. At summer's end, Limassol's gardens are transformed into a tribute to Dionysus for the Limassol **wine festival,** where participants are given a bottle to fill with as much of the local vintage as they can handle. The general intoxication is compounded by music, dance, and theater. (£1.50.) At the end of June, actors from around the world trek to Limassol for **Shakespeare Nights. Carnival,** which takes place in February, 50 days before Orthodox Easter, is celebrated with more vigor in Limassol than anywhere else in Cyprus. Details of these events are available at the CTO and in *This Month's Principal Events.*

🌊 BEACHES

The city's long stone beach might be a little too rocky for the discerning beach-goer, but a new breakwater has made the area more pleasant for swimming. **Dassoudi Beach,** 3km east of Limassol, is famous throughout Cyprus (take bus #6 from the Kanaris market, every 15min., £0.50.). The ebullient **Ladies' Mile Beach,** just west of the new port, is also popular (take bus #1). When making the excursion to Kourion, be sure to spend some time at the undiscovered **Kourion Beach.** (The bus to Kourion continues to the beach area; just ask the driver.)

🍸 NIGHTLIFE

Local bars and cafes are on Ag. Andreou and near the castle, while dance clubs are at the edge of town in the tourist district. For disco dance clubs, **The Hippodrome,** on Georgiou, is the place to get down as the neighboring bars dwindle after 1am. Well dressed twentysomethings congregate at **Graffiti,** Ag. Andreou 244, a tree-laden open-air bar with great live music. **Paradozo,** Irinis 140, has plenty of nooks for conversation. (Open Su-Th 8pm-2am, F-Sa 8pm-3am.) **The Green Movement,** Ag. Andreou 259, in a 200-year-old building is testament to Limassol's fine architectural past with its sand-white columns. (☎369 595. Open M-F 10am-midnight.)

PAPHOS Πάφος   ☎06

Paphos was the favorite city of Aphrodite, the goddess of love, and a cosmopolitan hotspot in Roman times. After being leveled by an earthquake in the 4th century BCE, it has reemerged as the tourist capital of Cyprus.

✴🛈 ORIENTATION AND PRACTICAL INFORMATION

Paphos is divided into two sections. The upper section, **Ktima Paphos** (or just "Paphos"), is centered around **Pl. Kennedy,** with its shops, budget hotels, and services. The lower section, **Kato Paphos,** is roughly one kilometer south, with luxury hotels and the city's nightlife. Unless noted, everything below is in Ktima Paphos.

City Buses: Bus #11 runs between Ktima and Kato (every 15min., £0.50). Catch them in Ktima up the road from the post office; in Kato at any of the yellow benches on the road to town. Bus #10 goes to **Coral Bay** (20 per day, £0.50).

Service Taxis: To **Limassol** (every 30min. M-Sa 5:45am-6:30pm, Su 7am-5:30pm; £2.50). Contact **Travel & Express** on Eagorou (☎233 181).

Moped Rental: There are several shops in Kato and Ktima Paphos. £2.50-6.50 per day.

Tourist Office: CTO, Gladstone 3, just outside of Pl. Kennedy (☎232 841; fax 232 841). Open M-Tu and Th-F 8:15am-2:30pm and 3-5:15pm, W and Sa 8:15am-1:30pm.

Travel Agency: Iris Travel, Gladstone 10A (☎248 933 or 237 585; fax 233 960), opposite CTO. Ferry tickets to **Rhodes, Crete,** and **Israel** (from £44; student discounts up to 20%). Airline tickets to **London** and **Greece** (about £40; student discounts up to 40%). Open M-F 8am-1pm and 4-7pm, Sa 8am-1pm.

Banks: Concentrated around Pl. Kennedy on Makariou. All have 24hr. **ATMs.** Open M-F 8:30am-12:30pm. ATMs can be found on any major road.

Police: (☎806 060) on Grivas Digenes, in Pl. Kennedy. English spoken. Open 24hr.

Hospital: Paphos General (☎240 111), on Neophytos Nicolaides, offers free first aid. English spoken. **St. George's Private Hospital,** El. Venizelou 29 (☎247 000), on the way to the youth hostel; casualty and ambulance services. English spoken. Open 24hr.

Telephone: CYTA (☎230 228), on Grivas Digenes. Open daily 7:30am-7:30pm.

Internet Access: Maroushia Fashion Cafe (☎247 240 or 247 241) is directly on Pl. Kennedy, No. 6. £2 per hr.

Post Office: Main branch, El. Venizelou. Open M-F 7:30am-1:30pm and 3-6pm, W 7:30am-1:30pm, Sa 8:30-10:30am. **Kato Paphos** (☎240 226) branch, Ag. Antoniou.

ACCOMMODATIONS AND FOOD

Finding affordable accommodations in Paphos is a chore. Solo travelers should stick to the youth hostel or the guest house; groups might try renting a flat. Prices are higher in Kato Paphos. The ideally located ▨**Triaron Hotel Guest House,** Makarios 99, is a brilliant choice. (☎232 193. Singles £5; doubles £7.) The **Youth Hostel (HI),** El. Venizelou 45, is a 15-minute walk from the *plateia* on Pallikaridi to Venizelou, on the right. (☎232 588. £5 for the 1st night, £4 each additional night.) **Violetta Flats,** Dionissiou 7, in Kato Paphos, has flats with kitchens and private baths, and is well situated for enjoying the nightlife. (☎234 109; fax 220 734. Singles £14; doubles £16; A/C £2 extra.) **Zenon Gardens Geroskipou Camping,** east of the tourist beach, 3km from the harbor, has a mini-market, restaurant, and kitchen. (☎242 277. Open Mar.-Oct. £2 per site; £2 per 3 people; £1 per small tent.)

Putting on pounds in Kato Paphos will cost a lot of them, but Ktima Paphos is affordable and elegant. Those craving the ultimate souvlaki should head to **Vasano Kebab House,** Agapinoros 25, Kato Paphos. (☎242 635. Souvlaki £1.) **Athens,** Pallikaridi 47, is the place for anyone who remotely likes sugar. (☎232 613. Pastries £0.40 and under.) **Peggy's Miranda Cafe,** in Pl. Kennedy, is run by and for British expats with a continental breakfast (£2) and a book swap. (Open M-Sa 8am-4pm.) **Euro Surfcafe,** Gladstone 1, has reasonably priced light meals (sandwiches £1-1.50, beer £0.80) and Internet access for £2 per hr. (☎239 239. Open daily until 9pm.)

SIGHTS

MOSAICS OF KATO PAPHOS. The mosaic floors of the House of Dionysus, the House of Theseus, and the House of Aion in Kato Paphos are the city's most dazzling ancient relics. Discovered accidentally in 1962 by a farmer plowing his fields, they were excavated by a Polish expedition that found mosaics covering 14 rooms of the **House of Dionysus.** Using the stones' natural varying hues, the floors depict vibrant scenes from mythology and daily life. Toward the water rests the **House of Theseus** (dating from the 2nd to 6th centuries CE), a decadent building with marble statues, columns, and mosaic floors. (☎240 217. Open daily 7:30am-7:30pm. £1.)

CATACOMBS OF AGIA SOLOMONI. The dark catacombs—decorated with Byzantine frescoes and containing a chapel dedicated to St. Solomoni—were built on the site of an old synagogue. Part of the deepest chamber is filled with water, which you may not notice until you're drenched in it. A tree that is said to cure the illnesses of those who tie a cloth to it marks the entrance to the catacombs. St. Paul was whipped for preaching Christianity to the Greeks at nearby **St. Paul's Pillar.** *(Opposite the Apollo Hotel on Ap. Pavlou. Open 24hr. Free.)*

OTHER SIGHTS. The remnants of an *agora* are north of the mosaics beside the 3000-person, Roman **odeon,** a roofed limestone theater that is still in use today. Built in the 7th century on a hill overlooking the harbor, the **Byzantine Castle** *(Saranda Kolones)* was intended to protect inhabitants from Arab pirates. When an earthquake destroyed the castle in 1222, the Lusignans built the **Paphos Fort** at the end of the pier. *(Open 7:30am-7pm. £0.50. The Byzantine Castle is on Sophia Vembo off Ap. Pavlou. Paphos Fort open 10am-5:45pm. £0.75.)*

◪ BEACHES

The two most popular beaches are the touristy **Geroskipou** to the east and the bigger, sandier **Coral Bay** to the north. For Geroskipou, take bus #11 from Ktima Paphos (3 per hr., £0.50); to reach Coral Bay, take bus #15 from Geroskipou (every 20min., £0.50). **Cape Lara** is host to lovely, sandy beaches and is a nesting site for Green and Loggerhead Turtles. The **◪Lara Sea Turtle Project** was conceived in 1971 to protect the turtles by ensuring that nesting continues. Turtle nests can be viewed in the Project's hatchery enclosure. There's no public transportation to Cape Lara; your best bet is a jeep excursion or motorbike. Follow signs for **Agios Georgios** from Coral Bay to find a tiny sandy beach that sits below the uninteresting church. On the road to Ag. Georgios, there are sea caves with limestone rocks peering over clear deep waters. Bask uninterrupted or explore the nearby caves. **Sundy Beach,** about 2km down the dirt road to Cape Lara, is a long stretch of practically untouched golden sand, and arguably the most secluded beach in the area.

◪ NIGHTLIFE

Virtually all of the area's nightlife centers around Ag. Napas and Ag. Antoniou, a couple blocks inland from the waterfront in Kato Paphos. **Club 12,** on Ag. Andreou, draws all the crowds after 1am with heavy bass and the latest techno tunes. (☎(0191) 230 4848. Cover £5.) **Summer Cinema** (☎247 747) on the waterfront, is a trendy open-air club just far enough from package hotels for the locals to call it their own. **Boogies,** on Ag. Antoniou across from the post office, is Paphos's favorite karaoke bar: after 2am, slurred but earnest Backstreet Boys renditions give way to equally enthusiastic dancing. (☎244 810. Open 9pm-4am.)

◪ DAYTRIPS FROM PAPHOS: KOUKLIA

Adjacent to the modern village of Kouklia are the ruins of the great **Temple of Aphrodite** and **Paleopaphos** (Old Paphos), once the capital of a kingdom encompassing nearly half of Cyprus. The temple itself was the kingdom's religious center and a destination for pilgrims from every corner of the Roman world. Built in the 12th century BCE, it thrived until the 4th century CE, when the edicts of Emperor Theodosius and a series of earthquakes reduced it to rubble. The scant remains—merely piles of rocks—make little sense without a guide. *A Brief History and Description of Old Paphos*, published by the Department of Antiquities, is available in the adjoining **Paleopaphos Museum.** *(☎432 180. Open M-F 7:30am-5pm, Sa-Su 9am-4pm. Admission to ruins, city, and museum £0.75.)* The sites are most easily seen from the excursion buses. Renting a moped is **not advisable**—the road is very dangerous; service taxis are a much safer bet.

APPENDIX

HOLIDAYS AND FESTIVALS

Islamic holidays are timed to local sightings of the moon, so dates are not set until the last minute and differ from country to country. **Jewish** holidays last from sundown one day until sunday the next day. For longer holidays, businesses are closed for the first day (in the case of Passover, the last day) but remain open the rest of the time. The **holy day** (when many business are closed) is Friday *(Juma'a)* in the Muslim world and Saturday *(shabbat)* in Israel. Businesses typically close on national holidays (listed below) as well. **Christian** holidays listed are those of the Eastern Orthodox or Maronite Church, and are celebrated among Christians in Syria, Lebanon, and Cyprus.

DATE	FESTIVAL	TYPE
Nov. 1, 2000	All Saints' Day	Christian
Nov. 22	Independence Day	Lebanese
Nov. 27	First Day of Ramadan (approximation)	Islamic
Dec. 22	Laylat al-Qadr	Islamic
Dec. 22-29	Ḥanukkah	Jewish
Dec. 25	Christmas	Christian
Dec. 27	'Eid al-Fitr (end of Ramadan)	Islamic
Jan. 7, 2001	Epiphany	Christian
Jan. 30	King Abdullah's Birthday	Jordanian
Feb. 9	Mar Maroun (Feast of St. Maron)	Christian (Lebanon)
Mar. 6	'Eid al-Adha (Feast of the Sacrifice)	Islamic
Mar. 8	Revolution Day	Syrian
Mar. 9	Purim	Jewish
Mar. 21	Women's Day (Mother's Day)	Syrian
Mar. 22	Arab League Day	Syrian
Mar. 26	Muharram (Islamic New Year)	Islamic
Apr. 4	Ashoura	Islamic
Apr. 8-14	Pesaḥ (Passover)	Jewish
Apr. 13	Good Friday	Christian
Apr. 15	Easter	Christian
Apr. 17	Evacuation Day (Independence Day)	Syrian
Apr. 20	Yom Ha-Shoah	Israeli
Apr. 23	National Independence and Children's Day	Turkish
Apr. 28	Yom Ha-Atzma'ut (Israel Independence Day)	Israeli
May 1	Labor Day	Cypriot, Jordanian
May 6	Martyr's Day	Lebanese, Syrian
May 19	Atatürk's Commemoration/Youth & Sports Day	Turkish
May 21	Yom Yerushalayim (Jerusalem Day)	Jewish
May 25	Independence Day	Jordanian
May 28	Shavuot	Jewish
June 3	Pentecost	Christian
June 4	'Eid Mawlid al-Nabi (Birth of the Prophet)	Islamic
June 10	Army Day and Anniversary of the Great Revolt	Jordanian
June 18	Evacuation Day (Liberation Day)	Egyptian
July 23	Revolution Day	Egyptian

DATE	FESTIVAL	TYPE
Aug. 15	Assumption of the Virgin Mary	Christian
Aug. 30	Victory Day	Turkish
Sept. 18-19	Rosh Ha-Shana (Jewish New Year)	Jewish
Sept. 27	Yom Kippur	Jewish
Oct. 2-9	Sukkot	Jewish
Oct. 6	National Day (Armed Forces Day)	Egyptian
Oct. 6	October War Day	Syrian
Oct. 9	Simḥat Torah	Jewish
Oct. 14	Isra' and Miraj	Islamic
Oct. 24	Suez and National Liberation Day	Egyptian
Oct. 29	Republic Day	Turkish
Nov. 1	All Saints' Day	Christian
Nov. 16	National Day	Syrian
Nov. 17	First Day of Ramadan	Islamic
Nov. 22	Independence Day	Lebanese
Dec. 10-17	Ḥanukkah	Jewish
Dec. 16	'Eid al-Fitr (end of Ramadan)	Islamic
Dec. 23	Victory Day	Egyptian
Dec. 25	Christmas	Christian

TIME ZONES

The Middle East spans three continents, so time zones vary. During standard time, **Egypt**, the **Levant** (Israel, The West Bank, Gaza, Jordan, Lebanon, Syria), **Cyprus,** and **Turkey** are two hours ahead of Greenwich Mean Time (GMT). Things get complicated during daylight savings, when countries switch over at different intervals.

MEASUREMENTS

The metric system is used throughout the Middle East.

MEASUREMENT CONVERSIONS

1 inch (in.) = 25.4 millimeters (mm)	1 millimeter (mm) = 0.039 in.
1 foot (ft.) = 0.30 m	1 meter (m) = 3.28 ft.
1 yard (yd.) = 0.914m	1 meter (m) = 1.09 yd.
1 mile = 1.61km	1 kilometer (km) = 0.62 mi.
1 ounce (oz.) = 28.35g	1 gram (g) = 0.035 oz.
1 pound (lb.) = 0.454kg	1 kilogram (kg) = 2.202 lb.
1 fluid ounce (fl. oz.) = 29.57ml	1 milliliter (ml) = 0.034 fl. oz.
1 gallon (gal.) = 3.785L	1 liter (L) = 0.264 gal.
1 acre (ac.) = 0.405ha	1 hectare (ha) = 2.47 ac.
1 square mile (sq. mi.) = 2.59km^2	1 square kilometer (km^2) = 0.386 sq. mi.

ARABIC (AL-'ARABI) العربى

Dialects of Arabic vary from country to country—it is not uncommon to see a Moroccan and a Palestinian speaking French because their dialects are so different. There may even be dialectal differences within countries. In Upper (south) Egypt, the Nubians (also called Sa'idis) replace the Classical Arabic q with a hard g. In Lower Egypt and in most other dialects, q is dropped completely and replaced with a glottal stop (a sound similar to that of the middle syllable of the word "butter" pronounced with a Cockney accent), indicated with a ' in transliteration. The main phonetic difference between the Egyptian and Levantine (includes the dialects of Jordan, Syria, Lebanon, the West Bank and Gaza) tongues is that the Levantine *j* sound (as in fu**dge**) becomes a hard *g* (as in **g**ulf) in Lower Egypt. Egyptian is the most widely understood dialect because of Egypt's prolific film and television industry. It's also considered to be the best dialect in which to tell jokes.

Arabic is read from right to left, but numerals are read from left to right. Arabic uses eight sounds not heard in English. *Kh* (خ) is like the German *ch*; *gh* (غ) is like the French *r*. There are two *h* sounds; one (ﻫ) sounds like the English "h" and the other (ح, in Muhammad) is somewhere between *kh* and plain *h*. The letter *'ayn* (ع) comes from the throat; it is indicated by ' in transliteration. *R* is pronounced as a trill, just as it is in Spanish. The sounds *dh* (as in **th**is), *d*, *t*, *k*, and *s* all have emphatic equivalents. Vowels and consonants can be either long or short (it means the difference between a *hammam*, bathroom, and a *hamam*, pigeon). The definite article is the prefix *al*. When *al* comes before the sounds *t*, *th*, *j*, *d*, *dh*, *r*, *z*, *s*, *sh*, or *n*, the *l* is not pronounced, and the *l* elides to become the letter which follows it (e.g., *al-noor* becomes *an-noor*).

ARABIC NUMERALS

0	1	2	3	4	5	6	7	8	9	10
٠	١	٢	٣	٤	٥	٦	٧	٨	٩	١٠
sifir, zeero	waahid	itnein	talaata	arba'a	khamsa	sitta	sab'a	tamaniya	tis'a	'ashara

EMERGENCY

ENGLISH	ARABIC
Help!	Saa'idoonee
Stop!	Wa'if (sg)/Wa'foo (pl)
I'm ill.	Ana marid (m)/Ana marida (f)
It hurts me here. (Levant/Egypt)	Bituja'ani hun/Bituga'ani hina
I'm tired.	Ana ta'aban (m), Ana ta'abana (f)
Water	Mayya
Hospital	Mustashfa
Doctor	Duktoor
Tourist police	Bolees as-seeyaaha
I'm calling the police. (Levant/Egypt)	Hakhabar al-bolees/Hagiblak al-bolees
Go away!	Imshee!
Passport	Basbor/Jawaz (Levant), Gawaz (Egypt)
Embassy	Safaarah

GREETINGS

ENGLISH	ARABIC
Informal hello; Formal hello (Response); Goodbye	Marhaba; As-Salaamu aleikum(Wa Aleikum as–salaam); Ma' as-salaama
Good morning (response)	Sabah al-kheir (Sabah an-noor/Sabah al-ishta)
Good evening (response)	Masa' al-kheir (Masaa' an-noor)
How are you? (Levant/Egypt)	Keefak?/Izzayyak? (m), Keefik?/Izzayik? (f)
I'm fine (Levant/Egypt)	Mabsuut/Kwayyis (m), Mabsuuta/Kwayyisa (f)
Yes; Yes (formal); No; Maybe	Eeh (Levant)/Aywa (Egypt); Na'am; La; Mumkin
Never mind, no big deal	Ma'alesh
Thank you	Shukran
Please (Levant/Egypt)	Min fadlak (m), Min fadlik (f)/Law samaht (m), Law samahti (f)
I'm sorry	Ana aasif (m), Ana aasfa (f)
Excuse me (to get attention)	'An iznak (m), 'An iznik (f)/'Afwan
God willing; Praise God	Inshallah; Al-hamdu lillah

APPENDIX

ENGLISH	ARABIC
I don't know (Levant/Egypt)	Ma Ba'raf /Mish 'aarif (m), Mish 'aarifa (f)
What is your name? (Levant/Egypt)	Shoo ismak/Ismak eh (m), Shoo ismik/Ismik eh (f)
My name is...	Ismee...
Student (m/f)	Talib/Taliba
Tourist	Saayih (m), Saayiha (f), Suwwaah (pl)
I don't understand (Levant/Egypt)	Ma bafham/Mish faahim (m), Mish faahma (f)
I don't speak Arabic (Levant/Egypt)	Ma bahki 'arabi/Mabatkallimish 'arabi
Do you speak English? (Levant/Egypt)	Bitihkee inglizi?/Bititkallim inglizi? (m), Bititkallimee inglizi? (f)
Please speak slowly	Kalimnee biraaha min fadlak
Whatis that? (Levant/Egypt)	Shoo hey/Eh da?
Where; What; Why; Who; When (Levant/Egypt)	Feyn/Wayn; Eh/Shoo; Leh/Leysh; Meen; Imta

DIRECTIONS

ENGLISH	ARABIC
Let's Go!	Yallah! or Yallah beena!
Can you tell me how to get to [Sesame] Street?	Shaari'a [Simsim] fein?, wayn Shaari'a [Simsim]?
Straight	Dughree or 'Ala tool (Egypt)
Right/Left	Yameen/Shimal or Yisaar
North/South/East/West	Ash-shamal/Al-ganoub/Ash-shar'/Al-gharb
I'm lost. (Levant/Egypt)	Ana daayi'a/Ana tuht.
Station	Mahatta (Mahattat when followed by name).
Public Square	Midan
I would like a ticket for... (Levant/Egypt)	Bidi bitaa'a ila/'Aayiz (f: 'Aayza) tazkara rayhah...
One way/Round-trip	Bass/Rayih gay
What time does the ___ leave?	Biyitla' imta ___
Bus	Al-Baas (Levant), Al-Autubees (Egypt)
Train	Al-Atr
Automobile	As-Sayyaara (Levant), Al-'Arabiyya (Egypt)
Airport	Mataar

SERVICES

ENGLISH	ARABIC
Room (Levant/Egypt)	Ghurfa (Levant); Oda (Egypt)
I'd like a (single/double) room.	'Aayiz (f: 'Aayza) ghurfa (bisrir wehid/litnein).
How much is a room?	Al-ghurfa bikam?
Is there ___ ?	Fee ___ ?
There is no ___	Mafeesh ___
Hotel	Funduq or (h)otel
Lunch/Dinner	Al-ghada/al-'asha
Coffee/Tea	Ahwa/shay
Bathroom	Hammam, twaleet
Restaurant	Mata'm
Telephone	Tilifon
I'd like call the US (Levant/Egypt)	Bidi khaber Amrika/'Aayiz (f: 'Aayza) atasil bi Amrika
Pharmacy	Saydaleeya or 'Agzakhena (Egypt)
Post Office (Levant/Egypt)	Maktab al-bareed/Bosta
Street	Shaari'a
Market	Souq
Museum	Mat-haf
Mosque	Masjid/jaame' (Levant), Masgid/gaame' (Egypt)
Church	Kineesa

DATE AND TIME

ENGLISH	ARABIC
What time is it? (Levant/Egypt)	Addeish as-saa'a?/Es-saa'a kaam?
Hour, Time	Saa'a
Day/Week/Month/Year	Yom/Usbuu'/Shahr/Sana
Yesterday/Today/Tomorrow	Imbaarih/Al-yom (Egypt: An-naharda)/Bukra
What time do you open/close?	Ayyeh saa'a bitiftah/bitsakker? (Levant); Bitiftah/Biti'fil as-saa'a kam? (Egypt)
Sunday/Monday/Tuesday/Wednesday	Yom al-ahad/Yom al-itnein/Yom at-talaat/Yom al-arba'
Thursday /Friday/Saturday	Yom al-khamees/Yom aj-juma'a (Egypt: Yom ig-guma'a/Yom as-sabt

MONEY

ENGLISH	ARABIC
How much is this? (Levant/Egypt)	Addaysh?/Bikam?
Will you take half?	Taakhud nuss? (m) Taakhdee nuss? (f)
I want... (Levant/Egypt)	Biddee/'Aayiz (m), 'Aayza (f)
Is there a student discount?	Fi takhfid lit-talaba?
Cheap/Expensive	Rikhees/ghaalee
No way!	Mish mumkin!
Money	Masaari (Levant), Fuloos (Egypt)
Change	Fraata (Levant), Fakka (Egypt)

HEBREW (IVRIT) עברית

The Hebrew language contains 22 characters, written from right to left. Although Hebrew is read from right to left, **numerals** are read from left to right. Vowels are generally left unwritten, but may appear underneath regular characters as smaller markings. Modern spoken Hebrew contains a large number of Hebraicized versions of English words that may be understandable to perky-eared English-speaking listeners. The transliterations ḥ (ח) and kh (כ and ך) are both guttural, as in the German word *ach*. The Hebrew *r* is close to the French *r*, although an Arabic (or even English) *r* is also understood. The definite article is the prefix *ha*. Feminine adjectives add an "-ah" at the end; feminine verbs usually add an "-at" or an "-et."

HEBREW NUMERALS										
0	1	2	3	4	5	6	7	8	9	10
efes	eḥad	shtayim	shalosh	arba	ḥamesh	shesh	sheva	shmoneh	teisha	eser

EMERGENCY

ENGLISH	HEBREW
Help!	Hatzeeloo!
Stop!	Tafseek! (m)/Tafseekee! (f)
Don't touch me	Al teegah bee
I'm ill	Anee ḥoleh (m)/Anee ḥolah (f)
I'm hurt	Anee patzoo'ah (m)/Anee ptzoo'ah (f)
Water	Mahyim
Hospital	Beit-ḥolim
Doctor	Rofeh
I need a doctor	Anee tzariḥ rofeh (m)/Ani tziriḥa rofeh
I'm calling the police	Anee kore (m) (f: koret) lamishtara
Leave me alone	Azov otee
Go away/Go to hell	Tistalek/Lekh l'azazel
Police/Fire fighters/Ambulance	Mishtara/Meḥabei esh/Ahmboolance

GREETINGS

ENGLISH	HEBREW
Hello/Goodbye	Shalom
Good morning/Good evening	Boker tov/Erev tov
Could you help me?	Atah yaḥol la'azor lee(m)/At yeḥola la'azor lee (f)?
How are you?	Ma nishma?
Excellent/Fine/Not good	Metzuyan/Be-seder/Lo tov
Yes/No/Maybe	Ken/Lo/Oolai
Thank you	Todah
Please/You're welcome	Bevakasha
Excuse me/I'm sorry	Sliḥa
I don't know	Anee lo yodeah (m)/Anee lo yoda'at (f)
What is your name?	Eikh korim lekha? (m) Eikh korim lakh? (f)
My name is...	Shmee...
I'm a student	Anee student (m)/studentit (f)
How do you say...?	Eikh omrim...
I don't understand	Anee lo mevin (m)/Anee lo mevinah (f)
I don't speak Hebrew	Anee lo medaber (f: medaberet) ivrit
Do you speak English?	Ata medaber ivrit? (m)/At medaberet ivrit? (f)
Please repeat	Tagid (m) (f: tagidi) od pa'am, bevakasha
Please speak slowly	Tedaber (m)/(f: tedabri) le'at bevakasha

DIRECTIONS

ENGLISH	HEBREW
Where is... ?	Eyfoh... ?
Straight	Yashar
Right/Left	Yameen/Smol
North/South/East/West	Tzafon/Darom/Mizraḥ/Ma'arav
I'm lost	Ne'ebadetee
Do you know where... is?	Ata yodeah (f: Aht yoda'at) eifoh nimtzah... ?
Do you stop at...?	Ata otzer b'...?
From where does the bus leave?	Mi'eifo ha-otoboos ozev?
Center of town	Merkaz ha'ir
Central bus station	Taḥana merkazit
Bus stop	Taḥanat otoboos
I would like a ticket for...	Ani rotzeh kartees le...
One-way/Round-trip	Keevoon eḥad/Haloḥ ve'ḥazor
Please stop	Atzor, bevakasha
What time does the ___ leave?	Matai ha___ ozev?
Bus	Otoboos
Taxi	Monit/Taxi
Automobile	Mekhonit
Train	Rakevet

SERVICES

ENGLISH	HEBREW
Do you know of a cheap hotel?	Ata makeer (m) (f: makeera) malon zol?
Do you have a single/double room?	Yesh laḥem ḥeder le'yaḥeed/kafool?
How much is the room?	Kama oleh haḥeder?
Hotel/Hostel	Malon/Aḥsania
Breakfast/Lunch/Dinner	Aruḥat boker/Aruḥat tzohora'im/Aruḥat erev
Do you have vegetarian food?	Yesh laḥem oḥel tzimḥonee?

ENGLISH	HEBREW
I am vegetarian	Ani tzimḥonee/tzimḥoneet
Coffee/Tea	Kafeh/Teh
Bathroom	Sherutim
Room	Ḥeder
Restaurant	Mees'ada
Telephone	Telephon
I'd like to make a call to the U.S.	Anee rotzeh (m) (f: rotzah) letalfen le'america
Passport	Darkon
Pharmacy	Beit Markaḥat
Post office	Do'ar
Street	Reḥov
Market	Shuk
Museum	Muzaion
Synagogue	Beit knesset
Church	Knessia
Mosque	Misgad
Beach	Ḥof
Grocery store	Makolet

DATE AND TIME

ENGLISH	HEBREW
What time is it?	Ma hasha'ah?
Hour, Time	Sha'ah
Day/Week/Month/Year	Yom/Shavuah/Ḥodesh/Shanah
Early/Late	Mookdam/Me'ooḥar
Today/Yesterday/Tomorrow	Ha-yom/Etmol/Maḥar
Morning/Afternoon/Evening/Night	Boker/Tzohora'im/Erev/Lyla
What time do you open/close?	Matai atem potḥim/sogrim?
Open/Closed	Patoo'aḥ/Sagoor
Sunday /Monday/Tuesday/Wednesday	Yom rishon/Yom shaini/Yom shlishi/Yom revi'i
Thursday /Friday/Sabbath (Saturday)	Yom ḥamishi/Yom shishi/Shabbat

MONEY

ENGLISH	HEBREW
Do you have... ?	Yesh lekha? (m) Yesh lakh? (f)
How much is this?	Kama zeh oleh?
I want...	Anee rotzeh (m)/Anee rotzah (f)
I don't want... (male/female)	Lo rotzeh (male) Lo rotzah (female)
Is there a student discount?	Yesh hanaḥa le'studentim?
Cheap/Expensive	Zol/Yakar
Do you accept credit cards/traveler's checks?	Atem mekablim kartisei ashrai/hamḥaot nos'im
Money	Kesef
Change (literally "leftovers")	Odef

TURKISH (TÜRKÇE)

Turkish is phonetic: each letter has only one sound that is always pronounced distinctly (save ğ, which lengthens the vowels adjacent to it). Special vowel and consonant pronunciations include: c (jacket); ç (check); ı (i without a dot, cousin); i (peace); j (zh, pleasure); ö (deux); ş (short); u (boot); ü (cue). Special letter combinations include: ay (pronounced eye); ey (play); oy (toy); uy (phooey).

TURKISH NUMERALS

0	1	2	3	4	5	6	7	8	9	10
sıfır	bir	iki	üç	dört	beş	altı	yedi	sekiz	dokuz	on
si-fihr	beer	ee-KEE	ooch	durt	besh	altih	ye-DEE	SEH-kuz	doh-KOOZ	ohn

EMERGENCY

ENGLISH	TURKISH
Help!	İmdat! (Eem-daht!)
Stop!	Ayıp! (Ah-yup!)
I'm ill	Hastayım (has-TA-yuhm)
Water	Su (soo)
Hospital	Hastane (has-ta-NE)
I need a doctor	Doktora ihtiyacım var (dohk-TOR-ah eeh-tee-YA-cum vahr)
Go away!	Haydı git! (Hah-dee git!)
Police	Polis (polees)

GREETINGS

ENGLISH	TURKISH
Hello /Goodbye (morning)/Goodbye (evening)	Merhaba (Mehrhaba)/İyi günler (eee-YEE goon-lehr)/ İyi akşamlar (eee-YEE ak-SHAM-lar)
How are you?	Nasılsın?(nah-sil-sihn)
Fine	İyiyim
Yes/No/Maybe	Evet (eh-veht)/Hayır (hyer)/Belki (behl-kee)
Thank you	Teşekkur ederim (tesh-ekur edeh-rim)
You're welcome	Bir şey değil. (beer shey dee-eel)
Please	Lütfen (loot-fahn)
Excuse me/I'm sorry	Pardon (pahr-don)/Özür dilerim (oz-oor deel-er-rim)
My name is...	İsmim (Ees-meem)
What is...?	...ne? (neh)
I'm a student	Oğrenciyim (OH-ren-jee-yeem)
I don't understand	Anlamadım (ahn-luh-mah-dim)
I don't speak Turkish.	Turkçe bilmiyorum. (Toork-che BEEL-mee-YOR-uhm)
Do you speak English?	İnglizce biliyor musun? (een-gul-EEZ-je beel-ee-YOR muh-SUN?)
Please speak slowly	Yavaş lütfen (yah-vash loot-fahn)
Are you a pimp?	Pesevenk misin? (pehs-seh-vehnk mih-sihn?)

DIRECTIONS

ENGLISH	TURKISH
Where is... ?	...nerede? (...nehr-eh-deh?)
How far is...?	...a ne kadar uzakta (a neh kahdahr oozakta?)
Straight	düz (dooz; to a taxi driver); doğru (doh-oo; said in all other instances)
Right/Left	Sağ (saa)/Sol (sohl)
North/South/East/West	Hangisi (han-gee-see)/Güneye (goo-ne-YE)/Doğuya (do-ghoo-YA)/Batıya (ba-tuh-YA)
I'm lost	Yolumu kaybettim (yol-oo-moo kay-bet-teem)
I'm going to...	...'a gidiyorum (ah geed-EE-yohr-uhm)
Central bus station	otogar (oh-tow-gar)
Bus stop	otobüs duraği (oto-boos doo-raa)
I would like a ticket.	Bir bilet alabilir miyim? (beer bee-let ala-bee-LEER mee-yeem?)

ENGLISH	TURKISH
One-way/Round-trip	Gidiş (gee-deesh)/Gidiş-dönüş biletin (gee-deesh doo-noosh bee-le-teen)
What time does the ___ leave?	Saat kaçta kalkiyor? (sah-at kach-tah kahlk-ee-yor?)
Bus	otobüs (oto-boos)
Taxi	Taksi
Automobile	Bir araba (beer ah-ra-bah)

SERVICES

ENGLISH	TURKISH
Is there an available room?	Boş odanız var mı? (bosh odaniz vahr mih?)
Single/double/triple	Tek (tehk)/Çift (cheeft)/Üç kişilik (ooch keesheeleek)
How much is the room?	Bir günlük fiyat ne kadar?
Hotel/Pension	Otel (oh-tell)/Pansiyon (pan-see-yown)
Breakfast/Lunch/Dinner	Kahvaltı (kah-val-tuh)/öğle yemeği (oo-le yeme-ee)/ akşam yemeği (aksham yeme-ee)
Do you have food without meat?	Etsiz yemek var mı? (eht seez yemek vahr mí?)
I am vegetarian	Vejetariyanım (vej-e-tar-iyan-im)
Coffee/Tea	Kahve (Turkish coffee, kah-veh)/Çay (chai)
Bathroom	Tuvalet (too-wallet) or Banyo
Restaurant	lokanta
Telephone	Telefon
Can I make a call to the US?	Amerika'ya nasıl telefon edebilirim (ame-REE-kaya nasul telefon ede-bee-lee-reem?)
Passport	Pasaport
Pharmacy	Eczane (ej-ZAH-ne)
Post office	Postane
Market	Çarşı (charshi), Bedesten (be-de-STEN)
Museum	Müze (moo-zeh)
Mosque	Camii (jamee-ee)

DATE AND TIME

ENGLISH	TURKISH
What time is it?	Saat kaç? (Sa-at ka-ch?)
Hour	saat (sa-AT)
Day/Week/Month/Year	Gün (goon)/Hafta (hahfta)/Ay (ay)/Yıl(yil)
Yesterday/Today/Tomorrow	Dün (doon)/Bugün (boo-goon)/Yarıin (yah-rin)
Are you open/closed?	Açık/kapalı mısın? (a-chik/kah-pah-li misin)
Sunday /Monday/Tuesday/Wednesday	Pazar (pa-ZAR)/Pazartesi (pa-ZAR-te-see)/ Salı (saluh)/Çarşamba (char-sham-ba)
Thursday /Friday/Saturday	Perşembe (per-shem-be)/Cuma (joo-ma)/ Cumartesi (joo-mar-tee-see)

MONEY

ENGLISH	TURKISH
How much is...?	...ne kadar? (NE ka-dar?)
I want...	Biraz .... istiyorum
I don't want...	...istemedim (eestemedim)
Is there a student discount?	Öğrenci var mı? (Oo-ren-jee var muh?)
Do you accept credit cards?	Kredi kartı alıyor musunuz? (kredee kartuh aluh-YOR moo-soo-nooz?)
Money	Para (pahrah)

TELEPHONE CODES

CYPRUS	357
Limassol, Paphos	05, 06
EGYPT	**20**
Alexandria	03
Aswan	097
Bahariyya	010
Cairo	02
Dakhla	092
Hurghada	065
Kharga	092
Luxor	095
Port Said	066
Sinai Peninsula (incl. Suez)	062
ISRAEL	**972**
Be'er Sheva	07
Eilat	07
Golan	06
Haifa	04
Jerusalem	02
Tel Aviv	03
Tzfat	06
JORDAN	**962**
Amman	06
Aqaba	03
Azraq (Desert)	06
Dead Sea	05
Irbid	02
Madaba	08

LEBANON	961
Ba'albeck	08
Bcharré	06
Beirut	01
Sa'ida (Sidon), Sur (Tyre)	07
Tripoli	06
SYRIA	**963**
Aleppo	21
Damascus	11
Hama	33
Homs	31
Lattakia	41
Palmyra	34
WEST BANK	**972**
All locations	02
GAZA	**972**
Gaza City	07
TURKEY	**90**
Ankara	312
Antalya	242
Bodrum	252
Göreme	384
İstanbul (Asia/Europe)	216/212
İzmir	232
Marmaris	252
Trabzon	462

APPENDIX

GLOSSARY

'ain: spring
ankh: Egyptian symbol for life, Coptic cross
bab: door, gate
bakhsheesh: tip, bribe
bir: well
booza: ice cream
caretta: donkey-drawn taxicart
corniche: from the Fr., long avenue along the water
dabke: Lebanese line dance
dakle: Lebanese dance in which themes from village life are enacted
deir: monastery
djinn: ghost
emir: prince
felucca: Egyptian sailboat
galabiyya: long gown worn by men
hammam: hot baths; bathroom
hantour: horse carriage
hibis: plow
hijab: traditional women's head-covering
hurriyya: liberty; freedom
iconostasis: icon-covered screen in a mosque that separates the nave from the sanctuary
imam: Muslim leader
irwan: arcaded porch in a mosque surrounding the central open courtyard
jabal: hill, mountain
kalish: from the Fr. calèche, a horse-drawn carriage.
kefyeh: traditional black-and-white checkered headscarf.
khan: caravanserai, courtyard inn
khanqah: home for sufi mystics
khedive: Turkish for viceroy
khuttar: tradition in which prominent Bedouin families host any visitors that cross their path
kuttab: Qur'anic school
lakaban: marble basin
madrasa: school or college of Islamic law
margunah: large, decorated woven basket
mashrabiyya: interlaced wooden screen
mawlid: festival celebrating events from the Qur'an or birthdays of Coptic or Muslim saints
mayda'a: ablution fountain
midan: square
mihrab: richly decorated prayer niche in a mosque pointing in the direction of Mecca
minbar: pulpit in a mosque next to the mihrab where sermons are delivered
muezzin: person who does the call to prayer
papyrus: ancient Egyptian paper made from reeds
pronaos: vestibule
qala'a: fortress, citadel
qasr: castle
Ramadan: Muslim holy month of fasting
rue: Fr. for street
sabil: water dispensary
saha: central open courtyard in a mosque
service: group taxi
siq: narrow passageway in rock (see **Petra** p. 491)
souq: market
tarfudit: veils

umm: mother
wadi: small river or riverbed

FOOD & DRINK

ahwa: Arabic coffee
'araq: strong anise liquor
argeilah, sheesha: water pipe, hookah
'asab: sugar cane juice
aseer: fruit juice
baba ghanoush: pureed eggplant with lemon juice, mayonnaise, and spices
ba'laweh: pistachio- or almond-filled filo dough (baklava)
basbouseh: wheat pastry with syrup
burma: shredded, fried dough with pistachios
farooj: roasted chicken served with chilis and onions
fattoush: salad of lettuce, tomato, and cucumber with small pieces of toasted pita mixed in.
falafel: fried chickpeas, shaped into balls
fuul: cooked, mashed fava beans with garlic, lemon, olive oil, and salt on bread and vegetables
halawat al-jibn: unsalted cheese with semolina, sugar, syrup, and sweet cream
hummus: ground chickpeas with oil and spices
jamid: tangy yogurt-based sauce
jellab: raisin syrup with pine nuts
kibbeh naye: raw beef and spices
kofta: spiced ground beef grilled on skewers
kushari: starch-laden Egyptian dish of pasta, rice, lentils, and dried onions in tomato sauce
lagbi: sweet, palm tree juice
mahshi: stuffed grape leaves (stuffed with mincemeat, rice, and onions)
mana'eesh: pizza with za'tar
marqooq: paper thin baked bread
mensaf: rice on a large tray of flat bread, topped with pine nuts, lamb or goat, and a tangy yogurt-based sauce
mezze: appetizers
musakhan: chicken baked with olive oil, onions, and spices, served on bread
mujeddra: lentil stew with sautéed onions and spices
mulukhiyya: green Egyptian vegetable
na'na': mint
shawarma: fatty lamb rolled onto pita
shay: tea
shish kebab: skewered lamb
shish tawouq: skewered chicken
ta'amiyya: Egyptian version of falafel, discuslike in both shape and hardness
tahina: sesame-based sauce
tabbouleh: parsley, cracked wheat, onions, tomatoes, lemon juice, and spices mix together.
tawila: backgammon
zaghrouta: ululations
za'tar: thyme mixed with sesame seeds and spices

INDEX

INDEX

INDEX

ABOUT LET'S GO

FORTY-ONE YEARS OF WISDOM

As a new millennium arrives, *Let's Go: Europe*, now in its 41st edition and translated into seven languages, reigns as the world's bestselling international travel guide. For over four decades, travelers criss-crossing the Continent have relied on *Let's Go* for inside information on the hippest backstreet cafes, the most pristine secluded beaches, and the best routes from border to border. In the last 20 years, our rugged researchers have stretched the frontiers of backpacking and expanded our coverage into Asia, Africa, Australia, and the Americas. This year, we've introduced a new city guide series with books on San Francisco and our hometown, Boston. Now, our seven city guides feature sharp photos, more maps, and an overall more user-friendly design. We've also returned to our roots with the inaugural edition of *Let's Go: Western Europe*.

It all started in 1960 when a handful of well-traveled students at Harvard University handed out a 20-page mimeographed pamphlet offering a collection of their tips on budget travel to passengers on student charter flights to Europe. The following year, in response to the instant popularity of the first volume, students traveling to Europe researched the first full-fledged edition of *Let's Go: Europe*, a pocket-sized book featuring honest, practical advice, witty writing, and a decidedly youthful slant on the world. Throughout the 60s and 70s, our guides reflected the times. In 1969 we taught travelers how to get from Paris to Prague on "no dollars a day" by singing in the street. In the 80s and 90s, we looked beyond Europe and North America and set off to all corners of the earth. Meanwhile, we focused in on the world's most exciting urban areas to produce in-depth, fold-out map guides. Our new guides bring the total number of titles to 51, each infused with the spirit of adventure and voice of opinion that travelers around the world have come to count on. But some things never change: our guides are still researched, written, and produced entirely by students who know first-hand how to see the world on the cheap.

HOW WE DO IT

Each guide is completely revised and thoroughly updated every year by a well-traveled set of nearly 300 students. Every spring, we recruit over 200 researchers and 90 editors to overhaul every book. After several months of training, researcher-writers hit the road for seven weeks of exploration, from Anchorage to Adelaide, Estonia to El Salvador, Iceland to Indonesia. Hired for their rare combination of budget travel sense, writing ability, stamina, and courage, these adventurous travelers know that train strikes, stolen luggage, food poisoning, and marriage proposals are all part of a day's work. Back at our offices, editors work from spring to fall, massaging copy written on Himalayan bus rides into witty, informative prose. A student staff of typesetters, cartographers, publicists, and managers keeps our lively team together. In September, the collected efforts of the summer are delivered to our printer, who turns them into books in record time, so that you have the most up-to-date information available for your vacation. Even as you read this, work on next year's editions is well underway.

WHY WE DO IT

We don't think of budget travel as the last recourse of the destitute; we believe that it's the only way to travel. Living cheaply and simply brings you closer to the people and places you've been saving up to visit. Our books will ease your anxieties and answer your questions about the basics—so you can get off the beaten track and explore. Once you learn the ropes, we encourage you to put *Let's Go* down now and then to strike out on your own. You know as well as we that the best discoveries are often those you make yourself. When you find something worth sharing, please drop us a line. We're Let's Go Publications, 67 Mount Auburn St., Cambridge, MA 02138, USA (email: feedback@letsgo.com). For more info, visit our website, www.letsgo.com.

If I had my life to live over again,

I would relax. I would limber up. I would take more chances.

I would take more trips.

I would climb more mountains, swim more rivers, and watch more sunsets.

I would go places and do things and travel lighter than I have.

I would ride more merry-go-rounds.

Excerpt from Nadine Stair, 85 years old / photo> John Norris

technical packs & apparel

Will you have enough stories to tell your grandchildren?

<u>Yahoo! Travel</u>

Do You YAHOO!?